The
Guide to
Britain 1998

Edited by Alisdair Aird

Deputy Editor: Fiona May

Associate Editors: Karen Fick, Robert Unsworth

Walks Consultant: Tim Locke

Additional Research: Fiona Wright, Marcus Hankinson,

Hannah Begbie

EBURY PRESS
LONDON

Please send reports to:

The Good Guide to Britain
FREEPOST TN1569
WADHURST
E Sussex
TN5 7BR

This edition published in 1997 by
Ebury Press
Random House, 20 Vauxhall Bridge Road
London SW1V 2SA

1 3 5 7 9 10 8 6 4 2

ISBN 0 09 185244 7

Typeset from author's disks by Textype Typesetters, Cambridge
Printed and bound in Great Britain by Cox & Wyman Ltd, Reading, Berkshire

CONTENTS

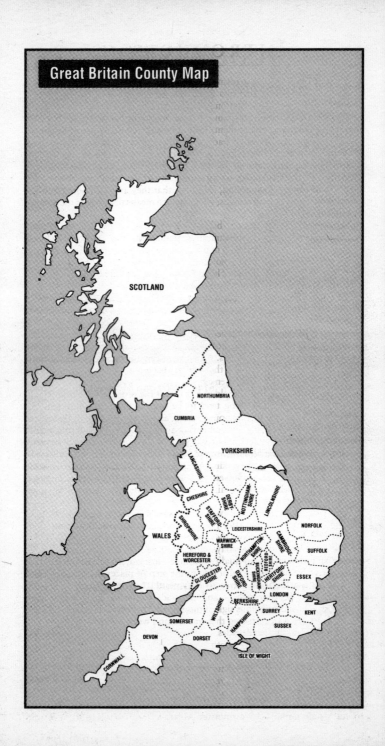

Great Britain County Map

SCOTLAND

NORTHUMBRIA

CUMBRIA

YORKSHIRE

LANCASHIRE

CHESHIRE

DERBY SHIRE

STAFFORD SHIRE

NOTTINGHAM SHIRE

LINCOLNSHIRE

SHROPSHIRE

WALES

LEICESTERSHIRE

NORFOLK

WARWICK SHIRE

NORTHAMPTON SHIRE

CAMBRIDGE SHIRE

SUFFOLK

HEREFORD & WORCESTER

BEDFORD SHIRE

BUCKINGHAMSHIRE

HERTFORD SHIRE

ESSEX

GLOUCESTER SHIRE

OXFORD SHIRE

LONDON

BERKSHIRE

WILTSHIRE

SURREY

KENT

SOMERSET

HAMPSHIRE

SUSSEX

DEVON

DORSET

ISLE OF WIGHT

CORNWALL

INTRODUCTION

Holiday Britain is on top form these days – it really is a good time to have a break here. There are two main reasons for this. One is the current strength of the £ in the international money markets. This is not good news for foreign visitors – it makes Britain more expensive for them. But for holiday-makers here at home it's excellent. First, it means that many places hoping to attract foreign visitors have had to set their prices low enough to look attractive even after conversion into foreign currencies. This means that for British people, with pounds in their pockets, these prices are now very attractive. At the same time, with people from abroad deterred by the – for them – expensive British pound, it follows that they aren't flooding into the tourist honeypots in such crowds, which in turn means that there's more space in which to enjoy things.

The second change is even bigger. Lottery money, particularly via the Heritage Lottery Fund, Millennium Commission, and Arts Councils of England, Scotland and Wales, is making a huge impact on many of the things that make Britain so special for holidays. Between them, these bodies will soon have funnelled £3,000 million of lottery money into a total of 6,747 individual projects, from the Millennium Commission's massive landmark projects in 14 regional centres, to a vast range of local initiatives. This is now having a tremendous impact on holiday Britain. All sorts of exciting new places to visit have been or are now opening, backed by lottery funding. A great many others are being expanded or redeveloped most attractively, thanks to lottery grants. Lottery money is allowing restoration (and subsequent opening) of some wonderful buildings and gardens. And it's backing the revitalisation of whole areas, particularly waterfronts, that are fast becoming the focus of a vibrant new holiday mood all around them.

One important but little-heralded fact is that the projects which succeed in attracting lottery-fund backing tend to be those which can show that the public will really get something out of them, as a result. In practice this means that, besides the few big or controversial grants that get all the media attention, a great many less publicised projects all over the country are now making a real difference to visitor pleasure. The results show all the way through the pages of this new edition of the *Guide*. It's fair to say that in the Editor's 25 years of close involvement in measuring holiday value for money, in this country and abroad, Britain's never before offered so much that's new, interesting and enjoyable.

After years in the doldrums, even Britain's seaside resorts have a new mood of confidence about them. After years of worrying about the British weather, and the fact that on that score they simply can't compete with places abroad, they've discovered that nowadays what most people want from the British seaside isn't Mediterranean-quality sunshine – instead, it's relaxation and fun. This year we've noticed a real spring in the step of places like Brighton and Torquay, a sparkle from Largs to Weymouth, a twinkle in the eye from Llandudno to Scarborough – and a good, roistering belly-laugh from Blackpool. The most obvious sign of this buoyant new seaside mood is that so many places are now restoring their piers – and work is even starting on the first new pier building for decades.

As we've said, prices – for both places to stay in and places to visit – are generally holding pretty steady. The big exception is that many places that used to be free (mainly museums and galleries) now charge for admission. Usually, places have done this reluctantly, knowing that it will cut visitors numbers but feeling forced into the change by shortage of public funds (as opposed to lottery money). Occasionally, the change is deliberately designed to cut visitor numbers: Westminster Abbey is the first place to have said publicly that this is the reason for its new charge, and in this case we think the charge entirely justified on crowd-control grounds – the abbey had sometimes been getting close to bedlam. But elsewhere we do sometimes detect an underlying attitude that visitors are a bit of a pain – an attitude that says 'We don't want you unless you pay' instead of 'We do want you to visit (but I'm afraid there's a charge)'.

The biggest sign of this fleece-the-customer approach is in the growing number of places now switching their telephone inquiry service to 0981 or equivalent numbers. These numbers charge people at a premium daytime rate of 49p a minute just for information – quite unjustifiable for a recorded message about prices, opening times and so forth. As we think this practice is so unreasonably grabby, in this edition we have substituted the ordinary office number for any place that normally publishes a premium rate number. It's a shame so very few places use the freephone 0800 number – as do Dobwalls Adventure Park in Cornwall, Monkey World in Dorset and the Severn Valley Railway between Worcestershire and Shropshire.

Another way in which more places could give customers better value is in really worthwhile family tickets. Too often the boast of a bargain family ticket turns out to be an almost negligible discount. Some places do offer much better family deals; we always point these out in the text, and the Seal Sanctuary at Gweek (Cornwall), Sulgrave Manor (Northamptonshire), Bodiam Castle (Sussex), and the Highland Wildlife Park at Kincraig (Scotland) deserve a special mention for this here. This year we have done our own bit to help. We approached all the places that we reckon are really good for family outings. Over 300 of them – about half – agreed to offer our readers a significant discount, usually allowing one child free admission for two adults paying. See **Using the Guide** and tear-out voucher card for details.

The tremendous range of excellent family outings now runs from quite simple and unpretentious places to immensely elaborate centres, and from ones that fascinate to ones that simply entertain. Whatever their nature, the best ones all share a dash of real enthusiasm that lift them right out of the ordinary.

Our choice as **Family Attraction of the Year** is Woburn Abbey and Safari Park (Bedfordshire), with masses to see and do for every taste, in lovely surroundings.

National Museum of the Year is the stunning Royal Armouries Museum in Leeds, a fascinating day out for people of any age.

Local Museum of the Year is the County Museum in Aylesbury (Buckinghamshire), where the new Roald Dahl Children's Gallery leaves most of its competitors behind by using verve and imagination (and £254,500 of lottery money) to put a really intriguing spin on the same subjects that other places deal with more prosaically.

We've mentioned the way that some museums and galleries that used to be free have now started charging. One man who has firmly resisted proposals to introduce charges – and has sometimes seemed to be carrying on a one-man war against them, is the Director of Glasgow's museums, which remain proudly free. It's for that thoroughly consumer-friendly reason that we name Julian Spalding as **Museum Man of the Year**.

Children's Outing of the Year is Legoland, near Windsor (Berkshire): guaranteed fun for anyone under 12.

Heritage Building of the Year is Fountains Abbey in Yorkshire, a romantic idyll in beautiful surroundings.

Garden of the Year is lovingly restored Hawkstone Park in Shropshire, its spectacular wooded parkland filled with extraordinary 18th-c follies.

Zoo of the Year is Chester Zoo, tireless in its quest to make life really enjoyable for its animals – and their visitors.

Guided Tour of the Year is the extremely appealing boat trip to see the seals off Blakeney Point, from Blakeney (Norfolk).

Scariest Ride of the Year is the horrific Vertigo sky-coaster at Oakwood, near Narberth (Wales), which would scare the wits out of anyone. Silliest Ride of the Year is a dead heat between Hoo Farm at Preston on the Weald (Shropshire), Big Sheep near Bideford (Devon) and Highgate Farm at Morland (Cumbria) for their sheep-racing – nobody actually rides the galloping sheep, but it is great fun.

Attraction Shop of the Year is the shop attached to Buckfast Abbey in Buckfastleigh (Devon); worth visiting on its own for the goods it brings in from other Benedictine abbeys all over Europe.

And finally, from the fascinating range of places that have opened recently, we choose as **New Attraction of the Year** the breathtaking London Aquarium.

Alisdair Aird

USING THE GUIDE

The Counties

England has been split alphabetically into county chapters. Scotland and Wales have each been covered in single chapters, and London appears immediately before them at the end of England.

Where to stay

In each section, hotels, inns and other places to stay such as farmhouses are listed alphabetically.

The price we show is the total for two people sharing a double or twin-bedded room with its own bathroom, for one night in high season. It includes full English breakfast (unless only continental is available, in which case we say so), VAT and any automatic service charge that we know about. So the price is the total price for a room for two people. We say if dinner is included in this total price. It is included in some of the more remote places, especially in Scotland and Wales, and may also be in some other places where the quality of the food is a main attraction; in these cases, the establishment concerned does not normally offer B & B on its own. In some of the places we list, some or occasionally even all the bedrooms share bathrooms; we say if this is the case.

An asterisk beside the price means that the establishment concerned assured us that that price would hold until the end of summer 1998. Many establishments were unable to give us this assurance; this last year, bedroom prices outside London have been holding very steady, but to be on the safe side it would be prudent to allow for an increase of around 5% by then. In London, allow 10%.

A few hotels will do a bargain break price at weekends even if you're staying for just one night. If so, that's the price we give, and we show this with a w beside the price. Many more hotels have very good-value short break prices, especially out of season, if you stay a minimum of at least two nights; if you plan to stay in one area rather than tour around, it's well worth asking if there's a special price for short breaks when you book. Many hotels also offer short-notice bargains which don't appear on their tariffs if they are underbooked on a particular night, so as to fill their rooms even at a discount. So, especially if you are not booking in advance, ask what price they can quote you for that particular night.

If there's a choice of rooms at different prices, we always give the cheapest, and if we know that maybe the back rooms are the quietest or the front ones have the best views or the ones in the new extension are more spacious then we say so. If you want a room with a sea view or whatever, you should always ask specifically for this, and check whether it costs extra.

If the hotel closes for any day or part of the year, we say so. But especially in outlying areas hotels have been known to close at other times if their business is very slack. And this last year or two we've found some go out of business altogether. So don't head off into an area where there are no nearby alternatives without checking by telephone first.

We always mention a restaurant if we know the inn or hotel has one. Note that we always commend food if we have information supporting a positive recommendation. So a bare mention that food is served shouldn't be taken to imply a recommendation of the food.

Where to eat

The price in **bold type** is for one person having a typical three-course restaurant meal with half a bottle of wine, including any automatic service charge. So double it to get a meal for two. The second price, in normal type after the l, is for a more informal single-dish meal, if that's available.

We list any scheduled closing dates. We have found quite a few instances of unscheduled closures in the last year or two, and recommend booking if your plans would be thrown into turmoil by finding a place unexpectedly closed. Moreover, many of the restaurants we list are very popular, and without a booking you may find there's no room for you.

If you want a good meal out in any area, look at the places to stay as well as the restaurants, especially in country areas. When we praise a hotel or inn for its food, that means it's well worth consideration as a place for a good meal out. In some parts of the country, it's in these hotel restaurants that you'll find the best food.

Our brief mentions of places to eat in the text of the **To see and do** sections are based on our own inspections or firm recommendations from readers.

Children

We asked all hotels, restaurants and other places to stay in and eat at which have full entries in the *Guide* whether they allow children. If the entry doesn't mention children, that means the establishment has told us that it welcomes them, with no restrictions. If there are restrictions (either an age limit, or segregated early evening meals for them), we spell these out. We have found that very occasionally establishments turn out in practice to be more restrictive about children than they claim. And of course managements change, and so do their policies. If you are travelling with children, to avoid misunderstandings it's always worth checking ahead that there will be no problem. Please let us know if you find any difference from what we say. Obviously, too, you should bear in mind the character of the hotel or restaurant, as described, and in relation to your own children. While some children might fit perfectly into the atmosphere of a dignified and old-fashioned country house, others might be fractiously ill at ease there – no fun for you, or for the other guests.

Locations

As far as possible, we list places to see (and hotels and restaurants) under the name of the nearest village or town. We use **bold type** to name the locality, and SMALL CAPITAL LETTERS to name the establishment. If the village is so small that you probably wouldn't find it on a road map, we've listed it under the name of the nearest sizeable village or town instead.

The maps use the same locality name as the text.

We include places in their true geographical locations – so if a village is actually in Buckinghamshire that's where we list it, even if its postal address is via some town in Oxfordshire.

Days Out – new this year

In each chapter except London, we have suggested several full days out, based around places or walks that we recommend in the main text, and which are close enough together to fit well into a single day. This is the first time we have done this, and we'd be very grateful for more suggestions.

Most of the itineraries we have suggested make very full days indeed – and while a determined and energetic sightseer might well pack everything into one long day, we expect most people would prefer to treat each day out as a sort of mini-menu, picking the things they'd enjoy most and skipping over the rest.

Prices and other factual details

Information about opening times and so forth is for 1998. In some cases establishments were uncertain about these when the *Guide* went to press during the late summer of 1997; if so, we say in the text. (And of course there's always the risk of changed plans and unexpected closures.) When we say 'cl Nov–Mar' we mean closed from the beginning of November to the end of March, inclusive; however when we say 'cl Nov–Easter', we mean that the establishment re-opens for Easter.

Where establishments were able to guarantee a price for 1998, we have marked this with an asterisk. In many cases establishments could not rule out an unscheduled price increase, and in these cases – i.e. no asterisk against the price – it's probably prudent to allow for a 5% increase around April 1998. If you find a significantly different price from that shown, *please let us know*.

🎫 Our discount voucher

Places to visit which have a 🎫 symbol immediately after their name have said they will honour our discount voucher until the end of 1998 (or, of course, the end of their season, if they close earlier). To get the discount, you must hand in one of the vouchers at the admissions kiosk; there are six vouchers on the tear-out card in the centre of the book. Usually, the discount is that one child will be admitted free for two adults paying the full price. Please check the text for that entry carefully. If there are any variations from the usual, or any special conditions, we spell them out in a bracket immediately after the 🎫 symbol. Please also note the general conditions on the voucher itself. As this discount voucher has taken some time and trouble to arrange, we'd very much appreciate hearing whether you think it's worthwhile, and would like us to repeat it in future years.

National Trust

NT after price details means that the property is owned by the National Trust, and that for members of the Trust admission is free. There is a similar arrangement for properties owned by the National Trust for Scotland (NTS); the two Trusts have a reciprocal arrangement, so that members of one may visit the properties of the other free. Membership is therefore well worthwhile if you are likely to visit more than a very few properties in the year – quite apart from its benefit to the Trusts' valuable work. NT membership is £27 a year (£46 for joint membership); details from National Trust, PO Box 39, Bromley, Kent BR1 1NH; (0181) 315 1111. NTS membership is £25 (£42 for a family); details from National Trust for Scotland, 5 Charlotte Sq, Edinburgh EH2 4DU; (0131) 226 5922.

Friends and Historic Houses

The Friends of Historic Houses Association has NT-style membership offering free entry to 283 historic houses and gardens in private ownership throughout Britain – including a high proportion of those we recommend which aren't NT, English Heritage or any other national equivalent. Membership is £28 a year (£40 for joint membership), so you only have to go to four or five houses and you've got your money back. Details from Historic Houses Association, Heritage House, PO Box 21, Baldock, Herts SG7 5SH; (01462) 896688.

English Heritage

A similar membership scheme now gives free access to those EH properties (about half) which charge admission. It costs £23 (£40 for a family). Details from English Heritage Membership Dept, Freepost 31 (WD214), London W1E 5EZ; (0171) 973 3000.

Other money savers

In the relevant sections we mention any notable travel bargains and other sightseeing bargains we know of, such as the London for Less discount card scheme – so popular in the three years it's been running that it's now been extended to Edinburgh, Bath and York, where the discount cards are particularly good value. You can save the cost of it almost straightaway, and it covers some of the main attractions rather than just peripheral ones. It's also worth knowing about the Slow Coach, especially if you're young and on a budget. Very popular with backpackers from overseas, it's a coach-run linking all the main tourist cities around the country – a £99 ticket gets you the whole circuit, though you can get on or off at any stage for as long as you like – there's no time limit; (01249) 891959.

Map references

Most place names are given four-figure map references, looking like this: NT4892. The NT means it's in the square labelled NT on the map for that area. The first figure, 4, tells you to look along the grid at the top and bottom of the NT square for the figure 4. The *third* figure, 9, tells you to look down the grid at the side of the square to find the figure 9. Imaginary lines drawn down and across the square from these figures should intersect near the locality itself.

The second and fourth figures, the 8 and the 2, are for more precise pinpointing, and are really for use with larger-scale maps such as road atlases or the Ordnance Survey 1:50,000 maps, which use exactly the same map reference system. On the relevant Ordnance Survey map, instead of finding the 4 marker on the top grid you'd find the 48 one; instead of the 9 on the side grid you'd look for the 92 marker. This makes it very easy to locate even the smallest village.

Disabled access

We always ask establishments if they can deal well with disabled people. We mention disabled access if a cautious view of their answers suggests that this is reasonable, though to be on the safe side anyone with a serious mobility problem would be well advised to ask ahead (many establishments made clear that this helped them to make any special arrangements needed). There may well be at least some access even when we or the establishment concerned have not felt it safe to make a blanket recommendation – again, well worth checking ahead. There are of course many places where we can't easily make this sort of assessment – particularly the less formal 'attractions' such as churches, bird reserves, waterside walks, viewpoints. In such cases (which should be obvious from the context) the absence of any statement about disabled access doesn't mean that a visit is out of the question, it simply means we have no information about that aspect. We're always grateful to hear of readers' own experiences. An important incidental point: many places told us that they would give free admission to a wheelchair user and companion.

Changes during the year – please tell us

Changes are inevitable during the course of the year. Managements change, and so do their policies. We very much hope that you will find everything just as we say. But if you find anything different, please let us know, using the report card in the middle of the book, the forms at the end of the book, or just a letter. For letters posted in Britain you don't need a stamp: the address is *The Good Guide to Britain*, FREEPOST TN1569, WADHURST, E. Sussex TN5 7BR.

Reports

This guide depends very heavily indeed on readers reporting back to it. In that sense it's very much a collaborative venture: and the more people that send us reports, the better the book will be. So please do help us by telling us about places you think should be added to the book, or removed from it, or even just confirming that places still deserve their entry. We try to answer all letters (though there may be a delay – and between the end of May and October we put all letters aside until after the end of the hectic editorial rush). People who help us do get a special offer discount price on the next edition. There's a note on the sort of information we need at the back of the book, with report forms; and a tear-out report card in the middle of the book.

Symbols

We have used the same symbols in the text and on the maps to pick out all the main types of places to visit. Though you don't need to pay any attention to the symbols, you can, if you like, use them to scan the text or a map quickly, to see what castles, say, or gardens a particular area has. These are what we have used the symbols to denote:

★ Attractive village or town

🏠 Interesting house – anything from an intimate cottage to the stateliest of stately homes

🏰 Castle, ruined abbey or other romantic ruin

🏛 More or less archaeological site such as Roman remains, Neolithic stone circles, early medieval maze, Iron Age hill fort

✝ Church, cathedral, minster, inhabited abbey

✸ Watermill, windmill or other type of mill

🌱 Nature conservation, including wildlife reserves

🐦 Bird reserve, bird centre (including falconry)

🐘 Zoo, safari park, anywhere keeping exotic animals

🐄 Farm animals, farm park, country centre, farm museum, also a vineyard

🐟 Anything to do with fish, including both fishing and aquariums

🦋 Butterfly park

🌼 Garden, plant centre, arboretum, landscaped park

🌳 Wood, forest

❋ Viewpoint

🍎 Orchard, fruit farm, pick-your-own

🕳 Cave, cavern

🏺 Museum

🖼 Art gallery, notable painting collections, sculpture park

⚓ Boat museum

✈ Air museum

🚗 Motor museum (including transport museums)

⚒ Open-air museum (including industrial museums)

🏛 Heritage centre such as Jorvik Centre in York

🚂 Steam locomotives, railway

⛵ Boat trip

☺ Amusement park, theme park, leisure park, permanent funfair

🎨 Craft centre or craft workshop: potters, glass-blowers, weavers, etc.

🏭 Factory visit (including power station visits and breweries)

! Anything odd, unusual or decidedly different

⊖ London Underground

⇌ Surface rail – former British Rail

🎟 Our special offer discount (see details on p.x and tear-out card)

Some places embrace all sorts of different attractions in just the one locality. With these, instead of cluttering the maps with all sorts of different symbols, we show a ✸ on the map.

On the maps, a bed symbol indicates recommended places to stay; a knife-and-fork symbol indicates recommended places to eat. A boot symbol shows the start of a walk mentioned in the **Walks** sections.

BEDFORDSHIRE

Some first-class family days out, and interesting quieter places.

Woburn Abbey is a splendidly managed complex of different attractions, from the exciting safari park to the quieter glories of the abbey and its collections, and deer park; plenty to keep all sorts of people interested, and more than enough for a day visit. Whipsnade is also excellent for a family day out. Much less well known, Woodside Farm at Slip End and Toddington Manor are both rewarding family outings. There's quite a wide range of other things for visitors, most notably gorgeous Luton Hoo, and the interesting collection of veteran aircraft at Old Warden. The Cecil Higgins gallery in Bedford has an exceptional collection of paintings, and the Stockwood craft museum near Luton is a bit different. There are some charming villages to stroll through.

Dunstable Downs have decent walking and remarkable views, though otherwise the county's scenery is generally not memorable. The brick-making which has so scarred the countryside south-west of Bedford has had its positive side – many towns and villages which might otherwise not be at all special have a sort of friendly glow from their warmly attractive masonry.

The county is flat enough to take the strain out of cycling; a tourist board leaflet details good circular cycle routes. You can get this from local tourist information centres, which stand out in this county for their wide range of helpful information. Another good leaflet is their timetable for 'Step This Way', a year-round programme of weekend guided walks and activities through some of the prettier villages and countryside.

Where to stay

Flitwick TL0335 FLITWICK MANOR Church Rd, Flitwick, Bedford MK45 1AE (01525) 712242 £125 room only, plus weekend breaks; 15 comfortable, thoughtfully decorated rms. 17th-c country house surrounded by interesting gardens; with log fire in the entrance hall, comfortable lounge and library, and a smart restaurant with fine French wines and delicious food using lots of fresh fish, home-grown and local produce; tennis, putting, croquet; children over 12; limited disabled access.

Leighton Buzzard SP9225 SWAN High St, Leighton Buzzard LU7 7EA (01525) 372148 *£87.50; 38 rms. Handsome Georgian coaching inn with pleasant lounge, relaxed bars, and an attractive restaurant with English cooking.

Sandy TL1749 HIGHFIELD FARM Great North Rd, Sandy SG19 2AQ (01767) 682333 *£45; 6 rms (2 in former stables), 4 with own bthrm. Neatly kept whitewashed house set well away from A1 and surrounded by arable farmland; friendly, helpful owner, open fire in the comfortable sitting room, and communal breakfasts in the pleasant dining room; cl Christmas.

Woburn SP9433 BELL Woburn, Milton Keynes, Bucks MK17 9QD (01525) 290280 £55; 25 attractively decorated rms, some with antiques. Lovely old inn, carefully restored, with a beamed restaurant, popular bar, and good food; also, residents' own lounge and bar.

To see and do

BEDFORDSHIRE FAMILY ATTRACTION OF THE YEAR

🐘 SP9433 **Woburn** WOBURN SAFARI PARK 📷 The drive-through safari is still the star draw at this superior park, attractively set in 300 acres of the grounds of Woburn Abbey (see below), but the surrounding activities stand out too. Rather than go down the theme park road, Woburn has kept most of its subsidiary features wildlife-related, and the mixture of hands-on animal attractions in the Wild World leisure section should easily fill a big chunk of the day for most families. The excitement of seeing lions and tigers through your own car windscreen can be hard to beat, but don't expect the animals to sit by the side of the road waiting for you to drive past; you may not see exactly what you'd hoped to first time round. Children love spotting rhinos, giraffes and the other usual suspects, but keep your eyes skinned and the guidebook handy and you may catch a glimpse of something a bit different, like the shy but distinctively marked bongo. Once out of the car you can feed elephants over the fence of their enclosure, go right up to the pygmy goats, or watch entertaining penguin-feeding and sealion shows. The walk-through aviary at Rainbow Landing is fun: carry a nectar cup in your hand and multicoloured lorikeets will swoop down for a taste. A well-constructed indoor adventure playground is shaped like Noah's Ark, and there's a separate play area for younger children – not to mention swan-shaped boats gliding across the lake. Several features are under cover but you'll definitely get more out of it on a dry day, especially in school holidays when there are extra events and activities for children. Meals, snacks, shop, disabled access; cl winter wkdys; (01525) 290407; £9 (£6 children, free for under-3s).

📷👤 **Bedford** TL0449 Really a straightforward modern town despite its long history, but there are decent riverside gardens and a few nice buildings. The River Festival around the spring bank holiday is always a lively time to visit. Its outstanding attraction is the very rewarding CECIL HIGGINS ART GALLERY & MUSEUM (Castle Close), which boasts the kind of paintings most other museums can only dream about, inc great works by Turner, Constable, Rembrandt, Matisse, Picasso and Dali. The Victorian mansion's beautifully furnished rooms make it look as if the family that lived here have just popped out – it's clear lots of thought has gone into the displays, and nothing seems unnatural or out of place. An award-winning extension has collections of local lace, glass and ceramics. Shop, disabled access; cl am Sun, all Mon (exc pm bank hols), 25–26 Dec, 1 Jan, Good Fri; (01234) 211222; free. The town MUSEUM next door is more traditional; cl am Sun and all Mon; free. John Bunyan lived

Days Out

Two very full family days

Day One: Walk on Dunstable Downs; Tree Cathedral, Whipsnade; lunch at Bell, Studham (or picnic at Whipsnade); Whipsnade Wild Animal Park or Woodside Farm, Slip End.

Day Two: Toddington Manor; lunch Rose & Crown at Ridgmont (or eat at Woburn); Woburn Abbey and deer park, or Woburn Safari Park.

Bedfordshire's quieter side

Elstow; Bromham Mill; lunch at Swan, Bromham, or the Bell in Odell; stroll in Harrold-Odell Country Park.

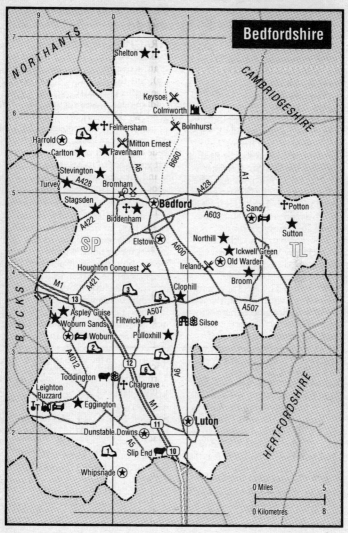

Bedfordshire

NORTHANTS

CAMBRIDGESHIRE

Shelton ★ ✝

Keysoe ✗
Colmworth

✝ Felmersham
Harrold ★
Bolnhurst
Carlton ★ ✗ Mitton Ernest
Pavenham ★
Stevington ★
Turvey Bromham
Stagsden ★
✝ ★ Bedford
Biddenham
Sandy ✝ Potton
SP
Elstow ★ Northill ★
Sutton ★
TL
Houghton Conquest ✗
Ickwell Green ★
Old Warden
Ireland ★
Broom ★
Clophill ★

M1 13
Aspley Guise ★
Woburn Sands
Woburn ★
Flitwick
Silsoe
Pulloxhill ★

Toddington
Chalgrave ✝
Leighton Buzzard
Eggington ★

Luton ★

Dunstable Downs 11
A5
Slip End 10

Whipsnade ★

BUCKS

HERTFORDSHIRE

0 Miles 5
0 Kilometres 8

around here for most of his life, and on Castle St there's a little MUSEUM on his life, adjoining the church of which he was minister. Open 2–4pm Tues–Sat Apr–Oct (am, too, July–Sept); (01234) 358870; 50p. There's also a trail around Bunyan-related sites. The Corn Exchange on St Paul's Sq has a bronze bust of Glenn Miller, who made many of his morale-boosting broadcasts from here. Lincolns (Goldington Green) is an interesting old place for lunch.

✗ ✗ **Bromham** TL0050 BROMHAM MILL (Bridge End) Picturesque, working 17th-c watermill on the River Ouse, with summer milling demonstrations, and a gallery with local art and crafts. Snacks, shop, disabled access to ground floor only (exhibitions here); open Sun, pm Weds–Sat, and bank hols, Mar–Oct; (01234) 824330; £1.50. The Swan is a popular food pub.

Colmworth TL1261 BUSHMEAD PRIORY Ruins of a late 12th-c

Augustinian priory, well preserved, with medieval wall paintings and timber-framed roof. Open wknds July and Aug; £1.60.

! 🚃 🏚 † Dunstable Downs TL0019 (see **Walks** section below) Very popular with kite-fliers and gliders at weekends or in summer. There's a countryside centre (cl Mon and winter wkdys), 2 car parks, and lots of space to run around. FIVE KNOLLS here is an important Bronze Age burial mound, excavated by Agatha Christie's husband Sir Mortimer Wheeler and Gerald Dunning. The Horse & Jockey (A5183) is a good family food pub. Dunstable itself has little to detain visitors, though the remarkable priory church incorporates part of a 12th-c abbey (where Henry VIII's first marriage was dissolved). The Old Sugarloaf (High St) is useful for lunch.

★ 🏚 † Elstow TL0546 The county's finest village, with a very attractive core of fine old timbered houses by the green. One of these is the MOOT HALL, an outstanding brick and timber, medieval market house with a collection of John Bunyan's works (he was born nearby), and a reconstruction of his writing room. Shop; cl am, all Mon (exc bank hols) and Fri, and Nov–Mar; £1. Bunyan was baptised in the attractive church, which has an unusual detached tower and a 'Pilgrim's Progress' window. The Three Tuns at Biddenham is the closest good place for lunch.

★ 🟤 🐦 Harrold SP9456 Pretty riverside village with a 13th-c church and packhorse-bridge, and an early 19th-c lock-up on the village green. Nearby, the HARROLD-ODELL COUNTRY PARK is highly recommended for birdwatching; it's especially good for waterfowl. Disabled access; visitor centre cl am Sun, all Mon (exc pm bank hols), and Oct–Mar exc pm wknds; (01234) 720016; free. The Magpie is useful for lunch, and in Odell the Bell is good.

🚃 ⛟ Leighton Buzzard SP9225 LEIGHTON BUZZARD RAILWAY 🏚 (Billington Rd; our discount vouchers not valid during Dec). Fine collection of over 50 locomotives from around

the world, with a fleet of 11 steamtrains to trundle you through gently varied countryside. The STONEHENGE WORKS terminus has industrial heritage displays. Snacks, shop, disabled access; open Sun and bank hols Easter–Sept, plus Weds Jun–Aug, Thurs and Sat in Aug, and wknds in Dec; (01525) 373888 for timetable; £4.50. The Globe in Linslade is a nicely set canalside food pub, with pleasant nearby walks.

🟤 🐝 ⛟ 🗡 🏠 Luton TL0921 Just south of this big, relatively modern industrial town, it's quite a surprise to find, tucked between the M1 and Luton Airport, a magnificent country mansion in 1,500 acres of parkland – LUTON HOO, started by Robert Adam, and grandly remodelled early this century for Sir Julius Wernher. As we went to press the family put the property on the market, which means its main draw for visitors, Wernher's incredible accumulation of art, furniture, tapestries and porcelain, may be rehoused elsewhere; the same goes for the unique Romian collection, which includes dresses and uniforms from the Russian court, Fabergé jewellery, and relics of the last generation of the imperial family. Meals, snacks, shop, disabled access; has been open pm Fri–Sun (and all day bank hols) Easter–mid-Oct, but best to check first; (01582) 722955; £5.75, garden only £2.50.

STOCKWOOD CRAFT MUSEUM AND GARDENS (Stockwood Country Park, Farley Hill) Ideal for a restrained and uncomplicated day out, with weekend demonstrations livening up the museum part, several lovely period garden settings (inc a 17th-c knot garden and a Victorian cottage garden), a refreshingly witty sculpture garden, and a children's play area. Also here, the MOSSMAN COLLECTION of restored old vehicles has plenty of vintage cars, and weekend rides through the park. Snacks, shop, disabled access; cl Mon (exc bank hols), and wkdys Nov–Mar; (01582) 738714; free.

★ † 🐝 Old Warden TL1343 An attractive village in its own right, built deliberately quaintly in the 19th c, but especially worth visiting for the SHUTTLEWORTH COLLECTION 🎫 (our discount vouchers not valid on flying display days). Nearly 40 working historic aeroplanes covering the early history of aviation, from a 1909 Blériot to a 1941 Spitfire in purpose-built hangars on a classic grass aerodrome. Several exhibits are the only surviving examples of their type, and it's worth trying to go on one on the days when some of them are flown (usually the 1st Sun of the month, May–Oct). Meals, snacks, shop, disabled access; cl 2 wks at Christmas; (01767) 627288; £6. The SWISS GARDEN nearby is an early 19th-c romantic wilderness garden, with pretty vistas and colourful trees and shrubs – a nice place for a stroll. Maybe evening opening or musical events in summer. Shop, disabled access; open Sun Jan–Oct, plus pm daily (exc Tues) Mar–Sept; (01234) 228671; £2.25. The village church has a number of European wood carvings, inc some from the private chapel of Henry VIII's wife, Anne of Cleves. The Hare & Hounds is a useful food pub.

🐾 ✙ ◔ **Sandy** TL1749 THE LODGE The elegant, 19th-c, Tudor-style house is the headquarters of the RSPB, and isn't open to the public, but is surrounded by a nature reserve covering 106 acres of heath, lake and woodland, with plenty of birds, animals and trails spread all over. Perfect for watching rare species undisturbed, but even if birdspotting's not your thing, this is a relaxing place to wander through, especially nice in spring when the woods are carpeted with bluebells. Summer meals, snacks, shop, some disabled access; cl Christmas; (01767) 680551; £2 (free for RSPB members). The Locomotive nearby is handy for lunch, and in the town the King's Arms is good.

🏠 🎱 **Silsoe** TL0835 WREST PARK (off the A6) Inspired by French châteaux, the 19th-c house has several ornately plastered rooms open to visitors, but it's the enormous formal gardens that are the main attraction. They go on for 150 acres and give a good example of the changes in gardening styles between 1700 and 1850. Perhaps best of all is the Great Garden, designed by the Duke of Kent between 1706 and 1740 and later modified by Capability Brown, with lovely views down the water to the baroque pavilion. Snacks, shop; open wknds and bank hols Apr–Sept; (01525) 860152; £2.75. The George Hotel is a friendly place for family lunches.

🐗 **Slip End** TL0818 WOODSIDE FARM AND WILDLIFE PARK 🎫 (Mancroft Rd) Very enjoyable for children, with plenty of friendly and feedable farmyard animals and a playground; you can handle rabbits and collect eggs straight from the hen house. Also rare breeds, poultry and wildfowl, and a farm shop. They sell pets and poultry, along with all the accessories you'll need to look after them. Meals, snacks, shop, disabled access; cl Sun, 25–26 Dec, 1 Jan; (01582) 841044; *£2.20. The Farmer's Boy at Kensworth is an appealing family-minded pub, not far.

🐗 🎱 **Toddington** TL0028 TODDINGTON MANOR 🎫 (Park Rd) Readers warmly recommend this well set place for its rare breeds centre and gardens, with pleached lime walk, herbaceous borders, herb and rose gardens. Children are given treasure hunt sheets, and fishing nets to use in the lake. Lovely woodland walks, vintage tractor collection, and weekend cricket matches in front of the house. Snacks, shop, plant centre, disabled access; open Weds–Sun May–Sept; (01525) 873924; *£3.50. The village green is attractive, there are unusual carvings on the church, and decent food is to be found at the Sow & Pigs.

🐘 🦛 ❗ **Whipsnade** TL0117 WHIPSNADE WILD ANIMAL PARK 🎫 Plenty of space for the animals at this splendid 600-acre zoo; the 17-acre elephant paddock is reckoned to be Europe's biggest. Altogether 2,500 creatures roam the beautiful downs-edge parkland, from tigers, lions, giraffes and rhinos to monkeys, wallabies, peafowl and Chinese water deer. You'll need a full day to see everything, and it's too big to get round completely on foot – you can drive round the perimeter road and walk from various stopping-points, or there's an open-topped tour bus, but the best way of getting around is on their railway, which takes you past herds of Asian animals. Younger visitors enjoy the penguin-feed and sealion demonstrations, and there's a hands-on Children's Farm, as well as indoor Discovery Centre with dwarf crocodiles, snakes and spiders. Play areas include a bear-themed maze. Meals, snacks, shop, disabled access; cl Nov–Feb; (01582) 872171; £8.50.

Tucked just off the village road is the TREE CATHEDRAL, trees planted in the plan of a cathedral in the 1930s, as a war memorial. The Bell at Studham is the best nearby place for lunch; the Old Hunter's Lodge is very handy.
🏠▣✟🐾★ **Woburn** SP9433
WOBURN ABBEY & DEER PARK ▣ One of England's grandest stately homes – everything from the lovely English and French 18th-c furniture to the splendid range of silver seems to have the edge over most assemblages elsewhere, and the art collection, taking in sumptuous paintings by Rembrandt, Van Dyck and Gainsborough, is outstanding (where else can you see 21 Canalettos in just one room?). The 3,000 acres of surrounding parkland were landscaped by Humphrey Repton, and today are home to several varieties of deer. Also a bird sanctuary, huge antiques centre, pottery and mature trees. Meals, snacks, shop, disabled access by arrangement; cl Nov–Dec and wkdys Jan–Mar; (01525) 290666; £7 (the antiques centre is 20p extra). *See separate Family Panel on p.2 for* adjoining WOBURN SAFARI PARK. The crowds come to Woburn for these 2 major attractions, but it's worth a look in its own right, with some

lovely 18th-c houses and good antique shops.
★ **Interesting villages** include Shelton TL0368, where the pretty little cottages, Hall and rectory are grouped around the quite delightful church, with 13th-c work inside, wall paintings, and a 14th-c font on 7 legs. Felmersham SP9857 has a lovely church by a medieval tithe barn, a fine old thatched pub and some other attractive old houses, with the River Ouse below. Nearby Pavenham SP9955 is also pretty, with a stroll down to the river. Sutton TL2247 is notable for its picturesque, steeply humped packhorse bridge, looking more like a part of Devon or Derbys; ironically, cars have to use a more ancient crossing, the shallow ford beside it. A decent pub nearby is named after John o' Gaunt, the village's former owner.

Other attractive villages include Aspley Guise SP9335, spacious Biddenham TL0249 (nice 12th-c church), Broom TL1743, Clophill TL0837, Eggington SP9525, Northill TL1546, Pulloxhill TL0634 and Turvey SP9452 (the interesting church has Saxon origins); all have pubs we can recommend for lunch. Carlton SP9555 and (with good wooded walks nearby) Woburn Sands SP9235 are also pleasant. Ickwell Green TL1545 nr Northill is well worth a look, too, with its colourful thatched houses around a broad green; Stagsden SP9849 is attractive, with a few thatched houses and strolls in the woods nearby. Stevington SP9853 has a handsomely restored windmill, and a holy well opposite the handsome church.
✝ **Other churches** worth investigating include Chalgrave TL0027 and Potton TL2449 (it's the gravestones that are worth the visit).

Walks
The **Dunstable Downs** TL0019 ◿-1 give great views from a spectacular escarpment path, amid ancient grasslands. The downs can be linked to a circuit incorporating Whipsnade village TL0018 and the nearby Tree Cathedral – the best walk in Beds. Elsewhere the predominant interest for walkers is in the greensand country, with the long-distance Greensand Ridge

Walk taking in **Woburn Abbey** SP9632 ⌂-2 (a right of way crosses the park) and the former hunting grounds of Henry VIII at **Ampthill Park** TL0337 ⌂-3 (surprisingly heathy but landscaped by Capability Brown, with lovely trees and a waterlily lake). The **Harrold-Odell Country Park** SP9657 ⌂-4 also has a lake, with waterfowl (especially in winter) and a nature reserve, and Bedfordshire County Council publish a circular route incorporating 3 waymarked walks up to 13 miles long; decent pubs in nearby Harrold and Odell villages. The ancient **Maulden Wood** TL0538 ⌂-5 has a picnic site, marked walks and muntjac deer. **Sundon Hills Country Park** TL0428 ⌂-6 is sheep-cropped downland with good views and marked walks (some quite steep). **Sharpenhoe Clappers** TL0630 ⌂-7 is steep-sided downland with chalkland flora and butterflies, and is crowned with a fine beechwood and an Iron Age hill fort; the area is owned by the National Trust and is laced with paths.

Where to eat

Bolnhurst TL0859 OLDE PLOUGH (01234) 376274 Pretty 500-year-old cottage, with a comfortably spacious lounge bar, woodburning stove in the public bar, dining room and upstairs restaurant; enjoyable daily specials, well kept real ale, seasonal mulled wine or buck's fizz; a pretty garden, and a light-hearted landlady. £17.40|£6.

Houghton Conquest TL0441 KNIFE & CLEAVER (01234) 740387 Civilised, 17th-c dining pub with a welcoming bar, blazing winter fire, friendly service, and stylish bar food; 24 good wines by the glass, well kept real ales, conservatory restaurant and neat garden; cl pm Sun, 27–30 Dec; disabled access. £19.85|£5.50.

Ireland TL1341 BLACK HORSE (01462) 811398 Busy, attractively refurbished beamed pub in a lovely setting; interesting, good-value food (fresh fish towards end of week), welcoming staff; cl Mon; disabled access. £16.50|£5.40.

Keysoe TL0762 CHEQUERS (01234) 708678 Attractive and friendly pub with comfortably modernised beamed bars, consistently good food and well kept beer; cl Tues, 25–26 Dec; disabled access. £17.85|£5.50.

Milton Ernest TL0156 STRAWBERRY TREE Radwell Rd (01234) 823633 18th-c thatched cottage with low beams and open fires, very good, interesting lunchtime and evening food (using the best ingredients) from a sensibly short menu, and very popular afternoon teas, too; cl Mon, Tues, all Jan; disabled access. £28|£6.

Special thanks to B M Eldridge, Ian Phillips, J Thompson, the Sandy family, Jenny and Michael Back.

We welcome reports from readers ...

This *Guide* depends on readers' reports. Do help us if you can – in return, we offer a discount on the next edition to people who've helped us with reports for it. Tell us what you think about places already in it, and anything extra you think we should say about them. And send us your ideas for inclusion in the next edition: places to visit, eat at or stay in, attractive drives or walks, maybe even unusual interesting shops you know of. Use the card in the middle, the report forms at the end, or just write – no stamp needed: *The Good Guide to Britain*, FREEPOST TN1569, Wadhurst, E Sussex TN5 7BR.

BEDFORDSHIRE CALENDAR

Some of these dates were provisional as we went to press.

FEBRUARY

24 **Toddington** Shrove Tuesday Ceremony: *just before midday* children gather on Conger Hill, with ears to the ground listening for the witch frying her pancakes (01582) 471012
28 **Bedford** Festival of Music, Speech and Drama – *till 7 Mar* (01234) 720481

MARCH

29 **Leighton Buzzard** Teddy Bears Outing at Leighton Buzzard Railway (01525) 373888

APRIL

10 **Leighton Buzzard** Easter Steam Weekend at Leighton Buzzard Railway – *till Mon 13* (01525) 373888

MAY

3 **Biggleswade** Shuttleworth Pageant: flying display at Old Warden Aerodrome (01767) 627502
4 **Ickwell Green** May Festival (01767) 640588; **Wilden** May Day Celebration (01234) 772295
16 **Bedford** Regatta (01234) 341171
23 **Bedford** River Festival – *till Mon 25* (01234) 21522; **Silsoe** Homes and Gardens Show at Wrest Park – *till Mon 25* (01525) 860152
25 **Luton** Carnival (01582) 8760056

JUNE

7 **Biggleswade** Shuttleworth Pageant: flying display at Old Warden Aerodrome (01767) 627502
13 **Toddington** South Bedfordshire County Show at Toddington Manor – *till Sun 14* (01525) 875170
14 **Luton** Festival of Transport at Stockwood Park (01582) 876005
20 **Flitwick** Carnival (01525) 875170

JULY

3 **Cranfield** Popular Flying Association Air Rally at the Airfield – *till Sun 5* (01273) 461616
5 **Bedford** 'Lazy Sunday': free festival with live bands, children's entertainments, street theatre and circus (01234) 360601; **Biggleswade** Shuttleworth Pageant: flying display at Old Warden Aerodrome (01767) 627502
12 **Bromham** Show (01234) 825684
18 **Luton** Fireworks Concert at Luton Hoo (0500) 66 1812

BEDFORDSHIRE CALENDAR

AUGUST

2 **Biggleswade** Shuttleworth Pageant: flying display at Old Warden Aerodrome (01767) 627502; **Leighton Buzzard** Model Event at Leighton Buzzard Railway (01525) 373888
8 **Bedford** Proms in the Park (01234) 269099
29 **Kempston** Fun Day (01234) 300848
31 **Biddenham** Show at St James School Field (01234) 211668

SEPTEMBER

5 **Leighton Buzzard** Autumn Steam-up at Leighton Buzzard Railway – *till Sun 6* (01525) 373888
6 **Biggleswade** Shuttleworth Pageant: flying display at Old Warden Aerodrome (01767) 627502
12 **Biggleswade** Bedfordshire Steam and Country Fair at Old Warden Park – *till Sun 13* (01462) 851711; **Luton** Country Show at Stockwood Park – *till Sun 13* (01582) 876005

OCTOBER

4 **Biggleswade** Shuttleworth Pageant: flying display at Old Warden Aerodrome (01767) 627502
7 **Bedford** Beer Festival at the Corn Exchange – *till Sat 10* (01234) 364796
18 **Bromham** Mill Apple Day: family activities (01234) 824330

NOVEMBER

25 **Bedford** Christmas Lights Switch-on (01234) 215226

DECEMBER

9 **Bedford** Victorian Fair – *till Fri 11* (01234) 215226

We welcome reports from readers . . .

This *Guide* depends on readers' reports. Do help us if you can – in return, we offer a discount on the next edition to people who've helped us with reports for it. Tell us what you think about places already in it, and anything extra you think we should say about them. And send us your ideas for inclusion in the next edition: places to visit, eat at or stay in, attractive drives or walks, maybe even unusual interesting shops you know of. Use the card in the middle, the report forms at the end, or just write – no stamp needed: *The Good Guide to Britain*, FREEPOST TN1569, Wadhurst, E Sussex TN5 7BR.

BERKSHIRE

Interesting days out, particularly in the east; quieter countryside in the west – good relaxing breaks.

Windsor Castle is an immensely powerful draw for visitors of all ages, and the town has plenty to fill a day or more of busy sightseeing. For a complete change of pace, nearby Dorney Court is a fine ancient building with the deep charm of a proper family home. Legoland near Windsor makes a very enjoyable family day out, and the Look Out discovery park in Bracknell also gets top marks for children. Some of the other places that children enjoy most here are much more informal – more on the lines of country parks, where they have plenty of space to let off steam.

In the west, rolling downland and civilised small villages linked by pleasant minor roads make for attractive drives – the Lambourn Valley and Lambourn Downs, the B4009 and B4494, and the back road from Pangbourne to Aldworth are among the best. This part of Berkshire has quite a good range of walking possibilities, from gentle strolls to long hikes, and with some comfortable and attractive places to stay in, as well as plenty of decent food, it makes for a relaxing short break. In tune with this quieter mood, Wyld Court Rainforest at Hampstead Norreys and Beale Park at Lower Basildon are most rewarding for anyone with an interest in wildlife, and the rejuvenated Kennet & Avon Canal is increasingly a focus for peaceful outings. Besides the county's great racecourses, horse-lovers can choose between opposite ends of the speed scale, at Lambourn and at Littlewick Green. The rural life museum on the edge of Reading is one of the best of its kind.

There's some glorious scenery in the east of the county – even if it's largely man-made. The lush stretch of the Thames between Marlow and Henley has rich surroundings, with easy towpath sauntering and plenty of boating activity. In holiday time the river does get very busy, but is idyllic on a fine early summer or autumn afternoon. Windsor Great Park, the Savill Garden and the Valley Gardens have memorable vistas, and can be returned to again and again without exhausting their possibilities.

Where to stay

East Ilsley SU4981 CROWN & HORNS East Ilsley, Newbury RG16 0LH (01635) 281205 £45; 10 rms, some in converted stable block. Lively and friendly old pub in horse-training country; with beamed rooms, pretty paved stable yard, interesting bar food, and lots of whiskies.

Hamstead Marshall SU4165 WHITE HART Hamstead Marshall, Newbury RG20 0HW (01488) 658201 £65; 6 beamed, comfortable rms in converted barn. Civilised country inn in a quiet village; with good food (Italian licensees), log fires, friendly service, and a very pleasant walled garden; cl 25–26 Dec, 2 wks Aug.

Hungerford SU3368 BEAR Charnham St, Hungerford RG17 0EL (01488) 682512 *£70w, plus special breaks; 41 comfortable, attractive rms with antiques and beams in older ones. Civilised hotel bar with fresh flowers, open fires, a stuffed bear, decent food, and a relaxing restaurant; disabled access.

Hungerford SU3368 MARSHGATE COTTAGE Marsh Lane, Hungerford RG17 0QX (01488) 682307 *£48.50; 8 individually decorated rms. Family-run, little hotel backing on to the Kennet & Avon Canal; with residents' lounge and bar, and seats overlooking water and marsh and more in the sheltered courtyard; children over 5; disabled access.

Lambourn SU3278 LODGE DOWN Lambourn, Newbury RG17 7BJ (01672) 540304 *£45; 3 rms. Country house in lovely grounds with views over the gallops of Lambourn Downs; open fire in the spacious, elegant sitting room, friendly owners, and good breakfasts around a communal table; visits to stables on request; tennis court and swimming pool.

Maidenhead SU8783 BEEHIVE MANOR Cox Green Lane, Maidenhead SL6 3ET (01628) 20980 *£58; 3 rms. Carefully preserved Tudor house run by two sisters; with huge beams, linenfold panelling, stained glass and latticed windows; home-baked bread for breakfast eaten around a big polished communal table, and light suppers by arrangement; cl Christmas; children over 12.

Maidenhead SU8783 FREDRICKS HOTEL & RESTAURANT Shoppenhangers Rd, Maidenhead SL6 2PZ (01628) 35934/24737 £188; 37 luxurious rms, many with garden views. Smart red-brick hotel close to the centre and next to the greens of Maidenhead Golf Club; complimentary glass of champagne on arrival in reception with its stylishly modern chandeliers and marble waterfall; plush cocktail bar, fine professional cooking in the luxurious restaurant, and good, formal service; lush wintergarden overlooking the gardens; cl 24 Dec–2 Jan; disabled access.

Pangbourne SU6376 COPPER Church Rd, Pangbourne, Reading RG8 7AR (0118) 984 2244 £105, plus weekend breaks; 22 rms, most overlooking gardens. Timbered and creeper-covered coaching inn, refurbished last year, with a comfortable sitting room, smart lounge, and good food and wine; disabled access.

Streatley SU5980 SWAN DIPLOMAT High St, Streatley, Reading RG8 9HR (01491) 873737 £102w, plus special breaks; 46 attractive rms, many overlooking the water. Well run, friendly riverside hotel with relaxed, airy lounges, and consistently good food in the waterside restaurant; popular leisure club, restored Magdalen College barge, and a flower-filled garden.

Windsor SU9676 MELROSE HOUSE 53 Frances Rd, Windsor SL4 3AQ (01753) 865328 £50; 9 rms. Friendly detached Victorian house, close to the town centre; with helpful resident owners, big breakfast room, and a snug lounge; no evening meals.

Windsor SU9676 OAKLEY COURT Windsor Rd, Water Oakley, Windsor SL4 5UR (01753) 609988 £130w, plus special breaks; 113 comfortable rms. Splendid Victorian country-house hotel in 35 acres of grounds by the Thames, with 9-hole golf course, croquet lawn, fishing and boating; log fires in the spacious lounges, a panelled library, and very good cooking in 2 restaurants; has featured in 200 films – notably the St Trinians series and Hammer House Dracula films.

Yattendon SU5574 ROYAL OAK The Square, Yattendon, Newbury RG16 0UF (01635) 201325 £90, plus special breaks; 5 pretty rms. Elegant and comfortable old inn in a peaceful village; with prettily decorated, panelled bar, lovely flowers, good food, and a walled garden.

To see and do

BERKSHIRE FAMILY ATTRACTION OF THE YEAR

☺ ! LEGOLAND (2m SW of Windsor town centre on B3022; shuttle-bus from the station at Windsor and Eton Riverside, which connects with London Waterloo) Don't be put off by the price: this is the country's most imaginative theme park, which just about manages to live up to its considerable hype – especially if you're under 12. It's quickly become one of the most visited attractions in the country, but far from resting on its laurels, in its second year has added 2 new rides (the Space Tower and the pedal-powered Sky Rider), and a guaranteed crowd-pleaser in the shape of an animated Lego Technic dinosaur. As at any theme park you can expect a fair amount of standing in line, though you can avoid this as much as possible by booking in advance – not only is this slightly cheaper, you'll also miss the long wait at the entrance, and be able to plan beforehand which bits you most want to see (essential for getting the best out of the place). It also removes the risk of not seeing anything at all – they close the doors when they feel there are enough visitors. The park is divided into several differently themed areas (all built using those amazingly versatile coloured building bricks), with the driving school at Lego Traffic one of the most popular; children who best negotiate the simulated roads and traffic systems earn their own driving licence. The Wild Woods is ideal for lively boys: its Rat Trap is a first-class labyrinth of wooden walkways, climbing nets and slides, and the Pirate Falls is an excellent steep water-chute. This section gets very busy mid-afternoon, so it's a good idea to head here straight away in the morning. Younger children enjoy the colourful Duplo Gardens, while My Town has some jolly fairground rides, a circus, and some splendidly put-together scenes and tableaux in the Explorer's Institute. Best of all though is Miniland, where 25 million Lego bricks charmingly re-create Amsterdam, Brussels, London and Paris in miniature, with moving people, vehicles and animals, and wonderful attention to detail (even down to the 'Mind the gap' on the London Underground). Plenty of other features, shows and activities – you'll need a full day to stand even a chance of seeing everything. Several snack bars and restaurants (and very good picnic area), decent shops, disabled access; open daily from the wk before Easter–end of Sept, plus Oct wknds and half-term; (01753) 626111; £15 (£12 children), £1 less if pre-booked.

Windsor SU9676 Well worth an expedition (though a tremendous magnet for visitors), the town is dominated by its famous castle, the largest inhabited one in the world. The little streets to the south have many pretty timber-framed or Georgian-fronted houses and shops. The High St, by contrast, is wide and busy. Legoland (*see separate Family Panel above*) is a huge draw for children. You can walk by the Thames (for example, from Home Park, beyond the station); or across to Eton. The good evening racecourse is best approached by boat – shuttle services run from Barry Avenue Promenade; (01753) 865234 for race dates. The Trooper in St Leonard's Rd and Two Brewers in Park St (handy for Royal Mews) are useful for a bite to eat, but for a better meal we'd recommend going out to the Thatched Tavern in Cheapside SU9469 – handy for the various Windsor Park attractions. Both the Union and Oxford Blue are decent pubs in the quieter nearby Thames-side village of Old Windsor.

🏰✝⛪! WINDSOR CASTLE A mass of towers, ramparts and pinnacles, this splendid palace is the official residence of the monarch, though it's changed considerably since William the Conqueror built his original wooden fort here. Henry II constructed the first stone buildings, inc the familiar Round Tower, from the top of which, on a good day, you can see 12 counties. For many the highlight is the magnificent St George's Chapel, a splendid example of Perpendicular architecture, with intricate carvings on the choir stalls, fine ironwork, an amazing fan-vaulted ceiling, and the arms and pennants of every knight entered into the Order of the Knights of the Garter. This is closed Sun mornings and occasional other dates, often at short notice – best to check on the telephone number given below. The State Apartments, used for ceremonial and official occasions, are decorated with carvings by Grinling Gibbons and ceilings by Verrio, and are full of superb paintings from the Royal Collection (inc notable Rembrandts and Van Dycks), porcelain, armour, and exceptionally fine furniture. This area (which may be closed when the Queen is in residence) was badly damaged by the disastrous fire in 1992, but you'd hardly know it now. Shop, disabled access; (01753) 831118 for full details of opening times; £8.80 (£6.60 on days when the Chapel or State Apartments are closed). The guards generally change on alternate days (not Sun), at 11am – again, telephone for exact dates. A separate charge (£1 in aid of charity) applies for Queen Mary's Dolls House, an exquisite creation by Edwin Lutyens, built for Queen Mary in the 1920s, with perfectly scaled furniture and decoration; it's open the same times as the State Apartments.

🏠 Frogmore House (Home Park) This lesser known former Royal residence is definitely worth catching on one of its few open days – usually spring and summer bank hols; (01753) 868286 ext 2235 for dates. It was a favourite with Queen Victoria, who is buried in a mausoleum in the grounds, alongside her beloved Albert.

🌼 Savill Garden (Wick Lane, Englefield Green – where the Sun is a good place for lunch break) On the eastern edge of Windsor Great Park, this is a very special place: the 35 peaceful acres include woodland, a formal rose garden, rock plants, herbaceous borders and so forth, and are punctuated with a number of rare trees, shrubs and perennials. The range of colours can be quite dazzling. Perhaps best in spring but enjoyable at any time of year. Meals, snacks, good shop with plant sales, disabled access; cl 25–26 Dec; (01753) 860222; £3.50.

🌼 🦢 Valley Gardens Lovely for a relaxing stroll, with over 400 acres of woodland – 50 of which are devoted

Days Out

The classy one
Windsor Castle (get there early to avoid the crowds); stroll into Windsor Great Park; lunch at Oakley Court, Windsor – or drive to the Fish in Bray (Old Mill Lane) or Thatched Tavern, Cheapside; Eton College.

The Thames
Boat trip from Maidenhead; Cookham (lunch at Bel & the Dragon, or Uncle Tom's Cabin); stroll by the Thames or on Winter Hill; Dorney Court, or Courage Shire Horse Centre (Littlewick Green).

Fresh air and nostalgia
Horse-drawn boat trip from Kintbury along Kennet & Avon Canal; picnic on Walbury Hill; stroll along crest to Combe Gibbet on Inkpen Hill.

Orchids and exotica
Walk by Thames at Streatley; Wyld Court Rainforest, Hampstead Norreys; lunch at White Hart there, or the unspoilt Bell, Aldworth; Beale Park, Lower Basildon.

to rhododendrons, making this the largest planting of the species in the world. Also an outstanding collection of trees and shrubs, a heather garden, waterfowl lakes, and attractive landscaping. It's free for pedestrians (the mile-long walk from Savill Garden is pleasant), though cars can enter by a gate on Wick Rd, Englefield Green, for a fee of £3.

🏠✝♿🅿 **Eton** SU9678 So close to Windsor it's pretty much part of it, this has a restrained and decorous High St with a mix of interesting old shops and houses. Its glory is ETON COLLEGE, the famous public school, whose stately Tudor and later buildings in graceful precincts are marvellously calm during the school's holidays. The chapel is an outstanding late Gothic building in the Perpendicular style, and a museum tells the story of the school from its foundation in 1440 up to the present, with fascinating videos on life for pupils here today (inc Prince William). Bizarre information is turned up by the various historical documents – in the 17th c, for example, smoking was compulsory for all scholars as a protection against bubonic plague. The Brewhouse Gallery has some good watercolour drawings and changing exhibitions, and next door there's an exhaustive collection of Egyptian antiquities. Shop, some disabled access; cl am in term-time, and all Oct–Mar; (01753) 671177; from £2.50 (more for guided tours). The College runs residential courses in summer on topics as diverse as rowing and choral singing. The Pickwick at Eton Wick has good-value food.

Other things to see and do

⛵ **Boating on the Thames** Though busy in summer, this is a lovely stretch of the river, flowing through lively towns and villages, past grand houses in imposing grounds to idyllic reaches by steep quiet woodland – with islets where you can picnic. A particularly pretty trip is from Wargrave to Henley to Medmenham Abbey to Hambleden, Hurley and Marlow Reach. A good shorter stretch is Cliveden Reach (the 2 miles

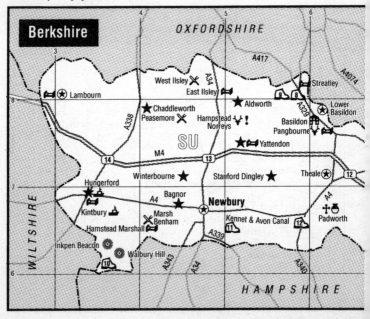

between Cookham and Boulter's Lock). As well as motor launches, you can hire very attractive (not to mention silent and quite environmentally friendly) electric launches, though for the purists – and the energetic – only a rowing boat will do. Bray Boats in Maidenhead, (01628) 37880, have small boats/motor launches ranging from £20 an hour to around £130 a day; they also run half-hour or 2-hour trips as far as Cookham. Kris Cruisers in Datchet have rowing boats from £5 an hour and electric launches from around £13 – they do good discounts during the week; (01753) 543930. A recorded information service (updated weekly) has details of events and estimated conditions on the river; (01734) 535520.

❀ **Arborfield** SU7567 HENRY STREET GARDEN CENTRE Specialist rose and bedding-plant grower, with a well stocked garden centre. From July-Sept you can wander through the fragrant rose fields. Meals, snacks, shop, disabled access; (0118) 976 1223; free. The George & Dragon over at Swallowfield is good for lunch.

! Ascot SU9268 ROYAL ASCOT Probably the most famous racecourse in the world, though most visitors spend as much time watching the people as the horses. The 4-day Royal Meeting in mid-Jun is still one of the highlights of the English season; to try for admission to the Royal Enclosure, British citizens should apply to Ascot Races (Royal Enclosure and Members' Stand), St James's Palace, London SW1; foreign citizens to their embassy. For the other stands contact the racecourse; tickets must be booked in advance and are available from 1 Jan. Plenty of other top-class races throughout the year, when ticket prices range from £7 to £34 depending on the enclosure (the Silver Ring is the cheapest). Meals, snacks, shop, disabled access; (01344) 22211 for dates. In town, Emperor House has an extensive display of antique and modern timepieces, with some wonderful longcase clocks; cl Sun. The Thatched Tavern at Cheapside is the best nearby place for lunch.

☺ 🍴 🏰 ❀ **! Bracknell** SU8769 Few find much to delight them in the town itself, but it's worth tracking down

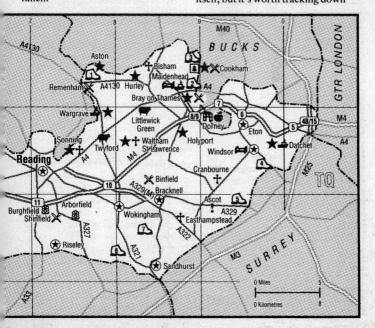

the LOOK OUT 🏛 on its southern edge (off the B3430), a lively centre that's the starting-point for 2,600 acres of woodland. Families love the hands-on science centre, now very much the main feature of the place, and a very full timetable of events includes some particularly well organised children's activities. Mainly conifer plantations, the forest is full of nature trails and wildlife (as well as an Iron Age hill fort); as the name suggests, there's an elevated platform with good views of the surrounding area. You can hire mountain bikes. Meals, snacks, shop, disabled access; cl 22–26 Dec; (01344) 868222; £3.50. Across the road, CORAL REEF is an unusually wacky swimming pool complex, great for younger members of the family; the Wild Water Rapids are the best bit. Meals, snacks, shop, disabled access; cl 2 wks before Christmas; £4.80. The Old Manor (Grenville Pl, High St) has decent food all day, and there's a dry-ski centre with toboggan run at the Leisuresport Complex at Amen Corner.

🕸 **Burghfield** SU6668 OLD RECTORY Plantsman's garden inc oriental rarities and cottage-garden plants. Plant centre selling plants from other gardens in the area, disabled access to most of garden; open last Weds of month Feb–Oct; (01734) 833200; £2. The Hatch Gate here is a friendly pub for lunch.

★ 🏛 **Cookham** SU8884 The village, leading down to the Thames, is attractive, and has several decent pubs of which the very smart if expensive Bel & the Dragon, and Uncle Tom's Cabin at Cookham Dean, are the current pick. STANLEY SPENCER GALLERY (King's Hall) Cookham really made its mark on Spencer and his art: it was his birthplace and he spent most of his working life here. This rewarding little gallery has a good range of his unique work, with highlights inc *The Last Supper* and the curious *Christ Preaching at Cookham Regatta*. Shop, disabled access; cl wkdys Nov–Easter; (01628) 520890; 50p.

🏚 🍴 **Dorney** SU9278 DORNEY COURT Engaging, partly 15th-c, timber-framed manor house with pleasant gardens and some very fine furniture, as well as the Elizabethan Palmer Needlework tapestry. The same family have lived here for over 450 years. In the 16th c they grew the first pineapple raised in England, and still have pick-your-own fruit and vegetables every day in season (usually daily Jun–Aug – discounts on Mon, Tues or Weds). Also plant centre, with plants from Blooms of Bressingham, and teas with their own honey. Open pm Mon–Thurs Jun–Aug; (01628) 604638; £4. The Pickwick at Eton Wick is handy for lunch.

! ❦ **Hampstead Norreys** SU5376 WYLD COURT RAINFOREST 🏛 (slightly out of village on the B4009) Very highly praised by readers, an unusual and quite fascinating tropical rainforest reconstructed under glass, with thousands of weird-looking plants currently in danger of extinction. They're spread over 3 different areas, Lowland Tropical, Amazonica and Cloudforest, each with its own climate and atmosphere. Particularly strange are the giant 8-ft lily pads (best from Jun–Oct), which start life the size of a pea, and the orchid collection is exceptional. Quite a few of these plants can't be seen anywhere else in Europe. Also squirrel monkeys, varied fish, and terrapins. As it's so warm, this is particularly handy on a cold day. Good shop (with plants for sale), mostly disabled access (though hard work over gravel in car park); cl 25–26 Dec; (01635) 200221; £3.50. The White Hart has good-value food.

★ 🚣 **Hungerford** SU3368 Attractive large village or small town with some interesting antique shops, some general, others specialising in items as diverse as fireplaces, kitchen furnishings and billiard tables; antique fairs in the town hall. CANAL TRIPS leave the wharf at 2.30pm wknds Easter–Oct (also Weds Jun–Sept, from £3; maybe also 4.30pm trips in July and Aug). The Tally Ho towards the motorway is a friendly place for lunch.

⚓ **Kintbury** HORSE-DRAWN BARGE TRIPS 1½-hour trips along the restored Kennet & Avon Canal, from Easter–Sept; (01635) 44154; £4.

! 🏠 ✝ **Lambourn** SU3278 Quiet streamside racehorse-training village below the downs. LAMBOURN TRAINERS' ASSOCIATION (Windsor House) Guided tours around this successful racehorse-training centre; you meet individual horses and see them put through their paces. Wear suitable shoes, and you must make an appointment. Shop, disabled access; open 10–12am, daily exc Sun and bank hols; (01488) 71347; £5 plus VAT. Up on the downs (OS Sheet 174 SU329828) SEVEN BARROWS is a Bronze Age cemetery with at least 32 barrows – a spectacle even for the uninitiated. The parish CHURCH OF ST MICHAEL AND ALL ANGELS is worth a look (originally Norman, with Perpendicular additions), and the Hare & Hounds (B4000 S), with strong racing connections, is useful for lunch.

🐄 **Littlewick Green** SU8379 COURAGE SHIRE HORSE CENTRE 🎫 (A4, 2m W of Maidenhead) You can go right up to the horses at this friendly place, and watch them being groomed and plaited up; also small animals and birds, working forge, and children's playground. Meals, snacks, shop, disabled access; cl Nov–Feb (though may be open half-term); (01628) 824848; £3.

✤ 🐦 ✱ ⚓ 🏡 🐛 **Lower Basildon** SU6078 BEALE PARK (Church Farm, Lower Basildon) Good, reliable and informative wildlife gardens, with a varied range of birds and mammals – many rare. Just about all their animals were born here in conditions as near as possible to the wild. The surroundings well deserve their listing as an Area of Outstanding Beauty, and there's a lot going on: added attractions include a narrow-gauge railway, the National Centre for Model Ships and Boats, and a children's playground. Readers get a great deal of pleasure from coming here. Meals, snacks, shop, disabled access; cl Christmas–Feb; (0118) 984 5172; *£4. In summer you can get a boat to here from Caversham Bridge in Reading (2 hours each way, £6.50 return). BASILDON PARK (A329) Elegant, Bath-stone, Palladian mansion with delicate plasterwork on the ceilings and walls, an unusual Octagon Room, and an intriguing collection of rare seashells in the Shell Room. Outside are old-fashioned roses, a pretty terrace, and pleasant grounds beyond. The classical frontage is particularly impressive. Older readers particularly enjoy coming here. Summer teas, light lunches wknds and bank hols, shop, disabled access (buggy rides avoid the long trek from the car park); open pm Weds–Sun and bank hols, Apr–Oct; (01734) 843040; *£3.70, £1.50 grounds only; NT.

✝ ⚓ ! 🏇 **Newbury** SU4666 Busy shopping town famed for its notorious bypass, but there are some nice parts, with interesting older buildings among the High St shops. ST NICOLAS is a fine, early 16th-c Perpendicular church with a magnificent pulpit. West Mills is the best evocation of the town's 18th-c prosperity, and leads to the attractively rejuvenated canal. BOAT TRIPS occasionally run from the old wharf, beyond the market square on the other side of the High St; (01635) 44154. The handsome DISTRICT MUSEUM (The Wharf) is good on the Civil War battles fought here, and on the development of ballooning (open pm Mon–Sat, exc Weds in term-time; free). The town has an excellent racecourse, with mid-week and weekend races all year; (01635) 40015 for dates; prices from £4–£17. DONNINGTON CASTLE (just N off the B4494) This is actually the tall, ruined medieval gatehouse of a much larger fortress destroyed in the Civil War. The Old Waggon & Horses (Market Pl) has a friendly, family dining area above the river, and the Lock Stock & Barrel (also waterside) an afternoon coffee shop as well as bar meals.

⚓ ✝ **Padworth** SU6166 KENNET & AVON CANAL VISITOR CENTRE (Aldermaston Wharf) Set in a nice little house beside the canal, exhibitions on the history and usage of the waterway, and useful information on things to do along its various stretches (of which some would say the Berks bits are the prettiest – see also Hungerford and Newbury entries for boat trips). Good trails and walks. Snacks (in picnic garden), shop, limited disabled access; cl am Sun, and all Nov–Mar; (0118) 971 2868; free. The quietly placed CHURCH feels very ancient and peaceful, and the Round Oak has decent food.

Pangbourne SU6376 PANGBOURNE MEADOW Traditional meadow by the Thames, scythed after flowering and seeding to preserve its wide range of wild flowers. The attractive riverside Swan has food all day, and the village has some decent shops; it was the home of Kenneth Grahame, who perhaps found inspiration around here for *The Wind in the Willows*.

Reading SU7272 Berkshire's county town, largely 19th-c red brick, and not really a tourist town, but with 3 museums worth visiting. The very well organised BLAKE'S LOCK MUSEUM (Gasworks Rd) concentrates on Reading's waterways, trade and industries, with reconstructed bakery (the town was well known for biscuit-making), barber's shop and printer's workshop, and a Victorian turbine house. Shop, disabled access; cl am wknds and bank hols, all Mon (exc bank hols), 25–26 Dec ; (0118) 939 0918; free. In a showy neo-Gothic building, the MUSEUM OF READING (Blagrave St) has hands-on displays and good reconstructions, and a unique Victorian copy of the Bayeux Tapestry. Meals, snacks, shop, disabled access; hours as Blake's Lock Museum; free. The abbey ruins round the corner in Forbury Gardens are worth a look if passing. In West St, Vicars & Sons is an old-fashioned game butcher's established in the 19th c, an interesting shop with good food. MUSEUM OF ENGLISH RURAL LIFE (University of Reading, Whiteknights Park; 2m SE on the A327, so you don't have to go into the busy centre). This has recently been short-listed by

the Heritage Secretary as one of Britain's top out-of-London museums. If life in the English countryside over the last couple of hundred years or so is your thing, you won't find a better exploration of it than this, taking in farm tools, rural crafts, and domestic room settings. Shop, disabled access; cl 1–2pm, all Sun and Mon, and 25 Dec–1 Jan; (0118) 931 8663; *£1. For the extravagant, a BALLOON TRIP gives a very different view of Berks; lift off from town-centre parks daily (weather permitting) in summer, dawn and dusk; (0181) 840 0108; £115. Sweeney & Todd in Castle St has excellent-value home-made pies, and the canalside Fisherman's Cottage (Kennet Side – walk through from Orts Rd off King's Rd) is also very popular for lunch.

Riseley SU7263 WELLINGTON COUNTRY PARK AND NATIONAL DAIRY MUSEUM (off the B3349 Reading–Basingstoke) Plenty for families in this big country park; the 350 acres of meadows, woodland and lakes include marked nature trails, a miniature steam railway, deer park, a collection of small domestic animals, and an adventure playground. The museum covers the history of the dairy industry, from attractive copper, pewter and wooden tools, to quaint milk delivery vehicles. You can fish, sail or row on the lake. Meals, snacks, shop; cl wkdys Nov–Feb; (0118) 932 6444; £3.50. The George & Dragon at Swallowfield does good lunches.

Sandhurst SU8361 TRILAKES COUNTRY PARK AND FISHERY (Yateley Rd) Not just for fishermen, these attractive lakes and surrounding park and woodland have lots of animals and birds, some of which you can feed. Shetland pony rides for children on summer Suns, and in spring you can bottle-feed the lambs. Also a model railway, and birds of prey some bank hols. Meals, snacks, shop, limited disabled access; cl wkdys Nov–mid-Mar; (01252) 873191; £2, fishing £7. The Bird in Hand at Little Sandhurst is useful for lunch.

🏠 🕸 ⚘ ⚘ **Theale** SU6371
ENGLEFIELD HOUSE (A340) The
striking house itself is open only to
groups, but the surrounding
woodland is attractive, with
interesting trees, water and formal
gardens, and deer park. Some
disabled access; open Mon all year,
plus Tues–Thurs Apr–July; (0118)
930 2221; £2. The Old Boot over at
Stanford Dingley has very good food
these days.

☛ **Twyford** SU7876 THAMES VALLEY
VINEYARD (Stanlake Park, B3018)
English wines made by a pioneering
blend of tradition and technology.
Snacks, shop; cl am Sun, 25 Dec–3
Jan; (0118) 934 0176; tours £6. Just
off the A4, ROCKS COUNTRY WINES
(Loddon Park Farm) produce a range
of country wines, liqueurs and mead,
with tastings and a walled herb
garden. Cl am wknds; (0118) 934
2344; free. The Bull nr the Thames at
Sonning is pleasant for lunch.

✎ 🍴 ⚘ 🕸 **Wokingham** SU8068
HOLME GRANGE CRAFT VILLAGE
(Heathlands Rd) Expanding craft
centre with paintings, sculpture, rugs,
and even a circus shop; play area and
animals for children. Meals, snacks,
disabled access; cl 25 Dec–1 Jan;
(0118) 977 6753; free. Heathlands
Rd has a couple of farm shops and
pick-your-own plots. Just S of town
on the B3016, turning right at Wick
Hill opposite the B3430, the woods

of CALIFORNIA COUNTRY PARK SU7864
are useful for children to let off steam.
Up to the N, DINTON PASTURES
COUNTRY PARK SU7872 (off the
B3030 S of Hurst – which has decent
pubs) has more for older children, inc
windsurfing and canoeing. The
Crooked Billet on Gardeners Green,
Honey Hill, just SE of Wokingham, is
a friendly place for lunch.

✝ The **church** at Bisham SU8485 is
worth a visit; sitting on a seat in the
churchyard by the Thames on a fine
evening is rather special. Also worth a
look is the magnificent 14th-c
Shottesbrooke Church in a park just
E of Waltham St Lawrence SU8276
(an attractive quiet village with an
ancient centre), while the churches at
Cranbourne SU9372 and
Easthampstead SU8667 have fine
stained glass by William Morris,
Edward Burne-Jones and others.

★ **Other attractive villages**, worth
looking at if you're near, and all with
reasonable pubs and pleasant local
walks, include Aldworth SU5579,
Aston SU7884, Bagnor SU4569 (with
a well regarded theatre in a lovely old
watermill), Bray SU9079,
Chaddleworth SU4177, Datchet
SU9876, Holyport SU8977, Hurley
SU8283, Sonning/Sonning Lock
SU7575 (lovely church, nice stroll
through churchyard and along the
Thames), Stanford Dingley SU5771,
Wargrave SU7878, Winterbourne

Walks

There's plenty of opportunity for pleasant strolling in the E of the county. In
particular, the Thames's nostalgic qualities of boating and Edwardian
England are seen to full effect from leisurely strolls along the towpath. A
notable stretch runs from Maidenhead SU8783 to Henley SU7882, sharing the
river with Bucks and Oxon; there are spectacular period riverside mansions
towards Maidenhead. There are lovely Thames walks from **Remenham**
SU7683 ⌂-1 in either direction. This reach is the course of the Henley Regatta;
you can instead start from Henley itself (coming back over the bridge – see
Oxon chapter) or Aston SU7884; the Flower Pots here is a useful halt. Another
good starting-point for river walks is **Boulter's Lock** SU9082 ⌂-2 (head
upstream).

There are few bridges across, and much of the hinterland is developed, but
opportunities for inland walks abound around **Cookham Dean** SU8785 and
Cookham SU8884 ⌂-3, with great views from the chalk escarpment of Winter
Hill SU8786. Cock Marsh (NT), by the Thames, is a fine lowland marsh, with
breeding wading-birds and wetland flora. Paths in this area are very well kept,
and it is hard to lose the way seriously, although woodland walking sometimes

means you have to keep your eyes skinned for arrow markers painted on trees.

Windsor Great Park ⌂-4 has miles of well kept parkland, so sensitively landscaped that it takes the occasional surprising find (statues, even a totem pole) to remind you that it's not natural. It's the only real prospect in this part of the county for walks that'll make you feel genuinely exercised. **Virginia Water** SU9768 ⌂-5 is very beautiful, particularly in autumn; and the Long Walk gives glorious perspectives of Windsor Castle. Best access via Valley Gardens or Savill Garden car parks.

Finchampstead Ridges SU8063 ⌂-6 is a steepish chunk of heather and pinewood, not big but with a natural character, good views and sheltered picnic spots; the fine avenue of Wellingtonias just above it is well worth seeing too. To the N, Simons Wood SU8163 is NT woodland, with a walk to Heath Pool and Devil's Highway Roman road, now a track. Not far off, the much broader stretches of pinewoods around **Caesar's Camp** SU8665 ⌂-7 between Crowthorne SU8464 and Bracknell SU8769 offer much longer but less varied walks, with many tracks inc some based on Roman roads; parking off the A3095/B3430 – the best start is the well organised and informative Look Out (see Bracknell entry, above).

W of Reading the countryside opens up. Around **Streatley** SU5980 ⌂-8 walks along the Thames contrast with more wind-blown tracks up on the downs. Just W of Streatley itself, **Streatley Hill** NT car park SU5880 ⌂-9 gives access to NT downland for fine views over the Thames valley. The long-distance, downs-top Ridgeway Path, one of the oldest tracks in England, follows surfaced farm roads in places hereabouts, but takes in some quiet countryside. More dramatic is **Inkpen Beacon** SU3562 ⌂-10 and the high escarpment between here and Walbury Hill SU3761, reached from a minor road S of Inkpen SU3564 (where the Swan is handy for lunch). The gibbet on top of the hill is a macabre relic from highwayman days. Immediately S lie some lovely rolling downlands laced with gentle and mostly well marked tracks, field paths and woodland paths overlapping into Hants and Wilts. Other paths tap quickly into sections of the Ridgeway, with good views from Aldworth SU5579 and West Ilsley SU4782 (both have decent pubs).

Thatcham Moor SU5166 ⌂-11 is, surprisingly, the largest area of inland freshwater reed beds in England; lots of birds (some rare), moths, and marshland and aquatic plants. Car park S of the A4.

The **Kennet & Avon Canal** ⌂-12 has been well restored in the last few years, and is now very pleasant to stroll or cycle along, from Thatcham SU5167, Aldermaston Wharf SU6067, Hungerford SU3368, Kintbury SU3866, Marsh Benham SU4267 or Woolhampton SU5767 (the Dundas Arms at Kintbury and Water Rat at Marsh Benham have reasonable food in civilised surroundings; the Rowbarge at Woolhampton is more of a family place). The railway makes a useful method of return – after a walk along the canal from Hungerford to Kintbury, for example.

Where to eat

Binfield SU8571 STAG & HOUNDS Little low-beamed rooms with log fires, interesting furnishings and pictures, and some fine sporting prints; a bustling atmosphere, real ales, decent wines, daily papers, and lots of good modern daily specials – plenty of fish and vegetarian dishes, too. £19|£6.75.

Bray SU9079 FISH (01628) 78111 Relaxed dining pub with 2 stylish rooms and a no smoking conservatory, candles and fresh flowers; friendly service, real ales and New World wines, particularly fine fish dishes and other adventurous food, and lovely puddings; cl pm Sun; children over 12 in evening. £25|£9.

Cookham SU8884 ALFONSO'S 19–21 Station Hill Parade (01628) 525775 Friendly, family-run restaurant with good, reasonably priced food inc

Mediterranean flavours and fish dishes, and quite a few Spanish wines; cl am Sat, Sun, 2 wks Aug and bank hols; disabled access. **£19.50|£7.50**.

Marsh Benham SU4267 Water Rat (01635) 582017 Comfortable, thatched pub-restaurant attractively decorated with 'Wind in the Willows' murals; interesting home-made food in the stylish bar, friendly staff, well kept real ales, and riverside gardens with children's play equipment; disabled access. **£24|£6.50**.

Peasemore SU4577 Fox & Hounds (01635) 248252 Tucked-away pub with a relaxed atmosphere, hunting prints and fox masks; decent home-made food, real ales, and a wide range of wines; cl Mon. **£10.50|£2.75**.

Remenham SU7683 Little Angel (01491) 574165 Cosy little restaurant with good seafood, a splendid range of wines by glass, and helpful service; also bar food in the old low-beamed and panelled bar; floodlit terrace. **£30|£6**.

Shinfield SU7368 L'Ortolan Church Lane (01189) 883783 Exceptional and innovative French cooking in a Victorian rectory with plant-filled conservatory extensions; delicious puddings, fine cheeseboard, and excellent wine list; cl pm Sun, Mon, 1st wk Jan. **£32.84**.

West Ilsley SU4782 Harrow (01635) 281260 Popular, white-tiled village inn overlooking the duck pond and green; good bar food (you can take the pies home, too), no smoking dining area, and real ales; notable children's play area with lots of animals; no food winter pm Sun; disabled access. **£22|£6.20**.

Special thanks to Joan Olivier, Heather Rhys, Jenny and Michael Back, Paul Winks, B and K Hypher.

BERKSHIRE CALENDAR

Some of these dates were provisional as we went to press, please check information with the telephone numbers provided.

JANUARY

3 **Savernake Forest** Icicle Hot-air Balloon Meet – *till Sun 4* (01672) 562277

26 **Bracknell** Berkshire Dance Festival at the Wilde Theatre – *till Sat 31* (01344) 427272

FEBRUARY

21 **Reading** Maidenhead and District Dog Show at Rivermead Leisure Complex (01734) 543939

MARCH

21 **Burchetts Green** Lambing Weekend at Berkshire College of Agriculture – *till Sun 22* (01628) 824444

APRIL

10 **Lambourn** Lambourn Racing Stables Open Day (01488) 71347

26 **Taplow** Horse Show (01628) 868196

MAY

1 **Reading** Real Ale Festival at King's Meadow – *till Sun 3* (01734) 390373

2 **Newbury** Steam Funtasia at the Showground – *till Mon 4* (01663) 732750; **Wokingham** Festival Week – *till Sat 9*: May fayre in the town centre on *Mon 4* with Green Man, Sun God, maypole dancing (01344) 423147

6 **Windsor** Frogmore Gardens and Mausoleum Open Day – *till Thurs 7* (01483) 211535

BERKSHIRE CALENDAR

MAY cont

9   **Newbury** Spring Festival – *till Sat 23* (01635) 32421

13 **Windsor** Royal Horse Show at Windsor Home Park – *till Sun 17* (01753) 860222

16 **Reading** Children's Festival: lots of free events – *till Sun 31* (01734) 390373

17 **Burchetts Green** Country Fair and Open Day at Berkshire College of Agriculture (01628) 824444

21 **Windsor** International Three-day Event at Windsor Great Park – *till Sun 24* (01753) 860222

25 **Sandhurst** Donkey Derby at Memorial Hall (01252) 879060

29 **Reading** Caversham Folk Festival: free event – *till Sun 31* (01734) 390373

30 **Burchetts Green** Open Day and Horse Show at Berkshire College of Agriculture (01628) 824444

JUNE

6   **Old Windsor** Carnival (01753) 862328

7   **Newbury** Summer Fair at Watermill Theatre (01635) 46044

8   **Windsor** Garter Ceremony at St George's Chapel after procession from Windsor Castle (apply by *1 Jan* for limited tickets to the Superintendent, Windsor Castle, SL4 1NJ)

13 **Woodley** Carnival (01734) 344117

16 **Ascot** Royal Ascot at the Racecourse – *till Fri 19* (01344) 22211

26 **Bracknell** Music Festival – *till Sun 28* (01344) 427272

27 **Chieveley** Garden and Leisure Show at Newbury Showground – *till Sun 28* (01635) 247111; **Hurst** Country Fayre and Horse Show – *till Sun 28* (01734) 793910; **Reading** Waterfest: free event (01734) 390373

JULY

3   **Bracknell** Festival at the Wilde Theatre – *till Sun 5* (01344) 427272

11 **Sandhurst** Royal Military Academy Open Days – *till Sun 12* (01276) 412273

16 **Reading** Real Ale and Jazz Festival – *till Sat 18* (01734) 883118

20 **Sunbury–Abingdon** Swan Upping on the River Thames: colourful 13th-c ceremony of swan-marking by Swan Masters and their assistants – *till Fri 24* (01628) 523030

25 **Ascot** Diamond Day at the Racecourse (01344) 22211

26 **Windsor** International Polo Tournament at Windsor Smiths Lawn (01753) 860633

AUGUST

1   **Pangbourne** River Thames Flower and Garden Show at Beale Park – *till Sun 2* (01283) 820548

8   **Knowl Hill** Steam Fair – *till Sun 9* (01628) 823393

15 **Basildon** Jazz Concert and Fireworks at Basildon Park (01494) 522234

28 **Reading** Rock Festival – *till Sun 30* (01734) 390373

30 **Spencers Wood** Swallowfield Horticultural Show – *till Mon 31* (01734) 883575

31 **Bray Wick** Littlewick Show (01628) 30622

SEPTEMBER

6   **Spencers Wood** Wokingham and Reading Agricultural Show (0118) 973 2232

12 **Windsor** National Horse-driving Championships – *till Sun 13* (01926) 815206

BERKSHIRE CALENDAR

SEPTEMBER cont

19 **Chieveley** County Show at Newbury Showground – *till Sun 20* (01635) 247111

26 **Ascot** Festival at the Racecourse: attractions and entertainments for the family – *till Sun 27* (01344) 22211; **White Waltham** Royal East Berkshire Ploughing Match and Show at Shottesbrooke Farm (01628) 822559

27 **Burchetts Green** Shrub Sunday at Berkshire College of Agriculture (01628) 824444

OCTOBER

4 **Wokingham** Victorian Day: arts, crafts and entertainments at the Holme Grange Craft Village (01734) 776753

NOVEMBER

7 **Reading** Fireworks at King's Meadow (01734) 390358

We welcome reports from readers ...

This *Guide* depends on readers' reports. Do help us if you can – in return, we offer a discount on the next edition to people who've helped us with reports for it. Tell us what you think about places already in it, and anything extra you think we should say about them. And send us your ideas for inclusion in the next edition: places to visit, eat at or stay in, attractive drives or walks, maybe even unusual interesting shops you know of. Use the card in the middle, the report forms at the end, or just write – no stamp needed: *The Good Guide to Britain*, FREEPOST TN1569, Wadhurst, E Sussex TN5 7BR.

BUCKINGHAMSHIRE

Beautiful countryside for walkers, some great houses and gardens, and a few rather special places for younger people; some excellent places to stay in, good eating out.

The Chiltern Hills give the south of the county a special charm: quiet valleys, lovely tucked-away villages with pretty brick and flint houses, and endless possibilities for rewarding strolls and longer walks in lovely surroundings. This scenery is at its best in spring and autumn through to November, when the beechwoods are at their most beautiful. Some of the most appealing stretches of the Thames are in this area – the finest reaches of all are best seen from a boat. The south also has the lion's share of this county's best accommodation (we have chosen places particularly for their surrounding scenery), and there are plenty of good places for meals, from attractive old pubs to grand hotel restaurants.

Outstanding places to visit include two sumptuous Rothschild stately homes, Waddesdon Manor and (re-opened in April 1998 after major works) Ascott at Wing. A favourite with readers is Bletchley Park, developing into a friendly and untouristy showpiece of World War II secret history despite trendier rivals beating it in the lottery money stakes. Other favourites are the Chiltern open-air museum at Chalfont St Giles, the medieval manor house at Chenies, and Claydon House at Middle Claydon. The great gardens of Stowe and Cliveden are memorable. The county also has two of Britain's oldest windmills, at Lacey Green and Pitstone, and a very strikingly placed one at Brill.

It's not so easy to find first-class family outings here, but the Roald Dahl Children's Gallery in Aylesbury and Odds Farm Park at Wooburn Common are both outstanding, and we'd also recommend the Bucks Goat Centre at Stoke Mandeville, the interesting zoo at Weston Underwood, and the Bekonscot model village in Beaconsfield.

Where to stay

Aston Clinton SP8712 Bell London Rd, Aston Clinton, Aylesbury HP22 5HP (01296) 630252 £76, plus special breaks; 20 comfortable rms, some in main building with antiques, some (more modern but spacious) in converted stables around a flower-filled courtyard. Early 17th-c coaching inn with an elegant panelled drawing room, flagstoned smoking room, restaurant with pretty murals and excellent modern French cooking, and formal but kind service; attractive, mature gardens; disabled access.

Aylesbury SP8213 Hartwell House Oxford Rd, Aylesbury HP17 8NL (01296) 747444 £208, plus special breaks; 46 rms, some huge and well equipped, others with four-posters and fine panelling, and 10 secluded suites in separate building with private garden and statues. Elegant, historic, Grade I listed building with Jacobean and Georgian façades, wonderful decorative plasterwork and panelling, fine paintings and antiques, marvellous Gothic central staircase, splendid morning room and library; exceptional service and excellent food; 80 acres of parkland with ruined church, lake and statues, and spa with indoor swimming pool, saunas, gym and so forth, as well as an informal restaurant; croquet; game fishing; children over 8; dogs accepted; good disabled access.

Fawley SU7586 Walnut Tree Fawley, Henley-on-Thames, Oxon RG9 6JE (01491) 638360 £50; 2 rms with showers. Popular dining pub in a lovely spot with the Chilterns all around; attractively furnished bars, and imaginative food and decent wines in the separate restaurant and no smoking conservatory.

Hambleden SU7886 Stag & Huntsman Hambleden, Henley-on-Thames, Oxon RG9 6RP (01491) 571227 *£48.50; 3 good rms. Little country pub surrounded by Chilterns beechwoods; with compact lounge, attractively simple public bar, good food, and pretty garden; cl 25 Dec.

Marlow SU8586 Compleat Angler Marlow Bridge, Marlow SL7 1RG (01628) 484444 £202, plus special breaks; 62 pretty, individually furnished rms overlooking garden or river. Famous Thames-side hotel with a comfortable panelled lounge, balconied bar, spacious beamed restaurant with a marvellous view, imaginative food, and friendly, prompt service; tennis, croquet, coarse fishing and boating; disabled access.

Mursley SP8128 Richmond Lodge Mursley, Milton Keynes MK17 OLE (01296) 720275 *£45; 3 attractive rms, some with own bthrm. Carefully run Edwardian house surrounded by a big neat garden, with tennis and croquet; open fire in the sitting room, lovely breakfasts (super dinner if ordered in advance), and friendly owners; no smoking; cl Christmas/New Year; children over 10.

Taplow SU9185 Cliveden Taplow, Maidenhead SL6 0JF (01628) 668561 £255 room only; 38 luxurious, individual rms with maid unpacking service and a butler's tray. Superb Grade I listed stately home with gracious public rooms, fine paintings, tapestries and armour, and a surprisingly unstuffy atmosphere; lovely views over the magnificent NT Thames-side parkland and formal gardens (open to the public); daily-changing, imaginative food in the 2 no smoking restaurants, very fine wines, friendly breakfasts around a huge table, and impeccable, bright staff; pavilion with swimming pool, gym and so forth, tennis, squash, croquet, riding, coarse fishing and boats for river trips; disabled access.

Winslow SP7627 Bell Market Sq, Winslow, Buckingham MK18 3AB (01296) 714091 £47; 39 rms. Elegant black and white timbered inn with beams and open fires, a plush hotel bar, all-day coffee lounge, decent bar food, good lunchtime carvery in the restaurant, and a pleasant inner courtyard; disabled access.

Wooburn Common SU9187 Chequers Kiln Lane, Wooburn Common HP10 OJQ (01628) 529575 *£87.50, plus special breaks; 17 stripped pine rms in mock-Tudor wing. Popular inn with a cheerful, traditional atmosphere in the cosy, low-beamed bar, standing timbers and alcoves, log fires, good often imaginative food in the busy dining room, and a spacious garden.

Please let us know what you think of places in the *Guide*. Use the report forms at the back of the book or simply send a letter.

To see and do

BUCKINGHAMSHIRE FAMILY ATTRACTION OF THE YEAR

👤! **Aylesbury** SP8213 County Museum (St Mary's Sq, Church St) Most county museums would hardly be of passing interest to children, let alone merit a special journey, but since the opening of its imaginative Roald Dahl Children's Gallery, this well refurbished place has proved so popular that at times they've had to turn people away. The delightfully constructed hands-on displays use Dahl's novels and characters to teach children about insects, light and any number of other topics. Visitors can crawl through the tunnel of Fantastic Mr Fox, discover Willy Wonka's inventions, and even go inside the Giant Peach to find out what things look like under the microscope. Most of the subject matter is essentially quite traditional – the difference is all in the presentation, which without them noticing encourages children to think and use their imagination. Even simple features are given a spin to excite younger visitors – why have an ordinary lift between floors when you can have a Great Glass Elevator? Children over 5 get the most out of it, though you might spot unaccompanied adults sneaking through too. It won't take a big chunk out of the day (an hour is probably all you'll need), but if you're coming from a distance it's worth ringing first to see how busy they are; the gallery only has room for around 85 people at a time, so at peak periods you may have to wait. Note too that on weekdays in term-time they restrict entry to pre-booked school groups until 3 o'clock. The Dahl theme is no gimmick; the author lived in Buckinghamshire most of his life, writing his books in a hut at the end of his garden. The rest of the museum has also been upgraded in recent years (there's a good collection of regional art and a walled garden), but despite its interactive displays isn't likely to appeal to children quite so much. Meals, snacks, shop, good disabled access; cl am Sun and bank hols (and until 3pm wkdys in term-time), and all Mon; (01296) 331441; £1.75 (£1.50 children over 3); the museum's other galleries are free.

👤 **Aylesbury** SP8213 *See separate Family Panel above* for the Roald Dahl Children's Gallery at the County Museum. The Bottle & Glass out on the A418 at Gibraltar is the closest good dining pub.

! **Beaconsfield** SU9490 Bekonscot Model Village 🎫 (Warwick Rd) The oldest model village in the world, with scaled-down churches, castles, zoo and even a racecourse, as well as a gauge-1 model railway. Snacks, shop, disabled access; cl Nov–Feb; (01494) 672919; £3.50. The Greyhound is handy for lunch.

🏠👤🎡 **Bletchley** SP8733 Bletchley Park (turn off the B4034 at Eight Bells pub, then turn right into Wilton Ave) During World War II 12,000 men and women worked in and around this Victorian mansion, cracking German codes. It now has a series of genuine and untouristy wartime exhibitions and displays, warmly praised by contributors. Some of the code-breaking bits are a little technical, but there's plenty more to see, inc a toy collection, landscaped grounds, and a working tank. It's a shame they've had such trouble trying to raise funds to develop the site. Snacks, shop, disabled access; open every other wknd, starting from 10–11 Jan; (01908) 640404; *£3.50. The Crooked Billet (Westbrook End, Newton Longville) has decent food.

! 🦆 **Boarstall** SP6214 Duck Decoy Displays and working demonstrations of one of only three remaining 18th-c working duck decoys. Also woodland walks and a nature trail. Open wknds and bank hols, plus 4–7pm Weds Apr–Sept; (01844) 237488; £2; NT. Brill (see entry below) is the nearest useful

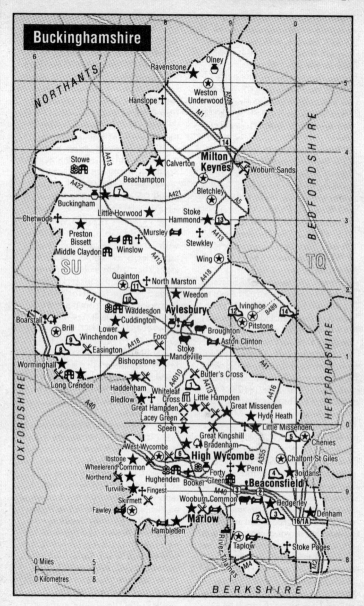

Buckinghamshire

place for lunch.

Booker SU8391 BLUE MAX
COLLECTION (Wycombe Air Park) The
15 or so aircraft here, inc a 1917
Sopwith Camel and 1940 Battle of
Britain Spitfire, are all veterans of
films or TV, from *Indiana Jones* to
Poirot. There are some displays of
film props and memorabilia. Shop; cl
Nov–Mar; (01494) 529432; *£2.75.
The Chequers at nearby Wheeler End
seems a very appropriately chatty sort
of place for lunch.

Brill SP6513 The WINDMILL

(open pm summer Suns) is in a magnificent position right on the edge of the Chilterns, with distant views across Oxford; there's been a mill on this site for over 700 years. In the distinctive and quietly attractive village, the Pheasant (with a view of the windmill) is good for lunch. There's a decent walk along the ridge and down to Boarstall (see entry above).

● **Broughton** SP8413 OAK FARM RARE BREEDS PARK ⊞ (off the A41, E edge of Aylesbury) Friendly little working farm, with animals to feed, walks and nature trails. Open Sun and Weds–Fri Easter–Aug, then wknds only in Sept and Oct; (01296) 415709; *£2. The Chequers in Weston Turville has enjoyable food.

★ ☉ **Buckingham** SP6934 Quite a lot of attractive early 18th-c brick buildings, and much of the nostalgic charm of a once-important town that has been eclipsed by rivals (in this case Aylesbury and Milton Keynes). OLD GAOL MUSEUM (Market Hill) Small local history museum in an extraordinary early Gothic Revival fort, with a good audio-visual show in an intact original cell. Shop; cl am Sun, and all Jan–Mar; (01280) 823020; £1. The thatched Wheatsheaf out at Maids Moreton does good steaks.

↓↑ ⌂ **Chalfont St Giles** SU9993 CHILTERN OPEN-AIR MUSEUM ⊞ (Newland Park, Gorelands Lane) A good few traditional Chilterns buildings that would otherwise have been demolished have found their way here in the last 20 years, painstakingly dismantled and rebuilt again piece by piece. Dotted about the 45 acres are structures as diverse as an Iron Age house, a Victorian farmyard, an Edwardian public convenience and a 1940s prefab, several containing displays on their original use; also a nature trail through the parklands and adventure playground. Usually extra events and activities on Suns and bank hols. Snacks, shop, disabled access (though terrain is quite difficult); open daily exc Mon Apr–Oct, from 11am wknds and bank hols, and 2pm during the

wk; (01494) 872163; *£3.50. MILTON'S COTTAGE (Deanway) The writer brought his family to this timber-framed 16th-c cottage to escape the Plague in 1665, and while here completed *Paradise Lost* and began *Paradise Regained*. Displays of first editions, other rare books and memorabilia, and a charming cottage garden full of plants and flowers mentioned by Milton in his poetry. Meals, shop, disabled access; cl 1–2pm, all Mon (exc bank hols), and Nov–Feb; (01494) 872313; *£2. The Ivy House (London Rd) and White Hart (Three Households, Deanway) have decent food.

⌂ ✿ † **Chenies** TQ0198 MANOR HOUSE ⊞ Rewarding 15th-c house with Tudor rooms, doll collection, tapestries, priest's hole, and 13th-c crypt; the gardens include a physic garden, herbs and a maze. Home-made teas, shop (good for dried flowers and herbs); open pm Weds, Thurs and bank hols Apr–Oct; (01494) 762888; £4.20 house and garden, £2.10 garden only. The neighbouring CHURCH has the rich family monuments of the Bedfords (viewed through a glass panel), 15th-c brasses, and a Norman font. The Red Lion is handy for lunch.

⌂ ☉ ✿ **Fawley** SU7586 FAWLEY COURT Not the typical English stately home it appears to be; though it does boast some fine Wyatt interiors and an elaborate ceiling by Grinling Gibbons, it's owned by a Polish religious group, and has a unique museum dedicated to their homeland, particularly strong on Polish military history. The grounds (landscaped by Capability Brown) run down to the river, and you can stay here, B & B or half and full board. Shop, limited disabled access; open pm Weds, Thurs and Sun Mar–Oct (exc wks of Easter and Whitsun); (01491) 574917; £3. The Walnut Tree has very good food.

⌂ **Forty Green** SU9292 The Royal Standard of England pub stands out as a quite remarkable old building, full of interesting furniture – crowded at weekends, it's well worth a quiet prowl during the week.

 ⊘ 🏵 **High Wycombe** SU8593 This sprawling, suburban-looking town grew around the furniture industry, starting with chair-making using beechwood from the Chilterns. The 18th-c CHAIR MUSEUM (Castle Hill House) has a comprehensive collection of the various styles produced nearby, as well as pretty landscaped gardens. Shop; cl Sun and bank hols; (01494) 421895; free.

🏠 🏵 **Hughenden** SU8695 HUGHENDEN MANOR The home of Benjamin Disraeli – the 'Dizzy' of our **Day Out** title – until his death in 1881, this imposing old house still has many of the former Prime Minister's books and other possessions, as well as related memorabilia, portraits of friends, and formal gardens; he's buried in the grounds. Snacks, shop, some disabled access; cl am, all Mon and Tues (exc bank hols), and Nov–Feb; (01494) 532580; £3.80, NT. The Red Lion at Great Kingshill does good fish lunches.

★ ✗ ✿ 🏠 **Ivinghoe** SP9416 Attractive old village with its 18th-c FORD END WATERMILL (Station Rd) the only remaining working watermill in the county. An unusual feature is the sheep wash, a special pool into which sheep were dropped and cleaned to make shearing easier. Shop; open pm Sun and bank hols May–Sept, with milling (water level permitting) 3–5pm on bank hols and 2nd Sun in May, Jun, July and Sept; £1. The Rose & Crown does fresh bar lunches. The village gives its name to a 760-ft high beacon, with splendid views (especially to the N) and an Iron Age earthwork on top. This enclave is almost encircled by Herts, so see that chapter for nearby attractions.

★ **Jordans** SU9791 Interesting as a quiet, tree-filled village built mainly this century in honour of the first 17th-c Quaker meeting-place here – a simple, evocative building. The nearby Mayflower Barn is built with timbers from the famous ship.

✗ **Lacey Green** SU8299 SMOCK MILL (off the A4010) The oldest surviving smock mill in the country, and indeed the third oldest windmill of any type, built in 1650 at Chesham and moved here in 1821. It's been well restored. Shop; open pm Sun and bank hols May–Sept; (01844) 343560; 70p. The Pink & Lily does decent food – and has kept its little tap room much as Rupert Brooke enjoyed it. Other well restored windmills can be seen at nearby Pitstone (see entry below), Loosley Row SP8100, and Ibstone SU7593, unusual for having 12 sides.

† ★ **Little Missenden** SU9298 The CHURCH of this pretty village has some wall paintings from the 12th c and some pre-Norman traces, and the village itself has charming old timbered and tiled houses. The attractive old Crown does good sandwiches.

★ 🏠 **Long Crendon** SP6908 The cottages in the High St are very pretty, some little changed since the village was a rich wool centre in the 15th c. A particularly lovely timber-framed building is the early 15th-c COURTHOUSE, probably built as a wool store. Open Weds, wknds and bank hols Apr–Sept; £1; NT. There are snacks in the nearby church house, and the Angel is a worthwhile dining pub.

🏠 **Middle Claydon** SP7125 CLAYDON HOUSE The wonderfully over-the-top rococo décor is the prime attraction of this mainly 18th-c house – quite a surprise given the classical simplicity of the exterior. Highlights are the carvings by Luke Lightfoot and the fantastic walls, ceilings and overmantels, though there are also portraits by Lely and Van Dyck, and mementos of Florence Nightingale, a frequent guest. The original owner's tastes were considerably richer than his pockets; though his ambitious plans for the house eventually bankrupted him, his family still live here. Snacks, disabled access to ground floor; open pm Sat–Weds Apr–Oct; (01296) 730349; £3.80; NT. The Seven Stars between Twyford and Calvert is a pleasant place for lunch.

⊘ 🍺 🏵 **Milton Keynes** SP8938 Britain's largest New Town is perhaps also the most successful example of the idea, with roads well laid out to keep traffic moving easily and well away from pedestrians, and a lot of greenery. Locals are proud of the remarkable number of public sculptures dotted around, from the endearing Wounded Elephant to the famous concrete cows in a field on the N side of the H3 road (Monks Way, or A422), nr the A5 junction. There's a very swish shopping centre at Midsummer Boulevard, named for its alignment with the summer solstice. The CITY DISCOVERY CENTRE (Bradwell Abbey, SP8339) tells you all you could need to know about the New Town development (lots of slides, maps and old photographs), in a 16th-c farmhouse in the 17-acre grounds of a former abbey. Also a 14th-c barn and chapel, medieval fishponds, herb gardens and a nature trail. Shop, disabled access; open wknds Apr–Sept; (01908) 227229; free. Not far from here WILLEN LAKESIDE PARK SP8241 (Brickhill St) has 2 lakes – one with water sports, hotel and restaurant, and the other for birdwatching; also a Japanese peace pagoda built by Buddhist monks, turf maze and a nature trail. Tucked around the city are various villagey corners, and the Swan (Broughton Rd in the Old Village) and the canalside Black Horse at Great Linford are both pleasant retreats for lunch.

☞ **Olney** SP8851 Pleasant, stone-built, extended village with a Thursday market and the enthusiastically run COWPER AND NEWTON MUSEUM (Market Pl), in the former home of hymn-writer William Cowper. Several of his personal possessions, manuscripts and poems are on display, along with some belonging to his friend John Newton, curate of Olney and composer of *Amazing Grace*. There's a notable lace-making exhibition, and a restored period summerhouse in the little gardens. Shop; cl 1–2pm, all Sun and Mon, and Christmas–Feb; (01234) 711516; *£2. There's a nice riverside stroll to the Robin Hood at Clifton Reynes; the Bull, HQ for the town's famous Shrove Tuesday

pancake race, is an alternative for lunch, as are the Swan and Two Brewers.

☞ **Pitstone** SP9415 As well as a decent little agricultural museum and an interesting old church, this small village has the oldest WINDMILL in the country, built in 1627. Open pm Sun Jun–Aug; £1. You can hire canal boats for a week or just a day from the wharf (over the B489), and there are pleasant canal walks from there to the Red Lion or White Lion at Marsworth.

☞ **Quainton** SP7521 BUCKS RAILWAY CENTRE ⚐ (Quainton Rd Station) One of the largest collections of engines and rolling stock we know of, with examples from all over the world attractively displayed in a restored country station; also vintage steamtrain rides, workshops, miniature railway, and a small museum. Regular half-day steam driving courses (not cheap at £125, but people come away converted for life). Shop; open Sun and bank hols Easter–Oct, plus Weds Jun–Aug; (01296) 655720; £3.50 (£4.50 bank hols). On the edge of the green is a particularly tall TOWER MILL; you can watch the continuing restoration work. Open am Sun and bank hols; (01296) 655348; donations. Waddesdon (see entry below) is the closest good place for lunch.

☞ **Stoke Mandeville** SP8310 BUCKS GOAT CENTRE ⚐ (Layby Farm, just off the A4010) Goats galore as well as a pig, poultry, sheep, donkeys and pets; you can feed the animals, and they often have kids (of the caprid kind) and other small animals for sale. Many animals are under cover, so fine for a rainy day. Donkey rides most weekends. Also a plant nursery, farm shop (with cheese and fudge made from goats' milk), and specialist mountain bike and golf shops. Meals, snacks, disabled access; cl Mon (exc bank hols); (01296) 612983; £2.50. The Chequers over at Weston Turville does decent lunches.

☞ **Stowe** SP6837 STOWE LANDSCAPE GARDENS Stunning gardens stretching over a staggering 580 acres, first laid out between 1713 and 1725.

Capability Brown was head gardener for 10 years, and the monuments and temples that adorn the grounds are by the likes of James Gibb, Sir John Vanbrugh and William Kent. Several suitably grand events throughout the year, but at any time this is a spectacular place to visit, the scale of its artistry quite staggering. Snacks, shop, disabled access (inc electric-powered cars at no extra charge). Open daily during school hols (inc over Christmas), plus Mon, Weds, Fri and Sun from mid-Apr to the end of Oct; (01280) 822850; £4.20; NT. The house itself (a public school since 1923) is open pm daily (exc Sat) during the Easter and summer hols (not bank hols or Easter wk); you may feel it's outclassed by its surroundings, though it is very elegant from the outside; £2. The Bull & Butcher at Akeley has a good-value buffet lunch (not Sun, when the Wheatsheaf at Maids Moreton would be a good substitute).

🏵 🐟 🏠 **Taplow** SU9185 CLIVEDEN Nearly 400 acres of lovely formal gardens, woodland and parkland overlooking the Thames. The magnificent house used to belong to the Astors and is now a luxury hotel (see **Where to stay** section), although visitors can see 3 of the rooms with their family portraits and elegant furnishings and décor. Meals and snacks (not Mon or Tues), shop, very good disabled access; gardens open daily Mar–Dec, house open only Thurs and Sun Apr–Oct from 3–6pm; (01628) 605069; £4.50, house £1 extra; NT.

🏠 🏵 **Waddesdon** SP7417 WADDESDON MANOR Back to its original grandeur after a 5-year, £10 million restoration, this late 19th-c Renaissance-style château is the most spectacular of the mansions built for Baron Ferdinand de Rothschild. Plenty of rooms to see, each as lavish as the last, and filled with a dazzling array of furnishings, porcelain, portraits and other objects; there's an unrivalled display of Sèvres china. Quite splendid late Victorian formal gardens surround the house, and there's a cast-iron rococo aviary (still in use). The fabled wine cellars have huge vintage bottles, and a collection of labels designed or painted by some of the century's greatest artists. A very satisfying place to visit, but it does get busy; they operate a timed ticket system for the house, so if you arrive too late it's possible you won't get in at all. Good meals and snacks, shop, disabled access; house open Thurs–Sun Apr–Oct, plus bank hols, and Weds in July and Aug; grounds open Weds–Sun Mar-20 Dec; (01296) 651282; £6 for house, £3 grounds (so £9 all-in); NT. No under-5s in house. The Five Arrows does very good lunches (and has some fine Rothschild wines in all price ranges).

★ 🏠 🏵 ☻ ! ✝ ❀ **West Wycombe** SU8394 The whole village was bought by the NT in 1929 when it was threatened with road-widening. It's still beleaguered by traffic, and you risk getting run over as you step back to admire the architecture along the village street – all the sites we mention are just off this street. WEST WYCOMBE PARK 300 acres of beautifully laid out parkland surround this splendid 18th-c Palladian house, unaltered since its completion. The magnificent rooms have a good collection of tapestries, furniture and paintings, and the Italianate painted ceilings are particularly notable. Snacks, shop; disabled access to grounds only; open pm Sun–Thurs Jun–Aug, plus grounds only pm Sun and Weds Apr and May; (01494) 524411; £4, £2.50 grounds only; NT. HELL FIRE CAVES 🏚 Great fun, these spooky old caves were extended in the 1750s by Sir Francis Dashwood to provide work for the unemployed. Legend has it that the Hell Fire Club he founded met in the tunnels for their drinking, whoring and sorcery. Once through the atmospheric Gothic entrance, the tunnels extend for about a third of a mile underground, and are filled with colourful models and tableaux. Snacks, shop; open wknds and bank hols all year, and wkdys Mar–Oct; £3. The interesting CHURCH OF ST LAWRENCE, on the site of an Iron Age fort, was again adapted by

Dashwood, and crowned with a golden ball so big that it too served as a meeting-place for the Hell Fire Club. The view from the top of the tower is impressive, and the church's interior has a number of unusual features. The busy George & Dragon is nice for lunch.

🐦 🏠 ★ **Weston Underwood** SP8650 FLAMINGO GARDENS AND ZOOLOGICAL PARK 🔢 Not just flamingos, but a notable collection of rare and endangered birds from all over the world, inc unusual pink-backed pelicans, vultures, cockatoos and toucans. Also mammals such as bison, llamas and a unique herd of white wallabies. William Cowper wrote many of his poems in the area now patrolled by peacocks and cranes, and extracts appear on several of the statues and urns. The staff are particularly helpful. Shop; open pm wknds and bank hols May–Jun and Sept, daily July and Aug; (01234) 711451; £4. The village is attractive, with Cowpers Oak good-value for lunch.

🏛 **Whiteleaf Cross** SP8203 A large, ancient hill cross dug out of the chalk on the Chilterns escarpment, above which is a Neolithic barrow. The Red Lion below is handy for lunch, and the houses of the surrounding hamlet are quite pretty.

🏠 🐝 † **Wing** SP8822 ASCOTT Another Rothschild mansion, its black and white timbers and jutting gables quite a contrast to the luxuriant opulence of nearby Waddesdon. Once again it's crammed full of treasures, but it feels more like a home and less like a museum; indeed it's still lived in. Ming and K'ang Hsi porcelain, paintings by Hogarth, Rubens and Gainsborough, Dutch art by Hobbema, Cuyp and others, and French and Chippendale furniture. The 260-acre grounds have extensive gardens with rare trees and shrubs, and some intriguing astrological topiary. The house is closed until April for major refurbishment, and at the time of going to press opening times after that were undecided; in the meantime the grounds are open pm Weds and last Sun of month Apr–Aug, and daily (exc Mon) in Sept; (01296) 688242; £3; NT. ALL SAINTS CHURCH has a fine monument to Sir Robert Dormer (died 1552), a 10th-c apse, crypt and nave, and 12th-c font. The Queen's Head has

---

Days Out

Ducks, trains and a Pheasant
Boarstall Duck Decoy; lunch at the Pheasant, Brill; walk from Brill to Muswell Hill; Bucks Railway Centre (Quainton).

Nature managed, manicured – and liberated
Odds Farm Park; Cliveden; picnic at Burnham Beeches; Church Wood Nature Reserve (lunch options: Cliveden for the grand, Blackwood Arms, Littleworth Common, for the merry).

A stroll into hellfire
Chilterns woodland walk from Bradenham to West Wycombe (National Trust village), lunch at George & Dragon here; West Wycombe Park, Hell Fire Caves.

Dizzy in the Chilterns
Hughenden Manor; drive through Chilterns; lunch at Rising Sun, Little Hampden (or picnic); stroll on Coombe Hill.

Some Chilterns history
Chiltern Open-Air Museum and Milton's Cottage, Chalfont St Giles; lunch at Red Lion, Chenies; walk in Chess Valley.

good-value home cooking.

🏠✝ Winslow SP7627 WINSLOW HALL Striking house almost certainly designed by Wren, and unusually surviving without any major structural changes. A modest but friendly place, with a collection of Chinese art. Open pm Weds, Thurs and bank hol wknds July and Aug, or by appointment; (01296) 712323; £5. Nr the market square, KEACH'S MEETING HOUSE is the oldest non-conformist chapel in the county; you'll need to get the key from Wilkinson's the estate agent on Market Sq, or from Mrs Williams, (01296) 712387. The Bell is useful for lunch.

🐾 Wooburn Common SU9387 ODDS FARM PARK Notably friendly farm developed with children in mind; they can go right up to the rare breeds, and join in bottle-feeding the lambs, hand-milking the goats, or collecting the chickens' eggs. Most pens and enclosures have signs written in a way that younger visitors will understand, and quite a bit of thought has gone into the play areas. Special events range from Christmas carols in the barn to a day when teddy bears drop down on parachutes. Meals, snacks, shop, disabled access; open daily Apr–mid-Sept, then Thurs–Sun mid-Sept–Mar (daily in school hols); (01628) 520188; £3.50. The Chequers Hotel does good food.

⛵ Boating on the Thames Marlow Reach is lively and attractive, and a good centre for trips in either direction (see **Berkshire** chapter): Bray Boats, (teel: 01628 37880), have small boats/motor launches ranging from £18 an hour to around £120 a day. If you don't want to picnic on the boat, the Compleat Angler right on the river is a fine place for lunch; on a humbler plane the Two Brewers back over the bridge and the Hare & Hounds out towards Henley are good bets.

✝! Interesting churches can be seen at Chetwode SP6429 which has fine Early English windows, Fingest SU7791 – famous for its huge Norman tower with a twin saddleback roof (the Chequers is nice for lunch), Hanslope SP8046 where the spire is higher than most in the county, Stoke Poges SU9983 where the churchyard inspired Thomas Gray's poem (he's buried here), and which has 17th-c stained heraldic glass in the 16th-c chapel, and at Stewkley SP8525 which has good examples of late Norman work; the village also has 2 decent pubs, and hour-long BALLOON TRIPS over the whole county – tel (01525) 240451, £125 per person. Also worth a look is the church at North Marston SP7722.

★ Attractive villages include Lower Winchendon SP7312, a secluded old place with carefully restored houses and a charming, simple church – the walk over the hill to Upper Winchendon gives interesting views. Bradenham SU8297 is pretty, and surrounded by ancient woodland, and Weedon SP8118 is a lovely little village with 17th- and 18th-c houses. Others, all with decent pubs, are Beachampton SP7737 (with a stream running alongside the main street), Bishopstone SP8010 (pleasant country walks), Bledlow SP7702 (which has a Norman church with early wall paintings), Calverton SP7939, Cuddington SP7311, Denham TQ0386, Great Missenden SP8901, Hambleden SU7886, Haddenham SP7408, Hedgerley SU9686, Hyde Heath SU9399, Ibstone SU7593, Little Hampden SP8503, Little Horwood SP7930, Marlow SU8586, Northend SU7392, Penn SU9193 (interesting church), Preston Bissett SP6529, Ravenstone SP8450, Speen SU8399, Stoke Hammond SP8829, Taplow SU9082, Turville SU7690 (perhaps the most lovely valley of all here) and Worminghall SP6308.

Please let us know what you think of places in the *Guide*. Use the report forms at the back of the book or simply send a letter.

Walks

The well wooded Chilterns offer plenty of easy-going walks, with a good scattering of rural pubs and pretty villages, though sometimes you have to choose your path carefully to avoid the numerous suburban developments. Even so, it's easy to escape into idyllic landscapes which some readers rate above all others for weekend walks. The escarpment where the hills drop sharply down to the plain gives some very distant views, for instance from above Bledlow SP7702 (good pub here). The signposted Ridgeway takes in the most dramatic features, inc **Coombe Hill** SP8506 ⌂-1, the highest point in the Chilterns, with its Boer War Memorial (an excellent place for views – and for kite-flying). Wendover Woods, with some well marked nature trails, are adjacent. The town of Wendover SP8607 (the Red Lion Hotel here is walker-friendly) gives nearby access, or you can follow paths from Ellesborough SP8306, and sneak views of Chequers, the Prime Minister's country retreat (emphatically private); an alternative path in is from Dunsmore SP8605.

Burnham Beeches SU9585 ⌂-2 is a supreme example of a Chilterns beechwood, splendid in spring and autumn colours, and with maybe a glimpse of deer; maps are posted throughout the forest, but it is quite easy to lose one's bearings. The main starting-point is at East Burnham Common car park SU9584, opposite the W end of Beeches Rd at Farnham Common. There are several decent pubs dotted around the forest.

Church Wood SU9787 ⌂-3, on the edge of the immaculate village of Hedgerley SU9686, is a nature reserve managed by the RSPB, with over 80 species of birds in 34 acres. **Hodgemoor Woods** SU9693 ⌂-4 W of Chalfont St Giles is an ancient woodland with 3 colour-coded nature trails.

The **Chess Valley** TQ0098 ⌂-5 shared with Herts is miniature and unspoilt, and handily reached from Chalfont & Latimer station on the Metropolitan Underground line; Chenies, Latimer and, just over the Herts border, Sarratt are the villages to head for.

A visit to the caves and village at **West Wycombe** SU8394 ⌂-6 can be easily combined with a walk into the beechwoods just N; the pretty village of Bradenham SU8297 makes a good objective for longer circular walks.

Other places to start a Chilterns walk from (or finish at – all these have decent pubs) include Bledlow SP7702, Bolter End SU7992, Botley SP9702, Bryants Bottom SU8599, Downley Common SU8495, Fawley SU7586, Fingest SU7791, Frieth SU7990, Great Missenden SP8901 (the George has walks' plans), Hambleden SU7886, Hampden Common SP8401, Hawridge Common SP9505, Ibstone SU7593, Lower Cadsden SP8204, Naphill SU8497, Northend SU7392, Penn Street SU9295, Prestwood SP8700, Skirmett SU7790, Turville SU7690, Wheelerend Common SU8093 (best for shortish ambles) and Whiteleaf SP8104.

There's a good footpath along much of the Thames here (on either this bank or the opposite Berks one). The footbridge over the weir at Hambleden is attractive and the best starting-point, and besides Marlow itself you can also get down to the river from Bourne End SU8985 (where Masons is popular for lunch) and Taplow SU9082 (the Feathers is a useful dining pub here).

Away from the Chilterns, the countryside tends to be rather too flat for walking to be very appealing in its own right, but there are some pleasant strolls passing particular features which add interest. Bucks County Council publish a series of circular walks, free from information centres, or from the County Hall, tel (01296) 382845. These include a 4½-mile route from **Thornborough Bridge** SP7233 ⌂-7 on the A421, taking in a mill, the site of a medieval village, and the Buckingham Arm Canal.

Shabbington Wood SP6210 ⌂-8 nr Oakley has been designated a Site of Special Scientific Interest because of its rich butterfly habitats; a special butterfly trail has been created to help you spot some of the 40-odd species here.

Some pleasant village-to-village walks include those around **Brill** SP6513 ⌂-9 and up nearby Muswell Hill, **Waddesdon** SP7417 ⌂-10 and **Quainton** SP7420 ⌂-11. The last 2 are on the 30-mile North Bucks Way from Chequers Knap above Great Kimble SP8205 to Wolverton SP8140 in Milton Keynes; this includes the prominent viewpoint of Quainton Hill SP7521.

Decent canalside walks are at **Marsworth** SP9214 ⌂-12, where there's an imposing flight of locks, and a family pub at Startops End SP9214; or nr **Stoke Hammond** SP8829 ⌂-13, where a pub is usefully placed between 3 locks.

Ivinghoe Beacon SP9617 ⌂-14 is a protruding finger of the Chilterns, and the finish of the long-distance Ridgeway Path which begins in Wilts. The slopes, too steep for ploughing, comprise woodland, scrub and unspoilt downland; from the beacon itself you look down over 8 counties. The Old Swan at Cheddington SP9217 has the nearest good pub.

Where to eat

For a special meal out, Cliveden, the Bell at Aston Clinton and (for its position) the Compleat Angler at Marlow are a fine choice – see **Where to stay** section above.

Butler's Cross SP8406 RUSSELL ARMS (01296) 622618 Although unremarkable from the outside and with a straightforward bar which has standard pub furnishings, this surprises with its very good fresh fish dishes and other inventive food, excellent puddings, real ales, decent wines, and friendly service; a pleasantly relaxed atmosphere and a small but light and airy dining room; no food pm Sun, Mon. £23.50|£10.

Easington SP6810 MOLE & CHICKEN (01844) 208387 Country dining pub with a very attractively furnished, beamed bar, winter log fires, and a nice mix of people; particularly good food served by neatly dressed young staff, a chatty atmosphere, and a fine range of drinks; cl 25 Dec; disabled access. £22|£5.

Ford SP7709 DINTON HERMIT (01296) 748379 Cosy, tucked away little stone pub with a log fire in the comfortable lounge and traditional public bar with inglenook; good, home-made lunchtime bar food and a more elaborate evening menu, and real ales; cl am Mon, no food 2 wks during July or Aug; disabled access. £23|£6.75.

Great Hampden SP8401 HAMPDEN ARMS (01494) 488255 Comfortable, little 2-room country pub by the cricket green; with a civilised atmosphere, decent choice of freshly cooked food, real ales, and friendly and efficient young licensees; handy for walks; disabled access. £15|£4.95.

Great Kingshill SU8798 RED LION (01494) 711262 Little brick and flint cottage with simple furnishings and remarkably good food from the friendly Spanish landlord; delicious fresh fish, decent house wines; cl Mon. £17.50|£4.50.

Great Missenden SO8901 GEORGE (01494) 862084 Attractive old place originally built as a hospice for the nearby abbey; with beams, alcoves, a big log fire, popular good-value food, quick, cheerful service, and a no smoking restaurant; pretty bedrooms; cl pm Sun, pm 25–26 Dec. £15|£4.75.

Haddenham SP7408 GREEN DRAGON (01844) 291403 Very civilised dining pub with particularly imaginative food in its 2 thoughtfully decorated, high-ceilinged rooms; a French brasserie-type atmosphere, well chosen wines, and real ales; winter log fire and a big sheltered terrace with seats. £25.50|£12.

Little Hampden SP8503 RISING SUN (01494) 488393 Secluded, upmarket dining pub with invariably good and interesting food, decent wines and real ales; attractive terrace, and rewarding walking country nearby; cl pm Sun, Mon. £23|£4.95.

Long Crendon SP6908 ANGEL Bicester Rd (01844) 208268 Friendly 17th-c dining pub, stylishly refurbished, with fresh, well prepared food (especially fish) in the conservatory, real ales, and friendly young staff. £25.30|£9.75.

Marlow SU8586 BURGERS The Causeway (01628) 483389 Long-standing family-run place serving breakfast, morning coffee, lunch and afternoon tea – as well as a spacious shop selling home-baked bread, cakes, pastries, scones, confectionery, and chocolates; take-away sandwiches, too; cl Sun, bank hols, Christmas; disabled access. £4.

Skirmett SU7790 OLD CROWN (01491) 638435 Charming village pub (completely no smoking) with imaginative food in both the bar and popular restaurant; log fires, cosy tap room, real ales, and a pretty garden; cl winter pm Sun, Mon exc bank hols; no children under 10. £25l£5.

West Wycombe SU8394 GEORGE & DRAGON High St (01494) 464414 Striking, partly Tudor inn in this handsome NT village; a cheerful, bustling atmosphere in the rambling main bar, big log fire, popular food inc very good home-made pies, and a large peaceful garden; bedrooms (not Christmas, New Year or Easter). £16.50l£5.

Wheelerend Common SU8093 CHEQUERS (01494) 883070 Pleasant old pub with welcoming licensees and a wide range of good-value bar food; cl pm Sun, Mon; disabled access. £18l£7.30.

Woburn Sands SP9235 SPOONERS 61 High St (01908) 584385 Smart, pretty restaurant with good-value French and English cooking, and a welcoming atmosphere; worthwhile snacks downstairs; cl Sun, Mon, 1 wk Aug, 2 wks Dec; disabled access. £23l£6.25.

Special thanks to Guy Press, Mrs Camilla Keeling, E G Parish.

BUCKINGHAMSHIRE CALENDAR

Some of these dates were provisional as we went to press, please check information with the telephone numbers provided.

FEBRUARY

8 **Milton Keynes** Brass Band Festival at Stantonbury Leisure Centre (01908) 510809

24 **Olney** Pancake Race: since 1455 (01234) 712176

APRIL

3 **Winslow** Jazz Festival at the Bell Hotel – *till Sun 5* (01296) 730575

12 **Quainton** Circus Fun Days at Bucks Railway Centre – *till Mon 13* (01296) 655720

25 **High Wycombe** Arts Festival – *till 31 May* (01494) 528226

MAY

1 **Quainton** May Day Fair (01296) 655348

2 **Chalfont St Giles** Live Craft Show at Chiltern Open-Air Museum – *till Mon 4* (01494) 871117

3 **High Wycombe** Carnival (01494) 522808

4 **Ivinghoe** Milling at Ford End Watermill, Ford End Farm (01582) 600391

10 **Chalfont St Giles** Transport Day at Chiltern Open-Air Museum (01494) 871117; **Ivinghoe** National Mills Day: milling at Ford End Watermill, Ford End Farm (01582) 600391

21 **High Wycombe** Mayor-making at the Guildhall (01494) 461000

25 **Ivinghoe** Milling at Ford End Watermill, Ford End Farm (01582) 600391; **Quainton** Bus Rally at Bucks Railway Centre (01296) 655720

31 **Pitstone** Pitstone Green Farm Museum Open Day (01296) 661997

BUCKINGHAMSHIRE CALENDAR

JUNE

12 **Great Linford** Waterside Festival: free theatre, music events and park entertainments – *till Sun 14* (01908) 608108; **Quainton** Thomas the Tank Engine and Friends at Bucks Railway Centre – *till Sun 14* (01296) 655720

14 **Ivinghoe** Milling at Ford End Watermill, Ford End Farm (01582) 600391; **Pitstone** Pitstone Green Farm Museum Open Day (01296) 661997

20 **Buckinghamshire** Art Weeks: artists' studios open throughout the county – *till July 12* (01628) 526605; **Marlow** Regatta (01491) 575478

28 **Pitstone** Pitstone Green Farm Museum Open Day (01296) 661997

JULY

3 **Milton Keynes** International Festival of Folk Art – *till Sun 5* (01908) 610564

4 **Prestwood** Chiltern Traction Engine Steam Rally – *till Sun 5* (01923) 262845

12 **Ivinghoe** Milling at Ford End Watermill, Ford End Farm (01582) 600391; **Pitstone** Pitstone Green Farm Museum Open Day (01296) 661997

18 **Burnham** Carnival at Burnham Park (01628) 605772

26 **Pitstone** Pitstone Green Farm Museum Open Day (01296) 661997

27 **Buckingham** Family Events and Entertainments in Bourton Park – *till 2 Aug* (01296) 585858

AUGUST

1 **Chalfont St Giles** Experience Medieval England: living history at Chiltern Open-Air Museum – *till Sun 2* (01494) 871117

27 **Weedon** Buckinghamshire County Show (01296) 83734

29 **Winslow** National Mare Show at Addington Equestrian Centre – *till Sun 30* (01296) 713663

30 **Chalfont St Giles** Children's Day at Chiltern Open-Air Museum – *till Mon 31* (01494) 871117; **Pitstone** Pitstone Green Farm Museum Open Day (01296) 661997

31 **Ivinghoe** Milling at Ford End Watermill, Ford End Farm (01582) 600391; **Quainton** Vintage Transport Rally at Bucks Railway Centre (01296) 655720; **Stony Stratford** Town Fair: stalls, Morris dancers, children's events (01908) 563143; **Winslow** Show: parade and horticultural show (01296) 712323

SEPTEMBER

5 **Aylesbury** Charter Day: free street events, parade (01296) 20411; **High Wycombe** Show – *till Sun 6* (01494) 463463

12 **Quainton** Thomas the Tank Engine and Friends at Bucks Railway Centre – *till Sun 13* (01296) 655720

13 **Chalfont St Giles** Farm Fayre at Chiltern Open-Air Museum (01494) 871117; **Ivinghoe** Milling at Ford End Watermill, Ford End Farm (01582) 600391; **Pitstone** Pitstone Green Farm Museum Open Day (01296) 661997

17 **Thame** Agricultural Show (01844) 212737

27 **Pitstone** Pitstone Green Farm Museum Open Day (01296) 661997

BUCKINGHAMSHIRE CALENDAR

OCTOBER

23 **Stoke Mandeville** Beer Festival: two dozen beers and live music – *till Sat 24* (01296) 2997519

NOVEMBER

5 **Downley** Torchlight Procession and Bonfire (01494) 421892

11 **Fenny Stratford** Firing the Poppers: since 1730 in celebration of St Martin, patron saint of Fenny Stratford Church; poppers are quart-size metal vessels filled with gunpowder and fired with a hot rod (01908) 372825

DECEMBER

11 **Chalfont St Giles** Christmas Live Craft Show at Chiltern Open-Air Museum – *till Sun 13* (01494) 871117

CAMBRIDGESHIRE

A couple of excellent family attractions, and Cambridge delights all but the very young; otherwise the county's appeal is largely to older people, quiet and civilised, with enjoyable hotels and inns.

The opening of the imaginative new American Air Museum at Duxford adds quite a bit to a place that's already an outstanding draw – enjoyable even if you're not plane-minded. Linton Zoo is another first-class family attraction. The M11 puts both these – and stately Wimpole Hall – within easy reach of London.

Cambridge itself is also an easy day out from London. Arguably Britain's most attractive ancient university city, it has lots of interesting places to visit, and a grace and charm that makes for delightful short stays. Three of its museums (Fitzwilliam, Archaeology & Anthropology and Whipple) are among the first two dozen outside London to be designated as of national importance by the Heritage Secretary – and they are by no means the only really interesting ones here. The city's at its best during the university terms, as it's the college students who put life and context into the medieval lanes, buildings and gardens. In summer, when it is host instead to foreign students, its popularity with coach tours means that particular places can suddenly overflow with visitors, so perhaps the best time of all is spring or autumn. In winter, like the rest of the county, it can be very chill.

Further afield, the Nene Valley Railway between Wansford and Peterborough, the Peakirk waterfowl garden, the Hamerton wildlife centre and the Sacrewell country centre at Thornhaugh are all enjoyable family destinations. Flag Fen just east of Peterborough is an intriguing window on prehistoric life around here – and on the intricate detective work needed to piece it together. Older people like quiet Ely with its graceful cathedral (and a decent museum), Anglesey Abbey at Lode, and Elton Hall. This is a good county for pottering around villages. Hemingford Grey is one of Britain's most attractive, and several others are very pretty, often with fine churches. In many more, subtle points of interest reward a patient stroller with an eye for detail.

The countryside is a touch monotonous for most people – especially the north's flat silt fens and vast level fields. But there are those who love the misty bleakness in autumn, say, and this area has a lot to offer birdwatchers. Wicken Fen has a much broader appeal, showing what the area was like before intensive agriculture took over; the Prickwillow Drainage Engine Museum gives another interesting slant on these fenland landscapes. To the west, the land's drier and more rolling, with stonebuilt villages more reminiscent of Leicestershire.

Cambridgeshire's Tourist Information Centres are among the best – very helpful with information, maps and trails.

Where to stay

Cambridge TL4658 ARUNDEL HOUSE 53 Chesterton Rd, Cambridge CB4 3AN (01223) 367701 *£59; 105 comfortable rms, 6 without bthrm, some overlooking the river. Carefully preserved terrace of fine early Victorian houses overlooking the River Cam and parkland, and refurbished this year: comfortable, attractive bar with 2 fires, elegant restaurant, large and airy plant-filled conservatory, good imaginative food, and seats in the pleasant garden; cl 25–26 Dec.

Cambridge TL4658 CAMBRIDGE LODGE Huntingdon Rd, Cambridge CB3 ODQ (01223) 352833 £70, plus wknd breaks; 13 rms, most with own bthrm. Mock-Tudor house on the outskirts of the city with open fire in relaxed and comfortable lounge, friendly service, and good freshly prepared food in popular restaurant; cl 25 Dec–2 Jan.

Duxford TL4745 DUXFORD LODGE Ickleton Rd, Duxford, Cambridge CB2 4RU (01223) 836444 £75w; 15 good-sized rms. Carefully run Victorian hotel in an acre of neatly kept gardens, with a restful little lounge, spacious bar, relaxed atmosphere, and enjoyable modern cooking in airy restaurant; cl 25–30 Dec; disabled access.

Ely TL5380 LAMB 2 Lynn Rd, Ely CB7 4EJ (01353) 663574 £80; 32 comfortable rms. Recently refurbished old coaching inn nr cathedral with 2 bars, enjoyable food in attractive restaurant, very friendly staff, and good car parking.

Huntingdon TL2371 OLD BRIDGE 1 High St, Huntingdon PE18 6TQ (01480) 452681 £89.50, plus wknd breaks; 24 excellent rms. Creeper-covered Georgian hotel with prettily decorated lounge, log fire in panelled bar, imaginative British cooking and extensive wine list in the partly no smoking restaurant and more informal lunchtime room (pretty murals), and quick courteous service; riverside gardens.

Little Gransden TL2754 GRANSDEN LODGE FARM Little Gransden, Sandy, Beds SG19 3EB (01767) 677365 *£38; 3 rms. Set on a working farm of 860 acres with pedigree Gelbwieh cattle, this friendly house has a big lounge, dining room, and gardens with fish ponds; no evening meals (plenty of pubs and restaurants locally).

Needingworth TL3472 PIKE & EEL Needingworth, St Ives, Huntingdon PE17 3TW (01480) 463336 £60; 9 rms. Very peaceful riverside spot with spacious lawns and marina, roomy plush bar, big open fire and easy chairs in smaller room, glass-walled restaurant, carvery, real ale, good breakfasts, and friendly staff.

Six Mile Bottom TL5757 SWYNFORD PADDOCKS Six Mile Bottom, Newmarket, Suffolk CB8 0UE (01638) 570234 £122, plus wknd breaks; 15 individually furnished rms with good bthrms. Gabled mansion in neat grounds with carefully furnished panelled rooms, fresh flowers and log fires, relaxed atmosphere, and friendly service; tennis, putting, croquet, and giant chess.

Stilton TL1689 BELL High St, Stilton, Peterborough PE7 3RA (01733) 241066 *£59, plus wknd breaks; 20 rms. Elegant, carefully restored coaching inn with attractive rambling bars, big log fire, generous helpings of good food using the famous cheese (which was first sold from here), and seats in the sheltered cobbled and flagstoned courtyard; limited disabled access.

Wansford TL0799 HAYCOCK Wansford, Peterborough PE8 6JA (01780) 782223 £115, plus special breaks; 50 attractively decorated rms. Old-fashioned golden stone inn with relaxed, comfortable, carefully furnished lounges and pubby bar; pretty lunchtime café, smart restaurant with good food, excellent wines and efficient friendly service; garden with boules, fishing and cricket; disabled access. The little village it dominates is attractive, with a fine bridge over the Nene, and a good antique shop.

To see and do

Cambridge TL4658 Quieter and prettier than Oxford (which the colleges here were founded to escape), the centre here is dominated by ancient and graceful university buildings: you get a real sense of centuries of study. It still has the character of a small old-fashioned market town (with an excellent market in Market Hill – emphatically not a hill even by Fenland standards), almost untouched by the modern world; Cambridge's hi-tech light industry is kept firmly on the outskirts. Between the colleges and university buildings are numerous less imposing but attractive old buildings, often grouped together quite picturesquely – a row of old-fashioned shops perhaps, or a cluster of very varied but harmonious houses. The architecture has a striking diversity, though isn't always shown off at its best, thanks to layers of muck and grime that rather spoil some of the libraries and faculty buildings. Happily, one of the most delightful parts of town, the river and its associated tracts of greenery known collectively as the Backs, never looks less than charming, with its delightful lawns, trees, college gardens, paths snaking in and out of the colleges, and punts gliding past the weeping willows. Don't try to drive around town; there really is no parking, and apart from the pedestrianised centre there's a frustrating tangle of one-way streets. Head for one of the big NCPs or a Park & Ride. If you don't plan to take a car at all, it's worth noting that the bus station's a good deal more central than the train station. For a first-time visit, the Tour Bus is good (about an hour), and it goes along the Backs. Walking tours set off from the Tourist Information Centre (Wheeler St) five times a day in summer. Quite a few shops are that bit different and worth popping into. In term-time, there are countless events; any college noticeboard will show what's on. In particular, the West Rd concert hall has outstanding acoustics.

♠ ❀ COLLEGES The colleges look private, but you can usually wander into the courtyards (not at exam time); several of the dining halls and chapels are worth seeking out. The finest college is Trinity, where the imposing Great Court is open to the public (the porters may intervene if you go into pretty Nevilles Court or New Court without looking as though you belong; the river's just beyond). King's is probably the best known, with its magnificent chapel (see below); pleasant to walk through and over the bridge. Gonville & Caius (pronounced 'keys') is small and slightly snooty, but very pretty. Queens' has a half-timbered courtyard and an eye-catchingly gaudy painted hall, as well as the famous Mathematical Bridge (built without any bolts or fastenings, until curiosity got the better of some engineers who dismantled it and found they couldn't put it back

together in the same way). Peterhouse is the oldest, founded in 1284; the buildings carry their years very gracefully and it has a park. St John's has the very photographed Bridge of Sighs. Jesus, a bit off the main beat, is huge and grandly impressive, and Emmanuel has notable gardens. Two charming smaller colleges are Clare and Trinity Hall, next to each other by the Backs. Tourism isn't exactly welcomed by the dons (they get terribly agitated if you even look at the grass let alone accidentally step on it), and, in an effort to keep the crowds down, some of the colleges charge £1 or slightly more for admission.
✝ KING'S COLLEGE CHAPEL The annual Festival of Nine Lessons and Carols has made the interior and something of the atmosphere familiar to most visitors, but you're still not fully prepared for the grandeur of the fan-vaulted ceiling, or the miraculously

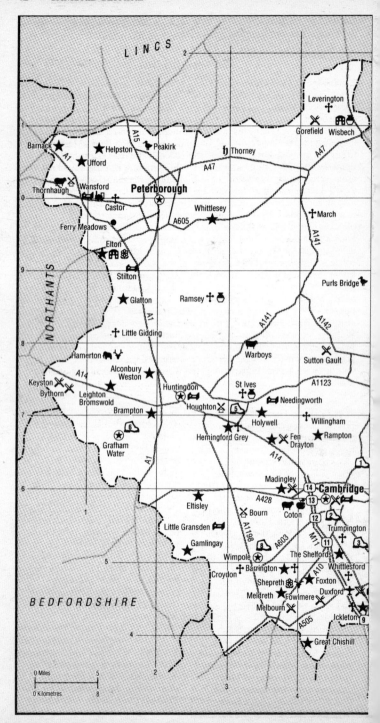

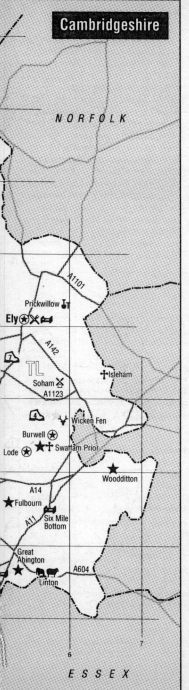

preserved 16th-c stained glass. The overall effect is marred slightly by the unique dark oak screen added by Henry VIII, but the chapel's other famous feature – Rubens's *Adoration of the Magi* – is quite breathtaking. Try to attend choral evensong at 5.30pm Thurs and Fri, or one of the Sun services (10.30am and 3.30pm). Shop, disabled access; cl most of Sun during termtime, and 22 Dec–3 Jan; (01223) 331155; £2.50.

University Botanic Garden (Cory Lodge, Bateman St) Much bigger than when founded in 1762, now covering 40 acres, with some marvellous mature trees, a geographic rock garden, scented garden, water and winter gardens, and many rare plants inc several National Collections. Rarely crowded, and very pleasant to stroll through. You can book guided tours. Snacks, shop, disabled access; cl 25–26 Dec, (01223) 336265; £1.50.

Fitzwilliam Museum (Trumpington St) This is a wonderful place, very grand and impressive, and crammed with more dazzling treasures than you could hope to examine in one visit. Downstairs are Greek, Egyptian, and Roman antiquities, European ceramics, English glass, carvings, and armour, while upstairs paintings include works by Titian, Canaletto and French Impressionists; if you've not been for a couple of years you'll be pleased to hear both galleries are now open all day. Decent café, shop, disabled access; cl Mon (exc bank hols), 24 Dec–1 Jan; (01223) 332900; free.

Most of the town's other museums have a rather academic bent, but are no less rewarding for that: the Sedgwick Museum (Downing St) is the university geology museum, with an outstanding collection of fossils, and rocks from Darwin's journey in HMS *Beagle*. The curator not so long ago proved that iguanadons were put together differently from how scientists had previously thought, and promised to rearrange the bones of his museum's 20ft specimen; theoretically, he claimed, it was currently in agony. Shop, limited disabled access; cl 1–2pm, pm Sat, all day Sun, Christmas–New Year, Easter; (01223) 333456; free. Down the same street is the MUSEUM OF ARCHAEOLOGY & ANTHROPOLOGY (open pm wkdys and am Sat; free), and a Museum of Zoology, where a 70ft whale skeleton hangs above the entrance inside (open pm wkdys; free). The MUSEUM OF CLASSICAL ARCHAEOLOGY on Sidgwick Ave has one of the few surviving collections of casts of Greek and Roman sculpture (cl wknds; free), while the various scientific instruments and apparatus at the WHIPPLE MUSEUM OF SCIENCE (Free School Lane) quickly make you thankful we need no longer rely on sundials and abacuses (open 2–4pm wkdys; free, though £2 charge for special exhibitions).

☕ CAMBRIDGE & COUNTY FOLK MUSEUM (2–3 Castle St) Useful exploration of local life in handsome 16th-c former inn near river. Shop; cl winter Mons; (01223) 355159; £1.

▣ KETTLE'S YARD (Castle St) Lively arts centre with temporary exhibitions in the gallery and permanent displays in the warmly welcoming house, taking in 20th-c paintings and sculptures (interesting St Ives connections), lovely 18th-c furniture and oriental carpets, and collections of shells and stones. Lots of activities and workshops, several designed especially for the blind or hard of hearing. Devotees say the sunlight on winter afternoons illuminates the exhibits to extraordinary effect. Shop, some disabled access; cl am, all day Mon

Days Out

Cambridge
Climb Great St Mary's Tower for the view; King's College Chapel and colleges; lunch in the Eagle, Bene't St; on sunny days punt (or walk) along the Cam to the tearoom at Granchester – otherwise the University Botanic Garden, and Fitzwilliam Museum.

For Flat-Earthers
Prickwillow Drainage Engine Museum; Isleham, Burwell and Swaffham fenland villages and churches; lunch at the Plough & Fleece, Horningsea; Anglesey Abbey at Lode or (20min drive via the A10/A1123) Wicken Fen.

A busy family day
Duxford Airfield/American Air Museum; lunch at the Pear Tree, Hildersham; Linton Zoo.

Country life
Willers Mill and Docwra Manor, Shepreth; stroll through Foxton and Barrington – lunch at the Royal Oak there; Wimpole Hall, Home Farm and/or stroll in the estate; if it's the last Sun of the month you may have time to fit in Bourn windmill.

Around St Ives
Hamerton Wildlife Centre; explore St Ives – lunch at the Lamb or Prince Albert there, or the Old Ferry Boat out at Holywell (or treat yourself at the Old Bridge, Huntingdon); riverside walk from Hemingford Grey to Houghton Mill, or walk, boat or cycle at Grafham Water.

Peterborough at its best
Nene Valley steam train from Wansford; Peterborough cathedral and railway museum or city museum; lunch on Charters; steam back to Wansford, tea at the Haycock there.

(except bank hols); (01233) 352124; free.

✝ ❀ Of many free churches here, it's worth noting ST BENE'TS, one of the city's oldest, the popular HOLY SEPULCHRE or Round Church, and GREAT ST MARY'S with its fine roof and good city views from the tower. Another place with good views is Castle Mound, beyond Bridge Street, which has an indicator to pick out the sights.

🏠 ✍ There are lots of secondhand bookshops worth a look. Heffers children's bookshop is particularly good, and the general bookshops are as fine as you'd expect from this university town. On the first Sat of the month there's a CRAFT FAIR on St John's Green.

Many attractive SNACK PLACES include Clowns (King St, off Sidney St), Roof Garden (top floor of Arts Theatre – side entrance in St Edward's Passage opposite King's), Boards (down a floor), the tiny Little Tea Room (All Saints Green), Copper Kettle (King's Parade), King's Pantry (King's Parade), and Browns (Trumpington St). Decent RIVERSIDE PUBS include the Anchor (Silver St Bridge), Boathouse (Chesterton Rd), Fort St George (Midsummer Common) and Mill (Mill Lane). The best pubs away from the river are the smoke-free Free Press (Prospect Row) and atmospheric Eagle (Bene't St).

🛶 PUNTING is the only way to travel, though if your skills in this department were picked up in Oxford you'll find they do things a little back to front here. You can punt right along the Backs, and even down to Grantchester, a pleasant little village still much as described in Rupert Brooke's poem of the same name, with the civilised Orchard Tea Gardens (lovely in summer – and does other drinks too, inc champagne) and three pubs. Hire punts from Scudamores on Mill Lane or other stations along the water; prices are generally around £5 an hour. Punters found themselves in unexpectedly deep water in 1997 when they were accused of disturbing students revising for their exams in colleges beside the river. Bumps races (several rowing eights start off in a line and have to catch up with the one in front) take place on the river in Feb, Jun and July.

Cyclists will enjoy the towpaths here; nettle-free, and safe if you have children with you.

Other things to see and do

CAMBRIDGESHIRE FAMILY ATTRACTION OF THE YEAR

✝ **Duxford** TL4846 DUXFORD AIRFIELD Very handy from Cambridge, this branch of the Imperial War Museum is home to Europe's best collection of military and civil aircraft, with over 140 flying machines from flimsy-looking biplanes to state-of-the-art Gulf War jets. There's a lot more to the place than just looking at planes, and easily enough to fill most of the day (the site covers more than a mile), but obviously it helps if some of the family have at least a passing interest in the subject. Children particularly enjoy the fun hands-on section, where they can go into the cockpits of some exhibits, and preserved hangars, control towers and operations rooms create something of the atmosphere Duxford must have had when it was a working World War II air base. A realistic hi-tech flight simulator (they prefer the more dramatic name dynamic motion theatre) recreates a Battle of Britain dogfight, and there's also the prototype Concorde, a summer narrow-gauge railway, pleasure flights, and an adventure playground. In August 1997 they opened a new wing, the American Air Museum, in a fantastic building designed by Sir Norman Foster; some of the planes here are suspended from the ceiling, as if in full flight. In summer they have half a dozen or so air shows or flying displays, so you may be lucky enough to see a Spitfire in action; otherwise, all year round you can watch the planes being restored. Not everything is flight-related: there are a few naval and army displays too, with tanks and other vehicles set in well put together battlezone tableaux. Enthusiasts won't find a better collection in the country, and don't worry about the weather – most exhibits are under cover. Meals and snacks (or plenty of space for picnics), shop, disabled access; cl 24–26 Dec; (01223) 835000; £6.40 (children over 5 £3.20); more on air show days. A family ticket covering two adults and three children is £18.

✗ **Bourn** TL3256 The working WINDMILL here is thought to be the oldest trestle post mill in the country. Usually open pm last Sun of month (or the Mon if that Sun is a bank hol wknd) Mar–Oct, but best to check first; (01223) 243830; *£1. The Duke of Wellington has good food.

🐃 🐄 **Coton** TL4054 COTON ORCHARD (Madingley Rd) Busy 60-acre site with garden centre, pick-your-own soft and top fruits, orchard, and small vineyard. Snacks, shop, some disabled access; (01954) 210234; free.

✝ **Duxford** TL4846 *See separate Family Panel above* for DUXFORD AIRFIELD.

🏠 ⚜ **Elton** TL0893 ELTON HALL 🔲 From the back a splendid 'gothick' fantasy, this is a fascinating lived-in house dating back to Tudor times, with lovely furnishings, porcelain and paintings, inc works by 15th-c old masters and Gainsborough and Constable. The library has a prayer book that belonged to Henry VIII (his writing is inside), and the gardens are especially pleasant in summer when the roses are in bloom. Snacks; open pm 24–25 May, then pm Weds Jun–Aug, pm Thurs and Sun July–Aug, and pm Aug bank hol; (01832) 280468; £4, £2 garden. The Black Horse is very handy for lunch.

✝ 👹 🏠 **Ely** TL5380 Busy little market town with good shops and some lovely old buildings; it well repays a leisurely stroll. The main feature is the CATHEDRAL, one of England's most striking, its distinctive towers dominating the skyline for miles; especially good views coming in on the Soham rd. Complete by the late 12th-c, it was restored in a surprisingly sympathetic manner mainly in the mid-19th c. The façade,

covered in blind arcading, is fantastic, but most remarkable perhaps is the Octagonal Tower, over 400 tons suspended in space without any visible means of support; it looks especially atmospheric from inside. The Lady Chapel has the widest medieval vault in the country, and there's a splendid Norman nave, seeming even longer than it really is because it's so narrow. Also not to be missed are a couple of elaborately sculpted medieval doors – and see if you can spot the railwayman's epitaph, with its unique imagery. Evensong every day except Weds, at 5.30pm. Meals, snacks, shop, disabled access; (01353) 667735; £3. Inside the cathedral the STAINED GLASS MUSEUM preserves fine medieval and more modern stained glass rescued from redundant buildings and churches. Good displays on how the windows are made, and a bonus is the unusual view down over the church; cl am Sun, and maybe Nov–Mar, best to check; (01353) 667735; £2.50. The Prince Albert, handy for the cathedral, has a nice garden. The town MUSEUM (Old Gaol, Market St) has displays on Hereward the Wake, who led the Anglo-Saxon resistance to the Norman Conquest from here. Shop; disabled access; cl Mon (exc bank hols); (01353) 666655; £1.80. OLIVER CROMWELL'S HOUSE Next to the unexpectedly grand church of St Mary's, this fine old house was the home of Oliver Cromwell and his family from 1636 until shortly before he became Lord Protector. Period furnished rooms, useful videos (one on the draining of the fens), and information centre in the downstairs front room. Shop; cl winter Suns, 25–26 Dec, 1 Jan; (01353) 662062; £2.30. The Cutter out at Annesdale off the A10 is an attractively placed riverside family pub.

♪ ♣ ❦ **Grafham Water** TL1468 Fishing and sailing (you can hire boats by the day – 01223 235235), cycle hire, nature reserve with birdwatching hides and trails (you'll see a lot more birds in winter), and good disabled access; car parking charge. The Wheatsheaf at West Perry is a popular refreshment stop, and if you're travelling on the B661 from here to Staunton, look out for the roadside stall at the Dillington crossroads – excellent pickled onions and the like, reasonably priced.

❦ ♞ **Hamerton** TL1379 HAMERTON WILDLIFE CENTRE 🔲 A favourite of several of our correspondents (some of whom seem to make monthly visits), an expanding centre providing sanctuary for over 120 different kinds of animal, some extinct in the wild. Enclosures of meerkats, wallabies, marmosets, gibbons and many more, inc the only breeding group of two-toed sloths in the country. Frequent exchanges with other zoos, so the inmates change quite often. Regular visitors recommend bringing wellies in winter, though there are concrete paths. Sensibly priced tearoom (cl winter), shop, disabled access; cl 25 Dec; (01832) 293362; £3.95. The Green Man over at Leighton Bromswold is a useful food stop.

★ † **Hemingford Grey** TL2970 Charming village with a peaceful view of the church over the willow-bordered river (the odd church tower is the result of its spire being lopped off by an 18th-c storm); one stone house among the thatched brick ones is Norman and said to be England's oldest. Nearby Hemingford Abbots is also pretty, and the Axe & Compass here is useful for lunch.

♨ ❀ ♠ **Huntingdon** TL2371 After considerable recent growth the old centre now feels a bit sidetracked, but has one or two fine buildings such as the George, a particularly handsome Georgian coaching inn. Two of Huntingdon's MPs can claim to have run the country for a while, and the CROMWELL MUSEUM (Grammar School Walk) commemorates the

first. The restored Norman building is where the future Lord Protector went to school (as did Pepys), and many of his possessions are on display. Shop; cl 1–2pm, all day Mon, am winter Sun and wkdys, 24–26 Dec; (01480) 425830; free. The Old Bridge is a good civilised place for lunch. A couple of miles W of town HINCHINGBROOKE COUNTRY PARK is good for a walk, a run-about, or a picnic. Guided walks and events start at the visitor centre most wknds, and there are water sports on the lake. Snacks, disabled access; (01480) 451568; free. Neighbouring HINCHINGBROOKE HOUSE (now a school) is where some reckon Cromwell and Charles I met as children; it's usually open bank hols and pm summer Suns (£2); the Olde Mill opposite is a delightfully set family dining pub.

♠ ♞ **Linton** TL5646 ZOOLOGICAL GARDENS (B1052, just off the A604) Well liked by readers, this friendly family-run zoo has a firm emphasis on conservation and breeding. Current residents include giant tortoises, snow leopards, a couple of Grevy's zebras, Sumatran tigers, and tarantula spiders, all housed in enclosures as close to their natural habitats as possible. Family quiz trails in school holidays, play area for smaller children, picnic areas around the prettily landscaped grounds (some under cover), and children's pony rides on summer wknds. Summer meals and snacks, shop, disabled access; cl 25 Dec; (01223) 891308; £4. Not far from here towards Balsham is the CHILFORD HALL VINEYARD, a friendly 18-acre winery with interesting old buildings and tours on the hour; cl Oct–Easter; (01223) 892641; £4.50 (inc tastings and a little souvenir glass). The Pear Tree in Hildersham does decent family food.

♠ ❀ ✕ **Lode** TL5362 ANGLESEY ABBEY All that remains of the original priory is a medieval undercroft, but the handsome 17th-c house has an eclectic collection of furnishings and paintings; not all engage the attention for long, but it's definitely worth pausing at Constable's view of the Thames and the landscapes by Claude. The bookshelves in the library are made from Rennie's Waterloo Bridge. The lovely gardens were laid out in Georgian style from 1926 by the first Lord Fairhaven, and a restored WATERMILL in the grounds still produces flour. Varied events and activities, inc highly regarded open-air theatre and opera. Meals, snacks, shop, some disabled access; house open pm Weds–Sun and bank hols late Mar–mid-Oct, grounds open at 11am and stay open all year exc Jan–7 Feb and mid-Feb–mid-Mar (and are also open Mon and Tues most of July and Aug). Shop, restaurant and plant centre; (01223) 811200; £5.60 (£6.60 Sun and bank hols), £3.30 grounds only; NT. The Red Lion at attractive Swaffham Prior does decent fresh food.

✝ **March** TL4197 Pleasant country town, market day Weds; a good base for exploring the Fens. St Wendreda's CHURCH with its wonderful angel roof was described by Betjeman as being 'worth cycling 40 miles in a headwind to see'. The Acre (Acre Rd) has good home cooking.

❧ **Peakirk** TF1606 PEAKIRK WATERFOWL GARDENS Most of the birds here were reared in captivity and can be fed by hand – always fun; they sell corn in the gatehouse but the birds seem to prefer bread, so take some along. The gardens have over 100 different species of waterfowl inc rare and unusual breeds, all in a lovely setting; a good outing even if you're not exactly a twitcher, fascinating if you are. Snacks, shop, disabled access; (01733) 252271; £3.50. The Ruddy Duck is popular for lunch.

✝☕♿🎦 **Peterborough** TL1999 The town has preserved much of its long history and fine old buildings, though it expanded hugely in the mid-1970s and is now a thriving industrial centre (with a good pedestrianised shopping area). The CATHEDRAL is one of the most dramatic in the country, its extraordinary west front a medieval masterpiece, with a trio of huge arches. Despite the damage inflicted

by Cromwell (he is said to have looked on approvingly as prayer books were torn up and the organ smashed), the richly Romanesque interior has preserved its original fabric to a remarkable degree; especially worth a look are the elaborately vaulted retrochoir and the fine early 13th-c painted wooden nave – though you'll probably need good light and glasses to see this at its best. Snacks, shop, some disabled access; £2 guided tour. The CITY MUSEUM AND ART GALLERY on Priestgate has some unusual models made by Napoleonic prisoners of war (cl Sun, Mon, Christmas wk, Good Fri; free), and there's a RAILWAY MUSEUM on Oundle Rd (cl wknds Nov–Feb; £2). ST MARGARET'S CHURCH in the suburb of Fletton has some exceptionally fine little Anglo-Saxon sculptures, and just W of the centre LONGTHORPE TOWER is a 13th–14th-c fortified house with rare wall paintings (now only open wknds and bank hols Apr–Oct; £1.10). FLAG FEN (2m E at Fengate) Fascinating and well organised prehistoric site, with excellent Bronze Age museum displaying finds from the ongoing excavations. In summer you should be able to watch archaeologists painstakingly uncovering more secrets, and a recreated Bronze Age farm puts the discoveries in context. Snacks, shop, disabled access; cl 25–26 Dec; (01733) 313414; £3.50. Charters (by Town Bridge) is an enjoyable floating pub/restaurant in a converted barge. The best place for lunch is some miles outside the town – the Haycock, along the A47 at Wansford. 4m W of town, FERRY MEADOWS COUNTRY PARK (off the A605) is useful for children to let off steam; 500 acres with children's play areas, two big lakes with watersports and boat trips, bird reserves, pony and trap rides, miniature railway, two golf courses and pitch and putt.

⬥✝ **Prickwillow** TL5982 PRICKWILLOW DRAINAGE ENGINE MUSEUM The story of water, pumping and fen drainage in the area since the last Ice Age, well displayed. Snacks, shop, disabled access; cl wkdys Nov–Mar; (01353)

688360; £2.

Purls Bridge TL4787 Highly recommended for diehard birdwatchers; there's an RSPB reserve off the B1093 with several hides (one with disabled access) and big mugs of coffee.

Ramsey TL2885 ABBEY GATEHOUSE The ruins of an ornate Gothic gatehouse with buttresses and friezes, along with the 13th-c Lady Chapel (all that's left of the abbey itself); cl Nov–Mar; free. Some of the stone from the abbey is thought to have made up the nearby local history MUSEUM (open pm Thurs and Sun Apr–Sept; £1). The Cross Keys at Upwood (where there's a windmill) has good-value food.

St Ives TL3171 Pleasant little town, with graceful church, small local museum, and walks by the curving river. There's an unusual tiny chapel on the old bridge, rising straight out of the water; key from museum. In the town, the Royal Oak does generous food, and the riverside Pike & Eel out at Needingworth is attractively placed for lunch.

Shepreth TL3947 WILLERS MILL WILDLIFE PARK Genuine little wildlife rescue centre with all sorts of unwanted or injured animals and birds. There's a monkey house, and fish farm where the koi will feed from your hand. The entrance isn't that well signed, so keep an eye out. Snacks (in elevated treetop café), shop, disabled access; cl 25 Dec; (01763) 262226; £4. Worth a visit nearby are the tranquil gardens of DOCWRA MANOR, at their best Apr–Jun but always with a variety of unusual plants grown and for sale. The highlight is perhaps the lovely intimate walled garden. Disabled access; open Mon, Weds and Fri, plus pm 1st Sun of month, or by appointment; (01763) 261557; *£2. The Plough is useful for lunch.

Thorney TF2804 The site rises from the flatlands like an island – which it was, when this was all half-submerged marsh. Much older than most villages in the area, it has a Norman-modified Saxon church on its green, and some interesting yellow-brick workers' houses put up by the Duke of Bedford. The friendly HERITAGE CENTRE has good displays, and organises tours of the village and abbey. Shop, some disabled access; open pm wknds Apr–Oct, or by appointment; (01733) 270908; the heritage centre is free, tours are £1. The Rose & Crown does freshly made food.

Thornhaugh TF0600 SACREWELL FARM AND COUNTRY CENTRE (off the A47) Based around an old working watermill, demonstrations and displays of rural crafts, tools and machinery, as well as gardens, maze and nature trails, lots of animals, and pick-your-own fruit in season. Pleasantly simple and undeveloped, this is a friendly place, well liked by visitors, and very organised as far as children are concerned. Snacks, shop, disabled access; (01780) 782254; *£4. Wansford (see entry below) is very handy for lunch.

Wansford TL0799 NENE VALLEY RAILWAY 15-mile round trip on steam trains through delightful countryside to Peterborough. Also a fine collection of steam locomotives and rolling stock, and small museum. The railway is a favourite with film-makers. Meals, snacks, shop, disabled access; best to phone for train times, (01780) 784444; £2.50 site admission (refundable against train fare), £7.50 for the train. It's easy to extend this into an all-day trip by breaking your journey at one of the country parks alongside stations en route, or by taking a stroll around Peterborough (see entry above). At the Wansford end, the Haycock is particularly good for lunch.

Warboys TL3080 GRAYS HONEY FARM (5m NE at Cross Drove, off the A141) Buzzing little place with bees at work in observation hives, an ingenious model railway, aviary, and guinea pig sty. Tearoom, shop (lots of honey-based products), disabled access; cl Sun, Mon (exc bank hols) and Nov–Mar (though shop usually open then); (01354) 693798; £1.

Wicken TL5670 WICKEN FEN (Lode Lane) The last of the undrained fens, and the most interesting scenery in

Cambs. Outstanding for birdwatching (there are hides), the marshy and open fen landscape is one of the oldest nature reserves in the country, originally safeguarded in 1899. Beautiful at all times of year, it's home to a wide variety of plants, birds and other wildlife, and has some good trails, along with the last fenland windpump (moved here from elsewhere). Snacks, shop, disabled access; cl 25 Dec; (01353) 720274; £3.50; NT. The Maid's Head overlooking the village green is a handy dining pub.

🏠 ⚙ 🍺 **Wimpole** TL3351 WIMPOLE HALL (off the A603) One of the most striking mansions in the whole of East Anglia, mainly 18th-c, with an imposing and harmonious Georgian façade, lovely *trompe l'oeil* chapel ceiling, and rooms by James Gibbs and Sir John Soane. Best of all are the 360 acres of parkland, designed by several different notable landscapers inc Capability Brown and Repton; the remains of a medieval village are under the pasture. Good programme of concerts and events in the hall or grounds. Meals, snacks, shop, disabled access; open pm wknds, Tues–Thurs, and bank hols late Mar–early Nov, plus pm Fri in Aug; (01223) 207257; £5.20; NT. Sir John Soane also designed the thatched and timbered buildings of adjacent WIMPOLE HOME FARM when the farm was at the forefront of agricultural innovation. Machinery and tools are displayed in a restored barn, and there are rare farm animals and heavy horse waggon rides. Snacks, shop, disabled access; open as Hall, plus mornings, winter wknds, and Fri in Jun and July; £4; NT. A joint ticket is £7. The surrounding park is open all year. The Queen Adelaide at Croydon is a good-value comfortable dining pub.

🏠 ♨ **Wisbech** TF4609 PECKOVER HOUSE Lovely early 18th-c house with rococo decoration, contemporary art exhibitions, and a 2-acre Victorian garden with kitchen garden and greenhouses – where orange trees are still fruiting after 250 years. Afternoon teas; open Apr–Oct, pm Weds, wknds and bank hols, plus garden only pm Mon and Tues; (01945) 583463; £2.50 (£1.50 on days when garden only). An honest local history MUSEUM on Museum Sq has several early manuscripts, and an exhibition on the slave trade (cl Sun, Mon; free). The North Brink along the River Nene has handsome Georgian houses (among them the Rose and – better for food – Red Lion are both decent pubs).

★ **Other attractive towns and villages** worth stopping at include – Barnack TF0704, which has interesting dotted-about clusters of stonebuilt houses, a windmill, a part-Saxon church, and a fine pub (the Millstone), Barrington TL3949, with its superb village green, pretty timbered houses, interesting church and a good pub, and nearby Foxton TL4148, especially interesting if you've brought *The Common Stream* by Rowland Parker as holiday reading (an intricate account of the village through the ages). Fulbourn TL5156 is an attractive, largely thatched village, with a windmill on the Cambridge rd, a good farm shop with pick-your-own fruit, and a pretty church; a path E takes you to the wooded line of the Fleam Dyke, a miles-long Dark Age defence earthwork. Ickleton TL4943 has a fine church, with Roman columns as bases for its arches, and interestingly carved pews. The churchyard is lovely, and around the church and small green are several beautiful old houses – often a good deal older than their Georgian refacing suggests. The Shelfords TL4652 will reward a slow stroll for those with an eye for architectural detail, and even a quick drive through will show up several delightful timbered houses. Other attractive villages include Brampton TL2170 (family dining pub in converted watermill, and nearby woods to explore), Burwell TL5866, Elton TL0893, Helpston TF1205 (John Clare's village), Meldreth TL3746, and, all with pubs doing decent food, Alconbury Weston TL1776, Eltisley TL2659, Fen Drayton TL3368, Gamlingay

TL2452, Glatton TL1585, Great Abington TL5348, Great Chishill TL4239 (well restored windmill), Holywell TL3370 (the riverside Old Ferry Boat pub here, just reopened after fire repairs, claims great antiquity), Leighton Bromswold TL1175, Madingley TL3960, Rampton TL4268, Swaffham Prior TL5764 (two windmills and two churches), Ufford TF0904 (the surrounding area can be lovely at bluebell time), Whittlesey TL2797 and Woodditton TL6659.

✗ This part of the country is particularly rich in **windmills and watermills**, and apart from the ones already mentioned fine examples can be found at Burwell TL5866, Houghton TL2871 (lovely building in pretty setting; the Three Horseshoes nearby has decent food), and Soham TL5973, which as well as a rather grand church has two surviving mills – you can buy flour ground here.

✝ **Some interesting churches** include those at Burwell TL5866 (handsome, airy building with fine oak roof), Castor TL1298 (two pleasant old thatched pubs here; it's an attractive, recently bypassed village), the quiet little country one at Croydon TL3149, Isleham TL6474 (wonderful roof), Leverington TF4411 (the tower and its spire are noteworthy, as is the 2-storey 14th-c porch), Little Gidding TL1382 (if closed ask at the farmhouse), Trumpington TL4455 (with the second oldest memorial brass in England), Whittlesford TL4748 (a rich interior; the Tickell Arms a little way off is a most unusual pub) and Willingham TL4070 (fine tower and spire, many early wall paintings, and some fine early screens).

Bike riding is a popular activity around here as the ground is so flat, and some safe places to ride with young children are at Ferry Meadows TL1497 and from St Ives TL3171 to Houghton TL2872.

Walks

From Magdalene Bridge right in Cambridge itself there's a pleasant **towpath walk** ⌂-1 out into the meadows – tranquil, with only punts as far as the lock. Beyond that, you could walk as far as Ely, with oarsmen setting an altogether more vigorous tone – though the Ancient Shepherds or Plough at Fen Ditton TL4860 might be a gentler target. Another pleasant stroll out – in the opposite direction – from Cambridge is the walk along the Cam to **Grantchester** TL4455 ⌂-2.

The surrounding countryside has little for walkers. The **Gog Magog Hills** TL4954 ⌂-3 S of Cambridge are worth a passing visit; among tall trees you can trace the main rampart and ditch of Wandlebury Iron Age fort, and there are good views of the city's distant towers and spires. The miles-long ancient embankment known as the **Devil's Ditch** ⌂-4 E of the city lets you fuel a walk with thoughts of whether it was built to fight off the Romans, or some centuries later to protect the riches of East Anglia from Midlands warlords. A good start or finish might be the Kings pub in Reach TL5666, at its N end: expert German cooking. It's not much of a topographical feature, and is crossed by one or two very busy roads.

Further N, the **River Ouse** ⌂-5 between St Ives TL3171 and Hemingford Grey TL2970 is a popular wknd stamping-ground, with Houghton Mill TL2872 as a charming set piece. **Grafham Water** TL1468 ⌂-6, the huge reservoir NW of St Neots, has an attractive waterside path along its northern shore.

Wicken Fen TL5075 ⌂-7 (NT) has a remarkable range of plants and insects, with good nature trails (one for wheelchairs); carefully preserved as an example of what the fens were like before they were turned over to intensive agriculture – see **To see and do** section above.

The **Wimpole Hall** estate TL3351 ⌂-8 welcomes walkers free of charge to the extensive paths and tracks through its farmland and woodland, past a folly and up to a surprisingly elevated ridge path. Start either from the main car park here, or walk over the hill from Great Eversden TL3653.

There are pleasant riverside walks from the Anchor at Sutton Gault TL4279 – see **Where to eat** section below.

Where to eat

Bythorn TL0575 WHITE HART (01832) 710226 Civilised dining pub with friendly welcome, several linked smallish rooms, magazines and cookery books to read, open fire, imaginative food, real ales, and sensible wine list; cl pm Sun, Mon, 26 Dec–1 Jan. £26.50|£6.

Cambridge TL4658 TWENTY TWO Chesterton Rd (01223) 351880 Simple and pretty evening restaurant with good modern cooking, lovely puddings, fine wine list and friendly service; cl Sun, Mon, Christmas–New Year; children over 10. £30.

Duxford TL4745 JOHN BARLEYCORN (01223) 832699 Pretty, early 17th-c thatched country pub, attractively furnished, with quietly chatty bar, good popular food, and courteous service; fine hanging baskets and flower-filled back garden; no children. £24|£8.70.

Ely TL5380 OLD FIRE ENGINE HOUSE 25 St Mary's St (01353) 662582 Former fire engine station next to cathedral with good English cooking, nice puddings, interesting wine list, simple furnishings, and large walled garden; can also have light lunch of soup and pâté; also, an art gallery; cl pm Sun, bank hols, 2 wks from 24 Dec; disabled access. £22.65|£4.

Fen Drayton TL3368 THREE TUNS (01954) 230242 Friendly thatched inn on banks of stream in pretty village, full of Tudor beams and timbers, 2 inglenook fireplaces, good bar food. £18|£7.20.

Fowlmere TL4245 CHEQUERS (01763) 208369 Civilised old coaching inn with smartly dressed waiters, ambitious food in galleried restaurant, good puddings, and excellent wines; log fire in bar, conservatory, and attractive garden; cl 25 Dec; disabled access. £21.

Gorefield TL4279 WOODMANS COTTAGE (01945) 870669 Very cheerfully run, busy village pub with up to 50 puddings as well as a wide choice of other good food; spacious modernised bar, comfortable eating area and separate restaurant; cl pm 25 and 26 Dec; disabled access. £22|£6.

Keyston TL0475 PHEASANT (01832) 710241 Pretty thatched former smithy, full of character, with a nice civilised atmosphere, a no smoking room, delicious imaginative food, a particularly good wine list, real ales, and friendly service; cl pm 25 and 26 Dec; disabled access. £24.50|£8.65.

Madingley TL3960 THREE HORSESHOES (01954) 210221 Smart thatched dining pub with open fire in charming bar, attractive conservatory, imaginative food, well kept real ales, and good wine list (many by the glass); pretty summer garden. £23|£5.

Melbourn TL3844 PINK GERANIUM Station Rd (01763) 260215 Very pretty 16th-c thatched cottage, pink inside and out, with consistently good sophisticated cooking, a cosy and relaxed atmosphere, carefully chosen wines, cottagey garden, and chauffeur service; cookery courses too; cl am Sat, pm Sun, Mon. £35|£7.

Sutton Gault TL4279 ANCHOR (01353) 778537 Popular dining pub with gas lamps and candles in 4 heavily beamed rooms (2 are no smoking), log fires, stripped pine furniture, delicious home-made food, real ales, very good wine list (10 by the glass), and riverbank tables; bedrooms; cl 25–26 Dec; no children under 5 after 8pm. £25|£5.50.

Special thanks to Jenny and Michael Back, Remi Smit, Nicki and Terry Pursey, Heather Martin, Paul S McPherson.

CAMBRIDGESHIRE CALENDAR

Some of these dates were provisional as we went to press, please check information with the telephone numbers provided.

JANUARY

1 **Wansford** "Thomas the Tank Engine" at Nene Valley Railway *also on Sun 4* (01780) 782854

9 **Whittlesey** Straw Bear Festival: folk song, music and dance *on Fri 9*, street procession and evening barn dance *on Sat 10*, straw bear burning on *Sun 11* (01733) 208245

17 **Alwalton** Sheepdog Nursery Trials at the East of England Showground (01733) 234451

FEBRUARY

7 **Lode** Snowdrop Weekend at Anglesey Abbey – *till Sun 8; also on 14, 15, 21 and 22 Feb* (01223) 811200

15 **Peterborough** Community Dance Festival: workshops and evening performance (01733) 263742

21 **Alwalton** Sheepdog Nursery Trials at the East of England Showground (01733) 234451

MARCH

14 **Alwalton** National Shire Horse Show at the East of England Showground - *till Sun 15* (01733) 234451; **Arrington** Lambing Weekend at Wimpole Hall and Home Farm – *till Sun 15* (01223) 207257

21 **Arrington** Lambing Weekend at Wimpole Hall and Home Farm – *till Sun 22* (01223) 207257

APRIL

4 **Thriplow** Daffodil Weekend: gardens open, crafts, rural pursuits – *till Sun 5* (01763) 208132

11 **Alwalton** Ponies (UK) Spring Championships at the East of England Showground (01733) 234451

24 **Alwalton** National Motorhome Show at the the East of England Showground – *till Sun 26* (01733) 234451

MAY

3 **Alwalton** Truckfest at the East of England Showground – *till Mon 4* (01733) 234451

4 **Stilton** Cheese Rolling Contest: wooden replicas are rolled down the high street; stalls and Mayday celebrations (01733) 241206

17 **Alwalton** British Motorcyclists Federation Rally at the East of England Showground (01733) 234451

24 **Waterbeach** Farm Animal Weekend at Farmland Museum and Denny Abbey – *till Mon 25* (01223) 860988

JUNE

6 **Cambridge** Strawberry Fair on Midsummer Common (01223) 463363

7 **Duxford** Air Display at the Airfield (01223) 835000

17 **Cambridge** Midsummer Fair on Midsummer Common – *till Mon 22* (01223) 463363

20 **Peterborough** Cathedral Festival: concerts, music, jazz and dance – *till 4 July* (01733) 343342

23 **Cambridge** Grass Roots 98 at the Cambridge Drama Centre: festival of new writing – *till 18 July* (01223) 322748

CAMBRIDGESHIRE CALENDAR

JULY

1 **Wisbech** Rose Fair: flower festival, jazz, musical entertainments, stalls and cream teas – *till Sat 4* (01945) 587476

4 **Cambridge** Camfest: arts festival at various venues – *till Sat 25* (01223) 359547; **Cambridge** Children's Festival Family Day: free theatre, entertainments and workshops (01223) 457000

5 **Ely** Riverside Gala and Raft Race at Willow Walk (01353) 662062

10 **Ely** Folk Weekend: family dance and music event – *till Sun 12* (01353) 740999

11 **Cambridge** Big Day Out: free family day with lots of events at Parker's Piece (01223) 463363; **Duxford** Air Display at the Airfield – *till Sun 12* (01223) 835000; **Witcham** World Pea Shooting Championships: stalls and games (01353) 778363

17 **Cambridge** Film Festival – *till Sun 26* (01223) 504444

18 **Arrington** Jazz & Blues Fireworks Concerts at Wimpole Hall and Home Farm – *till Sun 19* (01223) 207257

21 **Alwalton** East of England Show at the East of England Showground – *till Thurs 23* 234451

24 **Cambridge** Folk Festival: one of Europe's top acoustic festivals – *till Sun 26* (01223) 357851

28 **Cambridge** Town Bumps Rowing Races – *till Fri 31* (01223) 463363

AUGUST

1 **Alwalton** Faith 98: large gathering of mixed denominations at the East of England Showground – *till Sat 8* (01733) 234451

19 **Alwalton** Ponies (UK) Summer Championships at the East of England Showground – *till Sun 23* (01733) 234451

22 **Arrington** Open Air Concerts at Wimpole Hall and Home Farm – *till Sun 23* (01223) 207257

25 **Peterborough** CAMRA Beer Festival on the river embankment: over 200 real ales – *till Sun 30* (01733) 574331

29 **Ely** and District Horticultural Show at Paradise Sports Hall – *till Sun 30* (01353) 664004

30 **Waterbeach** '40s on the Farm' at Farmland Museum and Denny Abbey – *till Mon 31* (01223) 860988

SEPTEMBER

2 **Alwalton** British Show Pony Society Summer Championship Show at the East of England Showground – *till Sat 5* (01733) 234451

6 **Duxford** Air Show at the Airfield (01223) 835000

12 **Haddenham** Steam Rally inc heavy horse show – *till Sun 13* (01487) 841893

26 **Soham** Pumpkin Fair: pumpkins, sunflowers and large vegetables (01223) 236236

OCTOBER

11 **Alwalton** Rare Breeds Trust Exhibition at the East of England Showground (01733) 234451; **Duxford** Air Display at the Airfield (01223) 835000

NOVEMBER

5 **Cambridge** Fireworks at Midsummer Common (01223) 463363

15 **Ely** County Brass Band Championships (01353) 662062

CHESHIRE

Plenty of very varied interest, also unusual and attractive scenery and villages – and not too touristy; Chester itself is glorious.

Chester has beautifully restored and preserved medieval buildings, a partly Roman city wall, plenty of interesting places to visit from a first-class zoo to an unusual broadcasting museum, and a good deal of life. The city's tourist information department couldn't be more helpful.

From the wide range of other enjoyable places to visit we'd particularly pick out Catalyst in Widnes (the chemicals industry coming to life in a way that enthrals children), romantic Peckforton Castle (fun, too), the Styal industrial heritage site (gearing up for steam again, thanks to a Lottery grant), Jodrell Bank (far more than just radio telescopy now – even a fine arboretum), Tatton Park at Knutsford (stately home, lovely grounds, working historic farm), Lyme Park near Disley, and on a smaller scale the entertaining and friendly Mouldsworth motor museum (not just cars).

Other very rewarding places include the boat museum at Ellesmere Port, Tabley House, a vivid re-creation of medieval monastic life in Runcorn, the botanic gardens at Ness, Britain's most spectacular garden centre at Bridgemere, and a fine clutch of grand houses and grounds (notably Arley Hall near Northwich, Little Moreton Hall at Scholar Green, and Gawsworth Hall).

Cheshire's countryside is well worth exploring, with charming thatched and timbered villages, and a picturesque mix of steep wooded castle-topped sandstone hills and rich sheltered valleys in the west with altogether more rugged Peak District scenery in the east and north-east – small steep stone-walled pastures, shaggy sheep, deep twisty valleys, austere moorland. The central plain of rich farmland is well broken up by woods and hedges, with lush parkland, leafy lanes, a profusion of meres or lakes, and splendid black and white timbered buildings. Throughout the county, an intricate network of canals takes in some of the most interesting countryside, with well kept towpaths.

Away from the wild steep moors of the east, Cheshire's towns, villages and countryside leave a deep impression of well looked after solid comfort, which can give visitors a pleasantly pampered feeling. The modern industrial heartland is largely concentrated within a fairly self-contained and therefore easily avoidable area by the Mersey, with chemical works at Northwich and engineering around Crewe.

Macclesfield and Bollington have made the most of their mill-town past, with good walkways beside their surprisingly handsome industrial buildings set into tortuously steep hillsides.

Where to stay

Bickley Moss SJ5549 CHOLMONDELEY ARMS Bickley Moss, Malpas SY14 8BT (01829) 720300 *£57.50, plus special breaks; 6 rms with showers. Airy converted Victorian schoolhouse close to castle and gardens, with lots of atmosphere, very friendly staff, interesting furnishings, open fire, excellent imaginative bar food, and very good choice of wines; disabled access.

Brereton Green SJ7864 BEARS HEAD Brereton Green, Sandbach CW11 9RS (01477) 535251 £56.50w; 22 comfortable rms in attached modern block, with others in an older part leading off a courtyard. Run by the same family for 50 years, this civilised timber-framed old pub has traditional beamed bars, good food in bar and candlelit restaurant, decent Italian wines, courteous Italian staff, and summer barbecues.

Chester SJ4166 CASTLE HOUSE 23 Castle St, Chester CH1 2DS (01244) 350354 £42, plus special breaks; 5 comfortable rms, 3 with own bthrm. Small, carefully preserved 16th-c guest house in the middle of the city, with helpful, friendly owners, and fine breakfasts.

Cotebrook SJ5765 ALVANLEY ARMS Cotebrook, Tarporley CW6 9DS (01829) 760200 £60; 3 rms. Handsome creeper-covered Georgian inn with pleasant beamed bars (one area is no smoking), big open fire, a chintzy little hall, generous helpings of good food, and a garden with pond and geese.

Fuller's Moor SJ4953 FROGG MANOR Nantwich Rd, Fuller's Moor, Broxton, Tattenhall, Chester CH3 9JH (01829) 782629 £86, plus special breaks; 6 lavishly decorated rms. Enjoyable Georgian manor house full of ornamental frogs and antique furniture, open fires, restful upstairs sitting room, little bar, old-time music, and good English cooking in elegant dining room which leads to conservatory overlooking the gardens; dogs by arrangement.

Higher Burwardsley SJ5256 PHEASANT Higher Burwardsley, Chester CH3 9PF (01829) 770434 £70, plus special breaks; 10 rms in comfortably converted sandstone-built barn. Pretty half-timbered 17th-c inn on top of Peckforton Hills with marvellous views, interesting decorations, a huge fireplace, and a parrot called Sailor in the attractive old-fashioned bar, no smoking conservatory, good food, and friendly staff; lots of walks nearby; disabled access.

Higher Wych SJ4943 MILL HOUSE Higher Wych, Malpas SY14 7JR (01948) 780362 *£36; 2 rms, 1 with shared bthrm. Very welcoming and friendly B & B in former farmhouse on the edge of the Welsh/English border with relaxed atmosphere and good breakfasts – evening meals by arrangement; cl Christmas/New Year.

Hoole SJ4368 HOOLE HALL Warrington Rd, Hoole, Chester CH2 3PD (01244) 350011 £85; 97 rms, some no smoking. Extended and attractively refurbished 18th-c hall with good food in 2 restaurants, and friendly service; good disabled access.

Macclesfield SJ9271 SUTTON HALL Bullocks Lane, Sutton, Macclesfield SK11 0HE (01260) 253211 £90; 10 marvellous rms. Welcoming and secluded historic baronial hall, full of character, stylish rooms with tall black beams, stone fireplaces, suits of armour and so forth, friendly service, and good food; can arrange clayshooting/golf/fishing.

Macclesfield Forest SJ9772 HARDINGLAND FARM Macclesfield Forest, Macclesfield SK11 0ND (01625) 425759 £44; 3 rms. Neatly kept Georgian stone farmhouse set in the Peak National Park with wonderful panoramic views, an elegantly furnished lounge and Regency-style dining room; helpful owners, and delicious food using their own lamb and beef; cl Dec–Feb; no children.

Mobberley SJ7879 LABURNUM COTTAGE Knutsford Rd, Mobberley, Knutsford WA16 7PU (01565) 872464 *£50; 5 pretty rms, 3 with own bthrm. Neatly kept no smoking house set in flower-filled landscaped garden with croquet;

caring, welcoming owners, relaxed atmosphere in comfortable lounge, log fire and books, and generous breakfasts with home-made jams; children by arrangement.

Mollington SJ3870 CRABWALL MANOR Parkgate Rd, Mollington, Chester CH1 6NE (01244) 851666 **£148**, plus wknd breaks; 48 very comfortable, individually decorated rms. Partly castellated historic hotel in landscaped grounds with restful, attractive day rooms, open fires, very good modern British cooking in elegant restaurant, and friendly, professional service; disabled access.

Prestbury SJ9077 WHITE HOUSE The Village, Prestbury, Macclesfield SK10 4HP (01625) 829376 **£72.50w**; 11 individual, stylish and well equipped rms with antiques, in separate brick manor. Exceptionally friendly and pretty restaurant-with-rooms – lots of plants, silk and lace and very good modern British cooking; breakfast is taken in small conservatory lounge or in room; cl 24–26 Dec.

Rowton SJ4564 ROWTON HALL Whitchurch Rd, Rowton, Chester CH3 6AD (01244) 335262 ***£90**, plus wknd breaks; 42 attractive rms. 18th-c country house in 8 acres of award-winning gardens with conservatory lounge, comfortable bar, log fires and a relaxed atmosphere; leisure club with swimming pool, gym, sauna and solarium; may be closed over Christmas; disabled access.

Sandbach SJ7661 OLD HALL Newcastle Rd, Sandbach CW11 0AL (01270) 761221 **£70**, plus wknd breaks; 14 comfortable rms. Fine timbered Jacobean hotel with lots of original panelling and fireplaces, relaxing lounge, resident pianist, friendly welcome, and popular restaurant; disabled access.

Sandiway SJ6071 NUNSMERE HALL Tarporley Rd, Sandiway, Northwich CW8 2ES (01606) 889100 **£140** room only, plus wknd breaks; 32 individually decorated rms. Luxurious lakeside hotel on wooded peninsula with elegantly furnished lounge and library, oak-panelled cocktail bar, very good modern cooking, and a warm welcome from courteous staff; no children under 12 in the restaurant; disabled access.

Tarporley SJ5563 SWAN 50 High St, Tarporley CW6 OAG (01829) 733838 **£62.50**, plus special breaks; 20 rms. Well managed Georgian inn with a good mix of individual tables and chairs in attractive bar, well kept real ales, decent wines, and quite a few malt whiskies; good food from brasserie menu with lighter lunchtime choices, nice breakfasts, and friendly staff; disabled access.

Tilston SJ4651 TILSTON LODGE Tilston, Malpas SY14 7DR (01829) 250223 ***£55**; 3 thoughtfully equipped rms. Warmly friendly and beautifully restored Victorian house in 16 acres of grounds with collection of rare breed farm animals, comfortable and attractive public rooms, open fire in dining room, and good breakfasts; evening meal by arrangement.

Weston SJ7352 WHITE LION Main Rd, Weston, Crewe CW2 5NA (01270) 500303 **£59**; 16 comfortable rms. Pretty 17th-c timbered inn with low beamed rooms (several no smoking areas), a friendly, relaxed atmosphere, well kept real ales, and popular food; own bowling green; cl Christmas.

Wettenhall SJ6261 BOOT & SLIPPER Wettenhall, Winsford CW7 4DN (01270) 528238 **£44**; 5 attractive rms with showers. Cosily refurbished 16th-c coaching inn on small country lane with low beams and open fire in quiet bars, a relaxed, friendly atmosphere, and good breakfasts.

Worleston SJ6556 ROOKERY HALL Worleston, Nantwich CW5 6DQ (01270) 610016 **£95**, plus leisure breaks; 45 individually decorated rms. Fine early 19th-c hotel in 200 acres of lovely parkland with elegant lounges, log fires, intimate panelled restaurant with enjoyable food, and friendly service; disabled access.

To see and do

Chester SJ4166 One of Britain's most rewarding cities, Chester was the site of an important fort in Roman times, and later plentiful river traffic kept it rich. The old centre is ringed by a medieval TOWN WALL that's more complete than any other in Britain. You can walk the whole way round, enjoying marvellous views; there are summer exhibitions in some of the towers along the way. Partly because of the limit set by the wall, the centre of town is an easy place to get around on foot, not too big, and with the main streets pretty much free of cars (there may be a few buses). Guided walks leave the tourist information centre on Town Hall Square at 10.45am every day. If you're driving in, you'll be shunted round to one of the big car parks, and sometimes you may have to queue a while to get a space. Chester's racecourse, the Roodee, is the oldest in the world; it still has fashionable races in May, and a summer Sun meet that's become a lively event for families.

🏠 THE ROWS Giving the city's heart a magnificently Tudor look, these are sets of ornamentally timbered 2-storey shops – with open upper arcaded galleries – radiating from the central Cross. A particular charm of the Rows (parts of which are thought to be at least 700 yrs old) is that, besides being attractive to look at and charming to walk through, they include good shops (and a useful pub, the Boot, on Eastgate Row N). Watergate is one of the finest stretches, with some of Chester's most glorious timber-framed buildings, though more fine buildings jetty out over the pavement in Lower Bridge St (for instance, the late 17th-c

Falcon, once a house used by the Duke of Westminster's ancestors but now a good pub), and in St Werburgh St off Eastgate (built in the 1890s, despite their Elizabethan look). Several of the attractions described below are in the Rows.
✝ CATHEDRAL Not unlike an ordinary church at first glance, this is far more impressive inside, with some marvellous medieval carving in and above the choir stalls, and some fine vaulting. The old sandstone floor (highly regarded by some experts) has recently been replaced to install underfloor heating. Many of the former abbey buildings survived the Reformation, so the precincts still

---

Days Out

Chester and its zoo
Walk round city walls; look at the Rows; lunch at the Old Harkers Arms (Russell St), Francs (Cuppin St) or the Garden House (Rufus Court off Northgate St); Chester Zoo.

Gems of the South Wirral
Ellesmere Port Boat Museum; lunch at the Wheatsheaf, Raby; Ness Gardens; Parkgate, Little Neston and Burton villages, with walk along Dee estuary.

Romance of the Peckforton Hills
Peckforton and Beeston castles; lunch at the Cholmondeley Arms, Cholmondeley or Pheasant, Higher Burwardsley; Cholmondley Castle gardens or walk in Peckforton Hills.

Silk and Shakespeare's sonnets
Paradise Mill and Silk Museum, Macclesfield; lunch at Sutton Hall Hotel, just S; Gawsworth Hall; if you have any energy left, stroll in Teggs Nose Country Park (see **Walks** section below).

include peaceful arcaded flagstoned cloisters, a medieval chapter house, and older Norman parts inc a refectory – brought back into use as a café. There are quiet cobbled Georgian lanes around Abbey Square, behind the cathedral a little way down Northgate.

🏛 ⌂ ROMAN REMAINS These include some broken Roman columns in a neat and peaceful garden running along the town wall by the gate at the bottom of Pepper St. Nearby is the excavated part of a very large Roman amphitheatre – probably big enough to seat nearly 10,000 people. Other relics can pop up in unexpected places: Spud-U-Like and Miss Selfridge show off well preserved sections of hypocaust.

♌ DEWA ROMAN EXPERIENCE (Pierpoint Lane, off Bridge St) Recreation of Chester's Roman heyday, with the sights, sounds and smells of streets, fortresses, and even bathhouses. It starts off as though you're on board a Roman galley, and at the end is an exhibition of Roman, Saxon and medieval relics found on the site. Shop, disabled access; cl 25–26 Dec; (01244) 343407; £3.80.

♿ ♌ GROSVENOR MUSEUM (Grosvenor St) The surprising highlight is an award-winning gallery of huge Roman tombstones. A passage from here leads to a Georgian house with restored Georgian and Victorian rooms, an art gallery, and displays of locally made silver and furniture. Shop; cl am Sun, Good Fri, 24–26 Dec, 1 Jan; (01244) 321616; free. They also have a little outpost, the CHESTER HERITAGE CENTRE, in a former church on Bridge St Row; (01244) 317948; cl am Sun; £1, free if you're a Chester resident.

♿ 🐾 🎙 ON THE AIR 📻 (Bridge St Row) Evocative exhibition of radio equipment and broadcasts from the 1920s through to the 1990s, with reconstructed 1920s living room,

1930s shop, and wartime air raid shelter brought to life with period recordings. Displays of television and other broadcast equipment too – you can play on the cameras. Shop (sells vintage radios), good disabled access; cl Sun and Mon Dec–Apr; (01244) 348468; *£1.95. A candle shop near here usually has craftsmen at work.

🎙 TOY MUSEUM (Lower Bridge St Row) One of the best such collections we've come across, not least because of the hard-to-beat assemblage of Matchbox cars and toys (the company's HQ are here). Lots of Dinky toys and Hornby trains, as well as dolls, teddies, and some vintage amusement machines. Shop (good for dolls house furniture); cl 25–26 Dec; (01244) 346297; *£2.

❋ VIEWPOINTS The tree-shaded Groves look out to the medieval bridge over the River Dee – very photogenic. The bridge at the N end of Northgate gives a close view of the so-called Bridge of Sighs over the canal far below. Several companies operate ½hr boat trips along here.

🏛 CASTLE Though now largely moated by car parks, this has some impressive buildings, both medieval and grand-manner late 18th-c.

Besides places mentioned in the **Where to eat** section below, the trendiest restaurants in town are currently Nico's Brasserie (Dark Row) and Bensons (Lower Bridge St). Watergates (Watergate St) has good food in a lovely medieval crypt; the quaint Albion (Park St) and the Falcon (mentioned above), Old Custom House (Watergate St), Pied Bull (Upper Northgate St) and canalside Telfords Warehouse (Raymond St) are all useful for lunch. The ancient Blue Bell (Northgate St) has been licensed to sell alcohol since 1494.

See separate Family Panel below for Chester Zoo.

Please let us know what you think of places in the *Guide*. Use the report forms at the back of the book or simply send a letter.

Other things to see and do

CHESHIRE FAMILY ATTRACTION OF THE YEAR

🐘 CHESTER ZOO 🏰 (A41, 2m N) The biggest zoo in Britain, and undoubtedly one of the best. Its several thousand animals are housed in spacious near-natural enclosures spread over 80 acres of glorious gardens, with 11 miles of pathways. Over 200 of the species here are classed as rare or endangered, and they put a great deal of effort into successful breeding. Karha the baby elephant became such a draw she was added to the zoo signs on the A41, while they recently bred more than 30 Pacific island land snails from the last surviving example of its kind in the world. They work hard too at upgrading visitor facilities: the entrance was improved last year, and the guide book is exemplary, combining useful information and maps with itineraries to suit visits of various lengths. Everywhere is wheelchair-friendly, and they've recently added tactile maps and Braille guides. It's just as well they're so organised – on the busiest of summer days there can be 25,000 people here. Highlights include Chimpanzee Island (feeding time 2.15pm), the Tropical House, and the penguin pool with underwater viewing panels. The lions are fed between 1.30 and 3pm (not Fri) and the sea lions at 10.30am, 2.30pm and 3.40pm; times may change, so best to check at the information kiosk when you arrive. In summer a waterbus can ferry you between the attractions, or there's an overhead train that zips around the grounds; both cost £1 extra. You can spend the whole day here without feeling drained at the end, and there are lots of summer activities for children. Meals, snacks, shops, good disabled access; cl 25 Dec; (01244) 380280; £8 (£5.50 children 3–15). A family ticket for 2 adults and 3 children is £28.

🏠 🦋 🐚 **Arley** SJ6881 ARLEY HALL & GARDENS The dramatic-looking house is Victorian Jacobean, but the same family have lived on the estate for over 500 years, so there are older furnishings and mementos. Outside, the award-winning grounds include walled, scented, and herb gardens, shrub rose collection, a more informal woodland area, and craft workshops; also an interesting private chapel. Meals, snacks, shop and nursery, disabled access; cl am, all day Mon (exc bank hols), and Oct–Mar; (01565) 777353; £3.30 grounds and gardens, hall £2.30 extra. From the car park, tractor and trailer rides take you to nearby STOCKLEY FARM 🏰, a friendly working dairy farm that's ideal for children. Open pm Weds, Sat, Sun and bank hols Apr–Sept, plus daily exc Mon in Aug; (01565) 777323; £3.

🏰 ❀ **Beeston** SJ5459 BEESTON CASTLE Wonderful views from this ruined 13th-c fortress, perched atop dramatically rising crags, and said to be where Richard III left buried treasure. Good exhibition. Shop; cl 24–26 Dec, 1 Jan; (01829) 260464; £2.50. The pub of the same name, handy for the canal, does good-value generous food.

❀ **Bollington** SJ9377 Some fine old mill buildings and unchanged 19th-c shops and houses; overhead is a great stone canal aqueduct and its later rival the railway viaduct. In summer you can HIRE BIKES along a traffic-free 10-mile stretch of the Middlewood Way bordering the Peak District (£4.80 for 3 hours – £8.50 full day), or canoes on the Macclesfield Canal (wknds in July and Aug, from £6 for 2 hours); booking advisable, (01625) 572681. Just outside, the Cheshire Hunt at Pott Shrigley is a good place for lunch; and the Poachers (Ingersley Rd) or Redway (Kerridge) are good start points for the viewpoint Kerridge Hill (see **Walks** section below) just E of the town.

❀ **Bridgemere** SJ6352 BRIDGEMERE GARDEN WORLD (A51) A garden-lover's paradise – 25 acres of gardens (inc the WI cottage garden), plants, glasshouses, and garden furniture, with more plants in more varieties than anywhere else in Britain (indoor and outdoor), and professional help on hand for any sort of query. Best to visit in the morning before the coach parties arrive. Good meals and snacks, excellent shop, disabled access; cl 25–26 Dec; (01270) 520381; free (exc Garden Kingdom, £1.50).

🌶 🏠 **Burwardsley** SJ5156 CHESHIRE CANDLE WORKSHOPS Lots of improvements to the facilities here in recent years, but still the same popular demonstrations of candle-making and other crafts, and a big craft shop. Meals, snacks, disabled access; cl 25 Dec; (01829) 770401; free. The Pheasant is good for lunch, with great views.

🏠 **Capesthorne** SJ8472 CAPESTHORNE HALL 18th-c family home of the Bromley-Davenports, who have lived on the site since Domesday; fine paintings include Lowry's unusual interpretation of the house's striking exterior, and there's a good collection of Roman and Greek busts and vases. Also lovely Georgian chapel and 60 acres of gardens and woodland. Snacks, shop, disabled access; open pm Weds, Sun and bank hols Mar–Oct; (01625) 861221; £4, £2.25 garden only. The Blacksmiths Arms at Henbury (A537 towards Macclesfield) is a decent family dining pub, if you don't want the longer trip to the Dog over at Peover Heath.

🐾 **Cholmondeley** SJ5351 CHOLMONDELEY CASTLE GARDENS Very pretty to stroll through, with acres of colourful ornamental gardens around elegant castle buildings (not open). Famously, it's pronounced Chumley. Also fine woodland and lakeside walks, llamas and entertaining pygmy goats among the rare breeds, and an ancient private chapel. Snacks, shop and plant centre, mostly disabled access; open pm Sun, Weds, Thurs and bank hols Apr–Sept; (01829) 720383; £2.50. The Cholmondeley Arms is excellent for lunch.

🚂 **Crewe** SJ7055 A 19th-c railway town, smartened up a lot in the last decade or two, with bargains especially china in the market, a pedestrianised centre, colourful Queen's Park and useful foyer restaurant in the Victorian theatre. RAILWAY AGE (Vernon Way) Rapidly developing exhibition with one of the widest ranges of preserved electric and diesel locomotives in the country, along with models, miniature and standard gauge railways and other displays. Snacks, shop, disabled access; cl Nov–mid-Feb; (01270) 212130; £2.50 wkdys, £3.50 wknds (when there's more going on). The Crewe Arms is good value for a comfortable lunch.

🏠 🐾 **Disley** SJ9784 LYME PARK Wonderful country estate outside this pleasant hillside village. The Hall at its centre is a magnificent blend of Elizabethan, Georgian and Regency architecture and styles. Tours are unguided, so you can take your time looking at the intricate carvings, and lovely tapestries, paintings and furniture. There's a particularly grand staircase, and a fine collection of English clocks. Around the house (its exterior was used as Pemberley in the BBC's *Pride and Prejudice*) are 17 acres of Victorian gardens with orangery, sunken Dutch garden and wilderness garden, and a sprawling ancient park with herds of red deer and nature trails. Pleasant walk down to the canal, and the long-distance Gritstone Way (see **Walks** section below) starts here. Snacks, shop, disabled access (with notice); house and gardens open Sat–Weds Apr–Oct (house cl am), with the gardens also open some winter wknds – best to ring for dates; the park is open all year; (01663) 762023; £3.30 per car to go in the park, then £4 house and garden, £2 garden only; NT. The White Horse is a useful food stop (with OAP lunch days).

❄ 🐾 🏠 **Ellesmere Port** SJ4077 BOAT MUSEUM 🚢 (Dockyard Rd) Nicely set in a historic dock complex, a huge floating collection of canal boats, as well as steam engines, a blacksmith's forge, workers' cottages, stables, big indoor exhibitions, and boat trips. Meals,

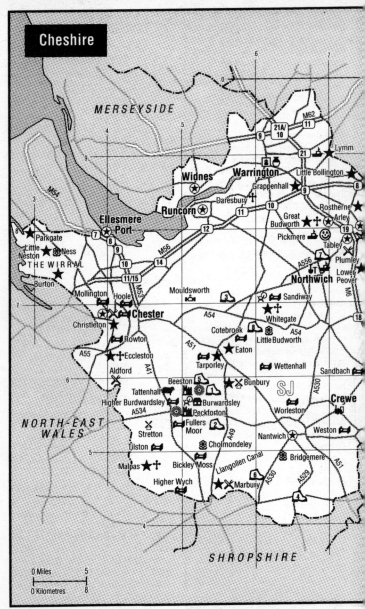

snacks, shop, disabled access; cl winter Thurs and Fri, 24–26 Dec; (0151) 355 5017; £5.20. Parts of the surrounding docks have been redeveloped with craft workshops and the like. The Woodland (Chester Rd) is a useful pub/restaurant (with its own bowling green). On the S edge of town (nr M56 junction 10) CHESHIRE OAKS claims to be Europe's biggest factory outlet shopping village, with familiar brands and good bargains.

🏠 **Gawsworth** SJ8969 GAWSWORTH

theatre has a well chosen range of concerts and plays; good gardens and park too. Snacks, shop; cl am, and all Oct–Mar; (01260) 223456; £3.80. The village has fine houses in parkland, ponds, an interesting church, and an unusual unspoilt farm pub, while the Sutton Hall Hotel over at Sutton Lane Ends is quite handy for lunch.

Jodrell Bank SJ7970 JODRELL BANK SCIENCE CENTRE AND ARBORETUM Plenty to do at this lively place, which has developed quite a lot over the last few years. The centrepiece is still the huge radio telescope, the second largest in the world and as big as the dome of St Paul's, but they also have a fun Science Centre, with hands-on displays and exhibitions examining subjects as diverse as plants, prisms and planets. Outside is an arboretum with 2,500 types of tree, as well as nature trails, picnic spots, and an Environmental Discovery Centre. Regular shows in the Planetarium. Meals, snacks, shop, disabled access; cl wkdys Nov–mid-Mar (exc school hols); (01477) 571339; *£4. The Dog at Peover Heath is quite handy for lunch.

Kettleshulme SJ9970 Dunge Valley Gardens (off the B5470) Colourful gardens in Peak District countryside, especially good for rhododendrons (May/Jun), and roses and unusual perennials. Teas, plant sales, limited disabled access; cl Sept–Mar; (01663) 733787; *£3 wknds and bank hols, *£2.50 wkdys (refundable if £10 spent on plants). The Crag nearby at Wildboarclough does decent food.

Knutsford SJ7578 Despite obvious present-day prosperity and some rather heavy traffic, this has a pleasantly old-world feel, with lots of striking Georgian and other period buildings. It quickly conjures up schoolday memories of reading Mrs Gaskell's *Cranford*, its alias. On the northern edge, TATTON PARK is a busy estate with a handsome neo-classical Georgian mansion at its centre. Magnificent collection of furnishings, porcelain and paintings (inc two Canalettos) in the opulent

HALL Exceptionally pretty timbered manor house dating back to Norman times, the former home of Mary Fitton, possibly the Dark Lady of Shakespeare's sonnets; plenty of fine furniture, stained glass, pictures and sculptures. In summer the open-air state rooms, and restored kitchens and servants' quarters; the more modest Old Hall hints at the long history of the site. The lovely grounds boast an Edwardian rose garden, Italian and Japanese gardens, orangery and fern house, leading to a big country park with mature trees, lakes, signposted walks and deer and waterfowl; you can fish, hire bikes, or take a carriage ride. There's also a Home Farm that works as it did 60 years ago, with vintage machinery and rare breeds of animals; children's playground. You could easily spend most of an undemanding day here (good family activities in summer school hols), or take a carload for a picnic in the park. Meals, snacks, shop, some disabled access; park and gardens open all year (exc winter Mons), rest cl Mon (exc bank hols), Oct wkdays, and all Nov–Mar (exc farm open Sun), mansion also cl am; (01565) 750250; entry to park *£3 per car (free for cyclists and pedestrians), then £2.80 for the mansion or gardens, and £2.50 for the farm or Old Hall. An all-in ticket is £8.50; NT (though as the site is managed by the county council members still have to pay for all exc the mansion and garden). Tabley House (see entry below) is just outside the town, over the M6.

🐝 Little Budworth SJ5965 CHESHIRE HERBS Award-winning specialist herb nursery growing and selling over 200 different varieties from agrimony to yellow melilot. Shop; cl 25 Dec–2 Jan; (01829) 760578; free. The Shrewsbury Arms has good-value food.

🐾✝ Lower Withington SJ8663 WELLTROUGH DRIED FLOWERS (signed off the A34) Well praised by readers, a helpful and friendly dried flowers specialist based on a working dairy farm, with waterfowl and calves for children; free. Further along the A34 at Marton SJ8568 is a simple 14th-c shingle-roofed black and white timbered CHURCH in unpromising surroundings; readers recommend the adjacent CRAFT CENTRE, where a farm shop sells home-made ice-cream.

☕🐝 Macclesfield SJ9273 Away from the modern shopping streets are plenty of fine old buildings associated with the early industrial revolution and the silk industry, and a more ancient core with quaint little cobbled alleys. The SILK MUSEUM on Roe St is the best place to learn about the industry, and has some fine examples of the end product. Snacks, shop, some disabled access; cl am Sun, 24–26 Dec, 1 Jan; Good Fri; *£2.50. Nearby PARADISE MILL is good fun; helpful guides (many of whom are former silk workers) demonstrate the silk production process on the mill's restored handlooms, and room settings give a good idea of 1930s working conditions. Shop, good disabled access; cl am, Mon (exc bank hols), 24–26 Dec, 1 Jan, Good Fri; (01625) 618228; *£2.50. A joint ticket with the Silk Museum is £4.40. The refurbished WEST PARK MUSEUM (Prestbury Rd) has a decent range of decorative arts and some interesting Egyptian antiquities. Shop; cl am, all day Mon, 24–26 Dec, 1 Jan, Good Fri; free. The Sutton Hall Hotel just S is best for lunch, and the moorland pubs mentioned in the **Walks** section below are in fairly easy reach. 3 or 4m W of town, HARE HILL (off the B5087) has acres of lovely parkland with walled garden, pergola and fine spring flowers. Some disabled access; open daily mid-May–June (for rhododendrons and azaleas), then only Weds, Thurs, Sat and Sun until end Oct; £2.50; NT. A footpath leads to Alderley Edge (see the **Walks** section below).

🐦 Mobberley SJ7879 HILLSIDE ORNAMENTAL FOWL 🦆 (Damson Lane) Excellent private collection of wildfowl with rare species such as magpie geese, white-headed stifftail and the Abyssinian black duck, as well as aviaries of softbills, flamingos and other exotic birds. Children should enjoy the penguin pool, and they have a pair of white wallabies. Snacks, shop; open Easter–Oct exc Thurs, (01565) 873282; £3.50. The Bird in Hand and Church Inn are useful for lunch.

🏛 Mouldsworth SJ5171 MOTOR

Museum (Smithy Lane) Splendid changing collection of cars, everything from vintage Bentleys to gleaming Ferraris, with several dozen other vehicles in between. It's a notably friendly place, and you really don't have to be a car fiend to enjoy it – the 1930s art deco building and its grounds are very attractive in themselves, and there's plenty to amuse children, with quizzes, play areas and space to run around. There's also a collection of unusual teapots, many from the 1920s and 30s. Disabled access; open pm Sun and bank hols Mar–Nov, plus pm Weds July and Aug; (01928) 731781; £2.50. The White Lion at Alvanley is a popular nearby dining pub.

✽ **Mow Cop** SJ8557 Right on the Staffs border is a shaggy steep hill with a castellated folly on top, and a rock pinnacle left by former quarrying; rich views over Cheshire (the village just behind, which is in Staffs, is a reminder of the contrast with Cheshire's richness). Worth a look if passing.

✝ ✽ ⬛ **Nantwich** SJ6552 A pedestrian-only centre protects the splendid 14th-c CHURCH, with its exceptional carved choir stalls; look out for the devil forcing open a nun's mouth, and the wife threatening her husband with a ladle. Much of the town, destroyed by a firestorm in 1583, was rebuilt then in intricate black and white timbering, and with countless window-boxes in flower in spring and summer is a fine sight especially around the centre. Quite a few decent antique shops, and the central Lamb Hotel does good snacks and lunches. As most of S Cheshire's roads seem to intersect at the town, traffic can be a problem. Off the A51 about a mile SE, STAPELEY WATER GARDENS ⬛ is the world's largest and best-regarded watergarden centre with display pools, fountains, waterfalls, gardens, coldwater and tropical fish, and a huge heated glasshouse full of over 350 water lilies (at their best Jun–Sept), piranhas, sharks, palms and parrots. Plenty of other gifts (lots for fishermen) as well as plants, and

frequent special events. Meals, snacks, shop, disabled access; (01270) 623868; gardens free, palm house £3.35. FIRS POTTERY (Aston; A530, about 5m towards Whitchurch) Friendly place organising one-day pottery workshops (half-days for children). Booking essential; (01270) 780345; £20 for a day course, inc lunch and tea and coffee (£10 children, during school hols). A good shop sells all sorts of useful pots, and the nearby Bhurtpore does good food.

✽ **Ness** SJ3076 LIVERPOOL UNIVERSITY BOTANIC GARDENS (NESS GARDENS) Extensive collection of specimen trees and shrubs, herbaceous plants, renowned heather, rock, rose and water gardens, with a slide show and other exhibitions; good children's adventure playground, and picnic area. Open till dusk in summer. Meals, snacks, shop, disabled access; cl 25 Dec; (0151) 353 0123; £3.80. Parkgate (see The Wirral below) is handy for lunch.

✖ **Nether Alderley** SJ8476 NETHER ALDERLEY MILL Lovely 15th-c watermill with carefully preserved atmosphere, and restored working waterwheels. The Victorian machinery still grinds flour (water supplies permitting). Open pm Weds, Sun and bank hols Apr–Oct, plus pm Tues, Thurs, Fri and Sat Jun–Sept; (01625) 523012; £1.80; NT.

⬩ ♨ **Northwich** SJ6674 Cheshire is the only British county to produce salt on a large scale, and much of it comes from here. The interesting SALT MUSEUM on London Rd has the industry pretty well covered; microscopes let you see the intricacy of each crystal. Snacks, shop, limited disabled access; cl am wknds, all day Mon (exc bank hols and in Aug), 24–26 Dec; (01606) 41331; £1.75. You can follow the Salt Heritage Trail around some of the other buildings. From the Quay there are cruises down the river. The Smoker at Plumley (A556 E) is a reliable dining pub.

⬛ ✽ **Peckforton** SJ5356 PECKFORTON CASTLE ⬛ It seems bizarre to talk about a medieval Victorian castle, but that's exactly what this is, built in 1840 using authentic medieval plans. It's the only intact medieval-style castle in the country, unique in showing what such a place was like in its prime. Rising majestically from its wooded hilltop, it has all the features you'd expect – forbidding gatehouse, ramparts, and broad battlements – as well as fine views over the Cheshire plain. There may be people in period costume, and readers tell us they have some quite outstanding cobwebs. Snacks, shop; cl 13 Sept–Easter; (01829) 260930; *£2.50. The Beeston Castle at Beeston is handiest for lunch, though there's a good hill walk over to the Pheasant at Higher Burwardsley.

♣ ☺ **Pickmere** SJ6877 has boat hire, lakeside funfair and plenty of open space. The Red Lion is useful for lunch.

🏵 ⛟ 🛶 **Poynton** SJ9283 BROOKSIDE GARDEN CENTRE (Macclesfield Rd) A splendid miniature railway chuffs its way through an authentically detailed circuit in a pretty garden setting; a replica West Country station is packed with railway memorabilia. Parking is not always easy. Meals, snacks, shop, disabled access (not train); railway runs wknds all yr plus Weds Apr–Sept and daily July and Aug; (01625) 872919; train 50p, garden centre free. A mile away at Higher Poynton, Coppice Fruit Farm has PICK-YOUR-OWN.

🏰 ⛟ 🏵 🛶 ✳ **Runcorn** SJ5183 The reason for visiting this New Town would be NORTON PRIORY MUSEUM & GARDENS (Tudor Rd, Manor Park), a lovely 12th-c priory that developed into a Georgian stately home, with exhibitions on medieval monastic life, and demonstrations of tile-making, carving and sculpture. Outside is an enchanting 18th-c walled garden, and beautiful woodland gardens. Snacks, shop, disabled access; cl am, 24–26 Dec, 1 Jan, walled garden cl Nov–Feb; (01928) 569895; £2.90. More centrally, the Sun pm MINIATURE TRAIN RIDES in the park on Stockham Lane are popular with children. There are views from the ruins of HALTON

CASTLE SJ5382 up on its grassy hill.

🐾 **Sandiway** SJ6171 BLAKEMERE CRAFT CENTRE (Chester Rd) Much better than average craft centre based around restored Edwardian stable block, with interesting range of goods in the 18 shops, small plant centre, and good food hall. Wknd craft fairs, meals, snacks, disabled access; cl Mon (exc bank hols); (01606) 883261; free.

🏰 ♣ **Scholar Green** SJ8356 LITTLE MORETON HALL (A34 N) One of Britain's best-preserved half-timbered buildings, its splendid black and white exterior pretty much unchanged since built in 1580, and covered with such a profusion of lines the effect is almost dizzying. The inside, though largely unfurnished, has some interesting features too, especially the wainscoted Long Gallery, Great Hall and chapel. There's a re-creation of a typical 17th-c knot garden. Regular open-air theatre and concerts. Meals, snacks, shop, disabled access to ground floor only; open pm Weds–Sun late Mar–Oct, then pm wknds up to Christmas; (01260) 272018; £3.80; NT. The Brownlow Arms nearby or Rising Sun in Scholar Green itself are popular for lunch. HERITAGE NARROW BOATS at Kent Green have electric narrow boats to hire by the day; cl Nov–Easter; (01782) 785700; £50–£75 wkdys for up to 12 people (£65–£90 wknds) – very satisfying, gliding along in silence.

✳ **Stretton** SJ4553 The working WATERMILL in lovely countryside here still produces corn, powered by two ancient wheels. Shop, some disabled access; cl am, all day Mon, and Oct–Mar (wknds only Apr and Sept); (01606) 41331; £1.75. The Cock o' Barton up on the A534 is quite useful for lunch.

⬇ 🏵 🏠 **Styal** SJ8383 QUARRY BANK MILL AND COUNTRY PARK ▣ One of the best and most extensive places in the country to get to grips with the Industrial Revolution – you can easily spend the best part of a day here. The 18th-c cotton mill that's the centrepiece still produces cloth (you can buy it in the shop), and as well as demonstrations of spinning and weaving has lively exhibitions looking at factory conditions for the millworkers and their bosses. The surrounding village has carefully preserved workers' cottages, chapels and shops; the house where the young pauper apprentices lived vividly illustrates the 12hr working days faced by young children (there are timed tickets in operation here, so it makes sense to see this bit at the start of your visit). Good woodland and riverside walks in the park, lots of events throughout the year. They hope that by Apr the mill will once again be powered by steam (until a Lottery grant it's been powered by water). Meals, snacks, shop, disabled access (recently improved through the park); cl winter Mons; (01625) 527468; all-in ticket £4.70, mill only £3.70, apprentice house only £3.20; NT. The Ship is pleasant for lunch. The PEACOCK FARM SHOP nearby is a notable family-run business, very welcoming, too, thanks to their colourful roadside flower plantings; meat and greengrocery as well as the farm produce, and their pony and donkey are extremely family-friendly.

Tabley SJ7378 TABLEY HOUSE (off the A5033) Probably the finest Palladian house in the NW, with a splendid collection of paintings. Sir John Fleming Leicester (whose family lived here for over 800 years) was the first great collector of British art, and though his plans to turn his home into a National Gallery came to nothing, most of the works he assembled are still here, inc pictures by Turner, Reynolds, Henry Thompson and James Ward. Snacks, shop, very good disabled access (though they prefer notice); open pm Thurs–Sun Apr–Oct; (01565) 750151; £3.50. TABLEY OLD SCHOOL CUCKOO CLOCK COLLECTION A unique collection of cuckoo clocks and other mechanical timepieces from all over the world. At the moment there are 500 rare and beautiful clocks, most of them working, but the number constantly increases as the owners nip off to Europe to track down more. Because

of this (and as it takes time to get them all going) the exhibition is open only by appointment. Shop, disabled access; (01565) 633039; *£3.50. The Smoker at Plumley is good for lunch.

Tattenhall SJ4858 CHESHIRE CHEESE EXPERIENCE (Drumlan Hall Farm) Demonstrations of cheshire cheese-making in purpose-built dairy; which stages of the process you see depends on the time of day you visit, but a museum fills you in on the rest. Shop, disabled access; cl 25 Dec, 2 wks in Jan; no cheese-making Tues or Weds; (01829) 770924; *£1. The adjacent CHESHIRE ICE-CREAM FARM has samples of another flavoursome dairy product, and you can see the cows being milked; cl 2 wks end Jan/Feb; (01829) 770995; free. The Egerton Arms down the A41 at Broxton is a good lunch stop.

Warrington SJ6188 Not an inspiring town for visitors, but its unusually lively MUSEUM & ART GALLERY (Bold St) has decorated skulls and shrunken heads, an Egyptian mummy and a toy-packed nursery, and a number of beetles and other creepy-crawlies. Shop, disabled access; cl Sun and bank hols; free. The Ferry at Fiddlers Ferry down by the Mersey off the A562 at Penketh is prettily placed for lunch.

Widnes SJ5185 Another place that rarely tops visitor itineraries, but well worth a special trip for CATALYST (Mersey Rd), an award-winning centre exploring the chemical industry and how it affects our lives. Put like that it doesn't sound too gripping, but children who enjoy museums where you poke, press and push things will really get a lot out of it. It's all presented in a splendidly enjoyable and entertaining way, with interactive games and displays such as Apples & Maggots, where you battle against maggots, gales and floods to grow a successful crop of apples, or the Game of Health, which involves travelling from the past to the present without falling victim to any deadly diseases. A glass lift whisks you up to a rooftop observatory with splendid views. There's an adjacent waterside park, with wildlife and brightly coloured fishing boats. Meals, snacks, shop, disabled access; cl Mon (exc bank hols), 24–26 Dec, 1 Jan; (0151) 420 1121; £3.95.

★ **The Wirral** The much built up right-hand side (the Merseyside part, inc Port Sunlight), with extensive dormitory villages and more industrial areas, is included in our Lancashire chapter. Its relatively unspoilt Cheshire part includes the charming village of Burton SJ3274 (strolls in wood of handsome old Scots pines just N), and nearby Parkgate SJ2878. This interesting village is the country's only inland seaside resort, the Dee estuary having retreated since its palmy days at the end of the 18th and early 19th c. Before that, it was a more important port than Liverpool, and there's an eerie charm in sitting in the Boathouse or Red Lion on the 'Promenade', looking out over the marshes to the distant waters and the Welsh hills on the far side. A similar sense of stranded time can be had at the Harp by the ruined marshside quay near Little Neston SJ2976; you can walk between the two (and on to Ness Gardens at Ness – see entry above) along the Dee estuary 'coastal' path.

† **Churches** of note include Astbury SJ8461 (graceful detached spire, spectacular roofing, rich carving; the village is very attractive, too), Daresbury SJ5983 (the Alice in Wonderland stained-glass window commemorates Lewis Carroll, who was born here; pleasant canalside strolls, and the Ring o' Bells is useful for lunch), and Mobberley SJ7879 (magnificently carved Tudor rood screen).

★ **Delightful villages** – all with decent civilised pubs that we can vouch for – are Barthomley SJ7752 (thatch, black and white timbering, up and down lanes, fine church); Bunbury SJ5758 (pretty cottages around 14th-c St Boniface's church at the NE end, and a well restored 19th-c watermill); Christleton SJ4465 (village green, pond, almshouses, medieval packhorse bridges); Eaton SJ5762

(unassuming picture-postcard combinations of thatch, stone and timbering); Grappenhall SJ6386 (ancient grinning cat on church tower, canal strolls); Great Budworth SJ6778 (quaint purpose-built estate village – imposing church and many pretty cottages); Little Bollington SJ7286 (peaceful hamlet by Bridgewater Canal and Dunham Massey deer park); Lower Peover SJ7474 (many people's Cheshire favourite: cobbled lanes, glorious 14th-c black and white timbered church, quiet watermeadows); Lymm SJ6786 (pretty cottages in the Dingle, boat trips on Bridgewater Canal, for example from the new Admiral Benbow pub at Agden Wharf, and strolls to the lake at Lymm Dam); Malpas SJ4947 (extraordinarily uplifting ceiling in 14th-c hilltop church nr fragmentary castle ruin, pretty cottages and some grander buildings); and Marbury SJ5645 (attractive church, lake, wood and canal surroundings). Other charming villages include Eccleston SJ4163 (romantically eclectic 19th-c estate village built for the Duke of Westminster, with richly expansive sandstone church that's a culmination of Victorian ecclesiastical architecture); Prestbury SJ9077 (very prosperous-feeling now, with good shops, the smart Legh Arms and homelier Admiral Rodney; pleasant riverside walks to the S, along the Bollin); Rostherne SJ7484 (charming brick cottages along cobbled pavement, and lovely view over one of the county's broadest meres from graveyard of attractive timbered church); Swettenham SJ8067 (rich paddocks with wrought-iron fences, daffodils in spring in a dell by an old mill; good dining pub behind partly 13th-c church); Tarporley SJ5563 (quietly attractive; very individual shops inc antique shops; the Rising Sun is a fine pub, Swan a well restored old coaching inn); and Whitegate SJ6369 (thatch, village green, fragmentary remains of biggest English Cistercian monastery opposite church, lakeside walk on nearby derelict railway).

Walks

The 30-mile Sandstone Trail offers very varied scenery, following the romantically wooded sandstone ridges, crags and outcrops stretching from Overton SJ5276 in the N (the church here is pretty, and the Ring o' Bells is a most attractive pub, with Mersey views) to the Shropshire border S of Malpas (the ancient Bell o' the Hill pub nr Tushingham down there is a useful stop). One particularly fine section is around the **Peckforton Hills** ⌂-1, with splendid views of real and real-looking romantic castles, and good pubs usefully placed at Bulkeley SJ5052 and Higher Burwardsley SJ5256. From the A534 nr **Harthill** SJ5055 ⌂-2, the Trail ascends Raw Head, the most spectacular natural feature of the central Cheshire ridge, with sandstone cliffs weathered into bizarre shapes, and a cave to explore.

The Trail passes through another very popular area for walks, the **Delamere Forest** ⌂-3: several square miles of mainly coniferous plantation, with some older oak and other woodland, inc plenty of open stretches and picnic places, and some small stretches of reedy water. There's good access from several places including Delamere SJ5669 and Hatchmere SJ5672, with decent prettily placed pubs in both villages.

The Shropshire Union Canal threads through the area, with interesting stretches for strolls, inc the flight of over a dozen locks near **Audlem Wharf** SJ6543 ⌂-4, the charming section through the richly wooded farming country below Beeston Castle at **Whartons Lock** W of Tiverton SJ5360 ⌂-5, and the pretty **Llangollen Branch** ⌂-6, with good access from Marbury SJ5645 and Wrenbury SJ5948 (there are decent pubs in all these places, and the Dusty Miller at Wrenbury has an interesting lifting bridge by it). There are canal walks from the Nag's Head at Wheelock SJ7559.

Marbury Country Park ⌂-7 has some quiet short walks, and gives on to the extensive Budworth Mere, with sailing, and herons, ducks, grebes and coots pottering around the rushes; good pubs nearby at Comberbach (pronounced Comberbatch) SJ6477 and Great Budworth SJ6778.

Little Budworth Country Park SJ5965 ⌂-8 is a strong contrast to most of this area's richly manicured countryside: poor wild heath with young bogs and scrawny birch woods.

Several more or less isolated pubs in the western part of the county make useful start or finish points for country walks: the Cock at Barton SJ4554 and below it the Farndon Arms in the attractive village of Farndon SJ4254 – where you can get down to the River Dee; the Copper Mine at Fuller's Moor SJ4954, the Bickerton Poacher at Bulkeley SJ5052, the Tiger's Head at Norley SJ6772 (Pytchleys Hollow), and the Fiddle i' th' Bag nr Burtonwood SJ5893 (Alder Lane off the A49; an unexpectedly remote-feeling spot between the disused St Helens Canal and the broad River Mersey).

The hilly eastern edge of the county forms part of the Peak District, and offers some grand views westwards towards N Wales. **Teggs Nose Country Park** SJ9573 ⌂-9 has a useful summer information centre, and good walks with far views, punctuated by relics of the former quarrying here. By the turn off the A537, the Setter Dog is a good pub.

From the park, a well marked track heads off S into the Macclesfield Forest, with steep deep green pine plantations around neatly walled small reservoirs; on the far side of this the isolated Leathers Smithy E of Langley SJ9471 is a warmly welcoming moorside refuge with superb views, and the Stanley Arms tucked away at Bottom of the Oven is also good. This track is actually part of the long-distance Gritstone Way, which is well marked and offers a few days' walking of the highest quality. It runs along these western flanks of the Peak from **Lyme Park** SJ9682 ⌂-10 (itself laced with gentle paths), to join the Staffordshire Way at Rushton Spencer SJ9462. Further N the Way can be picked up to track across high stone-walled pastures at either Pott Shrigley

SJ9478 (the Cheshire Hunt pub in Spurley Lane has good food) or, with fine views, Rainow SJ9576 (the Highwayman, a mile above the village, is a distinctive old pub). **Kerridge Hill** SJ9475 ⌂-11 above Bollington is topped by the curious folly known as White Nancy. Bollington is itself certainly worth a stroll: handsome stone milltown buildings, grand canal viaducts, attractive perspectives of the surrounding villages, and useful pubs such as the Church House and Vale.

These hills and moors SE of Macclesfield have many other good walks. A particular delight is that so many can be based around good civilised country pubs with decent food: the Crag in its untypically leafy sheltered valley at **Wildboarclough** SJ9868 ⌂-12 fits well with a walk to the Three Shires Head and the summit of Shutlingsloe, and the Ship at **Wincle** SJ9666 ⌂-13 is ideal for walks into the Dane Valley and along the exhilarating moorland tops of the Roaches (which are just over the Staffs border). Another well placed pub in this popular walking area is the Hanging Gate at Higher Sutton SJ9569 nr Langley; there's a good steep walk to it from the Ryles Arms at Higher Sutton SJ9469.

The **Middlewood Way** ⌂-14 is a sort of linear country park near Macclesfield, along a former railway; attractively bordered with wild flowers and trees, with tracks too for cyclists (bicycle hire at Lyme Park or Bollington) and horse rides (can also be hired by the hour, about £10); several decent pubs in Bollington SJ9377, one at Whiteley Green SJ9278. The pleasant stretches around the Poynton inclines SJ9283 are underrated, and the Boar's Head here is a good-value refreshment stop.

The **Macclesfield Canal** ⌂-15 tracks through good high countryside from the county boundary nr Disley to pass Bollington, Macclesfield and Congleton, with plenty of access points; S of the A54 just W of its junction with the A523, a staggering flight of 10 locks leads down to a sturdily elegant iron aqueduct.

Alderley Edge SJ8677 ⌂-16 (not to be confused with the straggling suburban settlement named after it, to the W) rises high out of the plain, with good walks through the woodland and fine views of the higher hills to the E. The local caving-club members are working towards opening some of the former copper mines which honeycomb the area.

The Cloud SJ9063 ⌂-17 has a craggy summit and drops steeply to the plain, with grand views; the Coach & Horses at Timbersbrook SJ9063 is a useful nearby pub.

Where to eat

Aldford SJ4159 GROSVENOR ARMS (01244) 620228 Sizeable Victorian pub, attractively decorated, with huge panelled library and several quieter rooms, airy conservatory, good interesting food from a daily-changing menu, well kept real ales, lots of New World wines (and malt whiskies), and large elegant sun-trap terrace and neat lawn; best to get there early. £20.50|£8.95.

Altrincham SJ7788 JUNIPER 21 The Downs (0161) 929 4008 cl am Sat, Sun, am Mon. Smart but informal-feeling restaurant with wooden floor and ceiling and an Italian mural, beautifully presented modern cooking (super fish), lovely puddings, good cheeses, a carefully chosen and interesting wine list, and efficient service; downstairs bar, too. £34|£9.50.

Bollington SJ9377 MAURO'S 88 Palmerston St (01625) 573898 Friendly Italian restaurant with lots of good pasta dishes, excellent fresh fish and lovely puddings; cl am Sat, Sun, 25–26 Dec, 1 Jan; disabled access. £27|£4.

Chester SJ4166 FRANCS 14 Cuppin St (01244) 317952 Cheerful timbered brasserie on 2 floors of old converted warehouse with very good French country food; partial disabled access. £20|£3.50.

Chester SJ4166 GARDEN HOUSE 1 Rufus Court, off Northgate St (01244)

320004 First-floor restaurant in handsome Georgian building with good interesting food; cl Sun, Christmas; children over 6. £30|£4.95.

Chester SJ4166 OLD HARKERS ARMS 1 Russell St, under Mike Melody Antiques, off City Rd (01244) 344525 Attractive conversion of an early Victorian canal warehouse with lofty ceiling, tall windows and well spaced tables and chairs, lots to look at, a comfortably busy atmosphere, friendly and efficient staff, a changing choice of nicely presented, sometimes unusual food (inc interesting sandwiches), well kept real ales, and New World wines; cl pm 25 and 26 Dec; no children; disabled access. £17.60|£5.95.

Knutsford SJ7578 BELLE EPOQUE BRASSERIE 60 King St (01565) 633060 Popular art nouveau restaurant-with-rooms; enthusiastic friendly staff and lovely modern cooking; cl Sat, bank hols; children over 9. £25|£11.50.

Marbury SJ5645 SWAN (01948) 663715 Friendly creeper-covered pub in attractive village, with open fire in neatly kept comfortable lounge, interesting food, good ales and whiskies and friendly service; nice walks to Llangollen Canal; cl am Mon, 25–26 Dec; disabled access. £18.85|£5.65.

Peover Heath SJ7973 DOG (01625) 861421 Busy pub in quiet lane with big helpings of interesting food, open fires, charming series of small bar areas with comfortable furnishings, and open fires; bedrooms. £17.50|£3.95.

Plumley SJ7175 SMOKER (01565) 722338 Popular thatched 16th-c pub with open fires and comfortable sofas in 3 well decorated connecting rooms, good swiftly served food, wide choice of whiskies, well kept real ales, and friendly service; big garden; disabled access. £20|£6.95.

Pott Shrigley SJ9478 CHESHIRE HUNT (01625) 573185 Isolated stone pub with several rambling small rooms, solid furnishings, beams and flowers, good bar and restaurant food and no noisy games machines or piped music; seats outside with country views; cl am Mon; disabled access. £15|£4.

Swettenham SJ8067 SWETTENHAM ARMS (01477) 571284 Tucked-away country dining pub with 3 spacious beamed bar areas, winter log fires, nice furnishings and huge range of very popular food; no smoking restaurant and real ales; disabled access. £17.50|£3.95.

Special thanks to Arthur and Margaret Dickinson, Derek and Sylvia Stephenson, Mr and Mrs A Barclay, E G Parish, Mark Hydes.

CHESHIRE CALENDAR

Some of these dates were provisional as we went to press, please check information with the telephone numbers provided.

Chester Ghost Walk 7.30pm, Town Hall – *every Thurs, Fri and Sat, May–Oct* (01244) 402445
Chester Guided walk of Roman Chester 11.30am and 2.30pm, Town Hall – *every Thurs, Fri and Sat, May–Oct* (01244) 402445
Chester Public Proclamations by the Town Crier 12 noon at the Cross – *every Tues–Sat, April–Oct* (01244) 402445
Chester Band Concerts by the River 3pm and 6pm at the Edwardian Bandstand in the Groves – *every Sun, May–Sept* (01244) 402445

JANUARY

4 **Knutsford** Dolls House Fair at Tatton Park (01270) 878519
24 **Nantwich** Holly Holy Day: celebration of the Battle of Namptwyche (01270) 610983

FEBRUARY

28 **Knutsford** Food & Country Shopping Fair at Tatton Park – *till 1 March* (01509) 217444

MARCH

14 **Chester** Film Festival – *till Sat 21* (01244) 380787
16 **Warrington** Fleadh: Irish Festival – *till Sat 21* (01925) 442362
21 **Knutsford** Arts, Crafts & Fashion Fair at Tatton Park – *till Sun 22* (01509) 217444

APRIL

10 **Ellesmere Port** Traditional Boat Gathering at the Boat Museum – *till Mon 13* (0151) 355 5017
11 **Knutsford** Easter Festival at Tatton Park: circus, fair, fun-on-the-farm, living history – *till Mon 13* (01565) 654822
24 **Chester** Pentice Court: full ceremonial and traditional gathering of Chester Guildsmen and procession to the Guildhall (01244) 320431

MAY

2 **Knutsford** Royal May Day: pavements are carpeted with elaborate sand patterns, procession, horse-drawn tableaux, morris dancers, maypole dancers, fireworks (01565) 633074; **Styal** Drama in the Yard at Quarry Bank Mill – *till Mon 4* (01625) 527468
3 **Styal** Maypole Celebrations at Quarry Bank Mill (01625) 527468
4 **Sandbach** Elizabethan Market (01260) 274821
5 **Chester** May Festival at the Racecourse – *till Thurs 7* (01244) 323170
9 **Marbury** Merry Days: falconry, raft racing – *till Sun 10* (01948) 663758
13 **Chester** Carnival – *till Thurs 14* (01244) 402446
16 **nr Nantwich** Reaseheath College Open Weekend: nature trails, gardening, tractor rides, animals and pets, sheepdog displays – *till Sun 17* (01270) 625131
17 **Knutsford** Dolls House, Teddies and Dolls Fair at Tatton Park (01270) 878519

CHESHIRE CALENDAR

MAY cont

22 **Kelsall** Chester Folk Weekend at the Morris Dancer Pub – *till Mon 25* (01244) 320424

23 **Styal** Drama in the Yard at Quarry Bank Mill – *till Mon 25* (01625) 527468

24 **Ellesmere Port** Model Tug Towing at the Boat Museum – *till Mon 25* (0151) 355 5017

25 **Audlem** Carnival (01270) 811467; **Knutsford** Street Fair (01565) 632611; **Northwich** Regatta (01606) 862862; **Runcorn** Town Park Show (01928) 576246

30 **Knutsford** Classic Car Spectacular at Tatton Park – *till Sun 31* (0161) 864 2906

JUNE

6 **Ness** Garden Festival at Ness Botanic Gardens – *till Sun 7* (0151) 353 0123

13 **Chester** Festival of Transport at the Roodee – *till Sun 14* (01244) 375283; **Ness** Open Air Concert at Ness Botanic Gardens (0151) 353 0123

16 **Chester** Lord Mayor's Parade *at 11am* and Fun Day at the Roodee (01244) 324324 or 402126

18 **Gawsworth** Open Air Festival: concerts and plays at Gawsworth Hall *every Wed-Sat till 15 Aug* (01260) 223456; **Neston** Ladies' Day: afternoon procession in period costume (0151) 336 3104

19 **Chester** St Werburgh Open Air Festival at the Cathedral: re-creation of medieval procession, concerts – *till Sun 21* (01244) 324756; **Middlewich** Folk & Boat Festival – *till Sun 21* (01606) 833946

20 **Appleton Thorn** Bawming the Thorn, traditional procession and festivities during which children bawm (dance round) a hawthorn tree, originated when a knight went on the crusades with an offshoot of the Glastonbury Thorn (01925) 266764

23 **Tabley** Cheshire Show at the Showground – *till Wed 24* (01829) 760020

27 **Macclesfield** Carnival (01625) 616097; **Northwich** Garden Festival at Arley Hall – *till Sun 28* (01565) 777353; **Willaston nr Nantwich** World Worm Charming Championships at the Primary School (01606) 552169

JULY

3 **Warrington** Walking Day: long processions wind round the town originally to draw people away from the races (01925) 444400 ext 2143

4 **Northwich** Fireworks Concert at Arley Hall (01565) 777353; **Northwich** Carnival (01606) 862862; **Runcorn** Carnival (01928) 580366; **Warrington** Street Theatre Festival – *every Sat in July and Aug* (01925) 442362

5 **Chester** River Carnival and Raft Race (01244) 324888

9 **Congleton** Open Air Theatre (local group) at Little Moreton Hall – *till Sat 11* (01270) 875944

10 **Chester** Summer Music Festival with international performers – *till Sat 25* (01244) 320722

11 **Chester** Fringe Festival and Youth Fringe Festival – *till Sun 26* (01244) 321497

CHESHIRE CALENDAR

JULY cont

16 **Congleton** Open Air Theatre (local group) at Little Moreton Hall – *till Sat 18* (01270) 875944

18 **Widnes** Halton Show at Spike Island – *till Sun 19* (0151) 424 2061

26 **Ellesmere Port** Classic Car Show at the Boat Museum (0151) 355 5017

29 **Nantwich** and South Cheshire Show at Dorfold Hall Park (01270) 780306

AUGUST

1 **Knutsford** Gun Dog Show at Tatton Park (01565) 654822

2 **Chester** Family Day at the Racecourse: children's entertainment, music and fun (01244) 323170

8 **Chelford** Astle Park Traction Engine Rally – *till Sun 9* (01751) 473780

9 **Knutsford** Volkswagen Rally: Beetles, Porsches, fair, children's entertainers at Tatton Park (01565) 654822

12 **Rainow** Rushbearing Ceremony at the Parish Church (01625) 572013

16 **Knutsford** Dolls House Fair at Tatton Park (01565) 654822; also Classic Triumph and MG British Sportscar Show at Tatton Park (01565) 654822; **Macclesfield** Forest Chapel, Rushbearing Ceremony (01625) 573915; **Macclesfield** free Family Fun Day at West Park (01625) 500500; **Over Peover** Country Sports Fair at Peover Hall: gun dogs, parade of hounds, fly-fishing demonstration, birds of prey (01565) 632611

22 **Knutsford** Steam Fair and Crafts at Tatton Park – *till Sun 23* (01565) 654822

29 **Crewe** and Nantwich Carnival at Queen's Park – *till Sun 23* (01270) 537777; **Poynton** Show at Poynton Park (01625) 260076; **Styal** Drama in the Yard at Quarry Bank Mill – *till Mon 31* (01625) 527468

30 **Ellesmere Port** Model Boat Convention at the Boat Museum – *till Mon 31* (0151) 355 5017

SEPTEMBER

12 **Chester** Cathedral Open Day (01244) 324756; **Crewe and Nantwich** Folk Festival – *till Sun 13* (01270) 663120; **Malpas** Yesteryear Rally – *till Sun 13* (01978) 780749

OCTOBER

3 **Chester** Literature Festival: guest authors, readings and workshops – *till Sun 18* (01244) 319985

4 **Ellesmere Port** Tugs and Pushers at the Boat Museum (0151) 355 5017

17 **Knutsford** Craft & Design Fair at Tatton Park – *till Sun 18* (01509) 217444

24 **Knutsford** Christmas Gifts Fair at Tatton Park – *till Sun 25* (01509) 217444

NOVEMBER

21 **Ellesmere Port** Christmas Craft Fair at the Boat Museum: Santa and narrowboat grotto – *till Sun 22* (0151) 355 5017

DECEMBER

12 **Lymm** Dickensian Christmas: locals in costume, craft fairs (01925) 753272

CORNWALL

Britain's best coastline – great variation from sandy family resorts to wild majestic cliffs, with intricate inlets, sheltered coves and picturesque fishing villages; masses of family attractions, some great gardens, a fine choice of places to stay.

Cornwall's magnificent coastal scenery is its greatest attraction. Readers like the south coast best – very sheltered and at its most gently picturesque, especially east of the Lizard Point, with plenty of interesting villages and little coves, winding estuaries and creeks rich in bird life, and boat and fishing trips from virtually every harbour. There are some dramatic cliffy stretches here too, interspersed with fine sandy beaches, especially west of the Lizard.

Prime places for an uncomplicated family beach holiday are around the attractive north coast town of St Ives, and between Padstow (appealing combination of fishing port and resort) and lively Newquay (Cornwall's biggest resort, increasingly a surfing centre). This stretch of coast is an almost continuous line of resort developments, with plenty of family attractions nearby.

From the county's great choice of enjoyable places to visit, the Seal Sanctuary at Gweek and friendly animal centre at Trecangate both have a disarmingly uncommercial appeal. Paradise Park in Hayle and the Dobwalls adventure park are very entertaining for children, while the excellent Flambards theme park near Helston has a happy knack of delighting adults too. Monkey World near Looe and the Goonhilly satellite station also have a very wide appeal. The lush almost subtropical gardens at or near Caerhays, Madron, Mawnan Smith, Mevagissey, Probus and Trelissick, spectacular in spring, are rewarding at any time. Cotehele, near Calstock, is Cornwall's most lovely house, and Lanhydrock House, Trerice, Antony House at Torpoint and the fairy-tale castle on St Michael's Mount off Marazion are also well worth visiting. More characteristic of Cornwall, though, is the charming profusion of quiet stone-built villages and delightful unspoilt country churches.

Cornwall also has a very different and much wilder side. The coast west of St Ives has rugged stretches of windswept empty moorland clifftops, with a hinterland exceptionally rich in well preserved visible archaeology – Bronze Age burial chambers and standing stones, Iron Age hill forts and village sites, ancient stone crosses. Small rather withdrawn-looking granite villages and farmsteads among wind-beaten pastures give this western part a rather clannish feel, almost like the more nationalistic parts of Wales; but though visitors are clearly seen as outsiders, the locals are far from unfriendly. Another stretch of wild grandeur is up towards Devon, north of commercialised Tintagel – towering precipices, dramatic surfing beaches and much completely unspoilt seaboard, with no development, little car access, just wildlife, wind, waves and the occasional walker. Port Isaac and Boscastle are the pick of this part's few settlements.

Away from the sheltered south-east, the inland parts are largely treeless, with rolling pasture and moorland. Windswept Bodmin Moor is the county's most untouched inland area. Some other parts have been left with a surprisingly industrial face by the defunct mining industry: the linked towns of Redruth, Pool and St Agnes are reminiscent of some towns in the industrial North. In the more exposed spots the towering alloy propellers of the new windfarms are becoming a striking landscape feature.

There's an excellent choice of distinctive places to stay. Generally, good dining places are most easily found in the south (plenty of fresh local fish), rarest in the west. The Isles of Scilly are ideal for a really quiet and relaxing holiday, with Penzance the quickest jumping-off point.

In high summer don't even think about a short break in Cornwall. It's so (justifiably) popular then for long holidays that the battle of getting there, jammed narrow roads, parking problems and the crowds at the most popular places can make a short break more of a frustration than a pleasure. But if you are there then for a longer holiday, it's surprisingly easy to escape the crowds that go with the big family attractions, honey-pot fishing villages and famous beaches. With 500 miles of coastal walks here, much of the land owned and beautifully preserved by the National Trust, you can always quickly escape into solitude. The relatively warm sea makes Cornwall popular bathing country in summer – but pick your beach carefully. The county has some of Britain's cleanest beaches, but some of the muckiest, too, with untreated sewage blighting many. We pick out reliably clean places in the text.

Out of high season, when its narrow roads are much less busy, Cornwall offers very substantial rewards to those prepared to spend the time getting there: lots to do, a very relaxed pace of life, and attractive prices. Late May and early June is an ideal time for a shorter break here, with the scenery at its best, and relatively few other visitors; in spring and early summer, the tall roadside hedged banks which block the view from many byroads compensate by being virtual walls of wild flowers. September and October is seal pup time.

This is not a good area for car touring or cycling: roads don't usually follow the coast and tend to be shut in by the very high hedges. Readers also baulk at petrol prices here (slightly higher than elsewhere); and a number of garages still don't have diesel. From London, you should allow about five hours' driving out of season to get well into the county; it's about three hours from Bristol – across just a couple of counties. The A30 is now a good fast long-distance route (much better than the A390).

If you'd rather avoid the roads altogether, a Cornish Rail Rover ticket is good value for a week's unlimited train travel throughout the county for around £35; you can also get a ticket for three days – which don't have to be together.

Where to stay

Bodinnick SX1352 OLD FERRY Bodinnick, Fowey PL23 1LX (01726) 870237 **£60;** 12 comfortable and roomy rms, most with own bthrm and river views. 400-year-old inn in a lovely situation overlooking the Fowey estuary; characterful back flagstoned bar partly cut into the rock and a comfortable lounge with French windows opening onto a terrace; real ales and decent food in the bar and little evening restaurant; pool in games room; quiet out of season.

Botallack SW3633 MANOR FARM Botallack, St Just-in-Penwith, Penzance TR19 7QG (01736) 788525 *£46; 3 rms. Blissfully quiet and friendly 17th-c local granite farmhouse on working farm, with a medley of furnishings in comfortable lounge; good breakfasts with home-baked bread; safe walled garden; no pets; marvellous walks along the cliffs, lots of ruined mines and small coves.

Buryas Bridge SW4429 ROSE FARM Chyanhal, Buryas Bridge, Penzance TR19 6AN (01736) 731808 *£36, plus winter breaks; 3 delightfully furnished rms. Relaxed, informal, friendly farmhouse tucked away down a remote country lane; excellent breakfasts around big wooden table; can see animals (working farm); children love it; cl Christmas for 3 days.

Calstock SX4368 DANESCOMBE VALLEY Lower Kelly, Calstock PL18 9RY (01822) 832414 *£125; 5 airy rms with river views. Lovely small Georgian house with first-floor verandah and fine views over a wooded bend on the River Tamar; warmly friendly owners, quiet relaxing atmosphere, open fires, flowers, books (no TV), and delicious food using fresh local produce; Cotehele House (NT) is just 15 mins' walk; cl Nov–Mar; children over 12.

Carne Beach SW9038 NARE Carne Beach, Veryan, Truro TR2 5PF (01872) 501279 **£206,** plus special breaks; 40 lovely rms to suit all tastes – some stylish ones overlook the garden and out to sea. Attractively decorated and furnished hotel in a magnificent clifftop position with secluded gardens, outdoor and indoor swimming pools; antiques, fresh flowers and log fires in the airy, spacious day rooms, very good food inc wonderful breakfasts, and run by staff who really care; is for quiet family hols, with safe sandy beach below; cl Jan; disabled access.

Constantine Bay SW8574 TREGLOS Constantine Bay, Padstow PL28 8JH (01841) 520727 **£108,** plus special breaks; 44 light rms, some with balcony. Quiet and relaxed hotel close to a good sandy beach (in the same family for 30 years); comfortable traditional furnishings, log fires, good food, friendly and helpful staff; sheltered garden, indoor swimming pool, pool and snooker, children's playroom; lovely nearby walks; self-catering apartments; cl 8 Nov-12 Mar; children over 7 in evening restaurant; disabled access.

Crackington Haven SX1396 MANOR FARM Crackington Haven, Bude EX23 0JW (01840)230304 **£60;** 5 pretty rms. Lovely Domesday-listed, no smoking manor surrounded by 25 acres of farmland and carefully landscaped gardens; antiques in 4 lounges, log fire, games room and a house-party atmosphere; big breakfasts, and fine 4-course dinner; cl 25 Dec; no children.

East Looe SX2654 WOODLANDS St Martin's Rd, East Looe PL13 1LP (01503) 264405 **£40;** 4 rms. Attractive Victorian country house overlooking the river estuary and set on the edge of quiet woodland; friendly, helpful owners; generous helpings of enjoyable food using home-grown and local organic produce where possible, and good breakfasts.

Falmouth SW8032 PENMERE MANOR Mongleath Rd, Falmouth TR11 4PN (01326) 211411 **£85,** plus special breaks; 38 spacious rms. Run by the same owners for 26 years, this quietly set Georgian manor has 5 acres of subtropical gardens and woodland; heated outdoor swimming pool, giant chess, croquet, and a leisure centre with indoor swimming pool, mini gym and sauna, and woodland fitness trail; particularly helpful and friendly staff; enjoyable food (inc menu dedicated to lobster dishes) in restaurant and informal bar; cl 24-27 Dec.

Fowey SX1252 CARNETHIC HOUSE Lambs Barn, Fowey PL23 1HQ (01726) 833336 ***£64,** plus special breaks; 8 rms. Warm and friendly Regency house in lovely gardens with heated swimming pool, badminton and putting; a relaxed and informal atmosphere and very helpful owners; attractive lounge, and good home-made food using local fish; cl Dec–Jan; disabled access.

Fowey SX1252 MARINA The Esplanade, Fowey PL23 1HY (01726) 833315 **£54,** plus special breaks; 11 rms, several with lovely views (some with balcony). Homely, friendly hotel in lovely position overlooking the River Fowey and the open sea (private access from secluded walled garden); comfortable lounge, dining room overlooking the water; good food, and helpful service; cl Jan and Feb.

Gerrans Bay SW8937 PENDOWER BEACH HOUSE Gerrans Bay, Ruan High Lanes, Truro TR2 5LW (01872) 501241 ***£104,** plus special breaks; 11 rms. Family-run hotel dating back to 16th c, in 8 acres of grounds on the edge of a lovely sandy beach, with superb sea and coastal views; a relaxed, friendly atmosphere in attractive and comfortable rooms; good food in cosy restaurant (super fresh local fish and shellfish); tennis court; cl Oct–Mar; disabled access.

Gillan SW6527 TREGILDRY Gillan, Helston TR12 6HG (01326) 231378 ***£55,** plus special breaks; 10 good rms with fine views over Falmouth Bay. Elegantly refurbished hotel in 4 acres of grounds with private access to the cove below; spacious airy lounges, fresh flowers and books, courteous, helpful service and a restful atmosphere; very good food in attractive restaurant; cl Nov–Feb.

Gunwalloe SW6522 HALZEPHRON Gunwalloe, Helston TR12 7QB (01326) 240406 ***£60;** 2 cosy rms. 500-year-old ex-smugglers' inn run by knowledgeable and friendly Cornish couple; good food in bar areas and bistro-style restaurant, open fire, and fine views of Mount's Bay; lots of walks, nearby beaches, golf and boating; cl 25 Dec; children over 12.

Lamorna Cove SW4524 LAMORNA COVE Lamorna Cove, Penzance TR19 6XH (01736) 731411 ***£69;** 12 well furnished rms, most with cove views. Comfortable, beautifully situated hotel overlooking gardens to the sea; homely rooms, light airy restaurant using fresh local food (especially seafood), very good attentive service; outdoor heated swimming pool; marvellous walks; cl Nov–Feb, but open 4 days at New Year.

Liskeard SX2564 WELL HOUSE St Keyne, Liskeard PL14 4RN (01579) 342001 **£105,** plus special breaks; 9 good rms, fine views. Light and airy Victorian country house with warm, friendly owner and courteous staff; comfortable drawing room, cosy little bar; particularly good food and fine wines in dining room overlooking a terrace and lawns; 3 acres of gardens with hard tennis court, swimming pool and croquet lawn.

Little Petherick SW9172 OLD MILL COUNTRY HOUSE Little Petherick, Wadebridge, PL27 7QT (01841) 540388 ***£60;** 7 rms. 16th-c corn mill in lovely riverside gardens with waterwheel and other original features; beamed dining room and lounges; freshly cooked food, and attentive service; cl Nov–Feb; children over 14.

Looe SX2251 TALLAND BAY Talland, Looe PL13 2JB (01503) 272667 **£98;** 19 charming rms with sea or country views. Down a little lane between Looe and Polperro, this restful partly 16th-c country house is set in lovely subtropical gardens just above the sea; comfortable drawing room with log fire, smaller lounge with library, fresh flowers, courteous service; good food in pretty oak-panelled dining room, and pleasant afternoon teas; heated outdoor swimming pool, putting, croquet; cl Jan; children over 5 in evening restaurant (high tea for younger ones); dogs by prior arrangement.

Mawnan Smith SW7728 MEUDON Mawnan Smith, Falmouth TR11 5HT (01326) 250541 **£130,** plus special breaks; 29 well equipped comfortable rms in separate wing. Run by the same caring family for 30 years, an old stone mansion with a newer wing, in beautiful subtropical garden laid out by Capability Brown; fine views from the dining room, comfortable lounge with log fire; good English cooking, and old-fashioned standards of service; cl 5 Nov–1 Mar; dogs by arrangement (not in public rooms); limited disabled access.

Mawnan Smith SW7728 NANSIDWELL COUNTRY HOUSE Mawnan Smith, Falmouth TR11 5HU (01326) 250340 *£115, plus special breaks; 12 individually decorated rms. Comfortable creeper-covered granite house in a wonderful woodland garden with sea views and direct access to a good beach; comfortably elegant rooms with log fires, fresh flowers, and books; fine food inc home-grown produce and home-made jams and breads in excellent restaurant; hard-working, enthusiastic owners; many gardens to visit nearby; cl 2 Jan–1 Feb; children over 6 in evening restaurant (high tea available); disabled access.

Maxworthy SX2592 WHEATLEY FARM Maxworthy, Launceston PL15 8LY (01566) 781232 **£42,** plus special breaks; 4 attractive rms with showers. In the same family for 5 generations, this working sheep and dairy farm has comfortable, pretty furnishings, log fires, a games room with table tennis and toys, animals to visit, pony rides, and a safe play area for children; self-catering cottages, too; cl Oct–Mar (open for Easter).

Mithian SW7450 ROSE-IN-VALE COUNTRY HOUSE Mithian, St Agnes TR5 0QD (01872) 552202 **£75,** plus special breaks; 19 pretty rms. Secluded and quietly set Georgian house in 4 acres of neatly kept gardens; comfortable spacious day rooms, a friendly atmosphere, helpful, long-standing local staff, and good food in enlarged dining room; ducks in ponds and trout stream, outdoor swimming pool, badminton and croquet; children over 7 in evening in public rooms and restaurant (high tea for smaller ones); well behaved dogs welcome; cl Jan and Feb; disabled access.

Mullion SW6719 POLURRIAN Mullion, Helston TR12 7EN (01326) 240421 *£172 inc dinner, plus special breaks; 39 rms, some with a memorable sea view. White, clifftop hotel in lovely gardens with a path down to the sheltered private cove below; civilised modern comfort and good breakfasts; leisure club with heated swimming pool, and heated outdoor pool, badminton, tennis, mini-golf, squash and croquet; good with children; cl Jan; disabled access.

Newlyn SW4628 HIGHER FAUGAN Newlyn, Penzance TR18 5NS (01736) 62076 *£93, plus special breaks; 11 attractive rms with garden and sea views. Country house in 10 acres of quiet gardens and grounds with outdoor swimming pool, tennis, and putting green; pleasantly old-fashioned sitting room, helpful owners, and good home-made food using fresh local produce; disabled access.

Pelynt SX2055 JUBILEE Pelynt, Looe PL13 2JZ (01503) 220312 £59, plus special breaks; 9 rms. Neat 16th-c inn with Queen Victoria mementoes, oak tables and a mix of seats under the beams in the relaxed lounge bar, log fire, gleaming brass and fresh flowers; good waitress-served bar food; well equipped children's play area; dogs welcome.

Pendeen SW3834 TREWELLARD MANOR FARM Pendeen, Penzance TR19 7SU (01736) 788526 £19; 3 rms, 2 with own bthrm. Victorian house in lovely coastal spot; log fire in the lounge, outdoor summer swimming pool, and fine walks all round; self-catering also; cl Christmas.

Penzance SW4730 ABBEY HOTEL Abbey St, Penzance TR18 4AR (01736) 66906 £85, plus winter breaks; 7 charming rms. Stylish little 17th-c house close to harbour, with marvellous views; a relaxed atmosphere in the comfortable drawing room full of flowers, fine paintings and antiques; a good set menu in the small restaurant; pretty garden; cl Christmas for 6 days; children over 6.

Pillaton SX3664 WEARY FRIAR Pillaton, Saltash PL12 6QS (01579) 350238 *£50, plus special breaks; 12 rms. Pretty 12th-c inn by the church in a pleasantly remote village; lots of charm and character in its 4 knocked-together rooms, attractive furnishings, and good food.

Polperro SX2051 LANDAVIDDY MANOR Landaviddy Lane, Polperro, Looe PL13 2RT (01503) 272210 *£48, plus special breaks; 7 pretty rms. Attractive and carefully furnished, a no smoking 18th-c manor house with fine views over the 2 acres of peaceful gardens and the bay beyond; comfortably furnished lounges, an open fire, and a relaxed atmosphere; Aga-cooked breakfasts in the beamed dining room; cl Nov–Feb; children over 14.

Port Isaac SX0080 PORT GAVERNE Port Isaac PL29 3SQ (01208) 880244 £96, plus special breaks; 17 comfortable rms. A lovely place to stay and an excellent base for the area (dramatic coves, good clifftop walks, and lots of birds); big log fires in the well kept bars, relaxed lounges; decent bar food, very good restaurant food, and fine wines; also restored 18th-c self-catering cottages; cl early Jan–mid-Feb; children over 7 in restaurant; dogs allowed.

Quintrell Downs SW8560 MANUELS FARM Quintrell Downs, Newquay TR8 4NY (01637) 873577 *£40; 3 rms, 2 with shared bthrm. Comfortable and relaxed 17th-c farmhouse with log fires, candlelit dinners, and pretty garden; good for children – bottle-feed calves, collect eggs and so forth (free babysitting, too); cl Christmas/New Year.

Ruan High Lanes SW9039 CRUGSILLICK MANOR Ruan High Lanes, Truro TR2 5LJ (01872) 501214 *£80, plus special breaks; 3 rms. One of the loveliest houses in Cornwall, this Queen Anne manor house was extended from a pre-Elizabethan farmhouse and is surrounded by a big quiet garden with wooded valley views; log fire in a drawing room with a Napoleonic ceiling; candlelit dinners in 17th-c dining room using home-grown produce where possible, fine breakfasts; charming owners; self-catering cottages in grounds with excellent disabled access, children welcome; cl Christmas and New Year; children over 12 in main house.

St Austell SX0553 BOSCUNDLE MANOR Tregrehan, St Austell PL25 3RL (01726) 813557 *£130, plus special breaks; 10 rms. Mainly 18th-c rambling manor with country house atmosphere in its low-beamed and carefully furnished rooms; enjoyable food, a good wine list, and breakfasts in the pretty conservatory; 2 acres of terraced gardens with croquet, outdoor heated swimming pool, indoor swimming pool, golf practice area with 2 greens and 2 all-weather teeing positions; barn with gym, snooker, table tennis, and darts, and outside badminton; woodland walks; self-catering cottage; cl Nov–mid-Mar.

St Blazey SX0654 NANSCAWEN HOUSE Prideaux, St Blazey, Par PL24 2SR (01726) 814488 *£70; 3 spacious rms overlooking the garden. Pretty creeper-covered, no smoking Georgian house in 5 acres of quiet grounds; helpful owners; big drawing room; good food using home-grown produce served in the airy conservatory; heated outdoor swimming pool and outdoor whirlpool bath; cl 25–26 Dec; children over 12.

St Hilary SW5531 ENNYS St Hilary, Penzance TR20 9BZ (01736) 740262 £55, plus special breaks; 5 pretty rms, 3 in converted barns. Warm, friendly 17th-c Cornish manor house on a working farm; grass tennis court and heated swimming pool in the sheltered gardens; log fire in the big comfortable sitting room; candlelit dinners using home-grown herbs and vegetables, local fish and shellfish, and breakfasts with home-baked bread; fishing in nearby lakes; self-catering studio.

St Ives SW5140 BLUE HAYES Trelyon Ave, St Ives TR26 2AD (01736) 797129

*£80, plus special breaks; 9 rms, most with own bthrm. Long-standing and friendly guest house in wonderful clifftop position overlooking the sea, with a quiet garden leading to the beach; comfortable rooms, and enjoyable food; cl end Oct–Mid-Mar; children over 5.

St Ives SW5140 COUNTRYMAN Old Coach Rd, St Ives TR26 3JQ (01736) 797571 *£55, plus special breaks; 6 rms. Small, friendly no smoking hotel in 2 acres of gardens; log fire in the comfortable lounge, a bright flower-filled breakfast room, and a cosy little restaurant; walks, golf and Tate Gallery nearby; children over 7.

St Ives SW5441 GARRACK Burthallan Lane TR26 3AA (01736) 796199 £46, plus weekend breaks; 18 rms, some in more modern wing. Friendly no smoking hotel in 2 acres of gardens with wonderful sea views; cosy lounges with antiques, books, open fires, a fine collection of paintings by Newlyn artists and a family room; restaurant with good food inc fresh shellfish; helpful staff, and an indoor leisure centre (heated outdoor swimming pool, too); disabled access.

St Ives SW5140 KANDAHAR 11 The Warren, St Ives TR26 2EA (01736) 796183 £46; 5 rms with sea views, some with shared bthrm. No smoking B & B in splendid water's-edge position overlooking the harbour and up the coast to Newquay; comfortable old-fashioned lounge and good breakfasts in a small dining room overlooking the sea; cl Nov–Mar; children over 5.

St Ives SW5140 SKIDDEN HOUSE Skidden Hill, St Ives TR26 2DU (01736) 796899 *£78; 8 rms. Small, warmly welcoming 16th-c hotel nr the beach; carefully cooked food in cosy dining room; quiet no smoking lounge with small library, and comfortable bar; you may be asked for a large deposit; dogs welcome by prior arrangment; cl Dec; disabled access.

St Keyne SX2564 OLD RECTORY St Keyne, Liskeard PL14 4RL (01579) 342617 £56, plus special breaks; 8 comfortable rms. Friendly family-run hotel in 3 acres of grounds, with an open fire in the comfortably furnished lounge, cosy bar, good homely atmosphere, and enjoyable food; cl Christmas and Jan; children over 12; disabled access.

St Martin SX2655 BUCKLAWREN FARM St Martin, Looe PL13 1NZ (01503) 240738; *£42, plus special breaks; 6 rms. Spacious farmhouse on 500-acre dairy and arable working farm; croquet and putting in the big garden; coastal and sea views, large homely lounge, south-facing sun lounge; farmhouse cooking using home-grown and local produce; cl Nov–Mar; disabled access.

St Mawes SW8433 RISING SUN St Mawes, Truro TR2 5DJ (01326) 270233 £59, plus special breaks; 8 rms. Small attractive hotel in popular picturesque waterside village; harbour views, large and comfortable, newly refurbished lounge bar area, airy conservatory, charming terrace.

St Wenn SW9665 WENN MANOR St Wenn, Bodmin PL30 5PS (01726) 890240 *£80; 3 rms. Carefully restored and friendly restaurant with rooms, tucked away among rolling hills in 4 acres of wooded grounds; panelled bar with inglenook fireplace and 42-ft well, candlelit dining room with 2 open log fires, and good, fresh food; croquet; cl Christmas; no children.

Sennen SW3425 LAND'S END HOTEL Sennen, Land's End, Penzance TR19 7AA (01736) 871844 £88, plus special breaks; 33 elegant airy rms, many with splendid sea views. Comfortable hotel right on the clifftop with fine sea views; good food in attractive conservatory-style restaurant, elegant seating areas, informal bar with lots of malt whiskies, and helpful staff.

Tregadillett SX2983 ELIOT ARMS Tregadillett, Launceston TL15 7EU (01566) 772051 *£40, plus special breaks; 2 rms, shared bthrm. Friendly, creeper-covered old house with lots to look at (such as 66 antique clocks inc 7 grandfathers); very good food with plenty of fish and interesting daily specials; dogs welcome.

Tregaswith SW8963 TREGASWITH FARMHOUSE Tregaswith, Newquay TR8 4HY (01637) 881181 *£44, plus special breaks; 4 pretty, homely rms. 18th-c house with beams and antiques on smallholding breeding horses (pony rides) and rare poultry; good breakfasts and proper country cooking; dogs welcome by arrangement.

Tregony SW9245 TREGONY HOUSE Tregony, Truro TR2 5RN (01872) 530671 *£66 incl dinner; 5 individually furnished rms, some with own bthrm. Partly 17th-c house with very friendly, helpful owners; big breakfasts and good evening meals in low-beamed dining room; cosy sitting room; and pretty cottagey garden; cl Nov–Feb; children over 7.

Trelights SW9979 LONG CROSS Trelights, Port Isaac PL29 3TF (01208) 880243 *£40; 12 rms, some with sea view. Well modernised Victorian house with an interesting period 'garden of secrets' – attractive plants in carefully restored, interlocking hedged enclosures snugged down against the winds (see To see and do sections, below); disabled access.

Trenale SX0688 TREBREA LODGE Trenale, Tintagel PL34 0HR (01840) 770410 *£78, plus special breaks; 7 pretty rms with views across fields to the sea. Handsome manor house with log fire and honesty bar in the comfortable smoking room, elegant first-floor drawing room; a good set dinner in the oak-panelled dining room; lots of walks; cl 4 Jan–13 Feb; children over 12; dogs welcome by prior arrangement.

Watergate SX2354 HARESCOMBE LODGE Watergate, Looe PL13 2NE (01503) 263158 *£20, plus special breaks; 3 cosy rms. Friendly and carefully modernised 18th-c house with waterfalls and old stone bridges in a quiet garden; good breakfasts; half an hour's walk along the river path into Looe; children over 12.

Widegates SX2858 COOMBE FARM Widegates, Looe PL13 1QN (01503) 240223 £46, plus special breaks; 10 comfortable rms. Warmly welcoming and relaxed no smoking country house in 10 acres of garden, meadows, woods and streams with distant sea views; an outdoor swimming pool, and a stone barn with table tennis and snooker; plants, log fires and antiques in the sitting room; hearty English breakfasts, enjoyable set evening meals, and an honesty drinks tray; cl Nov–Feb; children over 5; disabled access.

To see and do

CORNWALL FAMILY ATTRACTION OF THE YEAR

✤ ⏑ **Gweek** SW7027 NATIONAL SEAL SANCTUARY Very nicely set overlooking the Helford estuary, this is the biggest seal sanctuary in Europe, with plenty of seals and sea lions all year round. Part of the chain of Sea Life Centres, it's clearly a very sincere place, providing a home to dozens of injured or orphaned seals that they hope to be able to release back into the wild. They're very good at bringing out the character traits of individual animals – the one slapping his flippers against his side to attract attention is Scooby, and that big one is Carus, a bull sea lion weighing in at well over quarter of a tonne (600lb). They look a bit clumsy lumbering about on land, and underwater observatories let you see them in their element. Feeding times are fun, and there are useful talks and related displays, as well as guided woodland walks throughout the day. It's a relaxed and undemanding place, excellent for distracting under-12s for a couple of hours (it's not ideal for babies and very young children); children interested in animal conservation really get a lot out of it. Most things to see are outdoors (including all the seal pools), so it's best on a dry day, though some of the eating areas are under cover, and of course the audio-visual displays are inside. There's a play area too, as well as donkeys and sheep, an aquarium, and a nature trail well praised by several of our correspondents. Snacks (summer barbecues), shop, disabled access; cl 25

Dec; (01326) 221361; £5.50 (£3.50 children over 4); a family ticket for 2 adults and up to 4 children is very good value at £16.50. The Gweek Inn, with home-made food, is handy, and the Trengilly Wartha at Nancenoy is excellent for lunch, with a nice walk down to Scotts Quay on the creek.

★ **Attractive seaside villages** and towns are the highlight of the county. Snugged into the rocky coast, they are often really lovely, with friendly local people. Generally well sheltered, they can be pleasantly mild when other parts of the West Country are cold. In summer they manage to keep their charm, as the strolling crowds never quite override the natural local character. Favourites like Fowey, Mevagissey, Polperro, Portscatho and St Mawes are described below. Others with nothing specific to see and describe but immensely appealing in their way are Kingsand/Cawsand SX4350 (higgledy-piggledy charm, nr great cliff walks; the Halfway House and Rising Sun both have good local fish), Penryn SW7834 (pretty houses dropping down to the river), Porthtowan SW6948, Portloe SW9339 (tiny unspoilt village wedged into a precipitous cove; good teashop/small restaurant), Polkerris SX0952 (terrific view, almost even better in winter, across St Austell bay from well restored ancient quay), and Portreath SW6545 (the B3301 W of here has some good sea views). All these have decent pubs.

✝ ⌂ **Altarnun** SX2281 The CHURCH has an enchanting set of 16th-c carved bench ends, much humanity and humour. The unpretentious Rising Sun just N does decent simple food. Nearby WESLEY'S COTTAGE just off the A30 at Trewint, the world's smallest Methodist place of worship, has a primitive time-warp room used by Wesley in 1744.

⌂ ❀ ⌂ **Bodmin** SX0360 PENCARROW ▦ (Washaway, 3m N off the A389) Notable 18th-c house with fine paintings and furniture, rococo ceiling in the music room, and, perhaps the highlight, 50 acres of lovely formal and woodland gardens with over 600 different rhododendrons and an acclaimed conifer collection. Also marked trails, children's play area, pets' corner, craft centre, and ancient British encampment. Snacks, shop, disabled access; house open pm Sun–Thurs Easter–mid-Oct, garden open all day; (01208) 841396; £4, garden only £2. BODMIN & WENFORD RAILWAY (Bodmin General Station, St Nicholas St) Restored steam locomotives take you back to the glory days of the Great Western Railway when hordes of holiday-makers travelled this route to the sun. As well as enjoying the view, you can stop off for pleasant woodland walks. Regular trains connect with Bodmin Parkway station. Snacks, shop, disabled access; cl Jan–late Mar, and Nov, with a limited service in Oct and Dec – best to phone for train times; (01208) 73666; £5. BODMIN GAOL (Berrycombe Rd) The former county prison, built in 1778, with spooky underground dungeons; the Crown Jewels were stored here in the First World War. Meals and snacks (pub on site), shop; (01208) 76292; £3. There's a sacred well in the churchyard of St Petroc's church. The Borough Arms (on the A389 NW) is good value for lunch.

! ⌂ **Bolventor** SX1876 POTTER'S MUSEUM OF CURIOSITY Set in the little complex that's sprung up around Jamaica Inn, the pub immortalised by Daphne du Maurier, this is a bizarre Victorian collection of stuffed animals and other assorted oddities. Rather than simply displaying them in cases, Mr Potter constructed elaborate tableaux around the bodies brought to him by local farmers. Guinea pigs play cricket, rabbits sit in a classroom, and squirrels carouse in a pub in this weird little world – while the Kittens' Wedding has to be seen to be believed. Meals, snacks, shop, disabled access; cl 24–25 Dec and last 3 wks of Jan; (01566) 86838; £1.95. The pub itself is still atmospheric

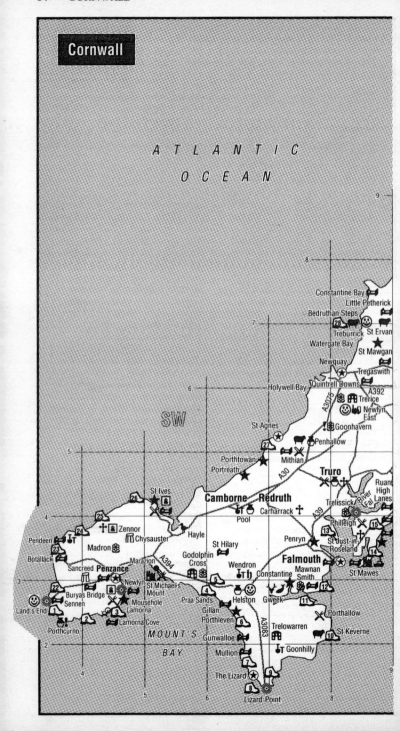

Cornwall

ATLANTIC

OCEAN

Constantine Bay
Little Petherick
Bedruthan Steps
Treburrick   St Ervan
Watergate Bay
St Mawgan
Newquay
Tregaswith
Quintrell Downs
A392
Holywell Bay
Trerice
Newlyn East
Goonhavern
SW
St Agnes
Penhallow
Porthtowan   Mithian
Portreath   A30
Truro
Ruan High Lanes
Camborne   Redruth
Trelissick
River Fal
Pool   Carharrack
St Ives
Philleigh
Hayle
St Just-in-Roseland
Pendeen   Zennor
St Hilary
Penryn
Chysauster
Madron   Godolphin Cross   Falmouth
Botallack   Wendron   Mawnan Smith
Sancreed   Penzance   Marazion   Constantine   St Mawes
Buryas Bridge   Newlyn   St Michael's Mount   Helston   Gweek   Porthallow
Sennen   Mousehole   Praa Sands   Gillan   Trelowarren   St Keverne
Land's End   Lamorna   Porthleven   A3083
Porthcurno   Lamorna Cove   Gunwalloe   Goonhilly
MOUNT'S   Mullion
BAY   The Lizard
Lizard Point

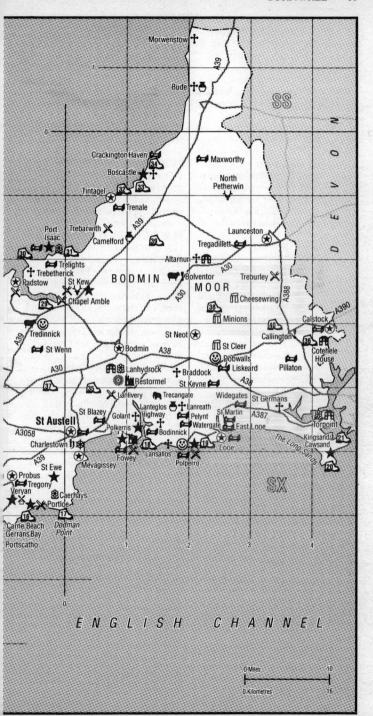

despite the developments. Just S on the A30, COLLIFORD LAKE PARK has plenty going on for families – rare breeds of birds, cattle, poultry, and sheep, indoor and outdoor pets, adventure play areas, undercover assault course, museum, and lakeside walks. Meals, snacks, shop, some disabled access; cl Oct–Easter; (01208) 821469; £3.50. About a mile away, Dozmary Pool is one of two Cornish lakes that claim to be where a legendary arm rose from the depths and reclaimed Excalibur (the other is Loe Pool near Porthleven), and it's an easy starting point for Bodmin Moor. The A30, incidentally, has better views of the moor than any of the byroads.

★ † **Boscastle** SX0990 Pretty harbour with 16th-c pier squeezed into a rocky creek, cottages converted from warehouses, gift shops, a witchcraft museum; the Cobweb and (a stiff climb) the Napoleon are useful for lunch. Not far from here at Trevalga SX0690, Tredole Farm will arrange coastal or country HORSE AND PONY TREKKING; non-riders welcome; (01840) 250495. Nearby St Juliot CHURCH SX1290 was restored by Thomas Hardy in his career as an architect; he described the area later in *A Pair of Blue Eyes*.

♿ † **Bude** SS2006 A popular area for surfing, with great beaches beyond the dunes; Sandy Mouth slightly N has clean water for bathing, and there's a nature trail close to surfers' favourite Duckpool. Otherwise it's an unremarkable resort, though the BUDE AND STRATTON MUSEUM (The Wharf) is a decent rainy-day retreat; cl Oct–Easter; 50p. The Falcon Hotel does good-value quick food. The carved bench ends up at POUGHILL CHURCH SS2207 (pronounced 'poffle') are entertaining; the Preston Gate is a decent pub here.

🏵 **Caerhays** SW9741 CAERHAYS CASTLE GARDENS Relatively undiscovered, these magnificent spring gardens are beautifully set around the back of a striking castle, with lovely coastal views. Renowned especially for their rhododendrons, magnolias and camellias, they're easily combined with a visit to the now better-known Lost Gardens of Heligan (they do a map showing how to get between the two). Good afternoon teas, some disabled access; open wkdys 16 Mar–late May – best to ring for exact dates; (01872) 501144; £3.50. The Crown over at St Ewe does good lunches, but depending on where you're coming from, the Kings Arms at Tregony up on the main road might be handier.

! **Callington** SX3669 Off the A388 S is DUPATH HOLY WELL, the best-preserved of Cornwall's many holy wells, its unappetising water said to cure whooping cough. The town is not in itself remarkable.

🏚 🏵 ✿ **Calstock** SX4167 COTEHELE (1m W by footpath, 6m by road) Tucked away in a network of twisting roads high above the Tamar, this rambling granite house has hardly changed since built in the late 15th c; there's no electricity, so the dark and atmospheric rooms – with fine furniture, armour and tapestries – have an authentically medieval feel. Outside are lovely terraced gardens, a medieval dovecot, restored watermill, and miles of peaceful woodland walks. Down at Cotehele Quay a National Maritime Museum outpost shows the quay's history, and the last of the Tamar ketch-rigged barges has been restored here. One of the most rewarding places to visit in Cornwall, but now so over-visited that to protect it the National Trust have had to limit entrance to 600 people a day. Best to come midweek out of high season, or at least early in the morning; at other times you'll have to wait, and may not get in at all. Meals, snacks (tearoom in pleasant riverside setting with good cream teas), shop; house and mill cl Fri and Nov–Mar, garden open daily all year; (01579) 351222; £5.60, £2.80 garden and mill only; NT. Pleasant walks along the Tamar from the village. The Carpenters Arms at Lower Metherell and unusual Who'd Have Thought It at St Dominick are good for lunch.

♿ **Camelford** SX1083 Locals will tell you this is the site of Camelot, and send you a mile N to the otherwise unremarkable Slaughter Bridge, where Arthur supposedly fell at his last battle. Far more worthwhile (though in the same direction) is the BRITISH CYCLING MUSEUM ⚏ (Camelford Old Station on the B3266 N), a comprehensive (and still growing) collection of over 400 bicycles, from an original 1819 hobby-horse through boneshakers and penny-farthings to the hi-tech bikes of today. The couple who run it met through cycling, and really know their stuff. Outside is a sculpture made up of old bicycles. Shop, disabled access; usually cl Fri and Sat, but they do occasionally open then so worth checking; (01840) 212811; *£2. NORTH CORNWALL MUSEUM & GALLERY (The Clease) Good exploration of regional life over the past century, with displays of cider-making and farming, and collections of pottery and even early vacuum cleaners. Shop; cl Sun and Oct–Mar; (01840) 212954; £1.25. The Masons Arms has good-value food.

† **Carharrack** The CHURCH SW7341 has an exhibition on Cornish Methodism and John Wesley, who preached at the chapel that used to stand here. Disabled access; open am Mon–Thurs, or by appointment; (01209) 820381; free. Wesley preached more regularly at nearby GWENNAP PIT SW7440, which still has services (2.30pm Sun in July and Aug), and a visitor centre. Centre cl Oct–Apr exc by arrangement, the peaceful amphitheatre itself is open all the time; free. The Fox & Hounds at Lanner is useful for lunch.

❀ **Charlestown** SX0351 A picturesque working china clay port, with sailing ships as well as modern cargo boats; it's been much used as a film/TV setting, eg for *Poldark*. There are always at least 2 out of a fleet of 5 tall ships in the harbour, and most of these offer tours by costumed guides; perhaps the most interesting is a reconstruction of Columbus's *Santa Maria*. The SHIPWRECK & HERITAGE CENTRE on Quay Rd is good for local history; cl Nov–Feb; £3.95; and the harbourside Rashleigh Arms is handy for lunch.

🏛 **Chysauster Ancient Village** SW4735 (off the B3311 N of Gulval) On a windy hillside overlooking the coast, these stunted remains of 8 courtyard houses give some impression of village life 2,000 years ago. The site is also notable for its large untreated meadow, popular with wild birds, and, depending on the season, bright with bluebells, heather or unusual orchids. Cl Nov–Mar; (01326) 212044; £1.50.

☺ **Dobwalls** SX2165 ADVENTURE PARK (off the A38) Good theme park with lively attractions inc steam and diesel train rides along a 2-mile stretch of miniature American-style railroads, aerial cableways, and lots of excellent play areas, with their Skydome – a complex climbing frame of latticed ropework – particularly unusual. Also weekly displays of falconry (Fri) and sheepdog trials (Weds) in the summer hols, and an interesting wildlife gallery, with period artwork brought to life by atmospheric interactive tableaux. Meals, snacks, shop, disabled access; open Weds–Sun Apr–Jun, daily July–Sept, wknds in Oct (daily half-term); freephone 0800 521812; £5.25. The Highway is worthwhile for lunch.

★ ❀ 🏔 **Falmouth** SW8032 The county's biggest town has a huge natural harbour full of sailing boats of every description, big sea-going ships, little passenger ferries (to St Mawes and Truro – great fun) and boat trips; it's also a busy but pleasant shopping centre with some nice old-fashioned streets, ships' chandlers and a good bustling atmosphere, though surprisingly few sea views. Broad avenues of spiky-leaved dracaena trees away from the centre give it a quite foreign feel. The A39 here from Truro can be tiresomely slow. A MARITIME MUSEUM opposite Marks & Spencer on Market St has lots of seafaring history; cl winter Suns; £1. It also administers a steam tug open to the public down in the little inner harbour. The Quayside and Chain Locker by the inner harbour do useful food, and the Warehouse is an enjoyable waterside restaurant. Superb views from well preserved PENDENNIS CASTLE (1m SE), one of Henry VIII's chain of coastal defences; cl 24–26 Dec, 1 Jan; £2.50.

★ 🏰 **Fowey** SX1252 (pronounced 'Foy') Steep, lively and bustling, in an exceptional riverside position, with pretty views from up the hill on either side, some interesting shops in its maze of quaint alleys and tiny lanes, and a choice of good-value food pubs – the King of Prussia, Ship and Galleon. The harbour has yachts to ocean-going ships, also a car ferry to Bodinnick SX1352, and a foot ferry to Polruan SX1251, the similarly steep little harbourside hamlet opposite – less interesting, but with lovely views of Fowey (both have decent pubs). ST CATHERINE'S CASTLE is a ruined stronghold built by Henry VIII, restored mid-19th c; free. The NT owns most of the coastline in these parts, so count on clean beaches; just around from the harbour, the secluded cove at Lantic Bay (reached by a steep coastal path) is particularly attractive.

🏠 **Godolphin Cross** SW6031 GODOLPHIN HOUSE 15th-c house of Earls of Godolphin, well known for its colonnaded front. Spinning and lace-making demonstrations most days, and gardens dating back to Tudor times. Teas, shop (plants and herbs for sale), disabled access to ground floor and garden only; open pm Thurs and bank hols May–Sept (all day in Aug, with a break for lunch) as well as pm Tues July–Sept; (01736) 762409; *£3, garden 50p. The Queens Arms down at Breage does decent food.

❗ **Goonhavern** SW7953 WORLD IN MINIATURE The world's landmarks at a fraction of the normal cost – and size. Beautiful gardens with thousands of plants, and lots for children. Meals, snacks, shop, disabled access; cl Nov–Mar; (01872) 572828; £3.99.

📡 **Goonhilly Downs** SW7221 SATELLITE EARTH STATION 🎫 Very un-Cornish, this space-age complex is one of the planet's foremost telecom centres. In the control room you can see information and images sent out and received from all over the world, while the visitor centre lets you operate one of the tracking dishes yourself. Also bus tour round the site (which is a nature reserve), audio-visual show, and adventure playground. The vast aerials rising out of the heath are an awesome sight. This is one of the most interesting and genuinely exciting places to visit in the whole of Cornwall, though probably not ideal for younger children. Meals, snacks, shop, disabled access; open Easter–Oct; (01326) 221333; £3.99. The B3293 past here and the byroad to Kuggar are unusual for Cornish roads, in giving some quite distant views. The White Hart at St Keverne is the best place around for lunch.

🐾 🦭 **Gweek** SW7027 NATIONAL SEAL SANCTUARY (*see separate Family Panel. on p.82*).

🦜 **Hayle** SW5537 PARADISE PARK 🎫 Headquarters of the World Parrot Trust, with the colourful birds showcased to spectacular effect in the huge Parrot Jungle, a splendid mix of waterfalls, swamps and streams. Plenty of other exotic and rare birds, and lots of animals too, some of which you can feed at the Fun Farm. Entertaining penguin and otter feeding displays, children's quiz trails, and a big play area, with bird of prey displays in summer (not Sat), and a narrow gauge railway gently rattling through the park. Adults may prefer the Victorian walled garden (lovely clematis arches in May), or the pub that brews its own real ale. Snacks, shop (with plant sales), disabled access; (01736) 753365; £4.95, with return tickets just £1. The Towans, just N in St Ives Bay, is a good clean beach.

🔔 😊 **Helston** SW6626 World-famous for its annual Furry Dance (see **Calendar** section, below), it has a popular Saturday market and a little FOLK MUSEUM in the Old Butter Market; cl Sun, pm Weds, Christmas week; free. The main draw is FLAMBARDS (off the A394, S edge of town), a beautifully kept leisure park.

The best bit is the very good reconstructed Victorian village; once just 3 period rooms, it now has over 50 houses, shops and settings, complete with cobbled streets, carriages and other period pieces. Also a state-of-the-art time travel exhibition from the Big Bang to the present day, a life-size 'Britain in the Blitz' street, a collection of aircraft, adventure playground and play areas, award-winning gardens, and rides to suit all age groups (inc a daunting rollercoaster). This is a clear cut above the average theme park, and one that adults get at least as much out of as children; you could easily spend most of a day here. Meals, snacks, shop, disabled access; cl Nov–Easter, and Mon and Fri at the start and end of season; (01326) 564093; £5.99 (less off-season or from mid-afternoon). The simple Blue Anchor pub has a 15th-c working brewhouse which you can usually look around at lunchtime; the best food nearby is at the Halzephron at Gunwalloe, off the A3083 S – a good road with views, and usually signs of action from the Culdrose helicopter base.

⚓ **Lamorna** SW4424 The cove is pretty, with good walks along the coast path. In school hols children can try their hands at the wheel at LAMORNA POTTERY, and all year as well as the pottery there's a garden with acclaimed cream teas. Meals, snacks, shop, disabled access; cl mid-Jan; (01736) 810330; free. There's a good view of the Merry Maidens stone circle from the B3315. The Lamorna Wink is useful for lunch.

🌼 ☺ **Land's End** SW3425 The most westerly point of England, with wild and blustery walks along dramatic clifftops, and on a clear day views out as far even as the Isles of Scilly. You may not be able to stand and contemplate it on your own – the 200-acre site has been extensively developed for families in the last few years, and it's become almost like a theme park, with 'multi-sensory experiences', gift shops, craft centres, farm animals and burger bars. It's not as bad as it sounds – the exhibitions and hi-tech displays are a useful enough introduction to the folklore of the area, and there's plenty to amuse children. An RSPB observation hide has information on the coastline's wildlife. Meals, snacks, neat shopping arcade, good disabled access; cl 25 Dec; (01736) 871501; £7.95 for all attractions, less off-season. A public right of way goes through here to Land's End itself, so you're not obliged to buy a ticket if you just want to walk to the end of England.

🏠 🦋 **Lanhydrock** SX0863 LANHYDROCK HOUSE A staggering 49 rooms to visit in this splendid old house, well liked by readers; the highlight is the Long Gallery, with its magnificently illustrated Old Testament scenes – it's one of the few original 16th-c parts left, as a disastrous fire in the 19th c resulted in major changes and refurbishments. The house can be seen in the film of *Twelfth Night*; the producers wanted one actor to dance on a table but were told the he was too heavy and the table too precious. Do leave time to explore the pretty formal GARDENS and grounds; it's a lovely walk down to the river and back through the woods. Good meals and snacks, shop and plant sales, disabled access; house cl Mon (exc bank hols) and Nov-Easter; (01208) 73320; £6, £3 grounds only; NT. The Crown down at Lanlivery is most enjoyable for lunch, in a Jane Austen village setting.

✝ ⛻ **Lanreath** SX1757 Pretty village with some remarkable woodwork in its exceptional medieval CHURCH. The FOLK MUSEUM is most fun for its summer demonstrations and workshops – corn dolly making (Mon), Cornish pasty crimping (Weds) and egg decorating (Fri); all activities 2–4pm. Snacks, shop, disabled access; cl Nov–Easter; (01503) 220321; *£2.50. The Punch Bowl has a fascinating old bar.

🚂 ⛻ 🐎 **Launceston** SX3384 The most attractive inland town in Cornwall, with winding old hillside streets and an untouristy feel; it was once Cornwall's capital. STEAM RAILWAY 🚃 2-ft gauge line on the trackbed of the old North Cornwall Railway, running through 2½ miles of scenic valley – on sunny days in an open carriage; also engine displays, model railway, and car and motorcycle museum. A recent extension provides access to the region's network of footpaths. Snacks, shop, disabled access; open Easter, then Sun and Tues until Spring bank hol, Sun–Fri Spring bank hol–Sept, Sun and Tues Oct, and some trains Dec wknds; (01566) 775665 for times; £5.20. The museum in Georgian LAWRENCE HOUSE (Castle St) has useful displays on the town's past; cl wknds and mid-Oct–Mar; free. The 12th- and 13th-c hilltop CASTLE is substantial and commanding, though ruined – it was captured 4 times during the Civil War. Shop, some disabled access; cl 1–2pm, and Nov–Mar; £1.30. The White Hart does popular food. TRETHORNE LEISURE FARM ▣ (Kennards House, 3m W, off the A30) 140-acre working dairy farm good for children, who can milk Daisy the cow, walk the miniature ponies, play with the rabbits, or bottle-feed the lambs. Also birds of prey, good 18-hole golf course, and big indoor play area. Meals, snacks, shop, disabled access; cl Sun (exc golf); (01566) 86324; £4.25, golf £16 round.

The Lizard This peninsula S of Helston is famous as the most southerly part of mainland Britain, and though the inland parts can be rather dull, the coastline is altogether more attractive; readers very much enjoy exploring its dramatic western and eastern edges. The W side has mighty cliffs, with roads down to beautiful Mullion Cove SW6719 and Kynance Cove SW6813 (which has a particularly fine beach below the spectacular cliffs – a long walk down from the car park but well worth it for the strange rock formations, caves and sandy coves – lovely views from the cliff walk S). The E side is more sheltered and lusher, with wooded creeks. Porthallow SW7923 is a snug little fishing harbour with a beautifully set pub, the Five

Pilchards; the beach is notoriously polluted, and swimming in the sea is not recommended. A friendly little VINEYARD here has self-guided tours, free samples of their wines and cider, and a particularly tasty birch country wine; cl 1–2pm, Sun, and Nov–Easter; (01326) 280050; free. CYCLING is a good way to explore – you can hire bikes at Atlantic Forge, Mullion; open all yr, but check first out of season; (01326) 240294; (£5 half-day, £7 day). As well as Mullion SW6719 (where the church has an unusual dog-flap, and the Old Inn is an enjoyable family pub), attractive coastal villages with decent pubs include Cadgwith SW7214 (fish stores, thatched cottages, pretty cove), Coverack SW7818 (good walks and view of the Manacle rocks), and St Keverne SW7921, which has a lovely little WORKING FARM just S at Tregellast Barton, undeveloped and tranquil, with pleasant walks through woods and meadows, afternoon milking (4.30pm), and a good farm shop with samples of their unusually flavoured ice cream; cl Nov–Jan and wkdys mid-Jan–Mar; (01326) 280479; free. KENNACK SANDS just E of Kuggar SW7216 is one of the cleanest beaches in Britain, with beautifully clear water; it can get crowded. The National Trust have improved the area around Lizard Point in recent years, though Lizard SW7012 itself is pretty uninspiring (there's a very civilised pub, and they sell interesting local serpentine rock carvings). On top and inland the Lizard is disappointing, a big flat peninsula; the Goonhilly satellite station (see entry above) is a remarkable landmark. The manor house at TRELOWARREN SW7223 is worth a look for its elaborate Strawberry Hill gothick chapel (open pm Weds and bank hols only), and the surrounding estate (open daily, free) has plenty going on, inc woodland walks, craft shops and pottery, campsite, summer Thurs evening concerts, and good meals and snacks in the Yard Bistro. **Looe** SX2553 Seaside resort packed with tourist shops, teashops and pubs, but with a nice easy-going atmosphere even in high season. The old fishing village with its picturesque harbour and narrow little back streets is now immersed in tourism, and is the main shark-fishing place (on 'shark-fishing' trips you watch others doing the catching). During the summer you may see a locally caught shark displayed in ice at the LIVING FROM THE SEA exhibition on Buller Quay, which also shows off local lobsters and shellfish in an aquarium. Disabled access; cl 12.30–1pm, Sat in low season, Nov–Easter; £1.50. From the quay there are summer BOAT TRIPS, the easiest out to nearby St Georges Island. One of the most fascinating places to visit in the entire county is the MONKEY SANCTUARY just E of town (signed off the B3253 at No Man's Land); established in 1964, its wooded grounds are home to the world's first colony of Amazon woolly monkeys to breed successfully outside their natural habitat. You can get right up to the animals, all of which were born here, and talks by staff give an intriguing insight into the dynamics and politics of the monkey community. Meals, snacks, shop, limited disabled access; cl Fri, Sat, Oct–Easter; (01503) 262532; £4. Back in town, the Olde Salutation has plenty of atmosphere and good simple food; the Smugglers is a decent friendly restaurant, and the quayside Trawlers has very good unusual seafood.

⚜ Madron SW4532 TRENGWAINTON GARDEN (on the B3312) The name in Cornish means 'Farm of the Spring' and it does always seems to be spring at this lovely place, the climate favouring plants not usually found outside in England. Magnolias, azaleas, rhododendrons, unusual southern hemisphere trees and shrubs inc a delightful tree-fern grotto, walled gardens, good views to Mount's Bay. Cream teas, shop, disabled access, interesting plant sales; open Sun–Thurs (and Good Fri) Mar–Oct (01736) 363021; £3; NT. The King William IV has good-value basic food. The road to Morvah passes a very photogenic prehistoric

burial chamber at Lanyon Quoit; a bit further along by a phone box, a signed path on the right takes you to a great Bronze Age stone hoop at Men-An-Tol, and the lane opposite leads to Chun Castle, an Iron Age fort with great views.

⛫ Marazion SW5130 ST MICHAEL'S MOUNT There's something particularly awe-inspiring about this medieval castle, rising majestically from the sea. On gloomy or stormy days the picturesque silhouette seems even more dramatic. The little island is reached by ferry, or at low tide on foot along a causeway; the walk up to the castle, still the home of the family which acquired it in 1660, is quite steep. Fine Chippendale furniture, plaster reliefs, armour and paintings, audio-visual show. Summer meals, snacks, shop; open wkdys and most wknds Apr–Oct, best to phone for winter opening; (01736) 710507; £3.90; NT (members may have to pay some wknds). The ferry crossing is 70p; it doesn't go in bad weather. The Cutty Sark has decent food.

⚜ Mawnan Smith SW7727 TREBAH GARDEN ▨ This steeply wooded ravine garden is widely reckoned to be one of the finest in the world. At times it really feels as if you've strayed into a benign, exclusive jungle. Huge subtropical tree ferns and palms, giant gunnera, lots of blue and white hydrangeas, 100-year-old rhododendrons, some fine rare trees. Several activities for children, and at the bottom end a private beach on the Helford River – good for a picnic or secluded swim. Snacks, shop (plants for sale); (01326) 250448; *£3.20. GLENDURGAN Lovely subtropical garden in valley above Helford River, started by Alfred Fox in 1820; fine shrubs from all over the world, mature trees, walled garden and restored laurel maze. Shop, snacks; cl Sun, Mon (exc bank hols), Good Fri, Nov–Feb; (01326) 250906; £3; NT. The village itself, handy for the coastal path, is pretty, and the Red Lion is good for lunch.

★ ⚜ ⚑☺ **Mevagissey** SX0145 This bustling place is a picturesque fishing village much expanded into quite a commercialised resort, but fun, with hillside cottages, narrow streets, gift shops, a busy working harbour. The Ship, Fountain and Harbour Lights are all worthwhile pubs, and the harbourside Mr Bistro mainly does fresh fish. LOST GARDENS OF HELIGAN (off the B2373, slightly NW) Forgotten and neglected between 1914 and 1991, these splendid gardens have now been fully restored. Some very fine mature trees, Victorian walled gardens, lots of rhododendrons, lakes, and big collection of tree ferns, bamboos and palms. It's a friendly place, and they're more than happy to talk about their work. Snacks, shop/nursery, part disabled access; cl 25 Dec; (01726) 844157; £3.40. The Crown at St Ewe is good for lunch. Back in town the WORLD OF MODEL RAILWAYS ▨ (Meadow St) has over 50 model trains trundling through a realistic little world that takes in Cornish china-clay pits, ski resorts, fairgrounds, towns and country. Shop, some disabled access; cl wkdys Nov–Easter; (01726) 842457; £2.65. There's a decent FOLK MUSEUM in an 18th-c boat-builder's shed on East Quay; cl am Sun and Oct–Easter; *50p.

† **Morwenstow** SS2015 The CHURCH, in an idyllic setting, has Norman arches and 16th-c bench ends, with shipwrecked sailors' headstones in the graveyard. A driftwood shack built for contemplation by a Victorian parson over the impressive cliffs is preserved by the NT. The Bush is an interesting old pub, and the rectory tearoom is delightful.

★ **Mousehole** SW4726 Attractive working fishing village with steep little roads – too many summer visitors, but lovely out of season, with spectacular Christmas lights in the little harbour; the harbourside Ship (with good-value bedrooms) is fun for lunch, though the Old Coastguard has more interesting food and a lovely garden. After the crew of TV's *Wycliffe* spent some of 1997 filming in Mousehole, the *Cornishman* newspaper published a furious editorial berating TV and film crews for clogging up the county – much to the horror of local tourism chiefs.

▣ **Newlyn** SW4628 Cornwall's busiest working fishing port; it's great fun watching the boats come in. There's an unusual art deco swimming pool, and an excellent and occasionally rather avant-garde ART GALLERY (New Rd) in a lovely coastal setting with fine views; cl Sun; (01736) 363715; donations. At Christmas the fishermen decorate the harbour and its boats with spectacular lights. The Dolphin and Fishermans Arms are useful for lunch.

▩☺ **Newlyn East** SW8356 LAPPA VALLEY STEAM RAILWAY AND LEISURE PARK ▨ 15-in gauge steam train trips through pretty countryside to an old lead mine, currently being restored. It's surrounded by parkland with lakes, woodland walk, a maze, and play areas; a section of the old branch line leads to a soft ball golf course. Meals, snacks, shop, some disabled access; cl Nov–Mar, limited opening in Oct – best to check train times; (01872) 510317; £5.25, covers fare and all attractions exc golf. The backstreet Pheasant has good home cooking.

▩☺♪🐄 **Newquay** SW8161 Now famed as England's surfing capital, a thorough-going seaside resort with excellent safe golden beaches below fine cliffs; Crantock Beach is the best and least crowded, with great views from the Bowgie family pub up on West Pentire headland. There's no shortage of souvenir shops, an alcohol-free zone declared on the streets, theme parks on the edge, and older houses around the harbour; there's decent food all day at the Fort Hotel (Fore St). Thanks in part to the surfers, the town has quite a cheery young feel these days. Fistral Beach is reckoned by some to be the best surfing beach in Europe; a couple of surfing schools here can get beginners started. NEWQUAY ZOO (Trenance Leisure Park, off the A3075 Edgcumbe Ave) The emphasis is very much on conservation here, with carefully designed enclosures for monkeys, penguins, lions and tortoises, as well as a maze, gardens, and summer activities. Feeding displays are well timetabled so there's something to see throughout the day. Also children's farm, play areas, and a maze. Meals, snacks, shop, disabled access; (01637) 873342; £4.50. You can get a joint ticket that includes entrance to WATER WORLD, a lively fun pool on the same site. SEA LIFE CENTRE (Town Promenade) Another in the reliable chain – a see-through tunnel creates the illusion of walking along the sea bed, and bubble windows bring you face to face with fish, eels and sharks. Meals, snacks, shop, some disabled access; cl 25 Dec; (01637) 872822; £4.95. Active children should enjoy the HOLYWELL BAY FUN PARK with go-karts, bumper boats, rides, golf; cl Oct–Easter; (01637) 830095; separate charges for various attractions. DAIRYLAND 🎫 (4m SE on the A3508) Much expanded since it first opened 20 years ago, this bustling dairy farm is a huge favourite with families. Its showpiece remains the daily milking sessions, when cows step aboard a bizarre merry-go-round milking machine and are milked to the strains of classical music. Also well labelled nature trails, farm park, rural bygones, brass rubbing centre and plenty of activities for children. Meals, snacks, shop, disabled access; cl Nov–Mar (exc around Christmas); (01872) 510246; £4.95.

✤ **North Petherwin** SX2889 TAMAR OTTER PARK Friendly place breeding otters then releasing them back into the wild; it's fun to watch the attractive Asian short-clawed otters playing. Three species of deer roam free, and there are waterfowl lakes, wallabies, and nature trails. The otters are fed at noon and 3.30pm. Snacks, shop, disabled access; cl Nov–Mar; (01566) 785646; £4.50.

★ 🏠 ✤ **Padstow** SW9175 Quaint streets, old buildings clustered around the working fishing harbour, and attractive slate houses; Rick Stein's restaurants are currently drawing the crowds (you'll need to book well in advance). The Camel estuary is popular for sailing: gentle dreamy scenery with lots of little boats. PRIDEAUX PLACE Still a lived-in family home, this fine old place has changed little since it was built in the late 16th c. Highlights include the elegant ceilings, atmospheric library and the intricate biblical tableaux in the Great Chamber. Notable concerts and special events in the grounds. Snacks, shop, disabled acess to ground floor only; open pm Sun–Thurs Easter–mid Oct; (01841) 532411; £4. SHIPWRECK MUSEUM (South Quay) Not far from the town's little harbour, a collection of relics and tales of the plentiful shipwrecks along this coast. Shop, disabled access; usually open Mar–Oct; (01726) 69897; £3.95. The Golden Lion, London Inn and Old Custom House are all handy for lunch. Plenty of good clean beaches near here; Constantine Bay is the best, and popular with surfers. The B3276 has the best roadside coastal views in this part of Cornwall.

↯T **Pendeen** SW3834 LEVANT MINE (1m W on the B3306) Unusual mine beneath the sea, powered by the oldest steam engine in Cornwall. Shop; open Easter and spring bank hols, Weds–Fri and Sun in Jun, Sun–Fri July–Sept; (01736) 786156; £3; NT. The nearby Pendeen Watch lighthouse is worth a look, and the Radjel is useful for something to eat.

🚌 👟 **Penhallow** SW7651 CALLESTOCK CIDER FARM Traditional working cider farm producing scrumpy, country wines and jam, with seasonal demonstrations, and friendly horses, rabbits, goats, pigs and donkeys. Also CIDER MUSEUM with ancient presses, and hives of the bees needed for pollination. Summer snacks, shop (with samples of everything they make); cl Sun (exc July–Aug), Jan, open late in summer; (01872) 573356; free, £2 for museum and tractor ride. The Miners Arms at Mithian is good for lunch.

👟 🖼 ✤ ⚓ **Penzance** SW4730 The area's main shopping centre, a pleasantly relaxed town by the sea. The prettiest part is Chapel St, where the extravagantly designed early 19th-c Egyptian House deserves a passing look, and the Turks Head is a good pub. Easy to spot thanks to the big buoys outside, the NATIONAL LIGHTHOUSE CENTRE (Old Buoy Store, Wharf Rd) has an excellent collection of lighthouse equipment, and a good audio-visual display on what it was like to live in one; a typical room is reconstructed, with original curved furniture. Many of the staff are ex-lighthouse personnel so a good source of information and anecdote. Shop, disabled access; cl Nov–Easter; (01736) 360077; £2.50. The paintings in the recently extended DISTRICT MUSEUM AND ART GALLERY (Morrab Rd) are worth a look, with pictures mainly by the Newlyn school. Snacks, shop, disabled access; cl pm Sat, and usually Sun; £1. There's a decent MARITIME MUSEUM on Chapel St. In summer you can take BOAT TRIPS around the coastline or across to the Isles of Scilly (see separate panel below), and there are regular HELICOPTER FLIGHTS to the islands. Harris's restaurant on New St has good local fish.

★ ☺ Polperro SX2051 Almost unbelievably pretty, tiny streets around a very quaint sheltered fishing harbour, little cottages perched on rocks – once a busy smuggling place, now some enjoyable craft shops tucked away, one or two tourist attractions, oddities like the shell-encrusted Shell House, and unspoilt harbourside fishermen's locals (the Blue Peter and Three Pilchards); the Crumplehorn Mill does good food. The beaches around here are some of England's cleanest. It gets very busy in summer – parking down in the village so difficult that in 1997 4 parking bays sold for the equivalent of £6 million an acre. The LAND OF LEGEND AND MODEL VILLAGE (The Old Forge, Mill Hill), with its model railway and scaled-down version of Polperro, is a useful enough distraction for children; cl Nov–Feb; (01503) 272378; *£2.20.

↓↑ ☺ Pool SW6641 CORNISH ENGINES (on the A3047) Developing site based around 2 big beam engines, originally used for pumping water from tin and copper mines. Shop, visitor centre; cl Oct–Mar; (01209) 216657; £2.50; NT. The Cornish Choughs (at Treswithian, just off the far end of the Camborne bypass) has interesting food inc good fresh fish. At Treskillard SW6739 a little way S, Lower Gryllis Farm has an uncommercialised SHIRE HORSE FARM; most displays are indoors, and there are working blacksmith's and wheelwright's shops. Meals, snacks, shop, disabled access; cl Sat; (01209) 713606; £2.99.

★ Porthleven SW6225 Pretty working fishing village; the Ship built into the cliffs is a good pub, and the long stretch of rocky beach S is a good walk if the surf's not beating in too fiercely.

! ☺ Porthcurno SW3822 MINACK THEATRE AND EXHIBITION CENTRE There are few better backdrops for plays than the one at this famous little open-air theatre – dramatic cliffs and blue sea stretching into the distance. Varied summer season, and an exhibition on the life of Rowena Cade, the remarkable woman who built the theatre with her own hands. Tickets go on sale a week in advance, but aren't for particular seats – if you've booked you'll still need to get there early to bag the best. Evening shows are more atmospheric. Shows are cancelled only in extreme conditions, so take a waterproof. Snacks, shop, disabled access; cl Nov–Mar, and exhibition cl during matinees; (01736) 810181; shows *£6, exhibition *£1.70. The secret wartime communications centre in the underground tunnels here has been opened as a MUSEUM OF SUBMARINE TELEGRAPHY. Don't let the name put you off – tours are a good deal more interesting than you'd think. Open Weds and Fri Easter–Oct, tours on the hour from 11am–3pm, meeting at Cable Hut at top of beach; (01209) 612142; £3. Porthcurno's lovely silver sands – among Cornwall's best beaches – are now the property of the National Trust, in common with so much of the coastline round here. If you walk their length, be careful not to get cut off by high tide. The Logan Rock at

Treen is handy for lunch and ideal for cliff walkers.

★ 🏰 **Port Isaac** SW9980 Delightful steep fishing village, a favourite with many: tiny streets, and houses hanging high over the pretty harbour – the Golden Lion's terrace overlooks it. Park at the top and walk down (at low tide you can park on the beach for £1). Slightly inland at Trelights SW9979 (but with good views down to the sea) the prettily restored LONG CROSS VICTORIAN GARDENS, intricately hedged against the sea winds, have interesting granite and water features, a maze, and playground and pets corner for children. Meals, snacks, pub, plant sales; (01208) 880243; *£1.40. Just up the coast Port Gaverne is a beautiful NT cove.

★ **Portscatho** SW8735 Very sheltered fishing village with a picturesque little harbour, lovely clifftop walks, and some fine nearby beaches – excellent for families. The Plume of Feathers is popular for lunch.

Praa Sands SW5727 A popular summer family beach.

🏛 🏰 † **Probus** SW8947 TREWITHEN (off the A390 between Probus and Grampound, where the Dolphin has good-value food) Justly famous landscaped gardens, with many rare trees and shrubs. The early 18th-c house is a little unfairly overshadowed by what's outside, and is an interesting obviously lived-in family home. Snacks, rare plants for sale, disabled access; gardens open Mar–Sept (cl Sun exc Apr–May), house open pm Mon–Tues Apr–July and Aug bank hol; (01726) 883647; gardens £2.80, house another £3.20. PROBUS GARDENS (Probus) How to choose the right plants/layout for your individual garden, propagation displays, herb, vegetable and fruit trials, historical plant collection, some outside sculpture. Probably best between Jun and Sept, but good for ideas at any time of the year. Snacks, shop, disabled access; cl 25–26 Dec; (01726) 882597; £2.65. The CHURCH has the tallest tower in Cornwall but is not special inside.

🏰 **Restormel** SX1060 CASTLE Very well preserved Norman castle with notable round keep and fine views over Fowey Valley. Lots of flowers in spring. Snacks, shop; cl Nov–Mar; (01208) 872687; £1.50. The Royal Oak in Lostwithiel is good for lunch.

★ 🏞 😊 ! **St Agnes** SW7150 A former mining town, now with a holiday role; some attractive steeply terraced cottages, fine cliff scenery nearby, and great views from the top of 630-ft St Agnes Beacon, just W of town. PRESINGOLL BARNS (Penwinnick Rd) Craft centre with demonstrations of pottery, candle and fudge-making, good picnic areas; cl 25–26 Dec; (01872) 553007; free, small charge for pottery tuition or candle-dipping. ST AGNES WONDERLAND (on the B3277, just S; on the way the interesting Railway Inn is worth a stop) Mature landscaped gardens with well known Cornish buildings in miniature, dinosaur replicas, an animated circus, haunted house, and fairyland; for younger children rather than older ones. Meals, snacks, shop, disabled access; cl Nov–Mar; (01872) 552793; £3.95.

† 🏰 ⚓ 🏛 **St Austell** SX0252 The centre of the china-clay industry and a busy modern shopping town. Holy Trinity CHURCH has a fine tower and interesting font, and you can tour the ST AUSTELL BREWERY on Trevarthian Rd (booking recommended); 01726 66022; £4, inc samples of beer. The area N is a strange bleak moonscape of whitish spoil heaps with metallic blue lakes dotted among them; the B3279 St Stephen –Nanpean road gives some of the best views over this. Up here off the A391 (so you don't have to go into the town) is the WHEAL MARTYN MUSEUM, an interestingly restored 19th-c clayworks showing the 200-year history of china-clay production. Working waterwheels and other equipment, horse-drawn waggons, steam locomotives, nature trails with a spectacular viewpoint over a huge clay pit, and children's adventure trail. Meals, snacks, shop; cl Nov–Mar; (01726) 850362; £4.25 (a good-value family ticket gets 2 adults and up to 4 children in for £11.50). AUTOMOBILIA (about 4m W of town at

St Stephen) Over 50 cars, motorcycles and other vehicles from 1904 to the 1960s, inc a vintage Bentley, Rolls-Royce and Aston Martin, with a permanent auto-jumble that vintage-car owners may find useful. Snacks, shop, disabled access; cl Sat in Apr, May and Oct, all Nov–Mar; (01726) 823092; £3.25.

🐖 **St Ervan** SW8970 TRENOUTH FARM RARE BREEDS CENTRE (off the A39) Friendly and unspoilt working farm with rare animals and poultry; lots of pigs (the piglets may race up to greet you) – even Iron Age ones descended from wild boar. Rarely crowded, and children really get a lot out of it. Some improvements are planned, but don't expect major redevelopment; one of the things that stands out here is the genuine and uncommercialised feel, and they've no intention of altering that. Teas, shop, mostly disabled access (but no facilities); open Easter–Sept, maybe cl Sat; (01841) 540606; *£3.50. The Ring o' Bells over at St Issey is useful for lunch.

✝ **St Germans** SX3557 The CHURCH has a wonderful Norman doorway and particularly fine east window; worth a look if you're passing this waterside village. There's a good view towards Port Eliot, a stately home designed by John Soane (not open).

★ 🖼 **St Ives** SW5141 A pretty place, despite the summer crowds, with its attractive working harbour and narrow streets and alleys (the cobbled Fore St is the prettiest). It has good wide beaches, and plenty of bird life along the Lelant Saltings (RSPB reserve). Its famous popularity with artists is best explored at the TATE GALLERY ST IVES, which can take a lot of the credit for the town's increasing popularity in recent years (in its first 18 months an extra £16 million was pumped into the local economy). Works by the familiar St Ives-school names are regularly joined by new displays of 20th-c art with a Cornish connection. It's an impressive building, outside and in, fully exploiting its spectacular cliffside setting – views are best from the café. Meals, snacks, shop, disabled access; (01736) 796226; cl winter Mon and

part of early Nov for re-hanging; £3.50. The adjacent BARBARA HEPWORTH MUSEUM & SCULPTURE GARDEN is a tranquil escape from the holiday hordes. Devoted to the artist's work and life, it has sculptures in the house, studio and subtropical garden, as well as photographs and letters. A joint ticket with the Tate is available, or a ticket for just here is *£3. Other works by Hepworth are dotted about the town. Besides the Pig 'n' Fish (see **Where to eat** section, below), the waterside Sloop (interesting pictures for sale) does reliable food. The best beach for surfers is Porthmeor slightly N, while in the other direction the B3306 to Land's End has great coast and moorland views.

✝ **St Just-in-Roseland** SW8435 An unspoilt spot, its CHURCH is in an idyllic creekside setting; the steep graveyard is like a lost subtropical garden – well worth a visit on a quiet sunny day, or in spring with the baby rooks blethering and the smell of wild garlic. The words on the inscribed stones by the path seem quite fitting.

✓ **St Kew** SX0276 Delightful quiet leafy village with old-fashioned feel, and agreeably low-key DONKEY AND PONY SANCTUARY; cl Nov–Easter; (01208) 841710; £3.50. The St Kew Inn is a nice place for a meal.

🏰 **St Mawes** SW8433 Very pretty harbourside and estuary views, a long waterfront to stroll along, clean bathing waters, a foot-passenger ferry to Falmouth and other boat trips (full of yachtsmen and others in summer, lots of guesthouses). The 16th-c CASTLE is remarkably well preserved; cl winter Mon and Tues; £2.20. The Victory does good-value lunches. Readers recommend taking the ferry across to St Anthony-in-Roseland for some remote and unspoilt views and walks; every half hour May–Sept; £1. The King Harry chain-drawn car ferry on the B3269 N of St Mawes is a favourite family crossing, and on the way the Roseland at Philleigh is one of Cornwall's nicest pubs.

✝ 🏛 🌳 **St Neot** SX1867 The parish CHURCH is well known for its early stained glass, and also has an unusual stone vault in the south porch. Nearby ancient remains include the 5 impressive BROWN GELLY BARROWS and some hut circles. CARNGLAZE SLATE CAVERNS are big long-abandoned mining chambers, with a lake at the far end of one; guided tours. The London Inn is good for lunch.

🏛 **Sancreed** SW4229 CARN EUNY ANCIENT VILLAGE Dating from the 1st c, substantial traces of a little village of stone courtyard houses, and a 66-ft underground passage leading to a circular chamber (some very minor roads to get here).

🏞🏛✝ **Tintagel** SX0588 A tourist trap since the 19th c, but well worth penetrating for TINTAGEL CASTLE. Forgetting the myths and legends, these dramatic 12th- and 13th-c ruins have a spectacular setting and unrivalled views. Try to come out of season, when the crowds are fewer and the mist and crashing waves add a touch of mystery. There's quite a lot of climbing involved, and the often steep steps among the crags can be slippery in wet weather. As for King Arthur, latest theories suggest he was a Shropshire lad, but a small exhibition makes the most of the Cornish case. Shop; cl 24–26 Dec; (01840) 770328; £2.70. A Land-Rover service can ferry you to the site from the village at regular intervals throughout the day. Arthurian legends are taken as fact at KING ARTHUR'S GREAT HALLS (Fore St), and while there's no denying the impressive craftsmanship (especially in the 72 stained-glass scenes), it's done too seriously to be anything more than a time-filler on a rainy day. Decent shop, disabled access; cl 25 Dec; (01840) 770526; £3. OLD POST OFFICE Small saggy-roofed 14th-c manor used in 19th c as a post office; shop; cl Nov–Mar; (01840) 770024; £2; NT. The Cornishman is handy for lunch, and the parish CHURCH worth a look.

🏛🐾 **Torpoint** SX4355 A pleasant ferry ride from Plymouth (it's a lot harder to get to by road). The car ferry from Devonport brings you closest to ANTONY HOUSE (2m NW), the finest Classical house in Cornwall, little changed since the early 18th c, with interesting contents and paintings in its panelled rooms; also riverside gardens redesigned by Humphrey Repton, and a dovecot. Snacks, shop, disabled access to ground floor only; open pm Tues–Thurs and bank hols Apr–Oct, plus Sun Jun–Aug; (01752) 812191; £3.80, woodland garden £1; NT. Further round the coast, and reached most easily by the Cremyll pedestrian ferry, is the mansion at MOUNT EDGCUMBE, reconstructed after World War II bombing, with period furniture and (the main attraction) acres of lovely gardens and parkland, divided into English, French and Italian sections. Great views to Plymouth. Meals, snacks, shop, disabled access; house cl Mon (exc bank hols), Tues, mid-Oct–Mar (but park and gardens open then, free); (01752) 822236; £3.50. The charmingly furnished Edgcumbe Arms by the ferry has good-value food.

✝ **Trebetherick** SW9377 ST ENODOC CHURCH Tucked well away from the roads under a seaside hill off the Rock road, looking out to Padstow Bay. A nice stroll from the village, it's the burial place of John Betjeman. Daymer Bay near here is a very clean and attractive beach, and as it's so shallow it's ideal for families wanting a paddle. The Carpenters Arms is useful for lunch, and down on the water at Rock the Mariners Hotel has lovely views over to Padstow.

🐾☺ **Treburrick** SW8670 TAMARISK LEISURE PARK (off the B3276) Friendly little place based around a farm with tame animals and rare breeds; various activities inc archery and scrumpy-tasting. Younger children love feeding the lambs – older brothers may prefer the free computer games. Snacks, shop, disabled access; (01841) 540829; £2.99. The Farmers Arms in St Merryn is a nearby family dining pub.

🐾 **Trecangate** SX1757 PORFELL ANIMAL LAND 🖼 Delightfully unspoilt and friendly, with deer, wallabies, goats, raccoons, ducks and chickens in 15 acres of sloping fields and woodland. More unusual are the 3 zebra and an ocelot. Readers very much enjoy the peaceful and remote feel. Snacks, shop, disabled access; cl Nov–Easter; (01503) 220211; £3.50. The Ship over at Lerryn SX1457 is fairly handy for lunch and often has good watercolours for sale; the stepping stones over the river there are a hit with children, and good circular walks are signposted from the car park.

🐎 ☺ **Tredinnick** SW9270 SHIRE HORSE ADVENTURE PARK Far more to this busy complex than just the magnificent horses: an owl sanctuary demonstrates night-time flight, there's a children's farm, an exhibition of rural antiquities, nature trails, watermill and working craftsmen, and a big adventure playground. The horses are displayed in an indoor arena (at noon and 3pm), and you can see them being groomed in their stables – along with Shetland ponies. Lots for all ages, but ideal for children. Meals, snacks, shop, disabled access; cl Nov–Easter; (01841) 540276; £5.50. The Ring o' Bells at St Issey is convenient for lunch.

🐝 **Trelissick** SW8339 TRELISSICK GARDEN (on the B3289) Woodland park with beautifully kept gardens of camellias, magnolias and hydrangeas, also subtropical garden and other unusual plants; wonderful views of the King Harry Passage and over to Pendennis Castle. There's a pretty orchard, and good walks in the surrounding woodland. Meals, snacks, shop, disabled access; cl am Sun, Jan–Feb; (01872) 862090; £4; NT. The NT have 4 holiday cottages on the estate. The Punch Bowl & Ladle at Penelewey on the King Harry Ferry road is popular for lunch.

🏠 🐝 **Trerice** SW8457 TRERICE Pretty Elizabethan house with unusual gables, and elaborate plasterwork ceilings in the magnificent Hall and Great Chamber. Fine furnishings from the 17th and 18th c, notable paintings, early embroideries, Oriental and English porcelain, and

in the grounds an unusual collection of lawnmowers; lovely colourful gardens with Cornish fruit trees. Snacks (in a barn with activities for toddlers), shop, very good disabled access; cl Sat (exc Aug–mid-Sept), Tues, and Nov–Mar; (01637) 875404; £3.80; NT. The Two Clomes at Quintrell Downs is quite handy for lunch.

♂ ✝ **Truro** SW8244 A busy but civilised town with good shops (market day Weds); Lemon St is a particularly fine Georgian street, and Boscawen St is cobbled. ROYAL CORNWALL MUSEUM (River St) Tales of local characters such as Black John of Tetcott, an 18th-c dwarf whose party piece was apparently tying mice together by their tails, swallowing them whole, and then pulling them up again. A new natural history gallery opened last year. Meals, snacks, shop, disabled access; cl Sun, bank hols; (01872) 72205; £2. The CATHEDRAL is one of the newer Anglican ones, designed in 1880 in Early English style and finished in 1910; the twin spires of the west front are handsome, and pop up dramatically from behind shops and houses. The Old Ale House, Globe, Wig & Pen and William IV are all good for lunch.

✗ **Veryan** SW9139 Lovely village famous for its 5 devil-proof, thatched, round houses; also a water garden sheltered by holm oaks. Nearby, 16th-c MELINSEY MILL is a nicely restored watermill in a lovely setting, with good afternoon teas; cl Mon, Oct–Mar. The prettiest approach is to walk along the streamside 'Secret Valley' from Pendower Beach (off the A3078 S) rather than go from the village itself.

↓ ✝ ♭ **Wendron** SW6731 POLDARK MINE AND HERITAGE CENTRE 🖼 A fun feature of this old tin mine is its underground post box, the deepest in Britain. More serious attractions include a tour of the mine, an 18th-c village, a film on the history of Cornish mining, old cottages, collection of working beam engines, and plenty of children's amusements. Varied enough to interest most members of the family. Meals, snacks, shop, limited disabled access; cl Nov–Easter; (01326) 563166; £5.50.

♂ ♱ **Zennor** SW4538 WAYSIDE FOLK MUSEUM Decent little local history

museum; you should be able to see the wheel of the adjacent watermill gently turning. Teas, shop (specialising in Cornish books and crafts); cl Nov–Easter, Sat in Oct; (01736) 796945; *£2. The CHURCH is

---

Days Out

Bodmin Moor exploits near the Tamar
Launceston; Altarnun church, Wesley's Cottage; lunch at Eliot Arms, Tregadillett; Cheesewring and The Hurlers stone circle, nr Minions; Cotehele House.

Medieval fortress and Victorian high life
Fowey; Golant church; Restormel Castle; lunch at Royal Oak, Lostwithiel; Lanhydrock House.

Fishing villages and an Arthurian mystery
Padstow; walk or cycle along Camel Trail; recover over lunch at Seafood Restaurant or St Petroc's, back in Padstow; Port Isaac, Tintagel – Boscastle if time.

Paradise on a rugged coast
St Ives; Paradise Park; lunch at Pig 'n' Fish, St Ives or Miners Arms, Mithian; stroll on coast path from Wheal Coates to St Agnes Head; Bedruthan Steps (on coast towards Newquay).

At the toe of Britain
Chysauster ancient village; Porthcurno theatre and beach; coast path to Treryn Dinas nr Treen; lunch at Logan Rock, Treen; Carn Brea (viewpoint inland from Land's End); Wayside Folk Museum, Zennor.

Island escapade
St Michael's Mount; Penzance – lunch at Turks Head; Flambards, nr Helston.

Space Age structure on the Lizard
Goonhilly Downs Satellite Earth Station; Lizard Point; lunch at White Hart, St Keverne; Mullion and Kynance Cove.

Garden exotica and a seal safari
Falmouth; Pendennis Castle; lunch at Pandora, nr Mylor Bridge; Trebah/Glendurgan gardens or Gweek seal sanctuary.

Lost gardens and a remote coast
Mevagissey; Charlestown; lunch at Crown, St Ewe; The Lost Gardens of Heligan; Portloe and Veryan villages.

Animal magic and a look at the past
Looe; Monkey Sanctuary; Polperro (walk in from Talland Bay), lunch at Crumplehorn Mill or Three Pilchards; Lanreath folk museum and church.

Cornwall's south-eastern corner
Mount Edgcumbe country park; Kingsand and Cawsand, lunch at Halfway House; stroll to Rame Point; Antony House.

best seen in its granite landscape from the hills above. The Tinners Arms is good for lunch.

★ **Attractive inland villages** with decent pubs include Constantine SW7229, St Ewe SW9746, and St Mawgan SW8765.

✝ As well as those mentioned above, **interesting churches** include Braddock SX1662 (wood carvings), Golant SX1155 (complete 15th-c fittings; waterside village), Lansallos SX1751 (carved bench ends) and Lanteglos Highway SX1543 (Perpendicular but not – subsidence has left the arches at drunken angles). ⋒ The northern part of Cornwall is full of interesting **prehistoric monuments.** Near Minions (Cornwall's highest village) the HURLERS STONE CIRCLES SX2571 is made up of 3 Bronze Age circles – the central one still has 14 stones standing. Close by is the RILLATON BARROW where the lovely Rillaton

gold cup (now in the British Museum) was found, along with other interesting relics. Not far off at St Cleer is TRETHEVY QUOIT SX2568, a very photogenic megalithic tomb. The Crows Nest SX2669 down nr Darite is handy for lunch. The strange CHEESEWRING SX2676 on Bodmin Moor, another appealing camera subject, is made up of several improbably overhanging granite slabs. (See also St Neot entry, above.) **Waterside pubs** in delightful settings include the Royal Standard at Flushing SW8033, Pandora on Restronguet Creek past Mylor Bridge SW8137; the best location of any Cornish pub – you can park in Mylor Bridge for leisurely 2-mile waterside walk there and back, or drive all the way), Shipwrights Arms at Helford SW7526 ('Frenchman's Creek' walk from here), Heron at Malpas SW8442 and New Inn at Manaccan SW7625.

Walks

Land's End ⌂-1 has fine cliff walks in both directions – the one to Sennen SW3425 is lovely, and the cove there is worth looking around. Some of the wildest and most formidable cliffs in Britain are between here and **Treen** SW3923 ⌂-2, from where you can walk from the Logan Rock pub (good food) to Treryn Dinas SW3922, which we think the most stunning of Cornwall's headlands, capped by the precariously balanced Logan Rock; a short mile west is the magical open-air Minack Theatre, cut into the steep cliffs above Porthcurno beach. **Lamorna Cove** SW4520 ⌂-3 (where there's another decent pub, a bit up the lane) also has some splendid cliff walks in both directions, and the eerie Nine Maidens stone circle just inland.

The coast walks tend to get easier (and less blowy) as you work along to the E. At **Rinsey** SW5927 ⌂-4 the coast path passes two magnificently sited ruined tin and copper mine buildings, Wheal Prosper and Wheal Trewavas, both now maintained by the NT; a few miles inland, **Tregonning Hill** SW6029 ⌂-5 takes only a few minutes to climb and has an impressive view; here in 1746 William Cookworthy made the first discovery of china clay in England, and went on to make porcelain. **Loe Pool** SW6425 ⌂-6, Cornwall's largest lake, is a haven for waterfowl and is blocked from the sea by an NT shingle bank called Loe Bar (only breeding place of the rare sandhill rust moth – and favourite place of worship of a German evangelical sect); a path leads round the lake. From here you can walk along the coast to Gunwalloe Fishing Cove SX0952. Dramatic **Mullion Cove** SW6617 ⌂-7 is best reached by a there-and-back walk along the cliff from Porth Mellin SW6618; the extension S to Kynance Cove is outstanding.

The most southerly point in England, **Lizard Point** SW7012 ⌂-8 is a good start for bracing cliff walks in either direction, with good views. Lizard village is well placed for longer walks encompassing Church Cove to the E and Kynance Cove to the W. Inland, the Lizard is largely flat and not really worth extended walks. A rewarding short stroll on the coast path from picturesque **Cadgwith** SW7114 ⌂-9 leads S to Chynhalls Point past the aptly named Devil's Frying Pan, where the waves foam into a spectacular collapsed cavern. There's a rewarding walk down from **Coverack** SW7818 ⌂-10 to Black Head SW7716 and maybe beyond, or to Lowland Point SW8019 (also reached from St Keverne), for dramatic views of the Manacles. The NE part of the Lizard around Helford SW7526 and **Dennis Head** SW7825 ⌂-11 is appreciably leafier, and has some intricate coves and an undemanding coast path. More blowy again is the fine stretch of coast path around **Rosemullion Head** SW7927 ⌂-12, from Mawnan SW7827, or from Maenporth SW7929, where there's a sheltered sandy cove with decent modern pub/restaurant.

A pleasant short seaside walk with a good finish is the stroll from **Mylor Bridge** SW8036 ⌂-13 round to the pub at Restronguet Passage. **St Anthony Head** ⌂-14 on the E side of the Fal estuary has superb views, and easy walks along low, level cliffs; parking at the head itself, SW8431, or nr Porth Farm on the way down. Virtually the whole of **Gerrans Bay** ⌂-15 is good easy walking, from Portscatho SW8735, Pendower Beach SW8938 (a good sandy stretch), or the handy Plume of Feathers in Gerrans SW8735 itself. **Portloe** SW9339 ⌂-16 has more rugged scenery, with stiffish climbs on to Nare Head. **Dodman Point** SX0039 ⌂-17 (reached from Gorran Haven SX0141, or one of the closer car parks – for instance, at Hemmick Beach) allows a round walk mainly along clifftops.

From **Fowey** SX1252 ⌂-18 a popular circular route takes you across on the Bodinnick car ferry, then takes the path through the steep creekside woods round to Polruan, and comes back on the other foot ferry. **Talland Bay** SX2251 ⌂-19 provides an easy 1-mile walk along the coast to enter Polperro's harbour the best way – a sensible alternative to sweating out summer traffic jams in Polperro village itself. **Rame Head** SX4148 ⌂-20 at the E end of Whitsand Bay juts far out and is capped by a primitive hermitage chapel – a worthwhile walk from the pretty village of Kingsand. Close by is the **Mount Edgcumbe Country Park** SX4552 ⌂-21, with woodland and parkland walks and some striking waterside views of Plymouth.

The north coast is generally more exposed and windy – but much of it is a good deal more deserted.

The long wonderfully clean beach below the cliffs at **Whitesand Bay** SW3527 ⌂-22 gives good walks, stretching away N of Sennen Cove SW3524 (very popular with surfers; the Old Success here has a great view). On a wild day **Botallack** SW3632 ⌂-23, with its ruined engine house right down by the sea, is very dramatic, and there are fine steep walks all around.

The moors nearly reach the sea around **Morvah** SW4035 ⌂-24, and in a few miles from here you can take in the cliff path, the moors close to the ruin of Ding Dong Mine, the prehistoric stone hoop of Men-an-Tol and the Iron Age hill fort of Chun Castle (close by Chun Quoit, a Bronze Age burial chamber). Around **Zennor** SW4538 ⌂-25 (decent pub) you can walk for miles without seeing another soul; Gurnards Head SW4338 juts dramatically into the Atlantic, and the hotel there (with unusual bar snacks) is a good base for cliff walks.

Out of season, when the caravan and camp sites are empty, the magnificent sands around **St Ives Bay** SW5440 ⌂-26 are well worth walking, with good cliff walks W.

Almost any stretch of the coast path E of here, right up to Trevose Head SW8576 (near Padstow), gives long bracing clifftop walks; a good base is Portreath SW6545, which has a decent pub. **Wheale Coates** SW6949 ⌂-27 is one of the most photogenic mine ruins on the Cornish coast, and the diversion up St Agnes Beacon SW7150 is well worth it for the commanding views. The **Bedruthan Steps** SW8469 ⌂-28 off the B3276 Newquay–Padstow road are really special with their dramatic rock pinnacles, cliffs and lovely sandy coves.

Much gentler, the **disused railway** ⌂-29 from Wadebridge SW9872 to Padstow SW9175 is a level 6 miles along the edge of the Camel estuary, with banks of wild flowers, birds, and lovely views between cuttings – you can walk or cycle (bike hire at either end), or picnic on the small beaches at low tide. Those with less energy could park at Wadebridge, walk to Padstow, have lunch and get the bus back (2.30pm from the old station). You might then walk on through scenic countryside beyond Bodmin (worth stopping at Helland pottery, just by the path at Helland Bridge). On the E side of the **Camel estuary** SW9376 ⌂-30 sand dunes suddenly give way to a rocky headland, Rumps Point, which can be walked round in an hour or so; or at low tide there's a pleasant sandy walk between Rock and Polzeath (which has one of Cornwall's best beaches, popular with surfers).

Some particularly fine stretches of cliff for walking are around **Port Isaac** SW9980 ⌂-31. A good start for **Tintagel** SX0588 ⌂-32 is from Rocky Valley, a craggy valley leading from the B3263 to the sea. **Boscastle** SX0990 ⌂-33 has fascinating clifftop views; **Crackington Haven** SX1396 ⌂-34, with a superbly sited dining pub, the Coombe Barton, has a good walk to High Cliff, Cornwall's highest.

Inland, from **Luxulyan** SX0558 ⌂-35 (which has a pleasant church) you can walk along the lush wooded valley to the S, strewn with huge granite boulders and crossed by an impressive viaduct; if you feel adventurous you can climb up the valley to the top of the viaduct. The **Tamar Valley** ⌂-36 has charming woodland paths close by Cotehele SX4268; it's otherwise short on good circular walks – we hope for early action on this, given its new protected status as an Area of Outstanding Natural Beauty. The rock at **Roche** SW9860 ⌂-37 is worth the short walk from the B3274, with a 14th-c ruined ivy-covered chapel built into it, and a ladder up (decent pub nearby, past the station).

Windswept Bodmin Moor is not as richly endowed as Dartmoor for walking, and much is boggy and rough. It does have its own bleak character, with strange tors, prehistoric traces, wind-bent trees, granite walls, lonely lakes, and, despite official denials, continuing tales of black panthers. For a taster start at **Minions** SX2671 ⌂-38 and explore the Hurlers stone circles SX2571 and the Cheesewring SX2676 (see **To see and do** section, above); there is a clear track between them. The nearby track from Sharptor SX2573 to Kilmar Tor SX2574 affords fine views. The summit of **Rough Tor** (pronounced Roe Tor) SX1480 ⌂-39, reached from a signed car park off the A39 nr Camelford, gives views of Brown Willy, the highest point in Cornwall. **Kit Hill** ⌂-40 off the A390 N of Callington SX3669, with a huge chimney stack and mine shafts, gives impressive views across to Dartmoor. Riding is popular on the moor, and quite a few stables on or around it cater for all levels of riding ability.

Where to eat

Several of the hotels and inns recommended as good places to stay are also good for diners eating out (see **Where to stay** section above).
Chapel Amble SW9975 MALTSTERS ARMS (01208) 812473 Popular family-run pub with attractively knocked-together rooms (one is no smoking), flagstones, beams and a big stone fireplace; good interesting food inc lots of fish, 20 wines by the glass, well kept real ales, and helpful friendly staff. £18.70/£7.95.
Fowey SX1252 FOOD FOR THOUGHT Town Quay (01726) 832221 Generous helpings of carefully presented food in a quayside evening restaurant – fine fish and some simple as well as other elaborate dishes, and lovely puddings; cl Sun, Jan–Feb; children over 10. £26.
Lanlivery SX0759 CROWN (01208) 872707 Pretty 12th-c inn with rambling series of rooms, chatty atmosphere, good food using home-grown and local

produce, and a nice garden; disabled access. £19|£4.50

Mithian SW7450 MINERS ARMS (01872) 552375 Secluded Tudor pub with lots of character, fine old furnishings and warm winter fires; popular food, real ales, and friendly service. £18.25|£4.50.

Mousehole SW4726 CORNISH RANGE (01736) 731488 Friendly restaurant, neatly kept, with a nice atmosphere; carefully cooked food inc good puddings and local fish; cl pm winter Sun, last 3 wks Jan; disabled access. £16|£6.50.

Padstow SW9175 ST PETROC'S 4 New St (01841) 532700 Attractive little hotel (under the same ownership as the Seafood restaurant) with good quickly served food from a short menu (mostly fish), a sensible wine list, and a friendly atmosphere; cl Mon, Christmas; disabled access. £15.50.

Padstow SW9175 SEAFOOD Riverside (01841) 532485 Wonderfully fresh seafood straight from the boats in this busy, airy quayside restaurant, good puddings, nice cheeses, a long, interesting and fairly priced wine list, and friendly service; conservatory for aperitifs; bedrooms; cl Sun, 21 Dec–6 Feb; children over 4; disabled access. £32.50 **dinner**, £26.50 lunch|£6.20.

Philleigh SW8639 ROSELAND (01872) 580254 Friendly little 17th-c pub with a good winter fire, lots of rugby and rowing prints and a relaxed atmosphere; well kept real ales, and good popular home-made food. £18|£7.50.

Polperro SX2051 KITCHEN The Coombes (01503) 272780 Cottagey, informal no smoking evening restaurant with really good interesting food inc vegetarian and daily-changing fresh fish dishes (lovely fresh lobster and crab), and good-value wines; cl Sun, Nov–Easter; children over 12. £23|£9.

Polperro SX2051 PLANTATION CAFE The Coombes (01503) 272223 Popular beamed tea shop with good cream teas, a wide choice of interesting teas inc herbal and fruit, lunchtime sandwiches, and evening meals; cl Sat, Nov–Easter; disabled access. £17|£5.95.

Porthallow SW7923 TARANAKI TEA ROOMS (01326) 280671 Lovely flower-filled tropical gardens with seats under a covered pergola or in the conservatory; home-baked scones and cakes, cream teas and light lunches (super crab sandwiches) all prepared by friendly owner; no licence but you can bring drinks from pub 50yds down road; cl Oct–Good Fri; partial disabled access. £6.50|£3.

Portloe SW9339 TREGAIN The Post Office (01872) 501252 Small friendly restaurant serving interesting well cooked food, specialising in local fish (lovely crab) and locally produced smoked fish; pasties, cider, ice-creams, and home-made cakes and scones for super cream teas; 2 bedrooms; cl pm Sun, Nov–Mar. £25|£4.

St Ives SW45140 PIG 'N' FISH Norway Lane (01736) 794204 Simply decorated restaurant serving interesting, very fresh fish dishes; cl Sun, Mon, mid-Dec–Feb; no children. £26.

St Kew SX0276 ST KEW (01208) 841259 Rather grand-looking stone pub with a friendly welcome, nice old-fashioned furnishings, good popular food, and a peaceful garden. £20.80|£4.85.

St Michael's Mount SW5130 SAIL LOFT The Harbour (01736) 710748 Converted boat house with enjoyable home-made cakes, Cornish cream teas, more substantial meals, and friendly service; cl Nov–Easter; disabled access. £14.25|£4.50.

Trebarwith SX0585 PORT WILLIAM (01840) 770230 Fresh fish from local fishermen in this marvellously placed old harbourmaster's house; other good food, too, nautical decor, and lovely sunsets; disabled access. £17.35|£8.

Treburley SX3477 SPRINGER SPANIEL (01579) 370424 Lovely relaxed atmosphere in main road pub with totally home-made interesting food inc delicious puddings; very friendly service, simply furnished bars, and attractive restaurant. £20|£4.50.

Truro SW8244 OLD ALE HOUSE 7 Quay St (01872) 71122 Appealing, bustling and friendly back-to-basics pub, popular with a good cross-section of people, with interesting bric-a-brac and engaging old furnishings; up to 24 real ales, and enterprising, freshly prepared and very cheap food from a spotless kitchen. **£12.65|£4.20**.

ISLES OF SCILLY

The islands, about 30 miles W of Land's End, are charmingly unspoilt and a great place for utter relaxation. They have beautiful scenery, an almost subtropical climate, and a variety of shore lines giving excellent coastal walks. In a lazy day you can comfortably walk round the largest, St Mary's, which is just 6 square miles. Tresco and St Agnes are the other main populated ones, though that means small undeveloped communities rather than any towns or big settlements. There are over 100 islands in all, some just strange-shaped rocks jutting out of the sea, their only visitors seals, dolphins and puffins.

You can get there from Penzance by ferry (around £30 day return) or more spectacularly by helicopter, a 20-minute ride with really beautiful views of the Cornish coast and of the islands (return fares start at around £60). The islands also have their own little airline Skybus which leaves from Land's End, Newquay or Exeter several times a day. The trip from Land's End is quickest and cheapest (from £55 return, maybe cheaper standby flights; no flights Sun). They also do packages in conjunction with InterCity – (01736) 787017 for details.

Where to stay

Tresco SV8915 ISLAND Tresco, Isles of Scilly TR24 0PU (01720) 422883 **£290 inc dinner**; 40 rms, many with balconies and terrace overlooking the gardens or the sea. Tiny private island, renowned for its wonderful subtropical Abbey Gardens and reached by helicopter or boat; the hotel tractor-drawn bus (no cars allowed though bike hire is available) takes you to a spacious, very friendly, modern hotel with a colonial-style bar, library, fine food and wine, panoramic views, swimming pool, and private beach; no dogs; cl Nov–Feb.

Hugh Town SV9010 TREGARTHENS Hugh Town, St Mary's, Isles of Scilly TR21 0PP (01720) 422540 **£138 inc dinner**; 33 rms, most with sea views. Magnificent views over the harbour and outer islands of Samson, Bryher and Tresco from this extended and modernised hotel, first opened in 1848; neatly kept rooms, good food and pleasant service; cl late Oct–mid-Mar; no dogs.

Pelistry Bay SV9311 CARNWETHERS COUNTRY HOUSE Pelistry Bay, St Mary's, Isles of Scilly TR21 0NX (01720) 422415 ***£94 inc dinner**; good-value weekly terms, too; 9 rms. Well run no smoking country guesthouse nr very fine beach, with an acre of lovely gardens, heated swimming pool, and croquet; lounge with helpful books about the islands, well stocked bar, good freshly cooked set 4-course dinner using local produce and a sound wine list; and games room with pool table and table tennis; sauna; lots of coastal walks; cl Oct–Apr; children over 8.

To see and do

As each of the islands is so small, few apart from Tresco have many specific attractions – visitors come mainly to 'get away from it all'. The total population is just 2,000, so there really can be a refreshing feeling of complete isolation. By far the best activity is walking – there are plenty of white sandy beaches to stroll along (the sea is clean but cold), or unusual plants and birds to track down. Hiring bikes is another good way of exploring and enjoying the scenery. Thanks to the climate – the name means Sun Isles – flowers come out early, and spring and autumn sunsets can be particularly beautiful. A good plan is to island-hop – there are regular ferries between the larger islands, though it can prove expensive. Every Fri evening and some Weds in summer you can watch the racing of the traditional six-oar gigs that used to dash out to shipwrecks.

Bryher SV8715 is a tiny quiet place, even by Scilly standards. The south bay has lots of wild flowers, and Watch Hill has wonderful views. The Hell Bay Hotel is good value.

St Agnes SV8807 has the most south-westerly community in the British Isles, and is joined to a smaller island called Gugh by a sandbar, awash at high tide. The sheltered cove here is especially popular. The 17th-c lighthouse is the second oldest in Britain. The views from here out to the rocks and islets are very atmospheric – especially when you remember more ships have been wrecked here than anywhere comparable in the world.

St Martin's SV9215 is a narrow rocky ridge with flowers stretching down to the main attraction – the extensive beaches, very popular for picnics. There's a diving school, and the St Martin's Hotel has lovely sunset views.

St Mary's SV9010 The hub of Scilly Isles life, though its centre, Hugh Town, is little more than a village by mainland standards. Most ferries and planes arrive here, and you can get PLEASURE CRUISES from the Old Quay out to the bird and seal colonies on the outer islets and islands; there are fishing trips from here too. There's a MUSEUM, and 9-hole putting green with fine views. The LONGSTONE HERITAGE CENTRE concentrates on the ecology and maritime history of the islands, with a huge collection of archive newspapers; open pm Tues–Fri; £1.95. The Bishop & Wolf is a pleasant pub, and the Atlantic Hotel has a good pub part. Up in the north at Bants Carn there's a burial chamber and ancient village. Back down south, walk out to Peninnis Head for good views of the Wolf and Bishop's Rock lighthouses. Just along the coast is STAR CASTLE.

Tresco SV8915 The highlight here is the amazing SUBTROPICAL GARDEN around the grounds of the Abbey, begun in 1834, which, despite storms, contains a magnificent collection of exotic plants, bananas even. Also in these grounds is VALHALLA, a collection of carved figure-heads from wrecked ships, many dating back to the 17th c. Helicopters from Penzance land just outside the garden gate, so it's possible (though not cheap) to come here for just a day. The southern parts of the island are mainly sandy, but in the north it's more wild and rugged, with the remains of castles of both Charles I and Oliver Cromwell, and a cave known as Piper's Hole. Cycling and walking are real pleasures – not least because there aren't any cars. The New Inn, embellished with a mystery cargo of pine planking which washed ashore recently, has good food inc seafood.

Where to eat

St Agnes SW7150 TURKS HEAD The Quay, Isles of Scilly (01720) 422434
Idyllically placed pub (a pleasant place to stay) with outstanding views over

sweeping bay, real ales, decent wines, good food inc fresh fish, cream cakes/ices all afternoon, evening barbecues; can take food down to beach; cl Nov–Mar; disabled access. **£16.50**|£5.

Special thanks to Mrs N Holtum, Yvonne Champion, David Wallington, Mrs E Hoare, Alan Reavill, Lisa Grey, Miss A Donoghue, Mrs P A Long.

CORNWALL CALENDAR

Some of these dates were provisional as we went to press, please check information with the telephone numbers provided.

This year **Cornwall** *will host the World Watersports Festival from April to August with tall ships, power boating, angling, surfing, trawler racing, as well as music, theatre, a classic boat festival and many more cultural events.*

JANUARY

1 **Mawnan Smith** Trebah Icicle: charity swim at Trebah Garden (01326) 250448

26 **Saltash** Music and Speech Festival – *till 6 Feb* (01752) 843073

FEBRUARY

2 **St Ives** Hurling the Silver Ball: the town and its people are divided in two, *at midday* a ball is thrown by the Mayor from the town hall into the crowd below who carry, fight or secrete the ball to their half of the town (01736) 797840

16 **Mawnan Smith** Children's Activities at Trebah Garden – *till Fri 20* (01326) 250448

24 **St Columb Major** Hurling the Silver Ball: town and country residents battle in the streets with shop windows boarded up, the town goal is a small stone trough and the country goal is 1m N on the road to Wadebridge (01872) 274057

27 **Wadebridge** Music and Speech Festival – *till Sat 28,* also *on 5–6 March* (01208) 812227

MARCH

Cornwall Festival of Spring Gardens: over 70 gardens open – *till 31 May* (01872) 74057

7 **St Columb Major** Hurling the Silver Ball (see above) (01872) 74057; **Truro** Cornwall Brass Band Association Contest (01762) 61042

9 **Truro** County Music Festival – *till Sat 14* (01872) 573338

14 **Perranporth** National Land Yachting Regatta – *till Sun 15* (0891) 22 1998

24 **St Austell** County Spring Flower Show at the Lost Gardens of Heligan – *till Thurs 26* (01872) 274057

26 **Roche** Music and Speech Festival – *till Sat 28* (01726) 890157

28 **St Mellion** Camellia Show at St Mellion Hotel – *till Sun 29* (01579) 352017

APRIL

5 **St Endellion** Music Festival – *till Sun 12* (01208) 850463

9 **Mawnan Smith** Easter Egg Hunt at Trebah Garden – *till Sun 26* (01326) 250448

CORNWALL CALENDAR

APRIL cont

10 **Bodmin** Thomas the Tank Engine at Bodmin General Station – *till Mon 13* (01208) 73666; **Hayle** International Sand and Surf Festival – *till Sun 19* 0891 221998; **Marazion** Windsurf National Racing Championships – *till Mon 13* (0891) 221998

11 **Penzance** Trials and Classic Car Display on the Promenade: end of 400 mile trial of motorcycles and cars (01359) 270954

13 **Helston** Easter Eggstravaganza at Flambards Village (01326) 573404; **Looe** National Youth Sailing Championships – *till Fri 17* (0891) 221998

24 **Mevagissey** Theatre of Flowers at the Heligan Gardens – *till Sun 26* (01726) 844157

25 **Camborne** Trevithick Day: traction engine rally, traditional Cornish dancing, street parades (01209) 712941

MAY

1 **Boscastle** Beer Festival – *till Mon 4* (01840) 250202; **Newquay** Great Cornwall Balloon Festival – *till Mon 4* (01637) 872211; **Padstow** Obby Oss Celebrations: May song, man in large full-skirted horse costume with other strangely dressed characters (01872) 274057

2 **Bugle** Music and Speech Festival – also *on Tues 5–Fri 8* (01726) 850535; **St Mary's** Isles of Scilly, World Pilot Gig Championships – *till Mon 4* (01872) 274057

3 **Newquay** English National Surfing Championships at Fistral Beach – *till Tues 5* (01726) 74466

7 **Wall** Music and Speech Festival – *till Sat 9* (01736) 850420

8 **Fowey and St Austell** Daphne du Maurier Festival – *till Sun 17* (01726) 74324; **Helston** Spring Festival: *from* Early Morning Dance *8.20am*, with Hal-an-Tow and ancient Furry Dance *later* (01326) 572082

10 **Bodmin Moor** Ten Tors Walk (01208) 72793; **Siblyback** Peninsula Classic Fly Fishing Competition at Siblyback Lake (0891) 221998

16 **Bude** March at 10.30am preceeding re-enactment of the Battle of Stamford Hill (1643) at **Stratton** *at 3.30pm*, and *on Sun 17 at 3pm* (01288) 354886

23 **Calstock** Festival – *till Sat 30* (01822) 832653; **Newquay** European Open Professional Surfing Championships at Fistral Beach – *till Mon 25* (01637) 879412

24 **Bodmin** Steam and Diesel Gala at Bodmin General Station – *till Mon 25* (01208) 73666; **Launceston** Steam Engine Rally – *till Mon 25* (01566) 776544

28 **Porthcurno** Minack Theatre Festival – *till mid Sept* (01736) 810181

JUNE

4 **Wadebridge** Royal Cornwall Show – *till Sat 6* (01208) 812183

7 **Mawnan Smith** D-Day Commemoration at Trebah Garden (01326) 250448

10 **Truro** Jazz Festival – *till Sun 14* (01872) 222202

12 **Penzance** Golowan Festival: traditional sea and land festival, with theatre, street theatre, Celtic arts, carnival and fireworks – *till Sun 21* (01736 331933

9 **Falmouth** World Power Boat Championships – *till Sun 14* (0891) 22 1998

CORNWALL CALENDAR

JUNE cont

15 **St Day** Feast Week – *till Mon 22* (01209) 820841
20 **Bugle** West of England Bandsmen's Festival at Molinnis Park (01446) 737232; **Saltash** Maritime Week – *till Sun 28* (0891) 221998
21 **Liskeard** Carnival Week – *till Sat 27* (01579) 341032
27 **Bodmin** Cornwall Theatre and Heritage Festival – *till 4 July* (01208) 76616; **Bodmin** Thomas the Tank Engine at Bodmin General Station – *till Sun 28* (01208) 73666
28 **Mevagissey** Feast Week – *till 4 July* (01726) 74014
29 **Penryn** Lady Jane Killiegrew Festival – *till 5 July* (01326) 374969

JULY

4 **Bodmin** Riding and Heritage Day (01208) 74121; **Sennen** European Surf Championships – *till Sun 5* (0891) 221998; **Padstow** Vintage Rally at Trevisker Farm – *till Sun 5* (01637) 876028
5 **Newquay** 1900 Week: Victorian entertainments inc processions, floral dance, fireworks – *till Sat 11* (01637) 878735
10 **Penzance** West Cornwall Maritime Festival – *till Tues 14* (0891) 221998
11 **Falmouth** Dragon Boat Challenge – *till Tues 14* (0891) 221998; **Lanhydrock** Jazz in the Park at Lanhydrock House (01208) 73320; **Merrymeet** Liskeard Country Show at Trengrove Farm (01579) 343125; **St Austell** White Gold Festival: street entertainment, clay dances, art and musical events – *till Sat 18* (01726) 74269
13 **Stithians** Show (01872) 240113
16 **Falmouth** Cutty Sark Tall Ships Race: rock and classical firework concerts at Pendennis Castle, marine show, live music and dance – *till Sun 19* (01872) 223527; **Launceston** Agricultural Show at Kennards House (01566) 777777
18 **Camborne** Show (01209) 714754
23 **Newquay** Surf Festival – *till 3 Aug* (0891) 221998
25 **Looe** Vintage Steam Rally at Bray Farm, Normansland – *till Sun 26* (01503) 240520
27 **Looe** Carnival Week – *till 1 Aug* (01579) 347701
28 **St Endellion** 40th Summer Music Festival – *till 7 Aug* (01208) 850463
31 **Tintagel** Re-enactment of the Battle of Camlann (450 AD): field opens 2pm, also *on 2 and 3 Aug* (01840) 770050

AUGUST

1 **Launceston** Garden Society Show (01566) 772333; **St Columb** Carnival *till parade on Sat 8* (01637) 880599; **Tredinnick** (nr St Issey) Cornish Steam Rally at Tredinnick Farm – *till Sun 2* (01208) 831293; **St Keverne** Ox Roast inc torchlight procession (01326) 280487
5 **Newquay** RAF St Mawgan International Air Day (01637) 850931
12 **Camelford** Agricultural Show (01840) 213761
22 **Bude** Carnival (01288) 355100, also Celtic Watersports Festival – *till Fri 28* (0891) 221998; **Penzance** St Mary's Art Festival – *till 6 Sept* (01736) 367659
24 **Marhamchurch** Revels: procession and country dancing (01288) 354240
28 **Wadebridge** Folk Festival – *till Mon 31* (01208) 831123

CORNWALL CALENDAR

AUGUST cont

29 **Bodmin** Thomas the Tank Engine at Bodmin General Station – *till Sun 30* (01208) 73666; **Bude** Jazz Festival: over 150 events, mostly trad jazz with street parades – *till 5 Sept* (01288) 356360; also **Bude** Lifeboat Day (01288) 355100; **Helston** Harvest Fair – *till Mon 31* (01326) 563167; **Merrymeet** Traction Engine Rally at Trengrove Farm – *till Mon 31* (01579) 342148; **Newquay** Surfers Against Sewage Ocean Festival – *till Mon 31* (0891) 221998; **Penryn** Town Fair (01326) 372911

30 **Stithians** Cornish Game and Country Fair (01872) 273366

31 **Bude** Horticultural Show (01288) 352114; **Ruan Minor** Kennack Sands Horse Show (01326) 290824; **Newlyn** Fish Festival (01736) 363499

SEPTEMBER

5 **Bodmin** Steam Gala at Bodmin General Station – *till Sun 6* (01208) 73666; **St Ives** Festival: folk, jazz and poetry – *till Sat 19* (01736) 795003; **St Just, Penwith** Cornish Gorsedd: celebration of the Cornish language with traditional dancing, recitation from new and old bards (01726) 833402

12 **Lanlivery** Vintage Rally and Country Fair – *till Sun 13* (01208) 873986

19 **Bodmin** Steam Gala at Bodmin General Station – *till Sun 20* (01208) 73666; **Mawnan Smith** Plant Sale at Trebah Garden – *till Sun 20* (01326) 250448

OCTOBER

7 **Callington** Honey Fair; ancient street fair (01579) 350230

14 **Perranporth** Lowender Peran Celtic Festival at Ponsmere Hotel: Cornwall's folk culture – *till Sun 18* (01872) 553413

26 **Mawnan Smith** Children's Activities at Trebah Garden – *till Fri 30* (01326) 250448

NOVEMBER

11 **Camelford** Carnival (01840) 212200

16 **Camborne** Music Festival – *till Sat 21* (01209) 711455

26 **St Austell** Music and Speech Festival – *till 5 Dec* (01726) 72982

DECEMBER

24 **Truro** Festival of Nine Lessons and Carols at Truro Cathedral (01872) 76782; also Midnight Mass

25 **Truro** Christmas Day Eucharist at Truro Cathedral (01872) 76782

CUMBRIA

England's highest mountains and most beautiful scenery, with outstanding access to the countryside, excellent places to stay in, and masses of interesting places to visit, for all ages.

There's tremendous variety among the lakes and the hills around them. Windermere, the longest and busiest lake, has always been a general favourite; it's picturesquely dotted with villas built by Victorian magnates, and has masses of accommodation on its east side. Ullswater approaches the grandeur of Scottish lochs, and has some excellent (if not cheap) places to stay right by the lake shore; Buttermere and Crummock Water also have scenery on the grand scale, perhaps without quite matching Ullswater's scenic perfection. Derwent Water wavers charmingly between highland and lowland in flavour, and its islands and manageable proportions make it a favourite for idle boating as well as for bankside strolls. Coniston Water, quite well wooded, also appeals to both boaters and walkers, with some fine views – in some ways it's a junior version of Windermere, smaller and quieter. Wast Water, England's deepest lake, is austere, surrounded by towering screes. Bassenthwaite Lake is altogether gentler, lowland in feel. Some much smaller lakes, notably Grasmere, Rydal Water and Elterwater, are idyllic.

The most beautiful landscapes are concentrated thickly around the central area, especially around Ambleside and Windermere. Both places are quite intensively developed for visitors and very busy indeed in summer; Keswick too has lots going on for all ages. These parts really come into their own at quieter times of year – you need a degree of peace and quiet to enjoy the beauty of the delicious central area between Windermere and Grasmere.

The National Trust controls over a quarter of the land in the Lake District National Park. So preservation of and access to the countryside here is first-class (and it's an area where membership of the Trust really pays off in terms of free admission).

The best coastal scenery is around Morecambe Bay in the south. The west coast is untouristy, with miles of unfrequented beaches (as well as some run-down looking places – and the big nuclear power plant at Seascale, which has an excellent visitor centre).

There are lots of interesting places to visit, including a great many good craft shops. We'd recommend a look at Hawkshead, Troutbeck and Cartmel, and among the many other places of interest we'd pick out the great houses and impressive gardens of Holker Hall at Cark-in-Cartmel, Levens Hall and Sizergh Castle (all in the south), Muncaster Castle in the west, and, towards the north, Dalemain House at Dacre, friendly Mirehouse near Bassenthwaite, and Hutton-in-the-Forest at Skelton. Many of these are given special charm by a degree of intimacy and personal contact that's missing from many places further south – and this is particularly true of smaller houses, such as Townend at Troutbeck, or those connected with literary figures. The Wordsworth trail at Grasmere and Rydal is heavily trodden in summer, but extremely well managed (the Wordsworth Trust here is among two dozen out-of-London museums designated in 1997 as outstanding by the Heritage Secretary); specially rewarding at quieter times. Ravenglass has a fine steam railway. The Maryport Steamships, now volunteer-run, are intriguing; and Whitehaven's heritage centre, the Beacon, is fascinating for anyone with a weather obsession – all too easy to acquire in Lakeland.

Cumbria is very good territory for children who get a kick out of doing outdoor things. Families who need more in the way of amusements laid on have tended to enjoy other areas more, but the growing list of enjoyable family attractions here is now reaching a level where there's really plenty to keep most children entertained. Some very good places (which many adults like too) are the Lakeside Aquarium, well organised farm centres at Morland, Southwaite and Bassenthwaite, the wildlife parks at Dalton-in-Furness and Milnthorpe, the very cheery sheep centre near Cockermouth, and perhaps the vast collection of reptiles at Amazonia in Bowness. Many young children very much enjoy the Beatrix Potter centre in Windermere, and the Lowther Leisure Park at Hackthorpe will keep most amused for the best part of a full day.

There's an excellent choice of places to stay, many of which serve really good food. We have gone out of our way to recommend places that are strong on peace and quiet; there's a splendid range of styles and prices.

For a quiet break with plenty of walking on your doorstep, the Langdales, particularly Great Langdale, and Borrowdale are outstanding. The west is even quieter, separated from the central Lake District by high ridges with tortuous roads over the few passes. British rock-climbing was born over here, with England's highest mountain, Scafell Pike, surrounded by other awesome peaks – serious walking country.

Another area where you can reckon on peace and quiet even in summer is the part east of the M6. This is one of England's least-known areas, and though overshadowed by the Lake District proper has a lot of charm, and some excellent-value places to stay in. Quiet river valleys shelter below more awesome open country and high moors, and there are some attractive and untouristy places to visit. Much of the high country is too bleak and boggy for most walkers, but moorland roads give drivers good views (e.g. the A683 Kirkby Lonsdale–Kirkby Stephen, B6260 Tebay–Appleby, B6413 Lazonby–Brampton, A689 Brampton–Alston roads). The railway crossing the moors between Carlisle and Settle is perhaps the best way of all of seeing this unusual part of England.

Lakeland generally is at its best out of season. May (sheets of wild flowers on the hills) and June are ideal: more sun, no crowds. The views are often clearest (and the ground firm and dry for walkers) in October and November, though afternoons are short then. In the summer holidays and at other peak times crowds make the best places less enjoyable, and indeed put a real strain on the environment. If you're determined to go at that time of year, you've more chance of finding peace in the west, or over by the Pennines east of the M6. For all but the hardiest expert outdoorsmen, winter up here is too bleak for pleasure – unless you plan to stay indoors. Whenever you come bring something waterproof – the Lake District has more annual rainfall than any other part of the country.

Plenty of civilised pubs (allowing children) do decent lunches, and most tourist attractions and all the main centres have refreshments. Many establishments are making determined efforts to hold down prices (generally speaking you get more for your money the further you go from the central Lakes). For this year's Guide we've found quite a few interesting new places.

Public transport in the Lakes is good and useful for round-trip long walks; information service (01228) 812812. Local information leaflets offer plenty of choice of well guided walks; information too from National Park visitor services (01539) 446601, and from the flourishing Cumbria Wildlife Trust (01539) 432476, which controls many reserves. Bicycles can be hired by the day in the main towns (considering the scenic grandeur, you can cycle for a surprisingly long way, at least in the central area, without having to struggle up steep hills). Many places offer riding: around £10 an hour for adults, £8 for children.

Where to stay

Alston NY7246 LOVELADY SHIELD Nenthead Rd, Alston CA9 3LF (01434) 381203 £114, plus special breaks; 12 rms. In a lovely setting with the River Nent running along the bottom of the garden (tennis and croquet), this handsome country house has a tranquil atmosphere, courteous staff and log fires in comfortable rooms (no smoking in sitting room or restaurant); very good food inc fine breakfasts; cl Jan; dogs by prior arrangement.

Ambleside NY3804 HORSESHOE HOTEL Rothay Rd, Ambleside LA22 OEE (015394) 32000 £49; 19 rms, most with own bthrm. Friendly stone house surrounded by lovely scenery; open fires in elegant lounge and cosy bar and enjoyable food in restaurant; plenty of sporting activities nearby.

Ambleside NY3804 ROTHAY MANOR Rothay Bridge (Coniston Rd), Ambleside LA22 0EH (015394) 33605 £172 inc dinner, plus special breaks; 18 attractive rms, many overlooking the garden. Family-run Regency-style country house in neatly kept mature grounds; log fires and fresh flowers in quietly civilised, comfortable day rooms; very good English food in no smoking dining room, a thoughtful wine list, super big breakfasts, and helpful friendly service; windsurfing/waterskiing, etc. close by, free use of nearby leisure club; cl Jan; good disabled access.

Ambleside NY3804 WATEREDGE Borrans Rd LA22 0EP (015394) 32332 *£104, plus special breaks; 22 good, comfortable rms. Beautifully placed warmly welcoming hotel with neat gardens running down to Lake Windermere (embarkation point for cruising the lake); light airy lounges, good meals in cosy beamed no smoking dining room, excellent service; cl mid-Dec–mid-Jan; children over 7; dogs by prior arrangement.

Appleby NY6921 APPLEBY MANOR Roman Rd, Appleby CA16 6JB (01768) 351571 *£108; 30 well equipped rms in original house (the nicest), coach house annexe or modern wing. Very friendly family-run hotel with fine views over Appleby Castle and the Eden valley; log fire in one of the 3 comfortable lounges, relaxed bar with wide range of whiskies, excellent service, good interesting food in panelled restaurant; leisure centre; cl Christmas; disabled access.

Barbon SD6383 BARBON INN Barbon, Carnforth LA6 2LJ (015242) 76233 £60; 10 simple but comfortable rms, some with own bthrm. Small friendly village inn in a quiet spot below the fells; relaxing bar, traditional lounge, good meals in candlelit dining room, and helpful service.

Bassenthwaite Lake NY1930 PHEASANT Bassenthwaite Lake, Cockermouth CA13 9YE (017687) 76234 £100, plus special breaks; 20 rms. Civilised hotel with delightfully old-fashioned pubby bar, restful lounges with open fires, antiques, fresh flowers and comfortable armchairs; interesting gardens merging into the surrounding fellside woodlands; cl 25 Dec; disabled access.

Borrowdale NY2413 SEATOLLER HOUSE Borrowdale, Keswick CA12 5XN (017687) 77218 £57; 9 spotless, comfortable rms. Friendly house-party atmosphere in 17th-c house that has been a guesthouse for over 100 yrs, self-service drinks and board games in comfortable lounges (no TV); good no-choice fixed-time hearty dinner (not Tues) served at 2 big oak tables and packed lunches; 2 acres of grounds and many walks from the doorstep as the house is at the foot of Honister Pass; cl Nov–Mar; children over 5; disabled access.

Bowland Bridge SD4289 HARE & HOUNDS Bowland Bridge, Grange-over-Sands LA11 6NN (015395) 68333 *£50, plus special breaks; 16 attractive rms, mostly with own bthrm. Friendly extended village inn below fells with welcoming landlord (ex-international soccer player); log fires, beams and stone walls in lounge bar, cosy residents' lounge, open fires, and sheltered garden.

Bowness SD4097 LINTHWAITE HOUSE Crook Rd, Bowness-on-Windermere, Windermere LA23 3JA (015394) 88600 £130, plus special breaks; 18 individually decorated rms, some with lake views. Stunningly set Lakeland house in 14 acres of immaculate gardens overlooking Lake Windermere, and with their own tarn fishing; comfortable, stylish furnishings in the engaging day rooms, an easy-going atmosphere, and very good service; most enjoyable modern British cooking in cosy candlelit restaurant; croquet, putting, golf practice hole; children over 7 in evening restaurant; disabled access.

Brampton NY5361 FARLAM HALL Hallbankgate, Brampton (on the A689 S) CA8 2NG (016977) 46234 £200 inc dinner, plus special breaks; 12 comfortable rms. Charmingly Victorian (though parts are much older) and very civilised country house with log fires in the spacious lounges, excellent attentive service, good 4-course dinner and marvellous breakfasts; peaceful spacious grounds with a croquet lawn and a small pretty lake; cl Christmas–New Year; children over 5; dogs welcome.

Brandlingill NY1626 LOW HALL Brandlingill, Cockermouth CA11 0RE (01900) 826654 £60; 5 pleasant rms. Beautifully sited partly 17th-c farmhouse below Whinlatter Pass and close to Cockermouth; big peaceful garden and log fires and books in lounges; real farmhouse breakfasts; no smoking; cl Nov–Feb; children over 10.

Buttermere NY1817 BRIDGE Buttermere, Cockermouth, CA13 9UZ (017687) 70252 £82, plus special breaks; 22 rms. Comfortable hotel surrounded by some of the best steep countryside in the county; with a beamed bar (the flagstoned part is popular with walkers), log fire and deep armchairs in the sitting room; good food in the bar and no smoking restaurant, real ales, decent malt whiskies, and friendly atmosphere; self-catering also.

Buttermere Valley NY1622 Pickett Howe Buttermere Valley, Cockermouth CA13 9UY (01900) 85444 *£118; 4 rms with thoughtful extras such as home-made biscuits and a torch. Standing at the end of its own track and surrounded by stunning mountain scenery, this 17th-c longhouse has a friendly relaxed atmosphere, lovely antiques, log fires, beams and slate floors; fine food in the candlelit dining room, a very sound wine list, and wonderful breakfasts inc home-made oatcakes, jam, marmalade and so forth; no smoking; cl mid-Nov–mid-Mar; children over 10.

Carlisle NY4056 Number Thirty One Howard Place 31 Howard Place, Carlisle CA1 1HR (01228) 597080 £50; 3 well equipped individually decorated rms. Carefully restored no smoking Victorian townhouse with a relaxed informal atmosphere, open fire and plenty of books in the cosy lounge; delicious interesting food using the best local products, breakfast with home-baked bread, home-made preserves and home-made Cumberland sausages; helpful courteous owners; cl Jan–Feb; no children.

Cartmel SD3879 Uplands Haggs Lane, Cartmel, Grange-over-Sands LA11 6HD (015395) 36248 £85, plus special breaks; 5 pretty rms. Comfortable Edwardian house in 2 acres of garden with views over to Morecambe Bay, attractively decorated rooms, and helpful service; the main draw is undoubtedly the richly imaginative food in the no smoking dining room; cl Jan–Feb; children over 8; well behaved dogs welcome.

Casterton SD6379 Pheasant Casterton, Carnforth LA6 2RX (015242) 71230 £64, plus special breaks; 10 comfortable rms, most with countryside views. Small civilised inn, recently refurbished, with a pleasant atmosphere, cosy residents' lounge, no smoking garden lounge and cheerful staff; good food in panelled dining room and small but sound wine list; dogs allowed; disabled access.

Catlowdy NY4677 Bessiestown Farm Catlowdy, Longtown, Carlisle CA6 5QP (01228) 577219 *£49; 4 rms. Friendly farmhouse on small beef and sheep rearing farm (mainly no smoking) close to the Scottish borders, with 2 comfortable lounges; good home-made food and big breakfasts in the attractive dining room; indoor heated swimming pool, and games room; self-catering also; well behaved children.

Crook SD4695 Wild Boar Crook, Windermere LA23 3NF (015394) 45225 £111; 36 rms. Comfortable, well run, extended hotel with period furnishings and log fires in its ancient core, and attentive service; good food in the no smoking dining room; free access to nearby leisure club and discounts on watersports.

Crosby on Eden NY4559 Crosby Lodge High Crosby, Crosby on Eden, Carlisle CA6 4QZ (01228) 573618 *£98, plus weekend breaks; 11 spacious rms (2 in stable conversion). Imposing and carefully converted country house with friendly, long-established owners, and set in attractive mature grounds, in nice countryside; with comfortable and appealing individual furnishings, and interesting food; cl 24 Dec–mid-Jan; limited disabled access.

Dent SD7187 Sportsmans Cowgill, Dent, Sedbergh LA10 5RG (01539) 625282 £40; 6 rms with shared bthrm. Unassuming, comfortable pub notable for its wonderful position in Dentdale by the River Dee, with the viaduct of the old Settle–Carlisle railway close by, and walks in all directions; open log fires and good-value home-made food; well behaved dogs allowed.

Dockray NY3921 Royal Dockray, Matterdale, Penrith CA11 0TT (017684) 82356 *£58, plus special breaks; 10 rms. Friendly and homely family-run hotel with open fires in spacious bars; good value hearty meals, and well kept beers; set in a fine spot between hill and lake with walks from the doorstep.

Elterwater NY3305 Britannia Inn Elterwater, Ambleside LA22 9HP

(015394) 37210 *£62, plus winter breaks; 13 rms, most with shower, some in quiet annexe opposite. Simple, charmingly traditional pub in fine surroundings opposite the village green; happy friendly atmosphere, and a comfortable no smoking lounge and bustling bar; and hearty home cooking inc superb breakfasts, and real ales; fine walks; cl 25–26 Dec; well behaved dogs allowed.

Eskdale Green NY1400 BOWER HOUSE Eskdale Green, Holmbrook CA19 1TD (019467) 23244 £64, plus weekend breaks; 24 comfortable rms, some in annexe. Relaxed and pleasantly isolated old stone inn with a nicely tended sheltered garden; log fires in a warren of rooms, and comfortable separate lounge; popular good-value food inc wonderful puddings; friendly staff; disabled access.

Far Sawrey SD3893 SAWREY Far Sawrey, Ambleside LA22 0LQ (015394) 43425 *£58; 20 rms, 18 with own bthrm. Friendly hotel well placed at the foot of Claife Heights, with simple pubby and smarter bars, and friendly staff; good straightforward food; seats on a pleasant lawn with good views of Lake Windermere; cl Christmas; kind to children, dogs allowed.

Garrigill NY7441 CROSSGILL FARMHOUSE Garrigill, Alston CA9 3HE (01434) 381383 £36; 3 rms, 2 with own bthrm. 18th-c ex-shooting lodge on a hill overlooking the River Tyne, with an open fire in the lounge; good home cooking, and friendly owners; no smoking; no evening meal Weds; cl April, Christmas.

Garrigill NY7441 GEORGE & DRAGON Garrigill, Alston CA9 3DS (01434) 381293 £37; 4 small rms, shared bthrm, but clean and comfortable. Friendly 17th-c pub on a dead-end road in beautiful countryside; with an informal flagstone bar, stone-and-panelled dining room, log fire in a smashing fireplace, and good service; not suitable for children.

Grasmere NY3406 MICHAEL'S NOOK Grasmere, Ambleside LA22 9RP (015394) 35496 £160 inc dinner, plus special breaks; 14 lovely rms. Beautifully furnished hotel with fine antiques, paintings and rugs (the owner is a former antique dealer), lovely flowers, comfortable sofas by open fires in the cosy bar or elegant drawing room; fine food; lovely garden with specimen rhododendrons, and good walks; great danes and exotic cats as well; free use of indoor pool and health facilities at nearby Wordsworth Hotel (under the same ownership, and listed below); children by arrangement but no under 7s in evening restaurant.

Grasmere NY3406 SWAN Grasmere, Ambleside LA22 9RF (015394) 35551 £118; 36 rms, most with fine views. Smart and friendly 17th-c inn in beautiful fell-foot surroundings; beams and inglenooks, an elegant no smoking dining room, and an attractive garden; lovely walks; partial disabled access.

Grasmere NY3406 WORDSWORTH Grasmere, Ambleside LA22 9SW (015394) 35592 £130, plus special breaks; 37 comfortable, pretty rms. Well run hotel, right in the village, with stylish lounges and an airy restaurant overlooking landscaped gardens; relaxed conservatory and popular pubby bar, friendly service; enjoyable food; heated indoor pool, mini-gym, and sauna; good disabled access.

Grizedale SD3494 GRIZEDALE LODGE Hawkshead Hill, Grizedale, Ambleside LA22 0QL (015394) 36532 *£75, plus special breaks; 9 no smoking rms. Friendly and comfortable hotel (carefully refurbished last year) in the middle of the magnificent Grizedale Forest with lots of walks from the front door, and a log fire in the lounge bar; imaginative fresh food in the attractive restaurant, and big breakfasts; cl 3 Jan–10 Feb; children under 5 provided with high tea at 5.30pm; disabled access.

Hawkshead SD3598 DRUNKEN DUCK Barngates, Hawkshead, Ambleside LA22 0NG (015394) 36347 £75, plus specials breaks; 9 rms. Very well run happy inn alone in 60 hillside acres; several cosy rooms, good fires, and views of Lake Windermere in distance; good interesting food inc fine puddings; fishing in private tarn; cl 25 Dec; limited disabled access.

Hawkshead SD3598 HIGHFIELD HOUSE Hawkshead Hill, Hawkshead, Ambleside LA22 OPN (015394) 36344 *£77, plus winter breaks; 11 good rms. Welcoming Victorian country house in spacious woodland garden with fine views (good walks from the door); open fire in comfortable lounge, cosy bar; generous food inc packed lunches and children's high tea; cl Jan.

Ireby NY2439 OVERWATER HALL Ireby, Carlisle CA5 1HH (017687) 76566 *£84, plus special breaks; 13 rms. Relaxed and friendly family-run hotel in 18 acres of gardens and woodland with lots of walks; log fire in the comfortable elegant drawing room; good imaginative food in the cosy dining room; children over 7 in restaurant (high tea 5pm); well behaved dogs welcome; cl 1st week Jan.

Kendal SD5293 LOW JOCK SCAR Selside (6m from Kendal), Kendal LA8 9LE (01539) 823259 £53; 5 rms, most with own bthrm. Relaxed and friendly little country guesthouse in 6 acres of garden and woodland; with residents' lounge, and good home cooking (picnic lunches on request); no smoking; cl Nov–Feb; children over 12.

Keswick NY2618 STAKIS KESWICK LODORE Derwent Water, Keswick CA12 5UX (017687) 77285 *£134, plus special breaks; 75 well equipped rms. Long-standing but well updated big holiday hotel with lots of facilities in 40 acres of lakeside gardens and woodlands; open fires in comfortable day rooms, and an elegant restaurant; leisure club, tennis and squash, outdoor swimming pool, games room and lots for children such as nursery with NNEB nannies, remote control cars, Sega computer games, babysitting, baby-listening service, high tea; spacious self-catering house too.

Keswick NY2624 SWINSIDE LODGE Newlands, Keswick CA12 5UE (017687) 72948 £88, plus special breaks; 7 comfortable rms. Victorian hotel in own grounds surrounded by wonderful unspoilt scenery at foot of Catbells, and few minutes from the shores of Derwent Water; helpful friendly service, and 2 relaxing sitting rooms; with hearty breakfasts and super home-made evening meals in candlelit dining room, cl Dec–Jan; children over 12.

Kirkcambeck NY5269 CRACROP FARM Kirkcambeck, Brampton CA8 2BW (016977) 48245 £50; 3 rms overlooking garden and open fields. Friendly Victorian farmhouse on 425 acres with stock and very good marked farm trails (they are keen on conservation); comfortable and homely rooms, good traditional breakfasts (other food arranged in advance) and games room and sauna; no smoking; cl Christmas; no children.

Lanercost NY5664 ABBEY BRIDGE Lanercost, Brampton CA8 2HG (016977) 2224 £60; 7 simple rms, most with own bthrm. Beautifully placed small country inn in quiet spot nr an ancient priory; decent food in an informal converted forge which also houses the cheerful bar; pleasant staff; cl 25 Dec; disabled access.

Langdale NY2906 OLD DUNGEON GHYLL Great Langdale, Ambleside LA22 9JY (015394) 37272 *£60, plus special breaks; 15 rms, some with shared bthrm. Friendly, simple and cosy walkers' and climbers' inn dramatically surrounded by fells; wonderful views and terrific walks; cosy residents' lounge and popular food – best to book for dinner if not a resident; cl 3 days over Christmas.

Lindale SD4280 GREENACRES Lindale, Grange-over-Sands LA11 6LP (015395) 34578 *£50, plus special breaks; 5 appealing rms. Charming 19th-c cottage with friendly atmosphere, a pretty sitting room, conservatory, and open fire; good home-made food and big breakfasts in the cosy dining room, and packed lunch on request; cl Dec.

Little Langdale NY3204 THREE SHIRES Little Langdale, Ambleside LA22 9NZ (015394) 37215 £70, plus special breaks; 10 rms. Stone-built country inn with beautiful views, comfortably old-fashioned residents' part, separate walkers' bar, and pretty gardens; cl Jan.

Lorton NY1525 NEW HOUSE FARM Lorton, Cockermouth CA13 9UU (01900) 85404 *£70, plus special breaks; 4 rms with wonderful hillside views. Friendly no smoking 17th-c house (not a working farm) in 15 acres of grounds; with beams and rafters, flagstones, open fires, and 2 residents' lounges; very good food inc game and fish caught by owner, home-made scones and preserves, and a thoughtful wine list; and lots of walks; children over 12.

Maulds Meaburn NY6217 MEABURN HILL FARM Maulds Meaburn, Penrith CA10 3HN (01931) 715205 *£50; 3 rms. 16th-c longhouse on 200-acre suckler beef and sheep farm; with beams, antiques and open fires in comfortable rooms and a well stocked library; farmhouse breakfasts; a large garden, orchard, and fine views; cl Dec–Mar; children over 10.

Mungrisdale NY3731 MILL HOTEL Mungrisdale, Penrith CA11 0XR (017687) 79659 £110 in dinner; 9 rms, most with own bthrm. Very friendly small streamside hotel beautifully placed in a lovely valley hamlet hidden away below Blencathra; an open fire in the cosy and comfortable sitting room; good imaginative 5-course evening meals, and a small carefully chosen wine list; cl Nov–Feb; dogs welcome by arrangment; disabled access.

Pooley Bridge NY4724 SHARROW BAY Pooley Bridge, Penrith CA10 2LZ (017684) 86301 £164; 28 lovely rms with antiques, books, and games, mostly with own bthrm. Country-house hotel in a quiet idyllic spot by Ullswater; lovely views of lake and mountains and showing the years of loving care the owners have put into its distinctive style, furnishings and décor; unobtrusively attentive service and excellent English cooking in the 2 contrasting dining rooms; cl Dec–late Feb; children over 13.

Ravenstonedale NY7204 FAT LAMB Cross Bank, Ravenstonedale, Kirkby Stephen CA17 4LL (015396) 23242 £60, plus special breaks; 12 comfortable rms. Welcoming moorland inn in beautiful open countryside; log fire in cheerfully modernised 2-room bar; in 17 acres of land, 7 of which is nature reserve; very good disabled access.

Rydal Water NY3606 WHITE MOSS HOUSE Rydal Water, Grasmere, Ambleside LA22 9SE (015394) 35295 £144 inc dinner, plus special breaks; 7 thoughtfully furnished rms in main house plus separate cottage let as one unit with 2 rms. Bought by Wordsworth for his son, this attractive stripped-stone country house – set in charming mature grounds overlooking lake – has a comfortable lounge; fine no-choice 5-course meals in the pretty, no smoking dining room and an excellent wine list; free use of hotel rowing boat, free fishing and free use of local leisure club; cl Dec–Feb; not suitable for toddlers.

Sedbergh SD6692 DALESMAN Main St LA10 5BN (015396) 21183 £50, plus special breaks; 6 comfortable and cheerful rms, most with bthrm. Friendly and nicely modernised old village pub, popular with walkers, and with quite a mix of decorations and styles; well kept real ales, and good-value food; limited disabled access.

Silloth NY1153 SKINBURNESS Silloth, Carlisle CA5 4QY (016973) 32332 £74, plus special breaks; 26 comfortable rms. Well equipped Victorian seaside holiday hotel away from the town, overlooking the sea and Scotland; comfortable lounge, popular food, and new leisure club; good provision for disabled.

Talkin NY5557 HULLERBANK Talkin, Brampton CA8 1LB (016977) 46668 *£40; 3 rms. Comfortable and very friendly no smoking Georgian farmhouse in unspoilt countryside; relaxed atmosphere in the homely lounge; good food using home-grown and local produce inc home-produced lamb (packed lunch on request); cl Christmas–New year; children over 12.

Thirlmere NY3116 DALE HEAD HALL Thirlmere, Keswick CA12 4TN (017687) 72478 *£75, plus special breaks; 9 pretty rms, most with lake views. Peaceful, partly 16th-c country house in lovely lakeside grounds; with comfortable lounges, log fire, and friendly owners; home-cooked food using produce grown in own walled garden; children over 10 for evening meals; cl Jan.

Tirril NY5126 QUEENS HEAD Tirril, Penrith CA10 2JF (01768) 863219 £42, plus special breaks; 7 lovely rms, most with own bthrm. The new licensees have redecorated to expose floorboards and flagstones, giving a good pubby atmosphere; spacious back restaurant, low beams, black panelling, inglenook fireplace and old-fashioned settles in the older part; good interesting food including snacks and OAP specials, well kept real ales; mostly no smoking.

Troutbeck NY4103 MORTAL MAN Troutbeck, Windermere LA22 3PL (015394) 33193 *£80; 12 rms. Spotlessly kept relaxing inn surrounded by marvellous scenery; partly panelled bustling bar, a big open fire, dark beams and picture windows in the restaurant; well kept real ales, good food, lovely breakfasts, and friendly staff; cl mid-Nov–mid-Feb; children over 5.

Wasdale Head NY1808 WASDALE HEAD Wasdale Head, Seascale CA20 1EX (019467) 26229 £68; 9 simple but warmly comfortable pine-clad rms. Old flagstoned and gabled walkers' and climbers' inn in a magnificent setting surrounded by steep fells; with civilised day rooms, and a cheerfully busy public bar; popular home cooking for 7.30pm dinner, a good wine list and huge breakfasts; self-catering cottages.

Watermillock NY4522 LEEMING HOUSE Watermillock, Ullswater, Penrith CA11 0JJ (017684) 86622 £120, plus special breaks; 40 cosseting rms, many with beautiful views. Well run extended hotel in 20 acres of quiet lakeside grounds; with log fires in comfortable lounges, cosy panelled bar, fine food in lovely no smoking dining room, and good courteous service; boating; high teas for young children; good provision for disabled.

Watermillock NY4522 OLD CHURCH Watermillock, Penrith CA11 0JN (017684) 86204 *£85, plus special breaks; 10 rms, some with lovely Ullswater view. Attractive 18th-c Lakeland house peacefully situated in waterside gardens; with log fires and individual furnishings in civilised day rooms and kind service; excellent English dinners at 8pm in no smoking dining room; rowing/windsurfing boats; cl Nov–Mar.

Water Yeat SD2989 WATER YEAT Water Yeat, Ulverston LA12 8DJ (01229) 885306 £51, plus special breaks; 5 chintzy rms with lovely views. Attractively converted and very neatly kept 17th-c farmhouse by Coniston Water in 3 acres of garden and woodland; with an especially relaxing atmosphere, log fire in lounge, generous breakfasts, wonderful food in heavily beamed dining room (much loved locally), and super hosts; cl mid-Dec–mid-Feb; children over 4.

Windermere SD4199 BEAUMONT Holly Rd, Windermere LA23 2AF (015394) 47075 *£52; 10 pretty rms. Attractively furnished and spotlessly kept no smoking Victorian house with friendly owners, open fire, home-made evening meals, and generous breakfasts in charming dining room; children over 10.

Windermere SD4199 FIR TREES Lake Rd, Windermere LA23 2EQ (015394) 42272 *£54; 8 attractive spotless rms inc 2 big family ones. Well run and comfortable no smoking Victorian house with an informal relaxed atmosphere, antiques, fine prints and fresh flowers, warmly helpful service (detailed suggestions of what to do), and good hearty breakfasts.

Windermere SD4199 HOLBECK GHYLL COUNTRY HOUSE Holbeck Lane, Windermere LA23 1LU (015394) 32375 *£150 inc dinner, plus special breaks; 14 individual rms, many with fine views. Charming and warmly friendly country house in mature landscaped gardens and 5 acres of woodland overlooking Lake Windermere, with tennis court, putting green, and croquet – their labradors like to walk with you; immaculate, comfortable lounges with antiques and wood panelling, log fires and a billiard room; very good food (vegetarian too) and wine in oak-panelled restaurant; newly opened health spa; children over 8 in evening restaurant.

Windermere SD4199 LANGDALE CHASE Windemere LA23 1LW (015394) 32201 £100; 30 rms, many with marvellous lake view. Welcoming family-run hotel in lovely position on the edge of Lake Windermere with water-skiing and bathing from the hotel jetty; tennis, croquet, putting and rowing and afternoon tea on the terraces; gracious oak-panelled rooms with antiques, paintings, fresh flowers, open fires; very good food (huge breakfasts, too), and friendly service; disabled access.

Windermere SD4199 MILLER HOWE Rayrigg Rd, Windermere LA23 1EY (015394) 42536 **from £150 inc dinner,** plus special breaks; 12 comfortable, well equipped rms, many with fine views. Splendid, immaculately kept Edwardian country house set high over the lake with unbeatable views from day rooms, conservatory and sloping garden, and run by well known chef John Tovey and his long-serving staff; an expectant theatricality about the excellent evening meals which adds to the special-event feel of eating here, a remarkably wide-ranging New World wine list with helpful tasting notes, and super breakfasts; children over 8; cl Dec–Feb.

Winton NY7810 BAY HORSE Winton, Kirkby Stephen CA17 4HS (017683) 71451 £35; 3 clean, good-value rms. Well kept unpretentious moorland pub in lovely setting, with welcoming low-ceilinged rooms, friendly owners, and good generous home cooking; well behaved children over 5.

To see and do

Ambleside NY3804 A busy holiday-oriented shopping centre inc excellent outdoor equipment shops strung along its central one-way system, with the quaintest information centre in the Lakes – the little NT shop in the tiny stone Bridge House over Stock Ghyll by the main car park. In the side lanes above here are one or two attractive older buildings. Traditional GLASS BLOWING at Adrian Sankey, Rydal Rd; good demonstrations and shop, but no pressure to buy; (015394) 33039. HAYES GARDEN WORLD (Lake Rd) is a big garden centre in landscaped gardens; café, disabled access. The Queens Hotel is good value for lunch.

STAGSHAW (just S, Waterhead) Hillside woodland garden with lovely lake views, mature camellias, rhododendrons, magnolias and heathers; best in spring. Open daily Apr–Jun then by appointment July–Oct; (015394) 35599; suggested donation £1.20; NT. Parking is very limited. There's little left of the ROMAN FORT in nearby Borrans Park NY3703.

BROCKHOLE (on the A591 S, or by launch from town pier) Exemplary National Park information centre in country house with well landscaped gardens and attractive lakeside grounds; also audio-visual show, exhibitions, and adventure play area. Special talks and events throughout the year. Meals, snacks, shop, disabled access; visitor centre cl Nov–Mar, gardens and grounds open all year; (015394) 46601; free, but charge for parking.

Kendal SD5293 A real town as opposed to a tourist centre, busy, with hectic traffic, but lots of small closes leading off the main street, some of them attractively restored to give a feel of what the place was like in the 18th-c heyday of the wool-weaving industry. The mint cake that takes its name comes in a surprising number of varieties. The Gateway (Crook Rd) is a good newish pub/restaurant. BREWERY ARTS CENTRE (Highgate) Good changing events and exhibitions, café, bar, and landscaped garden; (01539) 725133 for what's on. K Shoes have a FACTORY SHOPPING CENTRE at Netherfield; cl 25 Dec. Lakeland Canoes (Hollins Lane, Burneside) hire them by the day, and will take them to and fro for you. Webbs Garden Centre (Burneside Rd) is big, with lots of plants; decent café, disabled access.

🏛🖼⊘ ABBOT HALL (Kirkland)
Beautifully restored Georgian house
with period furniture, silver, china
and glass. The art collection reflects
Kendal's importance in the 18th c as
the centre of an artists' school, and
includes works by Ruskin, Turner,
Constable, and especially George
Romney. Meals, snacks, good craft
shop, disabled access; cl 24 Dec–15
Feb; (01539) 722464; £2.50 (or £1 if
you've visited one of the town's 2
other museums). The MUSEUM OF
LAKELAND LIFE & INDUSTRY behind has
lovingly recreated period rooms,
shops and workshops, and an almost
palpable feel of the past. Subjects as
diverse as shoemaking, Arthur
Ransome and Postman Pat. Some
disabled access; hours and price as
above.

⊘ KENDAL MUSEUM (Station Rd) Less
immediately appealing than the
town's other museums,
comprehensive but mostly
traditional; lots of realistically
mounted stuffed animals, and a
gallery devoted to the work of Alfred
Wainwright, the walkers' guru. Shop,
disabled access to ground floor only;
(01539) 721374; hours and price as
above.

🏛🏚 The ruined CASTLE On a small hill
on the E edge of town, the birthplace
of Henry VIII's wife Katherine Parr.
There's little more now than parts of
the outer wall with some towers – but
children enjoy it, and there are fine
views. A humble building associated
with it is the CASTLE DAIRY (Wildman
St), an unspoiled Tudor house with
some period furniture, inc the oldest
bed the V&A have ever recorded.
Open only 2–4pm Weds, Apr–Sept;
one of the best-value old houses in the
book, just 5p.

⊘ QUAKER TAPESTRY EXHIBITION
(Friends Meeting House,
Stramongate) Bayeux-style tapestry
history of the Quaker movement, also
embroidery demonstrations. Shop,
disabled access; cl Sun and Nov–Mar;
(01539) 722975; £2.50.

Keswick NY2624 The tourist centre of the northern Lakes, handy for Derwent
Water, with lots of Victorian villas (many of them now guesthouses and small
hotels) outside quite a traditional centre, with small cobbled closes running off
the main streets. It's full of breeches, boots and backpacks in high season, with
good outdoor equipment shops, and is a routine stop on coach tours. The Dog
& Gun and older-fashioned George Hotel are very popular for lunch, with the
Pheasant out towards Crosthwaite also good. The Wild Strawberry is a quaint
tearoom with an upstairs gallery; cl Tues and Weds. Lakeside Tea Gardens
(Lake Rd) have home baking, lots for children, pleasant modern furniture and
crockery inside and in garden with trees and chaffinches; cl about 5pm.
George Fisher (Borrowdale Rd) is a good big outdoors shop. The back road
around Swinside is pretty, and in clear weather is worth following up the
gauntly formidable Keskadale Pass.

! CARS OF THE STARS (Standish St)
Unusual collection of cars from film
and TV dating back to Laurel &
Hardy's Model T Ford, taking in
Chitty Chitty Bang Bang, the
Batmobile and cars used by James
Bond and Postman Pat along the way.
Shop, disabled access; cl Jan and part
of Feb; (017687) 73757; *£3.

⊘ KESWICK MUSEUM (Fitzpark, Station
Rd) Thoroughly traditional; the Poets
Corner stands out. Shop, disabled
access; cl Nov–Easter; (017687)
73263; £1.

⊘🏚 PENCIL AND TEAPOT MUSEUMS

Pencils and collectable teapots are
both made in Keswick; the museum
alongside the Derwent pencil factory
(Southey Works) is surprisingly
interesting, with some unexpected
exhibits; cl 25–26 Dec, 1 Jan; £2;
while the only shape you won't see
among the often ludicrous examples
at the Teapottery (Central Car Park
Rd) is the traditional one we all have
in our kitchens; cl 25 Dec, 1 Jan; free.

❀ From the boat pier, a short stroll
takes you up to Friars Crag for a fine
lake view; the car park on the B5289
just S gives access to another great

lake viewpoint, Castle Head.

🏛 CASTLERIGG STONE CIRCLE NY2923 (just E) This neolithic monument is well preserved, and gives photogenic perspectives of the mountains (the best times for pictures are morning and evening); take a map to identify the peaks it aligns with. The site is owned by the National Trust, and there's a brief explanation of the stones' history.

♨ **Penrith** NY5130 A real locals' rather than tourists' town, and the biggest in Lakeland. It's very much a northern country town, with solid stone streets, an unreconstructed traffic problem, farmers from far and wide descending on its Skirsgill agricultural market to beef about Brussels (Tues, sometimes Fri too in late summer/autumn), and genuinely traditional Lakeland shops selling real fudge and toffee, rich cakes (Birketts), local cheeses (Grahams), prize Cumberland sausage (Cranstons), local antiquarian books, and cheap and sturdy country clothes. John Norris (21 Victoria Rd) is the outstanding fishing/outdoor wear shop, with something for everyone; good prices. A MUSEUM on Middlegate is a useful introduction to the area (cl Sun exc summer pms; free), and the George does decent lunches. 6 miles out of town in Whinfell Forest is the Rank Organisation's Center Parcs-style OASIS HOLIDAY VILLAGE, which opened last summer (several months late). It's been very well thought out as far as visitors are concerned, and for small groups the lodges are pretty good value; (0990) 086000.

🏰 CASTLE Built in the 14th c as a defence against Scottish raids, and the home of Richard III when he was Duke of Gloucester. The ruins are surrounded by a park; free.

🏰 ⚔ BROUGHAM CASTLE NY5329 (off the A6 S) A sturdy Norman ruin on steep lawns above riverside sheep pastures; climb to the top of the keep for the best view. Traces of Roman remains too, with a small exhibition of tombstones. Snacks, shop; cl Nov–Mar; (01768) 862488; £1.30. BROUGHAM HALL CRAFT CENTRE nearby has silver and metal work, truffle-makers, and a smokehouse, in the attractive stone courtyard of a 15th-c Hall. Plenty to see around the house and grounds, currently undergoing a massive restoration. Meals, snacks, shop, disabled access; cl 25 Dec; (01768) 868184; £1 suggested donation.

⚔ ♨ WETHERIGGS POTTERY (Clifton Dykes NY5326, signed off the A6 further S) Interesting and very smart working pottery – one of the oldest in the country – with 19th-c steam engine and equipment; children can try their hands at the wheel, and there's a play area and rare breeds of pig. Restaurant, shop, disabled access; cl 25–26 Dec, 1 Jan; (01768) 892733; free.

Windermere/Bowness SD4199/SD4097 An extensive largely Victorian development of guest houses and small hotels spreads up between the older village of Bowness and the hillside station. It has a touristy feel right through the year, especially around the main street down to the steamer piers. In Bowness itself there is an inner core of narrower much older streets and buildings – one of the most ancient is the engaging Hole in t' Wall pub. HORSE-RIDING can be arranged from Wynlass Beck Stables (bottom of Patterdale Rd). The tourist information centre on Victoria St has a useful range of locally produced crafts if you haven't time to look properly, and the Birdcage (College Rd) is a good ANTIQUE SHOP – mostly small things, especially lamps.

❁ STEAMBOAT MUSEUM 🎫 (Rayrigg Rd) Nearly three dozen gleamingly restored graceful antique steamboats, inc the 1850 SL *Dolly*, the oldest mechanically powered steamboat in the world, and the record-breaker *Miss Windermere IV*. Also a few boats that comfortably predate steam, and events like vintage-boat rallies and model-boat regattas.

Snacks, shop, disabled access; cl Nov–Mar; (015394) 45565; *£2.90. For an extra £4.75, there are stately 50-minute tours of the lake on the silent steam launch *Osprey* or *Penelope*, weather permitting. Silvercrest Submarines hope to introduce mini-submarine trips; though not connected, the Steamboat Museum should have latest news.

ṭ ! WORLD OF BEATRIX POTTER ☷ (Old Laundry, Crag Brow, Bowness) Much enjoyed by young children, delightfully detailed recreations of characters and scenes from *Peter Rabbit* and other tales. Some bits have smells, so you can get more of the atmosphere of Mrs Tiggy-Winkle's laundry or nasty old Mr McGregor's potting shed. Meals and snacks (in the Tailor of Gloucester's kitchen), shop, disabled access; cl 25 Dec, last 3 wks Jan; (015394) 88444; £2.99.

🐍 AMAZONIA (Glebe Rd) Fascinating changing collection of reptiles – the only one in the country that's bigger is at their other branch in Great Yarmouth. All shapes, sizes and patterns, with snakes from 10cm (4in) long to others stretching 6m (20ft), rare species of crocodile, and plenty of brightly coloured lizards and the like, housed among koi and turtle ponds, waterfalls, and free-nesting tropical birds. Meals, snacks, shop, disabled access; cl 25 Dec, 1 Jan; (015394) 48002; £3.95.

Other things to see and do

CUMBRIA FAMILY ATTRACTION OF THE YEAR

🐗 **Morland** NY6022 HIGHGATE FARM AND ANIMAL TRAIL Though you'll find quite a few cheerful farms like this around the country (and even a couple around here), this one stands out as being particularly good value for money. There's plenty going on as well – last year they started having different activities on the hour (from cuddling bunnies and egg collecting to pony rides and pig feeding), so even though it's not that big or developed it can keep smaller children amused for quite a chunk of the day. Quite a few things are under cover (inc falconry displays and one of the picnic areas), so it's still a good bet when – as happens so often round here – the weather's not perfect. They recently introduced sheep racing just after lunch, with teddy bear jockeys; back the right runner and you could win a rosette. Ferrets may be put through their paces too, while plenty of sheep, goats, deer, pigs and chickens wander round at a more relaxed rate. An indoor play barn has go-karts and a sandpit. Last year entry tickets were valid for unlimited return visits for the next week – great for younger children staying nearby to make friends with the animals. Snacks, shop, disabled access; cl Nov–late Mar; (01931) 714347; £4.25 (£2.95 children); a family ticket for 2 adults and 3 children costs £14.60.

✝ **Abbey Town** NY1750 HOLME CULTRAM (on the B5302 Wigtown–Silloth) Remains of formidably rich Cistercian abbey – extraordinarily grand for this quiet village. The New Inn at Blencogo has good food – must book (016973) 61091.

🦽 ⚘ 🏛 **Alston** NY7246 Interesting little, well weathered Pennine town with a surprising number of pubs up and down its very steep cobbled main street (the Angel is best), and a craft shop with locally produced food, home-baked teas, and fresh coffee (cl Jan–mid-Feb). The chief attraction here is the SOUTH TYNEDALE RAILWAY, with diesel and occasionally steam vintage narrow-gauge train trips along a lovely winding valley. They plan to open a service up to Kirkhaugh in Northumberland. Teas, shop, disabled access by arrangement; open wknds and bank hols Apr–Oct, daily Jun–Sept (exc Mon and Fri Jun and Sept), and some

Days Out

Industrial time-warp by Windermere
Sculpture trail in Grizedale Forest; Hawkshead, lunch up at the Drunken Duck, Barngates; Stott Park Bobbin Mill; steamer trip on Windermere from Lakeside; Lakeside and Haverthwaite Railway; Lakeside Aquatarium

Over the steepest pass to the deepest lake
Drive over Wrynose and Hardknott passes from Langdale to Eskdale; Ravenglass & Eskdale Railway; lunch at Bower House, Eskdale Green; Wast Water; drive over Birker Fell to Broughton-in-Furness; Coniston Water (optional visit to Brantwood or trip on steam yacht Gondola if time allows).

Wordsworth's valley
Dove Cottage, Grasmere (get there early); lunch at the Travellers Rest; Rydal Mount; walk round Rydal Water.

A Cumbrian farmhouse and Ullswater's landscapes
Ambleside; Townend, Troutbeck – lunch at Queens Head; steamer from Glenridding to Howtown, and walk back along shore of Ullswater; Aira Force (with children, the afternoon could include Lowther Leisure Park at Hackthorpe instead of the walk, after lunch at the Punch Bowl, Askham).

Dawdling round Derwent Water
Keswick; explore Derwent Water (by launch service, stops round the lake; also walks and strolls, e.g. on shore past Friar's Crag, through Great Wood and up to viewpoints such as Catbells and Walla Crag); lunch at Coledale Inn, Braithwaite; Lingholm Gardens; Castlerigg stone circle, nr Keswick.

Romantic Borrowdale
Explore Borrowdale (inc stroll from Grange along the river to Castle Crag; the Bowder Stone beside B5289; Lodore cascade), or drive over Newlands Pass SW from Keswick; lunch at Bridge Hotel, Buttermere; walk round Buttermere, or march up Hay Stacks; Cockermouth.

Rainy day options
Levens Hall or Sizergh Castle; lunch at the Hare & Hounds, Levens; Kendal – especially Museum of Lakeland Life and Industry or Abbot Hall Art Gallery, and walk up to castle.

Exploring the fringes of Morecambe Bay
Holker Hall; Cartmel village – lunch at Cavendish Arms; for Morecambe Bay views stroll on to Humphrey Head Point or walk up from Grange-over-Sands to Hampsfield Fell.

From steam power to nuclear energy
Maryport steamships; Whitehaven; lunch there at Richmond Hotel, or Scawfell Hotel at Seascale; walk on to St Bees Head from St Bees; Sellafield Visitor Centre.

Railway adventure
Acorn Bank garden, Temple Sowerby; Appleby – early lunch at Royal Oak there; train trip from Appleby on Settle–Carlisle line – either Settle (great moors scenery), or Carlisle (to explore the city).

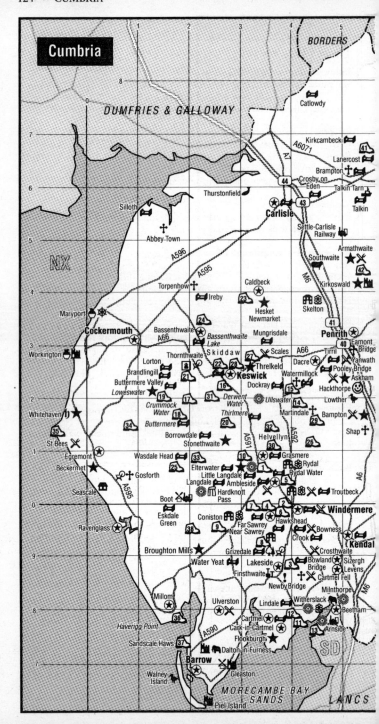

wknds in Dec – best to ring for timetable; (01434) 381696; fares from £2.50. GOSSIPGATE GALLERY (The Butts) Local art and crafts, with changing exhibitions and a good big shop. Their annual sheep show (spotlighting wool products) in Sept/Oct is popular. Snacks, disabled access (though no facilities); cl Jan–mid-Feb, and some wkdys Feb–Mar and Nov–Dec; (01434) 381806; free. HARTSIDE NURSERY (on the A686 W) Beautifully placed alpine nursery with small streamside garden and rare plants for sale; it's quite a draw for birds and wildlife. Shop, some disabled access with notice; cl am wknds and bank hols, and Nov–Feb (exc by appointment); (01434) 381372; free.

★ 👓 🏠 🐝 **Appleby** NY6921 An attractive riverside village; the main street, rising from the harmonious 12th-c church to the castle, is still a grand sight despite the cars, with a good few handsome buildings inc a lovely courtyard of almshouses. Pleasant strolls by the River Eden. APPLEBY CASTLE CONSERVATION CENTRE The castle itself is in remarkable shape for a partly 11th-c building, with one of the best-preserved keeps in the country; terrific views from the ramparts, and an unexpected collection of antique bicycles on the way down. The Clifford family lived here for nearly 700 years, though they moved later to the grander house next door, the great hall of which has antiques, paintings and Chinese porcelain on display. The main feature of the attractive grounds is the big collection of birds, waterfowl and rare farm animals, in a lovely setting above the river. Meals, snacks, shop, limited disabled access; cl Nov–Easter; (017683) 51402; £4. The National School of Falconry have displays here throughout the year; (017683) 51783. The Royal Oak is most enjoyable for lunch.

🚆 **Arnside** SD4678 A good start for the 20-minute BR train trip along the N shore of Morecambe Bay to Ulverston: long viaducts, stupendous views. The Ship at nearby Sandside also has glorious views.

★ **Barbon** SD6383 An unpretentious village given appeal by its fine setting, just below the fells; the road up to Dent, Dent Head and Deepdale reaches far into the hills. The Barbon Inn is good.

🏨 ⏚ † **Barrow** SD2069 The town shows the effects of the virtual collapse of shipbuilding in this country, on which it depended. The BR RAILWAY from here to Whitehaven hugs the coast and has good views, missed by the road, though in the other direction the A5087 to Ulverston has fine views across Morecambe Bay. DOCK MUSEUM (North Rd) Futuristic-looking museum exploring how Barrow developed from a tiny hamlet to the biggest iron and steel centre in the world, before becoming renowned for shipbuilding; displays range from simple fishing boats to Trident submarines. An extension includes interactive displays and an adventure playground. Snacks, shop, good disabled access; cl Mon (exc bank hols), Tues; (01229) 870871; free. FURNESS ABBEY (slightly N, off the A590) Impressive warm sandstone Norman remains of the one-time second richest monastery in England, with lovely arched cloisters, peaceful lawns, and views of pretty valley. Small museum, disabled access; cl winter Mon and Tues, 24–26 Dec, 1 Jan; (01229) 823420; £2.30. The Anchor out at Lindal has decent food.

★ 🏠 🏛 🐑 🚂 **Bassenthwaite** NY2228 Attractive close-set little village – the 12th-c parish church is 3m S; the Sun is an enjoyable pub. MIREHOUSE 🏷 (discount offer applies only to combined house/grounds tickets, not grounds only; off the A591 S) The family that still live in this modest 17th-c house once had excellent literary connections, so the fine rooms have mementoes of Wordsworth, Carlyle and Tennyson among others. There may be piano recitals in the music room, and on Weds in Jun, July and Sept they usually have displays of lace-making. Interesting garden (bee/butterfly plants), as well as peaceful lakeshore grounds, lakeside church, and woods with well thought-out adventure play areas. Lots to do, with a surprising number of activities for children. Good home cooking in ex-mill tearoom, shop, disabled access; house open pm Sun and Weds Easter–Oct plus pm Fri in Aug, grounds open Easter–Oct, plus wknds Mar and Nov; (017687) 72287; £3.50, £1.40 garden only. TROTTERS AND FRIENDS ANIMAL FARM (Coalbeck Farm) Excellent for families; children can join in feeding and milking, and there are plenty of other opportunities to get close to the animals. The 23-acre deer park is good for a picnic, and there are birds of prey and a reptile house. Indoor areas make it a good bet on drizzly days. Meals, snacks, shop, disabled access; cl wkdys Nov–Mar; (017687) 76239; £3.15. Escorted woodland HORSE-RIDING can be arranged from £11 an hour; (017687) 76949 for details. Readers tell us they know of few nicer sites for a caravan than the one at Englethwaite Hall near here.

✗ ⏚ † **Beetham** SD5079 HERON CORNMILL AND MUSEUM OF PAPERMAKING Well organised working watermill which dates back to 1096, though the current building is 18th-c. The big paperworks next door has displays of paper-making. Shop; cl Mon (exc bank hols), all Oct–Easter; (015395) 63363; *£1.50. Beetham itself is attractive, with an interesting CHURCH, and the Wheatsheaf is good for lunch.

✗ **Boot** NY1801 The steam railway (see Ravenglass entry, below) ends here, at Dalegarth Stn. ESKDALE WATERMILL Guided tours of attractively set 16th-c working 2-wheeled mill, with a picnic area nr woodland waterfalls. Snacks, shop; cl Mon (exc bank hols), all Oct–Mar; (019467) 23335; £1.25. Dalegarth Falls here are lovely. The Burnmoor Inn, very well placed for walkers, has extremely good-value food; the Bower House and King George IV further down Eskdale at Eskdale Green are also worthwhile.

† **Brampton** NY5361 LANERCOST PRIORY (signed away from town) Impressive and extensive remains of

Norman priory, built with stone recycled from Hadrian's Wall. Shop, some disabled access; cl Nov–Easter; £1. The nave, picturesquely framed by an arch, was restored in the 18th c as a red sandstone church, and now has stained glass by William Morris and Burne-Jones; it has candlelit Sun services. The Abbey Bridge Inn by the priory has decent food.

🏰 ⚔ Brough NY7915 CASTLE Classic ruined Norman fortress, in romantic setting on moors above village, with great views; free. Back in the village, CLIFFORD HOUSE CRAFT SHOP is good for handmade jewellery, and has a coffee shop with home baking (not Nov–Easter). The Golden Fleece is useful for lunch.

Caldbeck NY3240 John Peel's grave can be found in the churchyard here, and the Oddfellows Arms has good, generous food. There's a pretty drive to attractive Mungrisdale NY3731.

🏠 ⚘ ⛪ Cark-in-Cartmel SD3776 HOLKER HALL Opulently built and furnished mainly Victorian mansion with appealingly unstuffy feel despite the beauty. The glorious 25-acre formal and woodland gardens are among the best in the country, with spectacular water features, rose garden, rhododendron and azalea arboretum, and rare plants and shrubs. Also deer park, entertaining motor museum, toy and teddy exhibition, and adventure playground – enough to take up quite a lump of the day. Meals, snacks, shop, disabled access; cl Sat, and Nov–Mar; (015395) 58328; £3.50 gardens, grounds and exhibitions, Hall and motor museum extra. The nearby Engine is handy for lunch.

♫ † 🏰 🏠 ⚞ Carlisle NY4056 A sizeable town, not an obvious holiday destination, but there is plenty to interest the visitor, with several quietly attractive old buildings (and a very helpful visitor centre in one of them, the Old Town Hall). TULLIE HOUSE 🖼 (Castle St) Great fun: dramatic displays of Border history, using state-of-the-art techniques of sight, sound and smell. Children especially will find lots to do, from exploring mine tunnels to trying out a Roman crossbow. The ground floor has a more conventional art gallery/museum. Meals, snacks, shop, disabled access; cl am Sun, 25 Dec; (01228) 34781; £3.50 (get there between 10 and 11am and it's half price). The unpretentious little CATHEDRAL, founded in 1122 and severely damaged in the Civil War, has fine stained glass; try to go on a bright morning when the sunlight comes streaming colourfully through the east window. Also medieval carvings inc the Brougham Triptych, painted panels and stonework, and crypt treasury. Meals, snacks, good shop (some tasty local foods), disabled access (exc to restaurant); free. The extensive medieval CASTLE, rather gaunt and forbidding, is surprisingly well preserved considering its violent history. Interesting period furnished rooms, a portcullised gatehouse, lots of staircases and passages, and centuries of prisoners' carved graffiti in the dungeons; good views from the ramparts. Snacks, shop; cl 24–26 Dec, 1 Jan; (01228) 591922; £2.70. The GUILDHALL in Greenmarket is a handsomely restored medieval timbered hall; worth a look inside if you're passing – some displays (open pm Tues, Thurs and wknds; 50p). ST CUTHBERT'S CHURCH is remarkable for its mobile pulpit. The Crown & Mitre (English St) has a good-value lunchtime buffet, and there's good home cooking in the Black Lion out at Durdar, where the attractively placed racecourse has meetings every month exc July; (01228) 22973 for dates. The SETTLE–CARLISLE RAILWAY, up Ribbledale and into the Cumbrian Pennines, stopping at Dent Station, Garsdale Head, Kirkby Stephen, Appleby, Langwathby and other Eden Valley villages, is a memorable 70m of grand scenery, best from Appleby to Settle; (0345) 484950 for times and fares – it's described more fully under the entry for Settle in our Yorkshire chapter.

★ † ⚘ Cartmel SD3879 Picturesque little alleys lead off the delightfully harmonious central square – especially the one out through the former PRIORY GATEHOUSE. The PRIORY CHURCH, which towers massively over the village, is an interesting mix of architectural grandeur from 12th to 16th c, inc fine carving. Lots of arts and crafts in the village. CRAFT WORKSHOPS at Broughton Lodge Farm (N towards the A590), with demonstrations, and home baking in the vegetarianish cafe. The Cavendish Arms is good for lunch.

† **Cartmel Fell** SD4288 In a wonderful tucked-away country location, the CHURCH here has interesting early pews and a fine triple-decker pulpit. The Masons Arms is deservedly very popular indeed for lunch. The road here from Winster is very pretty.

🏠 † **Casterton** SD6379 Brontë fans will want to see CASTERTON SCHOOL; attractive pre-Raphaelite stained glass and paintings in the CHURCH result from enthusiastic Brotherhood holidays here. The Pheasant is good.

★ 🏠 🛢 🛢 🖎 🐎 **Cockermouth** NY1231 Quietly attractive riverside town, increasingly worth a holiday visit. WORDSWORTH HOUSE (Main St) The poet's happy childhood home, a handsome restored 18th-c town house with fine furniture, pictures by friends and contemporaries, good original panelling, and a walled garden above the river. Well worth a visit in its own right as well as for its Wordsworth associations, and interesting to see how different it is from the places he lived in later on. Snacks, shop; cl wknds (exc Sat July and Aug or before bank hol), and Nov–Easter; (01900) 824805; £2.60; NT. Next door, the PRINTING HOUSE is a working print museum, with a good range of historic presses and equipment; you can try out various printing methods. Disabled access; cl Sun; (01900) 824984; £2.50. The Norham opposite is a good teashop, and the comfortable Trout does decent food. JENNINGS BREWERY Tours of traditional Castle Brewery, where the water for brewing is still drawn from the well that supplied the Castle at the time of the Norman Conquest. Shop; tours 11am and 2pm wkdys

Mar–Oct (plus maybe 12.30pm in summer hols), and 11am Sat Apr–Sept – booking advisable; (01900) 823214; £2.90. No children under 12. A family-run motor museum, ASPECTS OF MOTORING, opened next door last summer, with a good changing range of vehicles, audio-visual displays, and a model race track for children. Snacks, shop, disabled access; open mid-Mar–Oct, plus wknds from Feb and Nov and Dec; (01900) 824448; £3. CASTLEGATE HOUSE GALLERY (Castlegate) Friendly lived-in Georgian house opposite the castle, with walled garden, Adam ceiling and sales of paintings and crafts. Cl Thurs, Sun, all Jan and Feb; (01900) 822149; free. TOY AND MODEL MUSEUM (Market Place) Good expanding collection of mainly British toys from the last century; shop, limited disabled access; cl Dec and Jan exc by appointment; (01900) 827606; £2. LAKELAND SHEEP AND WOOL CENTRE 🔤 (slightly S of the town towards Egremont) Entertaining live show starring 19 different species of sheep; they demonstrate shearing and sheepdog trials, and an adjacent exhibition is a good introduction to the area. Show times 10.30am, noon, 2pm, and 3.30pm. Meals, snacks, shop, disabled access; cl 25 Dec; show *£3, exhibitions free.

🏠 🌸 **Coniston** SD3195 Unpretentious village at the foot of its mountain, the Old Man. The Black Bull does filling food all day. BRANTWOOD on the opposite shore of the lake was Ruskin's rambling Victorian house. It still has lots of his furniture, books and paintings and is appealingly unstuffy, but the real attraction is the surroundings and setting, especially the very extensive informal hillside woodland gardens (best in late May/Jun). Good hour's walk on nature trail, and mouth-watering views of lake and fells. Meals, snacks, good shop, disabled access (grounds steep in places); cl winter Mon and Tues; (015394) 41296; £3.70. From Spoon Hall there's PONY TREKKING on the fells above; cl Nov–Easter; (015394) 41391; from £11 an hour.

🏠 🏵 † **Dacre** NY4626 DALEMAIN HOUSE 🏛 Largely Elizabethan despite the Georgian façade, and with a number of even older features, so an appealing variety of periods and styles. Some rooms are grand, others are charming, with splendid furnishings and paintings and a good deal for children to enjoy. Particularly interesting Chinese Room with hand-painted wallpaper. There's an adventure playground, and deer in the carefully landscaped PARK with lake and mountain views. Atmospheric restaurant, shop, plant centre, limited disabled access; cl Fri and Sat, and 2nd week Oct–Sun before Easter; (017684) 86450; £5, £3 grounds. The village CHURCH has pre-Norman sculpture, and quaint medieval stone bears in the graveyard. The Kings Arms in Stainton is good for lunch.

🐾 🏚 **Dalton-in-Furness** SD2374 SOUTH LAKES WILD ANIMAL PARK Rapidly expanding 14-acre wildlife centre, well placed for fine views of the entire Furness peninsula. Animals such as wallabies, antelope, raccoons, coatis and porcupines, and a 4-acre section with pheasants and ducks wandering free and waiting to be fed; also nature trail, lakeside walks, miniature railway, and pets corner. It's a very committed place, taking part in a number of international breeding programmes. Snacks, shop, some disabled access; cl 25 Dec; (01229) 466086; £3.75. The village also has a rather austere square CASTLE; the Anchor at Lindal has decent food.

★ 🐾 **Dent** SD7187 Inside the modern outskirts is a delightful steep cobbled village, a rewarding end to an attractive drive – though now on the tourist trail, so it's busy in summer. The welcoming Sun brews its own beer, and the church is well worth a look. E of the village, towards Denthead, Colin Gardner (Stone House, Cowgill; cl wknds) and Little Oak Furniture (Bridge End, Denthead) both make traditional furniture.

🏚 🏛 🔱 **Egremont** NY0111 Dominated by its very ruined Norman CASTLE; as so often, the gatehouse is the best preserved part. LOWES COURT GALLERY Georgian house with local arts and crafts for sale; cl Sun, and pm wkdys Jan/Feb; (01946) 820693; free. Just SE on the A595, the FLORENCE MINE HERITAGE CENTRE is based around what was the last working iron ore mine in Europe. Tours of the pit at 10.30am and 1.30pm, and visitor centre with reconstructions of pit life at the turn of the century. Snacks, shop, disabled access to visitor centre; cl Nov–Easter; (01946) 820683; £6.50 pit tour, £1 visitor centre.

★ 🌼 **Elterwater** NY3305 Idyllically placed village, with lake views. The Britannia is very popular for lunch. The B5343 past here gives awesome mountain views; you can keep on a poorer steeper road, passing near pretty Blea Tarn, and coming back down through the gentler Little Langdale.

🔱 **Finsthwaite** SD3788 STOTT PARK BOBBIN MILL (just N) Set in coppiced woodland, this former water-and-steam mill made wooden cotton reels from 1835 right up to 1971; good guides give excellent demonstrations of 19th-c industrial techniques. The mill is still powered by steam Tues–Thurs: the lathes look lethal. Snacks, shop, disabled access; cl Nov–Easter; (015395) 31087; £2.70. The Swan at Newby Bridge is attractively set for lunch.

✗ **Gleaston** SD2671 Well restored working WATERMILL in peaceful surroundings, with a working corn mill, and leather-making demonstrations. Meals, snacks, shop, some disabled access; cl Mon (exc bank hols) and winter Tues; (01229) 869244; *£1.50. The ruins of a partly built medieval castle are nearby.

† 🐾 **Gosforth** NY0703 The churchyard has a 10th-c carved CROSS, one of Britain's finest; there are more ancient carved hogback tombstones in the church. The working POTTERY may let you try making a pot; good shop. Cl Mon Jan–Mar, 25–26 Dec.

★ ⌂ ☉ 🅐 **Grasmere** NY3406 The pretty village swarms with visitors in summer, most of them here to see DOVE COTTAGE – still much as Wordsworth had it in his most creative years (he completed *The Prelude* here), with sister Dorothy's *Journals* and his extensive cottage garden. Informative guided tours cope well with the bustle, but in early morning (opens 9.30am) out of season you may get some space to yourself. The place always was crowded; barely big enough for two, with the poets' children and friends it often had a dozen or more people living here. The adjoining WORDSWORTH MUSEUM, included in the price, has changing exhibitions and possessions of the poet and his family and friends, as well as a reconstructed Lakeland kitchen. Meals, snacks, shop; cl 12 Jan–8 Feb, 24–26 Dec; (015394) 35544; £4.25. Wordsworth is buried in the graveyard of the robust old church, which has quite an unusual interior. The HEATON COOPER STUDIO has Lakeland watercolours and prints on display and for sale; cl am Sun. Sarah Nelson's gingerbread shop is wonderfully old-fashioned. The Travellers Rest (on the A591) is our current pick for lunch.

⌕ ✿ **Grizedale** SD3494 FOREST PARK Woodland trails from short strolls to half-day walks, punctuated by often hard-to-spot timber and rock sculptures. Lots of other activities too: craft centre, good information centre, bookable deer observation hides, orienteering, bike hire (it's an ideal area for cycling), and adventure play area. In all, 6 or 7 square miles of mainly coniferous hillside timber to get lost in. Some disabled access; (01229) 860373; parking charge, £1.20 for 4 hours. A highlight is the Theatre in the Forest; (01229) 860291 for what's on. The Eagle's Head at Satterthwaite (some winter closures) is good value for lunch, and the back roads through this area are quiet and pleasant.

☺ **Hackthorpe** NY5423 LOWTHER LEISURE AND WILDLIFE PARK 🅐 (signed off the A6 S of Penrith) Plenty to keep children up to around 11 amused for most of the day (the pace is too sedate for teenagers). Some features have a refreshingly old-fashioned appeal: there's a circus with trapeze and clown acts, and the rides are more along the lines of a traditional funfair than gravity-busting rollercoasters. The attractive parkland has a developing wildlife area, as well as puppet shows, boating, miniature train rides, challenging play areas, and an archery range. Meals, snacks, shop, disabled access; open wknds Easter–spring bank hol (plus Easter hols) then daily till early Sept; (01931) 712523; £6.25 (children too). The Punch Bowl at Askham does interesting food.

🏛 **Hardknott Pass** NY2101 HARDKNOTT ROMAN FORT Quite well preserved and interestingly restored, but most notable for its staggering lonely position high in the mountains; magnificent views to sea and even the Isle of Man. The drive up here is very steep and twisting, through this pass and Wrynose Pass, but the scenery makes it worthwhile; the Woolpack Inn at Bleabeck just W is worthwhile.

★ 🅐 ⌂ ✝ ✎ ☙ **Hawkshead** SD3598 Don't miss this virtually unchanged Elizabethan Lakeland village, with sturdy outside walls, and sheltered flower-filled inner courtyards. Though very popular with summer visitors, even at its busiest it has a pleasantly foreign 'different' feel, and the fact that cars are kept out helps a lot. The BEATRIX POTTER GALLERY (Main St) has a generous annually changing selection of the original illustrations of *Peter Rabbit* and other favourites, as well as rather different more acutely (almost acidly) observed drawings. A timed ticket system keeps it uncrowded – during holiday periods you may have to wait to get in. Shop; cl Fri, Sat, and Nov–Mar; (015394) 36355; £2.70; NT. The OLD GRAMMAR SCHOOL, now a museum, is only really worth poking your nose into to see where Wordsworth carved his name on a desk (he attended 1779–83); limited disabled access; cl pm Sun, and Nov–Easter; £2. The church next door has some eye-catching early 18th-c murals. The best nearby pub for lunch is the Drunken Duck up at Barngates. Trout FISHING and BOAT HIRE on nearby Esthwaite Water, the largest stocked lake in the region.

★ † ❀ **Kirkby Lonsdale** SD6278 Small and usually quiet town of considerable character, with interesting old yards and ginnels and good country shops; it's more lively on Thurs country-market day. Behind the fine CHURCH of St Mary is a pretty stretch of the River Lune, good for walking or just lazing about – even swimming if it's hot. Along here 87 steps lead up to Ruskin's View, a beautiful panorama over the Lune Valley, appealing countryside little visited by tourists. The Snooty Fox has good food.

▥ ♪ ✿ **Lakeside** SD3787 The steamer stop at the S end of Lake Windermere, and the starting point for the LAKESIDE & HAVERTHWAITE RAILWAY, a short steam trip running up to Haverthwaite. There's a small collection of steam and diesel locomotives. Meals, snacks, shop, disabled access; trains wknds Easter–Oct, daily from early May and around Easter; (015395) 31594 for times; £3.30 return. Beside here is the new LAKESIDE AQUARIUM, an imaginatively laid out aquarium-style centre which vividly demonstrates the story of a local river. You can walk in see-through tunnels along a recreated lake bed, with the area's animal, insect, bird and plant life all around, and there's a water lab with microscopes for close-up examinations of tadpoles, plankton and larvae. Snacks, shop, disabled access; cl 25 Dec; (015395) 30153; £4.50. GRAYTHWAITE HALL GARDENS SD3791 (2m N) Well kept late Victorian garden, strong on rhododendrons and late-spring-flowering shrubs. Open Apr–Jun only; (015395) 31248; *£2. At the Haverthwaite end you can watch CRYSTAL ENGRAVING by hand at Low Wood, and the White Hart at Booth does good food.

▦ ✿ ▥ **Levens** SD4985 LEVENS HALL ▨ (on the A6) Impressive Elizabethan mansion based around older core, with fine carved oak chimney-pieces, ceiling plasterwork, Spanish leather panelling, period furnishings and interesting paintings. The magnificent topiary GARDENS in their original layout of 1692 are perhaps the highlight, the fantastic shapes really standing out against the ancient grey stone of the house. Also model and other STEAM ENGINES (pm only; in steam bank hols and some summer Suns), play area, grand beech trees, and deer park. Snacks, plant sales, shop, disabled access to grounds only; open Sun–Thurs, Apr–mid-Oct (plus gardens open wkdys in Oct); (015395) 60321; £5, £3.70 grounds only. The Hare & Hounds is handy for lunch.

▥ **Little Salkeld** NY5736 There's access off the lane N to the quaintly named STONE CIRCLE Long Meg and her Daughters NY5737.

🦅 **Lowther** NY5323 LAKELAND BIRD OF PREY CENTRE Set in the huge Victorian walled garden at Lowther Castle, hawks, eagles, owls, buzzards and falcons, with flying displays at 12, 2 and 4pm. Also craft gallery. Teas, shop, disabled access; cl Nov–Feb; (01931) 712746; *£4.

❀ ◔ **Maryport** NY0436 Small port with 18th- and 19th-c streets; the harbour has been smartly redeveloped in recent years, though sadly has yet to revitalise the town's fortunes. SENHOUSE MUSEUM (The Battery, Sea Brows) Impressive collection of Roman military altar stones and inscriptions, dug from the former fort next door from the 1570s onwards, making it one of the oldest collections of antiquities in the country; also other artefacts inc a Celtic serpent stone. Snacks, shop, disabled access; open Fri–Sun all year, plus Tues and Thurs Apr–Oct, bank hols, and daily July–Sept; (01900) 816168; £1.50. There's a straightforward MARITIME MUSEUM on Senhouse St; cl Sun exc pm in summer, and maybe lunchtimes, especially in winter; free. The 2 fully restored STEAMSHIPS in Elizabeth Dock have been reopened by a group of enthusiastic volunteers, who bought them from the council for £1; best to check opening times on (01900) 815954; £1.90. The B5300 N has good views across to Scotland.

✝ 🏛 ⛵ 🍴 **Millom** SD1780 Not much of a town, but there's an interesting CHURCH, and RUINED CASTLE around what's now a farm (on the A5093 N: ask at the house for permission to look round the ruins). A decent FOLK MUSEUM on St Georges Rd (cl Sun, and mid-Sept–Apr, exc Easter; £1), and the Victorian station on Station Rd has been converted into craft workshops. S of the town a broad lagoon built to protect former mineworks is now a bird reserve, the loneliness exaggerated out of season when the nearby unsmart but enjoyable little resort of Haverigg SD1678 (great beaches, good sailing and fishing) has closed down; the Harbour Inn has good cheap food, good walks in the wildflower dunes.

🐾 ❀ 🦋 **Milnthorpe** SD4981 LAKELAND WILDLIFE OASIS 💷 (on the A6 S) Millions of years of evolution flash before your eyes at this lively jungle house, a fascinating cross between zoo and museum. Interactive displays alongside the brightly coloured and unusual fish, birds, insects and animals, and woodland where children can crawl into tunnels overlooking the meerkat enclosures. Snacks, shop, disabled access; cl 25 Dec; (015395) 63027; £4.50. The Wheatsheaf at Beetham and Blue Bell at Heversham are both good for lunch; the B5282 to Arnside has quiet estuary and mountain views.

🏠 **Near Sawrey** SD3796 HILL TOP Small, remote 17th-c farmhouse, kept exactly as it was when owned by Beatrix Potter, who wrote many of her stories here. Or at least as it was apart from the tourists; the NT (great beneficiaries of Potter's generosity) feel the place is over-visited, and are keen to reduce visitor numbers. One way they're doing this is by cutting down on publicity in Japan, where Peter Rabbit and his chums enjoy near-revered status. It's so small they don't allow many people in at once, so if you do decide to visit be prepared to queue. Shop (the

turnover is higher than at any other NT shop); cl Thurs, Fri, all Nov–Mar; (015394) 36269; £3.60; NT. The old-fashioned NT-owned Tower Bank Arms (with nicely furnished bedrooms) is pictured in *The Tale of Jemima Puddle-Duck*.

❗ **Newby Bridge** SD3786 From outside the well set Swan Hotel the Windermere Balloon Company run BALLOON TRIPS over the whole of this area (weather permitting); (01229) 581779; from £125.

🏛 **Piel Island** SD2364 Small island shared by a basic inn and a grand 14th-c ruined fortress commanding Barrow harbour and Morecambe Bay. It's reached by ferry (not winter exc by arrangement – 01229 833609) from Roa Island nr Barrow.

🚲 🏘 ⚙ 🍴 ✕ 🏛 **Ravenglass** SD0996 Pretty sailing harbour by the well sheltered Esk estuary; in summer a local fishing boat sells freshly caught fish on the shore. RAVENGLASS & ESKDALE RAILWAY 💷 England's oldest narrow-gauge steam trains, lovingly preserved, with open carriages chugging up 7 miles of unspoilt valley to Dalegarth; admirers say it's the most beautiful train journey in England. Cafés each end, and a small museum at Ravenglass. Shop, disabled access (with notice); cl most wkdys Dec–mid-Feb, but best to phone for train times and dates; (01229) 717171; £6.10 return. Good 3-hour summer walk back from Boot (walks booklets from stations). MUNCASTER CASTLE, GARDENS & OWL CENTRE (1m E on the A595) The same family has lived in this grand old house since 1208 – and will continue to do so as long as a magical glass drinking bowl remains intact. Extended over the centuries (especially 19th) from its original tower, its elegant rooms have rich furnishings and decor, inc fine Elizabethan furniture and embroidery. Entertaining Walkman tour, and glorious Esk and mountain views from the terrace. The lovely 77-acre grounds are particularly rich in species rhododendrons, and also have unusual trees, nature trails, adventure play area and lots of rescued birds of prey. Closed-circuit TV of nesting owls, along with talks and flying displays every afternoon at 2.30pm (Apr–Oct), weather permitting. Meals, snacks, shop and plant centre, good disabled access; house open pm daily (exc Sat), garden and owl centre open all year; (01229) 717614; £5.20, £3.50 garden and owl centre. A well restored working WATERMILL (on the A595 NE), has Victorian machinery and flour for sale. Cl Nov–Mar (exc wknds); (01229) 717232; £1.40. They also do good-value B & B. The so-called WALLS CASTLE just outside the village is actually a Roman bath house; its walls stand taller than any other building of its age so far north.

✝ 🌳 **Ravenstonedale** NY7203 The village is notable more for its pleasant riverside scenery than for its buildings – apart from the unspoilt CHURCH which escaped Victorian refitting; longitudinal pews, 3-decker pulpit, steeply pitched gallery (steep stairs up), and a fine E window memorial to the Fothergill family (one was the last female Protestant martyr to be burned at the stake). Choose a bright day for best light. Beckside Gallery makes hardwood traditional furniture. The Black Swan and Kings Head both have decent food.

🏚 🎡 **Rydal** NY3706 RYDAL MOUNT (on the A591) Wordsworth's sister Dorothy described Rydal as 'a paradise' when the family moved here from Grasmere in 1813; they stayed for the rest of their lives. The house itself is rather modest, with family portraits and period furniture, and it's what's outside that really stands out – the good-sized garden is still much as the poet laid it out, consciously picturesque, with original ideas that people are still rediscovering today. The setting is lovely, overlooking mountains and lakes, and they often have readings of the poetry it inspired. Shop; cl Tues Nov–Feb, and the first 3 weeks of Jan; (015394) 33002; *£3. Decent campsites nearby. The Glen Rothay Hotel does respectable lunches.

🏛 **Seascale** NY0401 SELLAFIELD (off the A595) Several million pounds have been lavished on the imaginative exhibitions and displays at this nuclear power visitor centre. Not everyone approves of the pro-nuclear PR, but children certainly enjoy the hands-on Disney-style approach to the industry, and there's still no entrance charge for any of the attractions. Meals, snacks, shop, disabled access; cl 25 Dec; (019467) 27027; free. Seascale itself has a pleasant beach, and a singularly scenic golf course, where every hole offers views of the sea or the mountains; the third tee ironically puts Sellafield into the same frame as a ring of prehistoric stones. The Scawfell Hotel, overlooking the sea, is a comfortable lunch stop.

🐄 🏛 **Sedbergh** SD6692 Hardy small town at the foot of the Howgill Fells (see ⌂-44 in Walks section, below), with a helpful Yorkshire Dales National Park Centre on Main St (cl Dec–Easter). It's recently replaced its picturesque cobbles with an ordinary surface – much to the chagrin of the National Parks and English Heritage, who only a few years ago paid for new cobbles. HOLME FARM (Middleton, just SW) 2pm tours of traditional hill farm, with plenty of young animals and nature trail. They do occasional evening tours with badger watch. Disabled access; cl Oct–Feb exc by arrangement; (015396) 20654; *£2. You may be able to camp here. PENNINE TWEEDS (Farfield Mill) is a factory shop for the riverside Victorian mill using 1930s looms (cl Sun Nov–Mar). The Dalesman is good for lunch.

✝ **Shap** NY5415 ABBEY (left towards Keld off the A6 going N out of village) The best feature is the unspoilt and undeveloped riverside seclusion; the abbey itself is very ruined, but you can trace the 13th-c layout in some detail. Nearby KELD CHAPEL is a lonely untouched shepherds' church in a riverside hamlet, and the gated Swindale road signed off the Bampton road nr Rosgill is pretty. The Greyhound is good-value for lunch.

🏚 🎡 🏛 🍽 **Sizergh** SD4987 CASTLE Lovely lakeside house, over the centuries harmoniously extended from its original sturdy 14th-c tower by the family which has lived here for generations. Fine Tudor and Elizabethan carving, panelling and furniture, Jacobite relics, and terraced gardens surrounding a grand flight of steps to water. Lots to interest a gardener, inc an enormous rock garden, Japanese maples, water garden, wild flowers, and daffodils in the crab-apple orchard; the autumn colours are lovely. Snacks, shop, disabled access to garden; open pm Sun–Thurs Apr–Oct; (015395) 60070; £3.40, £1.80 garden only; NT. THE BARN SHOP (Low Sizergh Barn) Plenty of fresh farm foods (cheese, meat, ice-cream, sausage and bread), and other local produce inc Morecambe Bay shrimps. Also craft shop and pick-your-own strawberries. The tearoom overlooks the milking parlour. Cl Mon Jan–Mar; (015395) 60426; free. The Strickland Arms, owned by NT, is useful for lunch.

🏠 🏵 **Skelton** NY4435 HUTTON-IN-THE-FOREST (on the B5305) Some say this formidable mansion was the castle of the Green Knight of Arthurian legend. Grandly extended in the 17th c from its 14th-c peel tower core, then castellated more recently, it has a magnificent panelled gallery. A terraced garden runs down to the lake; there's an 18th-c walled formal garden, and a more romantic Victorian garden with grand trees, dovecot and woodland nature walk. Snacks, shop; garden open daily (exc Sat), house open pm Thurs, Fri and Sun Apr–Sept, plus Easter wknd, Weds in August, and all bank hols; (017684) 84449; £3.50, £2 garden only.

🐏 **Southwaite** NY4545 FOUR SEASONS FARM EXPERIENCE (Sceugh Mire) Friendly working farm, designed mainly for schools so well geared to children, who can touch and feed most of the animals (inc pigs, donkeys, ducks and horses), and, more unusually, have a go at making their own bread and butter. Good play areas. Snacks, shop, disabled access; (01694) 73753; £3.50.

⚓ **Talkin Tarn** NY5458 Lovely lake with partly wooded shores, peaceful mountain views, plenty of space for strolling, and nature trail; disabled access, teas. You can hire rowing boats (from £4.40 an hour) and mountain bikes. The village is pretty; the Blacksmiths Arms is popular for food.

🏵 **Temple Sowerby** NY6127 ACORN BANK Richly planted terraced and walled garden with 250 varieties of medicinal and culinary herbs, clematis, unusual old fruit trees, and herbaceous borders; the steep wild garden drops down to the stream. A mill down here has been restored, and the wheel turns at wknds. This is a lovely spot at daffodil time. Shop, disabled access; cl Nov–Mar; (017683) 61893; £2.10; NT. The B6412 to Lazenby and then the back road through the Eden valley to Armathwaite and on up to Wetheral gives delicious quiet views.

🎨 **Thornthwaite** NY2225 THORNTHWAITE GALLERIES Fine art, pottery and other crafts, as well as teas, summer try-your-hand-at-it demonstrations, and a play area. Snacks, shop, disabled access (but no facilities); cl Tues and Dec–Feb; (017687) 78248; free. The Coledale Inn at Braithwaite is good for lunch (and walkers).

🎣 **Thurstonfield** NY3257 Lough Fishery (on the B5307) Hire tackle and boats (one suitable for disabled) for TROUT FISHING on a well stocked sizeable lake in peaceful woodland; cl Nov–mid-Mar; (01228) 576552.

🏠 🏵 **Troutbeck** NY4103 Delightful settlement of ancient farms strung along a steep valley below high fells. One of these, TOWNEND, is the perfectly preserved home of a comfortably off, very traditional farming family who lived here for 300 years till the 1940s, the house showing little change over all that time. Solid, simple, unshowy comfort, and a sensible, down-to-earth and entirely self-sufficient layout. Cl am, all Mon (exc bank hols) and Sat, and Nov–Mar; (015394) 32628; £2.70; NT. The beautifully placed hillside village has several more such 'statesmen's' farms. HOLEHIRD (off the A592 S) The Lakeland Horticultural Society's hillside garden – 5 acres of well grown plants in wide variety, inc National Collections of hydrangeas and some other families; lovely views. Disabled access; open all year, but manned in summer only; (015394) 46008; donations (they rely on these to maintain the gardens). Rookin House Farm has accompanied HORSE-RIDING, beginners welcome; (017684) 83561; £9.50 an hour. The quaint Queens Head is an excellent place.

✻ **Ullswater** NY4020 AIRA FORCE Reached by a scenic mile or so's walk through lovely NT woodland overlooking the lake, this is a 20m (65ft) waterfall, at its best after rain or on a misty morning; restaurant and shop, £1.20 parking charge – see also **Walks** section below. The good Royal Hotel at Dockray is handy.

☎ ⚲ ☃ ♫ ☂ **Ulverston** SD2978 On wkdys you can visit the factory of CUMBRIA CRYSTAL (Lightburn Rd), and watch the craftsmen blowing, cutting and (Mon–Thurs) engraving; £1. The factory shop (cl 25–26 Dec, 1 Jan) is good value, with cheap seconds; disabled access. The Pork Pie Shop at the N end of Mkt Pl is very good indeed, while the Dolls House Man (Furness Galleries, Theatre St) makes doll's houses, farms, wooden animals and so on, and usually has examples on display (cl Sun, Mon, Weds). Lots more local crafts at ULVERSTON POINT, a converted granary by the old watermill (not Sun). LAUREL & HARDY MUSEUM (Upper Brook St) The owner of this unique exhibition (a former mayor) really knows his subject, and it's his obvious enthusiasm that makes this one of Lakelands's best-loved attractions. Fittingly in Stan Laurel's home town, with delightfully informally presented mementoes and all-day films. Shop, disabled access; cl Jan; (01229) 582292; £2. The HERITAGE CENTRE on Lower Brook St has local history displays (cl Sun, and Weds in winter; free), and there's a MOTORCYCLE MUSEUM on Victoria Rd, unusual in that you can buy many of the changing exhibits (cl Sun, Mon; £3). The Rose & Crown (King St) has decent food, and the Bay Horse out at Canal Foot is worth going to for lunch.

➷ **Walney Island** SD1868 Over the bridge from Barrow, this has some long roads of low houses but is mostly a windswept sweep of duney grass, very offshore-feeling; nature reserves at both ends, with excellent bird watching and interesting plants. The George has enjoyable food.

★ ♫ **Whitehaven** NX9718 Planned as an 18th-c industrial town and major port, this interesting place is being restored after a decline. The harbour is attractive at high tide (a bit dirty at low tide). The town's history is excellently covered at THE BEACON ▨ (West Strand), but what really makes this friendly new heritage centre worth a look is the Met Office Weather Gallery on the top floor, full of hi-tech monitoring and recording equipment, and excellent hands-on displays explaining how weather forecasts are put together. The building itself is striking, with good views over the town and harbour from the top floor. Shop, disabled access; (01946) 592302; £3.30. Michael Moon's BOOKSHOP (Roper St) has a vast and rewarding secondhand stock, the best in the Lakes; cl Sun, bank hols, and Weds Jan–Easter. There are some other interesting shops in side streets, and the Richmond (Hensingham) is useful for lunch. Just S at Sandwith, the Lowther Arms is recommended by readers for good homely food and accommodation, handy for the coast to coast walk.

▨ **Witherslack** SD4384 HALECAT GARDEN (on the A590) Good example of modern landscaping with fine views from the mainly herbaceous garden; plants for sale (especially hydrangeas). Mostly disabled access; cl wknds Oct–Easter; (015395) 52229; free.

☃ 🏛 **Workington** NX9928 HELENA THOMPSON MUSEUM (Park End Rd) Some antique and Georgian costumes, as well as pottery, silver, furniture and local history, in period surroundings; cl Sun; (01900) 62598; free. Cobbled Portland Sq is pretty. WORKINGTON HALL (Curwen Pk, N) Former mansion, now ruinous hulk around a Norman tower, in public park – an odd conjunction. A famous letter by Mary Queen of Scots to her cousin Elizabeth I was written here. Shop; cl 1–2pm, am wknds, all day Mon (exc bank hols), all Nov–Easter; (01900) 735408; 85p. The Alamin Indian restaurant (Jane St) is good.

🌶 We've already mentioned a good few local craftsmen. Others can be found at Curthwaite NY3249, where Ian Laval of Meadow Bank Farm is a very traditional CABINET-MAKER (cl wknds), and Michael King at Todd Close in nearby Oakleigh makes silver and gold JEWELLERY (cl Sun, Mon); at Ainstable NY5346, where Jim Malone has a traditional WORKING POTTERY; and at Staveley (the one NW of Kendal, SD4798), where at the workshop of CABINET-MAKER Peter Hall you can see furniture being made, and watch woodturners at work (cl wknds and bank hols exc showroom and shop).

✝ Country churches are generally simple here, though candlelit ST WILFRED'S NY5328 (on the B6262 E of Eamont Bridge) is an exception for its magnificent furnishings including Continental treasures; others worth stopping at include Watermillock NY4522 for its evocative photographs of all its 1930s parishioners; Torpenhow NY2039 (formidably Norman, inc some Roman masonry); and Martindale NY4419 (attractive primitive stonework).

★ Other attractive villages in fine scenery include Askham NY5123 (2 greens – each with a good pub), Broughton Mills SD2290 (the Blacksmiths Arms is good), Hesket Newmarket NY3438, Kirkoswald NY5641 (ruins of 13th-c castle, views towards the Pennines, and a useful pub for lunch), Stonethwaite NY2613 (the Langstrath is a good stop for thirsty walkers) and Threlkeld NY3325 (the Salutation is hard, and the B5322 to Thirlmere pretty, with a very photogenic view of Clough Head from the Brigham/Keswick side road turning off just past Yew Tree Farm). The comfortable Kirkstile Inn at Loweswater NY1222 deserves a mention for its glorious setting. Peaceful Flookburgh SD3676 has excellent local potted shrimps, and a decent craft shop. Other nice villages, all with decent pubs, include Armathwaite NY5146, Bampton NY5118, Beckermet NY0207, Crosby Ravensworth NY6215 (Maulds Meaburn is also pretty), Garrigill NY7441 and Langwathby NY5734.

🏛 🐄 For Birdoswald Roman Fort at Gilsland, see Northumbria chapter (the GOAT FARM at Holme View nearby sells prize-winning traditional cheeses).

Boating

Lake Windermere The most popular boating lake, so the easiest on which to hire rowing boats and other vessels. Lots of launches, of all sorts of shapes and sizes, run cruises of varying lengths from Bowness Bay, Ambleside, Waterhead and (not Nov–Mar) Newby Bridge. The pick of the sightseeing boat trips is the 45-min tour on the silent steam launch Osprey, though it's available only to visitors to the Steamboat Museum just N of Bowness Bay (see **To see and do** section; above); £4.75, plus £2.90 museum admission. The pier at the S end of the lake is the terminus for the Haverthwaite steam railway.

Rowing boats can be hired from the Bowness Bay Boating Company; from £2.50 per hour, £2 per extra person. They also have motorboats, and a number of launches – at least one of which is equipped to take disabled people; (015394) 43360 to check. Lake Holidays Afloat do motorboats too; around £50 for a full day. A pleasant place to hire rowing boats (not Nov–Easter) is FELL FOOT PARK nr Newby Bridge, an 18-acre park with plenty of room for lakeside picnics; café and shop (cl Nov–Easter), some disabled access;

(015395) 31273; parking – charges (around £2), rowing boats £5 per hour for two people; NT. They can provide details of boating and fishing on other NT waters. Lakeland Sailing at Ferry Nab, Bowness, do day, weekend or longer cruises and courses on large sailing yachts; from £50 a day. Windsurfing or waterskiing can be arranged at Low Wood Water Sports Centre, Windermere; windsurfing, canoeing or dinghy sailing Mar–Oct at Windermere Sailing Centre, Rayrigg Rd, Windermere.

The chain ferry linking the ferry road below Bowness with the Hawkshead road below Far Sawrey is a utilitarian way of taking to the water; but though it runs every 20 mins and saves miles of driving, queues mean that it saves time only out of season.

On **Ullswater** elegant Victorian steamers converted to diesel run between Pooley Bridge, Howtown and Glenridding; disabled access, cl Dec–Mar. Sailing dinghies can be hired by competent sailors from Ullswater Marina at Watermillock, (017684) 86415, or the sailing school at Glenridding (017684) 82541; cl winter. Rowing and other boats can be hired from Tindals in Glenridding; (017684) 82393; around £5 per hour, motorboats around £10.

Derwent Water, with all its inlets and little islets, is a pleasant place for pottering about in rowing boats. You can hire them, and launches, in Keswick (not Nov–Easter); from around £5 per hour. Regular launches run all year from Keswick to half a dozen points around the lake.

Coniston Water has an opulent Victorian steam yacht which sails daily end-Mar–Oct, from Coniston Pier, Brantwood and Park-a-Moor; (015394) 41288 for times – best to ring between 9 and 10.30am or you're likely to get the answerphone. Or hire rowing or other boats from the boating centre run by the National Park, 15 minutes' walk from the village; cl Nov–Mar; (015394) 41366; rowing boats from £4 an hour (£1 each extra person), motorboats from £10, electric boats £12.50.

You can also hire rowing boats on Bassenthwaite, Buttermere and Crummock Water.

Walks

You could stay here for weeks every year of your life and never walk the same path twice – so our suggestions are really just initial pointers. Also, many of the recommended places to stay here have been chosen for the grand walks right from their doorsteps.

Grasmere ⌂-1, Rydal Water and Elter Water are famous for their lovely settings, and there are pleasant walks all around; you can even link all three together in a long afternoon's trek filled with glorious views. The walk up the good track to Easedale Tarn from Grasmere quickly gets you away from the crowds, into a fine valley; the lake itself is romantically set below rocks.

Orrest Head SD4199 ⌂-2 is a short steep walk (half-hour each way) from Windermere (opposite the station); it gives spectacular views over the lake and the Pennines, lovely at sunset. **Gummers How** SD3988 ⌂-3 further S from Windermere is an easy 20-minute climb from the road, for a fine lake view. The cream of Windermere's waterside strolls are on the lake's western shore, between the ferry at **Far Sawrey** SD3995 ⌂-4 and northwards to the Wray Castle estate, a large NT tract with general public access. The forested slope rising from this shore has several well signposted routes, with Far Sawrey and Near Sawrey villages and Latterbarrow (see ⌂-6, below) worthwhile objectives for circular walks.

Wansfell Pike NY3904 ⌂-5 is gained by a path from Ambleside. It's toylike in size compared with the bigger fells, but the view is as good as many. An even smaller protuberance is **Latterbarrow** SD3699 ⌂-6 near Hawkshead, but it is elevated enough above a relatively low-lying area to give views over Windermere and Langdale. **Tarn Hows** SD3299 ⌂-7, an easy hour's walk from Hawkshead, is a gorgeously photogenic small lake; particularly beautiful on a still clear autumn day. The sculpture trail in **Grizedale Forest** SD3494 ⌂-8 (see **Other things to see and do** section, above) is good when rain cuts off more open views; the sculptures are set in various spots throughout the plantations (map from visitor centre).

Coniston Water SD3095 ⌂-9 has a lovely path on its W side, S of Coniston; you can combine this walk with one on a higher-level route along the Walna Scar 'road' (an ancient hard track closed to through traffic) beneath the Old Man of Coniston SD2797, the outstanding viewpoint of the vicinity. Climb the Old Man from Coniston, go up past the remains of copper mines, and return down the Walna Scar road.

Great Langdale NY2906 ⌂-10, dominated by the awesome Langdale Pikes, is the area's main centre for more serious fell-walking in grand scenery. One very popular shorter walk here is up the good track to Stickle Tarn, from the car park by the Stickle Barn (useful for refreshments); and Bow Fell and Crinkle Crags are two longer fell walks. Wainwrights, in the not specially graceful settlement of Chapel Stile off the B5343, another useful refreshment place, is particularly popular with many of our contributors as a base for walks along here.

The sedately old-fashioned resort of **Grange-over-Sands** SD4077 – ⌂-11 is the start for summer guided walks over Morecambe Bay Sands, oddly other-worldly; glistening tidal flats, quick-stepping patrols of wading birds, distant hills, grisly tales of people and horses sucked under – a guide really is essential; phone Cedric Robinson, the official guide appointed by the Queen, on (015395) 32165 for times. **Hampsfield Fell** SD3979 ⌂-12 is a pleasant walk up through the woods from Grange-over-Sands, giving terrific views over the Bay from its limestone pavements and summit 'hospice' inscribed with 19th-c words of wisdom. Further stunning views of the bay are from Humphrey Head Point SD3973, a ¾-mile-long headland protruding into the sea, and from **Arnside Knott** SD4577 ⌂-13, near Arnside, which looks across to the southern Lakeland fells.

Ullswater's eastern shore ⌂-14 is outstanding; there are many different views, with a rewarding combination of waterside stretches and higher ground – from which to see more sweeping vistas. On the best and most popular stretch, Howtown–Patterdale–Glenridding, you will meet quite a few other people in summer (when it can be combined with the steamer for a round trip; best to take the steamer on the way out in case the service is cancelled). The charmingly old-fashioned Howtown Hotel is a good break in a stunning setting, and Hallin Fell NY4319 nearby gives an aerial view of the lake. The main road runs along the western side, but over here there's a pleasant if more populated stroll from the car park on the A592 just NE of the A5091 junction through lakeside woods to the **Aira Force waterfall** NY3920 ⌂-15 and the 'gothick' folly of Lyulphs Tower, with Wordsworth's daffodils a bonus in spring; above here, Gowbarrow Park NY4021 has the best lake views on this side.

Derwent Water too has gorgeous lakeside scenery, romantic little islets, ancient woodland, and a variety of mountain backdrops. A boat service connects several points on the lake. From Keswick, the walk S to **Friar's Crag** NY2622 ⌂-16 and up to Castlehead Wood gains exquisite views. Walla Crag above Great Wood NY2721 (often teeming with red squirrels) gains loftier heights, though the view is not that different; a moorland path heads to the photogenic Ashness Bridge NY2719, from where a rewarding return walk is one down to the shore and back again. Walks along **Derwent Water's western shore** ⌂-17, best reached from car parks off the back road between Grange NY2517 and Swinside NY2421, can be combined with the more demanding walk up Catbells NY2419 for the best views of the lake.

Buttermere ⌂-18 has a splendid varied flat walk around its shore, with glorious views, plenty of safe opportunities for children aged 6 or more to let off steam, and even a tunnel; weather has to be really savage to spoil it. Parking at Gatescarth NY1915. The Bridge Hotel in the little village is good for lunch. The walk from this village up Low Bank to Rannerdale Knotts NY1618 above nearby Crummock Water gives good views, and another rather more challenging but rewarding walk is up Hay Stacks NY1913 and Fleetwith Pike NY2014. You can walk round **Crummock Water** ⌂-19, best from the car park by Lanthwaite Wood NY1520 off the B5289 towards Loweswater at the N end; the scenery is less rewarding than around Buttermere, but there's a pretty view from the hill above the wood, and if you're keen to swim in one of the lakes this is probably the best.

Borrowdale ⌂-20 is many people's favourite Lakeland base for walks, with good paths along or just above the River Derwent, especially from Grange NY2517 (useful teashop). (For lazier souls, the drive along the B5289 gives glorious views.) Other prized walks all giving or leading to fine views include mossy Johnny Wood (from Rosthwaite NY2514 or Seatoller NY2413, where there's an NT centre exc in winter), the two famous waterfalls, both best after rain, Taylorgill Force NY2210 and Lodore Falls NY2618 (behind Lodore Hotel), and a walk up (for instance from Rosthwaite) to the lovely 'lost village' of Watendlath NY2716 – little more than a tarn, a farm and a very modest café. The Scafell at Rosthwaite is a fine walkers' local.

More challenging walks with grand views include the path winding up the back of impregnable-looking Castle Crag NY2415 (terrific lake views) from Grange. From the summit of Honister Pass NY2213 you can tackle Brandreth NY2111, and perhaps head on via Windy Gap for the least taxing ascent of Great Gable NY2110. Determined fellwalkers enjoy the unspoilt packhorse track from Seathwaite NY2312 over Styhead Pass NY2210 down into Wasdale, and the summit of the pass is a starting point for a fiercely dramatic route up Scafell Pike NY2207.

Walks through **Thornthwaite Forest** ⌂-21, the first-ever Forestry Commission plantation, and up to the fells above it (with lake and mountain views) are best started with a visit to the Whinlatter Visitor Centre NY1924 (B5292 above Braithwaite); good explanatory forestry displays, shop, forest maps, teas.

Dodd Wood NY2427 ⌂-22 (off the A591 N of Keswick) has marked walks through the woods, or on open hillside, with Bassenthwaite views.

Further N the area is less interesting for walkers, though there's a pleasant stroll from **Caldbeck** NY3239 ⌂-23 to a peaceful spot with a waterfall called the Howk NY3139. **Binsey** NY2235 ⌂-24, a pathless lump of a hill, has splendid views of the Lakes and Solway Firth (and into southern Scotland) by virtue of its geographical isolation.

In the W, **Eskdale** ⌂-25 is excellent for walks, especially around Boot NY1801, to the Stanley Ghyll Force waterfall SD1799, approached by a series of bridges and visible from a dizzying viewing platform high above, or up towards the open fells (the landlord of the Burnmoor Inn is helpful with route suggestions); from Trough House Bridge car park near the waterfall you can walk along one side of the river to Doctor Bridge then return the other side for an easy route with delectable views throughout. There is a nature trail in the grounds of Muncaster Castle, and the fell above has good views. You can use the Ravenglass & Eskdale railway as part of a round trip.

Cumbria's great fell walks include **High Street** NY4411 ⌂-26 (a Roman ridge road), reached best from Hawes Water reservoir (the hotel here, under newish management, is a good stop); **Blencathra** NY3227 ⌂-27; **Skiddaw** NY2629 ⌂-28 (quite an easy haul up from Applethwaite, for far views); the walk up Martindale to **Dalehead** NY4316 ⌂-29 from Howtown, then up over the fells to Bedafell Knott NY4216 and down into Patterdale (gorgeous views, Herdwick sheep, buzzards, ring ouzels); and **Fairfield** NY3511 ⌂-30, climbed by a horseshoe layout of ridges from Rydal. The green slaty fells N of

Buttermere offer superlative routes along **high ridges** ⌂-31: Whiteless Pike NY1818, Causey Pike NY2120, Crag Hill NY1920 and Grasmoor NY1720 are among the most exciting points. **Helvellyn** NY3415 ⌂-32 is most easily (and crowdedly) tackled from Thirlmere NY3116, but much more exciting when reached from Glenridding NY3817 and Striding Edge NY3415, where the path follows a narrow rocky edge (mild scrambling needed – best ascended rather than descended) above a great post-glacial corrie; it's a day's severe walking, for perhaps the grandest and certainly the most popular of all Lakeland panoramas, with dramatic ridges leading off for miles.

Wasdale ⌂-33 is the start for many magnificent fell walks, including the ascents of Great Gable NY2110 and Scafell Pike NY2207; one less taxing walk is straight up the head of the valley to the summit of Black Sail Pass NY1811 and back. Apart from around the interesting churchyard, it's not so good for gentle strolls, and parking at Wasdale Head NY1808 can be a problem in summer or at holiday times. Besides the Wasdale Head Hotel, the Strands lower down is a useful stop for food.

Ennerdale Water ⌂-34 has gentler walks by the lake (no boating) and through forestry, with high peaks above; the Fox & Hounds at Ennerdale Bridge NY0716 is a good pub.

The coast has one particular lure for walkers and bird watchers: the **cliff path** ⌂-35 between Whitehaven NX9718 and St Bees NX9512 – each town has a railway station. From the beach car park NW of St Bees an easy walk takes you up the nature-reserve sandstone headland, famous for its bird life, and with magnificent sea and hill views.

There are lots of long beaches, deserted except in high season, from Ravenglass SD0996 down to Hodbarrow Point SD1878, good for breezy seaside walks – especially the huge stretch of impressive dunes on **Haverigg Point** SD1378 ⌂-36, nr Millom. The dunes at **Sandscale Haws** SD2075 ⌂-37, nr Barrow, are protected as a nature reserve.

The **Duddon Valley** ⌂-38 is a favourite starting point for rather more demanding walks, either by the river or up into the heights, with the Newfield Inn at Seathwaite SD2396 a good base.

The high Pennines over in the E have few walking routes and are extremely bleak: this is the reserve of the dedicated peat-bog enthusiast. But **High Cup Nick** NY7426 ⌂-39, a great scoop in the ridge, is one of the most dramatic features in the whole of the Pennine range. An easy way to get an idea of the remoteness of these hills is to walk along paths encircling Dufton Pike from Dufton NY6825 (the Stag has good food). The back road from Langwathby NY5733 on the A686 through Skirwith to Kirkland leads to a **Roman track** ⌂-40 which plunges northwards into the Pennines. There are other walks from the clusters of sheep farms along the foot of the Pennines between here and Appleby.

Surviving traces of **Hadrian's Wall** ⌂-41, not the famous bits, can be reached on well signed paths from the lanes between the A69 and B6318 N of Brampton NY5361.

The **Nunnery Walks** ⌂-42 at Staffield NY5443 are private paths through old woodland inc lovely Eden Valley river gorge with waterfalls and quiet pools; teas; 50p. There are other good free walks in this delightfully wooded sheltered valley, for instance from Armathwaite NY5146 and Wetheral NY4654. The valley has the reputation of staying dry when it's pouring over in Lakeland.

Dentdale ⌂-43 has easy to middling walks from Dent SD7187, in the shadow of Whernside. The **Howgills** ⌂-44 are bold 2,000-footers, empty and tough going; the easiest walks into them are up Winder from Sedbergh SD6692, and from the A683 N of Sedbergh to majestic Cautley Spout waterfall.

Where to eat

Ambleside NY3804 SHEILA'S COTTAGE The Slack (015394) 33079 250-year-old cottage and converted barn run by the same owners for over 30 years; with 2 menus – one for light lunches and snacks, another for more substantial meals; popular afternoon tea, too; cl Sun, Jan. £28.

Appleby NY6921 ROYAL OAK (017683) 51463 Warm and friendly, very popular partly 14th-c coaching inn with good imaginative food, huge breakfasts, a fine range of beers, and carefully chosen wines; comfortable bedrooms. £17.45|£6.95.

Appleby NY6921 WHITE HART 34–36 Boroughgate (017683) 51598 Friendly family-run hotel with a wide choice of enjoyable home-made food in snug restaurant; bedrooms; well behaved children only. £15|£4.95.

Armathwaite NY5146 DUKES HEAD (016974) 72226. Comfortable and friendly inn in attractive village; a civilised lounge bar, coal fire, good home cooking, and decent wines; bedrooms. £16|£5.

Askham NY5123 PUNCH BOWL (01931) 712443 Attractively set, busy pub with interestingly furnished rambling bar, an open log fire, a friendly atmosphere, generous helpings of good bar food, and well kept beers; children until 9pm; cl pm 25 Dec. £16.50|£5.65.

Bampton NY5118 ST PATRICKS WELL (01931) 713244. Imaginative food in unpretentious surroundings (also simple good-value bedrooms); no children later in eve; cl winter Mon lunch; £16|£5.25.

Bowness SD4097 HOLE IN T' WALL (015394) 43488 Bustling, intriguingly ancient Lakeland pub with a friendly welcome for all, lots to look at, a fine log fire, good home-made food, well kept real ales and home-made lemonade; can be busy in summer; no food pm Sun. £15.25|£5.75.

Bowness SD4097 PORTHOLE 3 Ash St (015394) 42793 Long-established bustling bistro with consistently good evening meals (mainly Italian), a genuine personal touch to their service, simple furnishings, and decent wine – a reliably enjoyable evening out; cl am Sat, Tues, mid-Dec–mid-Feb; limited disabled access. £28|£7.50.

Cartmel Fell SD4288 MASONS ARMS (015395) 68486. Old-fashioned building in unrivalled setting with wonderful views, superb range of beers inc own-brew and interesting continental real ales, and very popular food – 50% vegetarian; self-catering accommodation; cl 25 Dec. £21.60|£4.75.

Crosthwaite SD4491 PUNCH BOWL (015395) 68237 Prettily set Lakeland inn now concentrating very much on excellent sumptuous food in an interesting series of nicely furnished rooms; a good pubby atmosphere; bedrooms; cl 25 Dec. £20|£6.50.

Kirkby Lonsdale SD6278 SNOOTY FOX (015242) 71308 Rambling inn with plenty of interest to look at in the various relaxed, pubby rooms; good interesting food, no smoking dining annexe, well kept beers, and pretty garden. £18.90|£6.95.

Melmerby NY6237 SHEPHERDS (01768) 881217 Friendly place in unspoilt sandstone village with popular home-made food inc marvellous range of cheeses, delicious puddings, and lots of daily specials using only local produce; quick, friendly table service; cl 25 Dec; £16.30|£6.20.

Melmerby NY6237 VILLAGE BAKERY (01768) 881515 Converted stone barn selling wonderful organic bread and cakes for cream teas, super breakfasts (until 11am) and good home-made restaurant food using produce grown organically behind the bakery; craft gallery upstairs. £18|£6.50.

St Bees NX9611 SEACOTE HOTEL Beach Rd (01946) 822777 Lovely views and headland walks; decent food in the pleasant, roomy bar or restaurant; welcoming to children. £16|£4.

Scales NY3427 WHITE HORSE (017687) 79241 Cosy and isolated farmhouse inn in dramatic setting under Blencathra, perfect haven after walks; best to book as the generously served food, using fresh local produce, is very popular; cl Mon, Nov–Apr. **£18.40**|£7.70.

Troutbeck NY4103 QUEENS HEAD (015394) 32174 Gabled 17th-c coaching inn with rambling bar, some fine antique carving, 2 roaring log fires, and helpful friendly staff; extremely popular first-class bar food and well kept real ales; bedrooms; cl 25 Dec. **£19.50**|£4.95.

Ulverston SD2978 BAY HORSE Canal Foot, past Glaxo (01229) 583972 Civilised and nicely placed inn overlooking Morecambe Bay; beautifully presented and very innovative food (interesting vegetarian choices and well hung Scotch steaks), well kept real ales and a good wine list; bedrooms; children over 12. **£35**|£8.

Windermere SD4199 ROGERS 4 High St (015394) 44954 Popular but intimate little evening restaurant with beautifully presented and individualistic French-based cooking, candlelit tables, and helpful service; cl Sun. **£25.**

Yanwath NY5128 GATE (01768) 862386 Unpretentious village local with really good inventive food, well kept real ales, obliging service, a log fire in the simple chatty bar and a no smoking dining room. **£18**|£5.95.

Special thanks to: Dr and Mrs A K Clarke, Mary Ellen McSweeney, M J Brooks, Derek and Sylvia Stephenson, G Line, Ian Phillips, Arthur and Margaret Dickinson, D G Hughes.

CUMBRIA CALENDAR

Some of these dates were provisional as we went to press, please check information with the telephone numbers provided.

Medieval rushbearing ceremonies mark the fact that earthen church floors were covered with straw and sweet-smelling herbs for warmth and cleanliness. Rushes are carried into the church in a colourful procession, followed by children bearing flowers and garlands and the town or village band with merry-making and thanksgiving.

JANUARY

1 **Kirkby Stephen** Nine Standards Fell Race (017683) 71199
23 **Grasmere** Book Collectors Festival at Dove Cottage – *till Sun 25* (015394) 35544
24 **Ulverston** Open Week at Cumbria Crystal Ltd – *till Sat 31* (01229) 584400
30 **Ullswater** Classical Music Weekend Break: Leon McCawley at Leeming House – *till 1 Feb*, book in advance 0345 543555

FEBRUARY

6 **Keswick** Queens Hotel Jazz Festival – *till Sat 7* (017687) 73333
8 **Grasmere** Wordsworth Winter School at Dove Cottage: residential course of lectures, seminars, poetry – *till Fri 13* (015394) 35544

MARCH

14 **Ambleside** Spring Flower Show – *till Sun 15* (015394) 32252

APRIL

10 **Barrow-in-Furness** Model Railway and Transport Exhibition at Forum 28 Main Hall – *till Sun 12* (01229) 831937; **Penrith** Steam Rally at Wetheriggs Pottery (01768) 982733

CUMBRIA CALENDAR

APRIL cont

11 **Grasmere** Cumbria Local Artists Annual Art Exhibition and Sale - *till Sun 19* (015394) 32963; **Whittington** Point to Point (015242) 21175

MAY

1 **North Pennines** Countryside and Arts Festival – *till Sat 30* (01434) 382069

3 **Carlisle** Spring Show at Victoria Park – *till Mon 4* (01228) 810208

9 **Barbon** National Speed Hill Climb at Barbon Manor (01539) 740777; **Carlisle** Spring Orchid Show at Carlisle College (016977) 2476

10 **Gleaston** National Mills Day at Gleaston Watermill (01229) 869244

15 **Keswick** Jazz Festival – *till Sun 17* (017687) 73333

22 **Grizedale** International Piano Festival – *till Sun 24* (01229) 860291

23 **Coniston** Water Festival – *till Sat 30* (015394) 41707; **Workington** Fair inc historical pageant at Curwen Park (01900) 604078

24 **Calderbridge** Country Field Day (019467) 25340

25 **Kendal** Medieval Market (01539) 721154; **Penrith** Motor and Leisure Show at Greystoke Castle: music, fair, vintage vehicles, helicopter and hot air air balloon rides (01768) 890003

29 **Cark-in-Cartmel** Garden and Countryside Festival at Holker Hall and Gardens: festival gardens, lectures and demonstrations, steel band, children's play area – *till Sun 31* (015395) 58838

JUNE

3 **Appleby-in-Westmorland** Horse Fair at Fair Hill: gypsies from all over Europe gather on Fair Hill for 300-year-old event with fortune telling, racing and spectacular horse, carriage and van sales on last 2 days – *till Wed 10* (01325) 362933

6 **Barbon** Hill Climb at Barbon Manor (01539) 740777

13 **Castletown** Gala Day (01768) 865353

14 **Carlisle** Carnival (01228) 810208

20 **Appleby-in-Westmorland** Jazz Festival at Appleby Castle – *till Sun 21* (017683) 51052; **Cockermouth** Carnival (01900) 824173

21 **Barrow-in-Furness** Gala: dancing, vintage vehicles, stunt cars (01229) 835123; **Brough** Hound and Terrier Show at Castle Garth (017683) 51921; **Flookburgh** Charter Fair (015395) 58421; **Keswick** Carnival (017687) 73189

28 **Endmoor** Country Fayre: ring events, wrestling (015395) 67382; **Patterdale** Ullswater Country Fair (01539) 723531

29 **Warcop** Rushbearing (017683) 41379

JULY

1 **Cockermouth** Festival – *till Fri 31* (01900) 823608

4 **Flimby** Children's Carnival (01900) 813264; **Ambleside** Rushbearing (015394) 33205; **Musgrave** Rushbearing (017683) 41355; **Whitehaven** Carnival (01946) 66307

5 **Distington** West Cumbria Vintage Vehicle and Machinery Rally (01900) 871637

7 **Hawkshead** Free Concerts and Recitals (charity collection) – *every Tues eve till 25 Aug* (015394) 32274

11 **Alston** Gala (01434) 382786; **Grange-over-Sands** New Lakeland Rose Show – *till Sun 12* (015395) 32375; **Maryport** Carnival (01900) 813171

CUMBRIA CALENDAR

JULY cont

18 **Allithwaite** Carnival (015395) 33389; **Carlisle** Cumberland County Show at Rickerby Park: music, children's entertainment, vintage vehicles, air and animal displays (01228) 560364; **Cleator Moor** Sports (01946) 811656; **Workington** Dalemain Craft Fair – *till Sun 19* (01529) 414793

24 **Brougham** Shakespearean and Classical Music Season at Brougham Hall – *till Sun 26* (01768) 868184

25 **Barbon** Sprint Hill Climb at Barbon Manor: motorcycles (01539) 740777; **Dearham** Carnival (01900) 817142; **Egremont** West Cumbria Rose Society Annual Show (01946) 64438; **Flookburgh** Cumbria Steam Gathering: arena events, circus – *till Sun 26* (015242) 71584; **Penrith** Agricultural Show at Brougham Hall Farm (01931) 713325

29 **Ulverston** North Lonsdale Show at Bardsey Park (01229) 585140

26 **Coniston** Country Fair (015395) 52314

30 **Ambleside** Sports: traditional lakeland sports (015394) 45531

31 **Grasmere** Lake Artists Society Summer Exhibition – *till 10 Sept* (015394) 35628

AUGUST

1 **Beetham** Sports (015395) 63110; **Cockermouth** Agricultural Show (01946) 692798; **Grasmere** Rushbearing (015394) 35245; **Grasmere** Wordsworth Summer Conference at Dove Cottage: residential course of lectures, seminars and poetry – *till Sat 15* (015394) 35544

5 **Cartmel** Show (01539) 722777

6 **Ings** Lake District Sheepdog Trials at Hill Top Farm (015394) 33721

7 **Ambleside** Great Summer Flower Show and Craft Fair *till Sun 9* (015394) 32252; **Lowther** Horse Driving Trials and Country Fair at Lowther Castle – *till Sun 9* (01931) 712378

8 **Dalston** Agricultural Show (01228) 23034

11 **Kirkby Lonsdale** Lunesdale Show (015242) 71437

13 **Appleby-in-Westmorland** Agricultural Show (01931) 714571; **Ravenglass** English National Sheepdog Trials at Muncaster Castle – *till Sat 15* (01234) 352672

15 **Hutton-in-the-Forest** Skelton Horticultural and Agricultural Show at Old Park: vintage parade, equestrian and driving events, music (017684) 83032

16 **Langdale** Country Fair (01229) 837680

19 **Gosforth** Agricultural Show (019467) 24652

20 **Brough** Agricultural Show (017683) 71554; **Grasmere** Traditional Sports inc Cumberland wrestling, hound trails, mountain bike and fell races inc English Hill Championship (015394) 32127

26 **Kirkland** Ennerdale and Kinniside Show at Leaps Field (01946) 861391

27 **Carnforth** Burton, Milnthorpe and Carnforth Show (01524) 701066

28 **Kendal** Folk Festival at the Brewery Arts Centre – *till Mon 31* (01539) 725133; **Kendal** Gathering: music, theatre, vintage vehicles, torchlight procession – *till 13 Sept* (01539) 720040

29 **Dufton** Agricultural Show and Sheepdog Trials (017683) 62015; **Patterdale** Dog Day and Sheepdog Trials (017683) 61317

30 **Broughton-in-Furness** Millom and Broughton Agricultural Show (01229) 772556; **Eskdale Green** Fete (01946) 723242; **Cark-in-Cartmel** MG Rally at Holker Hall (015395) 58328

CUMBRIA CALENDAR

AUGUST cont

31 **Keswick** Show: show jumping, driving, wrestling (017687) 79737;
   Ravenglass Country Fair and Sheepdog Trials at Muncaster Castle
   (01229) 717608; **Silloth** Carnival (016973) 31257

SEPTEMBER

5 **Kirkby Lonsdale** Victorian Fair: vintage vehicles, street entertainers,
   fair, dancing – *till Sun 6* (015242) 71237; **Lowick** Show (01229)
   861420; **Ulverston** Market Charter Festival – *till Sat 19* (01229)
   462334

10 **Crooklands** Westmorland County Show: around 240 trade stands
   (015395) 67804

19 **Egremont** Crab Fair inc world gurning (pulling a face) championships,
   greasy pole, pipe-smoking contest (01946) 821554

20 **Rosthwaite** Borrowdale Shepherd's Meet and Show (017687) 77678

26 **Boot** Eskdale Show (019467) 23269; **Whitehaven** Cumbria Brass
   Band Association Annual Open Contest in the Civic Hall (01946)
   61955

27 **Urswick** Rushbearing (01229) 869402

OCTOBER

2 **Cartmel** Festival of Flowers – *till Sun 4* (015395) 63230

10 **Wasdale Head** Show and Shepherds Meet (019467) 25340

17 **Ravenglass** Thomas the Tank Engine at Ravenglass and Eskdale
   Railway – *till Sun 18* (01229) 717171

19 **Windermere** Powerboat Record Attempts at Low Wood Watersports
   Centre – *till Fri 23* (015394) 42995

NOVEMBER

7 **Seathwaite** Walna Scar Shepherd's Meet Annual Show (015394)
   41647

8 **Cockermouth** Firework Display (01900) 823608

15 **Cockermouth** Christmas Lights Switch On (01900) 823608

19 **Santon Bridge** Biggest Liar in the World Competition at the Bridge Inn
   (01946) 67575

DECEMBER

5 **Kirkby Lonsdale** Christmas Fair (015242) 71437

6 **Keswick** Victorian Fair (017687) 71337

We welcome reports from readers . . .

This *Guide* depends on readers' reports. Do help us if you can – in return,
we offer a discount on the next edition to people who've helped us with
reports for it. Tell us what you think about places already in it, and anything extra you think we should say about them. And send us your ideas
for inclusion in the next edition: places to visit, eat at or stay in, attractive
drives or walks, maybe even unusual interesting shops you know of.
Use the card in the middle, or the report forms at the end, or just write –
no stamp needed: *The Good Guide to Britain*, FREEPOST TN1569,
Wadhurst, E Sussex TN5 7BR.

DERBYSHIRE

Beautiful scenery, magnificent and appealing stately homes, interestingly restored survivals of early industry and other lively and unusual places to visit.

The dales country, which includes much of the Peak District National Park, is very rewarding both for walkers and for drivers, with charming villages as well as the pale stone buildings and walling that underline the natural beauty of the countryside. The remarkable underground caverns are well worth exploring – the Heights of Abraham in Matlock Bath perhaps best for families, Poole's Cavern in Buxton the showiest and most interesting, Treak Cliff Cavern the best of those around Castleton. Haddon Hall is a particularly engaging stately home, Sudbury Hall another real charmer, and Chatsworth, Hardwick Hall, Calke Abbey and Kedleston Hall are all magnificent; less touristy, ruined Wingfield Manor at South Wingfield is evocative. Other places we'd highlight include the tramway museum at Crich (fun even if you have no interest in trams themselves – and now on the Heritage Secretary's new 'excellence shortlist' of nationally important museums), the enjoyable Peak Rail at Darley Dale, Lea Gardens (gorgeous in late spring), and Bolsover Castle and Eyam Hall. Cromford is a fascinating survivor of the earliest days of the Industrial Revolution.

There's enough variety to fill a family holiday, particularly around Matlock Bath and Matlock (where the Riber Castle wildlife park is another strong draw). The Chestnut Centre at Chapel-en-le-Frith is a most enjoyable conservation park, and the American Adventure theme park at Ilkeston is good for a family day out.

In the north the scenery becomes increasingly austere, with far fewer rainy-day attractions: Castleton's the most popular base for this part. The further north you head into the High Peak, the bleaker it becomes – territory for the really serious long-distance walker, and very forbidding in winter. Drivers up here though have lots of great scenery, and not too much traffic – the A6024, A628 (rather slow), A57, A5002, A624 and A625 all have outstanding views.

There's a very good choice of places to stay in; eating out is rather good, too. In summer the most lovely dales do have almost a crocodile of walkers snaking along them, though even then you can find quiet areas. As with other particularly popular areas, Derbyshire is perhaps ideally suited to short breaks in autumn, late spring or very early summer.

Where to stay

Ashbourne SK1846 CALLOW HALL Mappleton Rd, Ashbourne DE6 2AA (01335) 343403 £105, plus special breaks; 16 lovely well furnished rms, excellent bthrms. Friendly and relaxed Victorian mansion up long drive through grounds with fine trees, surrounded by marvellous countryside; comfortable drawing room with open fire, fresh flowers and period furniture, very good traditional food using home-grown produce, excellent breakfasts, and kind hosts; good private fishing; cl Christmas, 1 wk Feb; disabled access.

Ashford in the Water SK1969 RIVERSIDE COUNTRY HOUSE Fennel St, Ashford in the Water, Bakewell DE4 1QF (01629) 814275 *£95, plus special breaks; 15 individually decorated, pretty rms. Creeper-covered Georgian house in delightful village, with pretty riverside gardens, quiet relaxed atmosphere, antiques and log fires in cosy sitting rooms, imaginative food (served all day) in 2 dining rooms using silver and cut crystal, and good service; disabled access.

Bakewell SK2272 HASSOP HALL Hassop, Bakewell DE45 1NS (01629) 640488 £96.90, plus winter breaks; 13 gracious rms. Mentioned in the Domesday Book, in lovely parkland surrounded by fine scenery, this handsome hotel has antiques and oil paintings, an elegant drawing room, oak-panelled bar, good food and friendly service; tennis and croquet; no accommodation 3 nights over Christmas; partial disabled access.

Baslow SK2572 CAVENDISH Baslow, Bakewell DE45 1SP (01246) 582311 £113.50, plus winter wknd breaks; 23 spotless, comfortable and individually furnished rms (varying in size). Charming hotel with magnificent views over Chatsworth estate, most attractive well furnished day rooms (some furnishings come from Chatsworth), open fires and fresh flowers, fine food in 2 restaurants, very courteous staff; limited disabled access.

Baslow SK2572 FISCHERS BASLOW HALL Calver Rd, Baslow, Bakewell DE4 1RR (01246) 583259 £95, plus special breaks; 6 comfortable, pretty rms. Handsome Edwardian manor house with individually chosen furnishings and pictures, open fires, fresh flowers and plants, beautifully presented fine food using the best ingredients (lots of game and fish) in airy dining room or in lunchtime Café Max, and courteous attentive service; cl 25–26 Dec; children over 12 in evening restaurant.

Biggin-by-Hartington SK0673 BIGGIN HALL Biggin-by-Hartington, Buxton SK17 0DH (01298) 84451 *£59, plus special breaks; 18 spacious rms with antiques, some in converted 18th-c stone building and in bothy. Lovely carefully renovated 17th-c house in quiet grounds with 2 comfortable sitting rooms, log fires, and imaginative food using free-range produce and seasonal veg; children over 12; limited disabled access.

Birch Vale SK0286 WALTZING WEASEL New Mills Rd, Birch Vale, Stockport SK12 5BT (01663) 743402 £65.95, plus special breaks; 8 lovely rms. Attractive traditional inn with open fire, some handsome furnishings, daily newspapers and plants in civilised bar, very good food using the best seasonal produce in charming back restaurant (fine views), excellent puddings and cheeses, obliging service; children over 7; disabled access.

Castleton SK1583 BARGATE COTTAGE Market Pl, Castleton, Sheffield S30 2WG (01433) 620201 £41; 4 well equipped rms. Lovely old cottage, beautifully restored by charming owners (who are full of local knowledge), with beams, inglenook fireplace, delicious breakfasts, enjoyable evening meals, super packed lunches, and pretty terraced garden; no smoking; cl 25 Dec; no children.

Dove Dale SK1452 PEVERIL OF THE PEAK Dove Dale, Ashbourne DE6 2AW (01335) 350333 £107.90, plus special breaks; 47 rms. Relaxing hotel in pretty village with comfortable sofas and log fire in lounge, modern bar and attractive restaurant overlooking the garden, and good English cooking; tennis; wonderful walking nearby; disabled access.

Grindleford SK2478 MAYNARD ARMS Main Rd, Grindleford, Sheffield S30 1HP (01433) 630321 £69, plus special breaks; 10 rms. Comfortable hotel with log fire and good Peak District views from the first-floor lounge, smart welcoming bar, good choice of food, particularly attentive service.

Hathersage SK2381 GEORGE Hathersage, Sheffield S30 1BB (01433) 650436 *£98.50, plus special breaks; 19 pretty rms (the back ones are quietest). Substantial and comfortably modernised old inn with attractive airy lounge, beamed friendly bar, popular food, and a neat flagstoned back terrace by rose garden; good walks all around.

Hope SK1783 UNDERLEIGH HOUSE Edale Rd, Hope, Castleton S30 2RF (01433) 621372 £60, plus special breaks; 6 thoughtfully decorated rms with own teddy bear. In unspoilt countryside, this spotlessly kept converted barn has fine views from the comfortable sitting room, hearty breakfasts and very good home-made evening meals enjoyed around communal table in flagstoned dining room, friendly, cheerful owners (who used to run a successful restaurant), and neat gardens; children over 12.

Hopton SK2553 HENMORE GRANGE Hopton, Wirksworth DE4 4DF (01629) 540420 £55; 14 rms, 12 with own bthrm. Friendly and carefully modernised stone-built farmhouse and renovated farm buildings with lots of original features, old-fashioned hospitality, and a garden designed to attract butterflies; disabled access.

Kirk Ireton SK2650 BARLEY MOW Kirk Ireton, Ashbourne DE6 3JP (01335) 370306 £42; 5 rms. 17th-c walkers' inn with lots of woodwork in straightforward series of interconnecting bar rooms, and solid fuel stove in beamed residents' sitting room; close to Carsington Reservoir with its water sports and fishing; cl Christmas wk.

Matlock SK3060 RIBER HALL Matlock DE4 5JU (01629) 582795 £124, plus special breaks; 11 lovely beamed rms with antiques, chocolates, and baskets of fruit. Elizabethan manor house in pretty grounds surrounded by peaceful countryside, with antiques in the heavily beamed rooms, fresh flowers, 2 elegant dining rooms with reliable food and fine wines, and tennis and clay pigeon shooting; children over 10.

Monsal Head SK1871 MONSAL HEAD HOTEL Monsal Head, Bakewell DE4 1NL (01629) 640250 £54; 8 very good rms. Comfortable and enjoyable small hotel in marvellous setting high above River Wye with horsey theme in bar (converted from old stables), Victorian-style restaurant, well prepared decent food, and good service; cl 25 Dec; partial disabled access.

Rowland SK2072 HOLLY COTTAGE Rowland, Bakewell DE45 1NR (01629) 640624 *£40, plus special breaks; 2 rms, shared bthrm; 200-year-old no smoking cottage on a quiet lane, surrounded by peaceful rolling countryside, with open fire in large lounge, wood-burning stove in panelled hall, attractive dining room, excellent breakfasts with home-made rolls, bread and preserves, and lovely gardens; cl Nov–Dec.

Rowsley SK2566 PEACOCK Rowsley, Matlock DE4 2EB (01629) 733518 £99, plus special breaks; 14 comfortable rms. Handsome early 17th-c hotel by lovely trout river (private fishing in season), with well kept gardens, friendly staff, interesting old-fashioned inner bar, spacious comfortable lounges, and very popular restaurant.

Shirley SK2141 SHIRLEY HALL FARM Shirley, Ashbourne DE6 3AS (01335) 360346 *£38; 3 rms, 2 with own bthrm. Timbered and part-moated farmhouse on family-run dairy/sheep/arable farm, with homely sitting room, fine breakfasts, and private coarse fishing and lots of walks; nearby pub for evening meals.

Shottle SK3149 DANNAH FARM Bowmans Lane, Shottle, Belper DE56 3DR (01773) 550273 *£70; 8 rms with old pine and antiques. Carefully restored and friendly Georgian farmhouse with 2 comfortable sitting rooms, and popular imaginative cooking in attractive no smoking dining room; calves, ducks, hens, lambs in spring, Vietnamese pot-bellied pigs and farm dogs and cats; cl 25–26 Dec; partial disabled access.

To see and do

DERBYSHIRE FAMILY ATTRACTION OF THE YEAR

✿ ❀ ♤ **Matlock Bath** SK2958 HEIGHTS OF ABRAHAM Derbyshire is full of stunning show caverns (several better for geologists, not all as good for families), but few can boast as thrilling an introduction as the one here: cable cars whisk you up from the Derwent Valley to a 60-acre country park, with dramatic views over the ancient limestone gorge (not to mention a railway and the busy A6). At the end of the 5 minute trip a multi-media show explains how the rock was formed 325 million years ago, then guides escort you into the two show caverns themselves. Displays are well thought out and instructive, and the caves atmospherically lit to create a suitably mysterious feel. One of the caverns used to be a lead mine, so has models and tableaux illustrating how 16th-c miners struggled to work by candlelight. Outside are nature trails, the Prospect Tower to climb, dinosaur displays and a few play areas (including a maze), as well as great views and nicely laid out woodland walks. They usually have Punch & Judy shows or similar entertainments, and there's a choice of places to eat – though the picnic areas fit in better with the natural tone. Most people spend around 2½ hours here before taking the cable car back down (check the times of the last one if you're visiting in the afternoon), though it's quite possible to stretch it out longer. Children might not take in all the information, but enjoy the combination of cable car, caves, and space to run around; the very young probably won't get as much out of it. You can visit the caverns without going on the cable car – though it really does add to the overall appeal. Don't forget it's never as warm underground as it is on the surface, so even on sunny days you may be glad of a jumper. Meals, snacks, shop, some disabled access; open daily Easter–Oct and some winter wknds (best to check first as dates can depend on the weather); (01629) 582365; £5.95 (£3.90 children).

🐖 **Alkmonton** SK1838 BENTLEY FIELDS OPEN FARM Unspoilt traditional livestock farm stretching over 245 acres; they milk their cows at 1 and 4pm. In spring you may see calving or lambing – or chicks pecking their way out of their eggs. Teas, shop, some disabled access; open daily Easter wk and May half term, bank hol Suns and Mons; (01335) 330240; *£1.50. The Holly Bush over at Church Broughton is quite handy for lunch.

✝ 🏰 **Ashbourne** SK1846 A good few interesting Georgian buildings in the streets off the hillside market place, especially leading to its elegantly proportioned CHURCH, which has a famous white marble statue of a sleeping child. DERWENT CRYSTAL CENTRE (Shaw Croft) Quality glassworks and engravers, with demonstrations and factory shop. Disabled access; cl winter Suns, 25–26 Dec, 1 Jan; (01335) 345219;

free. The Gingerbread Shop sells the town's long-standing speciality. Smiths Tavern and the White Lion are good for lunch. The B5056 towards Bakewell and B5053 to Wirksworth have characteristic views.

♿ ♨ **Bakewell** SK2168 Away from the traffic this is a civilised small town, especially around the church. You can still get those raspberry tarts here, though there has been some dispute over the original recipe – two shops have claimed rights to the authentic Bakewell Pudding, and the case even went to court. The folk collection at the OLD HOUSE MUSEUM (Cunningham Place) is in the 16th-c former home of pioneer industrialist Richard Arkwright, still with its original wattle and daub interior walls and open-timbered chambers; cl am, and Nov–Mar; (01629) 812231; £2. The Castle Hotel and Aitch's are useful for lunch. 3m W, the surface remains of MAGPIE MINE

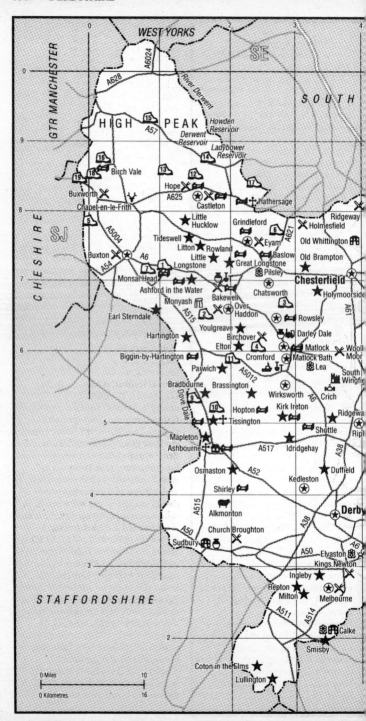

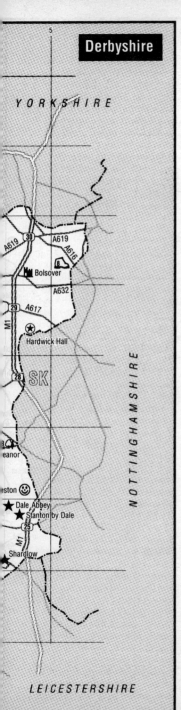

Derbyshire

YORKSHIRE

NOTTINGHAMSHIRE

A619 | 30 | A619

A616

Bolsover

A632

29 | A617

Hardwick Hall

SK

28

eanor

ston

Dale Abbey
Stanton by Dale

25

Shardlow

LEICESTERSHIRE

SK1768, last worked in 1958 and stabilised in the 1970s, give a good idea of a 19th-c lead mine; free.

🏰 **Bolsover** SK4770 The original ruined CASTLE dates back to the 12th c, but was rebuilt in 1613 as a spectacular mock castle – about 200 years ahead of this fashion. Battlements and turrets outside, and inside allegorical frescoes, fine panelling and ornate fireplaces. Snacks, shop, some disabled access; cl winter Mon and Tues, 24–26 Dec; (01246) 823349; £2.80, inc Walkman tour. Just on the other side of the M1 at Sutton Scarsdale SK4468 (and in fact looking down on the motorway), the ruins of a once-grand 17th-c hall are quite evocative.

🚬 🕿 🍴 ✳ **Buxton** SK0673 Much changed, but it still has some handsome buildings dating from its days as a flourishing spa, with Georgian terraces (the Crescent is a noble Georgian streetscape) and a restored Edwardian opera house. St Ann's Well is the only direct reminder of its water-based heyday. Many of the grander buildings come back to life during the town's excellent annual festival. A MUSEUM & ART GALLERY on Terrace Rd is a useful introduction to the area. POOLE'S CAVERN (Buxton Country Park, Green Lane) The best show cave in the Peak District and the longest in Britain, a spectacular natural limestone cavern in 100 acres of woodland, with well lit stalactites and stalagmites, and exhibitions on caves, woodland and Romans. As in other caverns, wrap up well. Snacks, shop, limited disabled access; cl Nov–Feb; (01298) 26978; *£3.80. GRIN LOW WOODS (just S of town) are well landscaped with mature woodland and the Victorian folly of Solomon's Temple (good views from the top); useful information centre, though it's not always open. The Columbine (Hall Bank) is good for lunch.

🏛 ✿ **Calke** SK3722 CALKE ABBEY One of the most rewarding NT properties in Britain, an unusual baroque mansion still in pretty much the same state as when the last baronet died here in 1924. You might expect the splendidly decorated rooms with their fascinating displays (inc an extensive natural history collection), but it's quite a surprise to find the more dilapidated corridors and areas where family possessions were just bundled together in heaps. This gives you a better appreciation of how the Abbey was a much-loved family home – and of how things forgotten in the attic can quickly become social history. Also extensive wooded parkland and walled gardens. Meals, snacks, shop, disabled access; cl Thurs, Fri, and Nov–Mar, house usually cl am; (01332) 863822; £4.85, £2.20 garden only – there's a £2 vehicle charge on entering the park, refundable on entry to the house (which has a timed ticket system); NT. The Hardinge Arms at Kings Newton is quite handy for lunch.

⛉ ▥ ❋ ⊖ ⛂ **Castleton** SK1582 Very much geared to visitors, and fills with walkers and cavers in summer; plenty of cafés, and shops selling expensive worked pieces of the Blue John fluorspar that's found only in the nearby mine workings. A small BLUE JOHN MUSEUM in one of the Cross St craft shops has some magnificent examples. The village's attractive dark stone buildings (one of the most impressive now a youth hostel) are dominated by the ruins of PEVERIL CASTLE, built high above in the 11th c – magnificent views. Shop; cl 24–26 Dec; (01433) 620613; £1.50. PEAK CAVERN ▣, right in the village, is the biggest natural cavern in the county and really does seem huge – the entrance hall is so large it used to house an entire village. From there it's a ½-mile walk along lighted subterranean passageways to the Great Cave, 45 x 27 metres (150ft wide, 90ft long). By the time you reach the Devil's Dining Room you'll be nearly 140 metres (450ft) underground. Snacks, shop; cl wkdys Nov–Easter; (01433) 620285; £4. BLUE JOHN CAVERN (Buxton Rd) Containing 8 of the 14 known veins of Blue John, this has been the main source of the precious stone for

nearly 300 years. It's an impressive example of a water-worn cave, over a third of a mile long, with chambers 60 metres (200ft) high. Snacks, shop; cl Jan; (01433) 620638; £4.50. SPEEDWELL CAVERN ▣ (Winnats Pass – the former A625 W) Very atmospheric former lead mine, with a long flight of steps down to a ½-mile underground boat trip along floodlit passages, finishing up in a cathedral of a cavern with an impressive 'bottomless pit'. Good fun, though you may have to queue. Shop; cl 25 Dec; (01433) 620512; £5. TREAK CLIFF CAVERN ▣ (off the former A625 W) Informative tours of the first Blue John mine, worked since 1750, with rich veins of the mineral and quite staggering stalactites and stalagmites. Well placed lights create spooky shapes and atmospheric shadows. The entrance is narrow, and it's quite steep, but readers prefer this to many of the other caverns nearby. Snacks, shop; cl 25 Dec, but worth checking first in winter; (01433) 620571; £4.50. The Rose Cottage, Castle, Olde Nag's Head and Peak all do decent food, and in the pretty nearby village of Hope the Cheshire Cheese is good. The B6061 to Sparrowpit (where the Wanted Inn has good-value home cooking) has fine views.

⋎ **Chapel-en-le-Frith** SK0580 CHESTNUT CENTRE ▣ (A625) Warmly recommended conservation park, concerned especially with breeding otters and barn owls, but other animals and birds of prey too. Good observation platforms. Snacks, shop; cl wkdys Jan and Feb; (01298) 814099; £4.50. The Cross Keys has decent food (all day Sun).

🏠 ▣ ❀ ★ **Chatsworth** SK2669 CHATSWORTH (off the B6012) Famously splendid home of the Duke and Duchess of Devonshire on the banks of the River Derwent. Sumptuously furnished, with a superb collection of fine arts, inc memorable paintings by Rembrandt and Van Dyck, and all sorts of intriguing decorative details. The lovely gardens cover over 100 acres and are full of surprises, while the surrounding park was landscaped by

Capability Brown. Also a farmyard (milking 3.30pm) and adventure playground. Meals, snacks, shops (inc one of England's best farm shops, towards Pilsley), garden centre, disabled access to garden only; cl Nov–Mar; (01246) 582204; house and garden £5.90, garden only £3.50, adventure playground and farmyard £2.30. The estate village of Edensor SK2469 opposite the main gate is a marvellous mix of styles, with fine views from the lane leading up out of it. Around Chatsworth are two more most attractive small estate villages, Baslow SK2572 and Beeley SK2667 (which has a good food pub). The B6012 (busy in summer) has pleasant views.

† ♂ 🏠 **Chesterfield** SK3871 Not a tourist town, but its largely 14th-c CHURCH has a really striking leaning spire, and is a rich building inside; the town MUSEUM (Corporation St) has the full angle on it. The Victorian market hall has flourishing markets every day exc Tues and Sun (junk Thurs, street entertainment summer Sats). Nearby GRASSMOOR COUNTRY PARK is a pleasant place to stroll. The Derby Tup (Sheffield Rd) is an enjoyable ale house with good-value simple food.

🏃 **Crich** SK3554 NATIONAL TRAMWAY MUSEUM 📷 A favourite of many correspondents: lovingly restored vintage trams from all over the British Isles and beyond, many of them in working order and running along a 1-mile period street overlooking the Derwent Valley. Unlimited rides on the vehicles, and very good indoor exhibitions and displays. The vehicles look especially good lit up – a late-afternoon bonus on one of their Dec wknd Santa specials. They have a guide book in Braille. Meals, snacks, shop, some disabled access; cl Fri in Apr–May and Oct (exc school hols), and all Jan–Feb; (01773) 852565; £5.70. The Derwent over at Whatstandwell on the A6 has good-value food. The village is pronounced 'Cry', not 'Critch', and is the setting for TV's *Peak Practice*.

🏃 ♣ **Cromford** SK2956 Good

example of an 18th-c cotton-milling village, little developed after its original building, and rewarding to stroll through. Carefully preserved North St, built in 1777, is the first true industrial street in the world. CROMFORD MILL (Mill Lane) is where Richard Arkwright established the world's first successful water-powered cotton mill in 1771; several craft shops. Wholefood restaurant, shop, disabled access; cl 25 Dec; (01629) 825776; site free, tours £2. The nearby restored CANAL is a quiet and attractive early Industrial Revolution setting with a restored steam-powered pumping house and a fine aqueduct over the river; pleasant walks along here, and horse-drawn barge trips in summer – also see **Walk** ◠-11, below. The HIGH PEAK JUNCTION WORKSHOPS out here have exhibitions and a film (cl winter wkdys; 40p). The Boat has well priced food. The A5012 to Grangemill gives evocative views.

🚂♂ **Darley Dale** SK2763 PEAK RAIL Blooming private railway, very popular with readers. Trains run between here and Matlock, then on to Rowsley (see entry below). The eventual aim is to run as far as Buxton. Wknd restaurant car, shop, disabled access; usually open wknds all year (not Sat in depths of winter), plus most days in summer hols, but best to check times; (01629) 580381; £5. The nearby RED HOUSE STABLES WORKING CARRIAGE MUSEUM has a collection of vehicles and equipment, some of which you can ride in. Also horse and pony rides – booking essential. Teas, disabled access; cl 25 Dec; (01629) 733583; £2.50. The Grouse (A6 N) is handy for a snack.

† ❀ 🏃 ♂ 🖼 🏠 🍴 ♫ **Derby** SK3536 A big busy city, but not too daunting for a visitor to penetrate, with several things worth visiting; it's got far more open spaces than you'd expect, and a pedestrianised centre. The 16th-c tower of the CATHEDRAL is the second highest in the country; the rest of the building was replaced in the 18th c. Bess of Hardwick is buried in the vaults, and there's a delightful early Georgian screen. Shop, disabled

access; cl 8–9 May for arts festival; £2 suggested donation. The tower is open this year on 27 June and 25 July (good views), with bell-ringing demonstrations then. The quaint nearby Olde Dolphin (Queen St) has bargain food all day. INDUSTRIAL MUSEUM (Full St) Restored early 18th-c silk mill and adjacent flour mill, with probably the world's finest collection of Rolls-Royce aero engines, and a Power Gallery with lots of hands-on displays. Shop, disabled access; cl am Sun and bank hols, 25–28 Dec; (01332) 255308; free. The town MUSEUM AND ART GALLERY (The Strand) stands out for its collections of porcelain and the paintings of local artist Joseph Wright (cl am Sun and bank hols; free), and you can get a very good idea of 18th-c domestic life at PICKFORDS HOUSE (Friargate), with its period furnished rooms and Georgian garden (details as town museum). ROYAL CROWN DERBY (Osmaston Rd) Cheerfully informative tours of bone-china factory (10.30am and 1.45pm, plus 1.15pm Fri, booking essential), with museum tracing the industry's development from 1748. Snacks, shop (lots of bargain seconds); cl 12.30–2pm, bank hols, no tours wknds (though shop open then); (01332) 712800; tour £3 – no children under 10. A Tudor grammar school in St Peter's Churchyard is now a HERITAGE CENTRE (cl Sun). Ghost walk tours through the city's tunnels leave here pm Mon–Thurs and Sun in summer, plus various other times; booking essential on (01332) 299321.

🐝 ⚜ Elvaston SK4132 ELVASTON CASTLE COUNTRY PARK (B5010) 200 acres of lovely 19th-c landscaped parkland, with formal and Old English gardens, wooded walks, and wildfowl on the ornamental lake. Also museum with traditional craft workshops, and nature trails. Meals, snacks, shop, disabled access; open all year, but museum cl Mon, Tues, and Nov–Apr; (01332) 571342; museum £1.20. Shardlow is convenient for lunch.

★ 🏛 ⚜ † Eyam SK2276 Attractive secluded village with a dark past: in the Great Plague sick villagers confined themselves here for fear of infecting people outside – plaques record who died where, and stones on the village edge mark where money was disinfected. EYAM HALL Sturdy-looking 17th-c manor house, still very much a family home, with furniture, portraits and tapestries, fine Jacobean staircase and impressive stone-flagged hall. Small craft centre in the stables. Meals, snacks, shop, disabled access to ground floor only; house open Weds, Thurs, Sun and bank hols Easter–Oct, craft centre open daily exc Mon Apr–late Dec, plus wknds in Mar; (01433) 631976; £3.50 – timed ticket system. The Miners Arms is very good for lunch. Just up the B6521 at Upper Padley SK2579, PADLEY CHAPEL is an interesting 15th-c revival, effectively restored in 1933.

🏛 🐝 ⚜ Haddon Hall 🏛 SK2366 One of the most perfectly preserved medieval manor houses in England, still with its 12th-c painted chapel, 14th-c kitchen, and banqueting hall with minstrels' gallery. Some rooms can seem rather bare (there aren't many furnishings or pictures), but a bright spot is Rex Whistler's painting of the house in the silver-panelled long gallery. It's a particularly pretty spot in summer when the long terraced rose gardens are in full bloom. Several films and TV adaptations have had scenes shot here in recent years. Meals, snacks, shop; cl August Suns (exc bank hol wknd), and all Oct–Mar; (01629) 812855; £4.75. In the pretty village of Over Haddon SK2066 the LATHKILL DALE CRAFT CENTRE (Manor Farm) has plenty of craft shops and demonstrations, and a café; cl 25 Dec; (01629) 813589; free. The Lathkil Hotel is good for lunch, and nearby roads have attractive views.

🏛 🐝 ✕ Hardwick Hall SK4463 HARDWICK HALL The marriages of the redoubtable Bess of Hardwick couldn't necessarily be described as happy but she certainly did very well out of them, the fourth leaving her enough money to build this triumphant Elizabethan prodigy house. The beautifully symmetrical towers are crowned with the monogram ES, and there's an amazing expanse of glass (her sight was dimming). Also fine tapestries and needlework, large park, and gardens laid out in walled courtyard. Meals, snacks, shop, limited disabled access; open Apr–Oct, house cl am, and all day Mon (exc bank hols), Tues and Fri; (01246) 850430; £2 vehicle charge to enter the grounds, refundable against full tickets – £5.80 house and garden, £2.50 garden only, operating on a timed ticket; NT. Not far from this 'new' house is the shell of Hardwick Old Hall, the first house that Bess built; (01246) 850431; £1.60 (though you'll have to pay the NT's vehicle charge on top of this). A joint ticket for both houses is £7. Also on the estate is a restored watermill (another £1.60). The park is attractive for walks, and at the end of it the Hardwick Inn, also NT-owned, is useful for lunch.

✝ **Hathersage** SK2381 Charlotte Bronte wrote *Jane Eyre* here. The CHURCH is the legendary site of Little John's grave. It's a good village for walkers and climbers, and besides the George, the Plough (A622) is useful for lunch. The B6001 S is a pleasant drive.

🐝 🐟 **Heanor** SK4346 SHIPLEY COUNTRY PARK Medieval estate developed and landscaped in the 18th c, with 600 acres of woodland, lakes and fields. A pleasant place to wander, with railway lines transformed into leafy walkways; you can hire bikes (daily Easter and July–Aug, wknds rest of year, £5 for 3 hours). Snacks, shop, disabled access; visitor centre cl 25 Dec; (01773) 719961; free.

☺ **Ilkeston** SK4642 AMERICAN ADVENTURE (Pit Lane) Excellent theme park with around 100 rides and attractions; all supposedly have an American theme, though this can be rather tenuous – ever so English Sooty stars in a Wild West show. Highlights include dropping 13 metres (42ft) at 62mph on the Nightmare Niagara triple log flume, and the Missile, a stomach-churning roller-coaster that twists and turns at unfeasible angles, before going the whole route again backwards. Live shows include a Wild West saloon and a Mexican fiesta, and there's a huge indoor play area for younger children. Meals, snacks, shops, good disabled access; cl Nov–late Mar; (01773) 531521; £11.99.

🏠 👵 🐝 **Kedleston** SK3041 KEDLESTON HALL This 18th-c Palladian mansion is thought by many to be the finest example of Robert Adam's work – it's certainly the least altered. Interesting *objets d'art*, original furnishings, good collection of paintings, and a museum of items collected by Lord Curzon when he was Viceroy of India. Adam designed a charming boathouse and bridge in the park outside, which also has extensive formal gardens with marvellous rhododendrons, and long woodland walks. Meals, snacks, shop, disabled access (best to phone in advance); open Apr–Oct, house pm Sat–Weds, grounds daily; (01332) 842191; £4.50, or £2 per vehicle for just the park; NT. We've had no suggestion of a closer place for lunch than the Black Cow at Lees, beyond the A52.

🐝 **Lea** SK3257 LEA GARDENS Beautiful woodland gardens with rhododendrons inc rare species and cultivars, azaleas and rock plants. Home-baked snacks, shop and garden centre, some disabled access; open 20 Mar–6 July; (01629) 534380; £2.50.

🐦 🖼 ❄ **Matlock** SK3060 RIBER CASTLE WILDLIFE PARK (off the A615 at Tansley) Specialising in rare breeds and endangered species of birds and animals (it's renowned for its lynx), a 25-acre park set high up on Riber Hill in the grounds of ruined Riber Castle. Excellent views; you find yourself looking *down* on the Heights of Abraham (*see separate Family Panel on p.149*). Wrap up well – even in summer the wind can make it feel rather chilly. Snacks, shop, disabled access; cl 25 Dec; (01629) 582073; £4. The Boat House is good value for lunch, with interesting walks. The A615 E and B5056 and B5057 W are good drives.

🏵⛵☺☀🚣 **Matlock Bath** SK2958
Pleasantly busy place, with lots to do;
for the HEIGHTS OF ABRAHAM *see
separate Family Panel on p.149.* A
spectacular wooded cliff looks across
the lower roadside town to pastures
by the Derwent; up the side of the
gorge, quiet lanes climb steeply past
18th- and 19th-c villas. PEAK DISTRICT
MINING MUSEUM AND TEMPLE MINE 🏛
(Temple Rd) Lively exploration of
mining, with a unique early 19th-c
water-pressure pumping engine, and
interactive display on the pitfalls of
working in a mine. Also tours of the
old Temple Mine workings, and the
chance to pan for minerals – they
found a tiny amount of gold not so
long ago. Snacks, shop; cl 25 Dec;
(01629) 583834; £2. GULLIVER'S
KINGDOM AND ROYAL CAVE (1m S off
the A6) Family theme park with chair
lift and hectic rides, cave tour, and
cowboy and ghost towns. Meals,
snacks, shops; open wknds and
school hols Easter–Oct; (01629)
580540; £5.25. Other family
attractions not worth a special
journey but useful enough if you're
staying in the area include the
AQUARIUM AND HOLOGRAM GALLERY
(cl winter wkdys; *£1.80), and the
MODEL RAILWAY MUSEUM attached to
a model shop, with a scale working
model of Mellorsdale as it was in
1906; best to check wknd and winter
opening, (01629) 580797. The
Temple Hotel (Temple Walk) has
great views and decent food.
✝🏛⛪🎋 **Melbourne** SK3825 This
pleasant small town has a good
relaxed feel and villagey lanes; the
White Swan and Railway Hotel are
good for lunch. The CHURCH of St
Michael and St Mary is impressive,
more like a cathedral than an
ordinary parish church. MELBOURNE
HALL Behind its 18th-c façade, this
grandly extended house dates back in
part to the 13th c, and has twice been
the home of British prime ministers;
fine pictures and furnishings.
Glorious formal gardens with
fountains, pools, and famous yew
tunnel; interesting craft centre (open
all year). Meals, snacks, shop,
disabled access; Hall open pm daily in

Aug (exc first 3 Mons), plus gardens
open pm Weds, Sat, Sun and bank
hols Apr–Sept; (01332) 862502;
*£4.50, *£3 for garden when house is
closed.
🏛 **Monyash** SK1566 Quiet village
with good-value home cooking at the
Bull's Head, and (2m S) the
mysterious ARBOR LOW STONE CIRCLE
SK1663.
🏠 **Old Whittington** SK3874
REVOLUTION HOUSE (High St)
Innocuous-looking thatched cottage,
300 years ago the birthplace of what
came to be known as the Glorious
Revolution. Good audio-visual
display, period rooms and furniture.
Disabled access to ground floor only;
open Good Fri–2 Nov, plus over
Christmas (when it's prettily decked
out with old-fashioned decorations);
(01246) 453554; free. The White
Horse is useful for lunch.
🌼 **Pilsley** SK2471 THE HERB GARDEN
Big main garden with lots of herbs
and old English roses, smaller
gardens specialising in rare medicinal
herbs, pot pourri or lavender. Teas,
shop; cl mid-Sept–mid-Mar; (01246)
854268; £1 suggested donation.
Pilsley itself is a charming village.
🚣🚂🏠 **Ripley** SK3950 MIDLAND
RAILWAY CENTRE 🏛 (Butterley
Station) Regular steam-train
passenger service through country
park, and developing railway
museum. Meals, snacks, shop,
disabled access; cl 25 Dec; best to ring
for train timetable, (01773) 570140;
£6.95 (more on bank hols). It's good
for families – not only are there a few
farm animals on the adjacent farm
(you can visit here free without
having to go on the railway), but two
children are admitted free with every
adult ticket. DENBY POTTERY VISITOR
CENTRE Guided factory tours
(10.30am and 1pm – not Fri or
wknds; booking essential) show the
intricate skills of potters and
craftsmen. Big factory shop, and
children's play area. Meals, snacks,
shop, disabled access; cl 25–26 Dec;
(01773) 743644; full tours £3.50,
otherwise £2.50. The Excavator on
the A610 out at Buckland Hollow is a
good-value family dining pub.

↓⊤ ⚡ ⬚ **Rowsley** SK2566 CAUDWELL'S MILL AND CRAFT CENTRE Working 19th-c flour mill, powered by water turbines, with crafts such as glass-blowing and wood-turning. Meals, snacks, shop; cl wkdys Jan and Feb; (01629) 734374; free. Rowsley also has an interesting STONE CIRCLE called the Nine Ladies. The Grouse & Claret does decent food (all day wknds).

★ **Shardlow** SK4330 CANAL BASIN Attractive, with some handsome former wharf buildings – one now an antiques warehouse, another, the Malt Shovel, a good pub.

⬚ **South Wingfield** SK3755 WINGFIELD MANOR (B5035) Substantial ruin with virtually complete banqueting hall, tower and undercroft. The 16th-c Babington Plot is thought to have been hatched here, leading to the final downfall of Mary, Queen of Scots. Shop; cl Mon and Tues; (01773) 832060; £2.75, inc Walkman tour. The White Hart at Moorwood Moor has reasonably priced food.

⬚ ☕ **Sudbury** SK1632 SUDBURY HALL Individual but attractive Stuart mansion with elaborate carving, frescoes, murals and plasterwork in splendidly elegant rooms; the interiors featured in the BBC's *Pride and Prejudice* as the home of Mr Darcy. It's worth a visit just for the excellent NATIONAL TRUST MUSEUM OF CHILDHOOD, which has a chimney climb for sweep-sized children. You can play with some exhibits, and at wknds the schoolroom is staffed by an Edwardian teacher. Meals, snacks, shop, disabled access; open pm Weds–Sun (and bank hol Mons) Apr–Oct, plus museum open pm wknds till Christmas; (01283) 585305; £5 for everything, or £3.50 house and grounds, £3 museum only; NT. The Boar's Head Hotel is useful for lunch.

★ **Tissington** SK1752 The Peak District's most beautiful village, its broad main street wonderfully harmonious, with wide grass verges, handsome stone houses inc a Jacobean hall (not open) and interesting church. The grey stone gardener's cottage is familiar from many calendars; craft centre, garden centre, decent homely café.

↓⊤ ♄ ⬚ **Wirksworth** SK2854 A lot of recent work has gone into restoring old buildings here. NATIONAL STONE CENTRE (Porter Lane) 330-million-year-old tropical lagoons and limestone fossil reefs, as well as an exhibition, guided fossil trails, and activities like gem-panning or fossil-rubbing. Snacks, shop, some disabled access; cl 25 Dec; (01629) 824833; *£1.80 for exhibition. WIRKSWORTH HERITAGE CENTRE (Crown Yard) Old silk and velvet mill, with displays on local customs like well dressing and clypping the church, and a few children's activities. Meals, snacks, shop; cl am Sun, Mon (exc bank hols and mid-July–mid-Sept), Tues (exc Apr–mid-Sept), and all Nov–mid-Feb; (01629) 825225; £1. Slightly N at Middleton SK2756, the MIDDLETON TOP ENGINE HOUSE is home to a beam engine built in 1829 to haul waggons up a steep incline on the Cromford & High Peak Railway. Snacks, shop, disabled access; engine in motion first wknd of month Apr–Oct, plus bank hols; (01629) 823204; *70p. The Knockerdown Inn out on the B5035 is pleasant for lunch, and the Carsington Reservoir (good visitor centre) out that way is beginning to tone into the landscape.

★ **Particularly appealing villages** are a strong attraction here, and besides those mentioned include Ashford in the Water SK1969, Bradbourne SK2152 (with an ancient Saxon cross outside its Norman church), Dale Abbey SK4338 (abbey ruins, Hermits Cave and remarkable All Saints Church, part of which was formerly the village inn; the Carpenters Arms has good-value food), Earl Sterndale SK0967, Elton SK2261, Hartington SK1360 (good cheese shop inc local Stilton, and pottery on Mill Lane), Little Hucklow SK1678, Little Longstone SK1971 (Great Longstone nearby is charming, too, and the back road from Baslow through here to Tideswell is a pretty drive), Litton SK1675, Old Brampton SK3372 (count the minutes between one and two o'clock on its church clock), Osmaston SK1944 (thatched cottages, pleasant path through lakeside park), Parwich SK1854, Repton SK3026, Tideswell SK1575 (where the spacious 14th-c church is known as the Cathedral of the Peak; good walking country, and the B6049 across Millers Dale has nice views) and Youlgreave SK2164 (another interesting church). Other attractive villages, all with good pubs, are Brassington SK2354, Coton in the Elms SK2415, Duffield SK3443, Holymoorside SK3469, Idridgehay SK2849, Kirk Ireton SK2650, Lullington SK2513, Mapleton SK1648 (domed church, nice riverside walk to Thorpe), Milton SK3126, Ridgeway SK3551, Smisby SK3419 and Stanton by Dale SK4638.

The RIVER TRENT impresses with its silent power; Ingleby SK3426 is one good access point – for example, from the big garden of the John Thompson pub, which brews its own beer.

This is a surprisingly good area for cycling, particularly on the Monsal or Tissington Trails (see Walks ◠-7 and ◠-10, below). You can hire bicycles by the half-day or day from Ashbourne Cycle Hire, Mapleton Lane, Ashbourne SK1846, Parsley Hay Cycle Hire, Parsley Hay SK1463, and Middleton Top nr Cromford SK2956; around £5 for 3 hours, from £7 a day. A bike shop at Hayfield SK0387 is handy for the Sett Valley Trail, about which there's an information centre nearby.

Days Out

Tram treat
Cromford village (or in spring/early summer Lea Gardens); lunch at the Derwent, Whatstandwell; Crich Tramway Museum.

Cave village and shivering mountain
Castleton caves and castle; lunch at Rose Cottage, the Castle Hotel, Peak or Olde Nag's Head in Castleton; climb up Mam Tor and walk along the ridge to Hollins Cross or Lose Hill.

An outing from the spa
From Millers Dale, walk on the Monsal Trail along Chee Dale to below Chee Tor; lunch in Buxton, at Columbine (Hall Bank) or the Coffee Bean Café (Spring Gardens); look round Buxton, especially Poole's Cavern.

Heights and depths
Matlock Bath, for Riber Castle Wildlife Park and the Heights of Abraham (including cable car); lunch at the Temple Hotel there, or the Boat House (A6 S); Peak District Mining Museum, Temple Mine, Peak Rail (see Darley Dale entry, above).

Aristocratic eye-catcher
Chatsworth house and gardens; lunch at the Devonshire Arms, Beeley; Edensor village; stroll by the River Derwent in Chatsworth estate.

Medieval manor, country crafts
Haddon Hall; lunch at the Lathkil Hotel, Over Haddon; visit the craft centre there, walk through Lathkill Dale; if time, visit Arbor Low nr Monyash.

Walks

The White Peak area, picturesquely cut by the intricate channels of the dales, has high, flat pastures with small fields of rich grassland enclosed by silvery stone walls, clusters of often very photogenic farm buildings, and small old-fashioned villages. It gives an abundance of generally gentle walking.

Winding **Monsal Dale** ⌂-1 is the outstanding valley in this central area, its pastoral quality emphasised by the disused limestone cotton mills along the way. It's especially lovely in May and June with wild flowers enriching the pastures along the broader stretches. Don't expect to have it to yourself. There's good access from the A6 a couple of miles towards Buxton from Ashford in the Water SK1969; and from Monsal Head SK1871 (handy hotel), where a disused railway viaduct adds interest. This viaduct forms part of the Monsal Trail – see below. The B6049 N off the A6 SE of Buxton gives access to Millers Dale SK1573, just past the little village of that name (the Anglers Rest is a decent pub); upstream of Monsal Dale, this is rather less visited but also lovely – as is its continuation Chee Dale SK1273.

Lathkill Dale SK1865 ⌂-2 has a charming combination of woods, steep pastures and more well weathered signs of old mines; its short tributary Bradford Dale is also very attractive.

The **River Derwent** ⌂-3 has pleasant stretches where Izaak Walton fished, either upstream from Rowsley SK2566, or from the B6012 N of there at the Calton Lees car park SK2568 – there's open access to Chatsworth Park on this W side of the river, which is particularly lovely.

Birchover SK2462 ⌂-4 is the starting point for an extraordinary walk over Stanton Moor, where among quarry workings and prehistoric burial mounds are the Nine Ladies stone circle, a folly tower and a huge boulder known as the Cork Stone, equipped with metal steps for the courageous and adorned with at least four centuries' worth of graffiti (the earliest we found was 1613); there are good views into Darley Dale from the edge of the escarpment. Behind the Druid Inn in Birchover are Rowtor Rocks, a gritstone outcrop into which one Rev Eyre cut steps, benches and a stone armchair for contemplation.

The well wooded **Goyt Valley** SK0177 ⌂-5 with its 3 miles of reservoirs is a man-made landscape, but none the less charming; reached off the A54 W of Buxton. Shining Tor SK1454 is a breezy but undemanding moorland walk from the summit of a minor road.

The E edges of the **Dark Peak** ⌂-6 include the abrupt ramparts of Curbar Edge SK2575 and Froggatt Edge SK2476, popular with rock-climbers and easily accessible from the road. Birchen Edge SK2772 and Wellington's Monument SK2673 are obvious objectives from the Robin Hood at Curbar SK2574.

The **Monsal Trail** ⌂-7 outshines the other former railway-track walks in the Peak District, though like them is in parts more exposed to the winds than walks down in the dales. It runs from Wye Dale SK1072 E of Buxton to Coombs Road viaduct SK2274 S of Bakewell. W of Millers Dale Station SK1573, the trail leaves the old railway and takes a stepping-stone route along the river beneath the towering cliffs of Chee Tor SK1273 before rejoining the railway track.

Further E, well out of the Peak District, **Creswell Crags** SK5374 ⌂-8 beside Crags Pond form the basis of a short but attractive there-and-back walk through woodland.

Dove Dale ⌂-9, shared with Staffs (the River Dove marks the boundary), is the most popular of all the dales. Partly wooded, it has a beautifully varied mixture of water, trees and pastures, and is lined with crags and curiously shaped outcrops of rock. To see fewer people, head for the upstream sections: the barer pastures and steep hillsides of Milldale SK1354, the wooded peace of Beresford Dale SK1259, or Wolfscote Dale SK1357, with its dramatic rocky gorge and still trout pools (best reached from Hartington SK1260, where the Devonshire Arms and Minton House are both reliable hotels). Other handy nearby refreshment places are the Okeover Arms at Mapleton SK1648, Coach & Horses at Fenny Bentley SK1750 and (to be found on the Staffs side) the Izaak Walton Hotel nr Ilam (cosier inside than it looks from out), Watts Russell Arms at Hopedale and George at Alstonefield.

The **Tissington Trail** △-10 follows a disused railway track from Ashbourne SK1846 up to Parsley Hay SK1463 on the A515, where it joins the similar High Peak Trail from Buxton SK0673 to nr Cromford SK2956. This has a particularly interesting finale from Middleton Top engine house to High Peak Junction, dipping down a great incline past old engine houses to reach the **Cromford Canal** △-11, along which it's a short walk to Cromford itself. Earlier, branching off at Roystone Grange is an archaeological trail.

Castleton SK1583 △-12 and Hope SK1783 have the most varied walks in the High Peak. The great walk here is to take in Castleton, the Lose Hill/Mam Tor ridge SK1383, the caves and Winnats Pass SK1382; Mam Tor is so shaly and prone to landslips that it's dubbed the Shivering Mountain. Cave Dale is an optional side trip from the back of Castleton. Quarrying has had an unfortunate effect on the local landscape in the area, and limits walks further afield, though there are some pleasant walks to be had in the gentler high pastures of the limestone country to the S.

Edale SK1285 △-13, famous as the start of the 256-mile Pennine Way into Scotland, has a good information centre and a couple of hikers' pubs. It tends to be packed with expectant long-distant walkers on Sunday mornings. For a taste of the Dark Peak proper, this can be the start for ½-day walks that quite quickly take you up through the stone-walled pastures of the valley on to the edge of the dark plateau above. The track signed as the alternative Pennine Way route up Jacob's Ladder is easier to find, and has more to see, than the official Pennine Way plod across a huge blanket bog.

The lane up past **Ladybower Reservoir** △-14 to the car park by the Derwent Reservoir (with a summer minibus service beyond to Howden Reservoir) gives plenty of easy waterside-forest walking on the relatively sheltered stone-walled slopes of the upper parts of Derwent Dale, with access to the higher moors for better views – for example, up on to Win Hill, or on a kind day on to the formidable Derwent Moors to the E. The Ladybower pub down on the main road is useful.

The dark moors of the real **High Peak** △-15 in the N of the area are one of England's great wildernesses. But they have few easy circular routes, are largely very bleak indeed, and often consist of private grouse moor with no right of public access. The car park at the top of Snake Pass (A57 Glossop–Hathersage) is near the centre of the biggest of the National Trust's moorland holdings here, giving free access to the miles of Hope Woodlands SK1091 (there aren't actually many trees).

The moorland village of **Hayfield** SK0387 △-16 and its attractive nearby smaller sister Little Hayfield have good walks around them, both up towards Kinder Scout SK0888 and to the Lantern Pike viewpoint SK0288 in the opposite direction. There's also a popular walk along a hillside former railway to New Mills SK0085, looking down on the mill buildings by the River Sett. The Lantern Pike Inn in Little Hayfield could hardly be more welcoming.

There are good walks in the countryside around **Hathersage** SK2381 △-17: for example, in the attractive moorland, pastures and woodland making up Longshaw SK2678, nr the Fox House Inn up on the Sheffield road; or, closer and gentler, down along the River Derwent towards Grindleford SK2478.

Torrs Riverside Park SJ9985 △-18 a deep gorge below New Mills, is a good place to potter among the ivy-covered remains of former mills and other industrial relics; the canal basin over at Buxworth SK0282 is interesting, with a very enjoyable pub.

The **Goyt Way** ⌂-19 between here and Marple SJ9588, partly following the Peak Forest Canal, is a pretty walk.

Derbyshire has lots of decent country pubs perfectly placed for walkers. These include the Miners Arms at Milltown, Ashover SK3561 (despite quarrying), Peacock at Barlow SK3474, Robin Hood at Baslow SK2572 (handy for the ridge of Baslow Edge), King's Head at Bonsall SK2858 (very child-friendly, by the Limestone Way), Bowling Green at Bradwell SK1781 in Smalldale, the restauranty Druid at Birchover SK2462, the Barrel on the ridge at Bretton SK2077, Beehive at Combs SK0478 (lovely valley), Chequers just below Froggatt Edge SK2476, Queen Anne at Great Hucklow SK1878, Maynard Arms and Sir William at Grindleford SK2478, Robin Hood at Lydgate nr Holmesfield SK3177 (for the Cordwell Valley), Royal Oak at Millthorpe SK3276, Bull's Head at Monyash SK1566, Grouse at Nether Padley SK2577, the unfashionably basic New Napoleon by Ogston Reservoir SK3761, Lathkil at Over Haddon SK2066 (for Lathkill Dale), Little Mill nr Rowarth SK0189 (particularly for Lantern Pike), Queen's Arms at Taddington SK1472 and Bull's Head at Wardlow SK1874 (for well wooded Cressbrook Dale).

Where to eat

Bakewell SK2168 Byways Water Lane (01629) 812807 Olde-worlde tearoom with several separate areas, roaring log fire, well presented good-value food from snacks to meals, and warmly friendly staff. |£3.40.

Birchover SK2462 Druid (01629) 650302 Pleasantly remote creeper-covered house with huge choice of very popular interesting food, well kept real ales, and good friendly service; children under 5 must leave by 8pm; cl 25 Dec. £22|£7.

Buxton SK0673 Coffee Bean Café 50 Spring Gardens (01298) 27345 Small bustling café, long and narrow, with old tea and coffee advertisements on the walls, 15 types of coffee, all-day breakfasts, savouries and light lunches, and delicious cakes; cl evenings; disabled access. |£4.

Buxworth SK0282 Navigation (01663) 732072 Very welcoming extended pub by former canal basin with low-ceilinged rooms, plenty to look at, good fires, well kept real ales, good-value generous food, and cheerful staff; tables on sunken flagstone terrace. £14.75|£5.

Castleton SK1583 Rose Cottage Cross St (01433) 620472 Friendly village cottage with lots of summer flowering baskets, pretty garden, lunchtime home-made snacks and meals and afternoon cream teas; cl Fri, Jan; disabled access. |£3.

Church Broughton SK2033 Holly Bush (01283) 585345 Neat brick village pub, nicely refurbished, with well kept real ale and good-value home-made simple but good food in bar and separate dining room; no food pm Sun; disabled access. £11.55|£3.80.

Eyam SK2276 Eyam Tea Rooms The Square (01433) 631274 Family-run teashop in village square with sandwiches, salads and good cream teas, and lots of speciality teas; cl Mon, weekdays Nov, Dec, Jan, Feb; partial disabled access. |£3.50.

Eyam SK2276 Miners Arms Water Lane (01433) 630853 Good restful dining pub in small village with lovely home-made food and decent wines; bedrooms; cl pm Sun, am Mon, first 2 wks Jan; disabled access. £20|£5.75.

Holmesfield SK3277 Robin Hood (01742) 890360 Rambling former farmhouse with a wide choice of consistently good food inc interesting daily specials, real ales, and friendly staff; good nearby walks. £20|£5.75.

Hope SK1783 Cheshire Cheese (01433) 620381 16th-c village pub with 3 cosy beamed rooms, each with its own coal fire, well kept real ales, a decent choice of house wines, good food (especially evenings), obliging service, and 2 small no smoking dining rooms. £18.40|£6.95.

Kings Newton SK3826 HARDINGE ARMS (01332) 813808 Good quickly served roasts, fish, salads and other food in comfortable, interesting, beamed and timbered 17th-c inn; disabled access. £11.50|£3.

Melbourne SK3825 BAY TREE 4 Potter St (01332) 863358 Small family-run cottagey restaurant with beams and simple furnishings, carefully presented popular food (Sun lunch is booked up weeks ahead), and thoughtful relaxed service; cl am Sat, pm Sun, Mon, 2 wks Aug. £40|£7.

Over Haddon SK2066 LATHKIL (01629) 812501 Busy, civilised pub in lovely spot with open fires, beams and comfortable furnishings, good food and well kept real ales, and helpful service; cl 25 Dec; children lunchtime only. £21.35|£6.75.

Ridgeway SK4081 OLD VICARAGE (0114) 247 5814 Big Victorian house in lovely gardens with a marvellously relaxing welcoming atmosphere, cosy sitting room for pre-dinner drinks and beautifully presented, quite exceptional cooking using home-grown produce in candlelit dining room or light and airy less formal conservatory; cl am Sat, pm Sun, Mon, 1–10 Jan; disabled access. £35.50.

Woolley Moor SK3661 WHITE HORSE (01246) 590319 Popular old pub run by very friendly people – and much liked by locals; very good food using best local produce, lots of daily specials, decent wines and beers, lovely view from garden, good play area. £13.65|£4.

Special thanks to Gill Sells, Rob and Anita Hill, Pam Goodfellow, Alan Reavill, J F M West.

DERBYSHIRE CALENDAR

Some of these dates were provisional as we went to press, please check information with the telephone numbers provided.

Many villages here decorate their wells and springs with flower-petal pictures in annual festive Well Dressings. Originally a pagan water-worshipping ceremony, this is now part of the Christian calendar. A procession led by the clergy and a blessing of the wells usually initiates a week of village celebrations. To avoid the crowds go a day or two before the actual ceremony for a good close view of the elaborate flower pictures which should stay fresh for almost a week. Some of the best are Chesterfield, Eyam and Tissington.

FEBRUARY

24 **Ashbourne** Shrovetide Football Game: free-for-all between unlimited number of Up'ards and Down'ards (from above and below Henmore Brook) who compete to get the ball to goals 3 miles apart along the brook – *till Wed 25* (01335) 343666

MARCH

28 **Ripley** Spring Diesel Gala at Midland Railway Centre – *till Sun 29* (01773) 747674

APRIL

13 **Chesterfield** Easter Market and Entertainment (01246) 207777

DERBYSHIRE CALENDAR

APRIL cont

14 **Flagg** Point to Point, A515 (01246) 345777

MAY

4 **Chesterfield** May Day Market and Gala (01246) 207777
9 **Chatsworth** Angling Fair at Chatsworth House – *till Sun 10* (01328) 830367; **Buxton** Antiques Fair at Pavilion Gardens – *till Sun 17* (01298) 25106
10 **Doe Lea** Airbourne Parade at Hardwick Hall and National Mills Day at Stainsby Mill (01246) 850430
16 **Chesterfield** Charter Exhibition: 400 years of Chesterfield's history at Chesterfield Museum – *till 31 Dec* (01246) 345727
17 **Borrowash** Derbyshire County Show at Elvaston Castle Country Park (01332) 571342
21 **Tissington** Well Dressing – *till Wed 27* (01335) 390246
23 **Ashbourne** Derbyshire Steam Fair at Hartington Moor Showground – *till Mon 25* (01663) 732750; **Brackenfield** Well Dressings: 5 displays – *till Tues 26* (01629) 534767; **Chester Green** Well Dressing (01332) 673210; **Middleton-by-Youlgreave** Well Dressing (01246) 345777; **Wirksworth** Well Dressing – *till Sat 30* (01246) 345777
25 **Bamford** Sheep Dog Trials (01433) 651624; **Chesterfield** Spring Bank Holiday Market and Street Entertainment (01246) 207777; **Crich** Mayday at the National Tramway Museum (01773) 852565
29 **Castleton** Ancient Garland Ceremony: ancient pagan fertility ceremony with Celtic origins now encompassing Oak Apple Day – King wears a beehive-shaped flower headdress and is accompanied by consort on horseback with girls in white dresses bedecked with fresh flowers; the procession stops and dances outside the 6 village inns (01433) 620560

JUNE

1 **Hartington** Flower Festival at St Giles Church – *till Sun 14* (01298) 84444
6 **Ashford in the Water** Well Dressing – *till Sun 14* (01246) 345777
7 **Crich** Tram Festival at the National Tramway Museum (01773) 852565
13 **Chelmorton** Festival and Well Dressing – *till Wed 17* (01298) 85381
14 **Crich** Working Horse Trams at the National Tramway Museum (01773) 852565
20 **Ripley** Well Dressing – *till Thurs 25* (01246) 345777
27 **Church Gresley** Festival of Leisure: free family event at Maurice Lea Memorial Park – *till Sun 28* (01283) 228094; **Derby** Cathedral Tower Open Day (01332) 341201; **Doe Lea** Elizabethan Fair at Hardwick Hall (01246) 850430; **Hope** Well Dressing – *till 4 July* (01433) 621312

JULY

4 **Ashbourne** Day of Dance at Sudbury Hall (01283) 585337; **Dove Holes** Beer and Jazz Festival – *till Sun 5* (01298) 814722; **Elvaston** Steam Rally at Elvaston Castle Country Park – *till Sun 5* (01332) 670346; **Glossop** Carnival and Country Fair at Manor Park (01457) 866233

DERBYSHIRE CALENDAR

JULY cont

5 **Buxton** Well Dressing Demonstration – *till Tues 7* (01298) 25106
8 **Buxton** Well Dressing *till Wed 15* (01298) 25106
10 **Buxton** Music Festival: operas, early music, jazz, cabaret and fringe – *till Sun 26* ((01298) 70395
11 **Baslow** Open Air Gala Concert and Firework Display at Chatsworth Park (01246) 345777; **Buxton** Carnival (01298) 25106; **Pleasley** Well Dressing and Flower Festival – *till Wed 15* (01623) 810775
12 **Crich** Children's Fun Day at the National Tramway Museum (01773) 852565
17 **Ashbourne** Jazz Concert at Sudbury Hall (01283) 585337; **Buxton** Festival of Morris Dancing – *till Sun 19* (01663) 742756; **Stainsby** Folk Festival at Brunts Farm – *till Sun 19* (01773) 834421
18 **Kedleston** Outdoor Concert at Kedleston Hall (01332) 842191
24 **Buxton** Jazz Festival inc parade – *till Sun 26* (01625) 528336
28 **Chesterfield** Medieval Market and Street Entertainment (01246) 207777; **Derby** Cathedral Tower Open Day (01332) 341201

AUGUST

1 **Tansley** Cromford Steam Rally at Highacres Farm – *till Sun 2* (01629) 824263
2 **Buxton** Gilbert and Sullivan Festival: competition, masterclasses, costumed parade – *till Sun 16* (01298) 25106; **Elvaston** Derbyshire Classic Car Event at Elvaston Castle (01484) 660622
5 **Bakewell** Show: biggest show in the county – *till Thurs 6* (01629) 812736
12 **Ashover** Agricultural and Horticultural Show (01246) 863412
14 **Barlow** Well Dressing – *till Wed 19* (0114) 289 0310
15 **Ashbourne** Show (01335) 330552; **Taddington** Well Dressing – *till Sat 22* (01298) 85736
16 **Ashhover** Vintage Car Rally at Rectory Fields (01246) 345777
19 **Holymoorside** Well Dressing – *till Thurs 27* (01246) 569177
22 **Castleton** Church Festival of Art, Craft and Music – *till Sun 30* (01433) 621148
29 **Ashbourne** Derbyshire Country Show at Hartington Moor Showground – *till Mon 31* (01663) 732750; **Bonsall** Well Dressing and Carnival Week *till* World Championship Hen Racing *on 1 Aug* (01629) 825685; **Eyam** Well Dressing and Carnival (01433) 630935; **Froggatt** Show (01246) 345777; **Matlock Bath** Illuminations – *till 31 Oct* (01246) 345777; **Wormhill** Well Dressing – *till 5 Sept* (01298) 871023
30 **Crich** Festival of Transport at the National Tramway Museum – *till Mon 31* (01773) 852565; **Eyam** Plague Commemoration Service in Cucklet Dell (01246) 207777
31 **Chesterfield** Market, Fair and Fireworks (01246) 207777; **Hope** Show and Sheepdog Trials (01433) 620905

SEPTEMBER

5 **Chatsworth** Country Fair at Chatsworth House – *till Sun 6* (01328) 830367; **Buxton** Healing Arts Festival – *till Sun 6* (01298) 25106; **Glossop** Victorian Weekend – *till Sun 6* (01457) 855920
6 **Crich** Working Horse Trams at the National Tramway Museum (01773) 852565; **Derby** Concert at Darley Park (01332) 255531

DERBYSHIRE CALENDAR

SEPTEMBER cont

8 **Chesterfield** Well Dressing Demonstration at Peacock Centre Courtyard – *till Sat 12* (01246) 345777

·12 **Buxton** Country Music Festival – *till Sun 13* (01298) 24658; **Chesterfield** Well Dressing at several locations inc Crooked Spire Church – *till Sat 19* (01246) 345777

13 **Crich** Free Entry for Visitors in Edwardian or Victorian Costume at the National Tramway Museum (01773) 852565

16 **Doe Lea** National Trust Free Day at Hardwick Hall (01246) 850430

19 **Little Hayfield** Sheep Dog Trials and Country Show at Spray House Farm – *till Sun 20* (01663) 733644

OCTOBER

26 **Crich** Children's Treasure Trail at the National Tramway Museum – *till 1 Nov* (01773) 852565

NOVEMBER

1 **Derby** Fireworks at Markeaton Park (01332) 255658

We welcome reports from readers . . .

This *Guide* depends on readers' reports. Do help us if you can – in return, we offer a discount on the next edition to people who've helped us with reports for it. Tell us what you think about places already in it, and anything extra you think we should say about them. And send us your ideas for inclusion in the next edition: places to visit, eat at or stay in, attractive drives or walks, maybe even unusual interesting shops you know of. Use the card in the middle, the report forms at the end, or just write – no stamp needed: *The Good Guide to Britain*, FREEPOST TN1569, Wadhurst, E Sussex TN5 7BR.

DEVON

Devon has a lot to please everyone, with a splendid range of places to stay in, and some very good food. There are lovely gardens, delightful thatched villages clustered around ancient church and equally ancient pub, glorious vistas of coast and moor, some decidedly unstuffy museums, all sorts of rustic pursuits, and vintage steamtrains puffing through gorgeous river valleys. The county is packed with so many enjoyable places to visit that we have divided it into three areas: Exeter and East Devon (classic family holiday country, with Exeter a charming small city); South Devon and Dartmoor (wonderful scenery, the widest range of interesting places to visit – good all year); and North Devon and Exmoor (a quieter appeal than other parts, less touristy but plenty of interest).

Devon is first-class for a summer holiday. For a shorter break spring, early summer, or autumn is better: no hold-ups on the roads, even richer colours in the countryside, a real sense of space and peace.

A particularly advantageous point for families is that even 'adult' places generally have a lot to entertain children too – Buckland Abbey in South Devon is a fine example. And vice versa – many family-orientated places can keep adults smiling too, such as the Big Sheep near Bideford or the Gnome Reserve near Bradworthy (North Devon), with its unexpectedly appealing plantings. There are, of course, places geared more exclusively to children: Crealy Country at Clyst St Mary (East Devon) is a prime example of these day-out-treat places; with the Plymouth Dome, Paignton Zoo and the Woodland Leisure Park at Blackawton all outstanding for families in South Devon. Devon also boasts the country's most enjoyable 'attraction shop' – the one attached to Buckfast Abbey at Buckfastleigh.

Some of the best views here are from trains; besides the steamlines, the standard railway Devon Rover is a good deal, with unlimited train journeys in the area at a reduced rate for either a week or any three days out of seven.

EXETER AND EAST DEVON

Attractive coast and beach resorts, interesting places to visit; Exeter is good for a quiet break.

Exmouth is the liveliest and biggest of this coast's four main family beach resorts, and doubles as a working port. Seaton, quieter, is a more typical family resort, with much less of a beach. Budleigh Salterton, the quietest, is rather retiring and genteel. Sidmouth is slightly busier, with a good deal of character as well as plenty for families – the broadest all-round appeal. Branscombe is the prettiest place on this coast.

Exeter is a gently attractive city with a lot to see; all its museums are interesting and particularly well organised. Served by fast trains and the M5, it can be reached quickly from far away – and good roads bring the other parts of Devon within comfortable reach for a day out. Very quiet at weekends, during the week it's active without being crowded or noisy.

Inland, coastal downs give a varied landscape of charming wooded valleys with views and high pastures between, and several attractive villages. North of the A30/A35 is more self-contained farmland, mainly well hedged traditional stock and dairy farms.

Besides places mentioned in the main introduction, our top shortlist here includes Killerton, the working mill museum at Uffculme, Bicton Park Gardens, and the village of Ottery St Mary.

Where to stay

Branscombe SY1988 Look Out Branscombe, Seaton EX12 3DP (01297) 680262 £92, plus special breaks; 5 pretty rms. Attractively converted, early 19th-c coastguards' cottages with lots of beams, antiques and flagstones; good food using local produce, secluded cottage garden and marvellous view, fine beach and cliff walks; cl 4 days over Christmas; children over 8; well behaved dogs by prior arrangement (away from public rooms).

Chardstock ST3004 George Chardstock, Axminster EX13 7BX (01460) 220241 £49.50; 4 rms. Neatly thatched old village inn with character furnishings, beams and old gas lamps; a quietly chatty feel, good food in both the bar and restaurant, and close to nice walks; children over 12.

Cullompton ST0107 Oburnford Farm Cullompton EX15 1LZ (01884) 32375 £40; 4 rms, most with own bthrm. Working mixed farm with Channel Islands dairy cows (lovely clotted cream) and beef cattle (guests can help feed the calves); attractive lounge, log fires, good breakfasts.

Exeter SX9292 Edwardian 30–32 Heavitree Rd, Exeter EX1 2LQ (01392) 276102 *£44, plus special breaks; 13 individually furnished rms, 3 with four-posters. Popular guesthouse close to the cathedral and city centre; with a pretty lounge, enjoyable breakfasts in the attractive dining rooms, and friendly and knowledgeable resident owners; cl Christmas/New Year.

Exeter SX9292 St Olaves Court Mary Arches St, Exeter EX4 3AZ (01392) 217736 £63w; 15 recently refurbished, well equipped rms. Handsome Georgian-style house just 400yds from the cathedral and standing in its own walled garden; with a warm welcome from the helpful and friendly staff, comfortable rooms, imaginative evening meals in the candlelit restaurant, and super breakfasts; disabled access.

Exeter SX9292 White Hart 66 South St, Exeter EX1 1EE (01392) 279897 £84, plus special breaks; 57 modern but slightly dated rms. Rather splendid, well run 14th-c inn with lots of different eating areas (wine bar-type as well as a proper restaurant); marvellous atmospheric bar, open fires, beams, antiques, good range of wines, and friendly service; attractive courtyard with proper barbecues; cl 24–26 Dec.

Gittisham SY1398 Combe House Gittisham, Honiton EX14 0AD (01404) 42756 *£105; 15 individually decorated, pretty rms. Peaceful Elizabethan country hotel in gardens with lawns and shrubbery; elegant day rooms with antiques, family portraits and fresh flowers; a happy relaxed atmosphere, good food using some home-grown produce, and fine wines; cl 2 wks end Jan–mid-Feb; dogs welcome by prior arrangement.

Higher Bulstone SY1988 Bulstone Higher Bulstone, Branscombe, Sidmouth

EX12 3BL (01297) 680446 £75, plus special breaks; 12 rms, 6 with own bthrm. Set in over 3 acres and surrounded by fields, this is a super place for family holidays – with both parents' and children's needs catered for; completely no smoking; lots of facilities and friendly staff.

Lympstone SX9984 RIVER HOUSE The Strand, Lympstone, Exmouth EX8 5EY (01395) 265147 £80, plus special breaks; 3 pretty rms. Warmly welcoming restaurant with rooms; marvellous river views from the big picture windows, good imaginative food (wonderful fresh fish and interesting vegetable dishes) in the first-floor restaurant using some home-grown produce, thoughtfully chosen wines, and kind service; practical cookery courses, too; cl 25–27 Dec, 1–2 Jan; restaurant cl pm Sun and Mon (though open if residents want to eat); children over 6; disabled access.

Membury ST2703 LEA HILL HOTEL Membury, Axminster EX13 7AQ (01404) 881881 £96, plus special breaks; 11 rms, inc 2 suites, in carefully converted barns, mostly with private garden areas or terraces. Set in lovely countryside and surrounded by 8 acres of grounds, this thatched 14th-c longhouse has comfortable beamed rooms, a convivial bar, relaxed and friendly owners; good evening meals, and nice breakfasts; well behaved dogs by special arrangement.

Sidford SY1390 BLUE BALL Sidford, Sidmouth EX10 9QL (01395) 514062 *£40; 3 rms with nice touches like free papers, fruit and fresh flowers; shared bthrm. Welcoming, thatched 14th-c inn run by the same family since 1912; very friendly service, decent food inc hearty breakfasts; dogs by arrangement.

Stockland ST2404 KINGS ARMS Stockland, Honiton EX14 9BS (01404) 881361 £40; 3 rms. Cream-faced, thatched pub with elegant rooms, first-class food in both the bar and evening restaurant (especially fish), and an interesting wine list; skittle alley, live music pm Sun; no accommodation 24 Dec–1 Jan; well behaved children only.

Tipton St John SY0991 GOLDEN LION Tipton St John, Sidmouth EX10 0AA (01404) 812881 £41; 2 rms with showers. Bustling village local with lots of fresh flowers in the softly lit bar, small no smoking restaurant, good food, and decent wines; several golf courses nearby; no baby facilities.

Whimple SY0497 WOODHAYES Whimple, Exeter EX5 2TD (01404) 822237 £95; 5 lovely spacious rms. Big Georgian country house in neat grounds, with comfortable, quietly decorated lounges, a small library, open fires, flagstoned bar and a pretty dining room; fine food, afternoon teas, and excellent breakfasts; tennis, croquet; cl 4 days over Christmas; children over 12.

To see and do

Exeter SX9292 Though large parts of the centre were devastated by World War II bombing, some choice streets and buildings survive, with picturesque, partly Tudor narrow lanes leading from the mainly pedestrianised High St into the serene, tree-shaded cathedral close. The atmosphere is distinctive – relaxed and liberal yet responsible, buoyed up by the thriving university. In the centre, modern shops are integrated into the old layout very discreetly indeed. With many smaller churches, decent book and other shops, pubs and so forth nearby, this is a very pleasant area for browsing around. Particularly attractive streets include Southernhay at the end of the close, and Stepcote Hill, a picturesque detour from Fore St.

The Quay, beyond the streams of fast traffic on the ring road (there are quiet underpasses), has become lively and entertaining, with handsomely restored buildings, resurgent cafés and pubs (the Prospect is good), and a growing number of craft shops and the like; the Old Quay House has a visitor centre with an audio-visual show.

Apart from the White Hart (see **Where to stay** section above), civilised pubs and wine bars with decent food include the sumptuous Imperial (New North

Rd), Chaucer's (High St, under C&A), the Ship (14th-c, Martins Lane), Well House (The Close; with cathedral view and Roman well), Papermakers (Exe St) and the Prospect (Quay).

There are £2.50 return boat trips down the ship canal to Exminster; or you can walk down, passing the Double Locks (a favourite pub) and ending at the Turf Hotel looking out over the estuary. The quickest way into the city from either the M5 or the A38 is to keep on round to the westbound A30 and go into the city from the Alphington roundabout.

✝ CATHEDRAL England's finest example of decorated Gothic architecture, with its magnificent nave soaring to the fan-vaulted roof, and intricately carved choir stalls; the misericords are thought to be the longest in the country. It also boasts the longest Gothic vault in Europe, superbly atmospheric. Lots of colourfully embroidered cushions, chronologically illustrating English and local history. The façade has 3 tiers of sculpted figures, inc Kings Alfred, Canute and William I. Meals, snacks, shop, disabled access; guided tours 11am and 2.30pm wkdys, just 11am Sat; £2 suggested donation.

! UNDERGROUND PASSAGES (entrance via Boots Arcade in High St) An unusual medieval attraction is this atmospheric network, built in the 13th c to bring water into the city; there's an introductory exhibition and video, then a guided tour of the tunnels themselves, still much as they were centuries ago. The guides can be very entertaining, and clearly enjoy their work. Flat shoes are recommended. On Sats they do longer tours for those who want to go into the more creepy and constricted parts – great fun, but be prepared to get muddy then. Snacks; shop; cl am wkdys (exc July–Sept and school hols), all Mon (exc school hols) and Sun; (01392) 265887; £2.50 (£3.50 July and Aug).

🏚 GUILDHALL This medieval municipal building with its ornately colonnaded Elizabethan façade is one of the oldest still in use; it has displays of civic regalia and so on. Cl 1–2pm, pm Sat, all Sun and bank hols, and during civic functions; free.

✝ 🏚 ST NICHOLAS'S PRIORY (Mint Lane) 11th-c Benedictine monastery with unusual Norman undercroft, Tudor room and a 15th-c kitchen. Shop, disabled access to ground floor only; open 3–4.30pm Mon, Weds and Sat Easter–Oct (guided tour last Tues of month); occasionally cl for private functions; (01392) 265858; free.

♿ ROYAL ALBERT MEMORIAL MUSEUM (Queen St) Wonderful Gothic exterior, and inside notable displays of regional silver, African carvings, archaeology, paintings and natural history. Snacks, shop, disabled access (new lift); (01392) 265858; free.

Other things to see and do

DEVON FAMILY ATTRACTION OF THE YEAR

🐘 ☺ **Clyst St Mary** SX9790 CREALY COUNTRY (Sidmouth Rd) This bustling family complex seems to get bigger every year – last summer they added the Magical Kingdom, a delightfully constructed area aimed mostly at under 7s, with play spaces and the High-Gliding Honey Swing. There's plenty to amuse older children too, from bumper boats and go-karts, to a farm where you can milk the cows (and always meet baby animals). Many of the attractions are indoors, inc some of the animals, and a very good and varied adventure playground, with lots of slides (one has a practically vertical drop) and things to swing on. As with the outdoor attractions, they've tried hard to make sure there's something in here for most age groups, and on some bits they don't mind adults joining in too. Other features include pony rides and lakeside walks, and they have a particularly wide range of special events and activities (usually on summer Suns) from pirates' treasure hunts to conker championships. It's obviously not the kind of place to come to without children, aimed unashamedly at fun and entertainment rather than anything more instructive, but families can easily end up staying here most of the day. Meals, snacks, shop, disabled access; (01395) 233200; cl 25–26 Dec; £4.50 (£3.75); several family tickets available. The only extra charges are for pony rides (around £1.25) and go-karts (about £1.75). Admission is slightly less in winter, when there isn't as much going on (no bumper boats or farm shows). They have an adjacent paintball site. If you don't want to eat in the park, the Half Moon has decent food.

ቴ 🕈 ⋔ **Beer** ST2389 Rather cottagey resort village, still with some fishing boats pulled up on the shingle beach, and a stream dug into the main street. PECORAMA PLEASURE GARDENS Fun for railway-lovers, with models and train collections in the house, and outside a miniature steam and diesel passenger line with stunning views of the bay. Also a putting green, aviary, and a children's maze and assault course. Meals, snacks, shop, mostly disabled access; cl pm Sat, Sun (exc Jun–Sept), and outdoor features cl Oct–Easter (exc half-term); (01297) 21542; £3.20 (less for just outside features). The village was famous from Roman times for its cavernous whitestone quarries, which can be visited, and the B3174 inland passes lots of Bronze Age burial mounds. The waterside Anchor Hotel has good, fresh, local fish, and readers have also praised the good-value bedrooms and breakfasts at the Dolphin.

🕸 🐾 ⋔ **Bicton** SY0684 BICTON PARK GARDENS 🆔 Busy place centred around 50 acres of lovely gardens, shrubs, lakes and woodland, with a rather jolly railway through the grounds. A futuristic-looking glass Palm House turns out to be early Victorian, and has a fine collection of tropical trees and plants. Also fuschia, geranium and orchid houses, bird garden, pinetum, magnificent Italian gardens, and – useful for families – crazy golf and adventure playground. Meals, snacks, shop and plant centre, disabled access; cl wkdys Nov–Mar; (01395) 568465; £4.95. Nearby, the entirely separate gardens of BICTON COLLEGE OF

AGRICULTURE are of great if more specialised appeal; long monkey-puzzle avenue through parkland, rich collection of magnolias, camellias and flowering cherries, national pittosporum and agapanthus collections, and a 17-acre arboretum with woodland garden. Snacks, plant centre; cl Christmas wk and Good Fri, plant centre cl winter wknds; (01395) 568353; £2. The Salterton Arms is handy, in nearby Budleigh Salterton SY0682 – a peaceful seaside resort, perked up last summer when another guidebook boobed by suggesting the entire beach was a haven for nudists (it's actually just the bottom end).

★ ✝ **Broadclyst** SX9897 Pretty thatch and cob village, with a marvellous old church, photogenic outside, interesting in. The Red Lion has good food – and the post office has a unique computer information kiosk.

🚌 ☺ **Clyst St Mary** SX9790 For CREALY COUNTRY *see separate Family Panel on p.169.*

🕸 **Dalwood** SY2499 BURROW FARM GARDENS (½m or so away from off the A35, turn off at signs for Taunton Cross) Part of this 5-acre site has been created from an ancient Roman clay pit, and there are spacious lawns, borders and unusual shrubs and trees as well as a woodland garden, pergola walk with old-fashioned roses, and super views. Cream teas, snacks, nursery; cl Oct–Mar; (01404) 831285; £2. The pretty Tuckers Arms is good for lunch.

★ ✝ **East Budleigh** ST0684 Attractive and quietly placed cob and thatch village; the pleasant CHURCH has fascinating Jacobean carved pew ends – some grotesque, some hilarious, some frankly rude. The Sir Walter Raleigh has decent food.

♣ ♪ 🏠 ♓ 🐎 ☺ ✦ **Exmouth** SY0080 Good family seaside holiday town, worth a visit for its lively harbour and marina, its long sandy beach and its stately church. Summer cruise trips go from the harbour up to Topsham, and there are sea fishing trips (they supply rod and bait); tel (01395) 222144 for both. A LA RONDE (2m N on the A376) Extraordinary 16-sided house, built around 1795 and decorated in part with feathers, seashells, seaweed and sand. A charmingly whimsical place, the outside looking not entirely unlike a giant biscuit barrel. Meals, snacks, shop; cl Fri, Sat, and Nov–Easter; (01395) 265514; £3.20; NT. GREAT EXMOUTH MODEL RAILWAY (Sea Front) Home to the world's biggest 00 gauge model railway, nearly 1½ miles of track indoors with outside trains running round a pond of koi carp. Some of the detail is amazing, right down to the birds in the trees. Shop, some disabled access; cl Nov–Easter; (01395) 278383; £2. WORLD OF COUNTRY LIFE (Sandy Bay) 40 acres of family-based activities, with friendly animals, adventure playground and undercover play areas, safari rides through deer and llama paddocks, a reconstructed Victorian street, classic

motorcycle collection, crafts, steam engines, and falconry centre (no displays Sat, exc July and Aug). Meals, snacks, shop, disabled access; cl Nov–Mar; (01395) 274533; £4.75 (less on Sat, exc in July and Aug). The Seafood Restaurant (Tower St) has nothing but the freshest fish and shellfish; the Grove (attractive seafront garden) and seafront Deer Leap are useful too.

♨ **Honiton** ST1500 Some handsome Georgian buildings along this country town's long high street, and some interesting shops. The Red Cow (High St) is good value for lunch. The 13th-c ALLHALLOWS MUSEUM (High St) has useful displays of Honiton lace, with lace-making demonstrations in Jun, July and Aug. Shop, disabled access to ground floor only; cl Sun, and Nov–Mar; (01404) 44966; £1. Fine views from the A375 S.

✤ 🏠 **Killerton** SS9700 KILLERTON Best of all in spring, 15 acres of beautiful hillside gardens, shrub borders and planted beds, with an impressive avenue of beech trees. The 18th-c house has an annually changing costume exhibition in the period-furnished rooms, but it's the gardens that really give the place its special appeal. Meals, snacks, shop and plant centre, good disabled access (with buggies round the grounds); house cl Tues, and Nov–mid-Mar; (01392) 881345;

Days Out

Exploring Exeter
Maritime Museum; Exeter Cathedral; lunch at White Hart (South St); Underground Passages tour.

Sheltered combes and dramatic undercliff
Sidmouth, inc Donkey Sanctuary; Branscombe – lunch at Masons Arms, look at church, smithy, NT bakery/tearoom; Branscombe Mouth – walk along Hooken Cliffs and through the undercliff.

A moated manor
Killerton; lunch at Red Lion, Broadclyst; Bickleigh Castle (see **North Devon and Exmoor** section).

Otter potter and Exe exploits
Bicton Park, or (at Ottery St Mary) Cadhay; Otterton Mill Centre; Topsham – lunch at Passage House; A La Ronde, Exmouth.

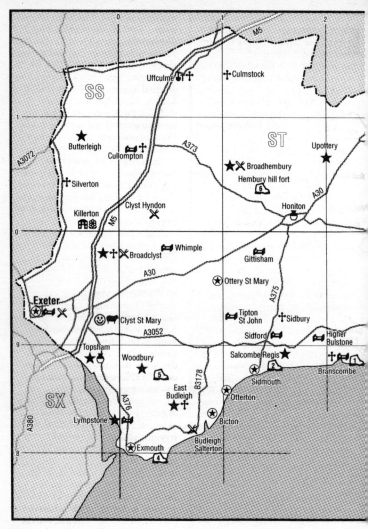

£4.80, £3.20 garden only; NT. The
Three Tuns in Silverton has decent
food, especially vegetarian, and
readers recommend the antiques
centre at nearby Hele (towards
Bradninch).

✗ ⚘ ★ **Otterton** SY0684 OTTERTON
MILL CENTRE Working watermill still
grinding flour for the bread, cakes
and pies sold on the premises. Also
craft workshops, display of East
Devon lace, and interesting evening
events. Meals and snacks (restaurant

cl winter wkdys), shop and garden
centre; cl 24–28 Dec; (01395)
568521; £1.75. The village is pretty,
and the King's Arms has a good
choice of food (with a lovely evening
view from the back garden).

🏠 ⚅ ♪ ✝ 🦋 **Ottery St Mary** SY0995
Restrained small town – or extended
village – with some attractive old
buildings around its interesting twin-
towered church. The London Inn is
useful. CADHAY (just NW) Beautiful
Tudor and Georgian manor house,

Exeter and East Devon

A303

3

A30

Chardstock

🐄 Stockland   🐄 ★

Tytherleigh ★

Membury 🐄

A358

❀✕ Dalwood

A35

SY

A3052

Lyme Regis

Seaton ★ Axmouth

‼️ 🟥

Beer

0 Miles   5

0 Kilometres   8

rose garden, wild boar enclosures, walks, views and parkland. Also wetlands and waterfowl park, and the pet centre has all you'll need for any kind of pet, inc the animals themselves. Meals, snacks, shop, disabled access; cl 25–26 Dec; (01404) 822188; £2.65. OTTER NURSERIES (Gosford Rd) Garden centre good for trees, shrubs and plants; the lavatories often win Loo of the Year awards. The circular TUMBLING WEIR by an 18th-c mill, signed off Mill St, is unusual and photogenic.

! 🚋 **Seaton** SY2490 MUSIC FUN CENTRE A unique place, where you can try your hand at playing any kind of musical instrument – you don't even have to have picked it up before. Woodwind, brass, percussion, keyboards, they've got the lot – though they tell us bagpipes are what most people want to have a go at. Disabled access; booking essential, (01297) 445803. Open-top trams run from Seaton to Colyton, where the Kingfisher is a worthwhile pub; back in town, the Fisherman's Inn (Marine Crescent) has decent cheap food all day. LYME BAY CIDER (Manor Farm, on the A3052 coast road) Vintage equipment and free tastings; cl Sun exc summer pm; (01297) 22887; free.

★ 🚋 👶 **Sidmouth** SY1287 Attractive old streets, very 18th-c, running back from the seafront, and grander Regency buildings facing the sea. It was a fashionable upper-class resort in the early 19th c, and many of the town's buildings show undoubted architectural verve – there's very little seaside tat. The pebbly beach has fishing boats pulled up on it, and the town is protected by warm red sandstone cliffs; it stretches back along the river valley, though away from the sea the buildings are less interesting. The Old Ship has good-value food. The dedicated DONKEY SANCTUARY is a useful free attraction for families. The local history MUSEUM (in a fine Regency house on Church St, open Apr–Oct only) organises summer walking tours round the town, Tues and Thurs at 10.15am.
★ 👶 **Topsham** SX9687 Old-world seaside village, well worth a quiet

with a fine, timbered 15th-c roof in its Great Hall, and unusual Court of Sovereigns – a pretty courtyard with statues of various monarchs. Disabled access to garden and downstairs; open pm Tues–Thurs July and Aug, plus Sun and Mon spring and Aug bank hols; (01404) 812432; *£3. ESCOT AQUATIC CENTRE & GARDENS 🔲 (Parklands Farm, Escot) Tropical and coldwater fish from koi carp to piranhas, as well as rabbits and other pets, otters (fed at 11.30am and 3pm), Victorian walled potter, its buildings showing its past importance as a port – as do its large number of good pubs and inns. The Passage House is currently the best for food, and readers like the fresh fish at the Galley restaurant. There's a small maritime museum.

† ⅃т **Uffculme** ST0612 A large pleasant village above the River Culm with a magnificent carved screen in the attractive CHURCH. COLDHARBOUR MILL WORKING MUSEUM Every stage in the production of wool, in a well restored 18th-c mill building. Also restoration of a steam engine, and one of the largest tapestries in the world. Meals, snacks, shop, limited disabled access; cl winter wknds, and at least a wk at Christmas; (01884) 840960; £5. The B3397 to Culmstock and then the turn to Hemyock is a pretty drive; beyond at Clayhidon, the Half Moon has good food, by a footpath to the Blackdown Hills visitor centre.

† As well as those mentioned above, **interesting churches** can be seen at Branscombe SY1988 (magnificently carved oak gallery, Norman tower with a distinctive stair-turret; the village is notably pretty – a series of largely unspoilt thatched hamlets strung along a lovely seaside valley), Cullompton ST0107 (remarkable painted screen; a busy little town), Culmstock ST1014 (which also has a nicely placed old pub and river walk to Uffculme), Sidbury SY1391 (an attractive village, with a very good pub nearby at Sidford) and Silverton SS9502 (another picturesue village).

★ **Other attractive villages**, all with decent pubs, include seaside Axmouth SY2591, Lympstone SX9984 and Salcombe Regis SY1488; and Broadhembury ST1004, Butterleigh SS9708, Chardstock ST3004, Otterton SY0684, Tytherleigh ST3103, Upottery ST2007 (over the A30, the Stockland Hill road has good views) and Woodbury SY0187 (the B3180, cutting through an Iron Age hill fort, also has fine views).

Walks

While this area does not have such consistently splendid walking as other parts of Devon, the cliffs E of Sidmouth take some beating. One of the most rewarding areas is around **Branscombe Mouth** SY2088 ◿-1, with a walk up on to Hooken Cliff using the coastal path, then down through the Hooken undercliff – a tremendous jumble of collapsed chalk. Branscombe SY1988, lying just inland, is linked to the coastal path by other paths and has the good Masons Arms in the main part of the village as well as the NT Old Bakery tearoom opposite the unique NT thatched smithy. There's a long stretch of **red sandstone cliff** ◿-2 between Sidmouth SY1287 and Branscombe, reached from either place (or, steeply but very prettily, from Salcombe Regis SY1488). The steeply tumbled, brambly wooded wilderness of **Dowlands Cliffs** ◿-3 SY2889, 3 miles E of Axmouth, has numerous small birds. The **High Land of Orcombe** SY0279 ◿-4, reached by the shore road E out of Exmouth SY0080 and protected against campsite encroachment by its National Trust ownership, is useful for a shorter stroll with sea views.

Off the B3180 E of Woodbury SY0187 are miles of **heathland** ◿-5 with some pinewoods, a place to get away from people even in high summer (red flags warn if there's firing on one section which is a shooting range). From the highest points, nr the road, there are far views along the coast and to Dartmoor. The wooded hill fort right by the road is worth a look, and it's a bit eerie tracing the ramparts through the beech trees.

Off the A373 NW of Honiton ST1500, you can walk up into **Hembury hill fort** ST1103 ◿-6 for good views.

Where to eat

Broadclyst SX9897 RED LION (01392) 461271 Ochre-washed pub in a quiet village setting, with popular food, very good wines, a heavy-beamed long bar, and skittle alley. **£16.40|£5.20**.

Broadhembury ST1004 Drewe Arms (01404) 841267 Friendly and efficiently run 15th-c pub with excellent, perfectly cooked, very fresh fish; also, lovely puddings, well kept beers, fine wines, and attractively decorated rooms; disabled access. **£20.80|£8.10**.

Budleigh Salterton SY0682 Salterton Arms (01395) 445048 Tucked-away but busy little pub with a wide choice of good food using lots of fresh fish, vegetarian choices too, and enormous salads; disabled access. **£15.25|£4.50**.

Clyst Hydon ST0301 Five Bells (01884) 277288 Charming, spotless, thatched pub, with very good food inc fresh fish in the long bar divided by standing timbers; warm and friendly service, and lovely cottagey gardens; cl pm 25 and pm 26 Dec; disabled access. **£23|£5.95**.

Dalwood ST2400 Tuckers Arms (01404) 881342 Delightful, thatched, medieval longhouse with well prepared, enterprising bar food and lots of colourful hanging baskets; bedrooms. **£19.15|£9**.

Exeter SX9190 Double Locks Canal Banks, Alphington (01392) 56947 Friendly and very relaxed lock-side country pub, popular with students; good, simple bar food (all day), summer barbecues, and up to 10 real ales on handpump; disabled access. **£4.20**.

Exeter SX9292 Lambs 15 Lower North St (under the iron bridge) (01392) 254269 Cheerfully run by knowledgeable staff, with a well balanced menu using fresh seasonal local produce – everything from nibbles to breads and puddings is totally home-made; thoughtful wine list; cl Sun and Mon. **£25|£15**.

South Devon and Dartmoor

Beautifully varied scenery, lovely villages, little harbour towns of real character, the riches of Torbay; very interesting places to visit.

The coast has an intricate mixture of small coves, stretches of cliff, and sheltered creeks and estuaries cut deeply into the coastal hills – very popular in summer with sailors. Several small towns along it, particularly Dartmouth and Totnes, have a strong allure – intimate, relaxed and unshowy. By contrast, there are the promenades, low cliffs, bright gardens and palm trees of Torbay and its English Riviera. Just inland are well hedged hilly pastures, steeply wooded valleys and occasional vivid red-earth fields. Dartmoor is a magnificent brooding wilderness, with excellent walking and all sorts of points of interest – especially its strange-shaped tors and its prehistoric remains. Around its edges are many lovely valleys and villages, delightful to explore. The area has some beautiful places to stay in.

Besides places mentioned in the main introduction, top attractions here are Morwellham Quay, the steam railway between Buckfastleigh and Totnes (perhaps combined with a river trip), magnificent Saltram near Plympton, Coleton Fishacre garden at Kingswear, Powderham Castle, Castle Drogo at Drewsteignton, Lydford Gorge, Buckland Abbey and the Garden House at Buckland Monachorum, Overbecks Garden near Salcombe, and the rare breeds farm at Bovey Tracey and the shire horse centre at Dunstone. Plymouth has plenty to fill a rainy day.

Where to stay

Aveton Gifford SX6947 COURT BARTON FARMHOUSE Aveton Gifford, Kingsbridge TQ7 4LE (01548) 550312 *£48; 7 rms, 6 with own bthrm. Pretty, creeper-clad, 16th-c farmhouse on 300 acres of arable land; with a cosy, homely lounge, log fires, warm welcome and a flower-filled garden; cl Christmas.

Bantham SX6643 WIDCOMBE HOUSE Bantham, Kingsbridge TQ7 3AA (01548) 561084 *£56; 3 well equipped neat rms. In lovely countryside with fine views down to the sea, this modern no smoking house is spotlessly kept and very relaxing, and offers very good breakfasts and delicious evening meals using home-grown produce; cl Nov–Jan; no children.

Blackawton SX8050 NORMANDY ARMS Blackawton, Totnes TQ9 7BN (01803) 712316 £48, plus special breaks; 5 pretty rms. Quaint, friendly pub in a quiet village; with a cosy main bar, log fire, some interesting displays of World War II battle gear, generous food in both the bar and restaurant, and real ales; also seats in the garden.

Bovey Tracey SX8178 EDGEMOOR HOTEL Haytor Rd, Bovey Tracey, Newton Abbot TQ13 9LE (01626) 832466 *£89.95, plus special breaks; 17 charming rms. Ivy-covered country house in neatly kept gardens on the edge of Dartmoor; with a comfortable lounge and bar, log fires, good food in the elegant restaurant, and high tea for children under 8; dogs welcome; cl 1st wk Jan; limited disabled access.

Burgh Island SX6443 BURGH ISLAND Burgh Island, Bigbury-on-Sea TQ7 4BG (01548) 810514 £220 inc dinner; 14 art deco seaview suites, most with balconies. Extravagantly decorated and restored 1929 hotel on a small island – access by hotel Land-Rover (or foot) at low tide, sea-going summer tractor-on-stilts at high tide, 300-yd crossing from Bigbury; domed palm court, sun lounge, classic cocktail bar, original art deco furniture, kind and helpful hosts, good food, and super breakfasts. Tennis, mini gym, snooker, water sports, natural pool and private beach, walks and sea fishing. Island also has a 14th-c pub – and summer day-crowds. No dogs; cl wkdys Jan–Feb.

Chagford SX7087 EASTON COURT Sandy Park, Chagford, Newton Abbot TQ13 8JN (01647) 433469 £45, plus special breaks; 8 rms. Creeper-clad, thatched 15th-c house with beams, an inglenook fireplace, granite walls, and a big library (literary connections include Evelyn Waugh writing *Brideshead Revisited* here); cosy bar, charming sitting room, good breakfasts, and delicious evening meals in the candlelit restaurant; cl Jan; children over 12; disabled access.

Chagford SX7087 GIDLEIGH PARK Chagford, Newton Abbot TQ13 8HH (01647) 432367 £350 inc dinner, plus winter breaks; 15 opulent and individual rms with fruit and flowers. Exceptional and luxurious, Dartmoor-edge, mock-Tudor hotel with a deeply comfortable panelled drawing room, wonderful flowers, and a conservatory overlooking the attractive grounds (of which there are 40 acres, with walks straight up on to the moor); log fires, particularly fine cooking, a superior wine list, and caring staff.

Dartington SX7862 COTT Dartington, Totnes TQ9 6HE (01803) 863777 *£60, plus special breaks; 6 character rms. Pretty, very warm and friendly ancient inn, with a fine thatched roof (the longest in southern England); heavy-beamed communicating rooms with open fires and flagstones, good lunchtime buffet and interesting evening food (lots of fresh fish), real ales and quite a few wines by the glass, and friendly cats; no smoking restaurant, seats on terrace also, and fine walks nearby; cl 25 Dec; children over 5.

Dartmouth SX8751 FORD HOUSE 44 Victoria Rd, Dartmouth TQ6 9DX (01803) 834047 £70, plus special breaks; 3 individually decorated rms. Close to the harbour, this Regency town house has a log fire in the comfortable drawing room, antiques, interesting food using fresh local produce eaten around a big table, delicious breakfasts, helpful service, and a sheltered garden; you can take over the whole house for a weekend party; cl Nov–Feb.

Dartmouth SX8751 ROYAL CASTLE 11 The Quay, Dartmouth TQ6 9PS (01803) 833033 £91, plus weekend breaks; 25 individually furnished rms. Well restored Georgian hotel overlooking the inner harbour – great views from most rooms – with a 16th-c core; lively and interesting public bar with open fires and beams, quiet library/lounge with antiques, a drawing room overlooking the quayside, winter spit-roasts in the lounge bar, an elegant, upstairs seafood restaurant, decent bar food, and friendly staff.

Doddiscombsleigh SX8586 NOBODY Doddiscombsleigh, Exeter EX6 7PS (01647) 252394 £59; 7 rms, some in a Georgian manor house 150yds down the road, and most with own bthrm. Friendly, atmospheric 16th-c pub with beams, heavy wooden furniture, and an inglenook fireplace in the attractively furnished 2-roomed lounge bar; an outstanding cellar running to 800 wines and 250 malts, and popular food in both the bar and restaurant inc a huge range of Devon cheeses; good views from the garden, and the church is worth visiting for its fine stained glass; cl 25–26 Dec; no children.

Galmpton SX6840 BURTON FARM Galmpton, Kingsbridge TQ7 3EY (01548) 561210 *£42; 9 rms, most with own bthrm. Welcoming working farm in lovely countryside with dairy herd and pedigree sheep (guests are welcome to look around and help); traditional farmhouse cooking using home-produced ingredients; no smoking; cl 25 Dec.

Goveton SX7546 BUCKLAND-TOUT-SAINTS Goveton, Kingsbridge TQ7 2DS (01548) 853055 *£120, plus special winter breaks; 13 luxurious period rms. Handsome Queen Anne mansion in 6 well kept acres of gardens with croquet and putting; relaxing rooms with antiques, fine panelling and plasterwork, chintzy furniture and a roaring log fire; imaginative food using good local produce in the lovely no smoking restaurant, notable wines, and excellent personal service; dogs by arrangement; cl Jan; no children under 6 in the restaurant.

Haytor SX7677 BEL ALP HOUSE Haytor, Newton Abbot TQ13 9XX (01364) 661217 £120, plus special breaks; 8 spacious rms. Handsome Edwardian country house with an elegant drawing room, comfortable sitting room, log fires, a friendly atmosphere, and fine, careful cooking in the pretty restaurant; wonderful views and peaceful garden; cl Dec–Feb; disabled access.

Haytor Vale SX7677 ROCK Haytor Vale, Newton Abbot TQ13 9XP (01364) 661305 £71, plus special breaks; 9 rms. Civilised old inn on the edge of Dartmoor National Park; with good food (inc fresh fish), a good mix of visitors and locals in the 2 rooms of the panelled bar, open fires, no smoking restaurant, courteous service, and a big garden; walking, fishing, riding and golf nearby; disabled access.

Hazelwood SX7148 CRANNACOMBE FARM Hazelwood, Loddiswell, Kingsbridge TQ7 4DX (01548) 550256 *£36; 2 rms. Quietly set and comfortable Georgian farmhouse on a working stock farm in a lovely unspoilt valley; with prize-winning cider, and hearty food; no smoking; babysitting; cl Christmas.

Holne SX7069 CHURCH HOUSE Holne, Newton Abbot TQ13 7SJ (01364) 631208 £50, plus special breaks; 6 rms, most with own bthrm. Medieval, Dartmoor-edge inn with a comfortable and interesting pine-panelled lounge bar, freshly prepared food using local produce, restaurant, decent wine list, pleasant service, and lots of good walks close by.

Holne SX7069 WELLPRITTON FARM Holne, Ashburton TQ13 7RX (01364) 631273 £36; 4 pretty rms, 3 with own bthrm. Small, friendly, Dartmoor farm with lots of animals; comfortable sitting room, good food (packed lunches on request), and a small swimming pool; children over 5 (younger by arrangement, out of season).

Hope Cove SX6739 HOPE COVE Hope Cove, Kingsbridge TQ7 3HH (01548)

561233 £44, plus special breaks; 7 rms with fine sea views. Neatly kept and welcoming little hotel in a tranquil spot, with sandy beaches and plenty of nearby walks; lovely views from the lounge or dining room, helpful owners and staff, and enjoyable food; cl Nov–Easter; children from 6; no dogs.

Kingston SX6347 Dolphin Kingston, Kingsbridge TQ7 4QE (01548) 810314 *£49; 3 rms. Peaceful 16th-c inn with several knocked-through beamed rooms, and a warmly welcoming atmosphere; small no smoking area, very good home-made food, and real ales; tracks lead down to the sea.

Lewdown SX4486 Lewtrenchard Manor Lewdown, Okehampton EX20 4PN (01566) 783256 £145, plus special breaks; 9 well equipped rms with fresh flowers and period furniture. Lovely Elizabethan manor house in a garden with a fine dovecot, surrounded by a peaceful estate with shooting, fishing and croquet; dark panelling, ornate ceilings, antiques, fresh flowers and log fires; a friendly welcome, relaxed atmosphere, and the candlelit restaurant has very good food; children over 8 by arrangement – ditto dogs; disabled access.

Lifton SX3885 Arundell Arms Lifton PL16 0AA (01566) 784666 *£108, plus special breaks; 28 well equipped rms, 5 in annexe over the road. Carefully renovated old coaching inn with 20 miles of its own waters – fishing is the main thing; comfortable lounge, log fires, good food in the smart restaurant, decent wines, and kind service; cl 2 days over Christmas; dogs welcome away from restaurant and river bank.

Lydford SX5184 Castle Lydford, Okehampton EX20 4BH (01822) 820242 *£59; 10 rms (inc 2 lovely new ones), most with own bthrm. Very well run, charming Tudor inn with particularly friendly staff; lots of interesting antiques and furnishings in the lounge areas (new one overlooks a nice garden with covered terrace), log fires, beams and flagstones; lovely food, well kept real ales and 13 wines by the glass; pets corner; next to castle and nr attractive gorge; cl pm 25 Dec.

Malborough (2m S) SX7037 Soar Mill Cove Malborough, Salcombe TQ7 3DS (01548) 561566 *£130, plus special breaks; 18 comfortable rms, some opening on to garden. Neatly kept, single-storey building in an idyllic spot by a peaceful and very beautiful cove on NT coast (excellent nearby walks); with lovely views, extensive private grounds, tennis, putting, and a warm indoor pool; outstanding service, log fires, very good food (marvellous fish), and thoughtful, early evening children's meal; cl Nov–Jan, but open at Christmas and New Year; small, mature, well behaved dogs welcome by arrangement; disabled access.

Moretonhampstead SX7586 Great Sloncombe Farm Moretonhampstead, Newton Abbot TQ13 8QF (01647) 440595 *£40; 3 rms – the big double is the favourite. Lovely 13th-c farmhouse on a working dairy and stock farm, with friendly owners; carefully polished old-fashioned furniture, decent food, log fires, a relaxed atmosphere, and good nearby walking and birdwatching; a no smoking area; children over 8; dogs by arrangement.

Moretonhampstead SX7585 White Hart Moretonhampstead, Newton Abbot TQ13 8NF (01647) 440406 £60, plus special breaks; 22 rms. Comfortable former Georgian posting house, with interesting furnishings in both the civilised lounge bar and hall, a lively back bar, good bar food, and a no smoking restaurant; well placed for Dartmoor; children over 10; disabled access.

Preston SX8574 Sampsons Farm Preston, Newton Abbot TQ12 3PP (01626) 54913 £45; 10 rms, most with own bthrms. Thatched, 14th-c longhouse with beams, panelling and big open fires in the cosy sitting rooms, and a very relaxed, welcoming atmosphere; most enjoyable food in the popular restaurant, and lots of nearby walks; children over 3; disabled access; self-catering too.

Salcombe SX7337 Tides Reach South Sands, Salcombe TQ8 8LJ (01548)

843466 **£126,** plus special breaks; 38 rms, many with estuary views. Unusually individual resort hotel run by long-serving owners, set in a pretty wooded cove by the sea; with airy, luxurious day rooms, big sea aquarium in the cocktail bar, good restaurant food using fresh local produce, and friendly, efficient service; squash, snooker, leisure complex, health area, and a big heated pool; windsurfing etc, beach over the lane, and lots of coastal walks; cl Dec and Jan; children over 8; disabled access.

Sandy Park SX7189 MILL END Sandy Park, Chagford, Newton Abbot TQ13 8JN (01647) 432282 *£75, plus special breaks; 17 neat rms, most with views. Quietly set, former flour mill with a waterwheel in the neatly kept grounds below Dartmoor; comfortable lounges, carefully prepared, interesting food and fine breakfasts, and good service; well behaved dogs welcome away from public rooms; partial disabled access.

South Zeal SX6593 OXENHAM ARMS South Zeal, Okehampton EX20 2JT (01837) 840244 *£60, plus special breaks; 8 rms. Grandly atmospheric old inn dating back to the 12th c and first licensed in 1477 (a Neolithic standing stone still forms part of the wall in the TV room); elegant beamed and panelled bar with a chatty, relaxed atmosphere and an open fire, decent food and wines; and charming, ex-monastic, small garden; well behaved dogs welcome.

Staverton SX7964 SEA TROUT Staverton, Totnes TQ9 6PA (01803) 762274 **£64;** 10 cottagey rms. Comfortable pub in a quiet hamlet nr the River Dart; 2 relaxed beamed bars, log fires, popular food in both the bar and airy dining conservatory, and a terraced garden with fountains and waterfalls; cl Christmas.

Stoke Gabriel SX8457 GABRIEL COURT Stoke Gabriel, Totnes TQ9 6SF (01803) 782206 *£77, plus special breaks; 19 rms, some in former hay lofts. Standing in a walled Elizabethan garden, this attractive, family-run old manor has quiet, relaxing lounges (winter log fire), enjoyable, traditional English food, and courteous, helpful staff; outdoor heated swimming pool and grass tennis court; dogs welcome.

Teignmouth SX9473 THOMAS LUNY HOUSE Teign St, Teignmouth TQ14 8EG (01626) 772976 *£70, plus special breaks; 4 pretty rms with flowers and books. Lovely little Georgian house close to the fishing quay; with open fires in both the spacious, comfortable drawing room and elegant dining room, a relaxed friendly atmosphere, enjoyable food around the big dining table, and a sunny walled garden; cl mid-Dec–Feb; children over 12.

To see and do

Dartmouth SX8751 Charming waterside small town with many exceptional buildings, especially around the inner harbour. Though so popular, it's kept its own strong character, and stays very much alive through the winter. Cobbled Bayards Cove, with old fort and steep wooded hills behind, is particularly photogenic, as is pedestrianised Foss St. Markets on Tues and Fri: Old Market is picturesque. The Royal Naval College is a striking building. Interesting shops, plenty of waterside seats, lots of action on the river. Parking in summer can be trying: best to use the good Park & Ride on the B3207 Halwell Rd.

🚣 RIVER TRIPS to Totnes pass some of Devon's prettiest scenery, much of which can't be seen on foot or by car; you can combine this with steamtrains (see Buckfastleigh entry) or a connecting bus back – which saves hearing the commentary a second time. You can also go on circular tours of the surrounding area. There may still be boats in winter – tel (01803) 832109 to check; £6 return to Totnes. Also quaint car and pedestrian ferries to Kingswear and the A379 (can be a 2-hour car wait at peak summer times).

🏰 ❋ CASTLE (slightly SE of town, off the B3205) Classic, late 15th-c battlemented fortress, virtually

intact, with cannon and later gun batteries, and great views out into the Channel. Snacks, shop; cl winter Mon and Tues (and maybe lunchtimes then); (01803) 864406; £2.40. In summer a little ferry leaves the South Embankment for here every 15 minutes or so – otherwise be prepared for a 20-minute walk.
✝ ST SAVIOUR'S Lots of charming detail, well worth a close look, inc altar, pulpit, painted rood screen, brasses on chancel floor, and elaborate 14th-c hinges on the south door.

✵ ♙ DARTMOUTH MUSEUM (Duke St) Well restored, 17th-c timbered house, with mainly nautical displays; cl Sun, 25–26 Dec; *£1. HENLEY MUSEUM (Anzac St) Smaller, but interesting too, with local history and botany; cl Oct–May; free.
♨ NEWCOMEN ENGINE HOUSE (Royal Ave Gdns) Huge, steam-powered, atmospheric beam-engine pump, thought to be the world's oldest, worked 1720–1913. Shop, disabled access; cl Sun from Oct–Mar; (01803) 834224; *50p.

Paignton SX8960 Largely a typical resort, with a long promenade between the good sandy beach and the green; the little harbour is pretty, with working fishing boats as well as yachts. The original inland core has an attractive red sandstone church with some interesting buildings nearby, especially KIRKHAM HOUSE, a handsome, sandstone, Tudor merchant's house with a lofty hall. The formal and subtropical lakeside gardens at OLDWAY are colourful; on summer weekday mornings there may be guided tours of the Versailles-style colonnaded mansion at their centre. Attractive Elberry Cove between Paignton and Brixham is altogether quieter. Decent places for lunch include the Blagdon Inn (off the A385) and the Ship (Totnes Rd).

🐾 ! PAIGNTON ZOO (St Michael's; SX8859) Well run and shown, with over 1,300 animals and birds (many of them breeding) in 75 acres of beautifully planted surroundings; it's perhaps the country's most visually appealing zoo. Recent improvements have included new ape, giraffe and elephant enclosures, and more additions are planned during the next couple of years. Also a lakeside miniature railway, and a splendid hands-on animal education centre for children. Lots of events and feeding displays throughout the day. Meals, snacks, shop, good disabled access; cl 25 Dec; (01803) 557479; £6.60.
♨ PAIGNTON & DARTMOUTH STEAM RAILWAY (Queen's Park Station, Torbay Rd) One of the nicest such steamtrain trips we know of – GWR steamtrains run from here right by the sea along Tor Bay (halts at Goodrington Beach, which has closer parking, and Churston), then along the Dart estuary to Kingswear. The front Pullman coach is less crowded, and there's a model railway at the Paignton end. You can combine this with a boat Dartmouth–Totnes, and bus Totnes–Paignton. Snacks, shop, disabled access; cl Nov–Feb (exc parts of Dec), and some wkdays out of season, (01803) 555872 for timetable; *£6 return.

Plymouth SX4755 Apart from the area round the Barbican (see below) most of the old quarters of the city were destroyed in the war, and in parts it is like lots of other busy modern towns. There are some interesting escapes from the bustle, and in places The Hoe has something of the feel of smaller seaside promenades, with great views out over the Sound; decent food from the Yard Arm (looking out in suitably nautical style) and the Waterfront bar/restaurant. A statue of Drake is a reminder that he's supposed to have played his famous game of bowls here; there's still a bowling green close by. A tour bus can take you to the main attractions, though it's perhaps more fun on one of the BOAT TRIPS run by Tamar Cruises from Mayflower Steps, off Madeira Rd, Barbican; (01752) 822105. The ferries over to Torpoint in Cornwall put Antony House and Mt Edgcumbe in very easy reach – see **Cornwall** chapter. The Bank (behind Theatre Royal) does good-value food all day, and the Tourist Information Centre is one of the most efficient we've come across.

🏛 BARBICAN Carefully restored since the war, a series of narrow twisty streets of old buildings west of working Sutton Harbour; photogenic – and evocative even in wet weather. New St is its oldest core. The next 5 attractions are all round here.

🏛 PRYSTEN HOUSE (Finewell St) The city's oldest house, an austere, late 15th-c granite building with a galleried courtyard. Unpretentious but quite atmospheric restored rooms feature a model of 17th-c Plymouth, and several yards of an ambitious tapestry showing American colonisation. Cl Sun, and Nov–Mar; (01752) 661414; 75p.

✝ ST ANDREW'S (St Andrew St) Bombed but lovingly restored, with stained glass by John Piper illustrating the city's history.

👃 MERCHANT'S HOUSE (St Andrew St) Well restored, 16th-c jettied house, telling the city's day-to-day history in displays themed on tinker, tailor, soldier, sailor; also early Victorian apothecary's shop and schoolroom. Shop; cl 1–2pm, Sun, Mon (exc bank hols), and Oct–Mar; (01752) 264878; 90p.

🍷🏛 BLACK FRIARS DISTILLERY (60 Southside St) Photogenic home of Plymouth Dry Gin, now the only English gin still made in its original distillery, founded in 1793. The building itself dates back much further, and has had periods as a monastery and a prison; tours include demonstrations of production, a film of the town's history and of course a sample of the gin itself. Shop; cl Sun and Nov–Easter; (01752) 665292; £2.

🏛 ELIZABETHAN HOUSE (32 New St) Splendid, timber-framed, Tudor sea-captain's house, with period furniture; cl Mon and Tues; £1. There's an Elizabethan garden just down the road at number 39.

♄! DOME 💠 (The Hoe) State-of-the-art evocation of Plymouth's past and present, using feel-part-of-it technology – you can stroll along lively Elizabethan streets, dodge press gangs, meet Drake and the Pilgrim Fathers, and come bang up to date with satellite and radar monitoring of current harbour action and weather. Good fun as well as interesting, and well worth 2 hours (you may have trouble parking nearby for longer than that). Particularly good for families – children don't mind learning about a place's heritage when it's presented like this. Snacks, shop, good disabled access; cl 25 Dec; (01752) 603300; £3.95 (includes admission to Smeaton's Tower).

🏛❋ SMEATON'S TOWER (The Hoe) Colourfully striped, 18th-c former Eddystone Rocks lighthouse, moved here 110 years ago, with a good view from the top if you like steps. Cl Nov–Easter, and maybe in bad weather; (01752) 600608; *75p.

📷❋ ROYAL CITADEL (The Hoe) Unrivalled views of the city and sea from the ramparts of this magnificent, 17th-c battlemented fortress. The gateway is striking, and the barracked parade-ground is still in use; admission by guided tour only, at 2pm and 3.30pm May–Sept, starting from the main gate – get tickets at least 15 mins earlier from the Dome; (01752) 775841; £2.50.

🐟 AQUARIUM (just outside Citadel) Comprehensive collection of seafish, crustaceans etc, run by a scientific institution. Plenty to touch and do. Snacks, shop, disabled access; (01752) 633333; £2. A bigger more elaborate aquarium is due to open across from the Barbican nr the fish market in May; under the name NATIONAL AQUARIUM, it will include an intriguing collection of seahorses until last year based on Exeter's Quay.

👃 CITY MUSEUM (Drake Circus) Well shown collections of mostly West Country interest. Shop, disabled access; cl Sun, Mon (exc bank hols); (01752) 264878; free.

📷 CROWNHILL FORT 💠 (Crownhill Fort Rd) Just N of town, the biggest and least altered of Plymouth's Victorian forts, though from the road it looks little more than a wooded hill. Used by the army right up to 1986, it's been well restored by the Landmark Trust, with underground tunnels, secret passageways and lookout towers to explore; children can run around quite freely, and there's an adventure playground. You can stay here (all year) and have the run of the place after dark. Snacks, shop, limited disabled access (lots of steep steps); cl Nov–Mar; (01752) 793754; £2.75.

Torquay SX9264 The busiest of the area's resorts, good for evening strolling, with palm trees and rocks, promenades, colourful gardens, decorous guesthouses and huge hotels, broad Victorian streets and pricey shops. The sheltered beaches around here are cleaner than many along this coast. Summer bustle centres around the attractive harbour, with lots of shops, boat trips, and an aquarium. In summer a CLIFF RAILWAY takes care of a dizzy swoop from Oddicombe Beach to the high wooded clifftop (around 50p each way). The quaint Hole in the Wall (Park Lane) and smart new London (Strand) do good-value food.

✠ KENTS CAVERN (Ilsham Rd, Wellswood) The oldest directly dated archaeological site in Britain; continuing excavations often make scientists reconsider their theories about prehistoric life. Good guided tours really bring out the mystery of the caves, and colourful stalagmites and stalactites add to the eerie atmosphere. In summer they do spooky evening tours (booking essential). Very well presented, and definitely worth an hour or so if you're in the area. Special visits at Christmas. Summer snacks, shop, disabled access (with prior notice); cl 25 Dec; (01803) 215136; £3.75 (£4.50 evening tours).

! MODEL VILLAGE ▦ (Hampton Ave, Babbacombe; SX9265) Hundreds of one-twelfth scale buildings in 4 acres of miniaturised landscape, beautifully done. Try coming at dusk between Easter and Oct, when the scenes are prettily floodlit. Snacks, shop, good disabled access; cl 25 Dec; (01803) 328669; £3.80 – a little pricey, but it's probably the best of its type (you may also have to pay for parking). The beach here has safe bathing water, and the Cary Arms (Beach Rd) is good.

🏰🏛🖼🎴 TORRE ABBEY (King's Drive; SX9063) Some of the earlier parts of the abbey remain, inc the medieval sandstone gatehouse and ruined Norman tower, but they've been eclipsed by the later house with its 17th-, 18th- and 19th-c period rooms. The main feature now is the art gallery, along with a showy garden and palm house and an Agatha Christie room, full of possessions of the locally born author. Snacks, shop; cl Nov–Mar; (01803) 293593; £2.70.

♨ BYGONES (Fore St, St Marychurch; SX9166) Enthusiastically reconstructed, life-sized Victorian street, with well stocked period shops and rooms, model railway, and re-created World War I trench, replete with sound effects and cooking smells. Open till 10pm in summer. Café, shop; cl 25 Dec; (01803) 326108; *£2.95.

♙ MUSEUM (529 Babbacombe Rd) Finds from ancient local caves, and a cannon that turns out to be a clock, designed to fire its charge at midday. Shop; cl winter wknds; (01803) 293975; £2.

★ ❀ COCKINGTON SX8963 Winding lanes of olde-worlde thatched cottages and bric-a-brac/craft shops in a sheltered village with millpond etc, well preserved by Torbay Council; also, an adjoining 500-acre park. The Drum pub (a useful stop) was designed to match by Lutyens in 1934. Terribly pretty, and very touristy in season, with open horse-drawn carriages.

Totnes SX8060 Busy in summer, but still keeping most of its charm even then, particularly early in the morning. The picturesque Elizabethan area known as THE NARROWS is very atmospheric, especially along the High St down to the arch at the top of Fore St, with quaint pillared arcades. On Tues May–Sept many traders wear Elizabethan costume, and the main streets are closed to traffic then, delighting visitors but infuriating some local traders. There's a working harbour (see Dartmouth entry above for excellent river trips), and you can walk some way downstream on either side of the River Dart. Behind the church of St Mary's (which has a super rood screen), several rooms in the 11th-c GUILDHALL may be open; it was originally part of a Benedictine priory. Perhaps unexpectedly, Totnes has quite a New Age flavour; there's even a flotation tank to wash away city stresses. The Kingsbridge Inn (Leechwell St), Royal Seven Stars Hotel (Fore St) and Albert (Bridgetown) have decent food, though the Cott at nearby Dartington easily merits the extra distance. There's an excellent cheese shop on Ticklemore St. The SOUTH DEVON RAILWAY, which stops here, is described under Buckfastleigh entry below.

🏰 ❄ CASTLE Part Norman, part 14th-c, these classic circular remains were lucky enough to avoid any battles, so the keep is pretty much intact. There's a tree-shaded inner lawn, and lovely views of the town and down to the river. Shop; cl winter Mon and Tues (and maybe lunchtimes then); (01803) 864406; £1.50.

🏺 MUSEUM (70 Fore St) Stately Elizabethan merchant's house with a galleried courtyard, herb garden, and display on the inventions of Totnes boy Charles Babbage, creator of one of the earliest computers. Shop; cl wknds, and Nov–Mar; (01803) 863821; *£1.50.

🏺 DEVONSHIRE COLLECTION OF PERIOD COSTUME (43 High St) Period costumes and accessories from the 18th c to the present, from high fashion to ordinary work clothes, with changing annual exhibitions. Shop; cl wknds, and Nov–Apr (exc by arrangement); £1.20.

🏚🏺 BOWDEN HOUSE 🏰 (Ashprington Rd, S; SX8059) Tours by costumed guides of handsomely restored, grand Tudor and baroque rooms (plenty of weaponry, and well documented tales of ghosts), and a separate PHOTOGRAPHY MUSEUM with still and moving pictures (inc cartoons) in attractive grounds. Snacks, disabled access to museum only; open pm Mon–Thurs and bank hol Suns from mid-Mar–Oct, cl other Suns but usually car boot sales then; (01803) 863664; *£4.50.

Dartmoor Classic moorland, where distant vistas of changing greens and browns fade into the austere grey-blues of far shoulders and edges. The moor is punctuated with all sorts of interesting focal points and features: numerous, easily traceable prehistoric remains; strange, wind-sculpted, eroded granite tors which crown many of the slopes; the little streams that thread over boulders; tamed watercourses where leats or miniature canals (dating back to the 16th c, one cut by Drake to supply Plymouth) curl carefully around the contours; sheltered valleys cut into the moors, where white houses crouch among sycamores and oaks; occasional higher clusters of much more stunted oaks mark abandoned tin-mine workings with ruined wheelhouses, and shaggy ponies hope for a hand-out. Good roads over the moor are the B3212 and B3357, and the back road towards Ashburton, off the B3344 just NW of Manaton. The main information and visitor centres are at Princetown on Tavistock Rd, (01822) 890414, and at Postbridge on the B3212, (01822) 88272. Even if it looks sunny, it might be worth packing waterproofs along with your maps – mists can come down without warning, and there's no shelter. The surrounding villages are well worth exploring: typically, thatched, white-plastered, stone cottages clustered around an ancient stone church beside its church-house inn. The towns ringing the moor have useful facilities. A big chunk of NW Dartmoor is used by the Ministry of Defence for firing practice; it's marked by red and white posts, and you can go in when there are no red lights or red flags.

Other things to see and do

★ ⚭ ♪ **Ashburton** SX7569 Probably the best of the small towns around Dartmoor, with a distinct character. The RIVER DART COUNTRY PARK (Holne Park) is pleasant for walking or fishing, with adventure playgrounds for children. Snacks, shop; cl Oct–Mar; (01364) 652511; £4.30. The London Hotel is good.
❋ **Berry Head** SX9456 Tremendous coast, sea and shipping views from this ex-quarry, country park; squat lighthouse, formidable Napoleonic War battlements with cannon (and guardhouse café); the nature trail takes in kittiwakes and guillemots on cliffs, as well as uncommon plants.
🏰 † **Berry Pomeroy** (off the A385, just E of Totnes; keep on past the village) SX8362 CASTLE Reputedly Devon's most haunted castle, hidden away on a crag over a quiet wooded valley. Appropriately spooky Norman gatehouse and walls around the ruins of an imposing and

unexpected Tudor mansion, with an interesting 15th-c fresco inside. The lawns in front are ideal for a picnic. Snacks, shop, disabled access; cl Nov–Easter; (01803) 866618; £2. The red sandstone 15th-c village CHURCH is worth a look on the way; there's an odd monument in Seymour Chapel. The road through here from Ashburton via Littlehempston and on to Stoke Gabriel is a nice drive.
♄ ♘ **Bickington** SX7972 GORSE BLOSSOM MINIATURE RAILWAY AND WOODLAND PARK Unlimited rides on 7¼-in gauge steam railway through 35 acres of woodland; also nature trails, play areas, and an outdoor model railway in Swiss mountain setting. Meals, snacks, shop, some disabled access; cl Nov–Easter; (01626) 821361; £3.90. The Toby Jug is useful for lunch.
☺ 🐎 **Blackawton** SX8050 WOODLAND LEISURE PARK (off the A3122) One of the best family days

---

Days Out

The Dart's changing moods
Totnes; South Devon Railway to Buckfastleigh (via Butterfly Park and Dartmoor Otter Sanctuary, after lunch at Kingsbridge Inn, Totnes); or river trip to Dartmouth (lunch there at Carved Angel, Billy Budds, the Cherub or Royal Castle, then a town walk along the coastal path, S from the castle, to Bolt Tail and Bolt Head).

Family fun in Torquay
Torquay – model village, Cockington, then lunch at Hole in the Wall (Park Lane); Kents Cavern.

Teign landscapes below a Lutyens masterpiece
Walk along the Teign at Fingle Bridge; Chagford – lunch at Ring o' Bells (or treat yourself at Gidleigh Park); Drewsteignton – Castle Drogo, Spinster's Rock.

Dartmoor ponies, Uncle Tom Cobbleigh and all
Miniature Pony Centre, North Bovey; Widecombe in the Moor; lunch at the Rock, Haytor Vale; strolls from the road to Hound Tor and Haytor Rocks; North Bovey and Lustleigh villages – cream tea at Moorwood Cottage, Lustleigh.

out in Devon, especially for children who like to run around and let off steam. A highlight is the Twister, an exhilarating, spiralling and plunging water-coaster (be prepared to get wet), and there are lots of well thought out play areas, inc several for younger children. Also a honey farm with millions of bees behind glass, tractor yard, and a small zoo with wallabies, llamas and foreign birds. The parkland also has quieter areas for woodland walks. Meals, snacks, shop, disabled access; cl Nov–Feb; (01803) 712598; £4.50. The Normandy Arms is a decent pub.

⚘ 🐝 **Bovey Tracey** SX8078 An unassuming, small, Dartmoor-edge town; the Devon Guild of Craftsmen have a good, varied CRAFT CENTRE at Riverside Mill (cl winter bank hols; £1.25 for exhibitions). TEIGN VALLEY GLASS & HOUSE OF MARBLES (Pottery Rd) Demonstrations of glass-blowing at a factory specialising in marbles, with a fantastic array of these in its museum. Meals, snacks, shop, disabled access; cl Christmas; (01626) 835358; free. The LOWERDOWN POTTERY (off the B3344) does fine decorated pottery; it's open by appointment only, (01626) 833408; free. The Cromwell Arms does generous food.

✝ **Brentor** SX4780 CHURCH (above the back road Lydford–Tavistock, just S of North Brentor) 12th-c, one of England's smallest churches, notable for its lonely hilltop position with remarkable coast and Dartmoor views.

★ ♣ ✾ **Brixham** SX9256 Busy fishing port, perhaps the prettiest of the Riviera resorts, with some attractive narrow streets on the hill above. Lots of activity (and summer seaside shops and cafés) in the harbour, inc (for no apparent reason) a full-size reconstruction of Drake's *Golden Hind*, and summer boats around Tor Bay. The local history MUSEUM (Bolton Cross) has something of a maritime emphasis (cl Sun, and Nov–Easter; £1.20). The quaint Quayside Inn is handy for lunch, and Shoalstone beach nr here has some of the cleanest bathing water in the UK.

✝ ♓ ✤ 🦋 🚌 ➧ **Buckfastleigh** SX7367
BUCKFAST ABBEY Originally established in 1018 but after the Dissolution of the Monasteries left abandoned until 1882, when it was refounded by 4 remarkable monks, who then did most of the rebuilding work themselves over a period of 32 years. It's now one of the most visited religious sites in Britain, with an interesting exhibition, and several services each day. An excellent shop sells not just their own famous honey, but goods produced at other Benedictine monasteries around Europe, inc Bavarian beer, French cakes and Irish linen; many people feel this alone is worth a special journey. Good meals and snacks, disabled access; guided tours (01364) 642519; church free, exhibition 75p (and you may have to pay £1 to park). SOUTH DEVON RAILWAY GWR steamtrain trips through lovely, unspoilt scenery along the wooded River Dart (some of which is hard to see any other way). It now stops just outside Totnes as well as at Staverton, and they do tickets combining it with a Dartmouth–Totnes river trip. Usually every 1½ hours in summer, less often other times; open daily Easter hols and from mid-May to mid-Oct, best to check dates in between; (01364) 642338 for timetable; £6. The Dartbridge opposite is a popular family dining pub. The train calls at the BUTTERFLY PARK AND DARTMOOR OTTER SANCTUARY (Dart Bridge Rd), where you can watch otters swimming and playing from an underwater viewing tunnel, or see them on land in the 4 big landscaped enclosures; summer feeding times 11.30am, 2pm and 4.30pm. Also an undercover tropical garden with free-flying butterflies and moths. Meals, snacks, shop, disabled access; cl Nov–Feb; (01364) 642916; £4.45. PENNYWELL FARM CENTRE 🅿 (Lower Dean, off the A38 just S) Friendly and unfussy, with over 750 animals in 80 acres, as well as lovely scenery, wildlife viewing hides, and falconry demonstrations. Different events every half-hour, from milking and feeding to ferret-

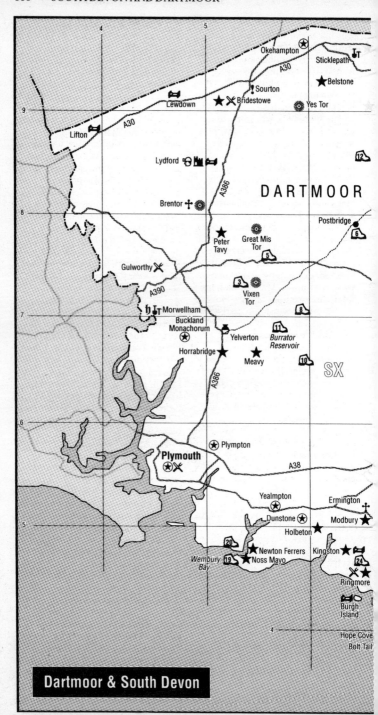

Dartmoor & South Devon

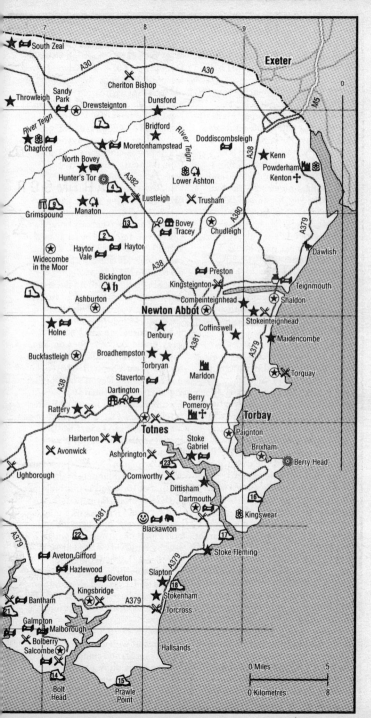

racing and worm-charming, so always something for children to get involved in. Meals, snacks, shop, disabled access; cl Nov–Mar (exc Feb half-term and Dec wknds); (01364) 642023; £4.95.

Buckland Monachorum SX4868 BUCKLAND ABBEY ⊞ The home of Francis Drake until his death in 1596, and of his family until 1946. They still have the famous drum said to sound whenever England is in danger, as well as craft workshops, herb knot garden, good walks, and entertaining summer activities for children. In Aug, for a small extra charge, you can play bowls on the lawn. Meals, snacks, shop, disabled access to ground floor only; cl Thurs, and Nov–Mar exc pm wknds; (01822) 853607; £4.30, £2.20 grounds only; NT. GARDEN HOUSE (towards Crapstone) Profusion of unusual plants beautifully laid out in a warm garden sheltered by the picturesque, partly ruined walls of former abbey buildings. They recently added a spring garden, quarry garden, rhododendron walk and wild flower meadow. Interesting plant sales, teas Apr–Sept; cl Nov–Feb; (01822) 854769; £3.50. The Drake's Manor is good for lunch. **Burgh Island** SX6443 Connected at low tide by a causeway to Bigbury-on-Sea (undistinguished for much save its clean sandy beaches); spectacular cliffs on the seaward side, a true island and quite remote-seeming when the tide's in. At high tide an odd giant tractor-on-stilts wades back and forth with passengers. The Pilchard is a quaint seaview pub, and you can windsurf or fish nearby.

★ **Chagford** SX7087 A large village, quite busy, and an attractive jumping-off point for the moor; even the bank is thatched, and the 2 old-fashioned general stores are fun. The Ring o' Bells is good for lunch, and the Bullers Arms is useful too. You can stroll round the lovely grounds of a luxury country house hotel GIDLEIGH PARK (see **Where to stay** section above) with colourful woodland walks and watergarden,

and immaculate more formal gardens. Excellent lunches, cream teas; cl bank hols and wknds; 50p.

★ **Chudleigh** SX8679 Despite the 1807 fire which destroyed lots of the buildings, this is a pleasant old wool town with pretty cottages in narrow, winding lanes. ROCK GARDEN AND CAVE 3 acres of wild gardens, populated by a good range of birds and wildlife. The cave has some interesting calcite formations, and from the pretty neighbouring waterfall it's a short walk up Chudleigh Rock for dramatic vistas of the surrounding countryside and moors. Snacks, nursery, craft shop, disabled access to nursery only; cl Christmas, and some bits may be cl in winter; (01626) 852134; *£2. You can arrange abseiling or caving on (01626) 852717. UGBROOKE PARK (just SE, off the A380) An interesting early example of the work of Robert Adam, in lovely Capability Brown parkland. Delightfully informal guided tours (2pm and 3.45pm). Teas, disabled access; open pm Sun, Tues, Weds, Thurs and bank hols mid-July–early Sept; (01626) 852179; £4.20. Devon's only organic VINEYARD can be visited at Farmborough House on Old Exeter St; cl Sun, and Oct–Easter, shop open all yr; (01626) 853258; £1.50 inc tastings (refundable against wine purchases).

Dartington SX8062 CIDER PRESS CRAFT CENTRE (Shinners Bridge) Cluster of 16th- and 17th-c buildings with craft shops, farm foods, herbs and such, and restaurants, inc a good vegetarian one. The surroundings add a lot to the attraction, with a nearby medieval Great Hall on a photogenic lawned courtyard, sculpture gardens, and a streamside nature trail. Disabled access; cl Suns Christmas–Easter; (01803) 864171; free. The Cott, excellent for lunch, is close by.

Dawlish SX9676 Old-fashioned small resort with modern developments and campsites outside; red sandstone cliffs, good beach, waterside parks with black swans, a small summer museum, promenade and pier; the mainline railway cut through the cliffs right by the water is striking. DAWLISH WARREN SX9879 Sandy grassy spit (with golf course) largely blocking in the Exe estuary, with glistening tidal flats full of wading birds, and dunes with some rare plants. In summer get well out to the point, to avoid the crowds and caravan parks at the station end; in winter it's splendidly wild and blowy, with thousands of ducks, brent geese and waders (even avocets) congregating at high tide to wait till the mudflats show again. Free, but they do guided summer nature walks for about £1.50; (01626) 863980 for times. The Mount Pleasant out here has decent food.

★ 🏰 🐝 ✿ 🏛 **Drewsteignton** SX7390 Above the charming village is the impressive granite CASTLE DROGO, designed by Lutyens and built earlier this century as a bizarre and brilliantly inventive mixture of medieval style and 20th-c luxury, with cunningly disguised radiators and amazing details even in the kitchen and lavatory. Lovely grounds with yew hedges form an outer barbican. Good guided walks through the surrounding woodland, and super views – it's 275 metres (900ft) up overlooking the gorge of the River Teign. Meals, snacks, shop; cl Nov–Easter, plus castle cl Fri (though garden, shop and tearoom still open); (01647) 433306; £4.90, garden and grounds only £2.30; NT. A well signposted minor road W of the village takes you to SPINSTER'S ROCK, a well preserved Neolithic burial chamber and the most easily accessible prehistoric feature in the area.

🐖 🦋 ✦ **Dunstone** SX5951 NATIONAL SHIRE HORSE CENTRE 🖼 Good, fine-weather family outing, with around 40 shire horses and foals, waggon rides, smithy and saddlery, butterfly house, falconry displays (pm only), adventure playground and pets corner. Meals, snacks, shop and craft centre, disabled access; cl 24–26 Dec; (01752) 880268; *£5.50, reduced rates and displays in winter. The Dartmoor Union in Holbeton is quite

handy for lunch, and the road from there to Noss Mayo has fine views.

★ 🏺 🍺 👹 † **Kingsbridge** SX7344 Small town of character, with pretty cobbled lanes diving off steep Fore St, arcaded shops, a pillared market house (market day Weds), interesting monuments in the church, boats on the tidal estuary (and ferry to Salcombe); the waterfront Crabshell is very popular for seafood. In a 17th-c grammar school, the COOKWORTHY MUSEUM (Fore St) re-opens in May after a major refurbishment; from then it will be cl Sun, and all Nov–Mar; (01548) 853235; £1.70. At the head of the nearby creek, pretty South Pool SX7740 has a fairly interesting CHURCH, with a delightfully ghoulish story attached, and a good pub.

🐝 **Kingswear** (3m E, off the Lower Ferry Rd at Tollhouse) SX8851 COLETON FISHACRE D'Oyly Carte's romantic and lush subtropical garden, with 20 colourful acres dropping down to a pretty cove; formal terraces, a walled garden with stream-fed ponds, unusual trees and shrubs, grassy woodland paths. Snacks, shop, limited disabled access; open Weds, Thurs, Fri and Sun Apr–Nov, plus bank hols and pm Sun in Mar; (01803) 752466; £3.30; NT. More ambitious marked paths beyond the gardens take you along the cliffs, showing how wild this part was before the garden was planted. See Paignton entry above for the Dart Valley Railway. The Ship is quite useful for lunch.

🐝 🐟 **Lower Ashton** SX8484 CANONTEIGN FALLS AND COUNTRY PARK Pleasant country park covering 80 acres of ancient woodland, with a spectacularly high waterfall; also lakes, wildfowl, miniature horses, and children's commando course. Meals, snacks, shop; cl mid-Nov–Mar (exc Sun and Feb half-term); (01647) 252434; *£3.50. The Manor pub in the village is useful for lunch (no children inside).

🖐 🏰 **Lydford** SX5184 LYDFORD GORGE 🖼 Spectacular gorge formed by the River Lyd cutting into the rock, causing boulders to scoop out potholes in the bed of the stream. Walks along the ravine take you to dramatic sights such as the White Lady Waterfall and the Devil's Cauldron whirlpool (summer crowds around this bit). Children like it but need to be watched carefully, and paths can be narrow and slippery. Snacks (in ingeniously designed tearoom), shop; most parts cl winter; (01822) 820441; £3.10; NT. The forbidding ruined CASTLE has a daunting 12th-c stone keep, its upper floor once used as a court, and the lower part as a prison; free. The Castle Inn is very good.

★ **Manaton** SX7581 A pretty village, with the private riverside woodland around BECKY FALLS 🈯 (off the B3344 to Bovey Tracey) useful enough for undemanding family walks if you don't plan to take advantage of the countryside proper. Meals, snacks, shop, some disabled access; cl Nov–mid-Mar (exc wknds, weather permitting); (01647) 221259; £2.75. The prettily placed Kestor has decent food.

🏰 **Marldon** SX8664 COMPTON CASTLE (1m N, off the A3022; or off the A381 at Ipplepen turnoff) Formidably fortified and rather picturesque 14th- and 16th-c manor around a courtyard with portcullised entrance, particularly interesting for its completeness. The exterior was used as Willoughby's house in the recent film of *Sense and Sensibility*. Very limited disabled access; open Mon, Weds and Thurs Apr–Oct, cl 12.15–2pm; (01803) 873314; £2.70; NT. The Church House Inn is handy for lunch.

★ **Modbury** SX6551 Attractive buildings especially in steep Church St, with a photogenic church at the top and pretty Exeter Inn at the bottom. Brownston St is quite interesting too, especially the ornate water conduit at the top.

� ṫ) **Morwellham** SX4469 MORWELLHAM QUAY Thriving and meticulously researched open-air museum in lovely countryside, with costumed guides convincingly re-creating the boom years when Morwellham was the greatest copper

port in the Empire. The restored cottages come complete with pigs in the backyard, and you can watch the work of a blacksmith, cooper, coachmen and quay workers. Also rides into the mines, horse-drawn carriages, and lovely walks. Very popular in school hols – a visit can easily last all day. Meals, snacks, shop; cl 24 Dec–2 Jan; (01822) 832766; £7.90 (reduced price and operations in winter). The Ship (part of the centre) is good, with period-costumed waitresses and traditional drinks.

🏰 🐾 🏠 **Newton Abbot** SX8671 A working town rather than a holiday centre, but several interesting places here or nearby. TUCKERS MALTINGS (Teign Rd) One of the few remaining working malthouses in the country, and the only one open to the public – every year they produce enough malt for 15 million pints of beer. Tours show all aspects of malting (you can touch the grain and taste the malt), and they've recently set up their own brewery. There's a hands-on section for children. Meals, snacks, shop; last guided tour starts 3pm (3.45p July–Sept and bank hols); cl Nov–Easter, exc by arrangement; (01626) 334734; £3.95 (inc sample of beer). PLANT WORLD (St Marychurch Rd, Coffinswell) Unusual 4-acre garden built and planted as a giant map of the world, with the countries containing their correct native plants, trees and flowers – many of them quite rare in this country, but flourishing in the mild Devon climate. Also has a plant centre (with seeds of some of the rarest plants), an old-fashioned English garden and fine views from the picnic area. Cl Weds; (01803) 872939; *£1. The Linny is a charming, old, thatched pub. BRADLEY MANOR (off the A381 S) Peaceful 15th-c house, nr a stream through extensive wood-fringed grounds, quiet walks. Open pm Weds Apr–Sept; £2.60; NT. ORCHID PARADISE (Forches Cross, A382 N) Colourful place, with lots of rare and endangered species in elaborate indoor reconstructions of their natural habitats. Snacks, nursery and shop, disabled access (but no facilities); cl winter bank hols; (01626) 52233; £1.50.

★ Newton Ferrers/Noss Mayo SX5447 Picturesque twin villages on a very sheltered, rocky and wooded creek of the Yealm estuary; besides modern development, there are some attractive whitewashed cottages. Lots of yachting in summer. The Old Ship, Dolphin and Swan are all pleasant places for lunch.

★ 🐴 North Bovey SX7483 A delightful, peaceful spot, not usually invaded by tourists: oak-shaded green with mounting block, stone cross, pump, ancient cottages and an attractive pub. MINIATURE PONY CENTRE 🎫 (Wormhill Farm) Lots of friendly and engaging tiny ponies, happy to give children steady rides. Also bigger horses, pigs, donkeys and chipmunks, bird garden, and a good adventure playground. The setting is lovely. Meals, snacks, shop, good disabled access; cl Nov–Mar; (01647) 432400; £4.50.

🏰 👃🏻 🐾 Okehampton SX5895 This Dartmoor-edge working town has a couple of things worth stopping for. The CASTLE tower on a steep grassy mound above the river is remarkable above all for the way it stays standing – a balancing act of ruined masonry zigzagging up into the sky. It's the biggest medieval castle in Devon, with sections dating from the 11th to the 14th c; good woodland walks. Snacks, shop; cl all Nov–Mar; (01837) 52844; £2.20. MUSEUM OF DARTMOOR LIFE (West St) Well converted old watermill with interactive displays on local life, Tourist Information Centre and working craft studios next door. Tearoom, shop, some disabled access; cl Sat exc Easter–Oct, and Sun exc Jun–Sept – best to check winter opening; (01837) 52295; £1.60.

🏚 🎫 ★ Plympton SX5255 SALTRAM (2m W, off the A38/A379 at Marsh Mills roundabout) Magnificent, mostly 18th-c mansion still with pretty much all the original contents, and especially notable for its unaltered Robert Adam rooms.

Georgian furnishings, decoration and paintings (strong on Reynolds, who as a regular guest advised on which other pictures to buy), interesting period kitchen, stately garden with orangery, and parkland by the wooded Plym estuary. The house has attracted lots of extra visitors since starring as Norland Park in *Sense and Sensibility*. Meals, snacks, shop, local art/crafts gallery, disabled access; house cl am, Fri, Sat, and all Nov–Mar; (01752) 336546; £5.30, garden only £2.50; NT. The old town around St Maurice Church is worth a look if you're here: attractive, partly arcaded streets, a very ruined motte and bailey castle, and decent food at the George.

🏰 🎫 Powderham SX9683 CASTLE 🎫 The ancestral home of the Earls of Devon, badly damaged in the Civil War but elaborately restored in the 18th and 19th c. The richly decorated state rooms were used in the film *The Remains of the Day*. Spectacular rose garden, home to Timothy the 155-year-old tortoise, spring woodland garden, and a broad deer park with views over the Exe estuary. Good guided tours and lots of special events. Meals, snacks, shop, some disabled access; cl Sat, and Nov–Easter; (01626) 890243; £4.95. The ancient waterside Anchor has good seafood.

★ 🎣 👃🏻 🎫 ❋ Salcombe SX7338 Steep fishing village with narrow streets, full of enjoyable holiday bustle in summer; lots of souvenirs, bric-a-brac, boating shops, teashops and pubs overlooking the sea, nearby beaches and coves. Also BOAT TRIPS and boat hire. Besides Foot in the Plate and Spinnaker restaurants, the Ferry, Victoria and Fortescue are all popular for food. OVERBECKS SX7237 (South Sands; also signed from Malborough) Named after the eccentric research chemist who lived here until 1937; among his possessions and inventions you can still see the Rejuvenator which he claimed 'practically renewed' his youth. For most the chief attraction is the luscious subtropical gardens, with terraced plantings among woodland, many rarities and plenty of palms and citrus fruits; outstanding in late May–Jun for the magnolias, but worth a trip any time of year. Glorious views out to sea, also a colourful statue garden, picnic belvedere and collections of dolls and lead soldiers. Snacks, shop; cl Sat and Nov–Mar; (01548) 842893; £3.60, £2.40 garden only; NT. Mill Bay nr here has one of the area's safest bathing beaches.

★ ➤ ✿ ❀ **Shaldon** SX9372 Interesting and colourful mix of seaside houses spanning 200 years of architectural fancy; some lovely corners especially down by the water away from the centre, also much older cottages in Crown Sq. The Clifford Arms has good local fish. High, grassy, sandstone Ness overlooks the sea and Teignmouth, with a tunnel cut by the 19th-c landowner to a sheltered beach; the beautifully set Ness House up here is useful for food. WILDLIFE TRUST (Ness Drive) Nicely low-key breeding collection of rare and endangered foreign birds, and small mammals inc monkeys; cl 25 Dec, 1 Jan; (01626) 872234; *£2.50. The BOTANIC GARDENS are pleasant, with lots of rare shrubs and trees and nice views; free. The A379 to Maidencombe has sea views.

! **Sourton** SX5390 HIGHWAYMAN An extraordinary pub, one bar recalling a galleon, the other a sort of fairy-tale fantasy, and the garden demonstrates yet more exuberant imagination – all meticulously done by the owners, not some brewery theme pub.

↓⊤ **Sticklepath** SX6494 MUSEUM OF WATERPOWER AND FINCH FOUNDRY No longer producing the sickles, shovels and tools for which it was known in the 19th c, but the waterwheels and machinery are all still working. Snacks, shop, disabled access; cl Tues, and Nov–Mar; (01837) 840046; £2.50; NT. The thatched Devonshire Inn in the village is good value.

★ **Stoke Gabriel** SX8457 Steep village above a sheltered side-pool of the Dart estuary, with a 14th-c church (with ancient yew) and

Church House (pleasant for lunch) perched prettily on a high cobbled terrace.

♨ **Teignmouth** SX9473 A popular resort for family holidays, with good beaches, windsurfing and so on, some handsome 19th-c streets and active docks, and a decent local history MUSEUM (cl Oct–Apr; £1). The beach-side Ship has enjoyable food all day in summer.

★ ⊤ **Widecombe in the Moor** SX7176 One of the most visited villages on Dartmoor, immortalised by the trip of Uncle Tom Cobbleigh and all to Widecombe Fair. The granite-carved village sign shows them all crowded on to their old grey mare. The CHURCH, known as the Cathedral of the Moors, has a distinctive, disproportionately high tower. The adjoining 16th-c CHURCH HOUSE is worth a look; open pm Tues and Thurs Jun–mid-Sept; free. Next door, the SEXTON'S COTTAGE is a NT and Dartmoor National Park information centre and gift shop; cl Jan–mid-Feb. The Post Office Stores has good ice-cream and local honey. The reconstructed Olde Inne in the village is very popular with tourists, but for more of a Tom Cobbleigh flavour try the Rugglestone Inn just S. The SHILSTONE ROCKS RIDING CENTRE organises horse-riding over Dartmoor, beginners welcome. Disabled access; (01364) 621281; from £12 an hour.

♻ ♧ ⚘ **Yealmpton** SX5751 KITLEY CAVES Tours of stunning illuminated caves, and above ground 50 acres of pretty woodland and riverside walks. Lots of varieties of plants, shrubs and trees, and displays on the creator of Old Mother Hubbard, who lived here. Snacks, shop; cl Nov–Mar; (01752) 880885; £3.50. The Rose & Crown does decent food. Nearby is a good farm shop, and seasonal PICK-YOUR-OWN fruit and veg (inc courgettes, spinach and pumpkins).

⚘ **Yelverton** SX5267 PAPERWEIGHT CENTRE (Buckland Terrace) Odd collection of over 800 glass paperweights, all sizes and designs, inc collector's pieces. Shop, disabled access; cl Sun (exc late May–mid-

Sept), and Nov–Mar exc Sat and pm Weds; (01822) 854250; free. The Rock (A386) is a good family pub.
★ One of the most **attractive villages** in the whole of England is Lustleigh SX7881, with charming riverside walks in utterly unspoilt woodland around it, or up to Hunter's Tor on Dartmoor. Primrose Cottage is hotly tipped for cream teas, and the Cleave Inn is good. Other noteworthy ones – all with worthwhile pubs – include Belstone SX6293, Bridestowe SX5189, Bridford SX8186, Broadhempston SX8066, Coffinswell SX8968, Combeinteignhead SX9071 (besides the Wild Goose in the village, the waterside Coombe Cellars is outstanding for families), Denbury SX8168, Dittisham SX8654, Dunsford SX8189 (traditional cider-making in summer), Harberton SX7758, Holbeton SX6150, Holne SX7069, Horrabridge SX5169, Kenn SX9285 (charming church), Kingston SX6347, Maidencombe SX9268, Meavy SX5467 (pronounced 'Mewy' locally; the parish still owns the pub), Moretonhampstead SX7585 (less secluded than the others, but more to see), Peter Tavy SX5177, Rattery SX7461, Ringmore SX6545, South Zeal SX6593, Stokeinteignhead SX9170, Stokenham SX8042 (sea views from the Stoke Fleming road), Throwleigh SX6690 and Torbryan SX8266 (unusual church). Slapton SX8244 and Stoke Fleming SX8648 have some of the best beaches in the country.
† **Other good churches** at Ermington SX6353, where there's a crooked, 14th-c stone spire above the tower (Victorian rebuilding kept the tilt; the B3210 from Totnes is pretty, the First & Last an attractive pub), and Kenton SX9583, its harmonious medieval sandstone masonry photographing well against a blue sky; fine carving inside.

Walks

Dartmoor is outstanding for walking, but mist can come down very suddenly, so on the open moor you must carry a compass. A lot of the moor is a long way from the road, hence rather inaccessible. There are more paths for walkers than the right-of-way network suggests, but don't assume a right of way marked on the OS map will be visible on the ground (the black dashed lines on these maps are generally more reliable). Old mineral railways and cart tracks make for some good walkers' routes. There are plenty of things to head for, to give a moorland walk a sense of purpose – most obviously, one of the many tors of naked rock rising out of the moor (beware: the rounded rocks can be a good deal more slippery than they look).

Among the finest paths is **Dr Blackall's Drive** ▵-1 from Bel Tor Corner to New Bridge: this specially created carriage drive gives splendid views of the Dart Valley.

The fortress-like collection of **Haytor Rocks** SX7577 ▵-2 make a striking and popular objective; nearby is an abandoned quarry served by an unusual 19th-c tramway with grooved-granite rails. In this same general area, the majestically monumental Hound Tor SX7478 is usually quieter, with an interesting, excavated, abandoned, medieval village nearby. Honeybag Tor SX7278 close by has marvellous views over Widecombe (though not shown on the OS map, there's a path to it along the spine of the ridge). A bit further N is the quaint Bowerman's Nose SX7480 looking snootily out over a patchwork of pastures.

In the W, the **Vixen Tor** SX5474 ▵-3 towering up from the bracken looks unclimbable, but is quite easily reached from behind; this area of the Walkham Valley is relatively lush and green, with old railway tracks from mineral lines which once served local quarries. Nr Lustleigh SX7881, a ridge path to

Hunter's Tor SX7682 ⌂-4 gives panoramic views of Lustleigh Cleave and the Bovey Valley. Up in the lonelier northern part of the moor, **Yes Tor** SX5890 and **Great Mis Tor** SX5676 ⌂-5 have great views over the moor. This is the highest terrain in southern England though, as throughout this northern area, access is often barred by army firing practice.

Two attractive, popular and easy-to-reach ancient packhorse **clapper bridges** ⌂-6 are those by the roads at Postbridge SX6478 and Dartmeet SX6773 – good centrepieces for strolling. From the Angler's Rest at **Fingle Bridge** SX7499 ⌂-7 there's a lovely 'Fisherman's Path' by a wooded stretch of the River Teign; you can return at high level on the 'Hunter's Path', passing nr Castle Drogo and gaining tremendous views. A path along the gently graded **Devonport Leat** ⌂-8 (a watercourse first engineered 200 years ago to give Devonport a water supply), in the western moors, takes in some remote scenery and makes getting lost quite difficult; it's easily reached off the B3212 NE of Yelverton.

Hundreds of ancient sites exist, but the large majority of those on the OS maps are invisible to all but the most astute archaeologist. One of the most impressive is by a stream at **Grimspound** SX7080 ⌂-9, with a fine old lichened granite cross nearby to mark the way for later medieval travellers; great views from the round walk to Widecombe. The upper valley of the **River Plym** SX5866 ⌂-10 has numerous visible hut circles, stone rows and cairns.

The **Burrator Reservoir** SX5567 ⌂-11 gives a 5-mile walk in beautiful woodland and moorland surroundings (Sheepstor church on the way has interesting memorials to the Brookes family, former rajahs of Sarawak). The open moorland expanses of **Shovel Down** ⌂-12 harbour some of Dartmoor's richest concentrations of antiquities. You'll need a map just to find the car park at Scorhill SX660877, SW of Gidleigh and W of Chagford; from there, a path brings you out on to the moor within sight of Scorhill stone circle. Close by are stone slab bridges over clear brooks; among the litter of rocks by one river is the Teign Tolmen, a natural boulder through which the water has gouged a perfectly circular hole. You can walk over to nearby Kes Tor, close to which is the Long Stone and a fine stone row of about 2500–1500BC. **Yarner Wood** SX7778 ⌂-13 nr Bovey Tracey is a National Nature Reserve and still has a good nature trail, despite hundreds of acres nearby being torched by arsonists in Spring 1997.

Another approach to Dartmoor walking is to use a pub or hotel as a starting- or finishing-point. The Tors at Belstone SX6293, Peter Tavy Inn SX5177, Elephant's Rest at Horndon SX5280, Forest Hotel at Hexworthy SX6572, East Dart Hotel at Postbridge SX6579, Warren House SX6780 E of there, Plume of Feathers in Princetown SX5873, Dartmoor Inn at Merrivale SX5475 and the Two Bridges Hotel at Two Bridges SX6175 are all right on the moor; and the Rock at Haytor Vale SX7677, Church House at Holne SX7069, the Tavistock at Poundsgate SX7072, Devonshire Inn at Sticklepath SX6494, the Highwayman at Sourton SX5390, Tradesmans Arms at Scorriton SX7068, Oxenham Arms Hotel at South Zeal SX6593 and the Northmore Arms at Wonson SX6789 are on the edges.

The finest part of Devon's south coast for walkers is between Plymouth SX4755 and Brixham SX9256 – much of it quite unspoilt. In summer, ferries cross the rivers (except the River Erme S of Ermington SX6353, which you have to cross at low tide). **Bolt Head/Bolt Tail** ⌂-14 is 6 miles of one of the best coastal path sections, with remote exposed clifftops, glorious coves, far views, and well preserved Iron Age earth ramparts on Bolt Tail; all NT. Best access is via Overbecks SX7237, Soar Mill Cove SX7037 or Hope Cove SX6739. **Prawle Point** SX7735 ⌂-15, further E, also has impressive scenery: wind-blasted gorse, grass and thrift above low but fierce cliffs, lending itself to a round walk, with a useful network of green lanes leading inland to the village of East Prawle SX7836 (good food at the Freebooters Arms).

Scabbacombe Head ⌂-16 is more of the same – a rewarding day's walk from Brixham SX9256 to Kingswear SX8851, 12 miles of stunning wild scenery (and some steep climbs), passing the oasis of Coleton Fishacre gardens. Dartmouth Castle and **Compass Cove** SX8849 ⌂-17 make an enjoyable milder excursion, though the immediate hinterland is unremarkable.

Slapton Sands ⌂-18 are 6 miles of almost straight shingle N of the lighthouse at Start Point SX8337, backed by hills in the S and by road, shingle bank, lake (Slapton Ley nature reserve, with a marked nature trail) and marsh, then low cliffs, in the N. Good for out-of-season desolation, sheltered from westerly winds, with a storm-ruined village at Hallsands SX8138, and a salvaged tank memorial to a US Normandy landings practice disaster at Torcross SX8242.

There are attractive walks by the wooded **Yealm estuary** ⌂-19 from Noss Mayo SX5447, then beyond to Gara Point SX5246 and exposed cliff; largely NT. This can be reached in sections via the Noss Mayo–Holbeton coastal ridge road. **Wembury Bay** ⌂-20 gives fine views, starting from Wembury SX5248, past the church at the start of NT clifftops; woods and pastures on opposite shore, Plymouth shipping in the distance.

Bantham Sands ⌂-21 allow a gentle walk from Bantham SX6643 through dunes (good picnic spots) to the broad stretch of rivermouth sand facing Burgh Island. You can go on above the rocks S, for views of Bolt Tail and the coves between.

Other worthwhile places for walks include **Loddiswell** SX7248 ⌂-22 (cross the river by the lane towards Woodleigh, then a quiet walk upstream by riverside pastures and woods towards Topsham Bridge); **Tuckenhay** SX8156 ⌂-23 (a pretty mile E along wooded Bow Creek from the Maltsters Arms – good food here); and **Kingston** SX6347 ⌂-24 (several walks down to an unspoilt beach). The Church House at Meavy SX5467 and the Skylark at Clearbrook SX5265 are pleasantly handy for the wooded River Meavy.

Where to eat

Ashprington SX8156 Durant Arms (01803) 732240 Friendly, gable-ended dining pub under new ownership; with 2 attractive bar rooms, family room, good, changing food, well kept beers, and pleasant service. £15.99|£5.25.

Avonwick SX7157 Avon Inn (01364) 73475 Popular dining pub with comfortable, fairly modern furnishings, a wide range of good food inc lots of interesting pasta dishes, plenty of fish, and lovely puddings; decent Italian wines, well kept real ales, and a pleasant riverside garden; restaurant cl winter pm Sun, pm Mon, 1 wk Jan. £20|£6.50.

Bantham SX6643 Sloop (01548) 560489 Nr a sandy beach (good for surfing), this 16th-c nautical village inn has nice bar food inc lots of fish, hearty breakfasts, and decent beers and wines; also self-catering cottages. £14|£5.45.

Bolberry SX6939 Port Light (01548) 561384 Popular even on dismal winter weekdays, this clifftop former RAF radar station (easy walk from Hope Cove) is warm and friendly with good home-made food in both the attractive bar and restaurant; super sea views, woodburning stove, and an outdoor children's play area; bedrooms; cl Tues in early part of year, cl Jan; disabled access. £19.95|£5.95.

Bridestowe SX5189 White Hart (01837) 861318 Friendly 17th-c village inn with consistently good food in the pleasant restaurant, and sound bar food too; bedrooms; fishing nearby; no children in bar (allowed in restaurant). £22|£4.50.

Cheriton Bishop SX7793 Old Thatch (01647) 24204 Welcoming 16th-c inn with good bar food from a big menu, interesting puddings, and friendly service; bedrooms. £16|£3.

Cornworthy SX8255 HUNTERS LODGE (01803) 732204 Quietly friendly country local, with a cottagey log-fire restaurant, popular bar food, well kept real ales, and tables on the big lawn. £24l£4.85.

Dartmouth SX8751 CARVED ANGEL 2 South Embankment (01803) 832465 Black and white timbered restaurant, airy and attractive, overlooking the quay, with wonderful meals using carefully chosen, absolutely fresh produce – superb fish, delicious puddings and lovely cheeses; fine wines in every price range, and a smart yet friendly atmosphere; no smoking; cl pm Sun, Mon, 6 wks from 1 Jan; children under 5 free. £52.50 dinner, £36.50 lunch.

Dartmouth SX8751 CHERUB 10 Higher St (01804) 832571 Interesting seafood specialities in one of Dartmouth's most ancient and picturesque buildings. Children in upstairs restaurant only. £23l£7.50.

Gulworthy SX4472 HORN OF PLENTY A390 just W of Tavistock (01822) 832528 On the edge of Dartmoor in quiet, flower-filled gardens, this relaxed Georgian restaurant has excellent, carefully cooked food using top quality local produce, inc lovely puddings and cheeses; wonderful breakfasts too, a good wine list, warm and friendly service, and a vine-covered terrace for aperitifs; comfortable bedrooms; cl am Mon, 25–26 Dec; children over 13, though any age allowed Sun lunch; disabled access. £35.50 dinner, £24 lunch.

Harberton SX7758 CHURCH HOUSE (01803) 863707 Ancient village pub with magnificent medieval panelling, and attractive old furnishings; generous helpings of interesting daily specials, well kept beers, and decent wines; children in family room; cl pm 25–26 Dec, 1 Jan. £14.75l£4.95.

Kingsbridge SX7344 CRABSHELL The Quay, Embankment Rd (01548) 852345 Famous old dining pub, very popular for its lovely waterside position and fresh local fish; quick, friendly staff, well kept real ales, decent wines, and a warm winter fire; disabled access. £20.25l£9.25.

Kingsteignton SX8773 OLD RYDON (01626) 54626 Cosy old pub with a wide choice of constantly changing, imaginative bar food; a winter log fire, well kept real ales, helpful service, and a prettily planted dining conservatory. £26 wknd, £19.65 wkdayl£6.40.

Lustleigh SX7881 PRIMROSE COTTAGE (01647) 277365 Thatched cottage by the old village church, with seats in the riverside garden, clotted cream teas, and lovely home-made cakes and pastries; cl end Sept–Easter; partial disabled access; £4.95.

Plymouth SX4755 CHEZ NOUS 13 Frankfort Gate (01752) 266793 Informal and friendly French bistro with careful cooking of good local produce – especially fresh fish and fine puddings; some distinguished wines, and a friendly atmosphere; cl Sun, Mon, 3 wks Feb, 3 wks Sept; partial disabled access. £42.

Plymouth SX4755 CHINA HOUSE Sutton Harbour (via Sutton Rd off the A374) (01752) 260930 Well converted, 17th-c waterside warehouse above the marina; very lofty and spacious, with beams, log fire, flagstones and bare slate, nautical decorations, and a first-floor dining area which becomes an evening restaurant; good disabled access. £18l£6.45.

Rattery SX7461 CHURCH HOUSE (01364) 642220 One of Britain's oldest pubs, with big open fires, friendly customers and staff, good bar food, decent wines and beers, fine malt whiskies, and nice dog and cats; peaceful setting; disabled access. £14.50l£3.85.

Ringmore SX6545 JOURNEYS END (01548) 810205 Partly medieval inn in a pretty setting, with a thatched servery in the panelled bar, open fire, a warm and friendly welcome, well kept beer, and nice fresh food; good-value bedrooms; cl 3–6pm daily. £20l£4.50.

Salcombe SX7338 FOOT IN THE PLATE Russell Court (01548) 842189 Bustling and enjoyable evening restaurant with a relaxed atmosphere, a good choice of pasta and Greek dishes, and music from around the world; cl Nov–Feb; well behaved children welcome; disabled access. £16.50.

Salcombe SX7338 Spinnaker (01548) 843408 Relaxed waterside restaurant with good fresh local fish and shellfish (some meat also), lunchtime bar snacks, and nice puddings; cl pm Sun, Mon (open July and Aug then), winter Tues, early Nov–mid-Feb; children welcome lunchtime but over 5 after 7.30pm. £19.75|£5.

Stokeinteignhead SX9170 Church House (01626) 872475 Picturesque, 13th-c, thatched dining pub with friendly staff, carefully restored, characterful bar rooms, decent bar food, and well kept real ales; nice back garden with a little stream; disabled access. £16|£5.95.

Topsham SX9264 Georgian Tea Room Broadway House, 35 High St (01392) 873465 18th-c house, with pretty embroidered tablecloths and fresh flowers, offering lunchtime meals inc a dish of the day and a popular roast on Tues, Thurs and Sun; snacks too, as well as cream teas, home-made cakes and cookies, and a wide range of teas and coffees, home-made lemonade and so forth. £3.90.

Torcross SX8242 Start Bay (01548) 580553 Notable and very popular fresh seafood, generously served in a busy thatched pub overlooking the 3-mile pebble beach; farm cider; family room; partial disabled access. £10|£5.

Torquay SX9264 Mulberry Room 1 Scarborough Rd (01803) 213639 Popular no smoking restaurant, with interesting food using good local produce, and very enjoyable home-made cakes and scones for afternoon tea; cookery demonstrations; bedrooms; cl Mon, Tues; disabled access. £16.50|£5.50.

Torquay SX9264 The Table 135 Babbacombe Rd (01803) 324292 Pretty little restaurant in a white terraced house, with excellent modern cooking (lots of fish and shellfish), a relaxed atmosphere, super bread, and good-value wines; cl 4 wks during Feb/Mar; children over 12. £35|£7.50.

Totnes SX8060 Greys Dining Room 96 High St (01803) 866369 No smoking Georgian house, with pretty china on a handsome dresser and partly panelled walls; many types of tea inc herb and fruit ones, sandwiches, salads and omelettes, as well as lots of cakes and set teas; cl Weds; no pushchairs. £5.

Trusham SX8582 Cridford Inn (01626) 853694 Friendly, atmospheric pub with a fine, early medieval window in the bar (oldest domestic window in Britain), flagstones, and a big woodburning stove; no smoking restaurant with an 11th-c mosaic stone, particularly good and interesting food, well kept real ales, a short, thoughtful wine list, and a suntrapping front terrace. £26|£6.50.

Ugborough SX6755 Anchor (01752) 892283 Friendly pub, with oak beams and a log fire, and a wide choice of very good food, inc unusual things such as ostrich, alligator, emu and bison; lots of fresh fish also, courteous service, and well kept real ales. £16.95|£5.95.

NORTH DEVON AND EXMOOR

Outstanding coastal scenery, particularly below Exmoor; a few traditional resorts, but mainly relatively untouristy – charming places to visit and to stay in.

This part of Devon is relatively untouristy, as until recently road access has been poor; the A361 now gives good fast access – but the crowds haven't quite caught up yet. Outside the few resorts and the famously pretty Clovelly and Combe Martin, the area is largely untouched by tourism, with long stretches of coast which are empty even in summer. Even Ilfracombe, the main resort, is not too tripperish; it's pleasant and distinctive, with plenty for families, and stays active all year. The lower-key beach resorts such as Woolacombe and Westward Ho! go into mothballs when the season's over, their marvellous beaches then ideal for lonely walks; elsewhere there are fine bracing cliff walks.

Exmoor has excellent walking, less busy than Dartmoor in summer. In some places it's been more tamed than Dartmoor – drained and resown with richer-growing grasses for better pasture. But it's still a wild place, with hawthorns and low oak trees bent and gnarled by the winds, and (unlike Dartmoor) wild deer. Where it drops away sharply to the sea, fast streams and rivers cut deeply into beautiful wooded valleys. Villages here are all rewarding, but Selworthy stands out. It's good driving country, with plenty of open views; the B-roads are generally less congested. Other inland parts are largely secluded farmland; the twisty wooded Taw Valley (A377) is pretty.

Among a broad choice of interesting places to visit we'd pick out Arlington Court, Bickleigh Castle, the woodland gardens at Rosemoor near Torrington, and Knightshayes Court at Bolham; Lynton and Hartland Quay; and for children, the Big Sheep near Bideford and Gnome Reserve near Bradworthy.

Though part of Exmoor lies in Somerset, we've covered the whole of the moor area in this chapter (some places such as Dunster, within the boundary of the National Park but outside the moor itself, are described in the Somerset chapter).

Where to stay

Ashwater SX3895 BLAGDON MANOR Ashwater, Beaworthy EX21 5DF (01409) 211224 *£110; 7 pretty rms. Carefully restored and tranquil 17th-c manor in 8 acres, surrounded by rolling countryside; beams and flagstones, log fires, fresh flowers, lovely food in a dinner-party atmosphere, and kind staff; cl Christmas; no children.

Bishops Tawton SS5630 HALMPSTONE Bishops Tawton, Barnstaple EX32 0EA (01271) 830321 *£120, plus special breaks; 5 pretty rms. Quietly relaxing, small country hotel with a log fire in the comfortable sitting room, enjoyable food in the panelled dining room, good breakfasts, caring service; attractive garden, nice views; cl Nov–Jan; no children.

Buckland Brewer SS4220 COACH & HORSES Buckland Brewer, Bideford EX39 5LU (01237) 451395 *£45; 2 rms above bar (could be noisy for children until 11.30pm). Welcoming, well preserved, 13th-c thatched village pub with a cosy beamed bar, log fires in inglenook fireplaces, truly home-made enjoyable food, dining room, and pleasant garden; children over 8; no dogs; cl pm 25 Dec.

Cadbury SS9005 BEERS FARM Cadbury, Exeter EX5 5PY (01884) 855426 £32; 2 rms. Former farm in quiet countryside with fine views, and 3½ acres of garden and grounds; homely lounge, English breakfasts in the dining room, and packed lunches on request; no smoking.

Chittlehamholt SS6420 HIGHBULLEN Chittlehamholt, Umberleigh EX37 9HD (01769) 540561 £110 inc dinner, plus special breaks; 35 comfortable and elegant, often spacious rms in main building and various attractively converted outbuildings. Victorian 'gothick' mansion set in huge wooded parkland and gardens with lots of wildlife, fishing on various beats, 9-hole golf course, indoor tennis court and swimming pool, table tennis, and squash court; consistently good food in the intimate restaurant overlooking the valley, a busy little bar, library, and relaxed, informal service (no reception, you ring a bell and wait); children over 8; no dogs.

Clawton SX3599 COURT BARN Clawton, Holsworthy EX22 6PS (01409) 271219 *£70, plus special breaks; 8 individually furnished rms. Charming country house in 5 acres of pretty grounds with croquet, 9-hole putting green, small chip-and-putt course, and tennis and badminton courts; comfortable lounges, log fires, library/TV room, good service, imaginative food and award-winning wines (and teas), and a quiet, relaxed atmosphere; dogs allowed away from public rooms.

East Buckland SS6731 LOWER PITT East Buckland, Barnstaple EX32 0TD (01598) 760243 *£70; 3 comfortable rms. Quiet, pretty stone farmhouse with a log fire in the cosy lounge, good, well presented food using herbs and veg from their own garden, simply furnished dining room and attractive conservatory; friendly service; no children; cl 25–26 Dec.

Hatherleigh SS5404 TALLY HO Market St, Hatherleigh, Okehampton EX20 3JN (01837) 810306 £60; 3 rms. Friendly and interesting old inn with genuinely old-fashioned fittings, good food and own-brew beers.

Hawkridge SS8530 TARR STEPS Hawkridge, Dulverton, Somerset TA22 9PY; off the B3223 towards Hawkridge, N of Dulverton; (01643) 851293 *£90, plus special breaks; 11 rms, most with own bthrm. Former Georgian rectory in 11 acres of gardens, surrounded by 500 acres of land with rough shooting and trout-filled river, riding and clay-pigeon shooting; carefully refurbished and comfortable drawing room with log fires and flowers, an oak-panelled bar, good food in the attractive dining room (popular locally) using own organic vegetables, a relaxed atmosphere, and friendly staff; self-catering cottage also; disabled access; well behaved dogs.

Heddons Mouth SS6549 HEDDONS GATE Heddons Mouth, Parracombe, Barnstaple EX31 4PZ (01598) 763313 *£75, plus special breaks; 14 comfortable rms named for their original use and many with views. Victorian country house hotel in interesting large gardens on the edge of Exmoor; a marvellously relaxed and friendly atmosphere, refurbished sitting room with lovely views, pleasant library/Victorian morning room, and an attractive dining room; very good home cooking inc 6-course dinners and proper afternoon tea, and friendly, helpful service; cl 3 Nov–Easter; children welcome if able to eat at 8pm (no special meals for them); dogs welcome by prior arrangement; disabled access.

Horns Cross SS3823 LOWER WAYTOWN Horns Cross, Bideford EX39 5DN (01237) 451787 £43; 3 rms. Beautifully converted barn and roundhouse in 5 acres of grounds with ornamental waterfowl on stream-fed ponds; round sitting room with beams and inglenook fireplaces, and lovely breakfasts in the big dining room; no smoking; self-catering cottages; cl Nov–Easter; children over 12; partial disabled access.

Knowstone SS8223 MASONS ARMS Knowstone, South Molton EX36 4RY (01398) 341231 £55w; 5 rms. Delightfully unspoilt, 13th-c thatched pub with very individual character; relaxed and friendly service, good homely bar food, restaurant, decent wines and nice garden; nearby walks; cl Christmas; dogs welcome.

Lynmouth SS7249 RISING SUN Mars Hill, Lynmouth EX35 6EQ (01598) 753223 *£79; 16 comfortable and cosy rms. Historic, thatched 14th-c inn with lovely views over the little harbour and out to sea; an oak-panelled dining room, a beamed and panelled bar with uneven oak floors, good food and wines, a charming terraced garden, and lots of nearby walks; children over 8.

Lynton SS7149 Bear Hotel Lydiate Lane, Lynton EX35 6AJ (01598) 753391 £48, plus special breaks; 11 rms. Warm and friendly hotel with caring owners; 2 comfortable and very neatly kept lounges, a blazing log fire, and a remarkably varied menu for both breakfast and the candlelit dinners (quite a few vegetarian dishes, too).

Lynton SS7149 HIGHCLIFFE HOUSE Sinai Hill, Lynton EX35 6AR (01598) 752235 *£80; 6 well equipped attractive rms. Carefully refurbished, no smoking Victorian house with wonderful views over Lynton, the sea and wooded countryside; comfortable sitting room with a log fire, conservatory, good food in the candlelit dining room, and kind staff; no children.

Martinhoe SS6648 OLD RECTORY Martinhoe, Parracombe, Barnstable EX31 4QT (01598) 763368 £80; 8 rms. Set on the edge of Exmoor in 3 acres of secluded gardens, this welcoming little hotel has a comfortable drawing room, small library and airy vinery (much of the furniture is made by the owners' son); very good English cooking in the elegant dining room, and carefully chosen wines; no smoking; lots of wildlife and fine walks; cl Nov–Easter; no children; disabled access.

Morchard Bishop SS7707 WIGHAM Morchard Bishop, Crediton EX17 6RJ (01363) 877350 *£70; 5 rms. Picturesque thatched longhouse on a 30-acre farm; with a house-party atmosphere, 2 sitting rooms, big log fires, snooker room, and a dining room with honesty bar; good set dinner and breakfasts using home-grown fruit and veg, home-made butter, breads and jams, and their own free-range eggs; no smoking and no pets (they have their own); outdoor heated swimming pool; children over 8.

Oakford SS9121 NEWHOUSE FARM Oakford, Tiverton EX16 9JE (01398) 351347 *£38, plus special breaks; 3 rms. 17th-c longhouse on the edge of Exmoor National Park, part of a working farm with beef suckler cows and a small flock of friendly sheep; cottagey sitting room, inglenook fireplace, beams, and a country dining room serving home-made food inc good bread, pâtés and puddings; cl Christmas; no children or pets.

Porlock SS8846 OAKS Doverhay, Porlock, Minehead, Somerset TA24 8ES (01643) 862265 *£85, plus special breaks; 9 airy and pretty rms. Particularly welcoming and spotlessly kept Edwardian country house looking down across the Exmoor countryside to Porlock Bay, with surrounding lawns and oak trees; a relaxed atmosphere and log fire in the attractive lounge, and good unpretentious cooking in the pleasant, no smoking restaurant; cl Jan and Feb; children over 8.

Porlock SS8846 WEST PORLOCK HOUSE Porlock, Minehead, Somerset TA24 8NX (01643) 862880 *£50; 5 rms. Nicely proportioned former manor house in 4 acres of gardens and grounds; with spacious, carefully furnished rooms (one lounge for smokers), kind personal service, and evening meals wknds only (if booked in advance); cl Dec and Jan; children over 6.

Selworthy SS9346 HINDON FARM Selworthy, Minehead, Somerset TA24 8SH (01643) 705244 *£40; 2 rms. Relaxed and friendly working farm with sheep, pigs, calves, goats and horses (you can help if you want to), lots of lovely walks around the farm or further afield, and a large lawn with stream and ducks; attractive sitting room and dining room, log fires, fine breakfasts, and a games barn with snooker, table tennis, darts and fancy dress; can arrange riding or bring your own horse; dogs welcome; self-catering wing also; cl Nov–Jan.

Sheepwash SS4806 HALF MOON Sheepwash, Beaworthy EX21 5NE (01409) 231376 *£75, plus special breaks; 16 rms. Civilised, heart-of-Devon hideaway in a colourful village square; with 10 miles of private salmon, sea-trout and brown-trout fishing on the Torridge; a neatly kept friendly bar, solid old furnishings and a big log fire, good wines, lovely evening restaurant, lunchtime bar snacks; dogs welcome; disabled access.

South Molton SS7226 PARK HOUSE South Molton EX36 3ED (01769) 572610 £88, plus special breaks; 8 comfortable rms reached by a fine staircase. In lovely countryside, and reached up a winding, tree-lined drive, this relaxed country house has very pretty gardens, friendly owners, open fires, books and magazines in 2 lounges (one is no smoking and has a little bar), and reliably good food in the attractive dining room; cl Feb; children over 12.

South Molton SS7125 WHITECHAPEL MANOR Whitechapel, South Molton

EX36 3EG (01769) 573377 **£130**, plus special breaks; 10 pretty rms. Carefully restored, Grade I listed Elizabethan manor in large grounds; with a magnificent Jacobean carved oak screen in the entrance hall, fine panelling, beams and log fires, and a relaxed atmosphere in both the cosy bar and comfortable lounge; excellent and thoughtful service, fine modern cooking as well as home-made breads, jams and marmalade, and carefully chosen wines; handy for Exmoor.

West Buckland SS6531 HUXTABLE FARM West Buckland, Barnstaple EX32 0SR (01598) 760254 ***£46**, plus special breaks; 6 rms. 16th-c farmhouse surrounded by carefully converted listed stone buildings, open fields, fine views, sheep, chickens, rabbits and Squeak the Shetland pony; candlelit dinner with wholesome home-made food using home-grown produce, home-made wine and bread, and a relaxing sitting room; sauna, fitness room, tennis court, games room and an outside children's play area with swings, sandpit and Wendy house; cl 20–29 Dec; disabled access.

Withypool SS8435 WESTERCLOSE COUNTRY HOUSE Withypool, Minehead, Somerset TA24 7QR (01643) 831302 **£69**, plus special walking breaks; 10 rms. Family-run, 1920s hunting lodge with moorland views and 9 acres of gardens and paddocks; comfortable lounges, a relaxed atmosphere, and good, interesting food using local produce; cl Jan and Feb; dogs welcome.

To see and do

★ ☼ ♨ 🐄 **Allerford** SS9047 Pretty stonebuilt village with a lovely packhorse bridge, and an enthusiastic local history MUSEUM (cl Sun and mid-Oct–Easter) with summer craft demonstrations. BOSSINGTON FARM PARK 🔠 Friendly place with rare breeds, pony rides, baby animals for children to feed, and birds of prey. B & B in the 15th-c farmhouse. Snacks, shop, some disabled access; cl Nov-Feb; (01643) 862816; *£3.40.

★ ✻ **Appledore** ST0614 A pretty centre of narrow cottagey streets off the quayside road which looks out over the Taw estuary, and ship- and boat-building in the yard just upstream. There's a pedestrian ferry over to Instow. The NORTH DEVON MARITIME MUSEUM (Odun House, Odun Rd) is good, exploring a different topic in each room. Shop, disabled access to ground floor only; cl 1–2pm, and Nov–Easter; (01237) 422064; £1. The Royal George has lovely views and decent food.

🏠☼ 🏛 **Arlington Court** (off the A39) SS6140 From its Victorian heyday up to 1949, Rosalie Chichester filled this early 19th-c house with model ships, stuffed birds, holiday souvenirs – in fact anything she could get her hands on; her assemblages have been watered down since, but there's still

quite a fascinating medley. Covering 3,500 acres, the grounds have attractive landscaped gardens and a number of Shetland ponies and sheep, along with a Victorian garden and conservatory, woodland and lakeside nature trails, and an unusual collection of carriages and horse-drawn vehicles (rides available). Meals, snacks, shop, disabled access; cl Sat (exc bank hol wknds), and Nov–Mar; (01271) 850296; £4.90, garden only £2.60; NT. The Pyne Arms at East Down is useful for lunch.

🦋 🏛 **Ashford** SS5335 BUTTERFLY HOUSE AND GARDENS Well looked after collection of tropical butterflies, with plenty of plants and birds, and 2 acres of landscaped gardens outside. Meals, snacks, shop, disabled access; cl Nov–Easter; (01271) 42880; £2, gardens free. The Ring of Bells at Pilton is handy for lunch.

🏠 🏛 ☼ ♨ 🐄 **Barnstaple** SS5533 The main regional shopping centre, with a good deal of unforced charm in the older parts. Interesting buildings include an imposing 18th-c colonnaded arcade on the Great Quay, a lofty Victorian market hall (market days Tues and Fri), almshouses behind the church, more off the square by the long old stone

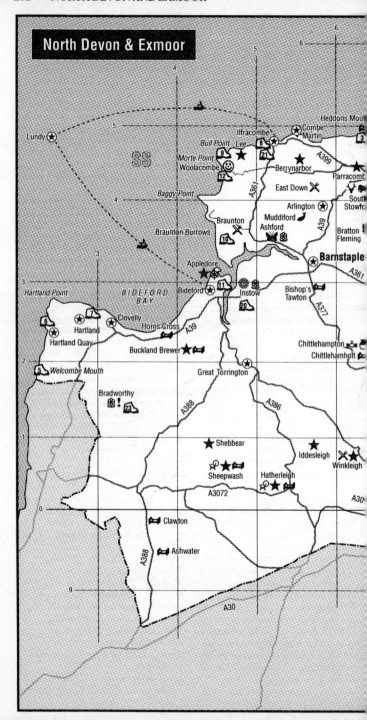

North Devon & Exmoor

SS

Lundy ★

Heddons Mou
Ilfracombe
Lee
Bull Point
Combe
Martin
Morte Point
Woolacombe
Berrynarbor
East Down ✗
Arlington ★
Parracomt
South
Stowfo
Baggy Point
Muddiford
Ashford
Braunton
Bratton
Fleming
Braunton Burrows
Barnstaple
Appledore
A361
Bideford
BIDEFORD
BAY
Instow
Bishop's
Tawton
A377
Hartland Point
Clovelly
Horns Cross
A39
Chittlehampton
Chittlehamholt
Hartland
Hartland Quay
Buckland Brewer ★
Welcombe Mouth
Great Torrington
A386
Bradworthy
A388
Shebbear ★
Iddesleigh ★
Winkleigh
Sheepwash
Hatherleigh
A3072
A30
Clawton
A388
Ashwater
A30

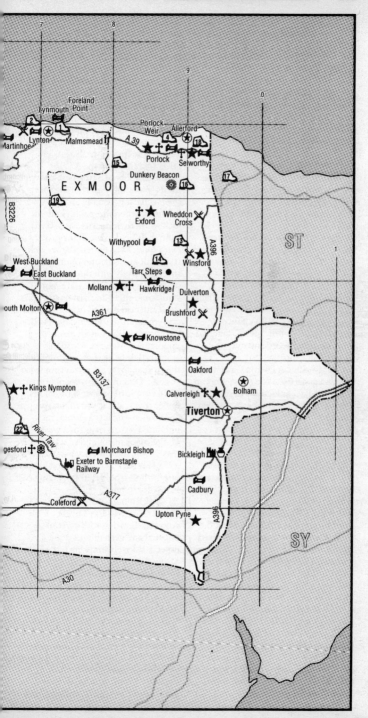

bridge, and some worthwhile shops. It's still a working port, though in a very small way now. The best nearby pub is the Chichester Arms up in Bishops Tawton. MARWOOD HILL GARDENS (Marwood; off the A361 towards Braunton) 18 well kept and colourful acres inc rare trees and shrubs, small lakes, extensive bog garden, clematis, camellias, alpines and eucalyptus, and national collections of astilbes (best in July) and tulbachia. Plant centre, some disabled access; cl 25 Dec; *£2. The New Ring o' Bells at Prixford is very handy for lunch. The MUSEUM OF NORTH DEVON (The Square) has some interactive displays, and an exhibition on the local environment. Shop, disabled access to ground floor only; cl Mon, 25–26 Dec, 1 Jan; (01271) 46747; *£1. BRANNAMS (Roundswell Industrial Estate) Guided tours of this big pottery (their terracotta pots are indispensable to many gardeners) with a chance to throw your own pot. Meals, snacks, shop, disabled access; no tours wknds, but shop open Sat; (01271) 43035; £3.50. On Pilston Causeway there's a good SHEEPSKIN SHOP; you can tour the adjacent factory. In summer you can hire bikes at the main railway station.

Bickleigh SS9407 BICKLEIGH CASTLE Charming moated and fortified manor house, still very much a family home; the 11th-c chapel is said to be Devon's oldest complete building. Also a medieval hall, armoury and guard room, Tudor bedroom, 17th-c farmhouse, and exhibitions on maritime history, the Civil War and the man who inspired Ian Fleming's 'Q' character. All done with great enthusiasm, and with a fair bit to amuse children. Good cream teas, shop, limited disabled access; open pm Weds, Sun and bank hols Easter–May then pm daily (exc Sat) till early Oct; (01884) 855363; *£4. The Fisherman's Cot is a beautifully placed riverside dining pub.

★ **Bideford** SS4526 quiet hillside town now bypassed, with a notable medieval bridge and some pleasant old streets, partly

pedestrianised, behind the Quay. The day-trip boat for Lundy (a good long day) sails from here year round, though not every day, and only rarely in Mar. One of the oldest streets is Bridgeland St, and up towards the top of Bridge St there are quite a few antique or antiqueish shops. The Joiners Arms (Market Sq) has decent food, and readers recommend the Vagabond Cavalier (Cooper St) for good-value Italian meals. THE BIG SHEEP ▨ (2m W on the A39) Exuberant sheep centre, best known for its splendidly entertaining sheep steeplechasing (usually around 3.20pm), when sheep with knitted jockeys on their backs race 200 yds from their field towards the prize of extra food. Even better are the duck trials half an hour later, miniature sheepdog trials with the sheep replaced by ducks; there are more traditional sheepdog demonstrations too. Other events and displays take in everything from shearing and bottle-feeding to milking, with plenty of opportunities to get close to the animals (lambs are born throughout the year, so there are always some to cuddle). Decent adventure play area, and a couple of puppet shows. Lots under cover, and it's particularly good value – tickets are valid for unlimited return visits for a week. Home-made meals and snacks (good teas), shop, disabled access; (01237) 477916; £4.25. The Thatched House family dining pub at Abbotsham is handy for lunch.

Bolham SS9514 KNIGHTSHAYES COURT Lovely woodland garden with acres of unusual and even unique plants, especially lovely in spring but a glory at any time of year. Alpine and more formal gardens, ancient yew topiary, attractive walks, and good Exe Valley views. The spooky-looking house itself is extravagantly ornate Victorian 'gothick', with elaborate painted ceilings and décor. The original plans were even more over-the-top, but when the horrified owner saw them he sent the architect packing. Meals, snacks, shop and plant centre, disabled access; cl Nov-

Mar, plus house cl Fri (exc Good Fri); (01884) 254665; £5, garden only £3.30; NT. The Rose & Crown over at Calverleigh is a pleasant place for lunch.

⚘ ! Bradworthy SS3515 GNOME RESERVE 🎦 (West Putford, 2¼m E) One of the most delightfully silly places in the area, woodland and wild flower meadows populated by hand-painted and individually modelled pixies. They lend you gnome hats and fishing rods so that the resident gnomes will think you're one of them. The setting is pretty (flowers and plants are labelled), and small children love it. Shop; cl Nov–mid-Mar (exc shop); (01409) 241435; £1.75. Coming from the N you could stop for something to eat at the thatched Farmers Arms, at Woolfardisworthy.

♄ Bratton Fleming SS6437 EXMOOR STEAM RAILWAY (Cape of Good Hope Farm) Enthusiastically run, family-owned, narrow-gauge railway with half-sized steamtrains winding through a mile of countryside, and a small display of traction engines. Meals, snacks, shop, disabled access; cl Sat, Fri (exc mid-July–Aug), and Nov–Mar (exc Dec specials); (01598) 710711; £3.50. The White Hart is useful for lunch.

🏚♿ Chittlehampton SS6325 COBBATON COMBAT COLLECTION 🎦 (off the A377) Growing private collection of over 50 British and Canadian World War II vehicles, quite tightly packed under cover but looking ready for action; also mock-ups of wartime scenes, wartime memorabilia, and play area with a Sherman tank. Summer snacks, shop, some disabled access; open daily Apr–Oct, best to ring for winter opening; (01769) 540740; £3.75. The Exeter Inn at Chittlehamholt has good food.

★ ❀ ⚘ 🐄 🐑 🏛 Clovelly SS3124 One of Devon's most famous views, down the very steep old cobbled street, free from traffic and with flower-covered cottages either side, to the tiny harbour below. It's a delightful village, best appreciated out of season. At any time of year you'll have to park up at the top, outside the village, then pay £2 to pass through a turnstile, and walk down. The Red Lion down by the quay is pleasant; if you can't face the climb back up, a Land-Rover can drive you back from behind here (summer only, 70p). You may be able to get boats to Lundy in summer. The parkland gardens of CLOVELLY COURT have tranquil sea views, and a fine walled garden. Open only pm Thurs Apr–Sept; (01237) 431200; *£1. THE MILKY WAY (Downland Farm) One of the biggest covered attractions in the region, losing a bit of its original character as it grows, but still friendly, and very good for families. They guarantee all children will be able to feed a lamb or kid, and there's also cow-milking, a working pottery, laser clay-pigeon shooting, birds of prey (twice-daily displays, not Sat), sheepdog training centre (no demonstrations Sun) and a little railway. Good play areas. Snacks, shop, disabled access; cl Nov–Mar; (01237) 431255; £5.50. Up towards the A39 is a big Iron Age hill fort, Clovelly Dykes, and along the coast the beachside hamlet of Buck's Mills is well worth a visit. The moorland road down from Stibb Cross on the A388 via Woolfardisworthy is good, and the woodland Hobby Drive toll road is the area's best coastal drive.

★ 🏚 ! ⚘ 🏚 Combe Martin SS5847 A string of former smallholdings and cottages scattered down a lovely sheltered valley, with an odd pub, the Pack of Cards, built to celebrate a cards win – 4 floors, 13 doors, 52 windows. There's a little fishing harbour in the shingly cove between the cliffs, and the Dolphin and Fo'c'sle are useful for lunch. COMBE MARTIN WILDLIFE AND DINOSAUR PARK (A399) Good range of animals and birds over 20 acres of woodland inc a pair of rare snow leopards, and meerkats in a huge desert enclosure. Also meticulously researched, life-size dinosaurs, some of which move and roar – like the towering Tyrannosaurus Rex. The gardens have rare and tropical plants, and there's a petting zoo for children.

Meals, snacks, shop, disabled access; cl Nov–Easter; (01271) 882486; £5.95. COMBE MARTIN MOTORCYCLE COLLECTION (Cross St) British bikes displayed against old petrol pumps, signs, garage equipment and other motoring nostalgia. Shop, disabled access; cl Nov–mid-May; (01271) 882346; *£2.50.

★ **Dulverton** SS9127 The main town for Exmoor is a civilised place, with a handsome old stone market house, and a fine bridge over the river which has cut this steeply wooded valley. The Lion Hotel is useful for lunch, and the area's main information centre is at the S end of Fore St, (01398) 323841.

✝ 🏛 **Eggesford** SS6811 This quiet Taw Valley village has a 14th-c CHURCH, and a garden centre prettily set in the walled garden of a ruined house; refreshments on a terrace with lovely views.

★ ✝ **Exford** SS8538 Attractively set in a sheltered valley by a small streamside green; the CHURCH up the hill a bit is well worth a look. The White Horse and Crown are handy for lunch.

🏠🍴🐾 **Hartland** SS2624 HARTLAND ABBEY Fine old house on the site of an Augustinian abbey, with elegant rooms (the drawing room is modelled on the House of Lords), an exhibition of old photography, and woodland walks in peacock-filled parkland. Snacks, shop; open pm Weds, Thurs, Sun and bank hols May–Sept, plus Tues July and Aug; (01237) 441264; £3.50, grounds only £1.50. Also in the village, CRAFT SHOPS inc a working pottery and Windsor chair-maker (children's sizes too).

🏛 🍴 **Hartland Quay** SS2224 Grand isolated spot at the foot of a toll road, on a jagged coast which looks like a dramatic cross between illustrations for geology textbooks and ones for a shipwreckers' manual. On the way down, detour to DOCTON MILL, an extensive, interestingly planted, sheltered streamside garden, largely naturalised, beside an ancient, restored watermill. It's especially attractive in spring. Snacks (good use

of local ingredients), plant sales; cl Nov–Feb; (01237) 441369; £2.50. They have a couple of bedrooms you can stay in. Down by the sea is a wonderfully maritime old inn, and the MUSEUM covers 4 centuries of shipwrecks – even big ships still go down here – and smuggling; cl Oct–Whitsun (exc Easter); 50p. Just S at Spekes Mill Mouth, the sea-eroded valley leaves the river spewing down the cliff in a seaside waterfall.

★ ☙ **Hatherleigh** SS5404 An attractive hillside village – even the church slopes – with fine inns (the Tally Ho, brewing its own beer, and the George) and a good POTTERY (20 Market St).

★🏛🍴✝🍴🏛☺ **Ilfracombe** SS5147 Picturesque resort around a busy harbour sheltered by high cliffs, with terraces of late Victorian boarding houses and small hotels looking out over it from their perches among the trees of the steep bay. There are period resort buildings and gardens, and even tunnels cut through the rock to a former Victorian bathing place. The 14th-c chapel above the harbour mouth has doubled as a lighthouse for over 450 years; the lifeboat station can be visited (donation requested). The town MUSEUM in Runnymede Gardens is cheerful and enthusiastic, if unsurprising (cl wknds winter; £1). The Royal Britannia (harbour) has good-value food, and we can also recommend the George & Dragon. In summer, the paddle steamer *Waverley* or the traditional cruise ship *Balmoral* run cruises from the pier to Lundy, Minehead and other places – even as far as Swansea. HOLY TRINITY CHURCH (Church St) is worth a look for its richly carved 15th-c waggon-roof, one of the most striking in the area. HELE MILL (A399, just E) Well restored, early 16th-c mill still producing wholemeal flour. Pottery demonstrations between 10 and 11am, and the chance to throw your own pot. Snacks, shop; cl Nov–Mar; (01271) 863185; *£2. Bicclescombe Park (A361, just S) has a restored 18th-c CORNMILL; the Coach House nearby has decent food. WATERMOUTH

CASTLE (off the A399, 3m E) Billed as 'Devon's Happy Castle', this is a fine 19th-c structure overlooking the bay, transformed into a world of gnomes, goblins, trolls and fairy tales, with slides, carousels and a musical water show. Very much for families, with young children the ones who'll enjoy it most. Snacks, shop, some disabled access; cl Sat, plus Fri at the start and end of the season, and Nov–Mar; (01271) 867474; £5.25.

❁ ❊ **Instow** SS4730 At the mouth of the Torridge estuary, this has an expanse of tidal sands, with dozens of moored boats beached on them at low tide. The Boathouse has good food and views. TAPELEY PARK (towards Westleigh) The very pretty Italianate garden with rococo features and a walled kitchen garden is the main draw, though there's also a pets corner, play area, and woodland walk. Lovely views down to the sea. Teas and snacks in period dairy, plant sales, disabled access; cl Sat, and Nov–Easter; (01271) 42371; £2.80.

★ ♨ ♤ **Lynton** SS7149 Merging into its harbourside extension, Lynmouth, down at the bottom of the cliff railway track, this delightfully situated steep village tucks into the wooded seaside gorge where the East and West Lyn tumble down to the sea. It clearly shows its origins as a Victorian resort in one of the many areas then known as Little Switzerland, with hillside villas now quiet boarding houses, photogenic corners and some older cottages. Pretty cottages down by the little tidal harbour, as well as craft shops and so forth (there's a friendly hands-on pottery); lots of trippers during the day in summer. In the old part of the upper village the simple LYN AND EXMOOR MUSEUM (Market St) is in an 18th-c cottage with a scale model of the former Lynton–Barnstaple narrow-gauge railway (you can still walk much of its track bed). Shop; cl 12.30–2pm, Sat, am Sun, and Nov–Easter; £1. GLEN LYN GORGE Carefully restored after the tragic flood of 1952, with pretty walks and an exhibition on water power.

Exhibition cl Nov–Easter, gorge cl 26 Dec and possibly in bad weather; (01598) 53207; £2. They have decent holiday flats and cottages in a peaceful setting. The Olde Cottage Inne (B3234 – lovely walk up The Lynway from Sinai Hill) is useful for lunch, and the Rising Sun down by the harbour has a good restaurant. The VALLEY OF ROCKS (see **Walks** section below) is an easy walk from the village. WATERSMEET HOUSE (1½m E) The 19th-c fishing lodge itself is not particularly remarkable (though it has interesting local wildlife displays), but the estate that surrounds it really is attractive – a perfectly relaxing wooded valley, with the house at the meeting-point of the rivers. Just right for an afternoon's pottering, though some of the walks can be steep. Meals, snacks, shop, disabled access by appointment only; cl Nov–Mar; (01598) 753348; free; NT.

♄ **Malmsmead** SS7947 The Exmoor Natural History Society run leisurely 2-hour strolls through the striking scenery around their NATURAL HISTORY CENTRE every Weds from mid-May–early Sept at 2pm. Very enthusiastically done, and especially worth knowing about as they're free (inc a cup of tea afterwards for a small donation); Mrs Waite has full details on (01643) 703470. The best way of finding the centre is from the County Gate National Park Centre on the A39. Jan Ridd brought his bride Lorna around here in *Lorna Doone*. The Exmoor Sandpiper at Countisbury, up towards Lynton, has decent food.

⏀ **Muddiford** SS5638 TROUT FARM Good for experts and beginners, with a little pool where you're practically guaranteed a bite; cl 25 Dec; (01271) 44533; *85p. More serious trout fishing in the carefully landscaped reservoir at ROADFORD LAKE SX4291 (cl Nov–Mar; £12.50 day permit).

★ ✝ **Parracombe** SS6644 A lovely little village worth visiting in its own right, but particularly interesting is ST PETROC'S CHURCH, one of the few churches to have a completely unspoilt medieval fabric with a

Georgian interior; locked Nov–Easter, but key available from the custodian then. The Fox & Goose is useful for lunch.

★ † **Porlock** SS8846 A lot of traffic, but some attractive cottages with distinctive, lighthouse-like chimneys and thatched roofs. The nearby harbour of **Porlock Weir** SS8647 is much quieter, tucked below wooded cliffs, with decent food at the thatched Ship; long walks along the coast, or through the woods up to the tiny and quite isolated CULBONE CHURCH.

★ † **Selworthy** SS9246 Gloriously unspoilt village, rated by a number of our contributors as the most attractive they've ever seen, with groups of white thatched cottages around a prettily planted hillside green looking out over Exmoor, and trees behind. The CHURCH is a gem, with a fine waggon-ceiling and roof bosses.

★ ℘ **Sheepwash** SS4806 Quiet village with cob and thatch houses around the green; the Half Moon is good for lunch. A mile N is Duckpool Cottage, a traditional wood-fired POTTERY.

🐖 ! ⌂ 🏠 **South Molton** SS7125 An attractive central square and an imposing church – and its farming roots show in the Thurs cattle market. The Castle at George Nympton has generous home cooking. QUINCE HONEY FARM (North Rd) The biggest wild bee farm in the world, with observatories linked by tunnels (to avoid disturbing the bees), and observation hives looking right into the centre of their colonies. Snacks, shop (lots of honey and their own beeswax skin and hair care products); cl Nov–Easter (though shop stays open); (01769) 572401; £2.95. The 18th-c Guildhall has a local history MUSEUM (cl Fri, Sun, and Dec–Feb), and monthly art and craft shows. HANCOCK'S DEVON CIDER (3m SW at Clapworthy Mill) Exhibition and film showing how they produce their good scrumpy. It's a nice spot for a picnic. Snacks, shop; cl 1–2pm, all Sun, and Oct–Easter; (01769) 572678; £1.95.

🐖 ✔ **South Stowford** SS6541 (off the B3226, N of Bratton Fleming) EXMOOR ZOOLOGICAL PARK Good-sized collection of rare and endangered creatures, many of which breed successfully throughout the year. Children can feed the smaller animals or play on the assault course, and there are nice views from the well landscaped grounds. Snacks, shop, disabled access; cl 25–26 Dec; (01598) 763352; £4.25. The Old Station House at Blackmoor Gate is a pleasant dining pub.

† 🏰 ⌂ ℘ 🐖 ♨ **Tiverton** SS9512 Formerly prosperous wool town, well worth wandering round; ST PETER'S CHURCH is magnificently decorated with rich carving, and other grand buildings include the Jacobean council offices. The handsome CASTLE was built in 1106 as a royal fortress

---

Days Out

Picture-book scenes on a wild coast
Rosemoor Garden, Torrington; Clovelly – Hobby Drive toll road, Buck's Mills village, Milky Way, lunch at the Red Lion; Hartland Quay, and walk along the cliffs in either direction; Hartland Abbey.

Village Exmoor
Allerford and Selworthy villages; stroll from the road up Dunkery Beacon; Exford; lunch at Royal Oak, Withypool; Winsford; Tarr Steps for a stroll by the river (good picnic spot); Dulverton.

Where moors meet coast
Lynmouth; walk from Lynton to Watersmeet along the river; lunch at Rising Sun, Lynmouth, or at the Olde Cottage, Lynton; Valley of Rocks; St Petroc's Church, Parracombe.

dominating the River Exe, and still has its Norman tower and gatehouse, as well as an interesting clock collection and one of the best assemblages of Civil War armour and arms. You can stay in apartments in the oldest parts of the building. Shop; open pm Sun and Thurs Easter–Sept, plus pm Mon–Weds July and Aug; (01884) 253200; £3. A 19th-c school on St Andrew St houses a local history MUSEUM with 2 waterwheels and an excellent railway gallery (cl Sun, and Christmas–early Feb; *£1), while the 4 showrooms of the TIVERTON CRAFT CENTRE showcase the work of over 170 local craftsmen; cl Sun; (01884) 258430; free. HIGHFIELD VINEYARDS (Longdrag Hill – B3137 W) Tours of working vineyard with free tastings; shop; cl Sun; (01884) 256362. In summer there are 2½-hour HORSE-DRAWN BOAT TRIPS along the attractively restored canal from the wharf; booking advisable, (01884) 253345; £6. They hire out rowing boats and motor-boat trips too, and can sort out fishing permits.

🏰†✹🐝🐾🎠 **Torrington** SS4919 Quiet dairy-farming town on a ridge above the River Torridge, with some attractive buildings inc 14th-c Taddiport Chapel (for a former leper colony), the imposing Palmer House, and a rather grand church built to replace the original that was blown up in the Civil War. There are good views from the neatly mown hill above the river, and other nearby strolls on the preserved commons surrounding the town. The Black Horse is useful for lunch. RHS GARDEN ROSEMOOR (off the B3220, just S) A wonderful place, constantly being developed and updated by the Royal Horticultural Society; marvellous rare trees, shrubs, and other plants in a charmingly landscaped, sheltered woodland setting; rose, stream and bog gardens, foliage and plantsman's garden, and trails for children. Meals, snacks, smart shop and garden centre, disabled access; cl 25 Dec; (01805) 624067; £3.20. On wkdys you can tour the factory of DARTINGTON CRYSTAL (Linden Close); there's a useful visitor centre and a shop with well priced goblets and decanters. Meals, snacks, disabled access (prior arrangement); (01805) 626262; £2.75. THE DOWNES (off the A386 towards Bideford, nr Monkleigh) Fine, big woodland garden with interesting flowering trees and shrubs and lovely landscaped lawns. Wknd teas, plant sales; open Easter–early Jun, then by appointment till Sept; (01805) 622244; £2.75. You can stay in a self-contained wing of the Georgian house.

★ **Winsford** SS9034 A quiet and attractive village below high hills, with the River Exe lacing through its countless bridges. The carefully restored Royal Oak is good for lunch.

☺ **Woolacombe** SS4543 The beach here is particularly nice, and its Atlantic breakers now draw quite a few surfers. The Rock at Georgeham and Mill at Ossaborough are pleasant for lunch, and the back road to Mortehoe is scenic. ONCE UPON A TIME (B3343 inland) Run by the same people as Watermouth Castle at Ilfracombe (see entry above), this is a super place for children up to about 11, with lots of rides and other activities; there's a driving school that even offers tests. Meals, snacks, shop, disabled access; cl Sat, plus Fri at start and end of season, and all Nov–Mar; (01271) 867474; £2.55 (£4.95 children).

♪ The ordinary British Rail EXETER–BARNSTAPLE line (known as the Tarka Line), mostly tracking along closer to the River Taw than the road does, is one of the finest of all for scenery.

★ **Other attractive villages** with decent pubs include Berrynarbor SS5646, Buckland Brewer SS4220, Calverleigh SS9214 (good church), Iddesleigh SS5708, King's Nympton SS6819 (another fine church), Molland SS8028 (yet another), Knowstone SS8223, Lee SS4846 (by the sea), Shebbear SS4409 (odd Devil's Stone by the green, and a working, wood-fired pottery), and Winkleigh SS6308. Readers particularly enjoy unspoilt Upton Pyne SX9197, the basis of Barton in

Sense and Sensibility.

♣ ✦ **Lundy day trips** (boat from Bideford or, in summer, Ilfracombe) Well worth considering if you're in Devon for more than just a few days. The island's best known for the migrant birds that come here in spring and autumn, but the remoteness and loneliness is also a powerful draw – the permanent population is around a dozen. Lovely walks along its 7 miles of formidably high cliffs and windswept rough pastures; there's also a small church, evocative castle ruins, 2 lighthouses (one the highest in Britain), wandering goats, small Soay sheep and ponies, and the chance of seeing seals (especially in autumn), the introduced small sika deer, and, in Apr and May, the island's trademark puffins. Accommodation can be arranged through the Landmark Trust (01628) 825925. The Marisco Tavern is a good place to eat. The return boat trip (about 2¼ hours each way) is about £25; (01237) 423365 for sailing times.

Walks

The coast is an enticing mix of upland, plunging wooded river valleys, wild clifftops and broad stretches of dune and estuary sand – ideal for super-varied walks. The cream of it is around **Lynton** SS7149 ⌂-1. To the E, paths run along the Lyn River to Watersmeet SS7448, where the Farley Waters tumble down to meet the East Lyn in a series of rocky cascades among steeply picturesque oak woods (there's a discreet NT refreshment pavilion here). Another scenic path leads high above the same valley along its S side, and riverside paths head on further upstream, to the prettily set Rockford Inn SS7547 (a good base for walks – food finishes at 2pm). Just N of Watersmeet, the Foreland Cliffs SS7551 are the highest in the country – a fine walk with dramatic views.

W from Lynton, the **Valley of Rocks** SS7049 ⌂-2 is a great valley bowl with steep crags and pinnacles of rock dividing it from the sea (and a dreadful, unscreened car park smack in the middle). It's reached by an easy coastal path, or by paths over Hollerday Hill SS7149 (wooded, but opens out dramatically on top). Further W are some rugged moorland hills by the sea, with secretive wooded combes: **Heddons Mouth Cleave** SS6549 ⌂-3 (there's a good walk down from the beautifully placed Hunters Inn SS6548 W of Martinhoe), and the terraced walkway known as the Ladies Mile SS6448 which runs along a charming valley nr Trentishoe. Heading W from **Porlock Weir** SS8647 ⌂-4 along the shore at the foot of the wooded cliffs, even the most avid pebble-hunter would find all he wanted.

More possibilities for wild coastal walks include the cliffs around **Welcombe Mouth** SS2117 ⌂-5 (rather a rough drive down); those around **Hartland Quay** SS2224 ⌂-6, much more dramatic than nearby Hartland Point SS2326 (toll gates to both); the woods, cliffs and clifftop farmland W of **Clovelly** SS3124 ⌂-7, reached from the village or from the NT's isolated farmhouses at The Brownshams SS2826; the cliffs between **Ilfracombe** SS5147 and **Lee Bay** ⌂-8 (the Grampus, up the sheltered wooded valley in the pretty village of Lee SS4846, is a good stop); and **Bull Point** SS4646 ⌂-9 and Morte Point SS4545 (the Ship Aground by the interesting church in Mortehoe SS4439 is a useful start). Baggy Point SS4240, reached from Croyde the surfers' centre (where the Thatch is a nice family pub), has a path good enough for wheelchairs.

The vast nature reserve expanse of great swelling dunes at **Braunton Burrows** SS4535 ⌂-10 is easily reached from the B3231 W of Braunton SS4836 (red flags warn if there's shooting on the range here; the Mariners Arms, in South St, in Braunton itself is a useful, pleasantly untouristy pub, and the Coffee Shoppe (Copperfields) has good local seafood); the dunes, sand slacks and meres behind the pebble ridge at **Northam Burrows** SS4430 ⌂-11, with the Atlantic rollers swinging in along the rock-strewn Saunton Sands beyond, are deserted out of season, but popular with families in summer; and the great surfy beach at **Woolacombe** SS4543 ⌂-12, is also a fine place out of season.

The peace of inland Exmoor is perhaps best appreciated from along paths by the rivers. A notable stretch is to be found along the **River Exe** ⌂-13 between Exford SS8538 and Winsford SS9034. The River Barle's most famous feature is the **Tarr Steps** SS8632 ⌂-14, the finest of all the stone and slab clapper bridges for packhorses; the path along the river, which runs between Simonsbath SS7739 and Dulverton SS9127, is uneven and surprisingly slow-going in places. **Badgworthy Water** SS7944 ⌂-15 can be taken in by a path from Malmsmead SS7947, getting into the heart of *Lorna Doone* country – it gets wilder and more remote with every step southwards (the surrounding moors provide a handful of return routes).

Exmoor's great ridge walk is **Dunkery Hill** ⌂-16, with Dunkery Beacon SS8941 as its high point surveying a huge chunk of south-west England and South Wales. It is easily walked from the nearby road; a splendid place to leave the car is Webbers Post SS9043 (which is also good for local pottering). It can also be incorporated into longer walks from Horner Woods SS8944 or Luccombe SS9144. Less well known but also recommended is **Grabbist Hill** SS9844 ⌂-17, which can be climbed from nearby Dunster SS9943. Above Selworthy SS9246, there are walks with excellent views on **Selworthy Beacon** SS9148 ⌂-18.

Note that some of Exmoor's moorland paths have a disconcerting habit of fizzling out without warning.

The Tarka Trail, not yet complete, will eventually run to nearly 200 miles linking Exmoor, Dartmoor and the north Devon coast, following the route of Henry Williamson's *Tarka the Otter* – and is most enjoyable with a copy of the book. One beautiful section is the route around **Pinkworthy Pond** SS7242 ⌂-19 and The Chains SS7342, reached from the car park a couple of miles along the B3358 E of Challacombe (where the Black Venus is good). The Trail is also rewarding around Watersmeet (see Walk 1 above).

Down at sea level, sections of **disused railways** ⌂-20 from Barnstaple SS5533 and Bideford SS4526 can be walked or cycled (local bicycle hire £5 a day, more for mountain bikes). The best section is the one from Barnstaple through Instow SS4730 and Bideford up to the Puffing Billy at the former Torrington Station SS4919. In autumn and winter particularly, this gives close views of the wading birds massed on the tidal sands of the estuary, and year-round the section up to Torrington is very attractive. The **Old Railway** ⌂-21 above Ilfracombe is another popular disused railway trail, with a tunnel, interesting plants, attractive scenery inc the lakes of Slade Reservoirs SS5045. For a one-way walk it's best to do it in reverse – for better views – and it's downhill all the way; Red Bus 31 or Filers 303 up from the town to Lee Bridge or Lee Cross (or to the Fortescue Hotel for a preliminary bracer).

Eggesford SS6811 ⌂-22 is a good base for inland walks (and a stop on the Barnstaple–Exeter railway line): in Flashdown Wood, up wooded Hayne Valley to Wembworthy SS6609 (the Odd Wheel is a decent family pub), or through Heywood Wood, where the mound of the former castle gives fine views (and there are picnic tables).

Bradworthy SS3214 ⌂-23 is another recommended jumping-off point, with some quiet local strolls on the common, or over by the Tamar Lake a couple of miles SW.

Where to eat

Braunton SS4836 Squires Exeter Rd (01271) 815533 Award-winning fish and chip take-away and restaurant with really excellent fish, decent wines, friendly service and attractive airy surroundings; cl Sun (but open school summer hols then), 25–26 Dec; disabled access. £7.50|£2.70.

Brushford SS9225 CARNARVON ARMS Brushford (01398) 323302 Good English bar and restaurant food, and friendly staff in this comfortable and individual sporting hotel with its own stabling, fishing and shooting; bedrooms; disabled access. £15|£5.

Coleford SS7701 NEW INN (01363) 84242 Comfortable thatched inn, 6 centuries old, with interesting food, extensive wine list, and well kept real ales; 4 nicely furnished areas, winter log fire, and an attractive garden with stream; bedrooms; cl 25–26 Dec. £20|£5.95.

East Down SS5941 PYNE ARMS (01271) 850207 Popular pub with lots of nooks and crannies in the low-beamed bar, a small, no smoking galleried loft, games area, nice food, and well kept real ales; cl 25 Dec; no children. £17|£4.95.

Lynton SS7149 LEE COTTAGE Lee Abbey (01598) 752621 Charming cottage run by members of the Christian community from Lee Abbey, and set in pretty terraced gardens with a stream and views of the north Devon coast; a few seats inside but plenty on the lawns and verandah; all the bread, scones, and cakes used in the filled rolls, ploughman's and cream teas are home-made; no smoking; cl Sun (Mon in Jun), cl end Sept–end May. £1.60.

Wheddon Cross SS9238 REST & BE THANKFUL (01643) 841222 Helpful staff and varied bar food in the comfortably modern 2-room bar with log fire and aquarium, and a restaurant; good bedrooms; cl pms 25/26 Dec; disabled access. £17.50|£5.

Winkleigh SS6308 POPHAMS Castle St (01837) 83767 Tiny, bustling place for morning coffee and lunch – bring your own wine – with particularly good, freshly cooked food, and a relaxed, happy atmosphere; cl Sun, Mon and Feb; no children. £22|£10.75.

Winsford SS9034 ROYAL OAK (01643) 851455 Prettily placed thatched inn with cosy bars, a smartly civilised atmosphere, log fire, and a wide choice of good, home-made bar and restaurant food; bedrooms; disabled access. £32.50|£7.

Special thanks to B and K Hypher, Dr and Mrs A Ewing, Fran Sturley, Karen McKeown, Juliet Rigbey, Mr and Mrs P M Healey, Dr P H Knight, E Robinson, N Brown, Louise Jowitt, Mr and Mrs D Evans, M P Scott, Mark Matthewman, Mr and Mrs P Tuszynski, Simon Barriskell, Rosemary Dabbs, W Elcock, Mr and Mrs Smith, Tina Rossiter, Mrs J H Mason, Miss A Donoghue, Louise Carlyle, E G Parish.

We welcome reports from readers . . .

This *Guide* depends on readers' reports. Do help us if you can – in return, we offer a discount on the next edition to people who've helped us with reports for it. Tell us what you think about places already in it, and anything extra you think we should say about them. And send us your ideas for inclusion in the next edition: places to visit, eat at or stay in, attractive drives or walks, maybe even unusual interesting shops you know of. Use the card in the middle, the report forms at the end, or just write – no stamp needed: *The Good Guide to Britain*, FREEPOST TN1569, Wadhurst, E Sussex TN5 7BR.

DEVON CALENDAR

Some of these dates were provisional as we went to press, please check information with the telephone numbers provided.

JANUARY

3 **Clyst St Mary** County Antiques Fair at Westpoint: about 500 stands – *till Sun 4* (01392) 446000

4 **Clyst St Mary** Baby Pets and Animal Day at Crealy Park (01395) 233200

10 **Exmouth** RSPB Cruise on the River Exe: to view the wintering Avocets – *also Sun 11, Sat 24, Sun 25* (01392) 432691

31 **Exeter** County Antiques Fair at Exeter Livestock Centre: about 430 stands (01392) 446000

FEBRUARY

7 **Exmouth** RSPB Cruise on the River Exe: to view the wintering Avocets – *also Sun 8* (01392) 432691

15 **Clyst St Mary** Baby Pets and Animal Day at Crealy Park (01395) 233200

MARCH

7 **Clyst St Mary** County Antiques Fair (see *3 Jan*)

21 **Clyst St Mary** South West Shooting and Game Exhibition at Westpoint – *till Sun 22* (01526) 398198

APRIL

3 **Lynton** Jazz Festival – *till Sun 5* (01271) 72064

4 **Exeter** County Antiques Fair (see Jan 31)

10 **Clyst St Mary** Easter Egg Hunt at Crealy Park – *also on Sun 12–Mon 13* (01395) 233200; **Exeter** Land's End Trial Start: 300-mile classic trial for motorcycles and cars (01359) 270954

12 **Paignton** Easter Egg Safari at Paignton Zoological Gardens – *till Mon 13* (01803) 557479

17 **Newton Abbot** Beer Festival at Tuckers Maltings: over 120 West Country real ales – *till Sun 19* (01626) 334734

26 **Clyst St Mary** Toy and Train Collectors Fair at Westpoint (01526) 398198

MAY

2 **Clyst St Mary** County Antiques Fair (see *3 Jan*)

3 **Clyst St Mary** Lost Toys Treasure Hunt at Crealy Park – *till Mon 4* (01395) 233200

4 **Uffculme** Sheep Show at Coldharbour Mill Working Wool Museum (01884) 840960

7 **Torrington** May Fair (01805) 622441

14 **Holsworthy** Agricultural Show (01409) 253979

21 **Clyst St Mary** County Show at Westpoint – *till Sat 23* (01392) 444777; **Torquay** Devon Art Society Spring Exhibition and Sale at St Anne's Institute Hall – *till 8 Jun* (01803) 328141

22 **Combe Martin** Hunting of the Earl of Rone *from Fri at 6pm*, then every day *till Mon 25* when the effigy is captured, seated facing backwards on a donkey and, after a procession with fool and hobby-horse, is thrown into the sea (01271) 882524; **Torquay** English Riviera Dance Festival: world champion cabaret, sequence and social dancing – *till 6 Jun* (01895) 632143

23 **Brixham** Heritage Festival: live music, dance displays and fireworks – *till Sat 30* (01803) 855262

DEVON CALENDAR

MAY cont

24 **Clyst St Mary** Treasure Hunt inc free canoes and abseiling at Crealy Park – *till Mon 25* (01395) 233200

25 **Stockland** Country Fair and Donkey Derby (01404) 881447

30 **Exeter** County Antiques Fair (see *31 Jan*)

JUNE

6 **Ilfracombe** Victorian Celebration: parades, steam fair, fireworks and music hall – *till Sun 14* (01271) 866708

13 **Beer** Steam and Model Festival at Pecorama Pleasure Gardens – *till Sun 14* (01297) 21542

14 **Cornwood** Vintage and Classic Vehicle Rally at Blachford Manor (01752) 491947

20 **Brixham** Trawler Race and Quay Festival (01803) 882325

21 **Ivybridge** Vintage Rally at Challonsleigh Farm (01752) 896253

27 **Ashburton** Carnival Week – *till 4 July* (01364) 652142

28 **Bovey Tracey** Devon Guild of Craftsmen Exhibition at Riverside Mill – *till Aug 30* (01626) 832223; **Clyst St Mary** Teddy Bears Picnic at Crealy Park (01395) 233200

JULY

2 **Exeter** Festival: cathedral concerts, open-air jazz, theatre, comedy, street entertainment and a fireworks concert – *till Sun 19* (01392) 265118

4 **Clyst St Mary** County Antiques Fair (see *3 Jan*); **Kenton** Horse Trials at Powderham Castle – *till Sun 5* (01626) 890243

8 **Dartington** Literature Festival at Dartington Hall: over 100 writers, talks, theatre and workshops – *till Sun 19* (01803) 867311

10 **Yealmpton** Wild West Living History at the National Shire Horse Centre – *till Sun 19* (01752) 880268

11 **Kenton** Historic Vehicle Gathering at Powderham Castle (01626) 890243

15 **Clyst St Mary** South-West Qualifier for Crufts at Crealy Park – *till Fri 17* (01395) 233200

18 **Kingsbridge** Traditional Glove-hanging Ceremony and Procession to open Fair Week – *till carnival on Sat 25* (01548) 856440

19 **Clyst St Mary** Treasure Hunt and Fireworks – *till Sun 26* (01404) 812252; **Dartmouth** Town Week – *till Sun 26* (01803) 835200

21 **Honiton** Hot Penny Ceremony and Fair (01404) 42836

24 **Kingsbridge** Town Criers' Competition – *till Sat 25* (01548) 853195

25 **Tiverton** Mid-Devon Show at Hartnoll Farm (01884) 821815

27 **Clovelly** Agricultural Show at Thornery Farm (01409) 241273; **Stoke Gabriel** Carnival Week with procession on *1 Aug – till 2 Aug* (01803) 782483

30 **Berry Pomeroy** Totnes and District Show (01803) 863168

31 **Sidmouth** International Folk Festival – *till 7 Aug* (01395) 515134

AUGUST

1 **Cornwood** Agricultural and Horticultural Show (01752) 837667; **Exeter** County Antiques Fair (see *31 Jan*); **Kenton** Fireworks Concert at Powderham Castle (01626) 890243; **Malborough** Carnival (01548) 853195; **Salcombe** Yacht Club Regatta – *till Sat 8* (01548) 843927; **Shaldon** Water Carnival (01626) 872842

5 **Landkey** North Devon Show at Plym's Farm (01769) 560205

6 **Honiton** Agricultural Show (01404) 891763

7 **Kenton** Open-air Concert at Powderham Castle (01626) 890243

DEVON CALENDAR

AUGUST cont

8 **Loddiswell** Show (01548) 853195; **South Zeal** Dartmoor Folk Festival
– *till Sun 9* (01837) 840162; **Yealmpton** Steam and Vintage Rally at
the National Shire Horse Centre – *till Sun 9* (01752) 880268

9 **Clyst St Mary** Toy and Teddies Tea Party at Crealy Park (01395) 233200;
Salcombe Town Regatta, with fireworks – *till Sat 15* (01548) 843927

13 **Torquay** Devon Art Society Spring Exhibition and Sale at St Anne's
Institute Hall – *till Mon 31* (01803) 328141

15 **Arlington** Folk Festival at Arlington Court (01271) 850296; **Dalwood**
Country Fair: costume parades, street market and medieval banquet
(01404) 881676; **Exeter** Heritage Weekend: medieval pageant and fair
– *till Sun 16* (01392) 265700; **Kingsbridge** Vintage Machinery Show at
Sorley Cross – *till Sun 16* (01548) 852939; **Malborough** Music
Festival – *till Sun 16* (01548) 853195

17 **Ilfracombe** Carnival Week – *till Mon 24*, procession *on Thurs 20 and
Sat 22* (01271) 863001

22 **Torbay** Royal Regatta – *till Weds 26* (01803) 299772

23 **Clyst St Mary** Toy and Train Collectors Fair at Westpoint (01526) 398198;
Clyst St Mary Pirates' Treasure Hunt at Crealy Park (01395) 233200

27 **Dartmouth** Royal Regatta: Red Arrows, fireworks and barrel rolling –
till Sat 29 (01803) 832435; **Hope Cove** Fun Weekend – *till Mon 31*
(01548) 853195; **Mortonhampstead** Carnival (01647) 440145

29 **Yealmpton** Medieval Field of Combat at the National Shire Horse
Centre – *till Mon 31* (01752) 880268

30 **Clyst St Mary** Adventure Sports Special inc free canoeing, abseiling
and archery at Crealy Park – *till Mon 31* (01395) 233200

31 **Brixham** Fish Market Open Day (01803) 859123

SEPTEMBER

5 **Clyst St Mary** County Antiques Fair (see *3 Jan*); **Kingsbridge**
Agricultural Show (01548) 853195

6 **Exe River** Struggle Raft Race (01884) 252336; **Yealmpton** Car and
Bike Show at the National Shire Horse Centre (01752) 880268

9 **Newton Abbot** Ancient Cheese and Onion Fayre: sample local cheese
and wines (01626) 53567; **Widecombe** Village and Agricultural Fair
(01626) 53567

19 **Barnstaple** Carnival (01271) 73311; **Exeter** County Antiques Fair (see
31 Jan)

OCTOBER

10 **Exeter** Grand Illuminated Procession (01392) 265700; **Exeter** County
Antiques Fair (see *31 Jan*)

16 **Lynton** Jazz Festival – *till Sun 18* (01271) 72064

18 **Exebridge** to **Tiverton** Exe River Struggle Raft Race (01884) 252336

29 **Bampton** Fair (01884) 255255

31 **Clyst St Mary** Halloween Party at Crealy Park (01395) 233200

NOVEMBER

5 **Ottery St Mary** Rolling of the Tar Barrels: since 1688 (01404) 812252

7 **Clyst St Mary** County Antiques Fair (see *3 Jan*)

15 **Clyst St Mary** Toy and Train Fair at Westpoint (01392) 444777

21 **Clyst St Mary** Kit Car Show at Westpoint – *till Sun 22* (01392)
444777; **Kingsbridge** Illuminated Carnival (01548) 853195

28 **Exeter** County Antiques Fair (see *31 Jan*)

DECEMBER

6 **Clyst St Mary** Father Christmas at Crealy Park – *also Sat 12 till Weds
23* (01395) 233200

DORSET

Very broad appeal, from civilised seaside resorts to unspoilt coast and countryside, from interesting towns to hidden villages, from stately homes and colourful gardens to lively family attractions

Dorset has a lot to offer families, with plenty to do around the interesting and rather elegantly old-fashioned resort of Weymouth. Smaller Lyme Regis has a similar traditional appeal. Children also particularly enjoy the Monkey World at Wool and the costume museum in Blandford Forum, while the tank museum at Bovington Camp appeals to many. The fact that Dorset is fossil country is reflected by a number of dinosaur centres; the one in Dorchester is the best.

Dorset's more adult side is very special. The inland countryside has a subtle understated appeal, with secluded valleys, narrow lanes threading through peaceful farmland and tucked-away villages (Milton Abbas is best of all). The central area's chalk uplands, cut by intricate valleys, give some splendid high viewpoints. The west's intimate farming country has the most sequestered feel. Many people get extra pleasure from the many direct memories of Thomas Hardy's books which particular villages and tracts of countryside conjure up. Forde Abbey at Thorncombe and the gardens and swannery at Abbotsbury are outstanding places to visit, and other rewarding places include Mapperton Gardens near Beaminster, Kingston Lacy near Wimborne, Athelhampton House, Compton Acres gardens in Poole, and Corfe Castle. Dorchester, Sherborne, Beaminster, Shaftesbury and Blandford Forum are interesting country towns.

The Bournemouth conurbation, stretching for miles along good beaches, dominates the east with its civilised and spacious spread of comfortably sedate resort areas and leafy suburbs (and Poole's bustling waterfront for contrast).

Further west the coast is lovely, with some marvellous views; you have to go right down to Cornwall to find its match. Much of it is quiet and unspoiled, especially along the rugged Isle of Purbeck. The tremendous sweep of the Chesil Beach, its pebbles and boulders immaculately graded by millennia of storms, is emphatically not for swimmers – the undertow will suck you straight down – but with its long lagoon behind is very interesting for beach-combers and nature-lovers. The heathland west of Poole Harbour, partly planted with conifers, has a quite different character – largely flat tank-training ground west of Weymouth, but a more interesting roaming ground for nature lovers towards Studland Bay.

An Explorer ticket is a good buy if you're going to be doing much travelling on buses.

Where to stay

Abbotsbury SY5785 ILCHESTER ARMS Abbotsbury, Weymouth DT3 4JR (01305) 871243 *£46; 10 comfortable rms. Handsome, old stone inn nr abbey with famous swannery; log fire in the rambling beamed bar decorated with hundreds of swan pictures, breakfasts served in attractive no smoking conservatory, restaurant, pleasant staff; plenty of coastal and country walks; no accommodation Christmas; disabled access.

Bournemouth SZ0991 LANGTRY MANOR 26 Derby Rd, Eastcliff, Bournemouth BH1 3QB (01202) 553887 £79.50, plus special breaks; 29 pretty rms, some in the manor, some in the lodge. Built by Edward VII for Lily Langtry, with lots of memorabilia, relaxed public rooms, and good food inc an Edwardian dinner every Sat evening; disabled access.

Bridport SY4692 BRITMEAD HOUSE West Bay Rd, Bridport DT6 4EG (01308) 422941 *£58, plus special breaks; 7 rms. Extended Victorian hotel with lots to do nearby; comfortable lounge overlooking the garden, attractive dining room, good food using fresh local produce, and kind, helpful service; self-catering bungalow; children over 5; dogs by prior arrangement; disabled access.

Chideock SY4292 PARK FARMHOUSE Main St, Chideock, Bridport DT6 6JD (01297) 489157 £46, plus special breaks; 6 attractively furnished rms. Partly thatched, Grade II listed former farmhouse, very neatly kept, with log fire in lounge; good breakfasts (inc vegetarian) and enjoyable evening meals (by prior arrangement) using much home-grown produce; and big garden; well-behaved pets welcome by arrangement.

Corfe Castle SY9681 KNITSON OLD FARMHOUSE Corfe Castle, Wareham BH20 5JB (01929) 422836 *£35; 3 rms, shared bthrm. Big, ancient cottage on working farm with sheep and Jersey cows, and a large garden with hens, pigs and horses; comfortable sitting room with flagstones and woodburner; good evening food by arrangement using home-reared pork and lamb served in the spacious kitchen; no smoking; cl Dec.

Cranborne SU0513 FLEUR-DE-LYS Cranborne, Wimborne BH21 5PP (01725) 517282 *£45, plus special breaks; 8 rms. Nicely placed, old creeper-clad pub in *Tess of the d'Urbervilles* country, not far from New Forest, with an attractively modernised, oak-panelled lounge bar, simply furnished, beamed public bar, and decent bar food; cl 24–26 Dec.

Dorchester SY6890 CASTERBRIDGE 49 High East St, Dorchester DT1 1HU (01305) 264043 *£60, plus weekend breaks; 15 rms. Small Georgian hotel in town centre, with modern annexe across little courtyard; elegant drawing room, cosy library, and attractive dining room and conservatory; no evening meals (lots of nearby restaurants); cl 25–26 Dec; disabled access.

Dorchester SY6890 KINGS ARMS High East St, Dorchester DT1 1HF (01305) 265353 £49.20w; 31 rms – the Lawrence of Arabia and the Tutenkhamun suites are extraordinary. Smart, thriving coaching inn made famous by Hardy's *Mayor of Casterbridge*; different menus in the restaurant, coffee shop and bar; old-fashioned public bar with real ales, live music twice a week; disabled access.

Dorchester SY6789 MAIDEN CASTLE FARM Dorchester DT2 9PR (01305) 262356 *£36; 6 rms, most with own bthrm. Victorian farmhouse on big working farm set beneath the prehistoric earthworks from which the farm takes its name; views of the castle and countryside, and comfortable traditionally furnished sitting room which overlooks the garden.

East Knighton SY8185 COUNTRYMAN East Knighton, Dorchester DT2 8LL (01305) 852666 *£50; 6 rms. Attractively converted pair of old cottages with open fires and plenty of character in the main bar, no smoking family room, generous food in carvery restaurant, and courteous staff; cl 25 Dec.

Evershot ST5403 SUMMER LODGE Evershot, Dorchester DT2 0JR (01935)

83424 **£155,** plus special breaks; 17 big, individually decorated rms. Beautifully kept and peacefully set former dower house with lovely flower displays in the comfortable and elegantly furnished day rooms, excellent food using the best local produce in the most attractive restaurant (with fine views of the pretty garden), delicious breakfasts and afternoon tea, and personal, caring service; outdoor swimming pool, tennis and croquet; dogs allowed by prior arrangement and away from public rms; partial disabled access.

Farnham ST9515 MUSEUM Farnham, Blandford Forum DT11 8DE (01725) 516261 ***£65;** 4 rms in converted stables. Traditional civilised old country inn in an attractive thatch and stone village; with inglenook fireplace and classical music in lounge bar, conservatory, decent food inc excellent breakfasts, and a sheltered terrace and garden; cl 25 Dec; disabled access.

Gillingham ST8026 STOCK HILL Wyke, Gillingham SP8 5NR (01747) 823626 ***£230 inc dinner,** plus special breaks; 10 lovely, very comfortable rms. Marvellously relaxing, carefully run Victorian manor house in 11 acres of wooded grounds; with antiques and paintings in the opulent day rooms, particularly welcoming service, and excellent food in the no smoking restaurant using home-grown herbs and veg, local meat and fish; all-weather tennis court, croquet; children over 7.

Halstock ST5407 HALSTOCK MILL Halstock, Yeovil BA22 9SJ (01935) 891278 ***£50;** 4 rms. Attractive 17th-c house quietly set in 10 acres and with lots of surrounding walks; log fire in cosy beamed lounge, pleasant little dining room, and good food using home-grown fruit and veg, local fish and cheese; stabling; cl Christmas; children over 5.

Loders SY4994 LODERS ARMS Loders, Bridport DT6 3SA (01308) 422431 **£40;** 2 rms. Carefully refurbished pub in a pretty village; friendly and unspoilt atmosphere, interesting food in small restaurant, comfortable bar with log fire and a nice mix of customers, good beers and wines, and a skittle alley.

Lower Bockhampton SY8290 YALBURY COTTAGE Lower Bockhampton, Dorchester DT2 8PZ (01305) 262382 ***£72,** plus special breaks; 8 rms overlooking garden or fields. Very attractive, family-run, 16th-c thatched house with a relaxed, friendly atmosphere; low beams and inglenook fireplaces in the comfortable lounge and dining room; carefully cooked, often imaginative food, good wines; cl 28 Dec–23 Jan.

Milton Abbas ST8001 HAMBRO ARMS Milton Abbas, Blandford Forum DT11 0BP (01258) 880233 **£55;** 2 rms. Pretty and popular old inn in a beautiful 1770s landscaped village; with beamed front lounge, log fire, popular food, and prompt, friendly service.

Osmington Mills SY7381 SMUGGLERS Osmington Mills, Weymouth DT3 6HF (01305) 833125 **£65;** 6 rms. Best out of season, this much-extended thatched stone pub – just above the sea – has cosy corners, log fires, appropriate woodwork and nautical decorations, good value bar food, and a partly no smoking restaurant; cl 25 Dec.

Poole SZ0590 INN IN THE PARK Pinewood Rd, Branksome Chine, Poole BH13 6JS (01202) 761318 **£50;** 5 comfortable rms. Small, friendly hotel well off the tourist track, with nice steep walks down to the sea; lots of pine in the residents' area, attractive dining room, decent small bar specialising in well kept real ales, good value bar food, and a small sunny terrace.

Poole SZ0190 MANSION HOUSE Thames St, Poole BH15 1JN (01202) 685666 ***£115,** plus special breaks; 28 cosy rms with lots of little extras. Close to waterfront, this civilised, old merchant's town house has a lovely sweeping staircase, antiques in the pretty residents' lounge, a cosy cocktail bar, good food in the attractive restaurant, and courteous, old-fashioned service.

Sherborne ST6316 EASTBURY Long St, Sherborne DT9 3BY (01935) 813131 **£72;** 15 pretty rms. Elegant Georgian townhouse with comfortable lounge, library, good food, a relaxing atmosphere, and walled garden; nr abbey and castles.

Sturminster Newton ST7814 Plumber Manor Hazelbury Bryan Rd, Sturminster Newton DT10 2AF (01258) 472507 *£130, plus special breaks; 16 very comfortable rms. Handsome 17th-c house in quiet countryside, with tennis and trout stream; warm fires, resident labradors, good and uncomplicated food, a relaxed atmosphere, and friendly, helpful service; cl Feb; dogs allowed away from public rms; disabled access.

Sydling St Nicholas SY6399 Lamperts Cottage Sydling St Nicholas, Dorchester DT2 9NU (01300) 341659 £38; 3 little attic rms, shared bthrm. Charming, mainly no smoking 16th-c thatched cottage in an unspoilt village; with friendly welcome from helpful owner, good breakfasts in a beamed dining room with huge inglenook fireplace and bread oven, and a pretty garden; children over 8.

Uplyme SY3293 Amherst Lodge Farm Uplyme, Lyme Regis DT7 3XH (01297) 442773 £46, plus special breaks. 4 rms. Comfortable Devon long house surrounded by 140 acres of gardens, woodlands, fields and 8 lakes – rod room, coarse and trout fishing; relaxed, friendly country-house atmosphere, oak-panelled lounge with fire, books and magazines, and enjoyable evening meals; also self-catering; cl Christmas; children over 10.

Wareham SU9287 Priory Church Green, Wareham BH20 4ND (01929) 551666 £135, plus special breaks; 19 very comfortable rms – the best being in the converted boathouse with its own landscaped gardens. Beautifully converted medieval buildings set in 4 acres of carefully kept riverside gardens; 2 elegant lounges furnished with antiques (pianist Sat evening), delicious English cooking served in the converted abbot's cellar (an exceptional English cheese board), and genuinely welcoming service; disabled access.

West Bexington SY5387 Manor West Bexington, Dorchester DT2 9DF (01308) 897616 *£86; 13 cottagey rms, most with own bthrm. Handsome and civilised old stone hotel mentioned in Domesday Book and in a pleasant setting not far from beach; relaxed, informal atmosphere, comfortable lounge, popular pubby cellar bar, log fires, good bar food, excellent restaurant food, and friendly service.

Wimborne Minster SZ0199 Beechleas Poole Rd, Wimborne Minster BH21 1QA (01202) 841684 £78, plus special breaks; 9 attractive, comfortable rms. Carefully renovated Georgian house with open fires in the cosy sitting room and charming dining room, airy conservatory; enjoyable, Aga-cooked English food using organic produce, nice breakfasts, and friendly, helpful owners; cl 24 Dec–12 Jan.

Yetminster ST5910 Manor Farmhouse High St, Yetminster, Sherborne DT9 6LF (01935) 872247 *£50; 3 rms. Fine, carefully modernised, no smoking 17th-c building with beams and oak panelling, inglenook fireplaces, helpful owners, and good traditional cooking; no children or dogs; partial disabled access.

To see and do

Bournemouth SZ0991 still has something of the 'very salubrious air' that Queen Victoria recommended to Disraeli. Neatly kept streamside gardens in the centre, a pier that's one of the few to look as fresh as when it was built, long promenades below the low cliff, and miles of well organised sandy beach (no dogs in summer, and children's activities then). All this, along with the mild climate and a good local orchestra, has made the town expansively popular both as a civilised place to retire to and as a centre for regular development, so it's a big, busy town surrounded by suburbs, with tall modern buildings and monumental traffic schemes. But down by the sea you're well insulated from all of that. And the western residential suburbs of Westbourne and particularly Branksome Park (it's virtually impossible to tell here when Bournemouth becomes Poole) are quiet, with pinetree valleys winding down to the sea. Besides our **Where to eat** entry for Bournemouth, Butlers Crab & Ale House (Old Christchurch Rd) is useful, and the Moon on the Square (Exeter Rd) is good value.

! DINOSAUR SAFARI (Expocentre, Old Christchurch Lane) A family favourite, full of computerised displays, fossils, and bones comparing the prehistoric beasts to more familiar mammals. Shop; cl 24–26 Dec; (01202) 293544; £2.95. Two other exhibitions in the same building offer a similar mix of fun and education: MUMMIES OF THE PHARAOHS looks at ancient Egypt and mummification, and BOURNEMOUTH BEARS takes in teddies of all ages, shapes and sizes; times and prices as above.

SHELLEY ROOMS (Boscombe Manor, Beechwood Ave) Small museum devoted to the life and work of the poet, especially the latter part of his life. Disabled access; cl am, all Mon, 25–26 Dec, Good Fri; (01202) 303571; free. Shelley's heart is buried beneath the impressive tombstone of Mary Shelley in St Peter's churchyard.
BEST BEACHES, with water safe for swimming, are at Durley Chine and Southbourne.

Poole SZ0190 merges indistinguishably into Bournemouth on the edges, but its centre is wholly distinct, with a more lively feel, especially around The Quay. The broad natural harbour is still busy with the comings and goings of boats and small ships (several decent pubs to watch them from – the nautical Portsmouth Hoy is best for lunch); launch ferries around the harbour, and out to Brownsea Island. There are interesting old buildings along here; the streets behind, some pedestrianised, are well worth strolling through. The Old Harry (High St) has good local fish.

WATERFRONT MUSEUM (High St) Well laid-out local history museum, with displays on smuggling, Scouts and sailing, and a reconstructed Victorian street. Teas, shop, disabled access; (01202) 683138; cl Nov–Easter; £3.25 (part of the ground floor may be open free in winter). During July and August a ticket includes entry to next door SCAPLEN'S COURT, a well restored, medieval merchant's home, with a craft gallery upstairs.

POOLE POTTERY (The Quay) Distinctive china has been produced here since 1873. Good factory tours, and a museum and film; you can have a go at throwing and decorating your own pot, and even smash up a few plates. Other craft demonstrations too. Restaurant with harbour views (open evenings), shop, disabled access; cl 12.30–1.30pm, 25 Dec, and poss some winter wknds; (01202) 666200; *£3.50.

AQUARIUM COMPLEX (Hennings Wharf, The Quay) Busy indoor centre with, as well as the aquarium, an enormous 00 gauge model railway, also smuggling and space exhibitions, and insectarium. Good for families on rainy days. Meals, snacks, shop; cl 24–25 Dec; (01202) 686712; *£4.75.

CHAIN FERRY This runs from Sandbanks, by the harbour mouth, to the Studland side – a spectacular entrance to Dorset proper; it's quickest to go as a foot passenger or by bus (they have priority). The beach at Sandbanks is regularly lauded as one of the best in Britain.

COMPTON ACRES GARDENS (Canford Cliffs) SZ0689 Perhaps Poole's outstanding attraction, with lovely statuary among fine plants landscaped in an eclectic variety of styles – the Japanese garden is the foremost in Europe. Good views of the hills and Poole harbour. Sat is the least busy day to visit. Meals, snacks (decent crêperie), shop and plant sales, disabled access; cl Nov–Feb; (01202) 700778; £4.50. The Nightjar has decent food.

☺ SPLASHDOWN (Tower Park, 2m NE on the A3049) Good for children, a water park with 8 rides and slides, inc a near-vertical drop in total darkness.

Snacks; cl Jan (and in peak periods they may have limits on how long you can stay); freephone (0500) 717000; £4.90.

✔ ✿ ✿ ♣ ✿ **Brownsea Island** SZ0187 Unspoilt 500-acre island in the middle of the huge natural harbour, famous as the site of the first Scout camp in 1907. Lots of birds (inc peacocks), animals and butterflies in heath and woodland (you may spot red squirrels), large heronry, nature reserve, and fine views back towards the coast from its beaches. It's a really splendid place to explore. Guided walks 2.45pm daily in July and Aug, and from mid-July to mid-Aug maybe open-air Shakespeare or opera. Snacks, shop, disabled access; cl Oct–Mar; (01202) 707870; *£2.20; NT. Ferries to the island run every half hour from Poole Harbour (£3.70 return, takes half an hour) or Sandbanks (£2.50 return, only takes six minutes); don't forget to check the time of the last one back.

Christchurch SZ1593 at the 'Hampshire' end of the Bournemouth complex has attractive Georgian brick buildings in its old centre, a restored watermill, and a quay looking out over the yachting harbour, busy in summer. Hengistbury Head, overlooking the harbour and reached from the Bournemouth side, is a popular place for strollers, with traces of an Iron Age hill fort (good beach here too). On the other side of the harbour mouth, long beaches stretch way into Hampshire from the vast Mudeford car park (the Haven House by the sea here is well worth knowing for its unrivalled position, and there's an excellent fishmonger nearby). Pleasant walking out of season.

✝ ☕ ✿ PRIORY Magnificent medieval monastic church, at well over 90 metres (300ft) the longest parish church in the country; very striking inside, with remarkable carving. The 'Miraculous Beam' apparently fitted in the roof only with divine assistance, so prompting the renaming of the borough to Christchurch (it used to be called Twynham). Free recitals most Thurs lunchtimes. Shop, snacks on recital days; disabled access; cl 25 Dec exc for services; £1 suggested donation. The church has a small museum open in the summer, and good views from the tower (50p) – though with 176 spiral steps you have to earn them.
🏰 🏚 CASTLE All that remains is a ruined keep, and the ruins of the Norman house probably used by the castle constable. It's quite well preserved, with one of the earliest chimneys in the country, and an ancient midden by a millstream; free.

☕ 🐂 RED HOUSE MUSEUM & GARDENS (Quay Rd) Georgian house with local history, dolls and costumes, and a walled herb garden. Shop, disabled access to ground floor only; cl Sun am, Mon (exc bank hols), Christmas wk; (01202) 482860; £1 during summer.
! BIG TOP JOUSTING (Arena, Stony Lane) A good distraction for children (especially in poor weather), a lively two-hour spectacle, under cover, with mock jousting displays. On tournament afternoons you can usually visit the horses in their stables. Shows at 3pm daily July and Aug, and other dates May, Jun and Sept, best to ring for dates, (01202) 483777; £5.

Weymouth SY6778 Elegant 18th- and 19th-c terraces along its curving esplanade, and some older buildings in the narrower, partly pedestrianised streets behind. The harbour is lively, with big ferries leaving from the outer quay, and the town's inner ring road running one-way around the inner harbour. The Old Rooms has good-value food and interesting harbour views. On the far side of the harbour the narrow streets of the old town are worth exploring; there's a TUDOR HOUSE on Trinity St. The resort has a good beach, and lots of lively family attractions.

♪ ☺ SEA LIFE PARK (Lodsmoor Country Park) One of the most elaborate in the excellent Sea Life Centres chain, and a reliable place for families. As well as the stunning marine displays and touch pools, new features include a Shark Academy, with fun interactive games and quizzes leading to a scholarship, and a splendid outdoor play area. Meals, snacks, shop, disabled access; cl 25 Dec; (01305) 788255; £5.95.

! ♦ DEEP SEA ADVENTURE 🔢 (Custom House Quay) Fascinating look at underwater exploration, shipwrecks, and the search for buried treasure, with lots of interactive displays. There's an exemplary exhibition on the Titanic, and a first-class indoor play area taking up most of the second floor (extra charge). Meals, snacks, shop, disabled access; cl 24–26 Dec; (01305) 760690; £3.

! 🐾 In the heart of the Old Harbour, BREWERS QUAY is a skilful conversion of harbourside Victorian brewery into shopping and leisure complex, with plenty of good year-round activities: the TIMEWALK 🔢 SY9788 imaginatively re-creates scenes from the town's history (limited disabled access), there's a craft market, 10-pin bowling, and a lively, hands-on science centre. They recently added a microbrewery, so the building has come full circle. Several places to eat, and good specialist shops; cl 25–27 Dec, and a couple of weeks late Jan; (01305) 777622; centre free, charges for some attractions (Timewalk £3.75).

🏰 ❄ NOTHE FORT (Barrack Rd) Interesting armed Victorian fort on 3 levels, spread over a staggering 70 rooms. Children can clamber over some of the vehicles and guns, and there are fine views of the harbour and coast. Snacks, shop, disabled access; open daily mid-May–Sept, plus pm Sun and bank hols rest of year; (01305) 787243; *£2.50. Good views too from the garden of the Nothe Tavern (with tasty fresh fish), and from the pleasant nearby Nothe Gardens.

Dorchester SY6890 Thriving country town, with busy shopping streets and Weds market, and several worthwhile antique and print shops. Though most of the more attractive Georgian buildings are just out of the bustle, there are a few distinguished buildings on the main streets, inc the timbered building of JUDGE JEFFREYS' LODGINGS in High West St; he stayed here during his notorious Bloody Assizes. The trial of the Tolpuddle Martyrs also took place on High West St, in the SHIRE HALL; the room is preserved as a memorial, and is open wkdys in summer hols, as are some of the cells. There are one or two traces of the Romans' occupation, including the fragmentary remains of a town house behind the County Hall, and of an amphitheatre on Weymouth Ave. Not far from here ELDRIDGE POPE'S VICTORIAN BREWERY has tours at 11am and 1pm on Weds, or you may be able to squeeze in on a pre-booked tour at other times, (01305) 251251 to check.

🏰 ❄ THOMAS HARDY lived here for most of his life, using the town as the centre of events in *The Mayor of Casterbridge* (the eponymous mayor supposedly living in what's now Barclays Bank). Among the places still associated with the author is MAX GATE (Alington Ave, 1m E on the A351), the house he designed and lived in from 1885 to his death in 1928, and where he wrote *Tess* and *Jude the Obscure*. You can see only the drawing room (the study has been moved to the County Museum), but the gardens are fascinating, not least because they inspired so much of Hardy's poetry. Shop, disabled access; open pm Sun, Mon and Weds Apr–Sept; (01305) 262538; £2; NT. The Trumpet Major food pub is very handy. HARDY'S COTTAGE (Higher Bockhampton, 3m E, just off the A35) The writer's 1840 birthplace is just outside town; the thatched house hasn't changed much since, though the heath's now largely forested (there is a stretch of open heathland much as he knew it just SE). House open by appointment Easter–Oct (not Fri and Sat); gardens open without appointment (though not much to see), with disabled access, or you can peer in from the public path; (01305) 262366; £2.50; NT. See **Walks** section below.

♿ COUNTY MUSEUM (High West St) Hardy's study from Max Gate has been reconstructed here, and there's a display on his namesake, Nelson's flag-captain at the Battle of Trafalgar. Quite a traditional museum, though very comprehensive. Shop, disabled access to ground floor only; cl Sun (exc July and Aug), 25–26 Dec, Good Fri; (01305) 262735; £2.75. Along in High East St the King's Arms Hotel, full of Hardy associations, is a good place for lunch.

! ♿ DINOSAUR MUSEUM (Icen Way) The best of Dorset's dinosaur-related exhibitions, a well displayed and entertaining collection very much designed with younger visitors in mind. Full-size skeletons and reconstructions, lots of opportunities to handle bones, fossils and the like (not many exhibits have barriers), and fun activities like Dinosaurs and You, where you put in your height and weight and the computer works out how you compare with a couple of dinosaurs. Look out for the intriguing Dinosaurid – a Canadian expert's idea of what dinosaurs would have evolved into if they hadn't become extinct. Shop, some disabled access; cl 24–26 Dec; (01305) 269880; £3.50 (£2.25 children). A similar approach is found at the TUTANKHAMUN EXHIBITION 🖼 (High West St), re-creating the discovery of ancient treasures using a mix of sights, sounds and smells; details as Dinosaur Museum.

♿ ❋ KEEP MILITARY MUSEUM (Bridport Rd) More interesting than most military museums, in handsome Victorian barracks gatehouse; splendid views from the battlements. Shop, disabled access; cl Sun exc July and Aug, 24 Dec–2 Jan; (01305) 264066; *£2.50

🏛 MAIDEN CASTLE (off the A354, S of Dorchester) One of the best examples of an Iron Age fort, a massive series of grassy ridges covering 47 acres.

Days Out

Fossils and the Dorset highlands
Boat trip from Lyme Regis; walk in Golden Cap estate from Stonebarrow Hill; lunch at the Anchor, Seatown; Pilsdon Pen; Forde Abbey.

Thomas Hardy's homeland
Dorchester; Maiden Castle; Hardy's Cottage, nature trail through Thorncombe Wood; lunch at the Ilchester Arms, Abbotsbury; visit subtropical gardens there, the swannery and Chesil Beach.

Lawrence of Arabia and the Tolpuddle Martyrs
Walk from Lulworth Cove to Durdle Door, or E through army ranges on cliffs when open; lunch at the Countryman, East Knighton; Bovington Camp, for Tank Museum and Clouds Hill; Tolpuddle.

Pottering around Purbeck
Corfe Castle, Swanage Railway; lunch at the Scott Arms, Kingston; explore cliff path from Worth Matravers, or walk up Ballard Down or into Durlston Country Park from Swanage; another option – Blue Pool and Studland (beach, Norman church).

Dorset's tranquil downlands
Beaminster, Powerstock, Eggardon hill fort; lunch at the Royal Oak or Red Lion, Cerne Abbas; Cerne Abbas giant, Mapperton gardens, Minterne Gardens.

A triangle of towns
Sherborne; Shaftesbury – lunch at the Two Brewers; Blandford Forum; if there's time, Milton Abbas village.

Poole and its unique island
Poole, Compton Acres garden; lunch at Portsmouth Hoy; boat trip to Brownsea Island; Sandbanks beach.

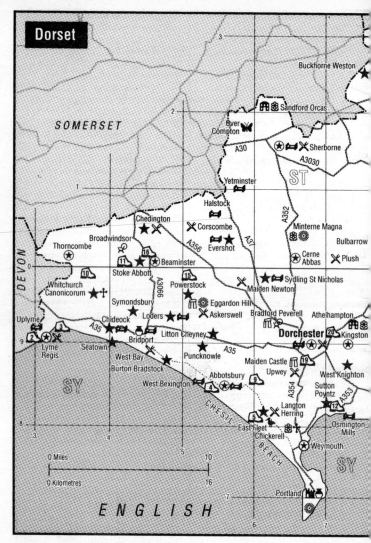

Other things to see and do

DORSET FAMILY ATTRACTION OF THE YEAR

! 🐾 ✙ **Wool** SY8486 MONKEY WORLD (off the A35 towards Bere Regis) This enthusiastic rescue centre for apes and chimps puts nearly as much care into looking after visitors as it does with the animals, so it's a very enjoyable as well as worthwhile trip. In addition to the biggest group of chimpanzees you'll see outside Africa, there's quite a range of play areas, with an extensive 15-stage obstacle course spread around the Pets Encounter, and mini-motor bikes and jet boats. Founded in 1987 to rehabilitate abused or injured chimpanzees, the centre now looks after all kinds of primates that are gradually reintroduced into natural surroundings: there are usually ring-tailed and ruffed lemurs, barbary macaques, capuchins and vervets, all roaming and climbing freely in decent-

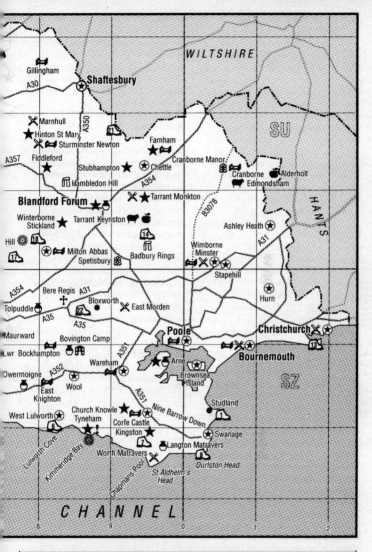

sized open enclosures. Keepers give useful talks, and you can see baby chimps playing in their nursery. There's the usual range of animals to fuss over, as well as woodland walks through the surrounding countryside. Last summer they had a clown on several afternoons throughout the holidays. Several bits are under cover or indoors, but it's not really ideal on a rainy day. Children from around 6 to 14 will probably enjoy it most (animal-minded adults will find it equally rewarding), and might not be as quick as parents to spot the wonderful irony of putting the obstacle course so close to the main chimpanzee enclosure; child and chimp seem to be clambering over not entirely dissimilar equipment. So much for evolution. Meals, snacks, shop, disabled access (a few steep paths); cl 25 Dec; freephone 0800 456600; £4.75 (£2.75 children). A family ticket is £13. The Seven Stars at East Burton has decent food (and a playground).

★ ⚘ ⚕ ⚘ ☨ ♈ ⛫ **Abbotsbury**
SY5785 Delightful Dorset village
with several worthwhile places to
visit – most famous is the unique
ancient SWANNERY 🅱, home to the
only sizeable colony of swans in the
world that can be seen during nesting
time, from decent paths. The swan
families quite happily come right up
to visitors, and during the cygnet
season (end of May–Jun) you might
see some of the hundreds of eggs
hatching right next to you. Also the
country's oldest working duck decoy,
children's activities, and interesting
reed-bed walks. Restaurant (reached
by a little bridge), shop, good
disabled access; cl Nov–Feb; (01305)
871684; £4.90. SUBTROPICAL GARDENS
20 acres of beautiful woodland with
very mild coastal climate letting rare
and record-breaking plants and trees
flourish; they claim the tallest
cultivated rose in the world. The
central walled garden in spring is a
mass of azaleas, camellias and
rhododendrons. Also a woodland
trail, aviary and play area. Meals,
snacks, shop and plant centre, some
disabled access; cl 25–26 Dec;
(01305) 871387; *£4 summer, less in
winter. The 14th-c hilltop CHAPEL (not
always open), with a bare earth floor,
belonged to the abbey, of which there
are a few medieval fragments around
the church. A huge medieval thatched
TITHE BARN now houses a museum of
rural life. Shop, disabled access; cl
Nov–Feb exc maybe Sun; (01305)
871817; £3. After visiting one of
Abbotsbury's attractions you get
discounts on the others. The village
also has an OYSTER FARM (cl am
winter), and the Ilchester Arms is
good for lunch. This is the best place
for access to Chesil Beach (see **Walks**
section below), and the B3157 W has
fine views, as does the Black Down
road passing the hideous Hardy
Monument (to the admiral) towards
Martinstown.

⛫ **Alderholt** SU1212 CRANBORNE
FARM Good for pick-your-own fruit.

⚘ ⚲ ⚘ ⛫ **Ashley Heath** SU1005
MOORS VALLEY COUNTRY PARK Good
for families, nearly 400 hectares of
forest, with river and lakeside walks,
fishing, nature trails, plenty of
wildlife, narrow-gauge steam
railway, unusual treetop walkway,
and 18-hole golf course. Meals,
snacks, shop, disabled access; cl 25
Dec; (01425) 470721; £3 car parking
charge (£1 after 4pm), free winter
wkdys (£1 wknds then).

♈ 🏵 **Athelhampton** SY7794
ATHELHAMPTON HOUSE (A35)
Magnificent 15th-c house, built on
the legendary site of King Athelstan's
palace. The Great Hall has a fantastic
roof. You'd never know now there
was a disastrous fire here in 1993 –
most of the beautiful furnishings and
contents (even much of the panelling)
were saved, and are back in their
original positions. An added bonus is
the acres of wonderful formal and
landscaped gardens with rare plants,
topiary and fountain pools. Meals,
snacks, shop, disabled access; open
daily (exc Sat) Mar–Oct, Sun only
Nov–Feb; (01305) 848363; *£4.80
house and gardens, £2.80 garden
only. The Martyrs at Tolpuddle has
decent home cooking.

♈ ♿ ⚘ 🏵 **Beaminster** ST4701
PARNHAM (A3066 towards Bridport)
Surrounded by 14 acres of lovely
gardens, this fine Tudor mansion is
famous as the home of John
Makepeace the furniture-maker. His
workshop is open, with completed
pieces shown around the house, along
with exhibitions by other craftsmen.
Meals, snacks, shop, mostly disabled
access; open Apr–Oct, Sun,
Tues–Thurs, and bank hols; (01308)
862204; *£4. The nearby woods of
Hooke Park are pleasant for a stroll;
you can get a combined ticket with
the house. MAPPERTON GARDENS (off
the B3163 E) Several delightful acres
of terraced hillside gardens in
grounds of a 16th-c manor house;
specimen trees and shrubs, fountains,
grottoes, fishponds, orangery, good
walks and views. Occasional musical
events in summer. Shop, some
disabled access; cl am, and all
Nov–Feb; (01308) 863014; *£3.
HORN PARK (off the A3066 N)
Unusual plants in a series of gardens
with bluebell woods, ponds, wild
flowers and nice views. They've

begun work on an arboretum. Teas, plant sales, some disabled access; open pm Tues, Weds, Sun and bank hols Apr–Oct; (01308) 862212; *£3. In the town, Pickwicks and the Greyhound are good bets for food.

† **Bere Regis** SY8494 The CHURCH here has the finest timbered roof in Dorset, with extraordinary carved figures; 20p in a slot lights these up to remarkable effect. It also contains the Turberville tomb and window mentioned in *Tess of the d'Urbervilles*. The Royal Oak is good value for lunch.

★ ♨ **Blandford Forum** ST8806 Georgian market town, rebuilt in 1731 after the older buildings were destroyed by fire – very interesting to walk round. MRS PENNY'S CAVALCADE OF COSTUME ▣ (The Plocks) Wide-ranging collection of clothes in Georgian Lime Tree House; children can try on copies of some of the exhibits. Snacks, shop, limited disabled access; cl Tues, Weds and 25 Dec; (01258) 450388; £3. The town also has a useful local history MUSEUM (cl Sun, Oct–Mar; *£1), and out at Blandford Camp the recently jazzed up ROYAL SIGNALS MUSEUM, looks at the history of army communications (cl wknds exc Jun–Sept, and 10 days over Christmas; £3). The Greyhound has a popular restaurant, and Nelson's has decent food.

♨ 🏠 **Bovington Camp** SY8388 TANK MUSEUM Over 260 armoured fighting vehicles from 23 countries, some of which you can go inside, as well as tank simulators (the screen can be a bit fuzzy), costumes, medals, weapons and videos. Many of the tanks are now put through their paces (complete with gunfire) July–Sept (not Sat), and their Battle Day, the last Sun in July, is quite a spectacle. There's an exhibition on Lawrence of Arabia, and an assault course for children. Meals, snacks, shop, disabled access; cl Christmas wk; (01929) 403463; *£5. A mile or so down the road, CLOUDS HILL is the cottage Lawrence lived in as a private in the tank corps, and his sleeping-bag, furniture and other memorabilia can be seen in the 3 ascetic little

rooms on display. Open pm Weds, Thurs, Fri, Sun and bank hols Apr–Oct; £2.20; NT. The very child-friendly Countryman at East Knighton has good food.

🏠 ♨ **Bradford Peverell** SY6593 NEW BARN FIELD CENTRE Authentic re-creation of an Iron Age homestead, complete with animals and so on; also a working potter, wildflower reserve and nature trails. Summer meals and snacks, shop, some disabled access; cl Oct–Easter; (01305) 268865; *£3.50. They run residential courses.

♨ **Bridport** SY4692 Still the country's main rope producer, and its old harbour is now the busy fishing port of nearby West Bay, a restrained small resort (where the West Bay Hotel has good local seafood). The old town centre has a local history MUSEUM in a fine Tudor building (cl Sun, Weds and Nov–Mar; £1). A HARBOUR MUSEUM, just S of town, has rope- and net-making displays (cl Oct–Mar; £1.50p). The Crown, out that way, also does decent food.

♨ **Broadwindsor** ST4302 Good CRAFT AND DESIGN CENTRE in former farm buildings; potters, woodworkers, hatters, gem-polishers and so forth. Meals, snacks, shop, disabled access; cl 23 Dec–1 Mar; (01308) 868362; free. The B3164 W to Birdsmoorgate and then the B3165 through Marshwood (good country pub) is an unspoilt scenic drive through a little-known valley.

❋ **Bulbarrow Hill** ST7705 Memorable viewpoint on the narrow lanes just S of Woolland, especially on a summer evening with the sun going down over Somerset. Around here, a scenic drive runs from Piddletrenthide through Plush (the Brace of Pheasants is a very good lunchtime stop) and Mappowder to Hazelbury Bryan, then through Ansty and Melcombe Bingham, to turn right at Cheselbourne for Piddletrenthide again.

★ † 🏠 ♨ **Cerne Abbas** ST6601 Attractive village with a fine church, fragments of the old abbey, a remarkable collection of good pubs (the Red Lion and Royal Oak are the best), and its famously indelicate prehistoric giant cut into the chalk above, best seen from the main road N. There's a working POTTERY (cl winter Mons) on the way up to the giant; above it, the old Dorchester–Middlemarsh ridge road has some bracing views.

🏠 ⛉ ✿ **Chettle** ST9413 CHETTLE HOUSE Fine baroque country house, with beautifully laid out gardens, vineyard and gallery; various craft wknds and special events. Snacks, some disabled access; cl Tues, Sat, and mid-Oct–Easter; (01258) 830209; £2. The Bugle Horn at Tarrant Gunville is handy for lunch.

⛉ † **Chickerell** SY6480 BENNETTS WATER GARDENS (Putton Lane) 8 acres of landscaped lakes renowned for their summer water lilies – over 100 varieties. Home-made teas, shop, disabled access; open Tues–Fri Apr–Oct, plus Sats Apr–Sept, and Suns Apr–Aug; (01305) 785150; £3.95. Neighbouring EAST FLEET SY6380 is interesting, particularly for the former church which was wrecked by a legendary 1824 storm. Swans nest on the nearby Fleet lagoon, and the vicinity's pleasant walks (see Walks section below) are especially interesting if you've read J M Faulkner's *Moonfleet*. The Elm Tree at Langton Herring is handy for lunch.

★ 🏰 ✿ ⚓ ⛉ ♨ **Corfe Castle** SY9681 The CASTLE is the most spectacular ruin in the area, and gives superb views from its dramatic hilltop position. The site is remarkably atmospheric considering how little of the castle is left, and it's great fun clambering over the ancient stones. Meals, snacks, shop; cl 25–26 Dec; (01929) 481294; £3.50; NT. The Swanage Railway (see entry below) now runs to here; a joint ticket is available. Set in attractive gardens, the MODEL VILLAGE has a faithful reconstruction of what the Norman castle looked like before the Parliamentarians destroyed it in 1646; cl Nov–Easter; (01929) 481234; £1.75. A Tudor building on nearby West St has a decent local history MUSEUM, with dinosaur

footprints; cl wkdys Nov–Mar exc some school hols; free. Parking can be a problem in the town in summer. The Halfway at Norden Heath (on the A351 towards Wareham) has good Cypriot food. The road W through Church Knowle is pretty.

⛉ **Cranborne** SU0513 A peaceful place, with the Fleur-de-Lys a good pub well known to Hardy and the subject of an entertaining poem by Rupert Brooke (framed inside). CRANBORNE MANOR Splendid 17th-c gardens originally laid out by Tradescant; Jacobean mount garden, herb garden, lovely river garden and avenues of beech and lime. Particularly attractive in spring. Snacks, shop and garden centre, disabled access; gardens open Weds only Mar–Sept, garden centre daily all year; (01725) 517289; *£3. The B3078 has good country views, as does the minor road crossing it to Three Legged Cross and the Gussages.

🐴 **Edmondsham** SU0611 DORSET HEAVY HORSE CENTRE 🖼 (well signed from Verwood) Cheery place with 6 different breeds of huge heavy horse, and miniature Shetland ponies at the other extreme. The shire horses are paraded at 11.30am, 2pm and 4pm. Snacks, shop, disabled access; cl Nov–Easter; (01202) 824040; £3.95, maybe less out of season. For an extra £12 an hour you can go for a tolt on an Icelandic horse (the tolt is said to be the most comfortable gait of all). The Albion is handy for lunch.

! ⛉ 🐴 ⚓ **Hurn** SZ1296 ALICE IN WONDERLAND MAZE (opposite Bournemouth Airport) Maze made up of 5,200 bushes cut into the shapes of Alice characters; also play areas, croquet lawns, herb gardens, theatre, a few rides, farmyard with rare breeds, and pick-your-own fields with berries, beans, potatoes, courgettes and sweetcorn. Lots of thought and effort have been put into the site. Meals, snacks, shop, some disabled access; open Easter–Oct (wknds only from mid–Sept); (01202) 483444; *£3. The Avon Causeway Hotel does decent food. **Kimmeridge Bay** SY9079 A lovely spot with intriguing rock strata, kept quieter than it might be by the toll. The New Inn up at Church Knowle is good for lunch.

🐕 🐘 🐄 **Kingston Maurward** SY7290 KINGSTON MAURWARD PARK Very close to Dorchester, but feels like the heart of the countryside, with peaceful woodland and lakeside walks, farm park (children can feed the animals), and plenty of garden variety inc Elizabethan and Edwardian gardens, *Penstemon* and *Salvia* national collections. Snacks, shop, some disabled access; cl Nov–Easter; (01305) 264738; £3.

♿ **Langton Matravers** SY9978 The village has a MUSEUM on the Purbeck stone industry; cl 12–2pm, all Sun, and Nov–Mar; free.

★ ♿ 🎣 ♿ 🐄 **Lyme Regis** SY3492 Enchanting old seaside town, with rather an elegant, steep main street and interesting side streets; the esplanade is pretty, and there's a lively little fishing and yacht harbour. The sea has been cleaned up by a new sewage treatment plant, tempting some quite varied animals to make the occasional visit. Pleasant coast and valley walks. The Pilot Boat on the front is the best place for lunch; the enjoyable old Royal Standard has a lighted terrace leading to the harbour and beach. DINOSAURLAND (Coombe St) has an excellent collection of fossils, and can tell you about any you may have at home. They do 2-hour fossil walks along the beach. Shop, disabled access to ground floor only; cl 25–26 Dec; (01297) 443541; *£3.20, guided beach walks *£4.50 (booking recommended). Right on the historic harbour wall (known as The Cobb) is a decent, family-run MARINE AQUARIUM, with local history exhibits too. Disabled access; cl Nov–Easter; (01297) 443678; *£1.30. They run entertaining scenic BOAT TRIPS around the coast; £3 an hour. The town gets very busy in summer, but it is worth braving the crowds; escape to the Jane Austen cliffside gardens for peaceful sea views.

★ 🐘 ✝ 🐄 **Milton Abbas** ST8001 Lovely thatched village built in the 18th c to replace an earlier one which had spoilt the view from the big house; the 17th-c almshouses were moved here at the same time. Pleasant stroll past the lake through the Capability Brown park to the fine 15th-c abbey church of a former Benedictine monastery (it now serves the public school in the nearby house). There's a signed walk over the lane to a former chapel in the wood. RARE POULTRY, PIG AND PLANT CENTRE 🐷 (Long Ash Farm, just W on the Ansty road) 10 breeds of pig and piglets, all sorts of unusual poultry inc hens laying eggs in dazzling blues and browns, baby chicks to touch, and local crafts. Snacks, shop, limited disabled access; cl Mon–Weds (exc bank hols), and Oct–Easter (exc Sun); (01258) 880447; *£2.

🐘 ❀ **Minterne Magna** ST6504 MINTERNE GARDENS (Minterne House, off the A352) Beautiful landscaped gardens, with lakes, cascades, streams, rare trees and impressive spring shows of azaleas, rhododendrons and spring bulbs; the autumn colours can be quite spectacular. Open April–Oct; (01300) 341370; *£3. The road W up Gore Hill and Batcombe Hill to Holywell has memorable views.

🦋 **Over Compton** ST5817 WORLDLIFE AND LULLINGSTONE SILK FARM Superb collection of butterflies, flying free in reconstructions of their natural habitat inside Elizabethan Compton Hall. The silk farm demonstrates production of English silk used for coronations and royal weddings. Snacks, shop, some disabled access; cl Oct–Mar; (01935) 474608; £4.

♿ 🏭 **Owermoigne** SY7685 MILL HOUSE CIDER MUSEUM Cider museum with fully restored 18th- and 19th-c equipment, and video demonstrating the process. Also collection of locally made 18th- and 19th-c clocks. Shop; cl Dec 25–mid-Jan; (01305) 852220; £1.50 cider museum, £2 clocks, £3 both. The beautifully placed Sailors Return at East Chaldon is good value for lunch.

❀ 🏰 ♿ **Portland** SY6870 This odd,

much-quarried promontory with its narrow neck and long naval connections gives tremendous views from its peak. Nearer at hand, the remarkable sea defences of Portland Harbour laid out below are a fine sight – and you may glimpse Britain's first prison ship for generations moored off here. The CASTLE was built under Henry VIII to defend the south coast. Snacks, shop, limited disabled access; cl Nov–Mar; (01305) 820539; £2.20. A cottage used by Hardy in *The Well-Beloved* (Wakeham St), is now a local history MUSEUM (cl 1–1.30pm, and all Weds and Thurs; (01305) 821804; £1.60). The Pulpit, handy for a stroll to the lighthouse and cliffs, is useful for lunch.

🏠 🅷 **Sandford Orcas** ST6220
MANOR HOUSE Interesting, lived-in Tudor manor house, largely unaltered since 16th c, with fine furnishings and family portraits, and pleasant gardens, at their best May and Jun. Open Easter Mon, then pm Sun and all day Mon May–Sept; (01963) 220206; *£2.50. The Queen's Arms at Corton Denham has decent food.

★ ❀ 🄫 ◔ **Shaftesbury** ST8622
Hilltop town with good views from Castle Hill and Park Walk; its most famous street is Gold Hill – thatched cottages stepped down a steep cobbled street, familiar from those Hovis TV advertisements. St James below (where the Two Brewers is the town's best family food pub) is attractive. You can still see the foundations of an ABBEY set up by Alfred the Great; excavated remains from the site can be seen at an adjacent MUSEUM, along with an Anglo-Saxon herb garden. Shop, disabled access; cl Nov–Easter; (01747) 852910; *90p. At the top of Gold Hill, the local history MUSEUM includes a mummified cat found during the rethatching of a local cottage. Shop, disabled access to ground floor only; cl Oct–Easter exc some wknds; (01747) 852157; 75p. There are several craft shops and workshops.

★ 🏠 ✝ 🄫 🅷 ◔ **Sherborne** ST6316

An attractive town to wander through, given a feeling of unchanging solidity by the handsome stone medieval abbey buildings that mix in with later ones of the public school here, and by many other fine old buildings in and nr the main street. The ABBEY itself is a glorious golden stone building with a beautifully vaulted nave; at the Dissolution the townspeople raised the money to buy it, and it's been the parish church ever since. Locals remain very much involved in its fortunes, recently winning their campaign to rid the church of a 19th-c stained-glass window by Pugin, in which Old Testament prophets were said to resemble Mr Blobby.
SHERBORNE CASTLE (1m E) Striking old house built by Sir Walter Raleigh in 1594, standing out particularly for its wonderful period furnishings, though there are also interesting paintings and porcelain. Outside are gardens designed by Capability Brown, and beautiful parkland with an enormous lake. Snacks, shop; open pm Thurs, Sat, Sun, and bank hols Easter–Oct; (01935) 813182; £4.80 house and gardens, £2.40 grounds only. Directly across the water, SHERBORNE OLD CASTLE is the original 12th-c castle, now a beautifully evocative ruin. Good for a picnic, and especially appealing in Apr when the dry ditch is full of wild primroses. Shop, disabled access (but no facilities); cl 1–2pm, winter Mon and Tues, 24–26 Dec; (01935) 812730; £1.50. The SHERBORNE MUSEUM (Abbeygate House) has a reconstruction of the old castle in its heyday, as well as Victorian dolls' houses and Roman remains. Shop, disabled access to ground floor only; cl am Sun, Mon (exc bank hols), and Nov–Easter; (01935) 812252; £1. The unspoilt Digby Tap (handy for the abbey but no food Sun) and Skippers (Horsecastles) are useful for lunch. Several craft shops include a working saddlery in the main street.
🄫 **Spetisbury** ST9102 OLD MILL Pretty, medium-sized riverside water garden, with lots of plants for sale. Snacks; open pm Weds and

occasional Suns Jun–Aug; (01258) 453939; *£2. The Charlton Inn at Charlton Marshall is a good food pub.

✝ ⚘ 🐜 🐦 **Stapehill** SU0500 STAPEHILL ABBEY 🔲 Just right for a relaxed, unhurried afternoon, a 19th-c Cistercian abbey with craft workshops and exhibitions on monastic life; acres of park and landscaped gardens with waterfalls and woodland walk, and a play area and farm animals for children. Meals, snacks, shop, disabled access; best to check winter opening; (01202) 873060; *£4.80. KNOLL GARDENS (Stapehill Rd) Rare and exotic plants in various colourfully themed gardens, with over 4,000 different named species, many of which can be bought in the rapidly developing nursery. Meals, snacks, shop and garden centre, disabled access; cl Dec–Feb, and Mon and Tues in Mar; (01202) 873931; *£3.25, OAPs £2.90. Adjacent Trehane Nurseries have a great range of camellias. The Barley Mow at Colehill is a good food pub.

🐚 🐜 🐦 **Swanage** SZ0278 Fairly quiet 19th-c resort, which, for reasons hotly disputed by locals, seems to be losing much of the sand from the northern end of its beaches. SWANAGE RAILWAY 🔲 Steamtrains now run along 6 miles of track to Corfe Castle (a joint ticket is available): a nice way of approaching the ruins – or you could walk there and ride back. The Swanage station has an exhibition of old railway memorabilia, and, more unusually, a travel agency where the commission goes to the railway's upkeep. Snacks, shop, disabled access; cl winter wkdys exc school hols, best to ring for timetable; (01929) 424276 for train times; £5.50. The seaview Mowlem Theatre restaurant (Shire Rd) is good. DURLSTON COUNTRY PARK 260 acres of spectacular clifftop scenery and unspoilt countryside; fine observation spots to watch seabirds, butterflies or deer (let them know if you see dolphins, seals or whales) – and see **Walks** section below. Snacks, shop, good disabled access (they have

a little buggy for bumpy ground); information centre cl wkdys Nov–Mar; (01929) 424443; free, though there's a parking charge of around £2 in summer (50p winter). The beach at nearby **Studland** SZ0382 is lovely – there's a charge to go on it in summer (less after 2pm), and car parking is expensive exc for NT members; behind is a nature reserve, with nearby a NT visitor centre with snacks and shop, and decent food at the Manor House Hotel (where Churchill and Eisenhower watched the D-Day rehearsals).

🐑 🍎 **Tarrant Keynston** ST9204 KEYNSTON MILL FRUIT FARM Interesting vineyard and farm shop, with 21 different kinds of pick-your-own. Meals and snacks; cl winter Mon; (01258) 452596; free. The True Lovers Knot has decent food and a big garden.

🐜 🏛 🐦 **Thorncombe** ST3504 FORDE ABBEY The extensive gardens here really are special, with glorious trees and shrubs, a fine collection of Asiatic primulas, many interesting plants, and sweeping lawns. The striking abbey buildings still retain some of the features of the original 12th-c Cistercian monastery, but it was modernised in 1500 by Abbot Chard, and it's his Great Hall and tower that remain. Cromwell's Attorney General later turned the abbey into a house, and the interior has changed little since, with magnificently furnished rooms, unusual plaster ceilings and a set of Raphael tapestries. Meals and snacks (in the 12th-c undercroft), shop, disabled access to gardens only; house open pm Weds, Sun and bank hols Apr–Oct, garden and nursery all year; (01460) 220231; £5, £3.70 garden only. Thorncombe Wood is awash with bluebells in spring. The George over at Chardstock is the closest good place for lunch.

🐚 **Tolpuddle** SY7994 Famous for the agricultural workers who united to improve their working conditions and terms of employment. The MARTYRS' TREE under which they supposedly met still remains, and a

MUSEUM spread over 6 cottages tells their story. Shop, disabled access by arrangement; cl Mon, Christmas wk; (01305) 848237; free. The Martyrs pub is useful for lunch.

! **Tyneham** SY8880 ABANDONED VILLAGE On the army's Purbeck firing ranges (open holidays and most wknds), this is quite poignant; there's an explanatory exhibition in the former church.

† ✠ 🐚 **Wareham** SY9287 This largely modern town has a few striking old buildings, inc the CHURCH of St Martin's, with a finely carved memorial to Lawrence of Arabia. The church of Lady St Mary not far from the Quay has the coffin of Edward the Martyr, murdered at nearby Corfe Castle in 978. There are 2 very traditional old inns, the Black Bear and King's Arms; another, the Quay, is in a fine position. BLUE POOL (Furzebrook, 3 miles S of Wareham) Peaceful beauty-spot with curious colour changes in the water whenever the weather alters, from light green to blue to suddenly a rich turquoise; it's bluest on an overcast day. Also 25 acres of heathland with rare plants and animals. Snacks, shop, some disabled access; facilities and museum cl Oct–Easter, site cl Nov–Mar; (01929) 551408; £2.40. The attractive road over the West Creech Hills may sometimes be closed for army firing practice.

🏰 ❀ 🐌 † ♭ **West Lulworth** SY8280 A lovely spot, though hardly undiscovered (parking can be a nightmare), just above a very beautiful cove with extraordinary nearby rock formations; the thatched Castle Inn is useful for lunch. 17th-c LULWORTH CASTLE has now been fully restored, and its South-east tower has splendid views over the wooded park; the formal gardens are a nice spot for a picnic. The Catholic chapel was the first to be built in England after the Reformation, and an Anglican church was built in part by Thomas Hardy, about whom there's an exhibition inside. Meals, teas, shop; best to check winter opening, (01929) 400352; *£1.50. Exhibitions on smuggling and country wines in the

LULWORTH COVE HERITAGE CENTRE (cl 25 Dec; free – may be a charge for parking nearby), and the Lulworth Equestrian Centre can arrange HORSE-RIDING; (01929) 400396; around £10 an hour. Slightly W, the unusually shaped rocks at Durdle Door are surrounded by particularly good beaches.

† 🐚 🏠 🖼 🐌 ✖ **Wimborne Minster** SZ0199 has Georgian houses (and decent antique shops and auctions) in the narrow central streets around the MINSTER – a fine, well preserved, largely Norman church with contrasting red and grey masonry, twin towers, and a brightly coloured jack striking the clock bell every quarter. Inside, is an interesting Norman crypt, a distinctive astronomical clock and the original chained library. PRIEST'S HOUSE MUSEUM (High St) Historic town house with carefully researched period rooms; regular cooking displays in the Victorian kitchen, and a charming walled garden. Summer teas, shop, disabled access to ground floor and garden; cl Sun (exc pm Jun–Sept and bank hol wknds), and Nov–Mar exc a couple of wks around Christmas; (01202) 882533; £2. Dormers (Hanham Rd) and the Cross Keys (Victoria Rd, W) are best for lunch. KINGSTON LACY (NW on the B3082) Impressive 17th-c mansion later remodelled by Charles Barry, with grand Italian marble staircase and superb Venetian ceiling; outstanding paintings such as the *Judgement of Solomon* by Sebastiano del Piamtino, and others by Titian, Rubens and van Dyck. The enormous grounds have landscaped gardens, a herd of Red Devon cattle in the park, and summer concerts and plays. Lovely snowdrops in Feb and early Mar. Meals, snacks, shop, disabled access to park and gardens; cl am, Thurs, Fri and all Nov–Mar; (01202) 883402; £5.50, £2.20 grounds only; NT. WALFORD MILL (Stone Lane) Former 18th-c flour mill with exhibitions and local crafts. Meals, snacks, shop, disabled access; cl 24 Dec–1 Jan, and Mon Jan–Mar; (01202) 841400; free. MERLEY HOUSE

Fine 18th-c mansion with interesting plaster ceilings and an excellent collection of 5,000 model toy cars, aeroplanes and railways. Snacks (July and Aug only), shop, limited disabled access; open for temporary exhibitions in spring and early summer (ring for exact dates) and daily July–Sept; (01202) 886533; *£1.75. Just W of town at Pamphill is a good big farm shop, and just E there are pleasant country walks around the Fox & Hounds at Little Canford SZ0499.

✤ **Wool** SY8486 In Hardy's Wessex this was the ancient seat of the d'Urbervilles. *See separate Family Panel on p.224 for* MONKEY WORLD.

★ **Attractive villages** with decent pubs include Buckhorn Weston ST7524, Burton Bradstock SY4889, Chedington ST4805, Chideock SY4292 (sadly ripped in half by the busy A35; nearby Seatown SY4291 has some charming stone cottages and a perfectly placed seaside pub – some local authority spending could turn this cove into a real honeypot), Church Knowle SY9481, Evershot ST5704, Farnham ST9515, Fiddleford ST8013, Hinton St Mary ST7816 (superb manor house, medieval tithe barn), Kingston SY9579, Langton Herring SY6182, Litton Cheyney SY5590, Loders SY4994, Powerstock SY5196, Puncknowle SY5388 (pronounced Punnel), Sutton Poyntz SY7083 (handy for White Horse Hill and coastal path), thatched Stoke Abbott ST4500, Sydling St Nicholas SY6399, Symondsbury SY4493, Tarrant Monkton ST9408, West Knighton SY7387, Whitchurch Canonicorum (fine church) and Winterborne Stickland ST8304 (the road through the Winterbornes to Okeford Fitzpaine has good downland views). Arne SY9788 is a relatively undiscovered little village, with a good toy museum, quiet beach and nature trail. You might also like to explore the bridleway from Stubhampton ST9114 along Ashmore Bottom to Ashmore (can be muddy in a wet spring).

🏛 Remains of once formidable **Iron Age hill forts** can be seen at Badbury Rings ST9602, just off the B3082 NW of Wimborne (associated by some with King Arthur), Eggardon Hill SY5494 (wonderful views and impressive ramparts), and Hambledon Hill ST8412 (in a commanding position just above Child Okeford).

Walks

The Dorset Coast Path, part of the 500-mile South-West Peninsula Path, follows the entire coastline where practicable, cutting in a bit to avoid some sheer unfenced drops from the clifftops (particularly on Purbeck).

Studland SZ0382 ⌂-1 provides the most remarkably varied short walk in the county. In a couple of hours you can take in Ballard Down (with huge views over Poole Harbour), Old Harry Rocks (tooth-like chalk pinnacles detached from the cliff) and the Agglestone (a rock standing solitary on Dorset's largest surviving heath). Nine Barrow Down SZ0081, the main Purbeck ridge, has far-ranging two-way views and makes a good goal for walks from Corfe Castle.

Lyme Regis SY3492 ⌂-2 has a path snaking W through an intriguing nature-reserve undercliff, still subject to landfalls, a celebrated area for fossils and flora. **Golden Cap** ⌂-3, the highest point on the county's coast, can be reached from Seatown SY4291 (friendly pub; nice walk too along to the New Inn at Eype SY4491). Just E of Charmouth a steep narrow road leads up to Stonebarrow Hill SY3893; good easy walking, fine sea and inland views, disabled WC, NT shop in season.

Abbotsbury SY5785 ⌂-4 is the start for strolls around Chapel Hill SY5784 and on to the massive shingle bank of Chesil Beach (exhausting to walk any distance along). Paths leading N from the village get lovely views from the chalk downs.

East Fleet SY6380 ◠-5 has a tiny ruined church close to the great lagoon enclosed by Chesil Beach, which was used for trying out the dam-busting bouncing bomb; it is a peaceful spot with a diverse bird population.

Lulworth Cove SY8280 ◠-6 has a classic mini-walk W along the cliffs to Durdle Door, a natural arch eroded by the sea; inland is prairie-like monotony, and it is best to return the same way. E of Lulworth Cove is army training land, which means high-security fences and dire warning notices, but you are allowed in most weekends and daily in Aug and during Easter (keep to the paths). Information boards by road junctions off the A351 and A352 nr Wareham give opening times; or ring (01929) 462721 ext 4824 and ask for the Guardroom. The coastal walk between Lulworth Cove and Kimmeridge Bay SY9078 is very strenuous but excellent, heading past the surreal 'fossil forest' (formed of petrified algae that once clung to tree-trunks) to Mupe Bay SY8479. Another path ascends Bindon Hill SY8380, looking down over the semi-circular cove.

Kingston SY9579 ◠-7 has an easy level path to Hounstout Cliff SY9577 (fortify yourself beforehand at the Scott Arms, a good family pub with superb views of Corfe Castle). Turn left at the end and you are into Dorset fossil country, presided over by the primitive hermitage chapel on St Aldhelm's Head SY9675; the path here is of the switchback sort, and the chalk mud can make it tough going. At Worth Matravers SY9777, the unpretentious Square & Compass (lovely views) is another good base for coastal walks in this area. Nr here, the rock pool at Dancing Ledge SY9976 is said to have been cut by a local schoolmaster.

Durlston Head Country Park SZ0377 ◠-8, on the edge of Swanage SZ0278, has fine views from the headland and the Great Globe, a 40-ton global representation in Purbeck marble.

Portesham SY6085 ◠-9 has high heathland above, with a view covering the entire sweep of the West Dorset coast. A track along Bronkham Hill SE from the car park by the prominent Hardy Monument feels truly ancient, with prehistoric burial mounds flanking it. **Lamberts Castle** SY3799 ◠-10 is an unspoiled hill fort, charming for strolls (especially late summer when the heather is out) but quite hard to spot the turning from the road. **Pilsdon Pen** ◠-11 ST4101 is less extensive as a strolling ground but even better for views – Dorset's highest point, capped by a hill fort and looking over Lyme Bay and N towards the Mendips; it is reached within minutes from a layby.

Sutton Poyntz SY7083 and **Osmington** SY7283 ◠-12 are thatched villages joined by paths with views of the White Horse – an equestrian portrait of George III etched into the hillside; you can walk back along the Dorset coastal path, which here leads along the top of the downs rather than along the coast itself.

The Bournemouth area doesn't have much walking of the sort that rouses appetites, but is only a short drive from Hampshire's New Forest. **Hengistbury Head** SZ1790 ◠-13 is by far the best closer place for a stroll: not a long walk, but the feeling of space and views are outstanding. **Badbury Rings** ST9602 ◠-14 is a hill fort, from where a Roman road lets you strike out for miles northwards.

Despite the ultra-English charm of much of inland Dorset – chalk downs, sleepy thatched villages, clumps of beechwoods and fine views – the area is surprisingly little walked, so field routes are often not obvious, careful map-reading is necessary, and even then sometimes the longer paths can be difficult to follow.

The best areas are those where agricultural improvement has been limited: the vicinities of **Nettlecombe** SY5195 ◠-15 and **Stoke Abbott** ST4500 ◠-16, for example, have delectable downland and valley landscapes, with a reasonably good path network (and both have decent pubs); another fine pub base for a country walk is the excellent Fox at Corscombe ST5105. **Binghams Melcombe** ST7602 ⌂-17 has attractive downland to the W; the dry ground of the Dorsetshire Gap ST7403 comes as a pleasant surprise on those days when you begin to think that all Dorset is turning to chalky mud.

Milton Abbas ST8001 ⌂-18 has attractive paths through the abbey estate and into Green Hill Down Nature Reserve; a longer walk continues NW to Bulbarrow Hill ST7605, which looks far into Somerset and Wilts. **Maiden Castle** SY6890 ⌂-19, nr Dorchester, is so vast that the tour of its grassy ramparts almost qualifies as a fully-fledged walk.

Higher Bockhampton SY7292 ⌂-20 gives a walk from the thatched cottage where Thomas Hardy was born into nearby forest plantations and on to Black Heath and Duddle Heath, parts of the 'untamed and untameable' Egdon Heath of Hardy's novels: further Hardyesque features abound locally, inc the church at Stinsford ('Mellstock') SY7191, where Hardy's heart is buried beside his first wife. A path from the river at Lower Bockhampton SY7290 leads to the village, and a nature trail leads through Thorncombe Wood to Hardy's cottage.

Cranborne Chase ⌂-21, shared with Wilts, offers good walking with some fine views, especially around Ashmore ST9217. **Bere Wood** SY8794 ⌂-22 at the W end of Bloxworth is a lovely bluebell wood; the track can be followed right through to Bere Regis. (There are even more bluebells at Delcombe Wood ST7805, but the only public track just skirts the W edge of the wood.)

Where to eat

Askerswell SY5292 SPYWAY (01308) 485250 Former smugglers' look-out with exceptional-value, very popular bar food, lots of salads and cheesecakes; nice views, a big garden, walks nearby; no children inside. £15.30|£5.40.

Bournemouth SZ0991 SOPHISTICATS 43 Charminster Rd (01202) 291019 Enjoyable, often elaborate food in this popular restaurant decorated with a cat theme; good-value wines and informal, friendly service; cl Sun, Mon, 2 wks Jan; disabled access. £27.

Chedington ST4805 WINYARDS GAP (01935) 891244 Comfortable pub with marvellous views and nearby walks; a wide choice of good bar food inc lots of fresh fish dishes, vegetarian choices, home-made puddings, daily specials, and children's menus; self-catering flats in a converted barn; disabled access. £14|£3.75.

Christchurch SZ1593 SPLINTERS 12 Church St (01202) 483454 Fine old building nr the priory with 3 attractively decorated rooms; good, imaginative modern cooking, lovely chocolatey puddings, a splendid British cheese choice, good-value wines, and friendly helpful owners; they also run Pommery's (next door) with a delicatessen on the ground floor and a lively café bar upstairs. £33.95|£4.95.

Corscombe ST5015 FOX (01935) 891330 Cosy thatched pub, very much a traditional family-run place, with lovely polished copper pots and pans, scrubbed pine tables, candles in champagne bottles, open fires in one room and woodburning stove in another; particularly nice food (especially daily specials), well kept real ales, local cider, and a good wine list; nice surrounding walks; well behaved children welcome; bedrooms. £23|£3.95.

Dorchester SY6890 POTTER IN 19 Durngate St (01305) 260312 Popular place in the centre of town, with all day food inc English breakfast, enjoyable lunchtime meals and snacks, and afternoon tea; a walled garden for summer, open fire and fresh flowers, and a friendly welcome; disabled access. £2.

East Morden SY9195 COCK & BOTTLE (01929) 459238 Popular dining pub with several beamed communicating areas, a nice mix of old furnishings and a log fire; enjoyable food inc interesting daily specials with plenty of fish and seasonal game, well kept beers, and good wines. £18.75|£6.75.

Langton Herring SY6182 ELM TREE (01305) 871257 Busy pub in a pretty thatched village with a good range of interesting home-cooked bar food, and children's menu; close to coastal path. £18|£7.55.

Lyme Regis SY3492 PILOT BOAT (01297) 443157 Welcoming place across from the beaches, with a bustling atmosphere, light comfortable dining bar decorated with fishing and nautical memorabilia, good food, and a no smoking restaurant; decent wines and liqueurs; disabled access. £11.50|£3.75.

Maiden Newton SY5997 PETIT CANARD Dorchester Rd (01300) 320536 Welcoming little restaurant with simple furnishings; good, interesting food – grilled kangaroo, quite a few Eastern influences, fine puddings, and a well chosen wine list; cl am Sun, Mon, 1st wk Jan; children over 6. £29.50.

Marnhull ST7718 BLACKMORE VALE (01258) 820701 Relaxed and friendly atmosphere in pleasant old pub with nice home-made bar food, decent beer and wine, and a log fire and interesting furnishings in the comfortably modernised bar; you can also eat in the garden where one of the tables is thatched; children over 14. £18|£3.75.

Plush ST7102 BRACE OF PHEASANTS (01300) 348357 Long, low, 16th-c thatched cottage with a civilised but relaxed atmosphere, good solid furnishings, fresh flowers and a log fire in the airy beamed bar; interesting food, well kept real ales, friendly labrador; swings and an aviary in the garden; children in the family room. £28|£6.75.

Sherborne ST6316 PHEASANTS 24 Greenhill (01935) 815252 Georgian restaurant with rooms in attractive town; with friendly staff, enjoyable modern English cooking, good breakfasts; cl pm Sun, Mon, 2 wks mid-Jan; disabled access. £27.50|£12.25 2 courses.

Sturminster Newton ST7814 RED ROSE Market Cross (01258) 472460 Long-standing, family-run, lunchtime restaurant with proper English cooking, a very relaxed, friendly atmosphere, and happy staff; very popular locally; cl evenings, Sun; disabled access. £5.

Tarrant Monkton ST9408 LANGTON ARMS (01258) 830225 Thatched 17th-c pub in a pretty village; wide choice of good, fresh home-made food (inc a popular children's menu), bistro restaurant, well kept beers, decent wines, and a comfortable bar; open fire, and skittle alley; comfortable bdrms; disabled access. £17|£5.

Upwey SY6684 OLD SHIP 7 Ridgeway (01305) 812522 Pretty, whitewashed cottagey pub with very good bar food, well kept beer, a fine range of wines, and friendly service. £18.50|£7.

Upwey SY6684 WISHING WELL (01305) 814470 Nice little restaurant, popular locally, with good, interesting lunchtime food and afternoon tea; friendly service; bring your own wine; open 10am–6pm; cl mid-Dec–1 Mar; disabled access. £12.50|£3.

West Bay SY4590 RIVERSIDE (01308) 422011 Delightfully situated and friendly restaurant with excellent, locally caught fish and shellfish (also a few meat dishes), and helpful service; cl pm Sun, Mon exc bank hols and Dec–Mar; disabled access. £20|£6.50.

Wimborne Minster SZ0199 CLOISTERS 40 East St (01202) 880593 Friendly restaurant with pleasant décor; enjoyable food inc breakfast with home-made marmalade, lunchtime snacks and meals, and afternoon tea; cl 4 days Christmas; disabled access. £17.50|£3.95.

Worth Matravers SY9777 WORTH CAFÉ AND CRAFT CENTRE (01929) 439360 Welcoming converted barn with enthusiastic staff, nice home-made lunches (lots for vegetarians), lovely cakes, and good quality, locally made craft items; walkers welcome; cl Tues, Jan; disabled access. £5.75.

Special thanks to G N Spencer, David Jack, R Kingsmill, Mr and Mrs A J Czainski, Paul Seligman, Claire Taylor, David Sainsbury, Heather Martin, Chris Foster, Mr and Mrs B Hindley.

DORSET CALENDAR

Some of these dates were provisional as we went to press, please
check information with the telephone numbers provided.

FEBRUARY

24 **Corfe Castle** Marblers' and Stonecutters' Day to enforce rules laid
down in 1651. At *noon* the church's pancake bell summons the
company from the Fox Inn to the town hall. After the meeting a
football is kicked along the old road to Ower Quay (each participant
carrying a pint of beer and loaf of bread) to preserve an ancient right of
way used in the shipping of marbles. (01929) 422885

28 **Bournemouth** Winter Car Rally (01656) 863888

MARCH

14 **Stinsford** Lambing Weekend at Kingston Maurward College – *till Sun
15* (01305) 264738

21 **Stinsford** Lambing Weekend, and also Antiques Fair at Kingston
Maurward College – *till Sun 22* (01305) 264738

APRIL

4 **Weymouth** Easter Festival at Brewers Quay – *till Sun 19* (01305) 785747

13 **Kingston Maurward** Teddy Bear Fair at Kingston Maurward House
(01305) 269741

14 **Sherborne** Abbey Millennium Commemoration: to mark 1000 years
since the arrival of the Benedictines in Sherborne and the foundation of
the monastery – *till 11 July* (01935) 815341

MAY

1 **Cerne Abbas** Wessex Morris Men dance on Giant Hill at *7am* (01305)
251481

2 **Bournemouth** Busking Weekend – *till Sun 3* (01202) 451718; **Corfe**
Medieval Archery at Corfe Castle – *till Mon 4* (01929) 481294

3 **Weymouth** International Beach Kite Festival: 175-ft kites, stunt kite
teams, children's workshop, firework and night kite flying display *Sun
eve – till Mon 4* (01305) 785747

10 **Stinsford** Plant Sale and Show at Kingston Maurward College (01305)
264738

13 **Abbotsbury** Garland Day inc blessing of the sea (01305) 251481

17 **Weymouth** Vintage Motorcycle Rally and Display (01305) 785747

21 **Sherborne** Ascension Day: abbey choir sing from the roof of the abbey
tower at *7am* (01935) 815341

24 **Athelhampton** Flower Festival at Athelhampton House – *till Thurs 28*
(01305) 848363; **Stinsford** Food and Drink Fair at Kingston
Maurward College (01305) 264738; **Weymouth** Oyster Festival at the
Olde Harbour (01305) 785747; **Weymouth** Dorset Tour: vintage and
classic vehicle rally (01305) 785747

25 **Blandford** Georgian Fayre and Town Criers' Competition (01258)
480808; **Bovington** Dorset Children's Show at the Tank Museum:
rare breeds, arena events (01929) 405096; **Sherborne** Country Fair at
Sherborne Castle (01935) 813182

JUNE

5 **Cerne Abbas** Music Festival at St Mary's Church – *till Sun 7* (01300)
341456

DORSET CALENDAR

JUNE cont

6 **Sherborne** Abbey Fête (01935) 815341; **Stinsford** Open Day at Kingston Maurward College (01305) 264738

10 **Weymouth** Jazz Festival at Brewers Quay – *till Sun 14* (01305) 785747

13 **Netherbury** Open Gardens – *till Sun 14* (01308) 488270; **Weymouth** International Military and Veterans Festival – *till Fri 19* (01305) 785747

14 **Bath to Bournemouth** Vintage Veteran Car Rally (01202) 451718

20 **Bournemouth** Music-makers Festival – *till 4 July* (01202) 451718; **Cerne Abbas** 30 Gardens Open – *till Sun 21* (01300) 341311

27 **Beaminster** Arts Festival – *till 7 July* (01305) 267992; **Cattistock** 20 Gardens Open, vintage cars and aeroplanes at Chalmington Manor (01300) 320226; **Stinsford** Church Flower Festival and Open Gardens (01305) 267992

28 **Beaminster** Gardens Open Day (01308) 862675; **Dorchester** Teddy Bear Fair at Borough Gardens (01305) 266861

JULY

2 **Bovington** Firepower Mobility: tank battles in the arena *every Thurs in July* (01929) 405096

3 **Lyme Regis** Jazz Festival – *till Sun 5* (01297) 442138

5 **Athelhampton** MG Owners Rally at Athelhampton House (01305) 848363; **Frampton** Village Fête (01300) 320394

11 **Puddletown** Carnival (01305) 848625; **Yetminster** Fair: Yetties concert, art exhibition, street market and dancing (01935) 872940

12 **Higher Melcombe** Open Garden (01305) 267992

18 **Stinsford** Antiques Fair at Kingston Maurward College (01305) 264738; **Weymouth** International Maritime Modelling Festival – *till Sun 19* (01305) 785747

19 **Tolpuddle** Rally: trade union banners, speeches (01202) 294333

25 **Dorchester** Thomas Hardy Conference: lectures, readings and walks – *till 1 Aug* (01305) 251501; **Stinsford** Book Fair at Kingston Maurward College (01258) 473561; **Lyme Regis** Lifeboat Week: Red Arrows, opera and fireworks – *till 1 Aug* (01297) 443724; **Sherborne** Craft Fair at Sherborne Castle (01935) 813182

29 **Portesham** Possum Fez Wik: traditional fair week (mentioned in Hardy's *Under the Greenwood Tree*) – *till 2 Aug* (01305) 871316

31 **Bournemouth** Fireworks – *every Fri till 4 Sept* (01202) 451718; **Weymouth** National Beach Volleyball Championships – *till 2 Aug* (01305) 785747

AUGUST

1 **Bournemouth** Carnival and Regatta – *till Sun 9* (01202) 451718; **Swanage** Regatta and Carnival – *till Sat 8* (01929) 422885

2 **Kingston Maurward** Teddy Bear Fair at Kingston Maurward College (01305) 264738; **Puddletown** County Arts and Crafts Association Exhibition at St Mary's School – *till Thurs 6* (01202) 553113

3 **Weymouth** Firework Display *also on Mon 10, Wed 19, Mon 24* (01305) 785747

6 **Bovington** Firepower Mobility: tank battles in the arena *every Thurs and Fri in Aug* (01929) 405096

8 **Yeovil** Festival of Transport – *till Sun 9* (01305) 267992

DORSET CALENDAR

AUGUST cont

9 **Bournemouth** Kite Festival (01202) 451718

15 **Bridport** Carnival Procession (01308) 422884

16 **Poole** Powerboat racing (01202) 707227

19 **Weymouth** Carnival: Red Arrows, procession, fireworks (01305) 772444

22 **Weymouth** Victorian Military Festival at Northe Fort – *till Tues 25* (01305) 785747

26 **Motcombe** Gillingham and Shaftesbury Agricultural Show (01747) 823955

27 **Bridport** Melplash Agricultural Show (01308) 423337

31 **Bournemouth** Festival of lights: light show set to music – *till Sept 4* (01202) 451700

SEPTEMBER

2 **Tarrant Hinton** Great Dorset Steam Fair: 30th anniversary, 500-acre site, steam funfair – *till Sun 6* (01258) 860361

3 **Bovington** Firepower Mobility: tank battles in the arena *every Thurs in Sept* (01929) 405096

5 **Dorchester** Agricultural Show at Came Park (01305) 264249

6 **Bournemouth** Historic Commercial Vehicle Run to Bath: starts in King's Park (01985) 214910

12 **Bovington** Heavy Military Vehicle Rally at the Tank Museum: arena events, stalls – *till Sun 13* (01929) 405096; **Corfe** Archaeology Weekend: activities and living history at Corfe Castle – *till Sun 13* (01929) 481294

20 **Bovington** Wessex Classic Car Show at the Tank Museum (01929) 405096; **Weymouth** Vintage Classic Car Rally Display (01305) 785747

OCTOBER

3 **Shaftesbury** Carnival (01747) 854327

12 **Sherborne** Pack Monday Fair (01935) 813343

24 **Corfe** Civil War Garrison at Corfe Castle – *till Sun 25* (01929) 481294; **Stinsford** Apple Day at Kingston Maurward College (01305) 264738; **Weymouth** Halloween Festival at Brewers Quay – *till Fri 30* (01305) 785747

25 **Stinsford** Teddy Bear Fair at Kingston Maurward College (01305) 269741

31 **Dorchester** and Weymouth Stamp Club Exhibition at the United Reformed Church Hall (01305) 786661

NOVEMBER

16 **Weymouth** Christmas Festival – *till Tues 24* (01305) 785747

21 **Stinsford** Antiques Fair at Kingston Maurward College – *till Sun 22* (01305) 264738

29 **Stinsford** Book Fair at Kingston Maurward College (01258) 473561

Please let us know what you think of places in the *Guide*. Use the report forms at the back of the book or simply send a letter.

ESSEX

Quietly attractive countryside and villages in the north and on the coast, some good days out; traditional seaside resorts too

Essex has more and more places to visit – ones new to the *Guide* are the animal rescue centre joining the extraordinary secret nuclear bunker at Mistley, farm parks at Billericay and Wethersfield, and the Mark Hall estate at charming Coggeshall. Top of our list for family visits is the double bill of toy museum and reconstructed Norman castle at Stansted, and Colchester's excellent zoo. That busy town has several more interesting and enjoyable attractions, too. Other places we'd pick out for children include the wildlife park at Widdington and the farm park at South Weald, while some will love the Heybridge barge basin at Maldon.

On the whole, there's more for adults to enjoy here. Saffron Walden is a most attractive small town, with magnificent Audley End nearby. Other charming villages include Finchingfield, Dedham, Burnham-on-Crouch, Coggeshall and Castle Hedingham. Many of the churches are well worth a look, and the county has quite a few good gardens to visit including Beth Chatto's at Elmstead Market, the Paradise Centre at Lamarsh (plenty to keep children occupied here), and the one at Rettendon. Other appealing places are St Osyth Priory and Layer Marney Tower – and in an entirely different way the nuclear bunker at Kelvedon Hatch.

North Essex has a real East Anglian flavour. Driving through, you pass lots of attractive houses right by the road, often with fine old timbering and distinctive colourwashed plasterwork – the intricate patterning on some is known as pargeting. The landscape gem is the Stour Valley, shared with Suffolk – a Countryside Commission special report in summer 1997 underlined growing concerns that Constable's famous landscapes here are endangered by mass tourism. The Blackwater/Crouch coast has a surprisingly remote feel, given London's closeness.

South Essex is pretty densely urban.

Where to stay

Broxted TL5726 WHITEHALL Church End, Broxted CM6 2BZ (01279) 850603 £110, plus special breaks; 25 pretty rms. Fine Elizabethan manor house in lovely walled gardens, with outdoor swimming pool and tennis court; restful, spacious lounge and a smaller, cosier one with log fire; pleasant bar, good food in big, timbered restaurant, and friendly service; cl 26–31 Dec; disabled access.
Burnham-on-Crouch TQ9595 WHITE HART Burnham on Crouch CM0 8AS (01621) 782106 £50.60; 19 rms, 11 with own bthrm. Old-fashioned, 17th-c yachting inn on quay overlooking the River Crouch with its own jetty; high ceilings, oak tables, polished parquet, sea pictures, panelling; residents' lounge, decent bar food, and restaurant.
Coggeshall TL8522 WHITE HART Market End, Coggeshall, Colchester CO6

1NH (01376) 561654 **£97**, plus weekend breaks; 18 attractive rms. Family-run, 15th-c hotel with beamed lounge bar and residents' bar, log fires, friendly staff, and good food in both the bar and restaurant.

Dedham TM0533 MAISON TALBOOTH Dedham, Colchester CO7 6HN (01206) 322367 ***£110**, plus special breaks; 10 luxuriously furnished rms. Tranquil Victorian country house in fine Constable country; deeply comfortable seating and fresh flowers in the elegant lounge; very good, imaginative food in the lovely timber-framed restaurant overlooking the river and gardens, and marvellous breakfasts; disabled access.

Dedham TM0533 MARLBOROUGH HEAD Dedham, Colchester CO7 6DH (01206) 323250 **£50**; 4 rms. Comfortable, old-fashioned, early 18th-c inn in heart of Constable's home village; interesting carved woodwork in central lounge, and a wide choice of interesting food; cl 25 Dec.

Duddenhoe End TL4636 DUDDENHOE END FARM Duddenhoe End, Saffron Walden CB11 4UU (01763) 838258 ***£36**; 3 rms. 17th-c, no smoking farmhouse with inglenook fireplaces and beams, visitors' lounge and separate dining room; cl Christmas; children over 12.

Maldon TL8506 BLUE BOAR Silver St, Maldon CM9 7QE (01621) 852681 **£80**, plus weekend breaks; 28 comfortable rms. 14th-c coaching inn with cosy little beamed and oak-panelled rooms, open fires, good food (nice breakfasts), and friendly staff; limited disabled access.

Rickling Green TL5029 CRICKETERS ARMS Rickling Green, Saffron Walden CB11 3YG (01799) 543210 ***£65**; 10 rms in modern block behind. Cheerful, family-run pub by the village green, with cricketing mementos and beamed saloon bar with open fires; home-made food in bar and attractive restaurant; handy for Stansted Airport; disabled access.

Saffron Walden TL5438 SAFFRON High St, Saffron Walden CB10 2AY (01799) 522676 **£72.50**, plus special breaks; 17 rms. Friendly, 16th-c hotel with panelled bar, beams, comfortable lounge, and good food in the conservatory restaurant.

Thaxted TL6130 SWAN Thaxted, Dunmow CM6 2PL (01371) 830321 **£50**; 21 comfortably modernised rms. Four-gabled, late 15th-c inn with views towards the church and almshouses; pleasantly pubby big bar area with nice warm atmosphere, well kept real ales, and good food.

West Mersea TM0112 BLACKWATER West Mersea, Colchester CO5 8QH (01206) 383338 ***£60**, plus special breaks; 9 pretty rms. Creeper-covered hotel with neat little sitting room, fresh flowers, an attractive beamed restaurant with good French food and fresh fish, and big breakfasts; cl 5–25 Jan.

To see and do

ESSEX FAMILY ATTRACTIONS OF THE YEAR

☉ ♉ ! **Stansted Mountfitchet** TL5222 TOY MUSEUM AND NORMAN CASTLE These two neighbouring places are our stand-out family draws in Essex this year. Though they're quite different in character, they're run by the same people, and visited together they make an appealingly varied half day out. The HOUSE ON THE HILL TOY MUSEUM is home to what we think is the biggest, privately owned toy collection in the world, with over 30,000 toys, games and playthings from Victorian times to the 1970s. Quite a few toy museums attract parents more than children (which might explain why so many have unfortunately closed over the last couple of years), but this one avoids that by making its very well thought out displays entertaining to look at; lots of them are animated, and it's great fun watching the soldiers, trains and Meccano in action. There are a few coin-operated slot machines and puppet shows, and a good collectors' shop. Cl mid-Dec–mid-Jan; (01279) 813237; £3 (£2.20 children). Five minutes walk down the hill is the intriguing MOUNTFITCHET CASTLE AND *1066* VILLAGE, an authentically reconstructed Norman castle and village, complete with thatched houses, and deer, sheep, goats and chickens wandering around between them. The castle includes a small chunk of the original, and there are dummies displaying gruesome examples of torture and punishment. Cheerful and enthusiastic rather than particularly sophisticated, it's a good introduction to life a thousand years ago, though you will need to visit on a dry day (the Toy Museum is all indoors, so good in any weather). Snacks (and space for picnics), shop, disabled access; cl mid-Nov–mid-Mar; £4 (£3 children). Our only real complaint is that there's no joint ticket available; though prices overall compare favourably with other places in the county, it's a little annoying when visiting both to have to fork out twice.

🐖 ⚓ **Billericay** TQ6794 BARLEYLANDS FARM (SE on the A129) Expanding series of attractions, from farm animals and rural life displays to working glassworks, craft studios and miniature railway (Sun only). Meals, snacks, shop, disabled access; open Easter–Oct; (01268) 282090; *£3. The nearby Duke of York (South Green) has decent food.

★ † **Bradwell-on-Sea** TM0006 Worth the long drive for the sense of being right out on the edge of things – the timeless emptiness if anything exaggerated by distant views of vast industrial installations. The walk eastwards down the old Roman road across the marshes takes you to a little restored SAXON CHAPEL right on the sea wall, the scene of an annual pilgrimage in July. The Green Man is a good traditional pub.

↓T ⚓ **Braintree** TL7622 WORKING SILK MUSEUM (South St) Silk production demonstrated from start to finish, in a well restored old mill building; the hand looms they use are over 150 years old. Shop, disabled access; cl lunchtimes, pm summer Sats, and bank hols; (01376) 553393; £3. The Green Dragon just S at Young's End has good food, and there's a decent CRAFT CENTRE at Blake End, a little W on the A120.

★ 🍺 ⚓ 🍴 **Burnham-on-Crouch** TR9595 Attractively old-fashioned yachting station, lively in summer (packed around the Aug bank hol for its regatta), but nice in winter too, with rigging clacking forlornly

against the masts of those yachts left to ride at anchor offshore. The White Harte on the quay is good for lunch. RAILWAY MUSEUM (Mangapps Farm, Southminster Rd) Friendly – and mostly under cover; open pm wknds exc Jan and Feb, daily in school hols; £3.50. Further along, The Limes is a decent FARM SHOP, with nature trails and PICK-YOUR-OWN fruit; cl Mon and pm Sun and Tues.

★ 🏰 † 🏆 ⚓ 🚂 **Castle Hedingham** TL7835 The town, which has some attractive buildings, is named for the Norman CASTLE which dominates it, the magnificent 4-storey keep towering above the surrounding trees. Exceptionally well preserved, it still has its roof, banqueting hall and minstrels' gallery. Teas, shop; cl Nov–Easter (exc some wknds Oct); (01787) 460261; £3. The CHURCH has grand Norman masonry and interestingly carved choir seats. There's a good working pottery in St James St, and the Bell is nice for lunch. COLNE VALLEY RAILWAY & MUSEUM Lovingly restored Victorian railway buildings with collection of vintage engines and carriages; short steamtrain trips pm Sun mid-Mar–mid-Oct, and pm Tues–Thurs in hols. Meals on Pullman coaches, snacks, shop, limited disabled access; cl 23 Dec–Feb; (01787) 461174; *£5, *£2 when trains not running. The B1058 towards Sudbury then left through Gestingthorpe and the Belchamps is a pleasant excursion.

⚓ **Chappel** TL8927 KNIGHTS FARM

(Swan St) Everything for the dried-flower enthusiast, plus other local crafts. The prettily sited Swan has good food, in sight of the Chappel Viaduct (reputedly the biggest brick structure in Europe), and there's a decent RAILWAY MUSEUM.

✝ **Chelmsford** TL7007 A big and busy city with little for visitors, but its 15th-c CATHEDRAL, consecrated as such only in 1914, has particularly harmonious Perpendicular architecture.

★ **Clacton** TM1715 Roomy, family seaside resort, with long stretches of gently shelving sandy beach and all the usual amusements. The Robin Hood (London Rd) is the best family dining pub in the area. Nearby FRINTON TM2319 is similar but quieter; beyond, the blowy open space of The Naze is pleasant for strolling, especially out of season when you're likely to have its 150 acres virtually to yourself.

★ 🏠 🕸 🏞 **Coggeshall** TL8522 Attractive small town with a good few antique shops, and PAYCOCKE'S (West St), a fine, timber-framed medieval merchant's home with unusual panelling and carvings, and a pretty garden behind. Open pm Tues, Thurs, Sun and bank hols Apr–Oct; (01376) 561305; £2; NT. The Fleece next door has decent food. There's a working POTTERY along the street, and the Woolpack out by the church is a magnificent timbered building. 12th-c GRANGE BARN (Grange Hill) is the oldest surviving timber-framed barn in Europe, originally part of a Cistercian monastery. Disabled access; hours as Paycocke's (see above); £1.50, or joint ticket with Paycocke's £3; NT. Gradually being restored, the MARK HALL estate is recommended by readers for an attractive and undemanding stroll. There's a massive 13th-c oak, and a developing arboretum. Snacks, shop, disabled access; cl Mon, and Nov–Easter; (01376) 563796; £3 per car.

🏛🗼♨✝🏠!✗ **Colchester** TM0025 Britain's oldest recorded town, the capital of Roman Britain. You can trace the Roman wall (the Hole in the Wall, Balkerne Gdns, is a decent pub built into the one surviving fragmentary gatehouse) – best armed first with a map-leaflet from the exemplary museum in COLCHESTER CASTLE 🔲. Ideal for families, at the museum they let you try on Roman togas and helmets and touch 2000-year-old pottery excavated nearby. Excellent collections of Roman relics (a Roman temple originally stood on this site). The castle itself has the biggest Norman keep in Europe. Shop, good disabled access; cl am Sun (all day winter), 24–26 Dec; (01206) 282931; *£3.50. A clutch of interesting museums nearby includes the NATURAL HISTORY MUSEUM and HOLLYTREES MUSEUM on the High St, the latter featuring lots of toys, costumes and curios from the last two centuries, and round the corner in Trinity St the TYMPERLEYS CLOCK MUSEUM, a particularly unusual selection in a lovely 15th-c house; there's something very special about coming here and hearing all the ticking. All 3 museums cl lunchtime, all day Sun and Mon, and 24–26 Dec, clock museum also cl Nov–Mar; (01206) 282931; all free. The High St has handsome buildings, some extravagantly timbered, and plenty more historical buildings inc ST BOTOLPH'S, the oldest Augustinian priory in the country; readers have enjoyed the contemporary ART GALLERY at no 74. Town tours leave the tourist information centre (Queen St) at 2pm in summer (11am Sun). Children like ROLLERWORLD (Eastgates), the only international-standard roller-skating rink in Britain; evenings only during the week, cl Mon; from £3.20. The Rose & Crown (East St) is popular for lunch. COLCHESTER ZOO 🔲 (Maldon Rd, Stanway, 2m E by the B1002) Not only is this one of the country's most satisfying zoos as far as animals are concerned, it also stands out in the value-for-money stakes; even extra activities such as face-painting and brass rubbing are included in the price. Over 170 rare and endangered species housed in glass-panelled enclosures as close to their natural

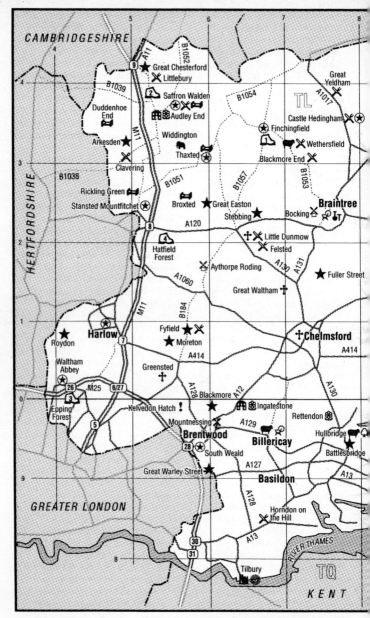

habitats as possible, with a particularly good timetable of events and demonstrations. Children can join in feeding the seals and elephants, and there are good play areas (best is the splendid Kalahari Capers under-cover complex). Meals, snacks, shop, some disabled access (a few steep hills; half-price entry); cl 25 Dec; (01206) 330253; *£6.95 (good value annual tickets). BOURNE MILL (just off the B1025 S) Delightfully

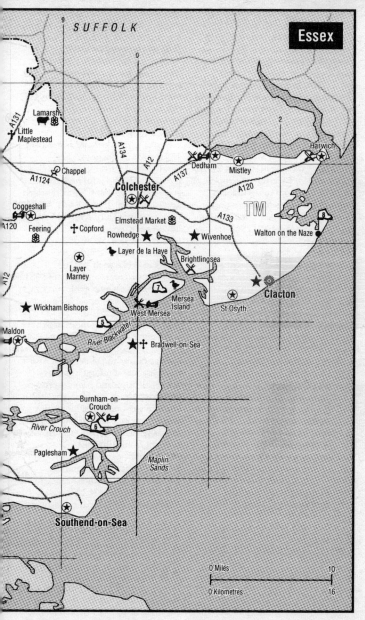

SUFFOLK

Essex

Lamarsh

A131

Little
Maplestead

Chappel

A1124

A134

A12

Colchester

A137

Dedham

Mistley

Harwich

A120

TM

Coggeshall

A120

Feering

Copford

Elmstead Market

Rowhedge

Wivenhoe

Walton on the Naze

A133

Layer de la Haye

Brightlingsea

Layer
Marney

A12

Wickham Bishops

West Mersea

Mersea
Island

St Osyth

Clacton

Maldon

River Blackwater

Bradwell-on-Sea

Burnham-on-
Crouch

River Crouch

Paglesham

Maplin
Sands

Southend-on-Sea

| 0 Miles | 10 |
| 0 Kilometres | 16 |

quaint restored watermill by pretty
millpond, worth a look from the
outside even when it's not open.
Open Sun and Mon bank hol wknds,
plus pm Sun and Tues July and Aug;
(01206) 572422; *£1.50; NT.

★ † ✿ 🐗 **Dedham** TM0533 Several
fine old buildings, especially the 15th-
c flint CHURCH, its pinnacled tower
familiar from so many Constable
paintings. There's also the school
Constable went to, and good walks

through the protected riverside meadows to his father's mill at Flatford (across the river lock, so in Suffolk, and described in that chapter). Worries about the hordes of visitors the Constable connection attracts have led local tourist boards to cut down on the publicity they give the village in their literature. The ART AND CRAFT CENTRE (High St) has a number of crafts, a growing collection of dolls houses, and a candle workshop; cl Mon, and Jan–Mar; *50p. DEDHAM RARE BREEDS FARM (Mill St) Nicely undeveloped, 16-acre farm, with two paddocks where children can feed the animals (bags of feed provided). Snacks, shop; open late Mar–Sept; (01206) 323111; £3.25. The handsome Marlborough Head, a wool merchant's house dating from 1475, has good food, and the partly medieval Sun here is useful too.

🐝 **Elmstead Market** TM0624 BETH CHATTO GARDENS A riot of colour in summer, these attractive gardens have been dramatically transformed from 4 acres of wasteland. Lots of gardening ideas, and unusual varieties of plants for sale. Cl Sun, bank hols and winter Sats, 2 wks over Christmas; (01206) 822007; £2.50. Over at Great Bromley, the Old Black Boy has good-value food.

🐝 **Feering** TL8621 FEERINGBURY MANOR (Coggeshall Rd) Fine, big riverside garden with ponds, streams, a little waterwheel, old-fashioned plants and bog gardens. Disabled access; open 8am –1pm wkdys May–July (exc bank hols), or by appointment; (01376) 561946; *£2. The Sun towards Kelvedon has interesting food.

★ 🏚 ✕ **Finchingfield** TL6832 The county's prettiest village, with charming houses spread generously around a sloping green that dips to a stream and pond; just off stands a pristine-looking small windmill. The Fox (one of the most attractive buildings) is nice for lunch.

✝ **Greensted** TL5303 ST ANDREWS CHURCH Recent tests have established that it was probably built around the time of the Norman Conquest – the oldest wooden church in the world. The nearby Green Man at Toot Hill has decent food (and fine wine).

🐚 🐝 🦋 **Harlow** TL4510 A New Town, and not perhaps top of most itineraries, but has a couple of surprisingly good museums. MARK HALL CYCLE MUSEUM AND GARDENS 🎫 (Muskham Rd) Bewildering assortment of bicycles, inc one that folds, another made from plastic – even one where the seat tips forward and throws its rider over the handlebars if the brakes are applied too hard. Also a Tudor herb garden and 3 walled gardens. Shop, disabled access; (01279) 439680; *£1.75. The town MUSEUM (Third Ave) has an important Roman collection, and a butterfly garden. Shop; open Thurs–Sat (exc 1–2pm); free.

🏰 🐚 ✿ ♣ ✕ **Harwich** TM2632 THE REDOUBT Circular fort built in 1808 in case of invasion by Napoleon, with 3 small museums. Shop; cl 1–2pm and Sept–May; (01255) 503429; *£1. Harwich's two lighthouses both have small museums, one a MARITIME MUSEUM, the other a collection of vintage radios and televisions. Also a small lifeboat museum (times as above; all 50p); and summer cruises around the harbour. From the A120 W there's an unusual sight for this part of Essex – a tall narrow WINDMILL (actually an interloper, as it was brought from Suffolk).

🐷 🐦 **Hullbridge** TQ8095 JAKAPENI FARM Small rare breeds park, specialising in pigs and sheep; you can fish on the lake (£2.50 a day). Snacks, shop, disabled access; open Sun and bank hols Easter–Oct; (01702) 232394; £1.75. The Bull nearby at Hockley has decent food, and is handy for walks in Hockley Woods.

🏚 🐝 **Ingatestone** TQ6499 INGATESTONE HALL Interesting old house, nothing too remarkable but enthusiastic tours by the family that live here, and lovely grounds. Teas, shop; open pm wknds Apr–Sept; (01277) 353010; £3.50. The Cricketers Arms out at Mill Green is a useful food pub.

❗ **Kelvedon Hatch** TQ5798 SECRET

NUCLEAR BUNKER 🏛 (off the A128) Who'd have thought that a 3-storey, Cold War underground complex lay beneath this innocuous 1950s bungalow? Knowledgeable tours take you through all parts of this clinically self-sufficient little world, and are done with real relish, but you can't help feeling relieved when you're back in the surrounding woodland. Snacks, shop; cl Mon–Weds Nov–Feb; (01277) 364883; *£5. The Black Horse in Pilgrims Hatch is a handy dining pub.

🐖 🎪 **Lamarsh** TM8835 PARADISE CENTRE (Twinstead Rd) Fun for children, with miniature goats, bantams and play area, and fascinating for gardeners, with a very wide variety of unusual plants (for sale) beautifully laid out, particularly woodland ones. Open wknds and bank hols Easter–Oct, or by appointment; (01787) 269449; *£1.50. The Lion is nice for lunch, and the Bures–Henny Street road is a pretty drive.

🌿 **Layer de la Haye** TL9619 ABBERTON RESERVOIR WILDFOWL AND VISITOR CENTRE (B1026) Popular wetland stop for wildfowl; observation room and hides, nature trails, and events for families in summer. Snacks, shop, disabled access; cl Mon, 25–26 Dec; (01206) 738172; £1 suggested donation (more for special events). The Donkey & Buskins (on the B1026) is handy for a meal.

🏰 🎪 🐖 **Layer Marney** TL9317 LAYER MARNEY TOWER The mansion here was never completed, but its 8-storey Tudor gatehouse is very impressive – one of the most striking examples of 16th-c architecture in Britain. Around it are formal gardens, a rare breeds farm, medieval barn, farm shop and deer park. Tearoom, shop, disabled access to grounds; cl am, all day Sat, and Oct–Mar; (01206) 330784; *£3.50.

⚜ 🏰 🌿 ✝ ⛵ **Maldon** TL8506 BOAT AND BARGE QUAY (Heybridge Basin, just outside) Full of life, and the best chance to see one of the classic Thames barges with its ox-blood sails in action. The Old Ship here has decent food and lovely views. Part of the old MOOT HALL is used to display an ambitious tapestry commemorating the 1,000th anniversary of the crucial Battle of Maldon. Cl Sun; £1. The MILLENNIUM GARDENS are named for the same event, and re-create what a garden might have looked like at the time of the battle. Also a CHURCH with an unusual triangular tower, some decent shops, a couple of small museums, and a riverside stroll past the golf course to the pretty weir by Beeleigh Abbey.

🌿 **Mersea Island** TM0413 Linked to the mainland by a little causeway, which can get covered by the tide; much of its coast is a National Nature Reserve for its shore life. It does feel very much an island, and away from the extended village of West Mersea, popular for retirement homes, there are few people about out of season (in summer the caravan parks bring in lots of families). The Willow Lodge has nice food; the Blackwater and Fox are good value too.

! 🌿 ✝ **Mistley** TM1231 ESSEX SECRET BUNKER 🏛 (B1352) Another of the newly opened nuclear war command centres; much of its original equipment has been returned by the government and other groups, so the operations centre looks especially authentic. Odd seeing something so contemporary consigned to history, especially when similar establishments are still in operation. Snacks, shop, disabled access; cl wkdys (exc Aug, Easter wk and bank hols) and all Dec–Jan; (01206) 392271; *£4.75. ANIMAL RESCUE CENTRE (New Rd) Very friendly; Ping and Pong the Vietnamese pot-bellied pigs may come to greet you as you go in. Snacks (not Mon, or winter wkdys), shop, disabled access; £2.50. (01206) 396483. The village has the remains of a Robert Adam church. If you come by train, don't miss the splendid station buffet at Manningtree.

🎪 **Rettendon** TQ7698 RHS GARDEN (Hyde Hall) 8 acres of year-round hillside colour, with woodland garden, big rose garden, ornamental ponds, shrubs, trees, and national collections of malus and viburnum. Meals and snacks in a thatched barn, plant sales, limited disabled access; cl Mon (exc bank hols), Tues, and all Nov–Mar; (01245) 400256; £3. The Barge at Battlesbridge is quite handy for lunch.

★ † ⚘ St Osyth TM1215 This pretty village is distinguished by the remarkable, crenellated flint gateway leading to St Osyth Priory. Surprisingly, few people seem to go any further, though the lovely towers and buildings on the other side cover a varied range of styles and periods, and the atmosphere is utterly peaceful and relaxed, with peacocks strutting across the wide shaded lawns. Notable paintings, and 20 acres of gardens. Disabled access to ground floor only; open May–Sept (and Easter wknd), grounds daily, house cl Sat; (01255) 820235; £3.50. The White Hart towards Point Clear has decent food and, not too far away, the beach at Brightlingsea TM0816 is probably the county's best.

★ † ☖ ⚘ 🏠 🖼 Saffron Walden TL5438 The finest small town in the region, with prime examples of warmly colour-washed pargeting throughout. Walking around to look at the buildings, you'll find it difficult to avoid being tempted into one of the many antique shops (or David Prue, the fine cabinet-maker in Radwinter Rd; cl wknds). The grand airy CHURCH has a magnificent spire, and the very ruined CASTLE, up on a grassy mound, is worth prowling around. Notable natural history section in the town MUSEUM. Good disabled access; cl am Sun and bank hols, 24–25 Dec; (01799) 510333; £1. BRIDGE END GARDENS Pleasant early Victorian gardens, spread over 3½ acres, with rose garden, formal Dutch garden, kitchen garden and an atmospheric wilderness leading to a little grotto. Disabled access; cl 25 Dec; free. You'll need a key from the tourist information centre (Market Pl) to explore the yew hedge maze beside the common. The Eight Bells does good food. AUDLEY END HOUSE (B1383, 1m W of Saffron Walden)

Spectacular Jacobean mansion and former Royal palace remodelled by Robert Adam, surrounded by splendid gardens landscaped by Capability Brown – from the town you can walk straight into the park. Nothing inside can compete with the quite breathtaking façade, but it's not for want of trying – there are around 30 rooms to see, crammed with fine furnishings and art. Suitably grand concerts and other events in the grounds. Snacks, shop, disabled access to gardens and ground floor; cl Mon (exc bank hols), Tues, and Oct–Easter; (01799) 522842; £5.50, £3.30 grounds only. The B184 to Chipping Ongar is a nice country drive; about 4m along Grace's Farm Shop at Wimbish is good, with PICK-YOUR-OWN in summer. Another good drive is the B1053 to Braintree.

! ☖ ⊌ ♪ ⚘ ♨ Southend-on-Sea TQ8885 Traditional seaside resort, long favoured by East Londoners, with many of the attractions you'd expect to find. Most famous is the pier, the longest in the world, excellent for fishing, with a museum and restored train service. Like many such resorts, Southend in winter has a special appeal for people who wouldn't like it in summer – seafront shops by the endless promenade looking closed for ever, the sea itself a doleful muddy grey. Readers enjoy the Westcliff part of town, with its decent art gallery. CENTRAL MUSEUM AND PLANETARIUM 🖼 (Victoria Ave) The only planetarium in the SE outside London, with local history too. Shop; cl Sun and bank hols (planetarium also cl Mon and Tues); (01702) 330214; £2.15 planetarium, museum free. SEA LIFE CENTRE (Eastern Esplanade) Fun way of exploring underwater life, with bubble-windows to make it seem as if you're in there with the sea creatures, and a walk-through tunnel along a reconstructed seabed. Children like the shark exhibition. Meals, snacks, shop, disabled access; cl 25 Dec; (01702) 462400; £4.75. A less expected find is SOUTHCHURCH HALL MUSEUM (Park Lane), a medieval moated manor house in an attractive park, with period room settings, and lute demonstrations every pm Sat. Shop, limited disabled access; cl 1–2pm, all day Sun and Mon; (01702) 467671; free. PRITTLEWELL PRIORY MUSEUM (Priory Park, slightly N of town centre) 12th-c Cluniac priory in nice grounds, with eclectic collections of local and religious history; details as Southchurch Hall. Summer BOAT TRIPS include occasional runs on a vintage paddle-steamer: (01634) 827648 for dates. There are year-round ferries to Felixstowe. LEIGH-ON-SEA TQ8385, though attached, has a quite distinct character, altogether more intimate, with wood-clad buildings and shrimp boats in the working harbour; Ivy Osborne's cockle stall here is justly famous, and the Crooked Billet overlooking the water has real, old-fashioned character.

★ 🐖 🐝 **South Weald** TQ5793 Attractive village; the Tower Arms is a decent food pub. OLD MACDONALD'S FARM PARK (Weald Rd) Very extensive range of animals, with 30 breeds of sheep alone. Demonstrations, nature trails and craft displays, and plenty of opportunities to stroke the animals. Meals, snacks, shop, disabled access; cl 25–26 Dec; (01277) 375177; *£2.75. Nearby is a COUNTRY PARK with deer enclosure, lakes, woods, and visitor centre.

🔥 ♄ ✗ **Stansted Mountfitchet** TL5222 *See separate Family Panel on p. 241* for the HOUSE ON THE HILL TOY MUSEUM and MOUNTFITCHET CASTLE AND 1066 VILLAGE. A well preserved 18th-c WINDMILL still has much of its original equipment (though it isn't working). Open pm 1st Sun of month Apr–Oct, plus pm every Sun in Aug, and pm bank hol Sun and Mons; 50p. The Cricketers Arms at nearby Rickling Green is nice for lunch.

★ ✝ 🏛 🔥 ✗ **Thaxted** TL6130 This engaging small town has a graceful, airy CHURCH with a tremendous spire, several handsome buildings inc nearby almshouses, a fine GUILDHALL (with a small local museum), and a restored WINDMILL. The RAVEN ARMOURY (on the B184 towards Dunmow) does hand-forged steel and weaponry. The 15th-c Swan has decent food.

🏰 ❀ **Tilbury** TQ6476 TILBURY FORT

Days Out

Pargeting extravaganza
Audley End; Saffron Walden – lunch at the Eight Bells there; Arkesden, Clavering.

The windmill on the green
Finchingfield, Castle Hedingham, Colne Valley Railway; lunch at the Bell, Castle Hedingham – or treat yourself at the White Hart, Great Yeldham; Thaxted; Paradise Centre, Lamarsh.

Constable's landscapes
Nayland; Dedham, Rare Breeds Farm, and lunch at the Marlborough Head there; walk from Flatford Mill over water meadows; harbour cruise at Harwich.

Inland from the Blackwater
Beth Chatto Gardens, Elmstead Market; Layer Marney Tower; Abberton wildfowl centre, Layer de la Haye; lunch at the Sun, Feering; Feeringbury Manor nr Feering; Thames barges at Maldon; Wivenhoe, Rowhedge, Wickham Bishops.

Woodland walk and a village tour
Stroll in Hatfield Forest; Fyfield (lunch at the Black Bull), Moreton, Great Easton and Stebbing villages.

Well preserved 17th-c fort with unusual double moat; good views of the Thames estuary. The most violent episode in its history was a 1776 cricket match that left three dead. Snacks, shop, some disabled access; cl Mon and Tues Oct–Mar, 24–26 Dec; (01375) 858489; *£2.20. For an extra £1 you can fire a 1943 3.7 anti-aircraft gun – irresistible for several children of our acquaintance.

✝☉🐄 **Waltham Abbey** TL3800 Despite the surrounding housing developments, the centre has some handsome buildings – especially the ABBEY CHURCH with its famous peal of 13 bells (and a museum in the crypt). Associated ruins include part of a Norman cloister, and the bridge dates back to the abbey's time. Lively holiday activities for children at the EPPING FOREST DISTRICT MUSEUM (Sun St), in 2 timber-framed old houses. Limited disabled access; open pm Fri–Tues, cl Christmas wk; (01992) 716882; free. LEE VALLEY FARM PARK (2m N on the B194) Takes in Hayes Hill children's farm, with plenty of traditional animals and Sun craft demonstrations, and Holyfield Hall working farm and dairy, with 150 cows milked every afternoon at 2.45pm, and seasonal events like sheep-shearing and harvesting. Snacks, shop, disabled access; (01992) 892781; £2.60.

🐂 **Wethersfield** TL7131 BOYDELLS DAIRY FARM Working dairy farm where you may be able to join in milking the goats and cows – or even the sheep. Also working beehives, various other animals, and ice-lollies made from their own sheep yogurt. Snacks, shop, disabled access; open pm Weds–Sun late May–Sept (pm daily in Aug); (01371) 850481; £2.50.

🐒 **Widdington** TL5331 MOLE HALL WILDLIFE PARK Family-run place with wide variety of animals around moated manor house. Otters are a speciality, but also free-roaming wildfowl, deer paddock, a butterfly house and insect pavilion. Summer snacks, shop, some disabled access; cl 25 Dec; (01799) 540400; £4 in summer, £1 in winter when the butterfly house is closed. The Fleur-de-Lys is a popular food pub.

✗ **Windmills** are quite a feature of inland Essex – given the relatively unhilly landscape, and they serve as attractive landmarks for miles around. As well as those we mention elsewhere, good examples can be seen at Aythorpe Roding TL5815, Bocking TL7524 and Mountnessing TQ6297.

★ **Other attractive villages,** all with decent pubs, include Arkesden TL4834, Battlesbridge TQ7894 (also a popular antiques and crafts centre, and walks to the head of the Crouch estuary), Blackmore TL6001, Fuller Street TL7416, Fyfield TL5606, Great Chesterford TL5143, Great Easton TL6025 (pleasant gardens at nearby Little Easton Manor; open pm Thurs May–Sept; £2), Great Warley Street TQ5890, Moreton TL5307 (pubs have leaflet detailing attractive village walk), Paglesham TQ9293, Pleshey TL6614 (ruined castle, charming churchyard, country walks), riverside Rowhedge TM0021 (nearby nature reserve among former gravel workings at Fingringhoe), Roydon TL4109, Stebbing TL6624, Wickham Bishops TL8412 and Wivenhoe TM0321.

✝ **Interesting churches** at Copford TL9222 (well restored 12th-c wall paintings), Great Waltham TL6913 (the village is pleasant, too), Little Dunmow TL6521 (surviving part of priory founded 1106; the Flitch of Bacon is a good pub), and Little Maplestead TL8233 (unusual round building modelled on the Holy Sepulchre in Jerusalem).

Please let us know what you think of places in the *Guide*. Use the report forms at the back of the book or simply send a letter.

Walks

For serious walkers, inland Essex lacks defined physical features and has too many vast arable fields. In places, a shortage of paths confines you to the road. That said, the prettiness of the villages, particularly in the N, encourages walks wherever there are connecting paths.

Finchingfield TL6832 ⌂-1 and Great Bardfield TL6730 both have windmills and charming cottages, with an easily followed path along the Finchingfield Brook leading from one to the other. **Saffron Walden** TL5438 ⌂-2 has a goodish network of tracks around it, extending into the parkland of nearby Audley End House. Longer rambles can take in Newport TL5234, where the houses have characteristic pargeted plaster walls, and Wendens Ambo TL5136.

Epping Forest TQ4197 ⌂-3 is a magnificent survival, an expansive tract of ancient hornbeam coppice, mainly tucked between the M25 and outer London. There are miles of leafy walks (and rides – you can hire horses locally), with some rough grazing and occasional distant views. There are so many woodland paths that getting lost is part of the experience; the long-distance Forest Way is, however, well marked. On the W side there's a pleasant diversion to High Beach TQ4097, from where a few field paths lead SW.

Hatfield Forest TL5320 ⌂-4 just S of Stansted Airport is more of the same, not on quite the same scale but still extensive enough, with a nature trail and boating lake.

The low-lying, much indented coast does have opportunities for walking, though the immediate hinterland is generally too dull to make circular walks worthwhile. The **Blackwater estuary** ⌂-5 has vast skies, with boats and bird life punctuating the flat sea and landscapes; the pick of local walks include paths along the dykes from Tollesbury TL9510, and towards isolated St Peter's Chapel from Bradwell-on-Sea TM0006. The Chequers at Goldhanger TL9009 is another good starting-point. **Burnham-on-Crouch** TQ9595 ⌂-6 provides walks along the Crouch itself, with more boats on view. The Ferryboat down nr the River Crouch at the end of the lane through North Fambridge TQ8597 is a good base for lonely waterside walks.

Mersea Island TM0413 ⌂-7 has a bracing coastal walk from East Mersea along the sea-dyke overlooking the Colne estuary. **Walton on the Naze** TM2623 ⌂-8 gives a walk from its N side northwards along the coast, round the tip of The Naze – with views of shipping entering and leaving Harwich and Felixstowe – to a nature reserve harbouring migrant birds; there is a nature trail here.

Inland, there are pleasant walks nr the White Hart at Margaretting Tye TL6800, the Viper at Mill Green TL6401 (in oak and chestnut woods), the Mole Trap on Tawney Common TL5001 and – despite surrounding urbanisation – from the Shepherd & Dog at Crays Hill TQ7192 between Billericay and Basildon.

Where to eat

Blackmore End TL7430 Bull (01371) 851037 Comfortable, tucked-away dining pub with pretty cottagey restaurant area, good snacks, excellent meals, and up to 10 wines by the glass; cl Mon exc bank hols; children allowed if eating. £14.75 lunch, £20 dinner.
Brightlingsea TM0815 Coffee Pot Victoria Pl (01206) 305738 Spotlessly clean place serving very good breakfast, lunch and tea – everything is freshly made daily; helpful friendly staff; cl pm, Sun; disabled access. £2.50.
Burnham-on-Crouch TQ9595 Contented Sole 80 High St (01621) 782139 Long-standing, family-run restaurant very popular for consistently good, imaginative food with an obvious emphasis on fine seafood; wine tastings all

year; cl pm Sun, Mon, 2 wks Sept and Feb; disabled access. **£12.95**/2 courses £10.95.

Burnham-on-Crouch TQ9595 CROOKED COTTAGE TEA ROOMS 1 The Quay (01621) 783868 17th-c beamed fishermen's cottages, with seats in the summer rose garden; nice cream teas with home-made cakes and a huge choice of teas, and friendly service; cl Mon (exc bank hols), mid-week Nov–Mar. /£4.

Castle Hedingham TL7835 BELL St James's St (01787) 460350 Interesting old coaching inn with a log fire in the beamed lounge bar, traditionally furnished public bar, quickly served decent food, and a lovely big walled garden behind; cl pm Mon exc bank hols; disabled access. **£15**/£3.50.

Clavering TL4731 CRICKETERS CB11 4QT (01799) 550442 Attractive and cosy L-shaped dining pub with low beams, 2 open fires, and a wide choice of imaginative, well presented food in the bar and restaurant; pretty bedrooms; disabled access. **£26**/£3.

Colchester TM0025 CLOWNS 61-62 High St (01206) 578631 Huge helpings of nice, straightforward food in this clean, spacious restaurant; good children's menu, too; cl 25–26 Dec; disabled access. **£12**/£3.

Dedham TM0533 MALLARD Riverside Cottage Mill Lane (01206) 322066 Unlicensed, little riverside restaurant with a homely, relaxed atmosphere and good, unpretentious food; cl pm Sun, Mon. **£17**.

Felsted TL6720 RUMBLES COTTAGE Braintree Rd (01371) 820996 Ancient cottage with interesting food, a relaxed atmosphere, and good-value wines; cl Mon, 2 wks Feb.**£25**.

Fyfield TL5606 BLACK BULL Prettily lit and vine-covered dining pub with nice interesting food served in low-beamed communicating rooms, well kept real ales, a welcoming atmosphere, and seats and an aviary in the garden. **£19**/£7.50.

Great Yeldham TL7638 WHITE HART Poole St (01787) 237250 Striking Tudor inn with an attractive garden, beams and oak panelling in refurbished rooms (one is no smoking), exceptionally good and inventive food, and fine wines; cl pm Sun, Mon; disabled access. **£20.40**/£7.95.

Harwich TM2632 PIER AT HARWICH The Quay (01255) 241212 Delicious fish and chips and smarter fish dishes in an attractive building overlooking the Stour and Orwell estuaries. **£20**/£7.

Horndon on the Hill TQ6683 BELL (01375) 673154 Flower-decked, medieval inn with welcoming licensees, an open-plan beamed bar with polished oak floorboards and flagstones; carefully prepared imaginative food, 5 real ales, and 13 wines by the glass, restaurant cl am Sat; no children. **£23.50**/£8.95.

Little Dunmow TL6521 FLITCH OF BACON (01371) 820323 Friendly pub with a nice mix of people; small, attractively furnished timbered bar, a sensibly small range of good, appetising bar food, popular Sunday buffet, and real ales; comfortable bedrooms. **£16.50**/£6.50.

Littlebury TL5139 QUEENS HEAD B1383 NW of Saffron Walden (01799) 522251 Unpretentious pub with friendly, connected beamed areas, good real ales (they hold an annual beer festival and have a monthly small brewery week), and excellent food; disabled access. **£16.50**/£5.

Saffron Walden TL5438 EIGHT BELLS Bridge St (01799) 522790 Handsome Tudor inn in good walking area, nr Audley End; lots of daily specials in the splendidly timbered weekend restaurant, well kept real ales, a good choice of wines by the glass, and friendly service; **£20**/£3.50.

West Mersea TM0112 WILLOW LODGE 108 Coast Rd (01206) 383568 Large, busy restaurant with a wide range of very good food inc lots of fresh fish; cl pm Sun, Mon; well behaved children welcome; disabled access. **£20**/£4.50

Wethersfield TL7131 DICKENS The Green (01371) 850723 Mainly 17th-c, popular restaurant in quiet country spot; lovely modern cooking, fine wines, very good service; cl pm Sun, Mon, Tues; disabled access. **£21**/£7.50.

Special thanks to Mrs J Hall, Geoff Meek, D A Ward.

ESSEX CALENDAR

Some of these dates were provisional as we went to press. Please check information with the telephone numbers provided.

JANUARY

11 **Lee Valley Park** Bird Race: who can spot the most birds in one day (01992) 717711

23 **Harwich** Film Festival – *till Sun 25* (01255) 553333

APRIL

10 **Chappel** Thomas the Tank Engine at East Anglian Railway Museum – *till Mon 13* (01206) 242524; **Stanford-le-Hope** Stationary Engine Rally at Walton Hall Farm Museum – *till Mon 13* (01375) 671874

12 **Billericay** Steam Rally at Barleylands Farm – *till Mon 13* (01268) 532253

21 **Benfleet** European Beer Festival at Runnymede Hall – *till Sat 25* (01268) 792711

MAY

3 **Billericay** Open Day at Barleylands Farm – *till Mon 4* (01268) 532253

6 **Chelmsford** Cathedral Festival – *till Sat 16* (01245) 359890

9 **Epping** Fighter Meet at North Weald Airfield – *till Sun 10* (01992) 522210

17 **Battlesbridge** Classic Car Show (01268) 575000; **Dovercourt** Tour de Tendring: cycle rally (01255) 256168; **Great Leighs** Essex Young Farmers Show at the Essex Showground (01245) 362411

24 **Billericay** Family Weekend at Barleylands Farm – *till Mon 25* (01268) 532253; **Southend-on-Sea** Air Show: free event – *till Mon 25* (01702) 215120

29 **Epping** Aerofair at North Weald Airfield – *till Sun 31* (01992) 522210

JUNE

5 **Thaxted** Morris Ring: annual meeting of over 200 Morris Men, massed dancing in the morning – *till Sun 7* (01371) 831024

6 **Braintree** Carnival (01376) 551969

7 **Great Braxted** Braxted Park Show (01206) 251790; **Chelmsford** Annual Open Day at Writtle Agricultural College (01245) 420705; **Colchester** Pipe Band Competition at Lower Castle Park (01376) 513076

13 **Colchester** History Fair: cannon, cavalry and infantry of the English Civil War from all over Britain –*till Sun 14* (01206) 794916

15 **Castle Hedingham** Thomas the Tank Engine at the Colne Valley Railway – *till Sun 28* (01787) 461174

18 **Great Leighs** Essex County Show at the Essex Showground – *till Sat 20* (01245) 362412

19 **Thaxted** Festival: classical and jazz concerts, workshops – *weekends till 12 July* (01371) 831421

20 **Brentwood** Strawberry Fair: vintage vehicles, swing orchestra, morris dancing at Shenfield Common (01277) 201111

21 **Southend-on-Sea** Open-air Concert (01702) 215120

26 **Old Leigh and Southend-on-Sea** Folk Festival: more than 350 free music and dance events – *till Sun 28* (01702) 215120

27 **Southend-on-Sea** Water Festival – *till Sun 28* (01702) 215120

28 **Canvey Island** Castle Point Show at Waterside Farm Showground (01268) 792711

ESSEX CALENDAR

JULY

5 **Battlesbridge** Motorcycle Rally and bike jumble (01268) 575000; **Southend-on-Sea** Open-air Concert (01702) 215120

11 **Manningtree** Tendring Hundred Show at Lawford Park (01206) 571517

12 **Clacton-on-Sea** Classic Vehicle Show (01255) 256155

16 **Cressing** Festival of Early Music at Cressing Temple Barns – *till Sun 26* (01376) 584903

19 **Southend-on-Sea** Open-air Concert (01702) 215120

25 **Harwich** Sea Festival (01255) 508408; **West Bergholt** Historic Vehicle Show: about 500 entries – *till Sun 26* (01206) 271253

26 **Brightlingsea** Pyefleet Week and Town Regatta: sailing, fun raft races, fireworks – *till 1 Aug* (01206) 303588

AUGUST

1 **Southend on Sea** Jazz Festival – *till Sun 2* (01702) 215120

4 **Takeley** Open-air Shakespeare in Hatfield Forest – *till Wed 5* (01603) 630944

6 **Coggeshall** Open-air Shakespeare at Marks Hall Estate – *till Fri 7* (01603) 630944

9 **Bulphan** Orsett Air Fête at Thurrock Aerodrome on the A128 (01992) 524233; **Great Leighs** Essex Heavy Horse Show at the Essex Showground (01787) 237880

14 **Southend-on-Sea** Carnival Week – *till* illuminated Carnival Procession and Fireworks on *Sat 22* (01702) 215120

15 **Maldon** Blackwater Barge Match: historic vehicles race on river Blackwater (01621) 851147

22 **Purleigh** English Wine Festival at New Hall Vineyards: country skills fair and family events – *till Sun 23* (01621) 828343

27 **Clacton-on-Sea** Air Show: Red Arrows – *till Fri 28* (01255) 423400

28 **Brentwood** Festival – *till 20 Sept* (01277) 201111; **Clacton-on-Sea** Jazz Festival – *till Mon 31* (01245) 423400

28 **Chelmsford** Outdoor Music Festival – *till Mon 31* (01245) 606985

29 **Burnham** Festival Week – *till 5 Sept* (01621) 782150; **Southend on Sea** Sailing Barge Race (01702) 215120

SEPTEMBER

5 **Orsett** Horticultural and Agricultural Show at the Orsett Showground (01708) 224666

9 **Chappel** Beer Festival: about 120 beers and ciders at the East Anglian Railway Museum – *till Sat 12* (01206) 242524

12 **Billericay** Essex Steam Rally and Craft Fair at Barleylands Farm: over 300 stands – *till Sun 13* (01268) 532253

18 **Brentwood** International Blues Festival – *till Sun 20* (01277) 201111

19 **Old Leigh** Regatta – *till Sun 20* (01702) 215169

20 **Brentwood** Town and Country Show (01277) 201111

27 **Battlesbridge** Vintage Vehicle Rally (01268) 575000

OCTOBER

4 **Colchester** Countryside Open Day at High Woods Country Park: historic re-enactments, rare breeds, activities (01206) 853588

9 **Maldon** Folk Festival – *till Sat 10* (01621) 859561

23 **Saffron Walden** Folk Festival – *till Sun 25* (01799) 528046

NOVEMBER

ESSEX CALENDAR

NOVEMBER cont

7 **Brentwood** Live Music and Fireworks inc children's rides (01277) 201111; **Canvey Island** Fireworks at Waterside Farm Showground (01268) 792711; **Harwich** Carnival and Fireworks (01255) 506139

12 **Southend on Sea** Christmas Lights Switch On and Gala Night (01702) 215120

27 **Brentwood** Christmas Parade (01277) 201111

28 **Southend on Sea** Victorian Christmas in the High St – *till Sun 29* (01702) 215120

DECEMBER

12 **Castle Hedingham** Santa Specials at the Colne Valley Railway – *till Sun 13,* also *Sat 19, Sun 20* (01787) 461174

GLOUCESTERSHIRE

Charming varied scenery, idyllic Cotswold villages and traditional small towns, lots of interesting places to visit, good food, excellent places to stay in.

This county's strongest appeal is to adults: its scenery, charming villages and small towns, good food, lovely places to stay in and interesting things to see make it one of the best parts of Britain for a relaxing short break. However, there are plenty of things to fill family days out too. Among the best of these are the farm parks at Blockley and Kineton, the country park at Tockington, steam railways at Lydney and Toddington, and for younger children the clever new Treasure Train at Coleford. Many children join adults in enjoying the birds of prey centre at Batsford near Moreton-in-Marsh; there's another good one near Newent. And the Slimbridge wildfowl centre is outstanding for all ages. For something a bit different, the Clearwell caverns are an adventure.

For adults, there's a very rich choice – the cream of the great houses being Stanway House, Snowshill Manor, Sudeley Castle near Winchcombe, the Chedworth Roman villa near Yanworth, and the never-finished Gothic mansion at Nympsfield. Some of the county's gardens and parks are unforgettable, especially Kiftsgate near Mickleton, the arboretums at Westonbirt and Batsford, and, particularly in late May, the gardens of Lydney Park. In the same sort of vein, the Nature in Art collection at Twigworth is very special.

Chipping Campden, Cirencester, Northleach, Painswick and Stow-on-the-Wold are all handsome Cotswold towns bulging with sightseeing possibilities – and antique shops; Tewkesbury too is attractive. Gloucester – a busy modern city – has a great deal to reward a day visit. Nearby Cheltenham still has a considerable degree of Regency elegance, and is a useful base for exploring the area; the tourism office does a good leaflet detailing how to get to most Cotswold attractions by public transport.

It's the countryside above all which delights here – especially the rolling hills of the Cotswolds, with their traditional dry stone-walled fields, occasional beechwoods, meandering streams, and beautiful villages of warm golden-tinted stone picturesquely roofed in heavy stone slabs. Many villages have handsome medieval churches, and their cottages and houses don't hide away behind gardens and high walls, but tend to be right by the road. Often, there's a strip of daffodil-planted grass between pavement and road (the area is particularly attractive in spring), and sometimes a little stream. The one snag is that the Cotswolds tend to be expensive – particularly in the north.

Other parts, besides being generally cheaper, have their charm too

– the tortuously steep hills and valleys around Stroud, the quiet watermeadows of the upper Thames, the unspoilt orchard and farming countryside around the Severn Valley (there are so few river crossings that the little villages down by the west bank, with few people passing through, have a very secluded and unchanging feel). The Forest of Dean has a unique landscape: hilly woodland, much of it ancient, that shows many traces of the way it has provided a livelihood for the people living around it. It's flanked by a spectacular stretch of the Wye Valley, and its woodland colours are at their best in late May and autumn.

In the summer the Cotswolds do attract a great many visitors, though even then you can find delightful villages that have escaped the crowds, especially in the south. For cyclists, the Cotswolds are great – quiet village-to-village lanes with ever-changing views.

Where to stay

Bibury SP1106 BIBURY COURT Bibury, Cirencester GL7 5NT (01285) 740337 £78; 19 individual rms. Lovely peaceful mansion dating from Tudor times, on the edge of a charming village and set in beautiful gardens, with an informally friendly atmosphere, panelled rooms, antiques, huge log fires, conservatory, and good imaginative food; cl Christmas.

Bibury SP1106 SWAN Bibury, Cirencester GL7 5NW (01285) 740695 £150, plus special breaks; 18 very pretty individually decorated rms. Handsome creeper-covered hotel on the banks of the River Coln with private fishing and attractive formal gardens, lovely flowers and log fires in carefully furnished comfortable lounges, a cosy no smoking parlour, good food in opulent dining room, nice breakfasts, and attentive staff; disabled access.

Bledington SP2422 KINGS HEAD The Green, Bledington, Chipping Norton, Oxon OX7 6HD (01608) 658365 *£60; 12 rms (2 over the kitchen can be noisy). Very nicely placed 15th-c Cotswold inn by duck-filled stream with cheery log fire in atmospheric bar, lounge overlooking garden, good food in bar and attractive, partly no smoking restaurant, and friendly service; cl 25 Dec; limited disabled access.

Broadwell SP2027 COLLEGE HOUSE Chapel St, Broadwell, Moreton-in-Marsh GL56 OTW (01451) 832351 £46; 3 lovely big rms, 2 with own bthrm. 17th-c house in charming village with large inglenook fireplace in flagstoned sitting room, good breakfasts, and delicious evening meals – which can be eaten on the terrace in summer; no children.

Brookthorpe SO8312 BROOKTHORPE LODGE Stroud Rd, Brookthorpe, Gloucester GL4 0UQ (01452) 812645 £40, plus special breaks; 10 rms, 7 with own bthrm, and most with country views. Family-run mainly no smoking Georgian guest house with a really warm welcome from owners, comfortable lounge, conservatory, light lunches (packed ones on request), and good evening meal; cl New Year; dogs welcome (with advance notice), disabled access.

Brookthorpe SO8312 GILBERTS Gilberts Lane, Brookthorpe, Gloucester GL4 0UH (01452) 812364 *£48; 4 rms. 400-year-old house with woodburner and games in sitting room, organic produce from the surrounding smallholding used for delicious breakfast (own honey and eggs), and relaxed atmosphere; non smokers preferred.

Buckland SP0836 BUCKLAND MANOR Buckland, Broadway, Worcs WR12 7LY (01386) 852626 £185, plus special breaks; 14 sumptuous rms. Really lovely 13th-c building in 10 acres of beautifully kept gardens; comfortable lounges with magnificent oak panelling, flowers and antiques, and elegant restaurant with fine food using home-grown produce; outdoor swimming pool, riding, tennis, croquet, putting; children over 12.

Charingworth SP2039 Charingworth Manor Charingworth, Chipping Campden GL55 6NS (01386) 593555 £170; 26 lovely rms with thoughtful extras. Early 14th-c manor with Jacobean additions set in fine grounds, with mullioned windows, antiques, log fires and heavy oak beams in relaxing sitting room, good modern cooking in charming restaurant, excellent breakfasts, and friendly staff; billiards, leisure spa with indoor swimming pool, and all-weather tennis court; dogs by arrangement.

Cheltenham SO9422 Hotel on the Park Evesham Rd, Cheltenham GL52 2AH (01242) 518898 *£106, plus special breaks; 12 lovely rms. Warmly welcoming and handsome Regency house with elegantly furnished drawing room and dining room, pretty flowers and antiques, and imaginative food in stylish restaurant – good breakfasts, too; children over 8.

Cheltenham SO9422 Lypiatt House Lypiatt Rd, Cheltenham GL50 2QW (01242) 224994 £68, plus wknd breaks; 10 attractive rms. Carefully restored Victorian house in its own grounds, with open fire, books and plants in light, comfortable drawing room, little conservatory bar, and friendly, personal service.

Chipping Campden SP1539 Eight Bells Chipping Campden GL55 6JG (01386) 840371 £48; 2 rms. Neatly restored heavy-beamed 14th-c pub by church; 3 log fires, interesting food with fresh local produce, decent wines and beers, friendly staff, and pleasant courtyard.

Chipping Campden SP1539 Noel Arms High St, Chipping Campden GL55 6AT (01386) 840317 £92, plus special breaks; 26 comfortable rms. Bustling 14th-c inn with comfortable, traditionally furnished small lounge areas, old farm tools and open fire in the bar, armour and antiques, conservatory, restaurant, and decent wines; disabled access.

Cirencester SP0201 Jarvis Fleece Market Pl, Cirencester GL7 2NZ (01285) 658507 *£85; 30 well equipped rms. Tudor coaching inn with oak beams and log fires in the comfortable lounge, good lunchtime food in relaxing restaurant, and pretty courtyard.

Clearwell SO5708 Tudor Farmhouse Clearwell, Coleford GL16 8JS (01594) 833046 £57, plus special breaks; 13 cottagey rms. Carefully restored Tudor farmhouse and stone cottages with landscaped gardens and surrounding fields, lots of beams, sloping floors and oak doors, delicious food in candlelit restaurant, and friendly staff; cl 1 wk over Christmas.

Clearwell SO5708 Wyndham Arms Clearwell, Coleford GL16 8JT (01594) 833666 £65, plus special winter breaks; 17 well equipped rms. Smart and neatly kept old country inn near Wye Valley and Forest of Dean, with comfortable beamed bar, open fire, particularly good food (much produce is home-grown), good service, and friendly dogs; cl 26 Dec; disabled access.

Corse Lawn SO8330 Corse Lawn House Corse Lawn, Gloucester GL19 4LZ (01452) 780479 £100, plus special breaks; 19 pretty, individually furnished rms. Magnificent Queen Anne building with comfortable and attractive day rooms, a distinguished restaurant with good interesting food and excellent wines (there's a less pricey bistro-style operation too), warmly friendly staff, a relaxed atmosphere, and 12 acres of surrounding gardens and fields; dogs welcome; disabled access.

Ewen SU0097 Wild Duck Ewen, Cirencester GL7 6BY (01285) 770310 £69.50; 10 rms. Attractive and very popular old-fashioned 16th-c inn with a particularly cosy atmosphere, consistently friendly service, high-beamed main bar with a talking African grey parrot and open winter fire, second bar with beams and a handsome Elizabethan fireplace, imaginative bar food (lots of fresh fish), and prize-winning garden; disabled access.

Great Rissington SP1917 Lamb Great Rissington, Cheltenham GL54 2LP

(01451) 820388 *£55*, plus special breaks; 14 pretty rms – several are suites with own lounge. Civilised 17th-c inn in pretty countryside with sheltered hillside garden, cosy 2-roomed bar, residents' lounge with log fire, good nearby walks; cl 25–26 Dec; dogs by prior arrangement.

Greet SP0230 MANOR FARM Greet, Cheltenham GL54 5BJ (01242) 602423 **£50*; 3 rms. Carefully restored 16th-c manor house on mixed farm, with fine views, big garden and croquet; also, self-catering cottages; cl Christmas.

Hazleton SP0818 WINDRUSH HOUSE Hazleton, Cheltenham GL54 4EB (01451) 860364 **£44*; 4 rms, 2 with own bthrm. Warmly friendly and neatly kept no smoking guest house with exceptionally good, imaginative food, lovely breakfasts, and traditional furnishings; cl Dec–Jan; no children, no dogs.

Kineton SP0926 HALFWAY HOUSE Kineton, nr Guiting Power, Cheltenham GL54 5UG (01451) 850344 **£36*; 3 rms, shared bthrm. Friendly little stone pub with a good mix of customers, a warm fire, farm tools and pictures in the unpretentious bar, tasty food inc themed nights, and well kept real ales.

Little Barrington SP2012 INN FOR ALL SEASONS Little Barrington, Burford, Oxon OX18 4TN (01451) 844324 **£80*; 10 rms. Handsome old inn with low beams, stripped stone and flagstones, a big log fire, old prints, particularly good fresh fish and other food, well kept real ales and wines, lots of malt whiskies, and a pleasant garden surrounded by good walks; cl 25–26 Dec.

Little Rissington SP1819 TOUCHSTONE Little Rissington, Cheltenham GL54 2ND (01451) 822481 **£34*; 3 rms with thoughtful extras. Attractive traditional-style Cotswold stone house with very friendly owners, good breakfasts in dining room with doors on to terrace, and lots of nearby walks; children over 7; cl Dec–Jan.

Lower Slaughter SP1622 LOWER SLAUGHTER MANOR Lower Slaughter, Cheltenham GL54 2HP (01451) 820456 *£135*; 15 luxurious rms with thoughtful extras. Grand 17th-c manor house on the edge of a particularly pretty village with 4 acres of neatly kept grounds, a 15th-c dovecot, all-weather tennis court, croquet, and indoor pool; lovely flower arrangements, log fires, fine plaster ceilings, antiques and paintings, excellent modern cooking and award-winning wines in the elegant restaurant, and attentive welcoming staff; children over 10.

Lower Swell SP1725 OLD FARMHOUSE Lower Swell, Cheltenham GL54 1LF (01451) 830232 *£72*, plus special breaks; 14 rms, some in main building but most in various barns, stables and outbuildings, and most with own bthrm. Peaceful and unpretentious 16th-c manor farm with log fire in lounge bar, good interesting food using fresh local produce, a thoughtful wine list, friendly staff, and walled rose garden; restaurant.

Moreton-in-Marsh SP2032 REDESDALE ARMS Moreton-in-Marsh GL56 0AW (01608) 650308 *£49*; 19 individually decorated rms, some in an annexe. Fine old coaching inn with big stone fireplace and prettily lit alcoves in comfortable panelled bar, lively public bar with well kept real ales, conservatory, good tasty food, and friendly helpful staff.

Moreton-in-Marsh SP2032 WHITE HART ROYAL Moreton-in-Marsh GL56 0BA (01608) 650731 *£65*; 19 good rms. Busy and comfortable partly 15th-c inn with interesting Civil War history, oak beams, stripped stone, big inglenook fire in lounge area just off main bar, friendly helpful staff, well kept real ales, decent food in bar and pleasant restaurant, and quick welcoming service; attractive courtyard.

Nailsworth ST8499 EGYPT MILL Nailsworth, Stroud GL6 0AE (01453) 833449 *£75*, plus special breaks; 18 comfortable airy rms. Carefully converted 16th-c watermill with original millstones and lifting equipment in the spacious lounge, a split-level restaurant, ground floor bar where 2 waterwheels can be seen, good freshly made food, friendly service, and seats in the waterside gardens; disabled access.

North Cerney SP0208 BATHURST ARMS North Cerney, Cirencester GL7 7BZ

(01285) 831281 £45; 5 rms. Civilised and handsome old inn with lots of atmosphere, notably friendly staff, a nice mix of polished old furniture, warm fires, very good food, good wines, and attractive garden running down to river.

North Nibley ST7496 New Inn Waterley Bottom, North Nibley, Dursley GL11 6EF (01453) 543659 £35; 2 rms, shared bthrm. Simple inn with character landlady, wholesome home-made food, plentiful breakfasts, several interesting ales, neatly kept garden, small orchard, and good nearby walks; cl Christmas–New Year; no children.

Northleach SP1114 Market House The Square, Northleach, Cheltenham GL54 3EJ (01451) 860557 £44; 4 rms, mostly shared bthrm. Pretty 400-year-old stone house with flagstones, beams and inglenook fireplace, and good breakfasts; cl Christmas; children over 12.

Oddington SP2225 Horse & Groom Oddington, Moreton-in-Marsh GL56 0XH (01451) 830584 £65, plus winter breaks; 7 quaint and comfortable rms. Attractive, well run inn in pretty Cotswold village with handsome old furnishings, big log fire, candlelit dining room, and lovely garden with watergarden and large play area; cl 24–25 Dec; limited disabled access.

Painswick SO8609 Painswick Hotel Kemps Lane, Painswick, Stroud GL6 6YB (01452) 812160 *£105, plus special breaks; 20 well equipped comfortable rms. 18th-c Palladian mansion – once a grand rectory – with fine views, antiques and paintings in the elegant rooms, open fires, good food using the best local produce, and a relaxed friendly atmosphere; garden with croquet lawn.

Parkend SO6208 Edale House Folly Rd, Parkend, Lydney GL15 4JF (01594) 562835 £45, plus wknd breaks; 5 rms. Georgian house opposite cricket green and backing on to RSPB Nagshead Nature Reserve, with comfortable sitting room, very good food in attractive dining room (overlooking the garden), and a relaxed atmosphere; self-catering cottages; cl Jan; children over 12.

Puckrup SO8836 Puckrup Hall Puckrup, Tewkesbury GL20 6EL (01684) 296200 *£100, plus special breaks; 84 comfortably spacious rms. Handsome Regency mansion in over 140 acres of parkland with its own par 71, 18-hole golf course, and new leisure club inc indoor swimming pool, crèche, gym and so forth; elegant lounge with fine plasterwork, relaxed bar overlooking croquet lawn, and good food in 4 different dining areas; disabled access.

St Briavels SO5605 George St Briavels, Lydney GL15 6TA (01594) 530228 £40; 4 rms. Pleasant old pub in particularly interesting village overlooking 12th-c castle, with 3 rambling rooms, big stone fireplace, a Celtic coffin lid dating from 1070 (found in a fireplace here and now mounted next to the bar counter), cosy dining room, and good food; outdoor chessboard.

Shurdington SO9218 Greenway Shurdington, Cheltenham GL51 5UG (01242) 862352 *£135, plus special breaks; 19 well equipped, spacious and pretty rms. Very well run, lovely 16th-c manor house with antiques, fresh flowers and comfortable seats in the attractive drawing room, cosy cocktail bar, particularly good modern British cooking, excellent wine list, attentive service, and neatly kept gardens; children over 7; cl 1st wk Jan; limited disabled access.

Stow-on-the-Wold SP1925 Grapevine Sheep St, Stow-on-the-Wold, Cheltenham GL54 1AU (01451) 830344 £120, plus special breaks; 22 well furnished rms. Warm, friendly and very well run hotel with antiques, comfortable chairs and a relaxed atmosphere in the lounge, a beamed bar, and good food in the attractive sunny restaurant with its 70-year-old trailing vine.

Stow-on-the-Wold SP1925 Old Stocks The Square, Stow-on-the-Wold, Cheltenham GL54 1AF (01451) 830666 £70, plus special breaks; 18 rms. Well run 16th/17th-c Cotswold stone hotel with cosy, welcoming small bar, beams and open fire, good food, friendly staff, and sheltered garden; cl Christmas; disabled access.

Stow-on-the-Wold SP1925 ROYALIST Digbeth St, Stow-on-the-Wold, Cheltenham GL54 1BN (01451) 830670 *£70; 12 rms. Ancient hotel with good claims to origins in 10th c, family-run, friendly and full of character; log fire in the charming lounge, cosy beamed bar, all-day coffee shop, good home-made bar food; disabled access.

Upper Slaughter SP1523 LORDS OF THE MANOR Upper Slaughter, Cheltenham GL54 2JD (01451) 820243 £125, plus special breaks; 27 rms carefully furnished with antiques, Victorian sketches and paintings. Warmly friendly hotel with mid-17th-c heart (though it's been carefully extended many times), lovely views over 8 acres of grounds from very comfortable library and drawing room, log fires, fresh flowers, fine modern English cooking in attractive candlelit restaurant overlooking the original rectory gardens, good breakfasts, and kind service.

Viney Hill SO6506 VINEY HILL COUNTRY GUEST HOUSE Viney Hill, Blakeney GL15 4LT (01594) 516000 *£46, plus special breaks; 6 well furnished, comfortable rms. Delightful old no smoking farmhouse in lovely countryside, with very pretty garden, 2 cosy lounges (one with TV), lots of books and local information, decent evening meals and good breakfasts, and friendly efficient service; very good walking all around.

Westonbirt ST8589 HARE & HOUNDS Westonbirt, Tetbury GL8 8QL (01666) 880233 £92, plus special breaks; 30 comfortable rms. Cotswold stone hotel in 10 acres of grounds with 2 tennis courts, squash court, and croquet; a pleasant old-fashioned bar, relaxed spacious and comfortable lounges, open fires, good food, friendly service, table tennis, and snooker; limited disabled access.

Willersey SP1039 OLD RECTORY Church St, Willersey, Broadway, Worcs WR12 7PN (01386) 853729 £60, plus special breaks; 8 attractive, well equipped rms. Quietly set and friendly 17th-c house opposite church (nice walks from the churchyard), with a log fire in dining/sitting room and pretty flower-filled walled gardens with an ancient mulberry tree; good breakfasts, but no evening meals – though several places nearby; cl Christmas; children over 8; disabled access.

Winchcombe SP0228 SUDELEY HILL FARM Winchcombe, Cheltenham GL54 5JB (01242) 602344 £44; 3 no smoking rms. Friendly 15th-c farmhouse on working mixed farm with log fires, guest sitting room, and dining room overlooking the large garden; cl Christmas; no dogs.

Winchcombe SP0228 WESLEY HOUSE High St, Winchcombe, Cheltenham GL54 5LJ (01242) 602366 *£65; 5 cosy rms with showers. Pretty half-timbered 15th-c house with quiet friendly atmosphere, log fire in comfortable lounge, and good food in attractive beamed restaurant; cl 14 Jan–12 Feb.

Winstone SO9509 WINSTONE GLEBE Winstone, Cirencester GL7 7JU (01285) 821451 £55; 3 rms. Small Georgian rectory in quiet countryside with 5 acres of gardens and paddocks, tennis, lots of surrounding walks, friendly hosts, traditional furnishings, and delicious food (by arrangement); dogs welcome.

Withington SP0315 HALEWELL CLOSE Withington, Cheltenham GL54 4BN (01242) 890238 *£83; 6 beamed and comfortable rms. Lovely old Cotswold stone house, dating back to the 15th c, with relaxed house-party atmosphere, beamed sitting room, late breakfasts, and good English food in the panelled dining room; high tea for children; 50 acres of grounds inc big garden with stone terraces, heated outdoor swimming pool, and fish in trout lake and on River Coln; riding can be arranged; dogs by arrangement; good provision for the disabled.

To see and do

★ **Cotswold villages** Lower Slaughter SP1622, with its sister village Upper Slaughter SP1523, is perhaps the prettiest village in Britain – a perfect harmony of stone, water, grass and trees. It's not as overwhelmed by summer visitors as its nearby rival Bourton-on-the-Water, though it certainly gets its fair share. By the same trout stream as over-visited Bibury SP1106, a pleasant drive links other villages that are just as engaging, but bypassed by most visitors, particularly Coln St Aldwyns SP1405 (the New Inn is excellent) and Quenington SP1404 (which has a decent village pub). On the far side of Bibury the back road tracking along the river passes through a string of pleasant little villages such as Coln Rogers SP0809, Coln St Dennis SP0810 and Yanworth SP0713, eventually reaching the pretty village of Withington SP0315 (where there is a delightful pub right on the stream).

Many lesser-known villages are almost as beautiful. We have picked out a short list which have the added attraction of a decent village pub: Alderton SP0033, Amberley SO8401, Bisley SO9005, Bledington SP2422, Blockley SP1634, Broad Campden SP1637 (the Bakers Arms), Broadwell SP2027, Chedworth SP0511, the Duntisbournes SO9707, Eastleach SP1905 (a lovely ancient clapper bridge links the two Norman churches, very photogenic when the daffodils are out), Ebrington SP1840, Ewen SU0097, Frampton Mansell SO9102 (nice short drive to Sapperton,) Great Barrington SP2013 (good cheap bedrooms at the Fox; lovely walks), Great Rissington SP1917, Lower Swell SP1725, Meysey Hampton SU1199, Naunton SP1123, Nether Westcote SP2120, North Cerney SP0208, Oddington SP2225 (interesting mural in 11th-c church; pleasant walks, especially from the Fox at Lower Oddington – very good food), Sapperton SO9403, Selsley SO8304 (William Morris, Ford Madox Brown, Burne-Jones and Rossetti all worked on the church's windows), Sheepscombe SO8910 (the cricket ground is so steep that fielders can scarcely see the bowler), Slad SO8707 (the setting for Laurie Lee's *Cider With Rosie*), Somerford Keynes SU0195, South Woodchester SO8302 (particularly for the views), Southrop SP1903 (another village that really comes into its own when the daffodils appear, with a charming riverside church), Stanton SP0734 (an absolute charmer), Todenham SP2436, Willersey SP1039, and – more small town than village – Wotton-under-Edge ST7593, with a fine Schreider organ in its church, a new little heritage centre, and some handsome old buildings; the B4058 is a good drive. Though there's no pub to recommend there, Saintbury SP1139 is a winner when the daffodils are out.

Parts of Avon now absorbed into Gloucestershire also turn up attractive villages: notably Almondsbury ST6084, Oldbury-on-Severn ST6092 (the church on the nearby knoll is unusual), and Wick ST7072; these last two have pleasant walks nearby. The B4060 N of Chipping Sodbury ST7282 and the side roads through Hawkesbury ST7786 and Hillesley ST7689 take you through attractive Cotswoldy scenery.

CYCLING is a good way to see some of these places at their best, and the Cotswold Cycling Company not only hire bikes but can arrange your route and accommodation too; (01242) 250642.

Gloucester SO8318 A busy modern city despite its long history – you have to search out the old buildings among today's big shops (for instance the splendid timber-framed house tucked down a passageway off 26 Westgate St). The Tourist Office at St Michael's Tower (itself a fine ancient building at the central Cross) is particularly good at sending you off well equipped for the hunt. The Waterfront (Llanthony Rd, S end of docks), and – all handy for the cathedral – Fountain, New Inn and Tailors House (Westgate St) are useful for a quick lunch.

✝ CATHEDRAL In 1330 the Abbot astutely purchased the remains of murdered Edward II, and the resulting stream of pilgrims paid for elaborate rebuilding in an early example of Perpendicular style, which towers majestically over the city's more recent buildings. Lovely fan-vaulted cloisters, the second largest medieval stained-glass window in the country, and a fine collection of church plate in the Treasury. Meals, snacks, shop, disabled access; (01452) 528095; donations. Not far from here are the remains of 9th-c ST OSWALD'S PRIORY, the city's oldest structure, and other ecclesiastical remains inc GREYFRIARS AND BLACKFRIARS, the latter pretty much unchanged since the 13th-c, with a rare scissor-braced roof.

♨ ♨ 🏠 GLOUCESTER DOCKS The revitalised waterfront deserves much of the credit for the city's tourism renaissance. The next two attractions are both located here, and there are also guided walks, summer boat trips along the canal or as far as Tewkesbury, the unusually interesting SOLDIERS OF GLOUCESTER MUSEUM (cl Mon exc summer and bank hols; £3.50), and a big ANTIQUES CENTRE, with 68 varied antique shops in Dickensian arcades (cl am Sun; free wkdys, 50p wknds and bank hols).

❀ NATIONAL WATERWAYS MUSEUM 🎫 (The Docks) The story of Britain's inland waterways, and the first heyday of these docks after the opening of the Gloucester & Berkeley Canal. It's a lively place, with a good deal to amuse children, who can even try their hand at steering a narrow boat. New galleries are to be added following a substantial Lottery grant. Snacks, shop, good disabled access; cl 25 Dec; (01452) 318054; £4.50.

♨ ROBERT OPIE COLLECTION MUSEUM OF ADVERTISING AND PACKAGING (Albert Warehouse, Docks) Great for nostalgia-lovers, an enormous and quite fascinating assembly of packets, tins, bottles, posters, street signs and more from Victorian days onwards. Also continuous showing of vintage TV commercials. Snacks, shop, disabled access; cl winter Mons, 25–26 Dec; (01452) 302309; *£2.95.

♨ PRISON MUSEUM (Barrack Sq) The only museum of its type attached to a fully operational prison (it's in the old Gate Lodge), with interactive videos and displays on life behind bars from the 19th c to the present. Shop (selling goods made by inmates of various jails), some disabled access; cl Sun, Oct–Easter; (01452) 529551; *£1.

♨ FOLK MUSEUM (Westgate St) Social history in a group of Tudor and Jacobean timber-framed houses; they recently opened a toy gallery. Shop, limited disabled access; cl Sun exc July–Sept, 25–26 Dec, 1 Jan, Good Fri; (01452) 526467; free.

♨ 🖼 🎻 CITY MUSEUM AND ART GALLERY (Brunswick Rd) Local history (inc the oldest known backgammon set), and paintings by Gainsborough and Turner. Shop, disabled access; cl Sun exc July–Sept, 24–26 Dec, 1 Jan, Good Fri; (01452) 524131; free. Guided tours of the ancient CITY EAST GATE leave here every hour on Sats May–Sept; 40p.

♨ HOUSE OF THE TAILOR OF GLOUCESTER (College Ct) Inspiration for Beatrix Potter's story, now with exhibition and shop. Disabled access downstairs; cl Sun and bank hols; free.

✝ HISTORIC AIRCRAFT (Airport, Cheltenham Rd E) The working surroundings make this collection seem more ready for action than some; children can climb into some of the cockpits. Usually only cl Tues, Thurs and Sat, but best to check first out of season, (01452) 330761; £3.

🎱 ❀ ROBINSWOOD HILL COUNTRY PARK (2m S) A little outcrop of the Cotswolds, with 250 acres of walks and trails, a wildlife information centre (fun talks and events), and wonderful views of the city from the summit. Snacks, shop, disabled access; (01452) 303206; free. Not far away is a dry ski slope.

🍎 FARM SHOP AT OVER (1m W) A good one, with local produce and PICK-YOUR-OWN in summer.

The Forest of Dean Still largely ancient oak woodland despite encroaching pine plantations, the forest rolls over many miles of hilly countryside, giving plenty of space – even in summer you can often have much of the woods to yourself. There are ponds, streams with stepping stones, cattle and maybe fallow deer, sudden distant views, the humps and gouges that mark ancient iron workings, the tracks of abandoned railways and tramways, and still one or two of the freeminers, who've been digging coal by hand from surface seams for hundreds of years. The forest scenery has most impact on those prepared to delve into its past a bit, perhaps at the heritage centre at Upper Soudley; good paths throughout.

🏛 🐟 🌱 ❋ **Forest sights** You can track the remarkably durable paving of a ROMAN ROAD just off the B4431 at Blackpool Bridge SO6508. There's a pleasant CONIFER ARBORETUM near Speech House SO6212. NAGSHEAD NATURE RESERVE SO6008 is a good place to see deer and other wildlife. SYMONDS YAT ROCK SO5616 Perhaps the most spectacular feature, where the River Wye rolls around a monumental wooded cliff barrier, a favourite spot with peregrine falcons; tremendous views in all directions from the top, and at the bottom a ferry runs between two inns. Around the edges of the forest the scenery changes to a patchwork of steep pastures – also very attractive. It's well worth getting a forest map, either from the Dean Heritage Centre or direct from the Forestry Commission in Coleford, (01594) 833057; these outline walks (inc an unusual sculpture trail), mark the best spots for views or picnics. The information centres can also provide details of canoeing, caving, cycling or fishing in the forest. The B4432 to Symonds Yat gives some good views, the B4228 down past St Briavels is a pleasant country road, and the little lanes around the edges of the Forest are rewarding drives – but need a large-scale map. See also Clearwell, Coleford, Lydney and St Briavels entries below; another useful food stop is the New Inn at Viney Hill SO6606.

Other things to see and do

GLOUCESTERSHIRE FAMILY ATTRACTION OF THE YEAR

🐦 **Slimbridge** SO7703 WILDFOWL AND WETLANDS TRUST (off the A38) The first of the Wildfowl and Wetlands Trust's 8 centres, and still the best, this enormous place is a lot more than just a bird and nature reserve. Thoughtfully upgraded in recent years (with more to come thanks to a hefty grant from the Millennium Commission), it shows off probably the world's most comprehensive collection of geese, swans and ducks, as well as 6 species of flamingo (you won't see so many anywhere else in Europe), rare and wild birds, and a tropical house that recreates the sights, sounds and smells of a rainforest. Last summer they added a new PondZone section, where children are encouraged to learn about wetland environments by taking part in pond-dipping and seeing what they help fish out of the water magnified on to TV screens. Also quite a few computer and video displays and games, and extra events and talks in the school hols. It's unusual in being somewhere that you might get more out of visiting in the winter, when up to 8,000 wild birds fly in; several of the excellent hides and viewing facilities are heated then. Some birds can be fed by hand, and you may be lucky enough to hear the amazing belch of the maccoa duck. There aren't any play areas or anything like that, but it's one of the most visitor-friendly bird reserves in the country, with plenty of activities specifically aimed at primary school aged children. They'll hire out binoculars if you've left your own at home. Meals and snacks, shop, disabled access; cl 25 Dec; (01453) 890065; £5 (£3 children over 4, free to WWT members). A family ticket for 2 adults and 2 children is £13.

🐂 **Arlingham** SO7010 ST
AUGUSTINE'S WORKING FARM 🎫
(B4071) Friendly working dairy farm
with cows, pigs, goats, hens, sheep
and rabbits, all of which children can
go right up to (quite a few feeding
opportunities). Snacks, shop,
disabled access; cl Nov–Mar and all
Mon (exc bank hols); (01452)
740277; *£3. The Ship at Upper
Framilode nearby has decent food in
an attractive setting.

🐝 **Barnsley** SP0705 BARNSLEY HOUSE
GARDENS (B4425) Lovely little herb,
vegetable and knot gardens, fruit
trees and decorative plants, laburnum
and lime walks and 18th-c
summerhouses; especially attractive
spring blossom and autumn colours.
Plant sales, some disabled access; cl
Sun; (01285) 740281; £3. The Village
Pub is good.
🏰 🐝 🦋 🍺 **Berkeley** ST6899 BERKELEY
CASTLE 🎫 (off the A38) Excellently

Days Out

Gems of the northern Cotswolds
Kiftsgate Court, Mickleton; Chipping Campden – lunch at the Eight Bells
or Noel Arms there, or the Crown at Blockley; Batsford Arboretum.

Abbey ruins and two contrasting manors
Hailes Abbey; lunch at Harvest Home, Greet; Stanway House or Snowshill
Manor.

Meet the animals and ride the train
Stroll up Cleeve Hill from Cleeve Common (good for kite-flying); lunch at
the Farmers Arms, Guiting Power or Halfway House, Kineton; Cotswold
Farm Park there; steamtrain trip from Toddington or Winchcombe.

Exploring the Coln valley
Fairford church; Bibury village – lunch at the Catherine Wheel; drive along
Coln valley; Barnsley Gardens, or Northleach for the mechanical music
show and church.

The Roman Cotswolds
Chedworth Roman Villa; lunch at the Seven Tuns there, or from a wide
choice in Cirencester; Corinium Museum, explore Cirencester, stroll in
Cirencester Park.

Secretive landscapes and a lost canal
Painswick, Painswick Rococo Garden, walk up Painswick Beacon;
Misarden Park, Miserden; lunch at the Daneway, Sapperton; walk from
the pub down the derelict Thames & Severn Canal; if time, explore
churches and villages inc Elkstone and Duntisbourne Rouse.

The great forest
Forest of Dean Sculpture Trail; lunch at the Wyndham Arms, Clearwell;
Clearwell Caves; Symonds Yat Rock, walk along Wye Gorge S to the
Biblins suspension bridge.

Sanctuaries along the Severn Estuary
Frampton Court, lunch at the Bell, Frampton on Severn;
Wildfowl and Wetlands Trust, Slimbridge, or Berkeley Castle.

Roses and trees
Hunts Court, North Nibley (cl Aug); lunch at Hunters Hall, Kingscote
(A4135); Westonbirt Arboretum.

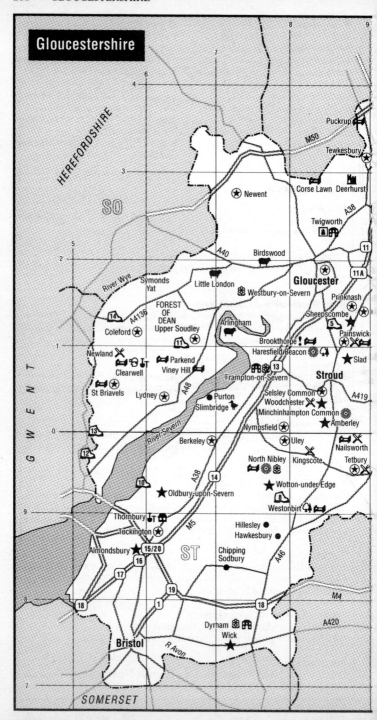

Gloucestershire

preserved castle, very much a family home, but still keeping a flavour of its days as a Norman fortress. Impressive paintings, furnishings and silver, fine old keep and Great Hall, terraced gardens, park, extensive butterfly farm – and the dungeon where Edward II was murdered in 1327. Snacks, shop, limited disabled access; open Tues–Sun Apr–Sept (cl am Sun, and am daily in Apr), plus Mon July and Aug, and pm Sun in Oct; (01453) 810332; £4.80, £1.75 gardens only, £1.75 butterfly farm. JENNER MUSEUM (High St) Largely unchanged Georgian home of Edward Jenner, who discovered the vaccine against smallpox here. He gave free vaccinations from the thatched hut in the attractive grounds. Shop, some disabled access; cl am, all day Mon exc bank hols, Oct exc Sun, and all Nov–Mar; (01453) 810631; £2. The Pickwick at Lower Wick is a popular dining pub.

★ ♪ ✕ Bibury SP1106 One of the most popular villages in the area, with lovely golden streamside houses; summer crowds can rather blunt its appeal. TROUT FARM Long-established working farm breeding rainbow trout in 20 ponds. You can feed the fish, or try to catch your own. Snacks, good shop, disabled access (though no facilities); cl 25 –26 Dec; (01285) 740215; £2. The 18th-c machinery of well restored ARLINGTON MILL nearby is demonstrated every day, with guided tours by arrangement. Meals, snacks, shop; cl 25 Dec; (01285) 740368; £2. Besides Bibury Court, the Catherine Wheel is the best place here for lunch.

🐖 Birdswood SO7418 OLD LEY COURT (Chapel Lane) Working farm producing double and single Gloucester cheese – you can watch them make it on Tues and Thurs, but best to tel first, (01452) 750225; £1.50. The Apple Tree at nearby Minsterworth is a pleasant dining pub, and the lane past it leads to a good quiet spot for watching the Severn Bore.

🐖 Blockley SP1634 SLEEPY HOLLOW FARM PARK 🔲 (Draycott Rd) Nicely unspoilt 25-acre farm park, with

particularly good collection of pigs, and unexpected animals such as alligators, tigers, a puma, jaguar and leopards. Plenty of demonstrations, and indoor pet centre. In 1997 they were open late on Fri and Sat nights in July and Aug, when you could see the animals behaving quite differently from the way they might during the hot summer days, but as we went to press they weren't sure yet whether they would be doing this again in 1998. Snacks, shop, disabled access (no facilities); cl mid-Nov–mid-Mar; (01386) 701264; £2.95. The Crown is a smart place for lunch.

🏵 🏠 Bourton-on-the-Hill SP1732 BOURTON HOUSE Unusual plants inc tender ones in attractive garden around fine old house (not open). Teas in 16th-c tithe barn, shop; open pm Thurs and Fri late May–Oct; £2.50. The Horse & Groom does decent food. SEZINCOTE SP1730 (off the A44 about 1m S) Exotic onion-domed forerunner of Brighton Pavilion, stunning from the outside, less interesting inside. Also classic early 19th-c watergarden, and a more recent Indian-style garden to match the building. Garden open pm Thurs, Fri and bank hols (cl Dec), house open pm Thurs and Fri May–July and Sept; £4.50, £3 garden only. Children are not allowed in the house.

★ 🐦 📷 ! Bourton-on-the-Water SP1620 One of the best-known Cotswold villages, but disfigured by sprawly crowds in summer unless you get there very early in the morning – when it's enchanting. There is a wealth of attractions aimed at visitors. BIRDLAND (Rissington Rd) Rare and exotic birds on banks of meandering River Windrush, inc the biggest colony of penguins outside America. Snacks, shop, disabled access; cl 25 Dec; (01451) 820480; £3. COTSWOLD MOTOR MUSEUM AND TOY MUSEUM In an old watermill, cars and motorcycles from vintage years to 1950s, along with advertising signs, automobilia, and toy collection. It's the home of Brum the children's TV character. Shop, disabled access; cl Dec–Jan, plus occasional winter wkdys; (01451)

821255; *£1.75. The price includes entry to the adjacent VILLAGE LIFE EXHIBITION, with re-created Edwardian rooms, village shop, and blacksmith's forge. MODEL VILLAGE Charming replica of the village, modelled from Cotswold stone in the 1930s to a scale of one-ninth, complete with working waterwheel and music in the church. Good home-made food (and lovely river view) in adjacent welcoming Old New Inn, shop; cl 25 Dec; (01451) 820467; *£1.50. PERFUMERY EXHIBITION (Victoria St) Aromatic displays and demonstrations of perfume-making and scent extraction, with scented garden. Shop, disabled access; cl 25–26 Dec; (01451) 820698; £2. FOLLY FARM WATERFOWL (3m W on the A436) Lakes and pools with 160 species of waterfowl, as well as friendly ducks, geese and poultry, and hand-reared animals. Good for children, and a nice spot for a picnic (or to camp). Their lavender fields are in full bloom July. Snacks, shop, disabled access; cl 25 Dec; (01451) 820285; £3. The Old Manse has decent food and garden tables overlooking the Windrush; the riverside Parrot & Alligator is good, too.

★ ♨ ⛲ ♨ 🖼 **Cheltenham** SO9422 Beautiful spa town useful for exploring Cotswolds, shopping, or admiring the elegant Regency architecture of its tree-lined avenues. PITTVILLE PUMP ROOM (Pittville Park) A short walk from the centre, this is generally regarded as the town's finest building, 19th-c Greek Revival with a colonnaded façade and balconied hall. It's easy to imagine the place's Regency heyday, especially strolling round the super park and gardens, or during concerts in the July music festival; on summer Suns they may have teas accompanied by live music. You can still sample the spa water – rather salty. The museum has local history and notable costume and jewellery collections. Shop, limited disabled access; cl Tues; (01242) 523852; *£1.50. HOLST BIRTHPLACE MUSEUM (Clarence Rd) Nr the Pump Room, this interesting

Regency house is where the composer was born in 1874; you can see his first piano. Worthwhile even if you're not mad about Holst, as the rooms are all carefully furnished in period style. Shop; cl Sun, Mon and bank hols; (01242) 524846; £1.50. ART GALLERY AND MUSEUM (Clarence St) Excellent Arts and Crafts collection inspired by William Morris, fine paintings inc 17th-c Dutch works, and rare porcelain and ceramics. Meals, snacks, shop, disabled access; cl Sun and bank hols; (01242) 837431; free. These days Cheltenham is best known for its races, and the racecourse at Prestbury Park (N on the A435) has an exhibition on Gold Cup winners; (01242) 513014; free. Lots of antique shops, especially around the Montpellier area. Taylors wine bar (Cambray Pl), the Restoration (Grosvenor St), Beehive (Montpellier Villas) and Beaufort Arms (London Rd) have decent food, and the well run café in the beautiful Imperial Gardens is suitable for families.

★ **Chipping Campden** SP1539 Extremely attractive town, with interesting old buildings inc an ancient covered open-sided market hall, a grand Perpendicular church typical of the area's rich 'wool churches', enjoyable shops, and fine old inns. Many of our contributors would put it among the country's most delightful small towns, though until they get the cars out of the centre not all would agree. Besides places mentioned in the **Where to stay** section above, the Lygon Arms and Volunteer are good for lunch.

★ ♦ ⛲ ♨ 🏔 ♨ **Cirencester** SP0201 A busy country town, particularly on its Mon and Fri market days, with a succession of fine Cotswold stone streets off the long market place. It has many attractive buildings, and interesting antique and other shops inc traditional country saddlers, etc. Though one of the most handsome of all the Cotswold towns, it isn't too touristy. The CHURCH of St John the Baptist (Market Pl) is wonderfully grand, and has a striking late Gothic tower. CORINIUM MUSEUM (Park St)

Cirencester was one of the most important cities in Roman Britain, and this spacious museum has one of the finest collections of antiquities from the period (all clearly displayed and labelled). Reconstructed period dining room and kitchen (complete with menus), with Saxon and medieval galleries too. Snacks, shop, excellent disabled access; cl am Sun, Mon Nov–Mar, Christmas; (01285) 655611; £1.75. BREWERY COURT 20 independent craft businesses and shops in former brewery (cl Sun), along with theatre, gallery and café. Also worth a look are the 12th-c remains of ST JOHN'S HOSPITAL, the NORMAN ARCH, and the various well preserved wool merchants' houses. Cecily Hill, one of the town's most attractive streets, gives on to the pleasant strolling-ground of Cirencester Park. Decent places for lunch include the Slug & Lettuce, Corinium Court, Tatyans (Chinese) and (very local but good value) Golden Cross.

☣ **Clearwell** SO5608 CLEARWELL CAVES ▨ (off the B4228) Tours of huge caverns, a source of ore from the Iron Age right up to 1945; deeper trips for the more adventurous. It's quite a labyrinth, with many miles of passageways, so stout shoes recommended. Lively themed displays down here at Christmas. Snacks, shop; cl Nov, and 24 Dec–end Feb; (01594) 832535; £3. The Wyndham Arms is good for lunch, and though the village is not in itself particularly pretty it's a very good centre for the lovely surrounding countryside.

⚑‼🏛 **Coleford** SO5710 GREAT WESTERN RAILWAY MUSEUM Converted Coleford GWR goods station with several large-scale model steam locomotives, relics, photographs and a Victorian ticket office; very much a private collection, enthusiastically presented, and manned by helpful volunteers. Open pm Sat all yr, plus 3.15–5pm Tues–Fri Easter–Oct; (01594) 833569; *£1.50. PUZZLE WOOD (just off the B4228) Pleasant for a stroll: wooded paths arranged in a puzzle, landscaped in the 19th c nr

remains of Roman iron mines. Snacks, shop; cl Mon (exc bank hols), and Nov–Easter; (01594) 833187; £2. Across the road is the TREASURE TRAIN, a new attraction that readers have already started to recommend for families; steam trains run along a ¾-mile stretch of narrow-gauge track, with children solving clues that lead to treasure along the way. There are 4 stops, with footpaths through the woods nearby. Snacks, disabled access; open wknds and bank hols Easter –Oct, maybe Weds too in summer hols; (01594) 834991; £2.90 for unlimited train journeys, plus £1.50 for the treasure trail. The Dog & Muffler at Joyford is a pretty place for lunch; good walks nearby.

🏛 **Deerhurst** SO8729 Ancient remains here include ODDA'S CHAPEL, a restored 11th-c chapel discovered as part of a farmhouse, and ST MARY'S PRIORY, a mainly Saxon church with a lovely atmosphere and some intriguing original carvings and features. The Farmers Arms at Apperley is a good dining pub (brewing its own beers).

🏠 🏵 **Dyrham** ST7475 DYRHAM PARK Set in an ancient park grazed by fallow deer, this fine William & Mary house has hardly changed since the late 17th c. The interiors have Dutch-style furnishings, Delft ware, Dutch bird paintings and a remarkable *trompe l'oeil* by Hoogstraten. Meals, snacks, shop, disabled access to ground floor; house cl am, all day Weds and Thurs, and all Nov–Mar, park open all year; (0117) 937 2501; £5.20, £2.60 garden and deer park only; NT. The Bull at Hinton Dyrham and Crown at Tolldown (A46) are handy for lunch.

✝ **Fairford** SP1501 Pleasant riverside meadows, and a wonderful 15th-c Perpendicular CHURCH, well known for its remarkable medieval stained glass (inc a fascinating depiction of Hell), and comical misericords. The Bull has decent food.

🏠 🏵 **Frampton on Severn** SO7407 FRAMPTON COURT Elegant lived-in Georgian house, with original furniture, porcelain and paintings, and fascinating gardens. The 18th-c orangery has been converted into self-catering holiday flats. Disabled access to garden only; personal tours all year by appointment, (01452) 740267; £4. The village green is said to be the largest in the country, with the orangery on one side, and the civilised Bell (good range of food) on another. Just outside the village the Gloucester & Sharpness Canal passes grand colonnaded lock-keepers' houses by pretty swing bridges.

🏠🚢🎈🌼 **Great Witcombe** SO9114 The outlines of a substantial ROMAN VILLA can still be traced here, around a courtyard, with several mosaics and evidence of an underfloor heating system. Nearby, the CRICKLEY WINDWARD VINEYARD produces up to 7 wines; cl am, all day Sun and Mon, and Christmas–Easter (exc by appointment); (01452) 863555; free. CRICKLEY HILL COUNTRY PARK (just N) has a few ancient sites, as well as nature trails, lovely clearly marked woodland walks, and fine views. Some disabled access; visitor centre cl winter; (01452) 863170; free. The Royal George Hotel at Birdlip has decent food, and the Golden Heart at Brimpsfield is good.

🌱🐚 **Hailes** SP0228 HAILES ABBEY (B4632) Graceful ruins of 13th-c Cistercian abbey, once a centre for pilgrims who flocked to see a phial containing what they believed to be Christ's blood. Walkman tour, shop, some disabled access; probably cl winter wkdys – best to check; (01242) 602398; £2.40; NT. The Harvest Home at Greet has the best food nearby, but Hayles Fruit Farm down the road is good for snacks, and has PICK-YOUR-OWN.

🐷 **Kineton** SP0926 COTSWOLD FARM PARK 🎫 (off the B4077, E) Full of delightfully odd-looking species of sheep, cattle, pigs, goats, horses and poultry, this is particularly well organised as far as children are concerned. Rabbits and piglets to cuddle and feed, good safe rustic-themed play areas, and a designated children's shop, with items from 5p to around £2 at the most. You can easily spend most of a day here; nature trails and woodland walks are ideal for a break from the animals, and there are 19 acres in which to picnic, kick a ball around, or relax on the grass. Lots under cover, so still good when the weather isn't perfect (best to wear wellies then). Meals, snacks, shop, disabled access; open Easter–wknd nearest end of Sept; (01451) 850307; £3.50. The Halfway House does decent food. Nearby Guiting Power SP0924 is attractive, sensitively restored and genuine, with pleasant walks; the Farmers Arms there is good.

★ **Lechlade** SU2199 Graceful village with one or two decent antique shops, good traditional toyshop, pleasant walks, and access to the quiet reed-fringed Thames for footpath walks – especially along to Kelmscot in Oxfordshire. The Trout along the A417 at St John's Bridge has lovely riverside tables.

🐚 **Little London** SO7019 ANGORA GOAT AND MOHAIR CENTRE (Blakemore Farm, Little London) Unusual goat farm with shop selling clothes made from their fleeces; other animals too. Snacks, shop, disabled access; cl Mon (exc bank hols), Tues, 24 Dec–late Jan; (01452) 830630; free. The Red Hart at Blaisdon is attractive for lunch.

🚂🏛️🏠🐚 **Lydney** SO6303 DEAN FOREST RAILWAY (New Mills, slightly N) Lots of locomotives, waggons and equipment at the station, and steam trips through the forest (mainly just wknds, best to ring for dates). Snacks, shop, disabled access; static displays open all year; (01594) 843423; £3.50. The Woodman at Parkend, handy for the stop there, has decent food and good nearby walks. LYDNEY PARK Extensive sheltered spring garden rich with flowering shrubs, rhododendrons, azaleas and magnolias; also lakes and deer park. Tucked away among the trees are the remains of a Roman temple, and a museum with finds from the site, inc the astonishingly intricate Lydney dog. Snacks, shop, plant sales; open Sun, Weds and bank hols Easter–early Jun; (01594) 842844; £2.

🏛️🌼 **Mickleton** SP1643 KIFTSGATE

COURT GARDEN (off the B4081)
Renowned for its old-fashioned roses
(best in Jun and July), inc the largest
rose in England, but with many other
rare plants, shrubs and trees, good
views across the Vale of Evesham,
and that special feel that comes from
generations of care by a gifted
gardening family. Snacks (Jun and
July, with teas in Aug), rare plant
sales; open pm Weds, Thurs, Sun and
bank hols Apr–Sept, plus pm Sat Jun
and July; (01386) 438777; £3.50.
HIDCOTE MANOR GARDEN (adjacent)
Series of small gardens separated by
walls and hedges of different species,
with rare shrubs, trees and roses.
Very popular even midweek, despite
the price. Meals, snacks, good shop,
some disabled access; cl Tues (exc
June and July), Fri and all Nov–Mar;
(01386) 438333; £5.30; NT. The
Kings Arms is good value for lunch.

🕷 🌼 ♘ ★ **Miserden** SO9308
MISARDEN PARK Views over the
wooded Golden Valley from
handsome gardens of 17th-c manor
house (not open), with Lutyens
topiary, mature shrubs and trees, and
colourful walled garden. Nursery,
some disabled access; open
Tues–Thurs Easter–Sept; (01285)
821303; £2.50. Also woodland trail
down by the river. The quiet village is
charming, with decent food in the
Carpenters Arms.

★ ✝ ♘ ✿ **Moreton-in-Marsh**
SP2032 Attractively bustling old
place, once an important linen
weaving centre and coaching town,
now with popular Tues market. For
food we recommend the White Hart
Royal, Black Bear, Redesdale Arms
and Bear. WELLINGTON AVIATION
MUSEUM (Broadway Rd) World War
II aircraft pictures, sculpture and
related material. Shop, disabled
access; cl 12.30–2pm, all day Mon,
25 Dec, Jan; (01608) 650323; *£1.
BATSFORD ARBORETUM (Batsford Park,
just NW) Well grown private
collection of over 1,000 rare and
beautiful species of tree spread over
50 acres; hundreds of maples, 90
different magnolias, flowering
cherries. Best in May and autumn,
but relaxing any time. Meals, snacks,

garden centre, disabled access; cl
Nov–Feb; (01608) 650722; £3. Also
in Batsford Park (home to plenty of
deer), the COTSWOLD FALCONRY
CENTRE 📷 has flying demonstrations
throughout the day, with a chance to
handle some of the birds. Closed-
circuit TVs give a bird's-eye view of
life in the nest. Snacks, shop, disabled
access; open Mar–Nov; (01386)
701043; £3.

♘ ✿ 🐖 **Newent** SO7226 Small
country town with some timbered
buildings which have a bit of a
Worcestershire or Herefordshire
look. SHAMBLES MUSEUM OF VICTORIAN
LIFE (Church St) Enthusiastic re-
creation of Victorian cobbled square,
with shops and furnished
tradesman's house. Shop, limited
disabled access; cl Mon (exc bank
hols), Jan–mid-Mar; (01531)
822144; £3.25. The George opposite
is handy for lunch. NATIONAL BIRDS OF
PREY CENTRE (Gt Boulsdon, just S)
Exceptional collection of birds of
prey, with flying displays and
breeding aviaries. Meals, snacks,
shop, some disabled access; cl
Dec–Jan; (01531) 820286; £4.50.
The Yew Tree at Cliffords Mesne a
bit further on this road has decent
food, and is handy for May Hill (see
Walk ⌂-11 below). You can tour 2
local vineyards: the THREE CHOIRS
VINEYARD (off the B4215 towards
Dymock), now one of the 6 largest in
the country (cl 23 Dec–10 Jan;
tastings free, tour and exhibitions
£2.75), and ST ANNES VINEYARD
(Oxenhall, off the B4221), who grow
– and sell – 150 varieties of vine (cl
some winter wkdys, best to check on
01989 720313; free).

🕷 **North Cerney** SP0208 CERNEY
HOUSE GARDENS Expansive old garden
behind 13th-c church, with old roses,
trees, shrubs, walled and herb
gardens, a few animals (they make
tasty goat's cheese), and a new
watergarden. The surrounding
woods are lovely at bluebell time.
Teas, shop, some disabled access;
open pm Tues, Weds and Fri
Mar–Sept; (01285) 831300; £3. The
Bathurst Arms is good for lunch.

🕷 🌼 **North Nibley** ST7495 HUNTS

COURT Informal gardens with over 400 varieties of old roses, plus unusual shrubs and other plants; fine views. Plant sales, mostly disabled access; open Tues–Sat (though cl Aug), plus spring bank hols and usually last 3 Suns in Jun and first in July; (01453) 547440; £1.50. The walk up to the Tyndale Monument gives even better views, and the Black Horse is handy for lunch.

★ † ! ⬤ **Northleach** SP1114 Fine example of an unspoilt small wool town, with a particularly interesting CHURCH, renowned for its collection of brasses. They recently installed an automatic winder to the church clock, allowing retirement for the man who'd faithfully wound it for the last 65 years. KEITH HARDING'S WORLD OF MECHANICAL MUSIC 🆔 (Oak House, High St) Quite captivating collection of clocks, musical boxes and instruments in old wool merchant's house, displayed and played in period settings. It's quite spooky watching the instruments work themselves. Shop, good disabled and blind access; cl 25 Dec; (01451) 860181; *£5. There's a decent enough COUNTRYSIDE COLLECTION on nearby Fosseway (cl am Sun, and all Nov–Mar; £1.60). The Red Lion and Wheatsheaf Hotel are both pleasant for lunch.

🏠 ※ **Nympsfield** SO8000 WOODCHESTER MANSION (B4066) Construction of this splendid unfinished Gothic mansion was inexplicably abandoned virtually overnight in 1870. It's being repaired but not finished, and you can usually see traditional building techniques like stonemasonry. Five species of bat add to the atmosphere. No children inside, for safety reasons. Snacks, shop, disabled access to ground floor only; open 1st wknd of month Apr–Oct, plus bank hol wknds; (01453) 860661; £3.50. You should be able to explore the surrounding valley, recently purchased by the NT. The Rose & Crown in the attractive village has good-value food (and comfortable bedrooms), and the walk up Coaley Peak gives tremendous views over the Severn Valley.

★ ※ 🏠 † ☆ 🐝 **Painswick** SO8609 Delightful little town sometimes referred to as the 'Queen of the Cotswolds'. There's been a settlement here since Celtic times, and if you climb up PAINSWICK BEACON to look at the remains of the earliest structures there are fine views towards the Malvern Hills. Plenty of old buildings to look at, such as the 15th-c POST OFFICE and the CHURCH OF ST MARY with its fine tombs and fascinating churchyard – 99 immaculately clipped yews forming gateways and canopies, interesting tombstones, drifts of wild cyclamen in Sept. Also antique shops and craft workshops, notably that of Dennis French who has a showroom of woodware (cl am Sun, 2 wks early Jan). PAINSWICK ROCOCO GARDEN (The Stables, Painswick House) Careful restoration of sizeable 18th-c garden to match a 1748 painting showing its fanciful mix of precisely trimmed hedging, paths and shrubs, unrestrained trees and slightly zany garden buildings. Pleasant vistas, children's walks – a cheery-feeling place. Snacks, shop, plant sales, some disabled access; cl Mon, Tues, and Dec; (01452) 813204; £2.90. The Royal Oak is popular for lunch.

† 🏠 🐝 🐦 **Prinknash** SO8614 PRINKNASH ABBEY AND POTTERY (off the A46) Unusual 20th-c Benedictine monastery and earlier house, now home to the world-famous pottery; you can watch production from the viewing gallery. Snacks, shop, disabled access; cl 25–26 Dec, Good Fri; (01452) 812239; £1 for pottery tours. The abbey grounds (as opposed to buildings) are attractive, with good views over the Severn Vale. Out here the PRINKNASH BIRD PARK 🆔 has exotic pheasants, peacocks and other birds, as well as deer, goats and waterfowl; most animals feed from your hand (the fallow deer are particularly friendly). Snacks, shop; cl 25–26 Dec, 1 Jan, Good Fri; (01452) 812727; *£3. The Black Horse in the very steep village of Cranham has enjoyable food.

★ 🏰 ※ ☆ **St Briavels** SO5605 Attractive and unusual small village focused on the ruins of its 13th-c castle (the inhabited part is a youth hostel), with a steeply grassy former moat and views from the ramparts of the curtain wall. Kathy Boy organises wknd WATERCOLOUR WORKSHOPS in one of its medieval rooms; (01594) 530026. The George is good for lunch, and there are various circular walks around the parish, devised by Mr McGubbin in the CRAFT SHOP (cl Tues, Weds and winter wkdys).

🎱 ❄ **Selsley Common** SO8304 The sizeable HERB GARDEN here has cream teas on Sun and bank hols, and a good nursery. Garden open pm Tues–Sun and bank hols Apr–Sept, or by appointment, nursery open Apr–Sept; (01453) 766682; £1. They also have a herb shop just up the A46 in Nailsworth ST8499 (which also has plenty of trails around its old mills). The grassland common itself is quite high, with good views and pleasant walks; the Bell is a handy refreshment stop.

➤ **Slimbridge** SO7703 *See separate Family Panel on p.264* for WILDFOWL AND WETLANDS TRUST. The Tudor Arms by the swing bridge across the canal is useful for food, and the village post office has details of pleasant little walks.

🏠🎱 **Snowshill** SP0933 SNOWSHILL MANOR It looks like an ordinary Cotswold manor house, but inside is one of those extraordinary collections of ephemera great eccentrics somehow amass. Each room is carefully themed, full of maybe toys, musical instruments, bikes hanging from the ceiling – even suits of Japanese samurai armour, spookily arranged to look like a group of warriors meeting in the gloom. There's a charming cottage garden, and you can stay in one of 3 cottages. Meals, snacks, shop; open pm Weds–Mon Apr–Oct; (01386) 852410; £5.40; NT. This is one of the Trust's busier properties, and there's a timed ticket system; try to come midweek or out of season. The nearby Snowshill Arms is popular for lunch (busiest 12–1.15pm), and the drive along the River Windrush to Ford, Kineton and Naunton is delightful.

♪ 🎱 ➤ ✡ 🐄 **South Cerney** SU0497 COTSWOLD WATER PARK 2,000 acres of lakes with facilities for angling, windsurfing, sailing and other watersports, country parks and walks, birdwatching and nature reserves. Snacks at some lakes, disabled access; some activities cl winter; (01285) 861459; £4 (£2 wkdys) car parking, free in winter. THE BUTTS FARM (1m NE on Northmoor Lane) Notably friendly, with a good range of animals for children to feed, and daily pony or cart rides. Snacks, shop, disabled access; (01285) 862205; £2.50. The Eliot Arms in the prettily preserved 16th-c village has good food.

🏠 🎱 **Stanway** SP0632 STANWAY HOUSE One of the most beautiful 16th-c manor houses in the country, a cluster of gabled buildings popping up unexpectedly from the countryside like something out of a Michael Innes crime mystery, with charming and clearly lived-in rooms. The early 18th-c grounds have fine trees and interesting buildings, inc a folly pyramid on a steeply wooded hill. Open pm Tues and Thurs Jun–Sept; (01386) 584469; £3.50, £1 garden only.

★ **Stow-on-the-Wold** SP1925 Handsome market town with fine stone buildings around its square and in the narrow lanes off, and a good few antique shops, bookshops and so forth. It's something of an antidote to the more sweetly pretty Cotswold villages, on quite a high plateau and altogether more austere in style – not for nothing was it known as 'Stow-on-the-Wold, where the wind blows cold', and the ancient stocks on the village green add a touch of quaint severity. In 1997 the town nearly caused a diplomatic incident when it refused to be twinned with the French town of Oudon, allegedly on the grounds that it was, well, French. The Queen's Head is the best pub for lunch.

🏠 ⚐ 🎱 **Tetbury** ST8993 A splendid raised MARKET HOUSE, some interesting little lanes, quite a few antique shops and craft workshops, and decent food in the Crown. CHAVENAGE ▣ (2m

NW) Friendly unspoilt 16th-c manor house with entertaining tours by the owner. It's a popular location for TV programmes, providing a backdrop for characters from Hercule Poirot to Mr Blobby. Shop, disabled access to ground floor only; open pm Easter Sun and Mon then pm Thurs, Sun and bank hols May–Sept; (01666) 502329; *£3. Out this way the Gumstool (A46/A4135) has very good food. 2m S of Tetbury, the pretty gardens of HODGE'S BARN at Shipton Moyne ST8989 are warmly praised by readers.

★ ♨ † **Tewkesbury** SO8932 Severnside town, site of the last battle in the Wars of the Roses in 1471, still full of attractive half-timbered medieval buildings in a maze of little alleyways. Two of these old places now house MUSEUMS. Most impressive is the ABBEY, its massively confident Norman tower one of the finest in existence. Also splendid vaulting, some 14th-c stained glass, and regular concerts. The historic Bell Hotel and (simpler) ancient Black Bear and Berkeley Arms are useful for lunch.

🏛 ↓⊤ **Thornbury** ST6390 OLDBURY POWER STATION Tours of nuclear power station, with hands-on displays, multi-media show, and nature trail. Shop, disabled access (not on tour); cl winter Sats, 24 Dec–1 Jan; (01454) 419899; free. The Anchor at Oldbury-on-Severn has good food.

❀ 🐾 ♣ **Tockington** ST2186 OLDOWN (B4461) Lively country park with good adventure play areas for older children – lots of rope bridges, tube slides and climbing nets. Play area for younger children too, though they'll probably get more out of the animals and demonstrations at the farm. Several picnic areas, pleasant walks, summer PICK-YOUR-OWN, and excellent farm shop – organic meat, local cheeses, home-made honey and so on. Meals, snacks, shop, disabled access; cl Mon (exc bank hols), and most parts cl winter (exc shop and restaurant); (01454) 413605; £3.50. The quiet village itself is attractive, with good-value food in the Swan.

🚂 **Toddington** SP0333 GLOUCESTERSHIRE–WARWICKSHIRE RAILWAY Steam and diesel train trips through around 6 miles of quiet countryside, departing from restored GWR stations either here or at Winchcombe (see entry below). Snacks, shop, good disabled access (though watch out for the potholes in the car park); trains wknds Mar–Oct, plus Tues–Thurs in Aug. (01242) 621405; £6.50. They stop nr the Harvest Home at Greet and Royal Oak at Gretton, both doing good food.

🏛🖼 **Twigworth** SO8422 NATURE IN ART (Wallsworth Hall, A38) In an imposing Georgian mansion, a growing collection of well displayed paintings, sculpture, and mosaics inspired by nature – more interesting than you'd expect, as artists represented include Picasso, Henry Moore and Graham Sutherland. Readers very much enjoy coming here. Good meals and snacks, shop, disabled access; cl Mon (exc bank hols), 24–26 Dec; (01452) 731422; £2.95.

★ 🏛🏛 ❀ ♣ ✳ **Uley** ST7898 Attractive former weaving village with some 18th-c or older stone houses; the Old Crown is good value (ditto its bedrooms), and a good base for walkers. ULEY TUMULUS (off the B4066 N) Quite daunting 55-metre (180-ft) long burial mound known as Hetty Pegler's Tump, with stone central passage and 3 burial chambers; key from nearby house. OWLPEN MANOR (B4066, just E) Charming Tudor manor house, with lovely formal gardens and peaceful woodland. Restaurant; open pm daily (exc Mon) Apr–Oct; (01453) 860261; £3.50. Good views from this road.

✕ ♨ ♣ ✿ **Upper Soudley** SO6513 DEAN HERITAGE CENTRE (Camp Mill) Useful introduction to the Forest of Dean, set around an old watermill in pretty wooded valley. Plenty going on, inc craft displays, adventure playground, and occasional traditional charcoal burning. Meals, snacks, shop, disabled access; cl wkdys Nov–Jan; (01594) 822170; £2.95.

❀ **Westbury-on-Severn** SO7114
WESTBURY COURT Formal Dutch
garden with canals, yew topiary, etc,
restored to its 1700s layout using pre-
18th-c cultivars inc old fruit varieties.
Disabled access; cl Mon (exc bank
hols), Tues, Good Fri, and all
Nov–Mar; (01452) 760461; £2.50;
NT. The Red Lion has good generous
food, by the CHURCH with its unusual
detached tower. This is a good spot
for catching the Severn Bore.

❀ **Westonbirt** ST8589 WESTONBIRT
ARBORETUM Over 18,000 numbered
trees and shrubs fill the 17 miles of
pathways at this magnificent
collection, begun in 1829.
Outstanding in spring and autumn,
but worth a stop any time, with lots
of wildlife hidden away amongst the
trees. Meals, snacks, shop, disabled
access; open all year, though visitor
centre cl late Dec–Feb; (01666)
880220; £3.20. The Hare & Hounds
is handy for food.

★✝🏰🏛❀🌳♨🌼 **Winchcombe**
SP0228 Very peaceful and
photogenic – once the capital of
Mercia, now worth a stop for a look
at the CHURCH with its grotesque
gargoyles, or just to soak up the
tranquil atmosphere. SUDELEY CASTLE
AND GARDENS (off the B4632)
Delightful old house, once lived in by
Catherine Parr, the luckiest of Henry
VIII's wives. The remains of the
original medieval castle were skilfully
blended into a 19th-c reconstruction.
Rich furnishings, porcelain and
tapestries, and notable paintings by
Turner, Van Dyck and Rubens. The 8
gardens are splendid, and include a
knot garden constructed using
flowers shown on a 16th-c tapestry
on view in the library. Meals, snacks,
shop and specialist plant centre,
disabled access to garden; cl Nov–Feb
(house also cl Mar); (01242) 604357;
£5.50, £4 gardens only. There's a
working POTTERY nearby (cl winter
Suns), and a FOLK AND POLICE MUSEUM
in the Old Town Hall, with a
collection of British and international
police uniforms (cl Sun, and all
Nov–Mar; 80p). RAILWAY MUSEUM
AND GARDEN (Gloucester St) Victorian
garden full of lovingly rescued

railway memorabilia inc booking
office, working signals and signal
box. Snacks, shop, disabled access;
usually open wknds Easter–Sept and
daily in school hols in between (exc cl
a wk or two in Aug); (01242)
620641; £2. The Plaisterers Arms
(High St) has good-value food, and
there are interesting craft and other
shops here. Splendid views of the area
from Belas Knap (see **Walk** ⌂-3).

★🏛👃 **Yanworth** SP0713 An
attractive village, especially at
daffodil time. CHEDWORTH ROMAN
VILLA The best example of a 2nd-c
Roman house in Britain, excavated in
1864 and nicely set in secluded
woodland. Well preserved rooms,
bath-houses and 4th-c mosaics, with
smaller remains in museum. Shop,
some disabled access; cl Mon (exc
bank hols), and Dec–Feb (exc 1st
wknd in Dec); (01242) 890256;
£3.20; NT. The Mill at Withington
and Seven Tuns in Upper Chedworth
are quite handy for lunch – and the
walk from each is very picturesque
and unspoilt.

✝ Many villages have most **attractive
churches**, few of them as yet locked.
Cirencester is a good base for
planning circuits of these. One such
group E of the town consists of
Ampney Crucis SP0602, Ampney St
Peter SP0801, Ampney St Mary
SP0802, Down Ampney SP1097
(Vaughan Williams was the vicar's
son), Hampnett SP1015 and
Northleach SP1114. Another group,
NW of Cirencester, has Elkstone
SO9612, Duntisbourne Abbots
SO9707, Duntisbourne Rouse
SO9806, Daglingworth SO9905
(with its finely preserved Saxon
carving of Christ on the cross),
Stratton SP0103, Baunton SP0204
and North Cerney SP0208.

❀🌼 The National Trust own quite a
bit of **attractive countryside** around
Stroud SO8602, notably HARESFIELD
BEACON SO8209 (3m NW), 450 acres
of woodland and grassland on the
Cotswold escarpment, with
spectacular views; and nearby
MINCHINHAMPTON and RODBOROUGH
COMMONS SO8600, 900 acres of open
land with fine views and a wide range

of wildlife; both free. The Old Lodge on Minchinhampton Common has good food, and the steep lanes all around are interesting drives.

Good riverside pubs can be found at Apperley SO8628, Norton via Wainlode Hill SO8523 and Twyning SO8936, though best of all is Ashleworth Quay SO8125, where there's a tithe barn of some note and the very traditional pub has been in the same family for centuries.

! The **River Severn** is well known for the Severn Bore, a tidal wave surging upstream at high tide, which can sometimes reach up to 6 ft in height around the spring and autumn equinox. The National Rivers Authority produces a calendar listing the best times and places to catch the phenomenon, with a rating of how spectacular it's likely to be; (01684) 850951. See also Birdswood and Westbury-on-Severn entries above. Another good quiet spot to get down to the river is from Purton SO6904, where the Berkeley Arms has a wonderful estuary view.

Ongers Farm at Brookthorpe SO8312 organise GUIDED HORSERIDING, (01452) 813344, from around £8 an hour.

Walks

The Cotswold Way, a 100-mile path from Chipping Campden SP1539 to Bath ST7464, carefully picks out some of the choicest scenery – a worthwhile aid for those planning a shorter stroll. **Stanton** SP0734 ⌂-1 is the start of a trio of timeless villages on this Way, going on to Stanway SP0632 – and Buckland SP0836; field paths and farm track let you detour to Snowshill SP0933, and from there it's a pleasant 3-mile walk to Broadway SP0937 just over the Herefs & Worcs border. **Lower Slaughter** SP1622 ⌂-2 is the start of another attractive village-to-village stroll – a leisurely mile or so following the river to Upper Slaughter SP1523. To make a longer walk for a circuit of a couple of hours, you can follow the signposted Warden's Way. The best way out of Bourton-on-the-Water SP1620 is the exit by the church, heading out W past the school and over the old railway line, then following the lanes and tracks S of Upper Slaughter to rejoin the River Windrush back to Bourton.

The steep grassy slopes of the W escarpment of the Cotswolds make for some of the area's best walking. **Cleeve Common** SO9925 ⌂-3, the highest point of the Cotswolds, has breezy, unkempt grassland on its open expanses and can be either reached from the nearby village of Cleeve Hill SO9826 on the A46, or integrated into a circular walk past Belas Knap long barrow SP0125 and through the Sudeley Castle estate into Winchcombe SP0228. There's also a pleasant walk up to Belas Knap from the Craven Arms (a decent pub, with a nice garden in a lovely setting) in Brockhampton SO0322; this could be tied in with a walk past some very surprising ruins of a Roman villa SP0425 tucked away in the woods.

Further S, the Cotswold Way takes in a series of excellent viewpoints. The **Devil's Chimney** SO9418 ⌂-4 is a rock pinnacle amid old quarries on Leckhampton Hill, perched above Cheltenham. **Painswick Beacon** SO8612 ⌂-5 and Haresfield Beacon SO8208 are two more great viewpoints, reached by short ascents from the road. The **Chedworth Woods** SP0513 ⌂-6 provide scope for short walks if you want the satisfaction of reaching Chedworth Roman Villa on foot.

The rich, steeply sheltered valleys around Stroud make up a complicated landscape, seen to best advantage for example between Chalford SO8903 and Sapperton SO9403. The derelict **Thames & Severn Canal** ⌂-7 here is atmospherically overgrown, although its towpath survives as an attractive wooded walkway; the Crown at Frampton Mansell, Butchers Arms at Oakridge Lynch (both SO9102) or Daneway at Sapperton are useful jumping-off points. In this same general area, the Amberley Inn and Black Horse at

Amberley SO8401 are set prettily for walkers.

Ozleworth Bottom ST7992 ⌂-8, a valley not far from Wotton-under-Edge ST7593, has a nostalgically forgotten quality about it, providing a walk between Lasborough Manor and Ozleworth Park, with its unusual Norman church endowed with a hexagonal tower.

The **River Coln** ⌂-9 gives an appropriately quiet approach to Bibury SP1106, along the path from the toll-house just S of Coln St Aldwyns. This route takes you in by the mill and bridge over the Coln itself.

Extended walks over the Cotswold plateau are not always rewarding, with unchanging views of arable fields often the rule.

The **Severn estuary** ⌂-10 makes for some lonely walks along the sea wall, with power station cooling towers and the vast Severn bridges emphasising the emptiness of the tidal flats. The White Hart in Littleton-on-Severn ST5990, Anchor in Oldbury-on-Severn ST6092, and right by the embankment the Windbound at Shepperdine ST6295 and Berkeley Arms at Purton SO6904 are useful starting-points. Further upstream Arlingham SO7010 is locked within a big bend of the Severn, about a mile from the river, with the river path looking across to the Forest of Dean.

The rolling **Forest of Dean** ⌂-11 itself is well equipped with car parks, picnic sites and forest trails. A good start is at the Heritage Centre at Upper Soudley SO6513. The Sculpture Trail takes a 4-mile route passing nearly 20 specially commissioned sculptures hidden deep in the forest (from the picnic site nr the comfortable Speech House Hotel SO6611). The Kidnalls Forest Trail is a good way of tracking down some early industrial sites. The Foundry Wood Trail passes Soudley fish ponds SO6212 and gains some fine views. The Wench Ford Forest Walk leads past a series of quite interesting rock outcrops. Signed paths ensure easy route-finding up to the open summit of May Hill SO6921, where on a clear day you can see the Cotswolds, Malverns, Welsh Marches and Severn Estuary.

The lower Wye Valley on the W side of the Forest of Dean cuts through a gorge giving some very picturesque views. As there are few crossing points, and the scenery away from the gorge is relatively unspectacular, walks along it are generally of the there-and-back sort. On this Gloucestershire side the valley is tracked by the Offa's Dyke Path (the Wye Valley Walk takes in the western bank). **Wintour's Leap** ST5496 ⌂-12 is a highlight: a sheer cliff N of Chepstow with dizzy views downwards. The **Devil's Pulpit** ST5499 ⌂-13, where trees frame a perfect vista of Tintern Abbey far below on the opposite bank, is another great viewpoint. The **Kymin** SO5212 ⌂-14 can be climbed from May Hill just across the river border opposite Monmouth; at the summit is the Naval Temple, a quaint rustic conceit put up in 1800 to commemorate admirals of the Napoleonic Wars. The stunningly placed Boat reached by footbridge over the Wye from Redbrook SO5309 and the Brockweir Inn in Brockweir SO5401 are both handy for Wye walkers. Other pubs that are well placed for walks include the Black Horse at Cranham SO8912 for Cranham Woods, the Edgemoor at Edge SO8509 (panoramic views), and the Fleece at Hillesley ST7689. In and around the Forest of Dean, useful pubs for walkers include the Wyndham Arms at Clearwell SO5708, Rising Sun at Moseley Green SO6308, Ostrich in the charming village of Newland SO5509, and White Horse at Staunton SO5412. The Glasshouse Inn at Glasshouse SO7122 is handy for Newent Woods.

Where to eat

Birdlip SO9214 KINGSHEAD HOUSE (01452) 862299 17th-c former coaching inn with lovely English/French cooking using the best fresh produce, helpful service, and good wines; cl pm Sun, Mon; disabled access. £30|£4.50.
Blockley SP1634 CROWN (01386) 700245 Smart and civilised Elizabethan

stone inn with very good food in bar or one of 2 restaurants (seafood specialities with up to 25 fresh fish main courses), lots of good wines, comfortable leather seating in lounge bar, and attractive split-level hotel bar; children allowed if well behaved; pretty bedrooms; disabled access. £20.50|£7.95.

Broad Campden SP1637 BAKERS ARMS (01386) 840515 Atmospheric former granary in tranquil village with very good-value bar food (inc children's menu), a fine range of real ales, cosy beamed bar, log fires, friendly cats, pleasant service, and nice garden; cl 25 Dec, pm 26 Dec. l£4.50.

Cheltenham SO9422 LE CHAMPIGNON SAUVAGE 24–26 Suffolk Rd (01242) 573449 Classic French cooking in quietly and simply decorated restaurant with helpful service and good thoughtful wine list; cl am Sat, Sun, 2 wks in summer, Christmas–New Year; disabled access. £23.25 lunch.

Chipping Campden SP1539 FORBES BRASSERIE The Square (01386) 840330 Fine 17th-c hotel with stylish and attractive brasserie offering good interesting meals and light snacks plus morning coffee and afternoon tea – more formal restaurant, too; pretty bdrms; cl 3 days Christmas; partial disabled access. £20|£6.50.

Cirencester SP0201 **Swan Yard Café** 6 Swan Yard (01285) 641300 Popular with shoppers, this small simple café is nicely decorated with dried flowers, china and knick-knacks (all for sale); friendly service, and tasty very good-value food (inc vegetarian); disabled access. 12.50|£4.50.

Coln St Aldwyns SP1405 NEW (01285) 750651 Civilised ivy-covered inn with beautifully presented restaurant-standard food served in a relaxed pubby atmosphere, attractively decorated rooms, a central log fire, well kept real ales and good wines, a no smoking restaurant, and split-level garden; nice surrounding countryside and walks; comfortable bedrooms; no children under 8 in restaurant. £22.50|£7.95.

Gretton SP0131 ROYAL OAK (01242) 602477 You can arrive at this popular pub by steamtrain at wknds, to enjoy the good-value food in the long series of flagstoned or bare-boarded rooms; beams, dim lighting from candles in bottles, entertaining medley of furnishings, and friendly young service; cl 25–26 Dec. £17.90|£5.95.

Kingscote ST8196 HUNTERS HALL (01453) 860393 Civilised creeper-covered old inn with some fine old furniture and big log fires in elegant series of high-beamed connecting rooms, good bar and restaurant food, excellent breakfasts, and quite a few wines by the glass; big garden with children's play area; bdrms; disabled access. £19.95|£6.50.

Lower Oddington SP2325 FOX (01451) 870555 Carefully restored elegant inn with well presented, imaginative food, a superb wine list, well kept real ales, fresh flowers and open fire in neat rooms, a lovely dining room, and a relaxed atmosphere; disabled access. £17.50|£5.95.

Nailsworth ST8499 WILLIAMS BISTRO 3 Fountain St (01453) 835507 Marvellous delicatessen with good-value bistro in a back extension; cheerful and informal atmosphere and decor, delicious interesting fish dishes (a few non-fishy things too), efficient service even when really busy, and fairly priced wines; cl Sun, Mon, Tues after bank hols, Good Fri, 2 wks over Christmas. £25.

Newland SO5509 OSTRICH (01594) 833260 Particularly attractive 13th-c inn in pretty village with big log fire, comfortable seating, attentive service, and freshly prepared good food; no children. £20|£5.

Northleach SP1114 RED LION Market Pl (01451) 860251 Good-value, well presented simple food in comfortable and friendly pub, popular Sun roast, open fire, no food pm Mon; disabled access. £16|£4.50.

Northleach SP1114 WICKENS Market Pl (01451) 860421 Cosy low-ceilinged restaurant with good modern English cooking, lovely puddings, pleasant service, and fine New World wines; cl Sun, Mon. £26.

Painswick SO8609 COUNTRY ELEPHANT New St (01452) 813564 Popular little restaurant open for morning coffee and summer afternoon tea as well as lunch and dinner; delicious, interesting food, good wines, and friendly service; no smoking in restaurant but you can do so in bar/lounge; big summer garden; cl Sun, Mon; disabled access. £17 lunch, £22 dinner|£5.

Southrop SP1903 SWAN (01367) 850205 Civilised creeper-covered old stone-tiled pub in pretty village, with good interesting food inc delicious ice-creams, a respectable wine list, no smoking restaurant, friendly service, and log fires; cl pm Sun. £18.50|£4.25.

Tetbury ST8993 GUMSTOOL (01666) 890391 Bustling pubby bistro (actually part of rambling Calcot Manor) with stripped pine, flagstones, and hop bines, neatly modern furnishings, a relaxed but civilised atmosphere, particularly good, interesting food, well kept real ales, a thoughtful choice of wines by the glass, and good service; comfortable bdrms. £20.50|£8.50.

Woodchester SO8302 RAM (01453) 873329 Bustling cheerful pub with spectacular views of valley from terrace, attractive beamed bar, good bar food, prompt friendly service, and lots of real ales; partial disabled access; cl 25 Dec. £12|£3.45.

Special thanks to Mrs L Norsworthy, Mrs M A Collis, Ivan Rickett, Fiona Watson, Peter Lloyd, Dave Irving, Peter Neate, A Lock, Peter and Audrey Dowsett.

GLOUCESTERSHIRE CALENDAR

Some of these dates were provisional as we went to press, please check information with the numbers provided.

JANUARY

1 **Cheltenham** Race Meeting at the Racecourse (01242) 226226

FEBRUARY

1 **Stow-on-the-Wold** Cotswold Antiques Festival – *till Fri 6* (01451) 831082
6 **Cheltenham** Folk Festival – *till Sun 8* (01242) 522878

MARCH

17 **Cheltenham** National Hunt Racing Festival inc Gold Cup – *till Thurs 19* (01242) 513014

APRIL

4 **Gotherington** Midland Hillclimb Championship at Prescott Hill – *till Sun 5* (01242) 673136
16 **Cheltenham** Jazz Festival – *till Sun 19* (01242) 521621

MAY

2 **Gotherington** British Hillclimb Championship at Prescott Hill – *till Sun 3* (01242) 673136; **Upton-upon-Severn** Folk Festival – *till Mon 4* (01684) 594200
3 **Coleford** Steam and Vintage Rally at Speech House (01989) 562602; **Randwick** Cheese Rolling – after church service *at 10.30am* three cheeses are blessed and rolled anticlockwise round the church three times. One cheese is cut and distributed, the other two are kept till the following Sat when they are rolled down a slope to open the Randwick Wap (see below) (01453) 766782
7 **Minchinhampton** British Open Horse Trials Championship at Gatcombe Park – *till Sun 10* (01454) 218272

GLOUCESTERSHIRE CALENDAR

MAY cont

9 **Randwick** Wap (see Randwick Cheese Rolling above): carnival, maypole and morris dancing (01453) 766782

10 **Gloucester** Stationary Engine Day at National Waterways Museum (01452) 318054

16 **Gloucester** Horses Weekend at National Waterways Museum – *till Sun 17* (01452) 318054

21 **Bisley** Blessing of the Wells at the Parish Church (01452) 770056

23 **Upton-upon-Severn** Oak Apple Day Celebrations – *till Mon 25* (01684) 594200

24 **Gloucester** Town and Country Show at the Showground – *till Mon 25* (01242) 256446

28 **Cheltenham** Ideal Home Exhibition at the Town Hall – *till Sun 31* (01242) 227979

29 **Chipping Campden** Robert Dovers Cotswold Olimpick Games at Dovers Hill: trad sports, bands, dancing, torchlight procession, then Scuttlebrook Wake with street entertainment, morris dancing and procession *on Sat 30* (01384) 274041

30 **Gotherington** Classic Car Hillclimb at Prescott Hill – *till Sun 31* (01242) 673136

31 **Brockworth** Coopers Hill Cheese Rolling (old custom) *from 6pm* (01452) 421188; **Tetbury** Woolsack Races: teams of men and women race up and down steep Gumstool Hill carrying 65lb woolsacks, medieval market and street entertainers (01452) 425673

JUNE

19 **Cirencester** Festival of Music and the Arts – *till 12 July* (01285) 657181

20 **North Nibley** Steam Rally at Nibley House – *till Sun 21* (01453) 546024

26 **Upton-upon-Severn** Jazz Festival – *till Sun 28* (01684) 594200

27 **Gotherington** Midland Hillclimb Championship at Prescott Hill – *till Sun 28* (01242) 673136; **Northleach** Charter Fair: procession, arena events, music (01451) 860971

JULY

3 **Moreton-in-Marsh** Opera and Open Air Picnic at Banks Fee – *till Sat 4* (01451) 830292

4 **Chedworth** Dry Stone Walling Competition and Church Fête (01242) 820482; **Cheltenham** International Festival of Music and Fringe – *till Sun 19* (01242) 521621; **Hailes** Music Festival – *till Sat 25* (01242) 602379; **Stroud** Show at Stratford Park (01453) 765381; **Tewkesbury** Carnival (01684) 295027

7 **Chavenage** Open Air Theatre – *till Sat 11* (01453) 833144

10 **Moreton-in-Marsh** Opera and Open Air Picnic at Banks Fee – *till Sat 11* (01451) 830292

11 **Tewkesbury** Medieval Fayre – *till Sun 12* (01684) 294939

15 **Cheltenham** Cricket Festival – *till Sun 26* (0117) 924 5216

17 **Moreton-in-Marsh** Opera and Open Air Picnic at Banks Fee – *till Sat 18* (01451) 830292

18 **Stroud** Rolling: international brick and rolling pin throwing competition (01453) 882039

24 **Postlip** Beer Festival – *till Sun 26* (01242) 522878

GLOUCESTERSHIRE CALENDAR

JULY cont

25 **Fairford** International Air Tattoo – *till Sun 26* (01285) 713300; **Gloucester** Festival – *till 8 Aug* (01452) 396620; **Guiting Power** Festival of Music: classical, jazz and opera – *till 1 Aug* (01242) 603912

AUGUST

1 **Gotherington** Vintage Sports Car Club Hillclimb at Prescott Hill – *till Sun 2* (01242) 673136

3 **Tewkesbury** Musica Deo Sacra at the Abbey – *till Sun 9* (01684) 850959

15 **Gloucester** Three Choirs Festival at the Cathedral – *till Sat 22* (01452) 421188; **Tibberton** Horticultural Society Show (01452) 790424

16 **Temple Guiting** Open Day at David Nicholson's Racing Stables (01386) 584209

22 **Fairford** Steam Rally and Show – *till Sun 23* (01285) 655011

29 **Upton-upon-Severn** Water Festival – *till Mon 31* (01684) 594200

31 **Berkeley** Hunt Agricultural Show (01453) 860352; **Moreton-in-Marsh** Horse Trials at Springhill Estate (01789) 720144

SEPTEMBER

4 **Cheltenham** Sequence Dance Festival – *till Sun 6* (01242) 522878; **Cirencester** Carriage Driving Trials at Cirencester Park – *till Sun 6* (01672) 861453

5 **Gotherington** British and Midland Hillclimb Championship at Prescott Hill – *till Sun 6* (01242) 673136; **Moreton-in-Marsh** Agricultural and Horse Show (01608) 651908

11 **Stroud** Fringe Festival – *till Sun 13* (01453) 832370

12 **Stow-on-the-Wold** Day of Dance: morris dancing around the town *from 11am* (01451) 831082

20 **Painswick** Ancient Clypping Ceremony at St Mary's Church (01452) 812334

26 **Cirencester** Cotswold Country Fair – *till Sun 27* (01285) 652007; **Gloucester** Modellers Weekend at National Waterways Museum – *till Sun 27* (01452) 318054

OCTOBER

3 **Stroud** Arts Festival – *till Sun 18* (01453) 764502

9 **Cheltenham** International Festival of Literature – *till Sun 18* (01242) 227979; **Tewkesbury** Mop Fair – *till Sat 10* (01684) 296010

NOVEMBER

22 **Cheltenham** Motor Rally – *till Tues 24* (01753) 681736

28 **Cheltenham** Festival of Christmas Lights (01242) 522878

DECEMBER

26 **Gloucester** Mummers and Morris Dancers in the Cathedral Precincts and New Inn Courtyard *at midday* (01453) 759921

HAMPSHIRE

Plenty of interest and attractions for all ages; the New Forest is particularly attractive, but less visited good countryside elsewhere too.

Two great NT properties here which have been closed for restoration reopen this year – Hinton Ampner, and The Vyne at Sherborne St John. They join a fine roster of great houses, with Beaulieu standing out for its wide range of attractions carefully organised to suit different tastes – and all ages. Broadlands near Romsey, Breamore and Stratfield Saye are also very rewarding. Some magnificent gardens include waterside Exbury (irresistible in late spring), the wonderful old-fashioned rose garden at Mottisfont Abbey, the Hillier Gardens at Ampfield, Spinners at Boldre and (new to the Guide) Houghton Lodge near Stockbridge. The Sandham Memorial Chapel at Burghclere is thought by some to be the greatest masterpiece of 20th-c British art.

Hampshire is particularly strong in museums dealing with military and naval history – among Britain's most interesting for specialists, but with a surprisingly broad general appeal too, for children as well as adults; many are concentrated around Portsmouth/Southsea, which could make an unusual but satisfying spot for a family break.

More specifically appealing to families, Marwell Zoo at Colden Common is one of Britain's most enjoyable. Other places almost guaranteed to delight children are Nature Quest near Ashurst, the farm park near Andover, the lovely Watercress Railway Line from Alresford, the Sea Life Centre in Portsmouth, the working Iron Age farm at Chalton, the Hollycombe Steam Collection near Liphook, and the Hawk Conservancy at Weyhill.

The New Forest countryside has great charm. Only parts of it are in fact wooded; the rest is unspoilt rolling heathland. Walkers can head off in virtually any direction without worrying about trespassing. Once away from the roads, it does give a great feeling of untrammeled space. Children like it: there are free-running ponies and deer, and plenty of scope for generally running riot without coming to grief. Its coast has sheltered yachting harbours, the pleasant waterside town of Lymington with warm Georgian buildings (the rest of Hampshire's coastline is largely built up), and the interesting Bucklers Hard.

There's good scenery elsewhere, in a broad belt of gentle countryside stretching from Andover, Stockbridge and Romsey along the Test Valley in the W, through Winchester and Alresford, to Alton and Petersfield in the E. This is a quietly charming mix of rolling blowy chalk downland, a patchwork of hedged fields and clumps of steep beechwood, the rich valleys of the clear chalk streams, and attractive small villages often of brick and flint.

Winchester has a charming old quarter around its cathedral, and plenty of opportunities for strolls nearby; a possibility for a quiet city break.

Where to stay

Beaulieu SU3802 MONTAGU ARMS Palace Lane, Beaulieu SO42 7ZL (01590) 612324 *£99, plus special breaks; 24 individually decorated rms. Attractive, creeper-clad hotel with lovely terraced garden, comfortable sitting room, and a conservatory lounge; very good food in beamed restaurant, and attentive staff; their health club is in the village; they also run the village shop, post office and bakery; children over 5 in evening restaurant (high tea for little ones).

Cheriton SU5828 FLOWER POTS Cheriton, Alresford SO24 0QQ (01962) 771318 £45; 5 rms. Unspoilt and quietly comfortable village local run by very friendly family; with 2 pleasant little bars, a log fire, decent bar food, own-brew beers, and old-fashioned seats on the pretty lawns.

Crawley SU4234 FOX & HOUNDS Crawley, Winchester SO21 2PR (01962) 776285 *£65; 3 well equipped rms. Striking almost Tyrolean small inn with elegant timbering and oak parquet, and a lounge with a log fire; good interesting bar and restaurant food; prompt unobtrusive service.

Eastleigh SU4518 PARK FARM Stoneham Lane SO5 3HS (01703) 612960 *£30; 3 rms, shared bthrm. Lots of country walks around these converted coaching stables, coarse fishing in their own lake, and evening meals by arrangement.

Hayling Island SU7201 COCKLE WARREN COTTAGE 36 Seafront, Hayling Island PO11 9HL (01705) 464961 £68; 5 pretty, well equipped rms. Carefully run and attractive tile-hung cottage hotel on the seafront; friendly courteous owners, log fire in the cosy lounge, and very good food in the conservatory dining room; heated swimming pool, and a pretty garden with pond, fountain and lots of pretty flowering tubs; well behaved older children only; disabled access.

Hurstbourne Tarrant SU3853 ESSEBORNE MANOR Hurstbourne Tarrant, Andover SP11 0ER (01264) 736444 £112, plus special breaks; 14 individually decorated rms. Small stylish Victorian manor with a calm relaxed atmosphere, comfortable lounge and snug little bar; good modern cooking, and friendly staff; neat gardens with tennis, croquet and golf; children over 7; disabled access.

Lymington SZ3094 EFFORD COTTAGE Everton, Lymington SO41 0JD (01590) 642315 *£42, plus special breaks; 3 comfortable rms. Spacious family home close to the New Forest; really marvellous 4-course breakfasts with freshly baked bread and home-made jams, and optional evening meal; good parking; children over 12; well behaved pets welcome by arrangment.

Lymington SZ3295 PASSFORD HOUSE Mount Pleasant Lane, Lymington SO41 8LS (01590) 682398 *£90; 55 neatly kept, pretty rms. Attractive hotel on the edge of the New Forest, with comfortable panelled lounge (3 others, too), cocktail bar, open fires, and excellent service; 9 acres of gardens and parkland with indoor and outdoor swimming pools, tennis, croquet, and putting.

Lymington SZ3295 STANWELL HOUSE High St, Lymington SO41 9AA (01590) 677123 £85; 29 pretty rms. Handsome town house with comfortable, attractively furnished lounge, cosy little bar, good imaginative food, and a pretty walled back garden.

Lyndhurst SU2908 PARKHILL Beaulieu Rd, Lyndhurst SO43 7FZ (01703) 282944 *£121, plus special breaks; 20 carefully furnished rms, some overlooking the lawns. 13th-c hunting lodge rebuilt by the Duke of Clarence in mid-18th c and set in parkland with fine views; comfortable lounges, antiques, flowers, and a civilised atmosphere; good food in attractive dining room, and friendly professional staff.

Middle Wallop SU2838 FIFEHEAD MANOR Middle Wallop, Stockbridge SO20 8EG (01264) 781565 £80, plus special breaks; 15 spacious rms. Friendly and comfortable old brick manor house in several acres of lovely gardens; restful atmosphere, pleasant small lounge and bar, good food in the candlelit restaurant, and enjoyable breakfasts; friendly staff; croquet; disabled access.

Mockbeggar SU1809 PLANTATION COTTAGE Mockbeggar, Ringwood BH24 3NQ (01425) 477443 *£50; 2 rms. Charming 200-year-old cottage in 3 acres of gardens and paddocks; nice breakfasts; no smoking; lots of pubs and restaurants nearby; self-catering cottage; no children.

New Milton SZ2495 CHEWTON GLEN Christchurch Rd, New Milton BH25 6QS (01425) 275341 £255; 52 really beautiful rms. Luxurious hotel in lovely grounds, with fine antiques in the sumptuous day rooms, excellent modern French cooking, and very good service; gardens include a 9-hole golf course, swimming pool, tennis (2 indoor courts as well) and croquet; also health club with indoor swimming pool, gym, saunas, treatment rooms; children over 7; disabled access.

New Milton SZ2495 YEW TREE FARM Bashley Common Rd, New Milton BH25 5SH (01425) 611041 *£55; 2 lovely spacious rms. Marvellously comfortable and well run traditional thatched smallholding on the edge of the New Forest; with small cosy hall and a friendly welcome; extensive breakfasts (taken in bedroom), and good home-made dinners (if required) using top quality produce; riding nearby; no smoking, children or dogs.

Portsmouth SZ6498 FORTITUDE COTTAGE 51 Broad St, Old Portsmouth, Portsmouth PO1 2JD (01705) 823748 *£44; 3 neat and attractive rms. Comfortable B & B in a cottage named after an old ship, with a pretty beamed breakfast room looking over the fishing boats; no evening meals but places nearby; cl 25–26 Dec; no children.

Portsmouth SU6498 SALLY PORT High St, Old Town, Portsmouth PO1 2LU (01705) 821860 *£59, plus special breaks; 10 rms. Beautifully kept 16th-c inn in a quiet position, with good food and very friendly, efficient service; said to have been a favourite of Nelson's.

Rockbourne SU1118 SHEARINGS Rockbourne, Fordingbridge SP6 3NA (01725) 518256 *£50; 3 rms plus garden annexe. Beside a winter stream, this warmly welcoming and pretty 16th-c thatched cottage has inglenook fireplaces, ancient beams (some nearly 1,000 years old), and a comfortable sitting room; good pub just up the road; cl mid-Dec–Jan; children over 12; no dogs.

Romsey SU3521 SPURSHOLT HOUSE Salisbury Rd, Romsey SO51 6DJ (01794) 512229 £44; 3 rms with antiques, fireplaces, and sofas. Lovely welcoming house with beautiful garden and a view of Romsey Abbey; open fire in the characterful sitting room, good evening meals (not wknds) in handsome Victorian-style dining room, and warm, friendly owners; cl 20 Dec–1 Jan.

Rotherwick SU7156 TYLNEY HALL Rotherwick, Basingstoke RG27 9AJ (01256) 764881 £130; 110 comfortable, well equipped rms. Grand Victorian mansion in 66 acres of gardens and parkland; gracious day rooms, ornate plasterwork, oak panelling, oil paintings, and log fires in big ornate fireplaces; interesting food in candlelit restaurant, and good attentive service; tennis, golf, indoor and outdoor swimming pools, gym and sauna.

Sparsholt SU4331 LAINSTON HOUSE Sparsholt, Winchester SO21 2LT (01962) 863588 *£157, plus special breaks; 37 spacious, individually decorated rms. Close to Winchester, this elegant William Mary hotel has 63 acres of fine parkland, a relaxing, elegant lounge, panelled bar and restaurant, and flowers and paintings; a fine wine list, and good British cooking; disabled access.

Sway SZ2798 NURSES COTTAGE Station Rd, Sway, Lymington SO41 6BA (01590) 683402 *£90 inc dinner, plus special breaks; 3 rms. Small, immaculately kept cottage with a comfortable lounge and dining room; enjoyable evening food using seasonal produce, a thoughtful wine list, and hearty breakfasts; very helpful owner, neat garden; cl 15 Nov–15 Dec; children over 10.

Wickham SU5711 OLD HOUSE The Square, Wickham, Fareham PO17 5JG (01329) 833049 £84, plus special breaks; 12 rms. Lovely early Georgian house under the same charming owners for 27 years; overlooking the village square, with beamed and panelled rooms, antiques, fresh flowers, and open fires; reliably good French cooking in the restaurant (once the timber-framed outhouse and stables); pretty back garden; cl 2 wks Aug, 2 wks Christmas, 1 wk Easter.

Winchester SU4829 HOTEL DU VIN & BISTRO 14 Southgate St, Winchester SO23 9EF (01962) 841414 *£75; 23 rms, real quality, and each sponsored by a well known wine company with relevant paintings, labels and old photographs. An engaging early 18th-c town house with enthusiastic owners and hard-working staff; a deeply comfortable sitting room, 2 relaxed and pretty eating areas with good bistro-style cooking and an exceptional wine list, and a lovely walled garden for summer dining; disabled access.

Winchester SU4829 ROYAL HOTEL St Peter St, Winchester SO23 8BS (01962) 840840 £83, plus special breaks; 82 well equipped rms, some in spacious modern wing. Quietly set but close to the centre, this friendly hotel has a big walled garden, comfortable, stylish lounges, and a busy little bar; good food in the attractive conservatory restaurant, and very helpful staff; partial disabled access.

Winchester SU4829 WYKEHAM ARMS 75 Kingsgate St, Winchester SO23 9PE (01962) 853834 £89.50; 13 well equipped attractive rms. Very well run, smart old town inn, close to the cathedral; the bars interestingly furnished with old school desks from the college, military and historical memorabilia, royalty pictures, mugs and so forth; 2 small dining rooms serving an excellent daily-changing menu (very good breakfasts, too), fine wines (lots by the glass), and prompt, friendly service; several no smoking areas; no children; cl 25 Dec.

To see and do

Portsmouth SZ6399 An island town, with just 2 roads and the motorway bridging it and its residential/resort part Southsea to the mainland – traffic can be very slow indeed on the main approaches. Its great claim on the imagination is its place at the heart of English naval history, and the 2 parts that are interesting to visitors are the Old Town and the Historic Dockyard, on either side of the ferry berths and well away from the traffic. Overlooking the narrow harbour neck, Georgian buildings on an old-fashioned cobbled hard give a good feel of the old days, and the little inner Camber Harbour still has fishing boats. From Apr–Oct a waterbus goes around the harbour, and over to Gosport. By the harbour, the Still & West is a beautifully placed food pub, and the Dolphin's a nice place in the old High St behind. The harbour is starting a huge redevelopment programme, centrepiece of which will be a 165-metre (540-ft) tower. The cathedral, dating from the 13th c to the present, is a delightful departure from the traditional layout.

✿ ♿ HM NAVAL BASE The main stop for most visitors, with lots to see. It houses HMS VICTORY, the MARY ROSE, HMS WARRIOR, and the ROYAL NAVAL MUSEUM. The flagship is of course HMS Victory, still in commission, and manned by regular serving officers. Guided tours bring those Trafalgar days very close, and include the spot where Nelson died.

The raising of the Mary Rose from the Solent silt where she had sat for 437 years provided a wealth of material and information about the Tudor period. The discoveries are well shown in an airy hall, while the great oak hull itself is in a separate shed, sprayed almost constantly to prevent the timbers from drying out; the Heritage Secretary now classes this as one of Britain's most important museums. HMS *Warrior* when launched 140 years ago was the most fearsome battleship in the world; she's been immaculately restored, and is manned by tars in period uniform. Again, tours are very vivid. The ROYAL NAVAL MUSEUM, in handsome 18th-c dockside buildings, has lively displays on the development and history of the Navy up to and beyond the Falklands War (or as it's called here the South Atlantic Campaign). Lots of Nelson memorabilia, and a very jolly gallery looking at popular images of the sailor. Each ship costs £5.50 to visit individually (though the HMS *Victory* ticket also includes entry to the museum, which on its own costs £3), so if you want to see more than one it's well worth getting the all-in ticket at £11, which covers all 3 ships and the museum. The site – which itself costs nothing to enter, after a security check – has a restaurant and shop, and there's disabled access to all the ships; ships cl 25 Dec, museum cl 25–26 Dec; (01705) 870999.

⊙ PORTSMOUTH'S FIGHTING HISTORY Several other places focus on this, notably the D-DAY MUSEUM ▣ (Clarence Esplanade, Southsea), which vividly recalls and explains the Normandy landings from the point of view of both sides. Very realistic in places – you almost panic when the sirens sound. There's a remarkable 272-ft D-Day embroidery. Snacks, shop, disabled access; cl am Mon Nov–Mar, 24–26 Dec; (01705) 827261; £4.50. The vigorous ROYAL MARINES MUSEUM ▣ (Royal Marines Eastney, Southsea) couldn't be more different from the usual military exhibitions – lively recreations of major amphibious actions, a junior commando assault course, and a jungle room with a real snake and scorpions. Meals, snacks, shop, disabled access; cl Christmas; (01705) 819385; £3.75.

🏰 ❄ HARBOUR FORTIFICATIONS The fortifications in defence of Portsmouth Harbour, here, around Gosport, and up on Portsdown, give a remarkably complete picture of the development of defensive strategy from Tudor times to the fears of French invasion in the 1860s, though they have more appeal to people interested in warfare than to those who like the romantic idea of a regular 'castle'. SOUTHSEA CASTLE AND MUSEUM is the best place to start, built in 1545 as part of Henry VIII's coastal defences. Good displays on Portsmouth's military history, and some splendid fish-bone model ships made by Napoleonic prisoners-of-war. Snacks, shop; cl wkdys Nov–Mar, 24–26 Dec; (01705) 827261; £1.70. On the seaward side of Southsea are sturdy Tudor and later towers, bastions and batteries, alongside the resort's gardens and entertainments, giving interesting sea views. Good guided walks around the Tudor fortifications and the best parts of the Old Town leave the Square Fort at 2.30pm on Sun (not late Sept–mid-Apr).

🏰 ⛴ SPITBANK FORT Wind up an exploration of Portsmouth's naval past with the boat trip from the Naval Base to this granite, iron and brick fortress a mile out to sea. Its 2 floors are linked by a maze of passages, and there's a 130-m etre (420-ft) deep well which still draws fresh water. The inner courtyard is now a sheltered terrace for summer refreshments from the cafe. Cl Mon (exc bank hols), Tues, Oct–Easter; (01329) 664286; £5.75 inc boat trip. Ferries leave the pontoon beside HMS *Warrior* at 12.15, 1.30 and 2.45pm (Sat), and you can stay overnight out on the Fort if you really do want to get away from it all (great views from comfortable rooms).

🐟 ⛴ SEA LIFE CENTRE (Clarence Esplanade, Southsea) Excellent for families, this is one of the most hi-tech of these centres, with all sorts of multi-sensory experiences and displays, and an exciting shark encounter. Children complete a scratchcard trail as they go round, and there's a good adventure playground. Snacks, shop, disabled access; cl 25 Dec; (01705) 734461; £4.95 (they'll stamp your hand and let you come back later in the day).

BOAT TRIPS round the harbour from nearby.

🐾 CUMBERLAND HOUSE NATURAL HISTORY MUSEUM (Eastern Parade, Southsea) Interesting collections, with a splendid butterfly enclosure in summer, and full-size dinosaur reconstructions. Shop; cl 24–26 Dec; (01705) 827261; £1.60 summer (butterfly season), £1.10 rest of year.

CITY MUSEUM (Museum Rd) Very good displays on the city's history, in an astonishing former barracks that looks rather like a French château. Also decorative art and crafts. Meals, snacks, shop, disabled access; cl 24–26 Dec; (01705) 827261; free.

DICKENS' BIRTHPLACE (Old Commercial Rd, in the main town) Restored to the modest middle-class style it had when the author was born here in 1812. Still has various Dickens-related objects such as the couch on which he died. Shop; cl Nov–Mar (exc 3 wks before Christmas); (01705) 827261; £2.

GUILDHALL (Guildhall Sq) Contains what's said to be the world's biggest glass mural. Free tours, usually 10 and 11.30am Mon, Weds and Fri Apr–Sept; (01705) 834092.

✝ ROYAL GARRISON CHURCH (French St) Roofless now, a once-grand place where Charles II was married in 1662; usually open Mon–Weds, but best to make an appointment, (01705) 527667.

Winchester SU4829 The compact and fascinating medieval centre still has 2 city gates intact; it was capital of England in Saxon times. Guided walks around the sights from the tourist information centre at 10.30am and 2.30pm Mon–Sat May–Sept (2.30pm only Apr and Oct). There's a multi-storey car park at the top of the High St, or a park and ride nr the junction with the M3. The most attractive part of the city is the glorious and peaceful CATHEDRAL CLOSE, surrounded by a very harmonious and distinguished collection of buildings; the handsome old Eclipse Inn nr the NE edge is a useful refreshment break. Anyone interested in military history will enjoy the 3 REGIMENTAL MUSEUMS, but of these only the Gurkha Museum (Romsey Rd) could be said to have a wider appeal; cl Sun, Mon; *£1.50. The Brooks Shopping Centre has a few jolly dioramas and displays on the city's history (cl Sun; free), with the chance for children to make their own Roman mosaic. There are pleasant walks up rounded ST CATHERINE'S HILL, which has a small medieval turf maze and traces of a hill fort.

✝ CATHEDRAL Awesome and full of interest – one of Europe's finest, with the longest of all Gothic naves, and quite a mixture of architectural styles. Among many rare books and manuscripts in its library is a wonderful 12th-c illuminated Bible, while the sculpture gallery contains some outstanding late Gothic work. William of Wykeham paid for much of the rebuilding, so his tomb is appropriately the finest; also memorials and monuments to Jane Austen, King Canute and St Swithin. Good guided tours, and first-rate visitor centre in 16th-c coach house, with very good meals and snacks (not cheap) and distinguished shop; £2.50 suggested donation. Close by are the appreciable remains of Wolvesey Castle, the original Bishop's Palace begun in the 12th c, and beside it (not open, but a handsome sight), the present Bishop's Palace of 1684. The best way out of the cloisters is through the medieval Kings Gate, which includes the upper-floor church of St Swithin. This takes you into Kingsgate St, calm and old-fashioned, with an excellent dining pub, the Wykeham Arms. Down on the left a lovely riverside path takes you along to the City Mill and a mighty statue of King Alfred.

WINCHESTER COLLEGE All along Kingsgate St are buildings connected with this, the oldest school in the country. Most of the original school buildings remain intact, especially around the grand 14th-c chapel and its calm, tilting cloisters with a delightful 2-storey chantry in their centre, and a glimpse of the Warden's garden through one gate. Good shop in former tuck shop, some disabled access; guided tours Apr–Sept, cl 1–2pm, am Sun (winter tours by appointment only); (01962) 621217; £2.50.

▟ CASTLE Now survives only in its huge 13th-c Great Hall, where Raleigh was tried and condemned to death; hanging off one wall is a round table they call King Arthur's (actually much the same date as the castle, and painted with its Arthurian scenes later). The roof, stone parapets and stained glass windows are being restored – work is due to finish in Jan. A small but interesting garden is laid out on the lines of what might have been there in the 13th c. Shop, disabled access; cl 25–26 Dec; (01962) 846476; free (summer guided tours 50p).

✿ WESTGATE MUSEUM (High St) Local history above a formidable medieval city gate – the panorama of the city and surrounding countryside is rewarding. Shop; cl 1–2pm Sat, am Sun, Mon in Oct, Feb and Mar, all Nov–Jan; (01962) 869864; *30p.

▣ GUILDHALL GALLERY (Broadway) Refurbished 19th-c building with changing exhibitions of fine art, crafts and photography. Snacks, shop, disabled access; cl am Sun and Mon (all Mon in winter), Good Fri, 25–26 Dec, 1 Jan; (01962) 848269; free.

♿ CITY MUSEUM (The Square) Well organised local history and archaeology, inc a telling Roman mosaic. Shop, limited disabled access; cl 1–2pm Sat, am Sun, Mon Oct–Mar, 25–26 Dec; (01962) 863064; free.

✕ CITY MILL (Bridge St) Restored 18th-c working watermill, with timbered and raftered ceilings and a pretty little island garden. Cl Mon (exc bank hols) and Tues, wkdys in Mar, all Nov–Feb; (01962) 870057; £1; NT.

▦ ST CROSS A short stroll along the watermeadows by the River Itchen. Very attractively set around 2 quadrangles, the quaint 15th-c almshouses still provide bread and ale to travellers who ask at the massive gate (you have to ask for 'wayfarer's dole'). 19th-c scandals here inspired Trollope's The Warden. Summer snacks, shop, disabled access; cl winter 12.30–2pm in winter, Sun, 25 Dec, Good Fri; £2. The Bell out here is useful for lunch.

The **New Forest** is an unchanging blend of woodland and heath, covering nearly 150 square miles, designated a royal hunting preserve by William the Conqueror not long after the Battle of Hastings. The two best drives are the slow back road from Brockenhurst N through Bolderwood and then round past Linwood to Rockford, and the road from Brockenhurst to Burley; main roads can get very busy around the more popular areas, especially on summer weekends. Still with quite a medieval feel, the ancient woodlands are very atmospheric to stroll through, especially when you come across an unexpected sunlit leafy glade. It's most fun just to potter around (it's a first-class walking area, as you can go pretty much wherever you please), but you'll also get a lot out of a guided tour with people who've lived or worked in the Forest all their lives; (01703) 282269 for details. Many of them have ancient forest rights and privileges, such as letting their pigs forage for acorns. It's a good place for cycling: bike hire at Brockenhurst SU2902. In summer you can usually go on guided badger-watch evenings; (01425) 403412. The Museum and Visitor Centre at Lyndhurst (see entry below) is a good place to start, and has details of watersports, riding and campsites. See **Walks** section, below for ideas for exploring the area on foot. Many people feel the New Forest and its wildlife would be better protected if it were designated a national park.

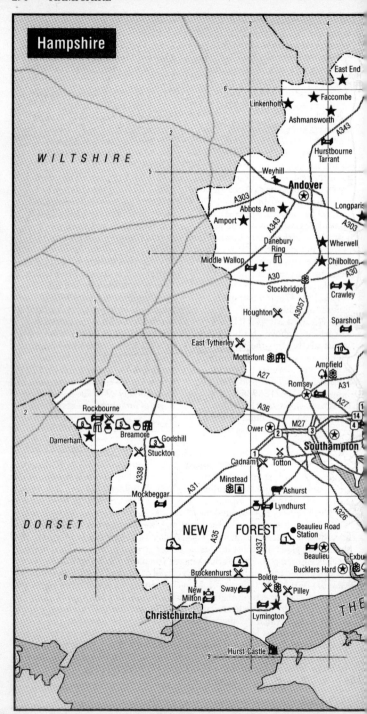

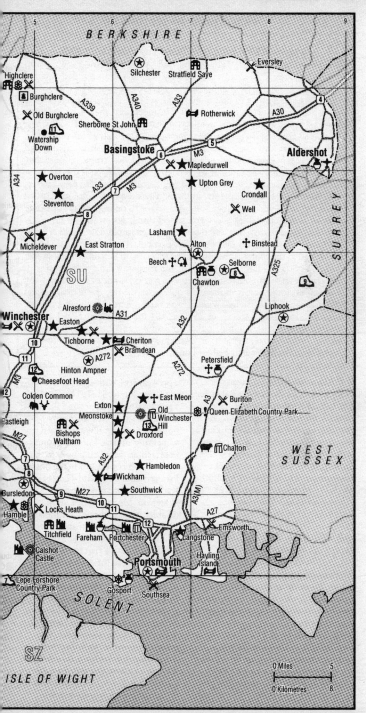

Other things to see and do

HAMPSHIRE FAMILY ATTRACTION OF THE YEAR

🐾 **Colden Common** SU5021 (off the A333 towards Bishop's Waltham) MARWELL ZOO Too many supposedly conservation-minded animal attractions still shove their animals into overcrowded cages or enclosures, so it's particularly nice to find one like this where – at least in places – the tables are turned; visit the lemurs for instance and they'll be enjoying plenty of space and freedom while you watch from covered walkways. Other well conceived viewing areas include a glass wall at the end of the tiger enclosure (so they can jump up at you perfectly safely) and underwater windows into the new penguin world. The tropical house they added last year may be familiar to dedicated zoo-watchers; it used to be at the late Windsor Safari Park, and was reconstructed here. It takes 2 hours each day to water the plants in here. Children can join in Animal Encounters during the summer holidays, maybe handling a snake or riding a camel, and touch tables allow you to feel things you wouldn't normally be able to get close to – lion and tiger skins for example. The 4,000 acres of parkland are attractively laid out, with particularly pleasant picnic areas; the old hall at the centre is the HQ of their successful breeding programme. There's a good adventure playground, and road and rail trains whisk you between the different enclosures, home to a good range of animals, many of which no longer exist in the wild. *Fierce Creatures*, the less successful follow-up to *A Fish Called Wanda*, was filmed here. Meals and snacks, shop, good disabled access; cl 25 Dec; (01962) 777406; £7.50 (£5.50 children aged 3 –14). A family ticket for 2 adults and 2 children costs £24. On the downs above, the Ship at Owslebury is good for a family lunch – quieter than the big nearby Fishers Pond.

✝ ♿ **Aldershot** SU8650 AIRBORNE FORCES MUSEUM (Browning Barracks) The best of Aldershot's profusion of military museums (most of which are of rather specialist appeal), looking at the parachute forces. Lots to take in, with very traditional displays. Snacks, shop, disabled access; cl Christmas; (01252) 349619; £2.50. MILITARY MUSEUM (Queens Ave) Quite well done, exploring the development of the local military camps and their impact on civilian and military life. Shop, disabled access; cl Christmas–New Year; (01252) 314598; *£2. The Aldershot/Farnborough area has quite a lot of open spaces in the surrounding pinewoods for children to let off steam, with boating lakes and so forth.

♿ ❀ **Alresford** SU5931 WATERCRESS LINE 🚂 One of the nicest steam railways in the country, with 10-mile trips between Alresford and Alton through wonderful countryside and its watercress beds. They try to create

a pre-war feel, with stations decked out accordingly. Their Thomas the Tank Engine weeks around Easter and in Aug are extraordinarily popular; several railways organise something similar, but the Thomas here is unusual in being built to the design and proportions in the books. Properly called the Mid-Hants Railway, it has connections to Waterloo. Meals, snacks, shop, disabled access; phone for timetable, (01962) 734866, cl Jan and Nov; £7.50. On some wkdys you can combine it with a visit to the modern Bass brewery at the Alton end, usually open only to groups. Alresford itself is a charming little town, from the Roman ponds teeming with wildfowl in Old Alresford to the so-called New Alresford founded around 1200; good antiquarian bookshop here. The Globe overlooking the ponds does decent lunches, and the Café Cressdon is good. The Itchen road W through Ovington and Easton is

pretty, the B3046 N shows high Hampshire farmland well, and the old road E past Ropley and Monkwood to Steep gives a fine downland impression.
🏛☕✝ **Alton** SU7139 One terminus of the Watercress steam line (see Alresford entry, above). ALLEN GALLERY (Church St) Superb collection of pottery, and a little herb garden. Some disabled access; cl Sun, Mon; (01420) 82802; free. The town brewery is commemorated in a MUSEUM on the High St; a CHURCH bears scars from one of the last battles of the Civil War. The French Horn (The Butts) is a friendly food pub.
🏵 🍴 **Ampfield** SU4023 SIR HAROLD HILLIER GARDENS AND ARBORETUM (Jermyns Lane, off the A31) Impressive collection of trees and shrubs, the biggest of its kind in Britain, covering 160 beautifully landscaped acres. Full of colour and surprises all year, and good walks and events (especially 1st Sun of month). Summer meals, snacks, nursery, disabled access; cl 25–26

Days Out

Army and Navy
D-Day Museum and Sea Life Centre, Southsea; lunch at the Still & West (Bath Sq, nr waterfront), Portsmouth; boat trip to Spitbank Fort; HMS *Victory* or *Mary Rose*; or spend full day at Portsmouth's Historic Dockyard.

Historic Winchester
Cathedral and precincts; Winchester College; lunch at Wykeham Arms (Kingsgate St), or the Cathedral Refectory; walk to St Cross Hospital and ask for Wayfarer's Dole; climb St Catherine's Hill for views.

Escape to the Forest
New Forest Museum and visitor centre, Lyndhurst; Furzey Gardens, Minstead; picnic in the New Forest, or lunch at the Trusty Servant, Minstead; stroll or mountain bike ride in New Forest, or Bolderwood/Rhinefield Ornamental Drives; Spinners garden, Boldre.

Hampshire's watery fringes
Bucklers Hard; lunch at Master Builder's House there; Beaulieu motor museum, or Exbury Gardens; if time, stroll in Lepe Country Park.

Back roads through the downlands
Queen Elizabeth Country Park; Butser Ancient Farm, Chalton; lunch at the Red Lion there; East Meon church; stroll on to Old Winchester Hill.

Ancient legacies
Rockbourne Roman Villa; lunch at the Rose & Thistle there; Breamore House, Saxon church and countryside museum; walk up through woods to find the Mizmaze.

Two abbeys and a hill fort
Romsey Abbey; Mottisfont Abbey garden; lunch at the Star, East Tytherley; tour through Nether Wallop, Chilbolton, Wherwell, Amport, Abbotts Ann villages; Danebury Ring (good walk up from Longstock).

Where Romans trod
Stratfield Saye; Silchester Roman town (Calleva); lunch at the Red Lion, Mortimer West End, or Yew Tree, Highclere; Sandham Memorial Chapel, Burghclere; Highclere Castle (summer).

Dec; (01794) 368787; £4 (£3 Nov–Mar). The White Horse nearby makes for a comfortable lunch break.

�`🖼`🚍 **Andover** SU3645 Nr the church at the top of the impressive High St of this very extended country town, the MUSEUM OF THE IRON AGE looks particularly at finds from nearby Danebury Ring, giving a vivid impression of life for the pre-Roman Celts. Snacks, shop, limited disabled access; cl Sun (exc pm summer), Mon (exc bank hols), Christmas; (01264) 366283; £1.50. There's an adjacent more general MUSEUM (open same hours, free). The local authority's conference room (Weyhill Rd) houses the remarkable TEST VALLEY TAPESTRY, each of its many panels embroidered by a different village to show a scene relating to that community; generally open Mon lunchtimes and pm last Thurs each month – best to phone (01264) 364144 ext 3453 to check; free. FINKLEY DOWN FARM PARK (just NE of town) Well laid out working farm with wide range of animals and poultry inc rare breeds; they encourage you to touch the tamer animals, and there are varied activities every half-hour. Also countryside museum, adventure playground and picnic site. Readers rate this very highly, and it has lots for children (inc space for them to run around). Snacks, shop, disabled access; cl Nov–Mar; (01264) 352195; £3.50. There are well stocked trout fishing lakes around Andover, for example at Rooksbury Mill, and Poplar Farm (on the A343 at Abbotts Ann SU3343) is a useful food stop.

🐗 **Ashurst** SU3510 NEW FOREST NATURE QUEST (Longdown; off the A326 nr Marchwood) Excellent redevelopment of the former New Forest Butterfly Farm by the people who do the chain of Sea Life Centres; this uses the same approach to look at British wildlife, with around 20 carefully recreated natural settings showing the kinds of animals that live in each. You go through back gardens, barns, riverbeds and ponds, with well designed viewing techniques offering a close look at prowling foxes, a swimming mink, and rats scurrying round a garage. Good woodland play area. Meals, snacks, shop, disabled access; cl Nov–Mar; (01703) 292166; £5.50. The friendly neighbouring LONGDOWN DAIRY FARM (Deerleap Lane) has plenty of animals to feed; their herd of Jersey cows is milked from 2.30pm every day. There's a small play area. Snacks, shop, disabled access; cl Nov–Easter; (01703) 293326; £3.80. The Pilgrim is an attractive thatched dining pub.

🚣`🏠`🎠 **Beaulieu** SU3802 Justifiably popular family day out, its centrepiece is still the National Motor Museum, a collection that has grown from humble beginnings to become one of the most comprehensive in the world – on the Heritage Secretary's new shortlist of national importance and excellence. Other features have a motoring theme, too, with Wheels probably the highlight for children – you sit in a pod-like vehicle and trundle through 100 years of motoring. For an extra £2 a simulator ride gives you a more robust driving experience. A monorail whizzes round the grounds, and in summer they usually have a daily Disneyland-style parade of vintage vehicles. Also go-kart style mini-bikes, radio-controlled cars, and some hi-tech arcade-style driving games. Meanwhile the Palace House is a fine old mansion based around the gatehouse of the huge Cistercian Abbey that stood here until the Reformation (still with what are thought to be the original monastic fan-vaulted ceilings). The surrounding lakeside parkland and gardens are rewarding to explore, with ruins of other abbey buildings, and an exhibition on the monks who lived here. Meals, snacks, shops, disabled access; cl 25 Dec; (01590) 612123; £8. In the village facing the Palace House gates, the Wine Press is popular for lunch, and a marked trail leads from it down to Bucklers Hard.

✝`🦌`🐝 **Beech** SU6938 ALTON ABBEY (signed off the A339) The home of a community of Benedictine monks, in peaceful woodland so a relaxing place for a stroll. The grounds have mature specimen trees and shrubs, especially rhododendrons and azaleas. The traditional Sun at Bentworth does good food.

† **Binsted** SU7740 CHURCH where Field Marshal Montgomery is buried; after the war he lived a mile away at Islington Mill SU7742 – a pretty spot. The Cedars has decent food.

🏛 **Bishop's Waltham** SU5517 PALACE Impressive ruins of the Bishop of Winchester's majestic 12th-c palace, with the remains of state apartments round a cloister court, and William of Wykeham's great hall and tower. Shop, disabled access to ground floor; cl Nov–Mar; (01489) 892460; £2. The Barleycorn (Basingwell St) has enjoyable food, and the downs N of here between Owslebury, Beauworth and Warnford give scenic drives.

🏵 **Boldre** SZ3198 SPINNERS (School Lane) Wonderful gardens created since the 1960s. The nursery is famed for its rare trees (especially maples and magnolias), shrubs and plants. Some disabled access; gardens open Tues–Sat mid-Apr–mid-Sept, or by appointment, nursery open all year exc Sun and Mon Sept–Apr; (01590) 673347; *£1.50. The Red Lion (no children) is good for lunch.

🏛🖙 **Breamore** SU1517 BREAMORE HOUSE 🔲 Late Elizabethan manor house, with fine furnishings, tapestries and paintings (mainly 17th- and 18th-c Dutch school), and better than average countryside museum. Children aren't left out – there's a mizmaze and an adventure playground. A recent version of Hardy's *The Woodlanders* was filmed here. Snacks, shop, disabled access; open pm Tues, Weds and Sun Apr–Sept, plus Thurs and Sat May–Sept, daily in Aug; (01725) 512468; *£5. The home cooking at the Horse & Groom at Woodgreen is good, and there are lovely wood and riverside walks.

★ ❀ ♄ ♣ **Bucklers Hard** SU4000 Very pretty little waterside village, with long red-roofed cottage rows flanking a wide, grassed waterside street. It was once an important centre for shipbuilding, and the MARITIME MUSEUM tells the story of the industry, right up to the voyages of Sir Francis Chichester. You have to pay to come into the village, though admission includes entry to the museum and the various other exhibitions and reconstructions dotted around, inc the carefully restored 18th-c homes of a shipwright and labourer, and a typical inn scene complete with costumed figures, smells and conversation. Meals, snacks, shop; cl 25 Dec; (01590) 616203; £3. There are summer boat trips, and the Master Builder's House is useful for lunch. A pleasant 2½-mile riverside walk takes you to Beaulieu, run by the same people.

🔲 **Burghclere** SU4761 SANDHAM MEMORIAL CHAPEL Stanley Spencer's moving masterpiece, built in memory of H W Sandham, killed in World War I. The final resurrection scene is especially dramatic, best on a bright day as the room is quite dark. Cl Mon (exc bank hols when cl following Weds instead), Tues, wkdays Nov and Mar, all Dec–Feb; (01635) 278394; *£2; NT. The Carpenters Arms opposite is pleasant for lunch, with superb views.

🖝 ♣ ✗ **Bursledon** SU4911 MANOR FARM COUNTRY PARK 🔲 (Pylands Lane) Woodland and riverside walks based around traditional working farm, with lots of animals, crafts and activities. Meals, snacks, shop, mostly disabled access; park open all year, farm cl winter exc Sun; (01489) 787055; £3.30. There may be BOAT TRIPS on some summer Sats from here along the Hamble. Bursledon also has a WINDMILL; open Sun and summer Sats. The Jolly Sailor is a beautifully placed food pub.

🏰 ❊ **Calshot Castle** SU4802 Down past the oil refineries and power stations, this Tudor fort stands on the end of the spit of land beyond the tidal mudflats at the end of Southampton Water; splendid views of the shipping and the Isle of Wight. The Jolly Sailor at Ashlett Creek nr Fawley is a pleasant waterside food pub.

🏛 🖿 **Chalton** SU7315 BUTSER ANCIENT FARM 🔢 (Bascombe Copse) Reconstructed Iron Age farm, with crops, animals, crafts and demonstrations. You can try your hand at grinding corn on a stone, and there's a Celtic maze (planted with period herbs). Shop, disabled access; cl Dec–Feb; (01705) 598838; £2. The ancient Red Lion is handy for lunch.

🏛 ♿ **Chawton** SU7037 JANE AUSTEN'S HOUSE Unpretentious 17th-c house where the author lived and worked between 1809 and 1817, still with some of her letters and possessions. Rooms are furnished in period style, and the pleasant garden is good for picnics. Good bookshop, disabled access to ground floor and garden; cl wkdys Jan–Feb, 25–26 Dec; (01420) 83262; *£2.50. The Greyfriar opposite has reasonably priced food, and there are good walks here. Just up the road, Chawton House, the former home of Jane Austen's brother Edward, is to become a Centre for the Study of Early English Women's Writing.

🖿 ✟ **Colden Common** SU5021 For MARWELL ZOO *see separate Family Panel on p.292.*

🏛 **Danebury Ring** SU3237 Iron Age hill fort rich in (excavated) remains, interestingly waymarked. The Peat Spade at Longstock to the E has good food.

🎇 ♧ **Exbury** SU4200 EXBURY GARDENS Wonderful 200-acre landscaped woodland gardens on the E bank of the River Beaulieu, with splendid rock garden, heather garden and river walk, and above all the Rothschild collection of rhododendrons, azaleas, magnolias and camellias – one of the world's finest, at its best in May and early Jun. Meals, snacks, shop, disabled access; cl Nov–Feb; (01703) 891203; price varies with the season, from £2.20 in summer when less is open, to £4.80 in spring. Nearby LEPE COUNTRY PARK is a nice place for a coastal stroll, with good views and lots of natural habitats. The Jolly Sailor (see Calshot entry above) is quite handy.

🖿 ♿ **Fareham** SU5706 FORT NELSON (Downend Rd) Built in the 19th c in response to fears of the French, this now houses the Royal Armouries museum of artillery, which they like to call the noisiest museum in the world. Certainly enough booms, blasts and crashes to please most children (guns are fired at noon and 3pm), and you don't have to be interested in weaponry to enjoy it. Wafting smells create a period atmosphere, and there are lots of underground tunnels to explore. Views of Portsmouth Harbour from the ramparts. Meals, snacks, shop, disabled access; cl winter wkdys; (01329) 233734; £3.95. You can get a joint ticket with Submarine World (see Gosport entry below). The Osborne View out at Hill Head has superb views, with pleasant walks nearby.

⚓ ♿ **Gosport** SZ6199 SUBMARINE WORLD 🔢 (Royal Navy Submarine Museum, Haslar Jetty Rd) The highlight here is the tour of beached World War II submarine HMS *Alliance*, still in full working order, and fascinating inside to small boys of any age. More conventional features include an audio-visual show giving the flavour of diving into the depths. Snacks, shop, some disabled access; cl 24 Dec–1 Jan; (01705) 529217; *£3.75. FORT BROCKHURST A good overview exhibition of how the various forts protected Portsmouth; the Dolphin (Fort Rd) has popular food. You can get a waterbus across to Portsmouth (Apr–Oct), and the sea at Stokes Bay is probably the county's cleanest for swimming.

★ 🎇 **Hamble** SU4806 This pleasant village in *Howards Way* country has interesting views of the yachts, and you can walk a long way up river or towards the Solent; the simple Olde Whyte Harte has decent food. There's a friendly little ferry taking about 10 people at a time (50p) to Warsash, where the riverside Rising Sun has good food, and there's a wildfowl nature reserve just N. Nearby Netley SU4508 has a coastal COUNTRY PARK and the extensive ruins of a 13th-c abbey.

🏛 🎇 **Highclere** SU4360 HIGHCLERE

CASTLE (best approached from the A34 rather than Highclere itself) Magnificent pastiche of a medieval castle, impressively grand inside and out. Elaborate saloon and main staircase, a desk that belonged to Napoleon, and a Van Dyck of Charles I. Exhibitions of Egyptian relics (the 5th Earl discovered Tutankhamun's tomb with Howard Carter), and horse-racing (the current Earl is the Queen's racing manager). The lovely gardens and grounds include a Victorian tropical conservatory and a walled garden. Meals, snacks, shop and plant centre; open Tues–Sun July–Sept, plus bank hols wknds; (01635) 253210; £5.50, £3 gardens only. The Yew Tree (on the A343 S of village) is a good-value dining pub.

🏠❀🏠 **Hinton Ampner** SU5927 HINTON AMPNER The Georgian house reopens this year after extensive rewiring, but it's the grounds that impress most, with tranquil 20th-c shrub gardens. Teas, disabled access; gardens open 15 and 22 Mar (good for daffodils), then pm Tues, Weds, wknds and bank hols Apr–Sept, house open only pm Tues and Weds; (01962) 771305; *£4 house and garden, *£3 garden only; NT. The Fox at Bramdean nearby is pleasant for lunch.

🏰 **Hurst Castle** SZ3189 One of the most sophisticated fortresses around when built by Henry VIII, on a little spit commanding the Solent, and best reached on foot or by boat from Keyhaven (there's a pleasant walk from the 17th-c Gun pub – good value food). Fortified again in the 19th c, it still has 2 huge 38-ton guns. Summer snacks, shop; cl wkdys Nov–Mar, 24–26 Dec, 1 Jan; (01590) 642344; £2.

★ **Langstone** SU7105 Thatched cottages, an old tidal mill, and a couple of decent pubs looking out over the thousands of acres of silted harbour – winter sunsets are memorable. Swans float up at high tide, with oystercatchers and droves of darting dunlins on the low-tide mud flats. Interesting walks along the old sea wall.

🏠 🕹 ⬆️ 🏰 **Liphook** SU8431 BOHUNT MANOR Lovely woodland gardens owned by Worldwide Fund for Nature, with water garden, roses and herbaceous borders, a lakeside walk, and unusual trees and shrubs. Disabled access; (01428) 722208; *£1.50 (usually free in winter). HOLLYCOMBE STEAM COLLECTION 🚂 (Midhurst Rd) Huge collection of steam-driven equipment, from paddle-steamers to an entire Edwardian fairground. Traction engine rides, and woodland steam train trips. Snacks, shop; open pm Sun and bank hols Easter–mid-Oct, usually daily July and Aug; (01428) 724900; £5.50. The nearest place for an enjoyable lunch is the Red Lion over at Fernhurst.

★ **Lymington** SZ3295 Handsome and relaxed waterside town, very popular in summer with yachting people; it has quite a number of attractive Georgian buildings and some good shops. The Chequers down Ridgeway Lane, S of Pennington, has decent food; the Angel (High St) and Toll House (on the A337) are also useful. You can get ferries to the Isle of Wight from here, and the B3054 to Dibden Purlieu is a pretty road.

👶 **Lyndhurst** SU2907 The tourist centre of the New Forest, as well as the main shopping town for people living here, so lots of tea shops, café, etc. NEW FOREST MUSEUM (High St) Very good themed displays and audio-visual exploration of the Forest's history and wildlife, and a 7½-metre (25-ft) embroidery. Decent children's features too. It looks like a modern supermarket from outside. Shop, disabled access; cl 25 Dec; (01703) 283914; *£2.50. The car park has a good information centre for the area. The Royal Oak in the pretty village of Bank just outside has a good choice of food.

✝ **Middle Wallop** SU2938 MUSEUM OF ARMY FLYING One of the country's best military museums, exploring man's efforts to fly. Kites, balloons, vintage aircraft, World War II gliders, and interactive displays. Some exhibits still soar occasional wknds.

Meals, snacks, shop, disabled access; cl Christmas week; (01980) 674421; £3.90. Nearby Nether Wallop SU3036 is an attractive sleepy village with an interesting Saxon church; surprisingly Leopold Stokowski died here, not in Hollywood. The Five Bells is a pleasantly modest place for lunch.

🕸 ▣ **Minstead** SU2711 Quiet and pretty, with a fine old church at the top of the hill; the Trusty Servant by the green has good food. FURZEY GARDENS 8 peaceful heather-filled acres, with developing young arboretum, around charming 16th-c thatched cottage with local craft gallery. Snacks, plant sales, limited disabled access; cl 25–26 Dec; (01703) 812464; £3 (£1.50 winter).

🏚 🕸 **Mottisfont** SU3226 MOTTISFONT ABBEY 12th-c priory salvaged from the Reformation as a delightful family house, in wonderful peaceful surroundings. The gardens are a delight, housing a national collection of old roses (largely scented). You can usually see a few of the rooms, inc one richly decorated by Rex Whistler. Meals, shop, good disabled access; open pm Sat–Weds Apr–Oct, daily during the rose season – this year 13–28 Jun (when they're open till 8.30pm); (01794) 340757; *£4, *£5 rose season; NT. The Bear & Ragged Staff up on the A3057 does decent food all day, and the road along the Test through Houghton and on to Wherwell is pretty.

🏄 **New Milton** SZ2495 SAMMY MILLER MUSEUM (Bashley Manor), Well regarded changing collection of fully restored motor cycles, many the only surviving examples of their type in the world. Snacks, shop, disabled access; cl 25–26 Dec; (01425) 620777; *£3.50. There's an adjacent craft shop.

🏚 🌼 **Old Winchester Hill** SU6420 HILL FORT This gives wide views of Hampshire, the Solent and Isle of Wight, with nature trails through natural downland that's never been ploughed and resown; fairly busy on fine wknds, wonderfully remote on a blustery spring or autumn weekday. The George & Falcon at Warnford is

popular for food.

♥ ! ☺ **Ower** SU3216 PAULTONS PARK Agreeable family theme park with 140 acres of rides, gardens, animals, birds and wildfowl, as well as moving dinosaurs, 10-acre lake with working waterwheel, miniature Rio Grande railway, go-karts, hedge maze, animated scenes from *The Wind in the Willows*, and unique Romany Experience with the sights, sounds and smells of traditional gypsy life. The flamingos breed only when they're surrounded by large numbers, so mirrors have been installed to make them think they're part of a bigger flock. Meals, snacks, shop, disabled access; cl wkdys Nov and Dec (exc Christmas specials), all Jan and Feb; (01703) 814442; £8. The White Hart at Cadnam is handy.

♦ † **Petersfield** SU7423 BEAR MUSEUM (Dragon St) Teddies, dolls and toys in a nursery setting. Children (or anyone else for that matter) can cuddle the exhibits; shop; cl Sun and Mon (exc Christmas); (01730) 265108; free. There's an interesting CHURCH on Market Sq, and the Good Intent does worthwhile lunches.

🏚 🏰 **Portchester** SU6105 PORTCHESTER CASTLE The imposing high walls and towers stretching right down to the waterfront were originally part of a 3rd-c Roman fort – they're the best example of their type in Europe. Other remains include a 12th-c church and 14th-c great tower, and what's left of a palace built by Richard II. Snacks, shop, disabled access; cl 25–26 Dec; (01705) 378291; £2.50. The nearby Cormorant has good-value food.

🕸 ! **Queen Elizabeth Country Park** SU7219 Lots going on all year, with woodland walks and rides (stables at the park), open downland, a new adventure play trail, and events like Easter egg rolling. You can hire bikes. Shop and café (cl wkdys Nov–Mar); (01705) 595040; *£1.50 parking charge Sun and bank hols, *£1 rest of wk. The excellent Five Bells at Buriton is nearby.

🏚 ♦ **Rockbourne** SU1118 ROMAN VILLA (off the B3078) Remains of largest known Roman villa in the area, found by chance 50 years ago by a farmer digging out a ferret. Interesting mosaics in the museum. Snacks, shop, disabled access; cl am wkdys exc July and Aug, all Oct–Mar; (01725) 518541; £2. In the charming thatched village, the Rose & Thistle is good for lunch.

🏠 ❀ ✝ **Romsey** SU3521 BROADLANDS (just S) Elegant Palladian mansion on the banks of the River Test, surrounded by beautiful landscaped grounds. Fine furnishings and paintings, and a good exhibition on former resident Earl Mountbatten. You can fish on an adjacent stretch of the River Test. Snacks, shop, disabled access; open pm mid-Jun–mid-Sept; (01794) 516878; *£5. The newly opened nearby Old Horse & Jockey and (afternoon teas too) Three Tuns have enjoyable food. Mountbatten is buried in the interesting 13th-c ABBEY, bought by the townspeople for their parish church at the Dissolution. There are some notable Saxon crosses and a 16th-c panel painting.

🏠 ❀ ⛁ **Selborne** SU7433 GILBERT WHITE'S HOUSE (The Wakes) Impressive 18th-c home of naturalist Gilbert White, furnished in period style. The extensive gardens are being restored to their original form, and separate galleries commemorate Captain Oates and Frank Oates. Teas and 18th-c style snacks, shop, plant sales, disabled access to ground floor and garden; cl winter wkdys, Christmas; (01420) 511275; *£3.50. Interesting walks trace White's steps, and the Queens Hotel is handy for lunch.

🏠 ❀ **Sherborne St John** SU6255 THE VYNE The Tudor mansion with its splendid 17th- and 18th-c embellishments is closed for major restoration until June, but you can still visit the gardens, which have much more to see than in previous years. They've opened a 19th-c walled garden, and there are pleasant woodland walks. Snacks, shop, disabled access; cl am, Mon (exc bank hols when cl following Tues instead), Fri, and Oct–Mar, best to check exact reopening date for house; (01256) 881337; £2; NT.

🏛 ✝ ⛁ **Silchester** SU6262 The site of the Roman town Calleva Atrebatum has been excavated nearby; 1½ miles of city wall to walk along (tricky in places), as well as a 9,000-seat amphitheatre, 12th-c church on the site of the Roman temples, and MUSEUM with small collection of finds from the site. The Calleva Arms (with a family dining conservatory) does cheap lunches, and sells helpful guides to the site; the Red Lion at Mortimer West End is a good dining pub.

🏠 ❀ ⛁ ✝ 🖼 **Southampton** SU4211 Known earlier this century (through its shipping importance) as the Gateway to the World, this huge bustling town rather unexpectedly has one of the 3 best-preserved medieval town walls in the country. The best stretch is along the western side of the old core, around from the magnificent partly Norman BARGATE (which has a small local museum); there are usually guided walks along here on Sun mornings, or you can walk it yourself at any time. Lots of other old buildings dotted around the less appetising modern townscape, though if you're short of time it's best to concentrate your efforts on the area around St Michael's Sq, Bugle St and perhaps the old High St. Parking around the centre is metered. The quayside nearest here has been cleaned up, with modern café-bars overlooking yachting berths. Just down the road the MARITIME MUSEUM (Bugle St) is a fine 14th-c warehouse with an impressive timber ceiling, and useful displays on the history of the port. Especially good on the great liners. Shop, disabled access to ground floor only; cl 1–2pm, am Sun, Mon (exc bank hols), Christmas; (01703) 635904; free. You may be able to visit the pretty 15th-c TUDOR HOUSE on the same road (it has been closed for restoration). The ancient nearby Duke of Wellington has decent food. GOD'S HOUSE TOWER (Winkle St) is an early 15th-c prototype gun battery, now housing an archaeology museum with displays on the city's Saxon forebear, Hamwic; details as Maritime

Museum. The nearby bowling green is said to be the oldest in the world. The HALL OF AVIATION (Albert Rd S) looks after various aircraft of local interest – inc prototype helicopters and the Spitfire. Shop, disabled access; cl Mon (exc summer, bank and school hols), Christmas; (01703) 635830; *£3. CITY ART GALLERY (Civic Centre, Commercial Rd) Extensive and distinguished collection of British and European paintings and sculptures from the last 600 years, particular emphasis on 20th c; highly praised by readers. Meals, snacks, shop, disabled access; cl am Sun, Mon, 25–27 and 31 Dec; (01703) 632601; free.

🏵 **Stockbridge** SU3535 HOUGHTON LODGE GARDENS (just SW) Pretty and very peaceful gardens running down to the River Test, with fine trees and lawns, and topiary peacocks. An intriguing hydroponicum demonstrates how to grow plants without soil. Wknd snacks, plant sales (especially good on fuchsias), disabled access; open wknds and bank hols and pm wkdys Mar–Sept, (cl Weds); (01264) 810177; *£4.50.

🏠 **Stratfield Saye** SU6861 STRATFIELD SAYE HOUSE (off the A33) A grateful nation granted the Duke of Wellington the money to buy this 17th-c house after Waterloo. Perhaps surprisingly, the Duke had a taste for French furniture, lots of which is still here. Also the Duke's splendid funeral carriage, and his hearing aid – needed after prolonged exposure to cannon-fire. Snacks, shop, disabled access; cl am, all day Fri, wkdys Sept, Oct–Apr; (01256) 882882; £5. The elegant Wellington Arms has good food. There are pleasant walks on Heckfield Heath E of the park, and Wellington Country Park in Berks is nearby.

🏚🏠 **Titchfield** SU5305 TITCHFIELD ABBEY Ruined 13th-c abbey, almost overshadowed by the grand Tudor gatehouse built after the Dissolution. Some of Shakespeare's plays were reputedly first performed here. Disabled access; free. The riverside Fishermans Rest opposite is a decent pub/restaurant, and there's a fine walk by the old canal to the coast at Meon Shore nr Hill Head.

✘ **Totton** SU3513 ELING TIDE MILL (Eling Toll Bridge) There's been a mill on this causeway for over 900 years, and the present one still uses tidal energy to produce flour. Heritage centre, snacks, shop, disabled access to ground floor only; cl Mon, Tues, 25 Dec – ring for milling times, which of course depend on the tide; (01703) 869575; *£1.40. In unpromising surroundings, the Anchor on Eling Quay is a good, cheap place for something to eat.

🦅 **Weyhill** SU3146 HAWK CONSERVANCY One of the best birds of prey centres we've come across; you can handle some of the birds, and there are regular flying displays (the best at 2pm). Snacks, shop, disabled access; cl Nov–Feb; (01264) 772252; £5.50. The Weyhill Fair is handy for lunch, and the lanes N take you into a particularly unspoilt corner of Hants.

★ ❀ 🦌 Among the county's many **attractive villages**, ones with decent pubs include Abbots Ann SU3243, Amport SU2944, Ashmansworth SU4157 (Hampshire's highest; good walks), Cheriton SU5828, Chilbolton SU3939 (the common is being carefully preserved), Crawley SU4234, Crondall SU7948, East End SU4161 (the one nr Highclere), East Meon SU6822 (splendid Norman church), East Stratton SU5440, Easton SU5132 (pleasant Itchen Valley walks), Exton SU6121 (beautifully set by the Meon under the downs, good walks nearby), Faccombe SU3858 (bright with daffodils in spring, great views from Pilot Hill), Hambledon SU6414, Lasham SU6742, Longparish SU4344, Mapledurwell SU6851, Meonstoke SU6119 (nice quiet road by the Meon down through Soberton, and the old Meon Valley railway line is now open as a footpath), Micheldever SU5142, Overton SU5149 (the B3400 to Hurstbourne Priors then the B3048 to Wherwell is a charming drive), Southwick SU6208 (good walks and views on Portsdown Hill), Tichborne SU5630 (pleasant walks), Upton Grey

SU6948, Wherwell SU3941 and Wickham SU5711 (huge village square; good farm shop with PICK-YOUR-OWN at nearby Droxford). In the N, Ashmansworth SU4157 and Linkenholt SU3658 are high enough to give fine views from many of their lanes (best explored by car). The 12th-c church in Steventon SU5447 has a memorial to Jane Austen, who was born in the village. In spring, it's worth visiting the churchyard at Damerham SU1016 to see the carpet of snowdrops.

Walks

The path network in the New Forest is remarkably comprehensive, and in most places there's no obligation to stick to rights of way (of which there are very few). The lack of major objectives can be a problem for purists: there are no obviously defined hills, and long walks in the eastern woodlands, many of which are coniferous, can become monotonous. Further W, the scenery is more intricate and a touch more varied. It is often a good idea to use routes which have plenty of landmarks to guide the way; the heath and forest can be fiendishly disorienting.

Besides the ponies, you may see fallow deer, especially at the Bolderwood Deer Sanctuary SU2308 (and in the woods, very occasionally, the smaller, shyer roe deer; even in some places red deer).

The best walks alternate mixed forest with heathland; isolated ponds and country pubs provide focal points. Good starting places include **Beaulieu Road** railway station SU3406 ⌂-1, for its surrounding remote-feeling heaths, **Burley Street** SU2004 ⌂-2, **Godshill** SU1714 ⌂-3 and **Brockenhurst** SU2902 ⌂-4.

Pubs handy for New Forest walks are the Royal Oak at Bank SU2807, Red Lion at Boldre SZ3198 (nr Raydon Woods nature reserve), Queens Head and White Buck at Burley SU2003, Royal Oak at Fritham SU2314, Foresters Arms at Frogham SU1713, High Corner Inn or Red Shoot nr Linwood SU1910, Royal Oak at North Gorley SU1611, Alice Lisle at Rockford SU1608, Sir Walter Tyrell at Upper Canterton SU2613, and perhaps the Turf Cutters Arms at East Boldre SU3700 and Filly at Setley SU3000.

Breamore SU1518 ⌂-5 is a thatched village just W of the Forest proper, within a pleasant walk of Breamore House and the mysterious Mizmaze, cut in the turf. **Bokerley Ditch** (or Dyke) ⌂-6 further W acted as a bulwark against raiders on Dorset in the 4th century; still impressive, it marks the county boundary and can be reached by walking up from Martin SU0619.

Lepe Country Park SZ4598 ⌂-7 E of the Forest allows mild saunters along the coast.

Selborne SU7433 ⌂-8 in E Hampshire has good scenic pockets – the countryside recorded in such detail by naturalist Gilbert White. The zigzag path he created with his brother in 1753 still climbs Selborne Hanger. The hangers hereabouts are beechwoods which cling to the abrupt escarpments; Noar Hill close by has been designated a nature reserve for its chalkland flora. From Selborne churchyard, a path leads into The Lythe, a wooded hillside that was another favourite haunt of White's.

Waggoners' Wells SU8535 ⌂-9 are a series of hammer ponds, a legacy of the medieval Wealden iron industry, set in charming heathy woodlands in a valley and perfect for a picnic. Paths skirt these NT-owned ponds, which are a haven for wildlife.

Farley Mount SU4029 ⌂-10 is an attractive downland and woodland area with good views.

Watership Down SU4957 ⌂-11 just S of Kingsclere was the home of the rabbits in the novel by Richard Adams – their final adventure was down at Freefolk SU4848, where the local pub often has live rabbits. Pleasant wooded walks through this area.

Cheesefoot Head SU5327 ⌂-12 (locally pronounced Chesford) is good for walks; a natural amphitheatre where Eisenhower and Montgomery addressed the troops before the Normandy invasion.

Old Winchester Hill SU6420 ⌂-13 is a good place for breezy strolls.

Many of the woodlands in this part of Hampshire fill with snowdrops in February; Warnford SU6223 is a good example. In May there are bluebells, for example at Froxfield SU7025, East Tisted SU7032 and Ropley SU6431.

Good pubs on which to base walks include the Milburys at Beauworth SU5726 (e.g. the Beacon Hill viewpoint), Dog & Crook at Brambridge SU4721, Fox at Bramdean SU6128 (downland, and nr Wayfarers Walk), Bat & Ball on Broadhalfpenny Down SU6716, Tally Ho at Broughton SU3032 (for high Broughton Down, and the Clarendon Way), Five Bells at Buriton SU7420, Red Lion at Chalton SU7315, Horse & Jockey at Curbridge SU5211 (NT parts of Hamble estuary), Queens Head at Dogmersfield SU7853, Mill Arms at Barley Hill, Dunbridge SU3126, Hampshire Bowman at Dundridge SU5718, George at East Meon SU6822, the Star at East Tytherley SU2929, Fox & Goose at Greywell SU7151 (canal), the Vine at Hannington SU5355, Hawkley Inn on Pococks Lane, Hawkley SU7429, John o' Gaunt at Horsebridge SU3430, Crown at Kings Somborne SU3631 (Test Way, Clarendon Way), Old House At Home at Newnham SU7054, the Bush at Ovington SU5531, the Ship at Owslebury SU5123, White Horse nr Priors Dean above Petersfield SU7129 (a lovely country pub), Selborne Arms in Selborne SU7433, Bold Forester at Soberton Heath SU6014 (Meon Valley), Coronation Arms in pretty St Mary Bourne SU4250 (Test Way), the Harrow at Steep SU7425 (the beechwood hangers), Elm Tree at Swanwick SU5109 (handy for the Hampshire Wildlife Reserve), the Woolpack at Totford SU5738, George at Vernham Dean SU3456 (Fosbury hill fort) and the Barley Mow at Winchfield SU7753.

Where to eat

Bishop's Waltham SU5517 TONY'S BRASSERIE The Old Granary, corner of Brook St and Bank St (01489) 896352 Cosy restaurant with friendly service, simple French and other international dishes, and decent wines; cl pm Sun, Mon, last 2 wks Jan. £20|£5.95.

Boldre SZ3198 RED LION (01590) 673177 Very busy, friendly pub on edge of the New Forest, with impressively good bar food, marvellous choice of wines by the glass, and well kept beer; prompt service; worth getting there early; no children; disabled access. £23|£5.50.

Bramdean SU6128 Fox (01962) 771363 Welcoming 17th-c dining pub with famous fox masks on the wall of the modernised and neatly cared for open-plan bar; lots of good fish dishes (and other food, too), an extensive wine list, well kept real ales, and obliging service; no children; cl 25 Dec. £25|£7.95.

Brockenhurst SU2902 LE POUSSIN The Courtyard, Brookley Rd (01590) 623063 Popular little restaurant with carefully cooked interesting food using the best local produce, good cheeses and puddings, friendly service, and chicken-themed decorations; cl Mon and Tues; disabled access. £35.

Brockenhurst SU2902 THATCHED COTTAGE 16 Brookley Rd (01590) 623090 Really charming, 400-year-old thatched cottage with a cosy beamed lounge, good dried and fresh flower arrangements, pretty restaurant, and enjoyable well presented imaginative food served by friendly staff; super cream teas in neat garden and morning coffee, too; cl pm Sun, Mon, Jan; children over 12. £42.50|£6.50.

Buriton SU7420 FIVE BELLS High St (01730) 263584 Popular, unpretentious country local with a genuine welcome, log fire and woodburner; very good bar food, and a good choice of well kept beers; children allowed in snug and restaurant; self-catering cottages; £18.95|£7.95.

Cadnam SU2913 WHITE HART (01703) 812277 Big multi-level dining lounge and good solid furnishings; a wide choice of interesting food inc fine daily specials and tempting puddings, well kept real ales and decent wines; goat, horses and dogs; cl 25–26 Dec; disabled access. £20|£5.

Droxford SU6018 HURDLES Brockbridge (01489) 877451 Pretty creeper-covered building with good traditional cooking, and friendly staff; cl 25–26 Dec; no children; disabled access. £11|£4.30.

East Tytherley SU2929 STAR (01794) 340225 Friendly country local by the village cricket field and with homely furnishings, log fires, a no smoking lower lounge bar, cosy, pretty no smoking restaurant, and a pleasantly informal atmosphere; enjoyable home-made food inc good daily specials, well kept real ales, and smart efficient staff; garden and skittle alley; bdrms. £16|£6.

Emsworth SU7406 36 ON THE QUAY South St (01243) 375592 Very good French cooking in charming quayside restaurant, with helpful service and sound wine list; cl am Mon and Sat, Sun, 2 wks Jan, 1 wk Oct; children over 2. £36.95|£16 for 2-course lunch.

Eversley SU7762 NEW MILL RESTAURANT AND GRILL ROOM New Mill Rd (0118) 973 2277 16th-c watermill by the Blackwater River with working waterwheel and corn grinding equipment; the main restaurant, with big windows overlooking the river and its wildlife, open fires and candlelit tables, has a good range of interesting, carefully cooked food; the beamed and flagstoned Grill Room is more informal and the menu simpler (and cheaper); thoughtful wine list with many by the glass; cl am Sat; partial disabled access. £26 **dinner**, £17 **lunch** in restaurant; £15 Grill Room.

Highclere SU4360 YEW TREE Hollington Cross, Andover Rd (01635) 253360 Plush L-shaped dining bar with a big log fire; enterprising food, friendly licensees, good unobtrusive waitress service, well kept real ales and decent wines; also restaurant; bdrms. £22|£6.50.

Houghton SU3432 BOOT (01794) 388310 Friendly, well run dining pub with simple decor, popular bar and restaurant food, well kept real ales, and pleasant service; cl Mon; disabled access. £18.95|£5.25.

Locks Heath SU5207 JOLLY FARMER (01489) 572500 Thriving old inn with plenty of character, a series of small rooms with lots of country bric-a-brac; a wide choice of quickly served food, well kept real ales; neat, friendly staff. £18.50|£6.

Mapledurwell SU6851 GAMEKEEPERS (01256) 22038 Interesting old pub in lovely thatched village, with wide choice of enterprising food, good-value wines, and friendly service; cl pm Sun, 25–26 Dec; disabled access. £26|£6.50.

Micheldever SU5139 DEVER ARMS (01962) 774339 Civilised country pub with calm simply decorated bar, beams, woodburners, and good solid furniture; generous helpings of interesting food inc lots of good daily specials, well kept real ales, and a thoughtful wine list; seats on terrace and by cricket green; disabled access. £19.40|£7.95.

Old Burghclere SU4758 DEW POND (01635) 278408 Beautiful 16th-c country house with log fires and a friendly atmosphere; imaginative food using fresh local produce on a frequently changing small menu – good game, fish and lovely puddings; no smoking; cl Sun, Mon, 2 wks Jan, 2 wks Aug; children over 5; disabled access. £31.

Pilley SZ3298 FLEUR DE LYS (01590) 672158 The oldest pub in the New Forest, this has plenty of atmosphere, with a huge inglenook fireplace; well kept real ales, good wines and farm cider, a wide range of carefully prepared interesting food inc vegetarian and fish dishes, and a thoughtful children's menu; pretty garden with popular barbecued fish. £18.50|£6.99.

Rockbourne SU1118 ROSE & THISTLE (01725) 518236 Very attractive thatched 17th-c pub with a smartly civilised feel; extremely good bar food, well kept ales, a good range of wines, and a thatched dovecote in the neat front garden. £23|£6.50.

Southsea SZ6498 A FISTFUL OF TACOS Albert Rd (01705) 293474 Evening restaurant with good Californian/Mexican food; cl 24–26 Dec, 1 Jan; partial disabled access. £18.

Stuckton SU1613 THREE LIONS (01425) 652489 Warmly welcoming restaurant with informal slightly pubby atmosphere, and a neat, airy bar with fresh flowers; very imaginative food inc lovely puddings, and a fine wine list; good atmosphere and friendly, efficient service; cl pm Sun, Mon, last 2 wks Jan, 1st wk Feb; disabled access; bedrooms. £35|£13.50 2-course lunch.

Tichborne SU5630 TICHBORNE ARMS (01962) 733760 Attractive thatched country pub in rolling countryside; very good imaginative bar food and delicious puddings; big garden; no children; disabled access. £14|£4.95.

Well SU7646 CHEQUERS (01256) 862605 Neatly kept and rather smart country pub with relaxed atmosphere, snug rooms, beams and lots of 18th-c country-life prints; very good bar and restaurant food; disabled access. £19|£6.50.

Winchester SU4829 CATHEDRAL REFECTORY Visitors Centre, Inner Close (01962) 853224 Excellent totally home-made food in bright, airy, modern conservatory, lovely breads and soups, afternoon cream teas, good children's menu, a friendly informal atmosphere, and nice staff; cl 25–26 Dec, Good Fri. £13.50|£4.75.

Special thanks to Phyl and Jack Street, E G Parish, Miss L S Willett, B and K Hypher, Mr and Mrs I Hughes, Carol Patton.

HAMPSHIRE CALENDAR

Some of these dates were provisional as we went to press, please check information with the telephone numbers provided

JANUARY

1 **Micheldever** Bangers and Beans: fly in at Popham Airfield (01256) 397733

FEBRUARY

24 **Sway** Shrove Tuesday Pancake Race: Station Rd (01590) 683402

APRIL

5 **Beaulieu** Boat Jumble at the National Motor Museum (01590) 612345

10 **Colden Common** Children's Easter Entertainments at Marwell Zoological Park – *till Mon 13* (01962) 777407; **Gosport** Easter Folk Festival at Thorngate Halls – *till Mon 13* (01705) 545294; **Havant** Easter on the Farm at Staunton Country Park – *till Mon 13* (01705) 453405

MAY

1 **Winchester** Folk Festival – *till Sun 3* (01703) 270292

2 **Aldershot** Show at Rushmoor Arena – *till Mon 4* (01264) 771055; **Micheldever** Microlight International Exhibition at Popham Airfield – *till Sun 3* (01256) 397733; – **Southsea** Heavy Horse Parade at Castle Field Arena *till Mon 4* (01705) 834146; **Portsmouth** Lord Mayor's Show (01705) 828112

4 **Micheldever** Aero Jumble, Fly In and Classic Car Rally at Popham Airfield (01256) 397733

9 **Beaulieu** Classic Auto Jumble at the National Motor Museum – *till Sun 10* (01590) 612345

HAMPSHIRE CALENDAR

MAY cont

25 **Havant** Countryside Skills: conservation at Staunton Country Park – *till Sun 31* (01705) 453405

JUNE

6 **Bishop's Waltham** Festival – *till Mon 15* (01489) 893197; **Sherborne St John** Jazz at the Vyne: open air jazz by the lake – (01372) 453401

7 **Hedge End** Teddy Bear Festival at Botleigh Grange Hotel (01305) 269741

13 **Middle Wallop** Air Show – *till Sun 14* (01264) 782086

20 **Wickham** Midsummer Weekend: street entertainers, carnival – *till Sun 21* (01329) 833808

27 **Fordingbridge** Carnival (01425) 657491

JULY

4 **Gosport** Carnival (01705) 522944; **Hedge End** Carnival and Gala Show (01489) 785041; **Southampton** Balloon and Flower Festival – *till Sun 5* (01703) 832755

11 **Horndean** Hampshire Country Fair and Sheepdog Trial at Queen Elizabeth Country Park (01705) 595040

17 **Sherborne St John** Music and Fireworks at the Vyne – *till Sat 18* (01372) 453401

18 **Fordingbridge** Show (01425) 652223

19 **Alton** Agricultural Show at Froyle Park (01420) 563492

24 **Stratfield Saye** Game Fair at Stratfield Saye House – *till Sun 26* (01256) 882882

25 **Damerman** Horticultural Show and Country Fair (01725) 518296

26 **Havant** World Music and Food at Staunton Country Park (01705) 453405

28 **Brockenhurst** New Forest and County Show at New Park – *till Thurs 30* (01590) 622400

AUGUST

1 **Winchester** Show – *till Sun 2* (01962) 866556

7 **Netley Abbey** Hampshire Show at Royal Victoria Country Park – *till Sun 9* (01703) 455157; **Portsmouth and Southsea** Show on Southsea Common: arena events, circus and farm trail – *till Sun 9* (01705) 834146

14 **Mottisfont** Open Air Jazz at the Abbey (01372) 453401

20 **Brockenhurst** New Forest Polo Club Summer Tournament – *till Sun 23* (01425) 473359

21 **Farnborough** Pro-Am Tournament at Southwood Golf Club (01252) 548700

27 **Southsea** Music Festival at Castle Field Arena: jazz, blues, rock – *till Sun 30* (01705) 834553

28 **Portsmouth** Festival of the Sea inc Dockyard Festival at HM Naval Base – *till Mon 31* (01705) 733060

29 **Southsea** International Kite Festival – *till Mon 31* (01705) 834553

30 **Catherington** Country Show: arena events, steam, show jumping, cars – *till Mon 31* (01705) 592520

31 **Emsworth** Show (01243) 378804; **Gosport** Vintage Vehicle Rally (01705) 351624

Hampshire Calendar

SEPTEMBER

5 **Alresford** Agricultural Show at Tichborne Park (01962) 733887; **Beaulieu** Classic Auto Jumble at the National Motor Museum – *till Sun 6* (01590) 612345

12 **Farnborough** International Air Show – *till Sun 13* (0171) 227 1000; **Fordingbridge** Patronal Festival Floral Carpet: around 10,000 flowers, church tower open – *till Sun 13* (01425) 653163; **Havant** Heritage Days: the story of the park at Staunton Country Park – *till Sun 13* (01705) 453405; **Romsey** Show at Broadlands Park (01794) 517521

13 **Southampton** International Boat Show at Western Esplanade – *till Mon 21* (01784) 473377

27 **Hedge End** Teddy Bear Festival at Botleigh Grange Hotel (01305) 269741

OCTOBER

16 **Sway** Wine Weekend – *till Sun 18* (01590) 683402

26 **Titchfield** Carnival (01329) 846166

30 **Havant** Hallowe'en: a theatrical fantasy trail at Staunton Country Park – *till Sat 31* (01705) 453405

31 **Beaulieu** Fireworks at the National Motor Museum (01590) 612345

NOVEMBER

4 **Cosham** Fireworks (01705) 834553

DECEMBER

26 **Crookham Village** Mummers Plays: *from midday* outside the Black Prince, Chequers and Queens Head (01252) 811151

HEREFORD AND WORCESTER

Classic unspoilt English countryside, very restorative for quiet breaks, with appealing small towns, lovely villages, great gardens.

The main appeal here is that there's so much unspoilt countryside, and that settlements and buildings are so unchanging. It's very good for quiet adult holidays. It has an exceptional number of fine gardens, and beautiful villages, with an interesting variety from the classic black and white timbering that is the area's hallmark to the Cotswold stonework around Broadway. For scenery, the Malvern Hills stand out, though as you head west the Herefordshire countryside becomes almost bewitchingly untouched – not at all showy, but the sort of peaceful world that elsewhere tends to survive only in people's memories. Not many tourists or country-cottagers have penetrated that part of the area, even at the height of summer, yet there's an abundance of art galleries and bookshops (Hay-on-Wye, that town-sized bookshop, is an attractive drive just over the Welsh border), and excellent natural cooking using local produce.

Hereford is engaging and relaxing, with plenty of varied attractions – the cathedral has a splendid display of its great treasures. Worcester is a much busier city, but has interesting finds among its more workaday bustle – the Commandery is exceptional. Ledbury, Broadway, Great Malvern and Evesham are all attractive, with several appealing places to visit. Kington, Leominster and Ross-on-Wye are also agreeable to wander around. Eastnor Castle, Berrington Hall at Ashton, Lower Brockhampton House at Brockhampton, Great Witley with its extraordinary ruin and splendid church, Croft Castle, Hanbury Hall (with several other places to visit nearby), Goodrich Castle and the nearby farm park, Dinmore Manor and the buildings museum at Bromsgrove make pleasant outings, and there are several enjoyable cider farms.

There's little in the west to entertain children: the very friendly farm park at Kington stands out. Another enjoyable farm attraction is the pig centre at Linley Green, and many children enjoy the Domestic Fowl Trust near Evesham. Bewdley in the east has quite a lot of family appeal – particularly the safari park and the terminus for Britain's most lively steam railway. Elsewhere there are not many family attractions, apart from farm centres.

The orchards make blossom time (usually April through early May) and harvest time (September) attractive: local tourist board trails make it easy to see the best of this, especially around the River Avon in the Vale of Evesham – rich farmland and orchard country, full of farm shops. Asparagus fanatics have a bonus in May, when there is an abundance of fresh local asparagus. In winter big log fires and generous central heating are the rule – people here really seem to appreciate their warmth.

Where to stay

Abberley SO7667 ELMS Stockton Rd, Abberley, Worcs WR6 6AT (01299) 896666 £110; 16 comfortable rms. Lovely Queen Anne mansion with fine views from the well kept grounds, elegant, restful drawing room with antiques, log fires and flowers; very good food and wines in airy restaurant, and friendly efficient staff.

Brimfield SO5368 ROEBUCK Brimfield, Ludlow S18 4NE (01584) 711230 £55; 3 rms. Civilised dining pub with good food in an elegant, modern, no smoking restaurant and panelled bar; open fires, caring pleasant staff, well kept real ales, and good wine list; cl 25–26 Dec.

Broadway SP0937 BROADWAY The Green, Broadway, Worcs WR12 7AA (01386) 852401 *£80, plus special breaks; 18 well kept rms. Lovely building dating from 1575, once a monastic guesthouse, with galleried and timbered lounge, and a cosy beamed bar; attractively presented food served by attentive staff in airy, comfortable restaurant, and seats outside on the terrace.

Broadway SP0937 COLLIN HOUSE Collin Lane, Broadway, Worcs WR12 7PB (01386) 858354 *£88, plus special breaks; 7 warm, comfortable and quiet rms. Golden-stone 16th-c Cotswold house in 3 acres of gardens, orchard and meadow; restful public rooms, oak beams, log fires, very good English food and carefully chosen wines in candlelit, beamed restaurant (views through mullioned windows on to the garden), and friendly, helpful service; outside swimming pool; cl 23 Dec for 5 days; children over 7 (unless by prior arrangement).

Broadway SP0937 LYGON ARMS High St, Broadway WR12 7DU (01386) 852255 £173.50, plus special breaks; 65 lovely period rms (some more modern, too). Historic, handsome hotel where Oliver Cromwell and King Charles I are said to have stayed, with interesting old beamed rooms, oak panelling, antiques, log fires; fine traditional food in the Great Hall with minstrels' gallery and heraldic frieze, excellent service, and a charming garden; health spa; disabled access.

Bromsberrow Heath SO7333 GROVE HOUSE Bromsberrow Heath, Ledbury HR8 1PE (01531) 650584 *£68; 3 spacious rms, 2 with 4-posters. Wisteria-clad, 15th-c manor house with dark panelling, open fires, beams, fresh flowers and polished antiques; good evening meals at a huge dining table using home-grown produce; 13 acres of grounds, hard tennis court, and neighbour's outdoor swimming pool; cl Christmas/New Year.

Bromsgrove SO9570 GRAFTON MANOR Grafton Lane, Bromsgrove, Worcs B61 7HA (01527) 579007 £105, plus special breaks; 9 individually decorated rms, some with their own open fires. Impressive early 18th-c mansion with an Elizabethan core, in lovely grounds; very good modern British cooking using home-grown produce in the splendid restaurant, comfortable lounge, attentive, friendly service; croquet and riding.

Carey SO5631 COTTAGE OF CONTENT Carey, Hereford HR2 6NG (01432) 840242 £48; 4 rms. Very pretty medieval country cottage in peaceful setting, with flagstoned and timbered bars, a friendly atmosphere, enjoyable food, well kept real ales, a good wine list, and seats on the flower-filled front and back terraces; cl 25 Dec.

Chaddesley Corbett SO8973 BROCKENCOTE HALL Chaddesley Corbett, Kidderminster, Worcs DY10 4PY (01562) 777876 *£120, plus special breaks; 17 individually decorated rms. Grand country-house hotel in 70 acres of grounds with half-timbered dovecot and lake; large, airy and attractively furnished rooms, conservatory lounge with garden views; elegant restaurant with nice, modern French and English cooking, and very good service; no dogs; disabled access.

Evesham SP0344 EVESHAM Coopers Lane, off Waterside, Evesham WR11 6DA (01386) 765566 *£118, plus special breaks; 40 spacious rms. Comfortably modernised and cheerfully run hotel with a warmly friendly, relaxed atmosphere, lots of facilities for children, very good food (especially the lunchtime buffet) from jokey menu, a huge range of spirits, indoor swimming pool, and croquet; cl 25–26 Dec; pets welcome (not in public rooms); partial disabled access.

Eyton SO4861 MARSH Eyton, Leominster, Herefs HR6 0AG (01568) 613952 £120, plus special breaks; 4 individually decorated, comfortable rms with garden views. Carefully restored 14th-c timbered country hotel with a quietly relaxing atmosphere in prettily furnished beamed rooms (fine medieval hall); enjoyable food using lots of home-grown herbs, good wines, and colourful big garden; cl 3 wks Jan; children over 12.

Fownhope SO5834 GREEN MAN Fownhope, Hereford HR1 4PE (01432) 860243 *£54, plus special breaks; 19 rms. Attractive and atmospheric Tudor inn close to the River Wye, with impressive oak-beamed lounge (the residents' lounges are no smoking), log fire, and generously served popular bar food; disabled access.

Frith Common SO6969 HUNTHOUSE FARM Frith Common, Tenbury Wells, Worcs WR15 8JY (01299) 832277 *£36; 3 rms. 16th-c timbered farmhouse on 180-acre arable and sheep farm in lovely countryside; friendly atmosphere, oak beams and open fires, and home-made cake served on arrival in the guest sitting room; cl Dec/Jan; children over 8.

Glewstone SO5622 GLEWSTONE COURT Glewstone, Ross-on-Wye, Herefs HR9 6AW (01989) 770367 *£85, plus special breaks; 7 rms. In lovely countryside and surrounded by 3 acres of grounds, this friendly hotel has open log fires, comfortable furnishings, and a high standard of food using the best local produce; croquet; cl 25–27 Dec; well behaved dogs welcome.

Grafton SO4937 GRAFTON VILLA FARM Grafton, Hereford HR2 8ED (01432) 268689 *£39, plus special breaks; 3 rms. Characterful early 18th-c farmhouse in an acre of grounds, with panoramic views, friendly dogs, open fire in the lounge, and enjoyable hearty breakfasts using their own free-range eggs; cl Nov–Feb; children over 2; disabled access (and self-catering cottage suitable also).

Harvington SP0548 MILL Anchor Lane, Harvington, Evesham, Worcs WR11 5NR (01386) 870688 *£92; 21 comfortable rms overlooking grounds. Handsome Georgian hotel in 8 acres of wooded parkland with 180 metres (600ft) of river, mooring for guests' boats, fishing, hard tennis court, and a heated outdoor swimming pool; carefully refurbished airy lounges with open fires, courteous helpful staff, fine imaginative food using fresh local produce, thoughtful wine list with helpful notes, and good breakfasts; cl 24–28 Dec; children over 10.

Himbleton SO9458 PHEPSON FARM Himbleton, Droitwich, Worcs WR9 7JZ (01905) 391205 *£40; 4 rms. Relaxed and friendly 17th-c farmhouse on 170-acre working farm with beef and sheep; comfortable lounge, good breakfasts in separate dining room; self-catering apartment; cl Christmas/New Year; partial disabled access.

Kemerton SO9437 UPPER COURT Kemerton, Tewkesbury GL20 7HY (01386) 725351 £75, plus special breaks; 6 rms, plus others in cottages. Lovely Georgian Cotswold manor with Domesday watermill, a lake (lots of wildfowl and free fly fishing in season), and dovecot in 15 acres of fine gardens; outdoor heated swimming pool, tennis court, croquet, and boating; relaxed atmosphere and many antiques (the owners run an antiques business and there is always something for sale) in elegant rooms; very good food using home-grown produce, and nice breakfasts; cl Christmas; dogs by arrangement; good disabled access.

Kington SO3057 PENRHOS COURT Kington, Herefs HR5 3LH (01544) 230720

£72.50, plus special breaks; 19 elegant rms. Beautifully restored 13th-c hall in 6 acres of grounds, with fine beams and flagstones; very nice, carefully cooked food using home-grown herbs and vegetables; medieval banquets, too; cl Jan/Feb; disabled access.

Kinnersley SO3449 UPPER NEWTON FARMHOUSE Kinnersley, Hereford HR3 6QB (01544) 327727 *£40; 3 prettily decorated rms with hand-crafted items. 17th-c farmhouse in the middle of a working farm, with log fires, beams, sloping floors, good food (inc vegetarian) using fresh farm vegetables, a colourful garden, and lots of walks; no smoking or pets; self-catering cottage.

Ledbury SO7138 FEATHERS High St, Ledbury HR8 1DS (01531) 635266 £85, plus special breaks; 11 carefully decorated rms making the most of the old beams and timbers. Very striking, mainly 16th-c, black and white hotel with a relaxed atmosphere, log fires, comfortable lounge hall (with country antiques, beams and timbers), particularly enjoyable food and friendly service in Fuggles bar, good wine list, and a fine mix of locals and visitors.

Ledbury SO7138 HOPE END Hope End, Ledbury, Herefs HR8 1JQ (01531) 633613 £123, plus special breaks; 8 rms. A marvellously peaceful place to stay, with a huge organic walled garden where most of the vegetables, fruit and herbs are grown for the lovely English cooking (roaming chickens provide the eggs); a fine Georgian landscaped garden which was important to Elizabeth Barrett Browning (the original house was her home), lots of books, woodburners, and comfortable seating in cosy sitting rooms, lovely breakfasts, and unobtrusive service; cl mid-Dec–early Feb; children over 12.

Leysters SO5663 HILLS FARM Leysters, Leominster, Herefs HR6 9HP (01568) 750205 *£48; 5 attractive rms, some in a converted barn. Traditional stone and brick, 15th-c farmhouse in 120 arable acres; rambling beamed rooms, a pretty sitting room, nice fresh food, fine views, and lots of walks; no smoking; cl end Oct–beg Mar.

Malvern SO7647 COWLEIGH PARK FARM Cowleigh Rd, Malvern WR13 5HJ (01684) 566750 *£46, plus special breaks; 3 rms. Carefully restored and furnished black and white timbered 13th-c farmhouse in its own grounds, surrounded by lovely countryside; with good breakfasts and light suppers or full evening meals (prior booking); self-catering also; cl Christmas/New Year; no children.

Malvern Wells SO7845 COTTAGE IN THE WOOD Holywell Rd, Malvern Wells, Worcs WR14 4LG (01684) 575859 £89, plus special breaks; 20 compact but pretty rms, some in separate nearby cottages. Family-run Georgian dower house with quite splendid views across the Severn Valley (marvellous walks from the grounds), antiques, log fires, comfortable seats and magazines in public rooms; modern English cooking and an extensive wine list in the attractive, no smoking restaurant.

Ombersley SO8463 CROWN & SANDYS ARMS Ombersley, Droitwich, Worcs WR9 0EW (01905) 620252 £45; 7 no smoking rms, most with own bthrm. Civilised and pretty Dutch-gabled inn with good views from the garden, a comfortable lounge bar with beams, timbers, log fires and maybe daily newspapers, and good popular food inc lots of fish; no dogs; cl 24–30 Dec.

Ross-on-Wye SO5923 BROOKFIELD HOUSE Ledbury Rd, Ross-on-Wye HR9 7AT (01989) 562188 £37; 8 rms, some with own bthrm. Part Queen Anne and part Georgian house with a sunny terrace and little garden with a view over the town; very friendly, welcoming owners, log fire in the lounge, and super breakfasts in big airy breakfast room; pets allowed.

Ruckhall Common SO4539 ANCIENT CAMP Ruckhall Common, Hereford HR2 9QX (01981) 250449 £62; 5 rms, some with river views. Smart country inn in pleasantly remote spot with good views of the River Wye and beyond from the terrace; beamed and flagstoned bar, good bar and restaurant food (not pm Sun or Mon); no children; disabled access.

Ullingswick SO5950 STEPPES Ullingswick, Hereford HR1 3JG (01432)

820424 *£80, plus special breaks; 6 spacious, pretty rms in barn and restored stone stable. Attractive 17th-c country-house hotel with heavy beams, flagstones, and inglenook fireplaces in the cellar bar, lounge and dining room, very good food, fine breakfasts, and hospitable owners; cl 2 wks before Christmas and Jan; children over 10.

Upton Snodsbury SO9454 COVENTRY ARMS Upton Snodsbury, Worcester WR7 4NN (01905) 381282 £45; 3 rms. Friendly, neatly kept inn with a cosy lounge bar, log fires and beams, and enjoyable food in the attractive dining room.

Upton Snodsbury SO9454 UPTON HOUSE Upton Snodsbury, Worcester WR7 4NR (01905) 381226 *£68; 2 well equipped, pretty rms. Carefully run, 12th-c village manor house with beams and log fires, comfortable sitting room, good food in unlicensed dining room, new conservatory, helpful owners, nice flower-filled garden, and outdoor heated swimming pool; cl Christmas/Easter; no children; kennel facilities for dogs.

Weobley SO4052 OLDE SALUTATION Market Pitch, Weobley, Hereford HR4 8SJ (01544) 318443 *£60; 4 rms. Friendly, 500-year-old inn looking down on attractive, half-timbered village; good bar and elaborate restaurant food, a quiet lounge with standing timbers and log fires, and small public bar; also self-catering cottage; children in cottage only.

Wickhamford SP0641 WICKHAMFORD MANOR Wickhamford, Evesham, Worcs WR11 6SA (01386) 830296 £50; 3 rms. Striking, timbered manor, first mentioned in the Domesday book and set in 20 acres of grounds with a 12th-c dovecot and lake; big log fire in the beamed drawing room, good breakfasts in the flagstone kitchen, dinner by arrangement, and a really warm welcome from the friendly owners; tennis and fishing; self-catering cottage.

Winforton SO2947 WINFORTON COURT Winforton, Herefs HR3 6EA (01544) 328498 £42; 3 rms, 1 with shared bthrm. In an attractive village of half-timbered buildings, this 16th-c house is run by a warmly friendly owner and has a pretty garden, an open fire in the small library, a comfortable drawing room, a choice of hearty breakfasts in former court room with huge stone fireplace and teacup collection, and lots of interesting bygones; cl Christmas week; children over 10.

Woolhope SO6136 BUTCHERS ARMS Woolhope, Hereford HR1 4RF (01432) 860281 £39; 3 neat, attractive rms with fruit and chocolates (shared bthrm). Family-run, 14th-c timbered building with low oak beams and log fires in bars, friendly staff, lots of flowers, and decent food (good breakfasts); lovely surrounding walks.

To see and do

★ **Hereford** SO5140 grew as a regional market centre, and still has its busy livestock and general market every Weds. For the rest of the week it feels very quiet-paced and old-fashioned, its streets (some pedestrianised now) lined with handsome Georgian and other buildings (Church St is almost wholly medieval). The many antique shops are by no means over-priced. Guided walks leave the tourist information centre every day from May–mid-Sept at 10.30am (2.30pm Sun). Wye-side walks give a pleasing view of the city, its spires and towers. Saxtys, the Green Dragon Hotel and Imperial Hotel are all useful for lunch.

† CATHEDRAL Nicely placed on the bank of the Wye, this largely Norman building has a lovely 13th- and 15th-c chapel, as well as the country's biggest chained library (the second biggest is at All Saints church, at the opposite end of the main st), and the famous Mappa Mundi, the largest surviving 13th-c world map. There's a splendid new interpretative exhibition, with some computer displays; the map itself is shown in a

specially dimmed room to preserve it. Meals, snacks, shop, disabled access; some parts cl Sun, and occasional lunchtimes, Good Fri, 25 Dec; (01432) 359880; cathedral free, exhibition £4. Guided tours at 11am, 1pm and 2.30pm (£1.50).

🕭 🐷 CIDER MUSEUM (Pomona Pl) Cider-making through the ages, with huge 17th-c French press, original cellars, and a working cider-brandy distillery – the first licensed for over 250 years. Shop, limited disabled access; in winter cl am and all day Sun, 25–26 Dec and 1 Jan; (01432) 354207; £2.20. The enormous modern BULMER'S CIDER MILL (Plough Lane) has tours and tastings; shop, cl wknds, bank hols, and mid-Dec–Feb, tours (10.30am, 2.30pm, 7pm) by appointment; (01432) 352000; *£2.95.

🏮 THE OLD HOUSE (High Town) Glorious Jacobean house with period furnishings and paintings. Shop, limited disabled access; opening times are under review so best to check

first; (01432) 364598; *£1.10.
🕭 CHURCHILL HOUSE MUSEUM (Venns Lane, northern outskirts) Regency house in fine grounds, with good local history, room settings, and 18th- and 19th-c furniture, costumes and paintings. Shop, some disabled access; cl am, all day Mon exc bank hols, and winter Suns; (01432) 267409; £1.10. You can get a joint ticket with the Old House (see above) for £1.75.

🕭 WATERWORKS MUSEUM (Broomy Hill) Restored Victorian pumping station, with giant steam-pumping engines, and smaller handpumps; you can try working some. Snacks, shop, disabled access; open pm last Sun of month, Apr–Sept, plus bank hols and second Sun in July, Aug and Sept; (01432) 361147; *£2.

🕭 🖼 CITY MUSEUM AND ART GALLERY (Broad St) Natural history and archaeology, interesting bee-keeping display, and changing art exhibitions. Shop, disabled access; cl Mon and winter Suns; (01432) 364691; free.

Worcester SO8555 Though it's a busy commercial centre, this has some splendid medieval buildings dotted about, with lots of half-timbered houses, particularly around Friar St and New St. Plenty of shops, inc some nice specialist ones and cafés in Hopmarket Yard, a former coaching inn; the King Charles House (New St) serves good meals, the Farriers Arms (Fish St, nr cathedral) has good snacks, and the Little Sauce Factory (London Rd) is an entertaining pub. You can tour the handsome Georgian Guildhall (not Sun).

🕭 🏮 ! THE COMMANDERY 🎴 (Sidbury) The only museum in the country wholly devoted to the English Civil War, in a striking, timber-framed 15th-c building. Lots of weaponry, spectacular audio-visual shows and life-size talking figures re-creating events from the war. Unusual special events and military displays, and brass-rubbing centre. Snacks, shop, limited disabled access; cl am Sun, 25–26 Dec, 1 Jan; (01905) 355071; £3.40.

🐷 🕭 MUSEUM OF WORCESTER PORCELAIN (Severn St) Reopening in spring after refurbishment, the country's oldest continuous producer of porcelain, with wkdy factory tours (no children under 11), and rare

18th-c porcelain in the excellent museum. Meals, snacks, shop, disabled access to museum only; best to check for exact date of reopening, then cl Sun; (01905) 23221; tour £3.50, museum and tour £4.95. The Potters Wheel opposite has decent food.

✝ CATHEDRAL Founded on the site of a Saxon monastery, in a calm and peaceful setting overlooking the river. It took from 1084 to 1375 to build, and has an attractive 14th-c tower, Norman crypt, and the tombs of Prince Arthur and King John, the latter topped by the oldest Royal effigy in the country. Lots of Victorian stained glass, and some monastic buildings. Guided tours in summer. Snacks, shop, some disabled access; £2 suggested donation.

🏠🔥 GREYFRIARS (Friar St) Beautiful and carefully restored medieval timber-framed town house (still lived in), with a delightful walled garden. Open pm Weds, Thurs and bank hols, Easter–Oct; (01905) 23571; £2.20; NT. Down the same street a 15th-c Tudor House is a MUSEUM OF LOCAL LIFE. Shop, some disabled access; cl Thurs, Sun (exc pm school hols); (01905) 722349; £1.50.

🔥🖼 CITY MUSEUM AND ART GALLERY (Foregate St) Local and natural history, with River Severn gallery and several children's activities. Meals, snacks, shop, disabled access; cl Thurs, Sun, 25–26 Dec, 1 Jan, Good Fri; (01905) 25371; free.

🐦 WORCESTER WOODS COUNTRY PARK (just E off the A442) 140 acres of ancient woodland on the edge of the city; not as interesting as woodlands elsewhere, but useful for strolling if you don't want to leave the city. Snacks, shop, disabled access; cl 25–26 Dec, 1 Jan; (01905) 766492; free.

🐄🔥🎵 BENNETTS FARM PARK (Lower Wick) Working dairy farm with animals, wknd milking parlour and vintage machinery museum in pretty 16th-c farm buildings. Walks and fishing in season. Snacks (inc their own ice-cream), shop, disabled access; cl Oct–Mar; (01905) 748345; *£3.

Days Out

Cider city
Hereford Cathedral; lunch at Saxty's (Central Sq), the Green Dragon Hotel (Broad St), or the Crown & Anchor at Lugwardine (off the A438 just E); Cider Museum, Waterworks Museum, Old House.

Porcelain heritage
Worcester Cathedral and museums; lunch at Browns (Quay St) or King Charles House (New St) – or the Bear & Ragged Staff, Bransford; Elgar's Birthplace, Lower Broadheath; Wichenford dovecot.

The great train ride
Trip on the Severn Valley Railway, Bewdley; lunch at the Little Pack Horse there; stroll around Bewdley; Witley Court.

Black and white villages
Weobley, Pembridge and Eardisland villages; lunch at the Riverside, Aymestrey; Croft Castle; walk through Leinthall Common to Croft Ambrey.

Church masterpieces around the Golden Valley
Kilpeck church; Abbey Dore; lunch at the Carpenters Arms, Walterstone; Clodock church; drive via Longtown (castle ruin) to Black Hill picnic site for walk on to Black Hill.

Elgar's beloved landscapes
Walk along Malvern Hills ridge and on to Herefordshire Beacon; Ledbury – lunch at Feathers; Eastnor Castle (limited opening).

Wye cornucopia
Ross-on-Wye; Hoarwithy church; lunch at the Cottage of Content, Carey; Brockhampton church; Weston's cider farm, Much Marcle; Goodrich Castle.

High in the sky
Clent Hills country park; lunch at the Holly Bush, Clent; West Hagley falconry centre.

Other things to see and do

**HEREFORD AND WORCESTER FAMILY
ATTRACTION OF THE YEAR**

🐖 ! **Kington** SO3055 SMALL BREEDS FARM PARK ▦ (Kingswood – off
A4111 S) Until recently called Oaklands Small Breeds Farm, this friendly
little farm will never be able to compete with the bigger wildlife parks or
zoos (it covers only 4 acres), but what it lacks in size and elaborate visitor
facilities it more than makes up for in its genuine enthusiasm and relaxed
atmosphere. Many of the animals – mostly miniature and rare or unusual
breeds – can be fed by hand, and there are plenty of rabbits and guinea pigs
to pet and fuss. The views and setting are a bonus, and the extensive
collections of owls and waterfowl are set in an attractively landscaped
garden. It's all very informal, and quite a few of the creatures have
distinctive characteristics and personalities. A particular favourite is
Dorrie the miniature Dexter cow, who even on tiptoe is just 81cm (32in)
high; she now has a strapping daughter, Delores. Numpy the giant Milky
Eagle owl likes to be stroked by visitors, while Flo-Jo the goose (easy to
spot by her luminous green beak) can take quite a fancy to male visitors
over 50. There are also pigs, goats, tortoises, poultry and pheasants. You
won't need to spend much of the day here, but it's the kind of place that
people like to come back to (they often spot parents returning without the
children). Father Christmas is usually here in December. Snacks, shop,
disabled access; cl Nov and Jan–Easter; (01544) 231109; £3 (£1.50
children).

✝ 🐝 ❋ **Abbey Dore** SO3830
Primarily the impressive surviving
part of a once-huge 12th/13th-c
Cistercian abbey church, with Early
English features and an awesome
stone altar. ABBEY DORE COURT
GARDEN Attractive riverside lawns
and gardens, with good views across
to the ruins. Meals and snacks (in
17th-c stables), unusual plant sales
and gift shop, teddy bear collection,
disabled access; cl Weds, and
Nov–Feb (though shop open up to
Christmas); (01981) 240419; *£2.
🏠 🐝 **Ashton** SO5164 BERRINGTON
HALL (A49) Elegant late 18th-c neo-
classical house, very elaborate inside,
with beautiful décor and furnishings
(mostly French), charming nursery,
and interesting examples of
'downstairs' life in the Georgian dairy
and laundry. The grounds were
landscaped by Capability Brown –
and in fact the house was built by his
son-in-law. Pleasant circular walk
through the park (July–Oct only).
Meals, tearoom, shop, disabled
access; open pm Fri–Sun and bank
hols Apr–Oct, plus pm Weds and
Thurs May–Sept, and daily July and

Aug; (01568) 615721; *£4, *£1.80
garden only; NT. The Stockton Cross
Inn (on the A4112 NE of Leominster)
is good.
🖋 **Beckford** SO9735 SILK SHOP Prints,
scarves and ties; processes
demonstrated, shop with good-value
seconds, café. The Gardeners Arms in
the attractive nearby village of
Alderton has nice food.
★ 🐎 🍺 🐖 ☺ **Bewdley** SO7875
Attractive small town, with riverside
walks and interesting side streets. The
Little Pack Horse (old High St) is full
of character. SEVERN VALLEY RAILWAY
Splendid steamtrain trips through the
Wyre Forest and the Severn Valley
between Kidderminster and
Bridgnorth in Shrops, with lots going
on – this railway is run with great
verve. The station has a fine model
railway. Meals, snacks, shop; trains
daily May–Sept and most other
wknds – (0800) 600900 for
timetable; fares from £4.50, £9.90 for
full trip. An 18th-c row of butchers'
shops has a local history MUSEUM (cl
Nov–Easter; *£2). WEST MIDLANDS
SAFARI AND LEISURE PARK (Spring
Grove, just E on the A456) Very

much a full day out, with the main attraction the drive-round animal reserves, home to over 40 species of rare and exotic animals. Some animals may come right up to your car, but others will watch nonchalantly from a distance; happily, you can go round as often as you like, so if you don't see what you want it's easy to give it another go later on. Admission also covers the sea lion show, reptile house, and pets corner, but you'll have to pay extra for the leisure park, which has around 30 rides from gentle carousels to a roller-coaster and popular log flume. The undercover Dome shows cartoons throughout the day. Meals, snacks, shop, disabled access; cl Nov–Mar; (01299) 404604; animals £4.50, leisure park £5 for limitless ride wristband.

🐄 ⚡ **Bishops Frome** SO6648 HOP POCKET HOP FARM Traditional hop farm, its hundred acres a hive of activity in the harvest season. Tours of kilns by arrangement, pretty gardens, and big craft shop – their hop pillows for poor sleepers are particularly popular. Snacks, disabled access; cl am Sun, Mon (exc bank hols), and Tues–Thurs Jan and Feb; (01531) 640323. The Green Dragon is a nice pub.

🎱 ⚑ **Blakeshall** SO8381 KINGSFORD COUNTRY PARK 200-acre park with pine forests, birch groves and plenty of walks and trails (inc one for the disabled). Very nice unspoilt feel – even the signposts and picnic tables are made at the saw mill here.

⚑ ✠ ❊ **Bodenham** SO5450 QUEENSWOOD COUNTRY PARK AND ARBORETUM 170 acres of woodland and arboretum with over 500 tree varieties; also wildlife displays and good views. Meals, snacks, shop and information centre, disabled access; shop and café cl 25–26 Dec; (01568) 797052; free, though car park 50p. The Three Crowns between Ullingswick and unspoilt Little Cowarne has very good food.

★ ✝ 🏠 **Bretforton** SP0943 One of the prettiest black and white thatched villages, with an interesting church and a splendid medieval pub, the Fleece, left to the National Trust after being in the same family for several centuries; a proper pub, it's kept just as it was, with a magnificent collection of Jacobean oak furniture and pewter.

★ ☕ 🏠 ❊ 🐄 ! **Broadway** SP0937 An exceptionally harmonious, stone-built Cotswold village, with the golden stone and uneven stone-tiled roofs perfectly blending the grand houses and the humbler cottages together, in a long, grass-lined main street. It's decidedly on the coach-tour trail, very busy indeed in summer. Fine things for sale in extraordinarily expensive antique shops, and a very grand old inn, the Lygon Arms, with a useful side wine bar. Our other **Where to stay** recommendations do good bar lunches; a good escape from the tourists is the Crown & Trumpet in Church St, an archetypal Cotswold pub, and the Buckland Manor does decent teas. BROADWAY TEDDY BEAR MUSEUM (High St) Recently restocked collection of old bears and toys. Shop; cl 25 Dec; (01386) 858323; £1.50. BROADWAY TOWER Above the village, this late 18th-c folly has marvellous views that on a clear day – with the help of the telescope – are said to stretch over 12 counties. There are some straightforward exhibitions on sheep and wool farming (and regular visitor William Morris), while the country park around it has farm animals and nature trails. Meals, snacks, shops, some disabled access; cl Nov–Mar; (01386) 852390; £3. Not everyone finds this good value, and you do get similar views from the public footpath through the park.

🎱 ❊ 🖼 **Brobury** SO3444 BROBURY HOUSE GALLERY 8 acres of semi-formal gardens with fine views; also watercolours and prints for sale. Disabled access (but no facilities); cl Sun, 25 Dec, 1 Jan; (01981) 500595; gardens £2, gallery free. They do B & B in the smart Victorian house, with fishing permits available. The Portway nr Monnington on Wye is a useful food stop.

🏠 ✝ 🎱 **Brockhampton** SO6955 LOWER BROCKHAMPTON Idyllic timber-

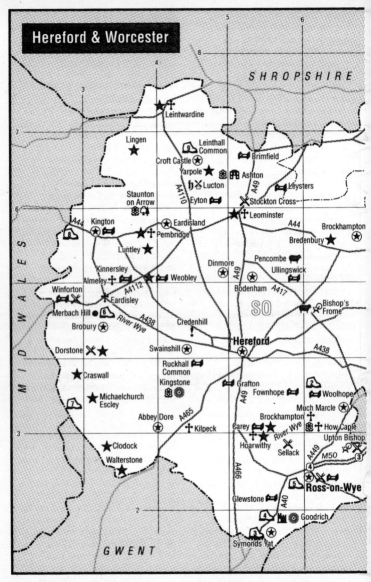

Hereford & Worcester

SHROPSHIRE

Leintwardine

Lingen

Leinthall Common

Brimfield

Croft Castle

Yarpole

Ashton

Leysters

Staunton on Arrow

Lucton

Eyton

Stockton Cross

Kington

Eardisland

Leominster

Brockhampton

Pembridge

Bredenbury

Luntley

Dinmore

Pencombe

Ullingswick

Kinnersley

Almeley

Weobley

Bodenham

Winforton

Eardisley

Bishop's Frome

Merbach Hill

River Wye

Brobury

Credenhill

Hereford

Dorstone

Swainshill

Craswall

Ruckhall Common

Kingstone

Grafton

Fownhope

Woolhope

Michaelchurch Escley

Much Marcle

Abbey Dore

Brockhampton

How Caple

Kilpeck

Carey

Upton Bishop

Hoarwithy

River Wye

Clodock

Sellack

M50

Walterstone

Ross-on-Wye

Glewstone

Goodrich

GWENT

Symonds Yat

framed and moated 14th-c manor house in attractive secluded countryside. Particularly interesting 15th-c gatehouse, and the ruins of a 12th-c chapel. Shop, some disabled access; cl Mon exc bank hols, Tues, and Nov–Mar; (01885) 488099; £1.60; NT. The Trust also owns the adjacent 1,700 acre BROCKHAMPTON ESTATE, with splendid views from its park and woodlands. The Talbot at Knightwick is a nice place for lunch.

Bromsgrove SO9468
AVONCROFT MUSEUM OF HISTORIC BUILDINGS (Stoke Prior; B4091 S) Threatened buildings of historical interest are carefully re-erected and restored here – anything from a 14th-c

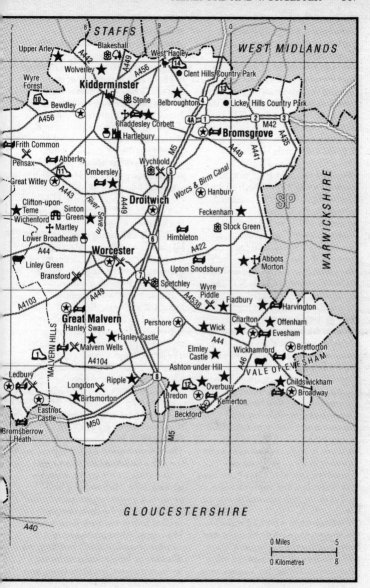

monastic roof through an 18th-c
dovecot and ice-house to a 1946
prefab. An interesting recent addition
is the National Collection of
Telephone Kiosks. Demonstrations
of traditional building techniques,
maybe wknd miniature train rides.
Meals, snacks, shop, disabled access;
cl Mon (exc Jul–Aug and bank hols),

Fri in Mar and Nov, all Dec–Feb;
(01527) 831363; £3.95, slightly less
out of season. The Country Girl here
does generous food and is handy for
walks on Dodderhill Common; the
parish council have mapped out other
walks too. Bromsgrove proper has a
thoroughly traditional local history
MUSEUM (cl Sun; £1.20) and DAUB AND

WATTLE'S POTTERY, a largely unchanged pottery building with displays and shop (cl Sun, Mon).

! **Credenhill** SO4544 ESCARGOT ANGLAIS (A480) Part of the National Snail Farming Centre, with snail trails showing various species (even hairy ones) and exhibitions. Shop, cl Tues, Weds, and winter wknds; (01432) 760218; *£2. The Bell at Tillington does more orthodox food.

Croft Castle SO4764 CROFT CASTLE The walls and turrets date from the 14th and 15th c, but the inside is mostly 18th-c, with an interesting staircase and plastered ceilings. Attractive parklands with an avenue of 350-year-old chestnuts, and footpath to CROFT AMBREY, an Iron Age fort. Shop, disabled access; open pm Weds–Sun and bank hols May–Sept, plus wknds Apr and Oct; (01568) 780246; *£3.20; NT. The picturesque Bell at Yarpole is handy for lunch.

Dinmore SO4850 DINMORE MANOR Hilltop manor house with spectacular views of surrounding countryside. Grand hall, good stained-glass collection, and farm animals in the grounds. Perhaps most interesting is the ancient chapel, incongruously placed between a rock garden and venerable yew tree. Summer teas, plant centre, disabled access; (01432) 830322; *£2.50. Nearby Green Acres has organically grown PICK-YOUR-OWN fruit and vegetables; DINMORE FRUIT FARM has a very wide choice of apple varieties, as well as more conventional PICK-YOUR-OWN.

! **Droitwich** SO9063 Famous as a spa town; you don't drink the water here, you float in it. The BRINE BATHS on St Andrews Rd are just the thing after an exhausting day's sightseeing; (01905) 794894 to book; £5.50. Interesting buildings include the timbered houses around the High St and the Sacred Heart CHURCH with its fine stained-glass mosaics. The HERITAGE CENTRE (Victoria Sq) has an unusual exhibition on radios and broadcasting. Shop, disabled access; cl Sun; (01905) 774312; free. The Firs out at Dunhampstead (just SE) is a pleasant dining pub.

★ **Eardisland** SO4258 is a gorgeous riverside black and white village; the spectacularly wonky weather vane on one ivy-clad dovecot has been at that angle for years. BURTON COURT (just outside on the A44) is an interesting old house with 14th-c great hall, and collections of ship models, costumes and natural history specimens. Also a working model fairground, and PICK-YOUR-OWN berries. Teas, shops, disabled access; open pm Weds, Thurs, wknds and bank hols May–mid-Sept, or evenings by arrangement; (01544) 388231; *£2.50. The friendly Cross Inn has decent food.

Eastnor Castle SO7336 (just E of Ledbury) Splendid neo-Gothic castle, especially dramatic in autumn, when the virginia creeper that all but envelops the stirring battlements turns a fierce red. Designed by Pugin, the richly decorated rooms are breathtaking, with fine collections of armour, tapestries, furniture and paintings. The attractive grounds have an arboretum and 300-acre deer park. Meals, snacks, shop; open pm Sun Easter–early Oct, plus bank hols, and wkdys in July and Aug; (01531) 633160; *£4. Eastnor village's thatched Post Office is lovely.

Evesham SP0344 The pedestrianised market square has some fine buildings around it inc a 12th-c ABBEY GATEWAY; the church's striking 16th-c bell tower is well preserved, and some altogether more ruined remnants in the town park beyond lead to riverside meadows. The tourist information centre is in another attractive abbey building, the Almonry, a Tudor timbered house with craft shows, small museum, and nice gardens. The Royal Oak (Vine St) is useful for lunch, and the Green Dragon (Oat St) visibly brews its own ales. TWYFORD COUNTRY CENTRE (just N on the A435) Busy little complex, with farm and craft shops, adventure playground, conservatory, and wildlife and falconry centre. They can arrange coarse fishing. Meals, snacks, shop, disabled access; cl 25–26 Dec, 1

Jan; (01386) 446108; free exc falconry and wildlife, £2.50. DOMESTIC FOWL TRUST (Honeybourne, E of Evesham) Rare breeds of hens, ducks, geese and turkeys, plus young chicks for children to handle (all year), and adventure playground. You'll need wellies on wet days. Summer snacks, shop, limited disabled access; cl Fri, 25–26 Dec; (01386) 833083; £2.50. In April or early May the orchard drive through Harvington, the Lenches, Badgers Hill, Fladbury Cross, Wood Norton and Chadbury is pretty.

🏰 ✳ **Goodrich** SO5719 GOODRICH CASTLE Proper-looking 12th-c castle built using the same red sandstone rock it stands on, so that it seems almost to grow out of the ground. Still plenty to see, with towers, passageways, dungeon and marvellous views of the surrounding countryside. Snacks, shop; cl 1–2pm, 24–26 Dec; (01600) 890538; £2.30. The Crown off the B4228 at Howle Hill is the nearest recommended place for lunch (not Mon).

★ ✳ † 🍺 🐾 ✳ **Great Malvern** SO7746 Elegant hillside spa town with easy access to inspiring hill scenery; the B4232 from Upper Colwall to Wynds Point has some of the best high views, while the B4218 on the E side gives several good views of the hills themselves. The beautifully symmetrical PRIORY has a notable collection of medieval wall tiles. Just along the road, the splendid former gateway of a Benedictine monastery houses a MUSEUM, with displays on Malvern spring water, and the life of Sir Edward Elgar. Shop; cl Weds in term-time, all Nov–Easter; (01684) 567811; *£1. A good few craft workshops include musical instrument-makers such as Hibernian Violins, Players Ave; cl lunch and wknds. The Foley Arms and Mount Pleasant Hotel have decent food and good views. On the E side of the hills BARNARDS GREEN HOUSE SO7945 has an attractive garden with a wide range of gardening ideas around a gracious half-timbered 17th-c house (not open). The owner is an authority on

dried flowers. Teas, plant sales, disabled access; open pm Thurs Apr–Sept, a couple of Suns in May and Aug, and other times by appointment; (01684) 574446; *£2. The nearby Bluebell is useful for lunch. On the W side (Walwyn Rd, Colwall), PICTON GARDEN at Old Court Nurseries has a nicely laid out cottagey collection of hardy plants and shrubs, best in summer, with a national collection of asters (late summer/autumn) and rock garden. Plant sales, disabled access; cl 1–2.15pm, all day Mon and Tues, and Nov–Mar; (01684) 540416); *£2. The Chase Inn at Upper Wyche is quite handy for lunch.

🏠 🏰 † ✳ **Great Witley** SO7664 WITLEY COURT Astonishing ruined shell of Jacobean house transformed into an Italianate palace by the Earl of Dudley, and partly destroyed by fire in 1937. It's an elaborate place, with ceiling paintings, enormous Perseus fountain, and balustraded garden – very atmospheric to wander through. Overlooking the lake beside it, a gloriously baroque church is no less dramatic, and one of the county's great finds; it has splendid paintings and stained glass around the largely papier-mâché interior. Snacks, shop, some disabled access; cl 1–2pm winter and all winter Mons and Tues, 25–26 Dec; (01299) 896636; £2.75. The Hundred House is handy for lunch. Slightly E at Sankyns Green (towards Shrawley), EASTGROVE COTTAGE GARDEN has interesting and unusual hardy and tender perennial plants in a cottage-garden setting by ancient timbered house (not open). Good plants for sale, disabled access; open pm Thurs–Mon Apr–July, then pm Thurs–Sat Sept–mid-Oct; (01299) 896389; *£2.

🏠 ✳ † ✳ 🐾 **Hanbury** SO9664 HANBURY HALL 18th-c country house with outstanding painted ceilings and staircase, fine porcelain, and contemporary ice-house and orangery in grounds. The formal gardens are being carefully restored. You can book rooms in the Lodge on the edge of the estate. Snacks, shop, some disabled access; open pm

Sun–Weds Apr–Oct; (01527) 821214; *£4.10, garden only ticket available; NT. The CHURCH, high on a hill, has superb views over the countryside. JINNEY RING CRAFT CENTRE (B4091 Droitwich Rd) Various craft workshops in beautiful timbered barns, from pottery to violin-making; some wknd courses. Meals, snacks, shop, some disabled access; cl Mon exc bank hols, Christmas; (01527) 821272; free. The Gate Hangs Well (Woodgate) has a good carvery.

🐾 ⛴ Hartlebury SO8371 HARTLEBURY CASTLE has been the official residence of the Bishops of Worcester since 850. A wing of it now houses the COUNTY MUSEUM; cl am Fri and Sun, all day Sat, and Jan–Feb; (01299) 250416; £1.90. The elegant STATE ROOMS are usually open Apr–Oct, pm Weds, bank hols and first Sun of month, possibly daily in Aug; 75p.

🏵 ✝ How Caple SO6030 HOW CAPLE COURT 11 acres of peaceful formal and woodland Edwardian gardens overlooking the river, with old roses and unusual herbaceous plants for sale. Snacks; cl Sun Nov–Mar; (01989) 740626; £2.50. Also an interesting medieval church and fabrics shop. The Green Man at Fownhope is popular for food.

★ ✝ 🏵 Kemerton SO9437 An attractively leafy village below Bredon Hill, with pretty stone-built houses among the trees. One of the most attractive is THE PRIORY, its big garden richly planted with colourful borders; also cool streamside plantings, handsome trees and shrubs. Plant sales; open pm Thurs May–Sept plus half a dozen Suns (when they do teas); (01386) 725258; *£2. The Crown is useful for lunch.

🚂 Kidderminster SO8376 Not an alluring place to visit, but a terminus of the excellent Severn Valley steam railway (see Bewdley entry, p.314), with a cheerful replica of Edwardian station refreshment rooms.

🏵 ❄ Kingstone SO4235 KINGSTONE COTTAGES (off the A40) Charming, exuberant cottage garden, not to be missed at midsummer for its profusion of old-fashioned pinks and border carnations. Also fine views, and tucked-away little grotto – looking out it seems as though you're waist-high in water. Unusual plants for sale; open wkdys early May–late Jun, or by appointment; (01989) 565267; £1. Not too far from the Ancient Camp Inn at Ruckhall, and worth the drive.

★ 🏵 🦋 🐗 Kington SO2956 Attractive border town by the River Arrow, well placed for walks (for example up the Hergest Ridge). The Queen's Head has good-value food and brews its own ales. HERGEST CROFT GARDENS (just W, off the A44) are the splendid result of inspired work by several generations of keen gardeners; some of the centenarian rhododendrons in the woods are of almost incredible size. Famous kitchen garden with colourful flowerbeds, and the national collections of birches and maples. Snacks, shop, some disabled access; cl am, and all Nov–Easter; (01544) 230160; £2.50. For the SMALL BREEDS FARM PARK see separate Family Panel on p.314. NE of the town at Bradnor Hill, the Kington Golf Club (set in 240 acres of NT-owned land) is the highest in the country, and has good views.

★ 🏠 ✝ 🎵 🐾 Ledbury SO7138 The spaciously leisured high street has some fine buildings: the old MARKET HOUSE, the FEATHERS HOTEL and LEDBURY PARK HOUSE are famous for their well balanced 15th and 16th-c timbering, and there are plenty of similar structures. From the Market House an exceptional alley of ancient jettied buildings leads to the partly Norman church of ST MICHAEL AND ALL ANGELS, with an unusual spire tower detached from the main building, and its carillon ringing out a well known hymn every third hour. The OLD GRAMMAR SCHOOL along here has been restored as a heritage centre (cl Nov–Easter). The council offices must be the only ones in the country decorated with medieval wall-paintings; you can see these free any wkdy between 11am and 2pm, or book a guided tour on (01531) 63545; *£1. There are craft workshops, antique shops, the national Playmobile specialist and a decent bookshop, and the Feathers has good food. The road N through Wellington Heath towards Mathon has some good views.

★ † Leominster SO4959 An attractive centre, the medieval streets almost lined with black and white timbered houses. The red PRIORY CHURCH still has many of its original Norman features, and the handsome old Talbot has decent food.

🐖 Linley Green SO7257 PIG PEN (Hareley Farm) Fun working pig farm, with lots of piglets to handle (lambs too in early spring), tours of pens and yards, play area, and woodland nature trails. Bring wellies when it's muddy. Snacks, shop, disabled access; open pm daily mid-Apr–mid-Oct; (01886) 884362; £2.50.

♉ Lower Broadheath SO8157 ELGAR'S BIRTHPLACE MUSEUM (Crown East Lane) Modest cottage where the composer was born in 1857; now, as he wanted, a museum of his life and work, with displays of musical scores and letters, and the desk where he did his writing. Shop, disabled access to ground floor; cl am winter, all day Weds, and mid-Jan–mid-Feb; (01905) 333224; *£3. You can pick up routes and information here about the Elgar Trail around the area, and the Bear & Ragged Staff over at Bransford is a nice place for lunch.

✗ ♭ Lucton SO4464 MORTIMERS CROSS MILL AND BATTLE CENTRE Charming watermill on banks of River Ludd, still in working order, with exhibition on the decisive Wars of the Roses battle fought here in 1461. Open pm Thurs, Sun and bank hols Apr–Sept; (01568) 708820; *£1.50. The Riverside at Aymestrey has decent food.

🐖 † 🏚 Much Marcle SO6633 WESTON'S CIDER FARM Still alongside the family house, this has an engaging combination of modern equipment and old-fashioned atmosphere. Enthusiastic guided tours, liberal tastings, interesting ciders and perries. Restaurant opening shortly, shop, tours by appointment; cl Sun;

(01531) 660233; *£3. The nearby Slip has good dishes of the day and outstanding gardens; the memorial monuments in the village church are unrivalled in the area. Just opposite, HELLEN'S is an unspoilt manor house dating back to the 13th c; you can see the portrait of Catherine of Braganza that convinced Charles II to marry her. Teas; open pm Sat, Sun, Weds and bank hols Easter–Sept; (01531) 660668; £3.50.

🐖 Pencombe SO5951 SHORTWOOD DAIRY FARM Working farm ideal for children, with hands-on afternoon activities like milking Daisy or feeding the pigs and calves. Good play area. Snacks, shop; cl Sun, and Oct–Easter, though open Oct half-term for cider-making; (01885) 400205; £2.75. The Three Crowns at Ullingswick has very good food.

★ † ! Pershore SO9445 Very much a working town, the 'capital' of the fruit- and vegetable-growing area around it. It's a pleasant place, largely Georgian, with an impressive ABBEY and walks by the River Avon. The Brandy Cask (Bridge St) has good-value food and brews its own beer. Heading out along the A4104 SW, when you've passed the Oak in Defford keep your eyes skinned for a group of cottages on your right; the last, surrounded by farm animals and without an inn sign, is the MONKEY HOUSE SO9143, a uniquely old-fashioned cider tavern (cl pm Mon, Tues).

★ 🏚 ♉ 🐾 Ross-on-Wye SO5923 Picturesquely perched on a sandstone cliff by the river, with twice-weekly markets at the striking 17th-c MARKET HALL. The lower riverside part has attractive waterside walks; the Hope & Anchor here has decent food. LOST STREET MUSEUM 🖼 (off Brookend St) Edwardian street with fully stocked walk-through period shops, and excellent collections of music boxes, gramophones, and advertising items. Snacks; cl Nov–mid-Feb and wkdys till Easter; (01989) 562752; £2. You can visit the workshop of C & J HUGHES CANDLEMAKERS on Old Gloucester Rd (cl Sun, 25–26 Dec), and there's a unique BUTTON MUSEUM on Kyrle St (cl Nov–Mar; £1.50).

🏵 ✝ **Spetchley** SO8953 SPETCHLEY
PARK GARDENS (A422) 30 acres of
lovely gardens, with sweeping lawns
and herbaceous borders, rose lawn,
and interesting trees and shrubs. The
adjacent park has both red and fallow
deer. Snacks, disabled access (but no
facilities); cl am Sun, all day Sat, Mon
(exc bank hols), and Oct–Mar;
(01905) 345213; £2.90. The Berkeley
Knot is handy for lunch.

🏵 🍴 **Staunton on Arrow** SO3660
STAUNTON PARK Big lakeside garden
with charming woodland walk, fine
trees, attractive herb garden, knot
garden and old-fashioned herbaceous
gardens. Nice teas with home-made
jams and chutneys, shop, disabled
access; open pm Thurs, Sun and bank
hols Apr–Sept; *£1.50. HORSEWAY
HERBS (Horsewayhead Cottage)
Friendly little place with lots of herb
plants, sold as both plants and crafts;
they also sell home-made pickles and
jams. Snacks, disabled access; cl
Weds, all Nov–Mar; (01544)
388212; free. The New Inn at
Pembridge has good food.

🏵 **Stock Green** SO9858 WHITE
COTTAGE (Earls Common Rd) A
profusion of interesting plants in
colourful borders, and a streamside
wild garden, pretty in spring.
Disabled access; cl Weds, Thurs,
second and fourth Sun in month, and
all Oct–Easter; (01386) 792414;
£1.50. The plant sales (inc rare
geranium species) are at the
Coneybury Plant Centre a little way
off. The Old Bull, the Archers' pub
over at Inkberrow, is appealing.

🏵 **Stone** SO8574 STONE HOUSE
GARDEN Unusual walled garden with
colourful plants, especially climbers
and tender flowering shrubs;
interesting plant sales. Disabled
access; open Weds–Sat Mar–Oct,
plus some summer Suns; (01562)
69902; *£2. The Fox at Chaddesley
Corbett has a popular carvery.

🏵 🍴 ❄ **Swainshill** SO4541 WEIR
GARDENS (Garden Cottage, off the
A438) Delightful riverside gardens, at
their best in spring, with displays of
bulbs set in woodland walks, and fine
views from clifftop walks. Paths can

be steep in places. Open Weds–Sun
(and bank hols) mid-Feb–Oct; £1.50;
NT. The Ancient Camp at Ruckhall is
quite handy.

✝ ❄ ! 🛏 🏵 **Symonds Yat** SO5616
Shared with Glos on the other side of
the river, this is a spectacular bend of
the River Wye through a steep,
wooded rock gorge, where peregrine
falcons nest (the RSPB have a
demonstration area); splendid Wye
views, nature trails; 2 inns on either
side of the river are linked by a hand-
pulled ferry, and there's ample
(walkers would say over-generous)
parking. Among other things to
amuse visitors here (it is a popular
tourist destination) is the JUBILEE PARK
🖼, with a hedge maze built for the
Queen's Silver Jubilee, and lively
maze museum telling the history of
similar labyrinthine creations. Meals,
snacks, shop, disabled access; cl Feb;
(01600) 890360; £2.80. On the same
site, the WORLD OF THE ORIENT has
indoor and outdoor oriental water
gardens including bonsais and
orchids. Snacks, shop, disabled
access; cl Dec 25–26; (01600)
890471; *£2.90.

🎨 **Upton Bishop** SO6527 WOBAGE
FARM CRAFT WORKSHOPS have several
potters, a furniture-maker, woodcarver and jeweller; open wknds only;
(01989) 780233; free.

✝ **West Hagley** SO9080 FALCONRY
CENTRE 🖼 (Hurrans Garden Centre,
Kidderminster Rd S) Frequent flying
displays of hawks, owls and other
birds of prey; some of their falconry
courses last only half a day. Shop,
some disabled access; cl Mon, 25–26
Dec; (01562) 700014; *£2. The
Holly Bush (on the A491 towards
Bromsgrove) has popular fresh food.

🕍 **Wichenford** SO7860 DOVECOT
Unusually constructed timber-framed
wattle and daub 17th-c dovecot with
nearly 600 nesting boxes; recently
restored. Open daily Apr–Oct, winter
by appointment; (01684) 850051;
60p; NT.

🏵 **Wychbold** SO9265 WEBBS GARDEN
CENTRE (A38 towards Bromsgrove) is
one of the best in the country,
attractively laid out, with a massive
choice of things to buy, fine

amusements for children and good disabled access. The thatched café is exemplary; cl 25–26 Dec; (01527) 861777.

★ The many **black and white villages** are a particular characteristic of the county. Besides Eardisland (see entry p.318), best of all is probably Pembridge SO3958, full of fine timbered buildings inc a medieval market hall, the ancient New Inn, and a lovely church. Dunkerton's small CIDER FARM (nearby at Luntley SO3956) uses ancient traditional local cider-apple and pear cultivars, for distinctive ciders and perries; free tastings, and good restaurant; cl Sun. Also in the very top rank is Weobley SO4052, with its long sloping green, and stroll out past the bowling green to the church; the Olde Salutation is good for lunch.

Other favourite villages, all with decent pubs, include Abbots Morton SP0353 (with a lovely church), Ashton under Hill SO9938 below Bredon Hill (many charming black and white timbered houses and a good Norman church), Belbroughton SO9277, Birtsmorton SO7936, Bredon SO9236 (magnificent medieval tithe barn, River Avon), Bredenbury SO6516 (despite the main rd), Carey SO5631, Chaddesley Corbett SO8973 (fine, partly Norman church), Charlton SP0145, Childswickham SP0738 (streamside, timbered stone cottages), Clifton upon Teme SO7162 (lots of quiet strolls above the orchards), Elmley Castle SO9841 under Bredon Hill (lovely church), Feckenham SP0061 (attractive green and some fine Georgian red brick), Fladbury SO9946 (walks by the River Avon, 9th-c Saxon cross, and a handsome Georgian village green), Hanley Castle SO8442 (rustic little place around a great cedar tree, with an unusually unspoilt pub), Hanley Swan SO8142 (pleasant traditional pub by the village green and a duck pond), brilliantly black and white Harvington SP0548 (one of the oldest in the area), Hoarwithy SO5429, riverside Leintwardine SO4174 (its church is much bigger than usual for this county), Lingen SO3767 (prettily set among hills, with Kim Davis's renowned alpine nursery and garden), Offenham SP0546 (original gaily striped maypole in its wide black and white main street), Overbury SO9537 (immaculate stone-built estate village with older buildings and a fine church), Ombersley SO8463 (attractive mix of handsome black and white timbered houses with elegant Georgian brick), Ripple SO8737 (finely carved choir seats in its imposing largely 13th-c church), Sinton Green SO8160, Upper Arley SO7680 (the Severn Valley Railway, see Bewdley and Kidderminster entries above, stops at a station over the River Severn footbridge), Walterstone SO3425 (peaceful walks), riverside Wick SO9645 (another good church), Wolverley SO8279 (steeply gabled cottages below a brick-built hilltop church, and the decent cliffside Lock Inn by the quaint Staffs & Worcs Canal), and streamside Yarpole SO4765 (with a free-standing medieval bell tower). Dorstone SO3141 has an impressive prehistoric burial mound nearby (and Herefs' oldest pub); this B4348/B4347 Golden Valley road is pretty, as are the remoter roads parallel to this, to the W, through Clodock SO3227 (delightful church) and Michaelchurch Escley SO3134 (another good pub down by the river), or passing Craswall SO2736.

✝ The area has many charming **churches**. The best-known is the small Norman one at Kilpeck SO4530 (a delightful little hamlet): amazing sandstone carving inside and out, beautifully preserved (except for the more uncomfortably pagan bits which prudish Victorians tried to remove). There are too many good churches in the county to list, but some wonderful curiosities include Almeley SO3351 (early 18th-c half-timbered Quaker Meeting House, contemplative feel; key in porch), Brockhampton SO6032 (extraordinary turn-of-the-century Arts and Crafts church designed by Lethaby; note that this is in the little village between Hereford and Ross-on-Wye), Eardisley SO3149 (12th-c font with wonderfully vivid carvings of sinner being wrested from clutches of evil), Hoarwithy SO5429 (Italianate, full of mosaics, etc), Martley SO7559 (13th-c wall paintings), and Pembridge SO3938 (unusual detached belfry where you can watch the clock mechanism). Quiet country drives can link several attractive churches, such as Bredwardine SO3344, Moccas SO3543, Tyberton SO3839 and Eaton Bishop SO4439; or perhaps Fownhope SO5834, Kings Caple SO5528 and even Foy SO5928 with Brockhampton and Hoarwithy.

☛ Vale of Evesham farm shops are good for all manner of local produce inc eggs, jams, pickles and trout as well as fruit and vegetables, but the highlights of the year are asparagus in May and apples and particularly plums in Sept. The A44 W of Broadway almost always has good pickings; Chapel Hill nursery, about ½m W of Broadway, has good-value plants for sale.

Walks

The **Malvern Hills** ⌂-1 form a splendid backdrop to the Vale of Evesham. From a distance they look a formidable mountain range, but seem to get milder and more welcoming as you approach. The gentle up-and-down path along their spine makes one of England's great ridge walks, with the Cotswolds and Midland plain on one side and wilder Wales on the other. The Herefordshire Beacon SO7640, capped by ramparts of an Iron Age hill fort, is easily reached from the car park on the A449 nr Little Malvern. Great Malvern is well placed for the Worcestershire Beacon SO7645, the highest point of the range (425 metres, 1,395ft), and for long, circular walks. The Chase Hotel at Upper Wyche SO7643 and the Malvern Hills Hotel by the British Camp car park on Wynds Point SO7641 are also useful start or finish points. Ledbury SO7138 and Eastnor SO7337 are good bases for rambles into the attractive western slopes.

Woolhope SO6136 ⌂-2 has rather similar elevated country around it, with good variety, and the views from Ridge Hill E and the more densely wooded hills nr Mordiford SO5737 among the highlights.

Symonds Yat SO5616 ⌂-3 in the Herefordshire part of the Wye Valley is something of a motorists' viewpoint over a tight meander of the Wye (there's a prominent car park), but with potential for more ambitious walks into the gorge, where an old railway line follows the river; to the SW an entertainingly rickety, wire-mesh suspension bridge at the Biblins gives access to the W bank, in addition to the chain ferry at Symonds Yat village. The formidable ruins of **Goodrich Castle** SO5719 ⌂-4 to the N, is a feasible objective or starting-point for gorge walks.

Ross-on-Wye SO5923 ⌂-5 in the more open stretches of the valley has pleasant woodland walks in Penyard Park, SE of the town.

There are particularly satisfying walks up the Golden Valley and the hills of the Welsh Marches to the W and NW of the area. **Merbach Hill** SO3044 ⌂-6 can be reached by driving up from Bredwardine SO3344, and then walking from the top of the lane; there's a view right over the Black Mountains, Herefordshire and Radnorshire, and a short stroll along the lane SE brings you to Arthur's Stone, a prehistoric burial chamber. The **Olchon Valley** SO2833 ⌂-7 is perhaps the remotest place in the county, a magnificent dead-end valley beneath the E flank of the Black Mountains. From the well signed picnic site nr Longtown SO3239 a path heads up the Black Hill, an exciting knife-edge ridge, its end-on aspect strikingly triangular – this bit is known as the Cat's Back; after the trig point you can make a circuit by dropping down from the very head of the Olchon Valley, or carrying on over peaty terrain to join the Offa's Dyke Path.

Hergest Ridge SO2556 ⌂-8, reached via a cul-de-sac from Kington, is NW Herefordshire's answer to the Malvern Hills – and like them (allegedly) inspired Elgar, in this case to write his *Introduction and Allegro for Strings*, as well as Mike Oldfield with his album *Hergest Ridge*; the less-known composer Moeran also walked here frequently, and his *Sinfonietta* was inspired by the area. It's another of those ridges for those who can't decide whether they prefer the gentle lowland textures of England or the more rugged offerings of Wales. The walk gets better with every step, as the wide ridge tapers into horseback width at the far end, above Gladestry in Powys.

Leinthall Common SO4467 ⌂-9, a brackeny expanse scattered with cottages, is a quiet corner of Herefordshire where you can walk around the estate of Croft Castle and scale the modest heights of Croft Ambrey, an Iron Age hill fort with a view into Shropshire.

The **Wyre Forest** SO7575 ⌂-10 is a major broadleaved woodland in the N, on the Shropshire border, with numerous ready-made Forestry Commission trails (leaflets available from the Visitor Centre; the Royal Forester nearby, if open, is useful for lunch). The **Abberley Hills** SO7567 ⌂-11 nr Stourport are far less trodden but rewarding, partly wooded, with good views and close to the extraordinary ruins of Witley Court (see Great Witley entry in **Other things to see and do**, p.319).

Bredon Hill ⌂-12 is the Vale of Evesham's one notable feature for walkers. It's an outlier of the Cotswolds, distinctively rounded and on cloudy days rather ominous. It's easily reached from Overbury SO9537, but the best walk over it is from Bredons Norton SO9339 to Elmley Castle SO9841.

Towards Birmingham, the topography is surprisingly interesting, with much of the land rising to over 300 metres (1,000ft). The **Lickey Hills Country Park** SO9975 ⌂-13 is densely wooded, a fragment of primeval forest, with the views suddenly opening out over the sprawling city; waymarking makes the maze of paths and tracks less confusing. **Clent Hills Country Park** SO9379 ⌂-14 is a fine hillscape, open and exhilarating, with waymarked routes. The Holly Bush at Clent SO9379 is a good lunch break.

Useful pubs for waterside walks are the Camp House at Grimley SO8359 on the River Severn, the Fox & Hounds at Lulsley SO7455 for quiet Temeside orchards (and on up through Ravenshill Wood to Crews Hill, or instead along to the attractive Talbot at Knightwick SO7355) and, on the Worcester & Birmingham Canal, the Firs at Dunhampstead SO9160, Navigation at Stoke Prior SO9468, Bowling Green at Stoke Works SO9468 (yes, it does have its own bowling green), and Queen's Head at Stoke Pound SO9667.

Other country pubs well placed for walks include the Penny Farthing at Aston Crews SO6723, Tally Ho! at Broad Heath SO6665, the Crown at Howle Hill SO6020 and Three Horseshoes at Ullingswick SO5949. The landlord of the Compasses at Wigmore SO4169 has his own leaflet of local walks.

Where to eat

Bransford SO7852 BEAR & RAGGED STAFF (01886) 833399 Stylish dining pub with cheerful atmosphere in interconnecting rooms, no smoking restaurant, helpful service, particularly good, interesting food inc quite a few fish dishes; well kept real ales, and New World wines; cl pm Sun. £18.55|£7.25.

Dorstone SO3141 PANDY (01981) 550273 Cosy, half-timbered ancient pub, very relaxed and friendly, with nice, imaginative food (lots of fresh fish and game), beamed and flagstoned rooms, well kept beers, and woodburning stove; cl Mon and Tues from Nov–Easter. £17.50|£3.50.

Ledbury SO7138 MARKET PLACE (01531) 634250 Pleasant bustling restaurant open all day for morning coffee, lunch and afternoon tea with home-made cakes, flans and puddings; cl pm, 25–26 Dec, 1 Jan. £12|£2.

Longdon SO8336 HUNTERS (01684) 833388 Friendly, rather civilised place with imaginative food in the smart, heavy-beamed restaurant and small dining room; 2 comfortable bars with flagstones and a woodburning stove, well kept beer and nice wines, and 6 acres of grounds with dogs, rabbits and ponies. £19.25|£7.75.

Malvern Wells SO7742 CROQUE-EN-BOUCHE 221 Wells Rd (01684) 565612 Boldly decorated Victorian house with delicious, carefully cooked evening food from a shortish menu, with marvellous puddings and cheeses, and an exceptional wine list – must book; open Thurs–Sat pm only; cl 1 wk May, 1 wk Sept, Christmas. £30.

Pensax SO7269 BELL (01299) 896677 Unspoilt and friendly 19th-c pub with good food, several changing real ales, open fires, and dining room extension with a fine view over the hills to Wyre Forest; cl am Mon except bank hols and summer holiday period; disabled access. £16.30|£6.95.

Ross-on-Wye SO6024 PHEASANTS 52 Edde Cross St (01989) 565751 Homely little restaurant with a cosy lounge, delicious food, nice cheeses, and relaxed atmosphere; cl Sun–Mon, 25 Dec–2 Jan, 1 wk early June; well behaved children welcome. £26.

Sellack SO5627 LOUGH POOL (01989) 730236 Attractive black and white timbered cottage in lovely countryside, with log fire in a cosy, beamed room and excellent, tasty bar food; cl 25 Dec; disabled access. £18.70|£3.10.

Stockton Cross SO5161 STOCKTON CROSS (01568) 612509 Heavy-beamed long bar with an old-fashioned feel, a huge log fire and woodburning stove, solid furnishings, a huge choice of enjoyable food, well kept beer, and welcoming service; seats in garden. £17.40|£5.95.

Upton Bishop SO6527 MOODY COW (01989) 780470 Merry place with several snug separate areas, a pleasant medley of stripped country furniture, big log fire, no smoking, rustic candlelit restaurant and a second small dining room; a good choice of changing, enjoyable food, and well kept beers. £19|£7.45.

Winforton SO2947 SUN (01544) 327677 Very friendly and neatly kept little pub with beamed rooms, woodburning stoves, particularly tasty, interesting food, ·and a sheltered garden; good bedrooms; cl winter Tues, pm Tues in summer; children over 10. £18.50|£6.99.

Worcester SO8555 BROWNS 24 Quay St (01905) 26263 Most attractive and spacious warehouse conversion with big windows overlooking the river; excellent modern cooking inc fish and vegetarian dishes, and good wines; cl am Sat, pm Sun, 1 wk Christmas; well behaved children over 6; disabled access. £18.50 lunch (£24 Sun), £33.50 dinner.

Worcester SO8555 KING CHARLES HOUSE 29 New St (01905) 22449 Historic inn from which King Charles II made his escape through the back door, closely pursued by Cromwell's forces; enjoyable food, open fires, and a relaxed atmosphere in the downstairs restaurant and upstairs bar; cl Sun, bank hols, 25–26 Dec; £13.95 lunch, £25 dinner|£7.50.

Wychbold SO9265 THATCH (01527) 861412 Part of Webbs Garden Centre, open 9am –7.30pm (till 5pm Sat, Sun and in winter) with wine licence, good-value snacks and meals in pleasant surroundings; cl 25–26 Dec; disabled access. £10|£5.

Wyre Piddle SO9647 ANCHOR (01386) 552799 Relaxing 17th-c pub with lovely views over lawn, river and on over the Vale of Evesham; friendly little lounge with log fire, comfortable bar, and good popular food; disabled access. £21|£6.75.

Special thanks to William Adams, Capt and Mrs G Tettant, J H Lawrence-Archer, Chris Reeve, Mrs K Gilbert, Mrs M Danks, Dr P Stephenson, Peter and Sarah Gooderham, Linden Milner, Fiona Watson.

HEREFORD AND WORCESTER CALENDAR

Some of these dates were provisional as we went to press. Please check information with the telephone numbers provided.

JANUARY

24 **Great Malvern** Worcs and Malvern Dog Show at the Three Counties Showground (01684) 584900

FEBRUARY

28 **Great Malvern** Mid-Western Gundog Show at the Three Counties Showground (01684) 584900

MARCH

13 **Tenbury** Festival – *till Sun 29* (01584) 810304
15 **Great Malvern** Gloucester Dog Show at the Three Counties Showground (01684) 584900

APRIL

10 **Ross-on-Wye** Real Ale Festival at the Crown & Sceptre – *till Mon 13* (01989) 562765
17 **Hereford** Classical Music Weekend Break at the Green Dragon – *till Sun 19*, brochure in advance from (01432) 272506
25 **Bromsgrove** Music Festival – *till 9 May* (01527) 575441

MAY

1 **Upton-on-Severn** Folk Festival – *till Mon 4* (01684) 593849
2 **Worcester** Living History at the Commandery *till Mon 4* (01905) 355071
3 **Eastnor** Spring Country Craft Fair at Eastnor Castle – *till Mon 4* (01531) 633160
4 **Kington** Flower Fair at Hergest Croft Gardens (01544) 230160; **Leominster** May Fair (01568) 616460
5 **Hereford** Spring Festival and May Fair – *till Thurs 7* (01432) 268430
8 **Great Malvern** Spring Garden Show at the Three Counties Showground – *till Sun 10* (01684) 584900
9 **Abbey Dore** Gilbert and Sullivan Society at Dore Abbey (01981) 240075
17 **Eastnor** Steam Fair and Country Show at Eastnor Castle (01531) 633160
23 **Worcester** Oak Apple Festival at the Commandery: celebration of the restoration of Charles II (01905) 355071
25 **Ross-on-Wye** Bank Holiday Festival (01989) 563164

JUNE

5 **Leominster** Festival – *till Sun 14* (01568) 612874
6 **Leominster** Beer Festival (01568) 610060
11 **Eastnor** Art of Living Decorative Arts Fair at Eastnor Castle – *till Sun 14* (01531) 633160
12 **How Caple** Open-air Music and Opera at How Caple Court Gardens – *till Sat 13* (01989) 740626; **Leominster** Fringe Festival – *till Sun 14* (01568) 610060
16 **Great Malvern** Three Counties Agricultural Show at the Three Counties Showground – *till Thurs 18* (01684) 584900
20 **Kidderminster** Carnival (01562) 751634

HEREFORD AND WORCESTER CALENDAR

JUNE cont

26 **Abbey Dore** Music Festival at Dore Abbey – *till Sun 28* (01981) 750315; **Upton-upon-Severn** Jazz Festival – *till Sun 28* (01922) 30779

27 **Bromsgrove** Charter Fair: starts festival week which runs – *till carnival procession on 4 July* (01527) 833981

JULY

3 **Ledbury** Poetry Festival – *till Sun 12* (01531) 636147

11 **Evesham** River Festival (01386) 442338; **Hereford** Carnival Jamboree (01432) 364619

12 **Kidderminster** 12 Gardens Open (01562) 755817

18 **Much Marcle** Steam Rally – *till Sun 19* (01531) 660464; **Romsley** Patronal and Flower Festival at St Kenelms Church – *till Sun 19* (01562) 710395

19 **Hereford** Summer Festival – *till Sat 25* (01905) 766375

25 **Pembridge** Show (01544) 388414

AUGUST

1 **Tenbury Wells** Show (01584) 810666

2 **Ross-on-Wye** Carnival (01989) 562768; **Wormbridge** Herefordshire Country Fair at Whitfield (01981) 240168

5 **Hereford** Street Entertainment in High Town – also *Wed 12, Wed 19, Wed 26* (01432) 268430

14 **Ross-on-Wye** International Festival – *till Mon 24* (01989) 563330

17 **Eastnor** Children's Fun Week at Eastnor Castle – *till Fri 21* (01531) 633160

26 **Hereford** Beer Festival at the Barrels – *till Mon 31* (01432) 268430

28 **Worcester** Living History at the Commandery *till Mon 31* (01905) 355071

31 **Ledbury** Street Carnival (01531) 633035; **Madresfield** Agricultural Show at Home Farm (01684) 576604; **Ross-on-Wye** Regatta (01989) 564100

SEPTEMBER

5 **Hereford** Photography Festival – *till 17 Oct* (01432) 344039

13 **Eastnor** Living History at the time of the Wars of the Roses at Eastnor Castle – *till Mon 14* (01531) 633160

18 **Bromyard** Folk Festival – *till Sun 20* (01531) 670249

26 **Great Malvern** Autumn Show at the Three Counties Showground – *till Sun 27* (01684) 584900

OCTOBER

3 **Eastnor** Christmas Craft Fair at Eastnor Castle – *till Sun 4* (01531) 633160

17 **Hereford** Apple Day Celebrations at the Cider Museum – *till Sat 31* (01432) 354207

24 **Worcester** One World Fair at Worcester Woods Country Park – *till Sun 25* (01905) 766493

NOVEMBER

7 **Ross-on-Wye** Bonfire and Fireworks (01432) 364619

20 **Hereford** Contemporary Crafts at the Town Hall – *till Sun 22* (01432) 364710

HEREFORD AND WORCESTER CALENDAR

NOVEMBER cont

25 **Hereford** Christmas Lights Ceremony (01432) 364619; **Hereford** Hop into Hereford: 5 weeks of country-theme events – *till 23 Dec* (01432) 364619

28 **Worcester** Green Fair at Worcester Woods Country Park – *till Sun 29* (01905) 766493

DECEMBER

7 **Worcester** Christmas Festival at the Commandery – *till Sun 20* (01905) 355071

We welcome reports from readers ...

This *Guide* depends on readers' reports. Do help us if you can – in return, we offer a discount on the next edition to people who've helped us with reports for it. Tell us what you think about places already in it, and anything extra you think we should say about them. And send us your ideas for inclusion in the next edition: places to visit, eat at or stay in, attractive drives or walks, maybe even unusual interesting shops you know of. Use the card in the middle, the report forms at the end, or just write – no stamp needed: *The Good Guide to Britain*, FREEPOST TN1569, Wadhurst, E Sussex TN5 7BR.

HERTFORDSHIRE

Not really a holiday area, but some good days out.

Hatfield House at Knebworth has all-round appeal for a day out. The Standalone Farm on the edge of Letchworth is also a good family outing, as is the friendly wildlife park at Broxbourne. The remarkable zoological museum at Tring intrigues most people – of any age. For older tastes, the Royal National Rose Society's garden just outside St Albans is a great summer spectacle, and the Henry Moore sculpture garden at Much Hadham may convert even sceptics. St Albans itself has other appealing points, including the well preserved remains of a Roman city.

Though much of the county is intensively built up, it has quite a few attractive villages and good pockets of pleasant strolling country.

Where to stay

Chipperfield TL0401 Two BREWERS The Common, Chipperfield, Kings Langley WD4 9BS (01923) 265266 £74; 20 comfortable rms. Comfortable and very neatly kept country hotel with relaxing views of the pretty village green, a dark-beamed main bar with cushioned antique settles, a bow-windowed lounge with comfortable sofas and easy chairs, and open fires; good bar and restaurant food; pleasant nearby walks; disabled access.

St Albans TL1507 WHITE HART Holywell Hill, St Albans AL1 1EZ (01727) 853624 *£60; 11 rms, most with own bthrm. Comfortable and civilised former coaching inn with 2 bar areas, antique panelling, handsome fireplaces and furnishings, the residents' lounge reached by a barleytwist staircase; courteous friendly service, and a good restaurant.

To see and do

St Albans TL1407 Though modern shops dominate your first impressions, corners of real antiquity are tucked away between and behind them. This was one of the most important Roman towns in Northern Europe, and has some fine well excavated remains in peaceful surroundings. A stroll through the town in search of other notable buildings (the tourist information office in the Town Hall, Market Pl, has helpful guide maps) is rewarded by the surprisingly large number of decent pubs here. Down between abbey gate and park, the Fighting Cocks is based on an ancient building which had some connection with the abbey, and its interesting layout includes the clearly discernible shape of a cockpit. In the quietly attractive largely Georgian St Michael's St, the Rose & Crown is very civilised, and the Six Bells is on the site of a Roman bath house, though not visibly so. The Cock (Hatfield Rd) is worth looking out because of its bizarre history; its floors were found to rest on thick foundations of human bones. Worth a look if you're nearby are the MUSEUM (Hatfield Rd), covering the town's post-Roman history (cl am Sun, 25 Dec; free), and GREBE HOUSE in the park nr Verulamium, the HQ of a regional nature trust, with recreated woodland setting, and tips on how to attract wildlife to your garden (cl wkdys Jan and Feb, am wknds; free). The B651 N towards Hitchin is quite a scenic country drive.

🏛🐾 VERULAMIUM This was the name of the Roman city; its remains are down in the SW corner of town, past the cathedral and attractive park (coming from outside, most easily reached by the A4147 off the Hemel Hempstead exit from the M1, junction 7). The place to start is the excellent VERULAMIUM MUSEUM (St Michael's St) 🚾, with its lively interpretation of everyday Roman life, as well as jewellery, wall paintings and domestic items found nearby. Shop, disabled access; cl am Sun, 25–26 Dec; (01727) 819339; £2.80. Follow signs from here into the adjacent playing fields: an unassuming brick building looking like a garage or changing rooms houses the carefully restored mosaic floor and hypocaust underfloor heating system of an excavated Roman villa; free. Further on is a well preserved section of the Roman town wall. Most impressive is the ROMAN THEATRE, not large by the standards of some others in England (room for 1,600) but, taking into account its good state of preservation, it's unique. Shop, limited disabled access; cl 25 Dec, 1 Jan; (01727) 835035; £1.50.

✝🏛 CATHEDRAL Up on a mound, this has good views; its 11th-c reddish exterior uses flint recycled from the Roman remains. Once the country's premier abbey, it suffered a little after the Reformation, and its fortunes didn't revive until Victorian times. It was touched up a lot then, but the majestic interior does have some earlier features, inc 13th- and 14th-c paintings in the long nave, and some Saxon transept pillars. Meals, snacks, shop, disabled access; cathedral free, £1.50 for audio-visual show. The great 14th-c ABBEY GATEHOUSE beyond leads down to a neat park, its lake and willow-edged stream packed with ducks.

🏛❀ MEDIEVAL CLOCK TOWER This striking free-standing stone building has a bell, striking on the hour, even older than the tower itself. Fine views from the top; open wknds and bank hols Easter–mid-Sept; 25p. Nearby, French Row is a narrow alley of striking timbered buildings jettied out over the street, right by a modern shopping centre. The Fleur de Lys pub here is a remarkable medieval building.

🐾 ORGAN MUSEUM (Camp Rd, 2m from centre) Tuneful collection of automatically operated organs and other musical instruments, inc Wurlitzer and Rutt theatre organs. Recitals every Sun 2–4.30pm, and concerts all year. Shop, disabled access (but no facilities); open pm Sun

---

Days Out

Distinctly East Anglian
Braughing; Westmill – lunch at the Sword in Hand there, or the Jolly Waggoner, Ardeley; Ardeley windmill (limited opening); Benington village and Benington Lordship (limited opening).

Romans and roses
St Albans Abbey; Verulamium Roman town, amphitheatre and museum; lunch at Waffle House (St Michael's St), St Albans; Gardens of the Rose.

Literary pilgrimage
Stroll along the River Lea from Ayot Green and past Brocket Hall; lunch at the Brocket Arms, Ayot St Lawrence; Shaw's Corner – or Knebworth.

Canalscapes and the N Chilterns
Wander along the Grand Union Canal towpath and beside Marsworth Reservoir; lunch at the Greyhound or the Valiant Trooper, Aldbury; walk in Ashridge estate at Ringshall, inc Bridgewater Monument, and Ivinghoe Beacon (described in Buckinghamshire chapter) – good picnic spots.

only; (01727) 869693; £2.

⚜ GARDENS OF THE ROSE (Chiswell Green; on the B4630 S of St Albans) The showgrounds of the Royal National Rose Society, with over 1,600 cultivars, many in mass plantings. Plenty of interesting cultivation trials going on, new roses from all over the world, lots of clematis, and other plantings. Meals, snacks, shop, disabled access; open 14 Jun–12 Oct; (01727) 850461; £4. The Holly Bush at nearby Potters Crouch has decent food (not Sun).

🗶 KINGSBURY WATERMILL 16th-c watermill half a mile from the city on the banks of the River Ver, still with one working waterwheel and a museum. Meals, snacks, shop; cl Mon, 25 Dec; (01727) 853502; *£1.10.

🏠 GORHAMBURY 2 miles out of town (the other side of Verulamium's park) but peaceful enough to make you think it's the heart of the country, an 18th-c house with extensive assemblage of 17th-c family portraits, and some 16th-c enamelled glass. Open pm Thurs May–Sept; (01727) 855000; *£4.

Other things to see and do

HERTFORDSHIRE FAMILY ATTRACTION OF THE YEAR

🏠 ⚜ **Knebworth** TL2520 KNEBWORTH HOUSE, GARDENS AND COUNTRY PARK
🎫 Thanks to its high profile gigs and concerts this is one of the few stately homes that children will have heard of, and thanks to its excellent extensive adventure playground it's also one that they very much enjoy visiting. Fort Knebworth has enough to keep active boys and girls busy for quite some time, and as there's no extra charge on top of what it costs to see the rest of the estate you can keep coming back during the day. In addition to the usual wooden climbing equipment and so forth there are quite a few exciting slides, including the monorail suspension slide (which basically means you hang on to a rope and then slide back down to the ground), and the twisting corkscrew. The house at the centre of the 250-acre park was originally a straightforward Tudor mansion, but was spectacularly embellished by Victorian author Sir Edward Bulwer Lytton; he wanted it to be a castle fit for the romantic characters in his novels. Still a lived-in home, the grand rooms include a splendid Jacobean great hall, and mementos of former guests like Dickens and Churchill. The gardens were designed by Lutyens, and include a herb garden laid out to plans by Gertrude Jekyll; there's also a deer park, a maze, and a miniature railway (90p extra). With plenty of space to run about or kick a ball around, there's enough here to occupy families for a good lump of the day. Meals, snacks, shop, limited disabled access; open wknds and school hols Easter–Sept, house cl am and all Mon, and occasionally for special events; (01438) 812661; £5 for everything (£4.50 children aged 5–16), £4 grounds only. A family ticket for the grounds (which includes the fort and play areas) is £14 for 2 adults and 2 children. Along the outer edge of the park is the pretty little hamlet of Old Knebworth; the Lytton Arms here is a very good pub.

⚜ ⛄ **Aldenham** TQ1398 COUNTRY PARK Plenty of space for children to run around in, with adventure play area, nature trails and a herd of longhorn cattle.

⚜ **Amwell** TL1613 GARDEN CENTRE (on the A1170) The Van Hage Garden Co has an unusually lively place here, good for an afternoon out, with children's farm, and plenty to look at in addition to their excellent range of plants and show gardens (inc an award-winning Japanese garden). Miniature railway some summer wknds. Meals, snacks, shops, disabled access; (01920) 870811; free.

★ 🗶 **Ardeley** TL3027 Attractive

thatched village with decent food at the Jolly Waggoner, and a pleasant quiet drive along the lane down through Wood End, Haultwick and Dane End.

CROMER WINDMILL (just NW) Partly 13th-c, lovingly restored, the last remaining post-mill in the county. Open pm wknds and bank hols mid-May–early Sept; (01438) 861626; £1.

★ † ♏ Ayot St Lawrence TL1916 Delightful little backwater, with a very picturesque 12th-c ivy-covered RUINED CHURCH; the existing CHURCH is an incongruously grand neo-Grecian affair. SHAW'S CORNER is much as it was when GBS lived here, 1906–1950; Shaw devotees will enjoy seeing his exercise machine, pen, spectacles, and even the soft homburg he wore for 60 years. The tiny writing shed at the bottom of the garden was designed to revolve and so maximise sunlight. Try and go on a weekday when more is open. Open air plays in July – (01494) 522234 to book. Open pm Weds–Sun and bank hols Apr–Oct; (01438) 820307; £3; NT. The Brocket Arms is an enjoyably old-fashioned inn.

★ ♏ ♏ Benington TL3023 One of the county's prettiest and most interesting villages, its church lovely when the snowdrops are out in late Feb. BENINGTON LORDSHIP Kept well up to date, 7 acres of Edwardian terraced gardens with many unusual plants, fine herbaceous borders, roses, a rock garden, and a particularly lovely splash of snowdrops. The grounds include a very picturesque early 19th-c 'Norman' ruined gatehouse, actually put together from stones of the genuinely Norman ruined moated keep. Plant sales; open pm Weds Apr–Sept and Sun Apr–Aug, pm bank hols, and some dates Feb/Mar for snowdrops – ring for details; (01438) 869668; £2.50. The lovely old Bell here has generous food.

♏ ☺ Broxbourne TL3707 PARADISE WILDLIFE PARK ▨ (White Stubbs Lane) Friendly little zoo and leisure park with lions, monkeys, camels and zebras, events from meeting the python to feeding the lions, and adventure playground, crazy golf, woodland walk and paddling pool. Meals, snacks, shop, disabled access; cl 25 Dec; (01992) 468001; £5.

♏ ♏ † Hatfield TL2308 This extensive modern built-up area includes on its edge a charming original core – Old Hatfield – with a fine old pub (the Eight Bells). Alongside is the extensive park of HATFIELD HOUSE, a great Jacobean house built in 1611 on the site of a childhood home of Elizabeth I; the splendid State Rooms include portraits of the queen, and even her silk stockings, perhaps among the earliest worn in this country. Also the National Collection of Model Soldiers, with over 3,000 exhibits. The scented garden and knot garden contain plants that were typical between the 15th and 17th c. Meals, snacks, shop, disabled access; open Apr–Sept, park and gardens every day, house cl am and all Mon exc bank hols. No guided tours Sun or bank hols; (01707) 262823; £5.50, £3 park and garden only. The nearby CHURCH has a window by Burne-Jones.

♏ ♏ ♏ Hertford TL3212 Some quiet older parts inc the old main Fore St, which has handsomely pargeted buildings – one of them the relaxing Salisbury Arms Hotel. There are several antique shops in St Andrew St (one in a fine 15th-c house). The so-called CASTLE is in fact the 15th-c gatehouse for Edward IV's original moated castle, carefully restored and now occupied by the council; open pm first Sun in month May–Sept, with a brass band outside. The extensive riverside grounds (with the massive flint walls of Henry II's castle) are always open. The cheery local history MUSEUM, in an elegant 17th-c building in Bull Pl, has a graceful Jacobean knot garden. Shop, disabled access to ground floor and garden; cl Sun and Mon; (01992) 582686; free. McMullens Brewery is a striking Victorian building on the river. The Old Barge by the Lee Navigation Canal has a wide choice of vegetarian food among other dishes, and the Silver Fox (on the

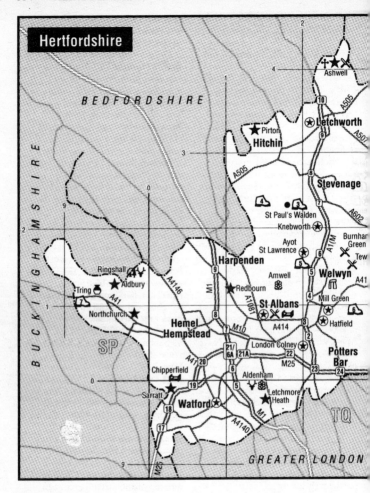

Hertfordshire

BEDFORDSHIRE

BUCKINGHAMSHIRE

GREATER LONDON

B1197, Hertford Heath) is very popular for lunch. Nearby Hertingfordbury is an attractive village, between river and beechwoods.

🏚 ⚙ ✌ **Knebworth** TL2520 KNEBWORTH HOUSE, GARDENS AND COUNTRY PARK *see separate family panel on p.332.*

ħ ☃ 🚜 **Letchworth** TL2232 The country's first garden city, begun in 1903. The FIRST GARDEN CITY HERITAGE MUSEUM (Norton Way South), set in the architects' charming Arts and Crafts-style thatched cottages, shows the thinking behind this uniquely 20th-c idea. Shop,

disabled access; cl Sun, 25–26 Dec; (01462) 482710; free. The nearby Three Magnets (Leys Ave) is a fine new pub. STANDALONE FARM (Wilbury Rd) Simple and unfussy working show farm, best for younger children with a genuine interest in animals. Milking demonstrations every day at 2.30pm, and in Mar and Apr (definitely the best time to come) you can bottle-feed new-born lambs (usually at noon and 4pm). Also pigs, free-range chickens and rare breeds of poultry wandering round the farmyard, exhibition barn with working beehive, model dinosaurs and various creepy-crawlies, outdoor

play area, and 170 acres of farmland, with walks and arboretum. Shire horse wagon rides wknds and school hols. Teas, shop, disabled access; cl Oct–Feb (exc autumn half term); (01462) 686775; £2.50 (£1.50 children).

✝ 🐀 ☕ **London Colney** TL1803 MOSQUITO AIRCRAFT MUSEUM (Salisbury Hall, off the B556) The Mosquito bombers were developed here in secret from 1939, and now the site houses a collection of 20 different de Havilland aircraft, as well as engines and other memorabilia. Snacks, shop, disabled access; open pm Tues, Thurs and Sat, all Sun and bank hols Mar–Oct; (01727) 822051; £4. There are pretty riverside gardens down by the bridge; the Green Dragon here is useful for lunch. AYLETT NURSERIES (on the A414 N) Enthusiastically run garden centre specialising in geraniums, fuchsias and especially their award-winning dahlias. Meals, snacks, disabled access; cl 25–27 Dec, Easter Sun; (01727) 822255. The trial grounds for the dahlias are at BOWMANS FARM, 5 minutes away by car – you can walk round free from Aug to the first frost of autumn. The farm itself has become quite a draw, not least because of its huge FARM SHOP, practically a supermarket (though cheaper for most things), with an enormous range of produce and a separate butchers' dept. Also animals, tractor rides, lakeside walks, and play areas. Meals, snacks, disabled access; cl 25 Dec; (01727) 821253; shop free, farm £3.50.

✗ ☕ 🐀 **Mill Green** TL2409 MILL GREEN MUSEUM Well restored working watermill with craft demonstrations most Suns Apr–Sept and Sats July and Aug, from paper-quilling to love-spoon carving. Shop, disabled access to ground floor only; cl am wknds, all day Mon; milling pm Sun, Tues and Wed; (01707) 271362; free.

🖼 ☕ 🐝 ★ **Much Hadham** TL4319 Henry Moore Foundation The excellent sculpture garden here is much enjoyed by readers. Several works are displayed in the studios where they were made, while the larger ones are shown off against a backdrop of woodland, pasture and hedgerows. Open wkdys only, with 90-minute guided tour at 2.30pm; (01279) 843333; £3. FORGE MUSEUM Based around a working blacksmith, the story of such craftsmen through the ages, with an unusual bee shelter in the Victorian-style garden. Snacks, shop, some disabled access; open Fri–Sun; (01279) 843307; *80p. The village is attractive, with fine Tudor and Georgian houses, a good specialist nursery (Hopleys), and an enjoyable family dining pub (Jolly Waggoners).

♨ ♈ **Ringshall** SP9814 Right on the county boundary and nr Whipsnade Zoo in Beds, the ASHRIDGE ESTATE has 4,000 acres of unspoilt woodlands and open spaces. Plenty of deer and other wildlife (inc the dormouse, though you won't see it in daylight), and a monument erected to the Duke of Bridgewater. Teas summer wknds, shop and information centre, disabled access; monument and facilities cl am, Fri, and Nov–Mar; (01442) 851227; monument £1; NT. The Greyhound and Valiant Trooper at Aldbury just below are pleasant for lunch.

🍖 🎣 **Sawbridgeworth** TL4814 KECKSYS FARM (off the A1184) Working farm with sheep, cattle, poultry, rabbits and rare breeds of pig; coarse fishing is available on the river, and they have a campsite. Disabled access; cl Oct–Easter (exc Sun); (01279) 600896; *£2. The George IV (nr station) has a good restaurant, and the Coach & Horses up at Thorley Street is an enjoyable family food pub.

🎣 **Tring** SP9211 ZOOLOGICAL MUSEUM 📧 (Akeman St, off High St) Part of the national Natural History Museum, this is primarily made up of the remarkably eclectic collections of the second Lord Rothschild, started when he was a little boy: thousands of preserved or stuffed mammals, insects, birds, fish and reptiles, inc domestic dogs, giant tortoises and even a display of dressed fleas. Probably more species on display than anywhere else in the world, and quite odd to see now-extinct creatures such as the zebra-like quagga or huge giant moa. Snacks, shop, limited disabled access; cl 25–26 Dec; (01442) 824181; £2.50 (free after 4pm on wkdys – shuts at 5). The Cow Roast (on the A4521 towards Berkhamsted) has worthwhile food (and popular family barbecues).

! **Ware** TL3514 SCOTT'S GROTTO (Scotts Rd) Built in the 1760s by the poet John Scott, this is one of the finest bits of romantic 'gothickry' in the world, extending 20 metres (67ft) into the hillside under a modern

housing development, with underground passages and chambers decorated with flints, shells, stones and minerals. Wear flat shoes and bring a torch. Open pm Sat and bank hols Apr–Sept, or by appointment; (01920) 464131; £1 donation requested. Several private gardens running down to the quiet River Lee have antique gazebos over the water, neatly restored with crisp white paintwork. The A10 N of here is quite a pleasant road, with decent food at the Sow & Pigs.

🦋 🎣 **Watford** TQ1196 CHESLYN GARDENS An unexpected pleasure in this largely modern urban area, with 3½ acres of woodland and formal gardens, and an aviary; free. From Cassiobury Park there are CANAL BOAT TRIPS along the Grand Union Canal pm Sun and bank hols Easter–Sept, plus Tues and Thurs in Aug; (01438) 714528; £4.50. The local MUSEUM (High St) has a display on the Watford Home Guard, the basis for the TV series *Dad's Army*. Shop, disabled access; cl 1–2pm Sat, all Sun, bank hols; free.

🏛 **Welwyn** TL2315 ROMAN BATHS (½m from the A1(M), junction 6, by the A1000 roundabout) Excavated before the construction of the A1 and since then rather ingeniously preserved within the motorway embankment, this Roman bath house is all that remains of a 3rd-c villa. Very good condition, with explanatory displays. Shop, disabled access; cl am wkdys Jan–Nov (exc bank and school hols), all Dec, and occasional other dates; (01707) 271362; *£1.

★ **Attractive villages** include Aldbury SP9612 (with a perfect village green, stocks, etc, teas, 2 good pubs), Ashwell TL2639 (unusually tall church tower; the Bushel & Strike just beside it and the Three Tuns are both useful for lunch), and Westmill TL3627 (a happy combination of neat green, tiled cottages and a fine old church; the Sword in Hand, well restored after fire damage, has enjoyable food). Others, all with decent pubs, include partly thatched Barley TL4038, Braughing TL3925 (pronounced Braffing; its 14th-c riverside church is pretty), Cottered TL3129, Great Amwell TL3712 (pretty conjunction of church, pre-Norman Emma's Well and pool with islets), Letchmore Heath TQ1597, Pirton TL1431 (the village green is actually the remains of a Norman motte and bailey), Redbourn TL1012 (despite motorway noise Church End with its workhouse and Norman church is pretty), Rushden TL3031 and Sarratt TL0499 (partly Saxon church – the Cock nearby is good). The thatch and timbering of Great Hormead TL4030 is attractive, and Standon TL3922 has some good timbered buildings in its curving High St. Northchurch SP9708 is notable for the ancient church where Peter the Wild Boy is buried; the George & Dragon is handy for lunch.

Walks

Large areas of this county are taken up by the northwards spread of London with continuous swathes of development, and also by the first early 20th-c New Towns, the garden cities of Letchworth and Welwyn, and their more modern successors Hatfield, Hemel Hempstead and Stevenage. But between and beyond these are good green windows of carefully preserved farmland and some more wooded countryside. These yield pockets of good walking terrain, though there is little that is really outstanding. A good point is that even in the prairie-like arable farmland that characterises large chunks of the county, the field paths are often in remarkably good condition and very adequately waymarked.

In the E, the villages and rolling farmland have an East Anglian flavour, quite rural in many places, such as around **Benington** TL3023 △-1, **Ardeley** TL3027 △-2, **St Pauls Walden** TL1922 △-3 (birthplace of the Queen Mother) and **Kings Walden** TL1523 △-4. **Ayot St Lawrence** TL1916 △-5 is conveniently close to link to a walk along the River Lea, which has been dammed at Brocket Hall to form a lake (in view from the public right of way). Shorter walks can start from Ayot Green TL2214, where an abandoned railway line is open to walkers and forms a useful link.

Essendon TL2708 △-6 has mildly hilly country around it, popular with weekend walkers for pleasantly varied village-to-village paths.

Tring SP9211 △-7 has a choice of canal towpath walks from nr the Grand Junction Arms pub (on the B488 at Bulbourne), where the Grand Union Canal has a part-abandoned offshoot, the Wendover Arm, and the still-operational Aylesbury Arm. There's also canal access from the Boat down Ravens Lane in Berkhamsted SP9807 and the Fisheries at Boxmoor TL0306.

Other pubs handy for walks include the Waggoners at Ayot Green TL2214, Clarendon Arms at Chandlers Cross TQ0698, Two Brewers on Chipperfield Common TL0401, Fish & Eels at Dobbs Weir TL3808 nr Hoddesdon, Bricklayers Arms and Green Dragon at Flaunden TL0100, Alford Arms at Frithsden TL0110, Huntsman at Goose Green TL3509 (for Hertford Heath), Cross Keys at Gustard Wood nr Wheathampstead TL1716, Five Horseshoes at Little Berkamsted TL2908, Two Brewers at Northaw TL2802 (the ancient Great Wood is very pretty), Cabinet at Reed TL3636, Harvest Moon at Thorley TL4718, Royal Hotel in Station Rd outside Tring SP9211 (on the Ridgeway long distance path which heads off W across southern England), White Lion at Walkern TL2826, Sword in Hand at Westmill TL3627 and Greyhound at Wigginton SP9410 (where the landlord's very helpful with suggestions; the 18th-c summerhouse in the woods is an odd find).

Scales Wood up nr Anstey TL4133 is also good for strolls, and in the woods above Hexton is an easily traced Iron Age hill fort, Ravensburgh Castle TL1029 (the Live & Let Live in nearby Pegsdon is handy for refreshment). There are pleasant unspoilt walks from Sarratt TQ0499 into the Chess Valley in Buckinghamshire.

Where to eat

Ardeley TL3027 JOLLY WAGGONER (01438) 832175 Friendly and pretty little pub with carefully prepared food in bars and restaurant, good range of wines, and well kept Greene King ales; lots of woodwork, a civilised relaxed atmosphere, and an attractive garden; cl Mon, 1st week Jan; children over 7. £25|£5.

Ashwell TL2639 BUSHEL & STRIKE (01462) 742394 Popular dining pub with cheerful open-plan bar, neatly laid tables, a wide choice of good food in the no smoking restaurant, and well kept real ales; friendly staff, seats on the terrace and in the garden; cl pm Sun. £20|£5.95.

Burnham Green TL2516 WHITE HORSE (01438) 798416 Thriving and civilised dining pub with attractive original black-beamed part by bar counter, and a big 2-floored extension (no smoking downstairs); very good-value food, friendly service from uniformed staff, and well kept real ales; well behaved children in restaurant only. **£20 dinner, £15 lunch**|£4.50.

Rushden TL3031 MOON & STARS (01763) 288330 Unspoilt and cottagey country pub with nice atmosphere in heavy-beamed bar with huge inglenook; enjoyable food served by friendly staff; pleasant garden; no food pm Sun, cl am Mon; children over 5 if eating. £19|£7.95.

St Albans TL1507 WAFFLE HOUSE Kingsbury Watermill, St Michael's St (01727) 853502 Little restaurant attached to 16th-c mill museum, serving delicious sweet and savoury waffles; terrace tables by the River Ver in summer; cl Mon exc bank hols; disabled access. **£9.50**|£4.95.

Tewin TL2714 PLUME OF FEATHERS (01438) 717265 Civilised, roomy dining pub with several low-ceilinged communicating areas, a pretty restaurant, and seats in the garden overlooking the golf course; interesting food, real ales, and decent wines by the glass. £17.90|£6.95.

Watton-at-Stone TL3019 GEORGE & DRAGON High St (01920) 830285 Civilised pub first licensed in 1603, with antiques, open fires, daily newspapers, and friendly, efficient service; first-class imaginative food in bar (good-value daily specials) and no smoking restaurant, and good house wines; cl 25–26 Dec. £19.30|£7.85.

Special thanks to Melanie H Stein.

HERTFORDSHIRE CALENDAR

Some of these dates were provisional as we went to press, please check information with the numbers provided.

St Albans Living Roman History at the Verulamium Museum *the second weekend in every month* (01727) 819339

JANUARY

1 **St Albans** New Year's Day Family Concert at the Cathedral (01727) 860780

MARCH

8 **Hitchin** International Traditional Country Dance Displays (01707) 390653

APRIL

26 **Hertford** Music Festival – *till May 31* (01992) 503129

MAY

3 **Sawbridgeworth** May Fair (01279) 724503
4 **Hertford** Art Society Annual Open Exhibition – *till Sat 16* (01438) 723535
7 **Hatfield** Living Crafts: over 500 crafts-people at Hatfield House – *till Sun 10* (01707) 262823
9 **Rickmansworth** Festival Week – *till Sat 16* (01923) 772325
10 **Knebworth** VW Rally at Knebworth House (01625) 575681
16 **Rickmansworth** Canal Festival – *till Sun 17* (01923) 778382
17 **Hertford** Dressage Show at Hartham Common (01920) 463430
23 **Knebworth** Living History at Knebworth House – *till Mon 25* (01625) 575681; **Redbourn** County Show – *till Sun 24* (01582) 792626
24 **New Mill** Canal Festival at Tring – *till Mon 25* (01442) 823378

JUNE

3 **Hatfield** Antiques Fair at Hatfield House: 50 stands – *till Sun 7* (01707) 262823
20 **Borehamwood** Carnival Parade, then Elstree Civic Week – *till 4 July* (0181) 207 1382; **Hatfield** Festival of Gardening: lectures, guided tours, flower marquee, arena events at Hatfield House – *till Sun 21* (01707) 262823
27 **Borehamwood** Elstree Film Festival (0181) 207 1382; **London Colney** Flying Weekend: vintage aircraft at Mosquito Aircraft Museum – *till Sun 28* (01727) 822051

JULY

4 **Borehamwood** Families Day: free event, arena, fair, stalls in Meadow Park (0181) 207 1382
18 **Chiswell Green** National Show of Miniature Roses at The National Rose Society – *till Sun 19* (01727) 850461; **Hatfield** Tudor Revels: reproduction at Hatfield House of a busy Tudor village inc jousting and working crafts to celebrate the 500th anniversary of the building of the Old Palace in Hatfield Park – *till Sun 19* (01707) 262823
26 **Knebworth** Firework and Laser Concert at Knebworth House (01625) 575681

HERTFORDSHIRE CALENDAR

AUGUST

7 **Hatfield** Pottery and Ceramics Festival at Hatfield House – *till Sun 9* (01707) 262823

23 **Knebworth** Last Night of the Proms Concert at Knebworth House (01625) 575681

29 **St Albans** Evening of Music and Family Fun inc mechanical organs, stalls at the Organ Museum (01727) 851557; **Watford** Show (01923) 213971

31 **St Albans** Carnival (01727) 853046

SEPTEMBER

2 **Hatfield** Antiques Fair at Hatfield House: 50 stands – *till Sun 6* (01707) 262823

5 **Letchworth** North Herts Festival: live music, classic cars, horse and dog shows at Standalone Farm – *till Sun 6* (01462) 442888

24 **Letchworth** CAMRA Beer Festival at Plinston Hall – *till Sat 26* (01462) 455976

NOVEMBER

5 **Borehamwood** Fireworks (0181) 207 1382

7 **St Albans** Firework at Verulamium Park (01727) 860780; **Welwyn Garden City** Fireworks at Stanborough Lakes (01707) 327655

13 **St Albans** Performing Arts Festival – *till Sat 21* (01727) 857827

20 **Hertford** Medieval Night: street entertainers, stalls (01992) 551214

DECEMBER

12 **Sawbridgeworth** Christmas Cruise to see Father Christmas (01279) 600848

We welcome reports from readers . . .

This *Guide* depends on readers' reports. Do help us if you can – in return, we offer a discount on the next edition to people who've helped us with reports for it. Tell us what you think about places already in it, and anything extra you think we should say about them. And send us your ideas for inclusion in the next edition: places to visit, eat at or stay in, attractive drives or walks, maybe even unusual interesting shops you know of. Use the card in the middle, the report forms at the end, or just write – no stamp needed: *The Good Guide to Britain*, FREEPOST TN1569, Wadhurst, E Sussex TN5 7BR.

ISLE OF WIGHT

Underrated as a holiday area: good family beach holidays with lots of interesting events and places to visit, attractive coast and countryside, quiet off-season breaks.

In high summer the main resorts and places to visit do get very busy, with coach parties descending in droves on the prettiest villages. But the many people who come here just for day visits tend to home in on just the obvious places. Away from these tourist haunts, much of the island is unspoilt and little visited. With good beaches, some of Britain's best weather, resorts, and plenty to interest families, it's rewarding for holidays. The most attractive scenery is in the west, the largest concentration of things to do in the east.

The emphasis is on tradition: the family attractions here don't really go in for the new-fangled displays and technology that you can find on the mainland, and for a holiday on the island it's better to think in terms of buckets and spades than computerised rides and gadgets. The most satisfying children's outings – Robin Hill nr Arreton, its stablemate at Blackgang Chine, and the Brickfields horse centre at Binstead – are firmly traditional.

Quite a few other enjoyable visits centre on animals or birds, particularly the Amazon Adventure at Newchurch and the bird and animal attractions at St Lawrence. Arreton has lots around it to entertain families. Osborne House at East Cowes is a highlight for many older people.

Outside the main holiday season the island has a great deal of potential for short breaks, feeling fresh, uncrowded and leisurely, with attractive countryside. The coastal walks are the finest in south-east England – worth coming just for these. In May and June the south coast is generally the sunniest place in Britain, and even in winter really cold weather is rare. Many of the more child-oriented places close for six months over winter.

The crossing takes about 30 minutes – half that for the Portsmouth–Ryde catamaran, even less for the Southsea Hovercraft. Readers like the Lymington–Yarmouth trip best (you'll need to book in summer). Foot fares start at £6.20, cars from around £30 – though the very cheapest fares are usually at pretty anti-social times: (01705) 827744 for bookings from Portsmouth to Fishbourne or Ryde, and Lymington to Yarmouth; (01703) 33033 for Southampton–Cowes; (01705) 811000 for Hovercraft Southsea–Ryde (from £7.90 day return).

Once you're there, prices are rather on the low side compared with the mainland, and for longer stays some hotels do good-value package deals that include the ferry fare.

The island bus service is excellent, especially between May and

September; a week's bus pass is good value, as is a daily Rover road/rail ticket.

Where to stay

Bonchurch SZ5778 LAKE Shore Rd, Bonchurch, Ventnor PO38 1RF (01983) 852613 *£52, plus special breaks; 20 rms. Early 19th-c country house in 2 acres of pretty gardens, with lots of flowers and plants in 3 light and airy lounges (one is an attractive conservatory); bar, restaurant and enjoyable food; cl Nov–Feb; children over 3; dogs by prior arrangement.

Bonchurch SZ5778 WINTERBOURNE Bonchurch, Ventnor PO38 1RQ (01983) 852535 £124 inc dinner; 14 rms, most with own bthrm, many with sea views and some in the coach house. Charming creeper-covered house with 4 acres of pretty grounds inc waterfalls, and a stream; a small heated swimming pool, and restful day rooms; good food in attractive restaurant, and friendly staff and resident owners; Charles Dickens wrote DAVID COPPERFIELD here; cl Nov–Mar; dogs welcome.

Chale SZ4877 CLARENDON Chale, Ventnor PO38 2HA (01983) 730431 *£70; 15 rms inc 3 suites, plus winter special breaks. Warm and friendly hotel (and very well run Wight Mouse family pub, attached) with engaging helpful owners, lots of charm and character; a comfortable sun lounge and cocktail bar, good food, wines and real ales, and an extraordinary collection of whiskies; excellent for families; disabled access.

Ryde SZ5992 RYDE CASTLE Esplanade, Ryde PO33 1JA (01983) 563755 £80; 21 rms, many with sea views, and some quite modern. 16th-c castle with a comfortable lounge, tapestries, a good bar, and friendly, helpful staff; enjoyable food in the restaurant designed to look like a galleon, and excellent breakfasts.

St Lawrence SZ5376 LISLE COMBE Bank End Farm, Undercliffe Drive, St Lawrence, Ventnor PO38 1UW (01983) 852582 *£34; 3 rms, shared bthrm. Elizabethan-style farmhouse in a 5-acre coastal garden with lovely sea views; friendly and courteous staff, and lovely paintings and furniture – it was once the home of poet Alfred Noyes and is still owned by his family; they keep their own rare breeds and waterfowl park, and are close to coves and beaches; must book months ahead (so popular with return customers); self-catering cottage; cl Christmas; no dogs.

Seaview SZ6291 SEAVIEW High St, Seaview PO34 5EX (01983) 612711 *£70, plus special breaks; 16 attractively decorated rms, some with sea views and private drawing rooms. Small, friendly and spotlessly kept hotel with fine ship photographs in the chatty and relaxed front dining bar, an old-fashioned characterful back bar, good imaginative bar food, and a highly regarded evening restaurant; proper high tea for children (must be over 5 in evening restaurant).

Shanklin SZ5881 LUCCOMBE CHINE HOUSE Luccombe PO37 6RH (01983) 862037 *£74, plus special breaks; 6 rms, all with four-posters and sea or garden views. Very friendly small hotel at the end of a long drive and surrounded by large wooded grounds where you can watch foxes and badgers at night taking food left for them on the lawn; homely lounge with help-yourself drinks tray, beams and inglenook fireplaces, very good food in the cosy dining room; good walks; cl Dec–Jan; no children.

Shorwell SZ4582 WESTCOURT FARM Shorwell, Newport PO30 3LA (01983) 740233 *£34; 3 rms. Fine Elizabethan manor connected to a farm of 250 acres; with a comfortable lounge/dining room, and a restful atmosphere; no smoking; lots of surrounding walks; cl Dec–Feb; children over 10.

Ventnor SZ5677 ROYAL Belgrave Rd, Ventnor PO38 1JJ (01983) 852186 *£120; 55 well equipped rms. Friendly Victorian hotel with fine views over the sea, and neat gardens with a heated outdoor pool; spacious and comfortable day rooms, good food in the attractive restaurant, and helpful service; disabled access, cl 5–26 Jan.

Yarmouth SZ3589 Bugle The Square, Yarmouth PO41 0NS (01983) 760272 £56; 10 rms, some with own bthrm (best to have one not above the lively bar). Bustling inn with a bar decorated like a galleon stern, and other panelled rooms; a friendly atmosphere, good bar and restaurant food (restaurant closed Sun, Mon), children's room, and sizeable garden.

Yarmouth SZ3589 George Quay St, Yarmouth PO41 0PE (01983) 760331 £110; 17 comfortable rms. Pleasantly relaxing panelled bars, one with a nautical theme, log fires, good food, prompt, courteous service, their own gardens leading to a private beach, and their own fishing operation in Yarmouth and St Vaast.

To see and do

ISLE OF WIGHT FAMILY ATTRACTION OF THE YEAR

☺ **Arreton** SZ5386 Robin Hill Country Park (Downend) By mainland standards this 88-acre site is a little tame, but it's a very useful retreat for families, particularly those with younger children who want to run around. And it's especially good value if you then feel like coming again within the next week: a return ticket costs only 50p. Like its stablemate Blackgang Chine it has a few rather dated-looking representations of trolls and the like, but it scores more highly for activities and play areas, inc quite a few new slides, underground tunnels and assault course style equipment. Paths and trails wind through the woodland, and there's a pitch and putt course, along with look-out tower, wooden maze (like walking round lots of high garden fences), and plenty of space for football, basketball or just wandering about. Children between around 5 and 11 will probably be kept interested longest, though the toboggan run is fun for older brothers (and dads); it's £1 extra a ride. Best in fine weather (most features are outdoors); easy to spend an undemanding half day here. Meals, snacks, shop, disabled access but rather hilly; cl Nov–Mar; (01983) 527352; £3.50 (£2.50 children 3–13).

! ❄ ✗ 🏠 🖼 **Alum Bay** SZ3484 The beach here is famous for its multi-coloured sands from the different rock strata in the cliff that runs down to it; 20 shades of pinks, greys and ochres, showing up brightest after rain. The otherwise unremarkable Needles Pleasure Park at the top of the cliffs stands out for its spectacular chairlift down to the beach, with wonderful views along the way. They sell little glass tubes with the sands carefully layered inside. Meals, snacks, shop, disabled access; cl Nov–Mar; (01983) 752401; park entry free (though car parking is £2, £2.50 July and Aug), then individual charges for attractions (return trip on the chairlift is £2), or all-in ticket for £5. This includes glass-blowing demonstrations at adjacent Alum Bay Glass (not wknds); there's also a good factory shop. From the park a minibus goes up to the 19th-c

Needles Old Battery (you can't go by car); the parade-ground of the fortress shows off two 12-ton gun barrels salvaged from the sea. A longish underground tunnel leads to a look-out spot that gives stunning views of the Needles themselves, a group of wave-battered chalk pinnacles, and their lighthouse. Snacks, shop, limited disabled access; cl Fri and Sat (exc July and Aug), and Nov–Mar; (01983) 754772; £2.40; NT. The High Down Hotel towards Totland has decent food.

✝ 🏠 ♿ ✗ ☺ **Arreton** SZ5386 A pleasant place with a delightful 13th-c church (which has a brass-rubbing centre). The White Lion is good for lunch, and the cross-island Wootton Bridge–Niton back road through here has quietly attractive views. Arreton Manor Lovely old mellow stone house, dating from around 1600, with splendid period furnishings and

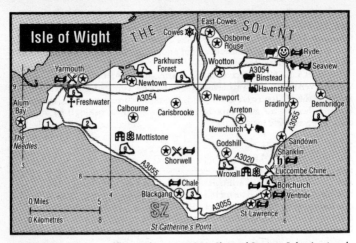

panelling, collections of lace and dolls, and the NATIONAL WIRELESS MUSEUM – Marconi made his pioneering experiments nearby. Meals, snacks, shop; cl am Sun, all Sat (exc bank hol wknds), and Nov–Mar; (01983) 528134; £3. The nearby COUNTRY CRAFT VILLAGE has craft workshops, a pub, and a restaurant with home baking. HASELEY MANOR The largest and oldest manor house open on the island, some parts dating from 1310. The enthusiastic owners have put a lot of effort into restoring the place, and the 20 or so rooms are carefully decorated in period style. Also reconstructed 18th-c farm with animals, herb gardens, pottery, play area, and craft centre, so a useful family day out. Snacks, shop, disabled access; cl Nov–Easter; (01983) 865420; £4.20. For ROBIN HILL COUNTRY PARK *see separate Family Panel on p. 343.*

✿ ✗ ❀ **Bembridge** SZ6488 Even in summer this is quiet for a coastal place, though with plenty going on in its yachting harbour, and a lifeboat station nearby. SHIPWRECK CENTRE AND MARITIME MUSEUM (Sherbourne St) 6 galleries of salvage and shipwreck items, and tales of pirates and mermen. Shop, disabled access ground floor only; cl Nov–Mar; (01983) 872223; £2.25. Nearby is the only surviving WINDMILL on the island, built in 1700 and used until

1913. Shop; cl Sat (exc July–Aug) and Nov–Mar; £1.20; NT. Out on the Foreland the magnificent rock pools would keep any beachcomber happy for hours. The clifftop Crab & Lobster (Forelands), an easy walk up from the beach has fabulous views.

🐎 **Binstead** SZ5791 BRICKFIELDS HORSE COUNTRY (Newnham Rd) 2 daily parades of horses in the indoor arena (noon and 3.30pm), livened up by the appearance of a medieval knight, and a cowboy and Indian, who chase each other around firing pistols and flinging tomahawks. Also tours of stables, waggon rides, rabbits and guinea pigs, and a collection of shetland ponies. Show-jumping displays from 7pm on summer Weds evenings (car boot sales Mon evenings), and on 3 evenings in mid-Dec they put on a spectacular Christmas show, which might include a pantomime and shetland pony Grand National. Meals, snacks, shop, disabled access; cl 25–26 Dec; (01983) 566801; *£4. The old White Hart at Havenstreet is handy for lunch.

☺ ⬩t ♟ ❀ **Blackgang** SZ4876 BLACKGANG CHINE FANTASY PARK Family leisure park, with gentle rides, a complete replica of a Victorian sawmill, traditional crafts, and a maritime museum down on St Catherine's Quay. The plentiful models of dinosaurs, goblins and the like are done with a fair bit of panache, but aren't really that exciting. The gardens are well illuminated on summer evenings. Meals, snacks, shop, some disabled access; cl Nov–Mar; (01983) 730330; *£5.50 (50p for return visit within seven days). The Wight Mouse at Chale SZ4877 is an excellent family pub, and the A3055 in both directions gives fine sea and coast views.

✝ 🏠 👑 ♨ 🐖 **Brading** SZ6087 Busy and attractive, with interesting monuments in its Norman CHURCH, and a pretty graveyard. The Bugle is a useful family food pub. The remains of a ROMAN VILLA have good mosaics (cl Nov–Mar; £2.25), and there's a little local history museum in the town hall; cl Sat and Oct–Apr; *50p. LILLIPUT DOLL AND TOY MUSEUM 💷 (High St) Excellent private collection, with over 2,000 exhibits dating from as far back as 2000 BC, and examples of almost every seriously collectable doll in Britain. Shop, disabled access (though there are 2 steps); cl 25 Dec; (01983) 407231; £1.45. MORTON MANOR 💷 (off the A3055) Friendly partly 13th-c manor house, set in lovely landscaped gardens with ornamental ponds and an Elizabethan turf maze. The little vineyard has an exhibition of winemaking relics. Meals and snacks in new tearooms, shop; cl Sat, and Nov–Mar; (01983) 406168; £3.50. NUNWELL HOUSE AND GARDENS (off the A3055) Lovely lived-in 16th-c house with charming gardens, Home Guard museum, and interesting furniture and family memorabilia. Charles I spent his last night of freedom here. Snacks, shop; cl am Thurs–Sun Oct–Jun, plus first 2 wks Aug; (01983) 407240; £4, £2.50 garden only. ISLE OF WIGHT WAXWORKS (High St) Set in the partly 11th-c Ancient Rectory Mansion, this is largely what you'd expect from a wax museum, with an adjacent collection of stuffed animals and birds. Shop, mostly disabled access; (01983) 407286; £4.50. The road out over Bembridge Down to Culver Cliff gives fine views, especially from the Culver Haven pub at the end.

★ ✝ 🐖 ❄ **Calbourne** SZ4286 Attractive village with photogenic streamside thatched cottages, a 13th-c CHURCH, and an enjoyable working POTTERY; cl Sun Jan–Easter, and 2 wks at Christmas; *40p. It's worth getting here early to avoid the coach tours. WATERMILL AND RURAL MUSEUM (on the B3401) A 6-metre (20-ft) waterwheel still powers this 17th-c mill, and the grounds have tame peacocks. Home-baked snacks, shop with stoneground flour, etc, some disabled access; cl Nov–Easter; (01983) 531227; £3. Fine views from the Blacksmiths Arms, a good family pub on the Carisbrooke road.

🏰 ❄ 🐑 🚃 **Carisbrooke** SZ4888 CARISBROOKE CASTLE Ruins of the only medieval castle on the island, between 1647 and 1648 home to the imprisoned Charles I (his daughter died here in 1650). Some later buildings behind the imposing gatehouse and walls, and entertaining demonstrations of how donkeys traditionally drew water from the 2 medieval wells. Snacks, shop, disabled access to ground floor; cl 24–26 Dec; (01983) 522107; £4. The Eight Bells above the waterfowl lake has decent food and good Solent views; there's also a DONKEY SANCTUARY nearby.

❄ **Cowes** SZ4995 Stylish and lively, very much centred on its yachting connections, with interesting buildings and shops inc fascinating ships' chandlers in the long narrow High St, and the battery of over 20 brass cannons used to start the yacht races down by the harbour. The Union (Watchhouse Lane) has good-value food. Seafaring collections at the small MARITIME MUSEUM in the public library on Beckford Rd (cl Sun, Christmas and bank hols; free), and at the pretty SIR MAX AITKEN MUSEUM (open Tues–Sat May–Sept; *£1).

🏠 ❄ 🐖 ✝ **East Cowes** SZ5095 OSBORNE HOUSE (1m SE) Queen Victoria's favourite residence, where she died in 1901; the state and private apartments haven't changed much since. Designed to resemble an Italian villa by Prince Albert, with professional help from Thomas

Cubitt, it's a striking place. Albert and his wife were also responsible for the original layout of the fine gardens, which seem filled with every conceivable English tree. A horse-drawn carriage conveys you in style to the Swiss cottage, where the royal children learnt cooking and gardening. Snacks, shop, disabled access to ground floor only; cl Nov–Mar; (01983) 200022; £6. Neighbouring BARTON MANOR GARDENS AND VINEYARD covers about 10 acres, with lovely gardens and plants, and a big rose-hedge maze. Snacks, shop, disabled access; open wkdys Jun–Aug; (01983) 292835; £3.75, inc 2 tastings and a souvenir glass. You can buy a combined ticket for the vineyards and Osborne House (you don't have to visit both the same day). WHIPPINGHAM CHURCH SZ5193 Said to have been another of Prince Albert's designs, and a good deal more eccentric than Osborne House: a bizarre mix of different styles. Down on the River Medina, the beautifully placed Folly Inn has an appropriately nautical atmosphere.

† **Freshwater** SZ3484 A very extended rather sprawling village, with a charming quiet core. The picturesque thatched CHURCH (built this century) includes quite a few Tennyson family memorials, and beyond it a causeway crosses the head of the Yar estuary. The Red Lion has good food, and the Vine has a pleasant terrace for warm days. There are fine walks nearby, and Hill Farm has riding.

★ † ! 🐛 👹 **Godshill** SZ5281 Best appreciated in winter, when the coach parties that descend on the teahouses and quaint little streets have gone home. Plenty of famously pretty thatched cottages, and a good 15th-c CHURCH, with an interesting 15th-c wall painting. The MODEL VILLAGE painstakingly recreates Shanklin, its Chine Valley, and Godshill in miniature, and is nicely floodlit summer eves. Shop, disabled access; cl Nov–Mar; (01983) 840270; £2.25. Based around a former blacksmith's forge, the OLD SMITHY TOURIST CENTRE has an aviary

of exotic birds, and a garden in the shape of the island itself. Snacks, shop (with local crafts), disabled access; cl 25–26 Dec, gardens cl Oct-Mar; (01983) 840364; 80p. The NOSTALGIA TOY MUSEUM has lots of pre-war toys and die-cast model cars (cl Nov–Easter; 95p), and there's a decent collection of fossils and minerals at the NATURAL HISTORY CENTRE (cl Nov–Mar; *£1.25). The Taverners has decent food.

🚂 **Havenstreet** SZ5690 ISLE OF WIGHT STEAM RAILWAY Well restored railway with very pleasant 10-mile trip from Wootton to Smallbrook Junction nr Ryde (where you can change directly on to BR). Vintage engines and rolling stock, and related memorabilia displayed in the old gasworks at Havenstreet Station. Meals, snacks, shop, disabled access if accompanied; open Apr–Oct, phone for timetable, (01983) 884343; £5.50. The Island Line day ticket (around £7) includes the steam railway with travel on all regular trains on the island. The White Hart does enjoyable and generous food.

🏠 👹 **Mottistone** SZ4083 Charming old village with a well in the centre of the green; even the bus shelter is stone-built. The Bluebell Wood opposite the church is lovely in spring. The fine gardens of MOTTISTONE MANOR are open pm Weds and bank hols Apr–Sept; (01983) 740552; £1.80; NT. The medieval and Elizabethan manor house itself is open Aug bank hol only. The Sun at Hulverstone nearby is lovely in summer (though we found it closed in late Aug 1997).

✌ 🏠 **Newchurch** SZ5685 A quiet village with a photogenic church; the Pointer beside it has decent home cooking. ISLAND AMAZON ADVENTURE Expanding collection of the kind of animals you'd find in an Amazon rain forest, with lively jungle and village settings; an effective mix of entertainment with environmental awareness. Meals, snacks, shop, disabled access; cl 25 Dec; (01983) 867122; £3.95.

★ 🏛 👹 † ✤ **Newport** SZ4989 The island's capital, with a good deal of character, some fine old Georgian houses, and warm red brick 18th-c buildings down by the quay. It's the main place on the island for antique shops. ROMAN VILLA (Cypress Rd) Well preserved baths and reconstructed rooms on the site of 3rd-c Roman villa, with an informative museum; also Roman garden. Shop; cl Nov–Mar; (01983) 529720; £1.75. The parish CHURCH OF ST THOMAS is worth a look – it has an interestingly carved Jacobean pulpit and a 19th-c memorial to Charles I's daughter. The 17th-c Wheatsheaf nearby is handy for lunch. The newly refurbished Quay Arts Centre (Sea St) usually has wknd antique and craft fairs, and in the Quay itself a restored PIRATES' SHIP (used in the filming of *The Onedin Line*) has variously priced summer activities and tours for children. There are usually other restored boats to visit nearby. The back road to Brading has pleasant views.

🏛 ✟ 🐄 Newtown SZ4290 For a while this was the island's capital, but it began a slow decline after a disastrous fire in 1377, and eventually faded out altogether – what used to be rich merchants' streets are now just grassy tracks. The OLD TOWN HALL, rebuilt in 1699 but now left stranded and unusually isolated from any houses, is all that's left to mark the once thriving town; open pm Mon, Weds and Sun Apr–Oct, plus pm Tues and Thurs in July and Aug; £1.10; NT. Rewarding walks for bird watchers at the nearby NATURE RESERVE. Just out of town the CLAMERKIN FARM PARK is a 30-acre working farm with friendly animals, fine views, craft demonstrations and a golf driving range. Meals, snacks, shop, disabled access (though no facilities); cl Nov to wk before Easter; (01983) 531396; £1.80. The New Inn at Shalfleet, open all day in summer, has good seafood.

☺ 🐄 Ryde SZ5992 Now the biggest town here, with a long triple pier, good sandy beaches, and a full set of holiday-resort amusements – just right for a straightforward family holiday. Free tours and tastings at the ROSEMARY VINEYARD on Smallbrook Lane; (01983) 811084.

🐖 🐄 ✟ 🐑 St Lawrence SZ5376 RARE BREEDS AND WATERFOWL PARK 🅱 (Lisle Combe, Undercliff Drive) Good rare breeds centre in a really lovely setting, covering 30 secluded coastal acres. Smaller animals for younger children (inc a guinea pig village). Meals, snacks, shop, disabled access (they prefer notice); cl winter wkdys; cl 25 Dec; (01983) 852582; £3.20. They do B & B in the attractive old house. TROPICAL BIRD PARK Over 400 birds in the beautiful grounds of Old Park, in the almost subtropical Undercliff. Snacks, shop, some disabled access; cl am winter, 25 Dec; (01983) 852583; £3. The Park also houses ISLE OF WIGHT GLASS, with demonstrations (not wknds), lovely displays, and shop. Disabled access; cl winter wknds; (01983) 853526; 50p. The St Lawrence Inn is a popular dining pub with superb Channel views.

♨ 🐄 🐘 ♨ Sandown SZ5984 All the usual things for a family beach holiday – pier, boat trips, canoeing lake, discos – and a fine beach. The ZOO has rare and endangered animals such as tigers, panthers and leopards, as well as a notable collection of poisonous snakes. Summer meals and snacks, shop; cl Nov–mid-Feb (exc wknds); (01983) 403883; £4.90. You can usually tour the partly underground winery of ADGESTONE VINEYARD on Upper Rd, but you'll need to book on (01983) 402503; free. MUSEUM OF GEOLOGY (High St) Small but interesting collection of local fossils and rocks, with recently excavated dinosaur fossils. Shop, some disabled access; cl Sun, 25–26 Dec; (01983) 404344; free. By 1999 the collection will be considerably more elaborate, thanks to a £1 million grant from the Millennium Commission.

🐦 Seaview SZ6291 A timelessly quiet retreat, with sedate streets of unassuming villas; the Seaview Hotel does very good lunches. Just W of town at Springvale, FLAMINGO PARK has hundreds of birds in spacious landscaped grounds; some can be fed by hand. Meals, snacks, shop, disabled access; cl Nov–Easter; (01983) 612153; *£3.95.

♄ **Shanklin** SZ5881 SHANKLIN CHINE Quite glorious natural gorge with magnificent 14-metre (45-ft) waterfall. A heritage centre gives details of rare flora, nature trails and life in Victorian Shanklin. Snacks, shop; cl mid-Oct–Easter; (01983) 866432; *£2. Down on the beach, the thatched Fishermans Cottage is useful for lunch (open all day in season, cl Nov–Mar), and up at the top the Chine Inn is a good-value family pub (no food Sun evening, Sat or Tues).

★ ✗ ➡ **Shorwell** SZ4582 One of the few really pretty villages on the island to have escaped a flood of tourist interest, with charming streamside thatched cottages and a fine church; the attractive Crown is very pleasant for lunch. YAFFORD MILL FARM PARK (just S) is fun: a seal lives in a special enclosure beside the millpond of the working 18th-c watermill, various species of waterfowl fill the pools of the stream, and rare breeds of sheep and cattle graze along its banks. Also nature trails, wagons and traction engines (sometimes in steam) and an adventure playground across the lane. Meals and snacks, shop, disabled access; cl 25 Dec; (01983) 740610; £3.80.

🏵 ☗ ★ † ❋ **Ventnor** SZ5677 Relatively untouristy little town up on the cliff, the fairly restrained and decorous seafront down below linked to it by a tortuously steep loop of road; between them perched on ledges among the trees are quite a few of Victorian villas – many of them still private houses rather than guesthouses. Its great pride is the BOTANIC GARDEN, where an exceptional collection of subtropical plants make the most of the mild climate; the Garden Tavern here has decent food and sea views. In the grounds (or more correctly under them) the MUSEUM OF SMUGGLING HISTORY demonstrates the tricks smugglers past and present have used to sneak in wool, brandy, tobacco or drugs. Meals, snacks, shop; cl Oct–Easter; (01983) 853677; £1.90. There are 2 decent local history museums: the HERITAGE MUSEUM on Spring Hill (cl 12.15–2pm, pm Weds and Sat, all Sun, and Nov–May; 50p), and the LONGSHOREMAN'S MUSEUM on the Esplanade (cl Jan and Feb; *50p). The Spyglass is an interesting pub with superb sea views. Nearby BONCHURCH is much quieter, with leafy lanes hugging the steep slopes and passing an unexpected tree-shaded pond; steep steps connect the different levels, and there's a quiet cove down below the cliff. The small 13th-c CHURCH has a lovely peaceful graveyard, and above the cliff St Boniface Down has tremendous VIEWS. The Bonchurch Inn is rather unusual, with its Italian landlord and food. For several miles along this

---

Days Out

Tennyson's strolling ground
Yarmouth; Newtown Old Town Hall and nature reserve; lunch at the Eight Bells, Carisbrooke; Carisbrooke Castle; Calbourne; walk on Tennyson Down from Alum Bay, or visit the Needles Old Battery.

Thatched cottages and a ruined mansion
Godshill; Appuldurcombe House, Wroxall; lunch at the Spyglass, Ventnor; St Lawrence Rare Breeds and Waterfowl Park, Appuldurcombe House; Shorwell.

Queen Victoria's retreat
Either Brickfields Horse Country, Binstead, and Isle of Wight Steam Railway (described under Havenstreet) or Bembridge windmill and a stroll on Culver Cliff; lunch at the Seaview Hotel, Seaview; Osborne House.

section of coast, the cliffs have been and to some extent still are subject to massive landslides. The UNDERCLIFF is formed from the irregular masses of earth which have come to rest below, with often rocky chasms between each other and the cliff itself. Sometimes planted and sometimes with profuse natural vegetation, the resulting scenery is unlike anything else on the island, with quite a subtropical aspect. Some of the attractions along it we've listed under St Lawrence.

🏠✝🦋🌳 **Wootton** SZ5492 A terminus for the STEAM RAILWAY – see Havenstreet entry, above. It has an attractive partly Norman CHURCH, and BUTTERFLY WORLD (Staplers Rd), next to a 5-acre garden centre (cl Nov–Easter; £3.50). The Sloop overlooking the creek is a reliable food pub.

🏠🌳 **Wroxall** SZ5480 APPULDURCOMBE HOUSE (W, off the B3327) Intriguing shell of a Palladian house, nestling among grounds beautifully landscaped by Capability Brown. You can still catch something of the atmosphere of the days when this was one of the grandest houses on the island. The stables have been converted into holiday cottages.

Snacks, shop, some disabled access; cl Nov–Mar; (01983) 840188; £2. The Star is useful for lunch.

🏰🌸🐾🏇⛵🏠 **Yarmouth** SZ3589 A lively place, its old harbour busy with yachts in summer. The CASTLE was built as part of Henry VIII's coastal defences; it's in an excellent state, and you can see the Master Gunner's surprisingly homely parlour and kitchen. Outside, the open gun platform has good views of the harbour. Shop; cl Nov–Mar; (01983) 760678; £2. Surrounding a rather later fortress, the FORT VICTORIA COUNTRY PARK also has good views over the Solent, as well as 50 acres of woodland and a mile or so of pebbly beach. In the grounds are a maritime heritage centre, excellent aquarium (£1.90) and planetarium (£2). Snacks, shop, disabled access (exc planetarium); not all parts open winter – best to check first; (01983) 760860; park free, guided ranger tours £1. The adjacent FORT VICTORIA MODEL RAILWAY is reckoned to be the biggest model railway in the country, and the only one completely controlled by computer. Good shop; open Easter–Sept; (01983) 761553; £3. The Wheatsheaf here is popular for lunch.

Walks

Tennyson Down SZ3285 ⌂1 on Wight's W tip is the best place of all for walkers here: a friendly grassy ridge and cliff walk rolled into one, with views over most of the island and across to the mainland. You pass the monument to Alfred Lord Tennyson (who lived nearby and loved this place), and the walk culminates in spectacular fashion above The Needles SZ2984. You can walk the entire ridge from Freshwater Bay SZ3485 (summer bus service from Alum Bay to bring you back), or make a round walk from Alum Bay car park SZ3085, past the Needles Old Battery and along to the monument, then up on to Headon Warren before going down to Alum Bay. The High Down Hotel (on the B3322) is another jump-off point.

Compton Down SZ3785 ⌂-2 is another good place for walks on this S coast, a hogsback grassy hill E of Freshwater Bay; circular walks can take in the coast path along Compton Bay – one of the island's best beaches, not touristy, with impressive cliff views (NT car park). **St Catherine's Hill** SZ4977 ⌂-3, capped by the ruins of a 14th-c oratory, is a short walk up from the coast path further E; you can walk on along a ridge to the prominent Hoy's Monument SO4978 at the far end of St Catherine's Down. The coast path meanwhile skirts the undercliff of St Catherine's Point SZ4875, the isle's southern tip, which has a modern working lighthouse; there are several other paths through the undercliff here. **Bonchurch Down** ⌂-4 above Ventnor SZ5677 has unsightly radar installations but gives fine views.

Godshill SZ5282 ⌂-5 is an inland starting point for a good walk via the Worsley Trail on to Stenbury Down (more masts, but redeemed by wide views), then back via the atmospherically ruinous Appuldurcombe House SZ5480 and passing through a huge estate gateway. The unspoilt reed-fringed **Yar estuary** ⌂-6 is skirted by a footpath along the former railway line S from Yarmouth SZ3589.

Newtown Nature Reserve SZ4191 ⌂-7 on the N coast has walks around the tranquil Norfolk-like creeks of the Newtown/Clamerkin estuaries, but there are few circular routes; from Newtown village SZ4290 a boardwalk leads out into the heart of the reserve within a few minutes.

The E coast is heavily developed; the coastal path sometimes follows roads and skirts large residential areas. **Bembridge** SZ6488 ⌂-8 does have opportunities for walks here, particularly S to Culver Cliff SZ6385.

Inland, the island is characterised by long curving chalk ridges (tracks often follow the crests) and forestry plantations (with many signposted woodland trails). The hills N of **Brighstone** SZ4282 ⌂-9 represent some of the pick of the scenery. The Countryman on Limerstone Rd is a good refreshment break, with fine views down to the sea. **Parkhurst Forest** SZ4890 ⌂-10, just W of the prison, is a couple of miles across, with plenty of paths and a good chance of seeing red squirrels.

Where to eat

Luccombe Chine SZ5879 Dunnose Cottage Tea Rooms (01983) 862585 16th-c thatched cottage in 3 acres of landscaped gardens; cream teas, snacks and simple lunchtime meals, speciality knickerbocker glories and nut sundaes, and lots of different teas; cl pm; wknds only Nov–Easter; bedrooms. l£5.

Shorwell SZ4582 Crown (01983) 740293 The big back garden with its trout-filled stream, ducks, doves and lilies is nice in summer, and there's an extended beamed lounge with a log fire, good food, and friendly staff; disabled access. £15l£3.95.

Yarmouth SZ3589 Jireh House St James's Sq (01983) 760513 17th-c guest house with friendly owners, a relaxed atmosphere, and a range of home-made meals, snacks and afternoon teas inc daily specials and fresh fish; cl Nov–just before Easter; disabled access (restaurant only). £9.50/special afternoon tea £5.50.

Yarmouth SZ3589 Wheatsheaf Bridge Rd (01983) 760456 Handy for the ferry, this inn has 4 comfortable and spacious eating areas inc an airy conservatory; a wide choice of good food (daily specials are the best), well kept beers and quick, friendly service; cl 25 Dec, pm 26 Dec; disabled access. £16l£3.

Special thanks to Liz Tuckey.

Please let us know what you think of places in the *Guide*. Use the report forms at the back of the book or simply send a letter.

ISLE OF WIGHT CALENDAR

Some of these dates were provisional as we went to press, please check information with the numbers provided

FEBRUARY

24 **Yarmouth** Pancake Races (01983) 760015

APRIL

11 **Yarmouth** Easter Egg Hunt in the High Street (01983) 760108
12 **Shorwell** Easter Egg Hunt – *till Mon 13* at Yafford Mill (01983) 740610
13 **Brook** Easter Steam-up and Vintage Ploughing Match at Compton Farm (01983) 740215

MAY

1 **Mottistone** Dance at Dawn by Morris Men at the Longstone, *5am* (01983) 822300
3 **Shorwell** Military Vehicles, Traction Engines and Tractors in Steam at Yafford Mill – *till Mon 4* (01983) 740610
10 **Shorwell** National Mills Day at Yafford Mill (01983) 740610
14 **Ventnor** Music for Fun Festival at the Winter Gardens – *till Wed 20* (01983) 854564
24 **Bembridge** Festival Week – *till Sun 31* (01983) 873087; **Shorwell** Children's Quiz Trail at Yafford Mill – *till Mon 25* (01983) 740610
25 **Whitwell** Crab Fair at the Rugby Club: stalls, fresh crabs (01983) 852771
30 **Arreton** Historical Re-enactments at Arreton Manor – *till 14 Jun* (01983) 528134

JUNE

12 **Binstead** Heavy Horse Festival at Brickfields Horse Country – *till Mon 15* (01983) 566801
20 **Cowes** Round the Island Yacht Race: over 1,000 yachts (01983) 296621
21 **Niton** Mackeral Fair (01983) 853625
27 **Shorwell** Isle of Wight Traction Engine Steam Up and Road Run at Yafford Mill – *till Sun 28* (01983) 740610

JULY

18 **Freshwater** Carnival (01983) 754335; **Northwood** County Show at the Showground – *till Sun 19* (01983) 740485
29 **Sandown** Carnival (01983) 402024

AUGUST

1 **Cowes** Week – *till Sat 8* (01983) 293303; **Shorwell** Traction Engine Rally and Vintage Ploughing Match at Yafford Mill – *till Sun 2* (01983) 740610
8 **Yarmouth** Carnival Week – *till procession on Sat 15* (01983) 760108
9 **Sandown** Regatta (01983) 403397
15 **Shorwell** Vintage Transport Rally at Yafford Mill – *till Sun 16* (01983) 740610
16 **Ryde** Carnival – *till Sat 22* (01983) 566461
19 **Shanklin** Regatta (01983) 862942

ISLE OF WIGHT CALENDAR

AUGUST cont

22 **Arreton** Garlic Festival at the Fighting Cocks Crossroads: biggest festival on the island with arena events, arts and crafts, circus, live bands – *till Sun 23* (01983) 865573; **St Helens** Jazz on the Quay (01983) 872519

23 **Newport** Carnival Week – *till Sat 29* (01983) 526595

26 **Sandown** Illuminated Carnival (01983) 402024

28 **Havenstreet** Summer Extravaganza at Isle of Wight Steam Railway - *till Mon 31* (01983) 882204

29 **Shorwell** Military Vehicle Rally at Yafford Mill – *till Mon 31* (01983) 740610

31 **St Helens** Carnival (01983) 873240

SEPTEMBER

12 **Shorwell** Festival of Country Ways and Vintage Threshing at Yafford Mill – *till Sun 13* (01983) 740610

OCTOBER

18 **Binstead** Cider-making Festival at Brickfields Horse Country (01983) 566801

NOVEMBER

5 **St Helens** Bonfire (01983) 522577

We welcome reports from readers . . .

This *Guide* depends on readers' reports. Do help us if you can – in return, we offer a discount on the next edition to people who've helped us with reports for it. Tell us what you think about places already in it, and anything extra you think we should say about them. And send us your ideas for inclusion in the next edition: places to visit, eat at or stay in, attractive drives or walks, maybe even unusual interesting shops you know of. Use the card in the middle, the report forms at the end, or just write – no stamp needed: *The Good Guide to Britain*, FREEPOST TN1569, Wadhurst, E Sussex TN5 7BR.

KENT

Masses to do and see for all ages, attractive, quite intricate countryside; good seaside resorts – old-fashioned without being jaded.

Canterbury has many fine buildings besides the cathedral itself, including two interesting heritage centres, and well shown Roman remains. Dover is also an excellent place for a day out, and more immediately appealing to most children; its castle is splendid, and the White Cliffs Experience is very well done indeed – a great family favourite. The zoos at Lympne and Bekesbourne are also outstanding family attractions, and there's lots more in the county to entertain children, including the new wildlife park at Blean. Many (boys, particularly) will love the historic Chatham dockyard, which also has a strong adult appeal. There are several enjoyable steam railways – the Romney Hythe & Dymchurch (with a model museum at New Romney) delightfully quaint.

Many excellent gardens are headed by grand Groombridge and Hever, romantic Sissinghurst and (near Lamberhurst) Scotney Castle, with the new gardens at Hadlow, the comprehensive Brogdale fruit tree collection near Faversham, and the unusual organic gardens at Yalding all fascinating in their way. Even the most avid appetite for stately homes won't be sated by the remarkable choice here, led by Leeds Castle, Knole near Sevenoaks, Penshurst Place, Squerryes Court and Chartwell near Westerham, Ightham Mote and Hever Castle. Among less conventional places, the extraordinary collections at Birchington, the Finchcocks collection of keyboard instruments at Goudhurst, the Hop Farm at Beltring, the bird park at Wingham, the ruined houses and new birds of prey centre at Eynsford, and the rare breeds centre at Woodchurch all stand out – and most have plenty to entertain children.

The north-east coast has some pleasant resorts dating from pre-railway Victorian days, when well-to-do Londoners came by boat. When the early coastbound railways took people further afield, these forerunners – most notably Broadstairs – settled into a tranquillity that at least to a degree they've kept till today.

Inland, the Weald (roughly west of the M20) has peaceful and intimate landscapes of little hills and valleys, small pasture fields and oak woods, and villages with attractive tile-hung and weatherboarded houses, early medieval stone-built churches, and a good smattering of antique shops, teashops and so forth – pleasant territory for pottering about by car. The North Downs between the M20 and the M2, also north of the M25/M26, are more open; the best parts are above Wye. The flatlands of Romney Marsh have a certain bypassed-by-time appeal. Incidentally, much of east Kent's orchard country tends to be lined by very high hedges that make country drives less interesting.

Where to stay

Benenden TQ8033 Crit Hall Cranbrook Rd, Benenden, Cranbrook TN17 4EU (01580) 240609 *£54; 3 thoughtfully equipped rms. Elegant no smoking Georgian house with lovely views over the pretty surrounding countryside (enjoyable walks), drawing room and conservatory opening on to garden, good breakfasts in spacious kitchen/breakfast room, imaginative dinner (optional) in separate dining room, and welcoming owners; cl mid-Dec–mid-Jan; children over 12; no dogs.

Boughton Aluph TR0247 Flying Horse Boughton Aluph, Ashford TN25 4HH (01233) 620914 £40; 4 rms. Notably friendly 15th-c pub opposite the cricket green, with an open-plan bar, hops and fresh flowers, 2 ancient spring wells covered and illuminated, a blazing log fire, good bar and restaurant food, well kept real ales, spacious rose-filled garden.

Boughton Lees TR0247 Eastwell Manor Eastwell Park, Boughton Lees, Ashford TN25 4HR (01233) 219955 £160, plus special breaks; 23 prettily decorated, spacious rms. Fine Jacobean-style manor (actually built in the 1920s) in 62 acres, with grand oak-panelled rooms, open fires, comfortable leather seating, antiques and fresh flowers, very good service and extremely good food in atmospheric restaurant; snooker, croquet, pitch-and-putt, riding, tennis and lots of walks; disabled access.

Boughton Monchelsea TQ7751 Tanyard Wierton Hill, Boughton Monchelsea, Maidstone ME17 4JT (01622) 744705 £100; 6 lovely beamed rms. Appealing medieval yeoman's house with fine views, beams and log fires in cosy day rooms, restaurant in 13th-c part of building (open to non-residents, too), and 10 acres of landscaped gardens; cl 3 wks late Dec–early Jan; children over 6.

Canterbury TR1557 Cathedral Gate 36 Burgate, Canterbury CT1 2HA (01227) 464381 *£75, plus special breaks; 24 rms, 12 with own bthrm and some overlooking cathedral. 15th-c hotel with bow windows, massive oak beams, sloping floors, antiques and fresh flowers, and a quiet restful atmosphere.

Canterbury TR1557 Falstaff 8–12 St Dunstan's St, Canterbury CT2 8AF (01227) 462138 £88; 24 rms. Partly 16th-c coaching inn nr Westgate Tower, with open fires and beams, polished oak furniture, comfortable lounge, and decent food; disabled access.

Canterbury TR1557 Thanington 140 Wincheap, Canterbury CT1 3RY (01227) 453227 *£68, plus special breaks; 15 rms linked to main building by Georgian-style conservatory. Thoughtfully run and warmly welcoming hotel with elegant little rooms, games room, walled garden, and indoor swimming pool; cl 24–26 Dec.

Charing TQ9549 Barnfield Charing, Ashford TN27 0BN (01233) 712421 *£38; 5 beamed rms, shared big bthrm. Delightful early 15th-c farmhouse with fine beams, big open fires, comfortable sitting rooms, lots of books, antiques and homely knick-knacks, good breakfasts, English home cooking (with home-brewed cider to accompany it), friendly owners, and big garden; cl Christmas.

Chartham TR1054 Thruxted Oast Mystole, Chartham, Canterbury CT4 7BX (01227) 730080 *£78; 3 charming rms. 4m from Canterbury, this carefully converted 18th-c oast house is surrounded by hop gardens and orchards, with pretty terrace and croquet; breakfast served in big farmhouse kitchen; picture-framing workshop and fine country walks; cl 25 Dec; children over 6.

Cranbrook TQ7835 Hancocks Tilsden Lane, Cranbrook TN17 3PH (01580) 714645 *£60; 3 lovely, thoughtfully equipped rms with home-made biscuits and fresh flowers. Lovely timbered 15th/16th-c farmhouse with particularly relaxed and friendly atmosphere, beamed rooms elegantly furnished with antiques, log fire in huge inglenook, super breakfasts, tea and cakes on arrival (tea and coffee at any time at no extra charge), and delicious evening meal by arrangement; pretty garden, friendly (not pesky) dogs, and lots of walks; cl Christmas; children over 9 (but they are flexible).

East Peckham TQ6648 ROYDON HALL East Peckham, Tonbridge TN12 5NH (01622) 812121 **£92**; 16 rms, 8 with own bthrm. Tudor manor offering vegetarian B & B (vegetarian lunch and light supper by arrangement); 10 acres of woodlands and garden, original oak panelling in the public rooms, and regular meditation courses. No smoking; cl 14 Aug–1 Sept; disabled access.

Frittenden TQ8141 MAPLEHURST MILL Mill Lane, Frittenden, Cranbrook TN17 2DT (01580) 852203 ***£58**; 3 rms with views over the water and surrounding countryside. Carefully restored 18th-c watermill attached to 15th-c mill house, with original machinery, millstones and waterwheel, big comfortable drawing room, and delicious, imaginative food served in beamed and candlelit dining room using home-grown organic produce; 11 acres of gardens and grounds and heated outdoor swimming pool. No smoking; children over 12; no dogs; disabled access.

Goudhurst TQ7238 STAR & EAGLE High St, Goudhurst TN17 1AL (01580) 211512 **£53**; 11 character rms, 9 with own bthrm. Striking medieval inn with comfortable Jacobean-style furnishings in heavy-beamed day rooms, pretty views, polite staff, good food, and well kept ales.

Groombridge TQ5337 CROWN Groombridge, Tunbridge Wells TN3 9QH (01892) 864742 **£38**; 4 rms, shared bthrm. Carefully preserved Elizabethan inn on the village green, with snug atmospheric timbered bar rooms, log fire in big brick inglenook, traditional furnishings, good popular food, well kept beers, good-value house wines, and quick service; children over 3.

Headcorn TQ8344 BLETCHENDEN MANOR FARM Headcorn, Ashford TN27 9JB (01622) 890228 ***£44**; 3 rms, 1 with own bthrm, 2 with shower. 15th-c farmhouse surrounded by own farmland in Weald of Kent, with big beamed dining room, own sitting room, and lots to do nearby; cl Dec; children over 10; self-catering in converted granary.

Littlestone TR0824 ROMNEY BAY HOUSE Coast Rd, Littlestone, New Romney TN28 8QY (01797) 364747 **£75**, plus special breaks; 8 rms with shower. 1920s house on a private road facing the sea with log fire in comfortable drawing room, first-floor 'look-out' with telescope, games and library, charming friendly owners and a relaxed atmosphere, enjoyable set evening meal, afternoon teas, and garden with tennis court and croquet; golf close by; cl 1 wk Christmas, 2 wks mid-June; no children.

Marden TQ7444 TANNER HOUSE Goudhurst Rd, Marden, Tonbridge TN12 9ND (01622) 831214 ***£42**; 3 rms with shower. Quietly set Tudor farmhouse on small family mixed farm with residents' lounge, inglenook dining room, large garden, and walks and picnic areas around farm; they breed shire horses; cl Christmas; children over 5; no pets.

Penshurst TQ5243 SWALE COTTAGE Old Swaylands Lane, Penshurst, Tonbridge TN11 8AH (01892) 870738 ***£52**, plus winter breaks; 3 beamed rms. Careful conversion of 13th-c Grade II listed barn and hayloft, with beams and an inglenook fireplace in the sitting room, good breakfasts, and cottage garden; not far from Hever. No smoking; children over 10; dogs by arrangement.

Plaxtol TQ6053 JORDANS Sheet Hill, Plaxtol, Sevenoaks TN15 0PU (01732) 810379 **£58**; 3 rms, shared bthrm. 15th-c no smoking house with leaded windows and beams, a warm fire in the inglenook fireplace, good breakfasts, and pretty garden; lots to see nearby; cl Christmas; children over 12.

Pluckley TQ9245 DERING ARMS Pluckley, Ashford TN27 0RR (01233) 840371 **£36**; 3 rms, shared bthrm. Dutch-gabled old inn with friendly and relaxed attractive bars, and wonderful food with emphasis on fish and game; monthly vintage-car rally; cl 26–27 Dec.

Pluckley TQ9245 ELVEY FARM Pluckley, Ashford TN27 0SU (01233) 840442 *£59.50, plus special breaks; 10 rms, some in the oast house roundel, some in original barn and stable block. 15th-c farmhouse in secluded spot on 75-acre working family farm with timbered rooms, inglenook fireplace, and French windows from lounge on to sun terrace; ample play areas for children; well behaved pets welcome.

St Margaret's at Cliffe TR3644 WALLETTS COURT St Margaret's at Cliffe, Dover CT15 6EW (01304) 852424 *£65, plus special breaks; 10 rms, 2 in converted stable block with gentle views. Fine old manor house with 13th-c cellars, beams, antiques, comfortable seating and open fires, helpful service, charming owners and marvellous food; very close to ferries; cl 4 days over Christmas; limited disabled access.

Shipbourne TQ5952 CHASER Stumble Hill, Shipbourne TN11 9PE (01732) 810360 £60, plus special breaks; 15 rms. Colonial-style building with porticoed front in a lovely spot by the village church and green; comfortable and homely atmosphere in well kept bar, and a wide range of attractively presented good food in both the bar and the beamed restaurant; pets allowed (£2.50); disabled access.

Sissinghurst TQ7937 SISSINGHURST CASTLE FARM Sissinghurst, Cranbrook TN17 2AB (01580) 712885 *£52, plus special breaks; 5 rms, some with own bthrm. Gabled Victorian farmhouse in the grounds of Sissinghurst Castle, with spacious rooms, pretty garden, and farm shop; farm is mostly arable with cattle and sheep; cl Christmas; children over 8.

Smarden TQ8842 CHEQUERS Smarden, Ashford TN27 8QA (01233) 770217 *£48; 5 rms, 3 with own bthrm. Comfortable olde-worlde pub full of character, with beams and log fire, a varied choice of good, reasonably priced food, and good breakfasts; cl 25 Dec.

Tenterden TQ8833 BRATTLE HOUSE Watermill Bridges, Tenterden TN30 6UL (01580) 763565 *£30; 3 rms. Partly 17th-c tile-hung house, said to have been the home of Horatia, illegitimate daughter of Nelson and Lady Hamilton, and set in 11 acres of garden, meadow and woodland; charming owners, low-beamed residents' sitting room, good breakfasts in conservatory, and delicious imaginative dinners in candlelit dining room. No smoking; cl Christmas and New Year; no children.

Tunbridge Wells TQ5839 SPA Mount Ephraim, Tunbridge Wells TN4 8JX (01892) 520331 £107, plus wknd breaks; 74 comfortable rms. Run by the same family for 3 generations, this Georgian hotel, in 14 acres of landscaped gardens, has a comfortable and quietly decorated, partly no smoking lounge, a popular and attractive bar, good food in Regency-style restaurant, a nice old-fashioned atmosphere and friendly long-serving staff; leisure centre with indoor heated swimming pool, gym, beauty salon, sauna, Jacuzzi, and solarium, and floodlit hard tennis court; disabled access.

West Malling TQ6757 SCOTT HOUSE High St, West Malling ME19 6QH (01732) 841380 *£55; 3 pretty little rms. No smoking Georgian town house (from which the family also run an antique business) with big comfortable lounge, good breakfasts in dining room, a friendly atmosphere, and helpful owners; cl Christmas; children over 10.

To see and do

Canterbury TR1557 One of Britain's most satisfying places to visit – but as around 100,000 visitors arrive each day in summer, you'll find it much more pleasant out of season. Redevelopment after World War II air-raid damage has been rather unsympathetic, but there's still a wealth of historic buildings tucked away in surviving narrow medieval streets. Much of the centre is pedestrianised, with good car parks on the fringes of the old centre (and a reliable Park & Ride). Interesting guided walks leave from the Visitor

Information Centre, 34 St Margaret's St; if you're making your own way, don't miss Palace St, Burgate with the Buttermarket Sq, and St Peter's St, all of which have fine buildings, and you can follow quite a lot of the ancient city wall on a walk passing the remains of the Norman castle (not open). The city's Roman and ecclesiastical heritage is well known, but there are other remains here too, notably a prehistoric tumulus in Dane John Garden. The Canterbury Tales (just off St Peter's St) is the best pub here for lunch.

✝ CATHEDRAL Dramatically floodlit in summer, it spectacularly lives up to expectations – for the most overwhelming first impression, it's best approached from Queningate. The earliest parts are Norman, with much added in the 15th c. Rewarding features are everywhere – an airily impressive nave, fascinating stained glass, the Bell Harry Tower, lovely cloisters, and the shrine of Thomas à Becket, murdered here in the 12th c. In the crypt are some wonderfully grotesque carvings, full of strange animals and fantastic fighting monsters. Shop, disabled access; may be closed for services at certain times, limited opening Sun; £2.50 – note this isn't a donation, you'll be charged this just to enter the precincts, and there are additional charges for everything from guided tours to visiting the lavatory (20p). This is intended to reduce the sheer pressure of numbers visiting, sometimes disruptive and according to the cathedral authorities even dangerous. It's even started charging on Sun – the first British cathedral to do so. In the precincts are fine buildings connected to the cathedral, inc the ruins of the former monastery in Green Court, and the impressive Norman Staircase. Not far outside is the medieval King's School (The Borough).

🏰 ST AUGUSTINE'S ABBEY (Longport) Founded at the end of the 6th c, but most of the remaining ruins date from the Benedictine rebuilding in the 11th c. A £1 million museum was added in summer 1997. Shop, disabled access; cl 24–26 Dec, 1 Jan; (01850) 293822; *£2.

♓ ♿ CANTERBURY HERITAGE MUSEUM 🖼 (Stour St) Housed in the medieval Poor Priests' Hospital (look out for the magnificent oak roof), a splendid interpretation of the city's history, told with deft use of lavishly up-to-date display technology inc holograms, leaving many vivid visual impressions – one of the most rewarding places in SE England. There's a gallery devoted to Rupert Bear. Shop, disabled access to ground floor only; cl Sun (exc pm Jun–Oct), Good Fri and Christmas wk; (01227) 452747; *£1.90. Hidden away through an arch beside the building, above the River Stour, is the charming Greyfriars, the remains of the first Franciscan settlement in the country.

♿ ROMAN MUSEUM 🖼 (Longmarket) Spendidly extended and updated underground museum, by the remains of a Roman town house; lively reconstructions of a market and aromatic kitchen, as well as lots of hands-on and hi-tech displays. The house's mosaic floor is very well displayed. Shop, disabled access; cl Sun (exc Jun–Oct), Good Fri and Christmas wk; (01227) 785575; *£1.90.

♓ THE CANTERBURY TALES (St Margaret's St) Chaucer's characters brought enthusiastically to life with smells, sound effects and lively celebrity voices; well put together. Meals, snacks, very good unusual shop, disabled access (prior notice preferred); cl 25 Dec; (01227) 454888; £4.85. The CHAUCER CENTRE on St Peter's St also has an interesting shop, and maybe displays; (cl Sun, 25 Dec; free).

♿ ✽ WEST GATE MUSEUM (where St Peter's St meets St Dunstan's St) The city's last remaining fortified gatehouse, built in the late 14th c, with interesting cells, and excellent views from the battlements. Children can do brass-rubbing or try on replica armour. Shop; cl 12.30–1.30pm, all day Sun, Good Fri, Christmas wk; (01227) 452747; *70p.

♿ 🖼 ROYAL MUSEUM, ART GALLERY

AND BUFFS REGIMENTAL MUSEUM (High St) Fine porcelain, glass, clocks and watches, Roman and Anglo-Saxon jewellery, and Victorian animal paintings by T S Cooper. Shop; cl Sun, Good Fri and Christmas wk; (01227) 452747; free.

✝ ST MARTIN'S CHURCH (North Holmes Rd) The country's oldest church in continual use; the Venerable Bede says it was built by the Romans, and there are certainly Roman bricks in the walls.

The Roman road S to the coast (B2068) is a good drive.

Days Out

Wealden tour
High Rocks nr Tunbridge Wells; Chiddingstone – lunch at the Castle Inn there; Penshurst Place or Hever Castle; Emmett's Garden S of Brasted.

The greensand country
Stroll in Knole Park, or along the Greensand Way from One Tree Hill nr Sevenoaks; lunch at the Harrow, Ightham Common or the (smart) Plough, Ivy Hatch; Ightham Mote; Westerham.

Weatherboarding and pantiles
Tenterden, and steamtrain trip on the Kent & E Sussex Railway; lunch aboard (Sun only), or at the Three Chimneys, Biddenden; Biddenden Vineyards; Sissinghurst; Cranbrook.

Treasures amid the Downs
Shoreham; light lunch at the Olde George there (or if driving at the Crown or the Horns, Otford); walk (or drive) along the Darent past the Lullingstone Park visitor centre at Eynford, and on to the Roman villa, the castle and maybe the birds of prey centre.

Journey to the end of the earth
Folkestone harbour and The Leas; lunch at the Clarendon, Sandgate; stroll from Hythe town centre to Saltwood Castle; Romney Hythe & Dymchurch Railway from Hythe to Dungeness.

The White Cliffs
Dover Castle; lunch at Blakes (Castle St); White Cliffs Experience, or walk along the cliffs to St Margaret's Bay.

Stepping back in time
Richborough Castle; Sandwich; lunch at the St Crispin, Worth; Deal.

Seaside delights
Ramsgate; lunch at Churchills (The Paragon); walk along the coast to Broadstairs.

Medway medley
Rochester – lunch at the Coopers Arms (St Margaret's St); Chatham Historic Dockyard and steamer trip.

From the Swale to the North Downs
Farming World, Boughton; Faversham – lunch at the Albion; Chilham; Wye, and stroll from the high-level road on to the Wye Downs.

A pilgrimage to Canterbury
Walk round the city walls; St Augustine's Abbey; St Martin's Church; lunch at Sully's (High St) or the Canterbury Tales (off St Peter's St); Cathedral; Heritage Museum.

Kentish harvest
Yalding Organic Gardens; lunch at the Woolpack, Benover; Hop Farm, Beltring.

Other things to see and do

✝ **Ash** TR2958 – A handsome, partly 12th-c church can be found on the Street.

✝ 🏛 **Aylesford** TQ7359 AYLESFORD PRIORY Often referred to as the Friars, these carefully restored 13th/14th-c buildings are once again the home of a group of Carmelite monks. Fine cloisters and chapels, sculptures and ceramics by modern artists and potters, and beautiful grounds. Snacks, shop; (01622) 717272; free. They do B & B. KITS COTY HOUSE (towards the A229) A massive Stone Age tomb chamber which 'mightily impressed' Pepys when he saw it; free. The Little Gem pub is very quaint and ancient.

🐖 **Barham** TR2050 ELHAM VALLEY VINEYARDS Friendly little vineyard in pretty sheltered valley; guided tours (£2.50). Tastings (20p) and sales, good craft shop, disabled access; cl am Sun, Christmas wk; (01227) 831266. The Duke of Cumberland has decent food, and the B2065

through this valley is a pretty drive.

🐟 **Bedgebury Pinetum** TQ7133 Lakeside landscaped valley full of magnificent conifers, with walks up through forest plots designed to try out the commercial possibilities of all sorts of little-known species. Snacks, shop; visitor centre cl Christmas–Feb; (01580) 211044; £2.50. The Bull at Three Leg Cross, Ticehurst is useful for lunch.

🐘 **Bekesbourne** TR1955 HOWLETTS WILD ANIMAL PARK The first of John Aspinall's two excellent wildlife parks (the other is at Lympne; *see separate Family Panel above*), well spread over lovely grounds. A highlight is the world's largest colony of breeding gorillas, though there are also deer, antelope, leopards, bison and a unique herd of breeding elephants. In 1997 Mr Aspinall won his battle with the local council over whether his keepers could enter the enclosures of freely roaming tigers (though his political ambitions have

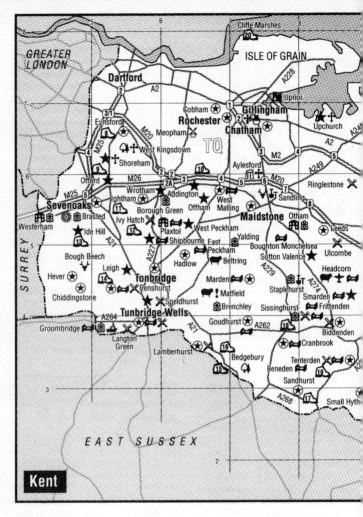

Kent

not yet met with the same success). Meals, snacks, shop, limited disabled access; cl 25 Dec; (01227) 721286; £7.99. The King William IV in nearby Littlebourne is good for lunch.

🪶 **Beltring** TQ6747 HOP FARM (off the A228) Recently sold by Whitbreads, but aiming to carry on as before, a popular and very well organised place for a family outing, based around the largest surviving group of Victorian oast houses and galleried barns. Clearly laid out exhibitions on hop-farming and rural bygones, easy nature trails, animals

(they have more than you'll find in quite a few farm parks), birds of prey, shire horses, pottery, and special events most summer wknds. Snacks, shop, some disabled access (not into oast houses); usually cl only 25–26 and 31 Dec, but as it's changed hands so recently probably best to ring for dates and prices; (01622) 872068. Brookers next door has decent food in a smart conversion of another oast house – used for drying hops (though usually now converted into homes), these buildings with their tall white cowls turning with the wind are a

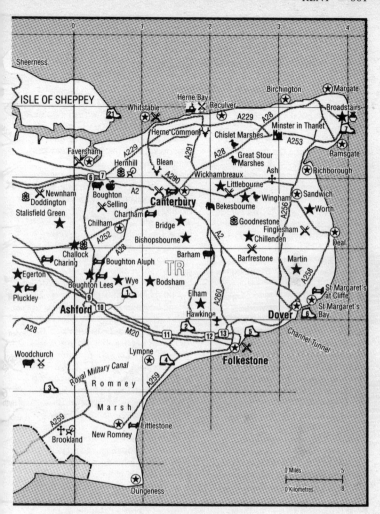

trademark of the Weald of Kent and E Sussex.

★ † 🚍 **Biddenden** TQ8438
Attractive village with several interesting old houses on the S side of the High St, and a handsome 13th-c CHURCH with a bold tower. BIDDENDEN VINEYARDS (towards Benenden) Thriving wine- and cider-producing vineyard. All-year tastings, harvesting in Oct and bottling in Mar. Meals, snacks, shop, disabled access (but no facilities); cl Sun Jan and Feb, 24 Dec–2 Jan; (01580) 291726; free. The Red Lion has decent food.

🏛 🏯 🕯 **Birchington** TR3069 QUEX HOUSE AND GARDENS AND POWELL-COTTON MUSEUM (off the A28) Fascinating museum attached to fine Regency house with furnished period rooms. 9 galleries display the collections of Victorian explorer and naturalist Major Powell-Cotton, with hundreds of well mounted animals, ethnic artefacts and oriental art. The walled gardens are being restored, and the grounds have an odd early 19th-c bell tower with bizarre wrought-iron spire (open odd Suns in summer). Summer snacks, shop, disabled access; open pm Tues, Weds, Thurs, Sun and bank hols Apr–Oct, plus gardens open Sun in Mar, Nov and Dec; (01843) 842168; £3.50, £2.50 in winter. The Morton's Fork Hotel inland at Minster does worthwhile lunches, and the Minnis Bay beach is good.

✣ **Blean** TR1260 DRUIDSTONE WILDLIFE PARK (A290) Run by the same family as the Brambles Wildlife Park nr Herne Bay, a smallish collection of farmyard animals, parrots and other animals and birds, with woodland trails, and a couple of adventure playgrounds (one for under 5s). Snacks, shop, disabled access; cl Nov–Easter; (01227) 765168; *£2.50. Nearby Blean Woods TR0860 are protected as a nature reserve, with well signed walks in the RSPB area.

✸ **Borough Green** TQ6157 GREAT COMP GARDEN (2m E at St Mary's Platt) Interesting collection of trees, shrubs, herbaceous plants and heathers with fine lawns and paths. Teas on Sun and bank hols, plant shop, disabled access; cl Nov–Mar; (01732) 886154; £3. The Plough at Ivy Hatch a few miles S is a good restaurant.

✣ **Bough Beech** TQ4846 NATURE RESERVE At the N end of the reservoir, with wildlife exhibitions in a 19th-c oast house. Open Weds, wknds and bank hols Apr–Oct; (01732) 750624; free. The Wheatsheaf has good food, and there are pleasant walks around here.

🐄 🗑 **Boughton** TR0459 FARMING WORLD 🏠 (Nash Court) Friendly farm with traditional and rare breeds, tractor and waggon rides, nature trails, adventure playground, walled garden, and PICK-YOUR-OWN fruit and veg (Jun–Oct). Meals, snacks, farm shop, disabled access; cl Nov–Feb; (01227) 751144; *£2.50. The White Horse at Boughton Street has decent food all day.

✸ 🌼 **Brasted** TQ4755 EMMETTS GARDEN (Toys Hill, 3m S) Charming hillside shrub garden with magnificent views – it's the highest garden in Kent. Full of bluebells in spring and a riot of colour in autumn. Teas, shop, some disabled access; open wknds, Weds and bank hols Apr–Sept; (01892) 890651; £3; NT. The quaint Fox & Hounds out here has good cheap snacks; back in the village are quite a few antique shops.

✸ **Brenchley** TQ6741 Some attractive old houses and a venerable village inn. MARLE PLACE Pretty garden around a fine 17th-c house (not open), with interesting scented plants in the walled garden, woodland walk, and showy bantams. Herbs and other plants for sale, teas, some disabled access; cl Nov–Mar; (01892) 722304; £3.

★ 🕭 **Broadstairs** TR3967 Appealingly unspoilt seaside resort, attractively meandering up among the trees on the low hill behind, with pleasant gardens, old-fashioned bathing-huts on its central beach, and a good relaxed atmosphere. There are fishing boats and yachts in the lively little harbour, 7 sandy bays (Joss Bay, slightly E from the centre, is excellent for families), refreshing clifftop walks and lots of Dickens connections 'Our watering place', he called the town). Bandstand concerts at 2.30pm on summer Suns. BLEAK HOUSE MUSEUM (Fort Rd) The author's favourite seaside residence, where he wrote *David Copperfield*, and which he used as the title for another novel. Lots of his belongings and related memorabilia, plus displays on local wrecks and smuggling. Shop, some disabled access; cl Dec–Feb; (01843) 862224; *£2.50. DICKENS HOUSE MUSEUM (Victoria Parade) Former home of Miss Mary Strong, the basis for Betsey Trotwood in *David Copperfield* – the parlour is furnished as in the book. Also more of Dickens's letters and possessions. Shop; cl am, all mid-Oct–Mar; (01843) 862853; £1.

🖉 ✝ **Brookland** TQ9825 PHILIPPINE VILLAGE (A259 SW) Unique centre selling crafts from the Philippines, with occasional special events; cl wkdys Oct–Apr, other times by arrangement; (01797) 344616; free. The Walland Marsh here is an extension of Romney Marsh (see

New Romney entry below); the sign off the A259 to the Woolpack leads you to a particularly good pub with the right sort of atmosphere for the area. Standing quite alone in the marshes not far away, FAIRFIELD CHURCH TQ9626 is a tent-roofed brick and timber building, remarkable for its utterly lonely surroundings and attractive inside.

❀ **Challock** TR0351 BEECH COURT GARDENS Peaceful gardens with traces of a medieval wall in the rockery, and lots of spring and autumn colour; the firs and pines reflect the designer's admiration for Inverewe in Scotland. Also a few animals and a nature trail for children. Teas in oast house, plant sales and craft shop, disabled access; cl am wknds, Mon (exc bank hols), all Nov–Easter; (01233) 740735; *£2.50. The 17th-c Chequers by the village green has good-value food.

❀ ✿ ♣ ♠ ❀ **Chatham** TQ7567 HISTORIC DOCKYARD ▣ Excellent 80-acre working museum set in the most complete Georgian dockyard in the world. Lots to see and do: the Wooden Walls exhibition uses sights, sounds and smells to show how 18th-c warships such as HMS *Victory* were built here, and there's an exhibition on the RNLI, with 15 lifeboats. Also restorations, rope-making demonstrations, craft workshops, and lively events. A visit here can easily fill most of the day. Meals, snacks, shop, disabled access; open daily Apr–Oct, plus wknds and Weds in Nov, Feb and Mar; (01634) 812551; £5.60. You can get a ticket that includes BOAT TRIPS on the paddle steamer *Kingswear Castle*, and may be able to tour the submarine *Ocelot* moored in Chatham Maritime. FORT AMHERST (Dock Rd) Perhaps the finest surviving 18th-c fort in the country, with massive ditches, gun emplacements, a warren of tunnels and a firing gun battery. 18 acres of parkland, and live re-enactments the first 3 Suns of each month. Meals, snacks, shop; cl 25–26 Dec, 1 Jan; (01634) 847747; £3.50. The Command House below by the water does limited but decent food.

★ ♠ ▣ ❀ ♪ **Chiddingstone** TQ5045

A favourite Kentish village, an unspoilt cluster of Tudor houses and buildings owned by the NT, in lovely countryside. The church and the mysterious stone which one story claims gives the village its name are worth a look. CHIDDINGSTONE CASTLE ▣ 17th-c house rebuilt in castle style at the start of the 19th c; renowned paintings and antiquities from England, Egypt and the Orient, inc fine collections of Japanese swords and Buddhist art. The landscaped grounds have been restored, and you can fish in the lake (£8 a day). Snacks, shop, some disabled access; open pm Weds, Thurs, Fri, Sun and bank hols May–Sept, Sun only in Apr and Oct; (01892) 870347; £3.50, £4 Sun. The Castle is good for lunch.

★ ☙ ✿ ♨ **Chilham** TR0653 The lovely village square is the prettiest in Kent, and several antique shops reflect its popularity with visitors – in summer, get there early to catch it at its most photogenic. The Woolpack just down the hill is useful for lunch. BADGERS HILL FARM AND CIDERY (New Cut Rd, towards Selling) Cheerily unspoilt spot, with cider-making, local crafts, free-roaming pigs (you may find them in the shop) and other animals, picnic and play areas, and PICK-YOUR-OWN apples (10 types, Aug–Oct). Farm shop, disabled access; cl 24 Dec–Feb; (01227) 730573; free.

❧ **Chislet Marshes** TR2366 Thousands of geese and ducks; duck food by the bag from the nice little Gate Inn at Boyden Gate TR2265.

★ † ♠ ❀ **Cobham** TQ6768 Another attractive village, with a good mix of unspoilt buildings from various centuries – an excellent place to walk round (as Dickens liked to do). The partly 13th-c CHURCH is worth examining, with its magnificent brasses and tombs, as is the 14th-c NEW COLLEGE, like a miniature Oxford college but far less known to visitors (cl Thurs; free). The Earls of Darnley once lived in the impressive COBHAM HALL, now a girls' school. The decor is quite splendid in parts (some notable marble fireplaces), and the lovely grounds are being restored.

Snacks, shop; open pm Sun, Weds and Thurs in Apr, July and Aug; (01474) 824319; *£3. At the S end of the village, OWLETTS is a modest 17th-c yeoman's house with an interesting staircase – and in the garden the grandest bird bath we've ever seen. Open pm Weds and Thurs Apr–Sept; (01892) 890651; *£2; NT. The Leather Bottle has decent food, interesting Dickens memorabilia and a good garden.

✗ ★ 🏠 ♨ **Cranbrook** TQ7735 A very good working WINDMILL, picturesquely set almost in the centre, still grinds corn. Open pm Sat and bank hols Apr–Sept, plus pm Sun mid-July–Aug; donations. The attractive miniature town, with largely unspoilt lanes of tile-hung buildings, also has a friendly local history museum, and for picnics Perfect Partners (Stone St) is the best delicatessen for many miles.

★ 🏰 🌐 ♨ **Deal** TR3752 Once the busiest harbour in SE England, and Caesar's landing point in 55 BC; now pleasantly understated seaside resort, full of pretty little streets and alleys – but beware of vigilant traffic wardens. DEAL CASTLE The biggest in Henry VIII's chain of coastal defences, uniquely shaped like a Tudor rose with every wall rounded to deflect shot. Good Walkman tour, shop, some disabled access; in winter cl Mon and Tues; (01304) 372762; £2.80. WALMER CASTLE (SW of Deal on the A258) Another of Henry VIII's coastal defence fortresses, later the official residence of the Lord Warden of the Cinque Ports (one was the Duke of Wellington, who left behind his famous boot). It became more stately home than fortress, with rooms furnished in 18th-c style, and pretty gardens laid out mainly by a niece of William Pitt (there's a new one dedicated to the Queen Mother). Snacks, shop, some disabled access; cl winter Mons and Tues, all Jan and Feb, and whenever the Lord Warden is in residence; (01304) 364288; £4. TIME-BALL TOWER (Victoria Parade) Museum of time, telegraphy and maritime communication, with time-ball dropping on the hour. Shop;

open July and Aug (not Mon); (01304) 360897; £1.20. The seaview King's Head (Beach St) has good-value food (and bedrooms).

🌐 **Doddington** TQ9357 DODDINGTON PLACE Grand garden with formal plantings, old-fashioned rock garden, rhododendrons in woodland, broad views, and delightfully peaceful atmosphere. Plant sales, café, disabled access; open Weds, bank hols, and pm Sun May–Sept; (01795) 886101; *£2.50. The George at Newnham is nice for lunch, with good walks nearby.

🏰 ✝ ❀ ! ♄ ♨ ✗ 🏛 **Dover** TR3141 The busiest ferry port in Europe, Dover is not in itself an attractive town but has several extremely interesting places to visit, reflecting the fascinating history it owes to its strategic importance. A useful way of exploring is with the Passport to Dover scheme, which gets you into the main attractions more cheaply. DOVER CASTLE Not to be missed, a magnificent and excellently preserved Norman fortress with its original keep, 74-metre (242-ft) well and massive walls and towers. There's a lot to see, inc a lively collection of secret-agent gadgetry, children's activity area, and Hellfire Corner, the atmospheric complex of underground tunnels that played a vital role in World War II. Also included are the Pharos Tower, a Roman lighthouse using a 4th-floor flaring brazier as a guide-light, and a restored Saxon church. Meals, snacks, shop, disabled access; cl 24–26 Dec, 1 Jan; (01304) 211067; £6. A walk along the battlements gives interesting views of the comings and goings down in the harbour, and out to sea. GRAND SHAFT An unusual spiral stone staircase which links top and bottom of the famous cliffs; open Tues–Sun July–Aug; £1.20. THE WHITE CLIFFS EXPERIENCE 🎦 (Market Sq) Refreshingly lively museum where children can press, poke and push things, and inadvertently learn about Dover's history while they're doing it. Splendid new Roman Encounter and World War II section, as well as 20min animatronic show bringing the town's history to life. In summer there may be outdoor activities like archery. Snacks (and picnic site), shop, disabled access; cl 25 Dec; (01304) 214566; £5.50. The same site also has a more conventional museum. OLD TOWN GAOL (High St) Hi-tech effects re-create courtroom scenes and life in a Victorian prison; they'll even lock you (albeit briefly) in a tiny cell. Shop, disabled access; cl am Sun, Mon, Christmas; (01304) 242766; *£3.40. CRABBLE CORN MILL (Lower Rd) Beautifully restored working 19th-c watermill. Snacks (made with their own flour), shop; open Sun all year, plus Sat and bank hols Easter–Sept, and Weds–Fri July and Aug; (01304) 823292; tours *£1.50. ROMAN PAINTED HOUSE (New St) Well preserved remains of Roman hotel with unique wall paintings and panels, and elaborate underfloor heating system. Shop, disabled access; cl Mon (exc bank hols), and Nov–Mar; (01304) 203279; *£2. Blakes (Castle St) is useful for lunch.

🏠 ⛵ ❀ **Dungeness** TR0916 Fascinatingly odd, a real curiosity and quite foreign-feeling, with acres of shingle colonised by fishing shacks and railway carriages converted into homes (Derek Jarman used to live here). It's a terminus for the little steam railway described under New Romney. One reader was quite taken aback at just how many pebbles there are. DUNGENESS INFORMATION CENTRE AND POWER STATIONS Tours of either the A or the B power station, with interactive displays, videos, and nature trail. Snacks, shop, disabled access to visitor centre only; cl Sat Nov–Mar, Christmas; no children under 5, as everyone has to wear a hard hat; (01797) 321815; free. RSPB NATURE RESERVE Interesting for its unusual plants and in late spring for the nesting terns on the shingle headland. Snacks, shop, disabled access; cl Tues, 25–26 Dec; *£2, RSPB members free. The friendly Britannia has fresh local fish and is by the OLD DUNGENESS LIGHTHOUSE, which has fine views from the top of its 167 steps; cl Nov–Easter; £2.

🏛 🏰 ❀ 🏚 ⛵ **Eynsford** TQ5465 A

clutch of interesting ruined houses here, starting with EYNSFORD CASTLE, a Norman knight's fortress with impressive 9-metre (30-ft) walls, and remains of the hall and ditch; cl 24–26 Dec, 1 Jan; free. LULLINGSTONE CASTLE Historic family mansion with fine state rooms, great hall, staircase and library, and beautiful grounds. The 15th-c gate tower was one of the first buildings to be made entirely of brick. Snacks, shop, disabled access; open pm wknds and bank hols July–Sept plus Sun Apr–Jun; (01322) 862114; *£3.75. LULLINGSTONE ROMAN VILLA (just SE, off the A225) Remains of rather well-to-do 1st- and 2nd-c family's villa, with exceptionally well preserved floor mosaics and an extensive bath complex. Also an early Christian chapel – the only one so far found in a private house. Snacks, shop, some disabled access; cl 24–26 Dec, 1 Jan; (01322) 863467; £2. Nearby Eagle Heights is a birds of prey centre, good in any weather as many displays are indoors (outdoor ones at 12 noon and 3pm). You can handle snakes and reptiles and meet the owls. Snacks, shop, disabled access; cl wkdys Dec–Feb; (01332) 866466; £3.50. The Malt Shovel has good seafood.

★ ♒ ⚓ 🐄 🏚 🎴 **Faversham** TR0161 Delightfully photogenic small town ideal for a stroll: plenty of colour-washed timbered old buildings such as the Elizabethan grammar school and the Guildhall (one of the few raised market halls still to shelter stallholders in the pillared market court beneath it – Tues/Fri/Sat). In another 16th-c building, the very good FLEUR DE LIS HERITAGE CENTRE, all the better for the impetus given it by enthusiastic volunteers, has colourful displays, reconstructions and a working vintage-telephone exchange. Shop (good for books on Kent), disabled access to ground floor only; cl Sun Oct–Mar; (01795) 534542; *£1.50 for museum. Walking tours of Faversham leave here at 10.30am every Sat Apr–Sept (£1). CHART GUNPOWDER MILLS (Westbrook Walk) Well restored old gunpowder mills, reputedly the last left in the country. Small shop; open pm wknds and bank hols Easter–Oct; donations. The Albion (Front Brents) has good food, and just N of the town, a track off the road to Oare leads to a remote waterside pub, the Shipwrights Arms: a charming setting on summer evenings. BROGDALE TRUST (Brogdale Rd, S of the A2) Mammoth fruit farm, beautiful but baffling to stroll through, its 30 acres of orchards producing hundreds of distinct varieties of every hardy fruit imaginable; there are 2,500 variants of apple alone. The shop sells trees, bushes and flowering plants, as well as crops from pears, plums and cherries to cobnuts, quinces and medlars. Meals, snacks, disabled access; orchards cl Dec–Easter, though shop and tearoom open then; (01795) 535286; £2.50. BELMONT (Throwley, 4m SW of Faversham) A pleasant 18th-c mansion in well placed parkland, with a walled garden, and collection of unusual clocks – one looks like a church steeple. Snacks, shop, disabled access; open pm wknds and bank hols Easter–Sept; (01795) 890202; £4.75, £2.75 garden only.

✝🏛☀🏠☺ **Folkestone** TR2336 Despite much development of this major cross-Channel port, there is an intact pre-19th-c area called the Bayle around the interesting old CHURCH – very pretty and Kentish. The part around the harbour, previously a picturesque warren, was badly bombed in World War II, but the fish stalls there contribute authentic local colour, the Old High St has a Cornish-type quaintness, and Carpenters (The Stade) has good fresh fish. The remains known as CAESAR'S CAMP in fact long pre-date the Roman invasion. Particularly pleasant is a walk along The Leas, a clifftop expanse of lawns and flower gardens with good views. You can watch sweet- and rock-making (exc Weds) at ROWLANDS CONFECTIONERY on the Old High St; free. The ROTUNDA AMUSEMENT PARK is a traditional fairground, with lots undercover, and a big market Sun and bank hols.

✝☺ **Gillingham** TQ7768 The town has a partly Norman CHURCH, and the ROYAL ENGINEERS MUSEUM (Brompton Barracks), more appealing than you might think, with sound effects, and art and oddities brought back from various countries. Snacks, shop, disabled access; cl Fri, 25–26 Dec, 1 Jan; (01634) 406397; £3. Off the A2 between here and Boughton Street village, any of the little lanes take you deep into orchard country, with foody pubs at Dargate, Selling and Eastling; blossom-time Apr and early May, many farm shops with local apples Sept onwards.

🌸 **Goodnestone** TR2553 GOODNESTONE PARK Old-fashioned roses in traditional walled garden recalling Jane Austen's stays in the fine 18th-c house (not open). Also woodland garden with good trees. Teas Weds and Sun May–Aug, nursery, disabled access; cl Tues, Sat, and all Nov–Mar; (01304) 840107; £2.50. The Fitzwalter Arms has good-value food.

★ 🌼 🏛 🌸 ☺ **Goudhurst** TQ7237 Charming Wealden village, with quite a few antique shops and so forth, and spectacular views from the graveyard of the 14th-c hilltop church (but during the day too much traffic for comfort). The Spread Eagle up by the church, one of the village's most handsome old buildings, is useful for lunch. FINCHCOCKS (off the A262 W) The early Georgian house and its lovely gardens are attractive, but the main draw is the big collection of working keyboard instruments from the 17th c onwards. Some of these are played whenever the house is open, the well organised recitals really adding to the atmosphere. Snacks, shop, some disabled access; open pm Weds and Thurs in Aug, as well as pm Sun and bank hols Apr–Oct; (01580) 211702; £5.20. The Green Cross Inn up by the main road has good home cooking.

🦢 **Great Stour Marshes** TR2262 Interesting for their thousands of geese and ducks; access from the good Grove Ferry pub just off the A28 near Upstreet TR2263.

❀ ⚓ **Groombridge** TQ5337
GROOMBRIDGE PLACE GARDENS
(B2110) Beautiful walled gardens,
among the country's most
spectacular, around 17th-c moated
mansion (not open), the parkland and
forest inspiring generations of artists
and writers. Drunken topiary garden,
oriental garden, rose garden,
sculpture garden, and lots more, the
paths patrolled by peacocks, the moat
guarded by black swans. Families are
better provided for than at most
gardens, with play areas, a few birds
of prey, and canal boat and tractor
rides. Snacks, unusual gift shop,
disabled access; cl Nov–Mar; (01892)
863999; £5. Near the entrance, the
prettily placed Crown does good
food.

❀ ✝ 🏠 **Hadlow** TQ6349 BROADVIEW
GARDENS Opened in spring 1997 after
several years' careful design and
planting, a good mix of traditional
and imaginatively themed gardens
put together by horticulturists at
neighbouring Hadlow College; the
atmospheric Heaven and Hell
Garden is one of our favourites.
National collections of hellebores
and Japanese anemones, and a well
stocked plant centre. Meals, snacks,
shop, disabled access; open
Weds–Sun mid-Mar–early Nov;
(01732) 850551; £2. Hadlow's
church has the interesting Hop
Pickers Memorial, dedicated to the
30 villagers who one wet day in 1853
drowned on their way back from the
fields; the enormously tall folly of
Hadlow Tower is worth a look, and
the Artichoke has decent food.

✝ **Hawkinge** TR2139 KENT BATTLE OF
BRITAIN MUSEUM Plenty of aeroplanes,
and extensive collection of relics and
memorabilia of British and German
aircraft involved in the fighting.
Snacks, shop, some disabled access; cl
Nov–Easter; (01303) 893140; *£3.
The Valiant Sailor at Capel le Ferne
(A20) saves you going into
Folkestone for lunch.

🐖 ✝ **Headcorn** TQ8344 HEADCORN
FLOWER CENTRE AND VINEYARD (Grigg
Lane) Enormous all-weather flower
centre and vineyard, with excellent
heated flower houses. Snacks, shop,

disabled access; cl 25 Dec–1 Jan;
(01622) 890250; £1.50 self-guided
tours, £2.95 guided tours (wknds
Easter–Oct plus wkdys Jun–Aug), inc
tastings. Watching the varied
activities at Lashenden aerodrome
(pleasure flights; also air warfare
MUSEUM open Sun Apr–Oct) will while
away a few minutes if you're passing.
The Bell towards Smarden is an
attractive place for something to eat.

⚓ ✗ **Herne Bay** TR1768 Not terribly
exciting, but a decorous and
spaciously laid out 19th-c resort.
Mike Turner runs BOAT TRIPS around
the bay and out to see seals from
May–Oct; best to book for the seal
trip, (01227) 366712. The Ship and
the Richmond, on or just off the
front, both have decent food. There's
an enthusiastically restored late 17th-
c WINDMILL, with much of the original
machinery still working. Shop,
limited disabled access; open pm Sun
May–Sept, bank hols, and pm Thurs
July and Aug; (01227) 361326; £1.
Other working windmills at Stelling
Minnis TR1446 (open pm Sun and
bank hols Apr–Sept; 50p) and
Willesborough TR0241 (open pm
wknds Easter–mid-Oct; *£1).

✯ **Herne Common** TR1865 BRAMBLES
WILDLIFE PARK 🔄 (Wealden Forest
Park) Cheery 20-acre woodland park
with lots of animals, small rare-
breeds farm, and indoor garden.
Children enjoy feeding the lop-eared
rabbits (bags of food are on sale near
the entrance – they don't like you
bringing your own). Snacks, shop,
disabled access; cl Jan–Mar; (01227)
712379; *£3.

❀ 🌿 **Hernhill** TR0660 MOUNT
EPHRAIM GARDENS 7 acres of pleasant
gardens, with Japanese rock garden,
topiary garden, watergarden,
woodland walk and small vineyard;
good views. Teas (not Tues), craft
shop; open pm mid-Apr–Sept;
(01227) 751496; *£2.50. There's a
craft centre on Sun (exc July). By the
church and small green of this
charming village, the ancient Red
Lion has decent food.

🏰 ❀ ! **Hever** TQ4745 HEVER CASTLE
AND GARDENS In 30 acres of beautiful
gardens, the double-moated 13th-c

castle has hardly changed externally since Anne Boleyn lived here as a child. Inside it's a different story, as the rooms were magnificently restored by the Astor family at the start of this century. Antiques, furnishings and art from all over Europe, and an exceptional collection of astonishingly detailed miniature houses, furnished and decorated in authentic period styles. The grounds are a draw in their own right, with lakes, Italianate garden with antique sculptures, walled rose garden and maze. Meals, snacks, shop, good disabled access to gardens; cl Dec–Feb, castle cl am; (01732) 865224; £6.50, £4.90 gardens only. The Henry VIII is popular for lunch.

🏰 ❀ ❦ Ightham TQ5956 IGHTHAM MOTE (2m S off the A227) Lovely medieval manor house, still with its surrounding moat, a unique survival that looks especially beautiful on a sunny day. Fascinating great hall, Tudor chapel and 14th-c crypt, while the drawing room has a striking Jacobean fireplace, frieze and windows. Pretty courtyard, garden and woodland walks. The house is halfway through the biggest programme of repair and conservation the NT has so far undertaken. Snacks, shop, some disabled access (more later in 1998); cl am Tues, Sat, and all Nov–Mar; (01732) 810378; £4; NT. The Plough at Ivy Hatch does good meals; the Harrow on Common Rd is cheaper, more informal.

🏰 ❀ 🐂 ♪ Lamberhurst TQ6736 The bypass now being built will make this an attractive village to stroll around. SCOTNEY CASTLE (A21 just S) Beautiful 19th-c gardens surrounding the ruins of a small 14th-c moated castle, with impressive rhododendrons, azaleas and roses – a really romantic place. Shop, some disabled access (they recommend a strong pusher); open Weds–Sun and bank hols Apr–Oct, castle open same times May–mid-Sept; (01892) 891081; £3.60; NT. OWL HOUSE GARDENS (NE off the A21) 13 acres of sweeping lawns, flowers, shrubs and fruit trees around timber-framed

16th-c wool smugglers' house; sunken watergardens and woodlands. Shop, disabled access; cl 25 Dec, 1 Jan; (01892) 890230; £3. BAYHAM ABBEY (2m W) Technically in Sussex but more handy from here, impressive ruins of 13th-c Premonstratensian abbey and gatehouse in pretty wooded valley. Snacks, shop, disabled access; cl Nov–Mar; (01892) 890381; £2. LAMBERHURST VINEYARD (Ridge Farm) Tours of one of the biggest vineyards in SE England, with tastings, nature trails and craft displays. Meals, snacks, shop, disabled access; cl Christmas wk; (01892) 890286; £4.50. BEWL WATER right on the Sussex border has good walks, boating and fishing, picnic areas, and cycle hire (and a great adventure play area); £3.80 parking charge summer Suns and bank hols, less at other times. The Brown Trout, on the B2169 nearly opposite Scotney Castle entrance, has good fish; the Elephant's Head at Hook Green out nr Bayham Abbey and Owl House is also useful.

🏰 ❀ ! 🐖 Leeds TQ8253 LEEDS CASTLE Long renowned as one of the loveliest castles in the country, perfectly placed on two little islands in the middle of a lake in 500 acres of landscaped parkland. It dates from the 9th c, and was converted into a royal residence by Henry VIII. Lots of paintings, furniture and tapestries, and a unique dog-collar museum in the gatehouse. The enormous grounds have gardens, a maze and grotto, duck enclosure and aviary (well liked by readers), golf course, and vineyard (with tastings); as this suggests, it's a busy place, not quite as idyllic as it appears from a distance, but very satisfying for a day out. Special events from wine festivals to open-air concerts. Meals, snacks, shop, good disabled access; cl 25 Dec, and the day prior to evening ticketed events (3 days a year, usually the last wknd in Jun, the first in July and the one nearest 5 Nov but best to check first); (01622) 765400; £8.50, £6.50 park and gardens only. The Pepper Box nr Ulcombe is the best nearby place for lunch.

🚐🏠❄ **Lympne** TR1135 *See separate Family Panel on p.359* for PORT LYMPNE WILD ANIMAL PARK. LYMPNE CASTLE Fortified medieval manor house remodelled in Edwardian times, with good views from Norman tower. Open Mon–Thurs and some Suns June–mid-Sept; (01303) 267571; £2. The Botolphs Bridge Inn just S has decent home cooking.

🏠☕✝🖼⚓ **Maidstone** TQ7555 Busy modern town, but worth penetrating on a Sun (when it's quieter) for its good museums. The striking ARCHBISHOP'S PALACE (Mill St) was used by the Archbishops of Canterbury as a stopping-place on their way from London. You can visit the Great Hall and other rooms; cl 25–26 Dec; (01622) 663006; free. In the Palace stables, the TYRWHITT DRAKE MUSEUM OF CARRIAGES is a notable collection of horse-drawn vehicles. Shop, disabled access to ground floor only; cl am winter, 25–26 Dec; (01622) 754497; *£1.50. The site also includes the old parish CHURCH of All Saints. The town MUSEUM AND ART GALLERY is in a handsome Elizabethan manor house on St Faith's St, with period original room settings. Snacks, shop, some disabled access; cl am Sun, 25–26 Dec; (01622) 754497; free. The Minstrel (Knightrider Rd) is a useful wine bar, and the Muggleton (King St) an exemplary new pub converted from a very grand Victorian building in conjunction with English Heritage. You may be able to go on a BOAT TRIP along to Allington.

★✝✤ **Marden** TQ7444 This attractive village has a 12th/14th-c ragstone CHURCH with a unique white weatherboarded tower, and other buildings going back to the 14th c. MARDEN MEADOW (Staplehurst Rd) A lovely unimproved hay meadow, alive with wild flowers and butterflies in late spring and early summer. The Wild Duck just S (Pagehurst Lane) has good food.

❗☕🏠☺✖ **Margate** TR3571 Often rather brash seaside resort, past its best, though huge grants from the European Union are having a noticeable effect, and there's plenty for families, inc excellent sandy beaches. An unexpected puzzle is the SHELL GROTTO (Grotto Hill), 185 sq metres (2,000 sq ft) of winding underground passages and exquisitely decorated tunnels leading to a mysterious ancient shell temple, thought to be the only one in the world. No one really knows its origins or what it was for. Shop; cl Nov–Mar; (01843) 220008; *£1.50. Similarly atmospheric are the MARGATE CAVES nearby, huge caverns with wall paintings and spooky shapes and shadows; times and price as Grotto. The Old Town Hall (Market Pl) has a local history MUSEUM (cl winter wknds; *£1), and nearby is a well preserved TUDOR HOUSE, open only on special occasions, but worth a look from outside. The euphemistically named DREAMLAND THEME PARK has been completely redeveloped by its current owners, and once through the inauspicious entrance is a very satisfactory and well laid out fairground. The soaring big wheel is Britain's biggest, and would be the town's most prominent landmark if it weren't for the unsightly tower block near the station. Buster Bloodvessel of Bad Manners fame runs a hotel called Fatty Towers. To the E of town on College Rd there's a working WINDMILL (open pm Sun Easter–Sept, 60p).

🐂❗ **Matfield** TQ6541 BADSELL PARK FARM 🐖 (Crittenden Rd) Run by a charity looking after disabled young people, this is an appealing place, with rare breeds of cattle, pigs, goats and sheep, free tractor and pony rides, maze, and nature trail. The ant house is home to the biggest colony of ants on view anywhere in the country. Meals, snacks, shop, disabled access; cl 25 Dec; (01892) 832549; £4.50. The Standings Cross Inn and Wheelwrights Arms both have decent food.

✖ **Meopham** TQ6466 The windmill here is unusual both for its 6 sides and for the fact that its base is a meeting-place for the parish council. Shop;

open pm Sun and bank hols May–Sept; 70p. The Cricketers prettily set on the green is a useful chain food pub.

🏰 Minster in Thanet TR3164 MINSTER ABBEY Site of one of the earliest nunneries in the country, with ruins and cloisters of the 7th-c building. The current house is still run by Benedictine nuns. Shop, some disabled access; open 11am–noon all year, then 2–4.30pm June–Sept; cl Sun and pm Sat; (01843) 821254; free.

🚂👹 ★ New Romney TR0624 ROMNEY HYTHE & DYMCHURCH RAILWAY 🚂 The world's smallest-scale public railway, with 13½ miles of 15in-gauge track between Hythe and Dungeness. The station has a toy and model museum with 2 magnificent model railways. Engines are often changed en route, and the carriages are comfortable. Well run and friendly, it's quite a favourite with readers. Snacks, shop, disabled access (they prefer notice); trains daily Apr–Sept, wknds Oct and Mar, and various days in Dec – ring for timetable; (01797) 362353; fares start at around £3, £8 full fare. HYTHE TR1634 This hillside town is well worth a look, with attractive old houses in its narrow High St and the pretty lanes around the church. Its beach stretches to Sandgate, also pleasant to stroll through (the Ship and, closer to Hythe, the Clarendon up a steep cobbled lane have decent food). ROMNEY MARSH The most unspoilt corner of Kent, flat country laced with drainage ditches and isolated farmsteads: St Mary in the Marsh has a small but attractive church (where E Nesbit – Mrs Edith Hubert-Bland – is buried), and a good flagstoned pub – the Star.

🏰 🌸 TQ7953 Otham STONEACRE Lovely half-timbered 15th-c manor house, restored in 1920s, with charming cottage garden. Open pm Weds and Sat Apr–Oct; (01622) 862871; £2.20; NT.

★ 🏰 🌸 🐾 Penshurst TQ5243 A pretty village, with antique shops, teas and so forth, and, above all, PENSHURST PLACE, a great medieval manor house, unchanged since the Sidney family first came here centuries ago. Interesting combination of architectural styles, huge chestnut-beamed baronial hall, extensive collections of portraits and furnishings, toy museum, and marvellous formal gardens with nature trails and adventure playground. Meals, snacks, shop, disabled access to grounds (inc a garden for the blind); house cl am, wkdys Oct and Mar, all Nov–Feb; (01892) 870307; £5.70, £4.20 grounds only. A VINEYARD (Grove Rd) has self-guided tours, tastings and various animals inc rare breeds of sheep; cl Christmas wk, and wknds Jan and Feb; (01892) 870255; £1.50 for animals. The Leicester Arms in the village is good for lunch, and above it up on Smarts Hill the Spotted Dog has lovely views down over Penshurst Place. The Bottle House and the Rock out in this direction are also both well worth tracking down if you're walking in this attractive area.

🏰 Plaxtol TQ6053 OLD SOAR MANOR An ancient oak door at this 13th-c knight's dwelling has graffiti spanning the ages, and there's also a very well preserved chapel and barrel-vaulted undercroft; cl Oct–Mar; free. This general area is attractive orchard country, not too hedged, with good-value apples from the farm shops from Sept onwards; many here also have fresh cobnuts in Sept. The old Kentish Rifleman (Silver Hill, Dunks Green) has enjoyable food and a good garden.

★ ❀ 🏖 Ramsgate TR3865 Quietly civilised seaside resort, with some elegantly colonnaded Georgian buildings and other fine houses up on the cliffs (Pugin, the architect of the Houses of Parliament, designed the church – where he's buried – and the house next door), and a historic harbour (bustling now with its yacht marina and Hoverport). The MARITIME MUSEUM, in a handsome early 19th-c clock-house in the harbour, has a good collection of historic ships and boats (cl wknds; £1.50), while above it the MOTOR MUSEUM (West Cliff Hall) has vintage cars, motorbikes and bicycles in cheerful period settings (cl Dec–Mar exc Sun; £2.50). Churchills (Paragon) has harbour views and good-value food.

🏠🎠🐾 **Reculver** TR2269 ROMAN FORT Built in the 3rd c, this was well preserved until the 18th c, when cliff erosion collapsed some of it into the sea; some parts remain, though it's the proud pair of tall Saxon towers of the former church on the mound above the beach that stay in the memory. Surrounding these remains is a COUNTRY PARK, with a visitor centre (cl Mon exc bank hols); free.

🎠🏠♿ **Richborough** TR3260 CASTLE Another evocative ruined Roman castle – lots of walls and foundations, and a small museum. Snacks, shop, disabled access; cl Nov–Mar; (01304) 612013; £2 (inc Walkman tour).

✝🎠♿🏠 **Rochester** TQ7468 A busy town, but well worth walking round, with several attractive buildings besides those we mention; one of the quaintest is Kent's oldest pub, the Coopers Arms (St Margaret's St; cheap lunches). The Norman CATHEDRAL is the most spectacular, with its original richly carved door, vaulted crypt, St Gundolph's tower, tombs and effigies and huge 15th-c window. The choir sings Evensong at 5.30pm wkdys, 3.15pm Sat. Snacks, shop, good disabled access; £2 suggested donation. The dramatic CASTLE is one of the best examples of 11th-c military architecture; it looks a little like the Tower of London, only more forbidding. Shop; cl 24–26 Dec; (01634) 402276; £2.70. CHARLES DICKENS CENTRE (High St) Late Tudor house used in both *Pickwick Papers* and *Edwin Drood*, with scenes and characters from the author's books brought vividly to life. Shop; cl Christmas; (01634) 844176; £3. GUILDHALL MUSEUM (High St) Impressive decorated plaster ceilings, and some hands-on exhibits for children. Disabled access to ground floor only; cl 24–26 Dec; free. GAD'S HILL SCHOOL (Higham, A226 NW of Rochester) Dickens fans should also try to visit this, the only house the writer ever owned. He wrote many of his novels here, and his first sight of the house, many years before he lived there, is described in *A Christmas Carol*. Meals, snacks, shop; open pm first Sun of month Easter–Oct plus bank hol Suns, during Broadstairs' summer and Christmas Dickens festivals, and other times – out of school hours – by arrangement; (01474) 822366; £2.50.

🐾♿🏠 **St Margaret's Bay** TR3844 PINES GARDEN AND BAY MUSEUM (Beach Rd) 6 acres of trees, shrubs, flowers and an ornamental lake, with small local history museum. Disabled access; museum cl am, all day Mon and Fri, bank hol wknds and Sept–May, garden only cl 25 Dec; (01304) 852764; *£1.50. The SOUTH FORELAND LIGHTHOUSE on top of the cliffs has an exhibition on Marconi, who used it in his early radio experiments. Open pm wknds and bank hols Easter–Oct; £1; NT. The spectacularly sited Coastguard is useful for refreshments.

✝🐄🐾 **Sandhurst** TQ7928 has a fine 14th-c CHURCH with good views from the graveyard. SANDHURST VINEYARD (Hoads Farm, Crouch Lane) has tours of vineyard and hop gardens; hop-picking in Sept. Tastings and shop; cl am, and Jan–Easter exc by arrangement; (01580) 850296; free. They do B & B in a 16th-c farmhouse. TILE BARN NURSERY TQ8031 (Standen Street, Iden Green) The only nursery in the world to specialise in wild cyclamen, with 4 greenhouses filled with over two dozen miniature species, most of them hardy, in flower Sept–Apr. Usually cl Sun–Tues, best to ring first to check they're open; (01580) 240221. The 17th-c Woodcock signed nearby has decent food.

⏳✔ **Sandling** TQ7558 MUSEUM OF KENT LIFE (Lock Lane) The story of the Kent countryside, entertainingly told over 27 acres, taking in farming tools, crafts, gardens, animals, and a working oast house. A fair bit for children, and special events at least every other wknd. Snacks, shop, disabled access; cl Nov–Easter; (01622) 763936; *£3.80. Nearby, a well restored 17th-c barn on Bluebell

Hill has information on the area's nature reserves; cl Jan; (01622) 662012; free. The Kings Arms in the pretty neighbouring village of Boxley does decent lunches, with pleasant walks nearby.

★ ✝ ☉ ✕ **Sandwich** TR3358 Pleasant quiet town with a surprising number of medieval remains, inc some sections of the old town wall and three handsome medieval CHURCHES, one part-Norman. In its day it was one of England's main commercial ports; the sea's now left it far behind. The best timbered buildings are in Strand St, with some by the attractive former quay on the River Stour (the old Bargate is very photogenic). There's a TOY MUSEUM on Harnet St (open Feb half-term, then daily Easter–Sept, and wknds Oct–mid-Dec; £1). A WINDMILL on the A258 just out of town has a little folk museum; open pm Sun (maybe am too) and bank hols Easter–mid-Sept; (01304) 612076; £1. The St Crispin in the pretty village of Worth just S, not far from the sands, is pleasant for lunch.

🏠 ✿ ✈ 🌲 ✲ **Sevenoaks** TQ5255 This commuters' town has little to see apart from the handsome old buildings of Sevenoaks School. KNOLE (just E of Sevenoaks) Originally a simple medieval manor house, this was transformed into a palace by a 15th-c archbishop, Henry VIII, and several generations of the Sackville family. It's now a magnificent set piece, the largest – some would say the grandest – still lived-in private house in the country. It's a calendar house, with 365 rooms, 52 staircases and 7 courtyards. Outside are 26 acres of attractive grounds and a 1,000-acre deer park. Wrap up well: some of the beautifully furnished rooms can get a little chilly. Meals, snacks, shop, some disabled access; cl am Thurs, Mon (exc bank hols), Tues; the garden is open only on the first Weds of each month May–Sept; (01732) 450608; £5, £2.50 car park; NT. The Buck's Head at nearby Godden Green has decent food. WILDFOWL RESERVE (Bradbourne Vale Rd) 135 acres of lakes, ponds, woodland and reedbeds, several

viewing hides and a satisfying nature trail. Snacks, shop, disabled access; open Weds, Sat, Sun and bank hols; (01732) 456407; *£3. RIVERHILL HOUSE GARDENS (A225 S) Hillside gardens with rose and shrub terraces, woodland walks among fine trees, rhododendrons, bluebells in spring, and fine views. Teas, plant sales; open pm Sun and bank hol wknds Apr–Jun; (01732) 458802; *£2.50.

✿ **Sissinghurst** TQ7937 SISSINGHURST GARDEN Several charming gardens themed according to season or colour and cared for by obviously loving hands, all offset by the lovely tall-towered Elizabethan gatehouse (not open). Get there early – a timed ticket system is in operation, and they may close once capacity has been reached. Meals, snacks, shop, disabled access; cl am wkdys, all day Mon, and mid-Oct–Mar; (01580) 712850; £6; NT. The Three Chimneys on the way to Biddenden is good for lunch.

🏠 ☉ 🐄 ✿ ✕ **Small Hythe** TQ8930 SMALLHYTHE PLACE (B2082) Handsome half-timbered house, now a museum of the life of former resident Dame Ellen Terry. Charming rose garden. Open pm Sat–Weds Apr–Oct; (01580) 762334; *£3; NT. TENTERDEN VINEYARD AND HERB GARDEN (Spots Farm) Acres of vines, attractive lakes ideal for picnics, winery, herb garden and agricultural museum. Meals, snacks, shop, some disabled access; (01580) 763033; free. WITTERSHAM WINDMILL (down the B2082) Open pm Sun and bank hols May–Sept; 50p. Further down the B2082 the Peace & Plenty at Playden is a good dining pub.

↧ ✿ **Staplehurst** TQ7843 BRATTLE FARM MUSEUM Country museum based around a working farm, with agricultural bygones, and a pair of working oxen called Stuff and Nonsense. Teas, shop, disabled access; open Sun and bank hols May–Oct; (01580) 891222; *£1.50. IDEN CROFT HERBS (Frittenden Rd) Peaceful walled herb gardens, thyme rockery, and gardens designed for the blind or disabled. Snacks, plant sales; cl winter Suns; (01580) 891432; £1 gardens. The Lord Raglan (Chart Hill

Rd) has reasonably priced food.

★ ⚘ 🏛 ✿ 🍴 **Tenterden** TQ8833
Busy but attractive small town with
lots of charming old buildings,
especially 17th- and 18th-c character
cottages on the N side of the very
broad High St. A few antique shops,
and the striking 15th-c Woolpack has
good food. KENT & EAST SUSSEX
RAILWAY 🚂 Steam train trips from
here to Northiam in Sussex, with
lovely Wealden views. They have
plans to extend the line. Meals,
snacks, shop, disabled access; no
trains Jan and Feb, and Suns only in
Mar and Nov – (01580) 765155 for
timetable; £6. There's a small local
history MUSEUM further up the road (cl
am, Fri, and Nov–Mar; 75p).

🏛 ✿ 🏛 **Tonbridge** TQ5846 A
commuter town perked up a bit by
the distinguished buildings of
Tonbridge School. In summer you
can hire rowing boats on the river.
TONBRIDGE CASTLE (just off the High
St) A splendid Norman castle with
good displays in 13th-c gatehouse,
dramatic views from the battlements,
and pleasant gardens. – Shop; cl
25–26 Dec, 1 Jan; (01732) 770929;
*£3.

♪ ✝ 🍴 📺 ⚘ 🏚 **Tunbridge Wells**
TQ5839 Very much a busy
commuters' shopping centre
nowadays, but parts still show its
former character as a genteel spa
town. The allegedly health-restoring
water still trickles through the
Pantiles, the former centre of the
town, full of elegant buildings and
interesting shops. You can try the
water at the Chalybeate Spring here,
25p a glass; cl Nov–Mar. The town's
Georgian heyday is elaborately
recreated at A DAY AT THE WELLS,
using very up-to-date display
technology. Shop, disabled access
(prior notice preferred); cl 25 Dec;
(01892) 546545; £4.50. The CHURCH
of King Charles the Martyr is an
interesting chapel built in the late
17th c for the gentry visiting the
Pantiles; it has a remarkable plaster
ceiling. The MUSEUM AND ART GALLERY
(Civic Centre) has examples of
Tunbridge ware, the area's speciality
small-scale woodware. Shop,

disabled access; cl Sun and bank hols;
(01892) 526121; free. Above the
Pantiles the hillside Common is
pleasant for strolls, with plenty of
trees and rocks. The best places for a
proper lunch are Sankeys fish
restaurant (Mount Ephraim) or
Thackeray's House (London Rd). SPA
VALLEY RAILWAY (Old West Station,
by Sainsburys off the A26 just S of the
centre) By late summer 1997 this
developing railway was running
wknd steamtrain trips via High
Rocks as far as Groombridge. Best to
ring (01892) 537715 for timetable.
HIGH ROCKS (off the A264 just W) On
the edge of town, this former Stone
Age camp has impressive sandstone
formations in scenic woodland; take
care when wet; cl 26 Dec; (01892)
515532; £2.

🏛 **Upnor** TQ7670 CASTLE Well
preserved Elizabethan castle famous
for failing to protect the Medway
from the Dutch in 1667; attractive
turrets, gatehouse and windows.
Snacks, shop, disabled access to
grounds only; open Apr–Sept (cl
lunchtime); (01634) 718742; £2.70.
Up towards the Thames marshes, the
Black Bull at Cliffe has authentic
Malaysian food.

★ ✝ 🏛 ✿ **West Malling** TQ6757
Attractive village, most of which is a
conservation area thanks to its many
old timbered houses and wells; lots of
nice alleyways to explore.
Particularly worth a look are the
ABBEY, one of the country's oldest
ecclesiastical buildings, and ST
LEONARD'S TOWER, a fine Norman
tower from an 11th-c castle.
Opposite here, MANOR PARK COUNTRY
PARK has a wide range of wildlife in its
lake and surrounding copses, and
space for children to run round.
Wknd snacks; cl 25 Dec; £1 parking
Sun and bank hols, 50p other days.

🏚 ✿ **Westerham** TQ4454 This
pleasant country town is perhaps best
known to visitors for Chartwell some
way off, but also has 2 handsome
houses on its doorstep. SQUERRYES
COURT Overshadowed by its more
famous neighbour but to some people
more satisfying, this fine 17th-c
manor house overlooks attractive

grounds and has excellent collections of paintings, china and furniture. The garden was first laid out in 1689 and is being painstakingly restored; some of the magnificent lime trees are as old as the house. Teas, shop; open pm Weds, wknds and bank hols Apr–Sept; (01959) 562345; £3.90, £2.40 grounds only. QUEBEC HOUSE Gabled boyhood home of General Wolfe with exhibitions on his life and the battle that made his name. Open pm Tues and Sun Apr–Oct; (01959) 562206; £2.20; NT. CHARTWELL (off the B2026 S of Westerham) The home of Winston Churchill until his death. Still much as he left them, the rooms are full of his possessions and reminders of his career, and the gardens are very attractive, with the famous black swans on the lakes. Though this is one of the NT's most popular houses (entry is by timed ticket), you need at least a passing interest in the statesman really to enjoy it. Meals, snacks, shop, disabled access; house and garden cl Mon (exc bank hols), Tues, and all Nov–Mar; (01732) 866368; £5 house and garden, £3 gardens only, 50p extra for studio with Churchill's paintings; NT.

🌳🐾♿ **Whitstable** TR1166 The focus here is still very much the busy working harbour, where the OYSTER FISHERY EXHIBITION (East Quay) looks at the traditional Kentish industry of oyster fishing, with live shellfish, and hands-on seashore exhibit for children. Shop, disabled access (though no facilities); cl Weds (exc July), and all Nov–Apr; (01227) 272003; £1. They sell fresh oysters (which you can order by mail), and a recipe book with ideas for cooking them. The town MUSEUM AND GALLERY (Oxford St) explores other maritime history and traditions. Shop, disabled access; cl 1–2pm, Sun, Weds, Good Fri, Christmas wk; free. Small but friendly, the wonderfully named CHUFFA TRAINS RAILMANIA MUSEUM (High St) is ideal for children, with model trains and other toys to play on. Model railway shop; cl Sun, Weds, bank hols; (01227) 277339; *£1.50. Pearsons fish restaurant is

good value.

🦤 **Wingham** TR2457 WINGHAM BIRD PARK 🔲 Endangered birds from all over the world, with the emphasis very much on breeding and conservation. Also raccoons, wallabies and other animals, and a good adventure playground (made from recycled materials). Snacks, shop, disabled access; cl 25–26 Dec; (01227) 720836; *£2.95. The village is attractive, with decent food in 2 medieval inns, the Dog and the Red Lion.

🐷🍖 **Woodchurch** TQ9434 SOUTH OF ENGLAND RARE BREEDS CENTRE Acres of Kentish farmland with one of the largest collections of rare farm animals in Europe; lots of pigs, cattle, horses, goats and poultry. All nicely undeveloped and friendly, with plenty for children to touch and fuss (and a sandpit and play area for letting off steam). In summer they occasionally have clown workshops – best to ring for dates. Meals, snacks, shop, disabled access; cl winter Mons, 24–25 Dec; (01233) 861493; £3.25. Nearby is a well restored WINDMILL, still grinding corn for demonstrations, and its sails turning whenever it's open. Shop; open pm Sun and bank hols Easter–Sept; (01233) 860043; *£1.

🎴 **Yalding** TQ7050 YALDING ORGANIC GARDENS (B2162 just S) Interesting series of gardens maintained by the Henry Doubleday Research Association, the organic farming and gardening organisation (see also Ryton Gardens entry in **Warwickshire** chapter); each looks at how people have cultivated land in a given period, from medieval physick gardens to modern organic vegetable plots; cl Mon (exc bank hols) and Tues Oct–Apr, plus wkdys Apr and Oct; (01622) 814650; *£2.50. The nearby Woolpack at Benover has good-value food inc vegetarian.

★ **Other attractive villages**, all with decent pubs, include Addington TQ6559, Bishopsbourne TR1852, Bodsham TR1045, Boughton Lees TR0247, Bridge TR1854, Challock TR0050, Chillenden TR2653, Egerton TQ9047, Elham TR1743,

Ide Hill TQ4851, Leigh TQ5446, Martin TR3346, Offham TQ6557, Otford TQ5359 (ruined archbishop's palace), Pluckley TQ9245 (a flood of visitors after *The Darling Buds of May* was filmed here; well marked walks), Shipbourne TQ5952, Shoreham TQ5161 (lovely church), Smarden TQ8842, Speldhurst TQ5541, Stalisfield Green TQ9553, Sutton Valence TQ8149, Upchurch TQ8467 (where the 13th-c church has a unique 'candle snuffer' tower), West Peckham TQ6452, Wickhambreaux TR2158, Worth TR3356, Wrotham TQ6159, and Wye TR0546 (the Downs road above through Hastingleigh, Bodsham Green, Sole Street and the Crundale Downs is a nice drive from here). West Kingsdown TQ5762 has a largely Saxon church, given great appeal by its unique tranquil setting, secluded in the middle of a wood. The yew tree by the west door looks very old indeed.

Walks

Some of Kent's nicest walks are on the North Downs – not that high, but steep enough along the escarpment to give some great views. The **Wye Downs** TR0745 ᴖ-1, designated a nature reserve for their chalkland flora that includes a variety of orchids, look across the orchards below to both the Thames Estuary and the Channel.

The long-distance Saxon Shore Way also gives some good views and interesting walks. **Etchinghill** TR1639 ᴖ-2 starts a section which crosses under an old railway line, heads up an unspoilt dry valley, and leads along the top of the slope for sightings of Dungeness and the French coast (Cap Gris Nez in Picardy). The **Royal Military Canal** TQ9630 ᴖ-3, built along the N fringe of Romney Marsh as a defence against Napoleon, forms another section; you can combine it with a path along the escarpment at Lympne Castle. From **West Hythe** TR1234 ᴖ-4 the canal's towpath takes you up into Hythe itself, where a path from the junction of Station Rd (B2065) and Mill Lane enters parkland and continues up to Saltwood Castle TR1634, which still has its impressive medieval curtain wall.

The Warren TR2437 ᴖ-5 is an intriguingly jungly tumbledown undercliff, reached from the East Cliff at Folkestone by a walk out past the Martello tower; once there you can cross a railway footbridge and reach the shore, or go up a flight of steps and on to the clifftop, to return along the cliffs past the Battle of Britain Memorial. The cliff path also makes for a good bracing walk from Folkestone all the way to Dover for the train or bus back.

The **White Cliffs of Dover** ᴖ-6 provide an exhilarating walk (and interesting views of the harbour – you can even see France on a clear day) from Dover Castle to St Margaret's at Cliffe TR3644, passing the Roman lighthouse above Dover, and a curious scaled-down windmill at St Margaret's at Cliffe. There's a bus back to Dover (no point making a circuit, as the inland scenery here is not worthwhile), or you can press on to Kingsdown TR3748 (the Rising Sun is a handy stop) or to Deal TR3752.

Broadstairs TR3967 ᴖ-7 on the Thanet coast gives a pleasant walk to Ramsgate TR3865.

The area around Sevenoaks TQ5255 has more walk potential than a glance at the OS map might suggest. The terrain is complicated, the Wealden villages unspoilt to a remarkable degree, and the path network dense and very well kept. Orchards, hop gardens, tile-clad timber-framed cottages and oast houses set the Kentish theme. Newcomers may be surprised to find such attractive and deeply rural countryside so close to London.

Lullingstone TQ5064 ᴖ-8 has organised trails from the countryside centre along the River Darent and into woods above the nearby golf course. **Shoreham** TQ5161 and **Otford** TQ5359 ᴖ-9 have attractive village centres linked by an easy track, with the downlands to the E giving scope for longer walks across Magpie Bottom and past Romney Street. **Trottiscliffe** (pronounced Trosley) TQ6460 ⌂-10 gives a good walk E to the Coldrum Stones TQ6560, a 4,000-year-old burial chamber, with an extension on to the North Downs (Trosley Country Park), densely wooded except on the steep slope itself. A problem elsewhere as you go E is that the farmland soon gets arable, with tedious slogs over ploughed fields.

Knole Park TQ5454 ⌂-11, just on the edge of Sevenoaks, is criss-crossed with paths and tracks encompassing the deer park and the great house of Knole itself.

One Tree Hill ⌂-12, reached from a National Trust car park TQ5553 S of Godden Green, has a grand view over the Weald. From here the Greensand Way (look for GW markers) follows the very edge of the lower greensand escarpment which dips gently down to Ightham Mote TQ5853, 2m E; Ivy Hatch TQ5854 and Stone Street TQ5754 have handily placed pubs to make this into a circuit. **Ide Hill** TQ4851 ⌂-13, with its pubs and picture-book green, is also on the scarp slope and on the Greensand Way: other targets for walks here include Toy's Hill TQ4751, French Street TQ4552, Chartwell TQ4551 and Westerham TQ4454.

Around **Penshurst** TQ5243 ⌂-14 are some of the Weald's most luscious lowlands, predominantly pasture, the cottages characteristically tile-hung, and the paths just elevated enough to gain charming views. As with much of the rest of the area, route-finding is fiddly and patient map-reading is in order. One of the best circular routes is Penshurst–Chiddingstone Hoath TQ4942–Chiddingstone TQ4945, which passes several good pubs on the way.

Bewl Water TQ6732 ⌂-15, dissected by the Kent/Sussex boundary, is skirted by a 14-mile path on the banks of the reservoir (can be very busy on bank hols; sailing, fishing etc too).

Scotney Castle TQ6834 ⌂-16 has a public footpath striding through the estate's woods and pastures, which can form a basis for circular walks from Kilndown TQ7035 to Lamberhurst TQ6736 and back; another useful if short path skirts the Lamberhurst vineyards. E of **Sandhurst** TQ7928 ⌂-17 an attractive round walk runs from Burnt House Farm on the A268, via Cledge Wood and Marsh Quarter Farm to the Kent Ditch and the River Rother, to take you round to Bodiam Castle in Sussex, and back via Northlands Farm and Silverden. The walk from **Cranbrook** TQ7735 ⌂-18 to Sissinghurst TQ7937 and back is a pleasant way of joining two very interesting places; **Rolvenden** TQ8431 ⌂-19 has more consistently appealing scenery around it, with a windmill and oast houses gracing the landscape.

The Thames Estuary and North Kent coast are not really of mainstream appeal. However, **Cliffe Marshes** TQ7278 ⌂-20, N of Rochester, are bounded by a long sea wall cum footpath which feels (and is) extraordinarily remote and not a little surreal. The **Isle of Sheppey** ⌂-21 has a brief moment of interest at its E end, where you can walk the dyke S from Leysdown-on-Sea TR0370 to Shell Ness TR0567 at the mouth of the Swale.

Pubs useful for walkers include the Bald Faced Stag at Ashurst TQ5038, Woolpack at Benover TQ7048, Pepper Box at Fairbourne Heath above Ulcombe TQ8550, Woodman on Goathurst Common TQ4952, Buck's Head at Godden Green TQ5555, Ringlestone Inn TQ8755 N of Harrietsham, Rock at Hoath Corner TQ4943, Cock at Ide Hill TQ4851, Cock at Henley Street nr Luddesdown TQ6766, Kentish Horse at Markbeech TQ4742, Horns and Bull at Otford TQ5359, Fox & Hounds at Toy's Hill TQ4751, Harrow at Warren Street TQ9253 and Rising Sun at Woodlands TQ5560.

Please let us know what you think of places in the *Guide*. Use the report forms at the back of the book or simply send a letter.

Where to eat

Barfrestone TR2650 YEW TREE (01304) 831619 Chatty and relaxed pub tucked away by pretty Saxon church in country hamlet, old pine and hops, second little bar with French windows on to garden, and cosy dining room; good bar food (daily specials inc local game), 7 real ales, and 7 fresh coffees; disabled access. £16|£5.75.

Biddenden TQ8538 CLARIS's High St (01580) 291025 Charming no smoking 15th-c tearoom and gift shop with beams and inglenook fireplaces, lace tablecloths, a little garden, and home-made cakes and savouries served all day; cl Mon, last 3 wks Jan. |£3.45.

Biddenden TQ8538 THREE CHIMNEYS (01580) 291472 Atmospheric country pub with small beamed rooms, log fires, and imaginative food from a large, seasonally changing menu; cl 25–26 Dec; children in garden dining room only. £16.50|£4.95.

Canterbury TR1557 SULLY's High St (01227) 766266 Part of the County Hotel, this slightly old-fashioned-looking restaurant offers good, imaginative, seasonally changing cooking inc 2- and 3-course set menus (plenty of choice), and a generous lunchtime roast; disabled access. £29.50.

Faversham TR0161 ALBION (01795) 591411 Creekside pub (nice walks) with a pleasant chatty atmosphere in airy open-plan bar, perfectly kept beer and a sensible choice of very imaginative food from French chef; lots of outside seats for summer evenings; disabled access. £19.9|£4.95.

Finglesham TR3353 CROWN (01304) 612555 Pleasant 16th-c country pub, attractively refurbished, with wide choice of reasonably priced bar food, popular old-world restaurant with inglenook fireplace and flagstones, and good, friendly service; cl pm 25 Dec. £15|£4.55.

Folkestone TR2336 PAULS 2a Bouverie Rd W (01303) 259697 Popular, enjoyable restaurant run by the same owners for over 21 years, with very imaginative food inc good fish, game and vegetarian options, and a decent wine list; disabled access. £22.20|£4.95.

Ivy Hatch TQ5854 PLOUGH (01732) 810268 Relaxed and friendly tile-hung house with good, imaginative and constantly changing food (inc separate fish menu), good wines and well kept beers, and efficient service; cosy bar areas, elegant conservatory restaurant, and nearby walks; best to book; disabled access; cl pm Sun. £19|£6.95.

Lamberhurst TQ6635 BROWN TROUT (01892) 890312 Very popular dining pub with small, relaxed bar and larger dining room, good fresh fish dishes (and non-fishy things, too), well kept real ales, and friendly prompt service; disabled access. £10.95 set 3-course meal|£6.95.

Langton Green TQ5538 HARE (01892) 862419 Popular, civilised dining pub with light, airy knocked-through rooms, a chatty atmosphere, imaginative, generously served food from a menu that changes twice daily, attentive waitress service, and decent wines and beers; outside terrace; children in restaurant (not in bar); disabled access. £21|£6.95.

Littlebourne TR2057 KING WILLIAM IV 4 High St (01227) 721244 Friendly inn with straightforward character and decor but with good, freshly prepared, interesting food like ostrich and kangaroo, very good service, well kept real ales, interesting wines; bdrms. £18|£7.

Newnham TQ9557 GEORGE (01795) 890237 Distinctive 16th-c pub with friendly staff, imaginative food using fresh local produce, well kept beers, and good wines; no food pm Sun, Mon; children allowed; disabled access. £19.65|£8.25.

Penshurst TQ5243 BOTTLE HOUSE (01892) 870306 Relaxed and friendly 15th-c pub with huge beams, stone pillars, and big windows in the unpretentious bars, lots of old sewing machines, excellent, popular food, efficient service, and well kept local ales. £25|£5.95.

Penshurst TQ5243 SPOTTED DOG (01892) 870253 Quaint tiled house with fantastic views from terrace, particularly good food from a constantly changing menu, very good wines and real ales, popular restaurant, and fine inglenook and bustling atmosphere in the neatly kept beamed and timbered bar; cl pm Mon, 25–26 Dec. £15|£4.45.

Ringlestone TQ8755 RINGLESTONE (01622) 859900 Welcoming atmosphere in interestingly decorated, deservedly popular country pub, with very good, interesting food, especially the hot and cold lunchtime buffet (no chips or fried food), and lots of real ales and country wines; bdrms. £24.50|£6.95.

Selling TR0455 ROSE & CROWN Perry Wood (01227) 752214 Quietly civilised tucked-away woodland pub (good walks) with a relaxed atmosphere, lots of beams, hops and interesting corn-dolly work, a huge fireplace, comfortably cushioned seats, friendly, helpful service, good, generously served food, well kept real ales, and decent wines; limited disabled access. £19.70|£4.

Sissinghurst TQ7937 RANKINS The Street (01580) 713964 Interesting, enjoyable food from a fixed evening and Sun lunch menu in pretty white clapboarded cottage inc lovely puddings and vegetarian choices; no smoking until food service has finished; cl Mon, Tues, 1st wk Sept; children by prior arrangement; disabled access. £32.50.

Speldhurst TQ5541 GEORGE & DRAGON (01892) 863125 Distinguished old pub based on a manorial great hall dating back to 1212, with good bar food, striking 1st-floor restaurant under the original massive roof timbers, and a splendid wine cellar. £21|£8.50.

Tenterden TQ8833 KENT & E SUSSEX RAILWAY Tenterden Town Station (01580) 765155 Steam-hauled and ornately decorated Pullman dining car with good English food (Sun lunch/afternoon tea/dinner) served by authentically dressed stewards; great fun; cl Jan–Feb; disabled access. £25|£4.

Tunbridge Wells TQ5839 SANKEYS 39 Mount Ephraim (01892) 511422 Excellent fresh fish and seafood cooked in all sorts of ways in several cosy and relaxed restaurant rooms, very good wines, real ales, and friendly service; cheaper lively downstairs cellar wine bar too (get there early for a seat), and seats in the walled garden; cl Sun. £30|£6.50.

Tunbridge Wells TQ5839 THACKERAY'S HOUSE 85 London Rd (01892) 511921 Civilised detached house with 2 beamed upstairs rooms, pretty paintings, a mix of tables with crisp white cloths, very relaxed, comfortable atmosphere, friendly but carefully professional service, interesting and enjoyable food, and very good house wines; downstairs, the small wine bar does simpler food; cl pm Sun, Mon, Christmas. £31|£9.25.

Ulcombe TQ8550 PEPPER BOX (01622) 842558 Cosy old country pub with low beams and standing timbers in friendly, homely bar, comfortable sofa and armchairs by splendid inglenook fireplace, very good, imaginative food, well kept real ales, and efficient, courteous service; nice views from the garden. £21|£8.50.

Whitstable TR1166 PEARSONS (01227) 272005 Consistently good very fresh seafood in homely upstairs restaurant; kind and quick service – even when very busy; bustling traditional pub downstairs; cl 25 Dec. £20|£5.

Special thanks to Jenny and Michael Back, Simon Barriskell, Tina Rossiter, B M Eldridge, Emma Reilly, E G Parish.

Please let us know what you think of places in the *Guide*. Use the report forms at the back of the book or simply send a letter.

KENT CALENDAR

Some of these dates were provisional as we went to press. Please check information with the number provided.

JANUARY

1 **Leeds** New Year's Day Treasure Trail at the Castle (01622) 765400

FEBRUARY

15 **Chatham** Boat Jumble at the Historic Dockyard (01634) 812551

19 **Canterbury** Festival of Science at the College – *till Fri 20* (01707) 283008

MARCH

28 **Penshurst** Armada: Penshurst Place in 1588 as it prepares for the Spanish invasion – *till Sun 29* (01892) 870307

APRIL

10 **Sandling** Easter Chicken Hunt at the Museum of Kent Life – *till Mon 13* (01622) 763936

11 **Leeds** Celebration of Easter at the Castle – *till Mon 13* (01622) 765400

12 **Chatham** Mad Hatter's Tea Party: characters from Alice in Wonderland, magic show, fun and games at the Historic Dockyard – *till Mon 13* (01634) 812551; **Penshurst** Easter at Penshurst Place: trailer rides, stories and eggs – *till Mon 13* (01892) 870307; **Woodchurch** Easter Bunny Hunt at the Rare Breeds Centre – *till Mon 13* (01233) 861493

17 **Woodchurch** Sheep Shearing at the Rare Breeds Centre (01233) 861493

19 **Sandling** St George's Day Celebrations: dragon hunt at the Museum of Kent Life (01622) 763936

MAY

2 **Hever** May Day Celebrations at the Castle – *till Mon 4* (01732) 865224; **Penshurst** Weald of Kent Craft Show at Penshurst Place – *till Mon 4* (01892) 870307; **Rochester** Sweeps Festival: processions, morris dancers, ceilidhs, street entertainment – *till Mon 4* (01634) 843666

3 **Detling** Spring Smallholders Show at the Showground: country and agricultural show – *till Mon 4* (01306) 741302; **Sandling** May Day Celebrations at the Museum of Kent Life – *till Mon 4* (01622) 763936; **Tonbridge** Garden Show at the Castle (01732) 770929

4 **Whitstable** May Day Celebrations (01227) 763763

9 **Chatham** Steam Special and Victorian Fair at the Historic Dockyard – *till Sun 10* (01634) 812551

10 **New Romney** Steam & Diesel Gala at Romney Hythe & Dymchurch Railway (01797) 362353

16 **Leeds** Festival of English Food and Wine at the Castle – *till Sun 17* (01622) 765400

17 **Ramsgate** Festival: jazz, concerts, street festival, fireworks – *till Sun 31* (01843) 580994; **Tonbridge** Carnival (01732) 770929

23 **Deal** East Kent Garden Show at Castle Community School – *till Mon 25* (01304) 201644; **Tunbridge Wells** High Street Music Festival: bands in High Street and Pantiles – *till Mon 25* (01892) 526121

KENT CALENDAR

MAY cont

24 **Goudhurst** Spring Fair at Finchcocks – *till Mon 25* (01580) 211702;
Penshurst Classic Motor Show at Penshurst Place – *till Mon 25*
(01892) 870307; **Sandling** Family Fun Weekend at the Museum of
Kent Life – *till Mon 25* (01622) 763936

25 **Penshurst** Wool Race: demonstration of sheep shearing, spinning,
weaving and knitting at Penshurst Place (01892) 870307; **Sellindge**
Steam Festival (01303) 813000; **Shepherdswell or Sibertswold** Teddy
Bears' Picnic at the E Kent Railway (01304) 832042

28 **Rochester** Dickens Festival: Victorian costumed parade, street
entertainers, *son et lumière*, fireworks – *till Sun 31* (01634) 843666

JUNE

6 **Leeds** Balloon & Vintage Car Fiesta at the Castle – *till Sun 7* (01622)
765400; **Wrotham** Vintage & Veteran Steam & Transport Rally – *till
Sun 7* (01732) 883733

7 **Herne Bay** Heavy Horse Parade (01227) 742690

13 **Chatham** Model Railway Exhibition at the Historic Dockyard – *till
Sun 14* (01634) 812551

14 **Lamberhurst** Vintage Car Rally at Bewl Water (01892) 890661; **Penshurst**
Tudor Dancing on the South Lawn at Penshurst Place (01892) 870307;
Sandling Summer Garden Party at the Museum of Kent Life (01622)
763936; **Tonbridge** Summer Festival – *till Sun 21* (01732) 770929

20 **Biggin Hill** International Air Fair – *till Sun 21* (01959) 572277;
Broadstairs Dickens Festival – *till Sat 27* (01843) 863453; **Lydd**
Carnival and Fireworks (01797) 320999

21 **Whitstable** Midsummer Madness (01227) 275482

22 **Sevenoaks** Summer Festival – *till 4 July* (01732) 740480

27 **Leeds** Open Air Concert at the Castle (01622) 765400; **Sittingbourne**
Carnival and High St entertainment (01795) 417478

28 **Woodchurch** Classic Car Show at the Rare Breeds Centre (01233) 861493

JULY

1 **Swale** Festival – *till Fri 31* (01795) 580068

4 **Hythe** Festival (01303) 268715; **Leeds** Open Air Concert at the Castle
(01622) 765400

5 **Penshurst** Falconry Displays at Penshurst Place – *also on Sun 12, Sun 19,
Sun 26* (01892) 870307; **Sandling** Historic Commercial Vehicle
Gathering at the Museum of Kent Life (01622) 763936; **Tonbridge** Band
Concert on Castle Lawn – *also on Sun 12, Sun 19, Sun 26* (01732) 770929

11 **Lamberhurst** Firework & Laser Concert at Bewl Water (01892) 890661

13 **Penshurst** Balloon Fiesta at Penshurst Place: balloons take off at 6am
and 6pm – *till Tues 14* (01892) 870307

16 **Detling** Kent County Show – *till Sat 18* (01622) 630975

18 **Hernhill** Fireworks Concert at Mount Ephraim Gardens (01795)
580068; **Penshurst** Fireworks Concert at Penshurst Place (01892) 870307

25 **Birchington** Fireworks Concert (01843) 225544; **Hever** Jousting
Tournaments at the Castle – *also on 1 Aug, 8 Aug, 15 Aug, 22 Aug, 29
Aug* (01732) 865224; **Dartford** Festival – *till Sun 26* (01322) 343242;
Lamberhurst Have-a-go Weekend at Bewl Water: sailing,
windsurfing, canoeing, archery and more (01892) 890661; **Penshurst**
Elizabethan Revelry at Penshurst Place – *till Sun 26* (01892) 870307;
Whitstable Regatta and Oyster Festival: landing of oysters and parade
– *till 2 Aug* (01227) 273570

KENT CALENDAR

JULY cont

26 **Hever** Longbow Demonstrations at the Castle – *also on 2 Aug, 9 Aug, 16 Aug, 23 Aug, 30–31 Aug* (01732) 865224

31 **Chatham** Garden Festival at the Historic Dockyard – *till 2 Aug* (01634) 812551

AUGUST

1 **Herne Bay** Festival – *till Sun 16*, carnival *on Sat 8* (01227) 361911; **Penshurst** Elizabethan Revelry at Penshurst Place – *till Sun 2* (01892) 870307; **Whitstable** Carnival (01227) 275482

2 **Sandling** Woodland and Traditional Crafts at the Museum of Kent Life – *till Mon 3* (01622) 763936

7 **Broadstairs** Folk Week – *till Sat 15* (01892) 782326

8 **Folkestone** Donkey Derby – *till Sun 9* (01303) 851100

15 **Folkestone** Carnival (01303) 222333

16 **Woodchurch** Rare Breeds Show and Country Fair at the Rare Breeds Centre (01233) 861493

22 **Rochester** Norman Re-enactments throughout the town – *till Mon 24* (01634) 843666

30 **Woodchurch** Classic Car Show: arena, helicopter rides at the Rare Breeds Centre – *till Mon 31* (01233) 861493

31 **Hythe** Day of Syn: parade and historical re-enactment (01303) 266024

SEPTEMBER

4 **Folkestone** Shepway Festival: airshow, fireworks and motoring pageant – *till Sun 6* (01303) 850388

5 **Faversham** Hop Festival – *till Sun 6* (01795) 417478; **Goudhurst** Finchcocks Festival: opera and chamber music played on period instruments – *every wknd till Sun 27* (01580) 211702; **Sandling** Beer & Hop Festival at the Museum of Kent Life – *till Sun 6* (01622) 763936

11 **Hever** Patchwork and Quilting Exhibition at the Castle – *till Sun 13* (01732) 865224

12 **Penshurst** Weald of Kent Craft Show at Penshurst Place – *till Mon 14* (01892) 870307

16 **Leeds** Flower Festival at the Castle – *till Sat 19* (01622) 765400

19 **Boughton** Farming Festival at Farming World – *till Sun 20* (01227) 751144

OCTOBER

9 **Goudhurst** Autumn Fair at Finchcocks – *till Sun 11* (01580) 211702

10 **Canterbury** Festival: classical, jazz, folk, blues, street entertainment, children's events, fireworks – *till Sat 24* (01227) 455600; **Sandling** Apple & Cider Festival at the Museum of Kent Life – *till Sun 11* (01622) 763936

25 **Chatham** Boat Jumble at the Historic Dockyard (01634) 812551

NOVEMBER

7 **Leeds** Fireworks at the Castle (01622) 765400; **Sandling** Fireworks at the Museum of Kent Life (01622) 763936

DECEMBER

5 **Rochester** Dickensian Christmas: street theatre, children's shows, carol singers – *till Sun 6* (01634) 843666

12 **Leeds** Christmas at the Castle – *till Thurs 24* (01622) 765400

LANCASHIRE

Lots of variety, from lively family entertainment to unspoilt moorland, from the rich choice of things to do in Manchester and Liverpool, and Blackpool's carefree summer fun, to charming peaceful villages.

With generally low prices and welcoming people, Lancashire offers visitors all-round good value. It has a rich and lively medley of interesting places to visit, with a very wide appeal. Most are concentrated in Manchester and Liverpool, which have grand Victorian buildings and are increasingly enjoyable to visit – best in summer, and best for day visits, particularly at the weekend, when traffic is very light and both are quite quick to get into by car, with easy parking. Both have very good public transport, too. Outside these cities, the re-creation of 1900s life at Wigan Pier is quite engrossing, and other choice places include the Birkenhead warships, Bury's steam railway, Hoghton Tower, Leighton Hall, the Martin Mere wildfowl centre, the safari park at Prescot, Rufford Old Hall, and the Leighton Moss nature reserve above Silverdale. Plans for Smithills Hall in Bolton look exciting.

Keeping children entertained is easy in this area. Particular favourites are the Camelot theme park at Charnock Richard, and in Manchester the Granada studios and the science and industry museum; there's a very wide choice of other good places, too.

There's magnificent countryside even just outside the big cities. The south Lancashire moors have plenty of scope for exhilarating drives and walks, bewitched Pendle Hill has always held the imagination, and other areas of fine countryside include the great whaleback of Longridge Fell, and the wooded Beacon Fell country park. The Forest of Bowland has magnificent Pennine moorland. It's less visited than most areas of comparable scenery, as much of the moorland, privately owned, is closed to walkers. Development in some of the villages (also in private hands) is controlled too strictly for any significant expansion of holiday accommodation – let alone a proliferation of camp sites and so forth. These restrictions make the area particularly appealing for people who want peace and quiet, and it's not impossible to find good walks.

Another little-visited peaceful oasis is the Silverdale/Arndale area, up beyond the attractive town of Lancaster: hilly countryside well suited both to walkers and to drivers, and a coastline that's particularly interesting to birdwatchers and naturalists.

There are some glorious stretches of sand in the area, and the famous traditional seaside resorts are a tremendous draw to some, but it's not really a place for family beach holidays. Blackpool, with more visitors each year than the whole of Spain, is now more a place for young adults to have summer fun, with lots of discos, fun pubs and so forth as well as its vivid array of entertainments. Out of season, when those long stretches of beach and dune are empty, they have a certain lonely charm, and there's an element of fascination about the treacherous tidal sands of Morecambe Bay.

Where to stay

Ashworth Valley SD8913 LEACHES FARM Ashworth Valley, Rochdale OL11 5UN (01706) 41117 *£36; 3 rms, shared bthrm. 17th-c hill farm with really wonderful views, massive stone walls, beams and log fires; cl 22 Dec–2 Jan; children over 8 and dogs by arrangement.

Bilsborrow SD5139 GUY'S THATCHED HAMLET Bilsborrow, Preston PR3 0RS (01995) 640010 *£49, plus wknd breaks; 53 smartly modern rms. Bustling complex alongside canal, thatched tavern, restaurant and pizzeria, outside terrace, children's play area and craft shops; good base for exploring the area; open all day; cl 25 Dec; disabled access.

Bilsborrow SD5139 OLDE DUNCOMBE HOUSE Garstang Rd, Bilsborrow, Preston PR3 ORE (01995) 640336 *£45; 9 rms. Friendly, traditional cottage with enjoyable breakfasts in beamed breakfast room; disabled access.

Blackpool SD3035 IMPERIAL North Promenade, Blackpool FY1 2HB (01253) 23971 £138; 183 well equipped rms. Fine Victorian hotel overlooking the sea with spacious and comfortable day rooms, lots of period features, full health and fitness club with indoor swimming pool, gym, jacuzzi, steam and sauna room and solarium free to residents; disabled access.

Bromley Cross SD7213 DROP INN Hospital Rd, Last Drop, Bromley Cross BL7 9PZ (01204) 591131 *£84.50, plus weekend breaks; 86 rms. Big well equipped Rank hotel complex cleverly integrated into old-world pastiche village complete with stone-and-cobbles street of gift and teashops, bakery, etc., even a spacious creeper-covered pub with lots of beamery and timbering; popular one-price hot and cold buffet, and heavy tables out on an attractive flagstoned terrace; disabled access.

Bury SD8010 NORMANDIE Elbut Lane, Birtle, Bury BL9 6UT (0161) 764 3869 £69; 23 attractive rms. Unpretentious hotel high on the Pennines with fine views, a homely lounge and snug bar; excellent French and English restaurant food, fine wine list, and friendly professional service; cl 2 wks from 24 Dec, Easter weekend.

Capernwray SD5371 NEW CAPERNWRAY FARMHOUSE Capernwray, Carnforth LA6 1AD (01524) 734284 £62; 3 comfortable rms. Pretty 300-year-old ex-farmhouse with helpful, friendly owners, cosy lounge, stone walls and beams, and candlelit dinner in what was the dairy; they offer personally conducted tours; children over 10.

Chipping SD6343 GIBBON BRIDGE Chipping, Preston PR3 2TQ (01995) 61456 £90, plus special breaks; 30 rms, inc 22 split-level suites overlooking the gardens. Family-owned country hotel with beautiful landscaped gardens (plus popular bandstand with local bands); attractively presented food in the spacious, airy restaurant and adjoining conservatory, a quiet relaxing atmosphere, fine wines, and helpful service; health and gym area; a good base for walking and short driving trips; they hold a marriage licence and have a thriving trade in civil weddings; good disabled access.

Colne SD8839 HIGHER WANLESS FARM Red Lane, Colne BB8 7JP (01282) 865301 £40; 2 rms, one with own bthrm. Warmly welcoming farmhouse with beams and log fires; lovely surrounding farmland used mainly for breeding of shire horses, as well as sheep; cl Christmas/New Year; children over 3.

Cowan Bridge SD6477 HIPPING HALL Cowan Bridge, Kirkby Lonsdale Carnforth LA6 2JJ (01524) 271187 £84, plus special breaks; 7 pretty rms, 5 in main hotel, 2 cottage suites across courtyard (can be self-catering). Relaxed country-house atmosphere and delicious food in this handsome small hotel, with help-yourself drinks in the conservatory, open fire, lovely beamed Great Hall with minstrel gallery where guests dine together, and 4 acres of walled gardens; fine walks from front door; cl Nov–Feb; children over 12.

Darwen SD6922 OLD ROSINS Pickup Bank, Hoddlesden, Darwen BB3 3QD (01254) 771264 £49.50, plus wknd breaks; 15 well equipped rms. Friendly old pub tucked below moors, ideal as a base for exploring the area; good views from the cosy, open-plan bar, and interesting bar and restaurant food; partial disabled access.

Hurst Green SD6838 SHIREBURN ARMS Hurst Green, Blackburn BB7 9QJ (01254) 826518 £60, plus special breaks; 20 rms. Lovely 17th-c country hotel with a refined but friendly atmosphere, airy and neatly modernised bar, comfortable lounge, open fires, good-value food in the restaurant, and a fine view of the Ribble Valley from the conservatory; disabled access.

Langho SD7034 NORTHCOTE MANOR Northcote Rd, Langho, Blackburn BB6 8BE (01254) 240555 £100; 14 attractive rms with antiques, bric-à-brac and board games, reached up a fine staircase. In pretty countryside, this neatly kept red-brick Victorian house is more of a restaurant-with-rooms, with beams and oak panelling, big log fires, and 2 comfortable lounges; wonderful breakfasts, and delicious food in the civilised dining room; cl 1–2 Jan; disabled access.

Manchester SJ8398 VICTORIA & ALBERT Water St, Manchester M3 4JQ (0161) 832 1188 £95w, plus special breaks; 156 rms, individually styled and named after TV programmes. Carefully converted Victorian warehouse opposite Granada TV studios (free entry if staying here), with original iron pillars, oak beams and exposed brickwork; particularly good service, a comfortable bar overlooking the river, and nice imaginative food in the restaurant and all-day brasserie; disabled access.

Slaidburn SD7152 PARROCK HEAD FARM Slaidburn, Clitheroe BB7 3AH (01200) 446614 £55; 9 rms – 3 in main house, 6 in garden cottages. Lovely converted 17th-c farmhouse in wonderful spot between Lakes and Dales; with a cosy low-beamed bar, hayloft carefully converted to create a comfortable lounge and an elegantly furnished timbered library, fresh flowers, delicious food in the spacious restaurant, well chosen wine list, generous breakfasts, and friendly staff; dogs allowed; partial disabled access.

Waddington SD7243 BACKFOLD COTTAGE The Square, Waddington, Clitheroe BB7 3JA (01200) 422367 *£40; 3 rms. Tiny 17th-c cottage in cobbled street, beautifully furnished with antiques; very good service, candlelit evening meals (bring your own wines), and interesting walks in the Forest of Bowland nearby; cl Christmas; children at owner's discretion.

Waddington SD7243 PETER BARN Cross Lane, Waddington Clitheroe BB7 3JH (01200) 428585 *£37; 3 lovely rms. Converted old stone tithe barn with beamed sitting room and antiques; lovely home cooking, warmly welcoming owners and gentle atmosphere; surrounded by a delightful garden, fine walking country; cl Christmas/New Year; children over 12.

Whitewell SD6546 INN AT WHITEWELL Whitewell, Clitheroe BB7 3AT (01200) 448222 *£75; 11 refurbished rms, some with open peat fires. Civilised stone inn in the Forest of Bowland, attractive setting and grounds with views down the valley; interesting period furnishings, plenty of room, good food, fine wines, and unusual facilities such as an art gallery and 6 miles of trout, salmon and sea-trout fishing; friendly dogs welcome; disabled access.

To see and do

Liverpool SJ4395 The fine 19th-c buildings which mark Liverpool's past as one of the world's great ports have in the last few years taken on a cleaner and prouder look. At the same time a good few varied family attractions have opened; the Maritime Museum is a must, and entry here also covers several of the area's other notable museums and art galleries. The Philharmonic (Hope St) is probably the country's grandest late Victorian pub; nearby the Everyman Bistro has good-value food. You can tour the city's trademark Liver Building on wkdys Apr–Sept by arrangement, (0151) 236 2748, though it's best viewed from one of the famous ferries across the Mersey, which leave regularly from Pier Head. The real commuter ferries operate half-hourly during rush-hours (£1.70 return); the rest of the day the boats are hourly and aimed at visitors, with a commentary (£3.10 return). Back on land, an hourly tour bus can take you between all the sights (May–Sept only, £4.75).

† CATHEDRALS Unusually, both Liverpool's cathedrals were built this century, in widely differing styles. Walk along Hope St (the heart of the city's 18th-c area, with many Georgian brick terraces) to the impressive and more obviously modern Metropolitan Roman Catholic cathedral, designed by Frederick Gibberd after a vast earlier scheme by Lutyens ran out of money; blue light from the 16-sided glass tower reflects evocatively on the marble inside. The Anglican cathedral looks much older, but was completed only in 1978. Britain's biggest, it's undeniably powerful, though its soaring proportions and cavernous scale make it impersonal. Both churches have good concerts.

🏠 ⚓ ALBERT DOCK Spectacular restoration of previously redundant warehouse buildings by the river, now a lively complex of shops, cafés and exhibitions, with regular entertainers, performers, events and boat trips. The Pump House, one of the renovated buildings on the dockside, is good for lunch, and the next few attractions are housed in the complex – you can easily base a whole day around a visit here.

🖼 TATE GALLERY (Albert Dock) The National Collection of Modern Art, with plenty of sculptures, paintings and various special events. Not for traditionalists, though there are only occasional blackspots. It's closed until May for a major refurbishment, and then will be cl Mon (exc bank hols). Snacks, shop, disabled access; (0151) 709 3223; free, though £2.50 for special exhibitions.

! BEATLES STORY (Albert Dock) Bouncy (and pricey) tribute to the local boys made good and the sights and sounds of the 60s. Shop, disabled access; cl 25–26 Dec; (0151) 709 1963; £5.95. Beatles fans can also go on a 2-hour tour around related city sites – it leaves the Albert Dock daily at 2.15pm, calling at the Clayton Sq shopping centre at 2.30pm; (0151) 708 8854.

✿ ⊙ MERSEYSIDE MARITIME MUSEUM (Albert Dock) Huge museum spread over 6 floors, with boats, ships, craft demonstrations and a lively interpretation of what it was like for the millions who travelled from here to the New World. It takes in the MUSEUM OF LIVERPOOL LIFE, vividly re-creating social history from the last century or so, and the Customs and Excise museum, ANYTHING TO DECLARE – a lot more fun than it sounds, with an intriguing look at concealment techniques, and even demonstrations by sniffer dogs. A gallery on transatlantic slavery has bitterly divided local historians, who disagree on Liverpool's true role in the slave trade. Meals, snacks, shop, disabled access; cl 24–26 Dec, 1 Jan; (0151) 478 4499; £3, though as one of the galleries included in the Eight Pass scheme, a ticket here will then allow a year's unlimited return visits to all 8 of the National Museums and Galleries on Merseyside (look for Eight Pass where we normally list the price for the other galleries covered).

🖼 WALKER ART GALLERY (William Brown St) One of the finest art collections outside London, with especially notable Italian, Dutch and Pre-Raphaelite works. The Walker hit the headlines in 1997 when art collector Sir Denis Mahon revealed his offer to bequeath 3 notable 17th-c paintings to the gallery depended on entrance remaining free – which isn't likely to happen. Meals, snacks, shop, disabled access; cl am Sun, 1 Jan, 24–26 Dec; (0151) 478 4199; Eight Pass (see Maritime Museum entry above).

⬧ LIVERPOOL MUSEUM (William Brown St) You could spend hours at this excellent museum and still not see everything. There's a particularly good planetarium (shows 3.15pm, plus 1.15pm, 2.15pm and 4.15pm wknds; cl Mon), and a hands-on natural-history centre (pm only, cl Mon). Meals, snacks, shop, disabled access; cl am Sun, 23–26 Dec, 1 Jan; (0151) 207 0001; Eight Pass (see Maritime Museum entry above). Just along the road you can tour one of the biggest public libraries in Europe (not Sun or bank hols); (0151) 225 5445 to book; free.

! 🏠 WESTERN APPROACHES (Rumford St) Evocatively restored underground command centre for the Battle of the Atlantic; it's the only World War II bunker of its kind open to the public. Snacks, shop; cl Fri, Sun, and most of winter (best to check exact dates); (0151) 227 2008; *£4.75.

! LIVERPOOL FOOTBALL CLUB (Anfield Rd) Behind-the-scenes Anfield tours, taking in the grounds, dressing room and pitch. The trophy room has cups, programmes and other treasured memorabilia, and a video of some of the club's greatest moments. They were adding a new visitor centre as we went to press, so tour times were undecided – best to ring; (0151) 260 1433. Shop, some disabled access; £4.

🏠 🐾 🅓 SUDLEY (Mossley Hill Rd) Interestingly unspoilt private Victorian house with good gardens, attractive furniture, and paintings by Turner and the Pre-Raphaelites. Wknd snacks, disabled access to ground floor only; cl am Sun, 23–26 Dec, 1 Jan; (0151) 207 0001; Eight Pass (see Maritime Museum entry above).

🏠 🐄 🐾 CROXTETH HALL AND COUNTRY PARK (5m NE) Period displays in Edwardian house, and working farm, Victorian walled garden, miniature railway, and country walks in the grounds – a pleasant family trip out. Meals, snacks, shop, some disabled access; house cl Oct–Easter, park open all year; (0151) 228 5311; park free, hall farm and garden £3.40, hall or farm only £1.70.

Manchester SJ8498 Ambitious plans for the redevelopment of the city centre, backed by huge Government grants, will greatly enhance Manchester's already significant appeal. It's packed with interesting places to visit; no less than 4 of the city's impressive museums were among the first two dozen places outside London on the Heritage Secretary's new shortlist of nationally important museums. On a fine wknd or summer evening strolling around the very impressive buildings is already a real pleasure; Albert Sq is one of the finest areas, with the great Albert Memorial (predating London's), several key cultural centres, and some lively café-bars. The Town Hall is a massively impressive piece of Victoriana, facing colourful summer gardens; there may be guided tours in summer. The CATHEDRAL is a very wide 15th-c church, with notable choir stalls; the small medieval centre around it, and Shambles Sq (not far from the bomb-blasted Arndale Centre, but sustaining only superficial damage itself), deserve a look, as do Exchange St and St Ann's Sq. Not far from here on Deansgate is one of the city's most remarkable buildings, the magnificent neo-Gothic JOHN RYLANDS LIBRARY; free tours by arrangement, (0161) 834 5343. Sinclairs Oyster Bar in Shambles Sq is good value (not just oysters), while Mash & Air (Chorlton St) is currently drawing in the young and fashionable, thanks to its unusual own-brew beers and equally distinctive food. Note that Shambles Sq and Sinclairs may be closed for a while during the Arndale rebuilding. The Castlefield area by the basin where the Bridgewater and Rochdale canals meet is interesting: restored warehouses, viaducts and the like, and lots of lively redevelopment inc a tramway and wonderfully light and airy new footbridge, also the good Dukes 92 pub (maybe street theatre outside) – and, not far off, on the other side of the GMEX exhibition centre, the very smart new Bridgewater concert hall. By contrast, the Rochdale canal towpath is a fascinating seamy-side walk. Chinatown here, incidentally, is the second largest Chinese community in England: lots of authentic restaurants and a Chinese Arts Centre. Young trendies head to Afflecks Palace on Church St for 4 floors of antique clothing, records, etc. It's surprisingly quick getting across the city, and the Metrolink trams quickly cover much of Greater Manchester. See also separate entries for Salford and Prestwich, in Other things to see and do section, pp 399 and 398.

☺ GRANADA STUDIOS TOUR (Water St) The behind-the-scenes studio tour at this lively place has quickly become eclipsed by the other attractions, and it's now practically a theme park. Most features are based on TV programmes that Granada produce, though there are exceptions: the *Alien* motion-master ride, for example, and the replica House of Commons. Other highlights includes an interactive mystery based on *Cracker*, and the exterior sets for both the *Sherlock Holmes* series and *Coronation Street*. You'll find plenty of people peering through the letterboxes of the latter, and there's usually an appearance by a member of the cast. The main shows and exhibitions each last around half an hour, so check the times of what's on as you arrive – some bits overlap, and you'll need to do a bit of planning (seeing everything once takes 7½ hours). Meals, snacks, shop, disabled access; cl Mon exc bank and summer hols, and 25 Dec; (0161) 833 0880; £12.99.

! ⅃T MUSEUM OF SCIENCE AND INDUSTRY (Castlefield) Enormous museum on the site of the oldest passenger railway station in the world, hours of things to do, and plenty to touch and fiddle with. Highlights include the power hall, air and space gallery (with an excitimg simulator), interactive science area, reconstructed sewer in the underground exhibition on sanitation, and the electricity gallery – this bit alone covers 4 storeys. Enough to keep most families intrigued and entertained for the bulk of the day. Meals, snacks, shop, disabled access; cl 24–26 Dec; (0161) 832 2244; £5, car parking £1.50. The nearby White Lion (Liverpool Rd) has good-value food.

⅃ GALLERY OF ENGLISH COSTUME (Platt Hall, Rusholme) The best museum of its kind, a Georgian mansion with comprehensive displays of fashion over the last 400 years. Displays change regularly – though like the styles themselves, eventually come back. Shop, disabled access to ground floor only; cl Sun, Mon; (0161) 224 5217; free.

◻ CITY ART GALLERIES (Mosley St) Outstanding collection of Pre-Raphaelite paintings, as well as decorative and applied arts. Meals, snacks, shop; cl am Sun, Good Fri, 24–26 Dec, 1 Jan; (0161) 236 5244; free. On nearby Gt Bridgewater St, the Britons Protection does good bar lunches.

◻⅃♪ WHITWORTH ART GALLERY (Oxford Rd) British watercolours from Sandby to Turner, plus modern paintings and sculpture, and unusual collections of textiles and wallpaper. Meals, snacks, shop, disabled access; cl am Sun, Good Fri, Christmas wk; (0161) 275 7450; free. The MANCHESTER MUSEUM next door has a good Japanese collection, as well as Egyptian relics, aquarium, and beehive. Shop, limited disabled access; cl Sun, Good Fri, Dec 25–26, Jan 1; (0161) 275 2634; free.

⅃ ❀ PANKHURST CENTRE (62 Nelson St, Chorlton on Medlock) Emmeline Pankhurst launched the Suffragette movement from this Georgian semi, now with period-furnished parlour and interestingly planted garden. Meals, snacks, shop, disabled access; cl wknds and bank hols; (0161) 273 5673; free.

⅃ MANCHESTER JEWISH MUSEUM (Cheetham Hill Rd, 1m N on the A665) In a former synagogue, the story of Manchester's Jewish community over the last 200 years, with fascinating recorded

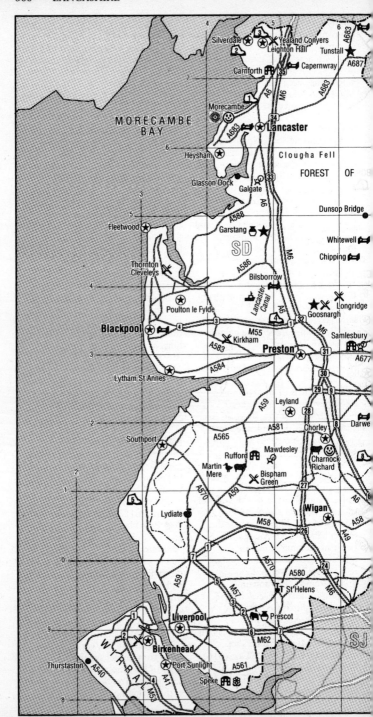

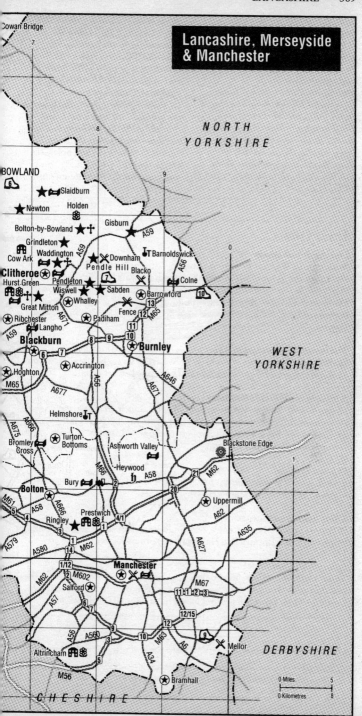

Lancashire, Merseyside & Manchester

recollections of life earlier this century. Shop, some disabled access; cl Fri, Sat and Jewish holidays; (0161) 834 9879; £2.50. The Derby Brewery Arms is a classic Mancunian pub, with good-value snacks.

MUSEUM OF TRANSPORT (Boyle St, Cheetham) Around 80 vintage local buses and other vehicles, as well as photographs, tickets and memorabilia – even historic bus stops. Snacks (Weds and Sat only), shop, disabled access; open Weds, Sat, Sun and bank hols; (0161) 205 2122; *£2.

MANCHESTER UNITED MUSEUM AND TOUR CENTRE (Old Trafford) Purpose-built football museum, covering the club's history from its foundation in 1878 to the more recent glory days. Hundreds of exhibits (changing almost as frequently as their strip) and tours of the ground (not match days, and limited on the days before); last tours at 2pm. Snacks, shop, disabled access; cl Mon (exc bank hols), 25 Dec; (0161) 877 4002; £5.50 tour and museum, £2.95 museum only.

Days Out

Liverpool walkabout
Museums in William Brown St, Roman Catholic cathedral; lunch at the Philharmonic (Hope St); Anglican cathedral; walk via Rodney St and Hanover St to Albert Dock; Tate Gallery or Merseyside Maritime Museum; walk to Royal Liver Building for ferry across Mersey to Birkenhead and back; walk back to William Brown St via Water St and Dale St.

The fringes of Morecambe Bay
Walk up Arnside Knott (Cumbria) or Wharton Crag; lunch at New Inn, Yealand Conyers; Leighton Moss nature reserve; Leighton Hall.

A drive in the Forest of Bowland
Gisburn and Bolton by Bowland villages; lunch at Assheton Arms, Downham; drive from Slaidburn to High Bentham via Great Harlow, then to Caton and back over the Trough of Bowland; optional walk from Dunsop Bridge up River Dunsop.

Pennine heritage
East Lancs Railway, Bury; lunch at the Lord Raglan, Nangreaves; Helmshore Textile Museums (cl Sat).

Sandy heights on the coast
Wildfowl and Wetlands Centre, Martin Mere; lunch at the Eagle & Child, Bispham Green; Rufford Old Hall; walk at Formby Dunes.

Industrious Manchester
Town Hall; walk along Rochdale Canal towpath from Princess St to the junction with Bridgewater Canal in Castlefield area; lunch at Dukes 92, Castle St; Museum of Science and Industry, or Granada Studios Tour.

Please let us know what you think of places in the *Guide*. Use the report forms at the back of the book or simply send a letter.

Other things to see and do

🖪 👟 🐘 **Accrington** SD7320 HAWORTH ART GALLERY AND MUSEUM (Haworth Park, Manchester Rd) Notable for its collection of Tiffany glass, said to be the biggest in Europe (an Accrington man used to manage the Tiffany studios). Nice setting, with nature trail through grounds. Cl am, all day Fri; (01254) 233782; free.

🏛 🐘 **Altrincham** SJ7687 DUNHAM MASSEY HALL 16th-c moated manor house extensively remodelled in the 18th c, with impressive silverware, paintings and furnishings, and restored kitchen, pantry and laundry. The largely unaltered grounds have plenty of deer, formal avenues of trees, and a working Elizabethan sawmill (usually Weds and Sun only). Concerts and events even in winter when the house is closed. Meals, snacks, shop, some disabled access; open Sat–Weds Apr–Oct, house cl am; (0161) 941 1025; £4.50 house and garden, £2.50 garden only; NT. In town the Old Packet House (Navigation Rd, Broadheath) by the canal does decent food.

🚂 **Barnoldswick** SD8746 BANCROFT MILL ENGINE The last working steam mill in the area – not that long ago Barnoldswick had 13. Snacks, shop, disabled access; open most Sats for static viewing, (01282) 813932 for dates of steamdays; *£1.50. The Fanny Grey (on the B651 towards Colne) has nice food.

ⓗ 🐘 🚂 ✝ **Barrowford** SD8539 PENDLE HERITAGE CENTRE 🔲 Growing local history centre, with 18th-c walled gardens, small farm, country trails, 14th-c barn with pot-bellied pig, and an exhibition on the Pendle witches – the house itself looks appropriately witchy. Snacks, shop, disabled access; cl 25 Dec; (01282) 695366; £2.75. This is picturesque, evocative countryside; the CHURCH at nearby unspoilt Newchurch SD8239 has the witches' grave, and there's good food at the Forest Inn at Fence and Bay Horse at Roughlee – a stone's throw from Alice Nutter's home.

🎰 ❊ ❄ 🖪 👟 🚙 🐘 **Birkenhead** SJ3288 Waterfront views over to Liverpool, of course, but a surprise in BIRKENHEAD PRIORY (Priory St), a ruined 12th-c Benedictine priory with notable visitor centre. Shop, some disabled access; open wknds all year, plus pm daily (exc Mon) in school

hols; (0151) 666 4010; free. Good views from the tower of the neighbouring church. The docks have a couple of HISTORIC WARSHIPS 🖼, HMS *Plymouth* and the submarine *Onyx*, both of which played a part in the Falklands War. You can peep up the periscope on the *Onyx*, and there's plenty for children to fiddle with. A few ladders to negotiate, but don't be put off – readers find this a very satisfying afternoon out. Snacks, shop; cl 25–26 Dec; (0151) 650 1573; £4.50 for both ships. The German U-boat displayed alongside spent the last 50 years on the seabed.
WILLIAMSON ART GALLERY AND MUSEUM (Slatey Rd) English watercolours and art by the Liverpool school, sculpture and ceramics, model ships, and a collection of cars and motorcycles in period garage setting. Shop, disabled access; cl am, and all day Mon; (0151) 652 4177; free. On summer Suns in Aug there are generally free concerts at either the museum or the priory. There's an unusual STEAM PUMPING STATION at Shore Rd, Woodside, nr the ferry terminal; an adjacent small transport museum has a working tram. Open pm wknds, and daily (exc Mon) in school hols; (0151) 650 1182; £1.70. Birkenhead Park laid out in 1853 was the world's first public park. The Shrewsbury Arms out in Claughton Firs is the best place for lunch.
🛉🛌🕇† 🐾 **Blackburn** SD6827 Put firmly on the map by the Industrial Revolution, this has bustling shops and market, some fine buildings, and lots of beautiful unspoilt countryside around. LEWIS MUSEUM OF TEXTILE MACHINERY (Exchange St) Period rooms well illustrate the development of the textile industry from the 18th-c. Shop; cl am (exc Sat), Sun, Mon, Christmas; (01254) 667130; free. MUSEUM AND ART GALLERY (Museum St) Quite a mixture – English watercolours, Japanese woodblock prints, Greek and Russian orthodox icons, and a fantastic collection of beetles, some pretty scary. Shop, disabled access to ground floor only; cl Sun, Mon, bank hols and Christmas; (01254) 667130; free.

The parish CHURCH (actually now a cathedral) is very handsome – grand yet elegant. WITTON COUNTRY PARK (off the A674 W of Blackburn) 480 acres of attractive countryside to explore; (01254) 55423; park free, small charge for visitor centre (cl Mon–Weds winter).
☺ 🎵 🖾 🐾 **Blackpool** SD3036 Britain's most loved and loathed seaside resort, in summer offering more bed spaces than the whole of Portugal. The atmosphere then is unashamedly boisterous (it's pretty dreary in winter), and though it's now more geared to young adults, most children love it, with plenty for them to do from donkey rides along the beaches to days at the SANDCASTLE leisure complex. BLACKPOOL TOWER The outstanding landmark has several lively attractions geared towards families, inc a circus, laser shows, aquarium (rare giant sea turtles), science gallery, dinosaur dark ride, and a lift to the top, perhaps most fun at night (they're open till 11pm in summer). Meals, snacks, shop, limited disabled access; cl winter wkdys; (01253) 22242; £5, more during the Illuminations. These famous autumn light displays are the best of their kind – if you don't mind travelling at a snail's pace along the Golden Five Hundred Yards (or Mile as they call it here). PLEASURE BEACH These days this dominates the town more than ever, thanks to its monster roller-coaster – at 72 metres (235 ft) high quite reasonably called the Big One, its coaches running at up to 85mph. Crowded and noisy, with a sprawling mass of over 145 other breath-taking rides, the amusement park is year after year Britain's most visited attraction. Meals, snacks, shops, disabled access; cl wkdys Mar, Nov and Dec, and all Jan and Feb; individual prices for rides, or books of tickets (around £20). Across the road Granada have built a reconstructed version of *Coronation Street*, with sets and props from the programme, and a 15-minute Sooty Show; cl winter wkdys; £5.99, so pretty much for fans only. SEA LIFE CENTRE 🖼 (Golden Mile Centre)

Broadly similar to others in the chain, but with a bonus: the biggest display of tropical sharks in Europe, with a walk-through tunnel underneath so you feel you're in there with them. Meals, snacks, shop, disabled access; cl 25 Dec; (01253) 22445; £5.95 (they stamp your hand so you can come back later that day). There's more to Blackpool than ice-creams and eyesores – away from the crowds is the decent GRUNDY ART GALLERY on Queen St (cl Sun and bank hols; free), and the ZOO (East Park Drive) has over 400 animals in 32 acres of landscaped gardens. The big cats are usually fed at 11.45am (not Fri), the sealions at 11am and 3pm, and the penguins at 2.30pm. Meals, snacks, shop, disabled access; cl 25 Dec; (01253) 765027; £5.50. The tram to Fleetwood is a must for tram freaks. The friendly Ramsden Arms opposite Blackpool North station is the best of the town's pubs and has good-value bedrooms.

✳ **Blackstone Edge** SD9716 PENNINE RIDING EXPERIENCE Guided rides along ancient packhorse routes through windswept moors and valleys; fantastic views. Trips last from 2 hours to a full wk, though you need at least some riding experience; (01706) 377061; from £20. For recovery, the White House has decent food – and great views.

🏠🍴🛏🖥🏫✿ **Bolton** SD7108 SMITHILLS HALL (Smithills Dean Rd) Interesting (though much restored) old manor house with 14th-c Great Hall and a splendid panelled drawing room. There are ambitious plans to develop the site as a 'living history' exhibition. Shop, disabled access to ground floor only; cl am Sun, Mon (exc bank hols), all Oct–Mar; (01204) 841265; £2. Nearby 15th-c HALL I' TH' WOOD (Crompton Way) is where Samuel Crompton developed his Spinning Mule in 1779; it was refurnished by the first Lord Leverhulme in 1902. Details as Smithills Hall, though a joint ticket is available. The MUSEUM AND ART GALLERY (Le Mans Crescent) is quite good, with Egyptian mummies, lots of watercolours and 20th-c sculpture.

Shop, disabled acces; cl Weds, Sun and bank hols; free. You can tour WARBURTONS BAKERY by arrangement, wkdys only; (01204) 523551; free. The King's Head (Junction Rd, Deane), with a bowling green behind, is useful for lunch, as is the restaurant of the Queen's Moat House – an interesting church conversion. Just outside town, at Bromley Cross, the LAST DROP VILLAGE is a pastiche of an 18th-c village, very rustic and quaint, with cottages, shops, decent pub and craft centre. The B6391 and the old Roman road through Edgworth N of here are fine moorland roads, as are the A675 N of Bolton itself (good detours off at Belmont), and the A666 to Darwen.

🏠🖥🐾 **Bramhall** SJ8984 BRAMALL HALL One of the finest houses in the area (particularly from the outside), a splendid timber-framed 14th-c hall with rare 16th-c wall paintings and furniture, and extensive parkland; there was a fair bit of prettifying restoration in the last century. Meals, snacks, shop, disabled access to ground floor; open pm wknds all year, plus pm wkdys Easter–Dec (exc Mon Nov–Dec); (0161) 485 3708; £2.95, park free. The Davenport Arms at Woodford does decent lunches.

🍴🏠🐦🦜 **Burnley** SD8432 The CANAL WHARF (Manchester Rd), which has a small museum, allows short towpath walks along the Leeds & Liverpool Canal, giving a vivid impression of the towering old weaving mills; the raised canal embankment across the valley is a remarkable sight. TOWNELEY HALL (A646 S of Burnley) A striking 14th-c building housing a decent museum (cl Sat, Christmas; free). ROCKWATER BIRD CONSERVATION CENTRE (Foxstones Lane, Cliviger – above Mereclough SE of Burnley) Expanding collection taking in pheasants, bantams, foreign birds and owls as well as rabbits, chipmunks and miniature sheep. Children can feed some animals. Snacks, disabled access (but no facilities); cl Mon (exc bank hols), wkdys Mar and Oct, all Nov–Feb; (01282) 415016; *£2.50. Nearby

CLIVIGER GORGE has pleasant walks, with stream, woodland and farmland; moors above. The Kettledrum at Mereclough has good home cooking, and the moorland roads around it are attractive – especially the old packhorse road from Mereclough up Stansfield Moor; good views from the back road angling off SE from the A52 to the junction of the A671 and B6238.

🚂 **Bury** SD8011 EAST LANCS RAILWAY (Bolton St Station) Well regarded by enthusiasts, a scenic 17-mile steam journey along the pretty Irwell valley; you can get on or off along the way. Meals, snacks, shop, disabled access; open wknds, bank hols, and other dates July and Aug; (0161) 764 7790 for timetable; £6 full return. The Lord Raglan up at Nangreaves (off the A56/A666 N) has great moorland views and hearty food.

🏠 **Carnforth** SD4970 The dilapidated station at this otherwise unremarkable little town starred in *Brief Encounter* in 1945. Railtrack has been developing the site to capitalise on the connection, and work could be finished by autumn – already the range of teas in the buffet puts that LMS cuppa rather to shame. A mile or so N are the ruins of a 14th-c manor house, WARTON OLD RECTORY.

☺ **Charnock Richard** SD5515 *See separate Family Panel for* CAMELOT *on p.391.*

🏠 🏵 🐦 **Chorley** SD5817 ASTLEY HALL (Astley Park) Unusual-looking timber-framed 16th-c house with particularly elaborate carvings and plasterwork, interesting pottery and paintings, and extensive gardens and woodland. It was used in the TV adaptation of *Moll Flanders*. Shop, disabled access to ground floor only; cl am, Mon (exc bank hols, and Mon–Thurs Nov–Mar); (01257) 262166; £2.50, free for Chorley residents. The Malt 'n' Hops behind the station in the town itself is useful for a bite to eat.

🏠 ♨ 🏵 **Clitheroe** SD7441 Bustling old market town: every Weds evening hundreds of poultry and small livestock enthusiasts come to the auctions, some from as far away as Scotland. The High St is dominated by the CASTLE perched on its limestone rock. One of the oldest buildings in Lancashire, it has one of the smallest Norman keeps in the country. The CASTLE MUSEUM has an extensive geology exhibition, and good views of the Ribble valley. Shop, limited disabled access; cl Thurs and Fri Mar–Apr and Oct–Dec, and all Jan and Feb; (01200) 24635; *£1.40. The Starkie Arms below is handy for lunch. There's a lovely drive through Bashall Eaves, the Trough of Bowland and Quernmore.

🏠 **Cow Ark** SD6745 BROWSHOLME HALL Unpretentious-looking Tudor house on the edge of the Forest of Bowland, with a surprisingly rich range of contents. Good guided tours by members of the family. Snacks, shop; open pm Easter and spring bank hol wknds, plus pm wknds in Aug and pm Sat in July; (01254) 826719; *£3. The Inn at Whitewell in one direction and Red Pump at Bashall Eaves in the other offer a choice of good places to eat.

⚓ ☕ 🏵 🐦 **Fleetwood** SD3348 Developed as a rather elegant 19th-c resort, with landscaping by Decimus Burton, plenty of smart buildings, lively harbour (summer boat trips), excellent market, 2 elegant if not entirely practical lighthouses (one's in the middle of the street), a decent summer museum (cl am Mon and Thur; *£1.25), factory shopping centre, and trams from Blackpool right through the town. The architecturally interesting North Euston Hotel by the terminus is a safe bet for food. The Marine Hall exhibition centre on the front has a decent bar (the Wyre – no food) with excellent views of the harbour and Morecambe Bay, while on Poulton St the Manzil is a good Indian restaurant. STANAH SD3542 Out on the Wyre estuary, this has a stretch of waterside country with reedbeds, birds and views, attractive despite the ICI chemical works in the background. On the opposite bank, over the toll bridge past Poulton, the Shard Bridge Inn at Hambleton

SD3741 is nicely placed for lunch.
SKIPPOOL SD3540 has lots of yachting
activity in an attractive boating area,
with a decent small café.

🏵 **Galgate** SD4855 CANALSIDE CRAFT
CENTRE Converted farm buildings
with various crafts inc woodturner
producing unusual clocks,
barometers and bowls. Covered
seating by canalside. Cl Mon;
(01524) 752223; free. The Plough
has good food.

★ ♨ **Garstang** SD4845 Quite an
attractive small market town, with a
good deal of canal activity (and a fine
aqueduct crossing the River Wyre).
The entertaining waterside Owd
Tithebarn (with a canal museum
upstairs) is fun for lunch, and the
DISCOVERY CENTRE (High St) is a
useful introduction to the area's
natural history.

Glasson Dock SD4456 Once an
important port for Lancaster, this still
has the occasional coaster berthing,
but is mainly a lively summer boating
place now, in pleasant countryside;
good Sunday car-boot sales. The
Victoria on the dock is a popular
dining pub, as is the 17th-c Stork up
on the A588.

♨T **Helmshore** SD7821 HELMSHORE
TEXTILE MUSEUMS (Holcombe Rd) 2
stone mills with comprehensive
collection of textile machinery, much
still in working order. Easily one of
the best textile museums in the
country, but if social history and
machinery aren't your things it's
unlikely to convert you. Snacks, shop,
disabled access; cl am, Sat, and
Nov–Easter; (01706) 226459; £3.
The Duke of Wellington on the
B6232 W of Haslingden is a reliable
family dining pub in fine
surroundings, with more views
further on that road.

♭ **Heywood** SD8513 CORGI HERITAGE
CENTRE (53 York St) Hundreds of die-
cast model vehicles from pre-war cars
to James Bond's Aston Martin – even
a turning *Magic Roundabout*; of
course it's all a huge plug for the
company that makes them, but
fascinating for collectors. Shop,
disabled access; cl Tues and Sun;
(01706) 365812; free. The Egerton

Arms off the B6222 Bury rd is a good
moorland dining pub.

♨T ♈ ♈ † **Heysham** SD4160 HEYSHAM
POWER STATIONS Hi-tech interactive
exhibition on electricity generation,
with tours of power station and
nuclear reactor, and 25-acre nature
reserve. This is the most elaborate of
Nuclear Electric's visitor centres.
Tours by arrangement (ring for
details); it may be worth booking in
summer. Snacks, shop, disabled
access; cl Sat, and Nov–Mar; (01524)
855264; free. A tremendous contrast
is the quaint squint-walled little
village CHURCH, partly Saxon, with
Norse-carved hogback tombstone
inside. The unusual waterside Golden
Ball at Heaton with Oxcliffe off the
Lancaster road (may be cut off by
very high tides) is fun for lunch.

🏠 🎱 ❀ **Hoghton** SD6125 HOGHTON
TOWER (A675) Splendid 16th-c
fortified hilltop mansion, with grand
state rooms and royal bedchamber,
and a collection of dolls and dolls'
houses. The gardens are lovely
(particularly the rose garden) and the
surrounding grounds offer wonderful
views of the sea, moors, Lakeland
hills and Welsh mountains. Meals,
snacks, shop; open pm Sun and Mon
Easter–Oct, plus Tues–Thurs
July–Sept; (01254) 852986; £1
parking and grounds, £2.50 house.
The Royal Oak at Riley Green has
decent food.

🎱 **Holden** SD7749 HOLDEN CLOUGH
NURSERY Old-fashioned nursery with
thoroughly up-to-date approach to
raising interesting plants in the
Victorian kitchen garden of Holden
Clough Hall; beds of alpines, trough
gardens, herbaceous perennials,
shrubs and rhododendrons. Disabled
access; cl 12–1pm, all Mon and most
Suns, 25 Dec–1 Jan; (01200) 447615;
free. The Copy Nook has good food,
and is a useful stop for walkers.

🏠 🎱 **Hurst Green** SD6838
STONYHURST COLLEGE Magnificent
16th-c manor house, now home to
the famous Catholic boarding school.
You can see the library, chapel, other
historic rooms and the extensive
grounds. Snacks, shop, limited
disabled access; open pm Aug exc Fri,

gardens usually open 20 Jul–24 Aug; (01254) 826345; £4, £1 garden only. The Punch Bowl and Bayley Arms have nice food, with fine Ribble Valley walks nearby.

🏕 🛏 ✝ 🏦 ✿ 🏠 🛍 🐟 ☼ 🌺 **Lancaster** SD4761 Friendly and relaxed despite the grandeur of many of its stone buildings; ambling down the cobbled streets and alleyways (much is pedestrianised), it's hard to believe this was once a major West Indies shipping port. These days the water traffic is more sedate, with punts for hire and canal cruises in summer. The Farmhouse Tavern (part of Scale Hall, on the A589 Morecambe rd) has good food, and other places worth knowing for lunch include the George & Dragon (nr the River Lune) and canalside White Cross. The dramatic 12th-c Norman CASTLE, famous for hangings and witch trials, is owned by the Queen as Duke of Lancaster. Part of it is still used as a prison, but the cells, tower and 18th-c Gothic Revival Shire Hall can all be visited. Shop; open wknds Apr–Oct, and wkdys when Court is not in session – usually around school hols but best to check; (01524) 64998; £3. The PRIORY CHURCH dates back to before the Conquest, though the present hilltop building is mainly 14th and 15th c; very interesting medieval choir stalls, needlework and Anglo-Saxon cross fragments. Snacks, shop, some disabled access; cl winter lunchtimes; free. Nearby are the remains of a Roman bath-house. MARITIME MUSEUM (St George's Quay) Up-to-date look at the local maritime trade and fishing industry; the audio-visual show is good fun. Snacks, shop, disabled access; cl am Nov–Easter, Christmas–New Year; (01524) 64637; £2 (free to local residents). JUDGES LODGING (Church St) 17th-c house with well restored period rooms, plenty of Gillow furniture, and museum of childhood. Open pm Easter–Oct (exc Sun), maybe all day summer hols; (01524) 32808; £2. Other decent collections at the firmly traditional CITY MUSEUM on Market Sq, in a very grand Georgian former town hall (cl Sun,

24 Dec–1 Jan; free), and at the COTTAGE MUSEUM opposite the castle, furnished in the style of an early 19th-c artisan's house (open pm Easter–Sept; *75p). ASHTON MEMORIAL 🏛 (Williamson Park) A magnificent folly clearly visible from the motorway, set in 38 acres of lovely landscaped parkland; splendid views from upper galleries. Displays on Edwardian life, and a butterfly house with a good collection of plants and lepidoptera, as well as free-flying birds and various creepy-crawlies. Meals, snacks, shop, disabled access; cl 25–26 Dec, 1 Jan; (01524) 33318; £2.75.

🏦 ✝ 🛍 **Leighton Hall** SD4974 A notably friendly welcome at this neo-Gothic mansion (more restrained inside), still the home of the Gillow family and with early examples of their furniture. The grounds have a collection of birds of prey (flying displays 3.30pm), nature trails, and beautifully kept gardens. The setting is lovely, with Lakeland hills rising up behind. Snacks, shop, disabled access; cl am, all day Sat and Mon (exc bank hols), Oct–Apr; (01524) 734474; £3.50. The nearby New Inn at Yealand Conyers has excellent food.

🏪 🍴 🖼 🐾 🛍 ✝ **Leyland** SD5422 BRITISH COMMERCIAL VEHICLE MUSEUM (King St) Now slightly jazzed up with sound effects, and over 90 perfectly restored British wagons, buses, trucks, vans and fire engines, shining so much you'd think they were new. Snacks, shop, disabled access; Open Sun, Tues, Weds and bank hols Apr–Oct; (01772) 451011; £4. The sturdy 16th-c OLD GRAMMAR SCHOOL (Church Rd) has changing local history displays; open pm Thurs, Tues and Fri, am Sat; free. WORDEN PARK has art displays and 9 varied craft workshops, and walks, gardens, a maze, and miniature golf. Leyland also has a pleasant little town trail, and the 15th-c church has some fine stained glass. The friendly Rose & Crown (A581 S) has decent basic food.

❌ ✿ 🐟 ✓ **Lytham St Anne's** SD3627 Decorous seaside town that seems a world away from nearby Blackpool. It has a splendidly restored WINDMILL by the prom in the centre of Lytham green (open daily Easter–Sept; free), and a small LIFEBOAT MUSEUM next door (open Tues, Thurs and wknds Jun–Sept; free). The Taps is a good real ale pub here. At the St Annes end, the TOY AND TEDDY BEAR MUSEUM in a Porritt-built Victorian building has a big collection of nostalgic children's items. Good shop, some disabled access; open Sun, school hols, and bank hol wknds all year, plus Weds–Sat late May–Oct; (01253) 713705; £2.50. A sand dune NATURE RESERVE runs alongside Clifton Drive North.

🐦🐄 **Martin Mere** SD4310 WILDFOWL AND WETLANDS CENTRE (off the A59) Thousands of wild geese, swans, ducks and flamingos regularly visit the re-created natural open water habitats at this important 376-acre centre. Some birds will feed straight from your hand. Good visitor centre, well organised walks, lively activities for children, and plenty of instructive and entertaining events. Meals, snacks, shop, disabled access; cl 25 Dec; (01704) 895181; £4.75. About 400 yards towards Holmeswood, the friendly 40-acre WINDMILL ANIMAL FARM has animals and their babies to feed (inc rare breeds), tractor rides, miniature railway, and an adventure playground. Snacks, shop, disabled access; cl wkdys mid-Sept–Easter, possibly wknds too Nov–Jan; (01704) 892282; £2.50. The canalside Ship at Lathom is very popular for lunch.

🐾 **Mawdesley** SD4915 CRAFT CENTRE (Back Lane) In former farm buildings, with animals and a play area for children; the tearoom has a good range of teas and coffees; cl Mon exc bank hols. The lanes around here are pleasant to drive through (though perhaps not quite justifying the local name of Wigan Alps), with lots of good eating houses – our favourite is the unusual Eagle & Child at Bispham Green.

☺🌼 **Morecambe** SD4364 5m of promenade and more of beaches to stroll along at this cheery resort, with pretty sunsets over the bay. The Dog & Partridge (Bare) has decent fresh food. FRONTIERLAND Wild West theme park with 30 family rides and attractions (inc circus), and spectacular views across the bay from the top of the bizarre Polo Tower, designed to look like end-to-end tubes of sweets. Meals, snacks, shop, disabled access; cl Nov–Easter; (01524) 410024; £10.

🏠🖼🐑 **Padiham** SD7933 GAWTHORPE HALL Early 17th-c manor house with fine panelling and moulded ceilings, minstrel gallery, and Jacobean long gallery. Important collections of costume, embroidery and lace, and paintings from the National Portrait Gallery. Snacks, limited disabled access; house cl am, Mon (exc bank hols), Fri, and Nov–Mar, grounds open all year; (01282) 771004; £2.90; NT. The hilly cobbled alleyways in the town's centre are now a conservation area.

★ 🖼 ♪ **Port Sunlight** SJ3384 The most famous of the garden villages built by 19th-c philanthropists, contriving something better than the appalling squalor of northern England's factory towns. Historically important as the precursor of garden cities, garden suburbs and New Towns, it's perfectly preserved, with groups of mock-Tudor cottages, swathes of greenery and parkland: no two groups of houses are alike. Lord Leverhulme, who had built his Sunlight Soap factory here, donated the village its outstanding LADY LEVER ART GALLERY. Recently refurbished, it has interesting Victorian paintings inc Turners and Pre-Raphaelites – many adapted for use in soap ads, to the fury of the artists. Meals, snacks, shop, disabled access; cl am Sun, 23–26 Dec, 1 Jan; (0151) 645 3623; £3 for an Eight Pass ticket, covering 7 other galleries in the area (see Merseyside Maritime Museum entry in To see and do section on p.385). PORT SUNLIGHT HERITAGE CENTRE sets the scene, with useful village trail leaflets; also period soap packaging (you can buy soap in replica wrappings). Shop, some disabled access; cl winter wknds and Christmas and New Year; (0151) 644 6466; *40p. Thornton Hough SJ3081 was built by Lord Leverhulme as a mock-Tudor estate village – Port Sunlight on a much smaller scale; the Seven Stars there is useful for lunch.

✝ ✗ ✿ **Poulton le Fylde** SD3539 Quite an attractive pedestrianised market square, with a lovely church (as others in Lancashire, looking a good deal older than in fact it is), and several useful places to eat – the Old Town Hall is particularly good value. THORNTON WINDMILL (B5412) SD3342 This restored working windmill has a good range of craft shops alongside; excellent tea shop, dried flower specialist, summer wknd entertainments, even a little clog museum.

🐘🐄 **Prescot** SJ4692 KNOWSLEY SAFARI PARK 5-mile drive through very natural-looking reserves of lions, tigers, rhinos, monkeys and other animals; they have the biggest herd of African elephants in Europe. Also pets corner and miniature railway. Meals, snacks, shop, disabled access; cl Nov–Feb; (0151) 430 9009; £10 per car – load in all your friends and it's very good value indeed. If you have to pass through the town, the MUSEUM (Church St) has an interesting collection relating to the area's former clock-making industry; cl 1–2pm, am Sun, Mon (exc bank hols), Tues, Good Fri, 25–26 Dec, 1 Jan; (0151) 430 7787; free. The Clock Face is a pleasant old mansion-house pub here.

🐄🏠♿✝🏰 **Preston** SD5329 The town has 2 decent museums: the impressive if rather dour Greek revival HARRIS MUSEUM AND ART GALLERY on Market Sq (cl Sun and bank hols; free), and the COUNTY AND REGIMENTAL MUSEUM on Stanley St (cl Thurs, Sun and bank hols; £1). There's a good big market (the space is used for car-boot sales instead on Tues and Thurs); Wall Street (Fishergate) has decent food. The RAILWAY CENTRE from Southport is due to move to Preston Marina early in 1998; (01704) 530693 (wknds only) for opening date. MOOR PARK OBSERVATORY is open most

Thurs evenings (exc the second of the month) Sept–Mar (not Dec); (01772) 257181 to check. The CHURCH OF ST MARY (Penwortham) has a 14th-c chancel, and the scant remains of a motte and bailey castle in the churchyard; nearby the Fleece (Liverpool Rd) is useful for lunch.

🏠🏛 **Prestwich** SD8104 HEATON HALL. Splendidly decorated 18th-c neo-classical house in extensive, well used public parkland; fine paintings, plasterwork and furniture, an unusual circular Pompeiian room, and various recitals and temporary exhibitions. Disabled access; cl 12–1pm, am Sun, all day Mon and Tues, and Oct–Apr; (0161) 236 5244; free. The Victorian Woodthorpe by the main gate has decent food.

★🏛♿✝🏛 **Ribchester** SD6335 Attractive little town, many of its buildings incorporating masonry plundered from the former Roman town here: the White Bull pub, with decent food, has a couple of Tuscan pillars for its porch and an excavated Roman bath-house behind. On the site of a fort occupied between the 1st and 4th c, a small ROMAN MUSEUM has lots of coins, pottery and the famous Ribchester helmet. Shop, disabled access; cl am wknds (exc Jun–Aug); (01254) 878261; £1.35. The 15th-c CHURCH also stands on the site of the Roman fort, and looks as if it uses much salvaged material from it. STYDD NURSERY (Stoneygate Lane) There are excavated Roman granaries behind this nursery which specialises in old-fashioned roses and hardy perennials; some disabled access; cl am (exc Sat), all day Mon; free.

🏠 **Rufford** SD4615 RUFFORD OLD HALL Lovely timber-framed Tudor house built by the Hesketh family in the 16th c, with an intricate hammerbeam roof in the Great Hall, and impressive collections of 17th-c Lancashire oak furniture, and 16th-c arms, armour and tapestries. Some later rooms too. Snacks, shop, limited disabled access; cl am, all day Thurs and Fri, and Nov–Mar; (01704) 821254; £3.30, £1.70 garden only;

NT. The Robin Hood just the other side of Mawdesley has good home cooking.

🍴 **St Helens** SJ5195 PILKINGTON GLASS MUSEUM (Prescot Rd) The surprisingly interesting history of glass production, well told via interactive displays and exhibitions. Snacks, shop, limited disabled access; cl am wknds and bank hols, all Christmas–New Year; (01744) 692014; free.

🔲👤🍴🏠 **Salford** SJ8197 Merging almost imperceptibly into Manchester, this owes its distinct place in the popular consciousness mainly to the works of L S Lowry. The city recently received a £64 million Lottery grant to build a giant arts centre, which as well as other features will be able to show its entire collection of his works. Half of these can already be seen at the MUSEUM AND ART GALLERY (Peel Park), which also has a nostalgic reconstructed industrial street scene, with some wonderfully over the top period advertisements. Snacks, shop, disabled access; cl Easter, 25–26 Dec; (0161) 736 2649; free. MINING MUSEUM (Eccles Old Rd) Georgian building with 2 reconstructed mines, and displays showing the history and development of coal-mining. Shop; cl 12.30–1.30pm, am Sun, Sat, Good Fri, 25–26 Dec; (0161) 736 1832; free. ORDSALL HALL MUSEUM (Taylorson St) Timbered Tudor manor house with local history and Victorian farmhouse kitchen. Shop, some disabled access; cl 12.30–1.30pm, am Sun, Sat, Good Fri, 25–26 Dec; (0161) 872 0251; free. The waterside Mark Addy (Stanley St) has a great choice of cheeses and pâtés.

🏠 **Samlesbury** SD6230 SAMLESBURY HALL Well restored half-timbered 14th-c manor house, with good changing exhibitions and craft demonstrations, and sales of antiques. Meals, snacks, disabled access; cl Mon exc bank hols, mid-Dec–mid-Jan; (01254) 812010; *£2.50. The Myerscough Hotel (A59) is good for lunch.

🏠 **Silverdale** SD4674 Looks out over the tidal sands to the Cumbrian hills, with streets of quiet houses and a church that looks 14th-c but was built barely a century ago. Various crafts are sold at the Georgian buildings of the WOLF HOUSE GALLERY, which also has an adventure playground. Snacks; cl 1–2pm, Mon, all wkdys 25 Dec–end Mar. There are good woodland walks behind the town, and the Silverdale Hotel on Shore Rd is worth knowing.

LEIGHTON MOSS NATURE RESERVE (off Yealand Redmayne Rd) RSPB reserve with several roomy hides looking out on to reedbeds where bitterns, bearded tits and marsh harriers breed; good walks and views. Guided wildlife outings on Tues and Thurs evenings in Jun and July. Meals, snacks, shop, disabled access; cl 25 Dec; (01524) 701601; *£3.50.

YEALAND CONYERS FRIENDS' MEETING HOUSE Unobtrusively charming, in a quiet and pleasant village; the New Inn here is an outstanding dining pub.

★ **Slaidburn** SD7152 A perfectly preserved Forest of Bowland village: charming stone cottages, a green with the River Hodder running by, and at the opposite end an early 18th-c schoolhouse and a church with a very 18th-c feel inside. The Hark to Bounty is good for lunch and has comfortable bedrooms. The B6478 and the narrow road N past Stocks Reservoir have appealing views.

☺🏠👤🔲👤🎯⛳ **Southport** SD3317 Smartish Victorian seaside resort, long famed as the most pleasant shopping town in the area, and as the place where the sea doesn't come in. In fact it comes in as often as anywhere else, but doesn't stay quite as long; this could be due to the famously mucky beach – for cleaner shores try slightly S at Formby. The promenade is set back quite a way from the sea, and looks over a man-made lake with boats. From here there are bracing trips down the PIER, either on foot or on the little train, and in summer you can get pleasure flights over the sands. Lord St is the elegant main shopping street; there's an excellent antiquarian bookshop down the Wayfarers Arcade just off it. Plenty of good summer activities: PLEASURELAND is a typical fairground, its wooden roller-coaster well regarded by connoisseurs. The zoo next door in Princes Park has one of the few snow leopards to be bred in captivity in the West; he was born last spring. Snacks, shop, some disabled access; cl 25 Dec; £3. There's a MODEL VILLAGE not far from here (£2.50). SOUTHPORT RAILWAY CENTRE (Derby Rd) Biggest centre of its type in the area, with plenty of old locomotives and other vehicles. They plan to move to Preston Marina early in 1998 – (01704) 530693 (wknds only) for latest info. ATKINSON ART GALLERY (Lord St) Specialises in 19th- and 20th-c watercolours, oil paintings, prints and sculpture. Shop, disabled access; cl pm Thurs and Sat, all day Sun, bank hols; (01704) 533133; free. BRITISH LAWNMOWER MUSEUM (Shakespeare St) Fully restored and often bizarre machines from the 1830s to the present, inc one of the first racing lawnmowers – the curator used to be a champion. Shop; cl Sun and bank hols; (01704) 535369; *£1. CHURCHTOWN SD3618 Southport's oldest part has a number of pretty thatched cottages, and the lakeside BOTANIC GARDENS, which are very attractive as well as being interesting to plantsmen; boats to hire, fernery, pets corner, and local history MUSEUM (open 11am–3pm Tues–Fri and pm wknds and bank hols; free). Just opposite, MEOLS HALL is worth a look for its paintings, inc works by Ramsey, Reynolds, Romney and Poussin. Disabled access; open pm 14 Aug–14 Sept; (01704) 28326; *£3. The Hesketh Arms across from the main gate is good for lunch.

🏠 🏵 Speke SJ4383 SPEKE HALL Built around a square courtyard, this is one of the most beautiful and richly timbered black and white houses in the country; the inside is mainly Victorian, though there's a vast Tudor Great Hall. The garden is being restored in Victorian style. Hard to believe the centre of Liverpool is just 6m away. Snacks, shop, disabled access; house open pm exc Mon Apr–Oct, plus wknds Nov–mid-Dec, garden open pm exc Mon all year; (0151) 427 7231; £3.80, £1.20 grounds only; NT. They do occasional roof tours to show how the timbers were put together.

🏠 👁 🏵 Turton Bottoms SD7315 TURTON TOWER 15th-c Renaissance house with Elizabethan buildings and earlier peel tower; mostly a museum inside, but there are a couple of period rooms, and a major collection of carved wood furniture. It was interestingly extended by followers of the Romantic and later Arts and Crafts movements. Formal Victorian gardens. Snacks, shop; open daily May–Sept (cl 12–1pm for lunch, and am wknds), pm Sat–Weds in Mar, Apr and Oct, and just pm Sun Nov and Feb; (01204) 852203; *£2. The Strawbury Duck just N at Entwistle is prettily placed for lunch.

★ 👁 🖼 Uppermill SD9905 This whole area of mill settlements in steep valleys cut through the moors is full of interest, and Uppermill itself is one of the most attractive places. The SADDLEWORTH MUSEUM AND ART GALLERY (High St) is based around an old mill, and volunteers occasionally dress up in appropriate garb. They've worked hard to liven up visits for families. Shop, limited disabled access; cl 25 Dec, and am Nov–mid-Mar; (01457) 874093; £1.20. Up above the town is a lonely moorland church, with good walks around it and an ancient pub opposite. Fine drives around here include the A635 over Saddleworth Moor, and the B6197 Delph–Grains Bar then the A672 or A640 over the moors.

🏰 🏠 ✝ Whalley SD7336 WHALLEY ABBEY Striking remains of 14th-c Cistercian abbey – the monks' quarters, rather than the church which has virtually disappeared – in the grounds of a 16th-c manor house used as a religious retreat (they do B & B). 2 gatehouses are intact, and there's a visitor centre. Snacks, shop, disabled access; cl Christmas and New Year; (01254) 822268; £1.50. The separate 13th-c parish CHURCH has interesting woodwork and 3 ancient Celtic-Scandinavian crosses.

The Freemasons Arms at Wiswell does good food.

ⓗ ⊛ ⚘ **Wigan** SD5805 WIGAN PIER 🔲 (Wallgate) Rather different from when Orwell knew it, this is now a dynamic and entertaining wharfside centre demonstrating local life in the early 1900s, with actors performing in a reconstructed mine, pub, school, music hall, houses and even seaside. An ingenious mix of museum and theatre, it's an enormously enjoyable family day out, and you really do get a tangible impression of life at the turn of the century. Meals, snacks, shop, disabled access; cl Fri (exc Good Fri), 25 Dec; (01942) 323666; £4.95 peak, £4.40 off-peak. The Old Pear Tree on Frog Lane does decent lunches; the atmospheric Orwell on Wigan Pier has quick food. Slightly N at Haigh, HAIGH HALL COUNTRY PARK is a 250-acre country park with guided walks, nature trails, a beautifully set golf course, craft centre, walled gardens and miniature railway. Meals, snacks, shops (one excellent for golfers), some disabled access; (01942) 832985; park free, charges for parking and attractions.

⊛ ⏻ **The Wirral** Its Merseyside parts aren't on the whole that appealing to visitors, especially on the built-up E side (with the notable exception of Port Sunlight). The NW corner can be rather more attractive, particularly along the edges of the Dee, looking across to the mountains of N Wales. The more interesting bits, inc unusual National Trust heathland, are linked by a 12-mile footpath, best joined at the WIRRAL COUNTRY PARK at Thurstaston SJ2584, and running down to the Cheshire parts of the Wirral. The Irby Mill at nearby Irby SJ2684 has decent food. The sweeping sands of HOYLAKE BEACH are beautiful, with an unusual, partly tidal nature reserve at Red Rocks SJ2088 N of the golf links. Nr here at low tide you can reach 3 tidal islands on foot from West Kirby SJ2187; the biggest, Hilbre, is a nature reserve, once popular with sunbathers, now

visited mainly by birds and occasional seals. Make sure you know the tide times – (0151) 648 4371 – as it's easy to be stranded out here.

⛵ The **Lancaster Canal** between Preston and Carnforth is ideal for boating – 40m without a single lock; often through quiet countryside, with herons and even occasional kingfishers – best in spring or early summer, with ducklings and cygnets bobbing about, and lambs in the fields alongside. In summer boats can be hired by the day at Catforth SD4735, (01772) 690232, where there's a decent teashop.

★ **Attractive villages**, all with decent pubs and great surrounding scenery, include Goosnargh SD5537, Tunstall SD6173 (Bronte church) and, on the slopes of Pendle Hill, Wiswell SD7437 and (linked by a scenic drive) Pendleton SD7539 and Sabden SD7737 (which has a decent antiques centre). Particularly pretty ones in or on the edges of the Forest of Bowland are Bolton by Bowland SD7849 (with a fine church), Gisburn SD8248, Grindleton SD7545, Newton SD6950 and Waddington SD7244 (fine church, and a lovely drive from Longridge SD6039). Below Pendle Hill, Downham SD7844 is outstandingly pretty, carefully preserved, on the side of a steep pasture valley with a stream winding along the bottom. There are unexpected corners even quite close to urban areas – such as Ringley SD7605 with its village stocks and ancient bridge over the Irwell (and a decent pub). Great Mitton SD7139 has an attractive church with an outstanding range of memorial tombs.

🍎 **Pick your own** is popular, with lots of places on the flat ground in the west of the area – soft fruit the speciality, late Jun–Aug; LYDIATE FRUIT FARM SD3604 (Pilling Lane) has a good farm shop in attractive 18th-c former stable buildings.

Walks

Morecambe Bay ◠-1 has vast mudflats and sands, home to 200,000 wading birds. Walks over them are described in the Cumbria chapter – foot access is easier from that side, though guided walks are also available from Hest Bank (details from local tourist information centres; the galloping tides and quicksand do make a guide essential). **Warton Crag** SD4973 ◠-2 just N of Carnforth gives fine views over the bay and coast, and enjoyable walking. **Leighton Moss Nature Reserve** ◠-3 is a short walk N, and is crossed by a public footpath.

The **Lancaster Canal** towpath ◠-4 allows pleasant walks, largely through quiet countryside; Catforth SD4735 is a good departure point.

Formby Dunes SD2809 ◠-5 reached from the NW edge of Formby is a large tract of sweeping sandy dunes which in some areas are being stabilised by pine plantations; broad beaches and good walks through the adjacent pinewoods, made interesting by the chance of seeing and even feeding red squirrels (you can buy nuts here). Best in spring and autumn – can be busy in summer; parking in some places may cost £1.50, but keep looking – a number of other spots are free.

The **Forest of Bowland** ◠-6 could be great for walkers but is largely barred to them, with only a few paths crossing the impressive massif that forms some of the county's most significant scenery; the Ramblers' Association has often organised mass trespasses as demonstrations against denial of access. There are, however, a few fine walks on rights of way – for instance, up Clougha Fell from Quernmore SD5259; above Tarnbrook Wyre SD5855; up Dunsop Fell from Slaidburn SD7152 or Dunsop Bridge SD6550; up Fairsnape and Wolf Fell from Chipping SD6143 or Bleasdale SD5745. Beacon Fell Country Park SD5642 is an atmospheric place to wander through. There are some pleasant walks around the Coronation Arms at Horton SD8550.

Pendle Hill SD7941 ◠-7 has an excellent network of paths, letting you walk round and almost all over it. Although Pendle's witch-persecuting days are happily over, the place still has a haunting, elemental appeal. The view that enraptured George Fox, the founder of the Quakers, is as good as ever. The quickest way up is from Barley village SD8240.

Rivington SD6214 ◠-8, just outside Horwich, lies close to attractive reservoirs. Lower Rivington Reservoir SD6213 has a waterside path along its eastern edge, and a curious mock-up of Liverpool castle built in 1912 as an adornment to the vast and atmospherically decayed gardens of Lever Park SD6313, which cover the hillside. A trail guides you around the undergrowth and up to the Pigeon Tower SD6314, within a few minutes of Rivington Pike, the summit. The Great House Barn SD6313 is the place to start, with a good information centre, maps and guides.

The **Peak Forest Canal** ◠-9 is reached from Marple SJ9588, the towpath soon leaving suburbia for green countryside; N is the famous set of Marple locks SJ9689 and aqueduct over the River Etherow. To the S, you can leave the canal at Strines SJ9868 and climb on to Mellor Moor SJ9987.

Wycoller Park SD9339 ◠-10 is Lancashire Bronte country (the ruined hall at Wycoller features in Jane Eyre), and has walks along a beck to Clam Bridge, an Iron Age slab, and up to Foster's Leap SD9439, a finely placed crag.

This area is outstanding for the number of pubs which are well placed as good jumping-off points for walks – or places to look forward to getting back to. Up on the moors, many of these are closed during lunchtime Mon–Thurs. Good pubs for walkers include the Hare & Hounds at Abbey Village SD6422, Pack Horse at Affetside SD7513, Black Dog at Belmont SD6716, Dog at Belthorn SD7224, White House on Blackstone Edge SD9716, Owd Betts at Cheesden on Ashworth Moor SD8316, Rams Head nr Denshaw SD9710, Diggle Hotel at Diglea Hamlet above Diggle itself SE0008, Wright Arms at

Egerton SD7114, Strawbury Duck by Entwistle Station SD7217, Bull's Head on Grains Bar SD9608, Duke of Wellington on the B6232 W of Haslingden SD7522, Egerton Arms off the narrow Ashworth rd above Heywood SD8513, Green Man at Inglewhite (nr Beacon Fell) SD5440, New Drop on Longridge Fell SD6439, Romper at Ridge End above Marple SJ9686, Kettledrum at Mereclough SD8632, Highwayman at Nether Burrow SD6275 (pretty stretch of the Lune Valley), Old Rosins at Pickup Bank, Old Hoddlesden SD6922, Roebuck on Roebuck Low SD9606, Royal Arms at Tockholes SD6623 (for Roddlesworth Valley woodlands, maybe on to the ruins of Hollinshead Hall and its restored curative well; the Victoria and Rock are also good, though slightly less well placed), and Railway at White Coppice SD6118.

Where to eat

Manchester and Liverpool both have plenty of good ethnic restaurants.

Birkenhead SJ3289 PASTIME RESTAURANT 42 Hamilton Sq (0151) 647 8095 Popular restaurant in a handsome Victorian building with good food (the fixed-price menu is good value), a relaxed atmosphere, and friendly, helpful service; cl Mon. £25|£6.

Bispham Green SD4914 EAGLE & CHILD (01257) 462297 Striking, 3-storey, dark brick pub with civilised mainly open-plan bar, fine old stone fireplaces, oriental rugs and some coir on the flagstones, handsome oak settles; imaginative daily specials like goat, buffalo, ostrich, kangaroo and so forth, popular curry night last Mon of month, well kept real ales, and friendly service; bowling green and croquet behind. £17.50|£5.

Blacko SD8541 MOORCOCK (01282) 614186 Isolated old stone inn with wonderful views from its big picture windows in the spaciously comfortable lounge bar; good, generously served food (lovely lamb dishes), efficient friendly service; disabled access. £14|£4.95.

Downham SD7844 ASSHETON ARMS (01200) 441227 Popular pub among peaceful pastures in a prettily preserved village; with a rambling, beamed bar, reasonably priced and generous bar food (lots of good fresh fish dishes), well kept real ales, and decent wines; disabled access. £19|£6.25.

Fence SD8237 FOREST (01282) 613641 Comfortable, with heavy panelling, lots of paintings, vases, plates, books and a big open fire; no smoking restaurant, varied and inventive food, a good choice of wines, and friendly, helpful service. £21|£8.50.

Goosnargh SD5537 BUSHELLS ARMS Church Lane (01772) 865235 Friendly modernised pub close to Chingle Hall, with an excellent range of imaginative food from a constantly changing menu, and good choice of wines; cl occasional Mon, 25 Dec; well behaved children only; partial disabled access. £14.50|£5.

Kirkham SD4231 CROMWELLIAN 16 Poulton St (01772) 685680 Tiny evening restaurant in 17th-c house, with consistently good and interesting food from a fixed-price menu – thoughtful wine list, too; cl Sun–Mon, 2 wks May, 2 wks Sept. £22.75.

Longridge SD6037 PAUL HEATHCOTES 104 Higher Rd (01772) 784969 Pretty restaurant with flowers, beams and candlelit tables; exceptional modern British cooking, marvellous puddings, and exemplary service; cl Mon, am Tues, Wed, Thurs, Sat. £55 dinner, £35 lunch.

Manchester SJ8398 LITTLE YANG SING 17 George St (0161) 228 7722 – Very busy and popular basement restaurant with super Chinese food (very good casseroles, vegetarian dishes, and dim-sum), a children's fixed menu, decent wines, and friendly service; cl 25 Dec; reasonable disabled access. £24|£2.50.

Manchester SJ8398 MARK ADDY Stanley St Salford (0161) 832 4080 Smart pub in converted boat waiting-rooms with a good range of food – though its choice of 50 different cheeses is the main feature; extremely big helpings, doggy-bags provided; bread and cheese £3.20.

Manchester SJ8398 ROYAL OAK 729 Wilmslow Rd, Didsbury (0161) 445 3152 Busy pub with exceptional choice of cheeses from around the world – rare to be given less than a pound; bread, cheese and salad £3.30 (not wknds).

Manchester SJ8398 YANG SING 34 Princess St (0161) 236 2200 Exceptionally good Chinese food using the best fresh ingredients (tanks of live fish, too), wonderful dim-sum, some unusual dishes among traditional Cantonese specialities, good-value set meals, a bustling atmosphere, and efficient service; must book ahead; cl 25 Dec; disabled access. £20|£9.

Mellor SJ9888 DEVONSHIRE ARMS Longhurst Lane (0161) 427 2563 Friendly, relaxed and distinctive pub on the edge of the Peak District with a cheerful little front bar, 2 other Victorian rooms, and nice, interesting and popular lunchtime food (they also serve food pm Mon). £17.40|£5.75.

Mellor SJ9888 ODDFELLOWS ARMS (0161) 449 7826 Fine old building with low ceilings and open fires in 2 flagstoned rooms; no smoking restaurant, a wide range of interesting food and lots of different types of fresh fish. £17.25|£7.25.

Thornton-Cleveleys SD3342 RIVER HOUSE Wyre Rd, Skippool Creek (01253) 883497 Delightful restaurant with very good, honest cooking using the freshest local ingredients, a decent wine list, fresh flowers and log fires, and fine views (they also have lovely bedrooms); cl pm Sun, 25–26 Dec, 1 Jan; children must be well behaved. £40|£20.

Yealand Conyers SD5074 NEW INN (01524) 732938 Ivy-covered stone dining pub with log fire in the little, beamed bar, 2 communicating cottage dining rooms, novel daily specials, fine salads served with meals, friendly professional service, decent wines, well kept ales and home-made lemonade, and a sheltered side lawn. £18.35|£6.95.

Special thanks to Mrs Tina Dowson, E G Parish, Phil and Dilys Unsworth, Arthur and Margaret Dickinson, Peter Baron, Mrs P Smith, Liz Bell.

LANCASHIRE CALENDAR

Some of these dates were provisional as we went to press. Please check information with the numbers provided.

JANUARY

1 **Liverpool** Great Model of Lutyens Design for Liverpool Catholic Cathedral at the Walker Art Gallery – *till 31 Dec* (0151) 4784616; **Manchester** Pre-Raphaelite Women Artists at Manchester City Art Galleries – *till 22 Feb* (0161) 236 5244

11 **Lancaster** New Year's Eve Calendar Walk: torchlit walk round the historic town with re-enactments, *starts 7pm* from John o'Gaunt Gateway (01524) 32878

13 **Manchester** Torvill and Dean at the Nynex Arena – *till Sat 17* (0161) 930 8000

28 **Manchester** Chinese New Year Celebrations in Chinatown (0161) 237 1010

29 **Liverpool** Chinese New Year Celebrations in Chinatown (0151) 708 8833

FEBRUARY

25 **Lancaster** Valentine's Day Calendar Walk (see 11 Jan for details)

APRIL

2 **Aintree** Race Meeting inc Grand National – *till Sat 4* (0151) 523 2600

LANCASHIRE CALENDAR

APRIL cont

10 **Lancaster and Morecambe** Maritime Festival at the Maritime Museum and St George's Quay: sea songsters, shanty men and entertainments – *till Mon 13* (01524) 582394

11 **Bacup** Britannia Coconut Dancers – colourful, elaborately costumed black-faced clog dancers *from 9am*, thought to be pirate dances brought with miners moving N from Cornwall (01706) 356592

13 **Castlefield** Street Market and Fun Fair (0161) 234 1281; **Preston** Egg and Orange Rolling in Avenham Park (01772) 253731

17 **Manchester** Food and Wine Fair at G-Mex – *till Sun 19* (0161) 832 9000

MAY

2 **Manchester and surrounding districts** – International Festival of Street Arts: inc steel bands, outdoor theatre, torchlight procession – *till Mon 25* (0161) 224 0020

4 **Castlefield** Street Market and Fun Fair (0161) 234 1281

6 **Liverpool** Town Hall Open to the Public: grade I building with 3 of the finest chandeliers in Europe – *till Sat 16* (0151) 707 2391

13 **Lancaster** May Day Calendar Walk (see 11 Jan for details)

23 **Liverpool** Show at the Wavertree Playground – *till Mon 25* (0151) 225 6351; **Manchester** England v South Africa, One Day International at Lancashire County Cricket Club (0161) 282 4000

25 **Castlefield** Street Market and Fun Fair (0161) 234 1281

27 **Preston** Caribbean Carnival Procession (01772) 461120

JUNE

6 **Burnley** Horse Show at Towneley Park (01282) 435411

7 **Burnley** Classic Car Show at Towneley Park (01282) 435411; **Garstang** Myerscough College Open Day (01995) 640611; **Morecambe** Carnival (01524) 414379

14 **Burnley** Agricultural Show at Towneley Park (01282) 435411; **Uppermill** Vintage Vehicle Gala at Saddleworth Museum (01457) 870336

20 **Lancaster and Morecambe** National Music Weekend – *till Sun 21* (01542) 582801

27 **Southport** Vintage Vehicle Rally at Meols Hall – *till Sun 28* (01704) 28326

JULY

2 **Carnforth** Fireworks and Candlelit Concerts at Leighton Hall – *till Fri 3* (01524) 734474; **Manchester** England v South Africa, Third Test Match at Lancashire County Cricket Club – *till Mon 6* (0161) 282 4000

4 **Altrincham** Festival and Parade (0161) 926 8336; **Lancaster** Midsummer Eve Calendar Walk (see 11 Jan for details); **Preston** Maritime Festival: rally of yachts and canal boats, Royal Navy displays, fireworks, live music – *till Sun 5* (01772) 558111

5 **Southport** Open-air Theatre at Meols Hall (01704) 28326

11 **Lancaster** One-Man-Band Shebang – *till Sun 12* (01524) 582803

12 **Whalley** Abbey Open Day (01254) 822268

18 **Morecambe** Music Festival: light music, jazz, blues – *till Sun 19* (01524) 582803

LANCASHIRE CALENDAR

JULY cont

19 **Fleetwood** Tram Sunday: large transport festival, bands and side shows (01253) 876525

24 **Chorley** Royal Lancashire Show at Astley Park – *till Sun 26* (01254) 813769

25 **Lancaster and Morecambe** Street Theatre Festival – *till Sun 26* (01524) 582803; **Southport** North West Country Music Festival and Line Dance Competition at Meols Hall (01704) 28326

26 **Southport** Proms in the Park at Meols Hall (01704) 28326

31 **St Helens** Show at Sherdley Park: circus, live bands, stalls – *till 2 Aug* (01744) 456991

AUGUST

1 **Garstang** Agricultural Show (01772) 717418; **Lancaster and Morecambe** Street Bands Festival – *till Sun 2* (01524) 582803; – **Southport** Woodvale International Rally: inc model aircraft, military vehicles, classic cars, country market – *till Sun 2* (01704) 578816; **Wigan** Pier Cross-Country Boat and Steam Rally – *till Sun 2* (01942) 323666

8 **Morecambe** Festival of Light and Water – *till Sun 9* (01524) 582801; **Rochdale** Rushbearing Ceremony – *till Sun 9* (0161) 236 2111

16 **Morecambe and Lancaster** Caribbean Folklore Festival and Carnival – *till Wed 19* (01524) 582803

20 **Southport** Flower Show at Victoria Park – *till Sun 23* (01704) 547147

22 **Saddleworth** Rushcart Festival: Morris dancing – *till Sun 23* (01457) 834871

24 **Preston** Flower Show (01772) 203456

26 **Liverpool** International Beatles Festival – *till 1 Sept* (0151) 236 9091

27 **Carnforth** Burton and Milnthorpe Show at Mason's Field (01524) 701066

28 **Colne** Rhythm and Blues Festival: over 700 bands on 7 stages – *till Mon 31* (01282) 864721; **Lancaster** Georgian Legacy Festival: re-creation of 1803 characters and events, sedan chair carrying championships – *till Mon 31* (01524) 32878; **Morecambe** WOMAD Festival – *till Sun 30* (01524) 582803

29 **Southport** Airshow – *till Sun 30* (01704) 5333333

31 **Castlefield** Street Market and Fun Fair (0161) 234 1281; **Hoylake** Lifeboats Open Day inc aircraft displays at the Promenade (0151) 647 6780

SEPTEMBER

3 **Preston** Historical Fair: crafts and entertainment at the Flag Market (01772) 203456

4 **Blackpool** Illuminations – *till 8 Nov* (01253) 25212

5 **Southport** Jazz Festival at Meols Hall (01704) 28326; **St Michael's on Wyre** Lancashire Vintage and Country Show – *till Sun 6* (01772) 687259

13 **Morecambe** Heritage Gala: traditional entertainments, vintage vehicles, aerial displays – *till Sun 13* (01524) 582803

19 **Parkgate** Horse Trials and Country Fair – *till Sun 20* (0151) 336 4169

OCTOBER

10 **Lancaster** Michaelmas Day Calendar Walk (see Jan 11 for details)

LANCASHIRE CALENDAR

NOVEMBER

7 **Lancaster** Fireworks and Beacon Lighting (01524) 32878; **Southport**
Fireworks at Meols Hall (01704) 28326

10 **Lancaster** Hallowe'en Calendar Walk (see 11 Jan for details)

DECEMBER

17 **Lancaster** St Nichola's Day Calendar Walk (see 11 Jan for details)

We welcome reports from readers . . .

This *Guide* depends on readers' reports. Do help us if you can – in return, we offer a discount on the next edition to people who've helped us with reports for it. Tell us what you think about places already in it, and anything extra you think we should say about them. And send us your ideas for inclusion in the next edition: places to visit, eat at or stay in, attractive drives or walks, maybe even unusual interesting shops you know of. Use the card in the middle, the report forms at the end, or just write – no stamp needed: *The Good Guide to Britain*, FREEPOST TN1569, Wadhurst, E Sussex TN5 7BR.

LEICESTERSHIRE AND RUTLAND

Sweeping country views, grand houses and castles, some unusual places to visit – and not too many tourists.

Attractively varied countryside and plenty of enjoyable places to visit make this a pleasant area for a civilised break. There's a lot for children to enjoy, too. Among several good farm parks, the friendly, well organised one at Oadby stands out, and people also very much like the one near Oakham. The Coalville discovery park captivates many young people, and other family favourites include Twycross Zoo (good for apes) and the steam railway running near Market Bosworth, from Shackerstone past the battlefield of Bosworth Field.

It's older people, though, who really get the most out of Rutland and Leicestershire. The countryside particularly suits scenic drives or cycle rides, especially in the east: graceful patches of woodland, plenty of charming stonebuilt villages to potter through, delightful churches. Many of the less busy roads stride along old coach routes, with sweeping views. There are quite a few worthwhile walks, too – and you get out into unspoilt countryside very quickly from the built-up areas, even from busy Leicester itself. Rutland Water is a reservoir, but now has the look of a huge natural lake, pleasant to walk around, with nature reserves at the western end, bicycle and boat hire, and even launch trips.

There are several fine houses to visit, often surrounded by handsome parkland; the one at Swinford has the widest appeal. Oddly enough, given the great houses, this is not an area for great gardens: the late Geoff Hamilton's garden near Exton is popular. Leicester has plenty of attractions (most free) and is good for day visits.

Information centres here are very helpful, and bus services excellent.

Where to stay

Castle Donington SK4427 PRIEST HOUSE Kings Mills, Castle Donington DE74 2RR (01332) 810649 **£99w;** 45 good rms, some in annexe. At the end of a country lane and in a pretty spot by the River Trent, this extended, partly 11th-c hotel has a Gothic tower and arched windows and doors; there's a huge Adam fireplace in the comfortable library, a cheerful bar, and a restaurant overlooking the river; disabled access.

Empingham SK9408 WHITE HORSE Main St, Empingham LE15 8PS (01780) 460221 **£49,** plus special breaks; 14 pretty rms, some in a delightfully converted stable block, and most with own bthrm. Popular, refurbished old pub handy for Rutland Water; relaxed and friendly atmosphere, big helpings of excellent food inc fine breakfasts, coffee and croissants from 8am, and cream teas all year round; log fire, an attractive restaurant and efficient, friendly service; cots/highchairs.

Glooston SP7595 OLD BARN Main St, Glooston, Market Harborough LE16 7ST (01858) 545215 *£49.50; 3 rms. Attractively restored 16th-c pub with civilised décor and an open fire in the beamed main bar; a charming little restaurant, super inventive food (some produce from their kitchen garden), good breakfasts, and decent real ales; pleasant walks nearby; well behaved children and dogs allowed.

Hambleton SK9007 HAMBLETON HALL Hambleton, Oakham LE15 8TH (01572) 756991 £165, plus winter weekend breaks; 15 luxurious rms. Set in beautiful grounds on the edge of Rutland Water, this grandly restored Victorian manor house has elegant day rooms with fine views, antiques, open fires and exceptional flower arrangements; professional and friendly staff, wonderful food, a stimulating wine list and a marvellously pampering atmosphere; disabled access.

Ketton SK9704 PRIORY Church Rd, Ketton, Stamford PE9 3RD (01780) 720215 £75, plus winter breaks; 3 rms. Lovely 17th-c house, carefully restored, with delightful gardens running down to the River Chater; particularly friendly, helpful owners, lots of fresh flowers, a comfortable lounge, an airy and attractive conservatory, good hearty breakfasts, and enjoyable evening meals; fine 12th-c church next door; cl Christmas wk.

Market Harborough SP7387 THREE SWANS 21 High St LE16 7NJ (01858) 466644 £75w; 36 rms. Fine old coaching inn with a plush lounge bar, attractive conservatory and a glorious courtyard; very friendly, helpful staff, and good food; disabled access.

Medbourne SP7993 NEVILL ARMS Medbourne, Market Harborough LE16 8EE (01858) 565288 £50; 3 rms. Bright and busy, old mullion-windowed inn just across a footbridge over the stream; excellent food, lots of bar games, friendly and prompt service, a log fire in the inglenook fireplace, and a paddock for visiting horses; cl 25 Dec; disabled access.

Oakham SK8609 WHIPPER-IN Market Pl, Oakham LE15 6DT (01572) 756971 £71, plus special breaks; 24 rms. Attractive and well run, 17th-c stone coaching inn with an oak-beamed and panelled lounge opening into a pleasant eating area; log fires, good food in the cosy restaurant, and well kept ales; disabled access.

Packington SK3614 SPRINGS HYDRO Packington, Ashby-de-la-Zouch LE65 1TG (01530) 273873 £130 inc massage and free use of all facilities, plus special breaks; 57 rms. Britain's first purpose-built health hydro with all the amenities; good healthy food, and friendly staff; cl 24–26 Dec; no children; disabled access.

Rothley SK5812 ROTHLEY COURT LE7 7LG (0116) 237 4141 £107.90; 34 rms (the ones in the main house have more character). Mentioned in the Domesday Book, this carefully run manor house, with its beautifully preserved 13th-c chapel, has some fine oak panelling, open fires, a comfortable bar, conservatory, a terrace and garden; courteous staff; disabled access.

Saxelbye SK7021 SAXELBYE MANOR HOUSE Church Lane, Saxelbye, Melton Mowbray LE14 3PA (01664) 812269 £40; 3 rms, 1 with own bthrm. Attractive old house (parts are several hundred years old) with a marvellous collection of Victoriana, and a long passage leading to a fine Elizabethan oak stairway built in the old stone stairwell; helpful, friendly owner, and very good traditional evening meals and breakfasts; cl Nov–Mar.

Stapleford SK8018 STAPLEFORD PARK Stapleford, Melton Mowbray LE14 2EF (01572) 787522 £193.87; 51 lavishly decorated rms, plus cottage. Luxurious country house, extravagantly restored, in lovely large grounds, with lots of mahogany, opulent furnishings, fine oil paintings and an impressive library; good restaurant food, an enthusiastic American owner, and warmly welcoming staff; health spa, indoor swimming pool, riding, stabling, tennis, croquet, miniature golf, coarse fishing, clay-pigeon shooting, hunting; cots/babysitting; dogs welcome; disabled access.

Stretton SK9416 RAM JAM INN Great North Rd, Stretton LE15 7QY (01780) 410776 £65; 7 comfortable and well equipped rms. Actually on the A1, this civilised place has a comfortable, airy modern lounge bar blending into a wine-bar-like eating area; a good choice of food quickly served all day, and a useful small wine list; cl 25 Dec.

To see and do

LEICESTERSHIRE FAMILY ATTRACTION OF THE YEAR

🐂 **Oadby** SK6200 FARMWORLD 🎫 (Gartree Rd) Nicely set in charming countryside (but very quick to get to from Leicester), this is a particularly well organised working farm with a good range of traditional farm animals and rare breeds. As with most farms, it's children between around 3 and 10 who'll probably appreciate it best, though we often hear from adults who've gone without children and enjoyed it immensely. Imaginatively named Ducky (no surprise as to what sort of creature he is) is a particular favourite, waddling after visitors much as he's done for the last 8 years. You can feed most of the inhabitants (they sell food, but don't mind you bringing sensible offerings from home), and they usually have some kind of baby or young animals all year round. There are milking displays most days, and good play areas for younger children. Some areas are under cover, but it's better in fine weather. The pub is an unusual feature – it's an enjoyable pastiche of an Edwardian alehouse, with plenty of period memorabilia. Meals, snacks, shop, disabled access; cl 24 Dec–3 Jan; (0116) 271 0355; *£4 (children 3–16 £2.25). A family ticket for 2 adults and 2 children is £11.50.

🏰♨️⚓🐾🏵️★✝ **Ashby-de-la-Zouch** SK3516 CASTLE The Norman core and its 15th-c extension were largely destroyed in the Civil War, but the ruins are impressive, and the adjoining fields were the setting for Sir Walter Scott's *Ivanhoe*. Bring a torch for the underground passage. Shop, limited disabled access; cl 24–26 Dec, and winter Mon and Tues; (01530) 413343; £1.60. There's a little MUSEUM next to the tourist information centre on North St, and the Royal Hotel has a good-value carvery. MOIRA FURNACE (Moira, on the B5003, W of Ashby) 19th-c blast furnace and foundations of an engine house and casting shed, with a few craft workshops in the grounds. Snacks, shop, disabled access; cl Sat, and Nov–Mar; (01283) 224667; free. The Rawdon Arms out here is useful for lunch, and the towpath of the Ashby Canal links the furnace to the attractions listed under Market Bosworth (see entry below).

STAUNTON HAROLD (off the B587, N of Ashby) In this pretty village, the FERRERS CENTRE has good craft shops around a striking Georgian courtyard (cl Mon exc bank hols; free). The CHURCH out here (owned by the NT) was one of the few built during the Commonwealth; open pm Sat–Weds Apr–Sept, plus wknds in Oct.
❄️ **Beacon Hill Country Park** SK5114 The hill itself (above Woodhouse Eaves) is one of the best viewpoints in the area – an intriguing mix of the industrial and the very rural; it's a popular local beauty-spot, rising almost like a volcano above its lower woodland slopes (good for a stroll). The Wheatsheaf is handy for lunch.
🏰🏵️ **Belvoir Castle** SK8133 Pronounced Beaver, this is best from the outside, a glorious fantasy of turrets and battlements, pinnacles and towers, surrounded by terraced gardens peopled with sculptures. Inside, only a couple of rooms are

grand enough to impress, and some of the contents are starting to look a little shabby. Meals, snacks, shop, limited disabled access – it's quite a walk up the hill; cl Mon (exc bank hols), Fri, and Oct–Mar; (01476) 870262; *£4.50. The Peacock at Redmile, not far off, is excellent for lunch. Good drives on fine old coach roads centre on Belvoir: for instance, from Long Bennington (in Lincs) through Bottesford, Harby and Hose, or via Knipton down through Eastwell and past Grimston all the way to Barrow upon Soar.

🛞 🏚 ✝ **Bradgate Country Park** SK5209 On the edge of Newtown Linford, this extensive tract of a former hunting park is little changed over the last 750 years. At its heart are the ruins of the 15th-c home of Lady Jane Grey, and a visitor centre tells her sad story. Shop, limited disabled access; visitor centre cl am, Mon, and all winter wkdys; (0116) 234 1850; pay and display parking, visitor centre £1.20. The entrance off the B5328 N of Cropston has better lavatories than the main entrance on the B5327. Fallow deer still roam these heathy slopes among the rock outcrops, and nearby Cropston Reservoir has waterfowl. The Pear Tree in Woodhouse Eaves has good food.

🛞 **Burrough on the Hill** SK7510 BURROUGH HOUSE The gardens here are well worth visiting – by appointment only (Apr–Aug). They include – moved from its original site – the summerhouse where Edward met Mrs Simpson for the first time; (01644) 454226; *£2.

! 🐦 **Clipsham** SK9616 YEW TREE AVENUE (just E, off Castle Bytham Rd) Delightfully quirky avenue of 150 yew trees, clipped in sometimes bizarre shapes to represent animals, characters and events; free. The surrounding woods are full of deer (not to mention bluebells in spring), and the Olive Branch has decent food.

☺ ⌷ ✝ ♪ **Coalville** SK4214 SNIBSTON DISCOVERY PARK (Ashby Rd) Busy 100-acre centre based around a former colliery (the first shaft was sunk by George and Robert Stephenson), with fun exhibitions and interactive displays on a hugely varied range of topics connected to science and industry. Children like the Science Alive gallery best, with plenty of hands-on experiments and activities (inc the illusion of cycling with a skeleton), while similarly organised galleries look at transport, mining, and fashion. The landscaped grounds include a huge play area and nature reserve, with extra charges for golf, fishing and tours of the mine workings by former pitmen. Meals, snacks, shop, disabled access; cl 25–26 Dec; (01530) 510851; *£4. The Bull's Head, above Whitwick, is a popular family food pub, with great views and quite a menagerie of farm animals.

⌷ ⌷ **Cottesmore** SK9013 RUTLAND RAILWAY MUSEUM 🚂 Nearly 40 industrial steam and diesel locomotives, and 60 other wagons and vehicles used in the ironstone quarries and industry. Occasional steam rides, and quite a nice lineside walk to the old Oakham Canal. Open wknds and bank hols Easter–Sept, plus over Christmas – best to tel (01572) 813203 for dates of steamdays; £2.50. The Sun is useful for lunch.

🐦 **Desford** SK4703 TROPICAL BIRD GARDENS (Lindridge Lane) Pleasant 5-acre woodland garden with over 50 different species, many in walk-through aviaries; the free-flying macaws are particularly spectacular. Cl mid-Oct–Mar; (01455) 824603; £3.

🏛 **Donington le Heath** SK4112 DONINGTON LE HEATH MANOR HOUSE One of the very rare examples of an almost untouched medieval manor house, pretty much unaltered since it was built in 1280. Snacks, shop; disabled access to ground floor only, cl am, all Mon and Tues, and Oct–Easter; (01530) 831259; free.

🏎 **Donington Park** SK4427 DONINGTON COLLECTION Largest private collection of single-seat racing cars in the world, with vehicles driven by all the greats, and related memorabilia. The price means you

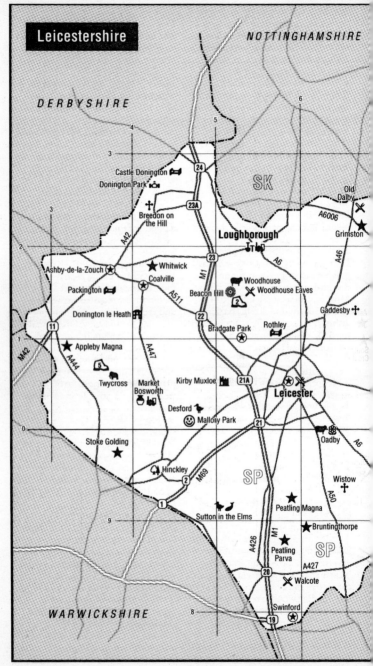

Leicestershire

NOTTINGHAMSHIRE

DERBYSHIRE

SK

Castle Donington
Donington Park

Old Dalby

Breedon on
the Hill

A6006

A42

Grimston

Loughborough

Ashby-de-la-Zouch   Whitwick
Coalville

A6

A46

Woodhouse
Woodhouse Eaves

Packington

Beacon Hill

Donington le Heath

A511

Bradgate Park

Rothley

Gaddesby

M1

A42

M42

Appleby Magna

A447

Twycross

Market
Bosworth

Kirby Muxloe

Leicester

Desford

Mallory Park

Oadby

A6

Stoke Golding

Hinckley

M69

SP

Wistow

A50

Peatling Magna

Sutton in the Elms

Bruntingthorpe

M1

Peatling
Parva

SP

A426

A427

Walcote

Swinford

WARWICKSHIRE

really have to be a racing fan to appreciate it. Meals, snacks, shop, disabled access; cl 25–26 Dec, 1 Jan; (01332) 811027; £7. The Nag's Head

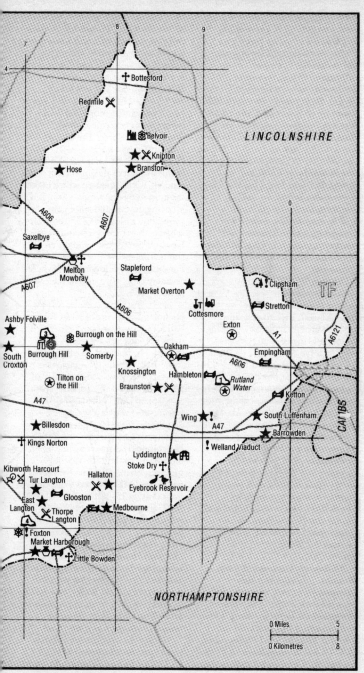

village of thatched houses around a
tree-studded green; the attractive

CHURCH is beautifully placed in a park, and the Fox & Hounds has decent home cooking. BARNSDALE PLANTS AND GARDENS (The Avenue) will be familiar to viewers of *Gardeners' World*; they were developed on the programme by the late Geoff Hamilton. The interesting plants are grown organically using peat-free compost, and there are plenty of useful ideas and techniques. Nursery, disabled access; cl 21 Dec–2 Jan; (01572) 813200; £4.50. Beyond here, towards the A606, the Barnsdale Lodge Hotel has fine food, comfortable bedrooms and a neighbouring antiques centre.

❦ ⏌ **Eyebrook Reservoir** SP8595 Rewarding for birdspotters and fishermen, though as it has no hides or facilities appeals mainly to true enthusiasts.

✸ ! **Foxton** SP7090 CANAL MUSEUM Next to an interesting staircase flight of locks, and based around the extraordinary, Victorian, steam-powered boat lift built to avoid using the lock and so save water; it's now being restored. Shop, some disabled access; cl winter Mon and Tues; (0116) 279 2657; site free, museum £1.50. Bridge 61 at the bottom of the locks has basic food and welcomes children (lots of ducks – take plenty of bread). The reservoir over at Saddington is a pretty spot, and the Queen's Head there is a popular dining pub.

◔ **Hinckley** SP4294 BURBAGE COMMON AND WOODS (off the A47, just E) Ancient forest with lots of footpaths (some accessible by wheelchair), observation hides, and spectacular ground flora. Visitor centre open Sun, pm Sat, and pms summer exc Weds; (01455) 633712; free.

❁ ♱ **Kibworth Harcourt** SP6894 WINDMILL The county's only remaining post mill, a fine example from the early 18th c. The Three Horseshoes is useful for lunch. Other well preserved WINDMILLS can be found at Arnesby SP6192, Shepshed SK4719 and Wymondham SK8518 – one of only four 6-sailed mills in the country, with a tearoom and craft shops (cl Mon, and winter wkdys);

free. The old coach road through Kibworth from Uppingham (another nice little town with a well known school and old church) and on to Kilby, Countesthorpe and Cosby is a rewarding drive.

🏰 **Kirby Muxloe** SK5104 KIRBY MUXLOE CASTLE Peaceful 15th-c ruins, barely used by their original owner before he was executed. Shop, disabled access; free. The Royal Oak is handy for lunch.

🏛🍴🏠🎡🖼⚓🚗 **Leicester** SK5804 In this busy city's mix of ancient and modern, it's the modern which makes the most immediate impression. But a bit of digging around among the shops, office blocks and traffic schemes does turn up reminders of its long and varied past – and the city's staunch defence of free entrance to museums etc, while places elsewhere are increasingly demanding a fee, is most attractive.

JEWRY WALL MUSEUM AND SITE (St Nicholas Circle) Site of 2nd-c Roman baths, the courtyard now excavated to reveal porticoes and shops sheltered by the remains of a massive stone wall. Excellent collections of mosaic pavements and painted wall plaster. Shop, disabled access; cl am Sun, 25–26 Dec; (0116) 247 3021; free. A short walk away on Applegate, WYGSTON'S HOUSE MUSEUM OF COSTUME has entertainingly displayed English costume from the 17th c to the present; you may be able to try some on. Shop, disabled access to ground floor only; cl 25–26 Dec; (0116) 247 3056; free. A stroll around here reveals a few other fine old buildings, notably the 14th-c Guildhall. The pick of the other museums includes NEWARKE HOUSES (The Newarke), where there's a quiet period garden, and the LEICESTERSHIRE MUSEUM AND ART GALLERY (New Walk), which has a collection of German Expressionist art that for this country must be unique; both open as Jewry Wall.

The JAIN CENTRE (Oxford St) has some fantastic examples of traditional Indian architecture; open 9–2pm wkdys; (0116) 254 3091; donations. The Hindu temple on

Narborough Rd is reckoned to be one of the finest outside India. Towpath walks along both the Grand Union Canal and the River Soar give a relatively tranquil back view of the city's industrial life. The Welford Place (on Welford Pl) serves good food all day.

BELGRAVE HALL (Church Rd, on the city's N edge) A fine example of 18th-c architecture, furnished with period pieces. Charming gardens. Shop, limited disabled access; (0116) 266 6590; free. Nearby, the Melton (A607/Gipsy Rd) is fascinating for its authentic on-view Bombay cooking (Thurs–Sun evenings). Also out here, the ABBEY PUMPING STATION (Corporation Rd) has been redeveloped as a museum of public health; in the Flush With Pride exhibition, you flush imitation faeces down a see-through loo to follow their progress through the drains. Shop, disabled access (exc to engine house); cl am Sun, 24–26 Dec; (0116) 266 1330; free (maybe small charge on days when beam engines in steam). GAS MUSEUM (Aylestone Rd) Comprehensive study of the industry and its application, from cookers and washing machines to hairdryers and magic lanterns. Shop, disabled access to ground floor only; open pm Tues–Fri (though cl Tues after bank hols); (0116) 253 5506; free. ECO HOUSE (Hinckley Rd) An ordinary house converted to show over 100 ways to make the modern home more environment-friendly, redeveloped with a greater emphasis on hands-on displays; open wknds and pm Weds–Fri; (0116) 285 4047; free. GORSE HILL CITY FARM (Anstey Lane) Friendly little community farm with the usual animals and activities, and a developing organic garden. Meals, snacks, shop, disabled access; cl Weds; (0116) 253 7582; £1 suggested donation. FRAMEWORK KNITTERS MUSEUM (Bushloe End, Wigston) A restored 18th-c knitters' house and workshop, with original hand frames. Open pm Sun and 1st Sat of month, plus May and Aug bank hols; £1. ⬆⬇ 🏠 Loughborough SK5354 BELL FOUNDRY MUSEUM (Freehold St) Part

of the largest working bell foundry in the world, with a quite remarkable array of bells in the tuning room. Shop, disabled access; cl 12.30–1.30pm, Mon (exc bank hols), and Sun and winter exc by arrangement; (01509) 233414; £1. GREAT CENTRAL RAILWAY (Great Central Rd) Main line steam railway to Leicester, with a museum this end. Meals, snacks, shop, disabled access; no trains wkdys Oct–Mar; (01509) 230726; £7. The Swan in the Rushes (A6) has nice home cooking.

★ 🏠 Lyddington SP8797 An attractive stonebuilt village. Handsome 15th-c BEDE HOUSE was a residence of the Bishops of Lincoln until the Reformation. Notable carved ceilings, 15th-c glass, and a tranquil garden. Shop, disabled access to ground floor only; cl 1–2pm, and Nov–Mar; (01572) 822438; £1.60. The Old White Hart is good for lunch. ☺ Mallory Park SK4500 Motorsport meetings every wknd Mar–Oct, a splendid spectacle if your idea of a day at the races doesn't involve horses – only horsepower. Meals, snacks, shop, disabled access; from £7.50. The Royal Arms at Sutton Cheney is the nearest good eating place.

👶 📢 Market Bosworth SK4003 Best known as the site of the deciding action in the Wars of the Roses, when Richard III's defeat led to the Tudors' seizing the English throne. The BOSWORTH BATTLEFIELD VISITOR CENTRE AND COUNTRY PARK has explanatory films and exhibitions, as well as a detailed trail following the sites of the fighting (now thought to be ever so slightly out). Meals, snacks, shop, disabled access; cl am wkdys (exc bank hols and during July and Aug), and all Nov–Mar; (01455) 290429; £2.30. The village itself is interesting to walk through, and Softleys and the Black Horse (by the market square alms houses) have good-value food. BATTLEFIELD STEAM RAILWAY LINE 🚂 Runs from Shackerstone SK3706 through Market Bosworth to Shenton SK3800 by the battlefield, a rather nice return trip of just over 9 miles. There's a Victorian tearoom at the

Shackerstone end (open Tues–Sun), and some displays. Trains usually wknds and bank hols Mar–Oct, plus Weds and Fri in summer; tel (01827) 880754 for timetable; £4.70 return. At the battlefield end, the Royal Arms at Sutton Cheney has decent food.

★ ♿ **Market Harborough** SP7387 An attractive market town which used to specialise in the production of corsets; bizarre, florid and even agonising examples can be seen in the town MUSEUM (cl am Sun; free). The centre has some fine old Georgian buildings, and above them the gracefully soaring 14th-c spire of the church. The Three Swans Hotel does good lunches.

✝ ♿ **Melton Mowbray** SK7518 Stilton cheese, pork pies and the Quorn hunt all originate in this little town, which also has a particularly distinguished church, St Mary's. The MELTON CARNEGIE MUSEUM (Thorpe End) celebrates the town's fashionable 19th-c days (cl Sun exc pms summer; free), and Dickinson & Morris (Nottingham St) still make the pies to a traditional recipe. SAXELBYE SK7021 Websters' 19th-c dairy here is a good place to buy Stilton. In the next village of Grimston, the Black Horse has decent food and a remarkable collection of cricket memorabilia.

🐄 ✿ **Oadby** SK6200 For FARMWORLD *see separate Family Panel on p.410.* BOTANIC GARDENS (Stoughton Drive South) Set around student halls of residence, these university gardens are 16 acres filled with a wide variety of plants in different and delightful settings, inc a hardy fuchsia collection. Plant sales, disabled access; cl wknds and bank hols; (0116) 271 7725; free. The Grange Farm (Florence Wragg Way) has imaginative food.

★ 🏛 🏚 ♿ 🐄 ♿ **Oakham** SK8609 Now that Rutland has won its battle for independence from Leicestershire, this is a county town again – most local people feel any resulting increase in council tax is well worth while. It's an attractive small town with a good sense of country bustle about it, one or two interesting antique shops, and bargain casual clothes at Land's End warehouse shop (Pillings Rd). The magnificent Norman banqueting hall is all that's left of the late 12th-c CASTLE, but earthworks and walls give a good idea of what it must have been like. The hall itself is decorated with a droll collection of extraordinary horseshoes, some grossly opulent, some simply enormously oversized. Shop, disabled access; cl am Sun, Mon (exc bank hols), 25–26 Dec, Good Fri; (01572) 723654; free. The emphasis at the RUTLAND COUNTY MUSEUM (Catmos St) is on rural life, though there are some Roman and Saxon finds. Snacks, shop, disabled access; cl am Sun, 25–26 Dec and Good Fri; (01572) 723654 free. RUTLAND FARM PARK (Uppingham Rd) Well liked by readers, with various breeds of cattle, pig, sheep and poultry, as well as old farming equipment, a play area, and shortish but pretty strolls round the woodland and stream, with fine trees and Victorian rockeries. Snacks, shop, disabled access; cl am out of season, all Mon (exc bank hols), and Oct–Mar; (01572) 756789; *£2.50. By the church, the 17th-c Wheatsheaf has decent food, and Barnsdale Lodge Hotel (just off the A606 E) does good lunches. There's a fine drive through Ashwell, Wymondham and Waltham on the Wolds to Harby.

🐦 🦋 🐌 🦋 🐟 ♿ ✝ **Rutland Water** Europe's biggest man-made lake, oddly shaped, with a number of attractions around its shores. The RUTLAND WATER NATURE RESERVE, stretching 9 miles, is divided into two parts. The Lyndon reserve SK8905 off the Lyndon–Manton road is for the general public (with a useful visitor centre, and maybe summer Sun crafts), while the one at Egleton SK8707 is aimed at the more serious birdwatcher (with a comfortable, purpose-built observation centre – several breeding pairs of ospreys have now been settled here, the first in England for generations). Both have varied talks, walks and events; (01572) 770651; Lyndon reserve open wknds all year, plus wkdys exc Mon in summer; £1.20; Egleton usually open every day; £3, less after 2pm. On the N side of the lake are nature trails, an unusual drought garden created by the late Geoff Hamilton, places to hire bikes, and hourly BOAT TRIPS. BUTTERFLY & AQUATIC CENTRE (off the A606 Empingham –Whitwell) Next to the main information centre, there's a butterfly house with a good water feature, and various other insects and reptiles; also a video on the reservoir's construction in the 1970s. Meals, snacks, shop, disabled access; cl Nov–Mar; (01780) 460515; £2.95. The White Horse at Empingham is good for lunch, and other handy dining places are the Finches Arms at Upper Hambleton (the best views over the water), and the Noel Arms at Whitwell. You can fish in various parts of the lake, and there's a fishing centre down at Normanton SK8141, as well as a small MUSEUM in a church modelled on London's St John's, Smith Sq (cl Nov–Mar; 60p). The refreshingly informal Normanton Park Hotel here has decent food.

↘ ♪ Sutton in the Elms SP5194 FALCONRY CENTRE ▣ (Mill on the Soar, Coventry Rd) Flying demonstrations of owls, hawks, falcons and buzzards; they really try to get the audience involved. On the same site are a fishing lake and thriving family dining pub. Meals, snacks, shop, disabled access; cl Mon, and 25 Dec; (01455) 285924; *£2.

🐗 🏛 ♪ ▣ 🌱 Swinford SP5779 STANFORD HALL AND MOTORCYCLE MUSEUM 5,000 books line the library of this handsome 17th-c house, an elegant place that still keeps a cosy lived-in atmosphere. Highlights are the painted ceiling in the ballroom, the portraits that accompany the winding grand staircase, and a good costume collection. The excellent motorcycle museum is in the grounds, which also have a lovely 14th-c church with splendid stained glass, walled rose garden, Sun craft centre, and a replica of the first successful flying machine in the country. Meals, snacks, shop, limited disabled access; open pm wknds, bank hols and Tues after bank hols, Easter–Sept; (01788)

860250; £3.80 house and grounds, £2.10 grounds only, motorcycle museum £1 extra. The Cherry Tree at Catthorpe (cl Mon/Tues lunchtime) has good-value food.

🐖 ♪ 🐝 † Tilton on the Hill SK7405 HALSTEAD HOUSE FARM ▣ (Oakham Rd) Specialist poultry farm, with a few animals as well as the birds, nature trail, fishing lake and gardens. They recently added miniature ponies, and they do tractor rides. Meals, snacks, well stocked farm shop (game and other fresh meats), disabled access; cl Mon, and all Oct–Easter; £2.70. The village CHURCH is notable, and the Rose & Crown is handy for lunch.

🐒 Twycross SK3305 TWYCROSS ZOO PARK ▣ Specialises in primates, with an enormous range of apes, gibbons, orang-utans, and chimpanzees – every shape, size and species. Plenty of other animals too, inc giraffes, sealions, elephants and penguins. Can be crowded in the afternoons. Meals, snacks, shop, disabled access; cl 25 Dec; (01827) 880250; £5. The Cock at Sibson is attractive for lunch.

! Welland Viaduct SP9197 (nr Seaton) One of the county's most striking sights: nearly a mile long, swooping across the pastures of the valley, it is the country's longest viaduct.

🐖 Woodhouse SK5315 WHATOFF LODGE (E towards Quorn) A decent nature trail starts from this working farm, where there's an exhibition of rural bygones and some farm animals. Snacks, shop, disabled access; cl Mon (exc bank hols), and Nov–mid-Mar; (01509) 412127; £2. The Pear Tree at Woodhouse Eaves is the best nearby place for lunch.

† Though not to quite such a degree as neighbouring Lincolnshire, this is church country, with many **fine churches** in both towns and villages. Besides those already mentioned, we'd pick out those at Breedon on the Hill SK4022 (on an interesting, partly quarried Iron Age hill fort, and with some unique Anglo-Saxon carvings), Gaddesby SK6813 (elaborate 13th-c workmanship), King's Norton SK6800 (graceful Gothic Revival), Little Bowden SP7487 (12th-c; fine old rectory), Stoke Dry SP8596, and Wistow SP6496. The one at Bottesford SK8038 is full of elaborate tombs and monuments; they had to raise the roof to fit them all in.

★ **Other attractive villages,** all with decent pubs, include Appleby Magna SK3109, Ashby Folville SK7011, Barrowden SK9400, Billesdon SK7202, Branston SK8129, Braunston SK8306, Bruntingthorpe SP6089, East Langton SP7292, Grimston SK6821, Hallaton SP7896, Hose SK7329, Knipton SK8231, Knossington SK8008, Market Overton SK8816, Medbourne SP7993 (interesting church too), Peatling Magna SP5992 and Parva SP5889, Somerby SK7710 (the Old Brewery pub brews very fine ales), South Croxton SK6810, South Luffenham SK9402, Stoke Golding SP3997, Tur Langton SP7194, Whitwick SK4316, and Wing SK8902, notable for its small medieval TURF MAZE.

The Cap & Stocking in Kegworth SK4826 is an interesting old tavern, at the start of a pleasant country drive through the Leakes, Wysall, Widmerpool, Kinoulton, Colston Bassett (just over the Notts border – the Martins Arms is the best lunch stop of all), Granby and Orston. The Cove Inn, spectacularly overlooking the Stoney Cove diving centre nr Stoney Stanton SP4994, is an attractive spot for something to eat.

Days Out

The Leicestershire highlands
Walk in Bradgate Country Park; lunch at the Pear Tree, Woodhouse Eaves; Whatoff Lodge at Woodhouse; stroll up Beacon Hill.

Leicester city freebies
Jewry Wall museum; Wygston's House costume museum; lunch at Welford Place (Welford Pl); Leicestershire Museum and Art Gallery; Belgrave Hall.

Midlands curios
Welland Viaduct; Bede House at Lyddington; lunch at the Old White Hart in Lyddington; turf maze at Wing; Rutland Water for boat trip, or a walk along the water's edge – and visit the Butterfly and Aquatic Centre there.

The miniature county
Oakham, inc Rutland Farm Park; Rutland Railway Museum at Cottesmore; lunch at Barnsdale Lodge Hotel (off the A606); antiques centre there; Barnsdale Gardens towards Exton, then Exton village.

Canal age wonder
Stroll along Burrough Hill (perhaps visiting Burrough House gardens); Halstead House Farm at Tilton on the Hill; Billesdon, Kibworth Harcourt and East Langton villages – lunch at the Bell, East Langton; Foxton Locks and canal museum.

Walks

Rutland Water ⌂-1 has a path totalling 24 miles around its edges – information centres have details of shorter trails. The little-publicised walk from Upper Hambleton SK9007 touring the peninsula, which protrudes into the reservoir, is the best.

Charnwood Forest ⌂-2, formerly a vast hunting park, has 2 good surviving chunks here: Bradgate Park SK5209 and nearby Beacon Hill SK5114 – see entries in **To see and do** section above. Surprisingly for the East Midlands, both have miniature patches of moorland with suitably scaled-down crags.

Both are part of country parks, with general access, plenty of waymarked paths, and lots of opportunities for picnics. From the 245-metre (800-ft) summit of Beacon Hill, the Jubilee Walk heads N and E through partly wooded country. A trail S makes a small circuit around Broombriggs Farm SK5114, with boards explaining farming methods by the path. The friendly Bull's Head (on the B587 Whitwick–Copt Oak), with a big garden and lots of animals, has fine views over the forest, and the Copt Oak pub itself at SK4812 is also useful.

Burrough Hill SK7611 ⌂-3 S of Melton Mowbray SK7518 has an enjoyable path along its escarpment. The summit has splendid views, and an imposing Iron Age hill fort, its high ramparts still largely intact (50p parking charge).

Foxton Locks SP7090 ⌂-4 are a good focus for Grand Union Canal towpath walks.

The **Ashby Canal** ⌂-5 towpath has nice countryside walking, with green fields and stone-arched bridges, as well as coots, moorhens, herons and maybe even the flash of a kingfisher. The best parts run from the tunnel under Snarestone SK3409 past Gopsall Park SK3505, and then on through Shackerstone SK3706 and Congerstone SK3605 to pass Shenton Park SK3800 on an embankment, before heading into Warwicks and its junction with the Coventry Canal. It also makes an ideal link between Bosworth battlefield and the steam railway to the N.

Pubs useful for walkers here include the the Pear Tree and Bull's Head in Woodhouse Eaves SK5214; and, all handy for canals, the George & Dragon at Stoke Golding SP3997, Soar Bridge in Barrow upon Soar SK5717, the Griffin at Congerstone SK3605, and the Navigation at Kilby Bridge SP6097. The Priest House Hotel at Kings Mills nr Castle Donington SK4427 is handy for the River Trent.

Where to eat

Braunston SK8306 Blue Ball (01572) 722135 Said to be Rutland's oldest pub, this popular place puts much emphasis on the well presented, imaginative food; well kept real ales, 8 wines by the glass, interesting furnishings, a pleasant informal atmosphere, and very good service, even when busy. £18.95|£5.95.

Braunston SK8306 Old Plough (01572) 722714 Attractive place with a pubby atmosphere; traditional bar with heavy beams, stylishly modern, no smoking conservatory, a decent choice of well presented meals, decent beers and a well noted wine list; also seats out under fruit trees; boules. £20.20|£8.75.

Hallaton SP7896 Bewicke Arms (01858) 555217 Thatched cottage by the village green; with a warm welcome and traditional feel in its 2 beamed bar rooms, generous helpings of popular food inc fine puddings, well kept real ales, and friendly service; bedrooms; no dogs. £19.35|£7.20.

Knipton SK8231 Red House (01476) 870352 Fine Georgian hunting lodge with a friendly atmosphere and woodburning stove in the roomy bar, as well as a no smoking conservatory and restaurant; rewarding and interesting bar food (inc good vegetarian dishes), well kept beers, a decent choice of wines, and friendly, obliging service; limited disabled access. £17.50|£5.65.

Leicester SK5804 Welford Place 9 Welford Pl (0116) 247 0758 Once a Victorian gentlemen's club, this friendly place offers full meals in the civilised, high ceilinged restaurant, as well as a spacious bar with good and enjoyable food served all day – breakfast, snacks, light meals, morning coffee and afternoon tea; efficient service. £17.50|£7.50.

Old Dalby SK6723 Crown (01664) 823134 Rather smart ex-farmhouse with a wide range of drinks (a dozen real ales, lots of malt whiskies, and an interesting wine list), and imaginative and completely fresh food (no freezers, microwaves or chips); several little black-beamed rooms, open fires, and a big, no smoking dining room; plenty of tables on a terrace and a large sheltered lawn; disabled access. **£27.75|£6.75.**

Redmile SK7935 PEACOCK (01949) 842554 Atmospheric little village house below Belvoir Castle, with extremely popular, imaginative and enjoyable food in the bar or pretty, no smoking restaurant; well kept real ales, fine wines, and courteous, friendly service; open fires and an attractive conservatory. **£22.40|£8.95.**

Thorpe Langton SP7492 BAKERS ARMS (01858) 545201 Extended thatched pub with a warm and friendly welcome, simple furnishings, and very good, nicely presented food (need to book well ahead); helpful service, well kept beer, decent choice of wines, and a no smoking snug; cl Mon, am wkdys, pm Sun; children over 12. **£20.90.**

Walcote SP5683 BLACK HORSE (01455) 552684 Big helpings of authentic Thai food cooked by the Thai landlady; unusual drinks, a chatty, unpretentious atmosphere, big open fire, a no smoking restaurant, and outside seats for summer; must book; cl am Mon–Tues (open bank hols); disabled access. **£15.50 for 5-course meal|£5.95.**

Woodhouse Eaves SK5214 PEAR TREE (01509) 890243 Full of Edwardian character, with a comfortably furnished and attractively decorated bar and a dining area serving very good food; a friendly landlord, open fires, and pleasant nearby walks; cl pm Sun. **£18.15|£6.75.**

Special thanks to Jenny and Michael Back, Mrs M A Dornan.

LEICESTERSHIRE CALENDAR

Some of these dates were provisional as we went to press, please check information with the number provided.

JANUARY

3 **Castle Donington** Antiques Fair: 200 stands at the International Exhibition Centre – *till Sun 4* (01332) 812919

MARCH

1 **Castle Donington** Toy and Train Fair: 350 stands at the International Exhibition Centre (01332) 812919

14 **Castle Donington** Lotus Show: 50th Anniversary at the International Exhibition Centre – *till Sun 15* (01332) 812919

28 **Loughborough** Food and Country Shopping Fair at Beaumanor Hall – *till Sun 29* (01509) 217444

29 **Leicester** Doll Fair at Aylestone Leisure Centre (01480) 216372

APRIL

13 **Hallaton** Bottle Kicking and Hare-pie Scrambling: teams compete to get 3 small kegs of beer across 2 streams a mile apart (01858) 468106

18 **Castle Donington** Antiques Fair: 200 stands at the International Exhibition Centre – *till Sun 19* (01332) 812919

MAY

3 **Loughborough** County Show at Dishley Grange Farm – *till Mon 4* (01509) 646786

4 **Bruntingthorpe** Open Day at the Airfield (0116) 247 8040; **Castle Donington** Medieval Street Market (01332) 810432

17 **Castle Donington** Toy and Train Fair at the International Exhibition Centre (01332) 812919; **Leicester** Historic Transport Pageant at Abbey Park (0116) 222 4040

23 **Belvoir** Civil War Siege Group at the Castle – *till Mon 25* (01476) 870262; **Burley on the Hill** Rutland County Show (01664) 454144

25 **Melton Mowbray** Show: arena events, Royal Air Force and bands (01664) 480992

LEICESTERSHIRE CALENDAR

MAY cont

30 **Castle Donington** Antiques Fair: 200 stands at the International Exhibition Centre – *till Sun 31* (01332) 812919; **Lutterworth** National Hovercraft Racing Championships at Stanford Hall – *till Mon 25* (01788) 860250

JUNE

1 **Little Casterton** Stamford Shakespeare Company Summer Season at Rutland Open-air Theatre, Tolethorpe Hall – *till 29 Aug* (01780) 754381

13 **Empingham** Water Show: arena events, crafts and activities on the water at Rutland Water – *till Sun 14* (01480) 846417; **Market Harborough** Carnival (01858) 462626

20 **Blackfordby** Vintage Rally – *till Sun 21* (01283) 212250

28 **Belvoir** Jousting at the Castle (01476) 870262; **Swinford** American Civil War Society at Stanford Hall (01788) 860250

JULY

4 **Breedon on the Hill** Open Gardens – *till Sun 5* (01332) 862099

5 **Market Bosworth** Show and National Sweetpea Society Show (01530) 271169

11 **Wymeswold** Steam and Country Show – *till Sun 12* (01509) 213102

12 **Measham** Ashby Agricultural Show at Measham Lodge Farm (01283) 704801

26 **Belvoir** Jousting at the Castle (01476) 870262

AUGUST

1 **Leicester** Caribbean Carnival at Victoria Park (0116) 253 0491

2 **Castle Donington** Toy and Train Fair: 350 stands at the International Exhibition Centre (01332) 812919

8 **Lutterworth** Fireworks Concert at Stanford Hall (01788) 860250

15 **Ashby-de-la-Zouch** Fireworks Concert at Calke Abbey (01332) 863822

21 **Egleton** British Birdwatching Fair at Rutland Water – *till Sun 23* (01780) 460321

29 **Castle Donington** Antiques Fair: 200 stands at the International Exhibition Centre – *till Sun 30* (01332) 812919

30 **Belvoir** Jousting at the Castle – *till Mon 31* (01476) 870262

31 **Packington** Open Gardens (01530) 412012

SEPTEMBER

5 **Bosworth** Battle Re-enactment at the Battlefield – *till Sun 6* (01455) 290429

26 **Loughborough** Food and Country Shopping Fair at Beaummanor Hall – *till Sun 27* (01509) 217444

27 **Castle Donington** Toy and Train Fair at the International Exhibition Centre (01332) 812919

OCTOBER

10 **Castle Donington** Antiques Fair: 200 stands at the International Exhibition Centre – *till Sun 11* (01332) 812919

NOVEMBER

14 **Castle Donington** Antiques Fair: 200 stands at the International Exhibition Centre – *till Sun 15* (01332) 812919

22 **Leicester** Doll Fair at Aylestone Leisure Centre (01480) 216372

DECEMBER

29 **Castle Donington** Toy and Train Fair: 350 stands at the International Exhibition Centre (01332) 812919

LINCOLNSHIRE

Undiscovered England, with lovely houses, castles and villages, well away from the crowds – and the sandy coast has a string of cheerful seaside resorts.

One of England's biggest counties, Lincolnshire is famous for its traditional family beach resorts, but has another very appealing and largely undiscovered side. With a very distinct character, it offers adults a lot for a get-away-from-it-all break – good value, with generally low prices; and tourist information centres here tend to be particularly helpful.

Lincoln itself is an interesting city with plenty to see; Stamford and Boston too have a good deal of character. North and east of Lincoln, the rolling Wolds countryside makes for enjoyable drives on uncrowded roads, punctuated by attractive villages and small towns, and by soaring church spires. Two unique places to visit are the cheerful entertainment museum at Whaplode St Catherine's, and the fishing heritage centre in Grimsby – a real eye-opener.

There are some very striking houses and castles – Burghley House on the edge of Stamford, Belton House, and Tattershall and Grimsthorpe castles. The Normanby Hall country park is a pleasant spot, and the ruined abbey at Thornton Curtis is a little-known romantic gem.

For families, Fantasy Island at Ingoldmells stands out – with plenty under cover, for days that are cooled by east winds off the North Sea (more common in recent summers). The seal sanctuary at Skegness is another family favourite, and adults as well as children really enjoy the butterfly park at Long Sutton and the owl centre at Weston.

Around the Wash and up the coast towards Wainfleet and Coningsby, the land is very flat, reclaimed from the sea: pretty dull, except in springtime when the endless bulbfields around Spalding burst into spectacular bloom. Throughout the county's farmland, huge fields of arable crops can be rather tedious for walkers; speeding past more quickly in a car, bus or train, you're more aware of the shape of the countryside, giving it more appeal. In winter, Lincolnshire can be very chilly.

Where to stay

Alford TF4576 WHITE HORSE 29 West St, Alford LN13 9DG (01507) 462218 **£40**, plus special breaks; 9 prettily furnished and comfortable rms. Picturesque thatched 16th-c inn, carefully restored over the years, with a plush beamed lounge; good range of well prepared reasonably priced food.

Aswarby TF0639 TALLY HO Aswarby, Sleaford NG34 8SA (01529) 455205 **£45**; 6 rms. Handsome 17th-c stone country inn with a quietly enjoyable civilised atmosphere, log fire and pretty flowers in the bar; good food in the bar and the attractive, popular restaurant, well kept ales and wines, and tables behind the building among fruit trees.

Barkston SP9241 BARKSTON HOUSE Barkston, Grantham NG32 2NH (01400) 250555 £42; 3 rms. Warm and comfortable restored 18th-c house in 7 acres of grounds, with open fires and beams, and a relaxed atmosphere; nice breakfasts, cl 3 days at Christmas.

Binbrook TF2193 HOE HILL Swinhope, Binbrook, Lincoln LN3 6HX (01472) 398206 £50; 3 rms. Comfortable late 18th-c farmhouse in attractive countryside, with a big sitting room, its doors opening on to a terrace and croquet lawn; hearty breakfasts with home-made bread and marmalade in the elegant dining room, and particularly good evening meals (by prior arrangement); cl Jan; children over 5.

Bourne TF0920 BOURNE EAU HOUSE 30 South St, Bourne PE10 9LY (01335) 350287 *£70; 3 rms. Handsome house, partly Elizabethan, partly Georgian, with beams and inglenook fireplaces; good dinner in the elegant dining room, and enjoyable breakfasts; friendly owners; cl Christmas and Easter.

Buslingthorpe TF0885 EAST FARM HOUSE Middle Rasen Rd, Buslingthorpe, Lincoln LN3 5AQ (01673) 842283 *£40, plus special breaks; 2 rms. 18th-c farmhouse surrounded by family farm; beams, stripped pine, log fires, a relaxed atmosphere, and splendid breakfasts; tennis and lots of walks; self-catering cottage.

Dyke TF1022 WISHING WELL Dyke, Bourne PE10 0AF (01778) 422970 *£45; 7 rms, most with own bthrm. The wishing well is at the dining end of the long rambling bar – heavy beams, dark stone, brasswork, candlelight and a big fireplace; good popular food, helpful service, and a friendly atmosphere; disabled access.

East Barkwith TF1781 BODKIN LODGE Grange Farm, Torrington Lane, East Barkwith, Lincoln LN3 5RY (01673) 858249 £40; 2 pretty ground-floor rms. Run by the same warm and friendly family as George Farm, this carefully extended bungalow has a comfortable sitting room with books, fresh flowers, an open fire and a baby grand piano; good breakfasts in the big dining room (evening meals by arrangement); award-winning wildlife farmland trails from the door, and marvellous country views; cl Christmas–New Year; children over 10.

Fulletby TF2973 OLD RECTORY Fulletby, Horncastle LN9 6JX (01507) 533533 *£58, plus special breaks; 3 rms. In lovely unspoilt countryside with lots of outside pursuits, this fine no smoking country house is set in over 4 acres of grounds and gardens with marvellous views; open fire in the comfortable sitting room; good breakfasts, enjoyable home-cooked evening meals in separate dining room, and a warmly welcoming and relaxing atmosphere; cl Christmas–New Year; no children.

Holbeach TF3426 PIPWELL MANOR Washway Rd, Saracen's Head, Holbeach, Spalding, PE12 8AL (01406) 423119 *£40; 4 rms. Handsome 18th-c farmhouse, welcoming and spotless, with a log fire in the comfortable sitting room, a pretty panelled dining room, and a conservatory; good breakfasts with their own eggs and home-made preserves; no smoking and no pets; cl Christmas.

Lincoln SK9872 CARLINE 1–3 Carline Rd, Lincoln LN1 1HL (01522) 530422 *£40; 12 well equipped rms, 10 with own bthrm. Spotlessly kept and comfortable double-fronted no smoking Edwardian guest house 5 minutes from the cathedral, with helpful and cheerful long-standing owners, quiet sitting rooms, and fine breakfasts; cl Christmas and New Year; no baby facilities.

Lincoln SK9872 D'ISNEY PLACE Eastgate, Lincoln LN2 4AA (01522) 538881 £69, plus special breaks; 17 charming rms. Friendly 18th-c hotel with lovely gardens, close to the cathedral; fine furniture, friendly owners, and a relaxed and homely atmosphere; good breakfasts served in the rooms; disabled access.

Stamford TF0207 GEORGE 71 St Martins, Stamford PE9 2LB (01780) 755171

*£105, plus special breaks; 47 rms. Historic, ancient former coaching inn with a quietly civilised atmosphere, and welcoming staff; sturdy timbers, broad flagstones, heavy beams and massive stonework, and open log fires; wonderful food in the garden lounge (tempting help-yourself buffet), restaurant and courtyard (in summer), excellent range of drinks – very good-value Italian wines; well kept walled garden and sunken lawn where croquet is played.

Whaplode TF3224 GUY WELLS Eastgate, Whaplode, Spalding PE12 6TZ (01406) 422239 ***£42**; 3 rms, 1 with own bthrm. Set in a country garden, this Queen Anne house is surrounded by the friendly owners' daffodil and tulip fields and glasshouses (cultivated spring flowers) – you can buy bulbs; low beamed ceilings, a woodburner, and pretty furnishings in the sitting room; very good food using their own vegetables and free range eggs; no smoking; cl Christmas; children over 5.

Winteringham SE9322 WINTERINGHAM FIELDS Winteringham, Scunthorpe DN15 9PF (01724) 733096 ***£85**; 7 pretty, chintzy rms with period furniture (3 are in the courtyard). Thoughtfully run restaurant-with-rooms in a 16th-c manor house with comfortable and very attractive Victorian furnishings, beams, and open fires; really excellent inventive food in no smoking dining room, fine breakfasts, and warm, friendly service; cl 1 wk Aug, 2 wks Christmas, bank hols; children over 8 (babies allowed).

To see and do

Lincoln SK9872 The cathedral and castle, both very striking, share the central hilltop, with enough old buildings around them to keep a sense of unity. There's a lot to appeal up here, and in the steep streets (Steep Hill, and Strait St) of ancient buildings running down from them to the 15th-c Stonebow Gate at the top of the High St below. This lower part of the town is much more of a normal bustling shopping and working centre, though even here there are a good few interesting old buildings – inc several Saxon churches and the Norman guildhall. The CITY AND COUNTY MUSEUM (Broadgate) is still closed for refurbishment. The Wig & Mitre and Browns Pie Shop, both on Steep Hill, and the Lincolnshire Poacher (Bunkers Hill) are good for lunch, and behind the cathedral and castle the Adam & Eve is a nice old pub. There are some good views from the A607 to Grantham.

✝ CATHEDRAL Many people reckon that this is England's finest. The original building was largely destroyed in an 1185 earthquake, but the magnificent west front survived, and after nearly a century of rebuilding it was complete by 1280. The triple towers rise spectacularly above the nearby rooftops, and are beautifully lit at night. Inside, the carvings and stained glass are stupendous, and the architecture gracefully harmonious. Snacks, shop, disabled access; donations. The ruins of the once formidable Bishop's Palace are close by.

◪ CASTLE In beautiful surroundings on a formidable earthwork, this was originally built in 1068 for William the Conqueror, but only 2 towers and 2 impressive gateways date back to then. One of only 4 remaining originals of Magna Carta is on display, and there are super views from the ramparts. A 19th-c prison has suitably gruesome exhibits; its chapel is unusually designed so that none of the congregation could see each other. Snacks, shop, disabled access; cl 25–26 Dec, 1 Jan; (01522) 511068; *£2.

▥ ROMAN REMAINS These include the high wall along Westgate, and the largely reconstructed Newport Arch N of the cathedral (it had survived intact until a 1964 disagreement with a lorry); the canal between Lincoln and the River Trent is also Roman – you can walk out into the country along it from the city.

ᛏ⚒ Museum of Lincolnshire Life (Burton Rd) County life over the last couple of centuries, well illustrated in big former barracks. Summer snacks, shop, disabled access; cl am winter Suns, 24–27 Dec, 1 Jan, Good Fri; (01522) 528448; £1.20. A lawn in the courtyard makes a good picnic area.

⬛ Usher Gallery (Lindum Rd) Attractive gallery with fine watches, porcelain and miniatures, Tennyson memorabilia, and Peter de Wint watercolours. Snacks, shop, disabled access; cl am Sun, 25–26 Dec, 1 Jan, Good Fri; (01522) 527980; £1.20, free on Fri.

! Incredibly Fantastic Old Toy Show 🚻 (Westgate) Old toys and end-of-pier amusements, close to both the cathedral and the castle, so a good treat for unwilling culture buffs. Shop, disabled access; open Tues–Sat plus pm Sun and bank hols Easter–Sept, wknds plus Tues–Fri in school hols Oct–Dec; (01522) 520534; *£1.90.

⚒ 🎎 🎵 The Lawn In 1820 this was the county's first lunatic asylum; now its landscaped grounds include hands-on history and archaeology, an aquarium and an exotic glasshouse, and a restaurant, coffee shop and bar. Cl 25–26 Dec; (01522) 560330; free.

Days Out

The best of Lincoln
Lincoln Cathedral; Castle; explore Steep Hill area – lunch at the Wig & Mitre or Browns Pie Shop there; Usher Gallery; Museum of Lincolnshire Life; Incredibly Fantastic Old Toy Show.

Family fun on the Gold Coast
Natureland Seal Sanctuary, Skegness; lunch at Vine Hotel there; Fantasy Island, Ingoldmells.

Fish, fuchsias and froth
Fishing heritage centre and trawler visit, Grimsby; fish lunch at Leons there, or eat on *Lincoln Castle*; Fuchsia Fantasy and Discovery Centre, Cleethorpes; try some of Willys beer there.

Romantic ruins and Humber wildlife
Thornton Abbey, Thornton Curtis; Barton Clay Pits, Barton-upon-Humber; if time, walk along The Cliff from Alkborough (see **Walks** section, below); lunch at Sheffield Arms, Burton upon Stather; Normanby Hall country park.

Wars across the centuries
Browse round Horncastle; lunch at the Magpies (see **Where to eat** section, below) there, or Abbey Lodge Hotel, Woodhall Spa; Tattershall Castle; Battle of Britain memorial flights, Coningsby.

Showpiece stone-built town
Stamford; lunch at the George there; Burghley House, or Grimsthorpe Castle.

Tropical adventure
Spalding, inc Tropical Forest (or Baytree Owl Centre, Weston); lunch at Chequers, Gedney Dyke (see **Where to eat** section, below); Long Sutton butterfly park; cool off with a stroll along the sea wall from Gedney Drove.

Other things to see and do

LINCOLNSHIRE FAMILY ATTRACTION OF THE YEAR

☺ **Ingoldmells** TF5669 FANTASY ISLAND 🔢 (Sea Lane) More elaborate than your average fairground, ideal in any weather, and with a customer-friendly pricing system – it's easy to see why we're highlighting this dynamic place for the second year running. Standing out particularly in a county with very few attractions specifically aimed at families, it impresses too with its unusual design; 95% of the rides and other features are inside, with thatched buildings and palm trees nestling under a giant pyramid. It doesn't cost anything to wander around, and you pay for rides (with tokens) only as you go on them, so it's easy to come in and out all day, rather than rush round trying to do everything at once; the beach is just opposite. The building work you'll see this year heralds the arrival of what's expected to be Europe's longest roller-coaster, due to open in 1999. The length of the Humber Bridge, it will run outside next to the pyramid and the beach, with four 21-metre (70-ft) high loops. In the meantime highlights include the IMAX simulator's 3 roller-coaster type experiences (the screen is all around you, and your seat slides towards it as well as shaking about all over the place), the balloon flight, with authentically created computer-controlled balloons soaring around the pyramid, a sail-through aquarium, and 2 water rides – one quite long, the other rather wet. Outside are a big play area for under-5s, and a huge market, with around 780 stalls. Lots of places to eat, mostly fast food from high street names, but full meals too (or of course you can nip out for lunch and come back later). Easily enough to keep children happy for most of the day – or for several trips during a holiday. – Meals, snacks, shop, disabled access; open wknds early Mar–early Nov, daily in Easter hols and May–Oct; (01754) 872030; free admission to park, then rides separately charged (from 50p; most cost £1, the IMAX is £2). Here our discount offer is a special one – if you buy £10 worth of ride tokens, on production of the voucher they will issue a further £10 worth free.

✗ 🐾 ♈ **Aby** TF4178 CLAYTHORPE WATERMILL AND WILDFOWL GARDENS Pretty spot around 18th-c watermill, the grounds full of ornamental wildfowl and poultry, and animals such as rabbits and a miniature pony. Fun to wander through the woods. Meals, snacks, shop, mostly disabled access; cl Nov–mid-Mar; (01507) 450687; £2.85. The Vine at South Thoresby is a civilised place for lunch.

🏠 ☗ ✗ **Alford** TF4575 Pleasant town with some attractive brick and thatch buildings, inc the 17th-c ALFORD MANOR HOUSE on West St, now a folk museum; cl Nov–Mar; £1.25. The town has a summer craft market (Fri). There's a tall restored 5-sailed WINDMILL on the road towards Sutton on Sea (open Tues, Sat, pm Sun, and bank hols all year, plus Weds–Fri Aug–Sept; £1.50), and

another a little further along at Bilsby. The White Horse Hotel is useful for lunch. W of here, just N of the A16/A1104 junction, the Bluestone Heath hill road past South Ormsby and on to the A157 W of Louth is a splendid scenic drive.

🐾 ✗ ♪ 🏠 **Barton-upon-Humber** TA0322 BARTON CLAY PITS Informative country park based around former clay pits, with nature reserves, walks, fishing (extensive reed beds), sailing – and good views of the Humber Bridge. Disabled access; visitor centre cl Mon, Tues and Oct–Mar; (01652) 633283; free. BAYSGARTH HOUSE (Caistor Rd) This handsome 18th-c house has well displayed local history, especially good on rural crafts. Shop, some disabled access; cl Mon (exc bank hols)–Weds, 25–26 Dec, 1 Jan; (01652) 632318; free.

🏠 🕸 **Belton House** SK9339 Splendid Restoration-period mansion with wonderful carvings, ornate plasterwork, and sumptuous furnishings, paintings and ceramics. The thousand-acre deer park has an orangery and a formal Italian garden. Meals, snacks, shop, disabled access to gardens only; open pm Weds–Sun and bank hols Apr–Oct, grounds open 11am; (01476) 566116; *£4.80; NT. The relaxing Brownlow Arms in picturesque Hough on the Hill has good-value food.

✝ ✗ 🍴 **Boston** TF3244 Once the country's second-largest seaport, this little town has a number of pretty spots and handsome historic buildings. Most famous is the BOSTON STUMP, the graceful tower of the magnificent 14th-c church St Botolph's. Climb to the top for far views over this flat landscape – it's the second-tallest parish church in the country (the tallest is in Louth – see Churches entry, p.433); the inside is spectacular too. Another prominent feature of the skyline is the MAUD FOSTER MILL, the tallest working windmill in the country, and surely one of the most photogenic. The Kings Arms opposite has lovely views of it, and cheap food; Goodbarns Yard (Wormgate) is a popular central pub/restaurant. In 1607 what's now the GUILDHALL MUSEUM (South St) was the prison of the Pilgrim Fathers after their unsuccessful attempt to flee to Holland (they did, of course, eventually escape further afield, taking this town's name with them). Displays cover this and the rest of the town's history. Shop, disabled access to ground floor only; cl Sun (exc pm Apr–Sept); (01205) 365954; £1.20. The surroundings (and the Lincs coast generally) are too flat for driving to be very interesting around here, and side roads which look clear on a map can turn out to be tryingly slow in practice, with agricultural vehicles trundling along slowly and muddily; the B1183 and B1192 aren't bad. Sibsey TF3550, up the A16 N of Boston, has a couple of WINDMILLS, one of them a splendidly restored 6-sailed model with fine views from the top.

🐟 **Bourne** TF0920 BOURNE WOOD (just outside on the A151) Sheltered woodland good for a gentle stroll, especially welcome as so much of the country is flat, treeless fen. Plenty of bird life, busy at wknds with locals exercising their dogs; £1 parking charge. In the town's market place, there's decent food in the Angel Hotel, opposite an interesting antique shop.

🍺 🍴 **Brandy Wharf** TF0197 CIDER CENTRE (on the B1205 SE of Scunthorpe) Pleasingly zany 18th-c riverside cider house with up to 60 different varieties; also orchard and small museum. The enthusiastic owner really knows his stuff. Meals and snacks (not Mon), shop, disabled access; open licensing hours, though cl winter Mon lunchtimes; no chidren under 14; (01652) 678364; free.

✝ ✗ **Burgh Le Marsh** TF5065 has a notable CHURCH, and a WINDMILL nearby has unusual left-handed sails.

🕸 🏡 **Candlesby** TF4567 CANDLESBY HERBS (Cross Keys Cottage) Good range of herb plants for sale and on display in the garden; cl Mon (exc bank hols); free. There's a specialist cactus grower at nearby Candlesby House.

✝ 🕸 ✔ 🦌 **Cleethorpes** TA3008 Big traditional seaside resort with extensive, gently shelving tidal sands, and a surprisingly ancient CHURCH among some attractive older houses in its original core. Willys (which brews its own beer) is useful for lunch. Varied attractions down by the waterside include FUCHSIA FANTASY (Kings Rd), selling hundreds of varieties of fuchsia, and other plants according to season; limited winter opening, best to check on (01472) 883075. A hands-on DISCOVERY CENTRE (Kings Rd) looks at local wildlife; its unusual spiral shape was inspired by a seashell. Teas, shop, disabled access; cl 25–26 Dec, 1 Jan; (01472) 200648; £1.50. The CLEETHORPES COAST LIGHT RAILWAY (Kings Rd) starts its trip around the local scenery from here; not winter wkdys; £1.40.

✝ ✝ **Coningsby** TF2258 BATTLE OF BRITAIN MEMORIAL FLIGHT VISITOR

CENTRE (on the A153) Subject to operational commitments you can see the aircraft of the Battle of Britain Memorial Flight – inc the only flying Lancaster in Europe. A visitor centre has exhibitions. Summer snacks, shop, disabled access; cl wknds, bank hols, and 2 wks over Christmas; (01526) 344041 – check first if you hope to see a particular aircraft; £3. The CHURCH has what's said to be the biggest dial of any clock with just a single hand. Just out of town, the interesting old Leagate Inn is useful for lunch.

🏠 **Doddington** SK9070 DODDINGTON HALL (on the B1190) Striking, lived-in Elizabethan mansion, unchanged externally since it was built, and still with its original walled gardens, gatehouse and family church. The elegant rooms are mostly Georgian. Regular concerts in the Long Gallery. Teas, shop, disabled access to ground floor; open pm Weds, Sun and bank hols May–Sept, garden also open Sun mid-Mar–Apr; (01522) 6943098; *£4, garden only £2. The Stones Arms prettily placed in nearby Skellingthorpe has good-value food.

☺ 🐾 **Elsham** TA0312 ELSHAM HALL COUNTRY PARK 🎫 (discount offer not valid on bank hol wknds; not with any other offer, only 1 per family) Lots for families – farmyard animals, arboretum, adventure playground, puppet shows, craft and garden centres, and falconry with regular flying displays. Carp will feed from your hand at the jetty. Meals, snacks, shop, disabled access; cl mid-Sept–Mar, and Good Fri; (01652) 688698; £3.95.

★ 🏠 **Epworth** SE7803 Pleasant village, the centre of the Isle of Axholme, with Georgian houses around the market place. OLD RECTORY (Rectory St) The childhood home of John and Charles Wesley, built in 1709 by their father. Restored in 1957, with rooms furnished in period style. Shop, some disabled access; cl 12–2pm, am Sun, Nov–Feb; (01427) 872268; £2. They do B & B. Thanks to the Wesley connection, the whole village has become something of a Methodist centre; the friendly

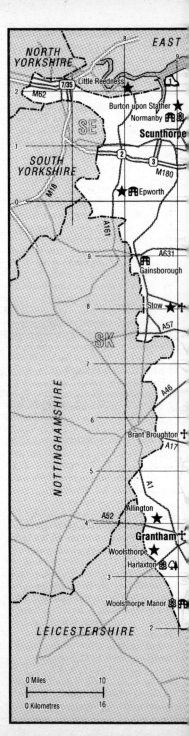

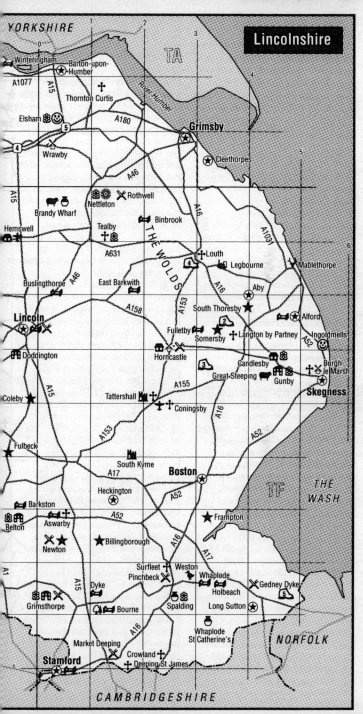

Lincolnshire

YORKSHIRE

Winteringham
Barton-upon-Humber
A1077
A15
Thornton Curtis
Elsham
A180
Wrawby
A46
Grimsby
Cleethorpes

TA

River Humber

A15
A4
Hemswell
Brandy Wharf
Nettleton
Rothwell
Binbrook
Tealby
A631
THE WOLDS
Louth
Legbourne
Mablethorpe
Buslingthorpe
A46
East Barkwith
A158
A153
South Thoresby
Aby
Alford
Lincoln
Fulletby
Somersby
Langton by Partney
Ingoldmells
Doddington
Horncastle
Candlesby
Burgh le Marsh
Coleby
A155
Great Steeping
Gunby
Skegness
Tattershall
Coningsby
A16
A15
A153
Fulbeck
South Kyme
A17
Boston
Heckington
A52
Barkston
Aswarby
Belton
Newton
Billingborough
Frampton
Surfleet
Weston
Pinchbeck
Whaplode
Gedney Dyke
Dyke
Holbeach
Grimsthorpe
Bourne
Spalding
Long Sutton
A16
Market Deeping
Whaplode St Catherine's
NORFOLK
Stamford
Crowland
Deeping St James
A1

THE WASH

TF

CAMBRIDGESHIRE

Red Lion has decent food, especially vegetarian.

🏠 **Gainsborough** SK8189 OLD HALL (Parnell St) Restored medieval manor house with interesting great hall and original kitchen. Good Walkman tour. Snacks, shop, disabled access to ground floor only; cl Sun (exc pm Easter–Oct), 24–26 Dec, 1 Jan, Good Fri; (01427) 612669; £1.75. The Trent Port is useful for lunch, and the lane N along the Trent embankment gives views of the flood plain of this powerful brooding river; the Jenny Wren at Susworth is another good stop.

🐂 **Great Steeping** TF4464 NORTHCOTE HEAVY HORSE CENTRE 🏇 Besides the gentle giants themselves (showcased at noon), this bustling place has other animals from rare breeds of cattle and sheep to miniature ponies and working dogs. Snacks, shop, disabled access; open Sun and Tues–Thurs Apr–Sept, plus Mon and Fri July and Aug; (01754) 830286; *£4 conducted tour. The Bell at Halton Holegate has enjoyable home cooking.

🍺 🌸 🐾 **Grimsby** TA2710 Though this declining fishing port has not yet made itself entirely appealing to visitors, it's making considerable strides in that direction. NATIONAL FISHING HERITAGE CENTRE (Alexandra Dock) Fascinating displays in this outstanding place provide the full experience of a trawlerman of the mid-1950s, taking you from the back streets of Grimsby to the fishing grounds of the Arctic Circle and back, complete with smells and sensations as well as sights and sounds. Good for families. Snacks, shop, disabled access; cl 25–26 Dec, 1 Jan; (01472) 323345; £3.30. Nearby Leons (Alexandra Rd) does good fresh fish. Additional tours of a real trawler, the *Ross Tiger*, are available, £3.50 on its own, £4.50 combined ticket with museum. The *Lincoln Castle*, a paddle-steamer moored in Alexandra Dock, is now a good-value floating restaurant. The Abbeygate Centre has reasonably priced antique shops, also upstairs craft workshops inc lace-making; café. Alfred Enderby's

smoked fish house (Fish Docks Rd) demonstrates traditional methods of smoking salmon, haddock and cod; cl Sun, and most Sats; (01472) 342984 to check.

🏠 🏵 **Grimsthorpe** TF0422 GRIMSTHORPE CASTLE 🏰 A patchwork of styles from its medieval tower and Tudor quadrangle to the baroque north front by Vanbrugh; the state rooms and galleries have especially fine furnishings. Outside are formal gardens and parkland with lake, and red deer tame enough for children to feed. Meals, snacks, shop, some disabled access; open Sun, Thurs and bank hols Easter–Sept, plus Mon–Weds in Aug, house cl am; (01778) 591205; *£6 all-in, £3 just castle or garden. The Five Bells at Edenham is a decent dining pub (and handy for walkers).

🏠 🏵 **Gunby** (the one nr Spilsby; off the A158) TF4666 GUNBY HALL Interesting neat red brick William III house, with fine oak staircase and clock collection; especially worth visiting for the 9 acres of splendid gardens, said to be Tennyson's 'haunt of ancient peace'. Open pm Weds (plus garden only pm Thurs) Apr–Sept; £3.50, £2.50 garden only. The Blacksmiths Arms at Skendleby does worthwhile simple lunches.

🏵 🌿 **Harlaxton** SK8832 HARLAXTON MANOR GARDENS (A607) Around 45 acres of classical gardens, built in the early 19th c to rival the finest in Europe, now being restored. Rose and herb gardens in 6-acre walled garden, and nature trails through surrounding woodland. The stunning mansion at the estate's heart takes on a gorgeous golden glow in the late afternoon sun. Snacks, shop, limited disabled access; cl Mon (exc bank hols), and Nov–Mar; (01476) 592101; £2.50. The Red House over at Knipton is a good dining pub.

✂ 🐾 ✝ **Heckington** TF1444 Understated but pleasant small town, its well restored WINDMILL the only one in Britain with 8 sails; open pm Sun mid-Sept–mid-Dec, Mon–Sat in summer; (01529) 461919; £1. Nearby the Pearoom is a decent CRAFT CENTRE, and the Nags Head is useful for lunch. The CHURCH still has many of its orginal 14th-c fittings.

✝ ☎ **Hemswell** SK9391 BOMBER COUNTY AVIATION MUSEUM Small but enthusiastic collection in former RAF base, where you can watch restoration work being carried out on Hunter, Vampire and Mystere planes. Snacks, shop, disabled access; open Sun; free. Collectors should find something to interest them at the HEMSWELL ANTIQUES CENTRE close by – 3 buildings with around 270 shops selling books, period furniture, ceramics, rugs and jewellery.

☎ ✗ **Horncastle** TF2669 Attractive market town popular for antiques, with 30 shops in the Bridge St Antiques Centre. You can still see parts of the town's ROMAN WALL. Old Nicks (North St) has a decent carvery, and the Fighting Cocks (West St) is also good value. Some 3 miles NW the 'High Street' (the B1225) forking off the A158 is a good drive, following an Iron Age trackway up to Caistor. The A153 to Louth gives rolling Wolds views. Another pretty drive here includes Scrivelsby and its vast deer park, Belchford (Blue Bell useful for lunch), Fulletby (perhaps a stroll on the footpaths here), Somersby (Tennyson's birthplace – his bust is in the church), Old Bolingbroke (castle ruins), Spilsby (worth-visiting delicatessen in the quiet market place with its statue of Sir John Franklin) and, if you've made good time, Wainfleet and Boston.

☺ **Ingoldmells** TF5669 For FANTASY ISLAND *see separate Family Panel on p.426.*

🐎 **Legbourne** TF3684 RAILWAY MUSEUM ▦ Varied local railway memorabilia at the oldest preserved Great Northern Railway station. Children can pull levers and press bells, and there's a model railway and pets corner. Likely to be the last year for this nice place, as the owners plan to retire. Snacks, shop, disabled access; cl Mon (exc bank hols), and Oct–Easter; (01507) 603116; £1.75. The nearby Queens Head has good cheap snacks.

🦋 ✿ ✝ **Long Sutton** TF4222

BUTTERFLY AND FALCONRY PARK One of Britain's biggest walk-through tropical houses, with hundreds of butterflies flying free. Also creepy-crawly little insectarium, wildflower meadows, and twice-daily falconry displays. A well organised place. Snacks, shop, disabled access; cl Nov–Mar; (01406) 363833; *£4.20. The parish CHURCH SPIRE is unusual for the hundreds of tons of lead sheathing it. The 17th-c Olde Ship has pleasant home cooking.

Ⅴ **Mablethorpe** TF5185 ANIMAL GARDENS AND SEAL TRUST (North End) Rescued seals unable to return to the wild find a permanent home here, along with monkeys, parrots, porcupines, llamas, emus and other animals. It's right by the beach. Snacks, shop, disabled access; cl Nov–Easter; (01507) 473346; £3.

❀ ❈ **Nettleton** TA1100 Potterton & Martin's NURSERY (Moortown Rd) has unusual and interesting plants - mainly alpines and small bulbs; (01472) 851792. Just S towards Normanby le Wold, Caistor Top is the highest point on the Wolds, at 550 metres (1,805 ft), with bracing walks. The Nickerson Arms over at Rothwell has decent food.

❀ 🏛 **Normanby** SE8816 NORMANBY HALL COUNTRY PARK (on the B1430) Pleasant spot with grazing deer, lots of wildfowl, nature trails, riding, some interesting sculptures, and a farm museum in its 350 busy acres. Period rooms in the Regency mansion. Meals, snacks, shop, disabled access to ground floor only; house and museum cl am, wkdys Apr, May and Sept, and all Oct–Mar, park open all year; (01724) 720588; free, though £1.50 charge for car parking (£2.50 –£3 wknds and bank hols). The Sheffield Arms at Burton upon Stather has enjoyable food.

Ⅴ 🐀 ⱵT **Skegness** TF3663 Built as a late 19th-c resort, this has been an archetypal one, with the first Butlin's Holiday Camp just up the coast; the beach has clean bathing water. The rewarding NATURELAND SEAL SANCTUARY ▦ (North Parade) is renowned for its seal rescuing activities. It's fascinating watching the seals performing tricks – they aren't trained in any way, they just like showing off. Also other animals inc crocodiles, snakes and a tarantula, aquarium, and free-flying tropical butterflies (May–Oct). Snacks, shop, disabled access; cl 25–26 Dec, 1 Jan; (01754) 764345; £3.60. CHURCH FARM MUSEUM (Church Rd Sth) Good recreation of daily farm life at the end of the 19th c, with craft demonstrations, and quite a few Lincoln longwool sheep. Snacks, shop, disabled access; cl Nov–Mar; (01754) 766658; £1. The comfortable old Vine Hotel on the southern edge of the town was here long before the resort, welcoming Tennyson among others; it's pleasant for lunch.

South Kyme TF1749 A fine 14th-c battlemented tower stands alone in a meadow quite nr the road.

Spalding TF2422 SPRINGFIELDS GARDENS (Camelgate) 25-acre garden with glasshouses; there's a fantastic bedding plants display in summer, and in spring over a million bulbs in bloom. Meals, snacks, shop, disabled access; open 21 Mar–mid-May and then probably cl for redevelopment; (01775) 724843; *£3. AYSCOUGHFEE HALL MUSEUM (Church Gate) Spooky-looking medieval manor house, with social history museum, and 5 acres of gardens and ancient yew hedges. Meals, snacks, shop, disabled access to ground floor only; museum cl winter wknds, gardens open all year; (01775) 725468; free. The riverside Lincolnshire Poacher is useful for lunch. TROPICAL FOREST (Rose Cottage Water Garden Centre, Pinchbeck, just N of Spalding) One of the biggest displays of tropical and subtropical plants in the country. Snacks, shop, water garden centre, disabled access; cl 25 Dec; (01775) 710882; £2.25. All around this area, the flat fields by the roadside are a mass of colour in spring, first daffodils and then a multicoloured sea of tulips – very Dutch.

Stamford TF0307 John Betjeman considered this England's most attractive town, though it's temporarily doomed to be thought of as the town of Middlemarch that it portrayed in the recent TV adaptation. Within the medieval walls are no less than 500 listed buildings, inc a good number of attractive medieval CHURCHES – particularly All Saints' in the centre, St George's with excellent 15th-c stained glass, and St Mary's nearby. The MUSEUM (Broad St) includes life-size figures dressed in the clothes of Tom Thumb (only 1 metre (3ft 4in) tall) and Daniel Lambert, a portly fellow who weighed 218 kg (50 stone) when he died on a racing outing here. Shop, disabled access to ground floor only; cl Sun (exc pm in summer), 25–26 Dec; (01780) 66317; free. The George, one of the town's grandest buildings with some parts going back to Saxon times, is excellent for lunch. BURGHLEY HOUSE A 20-minute walk from Stamford's centre leads to this splendid mansion, built by William Cecil and still the home of his family. The exterior is Tudor at its most solidly showy, but the state rooms inside are largely baroque, with wonderful frescoes by Antonio Verrio – the Heaven Room is astonishing. The peaceful grounds, where the Burghley Horse Trials are held, were landscaped by Capability Brown. Meals, snacks, shop, limited disabled access; cl early Oct–Mar (though gardens may open some dates in Apr for spring flowers display); (01780) 52451; £5.60. TOLETHORPE HALL (off the A6121 N of Stamford) This has Europe's biggest OPEN-AIR THEATRE in its grounds, with a covered auditorium and a good Shakespeare season; (01780) 54381.

Tattershall TF2157 The 15th-c CASTLE has a magnificent 30 metre (100 ft) turreted keep, with fine heraldic chimneypieces on each of the 4 storeys; there's a double moat with peacocks and waterfowl. Snacks, shop (with food for the birds), some disabled access; open Sat–Weds Apr–Oct, wknds Nov and Dec; (01526) 342543; £2.50; NT. The airy 15th-c CHURCH is also attractive, and just off the A153 towards Sleaford, on the left before you reach Tattershall Bridge, is a preserved steam engine which worked at keeping this area of the fens drained for nearly a century. The Abbey Lodge Hotel (on the B1192 towards Woodhall) has good food.

✝ **Thornton Curtis** TA1118 THORNTON ABBEY (on the East Halton road) Ruins of 12th-c Augustinian abbey, very atmospheric with its worn spiral stone stairs and dark corridors, well worth a visit. Also small exhibition in magnificent 14th-c gatehouse. Disabled access (not into gatehouse); grounds open daily, gatehouse open only pm 3rd Sun in month, plus pm 1st Sun Apr–Sept; free.

🦉 **Weston** TF2924 BAYTREE OWL CENTRE 🎫 (on the A151) Expanding collection of owls and other birds, with displays in a big arena (12 and 3pm); some birds can be handled. They plan to add red squirrels. Good meals and snacks, shop, disabled access; cl 25–26 Dec, 1 Jan; (01406) 371907; £2.60. It's part of a busy little complex, with ducks and rabbits in a landscaped glasshouse, good garden centre, and play area; also donkeys and a mule in a paddock by the car park – regular visitors tell us the latter can't resist carrots.

🔔 **Whaplode St Catherine's** TF3219 MUSEUM OF ENTERTAINMENT 🎫 (Millgate, off the B1165) Unusual and quirky collection tracing the development of entertainment from barrel and church organs to puppets and phonographs, taking in a history of the fairground along the way. Many exhibits are working, and the owners clearly love their subject. Snacks, shop, disabled access; open pm Sun–Thurs July–Sept, plus Easter wknd; (01406) 540379; £2.50.

🏛️🌸 **Woolsthorpe** SK9224 (the one nr Colsterworth) WOOLSTHORPE MANOR The birthplace of Isaac Newton, where he later conducted some of his more important experiments. Geometry workings said to be in his handwriting are scratched into the plasterwork – and of course the garden has a venerable apple tree. Open pm Weds–Sun Apr–mid-Nov; (01476) 860338; £2.50; NT.

🌀 **Wrawby** TA0209 The village has a WORKING WINDMILL, open special days Apr–Aug – ring Mrs Day to check, (01652) 653699; £1.

✝ This county has a remarkable collection of great **churches**. Even villages which are tiny now and can never have been very large are graced by buildings of often impressive power. The height of the spires is a particular feature, with the tallest of any parish church in Britain being the very elegant 16th-c church in Louth TF3387 (the tower can be climbed on summer afternoons; hundreds of steps for a fabulous view). Other notable spires are those in Grantham SK9135 (the early 19th-c jingle about it, 'Grantham, now two rarities are thine, A lofty steeple and a living sign', refers to the hive with living bees still used as an inn sign by the good Beehive pub there) and Brant Broughton SK9154.

Other country churches worth seeing if you're near include those in the park at Aswarby TF0639, Deeping St James TF1609, Langton by Partney TF3970 and Stow SK8882 (fantastic Saxon arches), while at Crowland TF2410 you can see the remains of a once-great abbey, part still used as the parish church. The church tower and spire at Surfleet TF2528 lean alarmingly.

🌺 Many **village cottage gardens**, easily seen from the road, add a welcome splash of colour that seems a particular Lincolnshire characteristic. Tealby TF1590 is the best example: a great variety of neat and charmingly planted gardens front the stonebuilt cottages, some thatched, on its main street, running down from the 12th-c church to a watersplash near a watermill, and there is more colour in the quaintly named side lanes. The 14th-c Kings Head has excellent food.

★ Other **attractive villages**, all with decent pubs, include Allington SK8540 (despite the A1 being so near), Billingborough TF1134, Burton upon Stather SE8717, Coleby SK9760, Frampton TF3239 (perhaps the prettiest Fenland village), Fulbeck SK9450, Little Reedness SE8023

(14th-c church, Ouse walks, nr RSPB nature reserve at Blacktoft Sands marshes just E), Newton TF0436, South Thoresby TF4077, Stow SK8882 and Woolsthorpe SK8435 (the one nr Belvoir). Readers recommend the woods near Woodhall Spa TF1963 for picnics, or those at Stapleford SK8857 (especially when the rhododendrons are in bloom). There are decent views and a duckpond at Castle Bytham SK9819, with nature trails in the woods nearby.

Walks

The county's mostly too flat for interesting walks. The Wolds are gentle chalk hills in the E, with mainly large fields (some like prairies) and patches of woodland. **Alkborough** SE8821 ⌂-1 overlooks the confluence of the Trent and Humber from a high (for this area) scarp called The Cliff, along which a path leads to Burton upon Stather.

The **Viking Way** ⌂-2 is a long-distance path helping village-to-village walks, with 'Tennyson country' a popular focus (Tennyson was born at the rectory in Somersby TF3472, when his father was rector at Bag Enderby nearby); the Black Horse at Donington on Bain TF2382 and the 2 Tealby pubs TF1580 are handy stops.

Snipe Dales TF3268 ⌂-3 is a country park and nature reserve, managed by the county council, covering 210 acres rich in bird and plant life; the country park is a 90-acre area of pine woods, while the adjacent nature reserve has a trail leading through 2 valleys and to a viewpoint over the Wolds.

Hubbard's Hill TF3186 ⌂-4 is a walk SW from Louth TF3387: not in fact a hill, but a river valley – surprisingly deep for the Wolds.

A good way of seeing the Wash is by following the dyke forming the sea wall; access is from a car park nr Gedney Drove End TF4728, from which you can follow the dyke to the mouth of the Nene, with its twin lighthouses either side. The **Peter Scott Walk** ⌂-5 is a 10-mile walk E from here – Scott used to come here to study and paint wildfowl. It leads along the dyke into Norfolk, with access from a car park TF4925 on the Nene's E bank.

Where to eat

Gedney Dyke TF4125 CHEQUERS (01406) 362666 Warm, welcoming and spotlessly kept small pub with an open fire, and an elegant dining conservatory; lots of fresh fish and seafood and a wide choice of other good, interesting cooking, well kept beer, and decent wines; polite, helpful service. £20.35|£7.95.

Grimsthorpe TF0423 BLACK HORSE (01778) 591247 Large open fire and rustic atmosphere in a narrow bar, the cosy Buttery Bar with another open fire, and an intimate candlelit dining room – all with excellent food and decent wine; friendly staff; children over 10; disabled access. £18|£5.50.

Horncastle TF2669 MAGPIES 73–75 East St (01507) 527004 Popular, well run restaurant with a relaxed atmosphere and very good French cooking using top quality fresh local ingredients; cl Sun Mon, 2 wks Jan, 2 wks Oct; disabled access. £30.

Lincoln SK9771 BROWNS PIE SHOP 33 Steep Hill (01522) 527330 Spectacular, really interesting pies (and lots of other food), helpful staff, comfortable seats and pleasant traditional atmosphere. £20|£4.25.

Lincoln SK9771 JEWS HOUSE 15 The Strait (01522) 524851 Small, intimate and elegantly furnished restaurant in one of the oldest buildings in the city; very good imaginative food, well schooled friendly service, and an upstairs coffee lounge for those who want to smoke after the meal; cl Sun, Mon. £26|£8.

Lincoln SK9771 Wig & Mitre 29 Steep Hill (01522) 535190 Attractively restored 14th-c building with imaginative food served all day (breakfast too), excellent puddings, an elaborate restaurant menu, interesting wine list, and consistently efficient, prompt service; cl 25 Dec; disabled access. £16.50|£4.75.

Market Deeping TF1310 Caudle House (01778) 347595 Georgian house with 2 small dining rooms and a little bar area, and friendly, helpful staff (the waitresses wear Victorian dress); a good choice of carefully cooked food, and a thoughtful wine list; bdrms; open pm Thurs–Sat, am Sun – but will cater for residents at any time; children over 8. £26.

Newton TF0436 Red Lion (01529) 497256 Full of charm and character, this civilised pub specialises in imaginative choose-as-much-as-you-like salads using top-quality ingredients (lots of fish, tasty pies and so forth) – home-made soups and daily specials are excellent, too; cl 25 Dec; disabled access. £17.45|£6.95.

Pinchbeck TF2425 Ship (01775) 723792 Friendly pub with comfortable small lounge and dining area, helpful service, good-value bar food, smarter restaurant, and real ales; cl pm 25–26 Dec; disabled access. £18|£4.95.

Rothwell TF1599 Nickerson Arms (01472) 371300 Convivial place with fresh flowers in pleasant beamed bar, enjoyably relaxed civilised atmosphere; good, interesting bar food, well kept real ales and interesting bottled beers, decent wines by the glass, and 4 ciders. £17|£6.85

Special thanks to Mr and Mrs M J Lake, Stephen Waters, Andrew Eaton, Jenny and Michael Back, Nigel Sopp.

LINCOLNSHIRE CALENDAR

Some of these dates were provisional as we went to press. Please check information with the numbers provided.

JANUARY

6 **Haxey** Haxey Hood Game: created in the 13th c by Lady de Mowbray whose hood was blown away and retrieved by labourers, the game resembles rugby played with leather hoods. Procession of players, colourfully dressed 'Boggans', king and fool (01302) 735385

25 **Lincoln** Great Australian Breakfast: celebration of Australia Day inc fancy dress, music (01522) 511511

FEBRUARY

5 **Spalding** Horticultural Exhibition: indoor flower show, over 100 trade stands at Springfields – *till Sun 8* (01775) 713253

21 **Spalding** Motorbike '98: arena events at Springfields – *till Sun 22* (01775) 713253

28 **Grimsby and Cleethorpes** Lincolnshire Literature Festival – *till 7 March* (01472) 323004

MARCH

3 **Lincoln** Lincoln Shakespeare Company at the Lawn – *till Sat 14* (01522) 511511

21 **Grange-de-Lings** Lincolnshire Horse Trials at the Lincolnshire Showground – *till Sun 22* (01522) 750602; **Spalding** Spring Fair and Motor Show at Springfields – *till Sun 22* (01775) 713253

23 **Stamford** Mid-Lent Fair *till Sat 28* (01476) 591591

30 **Grantham** Mid-Lent Fair – *till 1 April* (01476 591591

LINCOLNSHIRE CALENDAR

APRIL

12 **Lincoln** Victorian Prison Open at the Castle: re-enactments – *till Mon 13* (01522) 511511

13 **Cleethorpe** Dance Festival (01472) 323004; **Wrawby** Windmill Open Day (01652) 653699

18 **Belton** Horse Trials at Belton House – *till Sun 19* (01775) 680333

20 **Lincoln** Outdoor Activities Day at the Castle: inc abseiling from the castle walls, canoeing *till Mon 21* (01522) 511511

MAY

1 **Alford** Morris Men Dance at Dawn at the Windmill (01507) 462136; **Lincoln** Folk Festival – *till Mon 4* (01522) 511511

2 **Normanby** Model Engineers Festival at Normanby Hall – *till Mon 4* (01724) 720588; **Spalding** Flower Festival and Country Fair: famous flower float parade through the town and at Springfields – *till Mon 4* (01775) 713253

3 **Gainsborough** Living History Weekend at Gainsborough Old Hall – *till Mon 4* (01427) 612669

4 **Wrawby** Windmill Open Day (01652) 653699

13 **Tallington** Beer Festival at Barholm Road Showfield – *till Sat 16* (01780) 763063

16 **Tallington** Steam and Country Festival at Barholm Road Showfield – *till Sun 17* (01780) 763063

23 **Ealand** Crowle Agricultural Show (01724) 710463; **Normanby** Horse Trials at Normanby Hall – *till Sun 24* (01724) 720588

24 **Gainsborough** Town and Country Fair at Gainsborough Old Hall – *till Mon 25* (01427) 612669; **Harlaxton** Open Day at Harlaxton Manor (01476) 564541; **Louth** Car Show: arena events – *till Mon 25* (01775) 640737

25 **Woodhall Spa** Agricultural Show (01526) 352896; **Wrawby** Windmill Open Day (01652) 653699

31 **Messingham** Show (01724) 763004

JUNE

7 **Lincoln** Vintage Vehicle Rally at the Castle (01522) 511511

12 **Lincoln** Vintage Motorcycle Rally – *till Sun 14* (01522) 511511

14 **Lincoln** Jousting Tournament at the Castle (01522) 511511; **Mablethorpe** Vintage Car Rally (01507) 473417; **Normanby** Motor Show at Normanby Hall (01724) 720588

20 **Grantham** Carnival – *till Sun 21* (01476) 574484; **Messingham** Carnival (01724) 762752

21 **Appleby** Country Fair: jousting, falconry (01724) 733602

24 **Grange-de-Lings** Lincolnshire Show at the Lincolnshire Showground – *till Thurs 25* (01522) 524240

27 **Belton** Fireworks Concert at Belton House (01775) 680333; **Boston** Carnival – *till Sun 28* (01205) 355570; **Waddington** RAF Waddington Air Show: foreign aircraft and display teams, Red Arrows, service displays, crafts, funfair – *till Sun 28* (01522) 720271

28 **Harlaxton** Open Day at Harlaxton Manor (01476) 564541; **Wrawby** Windmill Open Day (01652) 653699

JULY

2 **Grantham and South Kesteven** Folk & Food, Drink & Dance Festival lots of events at various venues – *till Sun 12* (01476) 593966

LINCOLNSHIRE CALENDAR

JULY cont

3 **Grimsby** International Jazz Festival – *till Sun 5* (01472) 323004
10 **Spalding** Country Music Festival at Springfields – *till Sun 12* (01775) 713253
11 **Lincoln** Water Carnival at Brayford Pool – *till Sun 12* (01522) 511511
12 **Normanby** Show: cricket, music, fairground at Normanby Hall (01724) 720588; **Skegness** Illuminations Switch On; fireworks (01754) 764821; **Spilsby** Show (01790) 752566
18 **Barton** Carnival – *till Sun 19* (01652) 635330; **Broughton** Agricultural Horse and Dog Show (01652) 656448
19 **Belton** Family Fun Day at Belton House (01775) 680333; **Louth** Grand Carnival Parade, crafts, art exhibition and music (01507) 472496; **Mablethorpe** Illuminations Switch On, also District Show (01507) 472496; **Spalding** Vintage Vehicle and Classic Car Show at Springfields (01775) 713253
23 **Sutton-on-Sea** Carnival and Parade – *till Sun 26* (01507) 472496
24 **Stamford** Fireworks Concert with Dancing Waters at Burghley House – *till Sat 25* (01625) 575681
25 **Heckington** Agricultural Show at the Showground – *till Sun 26* (01529) 304145; **Lincoln** Family Fun Weekend: arena events, music, entertainment at the Lawn – *till Sun 26* (01522) 511511
26 **Wrawby** Windmill Open Day (01652) 653699
31 **Cleethorpes** Carnival Parade (01472) 323004; **Lincoln** Family Fun Weekend at the Lawn – *till 1 Aug* (01522) 511511

AUGUST

1 **Partney** Sheep Fair (01754) 810477
2 **Revesby** Country Fair (01205) 365213
5 **Brigg** Fair and Horse Fair (01652) 656744
7 **Lincoln** Veteran Car Rally; also **Lincoln** Outdoor Concerts – *till Sun 9* (01522) 511511
8 **Lincoln** Medieval Re-enactment at the Castle – *till Sun 9* (01522) 511511
9 **Mablethorpe** Carnival Week *till procession on Sun 16* (01507) 472496
16 **Skegness** Carnival Week – *till procession on Sat 22* (01754) 764821
20 **Lincoln** Classic Car Rally – *till Fri 21* (01522) 511511
22 **Barkston Heath** National Model Flying Championships at RAF Barkston Heath – *till Mon 24* (0116) 244 0028; **Lincoln** Craft Fair at the Lawn – *till Sun 23*; also **Lincoln** Steam Spectacular at the Lincolnshire Showground – *till Sun 23* (01522) 511511
29 **Boston** Show at Central Park – *till Sun 30* (01205) 368966
31 **Epworth** Agricultural Show (01427) 872571; **Wrawby** Windmill Open Day (01652) 653699

SEPTEMBER

3 **Stamford** European Championships Horse Trials at Burghley House - *till Sun 6* (01780) 752131
5 **Spalding** Flower Show at Springfields – *till Sun 6* (01775) 713253
12 **Normanby** Stationary and Miniature Traction Engine Rally at Normanby Hall – *till Sun 13* (01724) 720588
20 **Epworth** Festival of the Plough (01427) 872659

LINCOLNSHIRE CALENDAR

SEPTEMBER cont

24 **Lincoln** International Clowns Convention: inc workshops, street theatre – *till Sun 27* (01522) 511511

26 **Brigg** Chrysanthemum and Dahlia Show – *till Sun 27* (01652) 656810; **Woodhall Spa** Festival – *till Sun 27* (01526) 353775

NOVEMBER

5 **Cleethorpes** Giant Bonfire and Fireworks (01472) 323111

7 **Lincoln** Fireworks at City Football Ground; **Spalding** Model Railway Exhibition at Springfields – *till Sun 8* (01775) 713253

28 **Alford** Christmas Market *also on 5 Dec* (01507) 601111

DECEMBER

3 **Lincoln** Christmas Market – *till Sun 6* (01522) 511511

4 **Brigg** Christmas Fair: street entertainment, bands, santa's grotto (01652) 657959

We welcome reports from readers . . .

This *Guide* depends on readers' reports. Do help us if you can – in return, we offer a discount on the next edition to people who've helped us with reports for it. Tell us what you think about places already in it, and anything extra you think we should say about them. And send us your ideas for inclusion in the next edition: places to visit, eat at or stay in, attractive drives or walks, maybe even unusual interesting shops you know of. Use the card in the middle, the report forms at the end, or just write – no stamp needed: *The Good Guide to Britain*, FREEPOST TN1569, Wadhurst, E Sussex TN5 7BR.

NORFOLK

Some marvellously timeless and unspoilt parts, good range of beach resorts, interesting places to visit; and there's boating on the Broads.

North Norfolk has a great deal of unspoilt charm, untouristy and traditional-feeling, with an appealingly individual character, and a real sense of style about even the simplest buildings. This coast gives you refreshingly broad sweeps of sea, saltings and sky, and often hundreds of birds in sight at a time, big enough and distinctive enough to excite even non-ornithologists. There's a real get-away-from-it-all feel, and inland too, this part has the same sort of appeal. Up here, Hunstanton and Cromer are civilised seaside resorts, and there are many attractive smaller places as well.

Further down, the coast is dotted with beach resorts, some large and lively (most obviously, Great Yarmouth), some relaxed and more individual.

Norwich is a distinguished yet lively cathedral city, not overly touristy, yet with plenty to see. Highlights elsewhere include Sandringham (less grand than other royal residences – people like its more personal feel), Blickling Hall, Holkham Hall, Houghton Hall and Felbrigg Hall; besides these great houses, there's a very broad spread of other things well worth tracking down, from the unique watergardens at South Walsham to the dinosaur park at Weston Longville or the prehistory at Cockley Cley and Grimes Graves, from the elderly fighting vehicles at Weybourne to the Welney wildfowl centre.

Many of the most enjoyable places to visit appeal to children as well as adults. Boat trips from Blakeney to see the seals sum up the timeless simplicity of North Norfolk's appeal. Other good family outings include The Village at Burgh St Margaret, the tropical centre in Great Yarmouth, and Bressingham's steam museum and gardens. Among the many wildlife, zoo and farm parks here, those at Filby, Banham and Snettisham stand out. Steam enthusiasts have plenty to keep them occupied at Aylsham, Sheringham, Wells-next-the-Sea, Forncett St Mary and (our own favourite) Thursford Green. On a smaller scale, families very much enjoy the craft centre outside Hoveton.

Away from the north, the countryside is not in itself a big draw – much is flat and repetitive. It's excellent for cycling, though, with quiet lanes, attractive villages and country churches, and fair views (and lots of roadside snowdrops in spring). Driving along the twisty coastal A149 is pleasant out of season – though not much fun in summer. The best parts – the winding rivers and reed-fringed meres of the Broads – are much better seen from a boat than from land. Broads cruising is generally a week-long affair, but could be worked into a short-stay holiday; the boats nowadays have every mod con and are easy for even a novice to handle, but it's a chilly pastime until summer's well established. Wroxham is a popular centre for this, though one of the quieter bases in the north might make a better choice for just a day on the water.

Where to stay

Blakeney TG0243 BLAKENEY HOTEL Blakeney, Holt NR25 7NE (01263) 740797 £128, plus special breaks; 60 very comfortable rms, many with views over the salt marshes and some with their own little terrace. Overlooking the harbour with fine views, this friendly hotel has appealing public rooms, good food, and very pleasant staff; indoor swimming pool, saunas, spa bath, billiard room, and a garden; good disabled access.

Blickling TG1728 BUCKINGHAMSHIRE ARMS Blickling, Norwich NR11 6NF (01263) 732133 £60; 3 rms with four-posters, one with own shower. Handsome Jacobean inn in the grounds of Blickling Hall; with a civilised atmosphere, helpful staff, interesting food in both the bar and restaurant (best to book), nice breakfasts, well kept ales and good wines.

Burnham Market TF8342 HOSTE ARMS The Green, Burnham Market, King's Lynn PE31 8HD (01328) 738777 *£86, plus special breaks; 20 comfortable rms. Handsome inn on the green of a lovely Georgian village; with a smartly civilised atmosphere, attractive bars, some interesting period features, stylish food in both the conservatory and restaurant, inc morning coffee and afternoon tea, well kept real ales and fine wines; professional and friendly staff.

Downham Market TF6103 CROWN Bridge St, Downham Market PE38 9DH (01366) 382322 £39.50, plus special breaks; 10 rms, most with own bthrm. 17th-c coaching inn (the stables are now the restaurant) with an interesting history, low beams, flagstones and a roaring log fire, and a welcoming, cheerful landlord.

Great Bircham TF7632 KINGS HEAD Great Bircham, King's Lynn PE31 6RJ (01485) 578265 *£57; 5 rms. Old-fashioned and rather grand-looking Victorian country inn with an unassuming lounge, a quiet pleasant atmosphere and a good log fire; cheerful Italian landlord, reliable and generous bar food (quite a few Italian specialities and tempting puddings), a no smoking dining area, decent wines and well kept beers; also a big side lawn with seats and playthings; cl 25 Dec.

Grimston TF7222 CONGHAM HALL Grimston, King's Lynn PE32 1AH (01485) 600250 *£130, plus special breaks; 14 individually decorated rms. Warmly welcoming and handsome Georgian manor in 40 acres of grounds, inc herb, vegetable and flower gardens (herbs for sale and garden open to the public), outdoor swimming pool, tennis court, paddock, orchards, and a cricket pitch – also, walks leaflets available; lovely drawing room, a pretty orangery formal restaurant with excellent modern cooking (lighter lunches in the bar), and exemplary service; children over 12.

King's Lynn TF6220 TUDOR ROSE St Nicholas St, King's Lynn PE30 1LR (01553) 762824 £50, plus special breaks; 13 refurbished rms. Attractive, half-timbered, 15th-c inn with an interesting medieval door; friendly and chatty atmosphere, decent food in the bar and no smoking raftered restaurant, and good breakfasts; disabled access.

Morston TG0243 MORSTON HALL Morston, Holt NR25 7AA (01263) 741041 £105, plus special breaks; 6 comfortable rms with country views. Attractive, 17th-c, flint-walled house in a tidal village; lovely quiet gardens, beams and open fires in the 2 small lounges, hard-working and friendly owners, very good modern English cooking, a thoughtful small wine list, and super breakfasts; croquet; cl Jan.

Mundford TL8093 CROWN Crown St, Mundford, Thetford IP26 5HQ (01842) 878233 *£49.50; 10 good rms, most with own bthrm. Friendly small village pub, originally a hunting inn and rebuilt in the 18th c; with an attractive choice of good-value, straightforward food, very welcoming staff, happy atmosphere, and well kept real ales; disabled access.

Northwold TL7596 GRANGE Northwold, Thetford IP26 5NF (01366) 728240 *£45; 5 rms. Lovely 18th-c rectory in 12 acres of garden behind the church; with a log fire in the drawing room, views over lawns with peacocks and ducks, and a heated swimming pool; cl Christmas.

Norwich TG2308 BEECHES 4–6 Earlham Rd, Norwich NR2 3DB (01603) 621167 £70, plus special breaks; 25 quiet rms. Two listed Victorian mansions and an extension, only 10 minutes' stroll from the city centre but standing in 4 acres of English Heritage Victorian gardens; with a relaxed and informal atmosphere, friendly resident owners, enjoyable food in the bistro-style restaurant, and good breakfasts; cl Christmas; no children; disabled access.

Norwich TG2308 EARLHAM GUEST HOUSE 147 Earlham Rd, Norwich NR2 3RG (01603) 454169 *£44; 7 mostly no smoking rms, some with own bthrm. Friendly, terraced Victorian house with a small residents' lounge, good breakfasts inc vegetarian choices, and helpful owners; cl Christmas.

Pulham Market TM1986 OLD BAKERY Church Walk, Pulham Market, Diss IP21 4SJ (01379) 676492 *£44; 3 rms. 16th-c, no smoking house with lots of beams and timbers, inglenook fireplace with a fine log fire in the lounge, good breakfasts, enjoyable evening meal, and a friendly atmosphere; cl Christmas and New Year.

South Lopham TM0481 MALTING FARM Blo'Norton Rd, South Lopham, Diss IP22 2HT (01379) 687201 *£40, plus special breaks; 3 well furnished rms, some with own bthrm. Welcoming, no smoking, Elizabethan farmhouse on a working dairy farm; with woodburners in the inglenook fireplaces in both the sitting and dining rooms, big breakfasts with home-baked bread and preserves around a large table, and small play area with toys; the owner's passion is embroidery, patchwork, spinning and quilting; cl Christmas and New Year.

Sprowston TG2411 SPROWSTON MANOR Wroxham Rd, Sprowston, Norwich NR7 8RP (01603) 410871 £112.90, plus special breaks; 94 individually decorated, spacious rms. Extended 16th-c manor house in 10 acres of parkland and surrounded by Sprowston Park golf course; comfortable day rooms, fine food in both the elegant orangery and attractive restaurant; leisure club with palms and stone balustrades, poolside bar, health spa; disabled access.

Stoke Holy Cross TG2301 SALAMANCA FARM Stoke Holy Cross, Norwich NR14 8QJ (01508) 492322 *£38; 4 rms. Mainly Victorian farmhouse (parts are much older) just a short stroll from the River Tas; with a guests' lounge, spacious dining room, a big garden, and farm shop; cl 15 Dec–15 Jan.

Swaffham TF8109 STRATTONS Ash Close, Swaffham PE37 7NH (01760) 723845 *£80; 7 interesting, pretty rms. Warmly welcoming, elegant Queen Anne house, with delicious English food using home-grown herbs and vegetables from a family smallholding, and a carefully chosen wine list illustrated with Mrs Scott's own watercolours; comfortable drawing rooms with open fires and lots of china cats, dried flowers and books; big cupboard full of toys and games for children; cl 25–26 Dec; dogs welcome.

Thornham TF7343 LIFEBOAT Thornham, Hunstanton PE36 6LT (01485) 512236 £60, plus special breaks; 13 pretty rms, most with sea views. Well placed on the edge of coastal flats, with a very cosy atmosphere – especially in winter, when there are 5 fires and antique paraffin lamps; good food in both the bar and elegant restaurant; disabled access.

Thorpe Market TG2335 ELDERTON LODGE Thorpe Market, North Walsham NE11 8TZ (01263) 833547 £75, plus special breaks; 8 rms. 18th-c shooting lodge and dower house for the adjacent Gunton Hall estate; lots of original features such as old gun cabinets and fine panelling, a comfortable lounge bar, conservatory, restaurant with good food using fresh fish and game from the estate, and 6 acres of mature grounds overlooking herds of deer on the 1,000 acres of Gunton Park; cl mid-Jan for 3 wks; children over 6; disabled access.

Titchwell TF7543 TITCHWELL MANOR Titchwell, King's Lynn PE31 8BB (01485) 210221 *£90, plus special breaks; 17 rms. Comfortable hotel, handy for the nearby RSPB reserve; with an open fire, magazines and good naturalists' records of the wildlife in the reserve, a cheerful bar, and pretty no smoking restaurant with French windows looking on to the sheltered, neatly kept walled garden; very good food (especially fish), and particularly helpful licensees and staff; lots of pleasant walks and footpaths nearby; dogs welcome (bedrooms only, £2.50); disabled access.

Warham TF9441 THREE HORSESHOES Warham, Wells-next-the-Sea NR23 1NL (01328) 710547 £48; 3 rms, some with own bthrm. Basic but cheerful local with a marvellously unspoilt, traditional atmosphere in its 3 friendly gaslit rooms; simple furnishings, a log fire, very tasty and generous helpings of bar food, decent wines, home-made lemonade, and very well kept real ales; bedrooms are in the Old Post Office adjoining the pub, with lots of beams and a residents' lounge dominated by an inglenook fireplace; cl 25–26 Dec; no children; disabled access.

Winterton-on-Sea TG4919 FISHERMANS RETURN The Lane, Winterton-on-Sea, Great Yarmouth NR29 4BN (01493) 393305 *£50; 3 characterful rms, shared bthrm. Traditional 300-year-old pub in a quiet village, close to the beach; with warmly welcoming owners, a relaxed lounge bar, open fire, good home-made food inc fresh fish (fine crabs), enjoyable breakfasts, and a sheltered garden.

To see and do

Norwich TG2308 Busy but civilised, the old centre has quite a concentration of attractive streets and buildings, with all sorts of surprises in the narrow streets and lanes that still follow its medieval layout; Elm St is especially handsome, and there are plenty of antique shops and so forth. Even the more commercial/industrial centre north of the River Wensum has fine patches (such as Colegate), and the main shopping areas are closed to traffic. Fortunately the visually disappointing university is hidden away out on the western edge, though in term-time its students do bring a good bit of life into the centre. Norwich is the home of Colman's Mustard, and the Mustard Shop (Bridewell Alley) has some varieties you may not have come across before. The ancient Adam & Eve (Bishopgate) is pleasant for lunch, and other pubs useful for a bite to eat without being overrun by students include the Unthank Arms (Newmarket St) and the riverside Ribs of Beef (Wensum St).

🏰 🕭 🎦 CASTLE (Castle Meadow) This impressive four-square Norman fortress dominates the city from its hill. Guided tours of the dungeons, battlements and 12th-c keep, and MUSEUM with displays of art (with particular emphasis on the Norwich School), silverware (for which the town was famous) and ceramics. Don't miss the natural history gallery if you like stuffed birds. Snacks, shop, disabled access; cl winter Suns, Good Fri, 25–26 Dec, 1 Jan; (01603) 223624; £3.10 July–Sept, otherwise £2.30. Linked to this museum via an underground passage is a former courtroom in the historic Shirehall, now a regimental museum.

✝ 🏛 The modern city is firmly shut out by the great medieval gateways of the CATHEDRAL. Basically medieval, the church has some fine features from later periods – the flying buttresses for example, and the late 15th-c vaulted roof, spire and west window with Victorian glass. The Norman cloisters are the largest in the country, rebuilt after a serious riot between city and cathedral in 1272, and remarkable for the 400 bosses carved with scenes of medieval life (there are hundreds more in the cathedral itself, though less easy to see). Snacks and shop (not Sun), disabled access. Free guided tours leave the Information Desk at 11am wkdys and Sat, and 2.15pm wkdys only. The extensive precincts make an awe-inspiring impression: great medieval gateways, medieval alleys and secluded gardens, with all sorts of varied buildings from the cottages of Hooks Walk through the finer houses in the Upper Close to the buildings of Norwich School. The best view of the cathedral is from the river by Pulls Ferry; it's not easy to see from other parts of the town.

🕭 BRIDEWELL MUSEUM (Bridewell Alley) 14th-c building used as a prison from 1583 to 1828, now with exhibits on the town's trade and industries, and reconstructed turn-of-the-century shops. Usually only cl Sun, Mon, and Oct–Mar, but it may be best to check first; (01603) 667228; £1.20.

🏚 DRAGON HALL (King St) Well preserved medieval merchant's hall, with a splendid timber-framed roof, intricate carvings, cellars, vaulted undercroft, and some finely painted roundels. Shop, limited disabled access; cl wknds exc summer Sats, 23 Dec–1 Jan, bank hols; (01603) 663922; *£1.50.

✝🕭 MEDIEVAL CHURCHES Literally dozens of them, in great variety, these are one of the city's joys. Perhaps the finest of all is St Peter Hungate (Princes St), an impressive 15th-c church with a grand hammerbeam roof, museum of church art and brass rubbing centre. St Michael's (Coslany St) now has a HANDS ON SCIENCE CENTRE, wittily called Inspire. Snacks, shop, disabled access; cl Mon; £3.

⚓ BOAT TRIPS From the River Wensum you can clearly see how some of the city's older buildings were designed for water-borne traffic, rather than road transport.

🔳 SAINSBURY CENTRE FOR VISUAL ARTS (University of East Anglia, off the B1108 W of centre) Striking Norman Foster building with notable 19th- and 20th-c European art, and a fascinating range of ethnographic art, inc African tribal sculpture, and Egyptian and Asian antiquities. Meals, snacks, shop, disabled access; cl Mon, 24 Dec–2 Jan; (01603) 592467; £2.

Other things to see and do

NORFOLK FAMILY ATTRACTION OF THE YEAR

⚓🏴 **Blakeney** TG0243 SEAL BOAT TRIPS Few of our trips out in Norfolk this year have been as enjoyable as these trips around Blakeney Point. They've been going for years of course, and for many visitors it's the timeless simplicity that's the appeal: we came across several families making their annual visit. Boats leave from Morston Quay, slightly W of Blakeney on the A149 coast road, once or twice a day from Mar–Oct (times depend on the tide), and on most winter wknds; when the tide allows you'll also find trips wending their way down the creek from the little harbour at Blakeney itself. Most last 2 hours, which takes in an hour or so exploring the National Trust-owned bird reserve at Blakeney Point. The highlight comes just before that, when the boat goes past the sandbanks at the end of the Point, where dozens of grey and common seals lie basking happily in the sun. They seem to enjoy looking back at the people eagerly photographing them from the boat, which usually runs backwards and forwards a few times so that everyone can get a close-up view. Children like watching the little animals waddling along the shore (or spotting the odd head bob up and down out of the water), and get real pleasure from seeing them in their natural environment rather than in a specially constructed pool. If your idea of a day out usually runs to something more dynamic and developed, then this won't be for you, but in that case you're hardly likely to have come to this stretch of coast anyway. Several different operators run boats, with the smaller ones owned by the Beans – our favourites. Booking is recommended (especially in summer, when there are crowds of visitors waiting on the quay), on (01263) 740038, and they also recommend you pick up your tickets half an hour or so before departure. Seats are £4 for adults (£3 children under 12) and you'll also have to pay £1.50 for the busy NT car park. Local information centres have full details of operators and times.

Days Out

Royal haunts
Sandringham – stroll in the country park, and visit house if open; lunch at the Feathers, Dersingham or the King's Head in Great Bircham; Castle Rising; King's Lynn.

Down on the farm
Norfolk Lavender, Heacham; lunch at the Rose & Crown in Snettisham; Park Farm, Snettisham; Great Bircham windmill (partly cl Sat).

Pilgrimage by rail
Wells & Walsingham Light Railway, Wells-next-the-Sea; Little Walsingham; lunch at the Moorings or the Crown in Wells-next-the-Sea; stroll in Holkham Hall park, visit mansion; beach at Holkham Gap (walk from car park, or longer walk from Overy Staithe).

Tanks, shells and fairground organs
Muckleborough Collection, Weybourne (or the more peaceable option: Kelling falconry centre); lunch at the White Horse or King's Arms, Blakeney; Glandford shell museum; Thursford Collection; Letheringsett watermill (if open).

Landscapes of the Broads
Fairhaven Garden Trust, South Walsham, or rent a boat from Wroxham; lunch at the Ferry, Reedham; walk along the River Yare, or take a boat or train from Great Yarmouth to Berney Arms windmill.

Breckland secrets
Grimes Graves; lunch at the Crown, Mundford; East Wretham Heath nature reserve, and/or walk the Pingo Trail (see **Walks** section below).

To the manor born
Walk in Mannington Hall/Wolterton Park estates, Saxthorpe; visit Mannington Hall gardens if open; lunch at the Saracen's Head, Wolterton, or the Buckinghamshire Arms in Blickling; Blickling Hall.

Village nostalgia, animal exotica
Horsey windmill, Horsey Mere and beach; lunch at the Nelson Head, Horsey; The Village, Burgh St Margaret, or Thrigby Hall wildlife gardens, Filby.

Stepping back in time
Castle Acre; lunch at the Twenty Churchwardens, Cockley Cley; Iceni village and museum there; Oxburgh Hall, Oxborough.

Cultural Norwich
Cathedral; castle; lunch at Adlards (Upper St Giles St) or the Adam & Eve (Bishopgate); Sainsbury Centre for Visual Arts.

✿ † **Attleborough** TM0495 PETER BEALES ROSE NURSERY A specialist in old-fashioned roses that you won't find for sale elsewhere. The 15th-c CHURCH is interesting, with an unusual round tower and a screen decorated with the arms of the 24 bishoprics in England when it was built. The White Lodge has decent food.

🚂 **Aylsham** TG1926 BURE VALLEY RAILWAY Steamtrain trips along 9 miles of narrow gauge track between here and Wroxham; you can combine the journey with a 1½-hour cruise on the Broads. The stock isn't very old, but the people are friendly and the journey is good value. Snacks, shop, disabled access; trains late Mar–Sept, best to ring for timetable; (01263) 733858; £6.90 full return (£10.50 inc Broads cruise).

🏰 **Baconsthorpe** TG1237 BACONSTHORPE CASTLE The gatehouses, curtain walls and towers are all that's left of this moated and semi-fortified 15th-c house, but displays show what it must have looked like in its glory. A very pretty, peaceful spot, with swans on the lake adding to its charm; free. You can find information booklets at the nearby post office. The Hare & Hounds on the way to Hempstead is useful for lunch.

🐘🐾 **Banham** TM0688 BANHAM ZOO (The Grove) Over 20 acres of parkland and garden with rare and endangered species, particularly monkeys and apes. Also an indoor activity centre, ice-cream parlour, play area, putting green and across the road a CRAFT CENTRE around a cobbled courtyard. Helpful explanatory notes beside the enclosures, and feeding times are spread throughout the day. Regular visitors tell us it gets better with every visit. Meals, snacks, shop, disabled access; cl 25–26 Dec; (01953) 887771; £5.95 (crafts free). The King's Head, opposite the medieval market hall in New Buckenham, has inexpensive home cooking.

⚓ **Blakeney** TG0243 *See separate Family Panel above* for the SEAL BOAT TRIPS from harbour. Crabbing is fun

from here too, and surprisingly successful. Also long breezy walks, unspoilt flint cottages, and a very good tea shop; besides the Blakeney Hotel, the Manor, White Horse and King's Arms are all worthwhile.

🏠🖼✿ **Blickling** TG1728 BLICKLING HALL (off the B1354) Magnificent house dating mainly from the early 17th c, though the hedges that flank it may be older. Dramatic carved oak staircase and splendid paintings (inc a famous Canaletto), but best of all are the 38-metre (125-ft) Long Gallery with its ornate Jacobean plaster ceiling, and the Chinese bedroom, still lined with 18th-c hand-painted wallpaper. The gardens and grounds are lovely, with several miles of footpaths. Meals, snacks, shop, plant centre, good disabled access (a lift in the house); open pm Thurs–Sun and bank hols Apr–Oct; (01263) 733084; £5.50, £6.50 Sun and bank hols; NT. There's free public access to the park on the W side of the pike-filled lake, with a pleasant walk from the Buckinghamshire Arms (which is good for lunch).

🐦⚓ **Brancaster/Scolt Head** TF8045 Miles of dunes, flat coastal saltings and broad tidal beaches: a fine lonely place, largely National Trust and full of birds – Scolt Head island is an important breeding ground, and in good weather a boat takes people across from Brancaster Staithe. Incidentally, all along this coast the wading birds, surprisingly approachable, are best seen on a falling tide. The Jolly Sailors is useful for lunch.

🌿🦋🐦 **Breckland** Around Thetford, this is a region of poor, flat, sandy heathland with scattered shallow meres and originally scrubby mixed woodland, extensively planted now with pines instead; there are forest walks, for example from car parks on the A134 NW of Thetford, where you may disturb roe deer. A good place to see it as it was is the East Wretham Heath NATURE RESERVE TL9188 off the A1075 NE of Thetford: plenty of wild flowers, nature trails, and hides for watching the birds and deer; free.

Bressingham TM0780
BRESSINGHAM STEAM MUSEUM AND
GARDENS (off the A1066) The
founder, Alan Bloom, has effectively
combined his two interests at this
rewarding site. The 6 acres of
informal gardens are planted with
5,000 species and cultivars of alpines
and perennials in island beds, with
lots of the dwarf conifers Bloom has
done so much to popularise. Then
there's the excellent steam collection,
inc 50 road and rail engines, mostly
restored to working order. 4 steam-
hauled trains run through the
charming countryside and parts of
the garden. Meals, snacks, shop,
disabled access; cl Nov–Mar, and
museum also cl wkdys in Oct;
(01379) 687382; £4. The Garden
House is handy for lunch.

Burgh Castle TG4805 CASTLE
You can still see sections of the
massive walls of this coastal Roman
fortress, built in the 3rd c to protect
the coast from Saxon marauders;
free. The Church Farm Inn
overlooking the Yare and Waveney
has decent food. Across the water
from here, and accessible only by
foot, by boat, or by rail from Great
Yarmouth, the 7-storey BERNEY ARMS
WINDMILL dates from the 19th c when
it was used to drain water from the
marshes. Cl 1–2pm, and Oct–Mar;
(01493) 700605; £1.10.

Burgh St Margaret
TG4414 THE VILLAGE (A1064)
Delightful pastiche of a 19th-c
village, but an idealised one rather
than an authentic set-up along the
lines of somewhere like Beamish up in
Northumbria. Old-fashioned
fairground rides (inc traditional
Victorian gallopers), candle-making
and other crafts, and amusing live
shows – the puppet show effectively
blends marionettes with people. Also
silent comedy films in the 1920s
concert hall, miniature railway,
steam-hauled trailer rides, working
sawmill, collections of vintage
motorbikes and other vehicles, woodland walks, and a decent adventure
play area. Meals, snacks, shops,
disabled access; cl Nov–Feb; (01493)
369770; *£4.95 (*£2.50 Sat, when

less going on: no crafts or live shows).

Burnham Thorpe TF8441 This
hamlet's strong Lord Nelson
connections include a pub named
after him, with interesting related
memorabilia. The lectern in the
village church uses wood from HMS
Victory, and the church has other
Nelson mementos.

Caister-on-Sea TG5212 Like
the other settlements down this coast,
Caister plays host to many summer
visitors, with all the usual attractions,
inc long sandy beaches. It's also got a
lifeboat station, right by the beach. A
ruined moated CASTLE is set back from
the town, a little way inland. Falstaff
(the original behind Shakespeare's
creation) built it on returning from
Agincourt; its walls surround a 30-
metre (98-ft) tower. The grounds
contain a MOTOR MUSEUM with a good
collection of vehicles from 1893
onwards. Snacks, some disabled
access; open daily exc Sat mid-
May–Sept; (01572) 787251; £4.50.
The town has various remains of an
excavated ROMAN FORT inc one
gateway and a town wall.

Castle Acre TF8115 A
delightful village, with an 18th-c feel
along the tree-shaded walk of Stocks
Green (the Ostrich here is handy for
lunch). Extensive ruins of a Cluniac
PRIORY built by William the
Conqueror's son-in-law include the
fine arcaded west front of the
11th/12th-c church, a chapel and
15th-c gatehouse; good Walkman
tour. Well laid out, and very
picturesque. Snacks, shop, some
disabled access; cl winter Mon and
Tues, 24–26 Dec, and maybe 1–2pm
for lunch; (01760) 755394; £2.75.
Beside these relics are the sparser yet
still awe-inspiring ruins of a great
CASTLE built at the same time. The site
is on the Peddars Way, a Roman road
following the track of an earlier
herding way. West Acre, 2 or 3 miles
W, has a few further priory remains,
and (like Castle Acre itself)
picturesque fords over the River Nar.
A few miles N, some private
woodland opens for 3 weeks in late
spring for its magnificent azaleas.

Castle Rising TF6624 CASTLE

Massive earthworks surround this fine Norman keep, a marvellous setting for the summer jousting they occasionally stage here. Shop, limited disabled access; cl winter Mon and Tues, 24–26 Dec; (01553) 631330; £2.10. In the attractive village, the Black Horse is a popular dining pub.

✝ ✠ 🌼 **Cley-next-the-Sea** TG0443 Handy for the bird-sanctuary marshes towards the Blakeney Point sandspit, a pleasant village with a magnificent CHURCH. The neatly restored WINDMILL is a more obvious landmark, and has great views from the top (open pm Easter–Oct; £1.50), as well as very good accommodation. *The Albatros*, Europe's last sailing cargo boat, makes the trip from Rotterdam every fortnight or so and has occasional berths – (0031) 1184 89450. There's a long pebbly beach.

🗗 ✈ ✝ ⌂ 🎦 **Cockley Cley** TF7904 Lots of interesting historical things to see around this village (pronounced to rhyme with 'fry'). There's a MUSEUM in a 17th-c cottage, nature reserve, carriage collection and 7th-c Saxon church, but most unusual is the ICENI VILLAGE, built as and where it was believed to exist 2,000 years ago. Snacks, shop, disabled access; cl Nov–Mar; (01760) 721339; £3.30 covers all attractions. The Twenty Churchwardens is handy for lunch.

✝ 🌼 🗗 ❀ **Cromer** TG2242 Popular seaside resort since Victorian times, with lovely sandy beaches, more sun than average, bustling markets, golf courses, interesting shops and galleries and lots of entertainments. The pier is one of the last in the country to present an end-of-pier show – very popular, so worth booking early. The tower of the imposing CHURCH on Church St – Norfolk's tallest – gives spectacular views of the surrounding countryside. A good local history MUSEUM next door is spread over 5 19th-c fishermen's cottages (cl Mon lunch, Good Fri, 23–26 Dec, 1 Jan; £1.10), and on the promenade a small LIFEBOAT MUSEUM looks at local lifeboatman Henry Blogg, who over 53 years saved 873 lives (cl Nov–Apr; free). Nearby you often find dressed

crabs for sale; the crab boats still work from here, and Cromer crabs are the best on England's east coast. The seafront Bath House has decent food and good bedrooms.

✝ 🗗 ⌂ **Downham Market** TF6103 HERMITAGE HALL (Bridge Farm, A1122 just W) Based around an old chapel used by pilgrims on the way to Walsingham, now with mementos of local boy Nelson (inc letters, birth certificate and death mask), small collection of cars, Victorian street, and gentle walks down to the Ouse. Snacks, shop, disabled acess; guided tours 1pm Sun Easter–Dec; (01366) 383185; £5 (inc tot of Norfolk punch). There's an adjacent animal sanctuary.

✈ **Earsham** TM3289 OTTER TRUST (off the A143) This charitable trust works towards reintroducing otters to rivers from which they've disappeared; they're displayed here in a natural environment. They're obviously cheerful and intelligent, but don't perform on demand and you may have to wait a while to see anything. Snacks, shop, disabled access; cl Oct–Mar; (01986) 893470; £4.50. The Green Dragon in Bungay is a heartening retreat if they don't show.

🐝 🗗 ⚘ **Erpingham** TG1931 ALBY CRAFTS AND GARDENS 4 acres of interesting shrubs, plants and bulbs, with a museum devoted to lace, another concentrating on bottles (over 2,000 of them, mainly from regional brewers), bee observation hive, and crafts inc woodturning and stained glass. Very good roses and lilies in July. Meals, snacks, shop, mostly disabled access; cl Mon (exc bank hols), all wkdys mid-Jan–mid-Mar (lace museum also cl Sat); (01263) 761226; crafts free, gardens and museums *£1.50. The Ark, and the Saracen's Head out at Wolterton (at the start of a pleasant 2- or 3-hour circular walk), are both very good for lunch.

★ ✈ ▣ **Fakenham** TF9229 A pleasant market town; the comfortable Wensum Lodge Hotel has decent food (as does the prettily set Sculthorpe Mill, off the A148 just

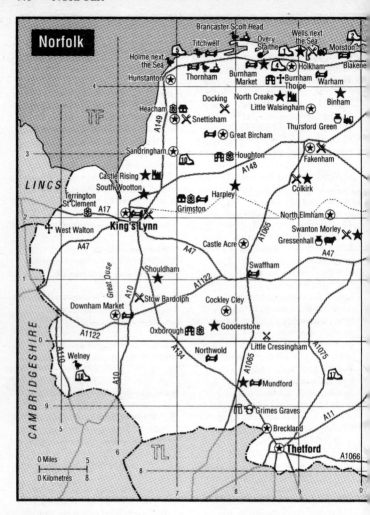

W), and the roads N pass through attractive villages. PENSTHORPE WATERFOWL TRUST (Pensthorpe, A1067) Good-sized collection of wild and exotic waterfowl, many of them rare. The visitor centre has displays of wildlife art and photography. Also woodland, meadow, lakeside and riverside nature trails, and very good talks and events. Meals, snacks, shop, disabled access; cl wkdys Jan–mid-Mar, 25 Dec; (01328) 851465; £4.45.

Felbrigg TG2039 FELBRIGG HALL Magnificent 17th-c house in splendid grounds, inc an orangery with a fine collection of camellias, and a colourfully restored walled garden overlooked by a dovecot. The house is decorated with paintings and furnishings from the 18th c, and has a wonderful Gothic library. Lots of events, with something going on at the stable block most Sun afternoons. Meals, snacks, shop, disabled access; hall and gardens cl Thurs, Fri, and Nov–Mar, hall also cl am, grounds cl 25 Dec only; (01263) 837444; £5.20, garden only £2; NT. There's public access to the woods and lake.

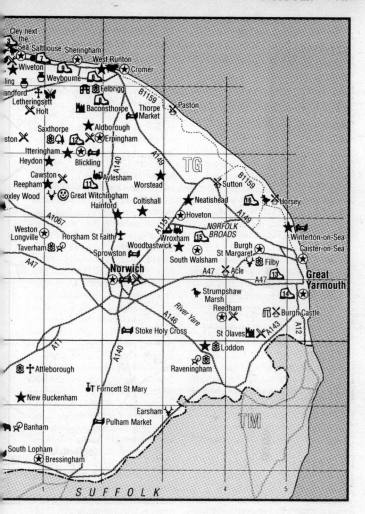

✿ 🏛 **Filby** TG4613 THRIGBY HALL
WILDLIFE GARDENS 18th-c park filled
with Asian animals and birds, with
tropical and bird houses, tree walk,
willow pattern garden, and
ornamental wildfowl on the lake.
Also a huge, jungly swamp hall where
crocodiles doze under water. Readers
enjoy coming here – though warn of
queues on summer wknds. Summer
snacks, shop, disabled access;
(01493) 369477; *£5.
⚙ **Forncett St Mary** TM1694
INDUSTRIAL STEAM MUSEUM Unusual
collection of stationary steam engines

rescued from all over the country, inc
one that used to open Tower Bridge.
Snacks, shop, disabled access; open
pm 1st Sun of month, May–Dec,
when the engines are in steam;
(01508) 488277; £3 (2 children free
with every adult). The Bird in Hand,
over at Wreningham, is a good-value
dining pub.
✿ **Foxley Wood** TG0321 A big block
of ancient woodland, mainly
deciduous and grown naturally for
many centuries; lovely woodland
spring flowers.
👁 **Glandford** TG0441 SHELL MUSEUM

Curious little museum housing the often very beautiful seashells and other interesting objects collected by Sir Alfred Jodrell, who lived in nearby Bayfield Hall. Shop, disabled access; cl lunchtimes, all Sun and Mon (exc bank hols), and winter exc by appointment; (01263) 740081; £1.50. The King's Head at Letheringsett is quite handy for lunch.

※ ❀ ★ 🅰 **Great Bircham** TF7732 WINDMILL Not far from Houghton Hall, this striking mill is on that Norfolk rarity, a hill – so one of the few places with views. They sell bread baked at the mill's own bakery. Snacks, shop, some disabled access; cl Oct–Easter, tearooms and bakery also cl Sat; (01485) 578393; £2. You can hire bikes. The village is attractive, with an art gallery, and the King's Head Hotel (unpretentious despite being a favourite with Sandringham shooting parties) is good for lunch.

✇ ☺ **Great Witchingham** TG1021 NORFOLK WILDLIFE PARK (A1067) 40 acres of attractive parkland with a good range of British and European wildlife; tame animals include a team of trained reindeer who take children for rides on a wheeled sledge. You can feed some of the animals (and carp), and there are big play areas. Meals, snacks, shop; cl Nov–Mar; (01603) 872274; *£4. The Old Brewery House in Reepham is the nearest decent place for lunch.

♪ ✇ ! 🏵 ☺ ☗ ⊕ 🏚 ❀ † **Great Yarmouth** TG5207 A cross between working town and resort, this still has a busy fishing harbour – used too as a port of call by the Broads cruising boats. There are lots of holiday entertainments; the first 3 attractions we list here are all good for families and holiday-makers (there's a decent fairground too), but the others might well tempt older visitors into the town if they were nearby. The best pubs here are the White Lion (King St) and Red Herring (Havelock Rd).

SEA LIFE CENTRE (Marine Parade) Displays of the kinds of marine life found on the Norfolk coast, as well as underwater tunnels through shark-infested oceans and tropical fish. Meals, snacks, shop, disabled access; cl 25 Dec; (01493) 330631; *£5.50.

AMAZONIA 🆓 (Sea Front) Recently opened cousin to a similar centre at Bowness up in Cumbria, an indoor tropical paradise with reptiles, insects, butterflies and birds; they have a 4-metre (13-ft) alligator, a python well over 7 metres long (24 ft), and an iguana named Levi. Snacks, shop, disabled access; cl 25 Dec; (01493) 842202; £3.95.

MERRIVALE MODEL VILLAGE (Wellington Pier Gardens) Attractive, landscaped gardens with children's rides and remote-controlled cars, and the exceptionally detailed village – featuring a railway, radio-controlled boats and over 200 models. Meals, snacks, disabled access; cl Nov–Easter; (01493) 842097; £2.80.

ELIZABETHAN HOUSE MUSEUM (South Quay) A patchwork of historical detail – built in 1596, it has a Georgian façade, 16th-c panelled rooms and, among features from later periods, some rooms decorated and furnished in 19th-c style, and a functional Victorian kitchen. Shop, disabled access to ground floor only; open 2 wks at Easter, then daily exc Sat Jun–Sept; (01493) 855746; £1.10 – entry to either here or one of the following 2 museums includes admission to the others. The MARITIME MUSEUM OF EAST ANGLIA (Marine Parade) looks at the local fishing industry exhibits, with some more incongruous features inc a mummified hand and an Indian scalp; times as Elizabethan house; (01493) 842267; 70p. The 13th-c TOLHOUSE MUSEUM (Tolhouse St) used to be the town's gaol and courthouse (you can still see the dungeons). It now has local history exhibits, and a brass rubbing centre; times and prices as Elizabethan house. The last surviving steam drifter, the *Lydia Eva*, can usually be visited in South Quay Easter–Oct; donations. OLD MERCHANT'S HOUSE (Row 117) 17th-c house standing among the narrow lanes or Rows nr the waterfront, with some well restored rooms. Shop; cl 1–2pm, and all Oct–Mar; *£1.60.

The 44-metre (144-ft) NELSON'S MONUMENT has fine views of the town at the top of its 217 steps; open pm Sun July and Aug, and 21 Oct, Trafalgar Day; 75p. The 14th-c CHURCH of St Nicholas, at the top end of the market place, has an exceptionally wide nave and an impressive west front.

🐑 ✿ **Gressenhall** TF9615 NORFOLK RURAL LIFE MUSEUM AND UNION FARM Re-creation of a typical 1920s farm, with rare breeds of sheep, pigs, cattle and poultry, and working reconstructions of agricultural life. Meals, snacks, shop, disabled access; cl am Sun, and Nov–Easter; (01362) 860563; £3.70. The White Horse at Longham has good-value food.

✿ 🏛 **Grimes Graves** TL8189 Bring a torch to this Breckland site, as you can climb into one of the 300 pits and vertical shafts which lead down into the galleries – some around 10 metres (33 ft) deep – where the Neolithic people mined their flint. No lavatories at the site, but there are some within a mile. Shop, disabled access; cl 1–2pm, all Mon and Tues Nov–Mar, 24–26 Dec, 1 Jan; (01842) 810656; £1.60.

✿ 🏠 **Grimston** TF7222 CONGHAM HALL HERB GARDEN In summer this has around 500 different herbs, in traditional layouts, with many unusual varieties for sale; open 2–4pm Apr–Sept (cl Sat); free.

✿ 🏠 **Heacham** TF6737 NORFOLK LAVENDER (Caley Mill) The largest lavender-growing and distilling operation in the country, along with a national collection of lavender species and cultivars. The guided tour (daily from spring bank hol–Sept) really adds interest, and at harvest time they may drive visitors out to the fields. Also rose and herb gardens. Snacks (inc their lavender and lemon scones), shop, disabled access; cl 2 wks after Christmas; (01485) 570384; tours £1.50 when distilling. The Gin Trap at Ringstead (with a decent nearby art gallery) and Rose & Crown at Snettisham both have good food.

🏠 ✿ 🖼 ✿ **Holkham** TF8944 HOLKHAM HALL Splendid Palladian mansion in delightful and very extensive tree-filled grounds, with an ornamental lake and 18th-c walled garden. Sumptuously furnished state rooms, with fine paintings by Claude, Rubens, Van Dyck and Gainsborough. An ancestor of the present owner was Thomas Coke, whose revolutionary farming techniques are described in an exhibition in the porter's lodge; there's also a pottery. Snacks, shop, limited disabled access; open pm Thurs, Sun, and bank hols Easter–Oct; (01328) 710227; £5 for everything, £3 hall only. The Victoria Hotel is handy for lunch. The beach has a bird reserve (and a nudist section).

✕ ✦ **Horsey** TG4522 A quiet corner of the coast, below sea level – among the places most at risk of flooding if the sea defences are breached. There's a good path to the dunes and the sea from the lane past the Nelson Head (nice food). On the other side of the main road, HORSEY WINDPUMP is a restored drainage windmill, now in full working order. Teas, small shop, some disabled access; cl Oct–Mar; £1.20; NT. A path from here goes round the N side of quiet Horsey Mere, and on up the New Cut to another former drainage windmill, from where you can walk back to the village; the marshes on the far side of the Cut seem alive with birds.

✦ **Horsham St Faith** TG2114 NORWICH AVIATION MUSEUM (Old Norwich Rd) Enthusiastic displays of local aeronautical history, with aircraft (there's a Vulcan bomber), engines and other paraphernalia; on the edge of Norwich Airport, so a good view of the live article too. Snacks, shop; open Sun and bank hols, and some other summer afternoons and evenings; (01603) 625309; £2.50. The thatched Chequers, prettily placed at Hainford, has decent food.

🏠 ✿ **Houghton** TF7927 HOUGHTON HALL 🔲 Built for Robert Walpole and obviously designed to impress, this is a spectacularly grand Palladian mansion set in charming parkland. The state rooms were decorated and furnished by William Kent, and house an important collection of 20,000 model soldiers and other militaria. Heavy horses, Shetland ponies and llamas in the stables. Snacks, shop, disabled access; open pm Thurs, Sun and bank hols Easter–Sept; (01485) 528569; £5.50. Driving along the C-road nr North Pole farm you may spot unusual herds of white deer. The 17th-c Duke's Head at West Rudham has good home cooking.

⚅ ⚘ ☛ Hoveton TG3018 HOVETON HALL GARDEN Large and attractive spring woodland garden with daffodils and rhododendrons, a lakeside walk, walled and old-fashioned herbaceous garden and a kitchen garden. You can stay in a wing of the house. Teas, plant sales, disabled access; open Weds, Fri, Sun and bank hols Easter–mid-Sept; (01603) 782798; *£3. Good for families, Wroxham Barns CRAFT CENTRE (Tunstead Rd) has several craft workshops in 18th-c restored farm buildings, as well as a children's farm and traditional fair. Meals, snacks, shop, play area, disabled access; cl 25–26 Dec; (01603) 783762; £2 for farm, otherwise free. The Black Horse is useful for lunch.

♨ ⚑ ☝ ⊚ Hunstanton TF6740 Clean, fresh and well kept resort with gently shelving tidal sands (donkey rides still), summer boat trips, and pleasant dune walks past the golf course up to the BIRD RESERVE on Gore Point. On a clear day you can see Boston's Stump across The Wash. An ocean tunnel at the excellent SEA LIFE CENTRE (Southern Promenade) brings you face to face with deep-water creatures as well as octopuses and toothy conger eels. Meals, snacks, shop, disabled access; cl 25 Dec; (01485) 533576; £5.25. Standing out among the typical resort entertainments is OASIS, a giant leisure park on the promenade, with tropically heated indoor and outdoor pools and both towering and toddler aquaslides (cl Dec and Jan; £3). The low cliffs around the town are quite colourful, with different rock strata. The Ancient Mariner (part of Le Strange Hotel, Old Hunstanton) is

good value, opposite an interesting craft gallery, and the Marine Bar (St Edmund's Terrace) has decent food all day.

⚑ Kelling TG0942 FALCONRY CENTRE (Weybourne Rd) Over a hundred or so kestrels, sparrowhawks and owls, as well as rarer peregrine falcons and redtail hawks; flying displays at midday, 2pm and 4pm (weather permitting). Meals, snacks, shop, disabled access; winter cl am and all Mon; (01263) 712235; £3. The attached Kelling Park Hotel is friendly and, reasonably priced.

✝ ⚏ ♒ ! ☝ King's Lynn TF6220 Once England's fourth largest town, it's quieter now, with pleasant corners, some attractive Georgian brick buildings and a few much older places such as the 17th-c Custom House on the quay by the River Purfleet, the 15th-c CHURCH of St Nicholas (Chapel Lane; attractive for festival concerts), the South Gates, Red Mount Chapel and the 2 medieval guildhalls. The first of these, the 15th-c ST GEORGE'S GUILDHALL (King St), is now the town's theatre, and home of the King's Lynn Festival; the tourist information centre has details of tours, (01553) 763044. The handsome Trinity Guildhall (Saturday Market Pl) is not open to the public, but the 14th-c King John Cup and other fabulous examples of civic paraphernalia housed in its undercroft are included in the tour of the OLD GAOL HOUSE (also Saturday Market Pl), a lively journey through the town's rich history. With spirited models, and spooky sights, sounds and smells, this is particularly good for children. Shop, disabled access; cl Weds and Thurs from Nov–Easter; (01553) 763044; *£2. The restored old fishermen's cottages at TRUES YARD (North St) give a good picture of life here in the last century, when families of up to 11 were often squeezed into 2 little rooms. Snacks, shop, disabled access; cl 25 Dec; (01553) 770479; £1.90. More social history at the TOWN HOUSE MUSEUM on Queen St (cl Sun exc pm May–Sept; £1.10), while the LYNN MUSEUM (Old Market Sq) includes the skeleton of a Saxon warrior, and a surprisingly interesting collection of medieval pilgrims' badges (cl Sun and Mon; *70p). On Tues the main market place has some good crafts stalls. The Tudor Rose between there and St Nicholas is handy for lunch, and the Globe Hotel on the market place itself is good value.

✝ 🦋 **Letheringsett** TG0538 The CHURCH has an unusual round tower, and the restored WATERMILL, in a pretty setting, still mills flour from local wheat. Cl 1–2pm, Sun (exc school and bank hols), Mon, and pm Sat in winter; demonstrations pm; (01263) 713153; £2.75 during demonstrations, otherwise £1.75. The King's Head is pleasant for lunch.

🏛 🏵 🏰🖐 **Little Walsingham** TF9336 Once as popular a centre of pilgrimage as Canterbury, thanks to a replica of the Virgin Mary's home in Nazareth. Things tailed off when Henry VIII destroyed the priory and its shrine in 1538, but picked up again earlier this century.
WALSINGHAM ABBEY GROUNDS still have plenty of remains of the 12th-c building, inc the abbey gates, great arch, part of the refectory and the holy wells. Pleasant gardens and woodland walks, with masses of snowdrops in early spring. Gates of site open Apr–Sept. You can also gain entrance through the estate office whenever it's open – generally weekday office hours; (01328) 820259; *£1.50. The nearby SHIREHALL MUSEUM has a particular emphasis on the pilgrimage to Walsingham; displays are in an almost perfect Georgian courtroom complete with original fittings. Shop, limited disabled access; cl Sun, and Nov–Mar; 60p museum only, £2 museum and grounds. The Bull Inn is a good place, with plenty of pilgrimage customers.

🏵 ★ **Loddon** TM3698 READS NURSERY (Hales Hall, off the A146 SE) Specialising for the last century in unusual conservatory plants, inc a good range of lemon, orange and other citrus fruits, also nut trees etc. Disabled access; cl Mon (exc bank

hols), Sun exc pm Jun–Sept, 25 Dec–5 Jan; (01508) 548395; nursery free, barn and garden £1.50. The village is attractive, and the 17th-c Swan has home-made food.

🏛 ★ **North Creake** TF8538 CREAKE ABBEY All that remains of this early 13th-c Augustinian priory is the crossing and east arm, but it's still worth a passing look, and the village is charming. Cartwrights at South Creake has good food.

✝ 🏛 🖐 **North Elmham** TF9820 CHURCH An attractive 13th-c building, odd in that there's a step down into it; a little further N are the interesting ruins of a SAXON CATHEDRAL, and there are pleasant walks. The King's Head has decent food, and a nearby vineyard can be visited.

🏰 🏵 **Oxborough** TF7401 OXBURGH HALL Henry VIII stayed in this pretty moated manor house in 1487, and the room is now decorated with wall hangings worked by Mary Queen of Scots. Unfortunately, most of the house was thoroughly refurbished during Victorian times, but the gatehouse remains as an awe-inspiring example of 15th-c building work, 24 metres (80 ft) high. The garden has a colourful French parterre. Meals, snacks, shop, disabled access; cl am, Thurs, Fri, and Nov–Mar; (01366) 328258; £4.60, £2.30 garden only; NT. The Bedingfeld Arms opposite has reasonable food.

🏵 🌿 **Raveningham** TM3996 RAVENINGHAM HALL GARDENS Interesting collection of rare shrubs, shrub roses, traditional kitchen garden, arboretum, and Victorian conservatory. Teas Sun and bank hols; gardens open pm Sun and bank hols May–Jun, arboretum open daily exc wknds Nov–Feb; (01508) 548222; £2. RAVENINGHAM CRAFT WORKSHOPS (Beccles Rd) Victorian farm buildings with furniture-making, antiques and other workshops; teas; free. Loddon's the best nearby place for a meal.

🌿 ☺ 🚶♿ **Reedham** TG4101 PETTITTS FEATHERCRAFT AND ANIMAL ADVENTURE PARK You can still watch the demonstrations of feathercraft, though they've become a little swamped by the other attractions here, inc aviaries, a gnome village, an American-style locomotive ride around the grounds, big adventure playground, miniature horse stud, a deer-petting park and crazy golf. Snacks, shop, some disabled access; cl Sat, and Nov–Easter (exc bank hols); (01493) 701403; *£6.50. The waterside Ferry is popular for lunch, and the little car ferry here is fun. ▓ **St Olaves** TM4599 ST OLAVE'S PRIORY Ruins of a 13th-c Augustinian priory; you can still see the fine brick undercroft in the cloister – a remarkable early use of this material; free. The riverside Bell is very old indeed, though much modernised. ⌂ ▩ † ⟠ ⌨ ⛵ **Sandringham** TF6928 Many people come to this part of the county for its connection with the royal family. SANDRINGHAM HOUSE was bought by Queen Victoria for her son Edward in 1862 and has become famous as the royal Christmas residence; the 19th-c building is filled with their portraits and those of their European counterparts, and has various gifts presented to the family over the years. Unlike at their other homes, you can see most of the rooms the family use, so there's a much more intimate feel than you'd get at Windsor or Buckingham Palace; expect queues though. The grounds and surrounding country park are lovely, with nature trails, adventure playground, and the parish Church of St Mary Magdalene, familiar from Christmas Day news programmes. Lovely rhododendrons in the woods May/Jun. Meals, snacks, shop, disabled access (a train runs between the entrance to the grounds and the house); open Easter–Sept, exc during summer Royal visit – best to check for dates; (01553) 772675; £4.50, £3.50 grounds and museum only. In summer, PICK-YOUR-OWN lets you sample fruit that might otherwise have graced the royal table. The Feathers towards Dersingham is useful for lunch. ▩ ⚘ **Saxthorpe** TG1130 MANNINGTON GARDENS AND

COUNTRYSIDE The most beautiful feature of these gardens is the summer rose display, but 20 miles of footpaths around the Hall and woodland are open all year. Snacks, shop, disabled access; gardens open pm Sun May–Sept, plus Weds–Fri Jun–Aug; (01263) 874175; £3. Paths lead to the pleasant grounds of Wolterton Park. The riverside Walpole Arms at Itteringham has good food. ⟠ ★ † ▩ ❀ **Sheringham** TG1443 The working fishing harbour has some old buildings around it, though there's a lot of more modern building up behind. The beach is nice, and the Two Lifeboats has fine sea views (as well as decent food inc fresh fish). NORTH NORFOLK RAILWAY Full-size steam railway, chugging through over 5 miles of lovely coastal scenery to Holt, a pleasant little town with some handsome Georgian buildings (Nicholsons in the High St sells anything from clothes to antiques and has a useful, continental-style licensed café). Plenty of railway memorabilia at the Sheringham station, and a collection of steam engines and vintage rolling stock. Meals, snacks, shop, disabled access; steamtrains Mar–Oct and Dec;, (01263) 822045 for timetable; £6.50 full return journey. The 14th-c CHURCH in the quiet flintstone village of Upper Sheringham nearby is very attractive, and the Red Lion makes a pleasant stop for refreshment. Footpaths from here lead to the extensive parkland of SHERINGHAM PARK, gloriously landscaped by Humphrey Repton (it was his favourite work), which gives excellent coastal views from its viewing towers. Also mature trees and fine rhododendrons (best late May/Jun), with good walks to the coast. Snacks, disabled access; (01263) 823778; free, but parking £2.60; NT. ⬛ ⚘ ✿ **Snettisham** TF6834 PARK FARM ▨ Working farm offering good insight into seasonal farming operations – lambing, shearing, and red deer calving. Lots of animals, plus an impressive adventure playground, craft centre and mini golf. Meals, snacks, shop, disabled access; cl some days in winter, so best to check first out of season; (01485) 542425; £3.95 for either farm or 45-minute guided ride around deer park, £7.90 for both. Pretty walks nearby, as well as a nature reserve along the beach. The Rose & Crown is a good dining pub.

South Walsham TG3613 FAIRHAVEN GARDEN TRUST Charming wooded watergardens set beside the private South Walsham Inner Broad, the waterways linked by little bridges. Rare plants, masses of rhododendrons among the flowers and a tree – the King Oak – said to be 900 years old. It's an extensive place, running to some 230 acres, inc a big BIRD SANCTUARY – to visit this part you need permission from the warden Mr Debbage. Boat trips every half-hour. Snacks, shop, disabled access – but paths are quite uneven; open Easter wk, then Tues–Sun plus bank hols May–Sept, cl am Sat; (01603) 270449; £3. The Ship has good home cooking.

Strumpshaw Marsh TG3306 (off Low Rd, Brundall) Partly drained watermeadows and fen between woodland and the River Yare, with RSPB hides for watching marsh birds inc harriers and bearded tits, winter geese, and maybe swallowtail butterflies in Jun; £2.50. The Yare Inn in Brundall is popular for food.

Taverham TG1513 There's a very large GARDEN CENTRE here, with an adjoining courtyard of CRAFT WORKSHOPS; teas.

Terrington St Clement TF5419 AFRICAN VIOLET CENTRE Wide range of plants besides the African violets it's developed so successfully as house plants; the owner is also a priest, and runs services in a former packing shed here. Good tearoom; (01553) 828374. The Woolpack at Walpole Cross Keys has decent food.

Thetford TL8783 ANCIENT HOUSE MUSEUM Early Tudor house with fine oak ceilings, now a local history museum with a small, period herb garden behind. Shop; cl 12.30–1pm, Sun (exc pm in summer); (01842) 752599; free exc July and Aug, when 70p. THETFORD PRIORY Ruins of a 12th-c Cluniac monastery; you can easily make out the full ground plan of the cloisters, and the 14th-c gatehouse still stands; disabled access; free. WARREN LODGE 15th-c flint former hunting lodge, worth a look. The Bell and Thomas Paine are both civilised places for lunch.

Thursford Green TF9833 THURSFORD COLLECTION Bouncy collection of musical organs, whether barrel, street or fairground. Most are demonstrated every day, and the Wurlitzer cinema organ also stars in concerts on summer Tues evenings. Showmen's steam engines too, and a 2-ft gauge steam railway, adventure playground, and Venetian Gondola switchback ride. Meals, snacks, shop, disabled access; cl am and Oct–Mar; (01328) 878477; £4.40.

★ **Wells-next-the-Sea** TF9143 Pleasant and rather gracious little village-sized town; don't be fooled by the name – the sea is a mile away these days. The Crown is good for lunch. WELLS & WALSINGHAM LIGHT RAILWAY Passing through delightful countryside, this railway is remarkable for being the longest in Britain to use a 10¼-inch-gauge track, with a steam locomotive built specially for it a few years ago. Snacks, shop, some disabled access; cl Oct–Easter; (01328) 856506 for times; *£4.50 return.

Welney TL5294 WILDFOWL AND WETLANDS TRUST (Hundred Foot Bank) Excellent 1,000 acre wild bird reserve, with numerous hides, spacious observatory, and a floodlit lagoon. In winter, the sights include up to 4,000 migratory Bewick's swans and numerous species of duck; it can be busy then, and you'll need to wrap up well. In spring, the emphasis switches to waders and other birds. There's also a summer nature trail, see **Walks** section below. Snacks, shop, disabled access; cl 25 Dec; (01353) 860711; £3. In winter some local roads can be flooded, and then you can approach it only from the E. The Jenyns Arms at Denver Sluice TF5800, with peacocks in its riverside gardens, is fairly handy for lunch, nr the towering hydraulic sluices which control water levels in these parts – quite a sight.

🐎 ★ **West Runton** TG1842 NORFOLK SHIRE HORSE CENTRE (West Runton Stables) Extensive collection of draught horses and moorland and mountain ponies (they have 9 breeds). You can hire riding horses by the hour, and there's a children's farm (though some readers feel the aviaries and hutches are a little crowded). Meals, snacks, shop, disabled access; cl Sat (exc maybe July and Aug), and Nov–Mar; (01263) 837339; £4. The seaside village itself is attractive, and the Village Inn is useful for lunch.

† **West Walton** TF4213 CHURCH A textbook example of early Gothic architecture; just about all of it dates from the mid-13th c, and there's a cool elegance throughout. The King of Hearts (good for lunch) holds the key.

🐾 ! ☺ **Weston Longville** TG1115 DINOSAUR PARK (off the A1067) 300 acres of unspoilt woodland with life-sized reconstructions of dinosaurs lying in wait around every corner – good for children to appreciate properly how big some of these beasts were. Also a maze, adventure playground and rural bygones. Snacks, shop, disabled access; cl Nov–Mar; (01603) 870245; £3.95. The Parson Woodforde (village signed off the A1067 in Morton) has popular food.

👃 **Weybourne** TG1042 MUCKLEBURGH COLLECTION (A149) World War II fighting vehicles and other soldierly relics on the site of a former military camp, once the lynch-pin of defences on this coast. Tank demonstrations every Sun, bank hols and wkdys during summer school hols. Meals and snacks (in NAAFI-style café), shop, disabled access; cl Nov–Feb; (01263) 588210; *£3.75. The Dun Cow overlooking the Salthouse marshes has decent food, with a nearby shack selling very fresh shellfish and samphire.

★ **Winterton-on-Sea** TG4919 One of the quieter seaside resorts on this coast, with a gentle villagey feel, and a particularly good beach over the dunes – nice for a wander by the sea; the 17th-c Fisherman's Return is very pleasant for lunch.

👃 🚤 **Wroxham** TG3017 BROADS BOAT CRUISING This is the main centre, with several boat hire firms. So it's a good place to watch the boating activities from dry land, or to use as the start of a longer cruising holiday. It can be very congested in summer. For more land-based transport, the BARTON HOUSE RAILWAY is a miniature railway through a big riverside garden; open 3rd Sun of month in summer, 30p. Boats leave for here from Wroxham Bridge (50p). The Bell has kept more character than many places around. ⌘ We've already mentioned several **windmills** around the area; other fine examples are at Acle TG3910, Little Cressingham TF8700, Paston TG3134 and, best of all, Sutton TG3823 (the tallest mill in the country, 9 floors high – cl Oct–Mar; £1).

🕊 **Bird watching** Norfolk's north coast is particularly rewarding for this. Besides places picked out with their own entries, observation points that have been firmly recommended to us include Holme-next-the-Sea TF7043, Thornham TF7343, and Titchwell TF7543 (a worthwhile RSPB reserve; besides the Manor Hotel, the Three Horseshoes has good-value food and bedrooms).

★ **Other attractive villages** here, all with decent pubs, include Aldborough TG1834, Binham TF9839, opulent Burnham Market TF8342 (also gatehouse and 13th-c priory remains), Colkirk TF9126, Coltishall TG2719, Gooderstone TF7602 (for its ancient church and nearby watergardens), Hainford TG2218, Harpley TF7825, Heydon TG1127 (very unspoilt, with good food at the Earle Arms), Itteringham TG1430, Mundford TL8093, Neatishead TG3420 (by Barton Broad nature reserve), medieval New Buckenham TM0890, Reepham TG0922 (the station has a nostalgia collection), Shouldham TF6708 (nature trails in pleasant woods just N), South Wootton TF6422,

Swanton Morley TG0116, Wiveton TG0342, Woodbastwick TG3315 (a picturesque thatched estate village) and Worstead TG3025.

Decent pubs in attractive coastal areas include the Red Lion at Stiffkey (pronounced 'Stukey') TF9743, Three Horseshoes at Warham TF9441, and Sandpiper at Wighton TF9340 (which has a good art gallery – Henry Moore lived there for 2 years).

The Broads

Norfolk's network of linking waterways is not easy to visit on foot or by car; the best way to see the Broads is undoubtedly by boat. Wroxham, with its neighbour Hoveton, is a major centre for boat hire, and like the other main centre Horning is probably better thought of as a base for longer spells afloat than short breaks or day trips. If you want a boat for just the day, the quieter reaches of the more northern Broads would probably suit you better – say, from Barton Turf TG3522, Hickling TG4123, Stalham TG3725 or Wayford Bridge TG3424. Or for a quick taste, you can combine a boat trip with the trains on the BURE VALLEY RAILWAY at Aylsham TG1926.

Good places to get down to the Broads but stay on land include Hickling itself (with a pleasant path along the north shore) and Ormesby St Michael TG4614, where the Eel's Foot pub has attractive waterside lawns. Other waterside pubs handy for watching boating activity include the Wood's End at Bramerton TG2904; the Rising Sun at Coltishall TG2719 (on a pretty bend of the River Bure; you can hire bikes from nearby Just Pedalling); the Crown at Dilham TG3325; the Swan or the Ferry, both busy Chef & Brewers pubs, at Horning TG3417; the quaint Walpole Arms at Itteringham TG1430; the Ferry House at Stokesby TG4310; the Ferry House at Surlingham TG3206 (there's still a rowing-boat ferry here), or nearby Coldham Hall (attractive riverside garden); the Sutton Staithe Hotel at Sutton Staithe TG3823 (a lovely quiet spot); or the Lock, a remote candlelit pub down by the River Waveney at Geldeston TM3991. For a sense of adventure you can take the long walk across the marshes from Wickhampton TG4205 or Halvergate TG4206, past former windpumps, to the Berney Arms on Breydon Water.

Ranworth Broad TG3514 is one of the few broads the cruise boats can't get to. A CONSERVATION CENTRE here has nature trails and displays of local and natural history; snacks, shop, disabled access; cl Nov–Mar; free. There are usually guided tours of the local wildlife on summer Suns, taking in a boat trip too; best to book, on (01603) 270479. The local church has the best painted rood screen in the county.

Walks

Dutch-gabled buildings, flint walls, huge skies, saltmarshes and the odd windmill give the north coast a real sense of place. The North Norfolk Coastal Path follows its length, although not always right next to the sea. The weather is often kinder on the coast, when conditions a few miles inland can be quite different. Going over sand can be tiring, despite the lack of contours. **Wells-next-the-Sea** TF9143 ➪-1 starts the best stretch, to Overy Staithe TF8444, where the sandy beach never quite looks the same from one day to the next. At Holkham TF8944 there is a car park quite close to the beach, where pine trees meet the sands; westwards the crowds rapidly thin out. From Overy Staithe, the path follows a zigzagging dyke – saltmarsh on one side, neat farmland on the other – to the dunes and beach. **Blakeney Point** TG0046 ➪-2 is another good stretch, which gets better as you walk along it, although the shingle bank needs patience and is hard on the ankles; pleasant dunes await at the far end. From **Blakeney** TG0243 ➪-3 the dyke walk to Cley-next-the-Sea TG0443 is less arduous, with the birds on the mudflats for company.

Holkham Hall TF8842 ☎-4 allows walkers on the driveways of its coastal estate; the parkland is a bit sombre, but impressively landscaped with a lake, temple and obelisk. **Holme-next-the-Sea** TF7043 ☎-5 gives access to a sandy beach for a 2-mile walk past a bird sanctuary and saltings to Thornham TF7343. The Peddars Way is an inland link from the coastal path, running from Holme-next-the-Sea down through Castle Acre TF8115 and then in a strikingly straight beeline right across the county to Knettishall Heath TL9480 nr Thetford, following ancient-feeling green ways and quiet lanes. Some may find there is a little too much road-walking to sustain interest.

Beacon Hill TG1841 ☎-6, nr Cromer, is the only place of any height (a humble 90 metres, 300 ft); the coastal path here detours over the sandy heath and through woodlands. **Salthouse** TG0743 ☎-7 and Kelling TG0942 back similar heathy hinterlands, where you can tie in a walk along the coast (here unvaryingly straight) as part of the same excursion. **Felbrigg Hall** TG1939 ☎-8 (1,700 acres with fine mature trees) and **Sheringham Park** TG1342 ☎-9 (waymarked walks, viewing tower, azaleas and rhododendrons) are parkland estates owned by the NT, both landscaped by Repton, and now with public all-year access.

Sandringham Country Park TF6727 ☎-10, with its majestic trees and glades, is a notable parkland walking area. **Blickling Hall** TG1728 ☎-11 has parkland with large tracts of woodland and pasture, as well as a disused railway line and a man-made lake with water birds – even kingfishers on the River Bure. There are circular walks within the park, and the long-distance Weavers Way can be used as part of a link to take in the paths through and around the **Wolterton Park** TG1631 ☎-12 and Mannington Hall estates (both owned by the Walpoles, who have opened up a network of paths extending NW to Holt Country Park TG0837).

Few paths get close enough to the Norfolk Broads themselves, often tantalisingly out of sight, and once away from the waterside and fenny woodlands you are immediately into the flat, humdrum agricultural landscapes found in much of the rest of the area. There is some scope for strolling along rivers, such as the reedy, estuarine River Yare nr Great Yarmouth, and the canalised parts of the **Bure** ☎-13, **Yare** ☎-14 (Breydon Water and the amazingly remote Berney Arms windmill with its nearby pub are worthwhile objectives), **Thurne** ☎-15 and others; pumping-mills, birdlife and the boating scene are the principal features. **Horsey** TG4522 ☎-16 gives a varied round walk: a path along reed-fringed Horsey Mere (NT, with wildfowl and otters) and the New Cut, then for a total contrast joining the beach for sea views nr Horsey Corner.

Elsewhere, the chief distinguishing marks are woodland plantations and parkland. Of the forests, the largest is Thetford Forest TL8783 – mainly conifers and more conifers. The **Pingo Trail** ☎-17, starting from Stow Bedon TL9596, is 8 miles through the unforested part of the adjacent Breckland grasslands, largely army training ground. It passes through 3 Sites of Special Scientific Interest (inc Cranberry Rough, an alder swampland), taking you along a disused railway line before joining the Peddars Way at Hockham Heath TL9292.

Welney Wildfowl Trust Refuge TL5993 ☎-18 has interesting conducted summer evening walks; tel (01353) 860711 for details.

Where to eat

Blakeney TG0243 WHITE HORSE 4 High St (01263) 740574 Small hotel close to the harbour (if that's not too grand a word), with a long cosy bar, a nice mix of customers, efficient and friendly service; good, well presented food inc local fish, reasonably priced wines, and an attractive evening restaurant; bedrooms. £16.50/£3.50.

Briston TG0532 JOHN H STRACEY (01263) 860891 Neatly kept, well run country dining pub with a wide choice of well cooked and fairly priced bar food; popular separate restaurant, speciality evenings, comfortable seats and log fire, well kept real ales, and friendly licensees; comfortable bedrooms; disabled access. **£12 in bar, £20 in restaurant**|£6.

Cawston TG1323 GREY GABLES (01603) 871259 Very good English cooking using fresh local produce in this little Georgian restaurant, with a log fire in the comfortable lounge, pleasant service, and a fine wine list; bedrooms; cl 25–26 Dec. £20.

Cawston TG1323 RATCATCHERS Eastgate (01603) 871430 Very much a dining pub, this popular place serves a huge choice of good, freshly prepared food (so there may be a wait) inc home-made bread, chutneys, stocks and herb oils, as well as fresh fish; open fires, real ales, country wines, an L-shaped beamed bar, and a cosy candlelit dining room, too; cl 25–26 Dec; disabled access. £20|£5.95.

Colkirk TF9126 CROWN (01328) 862172 Unpretentious, friendly village pub with open fires, solid country furniture, and a pleasantly informal, no smoking dining room; good, promptly served food (nice daily specials inc vegetarian choices), well kept real ales, decent wine list (they'll open any bottle you want – just for a glass), and a helpful landlord; own bowling green behind; no food 25–26 Dec; reasonable disabled access. £16.50|£6.50.

Docking TF7637 HARE ARMS (01485) 518402 Attractive and individually decorated pub with entertaining bric-à-brac; 2 smallish main bar rooms, a log fire, enjoyable and interesting food, well kept ales, and fine wines. £17.85|£7.25.

Erpingham TG1931 ARK The Street (01263) 761535 Lovely individual food, inc home-made bread and home-grown vegetables, in a simple, relaxed cottage with a log fire and courteous service; bedrooms; cl Christmas wk, Mon, am Tues–Sat, pm Sun; disabled access. £28.50.

Erpingham TG1931 SARACENS HEAD Wolterton (01263) 768909 Comfortably civilised inn with a simple, stylish 2-room bar, a nice mix of seats, log fires and fresh flowers; excellent and inventive food inc a good-value 2-course Sun supper and 3-course monthly feasts, very well kept real ales, interesting wines, and a charming, old-fashioned gravel stableyard; good bedrooms; cl 25 Dec; limited disabled access. £18|£4.50.

Fakenham TF9229 WENSUM LODGE (01328) 862100 Brick-built former grain store by the river, with a very roomy, relaxed and civilised bar, and 2 beamed dining rooms (one no smoking); interesting food inc sandwiches and filled baked potatoes served all day, real ales, and attentive service; bedrooms. £17.75|£7.25.

Holt TG0738 OWL TEA ROOMS White Lion St (01263) 713232 Georgian building with a bakery and tearooms behind; home-made bread, scones, quiches and pies served on plates made by the owners, organic local vegetables, daily specials and vegetarian choices; also home-made preserves, and good cream teas; cl Sun; disabled access. £10.55|£3.25.

King's Lynn TF6220 ROCOCO 11 Saturday Market Pl (01553) 771483 Delicious, imaginative modern cooking using fresh local produce, in a pretty dining room decorated with lots of flowers and paintings; also a cosy lounge area, relaxed atmosphere, good informal service, and decent wines; cl Sun, am Mon, Christmas–New Year; disabled access. £33.50 **dinner, £19.50 lunch**|£3.

Norwich TG2308 ADLARDS 79 Upper St Giles St (01603) 633522 Warm and friendly, quietly decorated restaurant serving delicious, carefully thought out food from a menu that changes daily; lovely puddings, fine service, and a good wine list; cl Sun, am Mon, Christmas wk. £36.25.

Reedham TG4101 FERRY (01493) 700429 Perfectly placed pub beside the River Yare, with plenty of tables from which to watch boats or swans (good moorings); a secluded back bar with a fine log fire, long front bar with big picture windows, a no smoking restaurant, and very popular, good food; disabled access. £17|£4.

St Olaves TM4599 PRIORY FARM (01493) 488432 Good interesting food inc fresh fish and a children's menu; right by St Olave's Priory; open all day Jun–Sept, cl 26 Dec; disabled access. £20|£4.95.

Snettisham TF6834 ROSE & CROWN (01485) 541382 Pretty white cottage, with a nice traditional layout to the 4 bustling bars; log fires, 5 real ales, 20 wines by the glass, good daily specials as well as the standard menu, afternoon teas, colourful garden, and an adventure playground; disabled access. £18|£4.50.

Stow Bardolph TF6205 HARE ARMS (01366) 382229 Good-value, quickly served, interesting lunchtime bar food in a pleasantly refurbished country pub with cheerful licensees; prompt and courteous service even when busy, fresh flowers, a separate, elegant evening restaurant, and a big conservatory for children (not allowed in main bar; must be over 10 in restaurant); cl 25–26 Dec. £21.50|£6.

Swanton Morley TG0117 DARBYS Elsing Rd (01362) 637647 Cosy, beamed country pub decorated with lots of farm tools and so forth; very well kept real ales, good, generously served and often interesting bar food, log fire, friendly staff, a children's room and an adventure playground; also bedrooms, self-catering, camping, caravan site, horse facilities, country trails; disabled access. £18.50|£7.50.

Wells-next-the-Sea TF9143 MOORINGS 6 Freeman St (01328) 710949 Pretty restaurant close to the harbour, with lovely locally caught seafood, good vegetarian dishes, and decent wines; cl Tues, Weds, pm Thurs, early Dec and early Jun; disabled access. £25|£11.50.

Special thanks to C Dowsett, Derek and Sylvia Stephenson, Mrs Y Champion, Jenny and Michael Back, Graham Spencer, E G Drain.

NORFOLK CALENDAR

Some of these dates were provisional as we went to press. Please check information with the numbers provided.

APRIL

10 **Blickling** Contemporary Crafts Show at Blickling Hall – *till Mon 13* (01263) 734711

19 **Norwich** Special Open Day at the Plantation Garden (01603) 455223

MAY

1 **King's Lynn** May Garland: large double hoop of flowers, ribbons and beads, with a doll in the middle, is carried through town accompanied by ox horns (01553) 768930

9 **Blickling** Norfolk Food and Drink Festival at Blickling Park – *till Sun 10* (01625) 575681

16 **Norwich and Norfolk** Artists' Open Studios: exhibitions and over 150 professional artists' studios – *till 7 Jun* (01603) 614921

23 **Felbrigg** Coast and Country Craft Show at Felbrigg Hall – *till Mon 25* (01263) 734711

24 **Downham Market** Festival – *till Sun 31*, with carnival on *Mon 25* (01366) 387440

30 **Walpole St Peter** Flower Festival: largest parish flower festival – *till 3 Jun* (01945) 780252

NORFOLK CALENDAR

JUNE

19 **Norwich** Open-air Theatre Festival: over 30 performances in parks and open spaces – *till 31 July* (01603) 666071
20 **Wymondham** Music Week – *till Sat 27* (01508) 533681
21 **Norwich** Special Open Day at the Plantation Garden (01603) 455223
27 **Sandringham** Country Show and Horse-driving Trials at Sandringham House- *till Sun 28* (01733) 234451

JULY

1 **Norwich** Royal Norfolk Show – *till Thurs 2* (01603) 748931
4 **Martham** Carnival, procession on *Sun 5* (01493) 842195; **Norwich** Fireworks Concert at Earlham Park (01473) 464007
5 **North Walsham** Carnival (01692) 407509
6 **East Dereham** St Withburga Week – *till Sun 12* (01362) 695333
10 **Norwich** Lord Mayor's Weekend Celebrations: carnival floats, music and fireworks – *till Sun 12* (01603) 666071
17 **Blickling** Outdoor Jazz and Blues at Blickling Hall – *till Sat 18* (01263) 731660; **King's Lynn** Festival – *till Sat 25* (01553) 774725; **Wheeting** Steam Rally – *till Sun 19* (01842) 810317
18 **Grimston** World Snail-racing Championships (01485) 600650
20 **Hunstanton** County Tennis Week – *till Fri 24* (01485) 532516
23 **Dersingham** Flower Festival at Saint Nicholas Church – *till Mon 27* (01485) 540865
26 **Weybourne** Family Fun Day at the Muckleburgh Collection (01263) 588210
29 **Sandringham** Flower Show inc arena events at Sandringham House (01485) 532516

AUGUST

1 **Blickling** Kite and Hot-air Balloon Festival at Blickling Hall – *till Sun 2* (01263) 731660
2 **Caister-on-Sea** Lifeboat Day and Fête (01493) 842195; **Norwich** Music Festival at Waterloo Park: 2 stages, entertainers, dance and children's area (01603) 212137; **Norwich** Special Open Day at the Plantation Garden (01603) 455223
6 **Cromer** Lifeboat Day (01263) 512503
9 **Hemsby** Lifeboat Day (01493) 842195
12 **Binham** Pageant and *Son et Lumière* at Binham Priory – *till Sat 15* (01263) 711736
14 **Blickling** Fireworks Concert at Blickling Hall – *till Sat 15* (01263) 731660
23 **Caister-on-Sea** Lifeboat Event (01493) 846107
29 **Filby** Fun Weekend – *till Mon 31* (01493) 846345
31 **Blickling** Aylsham Agricultural Show at Blickling Park (01263) 732432; **Sandringham** Craft Fair (01553) 772675

SEPTEMBER

6 **Hemsby** Herring Festival at Hemsby Beach (01493) 731606
13 **Norwich** Royal Norfolk Showground Spectacular: family entertainment, trade stands and arena events (01603) 748729

OCTOBER

7 **Norfolk and Norwich** Festival – *till Sun 18* (01603) 662661
26 **Norwich** CAMRA Beer Festival at St Andrew's Hall and Blackfriars Hall – *till Sat 31* (01603) 666071

Norfolk Calendar

NOVEMBER

10 **Norwich** Glyndebourne Touring Opera at Theatre Royal – *till Sat 14*
   (01603) 630000

DECEMBER

25 **Hunstanton** Christmas Day Swim (01485) 532516

We welcome reports from readers . . .

This *Guide* depends on readers' reports. Do help us if you can – in return, we offer a discount on the next edition to people who've helped us with reports for it. Tell us what you think about places already in it, and anything extra you think we should say about them. And send us your ideas for inclusion in the next edition: places to visit, eat at or stay in, attractive drives or walks, maybe even unusual interesting shops you know of. Use the card in the middle, the report forms at the end, or just write – no stamp needed: *The Good Guide to Britain*, FREEPOST TN1569, Wadhurst, E Sussex TN5 7BR.

NORTHAMPTONSHIRE

Good for a civilised short break, with charming scenery, fine houses and grounds; not so much family interest.

Little-known, this county has a lot to offer older people in search of a quiet, relaxing and comfortable break. It has gently appealing, partly wooded landscapes, villages built of red or honey-coloured stone, the fine churches of the Nene Valley that crosses the county from around the graceful small town of Oundle, past Northampton and Wellingborough to Badby, and an unrivalled concentration of great houses including Rockingham Castle, Althorp at Great Brington, Canons Ashby House, Deene Park, Cottesbrooke Hall and Boughton House. Most of these have lovely grounds to wander through, as do Castle Ashby, Holdenby House and Coton Manor.

The Sulgrave Manor living history events are most enjoyable for people of any age. Otherwise, the county does not offer a great deal to entertain families; Wicksteed Park on the edge of Kettering is a good treat for children. Other places with wide appeal are the canal museum at Stoke Bruerne, and in summer the dragonfly centre near Oundle.

Where to stay

Ashby St Ledgers SP5768 OLDE COACH HOUSE Ashby St Ledgers, Rugby CV23 8UN (01788) 890349 £60; 6 rms. In an attractive village full of thatched stone houses, this busy old inn has rambling atmospheric rooms, a winter log fire, and fine food in both the bar and partly no smoking dining room; also well kept beer, smiling service, and big gardens with a good play area.

Badby SP5559 WINDMILL Badby, Daventry NN11 6AN (01327) 702363 *£55, plus special breaks; 8 rms. Traditional, carefully modernised, thatched stone inn with beams, flagstones and a huge inglenook fireplace in the front bar; cosy comfortable lounge, good and generously served bar and restaurant food, and decent wines; fine views of the pretty village from the car park; disabled access.

Castle Ashby SP8659 FALCON Castle Ashby, Northampton NN7 1LF (01604) 696200 £77.50; 16 nicely decorated rms. Smart hotel in an attractive, preserved village, with stone walls and hops on the dark beams in the 16th-c cellar bar, an open fire, and real ales; restaurant overlooking the pretty garden, good breakfasts, and a welcoming landlord; children over 10 in evening restaurant; disabled access.

Culworth SP5446 FULFORD HOUSE The Green, Culworth, Banbury, Oxon OX17 2BB (01295) 760355 *£56; 3 pretty rms. Relaxing, 400-year-old stone house with lovely views over pastures with horses, and a charming garden; beams, log fire in the comfortable drawing room, and good food, around a circular Georgian table, using fresh home-grown vegetables (by arrangement); children over 5.

East Haddon SP6668 RED LION East Haddon, Northampton NN6 8BU (01604) 770223 £65; 5 rms. Welcoming and popular golden stone inn with attractive gardens; a neat, white-panelled lounge, small public bar, pretty restaurant, high quality, daily-changing food, and nice breakfasts.

Old SP7872 WOLD FARM Old, Northampton NN6 9RJ (01604) 781258 *£44;

6 rms, 4 with own bthrm. 18th-c house at the heart of a beef and arable farm; with spacious, interesting rooms, good food in the beamed dining room, inc hearty breakfasts, and attentive, welcoming owners; also a log fire, snooker table, and 2 pretty gardens.

Oundle TL0388 TALBOT New St, Oundle, Peterborough PE8 4EA (01832) 273621 £104, plus special breaks; 39 most attractive big rms. Mary Queen of Scots walked to her execution down one of the staircases now in this carefully refurbished 17th-c hotel; attractive cosy lounges, big log fires, good food in the timbered restaurant, and a garden.

Paulerspury SP7145 VINE HOUSE 100 High St, Paulerspury, Towcester NN12 7NA (01327) 811267 *£66; 6 individually decorated rms. 300-year-old building with carefully preserved original features, and a relaxed, welcoming atmosphere; cosy bar with an open fire, and very good modern English cooking in the attractive restaurant; pretty cottage garden; cl 24 Dec–6 Jan.

Sudborough SP9682 VANE ARMS High St, Sudborough, Kettering NN14 3BX (01832) 733223 £45; 2 rms. Welcoming, thatched pub on a picturesque village street; with a comfortable main bar, open fires, friendly, helpful staff, and a marvellous range of real ales.

To see and do

NORTHAMPTONSHIRE FAMILY ATTRACTION OF THE YEAR

! 🏠 🐾 **Sulgrave** SP5544 SULGRAVE MANOR 🏰 (off the B4525) The ancestral home of George Washington's family, this modest manor is exceptional value for families during their regular special events, when the whole place returns to how it would have been during a particular period. They seem less concerned with making money than with trying to spark real interest in the past in children, and of course the most direct way of doing that is to bring it to life around them. People in period costume go about their daily business, and children can take part in a wide range of activities from wassailing or helping in the kitchen at Christmas, to joining in the harvest during the Apple Day Festival. Since they started these Living History events, the number of visitors has shot up from 6,500 to around 35,000, and many families come back several times a year. The house is still worth a visit on non-event days, though it's mainly adults (and school groups) who get the most out of it then. There are several relics of Washington (he never lived here – it was his great-great-grandfather who emigrated to America), as well as elegant rooms and well kept gardens. The dates for this year's events are listed in the **Calendar** section at the end of the chapter. Snacks, shop; open wknds Mar–Dec, and pm wkdys (exc Weds) Apr–Oct (am too in Aug), cl 1–2pm for lunch; (01295) 760205; *£4.50 on special event days (*£2.25 children), less on ordinary days. Most visitors get the bargain family ticket, which admits 2 adults and 2 or more children for £12.

✝ 🐾 🏠 **Brigstock** SP9485 The CHURCH has a Saxon tower, and a bell that used to be rung 3 times a day to help anyone lost in the woods; the Olde Three Cocks is useful for food. BRIGSTOCK COUNTRY PARK A good place for a wander, especially around wildlife-filled Fermyn Woods on the edge; it can be a little muddy. LYVEDEN NEW BIELD Unfinished 'new building' started in 1595, but abandoned after the owner Sir Thomas Tresham's son died in the tower. Intriguing and unusual, it was intended to celebrate the Passion of Christ, and is shaped like a Greek cross; (01832) 205358; £1.70; NT. It's a half-mile walk from the car park.
🏠 🐾 ✝ **Canons Ashby** SP5750 CANONS ASHBY HOUSE (B4525) Exceptional little manor house, more

Northern-looking than Midlands, beautifully restored with Elizabethan wall paintings and glorious Jacobean plasterwork. The formal gardens have also been carefully restored over the last 20 years, and now closely reflect the layout of the early 18th c. A reasonably sized park has a hilltop 12th–14th-c priory church. Brewhouse café, shop, disabled access; open pm Sat–Weds Apr–Oct; (01327) 860044; *£3.50; NT – it's one of their busier properties. The Olde House at Home, at Moreton Pinkney, is handy for lunch.

♟ ✿ ✝ ✦ Castle Ashby SP8659 CASTLE ASHBY HOUSE Only the gardens can be visited, but the house is well worth seeing from outside – a splendidly palatial, Elizabethan building at the end of a magnificent, mile-long avenue planted nearly 300 years ago. The gardens include grand Victorian terraces, sweeping lawns, Italianate gardens with an orangery, and lakeside parkland that may well be the prolific Capability Brown's most enduring achievement. Disabled access; 125 De; (01604) 696696; £2.50. The CHURCH, within the park, is very attractive; there's a public path to it. Restored farm buldings nearby house a CRAFT CENTRE AND RURAL SHOPPING YARD (cl Mon). The Falcon, in the handsomely preserved estate village, has good food (and attractive bedrooms), and the drive through Cogenhoe, Whiston, Grendon and Easton Maudit is pleasant.

✿ ✦ ↷ Coton SP6771 COTON MANOR (off the A428) Attractive views from charming gardens around a 17th-c stonebuilt manor house (not open); interesting plantings, and watergardens with flamingos, cranes and ornamental waterfowl wandering freely. The neighbouring woods are lovely at bluebell time. Meals, snacks, plant sales, disabled access; open pm Weds–Sun Apr–Oct; (01604) 740838; *£3. Besides Grooms Cottage at Guilsborough, the Red Lion at East Haddon is good for lunch.

♟ ▣ ✿ Cottesbrooke SP7173 COTTESBROOKE HALL Very attractive Queen Anne house, reputedly the model for Jane Austen's *Mansfield Park*, with a renowned collection of mainly sporting and equestrian paintings. The lovely garden has formal borders, venerable cedars, greenhouses, an extensive wild garden and a separate cottage garden. Teas, unusual plant sales, disabled access to gardens only; open pm Thurs and bank hols Easter–Sept, plus pm Sun in Sept, garden also open pm Weds and Fri; (01604) 505808; £4, garden only £2.50. The George, in nearby Brixworth (see **churches** entry below), has decent food.

♟ ✿ ▥ Deene SP9492 DEENE PARK (off the A43) Lord Cardigan who led the Charge of the Light Brigade used to live in this beautifully presented, partly Tudor house; there's a high-spirited contemporary portrait of him in full-attack gallop. Extensive parklands with woodside and lakeside walks, and gardens reflecting continuing interest by the owners over the generations. Snacks, shop, some disabled access; open pm Sun Jun–Aug, plus Sun and Mon of bank hol wknds Easter–Aug; (01780) 450223; £4. KIRBY HALL (W of Deene) Splendidly ruined Elizabethan mansion with a bizarre mixture of styles and design; from some angles it still looks intact – even close up. The 17th-c gardens are being restored, and it's a tranquil spot for a picnic. Shop, disabled access; cl 1–2pm, all winter Mon and Tues, 24–26 Dec; (01536) 203230; £2.20 (inc Walkman tour). The Queen's Head, opposite the church in the pretty village of Bulwick, has good-value food.

★ ✝ ▥ Fotheringhay TL0593 Lovely village with interesting historical displays in the charming if slightly out-of-proportion 14th-c CHURCH, across a watermeadow from the River Nene. It was part of a small pre-Reformation college and doubles as a memorial to the House of York, with some interesting heraldry. There's only a fragment left of the CASTLE where Mary Queen of Scots was imprisoned, beside the castle mound. The Falcon is excellent for lunch.

★ ✝ ♟ ▣ ✿ Geddington SP8983 The

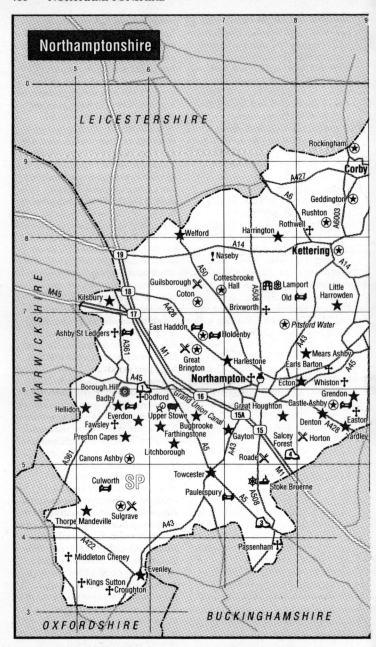

Northamptonshire

LEICESTERSHIRE

WARWICKSHIRE

Rockingham

Corby

A27

A6

Geddington

Rushton

Rothwell

Welford

Harrington

Kettering

A14

A14

Naseby

A50

Cottesbrooke Hall

Lamport

Old

Little Harrowden

Guilsborough

Coton

Brixworth

A508

Kilsbury

M45

A428

Ashby St Ledgers

East Haddon

Holdenby

Pitsford Water

A43

A45

Mears Ashby

Great Brington

Harlestone

Earls Barton

A45

Northampton

Ecton

Whiston

Borough Hill

Badby

Dodford

Grand Union Canal

Great Houghton

Castle Ashby

Grendon

Easton

Hellidon

Everdon

Upper Stowe

Bugbrooke

Denton

A428

Yardley

Fawsley

Farthingstone

Gayton

Salcey Forest

Horton

Preston Capes

Litchborough

A5

A43

Roade

M1

Canons Ashby

Culworth

SP

Towcester

Stoke Bruerne

Sulgrave

Paulerspury

A508

Thorpe Mandeville

A422

A43

Passenham

Middleton Cheney

Evenley

Kings Sutton

Croughton

OXFORDSHIRE

BUCKINGHAMSHIRE

very well preserved, elaborate 13th-c cross was erected by Edward I where Queen Eleanor's funeral cortège rested on its way to Westminster. The photogenic packhorse bridge is even older, and there's a 12th-c church. The Star has good food. BOUGHTON HOUSE (SE of Geddington)

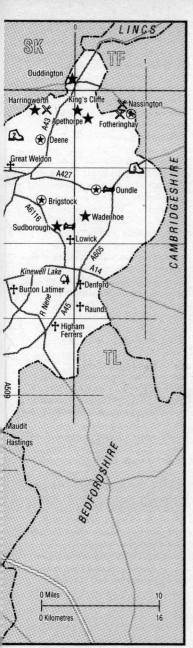

gorgeous mythical scenes painted on the ceilings, and works by El Greco, Murillo and Caracci lining the walls. Excellent armoury, beautiful parklands, and an adventure playground and garden shop. Snacks, shop, disabled access; grounds open pm May–Sept (exc Fri), house pm Aug only; (01536) 515731; £4, grounds only £1.50.

🏠▣✝🏵 ★ **Great Brington** SP6665 ALTHORP The home of the Spencer family since 1508 (though they don't spend much time here), remodelled several times, especially in the 17th and 18th c, and now the resting place of Diana Princess of Wales, on an islet in the Oval Lake, in a small arboretum just NE of the house. The house itself has a splendid collection of furnishings and porcelain, paintings by Rubens, Van Dyck and Lely. Snacks, shop, some disabled access; open pm daily July and Aug; (01604) 7702097; £6. The attractive CHURCH is on the edge of the park. Its graveyard has fine views. On the far side of the estate there's public access to a sandy-floored area of wildlife-filled pine woods and heathland known as Harlestone Firs SP7164, pleasant for walking – though there's a planning threat, of a possible new road through here to a proposed new town development. The village itself is charming, and the Fox & Hounds here has good food, and lots of character.

🏵 ✝🏠🛏🎠 **Holdenby** SP6967 HOLDENBY HOUSE GARDENS In Elizabethan times this was one of the biggest houses in the country, and the extensive gardens and grounds have been restored in the original style. Snacks, shop, disabled access; 1998 dates were undecided as we went to press – it has been open pm daily exc Sat Apr–Sept, but best to check; (01604) 770074; £2.75. An adjacent falconry centre is open the same times. The house itself (with its unique piano collection) is only open Easter, spring and Aug bank hol Mons; £4. NORTHAMPTON & LAMPORT RAILWAY SP7266 (Pitsford Rd, Chapel Brampton) Enthusiastic new little railway, with short Sun train

Impressively grand old place often compared to Versailles (some of its treasures were in fact made for there). Richly furnished and decorated, with rides (01604) 820327. Its name is a proud commitment to growth northwards, but for the time being the 14-mile walk and cycle way through pretty countryside by the line is a very pleasant foretaste. The Brampton Halt here has decent food.

☺ ♿ 🏛 **Kettering** SP8678 WICKSTEED PARK Big amusement park set up in 1921 when they introduced boating on the lake. Some older features still remain (an antique roundabout for example), though in the last few years they've been joined by more modern attractions, inc a monorail, roller-coaster, and films in the Cine 2000 dome. It's still low-key compared to other leisure parks – thrill rides here are mainly from the dodgems, ferris wheel and pirate ship school – but for many visitors that's precisely the appeal. Meals, snacks, shop, disabled access; open Easter–Sept; (01536) 512475; £4 parking charge (less wkdys out of high season), then you buy vouchers for the rides, or a wristband with unlimited rides for £9. The MANOR HOUSE MUSEUM (with its famous mummified cat) and adjacent ALFRED EAST GALLERY (Sheep St) are worth a look if passing; the former has free children's activities in school hols. Both cl Sun and bank hols; free.

🏰 ⚜ **Lamport** SP7574 LAMPORT HALL (off the A508) Mainly 17th- and 18th-c house in a spacious park, with tranquil gardens containing a remarkable alpine rockery – the home of the first garden gnomes, only one of which now survives. Frequent antique fairs, concerts and other events. Snacks, shop, disabled access to ground floor only; open pm Sun and bank hols Easter–Oct, plus in Aug guided tours daily at 4.30pm (exc Sun); (01604) 686272; £3.50. The Swan, with great views, has good-value food.

❗ **Naseby** SP6878 The owner of Purlieu Farm has set out a model of the Civil War's crucial BATTLE OF NASEBY, using many hundreds of model soldiers, with a 10-minute commentary; open by appointment, (01604) 740241; £1. The nearby Fitzgerald Arms is a good-value

dining pub. One BATTLE MONUMENT (Sibbertoft Rd) marks the position of Cromwell's New Model Army before his devastating counter-attack; there's another on the B4036 towards Clipston (this road from West Haddon and on to Market Harborough in Leics gives a good feel of rural Northants).

✝ ♿ **Northampton** SP7560 Daniel Defoe would no longer describe this prosperous shoe-making town as one of the most handsome in the country, but it has a few interesting buildings. There are several fine CHURCHES, most notably the 12th-c Holy Sepulchre (one of only 4 remaining round churches in the country), the very grand central All Saints, and the ornate Norman St Peters in Marefair, right by the dual carriageway. The Welsh House (now a china shop) and Hazelrigg House are also very handsome. The CENTRAL MUSEUM (Guildhall Rd) is home to a remarkable collection of boots and shoes, which includes an elephant's boot, Margot Fonteyn's ballet shoes, Roman sandals, and Queen Victoria's wedding slippers. Shop, disabled access; cl am Sun, 25 Dec, 1 Jan; (01604) 39415; free. A social history museum in Abington Park is set in the 15th-c home of Shakespeare's granddaughter; cl am, Sun; 25 Dec (01604) 39415; free.

★ ⚜ ❗ **Oundle** TL0388 Charming and elegant stonebuilt town with a graceful church and several antique shops. The ancient Ship does decent food. BARNWELL COUNTRY PARK (just S of Oundle) A good spot for a walk, with a variety of birds; the waterside Mill is a pleasant place for lunch. NATIONAL DRAGONFLY MUSEUM (just SE of Oundle – coming from town take a right at the A605 Oundle roundabout) At pretty Ashton Mill, this unique place has dramatic feeding sessions, several different habitats, and a TV microscope link to the larvae under the water. Fully grown dragonflies put on their best shows on sunny days, though it's a rewarding place in any weather. Teas, shop, disabled access; open wknds and bank hols 13 Jun–27 Sept;

(01832) 272427; *£2.50. Ashton itself is attractive.

🦆 🗡 🏵 **Pitsford Water** SP7669 Praised for birdwatching, especially in winter when wildfowl flock to the northern part of the lake; the southern part is popular for fishing. The White Swan at Holcot has decent food. Nearby SYWELL COUNTRY PARK SP8265 (off the A4500 towards Mears Ashby) has woodland and lakeside walks, play areas, and a little wildlife display; you can fish on the lake.

🏛 🏠 🄰 **Rockingham** SP8691 ROCKINGHAM CASTLE (A6003) Lovely old house still tucked away behind the curtain wall of the original Norman fortress – obviously quite an effective defence, as the castle was able to resist repeated assaults in the Civil War. The site of the original keep is now a rose garden, but the outline of the 2 baileys and the drum towers survive, and the later Elizabethan building has a good range of furnishings and art. Meals, snacks, shop, limited disabled access; open pm Sun, Thurs, and bank hols Easter–Sept, as well as Tues in Aug or after bank hols; (01536) 770240; *£4, garden only £2.60. Around here, pleasant back roads through the former Forest of Rockingham give quiet views of a particularly attractive part of the county.

🏠 🏵 🐾 **Rushton** SP8482 (1m W) TRIANGULAR LODGE Late 16th-c oddity designed by the same man as Lyveden New Bield, nr Brigstock: 3 walls, 3 windows and 3 gables on 3 levels, and a 3-sided chimney, to represent the Holy Trinity. Open pm Apr–Sept; (01536) 710761; £1.10. A few miles N at East Carlton SP8389 is a COUNTRY PARK with a few craft workshops nr the entrance.

❀ ⛵ **Stoke Bruerne** SP7449 CANAL MUSEUM 🄱 Close to a flight of locks on the Grand Union Canal, with fine old canal buildings (inc a popular pub, the Boat), and lots happening on the water, this is a handsome former corn warehouse housing a good collection of canal memorabilia, inc a reconstructed traditional narrow boat complete with immaculately packed-in, colourful furniture and crockery. Also boat trips through a nearby tunnel. Shop, limited disabled access; cl winter Mon, 25–26 Dec; (01604) 862229; £2.70. Pleasant towpath walks from here.

🏠 🏵 **Sulgrave** SP5544 *See separate Family Panel on p.464* for SULGRAVE MANOR. The Star is enjoyable for lunch.

🐖 🐾 **Upper Stowe** SP6456 OLD DAIRY FARM CRAFT CENTRE Sheep, pigs, peacocks, ducks and donkeys, as well as craft workshops, antiques, farm shop and a wool collection. Well organised, and with decent views – though be prepared for it to be muddy. Restaurant, snacks, shop, disabled access; cl 2 wks from 25 Dec; (01327) 340525; free, exc special wknds. The Narrow Boat and Globe at Weedon are good for lunch.

✝ The county is notable for its lovely stonebuilt **churches**, many with elegant spires visible a long way off and a memorable feature of the county's landscape – particularly along the valley of the River Nene. A shortlist might include Ashby St Ledgers SP5768, Brixworth SP7470 (a particularly fine Anglo-Saxon church, one of England's oldest – mostly 7th-c with much reused Roman material), Burton Latimer SP9075, Croughton SP5433 (14th/15th-c murals), Denford SP9976 (for its nature-reserve churchyard by the River Nene, waterside walks from here), Dodford SP6160 (striking memorials), Earls Barton SP8563 (fine Saxon tower), Easton Maudit SP8858, Fawsley SP5556 (above Capability Brown's lakes), Great Weldon SP9289, Higham Ferrers SP9669, King's Sutton SP4936, Lowick SP9780, Middleton Cheney SP4941, Passenham SP7739 (17th-c murals), Raunds SP9972, Rothwell SP8181 and Whiston SP8460. With many of these, the village is well worth seeing, too.

★ **Other attractive villages**, all with decent pubs, include Apethorpe TL0295, Bugbrooke SP6757, Denton SP8358, Duddington SK9800, Ecton SP8263, Evenley SP5834,

Farthingstone SP6155 (Knightley Way walks), Gayton SP7054, Great Houghton SP7958, Grendon SP8760, Harlestone SP7064, Harrington SP7780, Harringworth SP9197 (famous for its 82-arch railway viaduct), Hellidon SP5158 (pleasant walks nearby), Kilsby SP5671, Litchborough SP6354, Little Harrowden SP8771, Mears Ashby SP8466, Sudborough SP9682, Thorpe Mandeville SP5344, riverside Wadenhoe TL0383, Welford SP6480 and Yardley Hastings SP8656. Towcester SP6948 is a town not village (and pronounced 'toaster'), but despite some light industry on the edge has quite a pleasantly villagey feel and some attractive Georgian and Victorian buildings. We'd also recommend rather Cotswoldy King's Cliffe TL0097, and a trio of lovely, mellow, orange ironstone villages, Preston Capes SP5754, Everdon SP5957 and Badby SP5658 – the last has 2 good pubs.

❀ The **best views** in the region are from Borough Hill SP5862 above the golf course; an Iron Age hill fort shares the top with a formidable array of television and telecommunications masts, but on a clear day the views are tremendous.

🏠 The county's Enterprise Agency runs a very full programme of guided **factory visits**, most free, ranging from big shoe companies and places like Carlsberg or Barclaycard to helicopter-makers, narrow-boat-builders and blacksmiths; tel (01604) 671200 and ask for their 'Tours of the Unexpected' brochure; all tours must be pre-booked.

Days Out

Grand Union heritage
Walk the towpath and/or take a canal boat trip from Stoke Bruerne; canal museum, and lunch at the Boat Inn there; Canons Ashby; walk Knightley Way from Everdon, through Badby Wood and to Fawsley Park (see **Walks** section below).

Gardens after lunch
Lunch at Grooms Cottage, Guilsborough; Coton Manor gardens; then (depending on the actual day) choice of Cottesbrooke Hall gardens, Lamport Hall gardens, Holdenby House gardens or (half-hour drive) Boughton House gardens.

The house that never was
Brigstock country park; Lowick church; lunch at the King's Head, Wadenhoe; Lyveden New Bield, Brigstock.

Around the Nene
Stroll in Barnwell country park; Oundle (and National Dragonfly Museum if open); lunch at the Mill, Oundle, or at the Falcon, in Fotheringhay; Fotheringhay; Elton Hall (see **Cambridgeshire** chapter).

Please let us know what you think of places in the *Guide*. Use the report forms at the back of the book or simply send a letter.

Walks

The **Knightley Way** ⌂-1 takes a pleasant, 12-mile course from Badby SP5658, an area where gorgeous, orange-coloured stone adds to the charm of buildings; it's well waymarked to Greens Norton SP6649. The finest part is between Badby Wood SP5658 and Fawsley Park SP5657, where the path drops to landscaped lakes by the hall and estate church. In May, the Badby Wood bluebells are lovely.

Rockingham Forest SP9490 ⌂-2 has enough country houses scattered around it to spice interest, and grey-stone cottages are a local feature; on its NW edge, the Exeter Arms at Wakerley SP9599, a former hunting lodge, gives access to both Wakerley Woods (nice for a picnic) and the Welland Valley.

For **Grand Union Canal** walks ⌂-3 Stoke Bruerne SP7449 is a popular start, with its waterside pub and waterways museum. Other good pubs handy for the towpath are the Royal Oak at Blisworth SP7253, Admiral Nelson (Dark Lane) or Mill House (A45) at Braunston SP5366, New Inn at Buckby Wharf SP6065, the Navigation at Thrupp Wharf nr Cosgrove SP7942, Narrow Boat at Weedon Lois SP6046 (attractive Chinese restaurant) and the Wharf in Welford SP6480.

Salcey Forest SP8052 ⌂-4 is a couple of miles of ancient forest, largely oak, now managed for nature conservation, with well marked trails including one suitable for wheelchairs. **Kinewell Lake** SP9875 ⌂-5 is a well managed local nature reserve around former gravel-pit lakes by the River Nene.

Where to eat

Fotheringhay TL0593 FALCON (01832) 226254 Atmospheric and comfortable pub with good, imaginative bar food, well kept real ales, lounge and a simpler public bar, open fires, and a neat garden; cl Mon, 25–30 Dec; disabled access. £18|£5.20.

Great Brington SP6665 FOX & HOUNDS (01604) 770651 Golden stone, thatched village inn with lots of old beams, big flagstones and bare boards, an attractive mix of country tables and chairs, 2 fine log fires, and lots of bric-à-brac; a decent range of real ales, country wines, a sensibly short choice of good, freshly cooked food (especially the game), and sheltered tables in the paved courtyard and side garden. £18|£6.95.

Guilsborough SP6773 GROOMS COTTAGE (01604) 740219 Attractively converted stable block, serving good English food in the lovely gardens (open to the public) of Coton Manor (not open); open Easter–Oct for light lunches Weds–Sat, and from Sept–Easter, evening meals Fri, Sat, and for Sun lunch; disabled access. £16.50|£5.

Harringworth SP9197 WHITE SWAN (01572) 747543 Spotlessly kept, stonebuilt Tudor pub, with very large helpings of good food from the Spanish chef/patron; comfortable lounge/dining area, a quieter dining room, and friendly staff; disabled access, good-value bedrooms; cl pm 25 and 26 Dec and pm 1 Jan. £16.50|£4.

Horton SP8254 FRENCH PARTRIDGE (01604) 870033 Lovely little evening restaurant run by the Partridges for over 30 years; consistently excellent food (marvellous puddings), a relaxed atmosphere, and fine wines; cl Sun, Mon, 2 wks Christmas, 2 wks Easter, 3 wks July/Aug; children by arrangement; disabled access. £30 for 4 courses.

Nassington TL0696 BLACK HORSE (01780) 782324 Civilised, 17th-c dining pub with a splendid, big stone fireplace, easy chairs and settees in the beamed lounge; 2 comfortable restaurant rooms linked by the bar, well kept real ales, a varied wine list, and a wide range of interesting food inc children's helpings; a well tended garden. £22|£9.

Roade SP7551 ROADHOUSE 16 High St (01604) 863372 Very good food in this attractive and comfortable, popular restaurant; good wine list; cl pm Sun, am Mon; disabled access. £30|3-course lunch £6.

Sulgrave SP5545 STAR Manor Rd (01295) 760389 Hospitable, small, creeper-covered pub with good seasonal food, friendly staff, lots to look at, well kept real ales, and a no smoking restaurant; bedrooms; cl 25 Dec; no children. **£17.50.**

Special thanks to E G Parish, Jenny and Michael Back, Robert Owen.

NORTHAMPTONSHIRE CALENDAR

Some of these dates were provisional as we went to press. Please check information with the number provided.

APRIL

10 **Sulgrave** Festival of Easter Customs and Traditions at Sulgrave Manor – *till Mon 13* (01295) 760205

11 **Chapel Brampton** Easter Egg Special at Northampton & Lamport Railway – *till Mon 13* (01604) 820327; **Lamport** Garden Fair at Lamport Hall – *till Mon 13* (01604) 686272

25 **Lamport** Antiques Fair at Lamport Hall – *till Sun 26* (01604) 686272

MAY

1 **Daventry** Arts Festival – *till Sun 31* (01327) 302417; **Sulgrave** Georgian Living History at Sulgrave Manor – *till Mon 4* (01295) 760205

3 **Lamport** Crafts Festival at Lamport Hall – *till Mon 4* (01604) 686272

9 **Chapel Brampton** Easter Egg Special at Northampton & Lamport Railway – *till Sun 10* (01604) 820327

10 **Daventry** Country Day at Daventry Country Park (01327) 871100

15 **Wellingborough** 20th Waendel Walk: international walking event – *till Sun 17* (01933) 229777

16 **Moulton** Village Festival – *till Sun 17* (01604) 646818

23 **Braunston** Boat Show: historic boats, parade and fireworks – *till Mon 25* (01788) 890666; **Chapel Brampton** Friends of Thomas the Tank Engine at Northampton & Lamport Railway – *till Mon 25* (01604) 820327; **Rothwell** Street Fair – *till Sat 30* (01536) 710897; **Sulgrave** Festival of Needlework at Sulgrave Manor – *till Sun 31* (01295) 760205

24 **Lamport** Country Festival at Lamport Hall: field events, steam engines and vintage cars – *till Mon 25* (01604) 686272; **Northampton** British Falconry and Raptor Fair and Northamptonshire Game Fair at Althorp House – *till Mon 25* (01588) 672708

31 **Northampton** Horse Trials at Delaprey Park (01858) 525336

JUNE

12 **Northampton** American Auto Club: thousands of American cars, bands and side shows at Billing Aquadrome – *till Sun 14* (01948) 830754

13 **Kettering** Northamptonshire Motorshow at Wicksteed Park – *till Sun 14* (01536) 481111

20 **Corby** Carnival and Car Show at Corby Boating Lake (01536) 402551; **Flore** Flower Festival: 7 open gardens – *till Sun 21* (01327) 341264

NORTHAMPTONSHIRE CALENDAR

JUNE cont

27 **Northampton** Gala Centenary Concert at the Church of the Holy Sepulchre (01604) 22677; **Sulgrave** Tudor Living History at Sulgrave Manor – *till 5 July* (01295) 760205

JULY

4 **Hollowell** Steam and Heavy Horse Show – *till Sun 5* (01604) 505422; **Wellingborough** Carnival (01933) 623779

5 **Castle Ashby** Country Fair: over 100 stands and ring events (01604) 696521

10 **Oundle** International Festival of Music – *till Sun 19* (01832) 272026

11 **Corby** Highland Gathering at West Glebe Park (01536) 402551

12 **Silverstone** British Grand Prix (01327) 857271

16 **Northampton** Land-Rover off-road at Billing Aquadrome: arena events, largest off-road course in Britain – *till Sun 19* (01379) 890056

17 **Northampton** Town Show – *till Sun 19* (01604) 238791

25 **Cottesbrooke** Fireworks Concert at Cottesbrooke Hall (01604) 505808

AUGUST

1 **Lamport** Garden Fair at Lamport Hall – *till Mon 3* (01604) 686272

2 **Northampton** Dog Agility Stakes at Billing Aquadrome (01788) 817267

7 **Northampton** British Koi Carp Nationals at Billing Aquadrome – *till Sun 9* (01324) 626699

8 **Blakesley** Agricultural Show at Seawell Grounds (01327) 359821

14 **Sulgrave** Outdoor Theatre at Sulgrave Manor – *till Sun 16* (01295) 760205

14 **Northampton** Hot-air Balloon Festival – *till Sun 16* (01604) 238791

29 **Chapel Brampton** Teddy Bears Weekend at Northampton & Lamport Railway – *till Mon 31* (01604) 820327; **Sulgrave** American Civil War Re-enactment at Sulgrave Manor – *till Mon 31* (01295) 760205

SEPTEMBER

12 **Chapel Brampton** Steam Gala at Northampton & Lamport Railway – *till Sun 13* (01604) 820327; **Lamport** Crafts Fair at Lamport Hall – *till Sun 13* (01604) 686272; **Nassington** Knights of the Rose: 14th-c battle at Prebendal Manor House – *till Sun 13* (01780) 782575; **Sulgrave** Meet the Vikings at Sulgrave Manor – *till Sun 13* (01295) 760205

22 **Northampton** Festival of Music at the Church of the Holy Sepulchre – *till Sun 27* (01604) 754782

26 **Chapel Brampton** Friends of Thomas the Tank Engine at Northampton & Lamport Railway – *till Sun 27* (01604) 820327; **Lamport** Antiques Fair at Lamport Hall – *till Sun 27* (01604) 686272; **Sulgrave** Elizabethan Living History at Sulgrave Manor – *till 4 Oct* (01295) 760205

OCTOBER

11 **Oundle** World Conker Championships (01832) 272735

17 **Sulgrave** Apple Day Festival at Sulgrave Manor – *till Sun 18* (01295) 760205

24 **Lamport** Crafts and Gifts Fair at Lamport Hall – *till Sun 25* (01604) 686272

NORTHAMPTONSHIRE CALENDAR

NOVEMBER

5 **Corby** Fireworks and torchlight procession (01536) 402551

DECEMBER

5 **Chapel Brampton** Santa Specials at Northampton & Lamport Railway – *Dec wknds* (01604) 820327; **Sulgrave** Traditional Christmas Customs at Sulgrave Manor – *Dec wknds and 27–31 Dec* (01295) 760205

26 **Moulton** Mummers Play and Morris Dancing on Stocks Hill (01604) 646818

We welcome reports from readers . . .

This *Guide* depends on readers' reports. Do help us if you can – in return, we offer a discount on the next edition to people who've helped us with reports for it. Tell us what you think about places already in it, and anything extra you think we should say about them. And send us your ideas for inclusion in the next edition: places to visit, eat at or stay in, attractive drives or walks, maybe even unusual interesting shops you know of. Use the card in the middle, the report forms at the end, or just write – no stamp needed: *The Good Guide to Britain*, FREEPOST TN1569, Wadhurst, E Sussex TN5 7BR.

NORTHUMBRIA

Grand unspoilt scenery in both Northumberland and County Durham, a few outstanding places to visit, awesome castles and monuments – especially Hadrian's Wall; very good value.

This is one of the very best parts of Britain, if you want to be caught up in re-creations of times past. There's Hadrian's Wall, of course, striding right across England – staggering if you've not seen it before, nearly 2,000 years old, and dotted with interesting places to visit, including engrossing reconstructions and interpretations. Moving on a few centuries there's Bede's World in Jarrow (Anglo-Saxon life), then, among other things, the re-created 18th-c port at Hartlepool, and topping all of these the remarkable reconstruction of North of England life a hundred years ago at Beamish – a fascinating living museum.

Children really enjoy many of these places; a special treat for them is Newcastle Discovery – and it's free. Good days out for older people include that treasure trove, the Bowes Museum at Barnard Castle (one of Britain's top museums), Cragside at Rothbury (a magnificent stately home in glorious surroundings), and an abundance of classic castles. Alnwick, Warkworth and Lindisfarne are favourites, and Bamburgh, Raby at Staindrop and Chillingham (with its ancient white cattle) are much enjoyed too. The bird reserve at Washington is very enjoyable.

Durham is one of England's most rewarding cities for a short stay, with plenty to see besides its magnificent cathedral. Newcastle is becoming a really lively place to visit, with the bonus of good free museums and galleries.

Above all, though, is the great sweep of largely unspoilt scenery, quiet and uncrowded even in summer – prime spots are the beautiful landscapes of North Tynedale, Coquetdale and Teesdale, and the rolling empty grassy uplands of the Cheviot Hills. There are majestic stretches of rocky sandy coast, though its hinterland is less interesting. Kielder Water is developing as an attractive recreational area, in a part of Northumbria that's otherwise so little visited as to seem almost an undiscovered country. The area is very good both for walking and for driving, with little traffic (outside the Tyneside/Teesside industrial areas), peaceful lower landscapes enlivened by streams and woodland, solid stone country buildings, and unhurried small market towns.

People up here are among Britain's friendliest, and prices are low. May and June are the best months, with long evenings (stay away from inland waters in summer, unless you're midge-proof). September can be delightful, but autumn tends to set in quite fiercely in October, and winter is bleak.

Where to stay

Alnmouth NU2511 MARINE HOUSE 1 Marine Rd, Alnmouth, Alnwick NE66 2RW (01665) 830349 *£90 inc dinner, plus special breaks; 10 rms. 17th-c stone hotel on the edge of the golf links, with fine sea views, a log fire and plenty of books in traditional upstairs residents' lounge; cosy bar; and enjoyable, freshly prepared food in the cheerfully decorated, no smoking dining room; self-catering also; well behaved dogs welcome; children over 7.

Bamburgh NU1835 LORD CREWE ARMS NE69 7BL (01668) 214243 £74; 24 comfortable rms, 21 with own bthrm. Relaxing and comfortable old inn, beautifully placed in charming coastal village below magnificent Norman castle; entertaining bric-à-brac and log fire in the back bar, and no smoking plush lounge; good bar and restaurant food; cl end Oct–Easter; children over 5.

Cambo NZ2086 SHIELDHALL Cambo, Morpeth NE61 4AQ (01830) 540387 *£40; 5 well equipped suites, each with its own entrance. 18th-c stone house and carefully converted farm buildings around a courtyard, with antiques and other interesting furnishings (Mr Robinson-Gay is a fine cabinet-maker), a library, bar, and cosy lounge with French windows opening on to the neatly kept big garden; enjoyable, freshly produced food in the candlelit beamed dining room; cl Nov–Mar; children over 12.

Chatton NU0628 PERCY ARMS Chatton, Alnwick NE66 5PS (01668) 215244 *£50, plus special breaks; 7 rms, most with own bthrm. Partly creeper-covered stone inn with neatly kept, comfortable and spacious bar, and open fire; good-value food inc excellent fresh fish, and 12 miles of private fishing for residents; sauna, solarium, and keep-fit facilities; self-catering cottage also.

Chollerford NY9372 GEORGE Chollerford, Hexham NE46 4EW (01434) 681611 £110, plus special breaks; 46 well equipped rms. Quiet hotel with fine gardens sloping down to the river, and 17th-c bridge over the North Tyne visible from the candlelit restaurant; thoughtful, attentive service; swimming pool and leisure club; disabled access.

Cornhill-on-Tweed NT8639 TILLMOUTH PARK Cornhill-on-Tweed TD12 4UU (01890) 882255 £110, plus special breaks; 14 spacious, pretty rms with period furniture. Solid stone-built country house in 15 acres of parkland (fishing on the River Till, rod and drying room), with comfortable relaxing lounges, open fires, and a galleried hall; good food in the bistro or restaurant; lots to do nearby; dogs welcome.

Cotherstone NZ0119 FOX & HOUNDS Cotherstone, Barnard Castle DL12 9PF (01833) 650241 £50; 3 no smoking rms. Attractive building in lovely setting overlooking Teesdale village green; alcoves, local photographs, and an open fire in the comfortably furnished, cosy beamed bar; good food in the no smoking dining room, and courteous friendly service; handy for walks; cl 25 Dec.

Crookham NT9138 COACH HOUSE Crookham, Cornhill-on-Tweed TD12 4TD (01890) 820293 £46; 9 individual rms with fresh flowers and nice views, 7 with own bthrm. 17th-c farm buildings around a sunny courtyard; airy beamed lounge with comfortable sofas and big arched windows; good breakfasts, enjoyable dinners, and very warmly friendly and helpful owner; cl Nov–Easter; good disabled access.

Durham NZ2743 GEORGIAN TOWN HOUSE 11 Crossgate, Durham DH1 4PS (0191) 386 8070 *£50; 6 pretty rms. Attractive building with extravagantly comfortable sitting room, attractive, airy conservatory dining room, and a friendly atmosphere; cl Christmas.

Durham NZ2743 ROYAL COUNTY Old Elvet, Durham DH1 3JN (0191) 386 6821 £125, plus special breaks; 150 attractive, well equipped rms. Close to the city centre with views of the castle and cathedral, this extended hotel has attractively furnished rooms, several restaurants, and lots of leisure facilities; disabled access.

Gateshead NZ2662 ESLINGTON VILLA 8 Station Rd, Low Fell, Gateshead NE9 6DR (0191) 487 6017 ***£64.50,** plus weekend breaks; 12 rms. Extended, comfortable Edwardian house in a quiet residential area with some original features; lounge with comfortably modern furniture and bay windows overlooking the garden; good food in the conservatory restaurant, and a friendly atmosphere; cl Christmas; disabled access.

Greenhead NY6666 HOLMHEAD Hadrian's Wall, Greenhead, Carlisle CA6 7HY (01697) 747402 **£48,** plus special breaks; 4 cosy rms with showers. Family home, built of Wall stones, once a farmhouse but now a comfortable B & B with moorland, wildlife, Hadrian's Wall and Roman castles all nearby; airy lounge with TV at one end, small bar at the other, games and children's toys; nice, freshly prepared food using farm and local produce eaten family-style around candlelit oak table; pretty garden with a stream and games (table tennis and snooker in garage); also self-catering; cl 2 weeks in winter.

Greta Bridge NZ0813 MORRITT ARMS Greta Bridge, Barnard Castle DL12 9SE (01833) 627232 **£69.50,** plus special breaks; 18 rms. Smartly old-fashioned coaching inn where Dickens stayed in 1838 to research for *Nicholas Nickleby* – one of the interesting bars has a colourful Dickensian mural; comfortable lounges, fresh flowers, nice open fires, and a pleasant garden; coarse fishing; no children in evening dining room; pets allowed.

Haltwhistle NY7164 ALD WHITE CRAIG Shield Hill, Haltwhistle NE49 9NW (01434) 320565 **£42;** 2 rms. Homely and neatly kept 17th-c croft overlooking South Tyne valley, with prize-winning sheep, rare cattle, dogs, cats and poultry; coal fire and local information in the beamed sitting room, and good breakfasts around central table in the dining room; plenty of walks; cl Oct–Mar; no children, disabled access; self-catering cottages.

Headlam NZ1819 HEADLAM HALL Headlam, Darlington DL2 3HA (01325) 730238 ***£78,** plus weekend breaks; 28 pretty rms, in the main house and adjacent coach house, plus 2-bedroom cottage in the village. Peaceful Jacobean mansion in 4 acres of carefully kept gardens with a little trout lake, tennis court, small golf practice area, and croquet lawn; elegant rooms, a fine carved oak fireplace in the main hall, good traditional food in the 4 individually decorated rooms of the restaurant, and courteous staff; indoor swimming pool, snooker and sauna; cl 25 Dec; disabled access.

High Force NY8728 HIGH FORCE HOTEL High Force, Barnard Castle DL12 0XH (01833) 622222 ***£42;** 6 rms. Close to England's highest waterfall (for which it's named), this is a cheerful and friendly place with log fires in relaxing bars, good service, straightforward food, a micro brewery, and lots of malt whiskies; it includes a mountain rescue post.

Kirkwhelpington NY9984 CORNHILLS Kirkwhelpington, Newcastle Upon Tyne NE19 2RE (01830) 540232 ***£48;** 3 rms, some with own bthrm. Big, no smoking Victorian farmhouse on large stock-rearing farm with marvellous views towards the coast and Tyne valley; lots of original features, a comfortable lounge, good breakfasts (local pubs for evening meals), and indoor and outdoor games for children; self-catering also; cl Apr.

Longframlington NU1301 EMBLETON HALL Longframlington, Morpeth NE65 8DT (01665) 570249 **£75;** 10 comfortable, pretty and individually decorated rms. Charming hotel in lovely grounds surrounded by fine countryside; with a particularly friendly relaxed atmosphere and courteous staff; neat little bar, elegant lounge, log fires, excellent-value bar meals, and very good food in the attractive dining room.

Longhorsley NZ1595 LINDEN HALL Longhorsley, Morpeth NE65 8XF (01670) 516611 ***£130,** plus special breaks; 50 rms. Georgian hotel in 450 acres of landscaped park with coarse fishing, clay pigeon shooting, mountain biking (bike hire available), new 18-hole golf course, pitch and putt, croquet, jogging routes, giant chess, lots of leisure facilities inc a big swimming pool; pubby bar, elegant drawing room, and nice food in the attractive restaurant; disabled access.

Romaldkirk NY9922 ROSE & CROWN Romaldkirk, Barnard Castle DL12 9EB (01833) 650213 £80, plus special breaks; 12 rms – those in the main house have lots of character. Smart and interesting old coaching inn by green of this delightful Teesdale village; Jacobean oak settle, log fire, old black and white photographs, and lots of brass in the beamed traditional bar, a cosy residents' lounge; very good popular food in the bar and fine oak-panelled restaurant, and well kept real ales and wines; cl 25–26 Dec; disabled access.

Seahouses NU2232 OLDE SHIP Main St, Seahouses NE68 7RD (01665) 720200 £73, plus special breaks; 12 rms, plus 4 apartments, all newly refurbished last year. Thriving harbourside inn with small rooms full of nautical items and fishing memorabilia, windows looking out towards the Farne Islands, and a comfortable residents' lounge; popular bar food, 5 real ales, and friendly service; ideal for coastal walks; cl Dec–Jan; children over 10.

Slaley NY9858 ROSE & CROWN Slaley, Hexham NE47 0AA (01434) 673263 *£45; 3 attractively modernised rms. Traditional village inn with mugs hanging from the beams in the bar, popular food in bar and restaurant, and friendly service; lots to do nearby.

Staindrop NZ1320 GAZEBO HOUSE 4 North Green, Staindrop, Darlington DL2 3JN (01833) 660222 £40, plus special breaks; 2 rms. Attractive Queen Anne house in a charming village nr Raby Castle, with friendly, helpful owner; particularly good home-made food, fine breakfasts in the country kitchen and conservatory, and a walled garden; cl over Christmas.

Stannersburn NY7286 PHEASANT Stannersburn, Hexham NE48 1DD (01434) 240382 £56; 8 rms. Beautifully located, unpretentious 17th-c stone inn close to Kielder Water and its quiet forests; traditional and comfortable lounge, simple public bar, and a happy mix of customers; good food inc excellent fresh vegetables and enjoyable Sun lunch, well kept real ales, a fine choice of malts, welcoming service, nice breakfasts, and picnic-table sets in streamside garden.

Tynemouth NZ3669 HOPE HOUSE 47 Percy Gdns, Tynemouth, North Shields NE30 4HH (0191) 257 1989 *£49.50; 3 rms, 2 with sea views. Carefully refurbished, terraced Victorian house facing the sea, with an elaborately decorated drawing room, and an elegant dining room with lovely paintings; nice evening meals and a thoughtful wine list, and friendly, attentive service.

West Woodburn NY8987 BAY HORSE West Woodburn, Hexham NE48 2RX (01434) 270218 £40; 5 rms. Pretty, welcoming 18th-c coaching inn with a curious Roman stone in the garden which runs down to the River Rede (good for trout and salmon fishing); comfortable open-plan bar with open fire, and good-standard food (not lunch winter Mon–Fri) in the airy dining room.

Wolsingham NZ0737 GREENWELL FARM Wolsingham, Tow Low, Bishop Auckland DL13 4PH (01388) 527248 *£45, plus special breaks; 6 rms in comfortably converted stone barn. 300-year-old farmhouse with fine views, sitting and dining rooms; tasty food using naturally reared meats and locally grown produce; spring lambs, calves and chicks, nature trail and conservation areas; can bring own horse or mountain bike; self-catering cottage; cl Christmas and New Year; disabled access.

Please let us know what you think of places in the *Guide*. Use the report forms at the back of the book or simply send a letter.

To see and do

NORTHUMBRIA FAMILY ATTRACTION OF THE YEAR

☆ ! **Newcastle upon Tyne** NZ2464 NEWCASTLE DISCOVERY (Blandford Sq) Not so long ago this thriving complex housed a standard collection of displays on science and engineering – the kind of place that children were dragged to reluctantly and couldn't wait to leave. When the curators realised the problem they began a radical overhaul, adding new galleries and interactive features on subjects more likely to appeal to the whole family, and making sure that every section had something to please younger visitors. Now it's the biggest and busiest museum in the area, particularly worthy of praise because entrance to all sections is completely free. Pride of place goes to the 30-metre (100-ft) *Turbinia*, once the fastest ship on the seas, shown off in a splendid new multimedia gallery, but the area that children will like best is the interactive Science Factory, with plenty to push, press and poke: TV effects create the illusion of flying down the Tyne, there's a soft play area for very young children, and lots of mirrors, magnets and microscopes to fiddle with. Other galleries offer a similarly hands-on look at the history of the city (inc the early days of Newcastle United), fashion, shipbuilding, army life, and local inventors. Of course first and foremost it's still a museum, but one that can easily fill at least a couple of hours for most families passing through the area. There's a pay-and-display car park opposite, or Metro stations nearby. Meals, snacks, shop, disabled access; cl am Sun, Good Fri, 25–26 Dec, 1 Jan; (0191) 232 6789; free.

Durham NZ2743 The ancient core of the town stands on a crag defended by an almost complete loop of the River Wear, with a rewarding riverside path going from Prebends Bridge up to South St (with some of the best views of the cathedral's magnificent pinnacled towers), recrossing the river by Silver St bridge. The old part of town is largely pedestrianised, with attractive cobbled alleys and narrow medieval lanes, and fine medieval buildings among the Georgian and later ones, particularly around the 12th-c pedestrians-only Elvet Bridge (where the Regatta tea rooms have decent food). There are several medieval churches, and interesting little shops. You can hire rowing boats nr Elvet Bridge, which is also the departure point for launches.

✝ ⌂ CATHEDRAL Huge, and probably England's finest, a fiercely beautiful and unusually well preserved Norman building, breathtaking and very masculine inside; it was the first in Britain to use pointed arches. St Cuthbert's shrine is here, and they say that the Lady Chapel owes its odd position at the W end to his hatred of women; every time they tried to build it in the right place his spirit apparently caused the foundations to collapse. Try to spot the unique bronze knocker that seems to have a cheery grin. Rare books and manuscripts in the 15th-c monks' dormitory. Meals, snacks, shop, disabled access; monks' dormitory open 10am –4pm Mon–Sat, 12.30am –3.30pm Sun (80p), Treasury cl am Sun (£1). The close behind the cathedral has some handsome old houses. The Brewer & Firkin (Saddler St) is a handy central place for something to eat; the best-value food is out at the Duke of Wellington (on the A167 S of Nevilles Cross).

⌂ CASTLE Developed from an early Norman motte and bailey. Still a proud building, with original chapel and 13th-c Great Hall, it's now used for university accommodation, and you can stay here. Guided tours 2–4.30pm Mon, Weds and Sat in term time, usually every day in hols – best to check first; (0191) 374 3863; £2.75.

⚉ UNIVERSITY MUSEUM OF ARCHAEOLOGY On the river bank below the cathedral's SW corner, a former fulling mill with finds from the city and surrounding area. Shop; cl am, and in winter cl Tues and Weds; (0191) 374 3623; £1. Also along these banks is a sculpture of the Last Supper, carved by Colin Wilbourn from 13 trees that died of Dutch elm disease.

⚉ ORIENTAL MUSEUM (Elvet Hill) Unrivalled collections include remarkable displays of everything from plates, carvings, and paintings to costumes and mummies. Shop, some disabled access; cl 1–2pm, am wknds, Christmas–New Year; (0191) 374 7911; £1.50.

⚉ 🌂 UNIVERSITY BOTANIC GARDENS (Hollingside Lane) Hugely enjoyable 18-acre garden in mature woodland with exotic trees from America and the Himalayas, tropical house, cactus house and visitor centre, and unusual sculpture garden. Snacks, shop, disabled access; garden, glasshouses and visitor centre open all year; (0191) 374 2671; £1.

✝ ⌂ ST MARY LE BOW CHURCH (The Bailey) The heritage centre here has exhibitions on the city's history. Shop, disabled access; cl am (exc July and Aug), wkdys in Apr and May, and all Oct–Mar; 80p.

⚉ HOUGHALL COLLEGE GARDENS (Shincliffe Rd) The county's main horticultural training centre, with 10 acres of hardy plants, a water garden, woodland garden, Alpine rock garden, parterre and arboretum. This area records some of the lowest temperatures in the country so if it grows here, it'll grow anywhere. Snacks, plant sales, disabled access; (0191) 386 1351; free.

⌂ ⚉ DURHAM ART GALLERY (Aykley Heads) Good gallery with unusual temporary exhibitions, and adjacent regimental museum. Snacks, shop, disabled access; cl am Sun, Mon (exc bank hols), Christmas hols; (0191) 384 2214; £1.50.

✝ FINCHALE PRIORY (3m NE, minor rd off the A167) St Godric chose this site in 1110 as a place to meditate, and it's still a pleasant spot for contemplation, beside the graceful ruins of the 13th-c church.

Hadrian's Wall An amazing sight, if you've never seen it before. It's extraordinary to imagine those Roman military engineers, so far from their warm homeland, building this remarkable construction through such inhospitable surroundings. Many of its 73½ miles run along the natural crag of the great Whin Sills, making it that much more formidable; the overall sense of grandeur is a definite part of the appeal. The stone wall itself, with its turret watchtowers, milecastles and more sporadic forts, defines the northern side of a narrow frontier zone, bounded on its southern side by an equally remarkable ditch between turf ramparts; a military road runs between wall and ditch. It was this whole installation rather than just the wall itself which the Romans used to control trade and cross-border travel. The B6318 following the military road is a fine drive, with some of the best views of the wall.

We mention below some of the wall's more striking and accessible features, including the bigger behind-the-lines forts and camps; and see ⌂-3 in **Walks** section, p.496.

The section at Cuddys Crag NY7868 is perhaps the most beautiful of all, very photogenic and giving glorious views. English Heritage are cutting back on the publicity for some sites – thousands of marauding tourists have caused more damage than centuries of harsh weather and unstable politics ever managed.

In summer a tourist bus runs between Hexham and several of the main sites (and even as far as Carlisle), and you can get on or off at any of the stages along the way; check with the the information centre on (01434) 605225 for times. The best place to eat nr the main sites is the Milecastle Inn on the B6318 NE of Haltwhistle.

🏛⚬ **Bardon Mill** NY7868
VINDOLANDA Started well before the
Wall itself, this Roman fort and
frontier town soon became a base for
500 soldiers. Full-scale
reconstructions, and lots of well
preserved remains. The adjacent
museum has a fascinating selection of
hand-written letters and documents
found on the site, inc party
invitations, shopping lists and a note
that could have been written by many
a modern mother: 'I have sent you
socks and two pairs of underpants.'
Shop, snacks, disabled access to
museum but not site; museum cl late
Nov–mid-Feb, site open all yr (exc 25
Dec); (01434) 344277; £3.50, less
when museum cl in winter.

🏛 **Carrawbrough** NY8971 MITHRAIC
TEMPLE Three 3rd-c altars to Mithras
were found here, on the line of the
Roman wall near the fort of
Brocolitia. They're now in
Newcastle's Museum of Antiquities,
but you can see replicas in their
original setting.

🏛⚬ **Chollerford** NY9365 CHESTERS
ROMAN FORT (slightly W on the
B6318) The best-preserved example
of a Roman cavalry fort in Britain, in
an attractive riverside setting. In the
bath-house you can see exactly how
the underfloor heating system
worked, and a museum has
sculptures and inscriptions from here
and other sites. Snacks, shop,
disabled access; cl 24–26 Dec, 1 Jan;
(01434) 681379; £2.50. The Hadrian
Hotel at Wall (on the A6076 S) has
good-value food.

🏛⚬❀ **Corbridge** NY9964 is an
attractive village (or very small town)
above the Tyne; the Black Bull is good
for lunch. CORBRIDGE ROMAN SITE
(slightly NW) Granaries, portico
columns and what may be the
legionary HQ survive among these
3rd-c remains. The adjacent museum
has the magnificent Corbridge Lion.
Shop, limited disabled access; cl
winter Mon and Tues, and maybe
lunchtimes; (01434) 632349; £2.50.
Brocksbushes Farm (2m E) has PICK
YOUR OWN fruit and a farm shop;

(01434) 633400.

🏛❀ **Gilsland** NY6366 BIRDOSWALD
ROMAN FORT Overlooking the Irthing
Gorge (and, in fact, just over the
Cumbrian border), this is one of the
most impressive sites, partly because
it has so many features in such a small
area, and partly for its grand views.
Good visitor centre, and ongoing
excavations. Snacks, shop, some
disabled access; cl Nov–Mar (exc by
arrangement); (016977) 47602;
£1.95.

⚬ **Greenhead** NY6666 ROMAN ARMY
MUSEUM (Carvoran) Entertaining and
informative intrepretation of what it
was like to be a Roman soldier, with
everything you could possibly want
to know about his training, pay, and
off-duty hobbies. Snacks, shop,
disabled access; cl mid-Nov–early
Feb; (016977) 47485; £2.80.

🏛⚬ **Housesteads** NY7969
HOUSESTEADS ROMAN FORT AND
MUSEUM (B6318) The best-known
and most visited section of the Wall,
pretty much slap bang in the middle.
It owes its fine state of preservation
partly to the fact that while other
stretches were being used as a handy
source of free recycled quality
masonry, this fort was base camp for
a powerful group of border bandits;
woe betide anyone who tried to use
their fortifications as material for
cowsheds or churches. A museum has
altars, inscriptions and models, and
there are good walks in either
direction. Snacks, shop; cl 24–26
Dec; (01434) 344363; £2.50.

♭ **Steel Rigg** NY7667 ONCE BREWED
Very useful Northumberland
National Park Information Centre,
handy for Housesteads and
Vindolanda, with exhibitions and
audio-visual presentations. Guided
walks leave from here (though not
every day). Snacks, shop, disabled
access; cl Nov–Easter; (01434)
344396; free. The walk from here to
Housesteads offers some of the best
views of the Wall; it's only 3 miles but
is up and down so can take up to 2½
hours.

Newcastle upon Tyne NZ2464 This big industrial conurbation is far from being conventionally pretty, but has a strong vibrant atmosphere, and several excellent free museums (*see separate Family Panel on p.479* for Newcastle Discovery). Its best parts are grouped very compactly high above the River Tyne with its three great bridges – particularly what has become almost the city's trademark, the two-decker High Level Bridge for road and rail designed by Robert Stephenson in the 1840s. The Metro system makes it quick and straightforward to get around, and to the attractions noted under North and South Shields, Tynemouth and Whitley Bay; a one-day Day Rover ticket (available from stations or the tourist information centre) costs around £3 and is good for all Metro trips and stations (and the ferry between North and South Shields). You can still trace some stretches of the medieval CITY WALL, especially from St Andrew's Church along the cobbled lane W of Stowell St – Chinese restaurants around here – and past the Heber Tower along Bath Lane. The top of Grey's Monument offers a good bird's-eye view of the centre's lofty Victorian terraces; a steep climb, Sat only. Fitzgerald's down the street is useful for a bite to eat. Steep alleys and steps lead from the centre down to The Quay, the oldest part of town, with several unexpected and quaintly attractive timber-framed medieval buildings; one of the oldest, the Cooperage, is a good pub. Downstream, E of the 1920s Tyne Bridge, an area of refurbished 19th-c wharf buildings is enjoyable to walk through, with crafts and bric-à-brac on Sun, and a useful pub for food – the Baltic Tavern. This whole quayside area is gradually being redeveloped on a most impressive scale, with plans for a huge arts complex, and funding heading towards £200 million. Another stylish quayside warehouse conversion, the Waterline (by New Law Courts) has good food, as does the Fog on the Tyne overlooking St Peter's Basin marina.

† CATHEDRAL The 14th/15th-c Anglican cathedral is worth a look (cl most of Sun); plans are well advanced for a dramatic new stone sculpture to occupy the Chapel of the Incarnation.

CASTLE This Norman building gave the city its name; a lot still remains. It's a little spoiled by the main railway line which cuts the gatehouse off from the keep, but as much of the fortress was rediscovered only during the railway's construction it seems a little churlish to complain. Shop; cl Mon, 25 Dec, 1 Jan, Good Fri; (0191) 232 7938; *£1.50.

BESSIE SURTEE'S HOUSE (Sandhill) Well renovated timbered Jacobean house, with elaborate plaster ceilings and carved panelling. Open wkdys only (not bank hols); (0191) 261 1585; free.

LAING ART GALLERY (Higham Pl) Notable temporary exhibitions, and excellent children's gallery, the activities well designed to encourage young children to think about shapes, texture and patterns. Free guided tours of the main galleries 11.30am Sat. Cl am Sun, 25–26 Dec, 1 Jan, Good Fri; (0191) 232 7734; free.

HANCOCK MUSEUM (Barras Bridge) Very good natural history museum, with magnificent collections of stuffed birds and mammals. Again, lively temporary exhibitions, and plenty for children. Meals, snacks, shop, disabled access; cl am Sun, 25–26 Dec, 1 Jan, Good Fri; (0191) 222 7418; price varies according to exhibitions.

MUSEUM OF ANTIQUITIES (The University) Particularly good on Roman remains, with reconstructions of various points along Hadrian's Wall. The displays have been reorganised in a very user-friendly fashion. Shop, disabled access by arrangement; cl Sun, Good Fri, 24–26 Dec, 1 Jan; (0191) 222 7846; free.

Besides the pubs mentioned above, the handsome Crown Posada (The Side, off Dean St) and the Duke of Wellington (High Bridge) are pleasantly civilised.

Other things to see and do

★ 🏰 📷 🎠 ✝ **Alnwick** NU1813 Busy town at the heart of prosperous farming country, with some attractive old streets nr the market square. ALNWICK CASTLE The 'Windsor of the North' dates back to the 11th c, and is the second-largest inhabited castle in the country. Stone soldiers stand guard on the battlements, and inside all is Italian Renaissance grandeur, with a magnificent art collection taking in works by Titian, Van Dyck and Canaletto, and an outstanding

---

Days Out

Durham highlights
Walk past castle and through Palace Green to Durham cathedral; Lunch at Regatta tearooms (Elvet Bridge); walk along River Wear from Elvet Bridge (boat hire) to Framwelgate; cathedral view from South St.

The Great Wall of Northumbria
Birdoswald Roman Fort, Gilsland; Roman museum, Greenhead; lunch at Milecastle Inn, on the B6318 NE of Haltwhistle; Vindolanda, Bardon Mill; Housesteads, and walk along Hadrian's Wall; or skip the walk and look at Chesters Roman Fort, Chollerford.

Gems of Teesdale
Barnard Castle, and Bowes Museum; lunch at the Fox & Hounds, Cotherstone or Rose & Crown, Romaldkirk; nature trail from Bowlees visitor centre to Gibson's Cave; High Force; walk from Cow Green Reservoir to Cauldron Snout.

Coastal strongholds
Warkworth Hermitage (when boat is operating) and Castle; light lunch at the Jolly Fisherman, Craster; walk from Craster along coast path to Dunstanburgh Castle and back.

Castles and cattle
Walk in Hulme Park, Alnwick; see castle and town; lunch at the Tankerville Arms, Eglingham; Chillingham – castle, wild cattle, and stroll along escarpment to the hill fort.

Remote wilds of the Cheviots
Cragside, Rothbury; lunch at Newcastle Hotel there; drive up Coquetdale; walk from Alwinton.

Island eye-openers
Boat trip to Farne Islands from Seahouses; lunch at the Olde Ship, Seahouses; Bamburgh Castle; Holy Island (time visit to catch low tide).

Railway pioneers and the Tyne valley
Tanfield Railway, or Gibside, Burnopfield; lunch at the Feathers, Hedley on the Hill (wknd) or Manor House, Carterway Heads; Cherryburn, Stocksfield, or Prudhoe Castle; Stephenson's cottage nr Prudhoe.

Weardale drive
Hexham; lunch at the King's Head, Allendale or (more fun) Allenhead Inn, Allenheads; Killhope lead mining centre and Weardale Museum, Weardale; minor moorland roads to Blanchland.

Claude. Also famous collection of Meissen china, Roman remains, children's playground. Plans are now afoot for a multi-million-pound restoration of the previously magnificent gardens. Meals, snacks, shop; cl Fri, and Oct–Easter; (01665) 510777; £5.75, £4 grounds only. The hillside CHURCH of St Michael and All Angels above the river is a perfect example of a complete late Gothic building. The Market Tavern has bargain food.

🏰 **Aydon** NZ0166 CASTLE 13th-c, and remarkably well preserved, in a lovely setting. Snacks, shop, some disabled access; cl Nov–Mar; (01434) 632450; £1.80.

🏰 ★ ♨ † **Bamburgh** NU1735 BAMBURGH CASTLE Stunning huge square Norman castle on a cliff above the sea, its clock serving as timekeeper for the cricket green in the attractive village below. Despite the forbidding exterior, the inside is very much a lived-in stately home, with armour from the Tower of London. Snacks, shop; cl Nov–Mar; (01668) 214515; £3.50. GRACE DARLING MUSEUM (Radcliffe Rd) Pictures and mementos of the local heroine, inc the boat in which Grace and her father rescued 9 survivors from the wrecked SS *Forfarshire*. Shop, disabled access; cl Nov–Easter; free (donations to RNLI). There's a neo-Gothic shrine to Grace in the yard of the interesting 13th-c CHURCH. The Lord Crewe Arms is well placed for lunch.

★ 🏚 🖼 🏰 † **Barnard Castle** NZ0516 Pleasant market town, still coming to life on Weds market day, with several attractive buildings. BOWES MUSEUM 🖼 A beautiful French-style chateau in 20 acres of meticulously kept formal grounds. The 40 rooms are filled with sumptuous fine arts and an outstanding display of paintings by Canaletto, Goya, El Greco and others; also children's room and local history section. Relatively few people find their way to this treasure house, though it's one of the most worthwhile places to visit in the entire country; on a cold winter's day you'll have it and its frost-sparkling grounds virtually to yourself. Meals

Northumbria

Berwick-upon-Tweed
Horncliffe
Cornhill-on-Tweed
Crookham
Ford
Lindisfarne
NU
Bamburgh
Chatton
Warenford
Seahouses
Beadnell
Benthall
Chillingham
Newton by the Sea
Embleton
Craster
Rennington
Alnwick
Boulmer
Rothbury
Alnmouth
Longframlington
Warkworth
Amble
Longhorsley
West Woodburn
Woodhorn
Kirkwhelpington
Cambo
Bellingham
Whalton
Morpeth
Belsay
Carrawbrough
Chollerford Matfen
Wall
Housesteads
Ponteland
North Shields
Whitley Bay
Bardon Mill
Aydon
Corbridge
Haydon Bridge
Hexham
Newcastle
upon Tyne
Jarrow
Tynemouth
South
Shields
TYNE &
WEAR
Prudhoe
Gateshead
Stocksfield
Hedley on the Hill
Whitburn
Roker
Slaley
Rowlands Gill
Tanfield
Washington
Monkwearmouth
Burnopfield
Carterway
Heads
Beamish
Blanchland
WEARDALE
Lanchester
Durham
NZ
Wolsingham
Peterlee
Witton-le-Wear
Hamsterley Forest
Binchester
Hartlepool
TEESDALE
Middleton in
Teesdale
Bishop
Auckland
Shildon
High Force
Eggleston
Romaldkirk
Cotherstone
Staindrop
Stockton-
on-Tees
Barnard Castle
Bowes
Headlam
Darlington
Middlesbrough
Greta
Bridge
A66
BOWES
MOOR
NORTH YORKSHIRE

and snacks (summer only), shop, disabled access; usually only cl am Sun and over Christmas, but may be best to check in winter; (01833) 690606; *£4. CASTLE These dramatically set 12th-c ruins include the original keep and the 14th-c hall. Snacks, shop, disabled facilities; cl winter Mon and Tues, 24–26 Dec, 1 Jan; (01833) 638212; *£2. In the centre, the Golden Lion and Old Well have good-value food. EGGLESTONE ABBEY Downstream from Barnard Castle, this is reached by a couple of miles of enjoyable riverside walk – or by car. Substantial remains include gracefully arched windows, and some remnants of the monastic buildings; disabled access; free. ROKEBY PARK (just SE of Barnard Castle) Elegant 18th-c villa in a fine setting, most famous for its *Rokeby Venus* by Velásquez (though the original is now in the National Gallery). The best of the other pictures is probably Pellegrini's *Venus disarming Cupid*. Disabled access to ground floor only; open May bank hols, then pm Mon and Tues Jun–2nd Tues in Sept; (01833) 637334; £3.50. The Morritt Arms nearby does good meals. The B6278 to Stanhope and Edmundbyers is a fine drive.

ͱ ⵏ ! **Beamish** NZ2253 THE NORTH OF ENGLAND OPEN AIR MUSEUM Perhaps the most rewarding paid attraction in Britain, an amazingly ambitious 300-acre museum exhaustively re-creating life in the North of England at the turn of the century. No detail is overlooked, and there's something for everyone in the 5 main sections: a town with streets, shops, houses and businesses, colliery village with mine, chapel, cottages and school, manor house with formal gardens and orchard, railway station, and home farm with animals and craft demonstrations (ducks and geese wander round for extra authenticity). Costumed interpreters really bring the place to life. Children can wander round this authentic little world at their leisure, touching everything, and joining in most of the activities, from learning to play hoops and hopscotch to taking part in lessons in the schoolroom (bad handwriting is rewarded by a light rap on the knuckles). A Victorian fairground has rides including a Hall of Mirrors (small extra charge), and working trams and buses join up the different areas. Meals and snacks (inc period pub), good shops, some disabled access; cl Mon and Fri Nov–Mar, and two wks over Christmas; (01207) 231811; *£7.99 in summer hols, otherwise *£6.99, or *£2.99 late Oct–Mar when only the town and tramway are open (the plus side to a winter visit is there are fewer people then, so guides take more time to explain things). The Shepherd & Shepherdess not far from the gate is useful for lunch, as is the more individual Beamish Mary (follow sign from the A693 to No Place & Cooperative Villas).

✝ **Bellingham** NY8383 (pronounced Bellingjum) A small country town with an attractive 13th-c church, stone-roofed to protect it against arson-minded Border raiders; there's a pretty walk just N of the town, to the 9-metre (30-ft) cascade of Hareshaw Linn. Summer PONY-TREKKING from Brown Rigg Farm, (01434) 220272. The Cheviot Hotel does decent food. This is the main town in North Tynedale, one of the least-known and most unspoilt parts of Northumberland, with good scenic drives. Between the Pennines and the Cheviots, it's a peaceful river valley surrounded by wild moorland, with fine scenery and a particularly unrushed atmosphere – very relaxing.

🏠 ⛰ ❀ **Belsay** NZ1079 BELSAY HALL, CASTLE AND GARDENS (on the A696) The same family have lived here for nearly 600 years, first in a medieval castle, then a Jacobean manor house and finally a grand mansion designed to look like a Greek classical temple – all can still be seen. The 30 acres of landscaped parkland are especially agreeable, with rhododendron garden, formal terraces and woodland walks. Snacks, shop, disabled access; cl 24–26 Dec; (01661) 881636; £3.50. The Highlander has good food.

★ 🏠 ✝ ♨ ⵏ **Berwick-upon-Tweed**

NT9953 Largely unspoilt, this has some handsome 18th-c buildings and a fine 17th-c church; most people who come here seem to while away at least a bit of time watching the swans on the River Tweed. Alternatively, look out over the sea from the Rob Roy (Spittal Rd), which has good local fish. The town walls, partly grassed over and easy to walk, were a masterpiece of 16th-c military planning. BERWICK BARRACKS (The Parade) Britain's oldest surviving purpose-built barracks, now a local history museum and gallery, with an interesting exhibition on the British soldier. Snacks, shop, disabled access; cl winter Mon and Tues, 24–26 Dec, 1 Jan; (01289) 330044; *£2.30. WINE AND SPIRIT MUSEUM (Palace Green) The mainland base of Lindisfarne mead makers (see St Aidan's winery under Lindisfarne entry, p.490), with a collection of objects from the wine and spirits industries, working potter, home-made pot-pourri, and Victorian chemist shop. Snacks, shop, disabled access; cl Sun and Christmas wk; (01289) 305153; free.

🏛 **Binchester** NZ2332 ROMAN FORT Quite a lot left of this 1st-c 10-acre fort, inc the best-preserved military baths in the country, with an exceptional hypocaust system. Interesting events such as days when you can sample Roman food. Shop, disabled access; cl Oct–Easter; (01388) 663089; *£1.50. A 3rd-c fort can be seen a few miles S at Piercebridge NZ2116 (where the riverside George, with its famous grandfather clock which stopped when the old man died, is useful for lunch), and finds from both sites are shown at the Bowes Museum in Barnard Castle (see entry above, p.484).

🏰 † 🏛 † **Bishop Auckland** NZ2130 AUCKLAND CASTLE The main country residence of the Bishops of Durham, a grand series of buildings entered through a splendid Gothic gatehouse in the town's market place. Some rooms are relatively stark, but a highlight is the chapel, splendidly transformed from a 12th-c banqueting hall by John Cosin from 1660. The attractive grounds have an unusual 18th-c deercote. Shop; open pm Fri and Sun May–Sept, plus Thurs July–Aug, and Sat in Aug; (01388) 601627; £3. ESCOMB CHURCH (just N of Bishop Auckland) This interesting 7th-c church is built of stone from Binchester Roman fort.

★ **Blanchland** NY9750 The archetypal border village, every house looking a stronghold, alone in a great bowl of magnificent scenery; the Lord Crewe Arms here is an interesting hotel, in parts very ancient indeed.

🏛 **Bowes** NY9913 BOWES CASTLE Within the earthworks of a Roman fort, these remains include the great Norman keep, 3 storeys high; free. A few miles W, the Bowes Moor Hotel, one of England's highest, is a welcoming moorland oasis.

† 🏛 **Burnopfield** NZ1757 GIBSIDE Marvellous Palladian mausoleum for the Bowes family in 18th-c landscaped park, with the rather sad ruins of a hall and other estate buildings dotted around. Miles of pleasant walks. Snacks, shop, disabled access; cl Mon (exc bank hols) and Nov–Mar; (01207) 542255; £3; NT. The Highlander at White le Head has decent food.

🏰 🏛 **Cambo** NZ0285 WALLINGTON HOUSE Built in 1688 and altered in the 1740s, with fine plasterwork and porcelain, and works by the pre-Raphaelite circle, often found here in the house's 19th-c cultural glory days. Showpiece fuchsias in the conservatory, and 100 acres of lawns, terraces, lakes and woodland. Meals, snacks, shop, plant centre, disabled facilities; house cl am, all day Tues, and Nov–Mar, grounds and garden open all year; (01670) 774283; £4.80, grounds only £2.80; NT.

🏛 🏛 ¥ 🏛 ❋ **Chillingham** NU0525 CHILLINGHAM CASTLE Striking old castle dating back to 12th c, full of antiques, tapestries, arms and armour. Formal gardens, woodland walks, lake, and splendid views of the surrounding countryside; occasional concerts and special events. Brave souls can rent one of their haunted rooms. Snacks, shop, some disabled access; cl am, Tues (exc July and Aug), and Oct–Apr; (01668) 215359; £3.75. CHILLINGHAM WILD CATTLE PARK The famous large-horned white cattle have been here for the last 700 years, the only animals of their kind still pure and uncrossed with domestic breeds. As they're potentially aggressive, tours are conducted by a warden. Bring binoculars for a closer view. Snacks, shop, limited disabled access; cl 12–2pm, am Sun, all day Tues, and Nov–Mar; (01668) 215250; £2.50. ROSS CASTLE NU0825 Above the park, this hill fort has great views. The Percy Arms at Chatton is good for lunch.

Chollerford SY9372 HEXHAM HERBS (B6318, nr Chesters Fort) Over 800 varieties of herbs beautifully laid out in attractive walled gardens; also old-fashioned roses, many other plants, and woodland walk. Shop, some disabled access, plant sales; cl Nov–Mar (or by appointment only); (01434) 681483; £1.20.

Darlington NZ2419 RAILWAY CENTRE AND MUSEUM Interesting museum in carefully restored North Rd Station, part of which is still used for train services. Exhibits include the *Locomotion* built by Robert Stephenson in 1825, which pulled the first passenger steamtrain on a public railway. Steamtrain rides some summer wknds. Snacks, shop, disabled access; cl 25–26 Dec, all Jan; (01325) 460532; £2. An extraordinary BRICKWORK LOCOMOTIVE, a 40 metre (130 ft) approximation of the pre-war record-breaking *Mallard*, complete with clouds of bricky steam, was unveiled beside Morrisons supermarket in summer 1997; worth its £760,000? The friendly local history MUSEUM (Tubwell Row) is enlivened May–Sept by an observation beehive. Limited disabled access; cl 1–2pm, Weds, Sun, some bank hols; (01325) 463795; free. St Cuthbert's (Church Row) is an interesting Early English CHURCH. A Malaysian newspaper last year gave Darlington a bizarrely over-enthusiastic write-up, which even locals proud of their railway heritage

considered to be on the wrong track.

★ **Eggleston** NY9924 Attractive moorside Teesdale village, with EGGLESTON HALL GARDENS a good example of an updated 19th-c country-house garden, with rare and unusual trees, shrubs, perennials and other plants. They sell plants, organically grown herbs, and fruit and vegetables from the walled kitchen garden. Snacks, some disabled access; (01833) 650378; 50p, or £1 for a season ticket (money refunded if you buy a plant).

Embleton NU2322 DUNSTANBURGH CASTLE Screeching seagulls add to the atmosphere at these huge ruins, standing imposingly on the cliff above the North Sea. Turner painted the scene 3 times. Cl winter Mon and Tues, 24–26 Dec, 1 Jan; (01665) 576231; *£1.60; NT. The comfortable hotel named after the castle does good-value meals. The NT also own much of this stretch of coastline, inc the pleasantly bracing walk to Craster.

★ **Ford** NT9437 Built as a model estate-workers' village, for Ford Castle; very attractive, with one or two craft workshops, a well restored working corn mill (cl most of winter; £2), and the friendly Heatherslaw Bakery making good use of the resulting corn. HEATHERSLAW LIGHT RAILWAY Steam or diesel journeys on narrow-gauge railway along pretty valley of the River Till. Snacks, shop, disabled access; cl Nov–Easter, exc some wknds before Christmas; (01890) 820317 for times; £3.20. Trains go to nearby Etal NT9339, a pretty row of white cottages running down to a ford across the river, with a working forge and good thatched pub. ETAL CASTLE Good Walkman tours guide you round these evocative 14th-c ruins; also exhibition on Border history. Shop, disabled access to exhibition area; cl Nov–Easter; (01890) 820332; *£2.30. You can hire bikes on (01890) 820527.

Gateshead NZ2662 Not yet the area's most appealing stop for visitors, though work is starting on a £100 million Tyneside arts complex, partly funded by Lottery money, to include a massive contemporary arts centre – if you can wait till 2000. Meantime, the METRO CENTRE (on the A1 just W) is a useful rainy-day outing from Newcastle, a vast modern shopping and leisure complex with several different themed undercover areas, all sorts of fairground attractions (better for younger children than teenage thrill seekers), even a Roman Catholic church now. Do remember exactly where you put your car – there are 12,000 parking spaces. If you're in Gateshead, the SHIPLEY ART GALLERY on Prince Consort Rd is worth a look (cl am Sun; free); and the Keelmans riverside walk (off South Shore Rd) is quite pleasant. A monster much-criticised sculpture of an angel beside the A1 should have been completed by the time this edition hits the shops.

✿ Hamsterley Forest NZ0429 5,000-acre fellside forest with good walks, cycle routes, 4-mile forest drive, and visitor centre with local wildlife exhibitions (cl Nov–Easter); (01388) 488312; forest drive £1.50 a car. The Cross Keys at Hamsterley NZ1231 is a useful base.

✿ ♣ ⛴ ♨ Hartlepool NZ5133 Developing several lively new attractions likely to put it firmly on the tourist map. HISTORIC QUAY At the old docks, this is a vivid open-air re-creation of an 18th-c port, complete with painstakingly reconstructed furnished houses, market, prison, and fully stocked shops. Also a couple of film shows, and dramatic (and noisy) exhibition on fighting ships. Lots to see, exceptionally well done. Meals, snacks, shop, disabled access; cl 25 Dec, 1 Jan; (01429) 860888; £4.95. The next-door Jacksons Wharf has decent food. Berthed nr here is HMS *Trincomalee*, the world's second-oldest floating warship; cl 25 Dec, 1 Jan; (01429) 223193; £2.50. More reconstructions at the excellent MUSEUM OF HARTLEPOOL (The Marina), which again has something of a maritime emphasis. The well restored paddle steamer *Wingfield Castle* has now moved here (it's used in part as a café). Meals, snacks,

shop, disabled access; cl 25–26 Dec, 1 Jan; (01429) 222255; free. The town also has some remains of its medieval wall, and a factory shopping mall. HARTLEPOOL POWER STATION (3m S) The visitor centre has lively displays and tours (best to book). Shop, disabled access; cl 25–26 Dec, 1 Jan; (01429) 853888; free.

★ ☕ ✝ Hexham NY9364 A pleasant market town, not too big, with some attractive stone buildings. One, the country's first purpose-built prison, houses the BORDER HISTORY MUSEUM, colourfully charting the chequered contacts between the English and Scots. Shop; cl Weds–Fri in Oct, Nov, Feb and Mar, and every day Dec and Jan; (01434) 652351; £1.60. Founded around 674 by St Wilfrid, HEXHAM ABBEY was once the largest church north of the Alps. The bulk of what is seen today dates from the 12th c, though there are 2 splendid Saxon survivals – the superbly atmospheric crypt, and the throne of the Bishop (St Wilfrid's Chair or Frith stool). The choir still descend the unique Night Stairs for services. Summer snacks, shop, disabled access; free, but donations welcome. The County Hotel is a standby for lunch. WARDEN CHURCH NY6265 (just N of Hexham) Down a lane by the Tyne, this is a fine example of the sturdy northern churches that had to do double duty as holy places and watchtowers to warn of Border raiders. The B6305/B6295 through Allendale is a scenic drive; lots of walks up there, and very good stops at the King's Head in Allendale town and entertaining Allenheads Inn further up.

🐝 Horncliffe NT9350 CHAIN BRIDGE HONEY FARM 1,100 colonies of bees, a good visitor centre, and honey-based products for sale. Cl am Sun, and Nov–Mar; (01289) 386362; free.

✝ ☕ Jarrow NZ3065 ST PAUL'S CHURCH AND MONASTERY The Venerable Bede lived here for most of his 7th/8th-c life, producing the 37 books that encompass much of what is known of life in early Christian England. Along with the other half of the monastery, St Peter's, at nearby

Monkwearmouth, the site is still a major Christian shrine. Very little remains of the original monastery, but there's Saxon stained glass in the church, and the chancel incorporates one of the earlier chapels. A museum in adjacent Georgian Jarrow Hall has finely carved Anglo-Saxon stones, more stained glass, and excavated relics. The whole site is now known as BEDE'S WORLD, and is developing rather rapidly; there's an authentically re-created 11-acre period farm. Meals, snacks, shop, some disabled access; cl am Sun, all day Mon (exc bank hols), Christmas wk; (0191) 489 2106; £3.

✠ ⚓ 🐾 🐟 **Kielder Water** NY6688 This huge reservoir has done a lot to open up a remote part of the Borders; an attractive drive from Bellingham. It's an interesting shape, modelled by the steep folds of the land, and is already beginning to look as if it's always been tucked away in these pine-blanketed hills. TOWER KNOWE VISITOR CENTRE Down at the foot of the lake, with an exhibition and useful information about the area and its wildlife. Meals, snacks, shop, disabled access; cl Nov–Mar; (01434) 240398; centre free, exhibition £1. CRUISES start from here too, and call all around the lake (takes about an hour and a half). LEAPLISH WATERSIDE PARK (slightly round to the W) Another good starting point, with lots to do in summer, inc plenty of water sports, trails, and canoe and other BOAT HIRE; (01434) 250312. Reivers of Tarset also hire out boats and canoes: rowing boats from £4 an hour, motor boats from £15; (01434) 250203. Visitor centres can supply fishing permits for the lake. You can rent LOG CABINS by the week; (01502) 500500. BAKETHIN CONSERVATION AREA Up at the top of the lake, this is particularly rewarding for wildlife. CYCLING is fun round here – the very friendly Kielder Bikes company hire bikes from Hawkhope car park (they're good for repairs too); (01434) 250392; a good mountain bike costs around £8 for 3 hours. Their main shop is in the village of Kielder NY6293 itself, opposite

KIELDER CASTLE, an 18th-c hunting lodge built for the Duke of Northumberland. It's now a very good Forest Enterprise visitor centre with exhibitions and closed-circuit TV bird watching. Shop, meals and a play area; (01434) 250209; cl Nov–Easter; free. Regular guided walks from here into the surrounding Kielder Forest – miles of pine trees with a good chance of seeing red squirrels, as well as deer; some nice spots for picnics. There's also a 12-mile forest drive. The Pheasant at Stannersburn has good food.

🐖 **Lanchester** NZ1647 HALL HILL FARM ▦ (SW on the B6296) Friendly working farm with lots of animals, nature trails, riverside walk and trailer rides. Snacks, shop; cl Sat, and Sept–Mar exc Sun in Sept, Oct and maybe Dec – best to check; (01388) 730300; £3. The Queen's Head is good for food.

✝ 🏰 🐄 🏛 **Lindisfarne** NU1413 Otherwise known as Holy Island, this important centre for Christian pilgrims is linked to the mainland by a causeway which you can drive (or walk) over at low tide. Tide tables are posted at each end, or tel (01289) 389200; it really is worth checking these carefully – the causeway is impassable for 2 hours before high tide and 4 hours after. If you want to visit a particular attraction, make sure that the tide and the opening times match on the day you want to go. There are nature-reserve dunes, fishermen's huts made of upturned former boats, old lime-kilns, a small extended village with tourist cafés and pubs, and good views from the close-grazed grassy crags. The main draw is LINDISFARNE PRIORY, from where in the 7th c St Aidan and monks from Iona replanted the seeds of Christianity in Dark Age England. These early monks were driven out by Vikings, so it's the extensive remains of a later 12th-c church you can see today; a very peaceful and romantic spot, with graceful red sandstone arches bordered by incongruously neat lawns. Shop, disabled access to visitor centre; cl 24–26 Dec; (01289) 389200; £2.50. The rather lonely and austere exterior of LINDISFARNE CASTLE belies what's within; the 16th-c fortress was restored by Lutyens for the editor of *Country Life* in a suitably monolithic quasi-medieval style. Sumptuous furnishings include a fine collection of antique oak furniture, and there's a walled garden designed by Gertrude Jekyll to protect against the North Sea winds. Cl am, Fri (exc Good Fri), and Nov–Mar; (01289) 389244; *£3.80; NT. It's a mile's walk fom the car park. ST AIDAN'S WINERY Home of Lindisfarne Mead, a fortified wine made from grapes, honey, herbs and water from an island well. They make honey too, and the shop has British beers, ciders and cheeses, as well as local pottery and jewellery. Shop, cl winter wknds, 19 Dec–5 Jan, and other times according to tide; (01289) 89230; free. The Lindisfarne Hotel is useful for more conventional refreshment.

† Longframlington NU1201 BRINKBURN PRIORY Well preserved 12th-c church (thanks to some Victorian restoration), still with medieval grave slabs, font and double piscina. Occasional services and concerts. Shop, some disabled access; open pm Apr–Sept; (01665) 570628; *£1.40. The Granby is useful for lunch.

† 🏛 Monkwearmouth NZ4058 ST PETER'S CHURCH Sister church of St Paul's at Jarrow (see entry above, p.489), its early years equally well documented by the Venerable Bede. Much of the original Saxon church still remains, inc the west wall and tower. A striking Colin Wilbourn sculpture outside commemorates the church's 7th-c founder Benedict Biscop. Monkwearmouth Station has a RAILWAY MUSEUM, with as well as trains the chance to learn to drive a bus. Cl am Sun; (0191) 567 7075; free. N of here (on the A183 towards N Shields) the Grotto at Marsden is unique: a lift (or a hundred or so steps) down to a pub cut into the seaside cliffs.

🏛 ⚘ Morpeth NZ2086 The clock tower here is one of only 8 non-church bell towers in Britain; it has only one hand, but still rings the curfew every night. MORPETH CHANTRY BAGPIPE MUSEUM (Bridge St) Harmonious collection of small pipes and bagpipes from around the world. Headphones explain the difference between a rant and a reel. Shop; cl winter Suns, Easter Sun, and Christmas wk; (01670) 519466; *£1.50. Good CRAFT CENTRE next door (cl Sun). The Tap & Spile, open all day, has good-value food.

🏛 ☺ North Shields NZ3468 The excellent STEPHENSON RAILWAY MUSEUM (Middle Engine Lane) has steamtrain trips along a short section of the North Tyneside Railway, as well as displays on the development of steam and a collection of rolling stock, inc George Stephenson's *Billy*. Last year they were open wknds from May–Sept, but best to ring for 1998 opening, (0191) 262 2627; site free, charge for steam trips. WET 'N' WILD (Royal Quays) Children like this well heated indoor water park with 7 exciting flumes and slides (one has a *very* steep drop). Cl some days in Nov and Dec; (0191) 296 1333; £6.25 wknds and school hols, otherwise £4.95 (less after 6pm). The Magnesia Bank (Camden St) has good-value food.

🏛 ☘ Peterlee NZ4138 CASTLE EDEN DENE The biggest of Durham's wooded coastal ravines, now a picturesque nature reserve with 12 miles of footpaths over 550 acres; free.

🏵 🍃 Ponteland NZ1773 KIRKLEY HALL GARDENS (2m NW towards Morpeth) Attractive and thoughtfully maintained, with a big collection of herbaceous perennials, Victorian walled garden, pretty sunken garden, woodland garden and unusual trees and shrubs. The gardens are currently being remodelled, and a new water garden should be finished by the summer. Disabled access; (01661) 860808; £1.50. Nearby Milbourne has a good FARM SHOP with PICK-YOUR-OWN.

🏛 🏚 Prudhoe NZ0962 PRUDHOE CASTLE 12th/14th-c ruined castle on an impressive mound (the name means 'proud hill') overlooking the

Tyne, once the stronghold of the powerful Percy family. Remarkable restored gatehouse, and exhibition in nearby 19th-c manor house. Snacks, shop, disabled access; (01661) 833459; open pm Apr–Sept; £1.60. The Feathers at Hedley on the Hill does good weekend food.

STEPHENSON'S BIRTHPLACE NZ1265 (Wylam) The single room open here is the NT's least visited property, some days attracting nobody at all (open pm Thurs, Sat and Sun, 80p); the Fox & Hounds (a short walk along the old railway track) and Boathouse have good-value food.

✝ Roker NZ4159 has an interesting CHURCH, designed by leading members of the Arts and Crafts movement.

🏠 🏵 Rothbury NU0602 CRAGSIDE Opulent Victorian mansion of Lord Armstrong, the armaments king, with some spectacular rooms. Best of all are the miles of well wooded landscaped grounds, with lakes, glorious rhododendrons, showy formal garden, and a walk illustrating the various elements of the hydro-electric scheme he devised to light the house. Meals, snacks, shop, disabled access (inc fishing pier on trout lake); cl Mon exc bank hols, and Nov–Mar (though garden, grounds and visitor centre open wknds and Tues Nov and Dec); (01669) 620333; £5.80, £3.80 grounds only; NT. The Queen's Head and recently refurbished Newcastle Hotel have decent food. The B6344/B6341 into Coquetdale and then on to Alwinton is Northumberland's most scenic drive; picturesque walks around Holystone NT9508 (where the Salmon is a useful stop), and increasingly desolate up towards Blindburn.

🏠✝ Rowlands Gill NZ1759 DERWENTCOTE STEEL FURNACE (on the A694 between Rowlands Gill and Hamsterley, where the Cross Keys does good-value food) The earliest and most complete steel-making furnace to have survived, with an exhibition on steel production. Shop, disabled access; open pm 1st and 3rd Sun of month, Apr–Sept; (01207) 562573; free.

🏖 ⚓ Seahouses NU2232 An unpretentious seaside resort, with amusement arcades and so forth – and a busy fishing harbour, overlooked by an interesting pub, the Olde Ship. From Apr to Sept, weather permitting, boat trips around the FARNE ISLANDS let you see the eider ducks, thousands of other seabirds, and grey seals. Breeding season for the birds is usually around May–July, though perhaps a little later for the seals, whose plaintive-voiced pups stay on shore for only a few weeks. Most boats trips cost around £7. Landing on the NT-owned islands is extra (from £2.90, £3.80 breeding times). The NT has an information centre about the islands on Main St in Seahouses, (01665) 721099.

🏠✝ Seaton Sluice NZ3477 SEATON DELAVAL Vanbrugh's Palladian masterpiece, a splendid design of central porticoed main block and massive outer wings. Not all the interior has survived unscathed, and much of the original park and grounds has been submerged by surrounding developments. Snacks, shop; open pm Weds, Sun and bank hols, May–Aug, plus Thurs July–Aug; (0191) 237 3040; *£3. The buildings around the Norman CHURCH are attractive, and the Waterford Arms nr the low-key seafront does generous fresh fish.

🚂 Shildon NZ2326 TIMOTHY HACKWORTH RAILWAY MUSEUM (Hackworth Cl, just SE) Restored home of early railway pioneer, with working replica of Sans Pareil in the goods yard, and occasional passenger rides along 400 yds of original Stockton & Darlington track bed. Snacks, shop, limited disabled access; cl Mon (exc bank hols), Tues, and Nov–Easter; (01388) 777999; £1.50.

🏛 🕙 South Shields NZ3567 ARBEIA ROMAN FORT 🆔 (Baring St) Huge variety of remains, as well as re-created scenes of camp life, a museum with excellently displayed finds, and plenty for children to enjoy. Snacks, shop, some disabled access; cl Sun exc pm Apr–Sept; (0191) 456 1369; free, £1 for Time Quest (splendid hands-on archaeology exhibition). Just round the corner on Ocean St, the MUSEUM AND ART GALLERY also has some hands-on exhibitions; same hrs; (0191) 456 8740; free. Kirkpatricks (Ocean Rd) is a comfortable dining pub, and the Marsden Rattler (South Foreshore) is an enjoyable seafront bar complete with 2 original railway carriages.

▥ ⛊ Staindrop NZ1220 RABY CASTLE Imposing fortress with Saxon origins; vast medieval hall, 14th-c kitchen, and dazzling Victorian octagonal drawing room – now restored to its original splendour. From the outside – where there are walled gardens and a deer park – it looks just as a castle ought to. Snacks, shop (selling oven-ready game from the estate), disabled access to grounds only; open bank hol wknds from Easter, Weds and Sun May and Jun, and daily exc Sat July–Sept, castle pm only; (01833) 660202; *£4. The village is pretty. Up at Butterknowle the Malt Shovel has good-value food, evenings and wknd lunchtimes.

▥ ▦ ⚘ ❋ Stocksfield NZ0661 CHERRYBURN (slightly E at Mickley) Well preserved 18th-c farm, the birthplace of artist and naturalist Thomas Bewick, with an exhibition on his life. A nice spot, with farm animals running about the yard, craft demonstrations, and good valley views. Shop, some disabled access; cl am, all day Tues and Weds, and Nov–Apr; (01661) 843276; £2.70; NT. The Highlander at Ovington has good value food.

⚱ ⚘ ❀ Stockton-on-Tees NZ4419 GREEN DRAGON MUSEUM (Theatre Yard) Local history inc a good audio-visual presentation on the birth of the railways here in 1825. Shop, some disabled access (prior notice preferred); cl Sun and bank hols; (01642) 674308; free. There's a railway heritage trail around town. Slightly E along the river, the surprisingly graceful Tees Barrage keeps polluted tidal water from mixing with water from the hills, moors and valleys, which it's hoped will stimulate watersports in the area. PRESTON HALL MUSEUM (on the A135 Stockton –Yarm) Very well

constructed Victorian high street and other period rooms, plus working craftsmen, aviary, and woodland and riverside walks. Snacks, shop, disabled access to ground floor only; cl am Sun, 1 Jan, Good Fri, 25–26 Dec; (01642) 781184; free, though £1 for parking. On the same site BUTTERFLY WORLD has a re-created jungle environment with hundreds of exotic butterflies flitting between the trees, rocks and waterfalls. Shop, disabled access; cl Nov–Feb; (01642) 791414; £2.75.

🚋 Tanfield NZ1855 TANFIELD RAILWAY ⚏ (A6076) The world's oldest surviving railway, built in 1725 to carry coal to the Tyne, and set in a picturesque wooded valley. Steamtrains still chuff along the route, and you can get off by a wooded gorge spanned by CAUSEY ARCH, the earliest railway bridge. There's a collection of locomotives, and they often have a blacksmith forging new parts for restoration work. Summer snacks, shop, disabled access; trains usually run every Sun, plus Thurs and Sat in summer hols, and bank hols; (0191) 274 2002 for timetable; fares from £3.30.

Ⅴ Teesdale has the best of County Durham's scenery; the B6277 below its moors and on to Alston in Cumbria is one of the finest drives in England. Upper Teesdale is famous for its limestone flora, inc rare arctic alpine species and the unique Teesdale violet; Widdybank Fell is a National Nature Reserve. England's most powerful WATERFALL at High Force NY8728 (on the B6277) drops into a craggy cauldron at the end of a striking wooded gorge – though you'll have to pay around 50p (on top of parking) for the best view. The nearby High Force Hotel has decent food (and the highest brewery in England). The attractive villages of Middleton-in-Teesdale NY9526, Romaldkirk NY9922 (there's an especially distinguished church here), Eggleston NN9924 and Cotherstone NZ0199 all have good pubs and inns. Side tracks with rewards at their end include the cosy Strathmore Arms in Holwick NY9027 or the Cow Green reservoir (a short drive or walk above the pleasant Langdon Beck Inn NY8631, with the 60-metre (200-ft) cascade of Cauldron Snout below it); good fishing on the river or the reservoirs above it, and fine landscapes all the way along.

🏰 ♪ **Tynemouth** NZ3669 CASTLE AND PRIORY Evocative clifftop ruins, high above the Tyne estuary. Little remains of the once-rich 11th-c Benedictine priory beyond its stirring nave and chancel, and the spooky gravestones outside. Even less is left of the 11th/14th-c castle, but it's unusual to find 2 such ruins next to each other, and it's a great spot for picnics. Shop, disabled access; in winter cl 1–2pm, and all day Mon and Tues, 24–26 Dec, 1 Jan; (0191) 257 1090; £1.60. SEA LIFE CENTRE 🔲 (Grand Parade, Beaconsfield) The same reliable mixture as at their other centres, with a spectacular underwater tunnel surrounded by shark-infested water, and the unique Jelly Lab, demonstrating the life cycle of a jelly fish. Meals, snacks, shop, disabled access; cl 25 Dec; (0191) 257 6100; *£4.50. The Salutation (Front St) is comfortable for lunch.

† 🏰 **Warkworth** NU2403 The main street of this quietly picturesque small town rises attractively from the riverside 12th-c NORMAN CHURCH, with its finely vaulted chancel, to the striking CASTLE on its hill above the River Coquet. It's virtually complete, so wandering round the crooked passageways and dark staircases is wonderfully atmospheric. Events here were immortalised in Shakespeare's *Henry IV*. Shop; cl 1–2pm winter, 24–26 Dec, 1 Jan; (01665) 711423; £2.20. The Hermitage Hotel and Masons Arms are useful for lunch; there are one or two antique shops, and this stretch of coast has some lovely beaches. WARKWORTH HERMITAGE Prettily placed a short way upstream, this 14th-c cell of retreat is cut into the sandstone cliff, with some crude wall carvings and a tiny vaulted chapel; on Weds and Sun Apr–Sept a boat can take you there; £1.20.

🏯 ⅃⊤ ♥ **Washington** NZ3156 The unspoilt old village comes as a real surprise when you've penetrated the surrounding New Town. WASHINGTON OLD HALL (The Avenue) Well restored stone-built 13th-c manor, for several hundred years the home of George Washington's family, though his ancestors had been established elsewhere (notably Sulgrave Manor in Northants) for quite a while by the time he was born. They're re-creating a Jacobean formal garden. Snacks, shop, disabled access to ground floor only; open Sun–Weds Easter–Oct; (0191) 416 6879; £2.50; NT. The nearby Washington Arms is good-value for lunch, and there's a small MINING MUSEUM down Albany Way (free). WILDFOWL AND WETLANDS CENTRE (District 15, off the A1231 E of Washington) 100 acres with hides, well laid-out walks, adventure play area, and very good visitor centre. Some birds will feed from your hand (birdseed is 30p a bag – worth it to see the flamingos squabbling over every mouthful). Meals, snacks, shop, disabled access; cl 25 Dec; (0191) 416 5454; £4. In summer the River Wear Ferry from Sunderland stops here.

⅃⊤ � ★ **Weardale** This gave much of Co Durham's wealth, with lead and iron mining along its length and in the moors above. There's little reminder of those days now, but the A689 is a memorable drive. KILLHOPE LEAD MINING CENTRE NY8243 probably the best-preserved lead mining site in Britain, and unmissable if you're at all interested in industrial history. Equipped with hard hat and lamps, you're led through the mine's dark, chilly passageways to a huge underground waterwheel. Snacks, shop, limited disabled access; cl Nov–Mar; (01388) 537505; £3 for surface exhibitions, plus £1.60 for mine trip. A RIDING CENTRE at nearby Low Cornriggs Farm has lessons, guided rides along scenic former packhorse routes, and farmhouse B & B; (01388) 537600. WEARDALE MUSEUM at Ireshopeburn NY8639, nr the source of the river, re-creates life in the mining days, and has an exhibition on John Wesley, who often preached in the adjacent chapel. Shop; cl am, all day Mon and Tues (exc in Aug), and Oct–Easter; (01388) 537417; £1. Along the dale is a string of attractive villages like Stanhope NY9939 (the 'capital' of Weardale, with odd fossil tree stump in churchyard) and Wolsingham NZ0737 (good-value food at the Black Bull), as well as pleasant waterside and moorland walks. The diversion to Rookhope NY9342 is worthwhile: fine alpine plants nursery, small craft centre, decent pub, more good walks. The Golden Lion at St John's Chapel NY8838, open all day in summer, is another useful stop.

🏠 ✝ **Whitburn** NZ4262 SOUTER LIGHTHOUSE When built in 1870 this was the most advanced lighthouse of the day, and the first to be powered by electricity; it still has period rooms and equipment. Meals, snacks, shop, disabled access (but not to tower); cl Fri, all Nov–Easter; (0191) 529 3161; £2.50; NT. The Trust also owns the Leas, the spectacular stretch of coastline around here, leading to Marsden Rock with its colony of kittiwakes, cormorants and fulmars. The Jolly Sailor has decent food.

🏠 ❄ **Whitley Bay** NZ3572 ST MARY'S LIGHTHOUSE Out on St Mary's Island, reached by a causeway at low tide. Good views from the top – to tempt you up the 137 steps, a camera relays the image to a colour TV at the bottom. Shop, adjacent cafe; cl wkdys Nov–Mar (exc some school hols), and possibly other times depending on the tide; (0191) 565 0723; *£2. When the lighthouse is closed the island is worth a visit for the rock pools alone, and is visited all through the year by a wide range of birds. The Shiremoor House Farm up on Middle Engine Lane, New York (handy too for North Shields and Tynemouth) has some of the best food in this area – good value.

✠ **Witton-le-Wear** NZ1730 LOW BARNS NATURE RESERVE 100-acre reserve with nature trails, woodland, grassland, lake and lots of interesting wildlife. Snacks, shop, good disabled access; cl 25–26 Dec, 1 Jan; (01388) 488728; free. The village is attractive, with a tree-lined sloping green; the Victoria is useful for lunch.

🛏✝👤♿ **Woodhorn** NZ3088 WOODHORN COLLIERY MUSEUM (Queen Elizabeth II Country Park) Former colliery buildings re-creating life in the pit and the communities around it. Also short trips on narrow gauge railway, displays of art by local miners, craft workshops and woodland walks. Meals, snacks, shop, some disabled access; cl Mon (exc bank hols); (01670) 856968; free, though 70p for railway. The partly Saxon and Norman WOODHORN CHURCH close by is said to be the oldest on this coast; it has a local history museum and wknd craft demonstrations. Shop, disabled access; cl Mon (exc bank hols), all Nov–Mar; (01670) 817371; free.

★ A number of **attractive coastal villages** and towns dotted along the underpopulated N coast inc Amble NU2704 (solid old fishing harbour, new yacht marina; RSPB boat trips around nearby Coquet Island with its colourful eider ducks and puffins), Alnmouth NU2511 (attractive beaches, good coastal walks, a lot for summer visitors; the Saddle has good food), Beadnall NU2329 (boats on the beach, and an interestingly restored waterside limekiln at nearby Benthall, Boulmer NU2714 (active fishing boats), Craster NU2620 (tidal fishing harbour, good kippering factory, excellent pub) and Low Newton NU2424 (the Joiners Arms in High Newton is famous for its fish and chips; bird reserve nearby). Inland, Matfen NZ0372 is pretty, with a riverside village green; so is Whalton NZ1318.

Please let us know what you think of places in the *Guide*. Use the report forms at the back of the book or simply send a letter.

Walks

The Northumberland coast has much of interest along its sandy and rocky shores, but the hinterland is rather dull, so it's better for pottering and for there-and-back walks than for round ones. A coastal path covers the finest sections. **Dunstanburgh Castle** NU2521 ⌂-1 to Craster NU2620 is one such; **Ross Back Sands** NU1437 ⌂-2 is another – splendid windswept solitude, looking out to Holy Island. **Holy Island** NU1413 ⌂-3 itself has an easy but fascinating 3-mile walk around its shores.

Berwick-upon-Tweed NT9953 ⌂-4 has an extraordinary trio of bridges, and deserves to be approached along the Tweed: there are paths on both banks, starting from the East Ord picnic site by the A1 road bridge; the town ramparts, impressively intact, give good views. **Marsden Bay** NZ4065 ⌂-5 nr South Shields has a nature reserve providing one of the few reasonable coastal walks in industrial Tyneside.

The Cheviots, part of the Northumberland National Park, are strikingly empty and solitary, with only the characteristic local breed of hardy sheep for company in most places. **Windy Gyle** NT8515 ⌂-6 is the high summit by a fine ridge section of the Pennine Way, along the English/Scottish border – the best of the Way's long, lonely plod over these grassy moors. You have to walk some way from the road to reach this main ridge: start from Coquetdale NT8511 and walk along the Street, an ancient drovers' track. Gradients are mild but the peaty ground can get boggy after rain; not all routes are defined on the ground, but stone boundary walls and forest plantations are useful guides. **Clennel Street** NT9207 ⌂-7, another drove road leading from Coquetdale, can be followed from nr Alwinton NT9206, with much the same sort of scenery; there's a pretty way back, along a track by the River Alwin.

Chew Green Roman camps NT7808 ⌂-8 are little-visited spectacular earthworks alone in wild country, reached by a stiff walk up the Pennine Way through the Redesdale Forest above Byrness NT7602. The Pennines up here contain a great many more unspoilt prehistoric and other archaeological remains – useful goals for walkers in these magnificent hills, often yielding remarkable views. Some areas N of the A68 (which as it approaches the Scottish border is a remarkably dramatic drive) and W of the B6341 may temporarily be put out of bounds by Army training; current proposals to extend the Army area are being resisted by conservationists.

Rothbury Terraces NU0501 ⌂-9, nr Rothbury itself, and **Hulme Park** NU1414 ⌂-10 (dogs not allowed), just out of Alnwick's centre, are both excellent for gentler parkland walks; in the latter, don't miss the whimsical Brizlee Tower and hermit's cave.

The great tract of **Kielder Forest** ⌂-11 has been set up as a recreational area, with self-guided forest walks (easy to follow) from half a dozen or more points along the road through.

Wallington House NZ0184 ⌂-12 has free access to its huge estate, which is laced with footpaths and includes prehistoric sites and Capability Brown parkland (you have to pay for the house itself).

Hadrian's Wall ⌂-13 has easy access from the parallel B6318 and numerous car parks on the way. The best-preserved sections include those around Walltown Crags NY6666, Cawfield Crags NY7167 and Housesteads Fort NY7969. There's not a lot of point trying to make walks into circuits: all the interest is along the Wall itself, although in places you may prefer to drop down beneath the switchback Whin Sill (the ridge of hard rock on which the Wall stands), which itself can be quite tiring. The views are bleak and exhilarating. Even in fine summer weather the wind can be chilly on the Wall, so go well wrapped up.

Two NT estates S of Hadrian's Wall make pleasant strolling grounds, with year-round access to the paths: **Bellister** NY6963 ⌂-14 has a ruined castle and peel tower, while Allen Banks and **Staward Gorge** NY8063 ⌂-15 – frequented by roe deer – include the wooded River Allen and another ruined peel tower.

Upper Teesdale ⌂-16 has much of the best walking in the Durham Pennines. Most popular of all is the short path from the main road to the High Force waterfall NY8728. From Bowlees Visitor Centre NY9028 you can make more of a walk of it, first detouring N to Gibson's Cave NY9028, a pretty waterfall at the top of a gorge, and then heading S to cross the Tees for an easy 2 miles upriver, passing Low Force NY9028 on the way. Beyond High Force, the Pennine Way encounters some truly wild landscape as the Tees rushes along a gorge beneath Cronkley Scar NY8329 and tumbles down Cauldron Snout NY7930, a cascade which can be reached from the dam at Cow Green Reservoir NY8129 (where there is also a nature trail).

Barnard Castle NZ0516 ⌂-17 has more gorge scenery around it, here wooded, romantic and unmistakably lowland in character; the valley path W eventually climbs above the river and follows field routes as it leads towards Cotherstone NZ0119.

Where to eat

Bamburgh NU1734 COPPER KETTLE TEA ROOMS 21 Front St (01668) 214315 18th-c cottage nr castle, with beams, panelling, and copper implements; sandwiches, baked potatoes and salads, as well as home-made cakes and biscuits, a fine range of teas inc many fruit and herb teas, and a good choice of other drinks, too; no smoking; cl Nov–Mar; disabled access. £2.50

Berwick-upon-Tweed NU0053 FOXTONS Main St (01289) 303939 Lively bistro with imaginative and varied food that changes daily, good wine list, and friendly service; cl Sun. £19|£7.

Carterway Heads NZ0552 MANOR HOUSE Kiln Pit Hill (01207) 255268 Simple slate-roofed stone house with pleasant view over moorland pastures; plentiful, imaginative food with a menu that changes daily; cl 25 Dec; disabled access. £19.75|£6.40.

Corbridge NY9964 VALLEY Old Station House, Station Rd (01434) 633434 Extremely friendly Indian restaurant in attractively converted sandstone station house, with a wide choice of excellent Indian food and kind service; also, a special train service for parties from Tyneside with uniformed escort and free travel, and your order is phoned ahead to be ready on arrival – good fun; cl lunchtimes, cl Sun; partial disabled access. £20.

Craster NU2620 CRASTER RESTAURANT (01665) 576230 Upstairs restaurant overlooking the harbour with candles on tables, exceedingly welcoming staff, and huge helpings of fairly priced and really fresh fish – they have their own smoking yard, too; cl Oct–May; well behaved children. £6.95|£4.95 fish special.

Haydon Bridge NY8464 GENERAL HAVELOCK (01434) 684283 Very civilised old stone terraced house with stripped-stone back dining room overlooking the Tyne; nice if limited lunchtime food and interesting evening meals, well kept real ales, good wines by the glass, pleasant service, and friendly local atmosphere. £22|£8.50.

Hedley on the Hill NZ0859 FEATHERS (01661) 843607 Little stone local with 3 neatly kept traditional bars, woodburning stoves, straightforward furnishings, a charming, relaxed and welcoming atmosphere; imaginative weekend meals (no weekday food exc Christmas week and bank holidays), and well kept real ales. £15|£3.95.

Matfen NZ0372 BLACK BULL (01661) 886330 Striking, creeper-covered stone building by village green; fresh, well presented tasty bar food in the spacious turkish-carpeted main bar, particularly good restaurant menu, log fires, and efficient service; comfortable bedrooms; disabled access. £18|£5.25.

Rennington NU2118 MASONS ARMS (01665) 577275 Friendly pub with a wide choice of generously served bar food (fine puddings); comfortable lounge bar, cheery licensees, and decent breakfasts; bedrooms. £17.50l£4.95.

Warenford NU1429 WARENFORD LODGE (01668) 213453 Very individual old, though rather modern-feeling dining pub with stripped stonework, big stone fireplace, comfortable extension with woodburning stove; really good and attractively presented, interesting food, and decent wines; children in evening dining room only; cl Mon, am Tues–Fri; disabled access. £14l£5.

Whalton NZ1382 BERESFORD ARMS (01670) 775225 Civilised bar and dining room serving very nice, reasonably priced genuine home cooking; well kept real ales, and friendly staff; cl winter pm Sun; disabled access. £22l£7.

Special thanks to Simon Barriskell, Tina Rossiter, Nicola Wood, Miss J S Thomas, E Howbrook, D Isles, Mrs P Mowatt.

NORTHUMBRIA CALENDAR

Some of these dates were provisional as we went to press. Please check information with the number provided.

JANUARY

23 **Newcastle upon Tyne** New British Painting of the 1990s: 19 artists under 40 inc Damien Hirst, Fiona Rae, Ian Davenport – *till 19 April* (0191) 232 7734

FEBRUARY

1 **Newcastle** Chinese New Year: lion and unicorn dance procession and fireworks (0191) 261 0691

24 **Alnwick** Shrovetide Football at the Castle: ball is thrown from battlements and piped in procession to pastures where the game is played (01665) 574312

APRIL

11 **Gateshead** Spring Flower Show at Gateshead Central Nurseries – *till Sun 12* (0191) 477 1011

17 **Morpeth** Northumbrian Gathering: festival of Northumbrian traditions – *till Sun 19* (01670) 513308

MAY

1 **Berwick-upon-Tweed** Riding the Bounds: colourful groups of horse riders head out of town for an afternoon of fun and races (01289) 307384

3 **West Allerdean** Country Fair at West Allerdean Farm (01289) 387245

16 **Houghall** Farm and Garden Event at Durham College of Agriculture – *till Sun 17* (0191) 386 1351

17 **Berwick-upon-Tweed** Border Marches Festival: circular walks through the River Tweed valley (01289) 330733

20 **Barnard Castle** Carnival – *till* parade on *Mon 25* (01833) 637615

22 **Berwick-upon-Tweed** May Fair: music, stalls – *till Mon 25* (01289) 303677

23 **North Shields** Fish Quay Festival: international street theatre, world music stage, Irish stage, children's village, parade, fireworks – *till Mon 25* (0191) – 200 5157

25 **Corbridge** Northumberland County Show inc arena events at Tynedale Park (01434) 344443

NORTHUMBRIA CALENDAR

MAY cont

30 **Allendale** May Fair: carnival, bands (01434) 683269; **Stockton-on-Tees** Regatta (01642) 670067

JUNE

1 **Darlington** Cycling Festival – *till Tues 30* (01325) 388584

11 **Slaley** European Grand Prix Golf Tournament at Slaley Hall - *till Sun 14* (01434) 673350

13 **Stamfordham** South Tyne Engine Society Steam and Vintage Rally at Ouston Airfield – *till Sun 14* (01434) 321029

19 **Newcastle** Hoppings: funfair at Town Moor – *till Sat 27* (0191) 389 2787

20 **Ovingham** Goose Fair: Morris and country dancing, Northumbrian pipes (01661) 832822

22 **Stocksfield** Country Fair inc field sports at Bywell Hall (01665) 711210

27 **Darlington** Carnival – *till Sun 28* (01325) 483168

28 **Alnwick** Medieval Fair: costumed re-enactment, duckings, courts – *till 4 July* (01665) 605004; **Darlington** National Music Day: live bands in Market Square (01325) 388584

JULY

3 **Whitley Bay** Jazz Festival – *till Sun 5* (0191) 281 2935

4 **Lanchester** Show at Newhouses Farm – *till Sun 5* (0191) 373 4565; **South Shields** Cookson Country Festival: free family festival – *till 9 Aug* (0191) 427 1717; **Washington** International Kite Festival – *till Sun 5* (0191) 514 1235

8 **Barnard Castle** Shakespeare with Fireworks at Bowes Museum: *Much Ado About Nothing* – *till Sat 11* (01833) 650623

10 **Redcar** Festival of International Folk Music, Dance and Song – *till Sun 12* (01947) 840928

11 **Durham** Miners Gala: colourful march culminating in Trade Union rally on racecourse (0191) 384 3515

17 **Burnopfield** Open-air Concert: a tribute to the pop group Queen at Gibside (01670) 774691

18 **Burnopfield** Open-air Concert at Gibside (01670) 774691; **Rothbury** Traditional Music Festival (01669) 620718

19 **Middlesbrough** Mela: Asian Festival (01642) 263839

25 **Gateshead** Summer Flower Show at Gateshead Central Nurseries – *till Sun 26* (0191) 477 1011

31 **Stockton-on-Tees** Riverside International Festival – *till 2 Aug* (01642) 393906

AUGUST

1 **Alnwick** International Music Festival – *till Sat 8* (01665) 602398; **Sunderland** International Airshow – *till Sun 2* (0191) 510 9317

8 **Hartlepool** Headland Carnival (01429) 266105; **Slaley** Show: traditional agricultural show at Townhead Field (01434) 673530

9 **Billingham** International Folklore Festival: 10 countries represented – *till Sun 16* (01642) 393906

15 **Hartlepool** Show at Grayfield Recreation Ground: arena events, vintage vehicles – *till Sun 16* (01429) 266522

21 **Billingham** Show (01642) 670067

NORTHUMBRIA CALENDAR

AUGUST cont

25 **Blanchland and Hunstanworth** Show (01434) 675799

29 **Consett** Show at Allensford Park: festival of music and theatre – *till Mon 31* (01207) 218844; **St John's Chapel** Weardale Agricultural Show – *till Mon 31* (01388) 537398; **Stockton-on-Tees** Summer Carnival at Preston Park – *till Sun 30* (01642) 670067

SEPTEMBER

3 **Newcastle** Free Festival: carnival, mobile sculptures, comedy, dance, jazz – *till Sat 5* (0191) 275 0311

5 **Berwick-upon-Tweed** Military Tattoo – *till Sun 6* (01289) 307427; **Wolsingham** Agricultural Show and Country Fair – *till Mon 7* (01388) 527862

11 **Darlington** Railway Carnival at Darlington Railway Centre and Museum – *till Sun 13* (01325) 388584

12 **Bowes** Agricultural Show (01833) 637059; **Ingram** Agricultural Show (01665) 578361; **Stanhope** Agricultural Show – *till Mon 14* (01833) 650879

13 **Whitfield** Country Fair and Vintage Rally (01434) 345313

19 **Darlington** Championship Dog Show – *till Sun 20* (01325) 312484; **Eggleston** Agricultural Show (01833) 638749

OCTOBER

2 **Houghton-le-Spring** Festival: tournaments, parades – *till Sat 10* 0831 458774

10 **Alwinton** Border Shepherds Show (01669) 630246; **Middlesbrough** Writearound: festival for writers and readers – *till Tues 20* (01642) 243425; **Northumberland** Music Week: wide variety of traditional music and events at various venues – *till Sun 18* (01670) 533923

NOVEMBER

4 **Bishop Auckland** Fireworks and Music at Town Recreation Ground (01388) 765555

5 **Stockton-on-Tees** Fireworks (01642) 670067

7 **Darlington** Firework and Lazer Spectacular at South Park (01325) 388413; **Hartlepool** Firework and Music Display at Seaton Carew (01429) 869706

DECEMBER

31 **Allendale** Baal Festival: villagers parade in costume carrying burning tar barrels (01434) 683763

We welcome reports from readers . . .

This *Guide* depends on readers' reports. Do help us if you can – in return, we offer a discount on the next edition to people who've helped us with reports for it. Tell us what you think about places already in it, and anything extra you think we should say about them. And send us your ideas for inclusion in the next edition: places to visit, eat at or stay in, attractive drives or walks, maybe even unusual interesting shops you know of. Use the card in the middle, the report forms at the end, or just write – no stamp needed: *The Good Guide to Britain*, FREEPOST TN1569, Wadhurst, E Sussex TN5 7BR.

NOTTINGHAMSHIRE

Nottingham is well worth a visit; some good outings elsewhere, with interesting towns and villages, fine landscapes and generally low prices.

Nottingham has lots of good free museums, other interesting places to visit including the exceptional Galleries of Justice, and plenty of life. Elsewhere, the county has some charming and interesting villages, and Newark and Southwell are small towns of real character. Other highlights include Mr Straw's House in Worksop and Newstead Abbey outside Ravenshead (these two places in fascinating contrast at opposite ends of the housing spectrum). White Post farm at Farnsfield is a real treat for young children, and the World of Robin Hood at Haughton (excellent value) and Creswell Crags are also very enjoyable family outings.

There's some pleasant countryside, especially in the rewarding area known as the Dukeries in the north, with its extensive tracts of landscaped wooded parkland – though the grand houses and families which gave the area its name are long gone. Clumber Park is a choice example.

Where to stay

Drakeholes SK7090 GRIFF INN Drakeholes, Doncaster, South Yorks DN10 5DF (01777) 817206 **£45**; 3 rms. Handsome brick house with beautiful landscaped gardens and excellent views over the Chesterfield Canal basin and the flat valley of the River Idle; a wide range of food inc substantial breakfasts and good vegetarian meals, friendly helpful service; one dining bar is no smoking.

Gringley-on-the-Hill SK7391 OLD VICARAGE Gringley-on-the-Hill, Doncaster, South Yorks DN10 4RF (01777) 817248 ***£50**, plus special breaks; 3 rms. Pretty cottage in 3 acres with comfortable sitting room, delicious food, friendly owners, a flower-filled garden, tennis court and super views; cl 24 Dec–2 Jan; dogs by prior arrangement.

Langar SK7234 LANGAR HALL Langar, Nottingham NG13 9HG (01949) 860559 ***£85**; 10 lovely rms, some in wing and courtyard as well. Fine country house in spacious grounds with beautifully furnished elegant rooms, pillared dining hall with paintings for sale, antiques and fresh flowers, a relaxed informal atmosphere, a lively and friendly owner, and very good food; regular theatricals and murder weekends; cl 3 days over Christmas; dogs by arrangement.

Southwell SK7053 OLD FORGE Burgage La, Southwell NG25 0ER (01636) 812809 **£44**, 6 rms. 200-year-old former blacksmith's house with welcoming owner, interesting furnishings, super breakfasts in conservatory overlooking the Minster, light supper on request, and pretty terrace; well behaved dogs welcome.

Southwell SK7053 SARACENS HEAD Market Pl, Southwell NG25 0HE (01636) 812701 **£75.50w**; 27 well kept rms. Interesting old hotel (Charles I spent his last free night here) with ancient-feeling beamed main bar, pleasant staff, straightforward bar lunches, and restaurant.

To see and do

♂ ✝ **Nottingham** SK5739 At weekends and on summer evenings it quickly loses its big-city character, and is then easy to park in and stroll through, without the rush of traffic that otherwise swarms along its inner ring road. The parts around the parish church (which has some interesting carvings) and the Lace Market are particularly attractive. The tourist information centre on Wheeler Gate has a useful ½ hr audio-visual introduction to the town, which has an amazing number of decent pubs – handy for the thirsty work of serious sightseeing. You can buy an Explorer Pass covering entry to the main attractions, valid for a year. Besides museums we describe more fully, you might like the CANAL MUSEUM (Canal St, cl Mon, Tues, 25–26 Dec; free) and MUSEUM OF COSTUME AND TEXTILES (43–51 Castle Gate, cl 25–26 Dec; free). Useful lunch places are Fellows Morton & Clayton (Canal Rd; brews its own beer), the quaint old Bell (Angel Row), the Limelight (attached to the Playhouse) and the Lincolnshire Poacher (Mansfield Rd). There's an unusual NATURE RESERVE with good birdwatching down by Beeston at the extensive partly wooded Attenborough lakes SK5234; on the far side a path takes you along the narrow spit of land dividing them from the mighty River Trent. The Manor at Toton is a good nearby dining pub.

☝ CAVE TOURS The rock on which the old town once stood is honeycombed with hundreds of galleries, cellars and passageways (one attractive old pub, the Olde Trip to Jerusalem, has a fascinating bar tunnelled right into the rock face). Tours usually leave the Castle daily (exc Sun) at 2pm and 3pm (and 4pm in summer); as we went to press they had been suspended because of a rockfall, so it's always best to call (0115) 915 5330 first. They're quite strenuous;

£1. CAVES OF NOTTINGHAM 🎟 (Drury Walk) This is a tour with taped commentary of 700-year-old caverns beneath a busy modern shopping centre, through an underground tannery, Victorian slum, air raid shelters, and pub cellars. Shop; cl 24–26 Dec, Easter Sun; (0115) 924 1424; *£2.95.

🏰 ♂ 🏛 CASTLE Up on the summit, this dates from the 17th c, but the gateway is from an earlier 13th-c fortress. It now houses an appealing

---

Days Out

Children's day out in Nottingham
Tales of Robin Hood; Caves of Nottingham; lunch at the Lincolnshire Poacher, Mansfield Rd, or Fellows Morton & Clayton, Canal Rd; Galleries of Justice; Green's Mill and Science Centre.

Robin Hood country
Creswell Crags; Sherwood Forest Country Park, Edwinstowe; picnic there, or lunch at the Black Swan; walk or hire a boat or bike in Clumber Park; or the World of Robin Hood, Haughton; or Mr Straw's House, Worksop (timed ticket needed).

Curio tour
Winkburn church; Maplebeck village; Wellow's maypole and Rufford Country Park; lunch at the Olde Red Lion, Wellow, or Dovecote, Laxton; Laxton's medieval field system; Bygone Childhood Museum, Cromwell.

The mighty minster
Southwell Minster; lunch at the French Horn, Upton or Burnstump, Papplewick; Upton Hall or Newstead Abbey.

MUSEUM, with a history of the site and the subterranean passageways. Meals, snacks, shop, disabled access; cl am winter Fris; (0115) 915 5555; free wkdys, £1.50 wknds and bank hols. BREWHOUSE YARD MUSEUM (Castle Boulevard) Spread over 5 17th-c houses with period rooms and reconstructions, this has very good interactive displays on local life, and several features designed with children in mind (the Feely Boxes are fun). Award-winning historic roses in the cottage garden. Shop, some disabled access; cl 25–26 Dec; (0115) 948 3504; free wkdys, £1.50 wknds and bank hols.

ð⚡ LACE HALL (High Pavement) In a restored chapel with a Burne-Jones window, this has lace-making demonstrations – you can have a go yourself. It's a lively place, with a lot of commitment and interesting displays, touching on social conditions and child labour. Very good snacks and teas, shop (lots of classical music CDs), disabled access; cl 25–26 Dec; (0115) 948 4221; £2.85. LACE CENTRE (Castle Rd) This pretty 15th-c house has lace hanging from almost every beam, much of it for sale. Lace-making demonstrations pm summer Thurs. Some disabled access; cl 25–26 Dec; (0115) 941 3539; free.

ħ For the GALLERIES OF JUSTICE see separate Family Panel below.

🏠 🕸 ⬆r WOLLATON HALL (Wollaton Park, 3m W) Splendidly ornate Tudor house with the city's natural history collection. The 500-acre grounds are a delight. Shop, disabled access; cl am Fri Oct–Mar; (0115) 915 3900; free wkdys, *£1.50 wknds and bank hols. The adjacent INDUSTRIAL MUSEUM (Courtyard Buildings) looks once again at lace-making, along with other local industries.

ħ TALES OF ROBIN HOOD (Maid Marian Way) Cars carry you through the sights, sounds and smells of a recreated medieval Sherwood Forest, and a film looks at the truth behind the stories. Pretty much for insistent children only – otherwise you might be better going out to Haughton (see Other things to see and do, below). Meals and snacks (wknds and hols), shop, disabled access; cl 24–26 Dec; (0115) 948 3284; *£4.25.

✗ ! ▣ GREEN'S MILL AND SCIENCE CENTRE (Windmill Lane, Sneinton) Good for families: the restored tower mill still produces flour, and you can try grinding corn on part of an old millstone. Among the exhibits at the hands-on Science Centre next door is a weather satellite receiver showing pictures live from space. Shop, disabled access; cl Mon (exc bank hols), Tues, and 25 Dec – best to tel (0115) 950 3635 to check the mill is working; free. UNIVERSITY ART GALLERY (University Park, SW of centre) Good temporary exhibitions; opening times vary so best to check on (0115) 951 3189; free.

Other things to see and do

NOTTINGHAMSHIRE FAMILY ATTRACTION OF THE YEAR

ħ **Nottingham** SK5739 GALLERIES OF JUSTICE (Shire Hall, High Pavement) The grim realities of a 19th-c trial and prison life are re-enacted with real verve at this first-rate centre, set around 2 Victorian courtrooms in use right through to 1986. It's been open for only a couple of years but as we went to press was already beginning a major Lottery-funded extension, which they hope will help them realise their ambition of becoming the National Museum of Law. The award-winning centrepiece – designed very much to entertain children – is called Condemned, and begins with visitors being given a criminal identity number before being sent to trial in the Criminal Court. It's hardly giving the game away to say that the verdict is always guilty – but what will be the sentence? Public flogging, transportation to a penal colony, or execution? 'Prisoners' are then taken down to the cells, where costumed interpreters posing as prison warders lead them to their fate. Being locked in a cell or working on a treadmill is hardly the stuff of *LA Law*, so it's a real eye-opener for older children (it's not ideal for younger ones). In 1998 Condemned will close for 3 months from around mid-April, reopening much enlarged on 20 July. Earlier in April they'll also be opening a completely new attraction, Nicked, a police station experience at which vistors will be able to help solve a murder. When the two sections are open together (6–19 Apr and from 20 July onwards) it will make an enjoyable and informative ½- trip, or you can buy tickets for just one part if you don't have time for both; you'll still need at least 2 hours for Condemned if you want to do it justice. Meals (from July 1998) and snacks, shop, some disabled access; site only cl 24–26 Dec though see above; (0115) 952 0555; Condemned *£5.75 (£3.75 children 5–14), Nicked *£3.75 (£3.25 children), or *£8.50 (£5.50) combined ticket. A family ticket, admitting 2 adults and 2 children to both attractions, is *£23.95.

† ⚙ **Blyth** SK6287 An attractive small town, with interesting wall paintings in the CHURCH; the White Swan is good for lunch. HODSOCK PRIORY GARDENS (off the B6045 S) Especially lovely at snowdrop time; open 4 or 5 wks Feb/Mar, then Tues–Thurs Apr–May; (01909) 591204; plant sales; *£2.50.

⚙ **Clumber Park** SK6375 Nearly 4,000 acres of farmland, parks, lake and woodland, with interesting walled garden, and the longest lime avenue in Europe, almost 2m long. You can hire bikes (£3 for 2 hours, £7.50 for a tandem, bring ID), or boats on the lake. Meals, snacks, shop, disabled access; park open all year, some parts cl winter; (01909) 476592; £3 per car; NT.

🔱🏚 **Creswell** SK5274 CRESWELL CRAGS VISITOR CENTRE Stone Age man lived in the caves and rock shelters of this limestone gorge right by the Derbys border (the village is actually over in Derbys). Even on days when there aren't cave tours it's an intriguing prehistoric site, with a good visitor centre, reconstructions of Ice Age family life, and other displays and activities. They sometimes have children's stories in one of the caves (booking required). Picnic area, shop, disabled access; cl Nov–Jan exc Sun – best to check for cave tour dates (usually every wknd at least); (01909) 720378; site free, cave tours £1.95. Take a torch. The Greendale Oak at Cuckney has good-value food.

🔱 **Cromwell** SK7961 VINA COOKE MUSEUM OF DOLLS AND BYGONE CHILDHOOD (Old Rectory) Thousands of toys and objects related to childhood, in an imposing 17th-c rectory. Especially lively on Easter Mon, with morris dancers, crafts and the like. Teas, shop, limited disabled access; cl 12–2pm, all day Fri, 25–26 Dec; (01636) 821364; *£2.50. The Great Northern at Carlton-on-Trent has decent food.

🏚🔱✗ **Eastwood** SK4646 D H LAWRENCE BIRTHPLACE MUSEUM (8a Victoria St) The writer was born in this typical working-class house in 1885; it's been carefully restored to how he knew it. Shop, limited disabled access; cl 24 Dec–1 Jan; (01773) 763312; *£1.75. Craft workshops next door (not Weds, or pm Sat). Another home of Lawrence's, on Garden Rd, is furnished as he described it in *Sons and Lovers*; open by appointment with Mr Roberts on (0151) 653 8710 (or if no reply try asking the Birthplace Museum). The Yew Tree out at Brinsley has good-value food.

🔱🐾🐕 **Edwinstowe** SK6266 SHERWOOD FOREST COUNTRY PARK With an exhibition on Robin Hood, the visitor centre is a good springboard for the forest itself, only a fraction of what it once was but still miles across – and altogether more

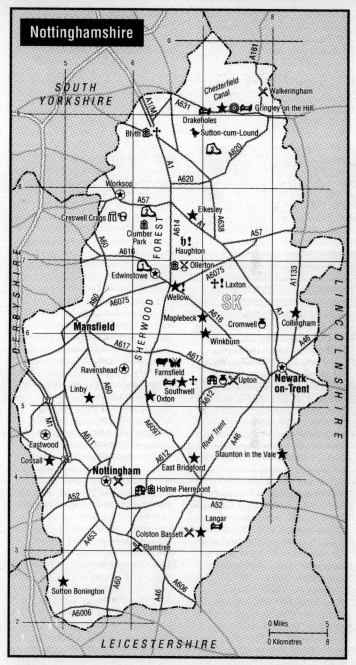

Nottinghamshire

SOUTH YORKSHIRE

Chesterfield Canal

Walkeringham

Gringley on the Hill

Drakeholes

Blyth

Sutton-cum-Lound

Worksop

Elkesley

Creswell Crags

Clumber Park

FOREST

Haughton

Edwinstowe

Ollerton

Laxton

Wellow

SK

Mansfield

Maplebeck

Cromwell

Collingham

Winkburn

SHERWOOD

Ravenshead

Farnsfield

Newark-on-Trent

Linby

Southwell

Oxton

Eastwood

Cossall

River Trent

Staunton in the Vale

Nottingham

East Bridgford

Holme Pierrepont

Langar

Colston Bassett

Plumtree

Sutton Bonington

LEICESTERSHIRE

DERBYSHIRE

LINCOLNSHIRE

0 Miles 5

0 Kilometres 8

forested than the heathland that Robin himself would have known.

Good waymarked paths and footpaths. Meals, snacks, shop,

disabled access; park free, car park £1 wknds, bank hols and all Aug, exhibition 50p. Near the village church (supposedly where Robin Hood and Maid Marian were married), the Black Swan is handy for something to eat; the Church Farm CRAFT WORKSHOPS here plan to move to nearer the forest in 1998. SHERWOOD FOREST FARM PARK (Lamb Pens Farm) Unusual breeds of traditional farm animals, foreign-bird aviaries, pets corner, and colourful waterfowl on a sizeable lake. Home-baked teas, shop, disabled access; cl Nov–Mar; (01623) 823558; £3.50. The best drive is the B6034 N towards Worksop, then the right turn to Carburton and Clumber Park. Sherwood Forest has one of England's three CENTER PARCS, a rewarding place to stay with excellent leisure facilities; (01623) 411411.

🐖 🦋 **Farnsfield** SK6456 WHITE POST MODERN FARM CENTRE 🖼 (1m W) Great for children, a bustling modern working farm with exhibits ranging from a mouse town to llamas, quails, snakes and fish. The pig-breeding unit is fun, and you may be able to watch eggs hatching in the huge incubator. The Farm Show in the barn is a highlight. Snacks, farm shop, disabled access; (01623) 882977; *£3.95. Their well stocked pet centre sells mice, gerbils, hamsters and rats, along with everything you'd need to look after them. WHITE POST WONDERLAND nearby is useful enough for families, with free-flying butterflies, a maze, indoor play area, mini golf, and wild flower meadow. Meals, snacks, shop, disabled access; cl Nov–Mar; (01623) 882773; *£3.25. Combs Farm Shop nearby is a good one (cl Sun and Mon). The Waggon & Horses at Halam is a popular dining pub.

♭ **! Haughton** SK6872 WORLD OF ROBIN HOOD 🖼 Splendidly enjoyable re-creation of medieval life, placing the Robin Hood stories in their historical context. They've meticulously constructed an entire medieval village, with moated drawbridge, cobbled streets and authentic shops and houses.

Costumed guides stay firmly in character, and there's plenty for children, inc a Disneyish version of the legends inside the castle for younger children, a small animal farm, and play area. Outside is a deer park and owl sanctuary, with summer activities such as archery. Meals, snacks, shop, some disabled access; cl Jan–mid-Feb; (01623) 860210; £3.95. The Robin Hood at Elkesley has good-value food.

🏠 ⚘ **Holme Pierrepont** SK6239 HOLME PIERREPONT HALL Early Tudor manor house with interesting early 15th-c timbers, and an elaborate parterre in the formal courtyard garden. Snacks, shop, disabled access to gardens only; open pm Sun Jun–Aug, plus Thurs July and Aug, Tues and Fri in Aug, and Easter hols; (0115) 933 2371; £3. The Round Oak in Radcliffe on Trent has decent food.

! † Laxton SK7268 Unique for having kept the pattern of its MEDIEVAL FARMING, with different villagers each owning strips of the 3 great fields. You can walk the grass paths or sykes which divide groups of these strips, and the Dovecote, a good village pub, has an exhibition in the yard explaining the system. The CHURCH has a fine 15th-c screen.

★ † ⚓ 🏰 ♭ ♋ † **Newark** SK7953 Attractive old market town with some interesting buildings in its side streets, a fine CHURCH, and walks by the River Trent with summer BOAT TRIPS. The Old Kings Arms (Kirkgate) is useful for lunch. The CASTLE ruins date from the 11th c, and there's still a fair bit to see; it was destroyed during the Civil War then had periods as a cattle market and a bowling green. Good explanatory displays at the GILSTRAP HERITAGE CENTRE in the grounds; cl 25–26 Dec, 1 Jan; free. Other useful town museums include the MUSEUM OF SOCIAL AND FOLK LIFE on Millgate (cl am wknds and bank hols; free), and the local history collection on Appletongate (cl 1–2pm, Thurs, and Sun exc summer pms; free). AIR MUSEUM (Winthorpe, NE of Newark) Over 40 assorted aircraft inc rare jet fighters and bombers; half the exhibits are under cover so fine all year round (and the Willow Tree over at Barnby in the Willows is handy for lunch). Snacks, shop, disabled access; cl 24–26 Dec; (01636) 707170; *£3.50.

✗ 🐝 **Ollerton** SK6667 OLLERTON MILL (Market Pl) The only working watermill in the county, still producing flour as it did in the early 18th c, in a pleasant setting on the edge of Sherwood Forest. Award-winning teas (teashop often open when mill isn't), shop; mill working pm Sun and bank hols Apr–Sept; (01623) 822469; £1.50. The Hop Pole in the pretty market place has good-value food. RUFFORD COUNTRY PARK SK6465 (off the A614 S of Ollerton) Pleasant lakeside spot on edge of Sherwood Forest, with the ruins of a 12th-c abbey, and family activities most summer weekends (£1 car park charge).

🏚 🐝 ⛵🎣⛴ **Ravenshead** SK5755 NEWSTEAD ABBEY (off the A60) Splendid former home of Lord Byron, in gorgeously romantic grounds; many of his possessions can still be seen. Rooms are decorated in a variety of styles from medieval through to Victorian, and there are substantial remains of the original abbey. Meals, snacks, shop, limited disabled access; cl Oct–Mar; (01623) 793557; £4 house and gardens, £2 gardens only. Mining below the house in 1999 may damage it, so be prepared for restoration closures then. In the town, the Little John has decent food. LONGDALE CRAFT CENTRE (Longdale Lane) Very good craft centre, partly set out as a Victorian village street, with rows of period workshops. Decent restaurant, disabled access; (01623) 794858; cl 25–26 Dec; *£1.95 for museum. PAPPLEWICK PUMPING STATION (off the Langdale Rd) A working Victorian waterworks with two beam engines; best to ring for steamdays, though open for static displays pm most Suns and Weds Easter–Oct; (0115) 963 2938; £1.50 (£3 steamdays). The Burnstump in the Country Park at Papplewick is a good-value family dining pub.

★ † **Southwell** SK7053 An attractive town around a magnificent 12th-c MINSTER, a fine sight from miles around (especially at night when it's floodlit), and glorious to walk through. Fine leaf carvings and lovely choir screen; it's worth catching one of the regular concerts. There's a smart new visitor centre. This small quiet town is the home of the Bramley apple, developed by Henry Merryweather in the last century. One of the original trees still prospers at his descendant's garden centre on Halam Rd, where there's a small exhibition on the subject. The Bramley Apple next door is good for lunch. There's a FRUIT FARM in the grounds of nearby Norwood Park.

🐦 **Sutton-cum-Lound** SK7285 WETLANDS WATERFOWL RESERVE AND EXOTIC BIRD PARK 🦜 (off the Loundlow Rd) Lagoons full of birds from ducks and swans to flamingos, and many more wild birds inc parrots in the surrounding countryside. Also owls, foxes, llamas and wallabies, and children's farm. Meals, snacks, shop, disabled access; cl 25 Dec; (01777) 818099; *£2. The canalside Boat at Hayton has decent food.

🏚 ⏰ **Upton** SK7354 UPTON HALL Includes a museum of clocks and timepieces from marine chronometers to the first telephone speaking clock. Some exhibits are over 300 years old, so don't expect them to keep perfect time. Snacks, shop, disabled access to ground floor; open pm (exc Sat) Easter–Aug; (01636) 813795; *£2.50. The French Horn and Cross Keys have good food.

★ ! **Wellow** SK6766 An attractive village, unusual for its permanent MAYPOLE – which used to be the trunk of a Sherwood Forest tree, but is now metal. It stands on the only genuine village green in the county, kept that way since the village was founded in the 12th c (all the others were just open spaces used by the villagers and itinerant traders for buying and selling, which have been grassed over since all that stopped). The Olde Red Lion is good for lunch.

🏚 ⏰ † **Worksop** SK5879 MR STRAW'S

HOUSE (7 Blyth Grove) One of the NT's most unusual properties, an ordinary 1920s semi, left untouched by 2 brothers who inherited it when their parents died. Even the calendar remains unturned. A fascinating time-capsule, it's open by pre-booked timed ticket only (Tues–Sat Apr–Oct), but it really is worth taking the trouble to get one – you'll have the place to yourself and get a much better feel of actually living there; (01909) 482380; £3. The town museum has a display on the Pilgrim Fathers (cl Sun and pm Thurs and Sat; free), and the PRIORY CHURCH is worth a look for the elaborate scrollwork on its 12th-c yew door; there's an art gallery and tearoom in the gatehouse. The Newcastle Arms (Carlton Rd) has good-value food.

The **River Trent** gives a tremendous sense of power even when it's on its best behaviour, sliding swiftly and massively along; its occasional floods are devastating, and most years it claims lives. Villages giving pleasant access to it include Laneham SK8076 and Thrumpton SK5031; decent pubs and inns in good riverside spots include the Hazleford Ferry at Bleasby SK7149, Lazy Otter in Wyke Lane, Farndon SK7651, Bromley Arms at Fiskerton SK7351 and Unicorn Hotel at Gunthorpe SK6844.

★ **Other interesting and attractive villages** include the delightfully rustic Maplebeck SK7160 (the Beehive is a classic country tavern; nearby Woodborough and Lambley are also worth a look), – Collingham SK8663, Cossall SK4842 (D H Lawrence country: he was once engaged to the girl who lived in Church Cottage), East Bridgford SK6943 (the Reindeer has good fresh fish), Elkesley SK6975 (working potter nr church; the Robin Hood is useful for lunch), Linby SK5351 (handy for Newstead Abbey; see Ravenshead entry above), Oxton SK6251 (the lane up the hill N below the power lines leads to an Iron Age hill fort), Sutton Bonington SK5025 (interesting spinning/weaving workshop on Bucks Lane; cl pm Weds, Sun and summer hols), Winkburn SK7158 (its simple 12th-c village church is a temple of the Knights Hospitaller), and, with their more 'Leicestershire-ish' character, Colston Bassett SK7033 (the Martins Arms is excellent for lunch, and the Haby Lane dairy makes lovely Stilton), and Staunton in the Vale SK8043 (the Staunton Arms is useful) over in the Vale of Belvoir. Beacon Hill, above the Chesterfield Canal at Gringley on the Hill SK7391, gives magnificent views in all directions; you can make out the towers of Lincoln cathedral on a clear day.

Walks

Though the county is far from being ideal for walkers, it does have some pleasant forest walks. **Sherwood Forest** ⌂-1 no longer covers a fifth of the county as in Robin Hood's day, and the heathland it once contained has been swallowed up into farmland. However, it is well endowed with trails, the most popular being to the Major Oak SK6267 (a huge tree in the heart of the forest).

Clumber Park SK6275 ⌂-2, one of the great former Dukeries estates, is outstanding for its walks, with enough paths through its woodland and parkland for a full-day excursion.

The **Chesterfield Canal** ⌂-3 has scope for towpath walks; one quiet stretch is by the Boat at Hayton SK7384.

Where to eat

Colston Bassett SK7033 MARTINS ARMS School Lane (01949) 81361 Civilised, rather smart pub with particularly good imaginative food in bar and restaurant (lovely puddings), well kept real ales, a good choice of malt whiskies, quite a few wines by the glass, an open fire, and smart uniformed staff; no children; disabled access. £27.50|£6.95.

Nottingham SK5739 LINCOLNSHIRE POACHER Mansfield Rd (0115) 941 1584 Cheerful town pub with really tasty home-made food using fresh local produce (inc lots of vegetarian dishes), interesting real ales, good ciders, lots of whiskies and a wine of the week, pleasant service, big wood-floored bar with breweriana, lively smaller bar, and chatty back snug; popular with young people in the evening. £13|£4.50.

Plumtree SK6132 PERKINS RESTAURANT AND BAR Old Railway Station (0115) 937 3695 Delightfully converted old railway station with very popular fresh delicious food (strong French influence), excellent service, and good wines; cl Sun, Mon, 2 wks Aug, Christmas, bank hols; children over 7. £22.70|£7.50.

Upton SK7354 CROSS KEYS (01636) 813269 Heavily beamed 17th-c pub with rambling bar, lots of interesting pictures, enterprising generous food inc good daily specials, well kept beers, decent wines, and welcoming efficient service; cl pm 25 Dec; children in tap room or restaurant only; disabled access. £21|£2.50.

Upton SK7354 FRENCH HORN (01636) 812394 Friendly and bustling dining pub with neat and comfortable open-plan bar, a nice relaxed atmosphere, imaginative food inc very good daily specials and lots of puddings, well kept real ales, several wines by the glass, friendly and efficient service, and a big sloping back paddock. £17.65|£7.25.

Walkeringham SK7792 THREE HORSESHOES (01427) 890959 Warmly welcoming distinctive pub, rather like a French *logis*, with quite amazing flowers and hanging baskets (using 9,000 plants); a wide choice of often inventive food, and well kept real ales. £15.75|£5.75.

Special thanks to Jenny and Michael Back.

We welcome reports from readers . . .

This *Guide* depends on readers' reports. Do help us if you can – in return, we offer a discount on the next edition to people who've helped us with reports for it. Tell us what you think about places already in it, and anything extra you think we should say about them. And send us your ideas for inclusion in the next edition: places to visit, eat at or stay in, attractive drives or walks, maybe even unusual interesting shops you know of. Use the card in the middle, the report forms at the end, or just write – no stamp needed: *The Good Guide to Britain*, FREEPOST TN1569, Wadhurst, E Sussex TN5 7BR.

NOTTINGHAMSHIRE CALENDAR

Some of these dates were provisional as we went to press. Please check information with the numbers provided.

FEBRUARY

2 **Winthorpe** Antiques Fair: largest in Europe at Newark Showground – *till Tues 3* (01636) 702627

9 **Newark** *Richard III* at Thoresby Park – *till Wed 11* (01636) 605111

22 **Newark** Doll Fair, Miniature & Teddy Bear Fair at Kelham Hall (01480) 216372

MARCH

8 **Winthorpe** Spring Exhibition: livestock show at Newark Showground (01636) 702627

20 **New Ollerton** CAMRA Beer Festival at Dukeries Leisure Centre – *till Sat 21* (01623) 862469

27 **Newark** Antique Fair at Thoresby Park: about 30 stands – *till Sun 29* (01636) 605111

APRIL

6 **Winthorpe** Antiques Fair: largest in Europe at Newark Showground – *till Tues 7* (01636) 702627

11 **Newark** Craft Fair at Thoresby Park: about 30 stands – *till Mon 13* (01636) 605111

17 **Sutton Bonington** National Folk Music Festival at the School of Agriculture – *till Sun 19* (01509) 672025

MAY

1 **Winthorpe** Nottingham County Show at Newark Showground – *till Sat 2* (01636) 702627

4 **Mansfield** May Day Market (01623) 656656; **Nottingham** Victorian May Day at Brew House Yard (0115) 915 5555

15 **Winthorpe** Americana: American show with cars and music at Newark Showground – *till Sun 17* (01636) 702627

23 **Newark** Endurance Horse & Pony Society at Thoresby Park (01636) 605111; **Nottingham** Free Music Festival at Wollerton Park – *till Mon 25* (0115) 915 5555

24 **Newark** Steam Fair at Thoresby Park – *till Mon 25* (01636) 605111; **Nottingham** Bus & Commercial Vehicle Rally at Wollerton Park (0115) 915 5555

25 **Nottingham** Shire Horse Show at Wollerton Park (0115) 915 5555; **Wellow** Maypole Dancing (01636) 605111

JUNE

1 **Winthorpe** Antiques Fair: largest in Europe at Newark Showground – *till Tues 2* (01636) 702627

5 **Newark** Jazz in the Gallery; also Antique Fair at Thoresby Park: about 30 stands – *till Sun 7* (01636) 605111

7 **Clipstone** Fun Day at Vicar Water Country Park (01636) 708265; **Nottingham** New, Vintage & Classic Car Rally at Wollerton Park (0115) 915 5555

20 **Winthorpe** Kit Car Show at Newark Showground – *till Sun 21* (01636) 702627

JULY

5 **Newark** Yesteryear Rally at Kelham Hall (01636) 605111

NOTTINGHAMSHIRE CALENDAR

10 **Winthorpe** Americana: American show with cars and music at Newark Showground – *till Sun 12* (01636) 702627

11 **Mansfield** Mardi Gras – *till Sun 12* (01623) 656656; **Newark** Vintage Tractor Rally at Thoresby Park – *till Sun 12* (01636) 605111

12 **Nottingham** Fishing Championship on Victoria Embankment (0115) 915 5555

AUGUST

1 **Nottingham** Riverside Festival: free event with street theatre, carnival, fireworks, world music, steam organs at Victoria Embankment – *till Sun 2* (0115) 915 5555

3 **Edwinstowe** Robin Hood Festival at Sherwood Forest Visitor Centre – *till Fri 7* – (01623) 823202

8 **Sutton in Ashfield** Show at Lawn Park – *till Sun 9* (01623) 450000

10 **Winthorpe** Antiques Fair: largest in Europe at Newark Showground – *till Tues 11* (01636) 702627

15 **Nottingham** Caribbean Carnival at Forest Recreation Ground – *till Sun 16* (0115) 915 5555

22 **Nottingham** Flower Show at Wollerton Park – *till Sun 23* (0115) 915 555

30 **Mansfield** Horticultural Show (01623) 656656

31 **Newark** Classic Car Show at Thoresby Park (01636) 605111; also Children's Festival Market in Market Square (01636) 708265

SEPTEMBER

25 **Newark** Antique Fair at Thoresby Park: about 30 stands – *till Sun 27* (01636) 605111

26 **Southwell** Bramley Festival – *till 4 Oct* (01636) 708265

OCTOBER

1 **Nottingham** Goose Fair: huge funfair – *till Sat 3* (0115) 915 5555

10 **Newark** Craft Fair at Thoresby Park: about 30 stands – *till Sun 11* (01636) 605111

19 **Winthorpe** Antiques Fair: largest in Europe at Newark Showground – *till Tues 20* (01636) 702627

29 **Nottingham** Robin Hood Pageant at the Castle – *till Sat 31* (0115) 915 5555

NOVEMBER

1 **Newark** Doll, Miniature & Teddy Bear Fair at Kelham Hall (01480) 216372

5 **Nottingham** Bonfire Night (0115) 915 555

DECEMBER

7 **Winthorpe** Antiques Fair: largest in Europe at Newark Showground – *till Tues 8* (01636) 702627

Please let us know what you think of places in the *Guide*. Use the report forms at the back of the book or simply send a letter.

OXFORDSHIRE

Richly varied countryside, plenty of delightful places for adults to visit, some good family days out; Oxford itself is a vibrant mix of medieval buildings and modern bustle.

Oxford has a great deal to fill a day visit or short break. It's full of uniquely striking buildings, and the colleges themselves, the art collections of the Ashmolean Museum, the unusual Curioxity, and the intriguing Pitt Rivers ethnology museum head a long list of rewarding places to see; the university's botanic garden is the oldest in the world.

Blenheim Palace by the attractive small town of Woodstock is the county's great showpiece, with memorable lakeside grounds, and all sorts of things going on to entertain families. The Cotswold Wildlife Park at Burford is another really good family day out. Children are also very fond of the friendly farm at Wigginton Heath, the bird and animal collection at Ipsden, the model landscape at Long Wittenham – and Thames boat trips.

Most of the county's other attractions are suited more to adults than to children. There are lots of rewarding old houses and other interesting buildings such as Broughton Castle, the newly opened Chastleton House, Dorchester Abbey, Rousham House, Stonor House, Buscot Park, Mapledurham House and Kelmscott Manor. The gardens at Waterperry and Greys Court near Henley are rather special. The countryside has Cotswolds charm over in the west, and good varied scenery in the prosperous south, including long rich reaches of the Thames, the edge of the Chilterns, and some sweeping downland. Many of the villages and small towns are very rewarding, with picturesque stone houses (up in the north-west corner many glow with a glorious golden stone), and plenty of antique and craft shops. Steam enthusiasts won't want to miss the railway collection at Didcot.

Oxfordshire is one of the more expensive places to stay in, though there's a fine choice of hotels and good food.

Where to stay

Asthall SP2811 MAYTIME Asthall, Burford OX18 4HW (01993) 822068 *£62.50 plus bargain breaks; 6 quiet rms. Attractive 16th-c Cotswold stone inn with comfortable relaxing dining bar, good food and decent wines, huge breakfasts; worth an early spring-morning walk through the pretty village, across the fields to Swinbrook and back along the river; disabled access.

Bampton SP3103 MORAR Weald, Bampton OX18 2HL (01993) 850162 *£43, plus special breaks; 3 rms. Warmly friendly and neatly kept modern stone house (no smoking) with helpful knowledgeable owners, separate lounge and dining room, lovely English cooking in winter using home-grown produce (home-made bread and preserves, too), pretty flower-filled big garden, and cats, a dog and goats (no visiting dogs allowed); cl Jan/Feb; children over 6.

Burford SP2512 BURFORD HOUSE High St, Burford, OX18 4QA (01993) 823151 £75, plus winter breaks; 7 cosy, individually decorated rms. Attractive 14th-c Cotswold stone beamed building, with 2 comfortable lounges (one for residents only), log fires, super breakfasts, and lots of plants in pretty stone courtyard; children over 10.

Burford SP2512 GOLDEN PHEASANT High St, Burford, OX18 4QA (01993) 823223 £80 plus special breaks; 12 pretty floral rms with bthrm or shower. Friendly partly 16th-c beamed coaching inn with attractive country furnishings, flowers, open fires, and interesting prints and pictures in flagstoned bar and candlelit dining room; comfortable sitting room, very good food, and a varied wine list.

Burford SP2512 LAMB Sheep St, Burford OX18 4LR (01993) 823155 *£100 plus special breaks; 15 rms. Very attractive 500-year-old Cotswold inn with lovely restful atmosphere, spacious beamed, flagstoned and elegantly furnished lounge, civilised public bar, bunches of flowers on good oak and elm tables, 3 winter log fires, antiques, good food in airy restaurant, and pretty little walled garden; cl 25–26 Dec.

Charlbury SP3519 BELL Charlbury, Chipping Norton OX7 3AP (01608) 810278 £75, plus special breaks; 13 comfortable rms. Small neatly kept 17th-c hotel with warm friendly atmosphere, quiet and civilised flagstoned bar, huge open fire, short choice of interesting bar lunches, decent restaurant, well kept real ales, and good breakfasts.

Church Enstone SP3724 CROWN Church Enstone, Chipping Norton OX7 4NN (01608) 677262 £45; 4 well appointed rms, most with own bthrm. Cotswold stone inn in pretty village, with attractive horseshoe bar, conservatory, friendly atmosphere and staff, good food in bar and restaurant, and decent breakfasts; no children. Heritage barn nearby can be viewed by appointment.

Clanfield SP2801 PLOUGH Bourton Rd, Clanfield, Bampton OX18 2RB (01367) 810222 *£95, plus special breaks; 6 lovely rms. Rose-clad 16th-c Cotswold stone manor house with armchairs and sofas in relaxed beamed lounge bar, open fire, friendly helpful staff and very good food in elegant restaurant; cl 27–29 Dec; children over 12.

Clifton SP4831 DUKE OF CUMBERLANDS HEAD Clifton, Banbury OX15 0PE (01869) 338534 £45; 3 rms with own showers in sympathetic extension. Pretty thatched 17th-c stone inn with friendly atmosphere, very good food in bar and back restaurant, enjoyable breakfasts, log fire, well kept beers and wines, helpful service; tables in garden.

Clifton Hampden SU5495 PLOUGH Clifton Hampden, Abingdon OX14 3EG (01865) 407811 £69.50; 6 rms with four-posters. Quaint little no smoking village pub close to the Thames, run by obliging and idiosyncratic Turkish couple, with marvellously relaxed friendly atmosphere, cosy bar with beams and panelling, 2 civilised lounge areas, and good fresh food in bar and restaurant.

Cropredy SP4646 OLD MANOR Cropredy, Banbury OX17 1PS (01295) 750235 £48; 3 rms, 1 with own bthrm. In a historic village, this lovely old place has 2 acres of garden and orchard, a moat with ducks and geese, and Gloucester old spot pigs in the fields bordering the Oxford Canal; guests' sitting room with games and books, breakfast in 15th-c dining room with antiques, clocks and more books, and 2 dogs and 3 cats; self-catering barn; private motor museum; cl Christmas/New Year; disabled access.

Dorchester SU5794 GEORGE High St, Dorchester, Wallingford OX10 0BS (01491) 836665 £82, plus special breaks; 39 characterful rms. Lovely 500-year-old building with medieval dining room, comfortably old-fashioned and civilised bar, ancient beams, big fireplace, good wines, interesting food, pleasant service; first used as brewhouse for Norman abbey opposite; cl 28–29 Dec; disabled access.

Great Milton SP6202 Le Manoir aux Quat' Saisons Great Milton, Oxford OX44 7PD (01844) 278881 £260; 19 opulent rms. Luxurious Jacobean manor in 27 acres of parkland and lovely gardens with heated pool and kitchen garden (providing many of the cooking ingredients); sumptuous lounges with fine furniture, beautiful flowers and open fires, exemplary service, and exquisitely presented superb food (at a price); residential cookery courses; disabled access. Has recently won planning permission for extension.

Henley-on-Thames SU7682 Hernes Henley-on-Thames RG9 4NT (01491) 573245 £65, plus special breaks; 3 rms. In big gardens and grounds surrounded by farmland, this peaceful no smoking family house has a 16th-c heart, comfortable sitting room with panelled ceiling, family portraits, and good breakfasts – dinner by arrangement; cl Dec–mid-Jan; no children.

Henley-on-Thames SU7682 Red Lion Hart St, Henley-on-Thames RG9 2AR (01491) 572161 *£120, plus special breaks; 26 rms, 23 with own bthrm, some with river views. Handsome family-run and neatly kept 16th-c riverside hotel with comfortable public rooms, very good interesting food in elegant Regency-style restaurant, and particularly helpful, warmly friendly staff.

Horton-cum-Studley SP5912 Studley Priory Horton-cum-Studley, Oxford OX9 1AZ (01865) 351203 £120, plus special breaks; 19 rms. Once a Benedictine nunnery, this lovely 12th-c Elizabethan manor stands in 13 acres of wooded grounds; fine panelling, 16th- and 17th-c stained-glass windows, antiques and open fires in the elegant drawing room and cosy bar, and seasonally changing menus in attractive restaurant; grass tennis court and croquet; no children.

Kelmscot SU2499 Plough Kelmscot, Lechlade, Gloucs GL7 3HG (01367) 253543 £45; 8 comfortable rms. Rather pretty little inn near the Thames with attractively traditional small bar (ancient flagstones, stripped stone walls and a relaxed chatty atmosphere), a larger cheerfully carpeted back bar, log fires, wide choice of food, separate restaurant, well kept real ales, and lots of nearby walks; no rooms 24–30 Dec; partial disabled access.

Kingham SP2523 Mill House Kingham, Chipping Norton OX7 6UH (01608) 658188 *£100 plus special breaks; 23 good rms. Carefully renovated 17th-c flour mill in 7 acres of grounds with its own trout stream, comfortable spacious lounge, open log fire in lounge bar, original features such as 2 bread ovens, a cosy, popular restaurant, and very good interesting food; disabled access.

Kingston Bagpuize SU3997 Fallowfields Southmoor, Kingston Bagpuize, Abingdon OX13 5BH (01865) 820416 £95; 10 rms. Delightful Gothic-style no smoking old manor house with elegant, relaxing sitting rooms, open fires, good Aga-cooked food in attractive dining room, and 2 acres of pretty gardens with outdoor heated swimming pool and tennis court; children over 10.

Little Wittenham SU5693 Rooks Orchard Little Wittenham, Abingdon OX14 4QY (01865) 407765 *£44; 2 rms. Comfortable 17th-c house in lovely gardens next to nature reserve and Wittenham Clumps, with beams, inglenook fireplaces, good breakfasts (evening meals by arrangement), welcoming owners, and baby-sitting service; cl Christmas week; dogs by arrangement.

Minster Lovell SP3111 Hill Grove Farm Minster Lovell, Witney OX8 5NA (01993) 703120 *£43; 2 rms. Friendly B & B on family-run 300-acre mixed working farm with homely lounge and sun room, good breakfasts, and nice views and walks; no smoking; cl Christmas.

Moulsford SU5983 Beetle & Wedge Ferry Lane, Moulsford, Wallingford OX10 9JF (01491) 651381 £120, plus special breaks; 10 pretty rms, most with lovely river view. Civilised riverside hotel where Jerome K Jerome wrote Three Men in a Boat and where H G Wells lived for a time (it was the Potwell in The History of Mr Polly); informal old beamed Boathouse bar and lovely conservatory dining room (both with first-rate food), a carefully chosen wine list, open fires, fresh flowers, riverside terrace and waterside lawn with moorings, and a warmly welcoming atmosphere; nice walks; no food 25 Dec; disabled access.

North Leigh SP3813 WOODMAN North Leigh, Witney OX8 6TT (01993) 881790 *£39; 1 comfortable rm. Friendly and roomy stone-built village pub with attentive licensees, good-value freshly prepared food, well kept real ales, decent wines, daily papers, and big garden.

Oxford SP5106 COTSWOLD HOUSE 363 Banbury Rd OX2 7PL (01865) 310558 *£61; 7 comfortable rms with showers. Beautifully kept modern Cotswold stone house with particularly helpful owners, residents' lounge, very good breakfasts, pretty flowers throughout, and neat back garden; cl 10 days at Christmas; children over 5.

Oxford SP5106 OLD PARSONAGE 1 Banbury Rd OX2 6NN (01865) 310210 £145; 30 lovely rms. Handsome and civilised 17th-c parsonage with very courteous staff, good breakfasts and excellent light meals in cosy bar/restaurant, small lounge, open fires and fine paintings, and pretty little garden; they have their own punt; cl 25–26 Dec.

Oxford SP5106 PINE CASTLE 290 Iffley Rd OX4 4AE (01865) 241497 £55, plus wknd breaks; 8 rms. Small family-run Edwardian hotel with comfortable cosy lounge, and good breakfasts in small restaurant; evening meals by arrangement; cl Christmas week.

Oxford SP5106 RANDOLPH Beaumont St OX1 2LN (01865) 247481 £180.50, plus special breaks; 109 rms. Fine neo-Gothic Victorian hotel facing Ashmolean Museum, with elegant comfortable day rooms, grand foyer, graceful restaurant with lovely plasterwork ceiling, and cellar wine bar; disabled access.

Shenington SP3742 TOP FARM HOUSE Shenington, Banbury OX15 6LZ (01295) 670226 *£40; 2 rms, shared bthrm. 18th-c farmhouse by village green, with oak beams, inglenook fireplaces, residents' sitting room, and good breakfasts.

Shipton-under-Wychwood SP2717 LAMB Shipton under Wychwood, Chipping Norton OX7 6AQ (01993) 830465 £68; 5 comfortable rms. Ancient Cotswold stone pub with relaxed and civilised atmosphere, open log fire, highly polished furniture and newspapers to read in beamed bar, good food in no smoking restaurant, and enjoyable breakfasts.

Shipton-under-Wychwood SP2717 SHAVEN CROWN Shipton-under-Wychwood, Chipping Norton, OX7 6BA (01993) 830330 £72, plus special breaks; 9 comfortable rms. Densely beamed ancient stone hospice built around striking medieval courtyard with old-fashioned seats on cobbles, lily pool and roses. Impressive medieval hall with a magnificent lofty ceiling, sweeping stairway and old stone walls, log fire in comfortable bar, intimate candlelit restaurant, well chosen wine list, good friendly service, warm relaxed atmosphere, and bowling green; children over 5 in evening dining room; disabled access.

Shipton-under-Wychwood SP2717 SHIPTON GRANGE HOUSE Shipton-under-Wychwood, Chipping Norton, OX7 6DG (01993) 831298 *£55; 3 rms. Carefully converted Georgian coach house and stabling with elegantly furnished sitting rooms, good breakfasts, a friendly welcome, and attractive walled garden; cl Christmas/New Year; children over 12.

South Leigh SP3908 MASON ARMS South Leigh, Witney OX8 6XN (01993) 702485 *£50, plus special breaks; 2 rms with country views. Charming thatched 15th-c inn with flagstones and open fire in cosy bar, good food in low-ceilinged restaurant, well kept real ales, and terrace and sheltered garden with peacocks; the nearby 12th-c church is famous for its fine wall murals; children over 7; disabled access.

Stonor SU7388 STONOR ARMS Stonor, Henley-on-Thames RG9 6HE (01491) 638345 £105, plus special breaks; 10 pretty rms. Carefully restored 18th-c hotel with good imaginative food in 2 elegant restaurants, each with a pretty conservatory; relaxed flagstoned bar, friendly staff; cl first 2 wks Jan; disabled access.

Uffington SU3089 CRAVEN Fernham Rd, Uffington, Faringdon SN7 7RD (01367) 820449 *£58, plus special breaks; 8 pretty rms, some with own bthrm. Most attractive 17th-c thatched house with beamed sitting room, log fire in inglenook, antiques, a friendly relaxed atmosphere, good food in beamed farmhouse kitchen, and lots of nearby walks; disabled access.

Wallingford SU6089 SHILLINGFORD BRIDGE Ferry Rd, Shillingford, Wallingford OX10 8LX (01865) 858567 £90, plus special breaks; 42 rms. Riverside hotel with own river frontage, fishing and moorings, spacious comfortable bars and attractive airy restaurant (all with fine views), squash, outdoor heated swimming pool, and Sat dinner-dance; disabled access.

Woodstock SP4416 FEATHERS Market St, Woodstock OX20 1SX (01993) 812291 *£105, plus special breaks; 16 individually decorated rms. Lovely old building with fine relaxing drawing room and study, open fires, first-class friendly staff, a gentle atmosphere, daily-changing imaginative food inc lovely puddings, and a sunny courtyard with attractive tables and chairs.

Woodstock SP4416 HOLMWOOD 6 High St, Woodstock OX20 1TF (01993) 812266 £65; 2 pretty rms, one with its own sitting room. Early 18th-c Cotswold stone house with oak beams and antiques, an attractive dining room, and friendly helpful owners; no smoking; cl Jan; no children.

To see and do

Oxford SP5106 On first impression this can seem quite a frenetic city: the ancient university buildings with their medieval lanes and scholarly corners are surrounded by a bustling largely industrialised town, with a formidable amount of traffic. The one-way system and difficulties in parking away from the NCPs combine to make it a driver's nightmare; if you don't come by train or coach, it may be best to leave your car at one of the Park & Rides around the ring road. Otherwise, the tourist information centre does a useful car park map, with times and prices. For first-time visitors, hop on and off TOUR BUSES from St Aldates, High St, Gloucester Green or Pembroke College take in all the best sites and last about 1½ hours (£7). Many of the city's oldest or most interesting buildings are grouped around the Bodleian Library, the Sheldonian Theatre and the splendid domed Radcliffe Camera (also a library). This partly cobbled central university area is most attractive, but does sometimes overfill with visitors – recently students have been complaining that the noise of tourists puts them off their exams. In the streets and lanes leading off, the honey-coloured stone makes for a harmony that unites different styles and different centuries. There are a few good shops dotted about; Blackwells is the main bookseller, with several branches around the Broad St area (the secondhand section in the main branch is well used by students, and their music shop on Holywell St is rewarding). Near the station, the OXFORD ANTIQUE TRADING CO has 80 dealers under one roof.

🏠 OXFORD COLLEGES Most allow visitors into at least some of their quads, and do have a wonderful timeless appeal. One of the few they failed to impress was William Cobbett, who wrote in his *Rural Rides* that he 'could not help reflecting on the drones that they contain, and the wasps they send forth'. Newcomers to the town are often surprised to discover that the colleges are all separate bodies with little in common, each firmly maintaining its own dons, rules and traditions; the university itself is little more than an administrative umbrella. Several now charge admission, notably Christ Church, New, Magdalen, Trinity and Brasenose; prices range from £1.50 to

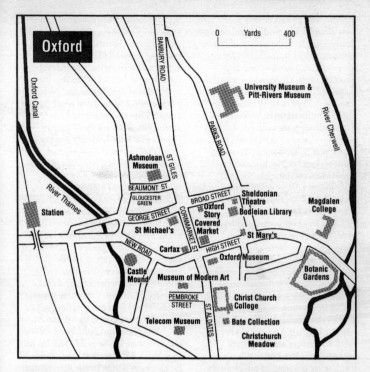

Oxford

Oxford Canal

River Thames

Station

BANBURY ROAD

University Museum &
Pitt-Rivers Museum

PARKS ROAD

River Cherwell

0   Yards   400

Ashmolean
Museum

ST GILES

BEAUMONT ST

GLOUCESTER
GREEN

GEORGE STREET

BROAD STREET

Sheldonian
Theatre

Oxford
Story

Bodleian Library

Magdalen
College

St Michael's

CORNMARKET ST

Covered
Market

NEW ROAD

Carfax

St Mary's

HIGH STREET

Oxford Museum

Castle
Mound

Museum of Modern Art

Botanic
Gardens

PEMBROKE
STREET

Christ Church
College

ST ALDATES

Telecom Museum

Bate Collection

Christchurch
Meadow

£3. Access may be more limited in term-time. A few may let you in only with a guide, so a good way of making sure you see a cross-section is to join one of the walking tours that leave the tourist information centre (Old School, Gloucester Green) every day at 10.30am, 11am, 1pm and 2pm; £4. Afternoon tours are the best, but get there early – places are limited. Guided walks also leave from the Catte St/High St corner; your guide might turn out to be an enterprising student. Ideally, though, it's worth trying to explore at your own pace away from the crowds – again, afternoons are best, with more colleges open then.

🏚 ♈ 🏵 MAGDALEN The most beautiful college, its tower a dramatic sight for visitors entering the city from the S. The quads and cloisters are very pleasant to stroll through, but the chief attraction is the DEER PARK, an unexpected haven in the heart of the bustling city. There's a circular path around this meadow

(you can't go in) called Addison's Walk; in spring it's mass of snowdrops and daffodils, then has hundreds of thousands of fritillaries in later spring, and after that the deer. Over a small bridge is the Fellows' Garden with a small ornamental lake – a very peaceful, sheltered spot.

🏚 ✝ 🔲 CHRIST CHURCH The best known college, a magnificently stately place begun by Cardinal Wolsey in the 16th c, but soon taken over by Henry VIII. The main entrance into the front quad is through Tom Tower, designed by Christopher Wren and named after its famous bell that rings out 101 times at 9 o'clock every night – in less liberal times the hour when students were due back in their rooms. The hall is worth a look, with its remarkable hammerbeam roof, paintings of alumni and benefactors by all the most expensive portrait-painters of the period, and the long tables laid out with silver for meals; there may be teas here some afternoons. The elaborate little CATHEDRAL is England's smallest, and doubles as the college chapel. It has some excellent stained glass by Burne-Jones, fantastic pendant vaulting in the choir, and some of the original Norman priory work. Entry into the college may be limited on Suns. A hidden treasure unnoticed by most visitors is the college's PICTURE GALLERY (Canterbury Quad), with an important collection of old master paintings and drawings, and various temporary exhibitions. Shop; cl 1–2pm, am Sun, and Christmas and Easter weeks, guided tours Thurs at 2.15pm; (01865) 276172; *£1.

♿✝⚲ Other interesting colleges are NEW, with its impressive chapel, atmospheric wisteria-covered cloisters, and remains of the city wall; MERTON, the most ancient buildings, with the country's oldest library (tours available); UNIVERSITY, which has an interesting monument to Shelley despite having thrown him out; the brightly Victorian, very red-brick KEBLE on Parks Rd (with perhaps the most famous Pre-Raphaelite painting of all, Holman Hunt's *Light of the World*, in its chapel); and ST EDMUND HALL, the only surviving medieval college, complete with Norman crypt. Amble down some of the town's prettiest streets and there are more, such as charming EXETER, JESUS and LINCOLN down Turl St, and CORPUS CHRISTI and ORIEL around Merton Lane and Oriel Sq. This last college has a very attractive and unusual entrance to its dining hall. TRINITY on Broad St is very grand. Around Radcliffe Sq BRASENOSE is quaint (and has good views of the surrounding skyline from its quads), and HERTFORD has its BRIDGE OF SIGHS over New College St, in itself worth exploring for some more unusual and less busy views and a good look at the gargoyles on the backs of some of the buildings. WORCESTER has particularly nice GARDENS, and many of the other colleges' private Fellows' gardens not usually open to visitors can be seen under the National Gardens Scheme. ♿▣ ASHMOLEAN MUSEUM (Beaumont

St) The country's first museum, and still one of its finest, opened in 1683 and rehoused in this imposing building from 1845. The well arranged galleries include marvellous European paintings, an extensive collection of Pre-Raphaelite pictures, a representative range of work by French Impressionists, and antiquities from ancient Egypt, Greece and Rome. Meals, snacks, shop, disabled access; cl am Sun, Mon (exc bank hols), Easter, 1st wk of Sept (St Giles Fair), Christmas week; (01865) 278000; free.

♿♿ BODLEIAN LIBRARY (Broad St) One of the oldest in Europe, its splendidly grand quad dominated by the Tower of the Five Orders. Most of it is closed to the public, but guided tours take in the beautifully vaulted 15th-c Divinity School, which shows some of the library's treasures, and Duke Humfry's Library, the oldest reading room. Tours (not pm Sat, Sun, or last wk in Aug) are generally 10.30am, 11.30am, 2pm and 3pm, but best to check first on (01865) 277165; tours stopped in 1997 so that they could tackle death watch beetle infestation, and there may well be further disruption in 1998. No children under 14. Excellent shop, limited disabled access (notice preferred); cl some bank hols and last wk of Aug; £3. Altogether the library houses over 5,500,000 books, going down 6 storeys under the centre of the city.

♿ SHELDONIAN THEATRE (Broad St) A grand classical building, with a lovely painted ceiling. In its time it's been used for parliaments, and nowadays university ceremonies are held here; you may see gowned students heading for these on some wknds, though the theatre is closed to the public then.

♿ PITT RIVERS MUSEUM (Banbury Rd) Shrunken heads, totem poles and fertility rites – a fascinating close-packed ethnological museum off the tourist track, with art and ingenuity from all cultures and periods. The million or so exhibits range from Captain Cook's Pacific Islands collection and 18th-c ship models to severed fingertips and an Eskimo coat made from seal intestines. Everything is displayed in firmly traditional cases or drawers, with neatly handwritten labels, and there's still something of the Victorian atmosphere it must have had when it originally opened. Shop, disabled access (with notice); cl am, Sun, a few days over Christmas and Easter; (01865) 270927; free. The adjacent BALFOUR BUILDING has a gallery of archaeology and a large collection of musical instruments. Other slightly scholarly but excellent collections, of the highest national importance, are to be found at the UNIVERSITY MUSEUM (Parks Rd), a Victorian Gothic structure specialising in natural history, with a working beehive in summer (cl Sun, some days over Easter and Christmas; free), and the HISTORY OF SCIENCE MUSEUM on Broad St, in one of the city's nicest old buildings (cl am, Sun, Mon, and a wk at Christmas and Easter; free).

🕸 OXFORD BOTANIC GARDEN (High St) Britain's oldest botanic garden, founded in 1621, with 8,000 species of plant from all over the world. It's a lovely place to sit for a while, or wander through on the way to the river. Disabled access; cl Good Fri and 25 Dec; (01865) 276920; £1.50 Jun–Aug, otherwise free. They also administer the University Arboretum at Nuneham Courtenay.

❄ CHRISTCHURCH MEADOW An unspoilt expanse of green astonishingly close to the busy city streets. You can gaze across the fields of grazing longhorn cattle to the spires in the distance, or walk under overhanging trees along the banks of the river to the boathouses; college eights row from here all year, in just about any weather.

🏠 THE OXFORD STORY (Broad St) Europe's longest dark ride, with cars designed as desks taking you through a cheerful and well researched re-creation of university history, complete with sights, sounds and smells. A useful introduction to the city (especially for families), though no substitute for the real thing. Good shop (you can just visit here using the entrance on Ship St), disabled access;

cl 25 Dec; (01865) 790055; £4.75. In summer you can get a ticket which also includes entry to Magdalen and New College (£7.75).

❗ COVERED MARKET (High St) A maze of stalls with something different at every turn; chic boutiques, speciality shops, cafés and old-fashioned butchers and poultry merchants. The Oxford Sandwich Co do excellent take-away sandwiches here, and Ben's Cookies are a favourite with students.

❗ GLOUCESTER GREEN (bus station) Interestingly rejuvenated, with trendy shops and cafés; you'd hardly believe this was once one of the less desirable parts of town. On Weds there's a bustling market here. The Old Fire Station complex houses a theatre and CURIOXITY, an interactive science gallery where visitors can experiment with the exhibits. The staff are helpful, and several sets of parents have told us it kept their children captivated for a full hour. Meals, snacks, shop; open daily during school hols, otherwise by appointment; (01865) 794494; £2.10. Not far from here among the fashionable shops and boutiques of Little Clarendon St, George & Davies is a good ice-cream parlour.

👂 BATE COLLECTION OF MUSICAL INSTRUMENTS (St Aldates) Outstanding – and constantly developing – collection of early keyboards, woodwind, brass, percussion and other instruments inc a complete Japanese gamelan. Shop, disabled access; cl am, wknds, 25 Dec, Good Fri; (01865) 276139; free.

🖼 MUSEUM OF MODERN ART (Pembroke St) Modern art museum with the sort of exhibitions and displays not often found in galleries outside London. They open till 9pm on Thurs. Meals, snacks, good bookshop, disabled access; cl am Sun, and 2 wks between exhibitions – may be worth checking first; (01865) 722733; *£2.50.

🖼❄ MUSEUM OF OXFORD (St Aldates) Interesting little local history museum, with recreated rooms, maps, and period music. Shop; cl Sun, Mon, and 13–24 Jan; £1.50, free for county residents. The museum organises occasional tours of the town's CASTLE MOUND; there isn't much of the Norman castle left save a tower and crypt of the castle church, and an underground well chamber, but the Mound gives quite good views over the city and its surroundings. Tours at least one Weds a month in summer: ring Mrs O'Neill on (01865) 815559 for dates; £2.

❊ † VIEWS The best are from the tower of Oxford's oldest building, ST MICHAEL AT THE NORTH GATE (Cornmarket St), a Saxon church with displays of silver, clocks and bells (cl during services; *£1.20), or from the interesting university church of ST MARY (High St), which also has a nice – if busy – café in the crypt (cl am Sun; £1.50). Right at the traditional centre of the city CARFAX TOWER, all that remains of a 14th-c church, also has good views, and the bells in the tower are interestingly designed. Shop; cl Nov–Feb; £1.20.

⚓ PUNTING Good fun in sunny weather; once you've got the knack it's a very nice way of spending a lazy afternoon. You can hire boats from Magdalen Bridge or Folly Bridge; usually £8–£10 an hour – you'll have to put down a big deposit. Salters run steamer trips from Folly Bridge to Abingdon.

♿ † 2 museums have more of a specialist appeal. TELECOM MUSEUM (Speedwell St) Unusual telephone and telegraph equipment (open by appointment, 01865 246601; free). ROTUNDA MUSEUM OF ANTIQUE DOLLS HOUSES (Grove House, Iffley Turn – 2m S of Oxford centre) Private collection of over 40 elaborate houses, dating from 1720 to 1900, with period furniture, carpets, and dinner services (no under-16s; open 1st Sun of month May–Sept; £2). Iffley's Norman CHURCH is one of the county's finest.

Days Out

Amble round Oxford
Walk through Christ Church quads and Meadow; Botanic Garden; Magdalen College; walk past Radcliffe Camera and Bodleian Library; lunch at the Turf Tavern; walk along Holywell St and Broad St; Ashmolean Museum – or spend the afternoon punting along the river from Magdalen Bridge or Folly Bridge, or walking out along Oxford Canal to Port Meadow, for an early evening drink at the Trout, Godstow.

The prehistoric horse and the magic smithy
Walk along the Ridgeway from the White Horse, past Uffington Castle to Wayland's Smithy and back; lunch at the White Horse, Woolstone; Great Barn at Great Coxwell; Buscot Park (limited opening).

Treetops and Thames gems
University of Oxford Arboretum at Nuneham Courtenay; Dorchester Abbey and village; lunch at the George or Fleur de Lys, Dorchester; walk across the Thames and up Wittenham Clumps (see Walks section, ⌂-8, p.531).

Regatta course and two Chilterns houses
Walk along the Thames between Henley-on-Thames and Hambledon Lock nr Mill End; lunch at the Anchor or Old White Horse on the river at Henley-on-Thames, or treat yourself at the Crooked Billet, Stoke Row; see the Maharajah's Well there; Stonor House or Greys Court (both limited opening).

Cotswolds tones
Walk in the park of Blenheim Palace, Woodstock, or hire a boat; lunch at the Feathers in the town; Roman villa, North Leigh; Minster Lovell; Burford; or spend the afternoon at the Cotswold Wildlife Park there.

A half-day dawdle around Thame
Eat well at the Sir Charles Napier above Chinnor; Thame; Rycote church; Waterperry gardens.

Other things to see and do

OXFORDSHIRE FAMILY ATTRACTION OF THE YEAR

🏠 🍴 🐶 ! ♿ ♪ **Woodstock** SP4416BLENHEIM PALACE Undoubtedly one of the most impressive stately homes in the country, this fantastically grand palace is also one of the most efficiently organised as far as visitors are concerned. It's just as well, as thousands flock through the gates each day in summer, and most people stay all day. Given to the Duke of Marlborough by Queen Anne as a reward for his military achievements, the house itself covers 14 acres, and the grounds stretch for well over 2,000. Highlights within the palace include the sumptuous state rooms and 56-metre (183-ft) Long Library, along with plenty of opulent furnishings and sculpture; tours leave every 5–10 minutes. The grounds, landscaped by Capability Brown, are no less grand, though not stuffily so; you can picnic just about anywhere, saving you venturing into the slightly expensive restaurants. Plenty of other features and attractions have been added to broaden the family appeal, but it hasn't moved too far down market: there's a butterfly house and miniature railway (useful for weary legs at the end of the day), and play areas with swings, ropes and slides. An extra £1 adds a hedge maze, putting green, and model village based on Woodstock and surroundings. You can hire rowing boats (£1 per person per half-hour) or arrange coarse fishing on the lake, and at weekends they have a bouncy castle (in quite a secluded spot, so not as out of place as it sounds). There's enough space to absorb the crowds (Sun is busiest, and Weds is popular with overseas students), but you'll find the house usually gets quieter after about 3pm. And you can avoid having to wait for tickets by arriving early; though most parts are closed till 10.30am, the gates and ticket office open at 9am. Those with quieter tastes may find the grounds at their most pleasant out of season, though the house is closed then, and there isn't so much for families. Churchill was born here in 1874, and there's a straightforward exhibition on his life. Meals and snacks (3 different restaurants), several shops and plant centre, some disabled access; house cl Nov–mid-Mar, grounds open all year; (01993) 811325; £7.80 house and grounds (£3.80 children 5–15). A family ticket for 2 adults and 2 children is £20; a grounds-only ticket is £5 a car.

★ † ⛪ 🏛 **Abingdon** SU4997
Attractive Thames-side town, until 1974 the county town of Berks. Much expanded around its old partly pedestrianised core, which still has a fine old gatehouse, several attractive old buildings and almshouses around the impressive 15th/16th-c Wren-style CHURCH OF ST HELEN off Thames St, a good MUSEUM in the 17th-c former county hall (cl Mon; free), and the unusual CHURCH OF ST MARY, wider than it's long. The remains of the partly Norman Benedictine ABBEY, once the second most powerful in England, have been restored, with part now housing a local theatre. The riverside Old Anchor is prettily placed for lunch, and there's decent food at the Mill House, built into the medieval Town Bridge.

⛪ 🍴 **Banbury** SP4540 The busy shopping town was actually without its famous cross for 250 years, between the Puritans' destroying it in 1602 and the construction of its replacement in 1859. In the church graveyard is the tomb from which Jonathan Swift borrowed the name Gulliver for his traveller. There's a decent local history MUSEUM (cl Sun and winter Mons; free), and the Reindeer and the Wine Vaults, both in Parsons St, are useful for lunch. The B4035 towards Sibford Ferris runs through attractive hilly farmland, with good summer PICK-YOUR-OWN; the loop N through North Newington, Shutford and Epwell is good too.

☕♨ **Benson** SU6191 BENSON VETERAN CYCLE MUSEUM Private collection of over 500 bicycles from between 1818 and 1930; open mornings Easter–Sept by appointment with Mr Passey, on (01491) 838414; free. Down by the river at the Cruiser station you can hire boats by the day or the hour; (01491) 838304. The footpath beyond the weir bridge leads to Wallingford. The Home Sweet Home at Roke is a charming dining pub.

✠ **Bix Bottom** SU7288 WARBURG RESERVE An extensive area of wild-flower-rich rough grassland and ancient beech wood, good for wild orchids and butterflies, besides birds and maybe deer. The Fox (A423) is good for lunch.

🏰☕ **Broughton** SP4138 BROUGHTON CASTLE 🏰 (B4035 SW of Banbury) Striking early 14th/16th-c house with proper moat and gatehouse, originally owned by William of Wykeham. Exceptional oak panelling, period furniture, and Civil War relics. Some rooms have bare stone walls under elaborately plastered ceilings, an unusual combination that works rather well. Snacks, shop, disabled access to ground floor only; open Easter, then mid-May–mid-Sept pm Weds, Sun and bank hols, plus Thurs July and Aug; (01295) 262624; £3.80. There's a decent village MUSEUM, and the Roebuck at North Newington is a good dining pub.

★✠☕🐎🌙🏛 **Burford** SP2512 Lovely little Cotswold town with interesting shops and teashops along its pretty main street. The CHURCH is particularly intriguing, with a super graveyard, and 17th-c graffiti by some of the 400 Leveller mutineers imprisoned here by Cromwell. The town also has an interesting little MUSEUM (open pm Apr–Nov; 50p), and is full of attractive pubs: the best for food and atmosphere is the Lamb, and the Mermaid serves food all day. Burford does get very busy indeed with visitors, and it's worth noting that several smaller and altogether quieter nearby villages are, in their way, as pretty: TAYNTON SP2313, the

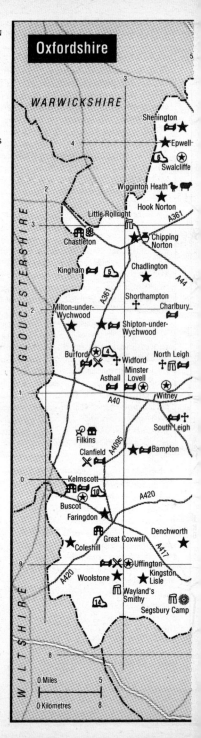

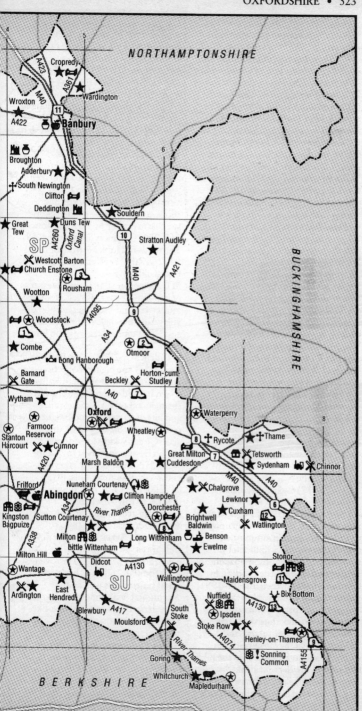

BARRINGTONS SP2013 (just over the Gloucs border), FULBROOK SP2513, SWINBROOK SP2712 and ASTHALL SP2811. All except the first have the additional attraction of a decent pub. You can walk between these, along the River Windrush for much of the way – the back roads along the Windrush Valley give pleasant drives, too. COTSWOLD WILDLIFE PARK (Bradwell Grove, A361 S of Burford) 🎫 A thoroughly reliable family day out, with animals, birds and reptiles from all over the world in re-creations of their natural environment. Also aquarium, tropical and insect houses, brass-rubbing centre, adventure playground and summer train rides, all set in acres of attractive parkland. Meals, snacks, shop, disabled access; cl 25 Dec; (01993) 823006; £5.10. 🏕🖼🐕🚂 Buscot SU2298 BUSCOT PARK (A417) What makes this 18th-c house really special is the amazing collection of art and furnishings amassed by its owners; paintings by Reynolds, Gainsborough, Rembrandt, Murillo and several of the Pre-Raphaelites (inc a splendid series by Burne-Jones), with some more recent pictures too. The attractive grounds have formal watergardens and a mouth-watering kitchen garden, and maybe PICK-YOUR-OWN in summer. Teas; open Apr–Sept, pm Weds–Fri and every 2nd and 4th wknd in the month; (01367) 240786; *£4.40, *£3.30 grounds only; NT. The Thames-side Trout (A417 towards Lechlade) is popular for lunch. 🏕🐕 Chastleton SP2429 CHASTLETON HOUSE (off the A44 NW of Chipping Norton) Opened in autumn 1997 after 6 years and £3 million of restoration, this handsome Jacobean manor house was little changed by the family who owned it 1605–1991, really feeling like a lived-in family house of that period, and not oversmartened despite the lovely plasterwork, beautiful oak and walnut furnishings, embroideries, Jacobite glassware, and even the Bible Charles I took to the scaffold. Peaceful Jacobean gardens inc topiary and first-class croquet lawn.

Car park up hill from house. Open Apr–Oct pm Weds–Sat; (01608) 674284; *£4.80, must have pre-booked timed ticket; NT. 🚆 Chinnor SU7698 CHINNOR AND PRINCES RISBOROUGH RAILWAY 4-mile train trips up into Bucks; trains most wknds Apr–Sept, some steam-hauled – best to ring (01844) 353535 for timetable and prices (you may need to book for special events). ★ 🐕 Chipping Norton SP3127 Pleasant old stone-built wool town with unusually wide market place, pretty church, some fine 17th-c almshouses, a good few antique shops, and a summer local history MUSEUM in the Co-op Hall (cl Mon; *£1). The Chequers has decent food. The roads to Hook Norton, or the B4026/B4022 to Witney, are good Cotswoldy drives. 🏰 Deddington SP4631 still has traces of its 12th-c CASTLE, as well as some attractive stone buildings around the village square; the Deddington Arms and Holcombe Hotel are good for lunch. 🚆 Didcot SO5290 DIDCOT RAILWAY CENTRE 🎫 The biggest collection anywhere of Great Western Railway stock, housed under cover, inc 20 steam locomotives, a diesel railcar and lots of passenger and freight rolling stock. Snacks, shop, disabled access; open wknds all year and wkdys Easter–Sept, best to ring for steamday dates, usually every Sun and Weds in summer hols; (01235) 817200; £3–£5.50 depending on event. The town itself more or less sprang up around the railway sheds. ★ ✝ 🐕 Dorchester SU5794 DORCHESTER ABBEY Impressive and well preserved old abbey, with 12th-c nave and rare lead font. The tower was rebuilt in 1605 and has a 14th-c spiral staircase, as well as an exceptional Jesse window from the same period, and some mosaic-like 12th-c glass in other windows. The adjacent former guesthouse now houses a little MUSEUM. In summer they do very individual ever-so-English teas (pm Weds–Sun), all home-made and quite addictive. Shop, disabled access; museum cl

12.30–2 pm, am Sun, and Oct–Apr; free. The whole Thames-side village is a lovely place to explore, with interesting antique shops. The George and Fleur de Lys do good lunches.

🎣 ⚓ 🦆 **Farmoor Reservoir** SP4407 Trout fishing, sailing, birdwatching, and other activities, though you'll need a permit; (01865) 863033 for details and prices.

🏛 ⚒ **Filkins** SP2304 COTSWOLD WOOLLEN WEAVERS Friendly working woollen mill with demonstrations of traditional production methods in 18th-c buildings. Snacks, well stocked shop, some disabled access; (01367) 860491; cl am Sun, 25–31 Dec; free. The Five Alls and Lamb are useful for lunch. Craft workshops in the village inc natural dyers (Filkins Farmhouse, appointment only (01367) 860253), traditional chairmakers (Calf Pens, Cross Tree) and saddlers (Oxleaze Farm).

🐑 🐄 **Frilford** SU4497 MILLETS FARM CENTRE PICK-YOUR-OWN fruit, animals, walks, and an unusually extensive farm shop which takes in a bakery, delicatessen, garden centre, and wine merchant; cl a few days over Christmas; (01865) 391555.

🏛 **Great Coxwell** SU2693 GREAT COXWELL BARN As noble as a cathedral according to William Morris, a 13th-c stone-built tithe barn 46 by 13 metres (152 ft long and 44 ft wide), with beautifully crafted timbers supporting the roof; *50p.

★ **Great Tew** SP3929 The most charming village in the area (some would say in all England). It's an outstanding series of golden stone 17th- and 18th-c cottages, some thatched and others with stone-slabbed roofs, around an attractive sloping green and among ancient trees, with wooded slopes above; the Falkland Arms here is a classic country tavern.

★ ♣ ✿ 🏛 🎋 ! † **Henley-on-Thames** SO7682 Pleasant well heeled Thames-side town famed for its summer regatta. You can usually see other rowing races or practices on the river throughout the year, or hire your own river boats on (01491)

572035 or (01494) 882210. A MUSEUM OF ROWING is due to open in 1998 by Mill Meadows, focusing as much on the river as on the sport itself; (01491) 410909 for opening details. The informal Anchor (Friday St) and comfortable beamed Old White Horse (Northfield End) are good-value riverside pubs, and the Three Tuns (Market Pl) does food all day. GREYS COURT (Rotherfield Greys, 3m W of Henley) An attractive gabled Jacobean house with interesting ruins of its medieval predecessor; the gardens are even more alluring, with white and rose gardens, ancient wisterias, a kitchen garden, wheelhouse and brick maze. They recently added an 1830s carousel. Teas, bookstall, some disabled access; open Apr–Sept, house pm Mon, Weds and Fri, garden pm daily exc Thurs and Sun; (01491) 628529; £4.20, £3 gardens only; NT. The village CHURCH is delightful, and the Maltsters Arms dining pub has lovely country views, and good nearby walks. The B480 to Watlington is a pleasant Chilterns drive.

🦆 🐖 ! **Ipsden** SU6385 WELLPLACE ZOO Mainly a bird park, but also animals such as lambs, goats, otters, donkeys and monkeys. You can feed several of them, so good for children. Snacks, shop, disabled access; cl wkdys Oct–Easter; (01491) 680473; £2. They have car boot sales on bank hols. The King William IV at Hailey is handy for something to eat. Ian Smith can arrange HORSE-DRAWN WAGGON RIDES through these pretty Chilterns fringes; most fine summer days he runs 2-horse waggons from Darkwood Farm, Park Corner on a local pub tour; (01491) 641324. Even by car, these are pleasant Chilterns drives – for instance the loop S of Nettlebed through Highmoor Cross, Stoke Row and Nuffield.

🏛 **Kelmscot** SU2499 A peaceful little village by the Thames; the Plough here is good. KELMSCOTT MANOR The summer home of William Morris until his death in 1896, now with one of the best assemblages of Morris memorabilia, standing out all the more for its domestic setting. Works by other Pre-Raphaelite artists include splendid paintings by Rossetti, who initially shared the lease. Snacks, shop, disabled access to ground floor only; open Weds (exc 1–2pm) and pm 3rd Sat of month Apr–Sept; (01367) 252486; *£6. We follow the Ordnance Survey spelling for the village, though many people now give it two t's.

🏠 🎡 **Kingston Bagpuize** SU4098 KINGSTON HOUSE (off the A415) Charming 17th-c manor house with lovely panelling, attractive furnishings and friendly unstuffy feel; peaceful garden with mature flowering shrubs, woodland walks, and Georgian gazebo over former Elizabethan cockpit. Snacks, shop; usually open pm bank hol wknds, and occasional other summer pms – best to ring for exact dates; (01865) 820259; £3.50, £1 garden only. The Hind's Head has good-value food.

🏚 **Little Rollright** SP2930 ROLLRIGHT STONES Dramatic and mysterious Bronze Age stones, chiefly in a circle about 30 metres (100 ft) across, now thought to date from between 1500 BC and 2000 BC; legend has it that the stones are a king and his men tricked by a witch into falling under her spell, and petrified. It's supposed to be impossible to count them as you can never tell where you started – which must have been frustrating for the estate agent when the stones were put on the market in 1997. The Gate Hangs High near here is useful for lunch.

🚌 **Long Hanborough** SP4214 OXFORD BUS MUSEUM Around 40 vehicles, from Oxford horse trams to more modern machines up to the 1960s, some roadworthy, others being restored. Disabled access; open Sun only; (01993) 883617; *£1.50. The Hand & Shears at Church Hanborough is now a very good dining pub.

👣 **Long Wittenham** SU5493 PENDON MUSEUM OF MINIATURE LANDSCAPE AND TRANSPORT 📷 Charming exhibition showing a highly detailed model railway and meticulously researched model 1930s village scenes; you can often see modellers working on the

exhibits, and they're always happy to chat. Snacks, shop; open pm wknds and bank hols Jan–Nov, plus pm Weds July and Aug; (01865) 820259; *£3. The Machine Man and riverside Plough are handy for lunch.

★ 🏡 🎿 🏠 🎡 ✕ **Mapledurham** SU6776 Very attractive little community with lovely beechwoods full of birds; the nicest way to reach it is by boat from the Caversham Promenade at Reading (summer wknds only). MAPLEDURHAM HOUSE An impressive Elizabethan mansion in pretty parkland running down to the Thames, with paintings and family portraits, great oak staircases, and moulded Elizabethan ceilings. In the grounds is the last WATERMILL on the Thames to use wooden machinery, still producing flour, bran and semolina. Also riverside walks and island with picnic area. Teas, shop, disabled access to ground floor only; open pm Sat, Sun and bank hols Easter–Sept; (01734) 723350; £4 house and watermill, £3 house only, £2.50 watermill only. You can stay in a number of lovely cottages on the estate (some thatched).

🏠 🎡 🍴 **Milton** SU4892 MILTON MANOR Elegant 17th-c manor house with splendid Strawberry Hill Gothic library, interesting chapel, walled garden, and unusual collections of teapots and fine china. Opening times were undecided at the time of going to press (they're usually concentrated around Aug), so best to ring (01235) 831287 for dates and prices. The Admiral Benbow has decent food. The CHERRY ORCHARDS around Milton Hill SU4790 are a fine sight when the white blossom is out in spring, and around July roadside stalls sell plump red-black fresh cherries – the Grove Farm Shop (A4130) is especially friendly.

★ ✝ 🏰 **Minster Lovell** SP3111 One of the prettiest and most unspoilt old villages in the area; there's an attractive 15th-c CHURCH and village green, and a 15th-c bridge over the River Windrush narrow enough for the Welsh drovers to use for counting the sheep in the flocks they brought this way each year. Imposing and attractively set 15th-c MINSTER LOVELL HALL was being used as ramshackle farm buildings until its 'restoration' as neat ruins in the 1930s. Macabre stories about the site usually involve people being shut up in various places and forgotten about until their skeletons are discovered much later. Open every day, free. There's a well restored medieval dovecot nearby. The smart Old Swan does good light lunches.

🏠✝ **North Leigh** SP3813 has the remains of a ROMAN VILLA Occupied between the 2nd and 4th c, when it was a very grand place with several dozen rooms, it's now just a few neat but poignant traces, in a very pleasant wooded setting; free. The medieval village CHURCH, with a Saxon tower, is lovely inside, and the Woodman is popular for lunch.

🏠✿ **Nuffield** SU6687 NUFFIELD PLACE The home of Lord and Lady Nuffield 1933 –1963, with the original 1930s furnishings. Very good gardens with mature trees and shrubs inc rhododendrons, lawns, pond and rockery, as well as Lady Nuffield's own Wolseley. Teas, limited disabled access; open pm 2nd and 4th Sun each month May–Sept; (01491) 641224; *£3. The Crown pub here has decent food.

🐾✿ **Nuneham Courtenay** SU5599 UNIVERSITY ARBORETUM (A4074) Fine conifers and other trees over 55 acres, as well as plants like rhododendrons that won't grow in the soil of Oxford itself. Some disabled access; cl wknds Nov–Apr, and 2 wks at Christmas; free. About ½m away, the roses at Notcutts Garden Centre are a blaze of summer colour easily seen from the road; decent meals here, though perhaps pricier than at some garden centres.

✦✿✿ **Otmoor** SP5615 Several square miles of flatland, so poorly drained that in very wet weather its river actually flows backwards. Because serious farming is virtually out of the question, it does have more natural wildlife than most places in the county; there are several paths through it. The Abingdon Arms at Beckley, with good food, is one good

starting point (and there's a good farm shop there on the B4027 from Stanton St John); the Nut Tree at Murcott does excellent steaks. On one edge, the PICK-YOUR-OWN fruit farm at Elsfield SP5410 has good views over the wilderness, as well as an unusually wide range of varieties.

🏠✿✝ **Rousham** SP4724 ROUSHAM HOUSE Nicely unspoilt 17th-c house embellished by court artists and architects, and remodelled in the 18th c by William Kent to give the external appearance of a Gothic Tudor mansion. It still has Civil War shooting holes in the door. Excellent 18th-c classically landscaped garden with buildings, cascades, statues and vistas in 30 acres of hanging woods above the River Cherwell, and walled flower and vegetable gardens. No children under 15. Some disabled access to grounds; house open pm Weds, Sun and bank hols Apr–Sept, gardens all year; (01869) 347110; £3 house, £3 garden. There's a 12th-c church. The Red Lion at Steeple Aston is very good for lunch (no children here, either).

✝ **Rycote** SP6604 RYCOTE CHAPEL (off the A329) Peaceful little 15th-c private chapel, later visited by both Elizabeth I and Charles I. Shop, disabled access; open pm daily, wknds and bank hols Apr–Oct; £1.50. The Bull at Great Milton has decent food.

🏠✿ **Segsbury Camp** SU3884 Extensive Iron Age hill fort, later used by the Romans, with good views; reached by the dead-end lane up past the Sparrow in Letcombe Regis.

✿! **Sonning Common** SU7080 HERB FARM (Peppard Rd) Extensive range of herb plants and products, with over 3,200 different species in the display garden. There's a maze (summer only), and agricultural displays in a restored granary. Summer snacks, shop, disabled access; cl Mon (exc bank hols and in Dec); (01734) 724220; free, £1 for maze. The Butchers Arms is a useful dining pub with wknd family entertainment.

★🏠✿ **Stanton Harcourt** SP4105 MANOR HOUSE The medieval Great

Kitchen has no chimney – the smoke from ovens and fireplaces collected in the cone of the roof and drifted out through wooden louvres. The gardens too are striking, with neat lawns and topiary, and a wilder wooded area. Teas, shop, disabled access; usually open pm Thurs and Sun fortnightly mid-Apr–Sept, plus bank hols – best to check first; (01865) 881928; *£4, *£2.50 garden only. The village is attractive, and the Harcourt Arms nearby does good meals.

🏠 🐝 **Stonor** SU7388 STONOR HOUSE AND PARK Even older than the stately Tudor façade suggests, with beautiful furnishings, paintings, sculptures and tapestries, and mementos of Jesuit scholar Edward Campion, one of the many Catholic recusants who found refuge here during the Reformation. The lovely gardens have an unusual exhibition of sculpture from Zimbabwe, and there's a wooded deer park. Snacks, shop, some disabled access; open pm Sun and bank hols Apr–Sept, plus pm Weds May–Sept, pm Thurs July and Aug, and pm Sat Aug; (01491) 638587; £4, £2 chapel and garden only. The smart Stonor Arms is useful for lunch.

★ 🏠 📖 **Swalcliffe** SP3737 SWALCLIFFE BARN (B4035) Another well preserved tithe barn, with much of its medieval half-cruck timber roof intact. There's a display of agricultural and trade vehicles. Disabled access; open pm Sun and bank hols Apr–Oct; free. The village is pretty, and the Stag's Head has good food.

🍺 **Tetsworth** SP6801 For many years an atmospheric coaching inn, the 16th-c Swan on the High St is now an unusual ANTIQUES CENTRE, with top-of-the-range antiques and furnishings well displayed in period rooms and meandering corridors. More like visiting a house than a shop, with the contents priced at anything from £15 to £5,000. Similarly stylish restaurant attached; cl 25–28 Dec; (01844) 281777. The Lion on the Green has good-value food.

★ † **Thame** SP7005 Well worth a look for its splendid range of unspoilt architecture. The very wide main street has escaped any significant development this century, and has medieval timber-framed buildings next to stately Georgian houses; the 13th-c CHURCH is attractive. The 15th-c Birdcage Inn used to be the town lock-up; the Rising Sun, Abingdon Arms and Six Bells are useful for a bite to eat – though the best nearby place for lunch is the Mole & Chicken at Easington out past Long Crendon.

★ † 🛏 📖 ❀ ! **Uffington** SU3089 Charming village, with decent food at the Fox & Hounds. Opposite here is John Betjeman's former home Garrard Farm, which you can rent in summer, (01328) 851155; as warden of St Mary's CHURCH, he made sure its oil lamps were preserved. TOM BROWN'S SCHOOL MUSEUM (Broad St) Young Mr Brown's schooldays were based on those the author Thomas Hughes passed here; there's an exhibition on his life and work, with a display on Betjeman too. Shop, disabled access; open pm wknds and bank hols (exc Aug bank hol) Easter–Oct; 60p. UFFINGTON CASTLE High above the village, this Iron Age fort covered 8 acres but had only one gateway; great views over the vale below. On the hillside a 115-metre (375-ft) WHITE HORSE carved into the chalk is now thought to be around 3,000 years old; it's a striking design, very Celtic. If you stand in the centre of the eye and turn around 3 times with your eyes closed, any reasonable wish will be granted. This is one good setting-off point for the Ridgeway (see **Walk** ⌂-14). The flat-topped little hill below is said to be where George killed the dragon. A bit over 1m E, off the B4507, the turning off up towards the downs opposite the Kingston Lisle road almost immediately passes a cottage on the left which has outside a huge pitted flint rock, locally known as the blowing stone: if you blow in the right hole and in the right way you can produce a splendid deep blast of sound.

🏰 🛏 ⛳ 🎣 **Wallingford** SU6089 Ruins of 13th-c CASTLE on a hill, the history of which can be found at the nearby

MUSEUM (High St), which also has a very good sight-and-sound history of the area. Shop; cl am (exc Sat), Mon (exc bank hols), winter Suns, and Dec–Feb; (01491) 835065; £1.75. The Little House Around the Corner by the Brook is a welcoming family pub in a lovely old streamside spot by the church. Plenty of places to hire boats or fish around here.

✝ ⚬ ✗ **Wantage** SU4087 Historic town where King Alfred was reputedly born; recently much expanded, though there's an attractive quiet corner by the 13th/15th-c CHURCH with its raised graveyard, and in Newbury St 17th-c almshouses have a courtyard cobbled with bones. The VALE AND DOWNLAND MUSEUM CENTRE (Church St) has well displayed local history and geology; in 1998 the main gallery will be closed until May. Meals, snacks, shop, disabled access; cl am Sun, Mon, Good Fri, Christmas; (01235) 771447; free. The downland roads S into Berks have fine views. VENN WATERMILL (A338 N of Wantage) Still the area's regularly used working corn mill; open 2nd Sun in month Apr–Oct; £1.

⚙ ✗ ✝ **Waterperry** SP6206 WATERPERRY GARDENS Peaceful gardens and nurseries, fine herbaceous borders, rock garden, riverside walk, shrub borders, lawns, trees and useful nurseries. The grounds include an arts and crafts gallery, and a wonderfully tranquil little CHURCH, mainly Norman, but incorporating some Saxon work. Meals, snacks, excellent garden shop, good disabled access; cl Christmas and New Year and several days in July; (01844) 339254; £2.40. The Clifden Arms in Worminghall just over the Bucks border is nice for lunch.

🏛 **Wayland's Smithy** SU2885 Midway along the Ridgeway between the Uffington White Horse and the B4000 above Ashbury (where the Rose & Crown is ideally placed for walkers), this was even in Saxon times reputed to be the forge of a magic blacksmith, who would invisibly shoe your horse overnight if you left it there with a silver coin – and exact horrid penalties if you tried to slip by without paying. It's an impressive place, alone on the downs, an excavated NEOLITHIC BURIAL CHAMBER rather more than 5,000 years old, made with massive sarsen stones each weighing several tons; free.

✗ ⊞ ✗ **Wheatley** SP5905 The unusual octagonal WINDMILL is open by appointment, (01865) 874610; free. Just S at Garsington SP5702 Jennings Farm Shop has a wide range of produce as well as craft workshops and a working blacksmith's forge. Garsington has decidely smart open-air operas (though spoilsport locals have occasionally tried to drown them out with strimmer and mower noise).

★ 🐄 **Whitchurch** SU6377 An attractive little village, with nice walks nearby; the Greyhound does good-value food. The BOZE DOWN VINEYARD (B471 N) has free tastings pm wknds, and guided tours by appointment; (01734) 844031. Path Hill Farm on Goring Heath nearby has a shop selling organic products.

🐄 ✔ **Wigginton Heath** SP3833 WATERFOWL SANCTUARY AND CHILDREN'S FARM Notably friendly family-run farm and rescue centre, standing out for its determinedly simple and undeveloped feel. Children love it, and can start cuddling and stroking animals practically as soon as they come through the door; the Baby Barn always has plenty of tiny chicks, rabbits, guinea pigs, kittens and the like. Also rare breeds, uncommon aviary birds, and 16 well set out (and carefully fenced off) waterfowl ponds, awash with ducks. Wear wellies in wet weather. Disabled access; cl 25 Dec; (01608) 730252; *£3.

★ ✝ 🏠 🐄 ⚬ **Witney** SP3510 Saxon kings used to hold their meetings, or witans, here – hence the name. It was a prosperous town in the Middle Ages, and is well known for its blankets, made here ever since. Quiet and relaxed, with picturesque stone buildings, market square still with its ancient butter cross and 17th-c clock, and quite a few interesting old buildings such as the 13th-c church and 18th-c blanket hall. The Three Horseshoes in Corn St is attractive for lunch. COGGES FARM MUSEUM (Church Lane) Entertaining and informative Victorian living farm museum, with period farmhouse kitchens and dairy, walled gardens, and local breeds of farm animals. Daily feeding, agricultural and craft demonstrations. Meals, snacks, shop, mostly disabled access; cl am wknds, Mon (exc bank hols), and Nov–Mar (exc Advent wknd when various seasonal events); (01993) 772602; £3. Just off Church Green you can see the excavated foundations of a 12th-c palace of the Bishops of Winchester (pm wknds only, free).

🥤 🏰 ✝ 🌟 **Woodstock** SP4416 Civilised and prosperous small town, with good antique shops and fine stone buildings. The Feathers Hotel, Bear Hotel and cheaper Black Prince are all good for lunch. *See separate Family Panel on p.521* for Blenheim Palace. OXFORDSHIRE COUNTY MUSEUM (Fletcher's House) Elegant town house with pleasant gardens and good displays. Snacks, shop, some disabled access; cl am Sun, Mon; (01993) 811456; £1.50. The graveyard of BLADON CHURCH, where Churchill is buried, has views over Blenheim Park.

✝ Among the county's **many fine churches**, one of the most interesting is at Widford SP2612 just outside Burford: very simple, but notable for 3 things – its medieval wall paintings, the remains of a Roman pavement at the west end of the chancel, and its surroundings, a former village that save one solitary house has now virtually disappeared. The churches at Shorthampton SP3220, South Leigh SP3908 and South Newington SP4033 also have fine wall paintings; the latter may be locked, but you can get the key from College Farmhouse next door.

★ **Other attractive small towns and villages** here, all with decent pubs, include Adderbury SP4635, Ardington SU4388 (several craft workshops in the Home Farm buildings), Bampton SP3103, Blewbury SP5385, Brightwell Baldwin SU6595, Chadlington SP3222, Chalgrove SU6396 (notable medieval wall paintings in the 11th-c church, which owns the pub), Church Enstone SP3724, Clifton Hampden SU5495, Coleshill SU2393 (NT; lots of good walks nearby), Combe SP4115 (walks into Blenheim), Cropredy SP4646, Cuddesdon SP5903, Cumnor SP4603, streamside thatched Cuxham SU6695, Denchworth SU3791, Duns Tew SP4528, East Hendred SU4588, Epwell SP3540, Ewelme SU6491 (particularly pretty and unspoilt), Faringdon SU2895, Goring SU6080, Hook Norton SP3533, Kingston Lisle SU3287, Lewknor SU7198, Marsh Baldon SU5699, Milton-under-Wychwood SP2618, Shenington SP3742, Shipton-under-Wychwood SP2717 (interesting bookshop, lovely green, 2 good inns – one very ancient), Souldern SP5131, Stoke Row SU6883 (with its unusual Maharajah's Well), Stratton Audley SP6026, Sutton Courtenay SU5093 (Asquith and Orwell unlikely bedfellows in their final rest in the graveyard), Sydenham SP7201 (lovely church), Wardington SP4945, Woolstone SU2987 (Thomas Hughes reputedly wrote *Tom Brown's Schooldays* in the bar here), Wootton SP4320, Wroxton SP4142, and unspoilt Wytham SP4708 (all houses owned and preserved by Oxford University).

Please let us know what you think of places in the *Guide*. Use the report forms at the back of the book or simply send a letter.

Walks

In Oxford itself there are countrified walks almost from the city centre. University Parks is the closest place for a good stroll – and you can watch first-class cricket matches for free.

The best outlying area is Port Meadow, an expanse of waterside common land with grazing horses and flocks of geese, which extends N from Jericho and can be reached on the far side of the Oxford Canal via Walton Well Rd, crossing the Thames and turning right along the W bank. Just beyond the far end of Port Meadow is the ruin of 12th-c Godstow Nunnery, where Fair Rosamund the mistress of Henry II is buried; nearby, the riverside medieval Trout pub is touristy but very attractive. A second well sited riverside pub, the thatched Perch at Binsey, is another popular objective in this direction. Iffley Meadows on the other side of the centre are conserved for wildlife, and in late spring are a sea of purple snakes-head fritillaries.

The Rivers Thames and Cherwell cut strikingly rural corridors through the city, though walks along the Cherwell may be impeded by closed college gates. They are most likely to be open in mid-afternoon.

From the big garden of the Fishes at North Hinksey SP4805 a footpath towards the town partly follows a causeway built originally by John Ruskin to give students experience of healthy outdoor labour.

Blenheim SP4416 ○-1 has plentiful paths and tracks through its huge estate – inc a public right of way if you don't want to pay admission. **Otmoor wilderness** SP5615 ○-2 is interesting to walk through.

Oxford Canal ○-3 towpath is shadowed by the railway, so you can walk from one village to another, for example from Lower Heyford SP4824 to Nethercott SP4820, and return by train. There's also access from the Jolly Boatman at Thrupp SP4815.

Over in the W, the Cotswolds offer a handful of good walks, such as along the **River Windrush** ○-4 from Burford SP2512 or Swinbrook SP2712; in the **village triangle** ○-5 comprising Adlestrop SP2426 (just over the Gloucs border), Cornwell SP2727 and Chastleton SP2429; and around **Sibford Gower** SP3537 ○-6 (the thatched Wykham Arms is good for lunch here). There are pleasant circular walks from the Plough at Finstock SP3616.

Forest Hill SP5807 ○-7 above Oxford gives several pleasant walks from the White Horse.

The **River Thames** ○-8 has pleasant walks starting and finishing at Dorchester SU5794; you can cross at Day's Lock SU5693, and a short walk brings you to Wittenham Clumps SU5692 (alternative access from adjacent car park), a pair of hillocks which look across the Chilterns and Berkshire Downs. The **Thames Valley** proper ○-9, shared with Berks and Bucks, has a classic, very English sort of beauty, with boating scenes, superb trees and riverside architecture. Riverside walks on the Oxon side are possible only in places, notably between Henley-on-Thames SU7682 and Sonning SU7575 – for instance to Shiplake Lock from the Plowden Arms at Shiplake SU7678; you can also get down to the Thames from the attractive Perch & Pike at South Stoke SU5983.

The **Upper Thames** ○-10 W of Oxford flows through low-lying country – the sort of walk you enjoy more for the people you're with than the scenery itself. But Cotswold villages here make good focal points: from William Morris's house at Kelmscot SU2499, for example, it is a straightforward 1½m E to the Swan at Radcot Bridge SU2899. Other useful pubs for pleasant if undramatic riverside strolls are the Trout on the unclassified road between Bampton and Buckland at Tadpole Bridge SP3300, Maybush on the A415 at Newbridge SP4001 (the Rose Revived here is worth knowing for its big Thames-side lawn), Ferryman off the B4449 S of Stanton Harcourt at Bablock Hythe SP4304 and Talbot on the B4044 nr Swinford Bridge SP4408.

The Chilterns have numerous possibilities for exploring the beechwoods and farmlands, though the chalk hills' more memorable viewpoints and landscapes mostly lie over in Bucks. **Stonor Deer Park** ⌂-11 is skirted by an attractive right of way from Stonor village SU7388, and you can link this with the famous Maharajah's Well at Stoke Row SU6883; or you can continue east to Turville SU7690 (see **Buckinghamshire** chapter). **Cowleaze Wood** SU7295 ⌂-12 between Christmas Common SU7193 and the M40 has forest art exhibits scattered around as part of a sculpture trail. Below here there are great views from Watlington Woods SU7093 – a mass of bluebells in spring. On the **Oxfordshire Way** ⌂-13, a short walk with a palpable sense of peace is the one from the lane out of Bix past Bix Hall to Valley End Farm SU7286. Useful pubs for walkers in and around the Oxfordshire Chilterns include the Fox at Bix SU7285, Black Horse or Four Horseshoes at Checkendon SU6683, Fox & Hounds on Christmas Common SU7193, Highwayman at Exlade Street SU6582, King Charles Head on Goring Heath SU6678, Five Horseshoes at Maidensgrove SU7288, Rising Sun on Witheridge Hill nr Highmoor SU6984, Olde Leathern Bottel at Lewknor SU7198 and Crown at Pishill SU7389.

Near the N crest of the downs, the Ridgeway tracks right across the county from Wilts to Berks. This broad grassy trackway was used as a herding highway for some 2,000 years before the Romans came, and after the break-up of the Roman empire came back into use for the same purpose, well into medieval times. It's now part of the long-distance path network, and gives good walking with fine views. **Compton Beauchamp** SU2787 ⌂-14 has a particularly atmospheric short stretch nearby, taking in the ancient sites of Wayland's Smithy, the White Horse and Uffington Castle.

Where to eat

Adderbury SP4635 RED LION (01295) 810269 Smartly civilised 16th-c coaching inn with comfortable and attractive rooms, lovely big inglenook, deep sofas, a pretty residents' lounge, an attractive no smoking back dining room, good home-made food, well kept beers, quite a few wines by the glass, and helpful licensees; bdrms; disabled access. £22.50|£10.50.

Ardington SU4388 BOARS HEAD (01235) 833254 Civilised and upmarket dining pub with 3 neatly kept and simply decorated rooms, low beams, bare boards, fresh flowers, particularly good wines, well kept real ales, imaginative regularly changing food, and friendly owners; good nearby walks; no food pm Sun, cl Mon; disabled access. £22.50|£5.50.

Barnard Gate SP4010 BOOT (01865) 881231 Friendly dining pub with an interesting collection of celebrities' boots, impressive choice of good generous food in bar and partly no smoking restaurant, prompt friendly service, decent wine, well kept beers, and big log fire. £20.25|£8.

Beckley SP5611 ABINGDON ARMS (01865) 351311 Busy, popular food pub with a sensibly short seasonal menu and really interesting food, well kept ales, a good range of wines, a comfortably modernised simple lounge with pretty flowers on tables, smaller public bar, pleasant garden and floodlit terrace; cl pm Sun for food; no children. £18|£6.25.

Burford SP2512 MERMAID (01993) 822193 Busy pub with handsome Tudor frontage, attractive long narrow bar with flagstones, stonework and some panelling, pretty dried flowers, no smoking dining conservatory and upstairs restaurant, good food inc cream teas usefully served all day, well kept real ales, and courteous efficient staff. £18.50|£6.95.

Chalgrove SU6396 RED LION (01865) 890625 Delightful pub owned by the local church since the 17th c, with a traditional atmosphere, stylish simple furnishings, a log fire and old woodburner, carefully collected prints and period cartoons, well kept real ales, decent wines, imaginative, very well presented bar food, a helpful landlord, and no smoking back dining room. £20.65|£8.95.

Chinnor SP7500 Sir Charles Napier Spriggs Alley, up on the escarpment (01494) 483011 Decidedly civilised, with excellent food in stylish back restaurant, champagne on draught, huge wine list, freshly squeezed pink grapefruit or orange juice; smartly relaxed little bar with homely furnishings, log fire, delicious food from a short bar menu, real ales; croquet lawn; cl pm Sun, Mon; children over 7 in evening; partial disabled access. £33|£9.50.

Clanfield SP2802 Clanfield Tavern (01367) 810223 Carefully refurbished place with new no smoking conservatory and new bar lounge, well kept ales, decent wines, imaginative home-made food, several flagstoned, heavy-beamed and stone-walled small rooms leading off main bar, and handsome stone fireplace; cottagey restaurant. £20.65|£8.95.

Cumnor SP4603 Bear & Ragged Staff (01865) 862329 Smart old pub with roaring log fires in comfortably rambling, softly lit bar, a civilised atmosphere, well presented good food (the dining area is no smoking), well kept real ales, several wines by the glass, and pleasant obliging service. £28.35|£13.95.

Maidensgrove SU7288 Five Horseshoes (01491) 641282 17th-c little brick house with log fire in rambling bar/bistro, good, often imaginative food, decent wine list, well kept real ales, and walkers' bar – the surrounding Chilterns beechwoods are popular; summer barbecues in nice garden; cl 25–26 Dec; children over 8 allowed only in club room or bistro; partial disabled access. £23.50|£6.50.

Nuffield SU6687 Crown (01491) 641335 Attractive brick and flint pub in fine countryside with roaring log fires, a wide choice of food, comfortable atmosphere, well kept beers, decent wines and prompt friendly service. £20|£7.

Oxford SP5106 Cafe Moma Museum of Modern Art, Pembroke St (01865) 722733 Clean, light and very popular self-service café in the museum basement, simple modern furnishings, exhibitions on walls, largely vegetarian food from a blackboard, excellent cakes, and efficient friendly service; open till 5pm (9pm Thurs); cl Mon, bank hols; disabled access. £7.85|£3.75.

Oxford SP5106 Gees 61a Banbury Rd (01865) 553540 Relaxed, airy atmosphere in genuine old conservatory, fresh herbs and spices to enliven interesting vegetarian pastas, wild mushrooms and so forth as well as good meat and fish dishes, good unusual wines; cl 25–26 Dec, service charge for groups of over 5. £20|£6.50.

Oxford SP5106 Le Petit Blanc 71–72 Walton St (01865) 510999 Very popular stylish and airy 2-room brasserie open all day for breakfast, lunch, afternoon tea and dinner; from the smarter room you can see into the kitchen and watch the preparation of the extremely good Mediterranean food; friendly service and helpful notes against each wine listed; cl 25 Dec; children very welcome; disabled access. £23|£9.20.

Oxford SP5106 Tiberio 260 Banbury Rd, Summertown (01832) 205117/205210 Welcoming Italian restaurant with good food and pleasant, efficient and friendly service; cl Sun, 25–26 Dec. £25|£4.75.

As well as these, the city is full of useful stop-offs. The ancient Turf Tavern in Bath Pl between Holywell St and New College Lane is the most interesting pub, and other decent pubs include the ancient Bear (Alfred St), enjoyably studenty Kings Arms (Holywell St), Eagle & Child (St Giles – Tolkien/C S Lewis connections), unspoilt old Rose & Crown (North Parade) and handily central White Horse (Broad St). The Victoria Arms at Old Marston, with a big garden on the Cherwell, is a popular punters' destination. The Pizza Express (Golden Cross) is in a surprisingly interesting medieval building.

South Stoke SU5983 Perch & Pike (01491) 872415 Attractive flint pub with a relaxed atmosphere, comfortable seats, open fires, a nice assortment of tables, civilised touches such as linen napkins, bone-handled cutlery and old napkin rings, and good innovative food; cl pm 25–26 Dec; no children in the bar; partial disabled access. £22|£4.95.

Stoke Row SU6883 Crooked Billet (01491) 681048 Open-plan country dining pub with log fires, a wide choice of good interesting food (changing daily; good vegetarian choice), jazz/classical guitar themed food evenings, decent wines and real ales, and big garden by Chilterns beechwoods. £27|£4.95.

Sutton Courtenay SU5093 Fish 4 Appleford Rd (01235) 848242 Good imaginative food in popular dining pub using daily fresh fish and local produce (vegetarian dishes, too), good wines, well kept real ale, friendly staff; bdrms; disabled access. £20.70|£5.

Tetsworth SP6801 Swan 5 High St (01844) 281777 15th-c former coaching inn with restaurant serving good traditional food inc fresh fish; candles on tables, a roaring log fire, and seats in landscaped gardens; antiques showroom next door with fine furniture, jewellery, longcase clocks, silver cutlery, and garden antiquities; cl pm Sun; disabled access. £19.50|£6.

Uffington SU3089 Britchcombe Farm (01367) 820667 Working farm in lovely spot below White Horse Hill, afternoon cream teas on Sat, Sun and bank hol Mon with home-made scones, cakes and so forth; very friendly service, log fire in winter, tables outside among the geese and sheep in summer; some fruit and vegetables, home-made mohair knitwear and crafts, mobile home for hire, and certified camping/caravan site; disabled access. £5 tea and scones for 2.

Wallingford SU6089 Annie's Tea Rooms 79 High St (01491) 836308 Prettily decorated and friendly no smoking 17th-c house serving morning coffee, lunches with a home-made daily dish, and afternoon tea inc a fine choice of home-made cakes and quite a few teas; cl Weds, Sun (except July–Sept for tea); disabled access. |£2.60.

Watlington SU6894 Chequers Love Lane (01491) 612874 Cheerful, cosy old pub with low beams, candlelight, nice old chairs and antique tables, conservatory, wide choice of good popular food, real ales, and pretty garden; cl 25–26 Dec; no children. £19|£4.

Westcott Barton SP4325 Fox (01869) 340338 Lovely stone-built village pub with enjoyable authentic Italian food cooked by the Italian licensee and his brother, a relaxed little bar with hops on low beams, open fires, high-backed settles and pews on the flagstones, an elegant restaurant, well kept ales, and espresso and cappuccino coffee; pleasant garden with wooden play fort. £15.50|£4.95.

Special thanks to Joan Olivier, Mrs E C Montague, B and K Hypher, M G Hart, David Jack.

OXFORDSHIRE CALENDAR

Some of these dates were provisional as we went to press. Please check information with the numbers provided.

FEBRUARY

1 **Oxford** Chinese New Year Celebrations at the Town Hall (01865) 204188

MARCH

13 **Didcot** Thomas the Tank Engine at the Railway Centre – *till Sun 15* (01235) 817200

APRIL

11 **Cogges** Lambing at Manor Farm Museum – *till Mon 13* (01993) 772602

13 **Steeple Aston** Spring Flower Show (01869) 340512

MAY

1 **Oxford** May Morning: Magdalen College choir sings from Magdalen Tower, morris dancing in Radcliffe Sq and Broad St (01865) 726871

2 **Wallingford** Regatta – *till Sun 3* (01491) 836517

9 **Wallingford** Music at St Peters – *till 26 Sept* (01491) 825421

21 **Oxford** Beating the Bounds: starts at the Church of St Michael at the Northgate (01865) 726871

23 **Woodstock** Fire Engine Rally: 200 engines at Blenheim Palace – *till Mon 25* (01993) 811091

24 **Cogges** Sheep Shearing at Manor Farm Museum (01993) 772602; **Woodstock** Celebrity Charity Cricket Match at Blenheim Palace (01865) 247427

25 **Oxford** Lord Mayor's Parade and Show at South Park (01865) 790260

JUNE

6 **Woodstock** Golden Jubilee Rally of the Morris Minor Owners Club at Blenheim Palace – *till Sun 7* (01993) 811091

13 **Woodstock** Fireworks Concert at Blenheim Palace (01993) 811091

14 **Banbury** and District Show (01295) 259855

20 **Abingdon** Election of the Mayor of Ock Street (since fight over an ox in 1700): new mayor is chaired down Ock St, morris dancing into evening (01235) 522711; **Wallingford** Carnival (01491) 836594; **Woodstock** Carnival at Quarry Park (01993) 811495

27 **Banbury** Steam & Vintage Vehicle Rally – *till Sun 28* (01295) 730272; **Thame** Festival – *till Carnival on 4 July* (01844) 215650

JULY

1 **Henley-on-Thames** Royal Regatta – *till Sun 5* (01491) 572153

5 **Hook Norton** Rural Fair (01608) 737336

8 **Henley-on-Thames** Festival of Music and the Arts – *till Sat 11* (01491) 410414

12 **Oxford** Horse Races and Craft Fair on Wolvercote Common (01865) 58845

15 **Wantage** Music Festival – *till Mon 20* (01235) 766078

16 **Waterperry** Arts and Crafts in Action at Waterperry Gardens: over 300 craftspeople and fine artists from around the world - *till Sun 19* (0171) 381 3192

OXFORDSHIRE CALENDAR

JULY cont

18 **Hook Norton** Beer Festival at the Pear Tree Inn (01608) 737482
20 **Sunbury–Abingdon** Swan Upping on the River Thames: colourful traditional ceremony – *till Fri 24* (01628) 523030

AUGUST

1 **Claydon** Vintage Fayre at Granary Museum – *till Sun 2* (01295) 259855
7 **Cropredy** Folk & Rock Festival with Fairport Convention – *till Sat 8* (01869) 337142
9 **Caversfield** Bicester and Finmere Show (01280) 848327
28 **Towersey** Village Festival: concerts, dance, street theatre – *till Mon 31* (01296) 394411
30 **Uffington** White Horse Show – *till Mon 31* (01367) 242191
31 **Bletchingdon** Heathfield Equestrian Show (01869) 350227; **Steeple Aston** Summer Flower Show (01869) 340512

SEPTEMBER

10 **Woodstock** Blenheim International Horse Trials at Blenheim Palace – *till Sun 13* (01993) 813335
12 **Hambleden** Henley Show (01491) 410948
13 **Abingdon** Works Car Show (01235) 522711
17 **Thame** Agricultural Show at the Show Ground (01844) 212737
19 **Cogges** Steam Threshing at Manor Farm Museum – *till Sun 20* (01993) 772602

OCTOBER

2 **Didcot** Thomas the Tank Engine at the Railway Centre – *till Sun 4* (01235) 817200
14 **Banbury** Michaelmas Fair (01295) 259855

DECEMBER

12 **Didcot** Thomas the Tank Engine at the Railway Centre – *till Sun 13* (01235) 817200
19 **Didcot** Thomas the Tank Engine at the Railway Centre – *till Sun 20* (01235) 817200

We welcome reports from readers . . .

This *Guide* depends on readers' reports. Do help us if you can – in return, we offer a discount on the next edition to people who've helped us with reports for it. Tell us what you think about places already in it, and anything extra you think we should say about them. And send us your ideas for inclusion in the next edition: places to visit, eat at or stay in, attractive drives or walks, maybe even unusual interesting shops you know of. Use the card in the middle, the report forms at the end, or just write – no stamp needed: *The Good Guide to Britain*, FREEPOST TN1569, Wadhurst, E Sussex TN5 7BR.

SHROPSHIRE

Distinctive really unspoilt countryside, interesting and unusual places to visit, charming places to stay in.

Shropshire's countryside is very special, the old-fashioned England which elsewhere exists only in memory and imagination, with pleasant drives through unspoilt scenery, attractive buildings in stone or black and white timbering, and sleepy views from a set of distinctive hills. Much is as it was when P. G. Wodehouse set his books here. The partly heather-covered Long Mynd, England's southernmost grouse moor, has great character (undimmed by a huge fire early last summer), with the much smaller but very striking Caer Caradoc facing it across the valley. The rather eerie Stiperstones west of the Long Mynd are outcrops of harder quartzy rock leaving strange-shaped boulders, tors and crests on the skyline – and strange tales among the people living nearby. Wenlock Edge, to the east, is long and smoother, wooded (and much quarried) along its flanks. Other notable hills are the rather volcanic-looking Titterstone Clee north-east of the picturesque town of Ludlow, the aptly named Brown Clee north of that, and the bold Wrekin towering over Telford.

Many family days out here fit well into this rustic pattern. There are quite a few appealing open farms: the one at Preston on the Weald is particularly good value, considering how long it holds people's attention, and the very traditional one at Acton Scott is also much enjoyed. But there's a wide range of other rewarding places to visit. The Ironbridge museums have been ranked among the top two dozen in Britain on the Heritage Secretary's new shortlist of national importance. They are among Britain's most enjoyable days out, with plenty to entertain children at lively open-air Blists Hill. Hawkstone Park is another exceptionally enjoyable place. Other outstanding attractions include Shrewsbury Quest (Shrewsbury is full of interest), the aerospace museum at Cosford, and the Severn Valley steam railway out of Bridgnorth. Wenlock priory, Boscobel House (good guided tour) and Benthall Hall at Broseley (charming garden) are favourites with older people.

Where to stay

Bishop's Castle SO3289 CASTLE The Square, Bishop's Castle SY9 5BN (01588) 638403 *£45; 7 rms with fine views, some with own bathrm. Standing on the site of the old castle keep, this 18th-c hotel has good fires, a relaxed and friendly atmosphere, lovely home-made food, well kept beers, and welcoming owners.
Bomere Heath SJ4819 FITZ MANOR Bomere Heath, Shrewsbury SY4 3AS (01743) 850295 *£50, plus special breaks; 3 rms, shared bthrm. Peaceful half-timbered no smoking Tudor house with a lovely big flower-filled garden, croquet, an outdoor swimming pool, and Severn fishing; attractive rooms with antiques, and traditional English meals in the candlelit dining room which has lots of paintings; cl Christmas.

Bourton SO5996 BOURTON MANOR Bourton, Much Wenlock TF13 6QE (01746) 785531 *£50, plus special breaks; 8 rms. In private landscaped grounds surrounded by pretty countryside, this extended 16th-c manor house has comfortably old-fashioned rooms with lots of panelling, a convivial bar, open fires, and very good service from friendly staff; most enjoyable food; partial disabled access.

Clun SO2881 NEW HOUSE FARM Clun, Craven Arms SY7 8NJ (01588) 638314 *£45; 2 rms. Remote 18th-c farmhouse nr the Welsh border with plenty of surrounding hillside walks, homely rooms with copper pans and decorative plates on the walls, plenty of books, a country garden, and helpful, friendly owners; enjoyable home-cooked evening meals, packed lunches, good breakfasts; cl Nov–Mar; no children.

Cressage SJ5604 CHOLMONDELEY RIVERSIDE Cressage, Shrewsbury SY5 6AF (01952) 510900 £60; 6 rms. Neatly converted 17th-c inn overlooking an exceptionally pretty stretch of the River Severn; with church pews, cushioned settles and oak tables in the civilised, roomy bar, wicker chairs in a new conservatory and more out on the terrace; good imaginative food, well kept beers, a fine choice of wines, and a relaxed friendly atmosphere; coarse fishing.

Diddlebury SO5185 DELBURY HALL Diddlebury, Craven Arms SY7 9DH (01584) 841267 *£85; 3 rms. Beautiful stately Georgian house in 80 acres of landscaped parkland with ornamental ducks on the lake, trout fishing, flower-filled gardens, and a hard tennis court; large hall with fine oak staircase, spacious drawing room, sitting room and snooker room; enjoyable food using their own vegetables, milk, eggs, hand-churned Jersey butter, a good wine list, and hearty breakfasts.

Gretton SO5295 COURT FARM Gretton, Cardington, Church Stretton SY6 7HU (01694) 771219 *£50; 5 rms. Large, comfortable stone-built farmhouse on 325-acre mixed farm; a warm welcome, with a big woodburner in the inglenook fireplace and good food using home-grown and local produce; no smoking; self-catering also in adjacent Stables; cl Nov–Jan; no children and no pets.

Hampton Loade SO7586 OLD FORGE HOUSE Hampton Loade, Bridgnorth WV15 6HD (01746) 780338 *£36; 2 rms. Homely family-run Georgian house close to the River Severn, with a log fire in the comfortable dining room; fine breakfasts, friendly owners, and a lovely quiet garden; cl Christmas–New Year.

Hanwood SJ4409 WHITE HOUSE Hanwood, Shrewsbury SY5 8LP (01743) 860414 *£56; 6 rms, 3 with own bthrm. Charming 16th-c black and white, half-timbered house with 2 sitting rooms; breakfasts using their own eggs, and enjoyable evening meals using some home-grown produce (must pre-book); 2 acres of garden; no children.

Hopesay SO3883 OLD RECTORY Hopesay, Craven Arms SY7 8HD (01588) 660245 *£64; 3 comfortable rms, 1 with own sitting room. 17th-c rectory with a lovely 2-acre garden overlooking Hopesay Hill (NT), a comfortable newly redecorated drawing room with a log fire and baby grand piano, and an attractive dining room; excellent home cooking, and hearty breakfasts with home-baked bread; no smoking; cl Christmas; no children.

Hopton Wafers SO6476 CROWN Hopton Wafers, Kidderminster, Worcs DY14 0NB (01299) 270372 *£75, plus special breaks; 8 rms. Attractive, creeper-covered, stone inn in pleasant countryside, with an interestingly furnished bar, and inglenook fireplace; enjoyable food, decent house wines, beers and malt whiskies, friendly efficient service; streamside garden.

Llanfair Waterdine SO2476 RED LION Llanfair Waterdine, Knighton LD7 1TU (01547) 528214 £45; 3 comfortable refurbished rms, 1 with own bthrm. In beautiful countryside overlooking the River Teme and landscaped river banks, this pub has a heavily beamed convivial lounge bar with a big open fire, a small black-beamed tap room, and a little dining room (a new terraced dining room with fine views is being developed this year); good big breakfasts, affable service and a determinedly traditional atmosphere – no noisy machines or music, children over 10.

Llanyblodwel SJ2423 HORSESHOE Llanyblodwel, Oswestry SY10 8NQ (01691) 828969 *£40; 2 rms, with shared bthrm. Lovely early 15th-c inn by a delightful stretch of the River Tanat (free fishing for residents), with a simple low-beamed front bar, traditional built-in settles and a black range in the inglenook fireplace, rambling rooms leading off, and an oak-panelled dining room; good, interesting food; no children; cl am Mon.

Longville SO5494 LONGVILLE ARMS Longville, Much Wenlock TF13 6DT (01694) 771206 £40; 5 comfortable rms in converted stables with fresh flowers and home-made biscuits. Warm and friendly inn with 2 spacious bars, well kept real ales, a wide range of enjoyable food, superb breakfasts, and a neat terraced side garden; cl 25 Dec; partial disabled access.

Ludlow SO5175 FEATHERS Bull Ring, Ludlow SY8 1AA (01584) 875261 *£88.50, plus special breaks; 39 comfortable rms. Striking hotel with exquisitely proportioned and intricately carved timbered frontage, Jacobean panelling and carving, and period furnishings; artistically presented restaurant dishes, decent food in the bar, and efficient pleasant service; limited disabled access.

Ludlow SO5175 UNICORN Lower Corve St, Ludlow SY8 1DU (01584) 873555 £40; 5 comfortable beamed and timbered rms, most with own bthrm. Pleasantly refurbished family-run inn with good popular food in the bar and relaxing restaurant (inc vegetarian and vegan dishes), excellent breakfasts, real ales; huge log fires, attentive service, and a riverside terrace; cl 25 Dec.

Ludlow SO5175 WHEATSHEAF Lower Broad St, Ludlow SY8 1PQ (01584) 872980 *£40, plus special breaks; 5 comfortable oak-beamed rms with showers. Attractively furnished, small 17th-c pub spectacularly built into the medieval town gate; traditional atmosphere, 2 log fires, lots of hops, timbers, and exposed stone walls; a wide range of good food in the bar and no smoking restaurant (super steaks), real ales and farm ciders; friendly owners.

Much Wenlock SO6299 TALBOT High St, Much Wenlock TF13 6AA (01952) 727077 £90 inc dinner, plus special breaks; 6 rms. Dating from 1360 and once part of Wenlock Abbey, this converted 18th-c malthouse is very civilised, with pretty flowers, log fires, prints, pleasant staff, good food in the no smoking restaurant and bar, and well kept real ales.

Norton SJ7200 HUNDRED HOUSE Bridgnorth Rd, Norton, Shifnal TF11 9EE (01952) 730353 *£80, plus special breaks; 10 cottagey rms (some with swing-seats and lavender scented sheets). Carefully refurbished mainly Georgian inn with quite a sophisticated feel; neatly kept bar with old quarry-tiled floors, beamed ceilings and oak panelling, and handsome fireplaces; elaborate evening meals using the inn's own herbs, friendly service, good popular bar food, excellent breakfast and afternoon tea; delightful garden, no dogs.

Rhydycroesau SJ2430 PEN-Y-DYFFRYN Rhydycroesau, Oswestry SY10 7JD (01691) 653700 *£73, plus special breaks; 8 rms. Built as a Georgian rectory, this handsome stone building stands in 5 acres with lovely views of the Welsh hills, and has log fires in both comfortable lounges, and a relaxed, friendly atmosphere; good food using the best local ingredients; trout fishing, hill-walking and riding (shooting can be arranged) dogs welcome; disabled access.

Shrewsbury SJ4917 ALBRIGHT HUSSEY Ellesmere Rd, Broad Oak, Shrewsbury SY4 3AF (01939) 290571 *£85, plus special breaks; 14 lovely rms. Fine moated medieval manor house, partly timber-framed and partly stone and brick, in 4 acres of gardens; particularly good food in the timbered and panelled restaurant, and excellent service; children over 3; disabled access.

Strefford SO4485 STREFFORD HALL FARM Strefford, Craven Arms SY7 8DE (01588) 672383 *£38; 3 rms. Stone-built Victorian farmhouse surrounded by 360 acres of working farmland; a woodburner in the sitting room, no smoking, lots of walks; cl Christmas–New Year.

Wenlock Edge SO5796 WENLOCK EDGE INN Hilltop, Wenlock Edge, Much Wenlock TF13 6DJ (01746) 785678 *£70, plus special breaks; 4 rms, showers only (served by 190-ft well). Popular and cheerfully welcoming, family-run inn by the Ippikins Rock viewpoint, with lots of walks through NT land that runs along the Edge, and a chatty and relaxed atmosphere; very good fresh home-made bar food inc old-fashioned puddings, fine breakfasts, and a wide range of drinks; 2nd Mon evening of month is story-telling night; cl Christmas; children over 8; disabled access.

Woolstaston SO4599 RECTORY FARM Woolstaston, Church Stretton SY6 6NN (01694) 751306 *£44; 3 comfortable rms. Lovely, half-timbered 17th-c farmhouse on the lower slopes of the Long Mynd, with fine views, a friendly welcome, a big beamed lounge, and a cosy TV room; hearty breakfasts; no evening meals; cl Dec–Jan; children over 12; no dogs.

Worfield SO7595 OLD VICARAGE Worfield, Bridgnorth WV15 5JZ (01746) 716497 £107.50, plus special breaks; 14 pretty rms. Restful and carefully restored Edwardian rectory in 2 acres, with 2 airy conservatory-style lounges, very good interesting food in no smoking restaurant, a fine wine list, and warm and friendly, helpful service; cl Christmas–New Year; good disabled access.

Wrockwardine SJ6212 CHURCH FARM Wrockwardine, Telford TF6 5DG (01952) 244917 £50; 6 rms, most with own bthrm. Friendly Georgian farmhouse, built on a very ancient site overlooking the attractive garden and church; with a relaxed atmosphere, beams and a log fire in the lounge; good home-cooked food in the traditionally furnished dining room; cl Christmas–New Year.

To see and do

SHROPSHIRE FAMILY ATTRACTION OF THE YEAR

🐃 **Preston upon the Weald** SJ6814 HOO FARM ANIMAL KINGDOM 🎟 Exceptionally good-value traditional working farm, with enough to keep families with very young children happy for a sizeable chunk of the day. All the ingredients you'd expect are here, from bottle feeding the lambs and milking demonstrations to a pets corner, egg collecting and nature trails, but they have several more unusual features too, such as ostriches, pheasant-rearing, and a big walk-in beehive, where a glass window lets you watch the bees at work. It's another place that does sheep-racing (summer afternoons at 3pm, not Fri), and they have a tiny Tote to put your bets on before the race. The sheep seem to enjoy their little sprint – even those not taking part that day have been known to try to join in when they hear the Tannoys. The farm also has a Christmas tree plantation, so there's a Christmas tree maze, with a story for toddlers to follow as they go round; Father Christmas is here in Dec. A few areas are under cover, but like most farms it's better on a dry day. There are picnic and play areas, and occasional spinning demonstrations. Snacks, shop, disabled access; cl 24 Dec–20 Mar; (01952) 677917; £2.95 (£2.50 children), slightly less in autumn. Different prices apply at Christmas.

🏰 **Acton Burnell** SJ5302 ACTON BURNELL CASTLE Ruined red sandstone manor house built in the 13th c, but almost abandoned by 1420; disabled access; free. The Plume of Feathers at Harley is fairly handy for lunch.
🐃 🐾 **Acton Scott** SO4589 ACTON SCOTT WORKING FARM (off the A49) Vivid introduction to traditional rural life, with plenty of rare breeds, and crops cultivated using old rotation methods; all the work is done by hand or horse power, with period farm machinery. Lots of craft

demonstrations, and daily butter-making. Unusually, this is a farm aimed just as much at adults (maybe more) as at children. Meals, snacks, shop, disabled access; cl Mon (exc bank hols), Nov–Mar; (01694) 781306; £3. The most convenient place for lunch is the Green Dragon at Little Stretton.

Atcham SJ5409 ATTINGHAM PARK Splendidly grand, late 18th-c house on the site of an old Roman villa, with an imposing 3-storey colonnaded portico. The extensive picture gallery was designed by Nash, who made imaginative use of early curved cast iron and glass for the ceiling; attractive mature gardens and deer park outside. Snacks, shop, disabled access by prior arrangement; open pm Sat–Weds Apr–Oct; (01743) 709203; house and grounds *£4, *£1.50 grounds only; NT. HOME FARM is nearby, with rare breeds and traditional farm machinery; you can watch the milking of the Jersey cows (3.30pm), and play with the pets. Farmhouse teas, shop, limited disabled access; cl am, Thurs and Fri (exc school hols), and Oct–Easter; (01743) 709243; £2.20. The Cholmondeley Riverside towards Cressage has good food.

Billingsley SO7185 RAYS FARM COUNTRY MATTERS Traditional farm in pleasant countryside with pigs, sheep, cattle, miniature ponies, llama, and a good collection of owls and other animals. Pleasant woodland walks, and indoor and outdoor picnic areas. Snacks, shop, disabled access; cl 25 Dec, 1 Jan; (01299) 841255; *£3. Both pubs in nearby Chelmarsh have decent food and lovely reservoir views; the Chelmarsh–Highley road is a nice drive.

Bishop's Castle SO3289 Historic little market town with some fine Elizabethan and Georgian buildings, railway and local history museums, good shops, and the curious House on Crutches. It's handy for exploring Offa's Dyke. The Three Tuns has a unique Victorian tower brewhouse, still in use – you can usually arrange a tour (01588) 638797.

Boscobel House SJ8308 Interesting old house renowned for sheltering Charles II after the Battle of Worcester, with an unusually well preserved 17th-c garden and cobbled courtyard, and 19th-c decor giving a romanticised view of the king's drama. Good guided tour. Meals, snacks, shop, disabled access to gardens only; cl winter Mon and Tues, 25 Dec, Jan; (01902) 850244; £3.75. The ROYAL OAK here is said by some to have been the hiding place of the king, by others to be a descendant, and by still others to be just a fine old tree. WHITE LADIES PRIORY (just SW) the ruins of an Augustinian nunnery destroyed in the Civil War; free. The Bell in Tong is good for lunch, and Weston Park at Weston under Lizard (Staffs) is nearby.

★ **Bridgnorth** SO7193 On the Severn, this old market town is picturesque without being touristy. It's divided into the High Town and Low Town, with steps between the two – though it's easier (and more fun) to take the hair-raising CLIFF RAILWAY. On the way down you pass some small caves that people lived in till 1856 (they're not open, but labelled). As well as some handsome red brick, High Town has lots of fine timbered buildings, such as the odd town hall built on a sandstone-arched base that straddles the road in the high street. CASTLE Largely destroyed in the Civil War, but part of the keep remains, left at a scary tilt by the constant bombardment; the grounds are now a park with good views – the best views are from Castle Esplanade. The unusual CHURCH on nearby East Castle St was designed by Thomas Telford. COSTUME AND CHILDHOOD MUSEUM (Newmarket Building) Lots of old costumes, dolls, and a Victorian nursery. Not open every day (usually cl Tues), but if you find them shut, next door Beryl's Pantry has a key and can let you in; *£1.25. SEVERN VALLEY RAILWAY The leading standard-gauge steam railway, with a great collection of locomotives, a splendidly lively atmosphere, and trips through beautiful scenery; for details see entry under Bewdley, in **Hereford and Worcester**. The Railwaymans Arms in the station is an atmospheric place for a snack. Other useful pubs for food here are the Bear (Northgate; not Sun) and Punch Bowl (on the B4364; good carvery, great views). DANIELS MILL (on the B4555, 1m S of Bridgnorth) Working cornmill still powered by its big waterwheel; a picturesque old place, run by the same family for 200 years. Snacks, shop; open pm wknds, Weds and bank hols Easter–Sept; (01746) 762753; *£2. MIDLAND MOTOR MUSEUM (off the A458 SE of Bridgnorth) Over 100 well restored sports cars, racing cars and motorcycles, in converted stables in the beautiful grounds of Stanmore Hall. Snacks, shop, disabled access; cl 25–26 Dec; (01746) 762992; *£3.50. The grounds also have a caravan site.

🏠 ⊛ **Broseley** SJ6602 BENTHALL HALL (just NW) Well liked by readers, an Elizabethan sandstone house with fine oak woodwork and panelling, decorative plasterwork, interesting garden, and 17th-c church (services 3.15pm most Suns). Some disabled access; open pm Weds, Sun and bank hols Apr–Sept; (01952) 882159; £3; NT. The Foresters Arms is useful for lunch.

✝ **Buildwas** SJ6204 BUILDWAS ABBEY (on the B4378) Beautiful remains of 12th-c Cistercian abbey – apart from the roof it's practically all still here. Shop, some disabled access; cl Nov–Mar; £1.60. It's right next to the gigantic cooling towers of a power station, which this close seem to have a geometrical beauty of their own. The Meadow coming out from Ironbridge has decent food.

🏛 ⊛ **Bury Ditches** SO3384 Iron Age ring fort, high on a hill, with superb views of S Shrops and N Herefords.

✝ ✗ **Cleobury Mortimer** SO6775 Civilised small town, most notable perhaps for its church's CROOKED SPIRE, though timbered Tudor buildings among its more elegant Georgian ones are picturesque. A restored WATERMILL produces its own stoneground flour. The 16th-c Kings Arms has good-value food (and

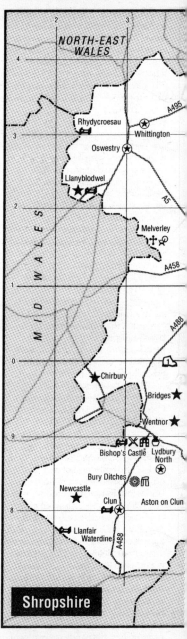

comfortable bedrooms).

★ 🛱 🏰 ⊛ **Clun** SO3081 Attractive stonebuilt village on the edge of the CLUN FOREST, a peaceful pastoral area

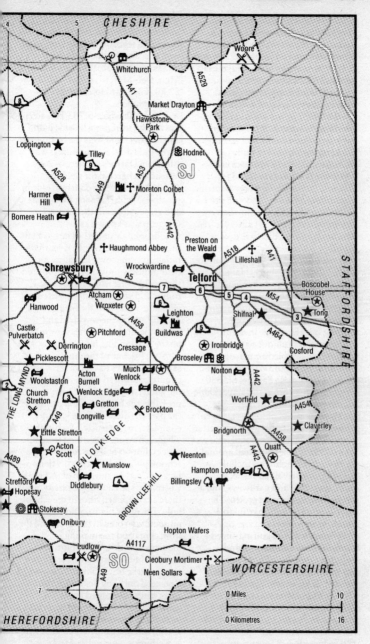

CHESHIRE

Woore

Whitchurch

A41

A529

Market Drayton

Hawkstone Park

Loppington ★

Tilley

Hodnet

A53

SJ

A528

Harmer Hill

A49

Moreton Corbet

Bomere Heath

A442

Haughmond Abbey

Preston on the Weald

A518

A41

Lilleshall

8

Shrewsbury

Wrockwardine

Telford

STAFFORDSHIRE

A5

7

6

5

4

M54

Boscobel House

Atcham

Wroxeter

Leighton

Shifnal

3

Tong

Hanwood

Buildwas

A464

Castle Pulverbatch

Pitchford

Cressage

Ironbridge

Cosford

Dorrington

Broseley

Picklescott

Woolstaston

Acton Burnell

Much Wenlock

Bourton

Norton

A442

THE LONG MYND

Church Stretton

Wenlock Edge

Worfield

A454

A49

Gretton

Brockton

Longville

Little Stretton

Bridgnorth

Claverley

A489

Acton Scott

WENLOCK EDGE

Neenton

A442

Quatt

Munslow

Strefford

Diddlebury

Hampton Loade

Hopesay

BROWN CLEE HILL

Billingsley

SO

Stokesay

Onibury

Hopton Wafers

Ludlow

A4117

A49

Cleobury Mortimer

WORCESTERSHIRE

Neen Sollars

7

0 Miles

10

HEREFORDSHIRE

0 Kilometres

16

of rolling partly wooded hills. The ruined Norman CASTLE gives fine views from its mound; free. Down by the River Clun, the 16th-c stone bridge is very picturesque. The Sun and White Horse are useful for lunch.
✝ **Cosford** SJ7904 AEROSPACE MUSEUM (on the A41) One of the

country's best aviation museums, a spectacular collection of carefully arranged aircraft inc the Victor and Vulcan bombers, Hastings, York and British Airways airliners, and the last airworthy Britannia, as well as lots of missiles and a display of engines. Snacks, shop, disabled access; cl 24–26 Dec, 1 Jan; (01902) 374872; £5. There's a decent farm shop on Holyhead Rd, and the Bell at Tong is a reliable family dining pub.

🐖 **Harmer Hill** SJ4921 PIM HILL FARM (Lea Hall, on the A528 S) Organic farm with rare breeds, picnic site, friendly donkey, and well priced produce shop. Snacks from their own bakery; cl Sun; (01939) 290342; free. The Bridgewater Arms has decent family food.

✝ **Haughmond Abbey** SJ5415 (off the B5062 E of Shrewsbury) HAUGHMOND ABBEY Extensive ruins of Augustinian abbey, inc a fine Norman doorway in the chapter house, some interesting sculpture, and well preserved lodgings and kitchens. In the grounds are some plants unique to the area. Shop, some disabled access; open Easter–Sept; (01743) 709661; £1.60.

🎱 🏠 ! **Hawkstone Park** 🎦 SJ5830 Created in the 18th c, this remarkable wooded parkland with its magnificent series of follies has been restored to its original grandeur, after a period of neglect; spectacular views from the monuments dotted around its 100 acres. Highlights include the ruins of a medieval red castle, intricate arches and pathways, and a fantastic underground grotto. The full circuit can easily take up to 3 hours, so sensible shoes are recommended (and you may need a torch for some of the caves and tunnels). The BBC filmed their *Chronicles of Narnia* here. Meals, snacks, shop, limited disabled access; cl Nov–Mar (exc wknds in Dec); (01939) 200611; *£4.50. The Caspian Bar of the Hawkstone Park Hotel has decent food.

🎱 **Hodnet** SJ6228 Several attractive half-timbered houses – here, and some interesting old books in the church. HODNET HALL GARDENS 60 acres of lovely landscaped gardens

with spacious lawns, lush pools, plants and trees; the astonishingly decorated tearoom is full of big-game trophies. Snacks, shop, disabled access (prior notice preferred); cl am, Mon, Oct–Mar; (01630) 685202; £2.80. The Bear Hotel opposite is good for lunch.

★ 🍴 🐾 **Ironbridge** SJ6703 This steep town, with intriguing hillside paths and narrow lanes, was the birthplace of the Industrial Revolution: it was Abraham Darby's use here of coke instead of charcoal for smelting which made mass-production of iron possible. Well set among the woods and grassy slopes of the Severn Gorge, it was known as Coalbrookdale until the Darbys built the IRON BRIDGE across the river that today gives the town its name. As their industry took off they produced the world's first iron rails, boats, trains, and wheels, and for quite some while the valley was the biggest iron-making area in the world. Many of the former industrial sites now make up the outstanding IRONBRIDGE GORGE MUSEUM 🎦, one of the most satisfying places to visit in the whole country, scattered over 6 miles along the gorge. 50-acre Blists Hill is probably the highlight, and certainly the part children like best – a complete, reconstructed Victorian village, showing everything from the offices, houses and machinery to the school, pubs and pigsties; it's the biggest open-air museum of its kind. Costumed staff add authenticity, and there are extra activities in the school hols. The other main sections include museums devoted to the river, and the iron, china and tile-making industries, with some beautifully restored houses (and wonderful echoes in the brick kilns at Coalport). You need only buy tickets for the parts you're interested in (useful leaflets suggest a variety of itineraries, from 3 hours to a whole day), but a special offer Passport Ticket covering everything is good value – and remains valid indefinitely until you've seen all the bits you want. On bank hols the sites are linked by a bus, otherwise it's best to drive (or walk –

see **Walks** section, below). Meals, snacks, shops, disabled access; cl 24–25 Dec, and some parts cl Nov–Mar – best to ring first then; (01952) 433522; £9 Passport ticket, or individual tickets to each museum available – Blists Hill is around £6.50. Across a footbridge from the Coalport tile museum, the big MAWS CRAFT CENTRE has 26 workshops selling things as diverse as pottery, puzzles and pictures (cl 25 Dec; free). Next to the Museum of the River, the TEDDY BEAR MUSEUM displays bears and other furry animals made here by the long-established Merrythought Co (cl 25 Dec; free). Attractively placed by the riverside, the Meadow, Woodbridge and Olde Robin Hood, and (all handy for Maws craft centre and the Coalport Museum) the Boat and Half Moon at Jackfield and Shakespeare at Coalport are all useful for lunch; there's a pleasant terraced walk between the river and the Golden Ball (Wesley Rd, off Madeley Hill). For a fuller restaurant meal, the Coracle in the village square is nice.

✝ **Lilleshall** SJ7315 LILLESHALL ABBEY Very impressive ruins of 12th-c abbey in pleasant setting surrounded by yew trees – it's a nice spot for a picnic, peaceful and undisturbed; disabled access; free.

★ 🏛 🎖 ✝ 🛡 **Ludlow** SO5175 Beautiful 12th-c town, its original grid plan still obvious today. The best road in is via Wigmore and Leinthall Starkes – lovely views as you approach. Dotted around are 500 listed buildings, with particularly good examples down Broad St, a charming mixture of Tudor and Georgian architecture. Book well in advance if you're planning to visit during the festival in early July. The most famous building is the lavishly carved and timbered FEATHERS HOTEL on the Bull Ring; some parts inside are almost as striking. The Broadgate, the only one of the town's 13th-c gates to have survived, is interesting. The splendid old CASTLE dates from around 1086, and lots of original parts survive, inc the Norman keep, and chapel with its unusual circular nave. The towers and battlements on

their wooded crag over the River Teme have a very properly 'castle-ish' feel; Shakespeare plays are performed here during the festival. There's a lovely view of it from over at Whitcliffe. Shop, disabled access; cl 25 Dec, Jan wkdys; (01584) 873355; *£2.50. Dominating the town almost as much is the PARISH CHURCH with its magnificent pinnacled tower; it's in an attractive, tranquil enclave behind the old buttermarket off King St, and has a wonderful sense of timeless peace inside. Magnificently intricate carvings, especially on the ceiling and the choir stalls. In winter it's open 12.30–3pm on Sun only, but in summer you can visit all day (exc am Sun). Quite a few antique shops in the town, as well as a good local history MUSEUM in Castle St (cl 1–2pm, Sun exc Jun–Aug, Nov–Mar; £1). The Unicorn is the nicest pub for lunch.

🏛 🎖 **Lydbury North** SO3485 WALCOT HALL Fine Georgian house built for Clive of India; free-standing ballroom, stable yard with matching clock towers, big walled garden, and arboretum with good rhododendrons, azaleas and specimen trees. Disabled access; usually open pm Sun in May, July and Aug, plus pm Fri May and Jun, and pm Weds in Sept, but may be best to check; 0171-581 2782; £2.50. You can stay in various wings of the house, and they can arrange fishing and riding.

🏛 **Market Drayton** SJ6734 The traditional home of gingerbread; the unique local recipe is locked in a bank. OLD COLEHURST MANOR SJ6631 (Sutton, to the S) 17th-c, beautifully restored by its Danish owner, though you need to stay here to get the full experience; (01630) 638833.

✝ 🏵 **Melverley** SJ3316 ST PETER'S CHURCH This beautiful black and white structure was rebuilt in 1406 after Owen Glendower burned the previous one; it has a fine Jacobean pulpit and chain bible. The stables of the Old Rectory have a CRAFT CENTRE open Sun –Tues. The Old Three Pigeons over at Nesscliffe has decent food and all-day coffee, with Kynaston Cave and good cliff walks nearby.

☖ ✝ Moreton Corbet SJ5623 CASTLE Destroyed by Parliament in 1644, but you can still see a small 13th-c keep and the substantial ruins of the once-grand Elizabethan house; free. There are some elaborate tombs in the adjacent CHURCH; the 18th-c Raven at Tilley up towards Wem is a good dining pub.

★ ✝ ☺ Much Wenlock SO6299 Lovely little medieval market town, with lots of timbered and jettied buildings. The famous PRIORY has its origins in the 7th c, but it's the magnificent remains of the 11th-c building and later additions you can see today. The chapter house has remarkably patterned interlaced arches. Shop; sometimes cl 1–2pm, winter Mon and Tues, 24–26 Dec, 1 Jan; £2 (inc Walkman tour). There's a local history MUSEUM in the Old Market Hall (cl 1–2pm, Sun exc Jun–Aug, all Oct–Mar; 50p), and the Talbot is good for lunch. The B4371 along Wenlock Edge has good views.

☛ Onibury SO4579 WERNLAS COLLECTION OF RARE POULTRY ▨ (Green Lane, W of the A49) Mostly large fowl, also rare breeds of pheasant, unusual European species, and several breeds of animal. About 6,000 chicks are hatched each year, so usually some for children to handle or feed. Snacks, shop; cl Mon (exc mid-July–mid-Sept and bank hols), 25 Dec; (01584) 856318; £2.75. The Hollybush is handy.

☖☺🏛❀ Oswestry SJ2929 CAMBRIAN RAILWAY MUSEUM and OSWESTRY CYCLE MUSEUM (Oswald Rd) Joint museum with lots of old bicycles and a history of cycling (especially good on Dunlop), as well as steam engines and railway memorabilia; some locomotives may be in steam bank hols and last Sun of month. Snacks, shop, some disabled access; (01691) 671749; *£1.50. OLD OSWESTRY (just N) Impressive Iron Age hill fort covering 68 acres. The elaborate western defensive entrance and 5 ramparts remain; free. The Butchers Arms has good-value food, the Wynnstay Hotel is a comfortable refuge. The OLD RACECOURSE (2 or 3m W on the B4580) is a high stretch of

common with splendid views into Wales.

☖☺❀ Pitchford SJ5403 GOLDING GARDEN Steeply terraced 16th-c gardens, with tender plants in sheltered corners, good views, and PICK-YOUR-OWN asparagus; open only by appointment, mid-Apr–mid-Jun; (01694) 731204; *£2. The new Cholmondeley Riverside up on the A458 has good food.

☛ Preston upon the Weald SJ6814 For HOO FARM ANIMAL KINGDOM see separate Family Panel on p.540. The Tayleur Arms over at Longdon upon Tern is a decent family dining pub.

🏠▣❀ Quatt SO7487 DUDMASTON (off the A442) 17th-c house with the old flower-painting collection of Francis Darby of Coalbrookdale, modern art, and lakeside and woodland walks in the extensive parkland. Meals, snacks, shop, disabled access; open pm Weds and Sun Apr–Sept; (01746) 780866; £3.50 house and garden, £2.50 garden only; NT. There's usually free pedestrian access to the woods all year. The Lion of Morfe over at Upper Farmcote is fairly handy.

★ ⚘ ☖ ✝ ☖ ♭ Shrewsbury SJ4912 The central street layout is still largely medieval, with oddly named streets (Shoplatch, Murivance, Wyle Cop), and plenty of quiet corners up narrow alleys and courtyards among its more modern shops and offices. It's rich in striking architecture, both Tudor timbering and Georgian brick. There's a signposted trail between some of the more interesting buildings. Around the Square numerous buildings reflect the town's medieval wool fortunes, inc the old market hall; in the adjacent High St, Owens Mansion and Irelands Mansion are fine half-timbered houses worth looking at from outside. Even McDonalds is in a medieval building. The original town is almost entirely ringed by a loop of the Severn (quiet waterside paths and parks, and you can hire boats along some stretches); only a narrow neck of land needed guarding by the 12th-c CASTLE. This was refurbished by Thomas Telford in 1790, though still has parts of the earlier building. The grounds are attractive. Shop, some disabled access; cl Mon (exc bank hols) and winter Suns; (01743) 358516; £2, grounds free. The walk up Castle St is worthwhile, passing the original Grammar School building and the half-timbered Council House Court. Nearby the church of ST MARY has one of the tallest spires in England. CLIVE HOUSE MUSEUM (College Hill) Old town house associated with Clive of India, with excellent displays of Coalport and Caughley porcelain, fine paintings in period rooms, and walled garden. Shop, disabled access to ground floor only; cl Mon (exc bank hols), winter Suns, 21 Dec–5 Jan; (01743) 354811; *£2. ROWLEY'S HOUSE MUSEUM (Barker St) Impressive timber-framed building with social and natural history, and some interesting Roman remains. Shop, disabled access to ground floor only; hours as Clive House; (01743) 361196; £2. A joint ticket for these 2 museums and the Castle is £4. Among other interesting shops in this part of town is an excellent CRAFT CENTRE in 12th-c St Julian's church (St Alkmunds Sq), with several cheery workshops, a bustling craft fair every Sat, and a good restaurant (especially useful for vegetarians). Some disabled access; cl Sun; (01743) 353516; free. SHREWSBURY QUEST 🎫 (Abbey Foregate) Delightful reconstruction of medieval monastic life, loosely based around the Brother Cadfael books by Ellis Peters (set in medieval Shrewsbury). You can create your own decorated manuscript or try your hand at ancient games and crafts. The carefully researched period herb garden is a draw in its own right – quite a few poisonous plants despite the lovely smell. Meals and snacks (some inspired by medieval recipes), shop, disabled access; cl 25 Dec, 1 Jan; (01743) 243324; £3.95. Just opposite, the impressive 14th-c ABBEY includes a statue of Edward III, and a memorial to Wilfrid Owen. Other places to mention for food include the riverside Boat House (New St/Quarry Park),

Coach & Horses (Swan Hill/Cross Hill), the cheery Dun Cow Pie Shop (Abbey Foregate), stately Lion Hotel (Wyle Cop), Cromwells (Dogpole) and Three Fishes (Fish St). Heading SW, the old coach road through Longden and Pulverbatch is an attractive drive – great views the further you go.

🏚 ❄ **Stokesay** SO4381 STOKESAY CASTLE (off the A49) One of the finest examples of a medieval manor house in existence, 13th-c, in a notably charming setting. The hall with its cruck-framed roof and early English windows is just as it was 700 years ago, and there's a timbered Tudor gatehouse. Good views from the top of the tower, and excellent Walkman tour. Summer snacks, shop; cl 1–2pm, all Mon and Tues Nov–Mar plus 24–26 Dec; (01588) 672544; £2.75. The Plough at Wistanstow is the nearest good place for lunch.

🖉 🐴 **Whitchurch** SJ5440 ROCKING HORSE WORKSHOP (Cottage Farm, Tilstock Rd) Here you can watch the production and restoration of traditional rocking horses. Shop; cl 25 Dec, check first at wknds; (01948) 666777; free.

🐎 ⬥ 🏭 **Whittington** SJ3331 PARK HALL WORKING FARM MUSEUM (off the A5) Powerful shire horses still work the land here as they have for decades. The Victorian stables have livestock from that period inc cattle, sheep and several breeds of pig, and there's lots of vintage farm machinery and equipment. Snacks, shop, disabled access; usually cl Fri (exc July–mid-Sept), and all Nov–Easter, but may change – best to check first; (01691) 652175; *£2.50. Nearby are the handsome remains of a 13th-c CASTLE, with good-value food at the Olde Boot alongside.

🏛 👶 🐎 **Wroxeter** SJ5608 ROMAN CITY One of the country's most important Roman sites, though the majority of the remains are buried under fields. There's a well preserved colonnade and municipal bath, with useful explanatory boards, and the MUSEUM has a good range of finds from the town (then Britain's fourth biggest) and the earlier fortress. Snacks, shop;

cl Mon and Tues Nov–Mar, 24–26 Dec, 1 Jan; (01743) 761330; £2.95. There's a Roman wall on the neighbouring ROMAN VINEYARD, a friendly little place producing several wines. Also lavender farm, rare breeds, and some interesting glacial stones. Teas, shop (with various lavender-based products), disabled access; cl Oct–Mar, shop open all year; (01743) 761888; £3. The Horseshoes at Uckington is a decent family dining pub.

! The local tourist information centres have details of imaginative trails around the region, centring on the work of Thomas Telford, haunted villages, the novels of Ellis Peters, and sites connected with King Arthur (recent theories suggest the mythical king was a 5th-c warlord ruling from a post-Roman city – possibly Wroxeter – in the heart of Shropshire). They can also give details of BALLOON TRIPS. ·

★ Other attractive villages, almost all of them with decent pubs, include Aston on Clun SO3982, Bridges SO3996 (handy for the Stiperstones and Long Mynd; nearby Picklescott SO4399 also has a delightfully placed ancient pub), Chirbury SO2698 (with its famously haunted graveyard), Claverley SO7993 (the church here has impressive medieval wall paintings), Leighton SJ6105, Little Stretton SO4392, Llanyblodwel SJ2423 (with an exuberantly decorated church), Loppington SJ4729, Lydbury North SO3586, Munslow SO5287, Neen Sollars SO6672, Neenton SO6488, Newcastle SO2582 (good local walks), Shifnal SJ7508 (another interesting church), Tilley SJ5027, Tong SJ7907, Wentnor SO3893 and Worfield SO7696.

Days Out

Follies and other surprises
Hawkstone Park; bar lunch at the Hawkstone Park Hotel or the Bear Hotel, Hodnet; Hodnet Hall gardens; Moreton Corbet castle; walk up Grinshill Hill (see **Walks** section, below).

Industrial Revelations in Ironbridge Gorge
Buildwas Abbey, with its strange view of the power station; stand inside Darby's furnace at the Coalbrookdale Museum of Iron; lunch at the Meadow, Ironbridge or the Woodbridge, Coalport; the Iron Bridge itself; Blists Hill open air museum.

Wander from Wenlock
Much Wenlock; lunch at the George & Dragon there; Benthall Hall, Broseley (limited opening); Bridgnorth; Severn Valley Railway.

Shropshire's highlands
Climb Caer Caradoc (if you're feeling energetic), or stroll in Cardingmill Valley (see **Walks** section, below); Acton Scott farm; lunch at Acorn Wholefood, Church Stretton (see **Where to eat** section, below) or Stiperstones Inn at Stiperstones; walk along Stiperstones ridge (see **Walks** section, below) from car park nr top of road.

The quintessential Marches
Stokesay Castle; Ludlow; lunch at the Unicorn, Olive Branch or Merchant House there; Clun; Bishop's Castle.

Medieval, Tudor and Georgian Shrewsbury
Walk up Bear Steps, along Butcher Row and Castle St to the castle; lunch at Poppy's (Milk St), Castle Vaults (Castle Gates) or the Armoury (Victoria Quay nr Welsh Bridge); walk via Dog Pole and Wyle Cop to Clive House Museum; walk via Kingsland Bridge then follow the path along banks of the River Severn; Rowley's House Museum.

Walks

South Shropshire's hills rise to nearly 550 metres (1,800 ft), and despite some quarrying have a real Welsh Marches feel. The **Stiperstones** ridge SJ3600 ⌂-1 is crowned by dramatic rocks and has a splendid view; reached from a nearby car park (you can make an interesting 8½ mile circuit with a stop at the More Arms at Hope SO3298), or you can take the longish walk up from the former lead-mining village of Snailbeach SJ3702. The **Long Mynd** SO4092 ⌂-2 is best reached from Church Stretton SO4593; this bracken-and-bilberry-clad massif has a flat plateau-like top, crossed by the Port Way, an ancient track dating from Neolithic times. Its sides are cut into by a series of narrow, remote-feeling valleys, of which Cardingmill Valley (NT) is best known because of its relative accessibility. **Caer Caradoc** SO4795 ⌂-3 E of Church Stretton SO4593 has a pleasingly compact summit, and the pick of the local views. The best start is Hope Bowdler SO4792, not far from the county's oldest pub, the Royal Oak at Cardington SO5095. **Brown Clee Hill** SO5985 ⌂-4, Shropshire's highest point, has a disappointingly flat top but a certain solitary grandeur.

The **Severn Gorge** ⌂-5 has such fascinating and picturesque (though not always exactly pretty) scenery that its industrial monuments cry out for a tour on foot. Steep lanes and paths connect Ironbridge SJ6703 and Coalbrookdale SJ6604, and an old railway track and a path along the base of Benthall Edge Wood SJ6603 assist routes along the gorge. A fine linear walk can be taken from Broseley SJ6701, descending NW into the gorge via Corbett's Dingle to Coalport SJ6902. From Coalport, you could follow the river all the way S to Bridgnorth SO7193.

The **Wrekin** SJ6208 ⌂-6 just W of Telford SJ6810 is no Everest (an easily attained 407 metres, 1,334 ft), but because it's so isolated on the edge of the Shropshire uplands it commands a huge panorama spanning places over 100 miles apart; just below, the Huntsman in Little Wenlock SJ6507 is handy for refreshment. The **River Severn** ⌂-7 offers walks further S; the Lion at Hampton Loade SO7586 is a good base.

North Shropshire is in general less interesting for walkers, but does have some places well worth seeking out. **Ellesmere** SJ3934 ⌂-8 has a number of meres or lakes nearby – the mere by Ellesmere itself, Blake Mere SJ4133, and Cole Mere SJ4333, which has a country park around it. This is close enough to the Shropshire Union Canal to include a walk along the towpath, with Colemere village SJ4332 a suitable starting place. **Grinshill Hill** ⌂-9, between Grinshill SJ5223 and Clive SJ5124, has much wider views than you'd expect from its modest height, and quite an atmospheric summit, where woods open out by sheer, quarried rock-faces.

Where to eat

Bishop's Castle SO3289 THREE TUNS (01588) 638797 Bustling lively atmosphere in simply furnished, beamed bar rooms, own-brewed beer from the Victorian brewhouse behind the pub, newspapers to read, a good mix of customers, and good home-made bar food. £16.50|£6.
Brockton SO5794 FEATHERS (01746) 785202 – Stylish, stone pub with charming atmospheric beamed rooms (one is no smoking), a restaurant atmosphere, and a conservatory; very good interesting food using fresh seasonal produce, and well kept real ales. £21|£8.95.
Castle Pulverbatch SJ4202 WHITE HORSE (01743) 718247 Bustling, welcoming country pub with beams and heavy timbering in several rambling areas, plates, pewter mugs and a collection of antique insurance plaques; well kept beers, decent wines by the glass, 115 malt whiskies, and good, homely good served by friendly, efficient staff. £20|£5.75.

Church Stretton SO4593 ACORN WHOLEFOOD 26 Sandford Ave (01694) 722495 Simple, unpretentious family-run restaurant with friendly service in several no smoking rooms; good filling food (mostly vegetarian), delicious puddings and soups, and cream teas with a choice of 25 teas; cl Tues, Weds in winter, Nov, Feb. £8|£1.75.

Dorrington SJ4703 COUNTRY FRIENDS (01743) 718707 Cosy half-timbered restaurant with good interesting food inc lovely puddings and British cheeses with home-made bread; cl Sun, Mon, two wks mid-July. £31.50|£8.50.

Ludlow SO5175 MERCHANT HOUSE Lower Corve St (01584) 875438 Two simply furnished and decorated rooms in friendly and relaxed Jacobean house; with exceptionally good food (wonderful fish and fine game) from a set 3-course (3 choices) menu, good-value interesting wines, and competent service; cl Sun, Mon, 2 wks spring; children must be well behaved. £35.

Ludlow SO5175 OLIVE BRANCH Old St (01584) 874314 Cheery wholefood restaurant in 17th-c former inn; changing range of good lunchtime meals and snacks inc often inventive vegetarian meals, and teas with home-made cakes and scones; cl pm. £12.80|£4.85.

Shrewsbury SJ4912 ARMOURY Victoria Quay (01743) 340525 Recently converted warehouse with big arched windows overlooking the river; lots of old prints and documents, cabinets with shells and explosives, corks and bottle openers; a good range of well kept real ales, 25 wines by the glass, 70 malt whiskies, and good, interesting bistro-style food. £21.75|£9.

Shrewsbury SJ4912 CASTLE VAULTS 16 Castle Gates (01743) 358807 Mexican restaurant attached to an ancient timbered pub, with generous helpings of good value food; cl pm Sun. £25|£4.95.

Shrewsbury SJ4912 POPPY'S 8 Milk St (01743) 232307 Lovely 17th-c building with really fine timbers in an upstairs room, plenty of space for shoppers on the ground floor and in the walled courtyard, and a little room for smokers; good enjoyable lunches and popular morning coffee and afternoon tea. £10|£4.25.

Woore SJ7342 FALCON (01630) 647230 Small, simple pub with a wide choice of generous well presented good food especially fresh fish, friendly service, and well kept beer; nr Bridgemere garden centre (see **Cheshire** chapter); children over 12 in restaurant. £19|£8.50.

Special thanks to M J Fowler, Arthur and Margaret Dickinson, Paul Kennedy, E P Smith, Mrs K Gilbert, Anna Corbett.

We welcome reports from readers ...

This *Guide* depends on readers' reports. Do help us if you can – in return, we offer a discount on the next edition to people who've helped us with reports for it. Tell us what you think about places already in it, and anything extra you think we should say about them. And send us your ideas for inclusion in the next edition: places to visit, eat at or stay in, attractive drives or walks, maybe even unusual interesting shops you know of. Use the card in the middle, the report forms at the end, or just write – no stamp needed: *The Good Guide to Britain*, FREEPOST TN1569, Wadhurst, E Sussex TN5 7BR.

Shropshire Calendar

Some of these dates were provisional as we went to press, please check information with the numbers provided.

MARCH

28 **Hawkstone Park** Mountain Bike Race *till Sun 29* (01939) 200300

APRIL

10 **Hawkstone Park** Easter Egg Hunt – *till Mon 13* (01939) 200300
11 **Ironbridge** Children and Animals Week inc gypsy caravans at Ironbridge Gorge Museum, Blists Hill – *till Sun 19* (01952) 433522
12 **Acton Scott** Eggs and Chicks at Acton Scott Working Farm (01694) 781306; **Newport** Driving Society Rally (01952) 291370
19 **Acton Scott** Goats and Kids at Acton Scott Working Farm (01694) 781306

MAY

 3 **Newport** Shropshire Game Fair at Chetwynd Park – *till Mon 4* (01588) 672708
 4 **Acton Scott** May Day Revels at Acton Scott Working Farm (01694) 781306; **Hawkstone Park** Circus Workshop (01939) 200300; **Telford** Kids International at the Town Park (01952) 202100
15 **Shrewsbury** Shropshire and West Midlands Show at Shropshire and West Midlands Showground – *till Sat 16* (01743) 362824
16 **Ironbridge** Ladies Day: Victorian wedding, traditional crafts and cooking at Ironbridge Gorge Museum, Blists Hill (01952) 433522
23 **Ludlow** Craft Fair at the Castle: dancing, children's tent, hands-on area – *till Mon 25* (01588) 650307
24 **Hawkstone Park** Arthurian Battle – *till Mon 25* (01939) 200300
25 **Acton Scott** Plant Sale at Acton Scott Working Farm (01694) 781306; **Ludlow** Carnival (01584) 875053
29 **Bridgnorth** Haydn Festival – *till 7 June* – (01952) 825235
31 **Acton Scott** Sheep Shearing at Acton Scott Working Farm (01694) 781306

JUNE

14 **Cosford** RAF Open Day (01902) 374872
20 **Bishop's Castle** Midsummer Rejoicing: rushbearing festival with morris dancing and procession – *till Sun 21* (01588) 638467; **Ludlow** Festival – *till 5 July* (01584) 875070; Fringe Festival (01584) 873611; **Shrewsbury** Carnival and Show (01743) 356934
22 **Acton Scott** Hay Meadow Flower Day at Acton Scott Working Farm (01694) 781306
27 **Shrewsbury** Abbey Fair (01743) 232723

JULY

 3 **Ledbury** Poetry Festival – *till Sun 12* (01531) 636147
 5 **Bishop's Castle** Carnival (01588) 638371
10 **Much Wenlock** Wenlock Olympian Games – *till Sun 12* (01952) 727615
12 **Acton Scott** Sheep Dog Day at Acton Scott Working Farm (01694) 781306; **Shrewsbury** World Music Day: open air bands at the Castle (01743) 231142
17 **Much Wenlock** Festival at the Edge: international storytelling – *till Sun 19* (01952) 883936

SHROPSHIRE CALENDAR

JULY cont

18 **Bridgnorth** Pageant and Carnival (01746) 763488

25 **Acton Scott** Herb Weekend at Acton Scott Working Farm – *till Sun 26* (01694) 781306; **Ironbridge** Transport Event: steam rally, horses, vintage cars at Ironbridge Gorge Museum, Blists Hill – *till Sun 26* (01952) 433522; **Wem** Sweet Pea Festival – *till Sun 26* (01948) 840779

AUGUST

1 **Oswestry** Show (01691) 654875

2 **Acton Scott** Falconry at Acton Scott Working Farm (01694) 781306

14 **Shrewsbury** Flower Show at Quarry Park – *till Sat 15* (01743) 364051

30 **Bicton** County Steam Engine Rally at Onslow Park – *till Mon 31* (01694) 723799; **Hawkstone Park** Victorian Fun Days – *till Mon 31* (01939) 200300; **Ironbridge** Victorian Street Theatre at Ironbridge Gorge Museum, Blists Hill – *till Mon 31* (01952) 433522; **Lydbury North** Traction Engine Rally at Walcot Hall – *till Mon 31*

31 **Ironbridge** Coracle (traditional boats) Regatta (01952) 813667

SEPTEMBER

6 **Oswestry** Marches Game and Country Fair at Halston Hall (01588) 672708

11 **Ellesmere** Festival – *till Sun 13* (01691) 622097

19 **Bishops Castle** Michaelmas Fair: vintage vehicles, morris dancing – *till Sun 20* (01588) 638467; **Ironbridge** Traditional Victorian Harvest Celebrations at Ironbridge Gorge Museum, Blists Hill – *till Sun 20* (01952) 433522

20 **Acton Scott** Traditional Harvest Festival at Acton Scott Working Farm (01694) 781306

27 **Acton Scott** Crafts in Action at Acton Scott Working Farm (01694) 781306

OCTOBER

17 **Acton Scott** Steam Threshing in Action at Acton Scott Working Farm – *till Sun 18, also Sat 31–1 Nov* (01694) 781306

24 **Acton Scott** in Action at Acton Scott Working Farm – *till Sun 25* (01694) 781306

NOVEMBER

7 **Ironbridge** Bonfire Night at Ironbridge Gorge Museum, Blists Hill (01952) 433522

Please let us know what you think of places in the *Guide*. Use the report forms at the back of the book or simply send a letter.

SOMERSET

Two contrasting cities packed with interest, some charming small towns and villages, varied, largely unspoilt countryside, and all sorts of places to visit – good value for a short or longer holiday.

Somerset is particularly good value these days, as most places here have been holding their prices steadier than elsewhere, and there's a great deal to see and do. It's the two main towns, Bath and Bristol, which have most to offer visitors. Bristol has all sorts of things to pack a day visit with interest, including the first-class hands-on science discovery centre and a splendid zoo, both excellent for families; it also has a full range of big-city problems, so isn't really appealing as a place to linger in. Bath, by contrast, is sophisticated, mellow, graceful and elegant – again, plenty to see, but also with the overall charm which makes it a very rewarding place to stay in. The Prior Park landscape gardens on the outskirts, opened in 1997, would be a new excuse for a return visit if you've been before.

There's also delightful countryside in Somerset. The best of the scenery is around the hills. In the east, Cheddar Gorge and the Wookey Hole caves bring summer crowds to the brooding Mendips and are best visited at quieter times of year – though even in summer there are much less populated parts of the Mendips (such as Ebbor Gorge, and the plateau of poor, windswept sheep pasture on top, pocked with unseen caverns used by potholers, and more visible Bronze Age funeral barrows). Over in the west the countryside feels more secluded and self-contained, with each small valley of the Quantocks seeming a private world, and the Blackdown Hills charmingly untouristy, too – classic quiet English countryside with some lovely villages. We describe the Somerset parts of Exmoor in the section devoted to Exmoor, in the Devon chapter (places like Dunster, off the moor though within the National Park, are included in this chapter).

The dead-flat, vivid green marshy pastures of the Somerset Levels provide an interesting contrast, rewarding for wildlife enthusiasts, and towards the east richer more rolling farmland with small valleys and wooded hillsides offers some gentle country drives.

There's a mass of interesting places to visit. Particular favourites include Dunster and its castle, Wells (a charming, largely unspoilt small cathedral city), magnificent Montacute House, the friendly animal centre at East Huntspill, the Fleet Air Arm museum at Yeovilton, Castle Cary (with Hadspen Gardens), Barrington Court with its lovely gardens, the famous manor garden at East Lambrook, the indoor jungle at Washford, the newly extended Hestercombe Gardens at Cheddon Fitzpaine, Hatch Court at Hatch Beauchamp, and one of the enjoyable cider mills at Dowlish Wake or Bradford-on-

Tone. There are plenty of craft centres, some of them unusual or even unique. Glastonbury has the pull of its Arthurian legends. On the coast, Minehead is a pleasant traditional resort, with a long steam railway line below the Quantocks. Weston-super-Mare is an undemanding family resort with some interesting places to go to, and Clevedon is also quite attractive.

Throughout, there are delightful villages, and the countryside is dotted with a profusion of landmark church towers, pinnacled, turreted and gargoyled. In the hillier parts, buildings are generally of stone, varying in colour and character from the Cotswold style of the north-east, through the pale limestones of the Mendips and the golden warmth of south Somerset's Ham stone, to the rugged and stolid greys of the hamlets tucked into the green folds of the Quantocks.

Somerset tourist information centres have a great deal of helpful material.

Where to stay

Barwick ST5613 LITTLE BARWICK HOUSE Barwick, Yeovil BA22 9TD (01935) 423902 £84, plus special breaks; 6 rms. Carefully run listed Georgian dower house in a quiet pretty garden; excellent food using local produce, a thoughtful wine list, super breakfasts, nice afternoon tea with crumpets; lovely relaxed atmosphere, log fire in the cosy lounge, and particularly good service; 2m S of Yeovil; cl Christmas–New Year; dogs by arrangement.

Bath ST7464 BADMINTON VILLA 10 Upper Oldfield Park, Bath BA2 3JZ (01225) 426347 *£56, plus special breaks; 4 rms. Big, no smoking Victorian house with marvellous city views, a comfortable lounge, good breakfasts, and helpful, friendly owners; cl 22 Dec–2 Jan; children over 7.

Bath ST7465 BROCKS 32 Brock St, Bath BA1 2LN (01225) 338374 £55, plus special breaks; 6 rms. Georgian house with fine breakfasts in the big dining room; lounge area, helpful staff, and good central position; cl Christmas, 2 wks Jan.

Bath ST7564 CHESTERFIELD 11 Great Pulteney St, Bath BA2 4BR (01225) 460953 *£60, plus special breaks; 19 rms. Comfortable Georgian house in notably handsome street beside park; residents' lounge, and good breakfasts (no evening meals); cl Christmas; disabled access.

Bath ST7464 DORIAN HOUSE 1 Upper Oldfield Park, Bath BA2 3JX (01225) 426336 £64, plus special breaks; 8 individually decorated rms. Gracious and neatly kept Victorian house with fine views of the city (only 10 minutes' walk); friendly owners, small bar, comfortable sitting room and elegant little dining room.

Bath ST7463 HAYDON HOUSE 9 Bloomfield Park, Bath BA2 2BY (01225) 427351 £60, plus special breaks; 5 good rms with sherry and home-made shortbread. Deceptively unassuming-looking Edwardian house with comfortable, elegant and restful rooms, antiques; excellent breakfasts (no evening meals), warmly welcoming owners, and a pretty garden; no smoking; children by arrangement.

Bath ST7565 OLD BOATHOUSE Bath Boating Station, Forester Rd, Bath BA2 6QE (01225) 466407 *£50; 4 rms. Edwardian boating station with black and white timbered verandah overlooking the river, free launch to Bath centre, punts and rowing boats for hire; sitting room with river views, and separate restaurant; partial disabled access.

Bath ST7464 PARADISE HOUSE 86–88 Holloway, Bath BA2 4PX (01225)

317723 *£67, plus special breaks; 8 rms (room 6 has a super view). Classically elegant early 18th-c hotel, lovingly restored, with marvellous views over the city, pretty breakfast room, restful drawing room, log fire, and spacious walled gardens; peaceful, though only 7 minutes' walk to the centre; cl 5 days over Christmas; no 1-night bookings Fri or Sat.

Bath ST7465 QUEENSBERRY Russel St, Bath BA1 2QF (01225) 447928 £129, plus special breaks; 22 lovely rms. 3 beautifully decorated Georgian town houses in quiet residential street, with comfortable, restful drawing room, open fire, attractive modern restaurant (Olive Tree, see **Where to eat** section, p.581) and professional service; cl 1 wk Christmas; disabled access.

Bath ST7465 ROYAL CRESCENT 16 Royal Crescent, Bath BA1 2LS (01225) 739955 £187, room only, plus special breaks; 45 luxurious rms. Elegant Georgian hotel in glorious curved terrace, with comfortable, antique-filled lounges, and very attractive garden room (with own menu), open fires and lovely flowers; excellently presented and very well prepared fine food in the Dower House Restaurant (see **Where to eat** section, p.581), impeccable service; outdoor pool and croquet; children over 7 in restaurant in the evening; disabled access.

Bathford ST7964 EAGLE HOUSE Church St, Bathford, Bath BA1 7RS (01225) 859946 £44, plus special breaks; 8 comfortable big rms, 2 in cottage. Lovely Georgian house with an informal and friendly atmosphere, particularly helpful owners, open fires, spacious drawing room and smaller sitting room; nice breakfasts, and a big garden with fine views; very good for families, grass tennis court in summer; cl 20 Dec–2 Jan. Like next entry, 3m from Bath.

Bathford ST7964 OLD SCHOOL HOUSE Church St, Bathford, Bath BA1 7RR (01225) 859593 £68, plus special breaks; 4 rms. Quietly relaxed, no smoking hotel in early Victorian village school house with winter log fires, a friendly atmosphere, and good nearby walks; disabled access.

Beercrocombe ST3220 FROG STREET FARM Frog St, Beercrocombe, Taunton TA3 6AF (01823) 480430 £50, plus special breaks; 3 rms. Peaceful 15th-c listed farmhouse deep in the countryside on big working farm; beams, fine Jacobean panelling, inglenook fireplaces, warmly friendly owner, delicious food (much produce from the farm, local game and fish; bring your own wine), and good breakfasts; cl Nov–March; children over 11.

Bleadon ST3357 PURN HOUSE FARM Bleadon, Weston-super-Mare BS24 OQE (01934) 812324 £40; 6 spacious rms, most with own bthrm. Working 400-acre family farm with dairy and beef cattle, sheep and family pets; nice food using home-produced meat and vegetables, comfortable sitting room, attractive, partly panelled dining room, games room with table tennis and so forth; riding, golf and fishing nearby; cl Dec–Jan; limited disabled access.

Cannington ST2438 BLACKMORE FARM Cannington, Bridgwater TA5 2NE (01278) 653442 *£40; 4 rms. Grade I listed manor house dating back to 15th c with garderobes, beams and stone archways; good breakfasts around a huge table in the Great Hall, and log fire in the comfortable sitting room; no evening meals; disabled access.

Dunster SS9943 LUTTRELL ARMS High St, Dunster, Minehead TA24 6SG (01643) 821555 £114, plus special breaks; 27 rms. Comfortably modernised ex-Forte hotel in ancient building of great character with individual atmosphere, friendly service, popular food and interesting evening meals; cannon emplacements in the garden date from the Civil War; close to Exmoor National Park; limited disabled access.

Emborough ST6151 REDHILL FARM Emborough, Bath BA3 4SH (01761) 241294 *£36; 3 rms, shared bthrm. Friendly old farmhouse high on the Mendips; with animals and poultry to amuse the children, residents' sitting room, and good fresh food; riding, sailing, fishing nearby; cl Christmas–New Year; no dogs.

Hatch Beauchamp ST3220 FARTHINGS Hatch Beauchamp, Taunton TA3 6SG

(01823) 480664 **£80**, plus special breaks; 9 rms with thoughtful extras. Charming little Georgian house in 3 acres of gardens; with open fires in quiet lounges, and nice food using fresh local produce; can arrange golf and other activities.

Hinton Charterhouse ST7759 HOMEWOOD PARK Freshford, Bath BA3 6BB (01225) 723731 ***£130**; 19 lovely rms. This charming Victorian hotel stands on the edge of the ruins of Hinton Priory; flowers, oil paintings and fine furniture in the graceful relaxing day rooms, an elegant restaurant with very good imaginative food (honey comes from their own bees – you can help them collect it), and 10 acres of gardens and woodlands; tennis, croquet; disabled access.

Holford ST1541 COMBE HOUSE Holford, Bridgwater TA5 1RZ (01278) 741382 ***£60**, plus special breaks; 18 rms. Warmly friendly former tannery (still has water wheel) in pretty spot; with comfortable rooms, log fires, tasty home-made food, and a relaxed atmosphere; heated indoor swimming pool, sauna, croquet, and tennis court; cl Nov–March.

Holford ST1541 QUANTOCK HOUSE Holford, Bridgwater TA5 1RY (01278) 741439 ***£40**; 3 rms. Thatched 17th-c house with a large cottagey garden, and big inglenook in the residents' lounge; delicious English cooking (evening meals by arrangement) and a friendly welcome; well behaved pets allowed; cl Christmas.

Horsington ST7023 HALF MOON Horsington, Templecombe BA8 0ED (01963) 370140 ***£35**; 4 rms, in chalets with showers. Nicely refurbished inn with stripped stone, oak floors, beams and inglenook fires; home-made food in the restaurant and bar, decent wines and real ales, and garden with play area; cl Christmas.

Hunstrete ST6462 HUNSTRETE HOUSE Hunstrete, Pensford, Bristol BS18 4NS (01761) 490490 **£160**, plus special breaks; 23 individually decorated rms. Classically handsome mainly 18th-c country-house hotel on the edge of the Mendips in 92 acres of grounds inc walled garden and deer park; comfortable and elegantly furnished day rooms with antiques, paintings, log fires, and fresh flowers from the garden; a tranquil atmosphere, excellent service, and very good enjoyable food using produce from the garden when possible; lovely gardens, croquet lawn, heated swimming pool, all-weather tennis court, and nearby riding.

Isle Brewers ST2224 BUSHFURLONG FARM Isle Brewers, Taunton TA3 6QT (01460) 281219 **£36**; 4 rms, 2 with own bthrm. No smoking hamstone farmhouse dating from early 1700s, on family-run arable farm with fine country views; breakfast room with access to garden, and guest lounge; no evening meals (pubs nearby), bikes for hire, fishing; cl Oct–Apr.

Kilve ST1442 MEADOW HOUSE Sea Lane, Kilve, Bridgwater TA5 1EG (01278) 741546 **£75**, plus special breaks; 10 rms, 5 of them in cottage in courtyard. Beautifully kept Georgian house with relaxed atmosphere, fresh flowers, antiques and comfortable seats; traditional English food using their own fruit and vegetables, a fine wine list, landscaped gardens, croquet, streamside walks, and sea fishing (5 mins); a smugglers' passage is said to run from the hotel to the church.

Langley Marsh ST0729 LANGLEY HOUSE Langley Marsh, Wiveliscombe, Taunton TA4 2UF (01984) 623318 **£105.50**, plus special breaks; 8 individually decorated, pretty rms. Spotlessly kept Georgian house with 16th-c heart, charming lounge and dining room, antiques, fresh flowers, log fires, and friendly service; excellent carefully cooked food using home-grown herbs and vegetables, and 4 acres of lovely landscaped gardens; croquet; dogs by arrangement.

Lower Vellow ST0938 CURDON MILL Lower Vellow, Williton, Taunton TA4 4LS (01984) 56522 **£60**, plus special breaks; 6 smallish but pretty and individually furnished rms. Charming and beautifully furnished no smoking hotel between the Quantocks and Brendon Hills with 200 acres of working farm to wander over, a lovely garden; very good evening meals in the antique-filled dining room, substantial breakfasts, and friendly staff (and other guests); the waterwheel and mill shaft have been carefully preserved and still work; outdoor heated swimming pool; they have a civil marriage licence; children over 8.

Luxborough SS9837 ROYAL OAK Kingsbridge, Luxborough, Watchet TA23 0SH (01984) 640319 *£45; 9 simple rms, most with own bthrm. Unspoilt and interesting old pub in idyllic spot, chatty and friendly atmosphere, beamed bar with log fire, a good choice of well kept real ales, good food in the bar and restaurant (plenty of game), and well liked breakfasts.

Middlecombe SS9645 PERITON PARK Middlecombe, Minehead TA24 8SW (01643) 706885 £84, plus special breaks; 8 rms (3 no smoking) with views of surrounding countryside. Fine Victorian country house on the edge of Exmoor with comfortable lounge, books, log fire, a relaxed atmosphere, friendly service, and good food in the panelled, no smoking dining room; pleasant walks and countryside nearby, and they can arrange shooting, fishing or riding at adjacent riding centre; dogs in one rm only; cl Jan; children over 12; disabled access.

North Perrott ST4709 MANOR ARMS North Perrott, Crewkerne TA18 7SG (01460) 72901 *£48, plus special breaks; 8 rms in restored coach house inc a fine panelled and beamed one. Comfortable and attractive 16th-c inn with friendly and helpful licensees, beams, exposed stone and inglenook fireplace, tasty home-made food in the small restaurant and bar, and a garden with play area; free coarse fishing, free entry into various South Somerset gardens; disabled access.

Polsham ST5142 SOUTHWAY FARM Polsham, Wells BA5 1RW (01749) 673396 *£38; 3 rms. Friendly Georgian farmhouse midway between Wells and Glastonbury; open fire in the comfortable lounge, an attractive dining room, good breakfasts and a pretty garden; cl Dec–Jan.

Roadwater ST0338 WOOD ADVENT FARM Roadwater, Watchet TA23 0RR (01984) 640920 *£45; 4 rms. Relaxed, spacious farmhouse on 340 acres of working farm within Exmoor National Park; log fire in the comfortable lounge, nice country cooking using their own produce in dining room with woodburning stove, grass tennis court, outdoor heated swimming pool, and fishing, clay-pigeon and pheasant shooting; children over 8.

Seavington St Mary ST4014 PHEASANT Seavington St Mary, Ilminster TA19 0QH (01460) 240502 £90, plus special breaks; 8 comfortably pretty refurbished rms. Carefully converted and spotlessly kept thatched 17th-c ex-farmhouse with open fire in the low-beamed bar, enjoyable food in an attractive candlelit restaurant, and a quiet landscaped garden.

Somerton ST4228 LYNCH COUNTRY HOUSE 4 Behind Berry, Somerton TA11 7PD (01458) 272316 *£49; 5 prettily decorated rms. Carefully restored, homely Georgian house with books in the comfortable lounge; good breakfasts (no evening meals) in airy room overlooking tranquil grounds and a lake with black swans and exotic ducks; also self-catering cottages; cl Christmas; no children.

Stanton Wick ST6162 CARPENTERS ARMS Stanton Wick, Pensford, Bristol BS18 4BX (01761) 490202 *£69.50; 12 rms. Warm and attractively furnished tile-roofed inn converted from a row of miners' cottages, with a big log fire, and woodburning stove; a wide choice of good food inc generous breakfasts, well kept beers, and friendly efficient staff.

Stogumber ST0937 HALL FARM Stogumber, Taunton TA4 3TQ (01984) 656321 £37; 6 rms. Old-fashioned B & B with optional evening meals (bring your own wine) – wonderfully unpretentious, with warmly friendly staff; cl Christmas; well behaved dogs welcome; disabled access.

Stoke St Gregory ST3527 ROSE & CROWN Woodhill, Stoke St Gregory,

Taunton TA3 7EW (01823) 490296 £38; 3 rms, 2 in cottage annexe, mostly shared bthrm. Very friendly 17th-c cottagey inn with a cosy and pleasantly romanticised stable theme; generous helpings of particularly good-value food in the no smoking dining room, excellent breakfasts, decent wine list, and efficient service from hard-working family in charge; popular skittle alley.

Ston Easton ST6253 STON EASTON PARK Ston Easton, Bath BA3 4DF (01761) 241631 £260 inc dinner, plus special breaks; 20 really lovely rms. Majestic Palladian mansion of Bath stone with beautifully landscaped 18th-c gardens and 26 acres of parkland; elegant day rooms with antiques and flowers, attractive no smoking restaurant with good food (much grown in the kitchen garden), fine afternoon teas, library and billiard room, and extremely helpful, friendly and unstuffy service; no dogs in rooms (though have kennels), babies and children over 7 welcome by prior arrangement.

Taunton ST2224 CASTLE Castle Green, Taunton TA1 1NF (01823) 272671 £120, plus special breaks; 36 lovely rms. Appealingly modernised partly Norman castle (its west front almost smothered in wisteria), with fine old oak furniture, tapestries and paintings in comfortably elegant lounges; really excellent modern English cooking, good breakfasts, a range of good-value wines from a thoughtful list, efficient friendly service, and a pretty garden; dogs by arrangement; disabled access.

Thornbury ST6390 THORNBURY CASTLE Thornbury, Bristol BS12 1HH (01454) 281182 £145; 18 opulent rms, some with big Tudor fireplaces or fine oriel windows. Impressive and luxuriously renovated early 16th-c castle with antiques, tapestries, huge fireplaces and mullioned windows in the baronial public rooms; 2 restaurants (one in the base of a tower), fine cooking, extensive wine list (inc wine from their own vineyard), thoughtful and friendly service, vast grounds; no children.

Wells ST5554 INFIELD HOUSE 36 Portway, Wells BA5 2BN (01749) 670989 £46, plus special breaks; 3 comfortable rms (the best view is from the back rm). Carefully restored, no smoking Victorian town house with period furnishings, an unusual paperweight collection, and an elegant lounge (with lots of local guides); nice breakfasts in dining room with Adam-style fireplace (no evening meals), and friendly personal service; no pets (they have a cheery labrador) and no children.

To see and do

Bath ST7564 For many this is England's most rewarding old town, though its throngs of summer visitors tend to mask its charms a bit then. Many places enjoyably recall the days of Beau Nash and the building of Bath as a fashionable resort; other draws go back to the Roman Baths, and come right up to date with the city's interesting and unusual shops. If ambitious plans come off, taking the spa waters won't just be something out of Jane Austen: the architect of Waterloo's Eurostar terminal has been commissioned to design a new spa building, likely to be ready in time for the Millennium. In the meantime our favourite places to visit are the Roman Baths, Pump Room, Museum of Costume at the Assembly Rooms, Building of Bath Museum, Industrial Heritage Centre, No 1 Royal Crescent, and Bath Abbey. The American Museum on the edge of the city at Claverton is very special.

Parts not to be missed include the great showpieces of 18th-c town planning, Queen Sq, The Circus and the Royal Crescent; the quieter Abbey Green and cobbled Abbey St and Queen St; and the great Pulteney Bridge (there's a fine view of it from the bridge at the end of North Parade, or the riverside Parade Gardens, where brass bands play in summer). The narrow little lanes between the main streets can be fascinating. In summer lots of informal eating places have tables outside. Good pubs with decent food include the Old Green Tree (Green St), Crystal Palace (Abbey Green) and

Saracen's Head (Broad St). Good street markets are in Bartlett St (daily), junk to top-drawer antiques, often buzzing with dealers from elsewhere; Guinea Lane (very early am Weds), antiques changing hands quickly; and Walcot St (Sat, occasional Sun) flea market, good bargains. The beautifully restored historic Theatre Royal presents more pre-West End productions than anywhere else in the country.

Don't try to drive around the city: Bath's streets were laid out for travel by sedan chair, not car, and a tortuous one-way system seems designed to deter drivers rather than to make traffic flow more easily. Inadvertently park your car in the wrong place and it may be quickly towed away, despite a lack of proper warnings. Walking around Bath is anyway a delight; there are flat parts, though to make the most of it you have to be prepared to slog up some of the steeper streets. Readers particularly enjoy the somewhat irreverent Bizarre Bath walking tours that leave the Huntsman Inn on North Parade Passage at 8pm daily, Apr–Sept (£3.50) – more street theatre than a typical tour.

The rush of a day trip doesn't do justice to the host of things worth seeing; it is best to stay, preferably out of season. On summer days crowds of trippers and school parties tend to spoil the best-known parts, and if you want to visit during Bath's early summer Festival, book accommodation well ahead.

If you're staying, the Bath for Less card is a good investment (£3.95 for 2 people for 4 days), with discounts on some attractions (inc the Baths) and restaurants; it's on sale at tourist information centres.

🏛️⛱️ ROMAN BATHS 💷 Founded by AD 75, and undoubtedly one of Britain's most remarkable Roman sites. They were built to service pilgrims visiting a temple to Sulis Minerva, which had been constructed around a sacred hot spring. After this the spring played a dual role – as both a focus for worship, and a reservoir supplying the baths with spa water. The baths were all but forgotten until the 18th c, when workmen chanced upon a bust of Minerva, and it was not until 1878 that most of what you see today was uncovered. The main baths are pretty much intact, though some of the columns are 18th- and 19th-c reconstructions; in August they're open at night and quite beautifully floodlit. A MUSEUM shows finds made during excavations, inc the bust of Minerva and a remarkable Gorgon's Head pediment, and a model of the site as it would have appeared in the 4th c. Meals, snacks, shop, some disabled access (though not to baths themselves); cl 25–26 Dec; (01225) 477000; £6, inc an elaborate audio-guide that rather resembles a mobile phone, and doesn't follow a predetermined route.

🏛️ PUMP ROOM This stylish 18th-c mecca for the fashionable was built directly above the Roman temple courtyard; you can catch a glimpse of the baths next door. It now houses a restaurant serving morning coffee, lunches and teas to the melodic strains of the Pump Room trio. You can sample the hot spa water, which always comes out at 46.5 deg C (116 deg F); (01225) 477000).

✝ BATH ABBEY Particularly renowned for its fan vaulting, the current building is the 3rd great church to be built on this site, begun in 1499. The Elizabethans called it the Lantern of the West because of its profusion of stained glass. Most impressive is the great east window, depicting 56 scenes from the life of Christ. On one side of this is a finely carved memorial to Bartholomew Barnes (1608), and on the other the beautiful medieval carving of the Prior Birde chantry. Restoration work has been returning the interior's gradually blackened Bath stone to its more appealing honey colour. Shop, disabled access; cl Good Fri, 25 Dec; £1.50 suggested donation. A very good exhibition on the abbey's history is in the adjacent carefully restored 18th-c vaults. Disabled access; cl Sun; (01225) 422462; £2. In summer there may be walking tours from the abbey churchyard (usually around 10.30am and 2pm).

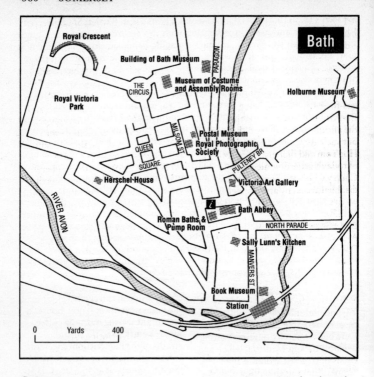

Bath

Royal Crescent
Building of Bath Museum
PARAGON
Museum of Costume and Assembly Rooms
THE CIRCUS
Royal Victoria Park
Holburne Museum
MILSOM ST
Postal Museum
Royal Photographic Society
QUEEN
SQUARE
PULTENEY BR
Herschel House
Victoria Art Gallery
RIVER AVON
Bath Abbey
Roman Baths & Pump Room
NORTH PARADE
Sally Lunn's Kitchen
MANVERS ST
Book Museum
Station

0   Yards   400

🏛 🏵 No 1 ROYAL CRESCENT The most splendid example of the architecture that sprang up in the town's Georgian heyday. In 1768 it was the 1st house built in Bath's most regal terrace, and now has 2 floors restored and beautifully furnished in the style of that time. Shop; cl Mon (exc bank hols), and Dec–mid-Feb; (01225) 428126; *£3.50. Between here and Queen Sq (another striking reminder of the period) a GEORGIAN GARDEN has been re-created in Gravel Walk, with the original layout, and the kind of plants that would have been used in a small town garden in the 1760s. Given the high ratio of walking-space to plants the emphasis back then was clearly on strolling and chatting rather than horticulture itself. Cl wknds and bank hols, and all Nov–Apr; free.

👶 🏛 BUILDING OF BATH MUSEUM (The Vineyard, Paragon) Fascinating displays on how John Wood and others transformed the town and its architecture, with full-scale reconstructions, original tools, and a fabulous model of the entire city, lighting up when you press the buttons. Shop, disabled access but no facilities – and those who have difficulty walking might notice the floor's slight unevenness; cl Mon (exc bank hols), and Dec–mid-Feb; (01225) 333895; £3.

🏛 👶 HERSCHEL HOUSE AND MUSEUM (New King St) Interesting Georgian home and workplace of William Herschel, the astronomer (and composer), with period rooms, models of his telescopes, and other scientific equipment. He discovered the planet Uranus from the back garden. Shop; cl am, and wkdys Nov–Mar; (01225) 311342; £2.50.

🖼 🏛 HOLBURNE MUSEUM (Gt Pulteney St) Fine old building displaying the decorative and fine-art collection of Sir Thomas William Holburne (1793–1874), as well as lots of 20th-c art and crafts. Meals, snacks, shop, disabled access; cl am Sun, winter Mons, and all mid-Dec–mid-Feb;

(01225) 466669; *£3.50.

♄ INDUSTRIAL HERITAGE CENTRE (Julian Rd) The highlight is the engaging MR BOWLER'S BUSINESS, an elaborate re-creation of a factory first established in 1872, providing various services from plumbing and engineering to gas-fitting and bell-hanging. Everything is just as it was then, inc the antique soda fountain that turned out such intriguingly named drinks as Hot Tom and that distant harbinger of today's gruesome alcopops, Cherry Ciderette. Snacks, shop, some disabled access by arrangement; cl wkdys Nov–Easter; (01225) 318348; *£3.50.

♨♦ MUSEUM OF COSTUME AND ASSEMBLY ROOMS (Bennett St) Dazzling – over 200 figures dressed in original costumes from the late 16th c to the present, one of the most impressive displays of fashion and fashion accessories in the world. It's housed in the Assembly Rooms, built in 1771 by John Wood the Younger, where the audio-guide (similar to the one at the Roman Baths) has a particularly entertaining commentary – listen out for the bun fight. Summer coffee, shop, disabled access; cl 25–26 Dec, and Assembly Rooms, may be cl under dates for functions; (01225) 477752; £3.60 (combined ticket with Roman Baths available). Along the same street is a small MUSEUM OF EAST ASIAN ART.

♨ POSTAL MUSEUM (Broad St) First-class exploration of the development of the postal system since the 16th c, inc a full-scale replica Victorian post office; it was from here that the world's first postage stamp was sent in 1840. Snacks, shop, disabled access to ground floor only; cl am Sun (all day Jan and Feb), 25–26 Dec, 1 Jan, Good Fri; (01225) 460333; *£2.50.

♨♧ BOOK MUSEUM (Manvers St) First and early editions of authors who lived or worked in Bath, especially Jane Austen and Charles Dickens; there's a reconstruction of Dickens's study at Gad's Hill, on the other side of England. A good chunk of the exhibition is devoted to the history and art of bookbinding, and

adjoining this is the shop of GEORGE BAYNTUN, who has been binding and selling antiquarian books for 50 years. Cl 1–2pm, pm Sat, all day Sun and bank hols; (01225) 466000; £2.

▣ ROYAL PHOTOGRAPHIC SOCIETY (The Octagon, Milsom St) 5 galleries with major international exhibitions and useful displays on photographic history, inc the first picture ever taken. Meals, snacks, shop, disabled access; cl 25–26 Dec; (01225) 462841; *£2.50 (free to members).

▥♨ SALLY LUNN'S KITCHEN (North Parade Passage) Reputedly the oldest house in Bath, a charming, partly timbered medieval structure, still preserving in its cellars the original kitchen of the legendary Sally Lunn, who in the 17th c created her famous brioche bread buns here. Meals and snacks (inc of course the buns, made to a secret recipe), shop; cl am Sun, 25 Dec; (01225) 461364; *30p.

▣♨ VICTORIA ART GALLERY (Bridge St) European Old Masters and 18th- to 20th-c British paintings and drawings, as well as decorative arts inc porcelain, glass and watches. Disabled access to ground floor only; cl am Sun, all day Mon, 25–26 Dec; (01225) 477772; free.

✽♨ BECKFORD'S TOWER (Lansdown Rd) Italianate tower with fine views from the top, and a little museum commemorating the well travelled collector William Beckford. Open pm wknds and bank hols Apr–Oct, possibly more in summer; (01225) 338727; *£2.

⚓ BOAT CRUISES These leave Pulteney Bridge landing stage at a quarter to and a quarter past the hour (not Oct–Easter). Boats and punts can be hired in summer from the Boating Station on the River Avon, Forester Rd, Bathwick: (01225) 466407. The revivified KENNET & AVON CANAL is one of Bath's pleasures, with quiet towpath walks along to Bathampton (where the George I is popular for lunch); it has quite a few colourful narrowboats in summer. You can cycle right into the centre along the Avon Cycleway, cycle tracks converted from the old Bath and Bristol railway.

! Hot-air BALLOON TRIPS give a good view of the city as it's shown in the great architectural drawings. They take off, subject to weather, from the Royal Victoria Park; (01225) 466888; from £110.

⊕ PRIOR PARK LANDSCAPE GARDEN (Ralph Allen Drive, off the A3062 S of Bath) In a sweeping valley, these striking 18th-c landscaped gardens are being comprehensively restored by the National Trust after a period of neglect. Capability Brown and Alexander Pope helped local entrepreneur Ralph Allen with the original design, and there are plenty of unique ornamental features (inc 18th-c graffiti on the Palladian bridge). Woodland walks offer unusual views over Bath. Note you can't drive all the way here: there's no car parking on site or nearby. You can walk from town, but the hill is very steep, so best to take the number 2 or 4 bus. Cl am, all day Tues, 25–26 Dec, 1 Jan; (01225) 833977; £3.80

(£1 off if you show bus or train ticket); NT. There's decent food at the Cross Keys over on Midford Rd.

⊙ ♭ ♠ ⊕ AMERICAN MUSEUM IN BRITAIN (Claverton Manor, just SE of the city at Claverton; ST7862) Quite a contrast to the rest of Bath's attractions, a fascinating illustration of American history and life, in lovely gracious surroundings. 18 rooms are fully furnished and decorated to re-create the style of American homes from the 17th to the 19th c, while the grounds include a replica of part of George Washington's garden at Mount Vernon, and an American arboretum. Collections of folk art and patchwork quilts, with sections on native Americans and Shakers, and good special events. Well liked by readers, it's the only museum in the country completely devoted to our colonial cousins. Snacks, shop, some disabled access; cl am, all day Mon (exc Aug and bank hols), and Nov–Mar; (01225) 460503; £5.

Bristol ST5872 Too busy an industrial city to use as a base for an enjoyable stay, Bristol has masses of things to fill a lively day visit. It's easily reached from Bath – or from one of the cosseting nearby country-house hotels we list, and day visits are made easy by good rail connections, and the motorway that plunges right into the city's heart. The city's prosperity still stems from its port, though aerospace now predominates among many other manufacturing interests. There are some striking buildings around the centre, notably the Corn Exchange and the Old Council House on Corn St, and on Broad St the Grand Hotel (1869), the Guild Hall (1843) and the art nouveau façade of the former Edward Everard printing house. The Theatre Royal, opened in 1766, is one of the oldest working theatres in the country. The best part for leisurely strolls is the elegant suburb of Clifton, with handsome Georgian terraces and its famous suspension bridge. Useful central places for a cheapish lunchtime bite are the Bridge (Passage St), Commercial Rooms (Corn St) and Le Chateau (Park St). In 1997 a 250-mile cycle way, developed at a cost of £43 million, was opened from here to Padstow in Cornwall, keeping off roads as much as possible.

⚓ ♠ ♭⊤ The DOCKS are being attractively restored, with distinctive blue and yellow FERRIES (Apr–Sept) linking several points. The old part around King St, between the waterfront and the Bristol Old Vic, has quiet cobbled streets of Georgian buildings, pleasant to wander through, and elsewhere some of the bigger warehouses (and even the boats) are being pressed into service

as museums, café-bars and the like; a former coaster has become the Old Profanity, an entertainment showboat popular with students. The ARNOLFINI, a big former tea warehouse, is now a contemporary arts complex with bar, restaurant, exhibitions, cinema, theatre and so forth. The INDUSTRIAL MUSEUM (Princes Wharf) is housed in a converted dockside transit shed, and is especially good on transport, with locally built steam locomotives and aircraft (inc a mock-up of Concorde's flight deck), and a good look at the development of the port. Shop, disabled access; cl Thurs, Fri, and in winter usually all wkdys; (0117) 925 1470; £1. You can get a ticket that also covers entry to the City Museum, Red Lodge, and Georgian House, all described below.

🚂 ⚓ ♿ ⛴ STEAM TRAINS AND SHIPS On the dockside a small steam railway on summer wknds will whisk you along the old cargo route to and from the SS *GREAT BRITAIN* 🔲. Isambard Kingdom Brunel designed this as the first iron, screw-propelled, ocean-going vessel, and a real departure from what had gone before. It's being restored, after a half century or so lying neglected in the Falkland Islands. Snacks, shop, some disabled access; cl 24 –25 Dec; (0117) 926 0680; £3.90. At the entrance to the ship (and sharing the same facilities) is the MARITIME HERITAGE CENTRE, with reconstructions and original machinery illustrating the city's long history of ship-building; free. Also moored here is the 1860s steam-tug *Mayflower*, which has interesting trips round the docks every hour most wknds in summer. It's only small so best to book with the Industrial Museum (see above); £2.50. The nearby diesel-powered firefloat *Pyronaut* (1934) and Fairbairn steam-crane (1876) also operate occasional summer wknds. From Apr to Oct the PLEASURE STEAMERS *Waverley* and *Balmoral* run fairly frequent day cruises from here, along the Avon and Severn or to Devon, Wales or Lundy; (0117) 926 0767 for programme. The *Balmoral* has surprisingly well kept real ale in its bar.

✝ CATHEDRAL On the other side of the water, this was originally an Augustinian monastery, founded on what's supposedly the spot where St Augustine met the Celtic Christians in the early 7th c. It's a real mix of architectural styles, and perhaps the country's most splendid example of a hall church, where the nave, choir.

and aisles are all the same height. Highlights include the Chapter House (one of the finest Norman rooms in Britain), and the candlesticks given in thanks by the privateers who rescued Alexander Selkirk (whose adventures inspired Daniel Defoe to write *Robinson Crusoe*). Snacks, shop, some disabled access. They usually have free concerts here at 1.15pm on Tues in term-time and during Aug.

✝ ST MARY REDCLIFFE (Redcliffe Hill) Elizabeth I described this as 'the goodliest, fairest and most famous parish church in England'. Most of the current building dates from the late 13th c, inc the wonderful hexagonal outer porch. Notable features include the tomb of Admiral Sir William Penn, who founded Pennsylvania, and the Handel Window, where 8 passages of the *Messiah* commemorate the great composer's ties with this church. Snacks Mon –Thurs, disabled access (through south door). Other interesting churches, plucked from quite a wide selection, include the LORD MAYOR'S CHAPEL on Park St (a rare civic church, with glorious 16th-c stained-glass windows, floor tiles and fan-vaulted ceiling; guided tours 11am and 2pm) and JOHN WESLEY'S CHAPEL, incongruously set in the Broadmead Shopping Centre. Still much as it was when Wesley preached here (from the double-decked pulpit upstairs), it's the oldest Methodist chapel in the world, built in 1739 and rebuilt in 1748. Guided tours by arrangement. Shop, disabled access to ground floor only; cl 1–2pm, and winter Weds; (0117) 926 4740; £2.50.

🏛 ✝ CHRISTMAS STEPS This famous old-fashioned alley is quaintly lined by steep buildings. At the top is the tiny late 15th-c CHAPEL OF THE THREE KINGS OF COLOGNE (the 'three kings' are the 3 wise men whose shrines are in Cologne cathedral); the warden of the nearby almshouses can let you in. And at the bottom is the lodge of ST BARTHOLOMEW'S – all that remains of the 13th-c hospital and almshouse which once stood on this site. This is a

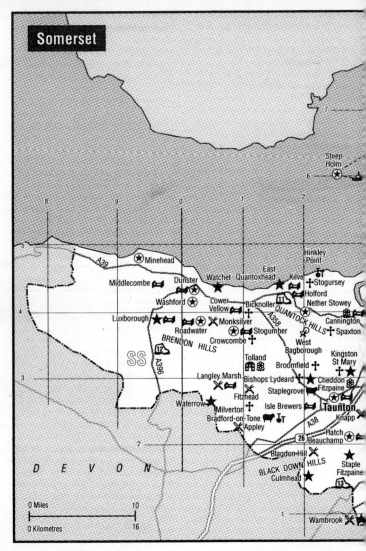

Somerset

good area for shops selling antiques, stamps and old books.

🏠 RED LODGE (Park St) The house was altered in the 18th c, but on its 1st floor it still has the last surviving suite of 16th-c rooms in Bristol, as well as a wonderful carved stone chimneypiece, plasterwork ceilings and fine oak panelling. They occasionally open the reconstructed Tudor-style garden. Cl am, occasional bank hols, and all Nov–Mar; (0117) 921 1360; £1, free on Suns. There are several elegant Georgian streets round here, notably Great George St, where the GEORGIAN HOUSE, built in 1790 for a wealthy sugar merchant, is a fine illustration of a typical town house of the day. 3 floors are decorated in period style, inc the below-stairs area with kitchen, laundry and housekeeper's room. Times and price as for Red Lodge; (0117) 921 1362.

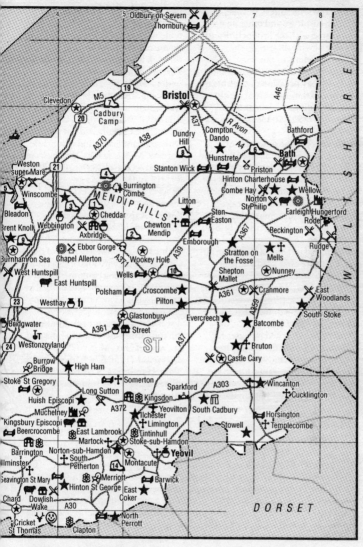

CABOT TOWER The attractive park at the end of Great George St is an urban nature reserve, and its tower rewards those willing to climb the hundreds of steps with probably the best views of the city. Snacks, cl 25 Dec; free. Nearby ST GEORGE'S has good Fri lunchtime concerts, usually with seats available on the day, but best to check on (0117) 923 0359.

CITY MUSEUM AND ART GALLERY (Queens Rd) Good collections of fine and applied art, archaeology, geology, and history – well worth a look. Snacks, shop, disabled access; cl Easter and Christmas bank hols; (0117) 922 3571; £2. The neo-Gothic Wills Memorial tower next door is a distinctive landmark.

! *See separate Family Panel below* for the EXPLORATORY HANDS-ON SCIENCE CENTRE.

HARVEY'S WINE MUSEUM (Denmark St) Unique collection of antique corkscrews, decanters, glasses, bottles, furniture and other items associated with the production and serving of wine, housed in the medieval cellars of this wine company. There's a very good shop, and you may occasionally be able to join one of the guided tours with tutored tastings. Cl Sun and bank hols; (0117) 927 5036; £4 (inc a glass of sherry).

🏠 🎨 CLIFTON The quiet side of Bristol, with some fine late 18th- and 19th-c terraces, an antiques market (Mall, cl Sun, Mon), a big park right on the spectacular Avon gorge facing the NT woodlands on the crags opposite, and the remarkably modern-looking Suspension Bridge, based on an 1836 design by Brunel and finished in 1864; a Victorian girl leapt off here after a tiff with her boyfriend, but was saved when her huge skirts acted as a parachute. The Somerset House (Princess Victoria St) is useful for something to eat.

🐾 BRISTOL ZOO GARDENS (Clifton Down; easily reached by buses 8, 9, 508 and 509 from the city centre) One of the most enjoyable zoos in the country, excellent value, lots to see, and plenty of well-thought-out children's activities. Highlights include the new Gorilla Island, Bug World, and Twilight World, with wide-awake rats, mice and other nocturnal animals – inc a walk-through bat enclosure. Good adventure playground, activity centre with face-painting, brass-rubbing and so on, and animal encounters well distributed throughout the day. A bonus is that everything is spread through beautifully laid out gardens, with spacious lawns and colourful borders. Meals, snacks, shop, disabled access; cl 25 Dec; (0117) 973 8951; £5.90.

🎨 ♿ 🐕 BLAISE CASTLE ESTATE (Henbury, 4m NW of city, off the B4047) A spacious and locally popular undulating park with some woodland and refreshments. The late 18th-c house is now a branch of the City Museum, with lots of carefully explained farming equipment, and collections of costume and dolls. The castle itself is a Gothic folly built in 1766 within the now scarcely discernible ramparts of an Iron Age hill fort. Shop; museum cl Thurs and Fri, and all Nov–Mar, park open daily; (0117) 950 6789; free. Nearby Blaise Hamlet is a NT-owned estate village designed by John Nash.

Other things to see and do

SOMERSET FAMILY ATTRACTION OF THE YEAR

! **Bristol** ST5972 EXPLORATORY HANDS-ON SCIENCE CENTRE (By Templemeads Railway Station) Probably the best of its kind, this hugely enjoyable science centre is as much fun for adults as it is for children. Altogether there are around 150 hands-on experiments (or plores as they call them), presenting science in an appealingly accessible and relevant way: light and vision are illustrated by walk-in kaleidoscopes and distorting mirrors, racing cars are operated by pulleys, and you can make your own electricity or launch a hot-air balloon. The sound and music gallery is fun: you stand inside a giant acoustic guitar and feel the vibrations as its strings are plucked. There are computers for surfing the Net, and plenty of staff on hand to help with any of the displays. A new gallery looking at the human body opens on 18 Mar. The StarDome planetarium (75p extra) is usually open wknds and school hols, but tickets for here sell fast and seats are limited; best to get your ticket for this bit as soon as you arrive. Bear in mind, too, that you'll crawl or crouch to get inside (disabled access to the rest of the building is excellent, with a wheelchair entrance round the back). You can keep going back and trying everything again, so a visit can easily last a few hours – and it won't necessarily be the children in the group that you have to drag away when it's time to leave. The centre is next to Templemeads Station (some of the buildings used to be engine sheds), with several car parks nearby; half the cost of parking at the NCP just before the Elf Garage opposite will be refunded on presenting the ticket at the Exploratory Centre. Snacks (wknds and school hols only), shop, disabled access; cl Christmas wk; (0117) 907 9000; £5 (£3.50 children); it's free for under 5s, though isn't ideal for them. A family ticket for 2 adults and 2 children is £15.

🏠 ☕ **Axbridge** ST4354 Pleasant small town with an appealing largely medieval square and narrow winding high street, unusual in this part of the world for its jettied timber-framed buildings. One of them is KING JOHN'S HUNTING LODGE, actually built around 1500 so having no connection with King John (nor in fact with hunting) – but no less attractive for that. It houses a local history museum. Disabled access to grounds; open pm Easter–Sept; (01934) 732012; donations; NT. The rambling old Lamb on the corner of the tranquil market square is good for lunch.

Days Out

Uniquely Bath
Building of Bath Museum; Museum of Costumes; No 1 Royal Crescent; lunch at Beaujolais (Queen Sq), Old Green Tree (Green St) or Crystal Palace (Abbey Green); Roman Baths; tea in the Pump Room.

Bristol-fashion
SS *Great Britain* and Maritime Heritage Centre; Exploratory Hands-on Science Centre; Bristol Zoo – picnic here; Clifton suspension bridge.

The timeless Quantocks
Dunster; Cleeve Abbey, Washford; Stogumber – lunch at the White Horse there; Crowcombe church; walk the track along spine of Quantocks from top of Crowcombe to Nether Stowey road; Coleridge Cottage, Nether Stowey.

Natural wonders of the Mendips
Burrington Combe (walk on to Dolebury Warren if time); Cheddar Gorge (take Jacob's Ladder steps up S side, hold on to something, and look down into gorge); lunch at Almshouse Bistro or the Lamb, Axbridge; Ebbor Gorge; Wookey Hole Caves.

Scissor arches and Arthurian tales
Wells; lunch at the City Arms or Fountain there; Peat Moors visitor centre, Westhay; Glastonbury.

Somerset's SE corner
Bruton; Hadspen Gardens (limited opening), nr Castle Cary; Castle Cary – lunch at the George there; walk up to Cadbury Castle; Haynes Motor Museum, Sparkford.

Mixed platter
Perry's cider mills, Dowlish Wake; Scotts of Merriott (nursery); Stoke sub Hamdon – lunch at the Fleur de Lis there; Montacute House or Tintinhull House garden; perhaps stroll in Ham Hill country park.

Barrington ST3918
BARRINGTON COURT In the grounds of
a splendid 16th-c house, a
magnificent series of gardens
influenced by Gertrude Jekyll, inc a
rose garden, and traditional walled
kitchen garden, the produce from
which is on sale in the shop. The
house shows off the reproduction
furniture of Stuart Interiors. Meals,
snacks, plant centre, disabled access;
open Apr–Sept exc Fri; (01460)
241938; £4, house extra £1; NT. The
village itself is attractive, and the
Royal Oak does good lunches.

Bradford-on-Tone ST1722
SHEPPY'S CIDER (Three Bridges) The
Sheppys have been making cider here
since the early 19th c, and you can
follow the entire process over the
370-acre farm. Tastings in the shop,
and a little museum. Snacks, shop,
disabled access; cl Sun, exc 12–2pm
Easter– Christmas; (01823) 461233;
£1.75. The White Horse has good
food.

Bridgwater ST3037 Once you're
through the industrial outskirts, some
central bits are worth seeing: Castle St
is the finest early 18th-c street in the
county. ADMIRAL BLAKE MUSEUM
(Blake St) Now the local history
museum, this picturesque house was
the birthplace of the Admiral in 1598,
and shows his personal possessions
(inc his sea chest) and a diorama of
his great victory over the Spaniards at
Santa Cruz. Shop; cl Sun, Mon,
25–26 Dec; (01278) 456127; free.

★ † **Bruton** ST6834 Fascinating little
town; worth looking out for are the
Bartons, narrow alleys leading down
from the High St to the river (which
you can cross either by footbridge or
by using stepping stones). ST MARY'S
CHURCH is on the site of a medieval
Augustinian priory and abbey – the
old abbey wall with its buttresses still
stands in Silver St. The church has a
spectacular altarpiece, and in the
chancel is a fine effigy of Sir Maurice
Berkely, a great survivor who was
standard-bearer to Henry VIII,
Edward VI and Queen Elizabeth.
Interesting and individual shops –
antiques, books and prints. The
Castle Inn is good for lunch. The

drive up towards Alfred's Tower
gives some open views, and below it
the Old Red Lion at North Brewham
has decent food.

† **Burnham-on-Sea** ST3050 In
summer a bustling inexpensive family
seaside resort, with wide beaches,
sandy dunes, and the usual holiday
facilities. Its plain-looking CHURCH
surprises with its collection of
Grinling Gibbons carvings from the
long-demolished Palace of Whitehall
in London. ANIMAL FARM COUNTRY
PARK and THE LAND OF LEGENDS (Red
Rd, N of Berrow) ST3054 Good fun
for children, with animals and
conservation trails, trampolines and
play areas, and tableaux based
around folk tales and other stories.
Meals, snacks, shop, disabled access;
cl 25 Dec (maybe other dates too in
winter); (01278) 751628; £3.50.
There's a small NATURE RESERVE in the
nearby sand dunes. The Red Cow at
Brent Knoll has good food.

Burrington Combe ST4758
This steeply wooded roadside combe
on the N flank of the Mendips has
good viewpoints above it; the B3134
is the best drive through these
limestone hills.

Burrow Bridge ST3630 SOMERSET
LEVELS BASKET CENTRE (Lyng Rd) Sells
baskets made from local materials cut
on the surrounding Levels; there may
be demonstrations, and they have
other crafts too. Shop, disabled
access; cl Sun, 25–26 Dec; (01823)
698688; free. The Rose & Crown at
East Lyng has good food.

Cannington ST2539 CANNINGTON
COLLEGE HERITAGE GARDENS Extensive
gardens inc over 10,000 different
types of plant, with 8 national
collections, display and ornamental
beds, tropical and sub-tropical
glasshouses, and gardens of bees and
butterflies. Unusual plant sales; cl am,
and Nov–Mar; (01278) 655000;
*£2.25. The Malt Shovel at Bradley
Green has decent food, and there's a
nice drive to Nether Stowey via
Combwich and Stogursey.

★ **Castle Cary** ST6332
Very attractive – basically a medieval
market town, now with a useful
range of traditional family-run shops

and crafts and antique shops. The 18th-c ROUNDHOUSE is Britain's smallest prison, and the local museum is worth a look if you've time. The George, a comfortable old thatched coaching inn, has good food. HADSPEN GARDENS (2m SE at Hadspen House, off the A371) Beautiful 8-acre gardens surrounding a fine 18th-c house; many old favourite plants, but also lots of exotics. A delightful 17th-c walled garden has all sorts of herbaceous plants and old-fashioned roses, and there's a lily pond and ancient flower meadow. Teas (Sun only), nursery, some disabled access; open Thurs–Sun Mar–Sept and bank hols; (01749) 813707; *£2.50. CASTLE CARY VINEYARD (Honeywick, just E of town) Produces award-winning wines and welcomes visits (cl am Sun and Nov–Apr).

✗ **Chapel Allerton** ST4050 ASHTON WINDMILL The only complete mill left in Somerset, built in the 18th c, with splendid views over the Cheddar Gorge and Somerset Levels. Open pm Sun and bank hols Easter–Sept, plus pm Weds July and Aug; (01934) 712694; free.

♨ ✗ 🏛 **Chard** ST3208 The local history MUSEUM (High St) has good displays on local industries such as lace-making, and a bizarre collection of artificial limbs. Shop, disabled access; cl Sun (exc July and Aug), Oct–May; (01460) 65091; £1.70. There are a couple of places to hire bikes; the local tourist board do good cycle routes. HORNSBURY MILL (just N of Chard) 200-year-old watermill, with landscaped watergarden, trout lake, and play area; you can stay here. Meals, snacks, shop, disabled access; cl Jan; (01460) 63317; free, £2 museum. Past here at Combe St Nicholas the Green Dragon has good-value food. FORDE ABBEY, just over the border so described under Dorset, is particularly worth visiting.

🍎 ✝ ❀ ⊞ ⅋ 🏛 ♪ **Cheddar** ST4754 In its older part, this extended village has a very fine market cross, with some interesting shops and a tall-towered 14th/15th-c CHURCH. The Galleries is quite useful for lunch, and outside are roadside strawberry stalls and PICK-YOUR-OWN in summer. CHEDDAR GORGE The area's big attraction, a magnificent limestone gorge with picturesque cliffs, formed when a cavern roof collapsed. The B3135 is a dramatic drive through, and the 274 steps of Jacob's Ladder climb to an excellent viewpoint (there's a slower but less exhausting alternative path). CHEDDAR SHOWCAVES Two beautiful caves beneath the Gorge; quite cathedral-like with spectacular stalagmites and stalactites joining to form columns. Also an exhibition devoted to 'Cheddar Man', Britain's oldest complete skeleton, with a re-creation of his world of 9,000 years ago. Good clifftop walks, and plenty of activities for children, inc the lively Crystal Quest. Meals, snacks, shop; cl 24–25 Dec; (01934) 742343; £6.50. The more daring can don hard hats and boiler suits for what they call Adventure Caving Expeditions; £7.50 (no under 12s). CHEDDAR GORGE CHEESE CO RURAL VILLAGE 🔲 (The Cliffs) Shops and traditional crafts based around a factory that, thanks to its location, claims to make the only genuine cheddar cheese in the world. You can watch each stage of the 7-hour process, and of course taste the matured product. Also fudge-making, scrumpy sampling, and less flavoursome crafts inc lace and candle-making. Meals, snacks, shops, disabled access; cl Nov–mid-Mar; (01934) 742810; *£3.50. There's an AQUARIUM near here too. Cheddar gets astonishingly busy in summer, when every building seems to be either a tearoom or a shop selling cheese or cider.

🏛 **Cheddon Fitzpaine** ST2428 HESTERCOMBE GARDENS Raised walks, sunken lawns and a water garden are all part of the grand design which Lutyens and Gertrude Jekyll created for this garden (now beautifully restored) set around the Somerset Fire Brigade Headquarters. In 1997 they reopened the intriguing landscaped secret gardens. Snacks, shop, limited disabled access; cl 25 Dec; (01823) 337222; £3. If you don't want to go into Taunton, the Bathpool Inn at Bathpool (on the A38) is a handy family dining pub.

🐾 † **Chewton Mendip** ST5953 CHEWTON CHEESE DAIRY (Priory Farm) Another traditional cheese dairy, one of the few to mature their cheeses properly, so producing not just the characteristic rind but also the true depth of flavour. They start at 7am and go on till 3pm, with the best time to watch between 11.30 am and 2.30pm. A video shows the stages you may have missed. Meals, snacks, farm shop, disabled access; no cheesemaking Thurs or Sun, cl 25–26 Dec, 1 Jan; (01761) 241666; £2.50 guided tour. The 15th-c CHURCH TOWER is perhaps the most magnificent in any village in the area. The Waldegrave Arms has decent food.

🎱 **Clapton** ST4106 CLAPTON COURT GARDENS (on the B3165) The country's largest ash grows in this series of formal gardens, spread over 10 acres right on the county border; spacious lawns, rockery, rose garden, and shrub-filled woodland garden. Open pm Tues–Thurs Apr–Sept; (01460) 73220; £3.

🏠🚲⚓🥤♪🐾 🎱 **Clevedon** ST4071 The Victorian PIER has been lovingly restored (it partly collapsed in 1970) and is pleasant for a stroll. Upstairs, above the tollhouse, a gallery sells paintings, and there are sailing and fishing from the pier itself. Shop, disabled access; cl Weds Oct–Mar, and 25 Dec; (01275) 878846; *60p. Round the corner in Waterloo House is a HERITAGE CENTRE; 60p (£1 joint ticket with Pier). Good views from Church Hill, and in Moor Lane the CLEVEDON CRAFT CENTRE has 15 varied workshops and a tearoom; some parts cl Mon. The Little Harp and Moon & Sixpence are seafront family dining pubs with sea views to Wales. CLEVEDON COURT (just E, on the B3130) Most of the original structure of this manor house, built in 1320, is still intact, though there are interesting additions from other periods inc a charming 18th-c garden. Thackeray wrote part of *Vanity Fair* here. Snacks, limited disabled access;

open pm Sun, Weds, Thurs and bank hols Apr–Sept; (01275) 872257; £4; NT.

🐾🏛✿ **Cranmore** ST6843 EAST SOMERSET RAILWAY 🚂 Steam trips along what's known as the Strawberry Line, as well as engine shed and workshops, with 9 steam locomotives and rolling stock, and an art gallery with wildlife paintings by David Shepherd. Meals, snacks, shop, disabled access; open daily, though trains don't run every day – best to ring for timetable; (01749) 880417; £5.50, less when no trains running. The Strode Arms in this quiet and pleasant village is very good for lunch, and there are good views from the top of CRANMORE FOLLY; cl Oct–Mar; £1.

♥☺ **Cricket St Thomas** ST3708 The leisure park on the great estate here, familiar from television's *To The Manor Born* and *Mr Blobby*, has lovely parkland, 600 wildlife park animals, and plenty more to amuse children – with a particularly unusual treat, a ride on one of the camels that arrived in 1997. In summer 1997 the estate was on the market (for £8 million), and seemed likely to be bought by a company interested in developing the leisure side even more. Meals, snacks, shop, disabled access (free for visitors in a wheelchair); cl 25–26 Dec, and maybe other dates in winter; (01460) 30755; *£8.50 (inc train, water ride and sea lion show), less in winter, when not so much going on (the wildlife area is still open then).

🐷🐾 **Dowlish Wake** ST3713 PERRY'S CIDER MILLS They've been making cider here for centuries, and between Oct and Nov you can watch it being produced. The cider mill is in a group of thatched 16th-c buildings around a yard with brightly painted old farm wagons and so forth. Enthusiastically run, with a new video on cider making, liberal tastings and half a dozen different ciders for sale, in old-fashioned earthenware flagons if you want. Shop, disabled access; cl 1–1.30pm, 25–26 Dec, 1 Jan; (01460) 52681; free. The nearby New Inn is very good for lunch.

★ † ☺ ⌂ ⊞ ☀ ✕ **Dunster** SS9943
Well worth a day of anybody's time,
with fine medieval houses along the
wide main street below the wooded
castle hill, as well as a handsome
former yarn market and market
cross, a lovely 15th-c priory CHURCH
with particularly tuneful bells, and a
well established DOLL MUSEUM in the
Memorial Hall (cl Oct–Easter; *50p).
If you plan to visit Exmoor the
National Park Information Centre is
a useful first stop. DUNSTER CASTLE
Dramatically set in a 28-acre park
rich with exotic flora and even
subtropical plants, the castle was
largely rebuilt in the 19th c, but has
older features inside such as the 17th-
c oak staircase and gallery with its
brightly painted wall hangings.
Excellent views. Shop in 17th-c
stables, limited disabled access (a
buggy avoids the steep climb up the
hill); castle cl Thurs, Fri, and all
Nov–Mar (gardens open all year);
(01643) 821314; £5, £2.70 garden
and park only; NT. In summer you
can go right up to the 12th-c OLD
DOVECOT, special for still having its
potence or revolving ladder, used for
harvesting the plump squabs from the
nesting boxes. A well restored 18th-c
WATERMILL continues to make and sell
flour, and has teas in a pleasant
riverside garden. Cl Sat (exc July and
Aug), and all Nov–Mar; (01643)
821759; *£1.60. The handsome old
Luttrell Arms Hotel is good for lunch,
and there's a wealth of tearooms.

🐾 **East Huntspill** ST3444 SECRET
WORLD ⊞ (New Rd Farm) Very
friendly family-run working farm,
with an emphasis on wildlife rescue
(especially badgers). The best feature
is the unique observation badger set
in the Nocturnal House, with glass
viewing panels to watch the
creatures' life underground. Also
farm trail, barn owls, lots of other
animals, adventure playground, and
special events. Meals, snacks, shop,
disabled access; cl 25–26 Dec, Jan;
(01278) 783250; *£4.50. You can
hire bikes here too (without having to
go into the farm). The Crossways Inn
over at West Huntspill is a popular
lunch place.

⊞ **East Lambrook** ST4319 EAST
LAMBROOK MANOR GARDEN This well
loved cottagey garden around a 15th-
c house (not open) is now Grade I
listed; it was started by Walter and
Margery Fish in 1937, and Mrs Fish
described the process in her book *We
Made A Garden*, which became
immensely popular. They keep a
National Collection of geraniums.
Plant sales, shop; cl Sun, and all
Nov–Feb; (01460) 240328; *£2.50.
The Rose & Crown opposite does
good-value food.

🎭 **Ebbor Gorge** ST5248 If you like
Cheddar Gorge but don't like the
souvenir stalls, coach parties and all,
then Ebbor Gorge is for you. It's the
same sort of thing, above Wookey
Hole, but altogether more unspoilt.
The Hunter's Lodge and New Inn up
around Priddy have sensibly priced
food.

⌂ **Farleigh Hungerford** ST8057
Extensive ruins of 14th-c CASTLE, with
monuments in the chapel to the
Hungerford family, who once owned
the land from here to Salisbury.
Snacks, shop; cl 1–2pm, winter Mon
and Tues, 24–26 Dec; (01225)
754026; *£2. The Hungerford Arms
has decent food.

⌂ ⊞ ☺ ☀ 🏛 🎭 **Glastonbury** ST4938
Tales of King Arthur can be found all
over the country, but are especially
prominent here; they like to say that
bones reinterred in the abbey in 1191
were those of Arthur and Guinevere.
The best approach is by the B3151,
showing the town below the famous
Tor. The noble ruins of GLASTONBURY
ABBEY are said to mark the location of
the birth of Christianity in this
country. The story goes that Joseph
of Arimathaea struck his staff into
Wearyall Hill, where it took root.
(Offshoots of the tree, the famous
Glastonbury Thorn, have flourished
to this day and there's a fine specimen
in the parish churchyard.) He is also
said to have brought with him the
Holy Grail (Jesus's Last Supper
platter, used by Joseph to receive his
blood at the cross), which Arthur's
knights heroically sought through so
many famous stories. The remains of
the church date mainly from 1524,

though the Lady Chapel is much older, and massive roof timbers and richly decorated gable ends and porches testify to the enormous wealth of the order who ran it. An interpretation area has a good range of stories connected with the site. Summer snacks, shop, disabled access; cl 25 Dec; (01458) 832267; *£2.80. Legend has it that the Holy Grail was hidden in the CHALICE WELL, now set in a colourful 2½-acre garden; the spring has apparently possessed healing powers ever since. True or not, it's a nice peaceful spot. Shop, disabled access; cl am Nov–Mar; £1. The Abbey Barn and outbuildings house the SOMERSET RURAL LIFE MUSEUM, with displays of traditional regional skills such as cider-making, peat-cutting and basket-weaving. Also orchard, rare breeds, and bee garden with hives. Summer snacks, shop, some disabled access; open Tues–Sat July and Aug – best to ring for other times; (01458) 831197; £2. Glastonbury was formerly an island rising from a vast inland lake, and you can almost see this from the top of the Tor, the highest point of the hills and ridges among which the little town nestles, with fantastic views. Excavations here have revealed a prehistoric LAKE VILLAGE covering 3 or 4 acres below it, consisting of nearly a hundred mounds surrounded by a wooden palisade. Lots of items and timbers from the village have been unusually well preserved thanks to the waterlogged state of the site, and some of the finds, providing a fascinating insight into the life of the settlement, are displayed in the GLASTONBURY TRIBUNAL, a fine 15th-c town house on the High St. The tourist information centre is here too, and there's some notable plasterwork in the lower back room. Shop, limited disabled access; cl 25–26 Dec; (01458) 832954; *£1.50. Glastonbury has quite a New Age feel, probably due to all those legends. The George & Pilgrims, its medieval carved façade one of the sights of the town, is quite useful for lunch, and the Who'd A Thought It

has good-value food. The bypass has made the town much more pleasurable.

🏠 🏯 **Hatch Beauchamp** ST3020 HATCH COURT Fine Palladian mansion with impressive hall, walled kitchen garden, deer park, plenty of china and small military museum. It's one of those places where the family take real care showing you round, enlivening the tour with lots of anecdotes. Teas (Thurs only); house open pm Thurs mid-Jun–mid-Sept, garden open all day Mon –Thurs mid-Apr–Jun, plus Fri July–Sept; (01823) 480120; £3.50, £2 garden only. The Hatch Inn is good value.

↓T **Hinkley Point** ST2646 POWER STATION The visitor centre has displays and interactive videos explaining how electricity is generated, with information on local ecology and wildlife (several nature trails nearby); tours by arrangement, (01278) 652461. Snacks, cl winter Sat, Christmas wk; free.

★ **Ilchester** ST5222 Charming, with a useful range of well stocked little shops. Used to be a Roman town, and one of the houses has a piece of Roman paving. The whole of the green fronting the Town Hall is said to be the burial ground of Plague victims. The comfortable Ilchester Arms has good food.

🐄 🏨 **Kingsbury Episcopi** ST4321 SOMERSET CIDER BRANDY CO England's first fully licensed cider distillery, with huge copper stills, oak vats and wooden presses, and traditional cider orchards to stroll through. Maybe tastings of their cider brandy. Shop, disabled access; cl Sun; (01460) 240782; free. The village green has an ancient lock-up, and the Wyndham Arms is useful for lunch.

🏠 🏯 **Kingsdon** ST5326 LYTES CARY MANOR Most of the surviving building dates from the 16th c, though there are interesting earlier features inc the 14th-c chapel, and the Great Hall with its 15th-c stained glass. The gardens were designed and stocked by Henry Lyte, a notable Elizabethan horticulturist, and are being brought back to their original state. Plant sales, disabled access to garden only; open pm Mon, Weds and Sat Apr–Oct; (01985) 847777; £3.80; NT. The Kingsdon Inn does good home cooking.

† **Martock** ST4619 The magnificent CHURCH has a splendid roof; also look out for the old Court House turned into a Grammar School by William Strode in 1661, with the inscription above the door 'Martock neglect not your opportunities' in English, Latin, Hebrew and Greek. The Fleur de Lis in Stoke sub Hamdon is useful for lunch.

❀ ⚘ **Merriott** ST4412 SCOTTS OF MERRIOTT Perhaps the last of the big general retail nurseries to raise and grow most of their own trees and shrubs, on 90 acres – a sea of colour when the 500 varieties of roses are in flower in July. Shop; cl 25–26 Dec, Easter Sun, (01460) 72306; free. In the village D B POTTERY (Highway Cottage, Church St) make attractive teapots and other stoneware; (01460) 75655; free. The Lord Poulett on the attractive main street of nearby Hinton St George is good for lunch.

🚃 ⚘ 🏖 **Minehead** SS9746 There's an easily missed area of sloping streets and thatched cottages around the church, with Church Steps a quaint, steep back lane. Around this original fishing village is a spacious resort, its beach and promenade sheltered by the wooded hills to the NE. It has the usual attractions, a lively harbour, a sizeable holiday camp, and a modern shopping area; there are plans to build England's first new pier for many years. The Old Ship Aground has good-value food and pleasant harbour views. There's an unusual POTTERY SHOP (cl 12–1.30pm) on Park St, and a little SHOE FACTORY you can visit on North Rd (cl 1–2pm and wknds exc am Sat). Minehead is the terminus for the WEST SOMERSET RAILWAY, whose steamtrains run along the coast to Watchet and then inland to Bishops Lydeard – a splendid long run stopping at several little stations. Meals, snacks, shop, very good disabled access, with a specially adapted coach; cl wkdys in Mar, Nov and Dec (exc Santa specials), and all Jan–mid-Mar, best

to ring (01643) 707650 for timetable; £8.20 full return fare. From the harbour you may be able to catch the *Waverley* (paddle steamer) or *Balmoral*, along the Bristol Channel or to Lundy Island. The clifftop Blue Anchor at the end of the B3191 has decent food and great views.

❀ ⚘ 🏛 **Monksilver** ST0736 COMBE SYDENHAM COUNTRY PARK (on the B3188) Half way through a 40-year restoration plan, 580 acres of Exmoor-edge woodland, with walks and trails, corn mill, play areas, and trout fishing. On summer Thurs they sometimes do tours of the 16th-c house. Cl Sat, and Nov–Mar; (01984) 656284, park free, charges for some features. The Notley Arms is excellent for lunch.

🏛 ★ 🖼 ❀ **Montacute** ST4917 MONTACUTE HOUSE Magnificent 16th-c honeyed stone house in beautiful little village, with a wealth of interesting tapestries, furniture, paintings and ceramics, set in rooms with decorated ceilings, ornate fireplaces and fine wood panelling. A highlight is the collection of Tudor and Jacobean paintings from the National Portrait Gallery. Impressive formal gardens. Meals, snacks, shop, disabled access to grounds only; cl am, Tues, Good Fri, and Nov–Mar; (01935) 823289; £5, £2.80 garden only; NT. In the village, features worth seeing include the Borough (a quite charming square of 2-storey houses), and Abbey Farm and the Monk's House – all that remains of the Norman priory destroyed during the Dissolution. The Phelips Arms is good for lunch.

🏚 ⚘ **Muchelney** ST4224 MUCHELNEY ABBEY The abbey was founded in the 9th c (perhaps earlier), but the well preserved ruins date from the 15th, inc part of the cloister, and the abbot's lodging with its splendidly carved fireplace. Shop, limited disabled access; cl 1–2pm, and Oct–Mar; (01458) 250664; £1.50. The tiny 14th-c priest's house opposite is worth a quick look; open pm Sun and Mon Apr–Sept; £1.50; NT. The JOHN LEACH POTTERY has a few items on display in the abbey, with the main showroom a couple of minutes' drive S; cl lunchtime, pm Sat, and Sun. Kingsbury Episcopi is handy for lunch.

★ ✿ ▥ **Nether Stowey** ST1939 An appealing large village with winding streets, handy for both Exmoor and the Quantocks, with good views over the Levels from the mound of the former Norman castle. The QUANTOCK HILLS INFORMATION CENTRE in Castle St is a valuable source of information, and the road up wooded Cockercombe gives a lovely sense of the Quantocks' feeling of peace and timelessness; it's generally the roads on the W side of the hills that give the best views. COLERIDGE COTTAGE (off the A39) Little changed since Coleridge moved here in 1796; he lived here with a pig or two, and his friends the Wordsworths resided in considerably more style not far away – the 2 families were regarded with suspicion by the local population. Open pm Tues, Weds, Thurs and Sun, Apr–Sept; (01278) 732662; £1.70; NT. The Cottage Inn at Keenthorne just E of the village is a useful lunch stop.

🚌 ✿ **Norton St Philip** ST7755 NORWOOD RARE BREEDS FARM ▣ (on the B3110) Friendly organic farm on high open land with plenty of traditional and rare breeds, nature trails, and good views. You can go right up to the animals, and watch the pigs being fed. Meals, snacks, good farm shop, disabled access; cl Oct–Mar; (01373) 834356; £3.50. The George is one of the most interesting ancient inn buildings in Britain. The B3110 has some steep, intricate views.

▥ ★ ✝ **Nunney** ST7345 CASTLE This 14th-c fort was reduced to ruins in the Civil War, but has one of the deepest moats in the country; it and its feeder stream running through the green of this quaint and quiet village are jostling with ducks. The castle's layout and round towers were supposedly modelled on France's Bastille; free. There's a small covered market place just above the stream, and nearby are 18th-c weavers' cottages. The CHURCH, as usual in so many Somerset villages,

is well worth a look.

✖ **Priston** ST6961 PRISTON MILL (Priston Mill Farm) Set in charming countryside, a working watermill once run by the monks of Bath Abbey. Good explanations of how it works, as well as play areas, pets corner, trailer rides, nature trails and a tithe barn. A relaxing place, good for families. Meals, snacks, shop; open Sun and Mon bank hols, plus pm Thurs in Aug; (01225) 423894; £2.50.

🐦 **Rode** ST8053 RODE BIRD GARDENS Huge collection of around 200 species of colourful and exotic birds flying through 17 acres of grounds, with ornamental lakes, ponds and masses of trees and shrubs. Also pets corner and woodland miniature railway (Easter–mid-Sept). Summer meals, snacks, shop (inc sales of clematis, of which they have a notable collection), disabled access; cl 25 Dec; (01373) 830326; £4.30. The Woolpack at Beckington has good food.

✝ **Somerton** ST4828 Built in light grey stone, this market town has a 17th-c market cross and fine old Georgian buildings in the quiet main square, where the Globe has decent food. ST MICHAEL'S CHURCH is stupendous, its roof supposedly created by monks of Muchelney from 7,000 fetter pieces, among which is a beer barrel – apparently a reference to Abbot Bere.

★ ▥ **South Cadbury** ST6225 An attractive scatter of golden cottages huddle around the church with its striking gargoyled tower; Waterloo Crescent is a distinctive row of farm workers' cottages built in 1815. CADBURY CASTLE and its Arthurian connection is the main draw. The legendary King and his knights are still said to sleep there, waking on Christmas Eve to ride down the hill, along what's long been known as King Arthur's Hunting Causeway, and through the village on their pilgrimage to Glastonbury. The castle, covering about 18 acres, is in fact a massive Iron Age camp: many relics have been found there – especially Roman artefacts. It's quite a steep climb, and can be muddy; stout walking shoes recommended. The nearby Sparkford Inn is a nice place for lunch. Compton Pauncefoot ST6425 just E is pretty.

✝ South Petherton ST4316 Global Village, a company importing ethnic art and low-technology products from over 30 countries, inc many in the Third World, has its HQ and 2 shops here. The CHURCH has the second-highest octagonal tower in the country.

🏠 Sparkford ST6026 HAYNES MOTOR MUSEUM (on the A359) Huge collection of gleamingly restored vintage and classic cars and motorcycles; you should be able to see some being test-driven outside. Meals, snacks, shop, disabled access; cl 25 Dec, 1 Jan; (01963) 440804; £4.50. The Sparkford Inn has a good carvery.

🐂 Staplegrove ST2126 STAPLECOMBE VINEYARDS Friendly little vineyard, with self-guided tours of the fields, then back at the house a cheery couple happy to chat. Open pm exc Sun Apr–Oct, or by appointment; (01823) 451217; free. Avoiding Taunton, the Lethbridge Arms at Bishops Lydeard does decent lunches.

✔ ❋ ⚓ Steep Holm ST2260 A small island a few miles off shore, its 50 acres a nature reserve teeming with rare plants, wildlife and historic remains. Terrific views from the rugged cliffs. You can get snacks out here, and there's a shop in former Victorian barracks, but it's not really suitable for the disabled. Boat trips to the island run from Knightstone Causeway, Weston, Apr–Oct – Mrs Rendell has dates and times on (01934) 632307; all-day trip *£12.

★ ✝ 🐂 Stogumber ST0937 Charming village with cottage gardens, an unblemished main street, and an interesting CHURCH; the White Horse has good food. BEE WORLD AND ANIMAL CENTRE 🏫 (just S of the station) Rather jolly bee farm with observation hives, useful enough exhibition, and plenty of rare breeds and farm animals, some of which children can stroke. Also play area, nature trails, and children's pony

rides. Staff are helpful and friendly, and you can see trains go past on the West Somerset Railway (combined tickets available). Good meals and snacks, shop, disabled access; cl Nov–Easter; (01984) 656545; £3.

✔ 🜲 ⚘ Stoke St Gregory ST3326 WILLOW AND WETLANDS VISITOR CENTRE (Meare Green Court, towards North Curry) shows how this area – the most important area of wetland in England – developed from marsh and swamp, and looks at its wildlife and industries, especially willow-growing and basket-making (of which there may be demonstrations). Shop, some disabled access; cl am Sun; (01823) 490249; free, guided tours (wkdys only) £2.50. ENGLISH BASKET CENTRE (Curload, towards Athelney) Produces baskets from its own willow plantations, as well as art charcoal. Also working blacksmith and display of willow sculptures. Shop, disabled access; cl pm Sat, Sun, bank hols; (01823) 698418; free. The Rose & Crown at Woodhill on the edge of the village is popular for lunch.

🏚 ⊛ ♿ ✔ ❋ Stoke sub Hamdon ST4419 The former 14th- and 15th-c PRIORY manor house has long since vanished, but its fine thatched barn and the screens, passage and Great Hall of the chantry can still be seen; free. The Fleur de Lis is a good place for lunch. Between here and Montacute is a striking folly, St Michael's Tower; it's one of three, all built by neighbouring friends in the 18th c – whenever one had a flag up it was an invitation for the others to go round for a hearty evening. HAM HILL COUNTRY PARK 140 acres of grassland and woodland, full of wildlife and plants. The hill has provided the stone for many of the villages in the area, producing that distinctive warm honey-coloured look; the views from the top of the hill are really quite splendid.

👠 🏚 Street ST4836 Clarks Shoes have been made here for quite some while now, and their SHOE MUSEUM on the High St has examples of footwear from Roman times to the present, along with machinery and advertising material. Shop, disabled access; cl

25–26 Dec; (01458) 443131; free.
Behind here CLARKS VILLAGE is an
attractively laid out factory shopping
centre, with well known names from
Jaeger to Black & Decker; some real
bargains, and plenty of snacks.

† � **Taunton** ST2324 Busy and
prosperous shopping country town
with a lively Sat cattle market. It's not
of great visual distinction; the best bit
is Hammett St, a short street of 18th-c
red brick terraces leading to the
county's biggest CHURCH, which has
an exceptionally ornate roof, lovely
pinnacled tower and lofty
Perpendicular chancel. The Tudor
house on Fore St is attractive. The
13th-c portcullised gatetower of its
former castle is now absorbed into
the County Hotel. Another part
houses the fine SOMERSET COUNTY
MUSEUM; shop, disabled access to
ground floor only; cl Sun, Mon (exc
bank hols), Good Fri, 25–26 Dec;
(01823) 355455; £2. Another old
building, thought to have been the
gatehouse for the priory that once
stood on the cricket ground, is now
the SOMERSET CRICKET MUSEUM (Priory
Bridge Rd), with bats, balls and
blazers, cards, cuttings and caps, and
a cricketing reference library too.
Snacks, shop, some disabled access;
open wkdys Apr–Sept, plus wknds
when there's a match on; (01823)
275893; 60p. Just behind Riverside Pl
the SHAKESPEARE GLASSWORKS have
demonstrations of glassblowing (not
Sun or Mon), and in Bath Pl MAKERS
is a decent craft shop selling local
hand-made crafts (cl Sun). There's a
good collection of antique shops on
East Reach (open pm Fri, Sat and
Sun). The Masons Arms in
Magdalene St is good for lunch (not
Sun).

† **Templecombe** ST7022 Ancient
village with stocks still in place; the
name comes from the medieval order
of Knights Templar, dedicated to the
protection of the Holy Sepulchre and
pilgrims to it. The CHURCH,
supposedly founded by King Alfred's
daughter, houses a 13th-c painting of
Christ, found by accident in an
outhouse 30 years ago; possibly an
early copy of the Turin Shroud,
which the Knights Templar may have
had in their possession for a while.

🏵 **Tintinhull** ST5019 TINTINHULL
HOUSE GARDEN Colourful and
attractive 1930s formal garden,
sheltered by walls and hedges, around
17th-c house with Queen Anne
façade (not open). Teas, some
disabled access; open pm Weds–Sun
May–Sept; (01935) 822545; £3.50;
NT. The Lamb has good-value food.

🏠 🏵 **Tolland** ST1131 GAULDEN
MANOR (off the B3224) Nicely
tucked-away medieval manor house
distinguished for its early
plasterwork. The gardens are
pleasant too, with a rose garden and
bog garden. Snacks, shop, plant sales,
disabled access; open pm Sun, Thurs
and bank hols May–Aug; (01984)
667213; £3.50. The Fitzhead Inn at
Fitzhead has good food.

🏠 🏵 ☖ † **Washford** ST0441
TROPIQUARIA 🔲 (on the A39 – easy to
spot by the tall radio masts) Amazing
transformation of 1930s BBC
transmitting station into an indoor
jungle with high waterfall, tropical
plants, free-flying birds and all sorts
of weird and wonderful animals – the
more dangerous ones caged. Also
radio exhibition, puppet shows (not
Fri or Sat out of high season),
landscaped gardens, and adventure
playground. Meals, snacks, shop,
disabled access (exc to aquarium); cl
winter wkdys, and all Dec and Jan
(exc school hols); (01984) 640688;
£4.25. The nearby station on the
steam line from Minehead has a little
RAILWAY MUSEUM devoted to the old
Somerset & Dorset Railway; cl
Nov–Feb; (01984) 640869; *£1.
CLEEVE ABBEY (signed S of Washford)
Remarkably well preserved 12th-c
Cistercian abbey, the gatehouse,
dormitory and refectory all in good
condition. Fine timbered roof,
detailed wall paintings and traceried
windows, and an exhibition on
monastic life. Snacks, shop, some
disabled access; cl 1–2pm, winter
Mon and Tues, 24–26 Dec, 1 Jan;
(01984) 640377; £2.40. The Notley
Arms at Monksilver is the closest
good place for a meal.

★ **Watchet** ST0743 This small

working port has fishing boats and coasters using its tidal harbour, and enough industry to keep it from being too touristy – though it's by no means unattractive. The West Somerset Hotel has good cheap food.

ᗧ **Webbington** ST3855 FORGOTTEN WORLD Romany museum and working wheelwright's shop, with brightly coloured carriages and caravans, and an Edwardian fairground. Snacks, shop, disabled access; open Fri–Sun Apr–Sept, daily July–Aug; (01934) 750841; *£2.25.

★ † 🏰 🐾 ᗧ **Wells** ST5445 With a population of only 9,500 this delightful place wouldn't normally even qualify as a big town, but in fact it's England's smallest city. The CATHEDRAL that grants it this honour is a stunning structure right in the centre, its 3 towers stretching up against the Mendip foothills. The spectacular west front is reckoned by many to be the finest cathedral façade in the country; dating from the 13th c, it carries 293 pieces of medieval sculpture. Unmissable oddities inside include the wonderful scissor-shaped inverted arches, the north transept's 14th-c clock where horsemen still joust every quarter of an hour, and the fine carvings in the south transept, inc various victims of toothache and 4 graphic scenes of an old man stealing fruit and getting what for. The embroidered stallbacks in the choir (1937–48) are a riot of colour, and the library, with documents dating back to the 10th c, at 51 metres (168 ft), is the longest medieval library building in England. Evensong is at 5.15pm wkdys (not Weds), 3pm Sun. Meals, snacks, shop, disabled access; £3 suggested donation. The 15th-c Chain Gate links the cathedral with the Vicars Close, where the Vicars Choral still live, in the original medieval houses. It's said to be one of the oldest complete medieval streets in Europe. The moated and fortified BISHOPS PALACE nearby can be approached only through the 14th-c gatehouse; it's quite dramatic going across the drawbridge. The beautiful series of buildings still has some original 13th-

c parts, notably the banqueting hall and undercroft, as well as several state rooms and a long gallery hung with portraits of former bishops. The grounds are the site of the wells that give the town its name, producing on average 150 litres (40 gallons) of water a second. Also a decent arboretum and a rather clever pair of swans, trained to ring a little bell under the gatehouse window when they're hungry (so many people feed them in summer that this isn't terribly often). Meals, snacks, shop, disabled access to ground floor; open Tues–Fri plus bank hols and pm Sun Easter–Oct, daily in Aug; (01749) 678691; £3, maybe more for special exhibitions. A Tudor building in Cathedral Green houses a good local history MUSEUM, with notable embroidery samplers, and stone figures originally on the west front of the cathedral, but now too fragile to be returned there. Disabled access to ground floor only; cl winter Mon and Tues; (01749) 673477; *£2 (ticket valid all year). There are a good few other attractive old buildings, many now used as offices and shops (inc several antique shops), and several grouped around the Market Place; the City Arms and Fountain nr here are good for lunch, and there's a big cheese shop not far away. The B3139 through Wedmore and side roads off it give a good feel of the dead flatness of the Somerset Levels.

ℛ **West Bagborough** ST1633 Tiny village well placed below the Quantocks, with a traditional working POTTERY, and fresh generous food (and comfortable bedrooms) at the Rising Sun.

ᗧ ♫ **Westhay** ST4341 PEAT MOORS VISITOR CENTRE (Shapwick Rd) In the heart of the peat-cutting area of the Somerset Levels, with an excellent exhibition on the topic, and a reconstructed Iron Age village. Craft demonstrations most summer wknds. Snacks, shop, disabled access (but no facilities); cl Nov–Mar; (01458) 860697; £1.95. You can get a joint ticket with the museums in Glastonbury. The Olde Burtle Inn over past Catcott Burtle has good fresh fish.

♨ ♄ ♪ ✝ **Weston-super-Mare**
ST3261 Friendly family seaside
resort, its Latin epithet added in the
19th c in an attempt to be one up on
the fashionable French resorts. The
dramatically named TIME MACHINE
(Burlington St) is actually a fairly
unsurprising local history museum,
focusing mainly on Victorian
domestic life, with reconstructed
shops and lots of seaside displays; it
includes adjacent Clara's Cottage, a
typical Westonian home of the 1900s
with period kitchen, parlour and
bedroom. Snacks, shop, disabled
access on ground floor only; cl 25
Dec, 1 Jan; (01934) 621028; £2
(which entitles you to as many return
visits as you like over the next year).
More local history at the HERITAGE
CENTRE on Wadham St (cl Sun; £1).
SEA LIFE CENTRE (Marine Parade)
Another in the reliable chain, right by
the beach, with walk-through
underwater tunnel, and plenty of
sharks. Meals, snacks, shop, disabled
access; cl 25 Dec; (01934) 641603;
£4.50. The seafront Pavilion
(Knightstone Parade) is a rather
stylish new family dining place, and
there are pleasant walks (and a toll
road) through the woods around the
Iron Age fort above the town. The
quietest beaches are to the N, around
Sand Bay. INTERNATIONAL HELICOPTER
MUSEUM 🔟 (on the B3146, which was
the A370) An unexpected find with
over 50 helicopters and autogyros on
display, and a realistic simulator. On
the second Sun of each month (exc
Jan and Feb) they have an Open
Cockpit Day, when some helicopters
are opened up for visitors to inspect.
Meals, snacks, shop, disabled access;
cl 25–26 Dec, 1 Jan; (01934) 635227;
*£3.

⌘ **Westonzoyland** ST3433 A pretty
village with a STEAM PUMPING STATION,
open Suns Apr–Oct, in steam first Sun
of month, static most other wks. Also
open pm Thurs Jun–Aug; £2.50
steam days, otherwise £2.

★ ✝ **Wincanton** ST7128 Fine
Georgian houses and many of the
multitude of inns and hotels survive
from the coaching era; many still have
old coach-entry gates. The CHURCH

PORCH has a medieval relief of St
Eligius. The cheerful Nog (South St)
has decent food.

♨ ⌘ ✖ **Wookey Hole** ST5347
WOOKEY HOLE CAVES AND PAPERMILL
🔟 Guided tours of half a mile of
dramatic subterranean tunnels and
caverns, using remote-controlled
lighting and special effects to
spotlight the geological features and
bring to life associated history and
myths. Just along the river the
papermill demonstrates paper
production, and also houses an
authentic Edwardian fairground,
Magical Mirror Maze and an Old
Penny Arcade. A bustling place, all
under cover, so ideal when the sun's
not shining. Meals and snacks
(readers find them a little pricey),
shop, disabled access exc to caves; cl
17–25 Dec; (01749) 672243; £6.50.
The Burcott Inn nearby is good for
lunch, and in Burcott itself there's a
working WATERMILL with several craft
shops and animals; cl Mon and Tues,
no milling tours wkdys; £2.

♨ ✝ **Yeovil** ST5516 Little to interest
visitors, but the MUSEUM OF SOUTH
SOMERSET (Hendford) is worth a look
if passing, with a good range of local
history and reconstructed Roman
and Georgian rooms (cl Sun and
Mon, plus winter Sats; free); there's
also a dry-ski centre and partly 14th-c
CHURCH.

✝ **Yeovilton** ST5422 FLEET AIR ARM
MUSEUM (Royal Naval Air Station, off
the A359) Big place concentrating on
the story of aviation at sea from
1908, and the history of the Royal
Naval Air Service. Lively displays on
the WRENS, the Falklands and Gulf
Wars, jets and helicopters, as well as
nearly 50 historic aircraft, and lots of
models, paintings, weapons and
photographs. Viewing galleries look
out over the aircraft using this busy
base. Also adventure playground,
and hi-tech flight simulator. You
could easily spend a good few hours
here. Meals, snacks, shop, disabled
access; cl 24 –26 Dec; (01935)
840565; £6.20. The Kingsdon Inn is
the best nearby place for lunch.

✝ Some of the **churches**, particularly
in the west, have very finely carved

15th- and 16th-c bench ends, with fascinating figures, beasts, fertility symbols and grotesques. The most interesting are at Bishops Lydeard ST1629 (attractive village), Combe Florey (Evelyn Waugh is buried outside), Hatch Beauchamp ST3220, Kingston St Mary ST2229 (a pretty village), Milverton ST1225 (where there's also a little pottery on the charming High St) and Stogumber ST0937; in the Quantocks Bicknoller ST1139, Broomfield ST2231, Crowcombe ST1336 and Spaxton ST2237 are all good. Many of these churches have fine oak waggon-roofs, brass candelabras and carved screens. The church at Ilminster ST3514 has a magnificent 15th-c tower, all turrets, pinnacles and gargoyles; Stogursey ST2042 has an exceptional Norman church with charming carved pew ends. Other interesting churches are at Cucklington ST7527 (13th-c, with a small side chapel dedicated to St Barbara, whose well lies further down in the village), and Limington ST5422 (with effigies of the Giverney family dating back to the 1300s).

★ Particularly **attractive villages**, all with decent pubs, include Batcombe ST6838, Brent Knoll ST3350 (another church with remarkable carved bench-ends), Combe Hay ST7359 (the road to Monkton Combe has good views), Compton Dando ST6464, Croscombe ST5844 (great 17th-c woodwork in its 15th-c church), East Coker ST5412 (T S Eliot's ashes are buried here), Evercreech ST6438, Hinton St George ST4212, Huish Episcopi ST4226, Litton ST5954, Luxborough SS9837, Mells ST7249 (marvellous church and graveyard, charming ancient inn, pleasant walks nearby), North Perrott ST4709, Norton sub Hamdon ST4615, South Stoke ST7641 (picturesque views from the steep nearby lanes), Wambrook ST2907, Waterrow ST0425, and Wellow ST7458. High Ham ST4320, Pilton ST5940, Stowell ST6822 and Winscombe ST4157 are also well worth a visit, and Stratton-on-the-Fosse ST6550 is notable for the spectacular modern (though not modern-looking) Downside Abbey. East Quantoxhead ST1343 with its archetypal duckpond, tiny church with fine oak carvings, and walks to the coast, is delightful. Staple Fitzpaine ST2618 is another pretty village with a fine pub; a quiet drive with good views loops along the S edge of Staple Hill then crosses the B3170 to run over Culmhead ST2216 (where the Holman Clavel is a good stop), along the Blackdown Hills and past the Wellington Monument.

The **lakes** in the Chew Valley – the Chew Valley Lake ST5656 itself and Blagdon Lake ST5159 – are more popular as breathing places for people living nearby than as places for visitors from afar; both are pleasant large stretches of water, with managed fishing, and the B3130 and B3114 have pleasant views. The New Inn at Blagdon ST5059 is nicely set for lunch.

Walks

Excluding Exmoor (discussed separately, in the Devon chapter), the Mendips have the county's most interesting walks – not on the top, which is mostly unremarkable farmland, but along its edges, particularly in the great limestone gorges. **Cheddar Gorge** ST4553 ☎-1 is a straightforward walk along the road. It rapidly loses its commercialised trappings, and when you reach the far end 2 worthwhile paths leave the road. On the E side is a quiet dale with 2 nature reserves, Black Rock ST4854 and Velvet Bottom ST4955. On the W side, the West Mendip Way climbs through woods and gives access to another path which skirts the top of the gorge (the views into it are hair-raising); you can also get up to this viewpoint via the Jacob's Ladder steps from the road at the west entrance to the gorge.

Ebbor Gorge ST5248 ⌒-2, altogether quieter than Cheddar Gorge, has an attractive nature trail. A good walk runs from Wookey Hole ST5347 through the Gorge to Pen Hill ST5548 for panoramic views. The **West Mendip Way** ⌒-3 (Wells to Weston-super-Mare) crosses the Mendip plateau and ascends some medium-sized hills: there are stunning views from Crook Peak ST3855, Compton Hill ST3856 and Wavering Down ST4055.

There is good walking on the northern edge, too. **Burrington Combe** ST4858 ⌒-4, an easy walk by the B3134, is a great limestone gorge which can be combined with walks up on to Black Down ST4757 for memorable views in all directions, and over the heather and cranberries to Dolebury Warren ST4558, where the site of an Iron Age hill fort marks a splendid Mendip viewpoint. Other useful starting points for the Mendips include the Crown at Churchill ST4459, the Swan at Rowberrow ST4558 (just over the Somerset border) and Ring o' Bells at Compton Martin ST5457.

Brean Down ST2958 ⌒-5, – protruding into the Bristol Channel between Weston-super-Mare and acres of holiday camps, gives the best coastal walk in east Somerset.

The **Kennet & Avon Canal** ⌒-6 has been attractively restored, with a good footpath alongside. It runs across the county from Bristol through Hanham ST6472 (where the Lock & Weir is a charmingly placed pub), Saltford ST6867 and Bath to the spectacular aqueduct at Avoncliff ST8059 (and beyond, across Wilts and into Berks).

Cadbury Camp ST4572 ⌒-7 is an Iron Age hill fort which can be reached from the Black Horse in Clapton-in-Gordano ST4773, by a lane past the church, which leads to a footbridge high over the M5. This should not be confused with the more famous Cadbury Castle down towards Yeovil.

Dundry Hill ST5566 ⌒-8 just S of Bristol's suburbs has views over the city, Chew Magna and Blagdon lakes and the Mendips. **Brent Knoll** ST3450 ⌒-9 has a path to its prominent summit from Brent Knoll village (the Red Cow here is useful).

The **cathedral walk** ⌒-10 from Croscombe ST5844 to Wells ST5445 gives unforgettable views of the cathedral.

The **Quantocks** ⌒-11 have the most for walkers in west Somerset (short of Exmoor). Their secretive quality is illustrated by the dense broad-leafed woodlands on the N side, where shady combes display splendid spring and autumn colours. The village of Holford ST1541 is a good starting point: the paths begin with helpful signposts, though you may soon get bemused by the complexity of the path junctions. Holford Combe ST1540 is reasonably easy to find, and a map will get you to the ancient hill fort site capping Dowsborough ST1639, from where a moorland track leads gently N to Holford. Another good approach is from Kilve ST1442, from where you can take a path to and along the coast, then through East Quantoxhead ST1343 to the N Quantock slopes for a remarkably varied circuit.

The less wooded western slopes have some attractive valleys enclosed by plunging slopes, with tracks along the bottom: Bicknoller ST1139 is an attractive start, and the Blue Ball at Triscombe ST1535 is another useful port of call. The moorland tops are quite a different world, where ancient trackways lead past prehistoric cairns and burial mounds; Exmoor, the Bristol Channel, South Wales and the Mendips are in sight. The tiny road from Nether Stowey ST1939 to Crowcombe ST1336 crosses the ridge and gives easy access to the moor.

The **Brendon Hills** ⌒-12 give breezy walks with long views; the Royal Oak at Luxborough SS9837 is a good base.

Castle Neroche ST2715 ⌒-13, an isolated ruined Norman fortification with more the aspect now of a hill fort than a castle, is the central feature of well marked woodland walks down towards the Blackdown Hills S of Taunton; fine views at the top. Further towards Chard, the Cotley Inn at

Wambrook ST2907 is in quiet countryside suiting both walkers and cyclists.

Ham Hill Country Park ST4817 ⌂-14 is an elevated area of old stone quarries with wide views; you can go E from here on paths past St Michael's Hill, topped by an 18th-c pepperpot tower, to Montacute ST4917, where the park of Montacute House is open to walkers.

Where to eat

Appley ST0621 GLOBE (01823) 672327 Cheerfully run unspoilt 15th-c pub with a relaxed chatty atmosphere; generous helpings of good interesting food inc adventurous daily specials and vegetarian meals, and super puddings; no smoking dining room; cl Mon lunch exc bank hols. £15|£5.

Axbridge ST4255 ALMSHOUSE BISTRO The Square (01934) 732493 Carefully restored 15th-c almshouse with flagstone floors, oak beams, stone walls, and attractive country furnishings; a good choice of imaginative food (especially the home-made pasta dishes), nice puddings, and friendly service; cl pm Sun, Mon; disabled access. £25|£5.95.

Bath ST7565 BEAUJOLAIS 5 Chapel Row, Queen Sq (01225) 423417 Bustling wine bar with naughty postcards and so forth on the walls, a conservatory area, and a small summer courtyard; enjoyable French food, and cheerful staff, cl Sun, 2 wks Jan; limited disabled access. £18.50 supper, £14.40 lunch|£5.80.

Bath ST7565 CLOS DU ROY 1 Seven Dials, Saw Close (01225) 444450 Big semi-circular room with French windows on to a balcony, and set next to the theatre; white baby grand piano (played in the evening) and a musical-theme décor; excellent French cooking (good-value set meals), lovely puddings, a proficient wine list, and pleasant service; disabled access. £27 dinner, £19.45 lunch|£5.95.

Bath ST7465 DOWER HOUSE Royal Crescent Hotel, 16 Royal Crescent (01225) 319090 Luxuriously decorated restaurant with delicious and innovative food, attractively presented, plenty for vegetarians, well chosen wine list, and excellent service; disabled access. £47 dinner, £15 2-course lunch.

Bath ST7565 HOLE IN THE WALL 16 George St (01225) 425242 Simply but attractively furnished main room plus another no smoking stylishly modern room; imaginative modern cooking from a varied menu, an excellent wine list, and good service; cl pm Sun. £31.50|£5.50.

Bath ST7565 OLD GREEN TREE 12 Green St (01225) 448259 Genuinely unspoilt pub with bustling, cheerful atmosphere in its 3 oak-panelled little rooms, a no smoking back bar, several well kept real ales, lots of malt whiskies, a nice little wine list with a dozen by the glass, and good home-made lunchtime bar food. £14.80|£4.80.

Bath ST7465 OLIVE TREE Russel St (01225) 447928 Light and airy no smoking basement restaurant in the Queensberry Hotel; stylishly simple modern décor, friendly and helpful service, super Mediterranean cooking (delicious fish and tempting puddings), and good-value wines; cl am Sun, 1 week at Christmas; partial disabled access. £35 dinner|£6.50.

Bath ST7565 RAJPOOT 4 Argyle St (01225) 466833 Exceptionally good, carefully cooked Indian food in attractively decorated restaurant, and particularly good service (you are met at the door by a colourfully uniformed doorman); used by stars of screen and stage; cl 25–26 Dec; disabled access (by arrangement). £20|£6.95.

Bath ST7565 TOXIQUE FISH 14 North Parade (01225) 445983 Elegant, stylish upmarket restaurant in vaults next to the River Avon, specialising in a superb range of fresh fish; shellfish bar and summer terrace, good service, and a comprehensive wine list; cl Sun, Mon (open all week in high season); disabled access. £35|£10 2-course lunch.

Bath ST7565 WOODS 9-13 Alfred St (01225) 314812 Handy for the Assembly

Rooms, bustling bright restaurant with horse-racing pictures; excellent set menus as well as interesting daily specials (good fish), and cheery staff; cl pm Sun, 25–26 Dec; disabled access. £19.50 dinner, £10 lunch|£6.

Beckington ST8051 WOOLPACK (01373) 831244 Relaxed and welcoming old inn with an attractive no smoking lounge, antique furnishings, a lively flagstoned public bar with a good log fire, and a cosy candlelit, no smoking dining room; good interesting food from a short, regularly changing menu, well kept real ales, decent and reasonably priced wines, and cheerful helpful, service; comfortable bdrms; cl Christmas; children over 5. £20|£7.50.

Blagdon Hill ST2217 WHITE LION (01823) 421296 Gently refurbished village pub with a wide choice of good home-made food, very pleasant service, nice china ornaments, log fire; cl pm 25 Dec; children in dining room. £15|£4.95.

Bristol ST5872 HARVEYS 12 Denmark St (0117) 927 5034 Comfortable restaurant in wine company's medieval cellars with marvellously imaginative food, good puddings, an exceptional cheese board, a great wine list, and friendly, knowledgeable staff; cl am Sat, Sun; children over 8. £42|£12.95.

Bristol ST5772 HOWARDS 1a–2a Avon Crescent, Hotwells (0117) 926 2921 Charming friendly restaurant in 2 Georgian terraced houses – smarter upstairs restaurant and more relaxed downstairs bistro, with enjoyable seasonal cooking inc set-priced meals too, and good-value wines; cl am Sat, Sun, bank hols and Christmas. £20 dinner, £18 lunch.

Bristol ST5873 MARKWICKS 43 Corn St (0117) 926 2658 Elegant restaurant in the vaults of an old bank building; delicious French and English cooking (first-class fish, lovely puddings), a carefully chosen wine list, and good friendly service. cl am Sat, Sun, Mon, 1 wk Christmas, 1 wk Easter, 2 wks Aug, bank hols. £20.50.

Bristol ST5873 MILLWARDS 40 Alfred Pl, Kingsdown (0117) 924 5026 Small candlelit, no smoking vegetarian evening restaurant with simple clean furnishings, excellent imaginative food, a decent wine list inc many organic choices, and smiling service; instead of choosing one particular dish you can have samples of each; cl Sun, Mon, 1 wk Christmas, 1 wk Easter; partial disabled access. £17.75.

Castle Cary ST6332 GEORGE (01963) 350761 Thatched coaching inn with a huge black elm mantlebeam, said to be over 1,000 yrs old, over the log fire in the beamed front bar; civilised, relaxed atmosphere, no smoking restaurant and inner no smoking bar, well kept ales, decent house wines, good-value and interesting food, and pleasant staff; bdrms. £16.50|£7.25.

Combe Hay ST7359 WHEATSHEAF (01225) 833504 Pleasantly old-fashioned rooms, sloping lawn looking down to church and ancient manor stables; wide choice of good food (lots of game and fish), and friendly staff; summer barbecues; cl 25–26 Dec; disabled access. £25|£5.50.

Cranmore ST6643 STRODE ARMS (01749) 880450 Neatly kept former farmhouse with charming country furnishings, newspapers to read, and log fires in handsome fireplaces; generous helpings of good interesting food in the bar and restaurant, well kept real ales, and decent wines; cl winter pm Sun; children in restaurant only; disabled access. £17.75|£4.25.

Dowlish Wake ST3713 NEW INN (01460) 52413 17th-c stone pub with hops and old-fashioned furnishings in a spotlessly kept dark-beamed bar, woodburning stove in inglenook fireplace, and a no smoking family room; good enjoyable bar food, well kept real ales and Perry's ciders, pleasant back garden; no food winter pm Sun; children in family room; disabled access. £18|£4.50.

East Woodlands ST7944 HORSE & GROOM (01373) 462802 Small civilised pub, on the edge of Longleat estate, with a small pleasant bar, comfortable little lounge, big no smoking dining conservatory; very well presented; particularly good food with up to 6 different vegetables served on a side plate, a fine choice of real ales, good wines by the glass, helpful service, and seats in the attractive garden. £17|£6.

Fitzhead ST1128 FITZHEAD INN (01823) 400667 Cosy village pub in peaceful countryside with consistently good and well presented food from an imaginative menu, well kept ales, a particularly good choice of wines, a pleasant relaxed atmosphere, and genial attentive service. £22|£11.

Knapp ST2925 RISING SUN (01823) 490436 Fine 15th-c longhouse with friendly atmosphere, stripped beams and stonework, and inglenook fireplaces; nice food with a strong emphasis on fish, wicked puddings; decent bedrooms; some disabled access. £25|£5.

Langley Marsh ST0729 THREE HORSESHOES (01984) 623763 Unpretentious red sandstone pub with short, changing choice of imaginative food (inc vegetarian dishes and always a game casserole), vegetables from their own garden, no chips or fried food, a wide choice of often unusual real ales, farm ciders; no fruit machines or pool tables; skittle alley, beer garden, and sloping back garden with play area and farmland views; good nearby walks; children must be well behaved. £15|£4.95.

Long Sutton ST4725 DEVONSHIRE ARMS (01458) 2411271 Imposing solid stone inn with tall gables and mullioned windows, a cosily old-fashioned front bar, smart restaurant with a friendly relaxed atmosphere, and a flagstoned back bar; well kept beers, decent wines, good coffee, and interesting, daily changing food; bdrms. £17.75|£5.75.

Monksilver ST0737 NOTLEY ARMS (01984) 656217 Relaxed and friendly pub with characterful beamed L-shaped bar, candles and fresh flowers, and woodburning stoves; particularly good popular food, interesting puddings, well kept beers, and neatly kept cottagey garden running down to a swift clear stream; cl last wk Jan/1st wk Feb; disabled access. £16.50|£5.95.

Norton St Philip ST7755 GEORGE (01373) 834224 Remarkable building that has been a pub for 600 years, with fine half-timbered and galleried back courtyard, an external Norman stone stair-turret, simple furnishings and lofty beams, open fires, and warmly friendly staff; very popular bar food (daily specials are the thing), and well kept real ales. £20|£9.95.

Oldbury-on-Severn ST6292 ANCHOR Church St (01454) 413331 Attractively modernised village pub with good-value daily-changing bar food, enterprising puddings, friendly service, no smoking dining room; busy wknds, cl 25–26 Dec; children in dining room and garden only; disabled access. £15|£5.50.

Rudge ST8251 FULL MOON (01373) 830936 Attractive rustic pub with friendly licensees, a lot of character in the different rooms, a gently upmarket atmosphere, small flagstoned dining room (and a separate plush restaurant); generous helpings of good bar food inc a bargain 3-course set lunchtime and early evening meal, and well kept real ales; disabled access; comfortable bdrms. £20|£5.

Shepton Mallet ST6143 BLOSTINS 29 Waterloo Rd (01749) 343648 Friendly little candlelit evening bistro with consistently good and interesting food inc lovely puddings, and fairly priced wines; cl Sun, Mon, 2 wks Jan, 2 wks Jun. £19.95.

Wambrook ST2907 COTLEY (01460) 62348 Bustling country pub with a relaxed, happy yet rather smart atmosphere, 2-room no smoking dining area, a no smoking separate restaurant, and open fires; good really enjoyable food (especially daily specials for large and smaller helpings), well kept real ales, a decent choice of wines; children's play area in the garden, and lots of nearby walks; nice bdrms; disabled access. £20.50|£4.95.

West Huntspill ST3044 CROSSWAYS (01278) 783756 Popular, spacious dining pub with buoyant atmosphere, good food (especially puddings), and decent wines; comfortable bdrms; cl 25 Dec; disabled access. £14|£4.50.

Weston-super-Mare ST3261 REFLECTIONS 22 Boulevard (01934) 622454 Informal family-run restaurant, a good but ordinary café at lunchtimes (exc Sun, when decent set lunch), but transformed Thurs, Fri and Sat evenings with elaborate and well presented high-quality meals; cl pm Sun–Weds, 1 Jan for 2 wks, 1st wk June; disabled access. £23.50|£4.25.

Special thanks to Claire Taylor, A Cartlidge, Rita and Brian Crawley, Dr and Mrs A K Clarke, M G Hart, Mr Bone, Mrs Yasmyne Thorner.

SOMERSET CALENDAR

Some of these dates were provisional as we went to press. Please check information with the numbers provided.

JANUARY

1 **Bath** New Year's Day Viennese Spectacular at the Forum (01225) 477761; **Dunster** New Year's Day Street Celebrations (01643) 821314

FEBRUARY

20 **Bath** International Literature Festival – *till Sat 28* (01225) 462231

APRIL

11 **Dunster** Easter Egg Hunt at Dunster Castle (01643) 821314

17 **Sparkford** Classic Cars at Haynes Motor Museum – *till Sat 18* (01963) 440804

30 **Minehead** Hobby Horse Celebrations: old May Day custom, Hobby Horse dances around the streets – *till 4 May* (01872) 74057

MAY

2 **Bath** Spring Flower Show at Royal Victoria Park – *till Mon 4* (01225) 462231; **Shepton Mallet** South West Custom and Classic Bike Show at the Royal Bath and West Showground – *till Sun 3* (01749) 823260; **Yeovil** Abbey Hill Steam Rally at the Showground – *till Mon 4* (01935) 863603

7 **Badminton** Horse Trials at Badminton House – *till Sun 10* (01454) 218272

8 **Cheddar** Fair and Folk Festival – *till Sun 10* (01934) 742320; **Minehead** Spring Steam Gala at West Somerset Railway – *till Sun 10* (01643) 704996

9 **Claverton** American Civil War Encampment and Drill Displays at the American Museum – *till Sun 10* (01225) 460503

15 **Bath** International Music Festival – *till Sun 31* (01225) 462231; **Bath** Balloon Fiesta at Royal Victoria Park – *till Sun 17* (01225) 396021

16 **Cannington** Agricultural and Horticultural College Open Day (01278) 655000; **Claverton** Shaker Furniture Exhibition at the American Museum – *till 18 Oct* (01225) 460503

17 **Dunster** Spring Plant Fair at Dunster Castle (01643) 821314

20 **Chard** Festival of Women in Music – *till Mon 25* (01935) 422884

23 **Bath** Classic Car Rally at Royal Victoria Park – *till Sun 24* (01225) 396021

24 **Dunster** Festival (01643) 821802; **Watchet** Spring Festival (01984) 631781

25 **Long Ashton** North Somerset Show at Ashton Court (0117) 964 3498

27 **Shepton Mallet** Royal Bath and West Show at the Royal Bath and West Showground – *till Sat 30* (01749) 822200

30 **Bath** International Kite Festival at Lansdown Playing Fields – *till Sun 31* (01225) 477761

SOMERSET CALENDAR

JUNE

6 South Petherton Folk Festival – *till Sun 7* (01935) 432966

10 Dunster Open-air Shakespeare at Dunster Castle – *till Thurs 11* (01643) 821314

13 Claverton North American Indian Weekend at the American Museum – *till Sun 14* (01225) 460503; **Crewkerne** Carnival – *till Sun 14* (01460) 76363

14 Long Ashton Bristol Motor Show and Historic Transport Pageant at Ashton Court Estate (0117) 934 3542

19 Great Elm Classical Music Festival – *till 5 July* (01373) 812383

26 Bath Balloon Fiesta at Royal Victoria Park – *till Sun 28* (01225) 396021; **Glastonbury** Festival – *till Sun 28* (01749) 890470

28 Weston-super-Mare Coast to Coast Vintage Motorcycle Rally (01934) 634993

JULY

4 Bristol St Paul's Carnival (0117) 944 4176; **Claverton** Independence Day at the American Museum – *till Sun 5* (01225) 460503; **Glastonbury** Anglican Pilgrimage at the Abbey (01458) 832267; **Minehead** Friends of Thomas the Tank Engine at West Somerset Railway – *till Sun 5* (01643) 704996; **Shepton Mallet** Truckfest at the Royal Bath and West Showground – *till Sun 5* (01775) 768661

5 Glastonbury Roman Catholic Pilgrimage at the Abbey (01458) 832267; **Watchet** Carnival (01984) 632291

10 Somerton Arts Festival – *till Sat 18* (01458) 273763

12 Castle Cary Cavalcade of Motoring (01963) 350700

17 Wells Open-air Concert: jazz, big band and fireworks at the Cathedral – *till Sat 18* (01749) 672986

18 Low Ham Somerset Steam Spectacular – *till Sun 19* (01458) 448638; **Yeovilton** Air Day at RNAS Yeovilton (01935) 471279

25 Langport Living History Day at Cocklemoor – *till Sun 26* (01458) 252180

31 Weston-super-Mare Helicopter Fly-in: static displays, flights, variety show, fair – *till 2 Aug* (01934) 822524

AUGUST

1 Minehead Vintage Steam Rally at West Somerset Railway – *till Sun 2* (01643) 704996

2 Ilminster Classical Guitar Festival at Dillington House – *till Fri 7* (01460) 55866

6 Long Ashton Balloon Fiesta Night Glow: fireworks and hot air balloons glowing in time to music at Ashton Court Estate (0117) 953 5884

7 Long Ashton Balloon Fiesta at Ashton Court Estate – *till Sun 9* (0117) 953 5884

8 Chippenham Opera in the Garden at Dyrham Park, *La Traviata* – *till Sun 9* (01985) 843601; **Claverton** French Indian Wars at the American Museum – *till Sun 9* (01225) 460503

15 Brompton Regis Show and Gymkhana (01398) 371438

16 Weston-super-Mare Raft Race: Grand Pier to Knightstone Causeway (01934) 634993

18 Bath Shakespeare Festival at the Theatre Royal – *till Sat 29* (01225) 477761

20 Priddy Sheep Fair: colourful event (01749) 677667

SOMERSET CALENDAR

AUGUST cont

21 **Dunster** Show (01398) 341490; **Glastonbury** Open-air Fireworks Concert at Glastonbury Abbey – *till Sat 22* (01749) 890470

28 **Glastonbury** Children's Festival – *till Mon 31* (01458) 834484

30 **Bristol** Jazz on King Street – *till Mon 31* (0117) 927 7137

SEPTEMBER

5 **Shepton Mallet** National Amateur Gardening Show at the Royal Bath and West Showground – *till Mon 7* (01749) 822200

7 **Weston-super-Mare** Golf Week – *till Sun 13* (01934) 634993

11 **Minehead** Steam Weekend at West Somerset Railway – *till Sun 13* (01643) 704996

12 **Claverton** Civil War Weekend at the American Museum – *till Sun 13* (01225) 460503; **Shepton Mallet** Countryside Cavalcade: country show at the Royal Bath and West Showground – *till Sun 13* (01458) 446645

13 **Ansford** Kite Festival (01963) 350408

15 **Brompton Regis** Show and Gymkhana (01398) 371438

16 **Frome** Cheese Show (01373) 463600

19 **Frome** Carnival (01373) 467271

26 **Wellington** Carnival (01823) 662339

30 **Bridgwater** St Matthew's Fair: sale of sheep and ponies *on Wed 30*, street traders and funfair daily – *till Oct 3* (01278) 427652

OCTOBER

3 **Castle Cary** Carnival (01935) 813101; **Weston-super-Mare** Speed Trials and Vintage Sprint – *till Sun 4* (01934) 626838

10 **Chard** Carnival (01460) 63576

16 **Bath** Beer Festival at the Pavilion – *till Sat 17* (01225) 477761

17 **Taunton** Illuminated Carnival and Cider Barrel Rolling Race (01823) 286137

29 **Dunster** Ghost Tour at Dunster Castle – *till Sat 31* (01643) 821314; **Hinton St George** Punkey Night – Lantern Parade (01460) 73500

NOVEMBER

3 **Weston-super-Mare** Western National Chrysanthemum Exhibition at the Winter Gardens – *till Wed 4* (01934) 510151

5 **Bath** Fireworks at the Recreation Ground (01225) 477761; **Bath** Mozart Festival – *till Sun 15* (01225) 477761; **Bridgwater** Guy Fawkes Illuminated Carnival: one of Europe's most spectacular parades with floats up to 30-metres (100 ft) long with thousands of lights (01278) 429288

7 **North Petherton** Guy Fawkes Illuminated Carnival (see Bridgwater above)

9 **Burnham-on-Sea** Guy Fawkes Illuminated Carnival (see Bridgwater above)

11 **Shepton Mallet** Guy Fawkes Illuminated Carnival (see Bridgwater above)

13 **Wells** Guy Fawkes Illuminated Carnival (see Bridgwater above)

14 **Glastonbury** Guy Fawkes Illuminated Carnival (see Bridgwater above)

16 **Weston-super-Mare** Guy Fawkes Illuminated Carnival (see Bridgwater above)

DECEMBER

4 **Bath** Handel's *Messiah* at the Abbey – *till Sat 5* (01225) 477761

5 **Dunster** Father Christmas at Dunster Castle (01643) 821314

STAFFORDSHIRE

Underrated and good value, with interesting and enjoyable days out and some lovely countryside.

Less well known as a holiday area than neighbouring Derbyshire, this county actually offers some very attractive days out. Alton Towers is enormous fun for families, with a very wide and constantly updated range of amusements, and children also enjoy the working farm at Amerton (which is free), the friendly steam railway at Blythe Bridge (good value) and – perhaps surprisingly – the garden centre at Eccleshall, which has lots going on for them. Shugborough and Weston Park at Weston under Lizard are splendid great houses in fine grounds, with plenty of family appeal. The Potteries around Stoke-on-Trent are full of industrial museums and showplaces that will fascinate anyone even remotely interested in china; one or two of these have a very wide appeal, even for children.

Some parts of Staffordshire's countryside are delightful. In the north-east, there are beautiful walks and drives in the Peak District, which here includes glorious Dove Dale, the Manifold Valley and Churnet Valley. Further south, industry is increasingly dominant, but even here Cannock Chase has miles of fine landscape, and the canal network has some particularly attractive stretches. The county has a good many charming villages.

Where to stay

Betley SJ7548 ADDERLEY GREEN FARM Heighley Castle Lane, Betley, Crewe CW3 9BA (01270) 820203 *£32; 3 rms, 1 with bthrm. Georgian farmhouse on a big dairy farm, with good breakfasts in the homely dining room, and a large garden; fishing on an adjoining farm; cl Christmas and New Year; children over 5.

Caverswall SJ9542 CAVERSWALL CASTLE Caverswall, Stoke-on-Trent ST11 9EA (01782) 393239 £70; 3 oak-panelled rms with four-posters. Historic castle dating from 1270, with turrets, dungeon, portcullis and moat; lots of atmosphere, fine panelling and paintings, comfortable, restful day rooms, grand dining room, and a big billiard room; indoor swimming pool and 2 lakes for fishing; cl Dec–Jan; disabled access; self-catering in restored stone turrets.

Cheadle SK0044 LEY FIELDS FARM Leek Rd, Cheadle, Stoke-on-Trent ST10 2EF (01538) 752875 *£18; 3 rms. Listed Georgian farmhouse on a working dairy farm, in lovely countryside with lots of walks; traditional furnishings in both the lounge and dining room, good home cooking, and a friendly welcome; cl Christmas and New Year.

Eccleshall SJ8328 ST GEORGE Castle St, Eccleshall, Stafford ST21 6DF (01785) 850300 *£70w, plus special breaks; 10 rooms. Friendly little hotel with an open fire in the relaxed bar, ales brewed in their own microbrewery, and good food in the bistro; quite a few things to do nearby.

Greendale SK0445 OLD FURNACE FARM Greendale, Cheadle, Stoke-on-Trent ST10 3AP (01538) 702442 £50; 2 big comfortable rms with good bthrms. Modernised farmhouse surrounded by lovely countryside; with a homely and relaxed atmosphere, log fire in the lounge, big tasty breakfasts, and very friendly owners; self-catering also; cl Christmas and New Year.

Oakamoor SK0544 BANK HOUSE Farley Lane, Oakamoor, Stoke-on-Trent ST10 3BD (01538) 702810 *£52; 4 lovely big rms. Carefully restored country home in neat gardens on the edge of the Peak District National Park and with lovely views; log fire in the comfortable drawing room, library, piano in the inner hall, and most enjoyable food using home-grown and local produce – super home-made breads, brioches, pastries, jams and marmalade at breakfast; friendly dog and cats; lots to do nearby; cl Christmas wk.

Oakamoor SK0544 TENEMENT FARM Three Lows, Ribden, Oakamoor, Stoke-on-Trent ST10 3BW (01538) 702333 £45; 8 rms with showers. Comfortable, no smoking house on a traditional beef and sheep farm surrounded by fine countryside; with an airy, homely lounge, licensed bar, and a sunny conservatory; also self-catering cottage; cl Nov–Mar.

Rolleston on Dove SK2327 BROOKHOUSE HOTEL Brookside, Rolleston on Dove, Burton upon Trent DE13 9AA (01283) 814188 *£99, plus wknd breaks; 21 comfortable rms with Victorian brass or four-poster beds. Handsome, ivy-covered, William and Mary brick building in 5 acres of lovely gardens; with comfortable, antique-filled rooms, and good food in the elegant little dining room; children over 12; disabled access.

Warslow SK0858 GREYHOUND Warslow, Buxton SK17 0JN (01298) 84249 £33; 4 clean and comfortable rms with shared bthrms. Warm, welcoming atmosphere in this slated stone inn handy for the Peak District; generous helpings of home-made food inc hearty breakfasts, and live Sat evening entertainment; cl 24–25 Dec; children over 12.

Wetton SK1055 OLDE ROYAL OAK Wetton, Ashbourne DE6 2AF (01335) 310287 *£35, plus wknd breaks; 4 rms. Shuttered, old stone village inn in lovely NT walking country; with a warm and cheerful welcome, an attractive older part that leads into a more modern-feeling area, open fires, country furniture, sun lounge overlooking a small garden, decent food, and nice breakfasts; children by arrangement.

To see and do

STAFFORDSHIRE FAMILY ATTRACTION OF THE YEAR

☺ 🎱 **Alton** SK0742 ALTON TOWERS (off the B5032) Every year this 200-acre giant is Britain's top paid attraction, and one of the reasons for its continued success is that they're never content to rest on their laurels. New attractions are added all the time, with the latest being a gondola ride called Ripsaw that spins you round 3 complete loops before leaving you dangling 15 metres (50 ft) above ground – accompanied by jets of water from handily placed fountains. They promise a new 'world first' ride when they re-open for this season, but weren't giving any clues as to what it might be. The last time they were so cagey the result was Nemesis, which whisks you round unfeasible angles at breakneck speeds, at a greater G-force than that faced by astronauts during a space shuttle launch. Younger children aren't left out: in the last few years they've deliberately set out to appeal to whole families rather than just daredevil teenagers, and succeeded in this rather well. Storybook Land for example has quite a range of gentler rides aimed at children of up to around 7; toddlers love the singing barn. Most of the thrill rides are located in Forbidden Valley, while in between are dozens of other distractions, from log flumes and live shows such as Peter Rabbit on Ice, to rowing boats and lovely extensive gardens. There's even a splendidly zany (but thoroughly comfortable) hotel, with a bizarre cross between a galleon and a hot-air balloon hanging in the lobby, and a room that keeps dishing out chocolate. Expect queues at some of the more popular rides – on a summer afternoon an hour's wait for Nemesis is not at all uncommon; best to leave it till as late in the day as you can, when the queues should have shortened. Other rides have an average wait of around 10 minutes. It's not a cheap place to visit, and you'll need the whole of the day and some fairly organised planning to get the most out of it, but the presentation and facilities are excellent – if you don't normally like theme parks you may be pleasantly surprised. Meals, snacks, shops, disabled access (for most rides too); cl early Nov–mid-Mar; (01538) 702200; £18.50 (£14.50 children 4 –13). A family ticket for 2 adults and 2 children is £56, a saving of £10, but it has to be booked and paid for a week in advance.

🏵 Biddulph SJ8858 BIDDULPH GRANGE GARDEN (Grange Rd) Notable High Victorian garden, extensively restored; divided by its founder into a number of smaller themed gardens to house specimens from all over world. Meals, snacks, shop; cl am wkdys, all Mon (exc bank hols), Tues, and Nov–Mar (exc wknds Nov–mid-Dec); (01782) 517999; £4 (£2 Nov and Dec); NT. You can get a joint ticket with Little Moreton Hall, 6 miles away in Cheshire.

🚂 Blythe Bridge SJ9540 FOXFIELD STEAM RAILWAY 5 miles through scenic countryside; a return ticket gives unlimited travel for the whole day (exc during special events). Staff are particularly friendly, and there's a collection of locomotives and rolling stock. Open wknds and bank hols Apr–Sept; (01782) 396210; £3.50. The Izaak Walton at Cresswell is handy for a good lunch.

↓T 🏚 🍴 Burton upon Trent SK2423 Dominated by its connections with the brewing industry, and the BASS MUSEUM (Horninglow St) explores this topic in some detail – with an emphasis on Bass and the company's shire horses (who can take you on a ride round the town). You can tour the brewery (no under-13s). Summer special events, and brass band concerts every 4th Sun lunchtime. Meals, snacks, shop, disabled access; cl 25–26 Dec, 1 Jan; (01283) 511000; £3.75. By contrast, the little Burton Bridge Brewery shows brewing at the very opposite end of the scale. The Queen's Hotel in Bridge Street is a comfortable place for lunch, as is the

Marquis Suite carvery at the New Talbot Hotel on Anglesey Rd; the Boat House at Stapenhill has river and wetland views (boat trips leave on the hour from the ferry bridge from midday onwards in summer). Nearby Rangemore SK1822 has a good GARDEN CENTRE, with farm animals for children.

🐾 ❋ Cannock Chase SK0017 Miles of lovely countryside and woodland, threaded with quiet side roads; dotted around the 17,000 acres are Iron Age hill forts, nature trails, streams, pools and springs, and lovely spots for picnics or dramatic views. There's an information centre at Marquis Drive, and decent campsites. See also **Walks** section below. The canalside Moat House at Acton Trussell SJ9318 does good food.

! Cauldon SK0749 Notable for its pub, the YEW TREE; a very unpretentious place packed with an extraordinary and delightfully higgledy-piggledy collection of remarkable bygones, especially mechanical music.

🏰 ❋ Chartley Castle SK0128 (just over 6m W of Uttoxeter) A fine old ruin, with good views.

✗ 🐾 🐾 Cheddleton SJ9752 FLINT MILL Fully preserved 17th- and 18th-c watermills, with a little museum; shop; cl am most wkdys, 25–26 Dec, 1 Jan; free. Readers praise the OLD SCHOOL CRAFT CENTRE nearby; it has a pleasant tearoom. CHURNET VALLEY RAILWAY (Station Rd) Small steam locomotive museum in a Victorian station building, with occasional short steam and diesel runs. Snacks, shop; open wknds Easter–mid-Oct,

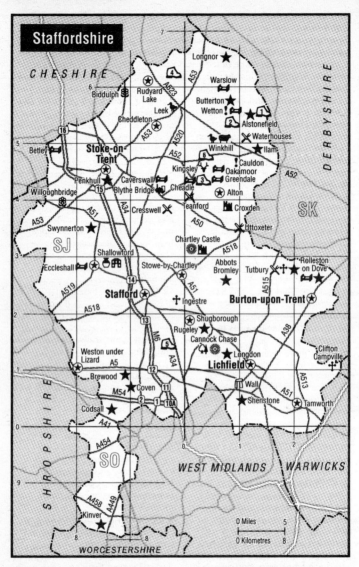

plus Weds in Aug and for various special events (inc in Dec); (01538) 360522; from £2.90 (£1 when no trains running). The Boat does decent lunches, with pleasant canal walks from it.

Croxden SK0639 ABBEY RUINS in quiet surroundings, with some towering arches surviving. The Raddle at Hollington is a good family country pub.

Eccleshall SJ8328 FLETCHERS GARDEN CENTRE (Bridge Farm, Stone Rd) Plenty to amuse children, inc an adventure playground, falconry displays, an aquatic centre, animals, crazy golf and (summer wknds and bank hols) a miniature railway. The St George (Castle St) has good home cooking, and on the other side of town, the Star, out at Copmere End, is prettily set overlooking the lake.

✌ **Kingsley** SK0147 WILDAID 🔳 (Sprinks Lane) Dedicated wildlife welfare centre, over the past few years saving the lives of hundreds of animals and birds. Conservation is their main priority, but there's plenty for visitors. Snacks, shop; open for guided tours only, 2.30pm Apr–Oct, plus 11am July–Sept, or by appointment (no under 5s); (01538) 754784; *£2.50. The Cross, in scenic surroundings along the A52 on Cauldon Lowe, does decent food.

🌿 **Leek** SJ9856 Nearby Coombe Valley has an RSPB BIRD RESERVE; shop, disabled access; free. The A53 high moorland road N has nice views, and E of here, the B5053 gives an excellent impression of the dales country (the Jervis Arms at Onecote is a good family stop).

★ ✝ ⸙ ♫ ❊ **Lichfield** SK1109 The attractive centre is largely pedestrianised, with many 18th-c and older buildings among the more modern shops (and antique shops). The CATHEDRAL, with its 3 graceful spires and close with lovely buildings around it, is magnificent inside, and its west front is memorable, especially at dusk or in the dark when shadows seem to bring the profusion of statues to life. Wonderful illuminated gospels in the chapter house. SAMUEL JOHNSON BIRTHPLACE MUSEUM (Breadmarket St) Dr Johnson was born here in 1709; the house is now furnished in period-style, with many mementos of him. Shop; cl Sun Nov–Jan; (01543) 264972; £1.20. There's a decent HERITAGE EXHIBITION in a sympathetically restored chapel site on Market Sq (cl 25–26 Dec, 1 Jan; *£1.30), and you may be able to go up to the viewing platform in the spire, which has splendid views of the surrounding countryside (£1). The Pig & Truffle (Tamworth St) is a good dining pub, while the Queen's Head (Queen St) has an amazing choice of cheeses.

⚓ 🏄 🌿 **Rudyard Lake** SJ9558 Though man-made it's perhaps one of Staffordshire's prettiest sights; you can hire a boat, there's a miniature railway (Mar–Oct), and the muddy marshland provides a haven for wading birds. The meadows and forested slopes above are pleasant for walks and picnics.

🏠☕ **Shallowford** SJ8729 IZAAK WALTON COTTAGE (Worston Lane) Smartly re-thatched home of the author of *The Compleat Angler*, with displays on the development of angling, a period herb garden and picnic orchard. Shop, limited disabled access; cl Mon (exc bank hols), and Nov–Mar; (01785) 760278; £1.60. The Worston Mill at Little Bridgeford is attractive for lunch.

🏠☕ 🐾 🐎 **Shugborough** SJ9922 SHUGBOROUGH ESTATE (off the A513) Imposing ancestral home of the Earls of Lichfield, begun in the late 17th c and enlarged in the 18th. Magnificent state rooms, restored working kitchens, an interesting marionette collection, and an exhibition of the present Earl's photography. The park has a variety of unusual neo-classical monuments, a working rare-breeds farm, and a restored corn mill. Meals, snacks, shop, disabled access; open Easter–Sept, plus wknds in Oct; (01889) 881388; entry to estate £1.50, museum and servants' quarters £3.50, house £3.50, farm £3.50; NT. An all-in ticket is quite expensive at £8 – better value on one of their special event days, when there are more activities (such as hands-on Victorian cookery displays) for no extra cost. The ancient Holly Bush, up in the pretty village of Salt (off the A51 N), is a charming place for lunch.

🏠 🏰 📷 ⚜ **Stafford** SJ9223 Greengate St has what's said to be the biggest timber-framed house in the country, built with local oak in 1595; period room settings and an information centre. Just SW of town are the remains of the Norman CASTLE, rebuilt in the Gothic Revival style in the early 19th c, then allowed to fall into disrepair. Good visitor centre, and a medieval herb garden. Teas Sun only, shop, disabled access to visitor centre; (01785) 57698; cl Mon (exc bank hols), 25–26 Dec, 1 Jan; £1.60. SHIRE HALL GALLERY (Market Sq)

Handsome former county hall with exhibitions of art, craft and photography, and a good craft shop. Cl Sun and bank hols; (01785) 278345; free. The Malt & Hops (A34/A449 roundabout) and Stafford Arms (nr the station) are useful for something to eat.

☎ ⛅ ✖ ⅃⊤ ▣ 🏠 **Stoke-on-Trent** SJ8745 THE POTTERIES These are 5 linked towns within this conurbation that still produce some of the finest china and pottery in the country. You can tour several of the factories, and most have museums or a visitor centre; a good local bus service connects them all, taking you through a memorable urban landscape, the buildings clinging to small steep hills. GLADSTONE POTTERY MUSEUM ▦ (Uttoxeter Rd, Longton) Particularly engrossing, a complete Victorian pottery made much more appealing to families over the last few years, with lively demonstrations and explanations. It's very much hands-on, and even hands-in – they're quite keen to get your fingers round the clay. It's quite possible to spend up to half a day here. Meals, snacks, shop, disabled access; cl Christmas; (01782) 319232; £3.75. ROYAL DOULTON VISITOR CENTRE (Nile St, Burslem) Potted history of the famous china company, with craft demonstrations, and a well displayed collection of Royal Doulton figures. Factory tours wkdys at 10.30am and 1.15pm, booking recommended; no under 10s. Good shop, disabled access to visitor centre only; cl Christmas, and no tours on factory and bank hols – best to check first; (01782) 292434; visitor centre and tour £5.50, visitor centre only £2.75. SPODE (Church St, Stoke) The birthplace of fine bone china, this is the oldest manufacturing ceramic factory in the Potteries. The museum has rare and precious pieces, especially in the beautifully laid out Blue Room, and you can have a go at making a piece yourself. Meals, snacks, factory shop, disabled access; no tours pm Fri or wknds, though shop and visitor centre open wknds; tours by appointment, (01782)

744011; £3.75 inc factory tour, or £2 just visitor centre and museum. WEDGWOOD VISITOR CENTRE (Barlaston) The story of that favourite item on wedding lists; art gallery, museum, and a reconstruction of Wedgwood's original 18th-c Etruria workshops. Meals, snacks, shop, disabled access; cl 25–26 Dec, 1 Jan; (01782) 204141; *£3.25. ETRURIA INDUSTRIAL MUSEUM (Lower Bedford St, Etruria) Based around the only surviving steam-powered potters' mill in the country, grinding materials right up to 1972. It's been well restored, and there's a working blacksmith. A new visitor centre is due to open this year. Museum open Weds–Sun all year (exc Christmas), engine in steam one wknd each month Apr–Dec, usually the 1st, but best to check; (01782) 287557; £1.50. CITY MUSEUM AND ART GALLERY (Bethesda St, Hanley) Excellent: more pottery and porcelain, plus other local history exhibits. Meals, snacks, shop, disabled access; cl am Sun, 25 Dec–1 Jan; (01782) 232323; free. FORD GREEN HALL (Smallthorne) An interesting little 17th-c house, open pm Sun–Thurs. On the 2nd Sun of the month Oct–Mar, they have informal performances of period music; (01782) 233195; £1.50. The Plough (off the A53, opposite the festival site in Etruria) is our current lunch recommendation.

🍴 ✖ ♈ 🐄 **Stowe by Chartley** SK0027 AMERTON WORKING FARM Working dairy farm with milking at 4pm, farm shop, trails, garden centre, craft workshops, Wildlife Rescue Centre and a little steam railway (Sun and bank hols Apr–Oct). Meals and snacks (with cream and ice-cream made on the premises), shop, disabled access; cl 25–26 Dec; (01889) 270294. This busy place stands out all the more because admission is free (£1 for wildlife centre and train). The Plough opposite is handy for lunch.

🏠 🏰 ✝ ☺ 🏠 **Tamworth** SK2004 A decent town trail links a number of historic buildings; there's also a unique indoor ski slope with real snow. TAMWORTH CASTLE (off Market

St) Glorious mixture of architectural styles from the original Norman motte and bailey walls through the Elizabethan timbered hall to the fine Jacobean state apartments. Perhaps more museum than historic home, but plenty to see, with a fair amount to please children. Shop, disabled access to ground floor; cl am Sun, 24–26 Dec; (01827) 63563; £3.40. ST EDITHA'S CHURCH nearby has windows by William Morris. DRAYTON MANOR PARK AND ZOO 🎟 (discount voucher valid not for admission but only to get 1 free ride wristband for every 2 bought at the full fee; off the A4091 S) Popular theme park, with 50 rides and attractions inc the zoo, and Europe's only stand-up roller-coaster. Meals, snacks, shop, disabled access; cl Nov–Mar; £3 entry to park, rides extra, or £9.50 for a wristband giving unlimited rides. The good Twycross Zoo is a few miles E, just over the Leics border.

🏛 **Wall** SK1006 ROMAN SITE (Watling St) An important military base from around 50AD; excavations began in the 19th c and revealed one of the most complete Roman bath-houses in the country. Good audio-tour, and finds from the area. Shop; cl 1–2pm, and all Nov–Mar; (01543) 480768; £1.50. The Black Bull at Shenstone is useful for lunch.

🏠 🖼 🏵 **Weston under Lizard** SJ8010 WESTON PARK (just off the A5) 🎟 (discount voucher not valid on bank hols, nor on any special event day noted in their leaflet) Striking, richly decorated, 17th-c house, with a fine collection of paintings inc works by Van Dyck, Rubens, Gainsborough and Constable, and letters by Disraeli that still somehow catch the imagination. The deer park and grounds, landscaped by Capability Brown, feature a restored 18th-c terrace garden, brightly planted broderie garden, and interesting trees and shrubs; in the last century it took 37 gardeners to look after it all. Also a play area, pets corner, and a miniature railway through the woodland. Meals, snacks, shop, some disabled access; open Easter, then wknds and bank hols May–mid-Sept, plus Tues–Thurs mid-Jun–Aug, and daily in summer hols (exc cl 17–18 Aug); (01952) 850207; £5, £3.50 park and gardens only. The Bell at Tong is a reliable food pub; there are several interesting places close by, just over the Shrops border.

🏵 **Willoughbridge** SJ7540 DOROTHY CLIVE GARDEN (A51) Woodland gardens created by the late Colonel Harry Clive in memory of his wife; at their best perhaps in spring and early summer, but lovely all year. Rhododendrons, azaleas, old roses, watergarden and rock garden. Snacks, disabled access; cl Nov–Mar; (01630) 647237; £2.70. The Falcon in Woore does good food.

🐾 🐦 **Winkhill** SK0651 BLACKBROOK WORLD OF BIRDS 🎟 Unusual species and aviaries, as well as waterfowl, insects and reptiles, and a children's farm – all much enjoyed by readers. Tearooms, shop, disabled access; cl wkdys Nov–Mar; (01538) 308293; £3.50. At pretty Waterhouses SK0850 nearby you can hire bikes from the Old Station Car Park, (01538) 308609; around £5.40 for 3 hours. The attractively set Cross there has decent food – or treat yourself at the Old Beams.

✝ **Interesting churches** at Clifton Campville SK2510 (practically perfect), and Ingestre SJ9724 (designed by Wren and reckoned by some to be the finest small 17th-c church outside London).

★ Quietly **attractive villages**, all with decent pubs, include Abbots Bromley SK0724 (pleasant countryside around), Alstonefield SK1355, Butterton SK0756, Coven SJ9006, Kinver SO8483 (the one right over in the W; some of Britain's only rock houses are nearby, still lived in 30 years ago; there are good views from the Iron Age fort on the ridge), Longdon SK0714, Penkhull SJ8644 (somehow undisturbed by the development of the Potteries around it), Rolleston on Dove SK2327, Rugeley SK0418 (with a beautiful 12th-c church), Shenstone SK1004, Swynnerton SJ8535, and Tutbury SK2128 (the Norman church has a notable west doorway and elaborate carvings; there are 2 crystal works, craft shops, an attractive, ruined castle with nice views, and the Olde Dog & Partridge with decent food). Longnor SK0864 is more of a small town, but despite its grand church has a pleasantly villagey feel (and a worthwhile craft centre). Brewood SJ8808 is another small charming town, with many attractive Georgian and older buildings. Codsall SJ8603 is notable in summer for its profusion of lupins (Moors Farm has a good farm shop and small country restaurant), and Ilam SK1350 is an attractive estate village (no pub). **!** Adventurous souls can learn to hang glide at the PEAK DISTRICT SCHOOL OF HANG GLIDING at Wetton SK1055; (01335) 310257; 2-day courses start at around £85. MOSELEY OLD HALL nr Wolverhampton is listed in the **Warwickshire** chapter.

Walks

Dove Dale ⌂-1, perhaps the finest of all the dales, is shared with Derbyshire (see the **Walks** section in that county's chapter). The **Manifold Valley** ⌂-2 also has many good walks, with fewer of the sensational rock features that abound in Dove Dale, but plenty of charm – more or less steep riverside pastures, ancient woodland in the narrower steeper gorges, waterside caves; there's good access to the hills above it, such as Wetton Hill SK1056, which have attractive views. The best viewpoint of all, not to be missed, is Thor's Cave SK0954, high above the dale. Wooded Ilam Park SK1351 shows the Manifold Valley at its most sheltered. The branch off up Hamps Dale SK0654 is also extremely pretty. There are decent pubs nearby at Warslow SK0858, Wetton SK1055 and Hulme End SK1059.

The **Churnet Valley** ⌂-3 gives lovely walks from Alton SK0742 or

---

Days Out

Landscape contrasts
Walk on The Roaches and/or to Lud's Church (see **Walks** section below); lunch at the Ship, Wincle (just in Cheshire); Rudyard Lake for a stroll or boating, and miniature railway; Biddulph Grange garden (limited opening).

The Dove's giant rockery
Walk into Dove Dale from Alstonefield; lunch at the George, Alstonefield; Ilam; drink at the Yew Tree, Cauldon.

A look at the Potteries
Gladstone Pottery Museum, Longton; lunch at the Plough, Etruria; Etruria Industrial Museum; visitor centre at Spode (factory tour most days), Royal Doulton or Wedgwood.

Green lungs and green fingers
Walk in Cannock Chase; lunch at the Moat House, Acton Trussell or the Holly Bush in Salt; Ingestre church; Shugborough Estate.

Transports of delight
Caldon Canal (Froghall Wharf) for a walk or horse-drawn barge trip (see **Walks** section below); or a trip on Foxfield steam railway, Blythe Bridge; lunch at the Izaak Walton, Cresswell; Chartley Castle (for the view); Amerton working farm, Stowe by Chartley.

Oakamoor SK0544; the best goes through Hawksmoor and Greendale to pass the broad fishponds in wooded Dimmings Dale and comes back down to the river past an old smelting mill – and a good café called the Ramblers Retreat (cl Mon). Hawksmoor Wood SK0344 is itself an attractive nature reserve, and the Talbot in Alton is useful for lunch.

The Roaches SK0062 ⌂-4 form an impressive western barrier at the edge of the Dark Peak; this is perhaps the most exhilarating of several moorland walks from the side roads off the A53 N of Leek. A walk here can be combined with the path through the unspoilt Dane Valley to Danebridge SJ9665 on the Cheshire border; hidden in the woods above the Dane is Lud's Church – not a church, but a miniature chasm reputed to have been a hiding place for religious dissenters.

Cannock Chase SK0017 ⌂-5 is the breathing space for the county's more industrial area: miles of forest and rolling heath, with fallow deer often seen. The large Castle Ring hill fort SJ0412 has fine views over the woods to the Trent Valley, and there are nice views towards the Welsh borders from the heights N of Broadhurst Green SJ9815. The German war cemeteries nr here are rather moving.

The county is liberally laced with canals, and their towpaths give many miles of pleasant, interesting walks. The **Caldon Canal** ⌂-6 and the Staffordshire & Worcester Canal have the best scenery. There's usually something happening at the Froghall Wharf SK0247 canal terminus (maybe inc horse-drawn barge trips – (01538) 266486), with an interesting walk along the canal to Consallforge SK0049 (unusual remote pub here). The nearby Nature Park continues this strange lost-valley scenery. There's also good canal access at Great Haywood SJ9922 (nr the longest pack-horse bridge in the country), and from the decent pubs at Amington SK2304 (the Gate), Armitage SK0716, Cheddleton SJ9752, Denford nr Leek SJ9553 (good-value food in the Holly Bush), Gnosall Heath SJ8220, High Offley SJ7826 (Bridge 42 on the Shropshire Union Canal – unusual pub specialising in ciders), Norbury Junction SJ7922, Filiance Bridge in Penkridge SJ9214, Shebdon SJ7625 and Wheaton Aston SJ8512. The Trent & Mersey Canal has little towpath here, but Fradley Junction SK1414, with a waterside pub and lots happening on the water, is an attractive place for a stroll. Other useful pubs for walks include the Cat at Enville SO8286 (Staffordshire Way path) and the Cock at Hanbury SK1727 (several attractive walks inc a poignant one to the vast crater left by the 1944 Fauld bomb dump explosion).

Where to eat

Cresswell SJ9739 Izaak Walton (01782) 392265 Very neatly kept, upmarket dining pub with 2 prettily decorated bar rooms and impressively good food (particularly the daily specials); mostly no smoking; cl 25–26 Dec; disabled access. £18|£2.95.

Teanford SK0040 Ship Cheadle Rd (01538) 722253 Busy little local with a generous choice of tasty, home-made food (particularly the bread and puddings), changing daily specials, and a good-value Sun lunch; friendly staff; cl Mon; disabled access. £15.95|£5.95.

Tutbury SK2128 Olde Dog & Partridge (01283) 813030 Popular carvery in a half-timbered dining inn with a stylish layout; well kept beers, good wines, and friendly, helpful service; nice bedrooms; cl pm 25–26 Dec, pm 1 Jan; disabled access. £17|£3.50.

Uttoxeter SK0933 Wellington High St (01889) 562616 Simply furnished, very individual pub run by an Orthodox priest whose family hails from Belgium – so there are Belgian beers, newspapers and some Belgian touches to the good, cheap food; upstairs restaurant; decent wines. £12.75|£3.75.

Waterhouses SK0850 Old Beams Leek Rd (01538) 308254 Very pretty cottage surrounded by flowers and creepers, with oak beams, antique furniture, and a cosy, friendly atmosphere; excellent; carefully cooked food, and good service; bedrooms; cl am Sat, am Sun, pm Mon and Tues; disabled access. **£29.65|2**-course meal £15.95.

Special thanks to Mrs F M Orchard, Mrs M Cooper.

STAFFORDSHIRE CALENDAR

Some of these dates were provisional as we went to press. Please check information with the numbers provided.

Many villages here decorate their wells and springs with flower-petal pictures in annual festivals called Well Dressings. For more information see the Derbyshire Calendar.

JANUARY
16 **Lichfield** Beer Festival at the Guildhall – *till Sat 17* (01543) 262223

FEBRUARY
6 **Stafford** Antiques Show at the County Showground – *till Sun 8* (01785) 258060
24 **Lichfield** Shrovetide Fair: pancake race and colourful procession in Market Sq (01543) 250011

MARCH
7 **Stafford** Bird Show at the County Showground – *till Sun 8* (01785) 258060
14 **Stafford** Sports and Kit Car Show at the County Showground – *till Sun 15* (01785) 258060
21 **Uttoxeter** Grand National at the Racecourse (01889) 562561

APRIL
4 **Stafford** National Terrier Club Championships at the County Showground (01785) 258060
11 **Burton upon Trent** Easter Festival inc steam engines at the Bass Museum – *till Mon 13* (01283) 511000; **Stafford** Classic Car Show at the County Showground – *till Sun 12* (01785) 258060
12 **Tamworth** Easter at the Castle – *till Mon 13* (01827) 59134; **Weston under Lizard** Festival of Transport at Weston Park – *till Mon 13* (01952) 850201
18 **Milford** Gamekeepers' Fair at Shugborough – *till Sun 19* (01889) 881388
23 **Lichfield** St George's Day Court: light-hearted gathering at the Guildhall (01543) 250011
24 **Tamworth** Folk Festival – *till Sun 26* (01827) 286001; **Weston under Lizard** Horse Trials at Weston Park – *till Sun 26* (01952) 850201
25 **Milford** Staffordshire Spring Flower Show at Shugborough – *till Sun 26* (01889) 881388; **Stafford** Classic Bike Show at the County Showground – *till Sun 26* (01785) 258060

MAY
2 **Leek** Arts Festival – *till Sun 31* (01538) 300492
3 **Milford** Classic Car Event at Shugborough – *till Mon 4* (01889) 881388
4 **Burton upon Trent** Classic Car Rally at the Bass Museum (01283) 511000; **Newborough** Well Dressing (01283) 575430

STAFFORDSHIRE CALENDAR

MAY cont

17 **Milford** Dressage Festival at Shugborough (01889) 881388

23 **Endon** Well Dressing (01782) 504085; **Milford** Spring Craft Show at Shugborough – *till Mon 25* (01889) 881388

25 **Burton upon Trent** Family Festival at the Bass Museum (01283) 511000; Lichfield Court of Arraye at the Guildhall: traditional ceremony to start Lichfield Bower Day: carnival and displays (01543) 879665

27 **Stafford** County Show at the County Showground – *till Thurs 28* (01785) 258060

30 **Wetton** World Toe Wrestling Championships at the Olde Royal Oak (01298) 84563

JUNE

5 **Weston under Lizard** Open-air Shakespeare at Weston Park – *till Sat 6* (01952) 850201

6 **Milford** Music from the Movies: concert with fireworks at Shugborough (01889) 881388

7 **Milford** Donkey Day at Shugborough (01889) 881388

12 **Lichfield** Jazz Festival – *till Sun 14* (01283) 762120

13 **Mayfield** Well Dressing – *till Sun 14* (01335) 342863; **Milford** Afternoon of Scottish Dancing at Shugborough (01889) 881388

17 **Lichfield** Shakespeare in the Park – *till Sat 20* (01543) 254808

20 **Tutbury** Arts Festival – *till Sun 21* (01530) 262272

21 **Milford** All About Pigs at Park Farm, Shugborough (01889) 881388; **Weston under Lizard** Model Air Show and German Shepherd Dog Show at Weston Park – *till Sun 21* (01952) 850201

25 **Lichfield** Real Ale, Jazz and Blues Festival at the Rugby Club – *till Sun 28* (01543) 262223

27 **Weston under Lizard** Hovercraft Championships at Weston Park – *till Sun 28* (01952) 850201

JULY

3 **Lichfield** International Festival – *till Sun 12* (01543) 257298

4 **Lichfield** Cajun Festival (01543) 262223; **Lichfield** Car Show at Beacon Park – *till Sun 5* (01543) 414000; **Milford** Gardeners' Weekend at Shugborough – *till Sun 5* (01889) 881388; **Uttoxeter** Festival Day (01889) 564085; **Weston under Lizard** English Civil War Re-enactment at Weston Park – *till Sun 5* (01952) 850201

5 **Lichfield** Community Arts Festival – *till Sat 11* (01543) 262223

11 **Burton upon Trent** Regatta and Riverside Show – *till Sun 12* (01283) 221333

18 **Milford** Fireworks and Laser Concert at Shugborough (01889) 881388; **Weston under Lizard** Balloon Festival at Weston Park – *till Sun 19* (01952) 850201

19 **Milford** Goose Fair at Shugborough (01889) 881388

25 **Tamworth** Festival (01827) 53092

AUGUST

2 **Draycott in the Clay** Agricultural and Horticultural Show (01283) 820721; **Milford** Victorian Street Market at Shugborough (01889) 881388

12 **Weston under Lizard** Music Festival at Weston Park – *till Sun 16* (01952) 850201

STAFFORDSHIRE CALENDAR

19 **Dove Dale** Sheepdog Trials

22 **Milford** Last Night of the Proms at Shugborough (01889) 881388

23 **Lichfield** Family Fun Day at Beacon Park (01543) 414000

29 **Ipstones** Agricultural Show (01538) 755646; **Milford** Craft Festival at Shugborough – *till Mon 31* (01889) 881388

30 **Weston under Lizard** Town and Country Fair at Weston Park – *till Mon 31* (01952) 850201

SEPTEMBER

5 **Lichfield** Sheriff's Ride: riding the boundaries (01543) 250011; **Weston under Lizard** All-wheel Drive Show at Weston Park – *till Sun 6* (01952) 850201

7 **Abbots Bromley** Horn Dance: ancient ritual dance (01283) 840405

11 **Tamworth** Beer Festival – *till Sun 13* (01827) 59134

18 **Burton upon Trent** Festival – *till Sun 27* (01283) 563761

19 **Weston under Lizard** Midland Game and Country Sports Fair at Weston Park – *till Sun 20* (01952) 850201

20 **Burton upon Trent** World Barrel-rolling Championships (01283) 511000

24 **Burton upon Trent** Beer Festival at the Town Hall – *till Sat 26* (01283) 569310

OCTOBER

9 **Weston under Lizard** Horse Trials at Weston Park – *till Sun 11* (01952) 850201

10 **Milford** Craft Show at Shugborough – *till Sun 11* (01889) 881388

15 **Tamworth** The Castle by Candlelight: evening openings, staff in period costume – *till Sat 17* (01827) 59134

22 **Tamworth** The Castle by Candlelight (see Oct 15 for details)

30 **Milford** Halloween at Shugborough – *till Sat 31* (01889) 881388

31 **Tamworth** Halloween at the Castle (01827) 59134

NOVEMBER

1 **Weston under Lizard** Bonfire and Fireworks at Weston Park (01952) 850201

DECEMBER

8 **Milford** Christmas at Shugborough – *till Fri 11* (01889) 881388

We welcome reports from readers . . .

This *Guide* depends on readers' reports. Do help us if you can – in return, we offer a discount on the next edition to people who've helped us with reports for it. Tell us what you think about places already in it, and anything extra you think we should say about them. And send us your ideas for inclusion in the next edition: places to visit, eat at or stay in, attractive drives or walks, maybe even unusual interesting shops you know of. Use the card in the middle, the report forms at the end, or just write – no stamp needed: *The Good Guide to Britain*, FREEPOST TN1569, Wadhurst, E Sussex TN5 7BR.

SUFFOLK

Charming quiet scenery, with some beautiful villages and unspoilt coast; good for a peaceful break.

Suffolk's strongest and most individual holiday appeal is to adults. Its gentle scenery inland and on the coast makes for a relaxing break, and several of its villages are really special – Long Melford, Lavenham, Cavendish and Clare are classic English villages which draw visitors from all over the world for their harmoniously colour-washed timbered buildings. The first two in particular have plenty of places to visit. Many other less famous villages and small towns have glorious churches, appealingly timbered and plastered buildings, and the abundance of antique shops that always seems to accompany such scenery. The county has several distinctive gardens, and rewarding buildings such as Euston Hall, Somerleyton Hall, Ickworth at Horringer and Framlingham Castle. The collection of music machines at Cotton is fun, the new small brewery at moated medieval St Peter's Hall in South Elmham makes for an unusual visit, and anyone interested in racehorses could spend a very enjoyable weekend based at Newmarket. The Anglo-Saxon site at Sutton Hoo will now be getting easier and more interesting to visit, and there's a good range of interesting places to see in Bury St Edmunds.

Constable country, around East Bergholt by the border with Essex, has had more than a comfortable share of summer visitors, but it is very pretty, and people interested in traditional British painting can easily combine visits to Flatford Mill there, Christchurch Mansion in Ipswich (free) and Gainsborough's House in Sudbury.

The open-air museum at Stowmarket is excellent for an undemanding family day out, and the wildlife park at Kessingland, particularly strong on African animals, is another family favourite. Children also enjoy the various attractions at West Stow, and there are several good farm and country centres.

Suffolk's coast is largely unspoilt. Even in summer you can walk for miles along fairly empty beaches and long stretches of bird country: these wide sea and skyscapes are very restorative. Southwold (and, across the water, Walberswick), Aldeburgh and Orford are ideal for a seaside stay in understated civilised surroundings. By contrast, Lowestoft, England's busiest fishing port, doubles as a summer beach and boating resort, and has plenty to do; Felixstowe is another place successfully combining commercial port with low-price family beach resort.

Walkers who want views and bracing contours will find much less for them here than those more interested in natural history. Suffolk is excellent for cycling, though – quiet back roads, lots of villages, gentle gradients without being dead flat, and accident figures suggest the county's roads are the safest in England.

Where to stay

Aldeburgh TM4656 WHITE LION Market Cross, Aldeburgh IP15 5BJ (01728) 452720 *£84, plus special breaks; 38 rms, some with sea view. Popular, rather smart 16th-c family-run hotel on the seafront with comfortable lounges, 2 bars, log fires, good food in panelled and beamed restaurant, and cheerful friendly staff.

Bildeston TL9949 CROWN Bildeston, Ipswich IP7 7EB (01449) 740510 £55, plus special breaks; 15 rms, most with own bthrm. Lovely timber-framed Tudor inn with comfortable, well furnished beamed lounge, open fires, good food in popular restaurant, welcoming courteous service, attractive 2-acre informal garden – and resident ghost; cl pm 25 Dec; disabled access.

Burstall TM0944 MULBERRY HALL Burstall, Ipswich IP8 3DP (01473) 652348 *£36; 3 comfortable rms, shared bthrm. Once owned by Cardinal Wolsey, this lovely old farmhouse has a fine garden, an inglenook fireplace in the big beamed sitting room, excellent food (ordered in advance) in pretty little dining room, very good breakfasts with home-baked bread, and helpful friendly owners; cl Christmas week.

Bury St Edmunds TL8564 ANGEL Angel Hill, Bury St Edmunds IP33 1LT (01284) 753926 £93, plus special breaks; 41 individually decorated rms. Thriving creeper-clad 15th-c country-town hotel with particularly friendly staff, comfortable lounge and relaxed bar, log fires and fresh flowers, and good food in elegant restaurant and downstairs medieval vaulted room (Mr Pickwick enjoyed a roast dinner here).

Bury St Edmunds TL8564 TWELVE ANGEL HILL 12 Angel Hill, Bury St Edmunds IP33 1UZ (01284) 704088 £70, plus wknd breaks; 6 rms. Warmly welcoming, mainly early 19th-c house (no smoking) with cosy bar, comfortable sitting room, good breakfasts in separate dining room, period furniture, and pretty little walled garden; cl Jan; no children.

Campsea Ashe TM3255 OLD RECTORY Campsea Ashe, Woodbridge IP3 0PU (01728) 746524 £55, plus special breaks; 11 comfortable and pretty rms. Very relaxed and genuinely welcoming Georgian house by church, with log fire in comfortable restful drawing room, lovely food from a set menu in summer conservatory or more formal no smoking dining rooms with more log fires, good wine list, and peaceful gardens; cl Christmas; dogs allowed (not in dining rooms).

Framlingham TM2863 CROWN Market Sq, Framlingham, Woodbridge IP13 9AN (01728) 723521 £80, plus special breaks; 14 comfortable rms. Bustling and friendly little black and white Tudor coaching inn with a pleasantly old-fashioned feel, a comfortable lounge and open fire, cosy bar with heavy beams and another log fire, good food in bar and restaurant, friendly helpful staff, and attractive small courtyard.

Great Glemham TM3361 CROWN Great Glemham, Saxmundham IP17 2DA (01728) 663693 £38; 3 tasteful rms. Welcoming and pleasantly placed old brick inn with beamed open-plan lounge, a huge double fireplace with woodburner on one side and logs blazing on the other, imaginative home cooking and super breakfasts, decent wines, well kept real ales, and neat garden.

Hadleigh TM0242 EDGEHILL 2 High St, Hadleigh, Ipswich IP7 5AP (01473) 822458 *£50, plus special breaks; 8 pretty rms. Friendly family-run Tudor house with Georgian façade, comfortable carefully restored rooms, personal service, traditional English cooking, and attractive walled garden with croquet; cl Christmas.

Hintlesham TM0843 COLLEGE FARM Hintlesham, Ipswich IP8 3NT (01473) 652253 *£38; 3 rms, 1 with own bthrm. Late 15th-c no smoking house on farm with neat garden, comfortably furnished rooms, lots of beams, log fire in inglenook fireplace, good Aga-cooked breakfasts in separate dining room, and friendly owners; walks around the farm (beef and arable), and riding and golf nearby; cl Christmas and New Year; children over 10; no pets.

Hintlesham TM0843 HINTLESHAM HALL Hintlesham, Ipswich IP8 3NS (01473) 652334 £115, plus special breaks; 33 lovely rms. Magnificent mansion, mainly Georgian but dating back to Elizabethan times, in 175 acres with big walled gardens, 18-hole golf course, outdoor heated swimming pool, tennis, trout fishing, snooker, croquet, sauna and steam room; restful and comfortable day rooms with books, antiques and open fires, fine modern cooking in several restaurants, a marvellous wine list, and exemplary service; well behaved children over 11 in evening restaurant; limited disabled access.

Hitcham TL9851 HILL FARMHOUSE Bury Rd, Hitcham, Ipswich IP7 7PT (01449) 740651 £36; 3 rms. Georgian/Victorian farmhouse with adjoining 15th-c timbered cottage in 3 acres of grounds with ducks on 2 ponds, croquet and badminton; residents' sitting room and separate dining room, dried flowers in inglenook fireplace, home-grown veg (where possible) and eggs used in the imaginative dinners (on Tues/Thurs, set meals only), bring your own wine, and good breakfasts; cl Nov–Mar.

Lavenham TL9149 ANGEL Market Pl, Lavenham, Sudbury CO10 9QZ (01787) 247388 *£65, plus special breaks; 8 comfortable rms. 15th-c inn in the heart of an excellently preserved medieval town, with original cellar and pargeted ceiling, several Tudor features such as a rare shuttered shop window front, a civilised atmosphere, good food in bar and restaurant (they smoke their own meat and fish), lots of decent wines, several malt whiskies, well kept real ales, thoughtful friendly service, and maybe live classical piano pm Fri; cl 25–26 Dec; disabled access.

Lavenham TL9149 SWAN High St, Lavenham, Sudbury CO10 9QA (01787) 247477 £139.80; 46 rms. Handsome and comfortable Elizabethan hotel, Forte as was, with lots of cosy seating areas, interesting historic prints and alcoves with beams, timbers, armchairs and settees, good food in lavishly timbered restaurant (actually built only in 1965), afternoon teas, intriguing little bar, and friendly helpful staff; disabled access.

Lawshall TL8654 BRIGHTHOUSE FARM Melford Rd, Lawshall, Bury St Edmunds IP29 4PX (01284) 830385 *£36; 3 rms. Homely B & B in timbered Georgian farmhouse with log fires, lounge and games room, and good breakfasts; self-catering and camping also.

Long Melford TL8645 BULL Hall St, Long Melford, Sudbury CO10 9JG (01787) 378494 £102.90, plus special breaks; 25 rms, ancient or comfortably modern. An inn since 1580, this fine black and white hotel was originally a medieval manorial hall, and has handsome and interesting carved woodwork and timbering, a large log fire, an old weavers' gallery overlooking the courtyard, old-fashioned and antique furnishings, a lovely calm atmosphere, good food, and pleasant friendly service; beautiful village.

Mildenhall TL7174 RIVERSIDE Mill St, Mildenhall, Bury St Edmunds IP28 7DP (01638) 717274 £80, plus special breaks; 21 rms. 18th-c country house on the banks of the River Lark with relaxed restaurant overlooking lawns, comfortable bar, welcoming staff, enjoyable food, real ales, croquet, and boats to hire; bridge wknds.

Needham Market TM0855 PIPPS FORD Norwich Rd, Needham Market, Ipswich IP6 8LJ (01449) 760208 *£55, plus winter breaks; 7 pretty rms with antiques and fine old beds, 4 in converted Stables Cottage. Lovely 16th-c farmhouse in quiet garden surrounded by farmland alongside attractive river, with log fires in big inglenook fireplaces and good imaginative food served in conservatory with subtropical plants (some meals can be communal); home-baked bread, home-produced ham and pork and own honey, eggs, and preserves with organically home-grown vegetables and herbs; cl mid-Dec–mid-Jan; children over 5.

Newmarket TL6463 RUTLAND ARMS High St, Newmarket CB8 8NB (01638)

664251 **£72.50**, plus special breaks; 46 rms. Imposing Georgian coaching inn built around lovely cobbled courtyard with elegant 2-room bar, open fires, good restaurant, friendly, efficient service and happy mix of customers.

Newmarket TL6463 WHITE HART High St, Newmarket CB8 8JP (01638) 663051 **£49.95**; 23 rms. Comfortable hotel with racing pictures and open fire in spacious lounge, traditional restaurant, reliable bar food, friendly staff, front bar where the trainers meet, and solid back cocktail bar where they take their more important owners.

Rougham TL9061 RAVENWOOD HALL Rougham, Bury St Edmunds IP30 9JA (01359) 270345 ***£85**, plus special breaks; 14 comfortable rms with antiques, some rms in mews. Tranquil Tudor country house in 7 acres of carefully tended gardens and woodland, with log fire in comfortable lounge, cosy bar (both newly refurbished this year), good food in timbered restaurant with big inglenook fireplace (home-preserved fruits and vegetables and home-smoked meats and fish), a good wine list, and helpful service; croquet, heated swimming pool and hard tennis court; disabled access.

Southwold TM5076 CROWN High St, Southwold IP18 6DP (01502) 722275 **£65**; 12 rms. Outstanding old inn with excellent imaginative food in no smoking restaurant and smart but relaxed main bar, inventive breakfasts, lots of interesting properly kept wines by the glass, well kept real ales, and friendly helpful staff; cl 2nd wk Jan.

Southwold TM5076 SWAN Market Pl, Southwold IP18 6EG (01502) 722186 **£95**, plus special breaks; 45 rms. 17th-c hotel with comfortable and restful drawing room, upstairs reading room, convivial bar, good food in elegant no smoking dining room, fine wines, well kept real ales (the hotel backs on to Adnams Brewery), and polite helpful staff; no dogs in main hotel; limited disabled access.

Stoke-by-Nayland TL9836 ANGEL Stoke-by-Nayland, Colchester, Essex CO6 4SA (01206) 263245 ***£59.50**; 6 comfortable rms. Civilised and elegant dining pub in Stour Valley with Tudor beams in cosy bar, stripped brickwork and timbers, fine furniture, a huge log fire and a woodburner, decent wines, and particularly good imaginative and reasonably priced bar food; cl 25–26 Dec; children over 10.

Wangford TM4679 ANGEL Wangford, Beccles NR34 8RL (01502) 578636 ***£49**; 5 rms. Neatly kept, solid 17th-c inn with a light and airy bar, no smoking restaurant, good-value dishes of the day and Sun lunch, well kept real ales, decent house wines, pleasant staff, and garden.

Westleton TM4469 CROWN The Street, Westleton, Saxmundham IP17 3AD (01728) 648777 **£76.50**; 19 quiet, comfortable bdrms. Smart extended country inn in a lovely setting with good nearby walks, an interesting comfortable bar, no smoking dining conservatory, restaurant, good food, log fires, several well kept real ales, good wines, and pretty garden with aviary and floodlit terrace.

Woodbridge TM2749 SECKFORD HALL Woodbridge IP13 6NU (01394) 385678 **£110**, plus special breaks; 32 rms. Handsome Tudor mansion in 34 acres of gardens and parkland with trout-filled lake, putting, and leisure club with indoor heated pool and gym; fine linenfold panelling, huge fireplaces, heavy beams, plush furnishings and antiques in comfortable day rooms, and good food and service; cl 25 Dec; well behaved dogs welcome; disabled access.

Worlington TL6973 WORLINGTON HALL Worlington, Bury St Edmunds IP28 8RX (01638) 712237 **£60**, plus special breaks; 9 comfortable rms with decanter of sherry, fruit and fresh flowers. 16th-c former manor house in 5 acres of grounds with a 9-hole pitch and putt course, comfortable panelled lounge bar with log fire, good food in relaxed candlelit bistro, and friendly staff.

To see and do

SUFFOLK FAMILY ATTRACTION OF THE YEAR

🏃 🐾 **Stowmarket** TM0458 MUSEUM OF EAST ANGLIAN LIFE (Iliffe Way) Children who've been on school trips to this excellent 70-acre open-air museum often come back with their parents, so though it might not be the first place to spring to mind when planning a family day out, it's clearly one that younger visitors can really enjoy. They look at the reconstructed buildings with a genuine sense of astonishment: did people really live like that? Even the room settings from the 1950s seem prehistoric to fresher eyes. The main buildings (which include a watermill, chapel, smithy and wind pump) are quite spread out, so there's a fair bit of walking involved, inc a nice stroll down by the river. There are a few animals dotted around; the most friendly are Remus the Suffolk punch horse and his friend Blackberry the Shetland pony, and you may be able to scratch the pigs' backs. On Suns they often have demonstrations of local crafts and skills like wood-turning and basket-making, some of which you can join in, though best to phone first to see what's on. In 1998 they're adding a rustic-style adventure play area. The museum's not great for under-5s, and teenagers might not find it that exciting (unless they like history), but otherwise in fine weather families can spend anything between 2 hours and a full day here; it's great for a picnic. Snacks, shop, disabled access; cl Nov–Mar; (01449) 612229; £3.85 (£2.25 children 5–16). The family ticket is only a saving if you have 3 children.

★ ☺ 🐾 **Aldeburgh** TM4656 Fishing village with quaint little streets running down to the shingle beach where the fishermen still haul in and sell their catch; touristy, but in a quiet way. Some newspapers had a field day in 1997 when the council voted not to erect a statue of composer Benjamin Britten, founder of the town's annual music festival, but it's hard to see how a statue would be better homage than the continued success of the festival itself. He and his companion the singer Peter Pears are now buried side by side in the churchyard. The 16th-c brick and timber MOOT HALL (reached by outside staircase), was the scene of the trial in Britten's *Peter Grimes*. It has displays on maritime history and coastal erosion, and finds from the Anglo-Saxon ship burial at Snape. Shop; open wknds Apr and Oct, daily May–Sept (cl am May and Jun); (01728) 452730 *£1. The attractively placed Cross Keys, the White Lion and the Mill are all good for lunch. There's an RSPB reserve just N at North Warren.

🐾 **Aldringham** TM4461 CRAFT MARKET 3 extensively stocked galleries of local crafts and fine art. Teas, disabled access; cl 12–2pm Sun (all am winter Suns), 25–28 Dec, 1 Jan; (01728) 830397; free. The Parrot & Punchbowl has good wines and decent food.

📞 🍎 **Ashbocking** TM1654 JAMES WHITE'S CIDER MILL (Helmingham Rd) Cider and apple-juice making and tasting, with PICK-YOUR-OWN in season. Snacks, shop, some disabled access; best to check first wknds and bank hols; (01473) 890111; free. The Barley Mow over at Witnesham has decent food.

☺ **Beccles** TM4289 WILLIAM CLOWES PRINT MUSEUM (Newgate) Interesting look at the development of printing from 1800 onwards, with wide range of machinery, woodcuts and books. Shop; open 2–4.30pm wkdys Jun, July and Aug, or by appointment; (01502) 712884; free. Down the same road is a decent local history MUSEUM; cl am, Mon (exc bank hols), Nov–Mar. The King's Head Hotel has good-value food.

🍺 ✿ **Brandon** TL7886 BRANDON HERITAGE CENTRE (George St)

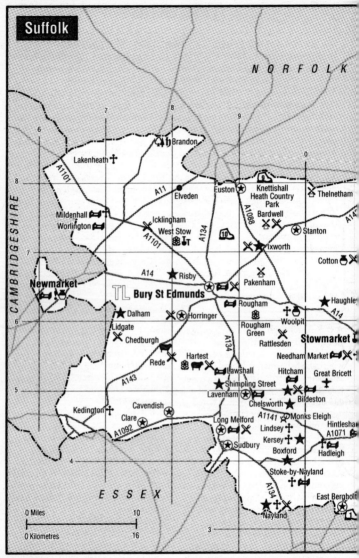

Suffolk

NORFOLK

CAMBRIDGESHIRE

Brandon
Lakenheath †
A1101
A11
Elveden
Euston ★ Knettishall Heath Country Park
× Thelnetham
Mildenhall
Worlington
Icklingham
West Stow
A134
A1088
Bardwell
× Stanton
A14
Ixworth
Cotton
A14
Risby ★
Pakenham
TL Bury St Edmunds
Haughley ★
Newmarket
Rougham
A14
Dalham ★
× ★ Horringer
Rougham Green
Woolpit
Lidgate
Rattlesden
Stowmarket
× Chedburgh
A134
Needham Market
Hartest
Great Brickett
Rede
Lawshall
Hitcham
Shimpling Street ★
A143
A134
Lavenham
Chelsworth
Bildeston
Kedington †
Cavendish
Long Melford
A1141
Monks Eleigh
Hintlesham
Clare
Lindsey †
A1071
A1092
Sudbury
Kersey † ★
Boxford
Hadleigh
Stoke-by-Nayland
A134
East Bergholt
ESSEX
Nayland

0 Miles 10
0 Kilometres 16

Brandon used to be the centre of the Stone Age flint industry, so among the local history here is a reconstructed flint-knappers' workshop; also displays on the fur industry and Thetford Forest. Shop, disabled access; open Sat, pm Sun, and bank hols, Easter–Oct, plus Thurs Jun–Aug; (01842) 813707; 50p. BRANDON COUNTRY PARK, largely pine woods, is pleasant to stroll around; for a car-borne impression of Thetford Heath, the best road is the B1106.

🐦 **Bruisyard** TM3266 BRUISYARD VINEYARD (signed off the B1119 Framlingham road) Picturesque 10-acre vineyard producing decent English wine, with herb garden, watergardens and woodland picnic area. Meals, snacks, shop, some disabled access; cl 25 Dec–15 Jan;

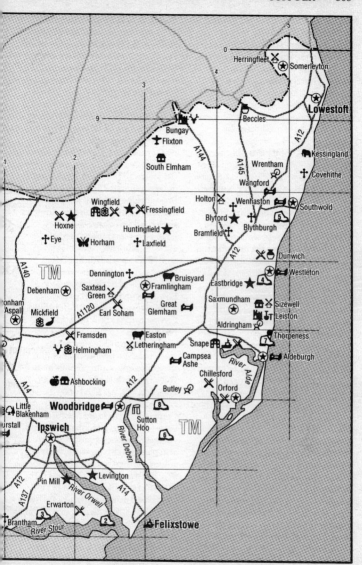

(01728) 638281; free, Walkman tours *£3.50.

🐗 ⋎ **Bungay** TM3389 Right in the centre of this historic little market town are the ruins of its Norman CASTLE, with twin towers and massive flint walls. Bungay straddles the county border, with the Otter Trust at Earsham close by in Norfolk. The Green Dragon has decent food and brews its own beers.

★ 🏰 🏛 ✝ ♨ 🏯 🖼 🏦 **Bury St Edmunds** TL8564 This busy shopping town has a good deal of character, with quite a few attractive Georgian and earlier houses, and several antique shops. The Linden Tree (Out Northgate St), Masons Arms (Whiting St) and Cupola House (Traverse) do decent food. The tranquil precincts of the former medieval abbey include little of its remains beyond the 12th- and

14th-c gatehouses, but the gardens are very pleasant, and a VISITOR CENTRE in Samson's Tower has a history of the site; cl Nov–Mar; (01284) 763110; free. Behind here is the old church building that in 1913 was given the status of CATHEDRAL; parts are 15th-c, but the hammerbeamed ceiling is 19th-c, and work still goes on. The nearby Queen's Head (Churchgate St) has good food. Another fine old church, ST MARY'S (Crown St), contains the tomb of Mary Tudor. An oddity near the abbey is the pretty little Nutshell (Traverse), probably the country's smallest pub, with long church connections – it closes on Suns and Holy Days. Jun–Sept walking tours usually leave the tourist information centre at 2.30pm wkdys and 10.30am Sun. MANOR HOUSE MUSEUM (Honey Hill) Georgian mansion with a marvellous collection of watches, clocks and other timepieces, and quite a few hands-on displays. A seemingly innocuous pair of breeches fell into this category not so long ago; they'd been worn by Mr Darcy in the TV adaptation of *Pride and Prejudice* and had to be put under guard when female visitors wouldn't stop stroking them. Snacks, shop, disabled access; cl Mon; (01284) 757072; £2.50, less for locals. MOYSES HOUSE MUSEUM (Cornhill) Unusual 12th-c flint and stone house with good range of Suffolk history, inc gruesome relics of the 'Murder in the Red Barn' – the murderer's account of his trial is bound in his own skin. Displays are firmly traditional, but there's lots to grab the attention. Shop, disabled access to ground floor only; cl am Sun, Good Fri, 25–26 Dec; (01284) 757488; £1.25. A handsome Robert Adam building is now the ART GALLERY (Market Cross), with changing exhibitions and a decent craft shop. Shop, disabled access; cl Sun, Mon, Christmas, and wk between exhibitions; (01284) 762081; *50p. Greene King have BREWERY TOURS at 2 and 2.30pm Mon –Thurs; booking essential, (01284) 714382; £3.50. The handsome THEATRE ROYAL on Westgate St is Britain's third oldest working theatre, built in 1819 by William Wilkins, the designer of London's National Gallery. It's owned by the NT, and you can look round when productions or rehearsals are not in progress (not Sun).

♣ **Butley** TM3650 BUTLEY POTTERY (Butley Barns, Mill Lane) Working pottery, with shop, tearoom and restaurant; cl Mon (exc bank hols and summer hols), Tues, and all Jan; (01394) 450785; free. The Oyster is good for lunch. The B1084 Woodbridge – Orford is a quietly attractive drive, and the even quieter back road S to Capel St Andrew passes the remains of a medieval abbey gatehouse.

★ † ☛ 🐑 **Cavendish** TL8046 A lovely sight, its green framed by colourfully plastered timbered houses, with the tower of the attractive medieval CHURCH behind. CAVENDISH MANOR VINEYARDS AND NETHER HALL (Peacocks Rd) 15th-c manor house nicely surrounded by vineyards; interesting old paintings in the house, tours and tastings in the vineyard. Shop; cl 25 Dec; (01787) 280221; *£2.50. The 16th-c Bull has good-value food. The A1092 from Clare goes on to Long Melford via a back road on to Lavenham – 4 lovely villages. The back roads N of here are also pleasant drives, with plenty of colour-washed old houses.

☛ **Chedburgh** TL7957 REDE HALL FARM PARK (A143 just E) Working farm based around agricultural life in the 1930s–50s, with rare breeds, huge working horses and seasonal activities; cl Oct–Mar; (01284) 850695; £3. A little further E, the Plough at Rede has good food.

★ † 🏰 🏚 🐄 **Clare** TL7645 Another of the area's very special timber and plaster villages, with a huge and beautiful CHURCH, the sketchy ruins of a CASTLE on an Iron Age earthwork above the River Stour, some remains of a 13th-c Augustinian priory, and little modern intrusion; nature trails around the castle. There's a 3-storey antiques warehouse, and the Clare Hotel and Swan have decent food.

⚓ **Cotton** TM0666 MECHANICAL MUSIC MUSEUM 🖼 Big collection of instruments and musical items taking in not just the expected organs, street pianos, polyphons and gramophones, but dolls, fruit bowls and even a musical chair. Their pride and joy is the Wurlitzer theatre pipe organ in the reconstructed cinema. Teas, shop, disabled access (but no facilities); open pm Sun Jun–Sept, plus the 1st Sun in Oct, a fair organ enthusiasts' day; (01449) 613876; *£3. The Trowel & Hammer is good for lunch.

★ ✝ 🎨 **Debenham** TM1763 This attractive village has a fine partly Saxon CHURCH, and a POTTERY (Carters Ceramics, Low Rd), specialising in teapots; cl Sun (exc pm summer), and they don't make pots at wknds; (01728) 860475.

⚓ **Dunwich** TM4770 Once quite a sizeable town, but it's slipping slowly under the sea – most is now submerged. Some say that on quiet nights, when there's a swell running after a storm, they can hear the bells of a submerged church tolling. There are some fragmentary ruins of a friary, and a small but very interesting MUSEUM (St James St) with exhibitions on the village's gradual erosion (open pm wknds in Mar, then daily Apr–Oct, free). Excellent coastal walks along the cliffs, beaches and heathland of Dunwich Heath, which has a National Trust tearoom (£1.50 parking charge).

⚓ 🎨 ✝ **East Bergholt** TM0733 BRIDGE COTTAGE, FLATFORD A 17th-c cottage near the mill immortalised by Constable, with a good interpretative centre for his paintings. Teas, shop; cl Mon and Tues (exc Jun–Sept), and Jan–Feb; (01206) 298260; free; NT. Guided walks through areas that inspired his work leave here several times a day May–Sept, but fill up quickly (£1.80). You can hire rowing boats for trips along the River Stour. The mill itself and its famous partner WILLY LOTT'S COTTAGE are both owned by the NT and leased by them to the Field Studies Council. You can see inside only by taking part in their arts courses or popular wildlife-watching wknds; (01206) 298283.

The King's Head nearby is attractive for lunch, and the church with its uncompleted tower has a unique 16th-c timber-framed bell cage. This Constable country is shared with Essex, around Dedham.

🐄 **Easton** TM2858 EASTON FARM PARK Friendly farm with milking demonstrations in the Victorian dairy and its more modern counterpart alongside, rare breeds, working blacksmith, adventure playground, and nature trails. Meals, snacks, shop, disabled access; usually cl Mon (exc bank hols) July–Aug, all Oct–mid-Mar; (01728) 746475; £4. The quaint White Horse has decent food, and the Wickham Market–Debenham back road through here via Brandeston and Cretingham has some attractive views.

Elvedon TL8279 One of Britain's 3 CENTER PARCS is close by, a relaxing place to stay with excellent leisure facilities; (01623) 411411.

🏠 🖼 ⚅ **Euston** TL9079 EUSTON HALL (A1088) Elegant old house built by Charles II's Secretary of State Lord Arlington. The highlight is probably the excellent art collection, with several portraits of the Merry Monarch and his family and court, inc works by Lely and Van Dyck. The grounds were laid out by John Evelyn, William Kent and Capability Brown, so reflect centuries of development, with stately terraced lawns, fine trees, a lake, lovely rose garden and classical temple. Teas in former kitchen, shop, disabled access to grounds and tearoom; open pm Thurs Jun–Sept; (01842) 766366; £3. The Pykkerel down at Ixworth and Six Bells at Bardwell both have good food.

⚓ **Felixstowe** TM2831 Quite a busy port, with a ferry (passengers, not cars) across to Harwich, and further afield to Zeebrugge. Thanks to its beaches and relatively dry climate it's developed into a popular low-price family resort. One of the main attractions, the Landguard Fort, is currently undergoing extensive repairs. Along the coast N, past another Martello tower, golf course and quiet sand dunes, is the gently attractive and altogether quieter little settlement of Felixstowe Ferry, with another foot-ferry across the estuary of the River Deben, and good local seafood in the waterside Victoria.

✙ **Flixton** TM3186 NORFOLK AND SUFFOLK AVIATION MUSEUM (Homersfield Rd) Aircraft and related items from the Wright brothers to the present day, with aeroplanes displayed outside and in the Blister Hangar. Shop, disabled access; open Sun and bank hols Easter–Oct, plus usually Tues–Thurs in summer hols; (01502) 896644; donations. The Green Dragon in Bungay is a useful nearby pub.

🏰 ❋ 🛏 ✙ **Framlingham** TM2863 The 12th-c CASTLE (B1116) is where Mary I heard that she had become Queen. Unusually the entire curtain wall has survived (you can walk all the way along it), and there are 13 towers, some 17th-c almshouses, and an array of Tudor chimneys. Good views, interesting museum. Snacks, shop, disabled access to ground floor only; cl 25–26 Dec; (01728) 724189; £2.60. The CHURCH has an excellent hammerbeam roof. The town's sloping market square is attractive, and the Crown at its head is useful for lunch. The B1116 to Fressingfield is quite a pleasant drive.

✙ **Great Bricett** TM0450 WATTISHAM AIRFIELD HISTORICAL COLLECTION (off the B1078) Small exhibition related to adjacent airfield (used mainly by helicopters now). Disabled access; open pm Sun Mar–Oct, or wkdys by appointment; (01449) 728933; free.

🐗 🛏 **Hartest** TL8352 The village green is attractive; at the end, the Crown is pleasant for lunch. GIFFORDS HALL (Shimpling, just SE of Hartest) 33 acres with vineyard and winery, wild-flower meadows, rare breeds of sheep and domestic fowl, and a rose garden. It's perhaps best known among gardeners for its sweet peas, and they have a Rose & Sweet Pea Festival the last wknd in Jun. Meals, snacks, shop, disabled access; cl Nov–Easter; (01284) 830464; *£2–£3, depending on season. They do B & B.

🛏 ❦ **Helmingham** TM1857 HELMINGHAM HALL GARDENS (B1077) Beautiful gardens pretty much as they were in Tudor times. The grand battlemented house they stand around (not open) is ringed by a moat, over which the drawbridge is still raised each night. Extensive deer park with hundreds of red and fallow deer, as well as Highland cattle and Soay sheep, and magnificent old oak trees. Constable painted a number of views of the woodlands. Teas, shop (inc Helmingham produce), disabled access; open pm Sun May–early Sept, and Weds by arrangement; (01473) 890363; *£3.50. The welcoming Dobermann at Framsden has good food.

🦋 **Horham** TM2072 The churchyard here has for generations been conserved as natural grassland around its older graves, just scythed for hay in the first week of July; so from spring onwards it's a mass of wild flowers, with plenty of butterflies (and beehives). The Ivy House in the quiet village of Stradbroke does good-value lunches.

★ 🏛 🖼 🛏 🐾 **Horringer** TL8161 A serenely attractive village with well spaced colour-washed buildings. ICKWORTH Very untypical stately home, an oval rotunda 30 metres (100 ft) high, with 2 curved corridors filled with a fascinating art collection (pictures by Gainsborough among others), and an exceptional array of Georgian silver. The gardens have a deer enclosure and adventure playground. Meals, snacks, shop, disabled access (there's a stair-lift); house open 21 Mar–1 Nov, pm daily exc Mon (though open bank hols) and Thurs, shop and restaurant also open wknds till Christmas, and park and gardens open all year; (01284) 735270; £5, £2 park and gardens only; NT. On Suns Mar–Dec you'll usually find various crafts in the Community Centre.

🏛 ✙ 🖼 🐾 🛏 🏚 **Ipswich** TM1644 After King John granted it a charter in the 13th c it flourished as a port, sending cloth to the Continent. Too busy now to consider as a place to stay in, it has quite a few things to look at on briefer visits (traffic schemes make getting in and out by car rather slow). Cardinal Wolsey set up a college here, but all that remains is the 16th-c gatehouse in College St. The Ancient House in the Butter Market (now a bookshop) has some 15th-c carvings and exceptionally neat pargeting (decoratively patterned external plasterwork). Dotted about the town are several attractive MEDIEVAL CHURCHES, especially the 15th-c St Margaret's (Constable Rd); St Mary at the Elms (Belstead Rd) has the town's oldest cottages behind it. If you're there on a winter's night 5 medieval churches are nicely floodlit. The port is quite busy. In the central pedestrian area the Great White Horse, a former coaching inn, is useful for snacks; the County (opposite County Hall), Old Rep (Tower St) and Greyhound (Henley Rd) have decent food. CHRISTCHURCH MANSION (Soane St) Perhaps the town's highlight; the original 16th-c house was altered in the following century after a fire, but since then it's escaped any further redevelopment. The rooms are furnished in period style, with a Victorian wing inc servants' quarters, and the Suffolk Artists' Gallery has the best collection of works by Constable and Gainsborough outside London. Shop, disabled access to ground floor only; cl am Sun, Mon (exc most bank hols), 24–26 Dec, 1 Jan, Good Fri; (01473) 253246; free. Another gallery is next door, and the surrounding park has play areas and a bird reserve. The natural history section of the town MUSEUM (High St) has been painstakingly restored to how it was in its Victorian heyday, and includes the first gorillas brought to Europe in the mid-19th c. Other parts have quite an emphasis on Roman Suffolk. Shop, disabled access to ground floor only; cl Sun, Mon, 24–26 Dec, 1 Jan, Good Fri; (01473) 213761; free. TOLLY COBBOLD BREWERY (Landseer Rd) Striking waterside Victorian brewery, with tours. Some particularly interesting old equipment, inc a Victorian steam engine, and tastings in the Brewery

Tap (which functions as a separate pub). Shop; tours daily May–Sept at noon, best to check winter times; (01473) 231723; £3.75 (inc drink). TRANSPORT MUSEUM (Lupin Rd) In an old trolley-bus depot, a developing collection of around 100 ancient commercial vehicles built or used in the area, from fire engines to buses and milk floats. Snacks, shop, disabled access; open Sun and bank hols Easter–Oct, and maybe pm wkdys in Aug; (01473) 715666; £2.25.

★ † Kersey TL9944 A very pretty one-street village, full of timbering and attractive and colourful plasterwork – though one or two buildings look ready for some attention. It runs from the fine 14th-c church down to a ford with ducks, and up the other side; several craft and antique shops.

🐾 Kessingland TM5286 SUFFOLK WILDLIFE PARK (A12) Quite an emphasis on African wildlife at this 100-acre park; some of the animals are the only examples of their type in the country, inc the wonderfully strange bonteboks (they look like a cross between a horse and a goat with a bit of cow thrown in). Lots for families in summer, with a bouncy castle beside the play areas, more animal demonstrations, birds of prey (usually only Tues and Weds), crazy golf, and games and activities in summer hols. Feeding times are spread throughout the day (meerkats and otters at 11.30am, lions and cheetahs at 3.15pm, and snake-handling at 4pm). The same people run Banham Zoo in Norfolk. Meals, snacks, shop, disabled access; cl 25–26 Dec; (01502) 740291; £5.50. Kessingland's beach is good, though busy in summer, and it's only 3 or 4m to Lowestoft.

★🏠👶🐾 🅿 Lavenham TL9149 One of the finest surviving examples of a small medieval town, this lovely little place has delightfully rickety-looking 14th- and 15th-c timbered buildings wherever you look; many now house teashops, banks or antique shops. The picturesque timber-framed 16th-c GUILDHALL dominates the Market Pl, and at various stages in its career has been a town hall, prison, workhouse and wool store; its beamed and oak-filled interior has interesting local history displays. Snacks, shop; cl Good Fri, and all Nov–Mar; (01787) 247646; £2.80; NT. LITTLE HALL (Market Pl) Delightful 15th-c house, attractively repainted, showcasing the Gayer–Anderson collection of books, pictures and antiques, with a pleasant enclosed garden. Shop; open pm Weds, Thurs, Sat, Sun and bank hols Easter–Oct; (01787) 247179; £1. There's a good small commercial art gallery nearby. The old wool hall has been incorporated into the Swan Hotel, itself well worth seeing. Both it (at a price) and the Angel are good for lunch. The A1141 through Monks Eleigh and then the B1115 through Chelsworth to Hitcham is a pretty drive.

🏭⛴ **Leiston** TM4462 A sizeable shopping town with the fragmentary remains of a 14th-c abbey off the B1122 just N. LONG SHOP MUSEUM (Main St) Big industrial museum in preserved buildings of Garrett Engineering Co, with steam engines, steam rollers, traction engines, and memorabilia from the nearby World War II air base. Shop, disabled access; cl Oct–Mar; (01728) 832189; £2. The Engineers Arms opposite has so much memorabilia it seems almost an extension.

🏵️ 🚣 **Little Blakenham** TM1048 BLAKENHAM WOODLAND GARDEN Woodland garden richly planted with camellias, rhododendrons, magnolias and the like; lovely in May when the bluebells are out. Lots of rare trees and shrubs. Open pm Mar–Jun; *£1. The Sorrel Horse over at Barham has decent food (and pleasant walks nearby).

★ ✝ 🏰 ! 🐎 🏵️ **Long Melford** TL8645 A very nice old place to stroll around: the fine green and exceptionally long main street (Hall St) are lined with buildings from varied eras, many with lovely timbering, and around 20 of them now antique shops (not cheap, but interesting). The CHURCH of Holy Trinity is glorious, with ornate carvings and dozens of

spectacular windows; especially attractive when floodlit at night. KENTWELL HALL (off the A134) Tudor manor house with genuinely friendly lived-in feel, best during their enthusiastic re-creations of Elizabethan life, usually wknds mid-Jun–mid-July, when everything is done as closely as possible to the way it would have been then – even the speech. It's surrounded by a broad moat, and the grounds have a brick maze and rare breeds farm. Meals, snacks, shop, disabled access; open pm Sun Apr–Sept, and daily Easter week and mid-July–Sept; (01787) 310207; £4.90 (quite a bit more on costumed days), £2.90 garden and farm only. MELFORD HALL Turreted Tudor house mostly unchanged since Elizabeth I with hundreds of servants and courtiers stayed here in 1578; it still has the original panelled banqueting hall. Displays include a collection of Chinese porcelain, and an exhibition on Beatrix Potter, who often stayed here; the gardens have a Tudor pavilion. Some disabled access; open pm wknds and bank hols Apr–Oct, plus pm Weds and Thurs May–Sept; (01787) 880286; £4; NT. The Bull Hotel, one of the finer old buildings here, does good light lunches, as does the comfortable Black Lion Hotel; the Crown and Scutchers Arms are also useful for food.

✝ 🚣 ❀ ☺ 🏰 **Lowestoft** TM5493 Britain's most easterly town, this is the area's main fishing port, so the harbour always has lots to see. It's developed as a resort thanks to its beaches (South Beach has the best bathing water) and proximity to the Broads. Cobbled streets of old buildings survive in the part known as The Scores, and the early medieval CHURCH is imposing and attractive. In the High St the Bayfields Hotel and Volunteer are useful for lunch, as is the seafront Jolly Sailors (Pakefield St). There are regular summer sea BOAT TRIPS, (01502) 523442 for details. The tourist information office on the Esplanade is housed in a rather grand old Pavilion, along with DISCOVERIG, a children's play area themed as a North Sea rig. Also in the harbour is the *Lydia Eva* STEAM DRIFTER, the last surviving herring drifter, with an exhibition on life aboard. Usually open July–mid-Oct (moored in Great Yarmouth Apr–Jun, when maybe a sidewinder diesel trawler is here instead); free. A MARITIME MUSEUM is housed under the lighthouse on Whapload Rd (cl Oct–May; 50p), and there's a small ROYAL NAVAL MUSEUM nearby (cl 12–2pm, all day Sat, and mid-Oct–mid-May; free). PLEASUREWOOD HILLS THEME PARK ▨ (Corton Rd) Lots of rides and family attractions; trains and chairlifts speed up travel round the grounds. Meals, snacks, shop, disabled access; open daily mid-May–Sept, and wknds in Apr and Oct; (01502) 508200; £9.95. EAST ANGLIA TRANSPORT MUSEUM (Carlton Colville; B1384 SW of Lowestoft) Lots of lovingly restored vehicles around 3 acres of woodland. The best part is the reconstructed 1930s street scene used as a setting for working trams, trains and trolley-buses. Snacks, shop, some disabled access; open Easter, then Sun May–Sept, Sat Jun–Sept, and pm wkdys in summer hols; (01502) 518459; *£3.50. The nearby Crown (A146) does good cheap lunches.

⊛ ♪ **Mickfield** TM1361 FISH CENTRE 2 acres of ornamental watergardens and working nursery, with displays of marine and freshwater fish. Wknd teas in summer, garden centre, disabled access; cl 25 Dec; (01449) 711336; free.

⚘ **Monks Eleigh** TL9647 CORN CRAFT (A1141) Traditional corn dollies and their production (demonstrations by appointment). In Aug and Sept you can walk through the fields and pick the flowers. Snacks, big shop, disabled access; cl 25–26 Dec; (01449) 740456; free. The Swan Hotel is handy.

★ † **Nayland** TL9734 Well rewards a stroll – its fine CHURCH has an altar painting by Constable; the old White Hart is now a smart pub-restaurant.

! ☗ **Newmarket** TL6463 Newmarket has been the centre of horseracing since James I used to slope off here

from 1605, and in the early morning people driving through are quite likely to have to give way to a string of racehorses. The NATIONAL HORSERACING MUSEUM (High St) tells the stories and scandals of the sport's development through the centuries, with trophies, videos of classic races, a display on the history of betting, and racing relics from saddles to skeletons. You don't have to be interested in racing to get something out of it. Meals, snacks, shop, disabled access; cl Mon (exc bank hols and July–Aug), and Nov–Feb; (01638) 667333; £3.30. They also organise informative tours of the local breeding and racing scene, with a look at horses at work on the gallops, and visits to a training yard, stud and to the handsome Georgian Jockey Club itself; booking essential, prices start at £15. NATIONAL STUD (A1304 W) Tours of this Mecca of horse-breeding by arrangement, (01638) 663464; guided tours are at 11.15am and 2.30pm wkdays, 11.15am Sat, and 2.30pm Sun, cl Sept–Feb (exc race days); £3.80. The Rutland Arms (across the road from the Jockey Club) and Bedford Lodge Hotel are useful for lunch; the King's Head out past the paddocks at Dullingham is also good.

▥ ▧ ❄ † ☗ ♥ ⚓ **Orford** TM4250 When Henry II commissioned the CASTLE here it was right on the shore, but since then the river has silted so much that it's now slightly inland. It has an amazing 18-sided keep rising to 27 metres (90 ft), supported by 3 extra towers. Good views from the top (as usual, at the end of a spiral staircase). Shop; cl 24–26 Dec, 1 Jan; (01394) 450472; £2.10. The CHURCH has the ruined chancel arches of a Norman predecessor in the graveyard. The process of coastal erosion is well illustrated at the DUNWICH UNDERWATER EXPLORATION EXHIBITION at the Craft Shop in Front St (cl 25–26 Dec; 50p). There's a long lane down to the shore with its quay and old smugglers' inn, the Jolly Sailor. The road through Iken Heath to Snape is a pleasant drive through quiet pinewoods. ORFORD NESS After years of belonging to the Ministry of Defence (who barred access to anyone who wasn't in uniform), this magnificently desolate shingle spit just opposite Orford quay is now owned by the NT and open to the public, though it's more for serious wildlife fans than day trippers. Ferries leave the quay every 20 mins between 10am and 12.20pm Thurs–Sat Easter–Oct – you can book if you want; (01394) 450057; *£5. HAVERGATE ISLAND TM4147 Birdwatchers can arrange whole day trips to this marshy RSPB reserve by writing to the warden, Mr Partridge, at 30 Mundays Lane, Orford, Woodbridge IP12 2LX (with SAE); permits available every Thurs and alternate wknds Apr–Aug, then in winter just the 1st Sat of the month; £5 inc boat trip from Orford quay.

★ **Pin Mill** TM2037 A nice spot below the wooded slopes by the River Orwell, with Thames barges on tidal moorings, and much favoured by artists; the Butt & Oyster here is attractively placed for a bite to eat.

🏶 **Rougham Green** TL9061 NETHERFIELD COTTAGE (Nether St, towards Hessett) Proof that you don't have to have a massive garden to make it very special indeed: hundreds of different herbs, beautifully yet sensibly grouped by how you'd use them, with 2 small knot gardens. Best May–Oct, but a peaceful haven at any time. The cheery owner is happy to chat. Plant sales; cl 25 Dec; (01359) 270452; free, guided tours by appointment. The Gardeners Arms over at Tostock is an appropriate place for lunch.

★ † ๕ **Saxmundham** TM3863 This attractive bypassed village has yet another fine CHURCH. The Poacher's Pocket at Carlton just N has decent food, and nearby Yoxford TM3968 has a couple of good craft workshops.

✗ **Saxtead Green** TM2564 SAXTEAD GREEN POST MILL (A1120) Traditional Suffolk windmill dating from 1854, meticulously brought back into perfect working order, but it's a steep climb up the staircase; cl 1–2pm, Sun, and Nov–Mar; (01728) 685789; £1.60. Attractive surroundings; the Old Mill House over the green has good home-made food.

🏠 ✗ **Sizewell** TM4762 SIZEWELL VISITOR CENTRE (B1353) Interactive displays and exhibitions on energy and nuclear power, with tours of both the Sizewell A and B power stations (booking essential); cl 25–26 Dec, 1 Jan; (01728) 642139; free. The aptly named Vulcan Arms opposite has good-value food. Nearby, the long Sizewell Beach is generally virtually deserted out of season, with agate and other semi-precious stones common among the pebbles, even sometimes amber after stormy E winds. THORPENESS At the S end of Sizewell beach, this curious place was built as a holiday village in a deliberately fanciful olde-worlde style, with quite a few attractive mock-Tudor houses (one even masking a watertower); it has a sizeable artificial but now thoroughly natural-looking picturesque lake, and the WINDMILL here was brought over from Aldringham.

🏠 ⚓ **Snape** TM3957 The converted 19th-c MALTINGS are home of the Aldeburgh Music Festival begun by Benjamin Britten, with other concerts throughout the year. The centre is pleasant to wander around, with unusual shops and galleries, and in summer there are 1hr BOAT TRIPS down the River Alde. The Plough & Sail just outside is good for lunch; up in the village, the Crown (with a bar recreated in *Peter Grimes*) and Golden Key are both good, too.

🏠 🏶 ! ⚓ 🐄 ♪ **Somerleyton** TM4997 SOMERLEYTON HALL 🎫 (B1074) Interesting Jacobean house rebuilt in the Anglo-Italian style in 1840, still very much lived-in, with period furnishings and paintings. The lovely gardens have a maze and miniature railway; live music in the gardens on bank hol pms. Snacks, shop, disabled access; open pm Sun, Thurs and bank hols Easter–Sept, plus Tues and Weds in July and Aug; (01502) 730244; £4.20. The Plough at Blundeston, home of Barkis the carrier in *David Copperfield*, is useful for lunch. N of here, with access from the Hall, is wooded FRITTON LAKE, which attracts numerous wildfowl, particularly in the autumn and winter. COUNTRY WORLD (Church Lane, Fritton) Good for families, with woodland walks, children's farm, fishing, heavy horse stables, miniature railway, birds of prey (displays 11.45am and 3.30pm, not Fri), rowing, and plenty of space for pottering. Snacks, shop, disabled access; cl Oct–Mar; (01493) 488208; £4.80.

☎ **South Elmham** TM3384 Medieval St Peter's Hall has in its outhouses the more modern ST PETERS BREWERY, whose excellent bitters, porters and fruit beers are made with water from their own source. Tours take in the whole brewing process, as well as parts of the Hall; a visitor centre is planned for one of the thatched barns. Shop, some disabled access; open Fri–Sun, best to ring for tour times; (01986) 782322; free entry to site, £5 tour.

★ † ☼ ❀ **Southwold** TM5076 Once an important fishing port, now a quite enchanting and civilised little resort with a distinctive lighthouse as its main landmark, an attractive unspoilt green by the sea, and no end of good pubs and inns supplied by the local Adnams brewery (their wholesale wine shop has interesting stock). For food, the Crown is outstanding, and though more straightforward the King's Head is good, as is the smart Swan Hotel; the Sole Bay and Lord Nelson have the most atmosphere. The Denes is the best beach. Southwold Jack on the tower of the interesting CHURCH is worth a look; he's an automaton that rings the bell for services. There are 2 decent museums: the town collections, housed in a 17th-c Dutch gabled cottage on Bartholomew Green (open pm Easter–Sept; free), and a LIFEBOAT MUSEUM on Gun Hill (open pm daily Jun–Sept; free). Across the golf course or along the breezy sea wall you come to the harbour, a tidal inlet, with its cheerful mix of beached fishing boats, multitudes of sailing boats, and tall black fishing shacks; the Harbour Inn

here is full of character. There's a footbridge over to WALBERSWICK on the other side of the water – an attractively decorous seaside village, popular with artists ever since Wilson Steer's days there in the 1890s. The Bell here is a striking old inn, and the 15th-c church, parts now destroyed and other bits looking shaky, is attractive. (The drive round by car between Southwold and Walberswick is several miles.)

❀ ◔ ☛ **Stanton** TL9673 WYKEN HALL GARDENS Formal herb, knot and woodland gardens, walled old-fashioned rose garden, copper beech maze, and woodland walk to 7-acre vineyard. A very nice unspoilt estate, just right for exploring. Meals and snacks in medieval barn, unusual country shop, disabled access; open Thurs, Fri, Sun and bank hols, and some evenings by appointment, cl 25 Dec–5 Feb; (01359) 250240; *£2. The Six Bells at Bardwell has good fresh food.

† **Stoke-by-Nayland** TL9836 The lovely 15th-c CHURCH has a tower familiar from several Constable paintings, and a few handsome Tudor buildings lurk among more ordinary ones; the Angel is excellent for lunch, but get there early.

☎ ⚘ ☙ **Stonham Aspal** TM1359 Around 30 small businesses based at Stonham Barns on the A1120, inc various craft workshops, bonsai shop, and garden centre. Also here is a BRITISH BIRDS OF PREY AND CONSERVATION CENTRE which has flying displays Apr–Oct, and every species of British owl; (01449) 711425; cl 25 Dec; *£4.50.

↓† ⚘ **Stowmarket** TM0458 See separate Family Panel on p.603 for the MUSEUM OF EAST ANGLIAN LIFE. The Kings Arms and Railway at Haughley both have good-value food.

★ 🏚 🏛 **Sudbury** TL8741 A pleasant market town (useful market stalls Sat); the Waggon & Horses (Acton Sq) has good plain food. GAINSBOROUGH'S HOUSE (Gainsborough St) The famous painter was born here in 1727, and the house now has an excellent collection of his work; unexpected finds include his efforts at sculpture. Plenty of period furniture and china too, and contemporary arts and crafts. Shop, disabled access to ground floor only; cl am Sun, all day Mon (exc pm bank hols), Christmas week, Good Fri; (01787) 372958; £2.80.

🏛 **Sutton Hoo** TM2849 One of the most famous archaeological sites in the country, where in 1939 the discovery of an Anglo-Saxon ship burial made historians completely reinterpret the Dark Ages. Most of the finds from here are in the British Museum, but you can see the burial mounds, and an exhibition explains the site's importance. At the moment tours are at 2pm and 3pm wknds and bank hols, Apr–early Sept; £2. The NT, who took over the site in 1995,

are embarking on a £4½ million Lottery-supported upgrade which by 2000 should include a new visitor and study centre with a reconstruction of the ship itself. A turn off the B1083 S takes you to the Ramsholt Arms at Ramsholt for lunch among waterside pine woods, with quiet walks along the Deben estuary.

🎲 ↓T **West Stow** TL8071 WEST STOW COUNTRY PARK is attractive, with 125 acres of heath and woodlands bordered by the River Lark. Over 120 different species of bird have been sighted here, and 25 species of animal; the visitor centre often has art exhibitions. The most interesting feature is the reconstructed ANGLO-SAXON VILLAGE 🏠, its buildings erected using the same methods and tools as in the 5th c. Occasional

---

Days Out

Stour Valley gems
Clare, Cavendish and Long Melford villages; lunch at the Bull, Long Melford; Gainsborough's House, Sudbury; Stoke-by-Nayland and Nayland churches; Kersey and Lavenham villages.

Britten's sea interludes
Boat trip from Snape Maltings on River Alde; Aldeburgh; lunch at the Cross Keys there; Thorpeness (you can walk from Aldeburgh along the beach, returning along the old railway track); Dunwich Heath and Minsmere RSPB reserve.

Sole Bay
Southwold (walk along shore and river, and across to Walberswick if there's time); lunch at the Crown or King's Head, Southwold; Blythburgh church; Kessingland wildlife park

The miller's tale
Letheringham watermill (limited opening); Easton Farm Park; Saxtead Green windmill (cl Sun); lunch at the Victoria, Earl Soham or Dobermann, Framsden; Helmingham Hall gardens (limited opening), and/or James White's cider mill, Ashbocking; tide mill and/or Buttrums Mill (limited opening), Woodbridge.

Anglo-Saxon chronicle
Bury St Edmunds; lunch at the Beehive, Horringer or Red Lion, Icklingham; Ickworth at Horringer, or West Stow country park and Anglo-Saxon village.

Straddling the Norfolk border
South Elmham brewery tour; Flixton air museum; Bungay – lunch at the Green Dragon there; Earsham otter trust, in Norfolk.

costumed days, and special events such as their Easter Sun market. Snacks, shop; cl 25–26 Dec; (01284) 728718; park free, village £3.20, inc excellent Walkman guide. The Red Lion at Icklingham has very good food.

★ ❀ ✔ **Westleton** TM4469 A pleasant village with an attractive green. The White Horse has good-value food, and just past it Fisks Clematis Nursery has many varieties of clematis on show and for sale; cl winter wknds. Minsmere Reserve Big RSPB reserve with lots of different species among the heath, woods, marshes and lagoons, and good observation hides. Meals, snacks, shop, disabled access; cl Tues, and 25–26 Dec; (01728) 648281; £3.50 for non-RSPB members. Nearby there are public walks over similar country, heath and pine woods; Dunwich is within quite an easy walk.

🏠 ❀ **Wingfield** TM2277 Wingfield College Quite a surprise to find a splendid medieval timber-framed building behind the Georgian façade. One of its 18th-c owners constructed the Palladian exterior to make his home more fashionable, using false ceilings, floors and windows so skilfully that for 200 years the house's earlier parts were forgotten. Striking great hall, and topiary and kitchen gardens. Snacks; open pm wknds and bank hols Easter–Sept; (01379) 384888; £2.50. They also organise Wingfield Arts, a varied programme of events in churches, halls and other everyday buildings all over the region; phone for programme. The De La Pole Arms has good food.

★ † ☗ ✗ **Woodbridge** TM2649 Quietly attractive and rather dignified market town, with many fine buildings and interesting book and antique shops, and a church of great style and interest. The local history museum (Market Hill) looks at the ship burial at nearby Sutton Hoo, as well as the recent Anglo-Saxon finds at Burrow Hill; cl am Sun, all day Mon (exc bank hols and summer hols), Tues (exc summer hols) and

Weds, and all Nov–Easter; (01394) 380502; *60p. Tide Mill Restored 18th-c mill on busy quayside, its wheel usually working when tides allow. Shop, disabled access to ground floor only; open Easter, then daily May–Sept and wknds in Oct; 80p. Buttrums Mill (Burkitt Rd) 6-storey tower mill, now fully restored, with displays of its history; open pm wknds and bank hols May–Sept; 50p. The Cherry Tree and Seckford Hall Hotel (both off the A12 N) do good lunches, and in the town the Seckford Arms (Seckford St) is good; so is the Wilford Bridge Hotel at Melton – well placed for river walks. The B1079 and then the B1077 up to Eye is a pleasant drive on an old coach road.

† ☗ **Woolpit** TL9762 The church here has a hammerbeam roof, and a translation of the village tale that in the 12th c 2 slightly strange-looking green-skinned children were found by a pit that was suddenly blasted in the earth one night; the boy soon died, but the girl lived, and grew up to marry a local lad and have children. She never said more about her origins than that she'd come from a land far far away. More on this at the small but interesting district museum (The Institute), which has annually changing local history displays. Shop, disabled access; open pm wknds and bank hols Easter–Sept; donations. The drive to Buxhall is pretty.

🜨 **Wrentham** TM4982 Wrentham Basketware (London Rd) They make and sell traditional willow baskets and hampers, with up to 320 styles; cl pm Sun, 25 Dec; (01502) 675628; free.

▣ Apart from the places already mentioned, lots of villages have **Constable and Gainsborough connections**, as both were raised in the area. Constable painted altarpieces for the churches at Brantham TM1034 and Nayland TL9734, and often painted the church at Stoke-by-Nayland TL9836, while Gainsborough painted the church at Hadleigh TM0242 (an old market town with some other striking buildings and nearby woodland RSPB reserve).

✝ **Other interesting churches** at
Blythburgh TM4475 (a magnificent
building in a lovely setting above the
marshes; there's a little working
pottery nearby), Bramfield TM3973
(unusual detached round tower),
Covehithe TM5282, Dennington
TM2867 (excellent sermons), Eye
TM1473 (beautiful stonework and
rood screen), Kedington TL7046
(Saxon crucifix), Lakenheath
TL7182, Laxfield TM2972 (nearby is
a charmingly preserved old pub, and
a useful enough museum), Mildenhall
TL7174, Needham Market TM0855
(where the marvellous hammerbeam
roof has been described as 'a whole
church seemingly in the air'), and
Wenhaston TM4276, where a 15th-c
wall painting in excellent condition is
full of lovely devils (it's a nice village
too). At Lindsey TL9745, St James's
Chapel is a charming little thatched
flint and stone chapel, built during
the 13th c but inc some earlier work
too.

❊ Suffolk is famous for its **windmills**;
many fell into disrepair earlier this
century, but quite a few have been
painstakingly restored. As well as
those already mentioned there are
good examples at Bardwell TL9473,
Pakenham TL9267, and Thelnetham
TM0178, all open at least summer
Suns; others at Herringfleet TM4797
and Holton TM4077, though you
can't often get into these.
Letheringham TM2757 has a pretty
watermill, surrounded by nice
gardens (open pm Sun and bank hols
Apr–May, plus daily July–mid-Sept,
*£1.50).

★ **Other attractive villages** here, all
with decent pubs, include Bildeston
TL9949, Blyford TM4277, Boxford
TL9640, Chelsworth TL9848,
Dalham TL7261, Eastbridge
TM4566, Fressingfield TM2677,
Haughley TM0262 (its Jacobean
manor house in lovely grounds),
Hoxne TM1777, Huntingfield
TM3374, Ixworth TL9370, Risby
TL8066 (with a decent antique
centre), and Shimpling Street
TL8752. Levington TM2339 is a
pleasant spot, with ancient
almshouses, a marina below, and the
Ship, a good pub (no children) with
estuary views.

Walks

From **East Bergholt** TM0734 ◰-1 the walk along the watermeadows by the
River Stour is East Anglia's most famous walk – picturesque views
immortalised by Constable, and well worth while. There is no real point in
leaving the path to make a circular route. Elsewhere, the Stour Valley's
attractive villages don't quite compensate for the humdrum scenery in
between, and although you can find field paths, it's difficult to work these into
circular walks.

Shotley Gate TM2433 ◰-2, at the meeting of the Stour and Orwell
estuaries, is at the hub of a rewarding walk with good views across to Harwich
and its shipping. Start inland at Shotley TM2335 and cross the fields either N
to the Orwell or S to the Stour, then follow the waterside.

Stutton TM1534 ◰-3 has another fine stretch of the broad Stour estuary
just S; on its N side, Alton Water is a reservoir recreation area.

Much of the flat formerly heathy land nr the coast further N is now covered
with pine plantations: pleasant for undisturbed walks, with the chance of
seeing red squirrels, and in summer with that lovely fresh foreign pinewood
smell. In some places the heath and marshy ground below it has been left
undisturbed, and these reserves are interesting for birdwatchers. **Minsmere
bird reserve** TM4369 ◰-4 is the best-known: the lake, surrounding
heathlands and woods, and the coast supply walks for all seasons. The reserve
is skirted by public paths, and a hide is available for public use, but you need a
permit to enter the rest of the reserve. Approach points are Dunwich TM4770
and Eastbridge TM4566.

The **River Blyth** ⌂-5 nr Southwold TM5076 (with marshy and heathy expanses to explore around nearby Walberswick TM4974) and the **River Deben** ⌂-6 nr Shottisham TM3144 are broad rivers close to the coast, with delightful waterside paths. **Beach walks** ⌂-7 around Thorpeness TM4759 and S to Aldeburgh TM4656 are pleasurable despite the rather graceless Sizewell nuclear power plant; heathland, an old railway track walk and the Meare (Thorpeness's lake) justify detours inland.

Tangham Nature Trail TM3450 ⌂-8 is a short walk among the plantations off the B1084 towards Woodbridge specially designed for disabled people; there are also longer walks through the pinewoods here, where red squirrels often show themselves. Further inland, there's little interesting walking. **Knettishall Heath Country Park** TL9480 ⌂-9 has some pleasant strolls. There's a nice shortish walk from **Great Livermere church** TL8871 ⌂-10 past the Ampton Water lake to Ampton church TL8671. A longer path leads up through farmland to Great Livermere from Ixworth TL9370.

Where to eat

Bardwell TL9473 Six Bells (01359) 250820 Quietly placed 16th-c pub with heavy beams, timbered walls and attractive decorations, a snug dining room and bigger restaurant with conservatory, a wide range of good interesting food, polite service, real ales, good wines, and seats in front of the building and on a back lawn; bedrms; cl 25–26 Dec. £17.50|£6.50.

Bildeston TL9949 Bow Window 116 High St (01449) 740748 Pretty pink-washed restaurant in attractive village square with beams, log fire in inglenook, pretty walled garden, good imaginative carefully cooked food, a fairly priced wine list, and friendly courteous service; cl Mon–Thurs, am Fri and Sat, Sun pm, 24–30 Dec; well behaved children allowed; partial disabled access. £21.45 dinner, £17.95 Sun lunch.

Bury St Edmunds TL8564 Mortimers Seafood Restaurant 31 Churchgate St (01284) 760623 Airy restaurant with artist Thomas Mortimer's sea pictures on the walls, lots of good fish dishes inc daily specials, and interesting wines from their shop next door; cl am Sat, Sun, 2 wks Aug, 2 wks Christmas, bank hols; disabled access. £20|£6.95.

Chillesford TM3852 Froize (01394) 450282 Heavy beams and lots of interesting things to look at in big comfortable open-plan dining bar and no smoking restaurant, very generous helpings of excellent food, especially wide choice of fresh fish, super schoolboy puddings, a fine choice of real ales and good range of wines by the glass, courteous service, hard-working owners, and seats in the garden; cl Mon, 20 Feb–10 Mar; disabled access. £22|£6.

Cotton TM0766 Trowel & Hammer Mill Rd (01449) 781234 Big friendly partly thatched and partly tiled white pub with spreading lounge, lots of dark beamery and timber baulks, a big log fire, good interesting food, and a large pretty back garden with swimming pool; restaurant cl pm Sun, Mon (exc bank hols); bar food available all week); well behaved children only; disabled access. £20|£5.

Dunwich TM4770 Flora Tearooms (01728) 648433 Extended former fisherman's hut right on the beach, with great views of the sea and fishing boats, famous for very good fish and chips but also other snacks, teas and home-made cakes; cl pm, Dec–Feb; disabled access. |£5.75.

Dunwich TM4770 Ship (01728) 648219 Delightful old pub by the sea with a good bustling atmosphere, friendly helpful staff who cope cheerfully with the crowds who come to enjoy the wonderfully fresh fish (straight from the boats on the beach), a traditionally furnished bar, conservatory, sunny back terrace, and well kept garden; the RSPB reserve at Minsmere is close by; bdrms; cl 25 Dec; disabled access. £15|£4.95.

Earl Soham TM2363 Victoria (01728) 685758 Unassuming, friendly pub with interesting own-brewed beers, simple country tables and kitchen chairs, an interesting range of pictures of Queen Victoria, open fires, and enjoyable, reasonably priced home-made food. £13.50|£4.50.

Erwarton TM2134 QUEENS HEAD (01473) 787550 Remote and unspoilt little pub with lovely views, a welcoming unpretentious atmosphere, cosy coal fire in beamed bar, good, well priced bar food inc fresh fish and game in season and decent-value Sun lunch, well kept real ales, and friendly service; cl 25 Dec; children in restaurant only; disabled access. £15|£3.25.

Framsden TM1959 DOBERMANN (01473) 890461 Charmingly restored thatched pub with twin-facing fireplace separating the friendly, spotlessly kept bars, good popular food, and a decent choice of beers and spirits; no children; disabled access. £16.50|£4.50.

Fressingfield TM2677 FOX & GOOSE (01379) 586247 Early 16th-c timbered inn by churchyard and duckpond, with good upmarket food (nice puddings), and fine wines; cl Mon, Tues, 2 wks July, 2 wks Christmas. £19|£6.95.

Hartest TL8352 CROWN (01284) 830250 Comfortably modernised and brightly lit pink-washed pub by village green and church (bell ringing practice pm Thurs), lots of space in 2 no smoking dining areas and large conservatory restaurant, reliably good, reasonably priced food inc take-away fish and chips and really good-value Weds and Fri 2-course lunches, quick friendly black-tie staff, a chatty local atmosphere, well kept real ales, and a big back lawn and side courtyard; disabled access. £13|£3.50.

Horringer TL8261 BEEHIVE The Street (01284) 735260 Particularly well run and pretty ivy-covered pub with extremely helpful service, friendly atmosphere, excellent imaginative food with lots of daily specials and a pudding board, attractively furnished little rambling rooms, a woodburner, well kept real ales, and decent wines. £17|£5.95.

Hoxne TM1777 SWAN (01379) 668275 Carefully restored late 15th-c house with heavy oak floors, fine fireplaces, lots of atmosphere, good bar food, well kept beer, decent wines, and tranquil back garden. £18|£5.95.

Icklingham TL7772 RED LION (01638) 717802 Civilised and rather smart thatched pub with a nice mix of wooden chairs, candlelit tables, fresh flowers, fishing rods and various stuffed animals, an inglenook fireplace and heavy beams in bar, very good food, well kept real ales, and country wines; disabled access. £20|£7.25.

Ixworth TL9370 THEOBALDS 68 High St (01359) 231707 Consistently good, imaginative food (inc vegetarian choice) in 17th-c restaurant with log fires, beams and standing timbers in cosy rooms, very good wine list, and kind service; cl am Sat, pm Sun, Mon, 2 wks Aug; children in evening over 8 only. £34|£8.

Lidgate TL7257 STAR (01638) 500275 Quaint old place with interesting small bar, big log fire, handsomely moulded heavy beams and polished oak and pine tables, a chatty Spanish landlady, big helpings of hugely enjoyable food with Mediterranean hints, good wines and ales, a cosy simple dining room, and tables in front and in the little rustic back garden; cl pm Sun. £21|£4.50.

Long Melford TL8645 CHIMNEYS Hall St (01787) 379806 Lovely beamed 16th-c building with very good, carefully prepared food and thoughtful wine list; the paintings are for sale; cl pm Sun; disabled access. £17.50.

Nayland TL9734 WHITE HART (01206) 263382 Smart 15th-c pub/restaurant with 18th-c coaching frontage, polished tables on wooden floors, comfortable sofa by log fire, glass-floored section over wine cellar, good, well presented cooking, a wide choice of wines, real ales in straight glasses, and a relaxed atmosphere; popular with businessmen and retired folk; cl 1–2 Jan; disabled access. £22.50 dinner, £19.50 lunch.

Needham Market TM0855 BONDS Bridge St (01449) 720265 Excellent fish and chip shop with enviable local reputation; you can buy fresh fish here too; cl Sun, Mon. |£2.25.

Orford TM4250 Butley Orford Oysterage (01394) 450277 Simple restaurant with its own oyster beds, fishing boat and smoke house; very popular locally and with yachtsmen for its wonderfully fresh fish, decent wines, and brisk friendly service; cl 25–26 Dec; disabled access. £17.50|£4.

Rattlesden TL9758 Brewers Arms (01449) 736377 16th-c pub with pleasantly simple beamed lounge and small lively public bar, very welcoming friendly service, imaginative food, decent wines, well kept ales, and magnificent old bread oven in main eating area. £18.50|£7.50.

Rede TL8055 Plough (01284) 789208 Welcoming, partly thatched cottage in lovely spot, with particularly helpful owners, lots of well presented fresh fish and game in season, imaginative daily specials, good evening restaurant, decent wine, and lovely sheltered cottagey garden; disabled access. £17.50|£5.95.

Snape TM3958 Crown (01728) 688324 Unspoilt smugglers' inn with a relaxed and warmly friendly atmosphere, old brick floors, beams, big brick inglenook and nice old furnishings, particularly good interesting and well presented food served by smiling staff, pre- and post-concert suppers, a thoughtful wine list (12 by the glass inc champagne), well kept real ales, and tables in pretty roadside garden; bdrms; cl 25–26 Dec; no children; partial disabled access. £21.40|£4.50.

Snape TM3957 Plough & Sail The Maltings (01728) 688302 Part of the Snape Maltings centre with a relaxed and friendly series of attractively furnished rooms, busy little restaurant, delicious food, well kept real ales, and a fine wine list; cl Sun, pm Mon Christmas–Easter; disabled access. £18.50|£7.50.

Wingfield TM2277 De La Pole Arms (01379) 384545 Carefully converted village pub with interesting bric-à-brac, comfortable traditional seats, a pleasantly civilised feel, good, enjoyable bar food, well kept ales, and prompt welcoming service. £17.50|£6.95.

Special thanks to Heather Martin.

SUFFOLK CALENDAR

Some of these dates were provisional as we went to press. Please check information with the numbers provided.

MARCH

8 **Long Melford** Lambing at Easter at Kentwell Hall – *also Sun 15* (01787) 310207

APRIL

10 **Long Melford** Easter Egg Hunt Quiz and Re-creation of Tudor Life at Easter at Kentwell Hall – *till Mon 13* (01787) 310207; **Needham Market** East Anglian Art and Crafts Exhibition and Sale: over 750 paintings – *till Mon 13* (01449) 722202; **Snape** Aldeburgh Easter Concert Series at the Maltings – *till Mon 13* (01728) 452935

12 **West Stow** Saxon Market: demonstrations and costumed Saxons at West Stow Anglo-Saxon Village – *till Mon 13* (01284) 728718

25 **Otley** Open Weekend at Otley College of Agriculture and Horticulture – *till Sun 26* (01473) 785543

MAY

2 **Long Melford** Tudor May Day Celebrations at Kentwell Hall – *till Mon 4* (01787) 310207

SUFFOLK CALENDAR

MAY cont

4 **West Stow** Archaeology Day at West Stow Anglo-Saxon Village (01284) 728718

8 **Bury St Edmunds** Festival – *till Sun 24* (01284) 757080

10 **Ingham** South Suffolk Agricultural Show at Ampton Park (01638) 750879

16 **Hadleigh** Agricultural Show (01473) 827920

23 **Long Melford** Re-creation of Tudor Life at Whitsuntide at Kentwell Hall – *till Mon 25* (01787) 310207; **Mildenhall** RAF Air Fête – *till Sun 24* (01638) 542995

24 **West Stow** Park Week at West Stow Anglo-Saxon Village: nature trails, costumed craftspeople – *till Sun 30* (01284) 728718

25 **Framlingham** Gala (01728) 723857

27 **Ipswich** Suffolk Show at Suffolk Showground – *till Thurs 28* (01473) 726847

30 **Bury St Edmunds** Carnival (01284) 701216

JUNE

1 **Southwold** Trinity Fair on South Green – *till Wed 3* (01502) 523002

5 **Suffolk** Open Studios: over 60 arts and crafts studios open to the public – *till Sun 21* (01728) 668327

7 **Euston** Country Fair and Vintage Rally at Euston Park (01359) 269265

12 **Snape** Aldeburgh Festival of Music and Arts at the Maltings – *till Sun 28* (01728) 452935

13 **Long Melford** Country Fair at Melford Hall – *till Sun 14* (01787) 280941; **Lowestoft** Maritime Week – *till Fish Fair and Smack Race on Sat 20* (01502) 562111

14 **Long Melford** Re-creation of Tudor Life at Kentwell Hall – *till 5 July* (01787) 310207

18 **Woolpit** Festival – *till Sat 27* (01359) 240655

21 **Bury St Edmunds** Nowton Park Country Fair (01284) 763666; **Bury St Edmunds** Open Gardens Day (01284) 754060

27 **Eye** 20 Open Gardens Weekend: 20 gardens – *till Sun 28* (01379) 870703; **Shotley** Classic Boat & Beer Festival: over 150 traditional boats at the Marina – *till 5 July* (01473) 788982

JULY

5 **Haverhill** Show (01440) 714448

9 **Bury St Edmunds** Open Air Concerts at Ickworth House – *till Fri 10* (01625) 575681

10 **Lowestoft** Rock and Folk Concerts at Sparrow's Nest Gardens – *till Sat 11* (01502) 523002

11 **Framlingham** Horse Show at Castle Meadow – *till Sun 26* (01473) 822790

12 **Hadleigh** East Anglian Summer Music Festival – *till 2 Aug* (01473) 822596; **Stowmarket** Carnival Week – *till procession on Sat 18* (01449) 676800

17 **Weeting** Steam Engine Rally at Fengate Farm – *till Sun 19* (01842) 810317

18 **Lowestoft** Family Day at Sparrow's Nest Gardens (01502) 523002

24 **Long Melford** Open Air Theatre at Kentwell Hall – *till Sat 25* (01787) 310207

SUFFOLK CALENDAR

JULY cont

26 **Cowlinge** Open Gardens Day: over 20 gardens (01440) 820204

30 **Lowestoft** Seafront Airshow (01502) 562111

31 **Beccles** Carnival Week – *till 3 Aug* (01502) 523002

AUGUST

1 **Haverhill** Thurlow Steam Rally and Show – *till Sun 2* (01440) 783457; **Long Melford** Re-creation of Tudor Life at Lammastide at Kentwell Hall – *till Sun 2* (01787) 310207; **Saxmundham** Carnival (01728) 602009; **Snape** Proms: folk, jazz, classical, opera, dance at the Maltings – *till Mon 31* (01728) 452935; **West Stow** Anglo-Saxon Festival at West Stow Anglo-Saxon Village: costumed Anglo-Saxons live in the village, traders, crafts, storytellers, guided tours – *till Mon 31* (01284) 728718

2 **Lowestoft** Carnival Week – *till Sun 9* (01502) 523002

8 **Ipswich** Carnival (01473) 743861

22 **Felixstowe** Fuchsia Festival at Orwell High School- *till Sun 23* (01394) 286374

28 **Long Melford** Re-creation of Tudor Life in High Summer at Kentwell Hall – *till Mon 31* (01787) 310207

30 **Eye** Show – *till Mon 31* (01379) 870224; **Walsham le Willows** Gardens Weekend: about 25 gardens – *till Mon 31* (01359) 259450

31 **Oulton Broad** Charity Gala Day (01502) 523000

SEPTEMBER

19 **Long Melford** Re-creation of Tudor Life at Michaelmas at Kentwell Hall – *till Sun 20* (01787) 310207

OCTOBER

3 **Otley** Open Weekend at Otley College of Agriculture and Horticulture – *till Sun 4* (01473) 785543

NOVEMBER

6 **Long Melford** Procession and Fireworks (01787) 379783

DECEMBER

12 **Long Melford** Christmas Concert at Kentwell Hall – *and Sun 13* (01787) 310207

We welcome reports from readers . . .

This *Guide* depends on readers' reports. Do help us if you can – in return, we offer a discount on the next edition to people who've helped us with reports for it. Tell us what you think about places already in it, and anything extra you think we should say about them. And send us your ideas for inclusion in the next edition: places to visit, eat at or stay in, attractive drives or walks, maybe even unusual interesting shops you know of. Use the card in the middle, the report forms at the end, or just write – no stamp needed: *The Good Guide to Britain*, FREEPOST TN1569, Wadhurst, E Sussex TN5 7BR.

SURREY

Some surprisingly unspoilt scenery, with very good walking; lots of enjoyable places to visit.

Good family days out here are headed by the Chessington zoo and theme park (its late evening opening in summer is a bonus), and Thorpe Park. Birdworld, near Farnham, is another excellent family day out, and the zoo at Charlwood, the children's farm west of Epsom, and the rural life centre at Tilford are also popular family treats. On a nice day, boat hire from Godalming or Guildford can be fun.

Adults really do even better in Surrey, with some first-rate places to visit. We'd include the NT properties at East and West Clandon (there's a good-value joint ticket), Denbies vineyard at Dorking, the gardens at Wisley, Brooklands (if you like motor racing), Polesden Lacey near Great Bookham, Claremont garden at Esher, Loseley House near Guildford, Winkworth arboretum at Hascombe and Painshill Park at Cobham. Some places few people have heard of turn out to be particularly enjoyable: the network of tunnels under Reigate castle grounds, the Watts picture gallery at Compton, Hannah Peschar's sculpture garden at Ockley, the Derby Day Experience in Epsom.

Though there are urban corridors, much of the countryside is beautifully preserved, and quite hilly. The National Trust owns several thousand acres in the finest parts, and walkers have an excellent choice, with relatively free access. Surprisingly, Surrey is the most heavily wooded county in England – and it includes some lovely villages, especially Shere, Outwood and Chiddingfold.

Where to stay

Abinger Hammer TQ1047 CROSSWAYS FARM Raikes Lane, Abinger Hammer, Dorking RH5 6PZ (01306) 730173 **£36**; 2 spacious rms, some with own bthrm. Interesting Jacobean farmhouse in lovely countryside, with a huge chimney, fine oak staircase, log fire in the comfortable sitting room, good home cooking using own-grown vegetables, and a small garden with croquet; cl 14 Dec–31 Jan.

Bagshot SU9062 PENNYHILL PARK Bagshot GU19 5ET (01276) 471774 **£181**, plus special breaks; 89 spacious, charming rms. Impressive Victorian country house in 120 acres of well kept gardens and parkland; with friendly and courteous staff, comfortable 2-level lounge with panelling and beams, a little bar, tapestries and fine paintings, and very good, imaginative cooking; outdoor swimming pool, tennis, 9-hole golf course, stabling, game fishing and clay-pigeon shooting – they can arrange riding too; disabled access.

Chertsey TQ0466 CROWN 7 London St, Chertsey KT16 8AP (01932) 564657 **£58w**; 30 comfortable modern rms. Bustling, friendly place with some original features and an open fire in the large bar; conservatory extension, good food, attractive restaurant, and a lovely big garden; disabled access.

Ewhurst TQ0940 HIGH EDSER Shere Rd, Ewhurst, Cranleigh GU6 7PQ (01483) 278214 ***£40**; 3 rms, shared bthrm. 16th-c, timber-framed farmhouse in lovely countryside; with a comfortable residents' lounge, friendly owners, and a tennis court in the grounds; cl Christmas and Easter.

Farnham SU8346 FARNHAM HOUSE Alton Rd, Farnham GU10 5ER (01252) 716908 £63w, plus special breaks; 20 comfortable rms. Attractive Victorian 'gothick' manor house with oak panelling and open fires in the comfortable public rooms, a split-level restaurant, and tennis court and outdoor heated swimming pool in the 5-acre gardens.

Godstone TQ3551 GODSTONE The Green, Godstone RG9 8DT (01833) 742461 *£45; 8 rms. Well run, late 16th-c hotel with an open fire in the comfortable residents' lounge, and good, popular food in the attractive, beamed restaurant; summer cream teas, and helpful service from the very welcoming owners; disabled access.

Haslemere SU8931 DEERFELL Blackdown Park, Fernden Lane, Haslemere GU27 3LA (01428) 653409 *£40; 2 rms with showers. Comfortable, no smoking, stone coach house with wonderful views and lovely surrounding walks; generous meals in the handsome dining room (ordered in advance), an open fire in the sitting room, good breakfasts, pictures, antiques and old rugs, a sun room, and friendly owners; cl mid Dec–mid-Jan.

Haslemere SU9032 LYTHE HILL HOTEL Petworth Rd, Haslemere GU27 3BQ (01428) 651251 £118, plus special breaks; 40 individually styled rms, a few in the original house. Lovely, partly 15th-c building in 20 acres of parkland and bluebell woods (adjoining the NT hillside), with a floodlit tennis court, croquet lawn and jogging track; plush, comfortable and elegant lounges, a relaxed bar, 2 no smoking restaurants (one with French cooking, the other with traditional English), and good, attentive service.

Holmbury St Mary TQ1144 BULMER FARM Holmbury St Mary, Dorking RH5 6LG (01306) 730210 *£42; 8 big comfortable rms, 5 in outbuildings with own showers. Attractive and welcoming 17th-c farmhouse on a 30-acre beef farm in lovely countryside; with oak beams and an inglenook fireplace in the attractive sitting room, breakfasts with home-made preserves in the neatly kept dining room, and a large garden; self-catering also; no children; disabled access.

Nutfield TQ3050 NUTFIELD PRIORY Nutfield, Redhill RH1 4EL (01737) 822066 £149.90, plus special breaks; 60 rms. Impressive, Victorian 'gothick' hotel in 40 acres of parkland; with lovely, elaborate carvings, stained-glass windows, gracious day rooms, a fine panelled library, cloistered restaurant, and even an organ in the galleried grand hall; extensive leisure club with indoor heated swimming pool; cl 24–31 Dec.

To see and do

SURREY FAMILY ATTRACTION OF THE YEAR

☺ 🎪 **Chessington** TQ1762 CHESSINGTON WORLD OF ADVENTURES (A243) Both of Surrey's huge theme parks are right up among the most popular, charged attractions in the country, though this one just has the edge on its rival as far as visitor numbers are concerned. Only 5 of the rides and attractions have any sort of height restrictions, so there's plenty for younger children to enjoy, from the Toytown area especially for them, through to the Dragon River log flume and Professor Burp's Bubbleworks. Of course no theme park would be complete without its thrill rides and this one has a corker: Rameses Revenge spins you round 360 degrees at speeds of up to 60mph while plummeting towards a rock-lined pit and water fountains. Another highlight, if you like that sort of thing, is the hanging roller-coaster, the Vampire, which flies above rooftops before diving underground. There's also a circus show with trapeze artists, clowns and stuntmen, and tucked away on the quieter, greener side of the park you'll still find the zoo from which it all developed – perhaps a little lost now among the other attractions, but still popular with children. A monorail takes you above some of the animals. You'll need a whole day here to get your money's worth, but there's easily enough to fill it, as well as patient staff to help you along. It's worth taking advantage of their later opening hours in the summer hols (till 9pm), as the park isn't quite so busy later in the day; weekends can be very busy. Meals, snacks, shop, disabled access; open late Mar–early Nov; (01372) 729560; £18 (£14 children 4–14).

🐾 ✝ 🦋 **Charlwood** TQ2340
GATWICK ZOO AND AVIARIES (Russ Hill) Hundreds of mammals and birds, many in big naturalistic settings – some of which visitors can walk through, inc the 2 big tropical houses with plants and butterflies from around the world. Meals, snacks, shop, disabled access; cl 25–26 Dec; (01293) 862312; £3.95. The Half Moon (Church Rd) in the attractive village has cheap home-made food; the Fox Revived at Norwood Hill is a bigger nearby dining pub.

🏛🍴💷☕♿ **Chertsey** TQ0466
Quite a few Georgian buildings in its main streets, the remains of a medieval ABBEY, and pleasant walks by the Thames. The late Georgian MUSEUM (Windsor St) has displays on the abbey, a good costume collection, and a pleasant little garden; cl am wkdys, all Sun, Mon and bank hols; (01932) 565764; free. GREAT COCKROW RAILWAY (Hardwick Lane, Lyne, W of Chertsey) A notable miniature steam railway, with a unique signalling system. Snacks, some disabled access; open pm Sun May–Oct; (01932) 565474; £1.20. The Golden Grove on St Ann's Hill, out towards here, is a nice spot for lunch. THORPE PARK (A320 N of Chertsey) The area's main draw, a well organised theme park covering 500 acres. Star ride is the bizarrely named X:/No Way Out, a roller-coaster hidden inside an enormous pyramid that not only soars up and down in total darkness, but does it all backwards. Tastes have clearly changed since the park opened with its models and rather gentle displays in 1979 (you can still see some of these in Model World, or dotted

around the grounds). Other lively features include Thunder River and Calgary Stampede, and there are quite a few water-based rides, inc the highest log flume in the country. Also more sedate play areas, a man-made beach and pools, and a traditional working farm with craft centre, reached by train or waterbus. Staff are friendly, and an extra bonus is that by booking in advance (even by a couple of days) you can knock quite a bit off the normal admission price. Meals, snacks, shop, disabled access; cl Nov–mid-Mar; (01932) 562633; £14.75. Grandad could very happily be dropped off in the nearby Red Lion on Ten Acre Lane.

☺ 🐾 **Chessington** TQ1762 *See separate Family Panel on p.623* for CHESSINGTON WORLD OF ADVENTURES. The Star (A243 towards Leatherhead) is a good place to fortify yourself before or after.

★ ✝ ⚜ **Chiddingfold** SU9635 Lovely village in fine surroundings, with one window of its church made up from locally excavated fragments of 13th-c glass made here. The old Crown is a handsome place for lunch or afternoon tea. RAMSTER (A283 S) has a splendid, Edwardian, woodland spring garden. Teas (May only), plant sales, disabled access; open 18 Apr–12 July; (01428) 644422; £2.50.

🏛 ✗ ⚜ **Cobham** TQ1060 Quite a busy shopping town, with some fine older buildings around the church and in Church St; just SW, Downside Common is a classic cricket green, with cottages scattered around it and an attractive pub – the Cricketers. BUS MUSEUM (Redhill Rd) Private collection of London buses from the 1930s to present. Open wknds and bank hols; free. The WATERMILL (Mill

Rd) has been authentically restored by enthusiastic locals and is once again working. Open pm 2nd Sun of month Apr–Oct; free. PAINSHILL PARK (A425 slightly W) These beautifully restored 18th-c landscape gardens are a continual surprise, with Gothic temples, Chinese bridges and other follies at every turn, and a lake with seemingly endless bays and inlets. Lots of unusual trees and shrubs. Snacks, shop, limited disabled access; usually cl Mon (exc bank hols), and winter Weds and Fri, but worth checking; (01932) 864674; £3.50. Almost opposite the gates, the Snail brasserie has decent food.

▣ † Compton SU9546 (nr Guildford) WATTS PICTURE GALLERY (Down Lane) Memorial gallery to Victorian painter and sculptor G F Watts; in his time he was one of the most celebrated artists in the world. Good tearoom, shop, disabled access; open am Weds and Sat, and pm Sun–Tues and Fri; (01483) 810235; free. Just down the road the Art Nouveau tomb built by his widow is worth a look, and the village church is attractive. The Harrow and Withies have nice but pricey food.

★ ☃ ❋ ! ☛ Dorking TQ1649 A pleasant market town with a lot of antique shops, and a local museum (West St, where the 16th-c King's Arms has decent food); the roads S of the A25, W of here, are the county's most rewarding drives, and the steep road up Box Hill N opens a great panorama. DENBIES (London Rd) Britain's biggest vineyard – at 250 acres, bigger than most in France. The tour is unique, with road-train rides round the winery, and a 3-D film, where 4 months of vine growth is condensed into 4 minutes, and grapes seem to fly out of the screen. You don't have to be a wine buff to enjoy it. Meals and snacks (in an unusually designed restaurant), big shop, good disabled access; cl am Sun, 25–26 Dec; (01306) 876616; *£4.50 (inc tastings). Fine views and walks nearby. CHAPEL FARM TRAIL (Westhumble TQ1651) Well organised working farm with lots of animals in lovely countryside, trailer rides (£1 extra), and pleasant walks. Snacks, shop, disabled access; cl Nov–mid-Feb; (01306) 882865; *£1.85.

🏠 🐾 East Clandon TQ0652 HATCHLANDS Handsome, 18th-c brick house with more floors than are visible from the outside, thanks to an ingenious use of false windows. The grand rooms are especially notable for their ceilings and fireplaces, early examples of the work of Robert Adam. A fine collection of keyboard instruments includes a piano once played by Mozart. The garden has a parterre by Gertrude Jekyll. Meals, snacks, shop, disabled access (with notice); open Apr–Oct, house pm Sun, Tues–Thurs and bank hols, plus pm Fri in Aug, park walk daily; (01483) 222482; *£4.20, *£1.70 garden and park walk; NT. A visit here is easily combined with Clandon Park at West Clandon (you can get a joint ticket). The Queen's Head is useful for lunch.

! ☛ Epsom TQ2259 Famous for its racecourse, where the Derby (first run in 1780) is still the most prestigious race for 3-year-olds – and a grand social event. DERBY DAY EXPERIENCE (Queen's Stand) Re-creates the excitement of the race, with the help of archive film, interactive displays and various relics and mementos. Worth a look even if you're not a racegoer – though it's usually open only one Sun a month; best to ring (01372) 726311 for dates; £3. Other famous racecourses in this area include Sandown Park TQ1364, (01372) 463072; Kempton Park TQ1168, (01932) 782292; and Lingfield TQ3843, (01342) 834800; all have good facilities. HORTON PARK CHILDREN'S FARM (B280 W of Epsom) Plenty of animals to feed and cuddle, tractor rides, and an adventure playground. Meals, snacks, shop, disabled access; cl 25–26 Dec; (01372) 743984; £3.15 per child (accompanied adults free).

🐾 🌳 Esher TQ1263 CLAREMONT LANDSCAPE GARDEN (off the A307) The oldest surviving landscaped garden in the country, laid out by Vanbrugh and Bridgeman before

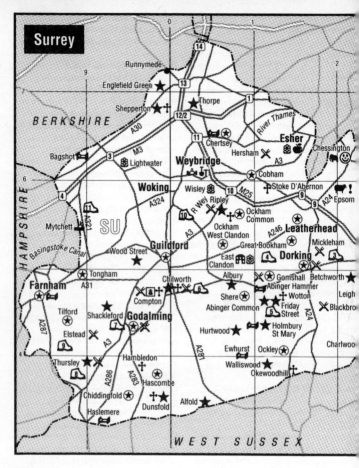

Surrey

Runnymede
Englefield Green ★
Shepperton ★ ✝
BERKSHIRE
A30
Bagshot
M3 ✿ Lightwater
Mytchett
SU
Basingstoke Canal
HAMPSHIRE
A321
Farnham
A31 Tongham
Tilford
Elstead
Shackleford
Thursley
Chiddingfold
Haslemere
Runnymede
Thorpe ★
12/2
11 Chertsey
River Thames
Esher ✿
Chessington ☺
Hersham ✗ A3
Weybridge
Cobham
Woking Wisley ✿ 10 M25 Stoke D'Abernon
A324 R Wey Ripley
10 Ockham Common
Ockham West Clandon
Leatherhead
A246
Great Bookham Mickleham
Guildford Wood Street East Clandon
Dorking ✗
Chilworth Albury Gomshall Betchworth ★
Compton Abinger Hammer
Godalming Shere ✿ Wotton ✝ Leigh
Abinger Common Friday Street Blackbro
5
Hurtwood Holmbury St Mary
Hambledon Ewhurst Ockley ✿ Charlwoo
Hascombe Walliswood ★
Dunsfold Okewoodhill
Alfold ★
WEST SUSSEX

1720 and extended and naturalised by Kent; 50 colourful acres to lose yourself in. Meals, snacks, shop, disabled access; cl Mon Nov–Mar, 25 Dec, 1 Jan, 7 July (the day before their annual fête); (01372) 469421; £3; NT. There's a farm shop with PICK-YOUR-OWN fruit on Winterdown Rd, just N.

★ ☗ 🏠 ⚥ ☙ ✿ ♪ **Farnham** SU8346 Handsome town that owed its Georgian heyday to the importance of local corn and hops. Many elegant buildings from this period remain, and there are some even older ones such as the early 17th-c Spinning Wheel. The area around Castle St is especially nice to stroll round. The Spotted Cow (Tilford Rd, Lower Bourne) is popular for lunch. The excellent local history MUSEUM (West St) has some William Cobbett memorabilia and a pleasant walled garden (cl Sun and Mon; free); Cobbett's picturesque birthplace in Bridge Sq is now a pub named after him. The CASTLE was for 800 years a residence of the Bishops of Winchester. Most of the buildings have been adapted to suit the briefing organisation based here, but the major rooms, inc the great hall, can be visited pm Weds; cl Christmas–New Year;(01252) 721194; £1.20. The Norman keep, administered separately, includes the massive foundations of a Norman tower; open daily Apr–Sept; (01252)

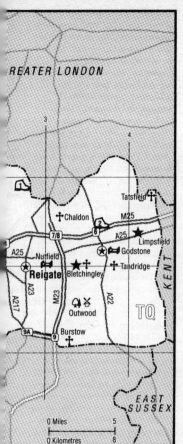

Attractive town with a quite a few interesting buildings and, because of its narrow streets (part cobbled and pedestrianised), a more old-fashioned feel than most in Surrey. Opposite the town hall, known affectionately by the locals as the Pepper Pot, is a 15th-c house with a local history MUSEUM and a Gertrude Jekyll-style walled garden (cl Mon, Sun, bank hols; free). The Inn on the Lake (A3100 S) is good for lunch, and the Star (Church St) has decent snacks. RIVER WEY & GODALMING NAVIGATION This 17th-c canal, passing through some fine scenery, was extended here in 1763, to link Godalming with the Thames. The wharf has some handsome Georgian buildings, and the locks and towpath have been restored for the NT. You can walk all the way to Weybridge, some 20 miles, or hire boats from Farncombe Boat House (01483) 421306. BUSBRIDGE LAKES SU9742 (Hambledon Rd, off the B2130) Very pretty spot with 3 lakes in pleasant parkland – exotic waterfowl, peacocks, ornamental pheasants and many other kinds of bird, as well as follies and grottoes throughout the grounds. Snacks, shop; only open 5–13 Apr, 3–4 and 24–25 May, and 23–31 Aug; (01483) 421955; *£3.40.

★ † 🐄 🏠 👺 Godstone TQ3551
Attractive despite its main roads, spread around a broad green with a duck pond, and a pretty group of houses around the imposing CHURCH, 14th/15th-c with a Norman tower. The Bell is an enjoyable dining pub. GODSTONE FARM (Tilburstow Hill) Friendly, 40-acre working farm; children are encouraged to touch the animals (and even climb in with some of them). Snacks, shop, disabled access; cl Nov–mid-Feb; (01883) 742546; £3.30 per child (accompanied adults free). PILGRIM HARPS (Stansted House, Tilburstow Hill Rd – a bit further S) Make and restore harps of all shapes and sizes; by appointment only, (01342) 893242. The ancient Fox & Hounds out this way has good food (no children inside). FLOWER FARM (Quarry Rd, just off the A22, E of

713393; £2, inc Walkman tour. The JOHNSON WAX KILN GALLERY in Bridge Sq has diverse arts and crafts; cl Sun and bank hols; free. BIRDWORLD (Holt Pound SU8143, off the A325, 3m SW of Farnham) A wide variety of birds in 18 acres of garden and parkland – all shapes and sizes from the tiny tanagers to the huge ostrich, with many rare species. Woodland walks and trails, and the adjacent UNDERWATER WORLD has tropical and other freshwater and marine fish. Meals, snacks, shop, disabled access; cl 25 Dec; (01420) 22838; £4.95 just Birdworld, £6.50 with Underwater World too. The nearby 16th-c Cherry Tree, at Rowledge, has good food.

★ 🏠 👺 ⚓ 🏵 🐦 Godalming SU9643

Oxted) Looking up to the downs, this has organically grown, PICK-YOUR-OWN produce and a vineyard. Meals, snacks, shop, disabled access; cl Nov–Apr (exc vineyard, open all year); (01883) 744590; free.

✕ ⛤ ⚘ 🅿 **Gomshall** TQ0847 GOMSHALL MILL (A25) Restored and working 2-wheeled watermill dating back to 1086, with riverside gardens, and various craft shops; restaurant (not pm Mon), disabled access; (01483) 202433; free. Next door, the GOMSHALL GALLERY has contemporary arts and crafts, as well as a French wine wholesaler, and house plants for sale; cl Sun and bank hols. The neighbouring Compasses (also with a streamside garden) does good-value lunches.

🏠🅿⛤ ♿ **Great Bookham** TQ1352 POLESDEN LACEY (S off the A246) Attractive Regency house once at the centre of Edwardian high society, now with photographs of some of the notable guests, as well as splendid tapestries, porcelain, old masters and other art. The spacious grounds have a walled rose garden and an open-air theatre. Meals, snacks, shop, disabled access; house open pm Weds–Sun Apr–Oct, plus pm wknds and Good Fri in Mar, grounds open all yr; (01372) 458203; £5, £3 grounds only; NT. Ranmore Common is handy for walks; nearby WALTON POOR sell herb, scented and foliage plants Weds–Sun Easter–Oct, and open their pretty garden by appointment (01483) 282273. On the other side of the extended commuter village, the Bookham Commons, with a mixture of thorny scrub (full of birds), small lakes, marshy bits and oak trees, are well wooded and attractive. In Effingham nearby, the Plough and Sir Douglas Haig are both reliable food pubs.

🏠♣✝🏰❀☼🍴🅿 **Guildford** SU9949 The biggest town in the area, Guildford is older than you might at first think; although many of the buildings are Georgian-fronted, what's behind often dates back much further. The sloping High St has attractive parts as well as its briskly modern shops, with interesting

buildings inc the ABBOTS HOSPITAL, the GRAMMAR SCHOOL with its notable chained library, and best of all the mainly Tudor GUILDHALL, which has one of the few existing sets of Elizabethan standard measures. Free guided tours at 2pm and 3pm Tues and Thurs; (01483) 444035. Tunsgate Arch opposite is the starting-point for free guided walks of the city – 2.30pm every Sun, Mon and Weds mid-May–Sept (plus 7.30pm Thurs till the end of Aug). The handsome GUILDFORD BOAT HOUSE (Millmead) is impressive; you can hire boats here for the Wey Navigation (01483) 504494. Nearby the White House and Jolly Farmer do decent food in a lovely riverside setting. The CATHEDRAL, begun in 1936, is one of the only two entirely 20th-c Anglican cathedrals in the country; it's quite austere, but has a cool elegance inside. The hill of the ruined 12th-c CASTLE has fine views of the town, and a garden in the former castle ditch. Shop; open Easter–Sept; (01483) 444702; keep 75p, grounds free. Nearby on Quarry St, the local history MUSEUM has a display on Lewis Carroll, who died here in 1898 (cl Sun; free). He's buried in the cemetery on the Mount, the continuation of the High St. LOSELEY HOUSE 🖼 (off the B3000, 3 miles SW of Guildford) Most people are familiar with the name from the yoghurts and ice-cream produced here (try the white chocolate and butterscotch versions), and you can tour the dairy farm that makes them. The stately Elizabethan country house was built in 1562, and has fine panelling, ceilings, paintings and tapestries. Trailer rides on Sats. Meals, snacks, shop, limited disabled access; house and farm open pm Weds–Sat and bank hols May–Aug, gardens open all day (from 11am); (01483) 304440; £4.50 for either house and grounds or farm, £6.75 both, £2.25 gardens only.

★✝♿ **Hascombe** SU9939 A lovely village with an interesting CHURCH; Dirk Bogarde's old local the White Horse is good for lunch (with a great garden), and the B2130 S and then the Dunsfold–Chiddingfold back road is a pleasant drive. WINKWORTH ARBORETUM (B2130, just NW of Hascombe) Nearly 100 acres of lovely hillside woodland, with fine views over the North Downs – especially nice in spring, and with unusual flaring colours in the autumn. Summer snacks and shop, disabled access; (01483) 208477; £2.50; NT.

♨▣🗯🗗⚘ **Leatherhead** TQ1656 LOCAL HISTORY MUSEUM (Church St) In a pretty, 17th-c, timber-framed building, and well worth a visit; open Sat, pm Thurs and am Fri Apr–Christmas; free. The Duke's Head in the pedestrianised High St is pleasant for lunch, and there are riverside walks nearby. FIRE AND IRON GALLERY (Oxshott Rd, A244 N) Unusual exhibitions of ornamental metalwork; cl Sun. BOCKETTS FARM PARK (Fetcham, A246 S of Leatherhead) 🎟 (discount not available 25 Mar–25 Apr) Working farm in a pretty historic setting, with traditional and rare breeds, cart rides, falconry and craft demonstrations. Meals, snacks, shop, disabled access; cl 25–26 Dec; (01372) 363764; £2.95.

🕸 **Lightwater** SU9362 LIGHTWATER COUNTRY PARK The exemplary visitor centre, which had displays on the area's rich natural history (in particular the sandy heathlands) recently burned down; they hope to have finished a new one by May, and there are plenty of nature trails. Snacks, shop, disabled access; park open all year; (01276) 479582; free.

⚓ **Mytchett** SU8855 BASINGSTOKE CANAL VISITOR CENTRE (Place Rd) Displays on the canal, with boat trips (wknds and bank hols, Easter–Nov); you can hire rowing boats and there are pleasant towpath walks. Teas, shop, disabled access; cl Mon (exc bank hols), winter wknds; (01252) 370073; information centre and play areas free, exhibition *£1.50.

🏚❀🕸 **Ockham Common** TQ0859 CHATLEY HEATH SEMAPHORE TOWER (entrance on Old Lane, off the A3 to Effingham) Unique tower rather like a lighthouse, the only surviving member of a chain that once sent messages between the Admiralty in London and Portsmouth; excellent views from the top of the 88 steps. Surrounding it are 700 acres of heath and woodland, with a nature trail and enjoyable walks (inc the 20-minute trek from the car park to the tower). Shop; open pm wknds and bank hols Apr–Sept, plus Weds in school hols; (01932) 862762; £2. The extraordinary 'gothick' Hautboy (Ockham Lane) has a good brasserie.

🕷▣🗯 **Ockley** TQ1439 Some attractive old houses along the Roman road here, with the 15th-c Cricketers Arms doing good-value food; the Scarlett Arms out at Walliswood is a delightful old place. HANNAH PESCHAR GALLERY AND GARDEN (Black and White Cottage, Standon Lane) Lush garden filled with contemporary sculpture: the watergarden is now more like a tropical rainforest than the cottage garden it started as, and the atmospheric sculptures and ceramics blend perfectly with its unusual design. Some disabled access (but no lavatory); open Fri, Sat and pm Sun and bank hols 2nd Sun in May–end of Oct, other times (exc Mon) by arrangement; (01306) 627269; *£5. There's a good big farm shop with PICK-YOUR-OWN fruit nearby.

✗🕸 **Outwood** TQ3245 Spread around an attractive common, with an antique shop, and adjacent National Trust woodlands ideal for a picnic. The Bell nr the common and Dog & Duck out towards Coopers Hill are good for lunch. The very well preserved POST MILL is England's oldest working windmill, built in 1665. It's a lovely spot, 120 metres (400 ft) above sea level, with ducks, goats and horses all wandering freely about its grounds. In Apr they do tours of the adjacent woods to see the bluebells. Shop, disabled access; open pm Sun and bank hols Easter–Oct; (01342) 843644; *£2.

⊖✗✝ **Reigate** TQ2550 Among the few surviving original buildings in this mainly modern town are one or two timber-framed houses around the High St. Below the peaceful castle grounds is a network of old tunnels, notably the intriguingly elaborate BARONS CAVE, a splendidly atmospheric passageway with all sorts of myths and stories attached. The tours are enthusiastic and entertaining; usually open at least one Sat a month Apr–Oct – ring the Information Office on (01737) 242477 for full details and dates; *75p. REIGATE HEATH (off the A25 W) The 220-year-old former windmill here was converted into a church in 1882. They still have services the 3rd Sun each month in summer. Disabled access; open all year – if cl, key at the golf club clubhouse. There are pleasant walks out here, and the Skimmington Castle is a nice country pub.

Runnymede SU9972 A field by a main road; not worth visiting unless you are quite fascinated by the Magna Carta, though up the hill beyond the trees, the nearby memorials to John F Kennedy and, with their names, to the aircrew who died during World War II, are dignified and touching.

★ † **Shepperton** TQ0867 One of the best places to watch the comings and goings on the RIVER THAMES, with the Wey Navigation joining the river here; the Red Lion (Russell Rd), Warren Lodge Hotel (Church Sq) and the handsomely refurbished Thames Court Hotel (Ferry Lane) all have riverside gardens, and there's a quiet and attractive 18th-c village square with a pleasant church.

★ † ☉ ❀ **Shere** TQ0747 Very picturesque village, with 17th-c timber-framed cottages, a grassy-banked stream with ducks and a ford, and lots of interesting corners. In the partly Norman CHURCH, a quatrefoil blocked hole in the chancel wall marks the spot where a 14th-c anchorite had herself walled in, being fed through another hole outside. The Malt House is a decent local history museum, and the ancient White Horse is a good place for lunch. The village is within reach of both the North Downs around Ranmore

---

Days Out

Surrey's greensand country
Ockley sculpture garden; lunch at the Stephan Langton, Friday Street; walk up to Leith Hill tower (from car park or from Friday Street – see **Walks** section below); Shere.

Exploring the North Downs
Chapel Farm Trail, nr Dorking; lunch at King William IV in Mickleham; stroll on to Box Hill or Denbies Hillside (see **Walks** section below); Denbies vineyard, or Polesden Lacey.

Wooded heights
Walk up St Martha's Hill to the summit chapel (see **Walks** section below); lunch at the White Horse, Hascombe; Winkworth Arboretum there.

Strolls on the heath
Devil's Punchbowl/Gibbet Hill (see **Walks** section below); lunch at Three Horseshoes, Thursley; Frensham Ponds (also see **Walks** section below).

A house and garden theme
Clandon Park, West Clandon; lunch at the Onslow Arms there, or at Michels in Ripley; Wisley gardens.

Sunday at the races
Brooklands museum, Weybridge; lunch at the Cricketers, Downside Common, Cobham; brasses in Stoke D'Abernon church (if open); Derby Day Experience, Epsom (limited opening).

Common and the greensand hills to the S; the view from the Ewhurst road is particularly memorable.

⬛🔱🅰🚂 **Tilford** SU8743 RURAL LIFE CENTRE (Reeds Rd, just W) Carefully displayed private collection of farm implements and machinery, spread over 10 acres of field and woodland, with an arboretum, children's playground, and a miniature railway on Suns. Snacks, shop, disabled access; cl Mon (exc bank hols), Tues, all Oct–Easter; (01252) 795571; £3. The village has a massive oak tree, thought to be 800 years old; the Barley Mow between the river and the goose-cropped cricket green is a pleasant spot for lunch, and it's not far from here to the remains of Waverley Abbey.

🏠🍺🍴 **Tongham** SU8848 HOGS BACK BREWERY (Manor Farm, the Street) Tours of this friendly little brewery, using traditional methods to produce its 6 distinctive ales. The shop has over 500 different English, Belgian and German beers (as well as their own), alongside English wines and farm ciders. Tours at 6.30pm Weds, 11am and 2.30pm Sat, 2.30pm Sun, other times by arrangement; shop open daily; (01252) 782328; tour *£4.75 (inc tastings). Manor Farm also has PICK-YOUR-OWN fruit on the same site Jun–Sept, and there is a CRAFT CENTRE in adjacent Seale SU8947 (cl am Sun, and Mon exc bank hols). The Crown at Badshot Lea does simple, good-value food.

🏠🅰🅱 **West Clandon** TQ0451 CLANDON PARK (just off the A247) Grand 18th-c house with an unusual collection of porcelain birds, and fine furnishings and paintings. Regular concerts in the grand 2-storeyed Marble Hall. The gardens have a Maori house brought over from New Zealand in 1892. Meals, snacks, shop, disabled access to ground floor; open Apr–Oct, house from 11.30am Sun, Tues –Thurs and bank hols, gardens every day; (01483) 222482; *£4.20 NT. The smart Onslow Arms is good for lunch, and the 16th-c Bull's Head is popular too.

🏠🔱 **Weybridge** TQ0662 BROOKLANDS MUSEUM (B374)

Exhaustive museum re-creating the racing circuit's 1920s and 30s heyday, with plenty of racing cars, motorbikes and bicycles displayed in the restored clubhouse. Also a restored Wellington bomber and a comprehensive collection of vintage Vickers and Hawker planes. This was the site of the first British Grand Prix, and the first 100mph motor ride. Demonstrations and events most wknds. Snacks, shop, good disabled access; cl Mon (exc bank hols), Good Fri, Christmas wk; (01932) 857381; *£6. In the town, the waterside Old Crown (Thames St) does good-value food.

🅱 **Wisley** TQ0659 WISLEY GARDEN (just off the A3) These 300-acre gardens have come a long way since they were set up in 1904 as experimental gardens for the Royal Horticultural Society; half the area is devoted to garden, inc vegetables, and the rest to farm, orchard and woodland, with lots of unusual plants, shrubs and trees; also exemplary glasshouses. The gardens get very busy (especially at weekends) but are quite big enough to cope. Meals, snacks, shop (lots of hard-to-get gardening/plant books), garden centre (decent plants from a wide range of nurseries, but expensive), disabled access; cl Sun (exc to RHS members), 25 Dec; (01483) 224234; £5. The canalside Anchor at Pyrford Lock (turn left down exit road) is useful for lunch if the queues at the good café here daunt you; and the pub is well placed for walks along the prettiest section of the Wey Navigation Canal.

★ **Other attractive villages,** all with decent pubs, include Abinger Common TQ1145 (pretty church and duck pond, woods around), Albury TQ0447 (where the Victorian mansion Albury Park is famed for its chimneys), Alfold TQ0334, Betchworth TQ2149 (village trail from the church where *Four Weddings and a Funeral* was filmed, a working blacksmith, and a nice drive via Brockham and Newdigate to Rusper in Sussex), Bletchingley TQ3250 (Norman church),

Chilworth TQ0247, Dunsfold TQ0036 (lovely green), Englefield Green SU9971 (handy for Savill Garden in Berks), Friday Street TQ1245, Holmbury St Mary TQ1144, Hurtwood TQ0845, Leigh TQ2246, Limpsfield TQ4053 (church where Delius is buried), Ripley TQ0556, Shackleford SU9345, Thorpe TQ0268, Thursley SU9039 (interesting church), Walliswood TQ1138 (delightful woodland walk from the pub to the 13th-c church) and Wood Street SU9550.

✝ Though Surrey's village **churches** are not as notable as those in, say, Somerset, Lincs or Suffolk, and though you'll usually have to get the key from a local keyholder, most are at least worth a look. A shortlist, for the intrinsic appeal of the churches themselves or for their surroundings, would include Burstow TQ3141, Chaldon TQ3155 (with its unique wall painting of the Ladder of Salvation), Chilworth TQ0247, Dunsfold TQ0036, Okewoodhill TQ1337, Ockham TQ0756, Tandridge TQ3750, Tatsfield TQ4156 and Wotton TQ1247. The one at Stoke D'Abernon TQ1259 has the earliest surviving brass in Britain, dating from the 13th c; set in the floor of the chancel, it's very well preserved. You can climb inside what's said to be a witch's tree in front of the church at Hambledon SU9638; walk round the tree 3 times and the witch may well appear.

❗ You can book BALLOON TRIPS over the county on (01252) 844222.

Walks

In this well wooded and surprisingly hilly county, it's easy to escape from the northern suburbia. Even quite close to the M25, the traffic is out of earshot at popular strolling-grounds such as **Banstead Wood** TQ2657 ⌂-1 and **Marden Park** TQ3655 ⌂-2.

Further W, the North Downs have a more untouched rural character. **Box Hill** TQ1850 ⌂-3 is the most popular viewpoint, with a summit car park and walks on its steep juniper and boxwood slopes: great views, wild orchids and butterflies in early summer, maybe field mushrooms in early autumn; the attractively placed King William IV at Mickleham T1753 is excellent for lunch. On the other side of the Mole Gap, the North Downs Way continues along **Ranmore Common** TQ1451 ⌂-4, chalk downland (inc Denbies Hillside, owned by the NT) with sheep, wild orchids and dense woodlands, within close range of Polesden Lacey.

The **upper greensand country** ⌂-5 to the S, though much wooded, displays some satisfying variety and is arguably Surrey's best walking territory. Paths are very well kept, but the landscape's intricacies may need more than the odd glance at the OS map. Leith Hill TQ1342 has heather, sandy walks, steep pine woods and tremendous views. An 18th-c tower on its top, the highest point in South-East England, is the best viewpoint of all, with a surprising view of South London – which feels a hundred miles away. It's open, with teas, on pm Weds and Sat, Sun and bank hols, but cl Oct-Mar exc fine weekends – 50p. Friday Street TQ1245, with a fine pub and a lake, is one starting-point for switchback routes S through a series of brackeny summits to the tower. Leith Hill can also be approached through attractive farmland from the S, from Ockley TQ1440 or from the Parrot at Forest Green TQ1241. There's a similarly open approach from Ewhurst TQ0940 to Pitch Hill TQ0842, where the Windmill has decent food and glorious views from its garden. Around Hurt Wood TQ0943 large areas of private forest are open to walkers; relatively unfrequented, so it's a good place to spot birds and wild animals. The Royal Oak at Holmbury St Mary TQ1144 is handy for walkers, too.

St Martha's Hill TQ0248 ⌂-6, E of Guildford, has a church on its summit that can be reached only on foot, and by starting from Chilworth TQ0247 (nearby, the Villagers at Blackheath has maps for walkers) you can see the long-abandoned gunpowder mills by the Tilling Bourne. **Winkworth Arboretum** SU9441 ☌-7, nr Godalming, SU9643 has unspoilt terrain around it, with Hydon's Ball SU9739 a fine viewpoint, though rather hard to find. The **Devil's Punch Bowl** SU8936 ☌-8, nr Hindhead, is a spectacular fold of the Downs, with nature trails through mixed woodlands, quiet valleys and sandy heaths with scattered ponds. The area is quite developed but the woods and intricacy of the landscape give it a wholesome rurality, and the footpath network is dense. Gibbet Hill SU9035, above the A3, gets a view over most of it.

Frensham Ponds SU8541 ☌-9, built in the 13th c as fishponds, are the major features of Frensham Common, a largish tract of heathland owned by the NT and leased to the local council as a country park. The heath and ponds attract a range of reptiles, birds and insects; the nearby Holly Bush has good food.

The **Wey Navigation towpath** ☌-10 in the W of the county has the best waterside walks. The **Basingstoke Canal** ☌-11, formerly derelict, has been undergoing a tremendous programme of rehabilitation over the last 15 years or so. In its Surrey section it does not pass through such fine scenery as the Wey Navigation, but its towpath has been well restored; there's good access from the canal centre at Mytchett SU8855.

Other country areas attractive for strolling include parts of wooded Netley Heath above Gomshall TQ0847; Headley Heath TQ2053 (sandy walks and rides through heather, birchwoods and rather too much bracken); Holmwood Common TQ1745 (undulating oak- and birchwoods, lots of decent paths; the Plough at Blackbrook is good for lunch); Horsell Common SU9959 (the sandpits which inspired and saw the start of H G Wells's *The War of the Worlds*; the Bleak House at the Anthonys and Red Lion in Horsell have nice food); and Thursley Common SU9040 (more heather, unusual birds, and boggy patches with shallow ponds where dragonflies breed; the Three Horseshoes at Thursley is useful for lunch).

The William IV at Little London TQ0646, the Sportsman at Mogador TQ2452, the Donkey at Charleshill SU8944, the Plough high on its hill at Coldharbour TQ1443 and Botley Hill Farmhouse at Warlingham TQ3759 (Limpsfield Rd) are popular starts or finishes for weekend walks, and the Thurlow Arms, at Baynards Station Yard nr Cox Green TQ0734, is handy for the disused railway Downs Link Path. Besides places already mentioned for the River Thames, the Swan at Staines TQ0371 (The Hythe) and the Swan, Riverside (both Manor Rd) and Anglers Tavern (off Manor Rd), and the Weir (Sunbury Lane) at Walton-on-Thames TQ1066 have good views and access to the river and towpath.

The County Council has -guided walks throughout the year, generally exploring some historical or, more usually, natural history theme; on a typical Sunday there might be 8 or more different walks to choose from. For the current programme, ring the Planning Dept, (0181) 541 9463.

Where to eat

Blackbrook TQ1846 PLOUGH (01306) 886603 Popular pub with colourful hanging-baskets and window-boxes, in attractive walking country; generous helpings of good, imaginative food, very friendly service, marvellous choice of wines by the glass, well kept real ales, and a pretty, cottagey garden with a Swiss play-house for children; no food pm Mon, cl 25–26 Dec, 1 Jan; limited disabled access. £14|£3.95.

Chilworth TQ0247 VILLAGERS (01483) 893152 Quietly set pub surrounded by woodland and plenty of walks, an attractive terrace and garden, and a path through trees to the cricket green (where Monty addressed thousands of

Canadian troups before D-Day – a shame there isn't a commemorative plaque); rambling, beamed main bar, a small flagstoned room with a big fireplace, good, home-made, often interesting food, well kept real ales, decent house wines, and pleasant young staff; bedrooms. **£18.25|£6.75.**

Compton SU9546 TEA SHOP Down Lane (01483) 811030 Well liked tea shop offering morning coffee, light lunches, and afternoon tea; home-made cakes, scones and jams, free-range eggs, a wide range of drinks inc interesting juices, seltzers and fruity mineral waters, lots of Indian, China, herbal and fruit teas, and different coffees; cl 24 –31 Dec; partial disabled access; **£2.90.**

Compton SU9546 HARROW (01483) 810379 Smart dining pub in an interesting village nr the North Downs Way; with little beamed rooms, nice furnishings, friendly service, a very good menu (book at weekends), and well kept real ales; cl pm Sun; disabled access. **£25|£6.**

Dorking TQ1649 PARTNERS & SONS 2–4 West St (01306) 882826 Heavily beamed, 16th-c building with dining rooms on 2 floors, very imaginative modern cooking, and a thoughtful wine list; newish owners; cl Tues, am Sat, pm Sun, all Jan; disabled access. **£29.**

Elstead SU9043 WOOLPACK (01252) 703106 Cheerfully old-fashioned pub, bustling and friendly, with huge helpings of good, interesting bar food, inc vegetarian choices and lovely home-made puddings; a fair amount of wool trade memorabilia, open fires, well kept real ales, and a play area in the garden; cl pm 25 Dec–26 Dec; children in family room or dining room only. **£20|£4.75.**

Godalming SU9643 INN ON THE LAKE Ockford Rd (01483) 415575 Comfortable and attractive country house inn surrounded by lawns, gardens and a lake; with a log fire in the friendly bar, and very good food in both the bar and restaurant. **£26.50|£4.95.**

Gomshall TQ0848 MULLIGANS Station Rd (A25) (01483) 202242 Friendly staff in this attractively decorated and relaxed fish restaurant, with live French café music on Thurs; disabled access. **£24.**

Hersham TQ1164 DINING ROOM Village Green (01932) 231686 5 little rooms with log fires, very good English food inc huge puddings, a relaxed atmosphere, and cheerful, friendly staff; also a shaded terrace garden; cl am Sat, pm Sun, 1 wk at Christmas, bank hols; disabled access by arrangement. **£23|£6.95.**

Mickleham TQ1753 KING WILLIAM IV (01372) 372590 Relaxed and unpretentious pub cut into the hillside; with fine views from the snug front bar, a spacious back bar with log fires and fresh flowers, a wide range of interesting daily specials inc good vegetarian choice, and well kept real ales; lovely terraced garden, and nice walks; no food pm Mon; cl 25 Dec; limited space for children. **£15|£6.**

Ripley TQ0556 MICHELS 13 High St (01483) 224777 Charming Georgian house, with carefully cooked seasonal food (inc some unusual dishes), a decent range of wines, and good service; cl am Sat, pm Sun, Mon; children over 5. **£21.**

Thursley SU9039 THREE HORSESHOES (01252) 703268 Rather civilised, tile-hung, partly 16th-c pub with beams and log fires in the dark, cosy bar, fine old country furniture, well kept real ales, good, home-made bar food, a separate back restaurant, and 2 acres of garden. **£18.45|£6.95.**

Special thanks to G T Gander, E G Parish.

Please let us know what you think of places in the *Guide*. Use the report forms at the back of the book or simply send a letter.

SURREY CALENDAR

Some of these dates were provisional as we went to press. Please check information with the numbers provided.

JANUARY

6 **Guildford** Wassailing: Twelfth night pub tour by morris men who perform a mummers' play and drink spiced beer from the wassail bowl (01483) 444007

27 **Elmbridge** Arts Festival – *till 15 Mar* (01372) 474566

MARCH

27 **Guildford** British Gymnastics Championships at Guildford Spectrum – *till Sun 29* (01483) 443322

APRIL

13 **Weybridge** Cycle Festival at Brooklands Museum (01932) 857381

19 **Woking** Dance Umbrella – *till Sat 25* (01483) 726448

25 **Esher** Gold Cup Racing at Sandown Park (01372) 470047

MAY

1 **Banstead** Arts Festival – *till Sun 17* (01737) 353738; **Guildford** May Day Ceremony: *at 5.30am* Pilgrim morris men dance to greet the sunrise on St Martha's Hill (01483) 444751

2 **Guildford** Procession carries maypole up High St to castle green, folk dancing around the pole and elsewhere throughout the day (01483) 444751

4 **Epsom** and **Ewell** Fun Day at Hook Road Arena (01372) 732463

8 **Guildford** Motor Show at Loseley Park – *till Sun 10* (01483) 304440; **Guildford** Lewis Carroll Centenary Celebrations – *till Sun 17* (01483) 444333

9 **Englefield Green** May Plant Fair at Savill Garden (01753) 860222

25 **Guildford** County Show at Stoke Park (01483) 414651; **Redhill** Fun Day at Memorial Park (01883) 743535; **Woking** Canal Festival at Woking Bridge Barn (01483) 743024

28 **Tilford** Bach Festival – *till Sat 30* (01252) 782167

29 **Guildford** Live Crafts at Loseley House and Park Farm – *till Sun 31* (01494) 450504

31 **Epsom** Derby Festival in the town and at the Racecourse – *till Jun 8* (01372) 470047

JUNE

5 **Epsom** Derby Day and Coronation Cup at Epsom Racecourse – *till Sat 6* (01372) 726311

13 **Abinger** Old Fair: Medieval fair with maypole dancing, knights, and traditional competitions (01306) 731083; **Caterham** Carnival (01483) 444007; **Great Bookham** Open-air Theatre at Polesden Lacey Open-air Theatre – *till Fri 27* (01372) 458203

20 **Redhill** Motor Show at Redhill Memorial Park – *till Sun 21* (0181) 661 2221

27 **Guildford** Summer Festival – *till 12 July* (01483) 444334

28 **Dorking** Country Day at Box Hill (01306) 885502

JULY

15 **Esher** Fête Champêtre at Claremont: music, dance, storytelling, street theatre, fireworks and themed costume – *till Sun 19* (01372) 451596

SURREY CALENDAR

JULY cont

20 **Sunbury–Abingdon** Swan Upping on the River Thames: colourful traditional ceremony – *till Fri 24* (01628) 523030

22 **Woking** Open-air Concert – *till Sun 26* (01483) 743024

24 **East Clandon** Open-air Concerts at Hatchlands – *till Sun 26* (01483) 222482; **Guildford** Garden Festival at Loseley House and Park – *till Sun 26* (01483) 304440

25 **East Molesey** Metropolitan Police Show and Tournament at Imber Court – *till Sun 26* (0181) 247 5480; **Reigate** Summer Music – *till Sun 26* (01737) 244407

26 **Tilford** Rustic Day: traditional crafts and entertainments at Old Kiln Rural Life Centre (01252) 792300

28 **Wisley** RHS Flower Show at RHS Gardens – *till Thurs 30* (01483) 224234

31 **Guildford** Classic Car Show and Country Fair at Loseley Park: over 1,000 vintage vehicles, arena events and bands – *till 2 Aug* (01483) 304440

AUGUST

1 **Lingfield** Steam and Vintage Show – *till Sun 2* (01293) 771980

2 **Cranleigh** Agricultural Show at the Showground (01306) 621505

7 **Guildford** Outdoor Music: at Loseley Park (01625) 575681

8 **Chertsey** Agricultural Show – *till Sun 9* (01932) 872272

29 **Englefield Green** Plant Fair at Savill Garden (01753) 860222

30 **Egham** Royal Show at Runnymede Meadows – *till Mon 31* (01784) 434833; **Lingfield** Edenbridge and Oxted Agricultural Show at Ardenrun Showground – *till Mon 31* (01737) 645843

31 **Guildford** Folk and Blues Festival – *till 2 Sept* (01483) 536270

OCTOBER

4 **Woking** Drama Festival – *till Sun 18* (01483) 755855

NOVEMBER

7 **Woking** Beer Festival – *till Sun 8* (01483) 743024

We welcome reports from readers . . .

This *Guide* depends on readers' reports. Do help us if you can – in return, we offer a discount on the next edition to people who've helped us with reports for it. Tell us what you think about places already in it, and anything extra you think we should say about them. And send us your ideas for inclusion in the next edition: places to visit, eat at or stay in, attractive drives or walks, maybe even unusual interesting shops you know of. Use the card in the middle, the report forms at the end, or just write – no stamp needed: *The Good Guide to Britain*, FREEPOST TN1569, Wadhurst, E Sussex TN5 7BR.

SUSSEX

Attractively varied scenery, sunny resorts, plenty of interesting places to visit.

A favourite county with our readers, with a great variety of places to visit, many of them ideal for families. Readers particularly like the town of Rye, Leonardslee gardens at Lower Beeding, Uppark at South Harting, Pallant House in Chichester, Beachy Head (good, well organised walks from the visitor centre), and, particularly those with children, the sheep centre at East Dean and Bentley at Halland. Bodiam Castle is one of the most fun for children in Britain, and other great family outings include Drusillas Zoo Park near Alfriston, the open-air museum at Amberley, the lively collection of rescued buildings at Singleton, the Bluebell steam line near Sheffield Park, the Foredown Centre near Brighton, and the llama farm at Wych Cross. Some of the smaller places such as Living World at Exceat can enthral children, too. And even the splendid Roman villas at Bignor and Fishbourne, appealing primarily to adults, are enjoyed by many children.

Sussex stands out for its spectacular gardens, with many of the finest specimen trees and shrubs to be found anywhere, and all sorts of rarities: besides Leonardslee, there's Wakehurst Place at Ardingly, Nymans at Handcross, Borde Hill near Haywards Heath and Sheffield Park, with many really worthwhile smaller places. Earnley Gardens is rather special for its unusual range of other attractions. The Goodwood sculpture park is most appealing (but very expensive), and some of the county's many vineyards are attractively geared towards visitors.

Sussex is rich in great houses to visit: besides Uppark, most notably Arundel Castle, Goodwood, Parham at Pulborough, and Petworth; Firle has some smaller gems around it.

The Sussex countryside has very varied yet very characteristic scenery: the South Downs with their attractive flint buildings and expansive views, culminating in Beachy Head and its nearby cliffs; the sparsely wooded high sandy heathland of the Ashdown Forest (the B2026 gives drivers the best views); and the intricate landscapes of the Weald, with its steep slopes and valleys, ancient woods and hedgerows punctuated by great oaks, pretty villages, tile-hung or weatherboarded oast houses and wood and tile barns with their long 'cats'-slide' roofs.

Much of the coast is developed. Brighton combines elegant Regency architecture, including the remarkable Royal Pavilion, with a more raffish side; it's a great place for antiques, and its museum is one of very few free museums to have won a place on the Heritage Secretary's new shortlist of excellence and national importance.

Eastbourne is an unusually civilised old-fashioned seaside resort; and sandy Bognor and Worthing have a restrained appeal. Chichester has its devotees – and the great sea inlet of Chichester Harbour has some very attractive places along its shore.

Where to stay

Alfriston TQ5103 STAR High St, Alfriston, Polegate BN26 5TA (01323) 870495 £111; 34 rms. Fine hotel with a fascinating, atmospheric front part, built in the 15th c as a guesthouse for pilgrims; lots of medieval carvings, a sanctuary post in the bar, decent food and drinks, and excellent service; disabled access.

Amberley TQ0111 AMBERLEY CASTLE Amberley, Arundel BN18 9ND (01798) 831992 £170; 15 very well equipped, charming rms. Magnificent, 900-year-old castle with day rooms filled with suits of armour and weapons as well as antiques, roaring fires and panelling; friendly service, imaginative food in the no smoking, 13th-c dining room, and exceptionally pretty gardens; children over 10.

Arlington TQ5507 BATES GREEN Tye Hill Rd, Arlington, Polegate BN26 6SH (01323) 482039 *£45; 3 rms. Originally an 18th-c gamekeeper's cottage, now a no smoking farmhouse on a 130-acre turkey and sheep farm; with beams and a log fire, home-made cake and tea on arrival, big breakfasts, good Aga-cooked evening meals, and a neatly kept garden; nr South Downs and Arlington Reservoir; cl Christmas; children over 10, no pets.

Arundel TQ0107 NORFOLK ARMS High St, Arundel BN18 9AD (01903) 882101 £90; 34 rms. Comfortable Georgian coaching inn with log fires in the pleasant bars, a comfortable lounge, good food and service, and a nice old-fashioned atmosphere; disabled access.

Battle TQ7217 NETHERFIELD PLACE Netherfield, Battle TN33 9PP (01424) 774455 £105; 14 lovely rms. Handsome, Georgian-style hotel in 30 acres of gardens and parkland; with light attractive day rooms, log fire, lovely flowers, a relaxed and friendly atmosphere, and imaginative food using produce from the garden; 2 hard tennis courts, croquet and putting green; cl 2 weeks over Christmas and New Year; disabled access.

Battle TQ7414 POWDER MILLS Powdermill Lane, Battle TN33 0SP (01424) 775511 *£90, plus special breaks; 35 rms, some in annexe. Attractive 18th-c, creeper-clad manor house set in 150 acres of park and woodlands with 4 lakes (trout fishing) and outdoor swimming pool; country house atmosphere, and log fires and antiques in the elegant day rooms; attentive service, and good modern cooking in the Orangery restaurant; children over 10 in evening restaurant; well behaved dogs by prior arrangement; disabled access.

Bepton SU8618 PARK HOUSE Bepton, Midhurst GU29 0JB (01730) 812880 *£95; 14 rms. Quietly set country house nr Goodwood and Cowdray Park, with a heated swimming pool, grass tennis courts, croquet and putting; comfortable drawing room, a convivial small bar, and good homely cooking in the elegant dining room; disabled access.

Bosham SU8003 KENWOOD Bosham, Chichester PO18 8PH (01243) 572727 *£45; 3 large rms. Comfortable and well kept Victorian house with harbour views, a plushly furnished lounge, and a pleasant dining room; heated swimming pool, croquet, and free-range poultry; disabled access.

Bosham SU8003 MILLSTREAM Bosham Lane, Bosham, Chichester PO18 8HL (01243) 573234 *£112, plus special breaks; 33 rms. Warm and friendly, small hotel in a charming waterside village; with an attractive bar and lounge, very good food using fresh local produce, decent wine list, and a streamside garden; disabled access.

Brighton TQ3004 DOVE 18 Regency Sq, Brighton, BN1 2FG (01273) 779222

*£58, plus special breaks; 10 rms, 4 with sea view. Lovely, neatly kept, bow-windowed Regency house with warmly welcoming and helpful owners; very good breakfasts in the light and airy dining room (enjoyable evening meals by prior arrangement); they are kind to families, with toys and babysitting available.

Brighton TQ3004 GRAND King's Rd, Brighton, BN1 2FW (01273) 321188 **£165**, plus special breaks; 200 handsome rms, many with sea views. Famous Victorian hotel with marble columns and floors and fine moulded plasterwork in the luxurious and elegant day rooms; exemplary service, very good food and fine wines, popular afternoon tea in the sunny conservatory, a bustling nightclub, and health spa with indoor swimming pool; disabled access.

Brighton TQ3004 TOPPS 17 Regency Sq, Brighton BN1 2FG (01273) 729334 *£79; 15 lovely comfortable rms, 11 with gas-effect coal fires. Carefully furnished and well kept Regency town house nr seafront; friendly, helpful service, good breakfasts and unpretentious dinners in attractive basement restaurant, and a library/reception room.

Burwash TQ6724 ASHLANDS COTTAGE Burwash, Etchingham TN19 7HS (01435) 882207 **£36**; 2 rms, shared bthrm. In a lovely spot nr Batemans, this pretty cottage has marvellous views, a homely sitting room, an attractive dining room (no full suppers but pubs nearby), and an appealing garden; children over 12.

Chichester SU8605 BEDFORD Southgate, Chichester PO19 1DP (01243) 785766 **£70**, plus special breaks; 20 attractive rms. Family-run Georgian hotel in the centre, with a friendly atmosphere, and a comfortable no smoking lounge and restaurant opening on to a quiet terrace.

Chidham SU7903 OLD RECTORY Chidham Lane, Chidham, Chichester PO18 8TA (01243) 572088 **£42**; 4 rms. Handsome country house with an elegant sitting room; friendly owners, and good breakfasts (good pub nearby for evening meals); and summer swimming pool in big garden; cl 2–3 wks in winter.

Climping TQ0000 BAILIFFSCOURT Climping, Littlehampton BN17 5RW (01903) 723511 **£125**, plus special breaks; 27 rms, many with 4-poster beds and open log fires in winter, and with super views. Mock 13th-c manor built only 60 years ago but with tremendous character – fine old iron-studded doors, huge fireplaces, heavy beams and so forth – set in 22 acres of coastal pastureland and walled gardens; elegant furnishings, enjoyable, modern English and French food, fine wines, and a relaxed atmosphere; outdoor swimming pool, tennis and croquet; limited disabled access.

Coolham TQ1222 BLUE IDOL Old House Lane, Coolham, Horsham RH13 8QP (01403) 741241 **£40**; 5 rms, shared bthrm. Lovely, no smoking, timber-framed house in quiet countryside, with a big garden (dogs welcome), a comfortable lounge, and enjoyable breakfasts.

Cuckfield TQ3024 OCKENDEN MANOR Ockenden Lane, Cuckfield RH17 5LD (01444) 416111 **£105**, plus special breaks; 22 pretty rms. Dating from 1520, this carefully extended manor house has antiques, fresh flowers and an open fire in the comfortable sitting room; good modern cooking in the fine panelled restaurant, a cosy bar, and lovely views from the neatly kept garden.

East Grinstead TQ3634 GRAVETYE MANOR Vowels Lane (off the B2110 SW), East Grinstead RH19 4LJ (01342) 810567 **£160** (minimum stay 2 nights at wkends); 18 lovely rms. Elizabethan manor house set in magnificent grounds and gardens – 400 years old this year, and also the 40th year the Herbert Family have been at the helm; antiques, fine paintings, and lovely flower arrangements in the spacious panelled public rooms, an excellent restaurant using home-grown produce (inc spring water and free-range eggs) and their own home-smoked fish and meats, an exceptional wine list, exemplary service, and a relaxed, almost old-fashioned atmosphere; children over 7.

East Hoathly TQ5116 OLD WHYLY Halland Rd, East Hoathly, Lewes BN8 6EL (01825) 840216 *£80; 3 rms. Handsome and historic 17th-c manor house set in a lovely garden with a tennis court and swimming pool, very close to Glyndebourne (hampers can be provided); fine antiques and paintings, and delicious food; plenty of walks.

Eastbourne TV6198 GRAND King Edward's Parade, Eastbourne BN21 4EQ (01323) 412345 £150, plus special breaks; 164 rms, many with sea views. Very well run, gracious Victorian seaside hotel with a tranquil atmosphere, opulent drapes, chandeliers and marble pillars, spacious lounges, and beautiful flowers; excellent, imaginative food in the elegant restaurant, and particularly good service; fine leisure facilities inc a gymnasium and snooker room; disabled access.

Eastbourne TV6097 HYDRO Mount Rd, Eastbourne BN20 7HZ (01323) 720643 £94, plus special breaks; 85 rms, many with fine sea views. Long-standing hotel with a loyal following, quiet gardens with croquet, putting, a heated outdoor pool, and sea views; comfortable, spacious lounges, a tranquil library, courteous helpful staff, and good reliable food in the elegant restaurant; disabled access.

Fairlight TQ8712 FAIRLIGHT COTTAGE Fairlight, Hastings TN35 4AG (01424) 812545 *£40; 3 rms. Comfortable and very friendly house in fine countryside, with views over Rye Bay and plenty of rural and clifftop walks; a big, comfortable lounge with nice views, good breakfasts in the elegant dining room, and generous, carefully prepared evening food (by prior arrangement); well behaved pets welcome.

Fittleworth TQ0118 SWAN Fittleworth, Pulborough RG20 1EN (01798) 865429 £50; 10 rms, most with own bthrm. Attractive 15th-c inn with a big inglenook log fire in the comfortable lounge, friendly service, decent food, an attractive panelled side room, and a sheltered back lawn; good nearby walks.

Five Ashes TQ5524 HUGGETTS FURNACE FARM Stonehurst Lane, Five Ashes, Mayfield TN20 6LL (01825) 830220 *£50; 5 rms, 2 in cottage. Lovely medieval house in quiet countryside, with 120 acres of farmland to walk around, a heated swimming pool, ponds and a river (coarse fishing); beams and inglenook fireplaces, a friendly atmosphere, dinner using home-grown produce (book in advance), and hearty breakfasts; self-catering also; children over 8; cl 24–26 Dec.

Frant TQ5835 OLD PARSONAGE Church Lane, Frant, Tunbridge Wells, Kent TN3 9DX (01892) 750773 *£62, plus special breaks; 3 very pretty rms, 2 with 4-posters. Just 2ms from Tunbridge Wells lies this carefully restored, imposing former Georgian rectory with antiques, watercolours and plants in the elegant sitting rooms and the spacious Victorian conservatory; good food in the candlelit dining room, and a balustraded terrace overlooking the quiet 3-acre garden; several nearby walks.

Hartfield TQ4837 BOLEBROKE MILL Perry Hill, Edenbridge Rd, Hartfield TN7 4JP (01892) 770425 *£57; 5 rms, some in the mill and some in the adjoining Elizabethan miller's barn. Used as a working mill up until 1948, this ancient place was mentioned in the Domesday Book, and is surrounded by mill streams and woodland; in the mill itself the internal machinery has been kept intact and the steep, narrow stairs lead to bedrooms that were once big corn bins; both this and the Barn have their own sitting room, breakfasts are marvellous, light suppers enjoyable, and the owners very friendly; excellent nursery nearby; no smoking; cl Christmas–Jan; children over 7.

Mayfield TQ5827 MIDDLE HOUSE Mayfield, TN20 6AB (01435) 872146 *£55; 8 spacious rms, most with own bthrm. Old-world Elizabethan hotel nr the church; with a lovely panelled restaurant, red leather chesterfields and armchairs by the cosy log fire, chatty locals' bar with a big open fire (maybe spit roasts), and a wide choice of good bar food; attractive back garden, and pleasant views.

Midhurst SU8821 SPREAD EAGLE South St, Midhurst GU29 9NH (01730) 816911 £115, plus special breaks; 39 pretty rms. Historic old inn dating back in part to 1430, with an impressive beamed and timbered lounge, a dramatic fireplace and imposing leaded-light windows; handsome furnishings, a neatly modernised, airy barrel-vaulted cellar bar, good food, fine wines and well kept real ales; limited disabled access.

Offham TQ4012 OUSEDALE HOUSE Offham, Lewes BN7 3QF (01273) 478680 £54, plus special breaks; 3 pretty rms with shower or bthrm. Victorian country house with good views, and 3½ acres of garden and woodland; friendly owners, a spacious lounge, and traditional cooking using home-grown seasonal produce; no children.

Rogate SU8023 MIZZARDS Rogate, Petersfield GU31 5HS (01730) 821656 *£52; 3 rms. 16th-c house in a quiet country setting, with a comfortable and elegant sitting room, and a vaulted dining room; outside swimming pool, landscaped gardens and lake, and fine farmland views; no evening meals, no smoking; cl Christmas; children over 8.

Rye TQ9220 JEAKES HOUSE Mermaid St, Rye TN31 7ET (01797) 222828 *£63, plus special breaks; 12 rms overlooking the rooftops of this medieval town or across the marsh to the sea, 10 with own bthrm. Fine 16th-c building, well run and friendly, with good breakfasts, lots of well worn books, comfortable furnishings, linen and lace, a warm fire, and a lovely peaceful atmosphere.

Rye TQ9220 LITTLE ORCHARD HOUSE West St, Rye TN31 7ES (01797) 223831 *£60; 3 rms. Beautifully furnished, fine old house with antiques and personal prints and paintings, Georgian panelling, and a big open fireplace in the study; good generous breakfasts (the friendly owners will make evening reservations at any of the many nearby restaurants), and an unexpectedly wonderful, secluded garden; children over 12.

Rye TQ9220 OLD VICARAGE 66 Church St, Rye TN31 7HF (01797) 222119 *£59, plus bargain breaks; 6 pretty rms with complimentary newspaper and glass of sherry. Charming, quietly placed, mainly 18th-c house with helpful and friendly owners; comfortable sitting room or small library, a log fire in the elegant dining room, and marvellous breakfasts with free-range eggs, freshly made scones and home-made marmalade; cl Christmas; children over 8.

Rye TQ9220 WHITE VINE HOUSE High St, Rye TN31 7JF (01797) 224748 £70, plus special breaks; 6 rms. Attractive Georgian house built over fine, medieval vaulted cellars; with a friendly relaxed atmosphere, plenty of books, pictures and flowers, and a cosy lounge; morning coffee, lunch and afternoon tea in the parlour (using the best local produce), and enjoyable breakfasts; no smoking; children over 12; self-catering cottage.

Shipley TQ1422 GOFFSLAND FARM Shipley, Horsham RH13 7BQ (01403) 730434 *£34; 1 family rm. Friendly, 17th-c Wealden farmhouse on a 260-acre family farm; good walks.

Slinfold TQ1131 RANDOM HALL Stane St, Slinfold, Horsham RH13 7QX (01403) 790558 £79.50, plus special breaks; 15 comfortable rms. Restored 16th-c farmhouse with lots of beams, flagstones, copper and brass and a fine inglenook fireplace in the lounge; a friendly relaxed atmosphere, good breakfasts, and enjoyable modern cooking in the candlelit restaurant (or on the terrace); cl 1st wk Jan.

Storrington TQ0814 LITTLE THAKEHAM Merrywood Lane, Storrington, Pulborough, RH20 3HE (01903) 744416 *£164.50, plus special breaks; 9 individually decorated rms with stylish fabrics and early antiques. Splendid combination of a magnificent Lutyens house, a delightfully restored Gertrude Jekyll garden, antiques and arts and crafts furniture and objets d'art; log fires, traditional English and French food using local produce, and good French wines; an outdoor swimming pool, tennis court, and croquet; cl Christmas and New Year.

Telham TQ7714 Little Hemingfold Farmhouse Telham, Battle TN33 0TT (01424) 774338 *£76, plus special breaks; 13 rms, most with own bthrm. Partly 17th-c, partly early Victorian farmhouse in 40 acres of woodland, with trout lake, tennis court, gardens, and lots of walks (the 2 labradors may come with you); comfortable sitting rooms, open fires, a restful atmosphere and very good food using home-grown produce – either in the style of dinner party or at one's own candlelit table; children can feed the farm animals; cl 6 Jan–10 Feb; dogs welcome.

Tillington SU9621 Horse Guards Tillington, Petworth, GU28 9AF (01798) 342332 *£62; 3 spacious clean rms. Neat, friendly and civilised 17th-c pub in a lovely village setting, with a beamed front bar, very good, imaginative food (fresh fish delivered 5 times a week, and excellent puddings), and up to a dozen wines by the glass; no children.

Trotton SU8322 Southdowns Country Hotel Trotton, Rogate, Petersfield GU31 5JN (01730) 821521 £99, plus special breaks; 22 rms. Close to Goodwood and Fontwell Park race courses, this extended Victorian hotel has spacious grounds, croquet, a leisure club with 2 all weather tennis courts, an indoor pool, and a multigym; comfortable, relaxed public rooms, and good food; disabled access.

Uckfield TQ4718 Horsted Place Little Horsted, Uckfield TN22 5TS (01825) 750581 *£100; 17 individually decorated spacious rms. Stately Victorian country house set in 23 acres; with antiques, flowers and log fires in the luxurious lounges, delicious food and good wine list in the no smoking dining room; croquet, tennis, an indoor heated swimming pool, and reduced green fees at East Sussex National; babies or children over 8 in restaurant; disabled access.

Wadhurst TQ6631 Newbarn Wards Lane, Wadhurst TN5 6HP (01892) 782042 *£44; 3 pretty rms, 2 with own bthrm. Carefully renovated, 18th-c tile-hung farmhouse in a marvellous position close to Bewl Water (walks, bike hire, boating, etc); very friendly, helpful owners, an inglenook fireplace in the attractive and comfortable sitting room, and good breakfasts with home-made preserves; lakeside gardens; self-catering cottages also; cl Christmas.

Wisborough Green TQ0526 Old Wharf Wharf Farm, Wisborough Green, Billingshurst RG14 0JG (01403) 784096 *£55; 4 rms with views over farmland and canal. Carefully restored, no smoking, canal warehouse with a fine old hoist wheel; comfortable sitting room with a log fire, breakfasts using free-range eggs from the farm, a walled canalside garden, and a friendly atmosphere; cl Christmas and New Year; children over 12; no pets.

To see and do

SUSSEX FAMILY ATTRACTION OF THE YEAR

🏰 ⛵ 🚣 **Bodiam** TQ7825 Bodiam Castle Children love this perfect picture-book castle, and though some people rush through in an hour, quite a few families easily stretch it out to half a day or more, a visit's length bound only by the limits of the imagination. It's a classic example of 14th-c fortification at its peak, with massive walls rising sheer and virtually complete from the romantic moat, and round drum towers steadfastly guarding each corner. Built to withstand attack from the French, it was only ever besieged by other Englishmen, and on both occasions was rather weedily handed over without a fight. The interior was destroyed about the time of the Civil War, and wasn't repaired until Lord Curzon bought it in 1916; he left the castle to the NT in 1925. It's great fun climbing the spiral staircases up to the battlements (splendid views from the top) and there are plenty of mysterious-looking nooks and crannies along the way. Also a couple of short videos on medieval castle life, and lots of space for picnics. They have several enjoyable special events, inc a fun day with donkey rides and Punch and Judy, a Christmas Cracker hunt, and children's story-telling. It's worth reading the leaflet they give you on arriving at the car park – most people fail to spot that the lavatories are at this end rather than at the castle itself, and have to trudge all the way back again. Meals, snacks, shop, limited disabled access; cl Mon Nov–Dec, 24–26 Dec; (01580) 830436; £1 car park, then castle £3 (£1.50 children 5–15); NT. The family ticket is good value: £7.50 for 2 adults and up to 3 children. Next to the castle, Knollys is a good tea shop, and the Salehurst Halt at Salehurst just W does good lunches. In summer you can put together a very enjoyable full day out by taking the 45-minute boat trip to the castle through peaceful countryside from Newenden (they don't run in bad weather); (01797) 280363 for times; £7 return. This can then link with a STEAM TRAIN on the Kent & East Sussex Railway (see Tenterden entry in our Kent chapter).

★ † 🎮 🏰 Alfriston TQ5103 In a sheltered spot below the Downs, this is one of Britain's most charming villages – at quieter times of year (in high summer the ice-cream eaters, teashops and curio shops somewhat blunt its appeal). Thatched, tiled and timbered houses, and a fine church built on a Saxon funeral barrow, by a large green just off the single main street. Nr here, the 14th-c CLERGY HOUSE was the first building to be taken over by the National Trust. Carefully restored, it now gives a faithful impression of medieval life. Open daily Apr–Oct (exc Tues and Fri); (01323) 870001; £2.20; NT. One of the most engaging buildings in the village is the Star Inn, with its Old Bill, a bright red figurehead lion on one corner taken as a trophy from a 17th-c Dutch ship, and some intricate painted 15th-c carvings among its handsome timbering. Besides the Star, the Market Cross is good for lunch. DRUSILLAS ZOO PARK 🎮 (up towards the A27) One of the best organised places for children in the entire country, a small zoo keeping only animals that they can provide with everything they'd have in the wild, so no lions, tigers or elephants, but plenty of smaller and arguably more entertaining creatures like meerkats, otters, beavers, and parrots in thoughtfully designed enclosures. You watch the meerkats through a little dome in the floor of their spacious enclosure, and underwater vantage points in Penguin Bay make it look as if the birds are flying above you. Excellent play areas (one especially for toddlers) and lots of opportunities for hands-on fun. Nearly half is under cover, and there's also a railway and pottery, with special events like birds of prey or knights, jesters, and jugglers in school hols. Shops and eating areas are just outside in Drusillas Village (along with some delightful gardens); you can visit here free without having to go in the zoo. The zoo changed hands last summer, but the new owners have been regular visitors for the last 14 years so aren't likely to spoil things. Good meals and snacks, shops, disabled access; cl 24–26 Dec; (01323) 870234; £5.95. Next door, the ENGLISH WINE CENTRE sells a good cross-section of wines made in this country, as well as regional foods and crafts. Snacks, shop, disabled access; cl 23 Dec–2 Jan; (01323) 870164; free, £4.95 tours and tastings. On the other side of the Cuckmere valley the small village of Litlington TQ5201 is notable for its CHURCH down a footpath – so small there can scarcely be room in it for a congregation of more than about 15. The Plough & Harrow here is useful.

★ ⬇️ Amberley TQ0313 A delightful thatched village; from the churchyard you can peer into the castle (now a good hotel), and there is public access to the Wild Brooks. The unspoilt Black Horse has good food, there are lovely Downs views from the Sportsman's conservatory, balcony and garden, and the riverside Bridge Inn at Houghton Bridge is great in summer; the B2139 is a pleasant drive. Beside here, handily placed next to the station, AMBERLEY MUSEUM is a carefully thought-out open-air museum covering 36 acres of former chalk quarry and limeworks, with plenty of traditional crafts and re-created workshops. Lots going on, from pottery and cobbling to a working village telephone exchange. Meals, snacks, shop, disabled access; cl Mon and Tues (exc school or bank hols), and Nov–mid-Mar; (01798) 831370; £5.

⊛ **Ardingly** TQ3331 WAKEHURST PLACE GARDEN (on the B2028) The 'Southern Kew', administered by the Royal Botanic Gardens, with a tremendous variety of interesting trees and shrubs inc many tender rarities. Lakes and water gardens, steep Himalayan glade, woodland walks and fine rhododendron species. Plenty to see throughout the year, and all very peaceful. Meals, snacks, plant and book sales, disabled access; cl 25 Dec, 1 Jan; £4.50 (free to NT members). Wknd guided walks usually start in front of the mansion at 11.30am and 2.30pm (2pm in winter); 0181 332 5585 to check. The Gardeners Arms (children in garden only), the Ardingly Inn and the Oak all do good lunches.

★ ☺ 🏛 🖼 ✝ ⚘ ⛄ ♨ **Arundel** TQ0106 Dating from pre-Roman days, this is dominated by the magnificent walls and towers of the castle on a mound high over the River Arun. Attractive buildings, inc antique shops and so forth, cluster along the sides of the steep main street climbing up from the bridge to the castle itself; a MUSEUM along here has local history (cl am Sun, and Oct–Mar; £1). The CASTLE has been the seat of the Dukes of Norfolk for over 700 years. It's a magnificent sight, a great spread of well kept towers and battlements soaring above the village and the trees around it. The keep is the oldest part;

the rest dates mainly from the 19th c. Excellent art collection, inc portraits by Van Dyck, Reynolds, Lely and Gainsborough, as well as 16th-c furniture, and personal possessions of Mary Queen of Scots. Meals, snacks, shop; cl am, Sat, and Nov–Mar; (01903) 883136; £5.50. The 19th-c Roman Catholic CATHEDRAL complements the castle well, giving rather a French feel to the whole small town. Also worth a look are the TOY & MILITARY MUSEUM (High St) housed in an attractive little Georgian cottage (open wknds all year, daily Jun–Sept and school hols, cl 1–2pm; £1.25) and ENGLISH COUNTRY CRAFTS in a converted chapel in Tarrant St – they sell a good range of local crafts and have another branch in Worthing. WILDFOWL AND WETLANDS TRUST (Mill Rd) 55 acres of well landscaped pens, lakes, and paddocks, home to over 1,000 ducks, geese and swans from all over the world. Hides overlook the various habitats, and there are children's activities in school hols. Meals, snacks, shop, disabled access; cl 25 Dec; (01903) 883355; £4.25. The lane past the Trust ends at a little cluster of houses by an isolated church and former watermill. On the way to the Trust, the Black Rabbit has a superb location and does food, and in summer there are BOAT TRIPS from it; in the town, the Swan and St Mary's Gate Hotel have decent food.

⊛ **Ashington** TQ1315 HOLLY GATE CACTUS GARDEN (Billingshurst Lane) Over 30,000 succulents and cactus plants from both tropical and arid habitats all over the world – a cactus enthusiast's prickly paradise. Plant sales, disabled access; cl Christmas; (01903) 892930; *£1.50. The Franklands Arms at Washington is a useful lunch stop.

✝ ☺ **Battle** TQ7415 Takes its name from certainly the most celebrated and perhaps the most disorganised skirmish in English history, thrashed out here in 1066. The BATTLEFIELD has a mile-long walk around it, with models demonstrating what happened. 4 years after the bloodshed William built BATTLE ABBEY 🏛 on the site as penance, the altar reputedly on the very spot where Harold fell. Not much is left of the original building, but later remains include the monks' dormitory and common room, and the great 14th-c gatehouse which looms over the small market square. There's an interactive video on daily monastic life. Snacks, shop, mostly disabled access; cl 24–26 Dec; (01424) 773792; £3.50. The main streets (carrying a fair bit of traffic, so not exactly peaceful) have a lot of attractive old buildings, some now antique shops and cafés; beyond them the town extends into spreading new estates. 2 decent local history museums on the High St: the MUSEUM has a diorama of the Battle of Hastings and a reproduction of the Bayeux Tapestry (cl Oct–Easter; 80p) and the old ALMONRY has a town model, teas, and a pretty little garden; cl Sun, 25–26 Dec; a few doors along from here, BUCKLEYS YESTERDAY WORLD has carefully reconstructed period shops, railway station and the like; lots of hands-on activities, and nostalgic film show. Snacks, shop; cl 25–26 Dec, 1 Jan; (01424) 775378; £3.75. The friendly Olde Kings Head has decent food, and the CHURCH of St Mary has some 13th-c wall paintings. The B2096 Heathfield road gives views S to Beachy Head from its highest points, nr Netherfield and just before Dallington. Off this road any of the narrow side roads N into the countryside between Burwash and Dallington take you into the most unspoilt part of the steep Wealden woods and pastures.

❀ ♫ **Beachy Head** TV5995 This towering abruptly cliffy end of the Downs is a landmark for miles around: an unspoilt spot with terrific views, inc the lighthouse dwarfed far below. The BEACHY HEAD COUNTRYSIDE CENTRE has unexpectedly enjoyable exhibitions, as well as indoor and outdoor play areas, and a full programme of guided walks (best to book for these) around cliffs, beaches and wildflower meadows. Usually open daily Easter–Oct, plus wknds Nov and Dec, with walks wknds and school

hols – ring for exact dates; (01323) 737273; free, walks £2.

🏠 ♨ **Bexhill** TQ7407 A low-key seaside town with a pebble beach interrupted by cumbersome groins – an unlikely setting for a gem of Bauhaus architecture, the shoreside De La Warr Pavilion designed by Mendelsohn and Chermayeff. The Italian-run café opposite is good value. BEXHILL MUSEUM OF COSTUME AND SOCIAL HISTORY Set in the delightful grounds of the Old Manor House up in the tiny 'Old Town', a good look at 18th- to 20th-c fashions, with accessories and other domestic items as well as the clothes. Shop, disabled access; cl Weds (exc Jun–Sept), Nov–Mar; (01424) 210045; £1.50.

🏛 ♨ **Bignor** SU9814 ROMAN VILLA AND MUSEUM One of the largest villas discovered so far, with marvellous mosaics inc the longest in Britain – 25 metres (82 ft) long, and still in its original position. Snacks, shop, some disabled access, and largely under cover; cl Mon (exc bank hols and Jun–Sept), Nov–Feb; (01798) 869259; *£3.25. The White Horse at nearby Sutton has enjoyable food (and good-value bedrooms).

➤ **Birdham** SU8200 SUSSEX FALCONRY CENTRE (Lockacre Aquatic Nursery, Wophams Lane) Originally set up as a breeding and rescue centre, then opened to the public with birds such as falcons, hawks, eagles and owls flown throughout the day. Shop, disabled access; cl Mon (exc bank hols), Nov–Feb; (01243) 512472; £2.50. This area S of Chichester is flat country, full of nurseries and huge glasshouses; the Lamb towards West Wittering is a popular dining pub.

🏰 ♨ ♨ **Bodiam** TQ7825 For BODIAM CASTLE, and how to combine it with a boat trip and steam train *see separate Family Panel on p.642*. Up the hill in Ewhurst Green, the White Dog has interesting food, and BODIAM BONSAI grow, show and sell these miniature trees.

Bognor Regis SZ9399 An old-fashioned seaside family resort, popular above all for its sandy beaches; the Alex (London Rd) has

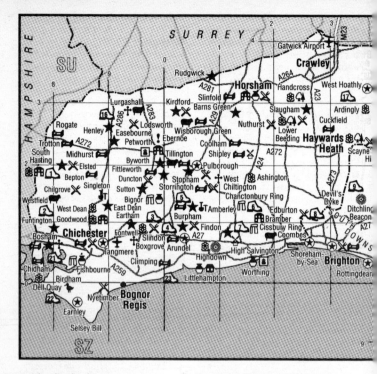

good-value food.

✝ ★ **Bosham** SU8003 The Saxon CHURCH here figures in the Bayeux Tapestry, and the village is a lovely cluster of old cottages around it, the green, and a broad, almost landlocked, inlet of Chichester harbour, busy with boating in the summer. Don't be tempted to park on the shore – the incoming tide is well known for its trick of lapping around parked cars. Very pleasant to stroll around, with good antique shops and craft galleries, especially on Bosham Lane. The Anchor Bleu, right by the water, is popular for lunch.

🏛 **Bramber** TQ1710 ST MARY'S Striking medieval house, with fine panelling, a pretty garden with topiary, and an unusual Elizabethan painted room. Concerts in spring and autumn. Teas, shop; open pm Sun, Thurs and bank hols Easter–Sept; (01903) 816205; *£3.80. The Bramber Castle has decent food. Adjacent Steyning has some attractive timber-framed and Georgian buildings (and a good Tudor pub, the Chequer).

★ 🏛 ♨ 🅿 ! ♪ ❀ ✝ ⚲ ✕ ❄ **Brighton** TQ3104 Despite its many more modern blocks, huge shopping centre and vast modern sports halls, Brighton still has plenty of glistening white Regency buildings dating from its fashionable days in the early 19th c, when the idea that sea-bathing was good for you sent London's finest scurrying to the coast. Still a thriving resort, its atmosphere gets a real kick from its vigorous young university and from its several language schools for foreign students; there's also a booming gay scene. The most lively part is the Lanes – 17th-c fishermen's cottages squeezed together in narrow twisting byways, now crammed with jewellery and antique shops, restaurants and bars; they're mostly closed to traffic. English's here is entertaining for lunch. The North Laine area is slightly more trendy, with good buskers and cool cafés. Throughout, there's no shortage of

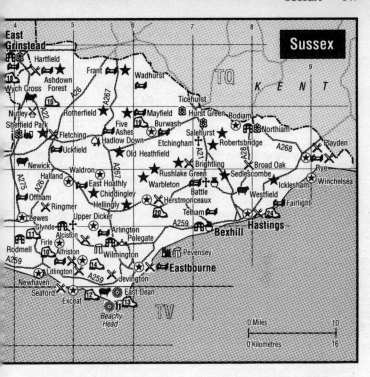

simple places to eat, inc the Cricketers (Black Lion St), Greys (Southover St, Kemp Town), Mary Packs Cliftonville (good local fish; Hove Pl), and, if you like sausages, Sussex Yeoman (Guildford Rd). ROYAL PAVILION Nash's flamboyant Indianesque confection should be top of anyone's itinerary: the most eccentric of all royal palaces, a riot of chinoiserie inside. Queen Victoria was the last monarch to own it, but was hardly its greatest fan; if the town council hadn't bought it from her she might well have demolished it. She would no doubt not have been amused to see her apartments restored to their full overblown glory. The gardens have also been returned to the original Regency plan, and they recently opened a previously unseen suite of rooms. The whole building is beautifully floodlit at night. It's less busy after 3pm – and better still out of season, when you may find more going on. Meals, snacks, shop, disabled access to ground floor only;

cl 25–26 Dec; (01273) 290900; £4.10. Around the corner, the Prince Regent's stables and riding school now house the town's excellent MUSEUM AND ART GALLERY (Church St), quite sumptuous in parts, with outstanding art nouveau and art deco objects ranging from vases, tapestries and sculpture to shoe heels and Salvador Dali's Mae West lips sofa. Snacks, shop, disabled access to ground floor only; cl am Sun, all Weds, 24–26 Dec, 1 Jan, Good Fri; (01273) 290900; free. Brighton was one of the earliest resorts to have a pier, and though that original is now a rusting wreck awaiting restoration (Lottery money is said to be in the offing), the PALACE PIER is a more than satisfactory replacement, and looks magnificent at night. Opposite here, the SEA LIFE CENTRE 🏛 (Marine Parade) has lively displays of creatures found off the British coast, with a walk-through underwater tunnel. Meals, snacks, shop, disabled access; cl 25 Dec; (01273) 604234;

£5.25. Nearby, the seafront arches across from the Old Ship Hotel used to be occupied by local fishermen, and a couple still are, the rest having been given over to little craftshops and artists. One houses a FISHING MUSEUM, with a collection of local boats, nets, models and pictures. Disabled access; cl 25–26 Dec, and any day Nov–Apr when the weather is poor; (01273) 723064; free.

A little inland, 2 particularly enjoyable museums are quite close together. BOOTH MUSEUM OF NATURAL HISTORY (Dyke Rd) A superb well presented collection of animal skeletons (inc some dinosaur bones), as well as the Victorian collection of birds the museum was first built to house. Shop, disabled access; cl am Sun, Thurs; (01273) 552586; free. PRESTON MANOR (on the A23) An entertaining and vivid illustration of life in Edwardian times, with fully furnished period rooms, and pleasant walled gardens soon to be restored. Shop; cl am Sun and Mon, 25–26 Dec, Good Fri; (01273) 292770; £2.95. On Sun mornings there's a good MARKET by the station approach; you do have to get there well before breakfast for the bargains, as it's become a major source of supply for the countless Brighton antique dealers. Nr here ST BARTHOLOMEW'S CHURCH (Anne St) is an odd building, like a huge brick barn. Film buffs will be well satisfied with the Duke of York's cinema at nearby Preston Circus, which shows the kind of movies not always found outside London. BRIGHTON MARINA (E of the centre) This modern place is lively in summer, with lots of boutiques, bars, tables out by the water and so forth. An electric train runs to here along the beach from the pier. BARLOW COLLECTION (off A27 N; University, just out of town at Falmer) Reckoned to be Europe's finest collection of Chinese ceramics. It's usually open 11.30am –2.30pm Tues (not Aug); (01273) 606755; free.

Hove TQ2804, the quieter half of the resort, is just W of Brighton proper. On the way you may be able to visit a REGENCY TOWN HOUSE in Brunswick Sq – you'll need to make an appointment on (01273) 206306; or pass ST ANDREW'S CHURCH (Waterloo St), designed by Sir Charles Barry – quite dull from the outside, but inside rather elaborate in places. HOVE MUSEUM AND ART GALLERY (New Church Rd) This grand Victorian villa houses a fine collection of British painting; cl am Sun, all Mon, and Christmas wk; (01273) 290200; free. BRITISH ENGINEERIUM (Nevill Rd) has all sorts of road, locomotive and marine steam engines, as well as tools, models, and a restored Victorian water pumping station. Shop, limited disabled access; cl wk before Christmas, engines in steam first Sun in month and bank hols; (01273) 559583; £3.50. Nearby on Holmes Ave is a WINDMILL with local history displays; open pm Sun and bank hols May–Sept; 70p. FOREDOWN TOWER COUNTRYSIDE CENTRE (Foredown Rd, Portslade) Very well done, with a CAMERA OBSCURA (best on bright days) as well as a weather station with satellite images, astronomy displays, and splendid views. They can arrange visits to Portslade Old Manor, a ruined medieval house a short stroll away. Snacks, shop; cl Mon, Fri, 23 Dec–2 Jan; (01273) 292092; £2.

★ 🏠 ⛲ ✗ **Burwash** TQ6724 The single main street of this ridge village has many attractively restored tile-hung cottages, inc a good antique centre and tea shop, with lime trees along its brick pavement. The graveyard of the Norman-towered church gives fine views over the Dudwell Valley, and the Bell opposite is useful for lunch. Just below the village, off the A265, BATEMANS was home to Rudyard Kipling from 1902 to 1936. His study is preserved much as it was then, as is the hefty pipework he installed for a hydro-electric plant to light the handsome early 17th-c stonebuilt house. The attractive gardens have a quaint operating watermill, grinding flour every Sat at 2pm. A couple of friendly donkeys are paddocked opposite. Snacks, shop, disabled access to ground floor only; cl Thurs, Fri (exc

Good Fri), and Nov–Mar; (01435) 882302; £4.50; NT. Good little-used walks up the wholly unspoilt valley from here, where you can look for Kipling landmarks such as Pook's Hill.

★ ✝ 🏛 🍺 🌳 ⚓ **Chichester** SU8604 Partly pedestrianised and easy to get around, this handsome former Roman city is one of the country's finest examples of Georgian town planning and architecture. The CATHEDRAL is mostly Norman, and unusual for rising straight out of the town's streets rather than a secluded close. The spire collapsed in the 1860s (the latest in a long line of structural problems), and was rebuilt, but even now the scaffolding always seems to be up. Highlights include the 14th-c choir stalls, John Piper's Aubusson tapestry, and the window by Chagall. Guided tours (not Sun) at 11am and 2.15pm Easter–Oct. Snacks, shop in the medieval bell tower (23 South St – unusual for being separated from the main building), disabled access; donations. The Bishop's Palace gardens are very pleasant. In St Martin's Sq, the 13th-c almshouse ST MARY'S HOSPITAL has some unique misericords in its chapel, and a pretty walled garden; usually open wkdys (exc Weds), but best to check first, (01243) 783377; free. The city's MUSEUM (Little London, cl Mon and Sun) houses its archaeological displays in the interesting former GUILDHALL in Priory Park, which began life as a Grey Friars church in medieval times; it's usually open pm Sat Jun–Sept, (01243) 784683 to check; free. Useful central pubs for food are the Bell (Broyle Rd), Jackson's Cellar (Little London; cl Sun) and Nag's Head (St Pancras). PALLANT HOUSE (North Pallant) Interesting Queen Anne town house with Edwardian kitchen and fine furnishings. The gallery has fine Bow porcelain, and an excellent range of carefully chosen 20th-c art – Sutherland, Klee, Leger, Ben Nicholson and the like. Shop; cl Sun, Mon, bank hols, and two wks in Jan; (01243) 774557; £2.50. MECHANICAL MUSIC AND DOLL COLLECTION 🔲

(Church Rd, Portfield) A multitude of barrel, fair and Dutch street organs, music boxes and phonographs – all restored and ready to play. Shop, disabled access; open pm exc Sat Easter– Oct, then just pm Sun (not Dec); (01243) 785421; £2. PAGHAM HARBOUR (off the B2145 S of Chichester) SZ8796 Peaceful nature reserve, largely silted marshy tidal flats, full of wading birds and wildfowl, particularly in spring and autumn; on the way the Blacksmiths Arms at Donnington, packed with bric-à-brac, has a good children's play area. BOAT TRIPS Peter Adams runs these around Chichester Harbour, full of yachts and dinghies in summer. They leave from Itchenor SU8001 and are best at high tide; (01243) 786418; £4. There's also an hourly passenger ferry between here and the landing at the end of the lane S from Bosham (daily Jun–Aug, wknds only Apr, May and Sept). Inland, cyclists have the Centurion Way, a short stretch of disused railway track converted to an easy route N of Chichester to Mid Lavant SU8508.

🚜 **Coombes** TQ1908 CHURCH FARM 🔲 Trailer rides over farmland and through conservation areas – you have to book, but it's great fun, especially in the lambing season. Snacks, shop, disabled access; cl mid-Oct–Feb; (01273) 452028; *£3. They also have a coarse fishing lake.

🏺 **Dell Quay** SU8302 Attractive waterside hamlet with remains of a Roman quay, harbour views (and fresh fish) from the Crown & Anchor. APULDRAM ROSES (Apuldram Lane) Over 300 kinds of old-fashioned and new roses in a harbourside field and gardens made from former orchards. The field is at its best from Jun–Sept, after which they have a good end-of-season sale. Snacks, plant sales; cl 24 Dec–7 Jan; (01243) 785769; free.

❋ **Ditchling Beacon** TQ3313 Right by the road, with superb views all around, especially out over the villages and towns to the N; a nice area of preserved sheep-cropped unimproved downland, with chalk hill blue butterflies in summer. The village below is pleasant, with a decent MUSEUM; the 14th-c Bull has good food. The B2116 to Offham has views of the South Downs.

🐄 🦋 🕊 ! **Earnley** SZ8196 EARNLEY GARDENS (Almodington Lane) This 5-acre site is these days quite a busy day out; as well as the long-established 17 themed gardens, exotic birds and free-flying butterflies, they now have a shipwreck display, small animal farm, and a refreshingly informal nostalgia museum, REJECTAMENTA. This takes in thousands of everyday objects from the last hundred years, collected over nearly a quarter of a century by an ex-art student who says she just can't stop. Meals, snacks, shop, disabled access; open mid-Mar–Oct; (01243) 512637; £5 everything, £3.25 just gardens and butterflies, £3 just nostalgia museum.

🐄 🌼 **East Dean** TV5596 SEVEN SISTERS SHEEP CENTRE 🎫 (Gilberts Drive) Very enjoyable family-run downland sheep farm with compact visitor centre, and paved paths between pens of many breeds of sheep. Lambing (mid-Mar–early May), demonstrations of shearing (Jun–mid-July), spinning, milking and cheese-making, and plenty of young animals to cuddle or bottle-feed. The farm shop sells sheep cheeses and yoghurts. Snacks, disabled access; cl am wkdys (exc school hols), all mid-Sept–mid-Mar, and some days in May – best to check first; (01323) 423302; £3. The village itself is prettily set around a sloping green, with an attractive pub, the Tiger. A lane past the farm continues to the BIRLING GAP TV5595, a cleft in the coastal cliffs famous since smuggling days, with a lighthouse and coastguard station (the Birling Gap Hotel is nicely set just above the shore); and on to Beachy Head.

🏠 🐄 **East Grinstead** TQ3938 STANDEN (off the B2110 W) A fine example of the many talents of the 19th-c Arts and Crafts Movement. Designed by Philip Webb (even down to the unusual light fittings), a friend of William Morris, and little changed since, the interior of the house is decorated with several different William Morris wallpapers, and many of the furnishings are of the period. Snacks, shop, limited disabled access; open pm Weds–Sun mid-Mar–Oct; (01342) 323029; £5, £3.50 garden only; NT. INGWERSENS (Birch Farm, Gravetye) Very long-established alpine plants specialist nursery; cl 1–1.30pm, wknds Oct–Feb, two wks at Christmas; (01342) 810236. Out this way, the White Hart at Selsfield (on the B2028), the Crown and the cheaper Red Lion at Turners Hill are useful for lunch. The town itself is really to be avoided, with long weekend traffic queues.

★ † 🕊 🏠 ❀ 🦋 **Eastbourne** TV6199 The Duke of Devonshire still owns much of this civilised and restrained seaside resort; as he prohibits seaside tat the place has a more dignified and solid feel than many of its livelier rivals – fun seekers should head elsewhere, but it's perfect for gentle seafront strolling. The CHURCH in the Old Town is lavish; next to it the Lamb is a nice old pub. MUSEUM OF SHOPS AND SOCIAL HISTORY (Cornfield Terrace) One of the most comprehensive collections of its type, 20 reconstructed and very well filled shops and rooms, inc an old seafarers' tavern. Shop, disabled access to ground floor only; cl Jan; (01323) 737143; *£2.50. The WISH TOWER (King Edward's Parade) is one of the 103 Martello Towers built in case of French invasion; there's a fascinating collection of puppets, some centuries old. Shop; cl Nov-Easter (exc school hols); (01323) 410440; £1.80. Another splendid tower, the REDOUBT FORTRESS (Royal Parade), houses a more interesting than average military museum. Open-air concerts (usually every Weds and Fri Jun–Aug) always end in a firework display. Snacks, shop; cl early Nov–Easter; (01323) 410300; *£2. There's an enthusiastic little LIFEBOAT MUSEUM on Grand Parade (cl Jan –Easter; free), and the handsome TOWNER MUSEUM (High St, Old Town) has good temporary exhibitions (cl am, Mon; charges for some exhibitions).

🐾 ❦ 🦋 **Exceat** TV5298 LIVING WORLD 🔲 (on the A259) Set in 2 18th-c barns in lovely countryside above Cuckmere Haven, a remarkable collection of small creatures and exotic insects, from snails through scorpions to marine life; most children love it. Meals, snacks, shop, disabled access; cl wkdys Nov–mid-Mar (exc school hols); (01323) 870100; £2.50. It's surrounded by the SEVEN SISTERS COUNTRY PARK, running down to the sea by the River Cuckmere – protected meadow, saltings, shingle and the flanking chalk headlands; you can hire bikes from the Cuckmere Cycle Co at Granary Barn, (01323) 870310. The roomy Golden Galleon does decent food.

🍺 🍴 † **Firle** TQ4707 An attractive quiet village, with a good pub, the Ram. FIRLE PLACE (off the A27) Beautiful house, essentially Tudor but remodelled in the 18th c, with some real treasures of European and English painting, and wonderful furnishings. Meals, snacks, shop, some disabled access; open pm Weds, Thurs and Sun Jun–Sept, as well as Easter, spring and summer bank hols; (01273) 858335; £4. There are longer unguided tours the 1st Weds in the month, when more rooms are open (and the price is higher). MIDDLE FARM (on the A27 E) Best known for its excellent farm shop, with a huge range of English ciders and perries, farmhouse cheeses, English wines, good sausages, organic meats, and other produce. Also children's farmyard, and always lots going on at apple harvest time; cl 25–26 Dec; (01323) 811411; small charge for farmyard. CHARLESTON FARMHOUSE TQ4906 (further along the A27 towards Selmeston) Delightful 17th/18th-c house which was the home of Duncan Grant and Clive and Vanessa Bell; decorated by them, it and its magical garden still evoke the atmosphere of those Bloomsbury days. Teas Sat, shop; open pm Weds–Sun and bank hols Easter–Oct (am too in summer hols), no guided tours Sun and bank hols;

(01323) 811265; £5. Longer tours on Fri (when children under 8 aren't admitted). Nr here at Alciston, the Rose Cottage has very good home cooking, and off the A27 a couple of miles E, BERWICK CHURCH TQ5105 has 1940s murals by the Bloomsbury Group (the Cricketers Arms here is another popular lunch place). See also Rodmell entry on p.656.

🏛 👌 **Fishbourne** SU8304 ROMAN PALACE (Salthill Rd) This magnificent villa with its 100 or so rooms was occupied from the 1st to the 3rd c, and is the largest known residence from the period in Britain. You can see 25 superb mosaic floors (a bigger collection than anywhere else in Europe), and a garden has been laid out according to its 1st-c plan. One theory about the site is that it was a high-class brothel. Snacks, shop, disabled access; cl mid-Dec–Feb (exc Sun); (01243) 785859; £3.80. The welcoming Bull's Head has a decent choice of food.

❀ **Fontwell** SU9507 DENMANS GARDEN (off the A27) Colourful series of vistas over 3½ acres, inc exuberantly oriental-feeling areas with a gravel stream, ornamental grasses, bamboos and flowering cherries, as well as a beautiful, richly planted walled garden. Meals, snacks, plant sales, disabled access; cl Nov–Feb; (01243) 542808; £2.50. The George at Eartham is a good nearby place to eat.

! **Gatwick Airport** TQ2841 SKYVIEW (S Terminal) Entertaining visitor gallery, with a multi-media show demonstrating a typical airport day, good explanation of cockpit controls, and excellent simulator rides. Splendid runway views. Shop, disabled access; (01293) 502244; £4.50.

🍺 † **Glynde** TQ4509 GLYNDE PLACE Elizabethan manor house in a beautiful setting, extensively remodelled inside in the 18th c, but outside left pretty much unchanged. Portraits and mementos give a good grounding in the family history, while outside are pleasantly wild parklands and lawns. Snacks, shop; open pm Easter, pm Sun and bank hols in May, pm Weds and Sun Jun–Sept; (01273) 858224; £3.50. There's a neat neo-Palladian CHURCH nearby, and the Trevor Arms has decent food. The Glyndebourne Festival, with its decidedly smart operas and marvellous new auditorium designed by Sir Michael Hopkins, takes place May–Aug.

🏠 🏛 **Goodwood** SU8808 GOODWOOD HOUSE Unusual-looking house in beautiful downland countryside, especially renowned for its paintings, inc works by Canaletto and Stubbs. There's quite a riding feel – it was acquired by the first Duke of Richmond in 1697 so that he could ride with the local hunt, and the stables added during 18th-c alterations seem grander even than the house. It closed last year for refurbishment but should be open again by Easter – best to ring for opening times, (01243) 774107; *£5. The adjacent RACECOURSE is the setting for Glorious Goodwood, and, as well as around 19 race days a year, has monthly antique markets; (01243) 774107 for dates. SCULPTURE AT GOODWOOD (Hat Hill Copse, towards East Dean) Excellent changing exhibitions of sculpture in 20 acres of beautiful wooded parkland; it's established an excellent reputation in the few years it's been open, so it's a shame the high admission price limits it to people with more than just a passing interest in the subject. Some disabled access; open Thurs, Fri and Sat Mar–Nov; (01243) 538449; £10. This is a good area for a country drive; the Anglesey Arms at Halnaker is the best nearby place for a meal.

🌳 **Hadlow Down** TQ5323 WILDERNESS WOOD (on the A272) Acres of working woodland, good for learning about forests and their wildlife, or for a pleasant stroll. Several picnic areas and a play area, occasional demonstrations of heavy horses and other traditional woodland working methods. Teas, shop (they make chestnut furniture and other goods), some disabled access; (01825) 830509; *£1.90. Just along the A272, Buxted has one of the oldest trees in Britain, a yew

thought to be 2,479 years old.

🏠 🏛 🐦 **Halland** TQ4815 BENTLEY WILDFOWL AND MOTOR MUSEUM Busy estate centred around Tudor farmhouse converted into Palladian mansion, filled with fine furnishings and paintings, inc 150 watercolours by local artist Philip Rickman. The motor museum has gleaming veteran, Edwardian and vintage vehicles, while the lakes and ponds that surround it are home to a countless variety of exotic wildfowl. There's also a narrow-gauge railway (summer wknds and bank hols, plus Weds in Aug), so plenty to keep families happy. Meals, snacks, shop, disabled access; open daily mid-Mar–Oct (house cl am), and all exc house also open wknds in Nov, Feb and Mar; (01825) 840573; £4.10, less winter. The Forge is useful for lunch.

🏛 🌿 **Handcross** TQ2629 NYMANS (on the B2114) Some very impressive rare trees here, inc magnificent southern beeches and eucryphias, as well as fine camellias, rhododendrons and magnolias, countless other interesting flowering shrubs, a secluded sunken garden, and an extensive, artfully composed wilderness. Meals, snacks, plant sales, shop, disabled access; cl Mon (exc bank hols) and Tues, Nov–Feb (exc wknds weather permitting); (01444) 400321; *£5; NT. Well worth a look nearby are the 20 acres of landscaped woodland at HIGH BEECHES GARDENS, with lots of rare plants, water gardens, and wild flower meadows. Plant sales; usually open pm daily exc Weds Apr–Jun and Sept–Oct, all Mon and Tues July–Aug; (01444) 400589; £3. The Chequers at Slaugham is a handy nearby dining pub.

❗🏛 🖼 🌸 ♪ 🐦 **Hastings** TQ8209 The Old Town up on the cliff at the E end is very attractive – 2 medieval churches, a couple of streets with raised pavements, lots of medieval buildings, and relatively unobtrusive more recent infilling. Down below, the fishermen still haul their boats up on to the beach and sell excellent fresh fish by the unusual tall, black, wooden net huts. The rest of the town is a busy shopping town, not smart (indeed rather run-down in parts), with 19th-c resort buildings nearer the seafront, seaside hotels and B & Bs, a good prom, and shingle beach. You can fish from the PIER (25p to walk along it), where a unique garlic shop sells garlic-flavoured ice-cream and chewing gum among other products. Bracingly set above crumbling cliffs (you can get a train up here from the beach), the evocative ruins of the Norman CASTLE are close to the site of William the Conqueror's first English motte and bailey castle. There's a lively audio-visual exhibition on the Battle of Hastings. Shop, some disabled access; (01424) 422964; £2.80. The town MUSEUM AND ART GALLERY (Johns Pl, Cambridge Rd) is a little out of the centre, but worth a look for its American Indian displays; children may prefer the dinosaur gallery. Shop, disabled access; cl 1–2pm Sat; (01424) 781155; free. Other useful museums include the FISHERMEN'S MUSEUM (Rock-a-Nore, Harbour), interestingly housed in a former fishermen's chapel (cl 25 Dec; free), and, a few doors along, the SHIPWRECK HERITAGE CENTRE; cl Oct–Easter; £1.95. Down the same road the SEA LIFE CENTRE is another in the lively chain, with walk-through underwater tunnel. Snacks, shop, disabled access; usually only cl 25 Dec, but best to check first in winter; (01424) 718776; £4.75. On wkdys the Town Hall (Queens Rd) shows off an ambitious 73 metre (240-ft) tapestry depicting great events in British history, created by the Royal School of Needlework; cl Christmas wk; £1.50. SMUGGLERS ADVENTURE ▣ A labyrinth of caverns and passages deep below West Hill, with models, museum and well done, life-size tableaux illustrating life for an 18th-c smuggler. Spooky lighting and sound effects in places. Shop, disabled access; cl 25–26 Dec; (01424) 422964; £4.20. At each end of the cliffs is an unusual sloping tracked lift down to sea level (60p). The First In Last Out in the Old Town has interesting food and brews its own beer.

🏵 🔌 **Haywards Heath** TQ3226 BORDE HILL (Balcombe Rd, N) Lovely 40-acre gardens with woodland walks through rare maples, oaks, conifers and many other fine trees, as well as a lake, herbaceous borders and magnificent rhododendrons. You can fish on the lake, and there's an adventure playground. Meals, snacks, plant sales, disabled access; cl 25 Dec; (01444) 450326; £2.50. The White Harte at Cuckfield does good-value simple lunches.

🏵 🏚 ! 🔌 **Herstmonceux** TQ6312 Extensive gardens around handsome 15th-c brick-built CASTLE ▣ (discount offer not valid for groups or on Special Event days; SE of village), with nature trails, hands-on science centre, and astronomy displays in the former buildings of the Greenwich Royal Observatory. You can tour the castle itself by arrangement. Snacks, shop, disabled access; cl Nov–Mar; (01323) 834444; £3. Nearby on Hailsham Rd, Thomas Smith demonstrates the local art of trug BASKET-MAKING; no demonstrations wknds (though shop open Sat); (01323) 832137. The Ash Tree over at Brownbread Street has popular old-fashioned home cooking.

🏵 🏵 **Highdown** TQ0904 HIGHDOWN HILL (on the A259) Excellent views from this famous garden, which differs from most of the other great Sussex gardens in that it's on very uncompromising chalk – laid out in and around a chalk pit high on the Downs above Angmering; many rarities, inc unusual Chinese plants. Some disabled access; cl wknds Oct–Mar; (01903) 501054; free. There is a nearby Iron Age hill fort, and the Spotted Cow at the foot of the hill does decent food.

🏵 🏚 **Horsham** TQ1730 The town's much developed, but a particularly attractive quiet corner is The Causeway, by the church. A timber-framed Tudor house here is now a well organised local history MUSEUM, with an extraordinary collection of early bicycles. The small but pretty garden has some unusual wild cyclamen. Shop, some disabled access; cl Sun; (01403) 254959; free. The Black Jug (North St) has good food. You may be able to join tours of the refreshingly egalitarian public school CHRIST'S HOSPITAL just outside town, where a remarkable painting by Verrio fills an entire wall of the Dining Hall. Meals, snacks, shop, disabled access; tours from £2.50 – booking essential; (01403) 263279 for dates.

❀ **Hurst Green** TQ7327 MERRIMENTS (Hawkhurst Rd) Developing, newish 4-acre demonstration garden with lots of planting ideas, some unusual plants, and a comprehensive nursery inc rare hardy plants. Tearoom, disabled access; garden open Easter–Oct, nursery all year; (01580) 860666; *£2.50.

★ ✿ ▨ ♨ ㈹ **Lewes** TQ4110 The administrative capital of East Sussex, this is a pleasantly unrushed country town below the quarried white edge of the South Downs. It has some attractive old buildings, mainly Georgian though with a few older stone-built or timber-framed specimens, particularly along its steep main street and in the little narrow alleys and other streets alongside. This is where you'll see Sussex tile-hanging at its best; there's also quite a lot of 'mathematical tiling' – sham bricks over timbered buildings to make them look more progressive. There are several decent antique shops, and an attractive complex of CRAFT SHOPS in a former candlemaker's factory in Market Lane; café, cl Sun. The Norman CASTLE is unusual for being built on not one but 2 artificial mounds (Lincoln is the only other such place we know of). The best view of the town is obtained from the roof of the keep, and there's a good archaeological museum. Shop; cl 25–26 Dec; (01273) 486290; £3.25. ANNE OF CLEVES HOUSE (Southover High St) Henry VIII's wife number 4 received this fine 16th-c house as part of her divorce settlement. She probably never came here, but its rooms give a good idea of regional life over the following 2 centuries. Shop;

cl am Sun, and all Nov–Feb exc Tues, Thurs and Sat; (01273) 474610; £2 (combined ticket with castle £4.25). Guided tours of the ruined Norman PRIORY leave here at 2.30pm Thurs and Sat mid-Jun–Aug; £1.50. Diarist John Evelyn's handsome boyhood home SOUTHOVER GRANGE (Southover Rd) is now the District Registry Office, but you can visit the attractive gardens free. The Dorset Arms (Malling St) and more bohemian Snowdrop (South St) are useful for lunch, and there's enjoyable Italian food at Tortellini's (High St). Local brewers Harveys have a good shop attached to the brewery on Cliffe High St. From Bell Lane on the SW edge you can follow the old Juggs Road track, used by the Brighton fishwives, up past Kingston and the downland nature reserve by Newmarket Hill to the outskirts of Brighton itself.

♨ ㈹ **Littlehampton** TQ0202 Little sign here of its age (it was an important port up to the 1500s), but its long sandy beaches make it a popular, simple family resort. There's a MUSEUM in an early 19th-c manor house on Church St; cl Sun and Mon; free. Towards the W, beyond the River Arun, there's quite an extensive area of unspoilt dunes between beach and golf course. You can visit the BODY SHOP FACTORY slightly out of town on the A259 at Watersmead; the 90-minute tours are interesting and informative, but you'll need to book, on (01903) 844044. No tours Sun, or pm Fri; £3.95. The 18th-c Arun View right on the river does decent lunches.

❀ ⌘ **Lower Beeding** TQ2225 LEONARDSLEE GARDENS (Mill Lane) Enormous Grade I listed garden set in a 240-acre valley with 6 beautiful lakes; marvellous rhododendrons, magnolias, oaks and unusual conifers, a delightful rock garden, extensive greenhouse and Japanese garden, a bonsai exhibition, and wallaby and deer. The gardens are on the edge of the ancient St Leonards Forest, and there's a summer wild flower walk. Readers get a great deal of pleasure from coming here. Meals, snacks, plant sales, limited disabled access; cl Nov–Mar; (01403) 891212; May £4.90, other times £3.90. The Crabtree does excellent food.

✝ ☛ **Lurgashall** SU9327 Attractive small village, with an unusual loggia outside the largely Saxon CHURCH where parishioners walking in from a distance could eat their sandwiches. The LURGASHALL WINERY produces a wide range of traditional country wines, meads and cordials. Tastings, shop, disabled access; cl 25–26 Dec, 1 Jan; (01428) 707292; self-guided tours wknds; *£1 per family. The Noahs Ark here is prettily placed for lunch.

🏰 ⚜ ♣ **Newhaven** TQ4401 NEWHAVEN FORT (Fort Rd) Built 120 years ago in case of French attack, this is a big place to explore, with underground installations and tunnels burrowing into the cliffs, super views from its ramparts, and an assault course for children. Snacks, shop; cl wkdys Oct and Mar, Nov–Feb; (01273) 517622; £3.25. PARADISE PARK AND PLANET EARTH (Avis Rd) Garden centre with exhibition on the last few million years of evolution, complete with earthquake experience and life-size moving dinosaurs. Also model village with miniaturised Sussex landmarks. Meals, snacks, shops, disabled access, cl 25–26 Dec; (01273) 512123; £3.99. You can take the FERRY TRIP to Dieppe in France from here. The harbourside Hope has enjoyable food.

🏠 ⚜ **Northiam** TQ8125 GREAT DIXTER (turn off the A28 at post office) Timbered 15th-c house, carefully restored and added to by Lutyens in the early part of this century. He designed the attractive gardens too; originally arranged as a series of distinct areas, they were later stocked more informally with interesting plants by the gardening writer Christopher Lloyd who lives here. Plant sales; house and gardens open pm Apr–mid-Oct (open earlier Sun in July and Aug), cl Mon exc bank hols; (01797) 252878; £4, £3 gardens only. Another fine old building here is the partly 15th-c

BRICKWALL HOUSE, with splendid 17th-c plastered ceilings and very pleasant formal gardens. Disabled access; open pm Sat and bank hols Apr–Sept; (01797) 223329; *£2.50. The Rainbow Trout down at Broad Oak is a popular dining pub.

🏠 ▣ **Petworth** SU9721 The magnificent rooms of splendid PETWORTH HOUSE are filled with one of the most impressive art collections in the country, inc Dutch old masters and 20 pictures by Turner, a frequent visitor. Other highlights include the 13th-c chapel, grand staircase with frescoes, and the carved room, elegantly decorated by Grinling Gibbons. You can see extra rooms on Tues and Weds, and they recently opened up more of the servants' block. Meals, snacks, shop, disabled access; cl am, plus Thurs and Fri, Nov–Mar; (01798) 342207; £4.50; NT. The deer park, with stately trees and prospects still recognisable as those glorified by Turner, is free. The village has narrow streets of attractive old houses, inc a good few antique shops. The Angel Hotel fits in well, and has a good weekend carvery; the Stonemasons has decent food too.

🏰 ⚏ **Pevensey** TQ6404 PEVENSEY CASTLE Formidable castle based around huge 4th-c Roman fort, with massive bastions and walls of Roman masonry still up to 9 metres (30 ft) high in places. The Norman keep was built by William the Conqueror, and you can see interesting interior details inc fireplaces, dungeons and an oubliette. Shop, some disabled access; cl winter Mon and Tues, 24–26 Dec; (01323) 762604; £2. The Castle Cottage restaurant does nice food, inc light summer lunches in the castle garden.

🚗 🏠 **Polegate** TQ5703 FILCHING MANOR MOTOR MUSEUM (Jevington Rd, Wannock) Gleamingly restored vintage cars, shown to great effect in the grounds of a striking manor house. Unique panelling in the minstrels' gallery, acres of woodland, Donald Campbell connections, and a go-karting track. Snacks, disabled access; open Thurs–Sun plus bank hols Easter–Sept; (01323) 487838; *£3.50. The CUCKOO TRAIL, following the route of a former railway from here to the lack-lustre town of Heathfield, is pleasant for traffic-free walking or cycling; the mileposts, sculpted by local artists, each have a cuckoo hidden in their design.

🐾🏛🐾🚌 **Pulborough** TQ0614 The town has some attractive buildings down towards the river; the Waters Edge, with lake views, has a wide choice of food. There's an RSPB Reserve nearby. PARHAM HOUSE Charming Elizabethan house, still a family home, its panelled rooms full of notable portraits, furniture, oriental carpets and rare needlework. The surrounding grounds are really very special – popular with birds, they include a rose garden and a vegetable garden, the produce from which is sold in the shop. Also deer park, and maze designed with children in mind. Teas, shop, plant sales; open pm Weds, Thurs, Sun and bank hols Easter–Oct; (01903) 744888; £4.50, £3 garden only. NUTBOURNE VINEYARDS (Nutbourne Manor) 18-acre vineyard with tours and tastings, and visitor centre in a former windmill; shop; no tours mid-Oct–May; (01798) 815196; free. The charmingly placed White Hart at Stopham has good food.

🏛 **Rodmell** TQ4106 MONKS HOUSE Just a quiet lived-in house, in a pleasant village, but a beautifully kept place of pilgrimage for followers of the Bloomsbury Group, as Leonard and Virginia Woolf lived here from 1919 until their deaths. Open pm Weds and Sat Apr–Oct; £2.20; NT. The Juggs at Kingston on the way from Lewes, is handy for lunch.

🍴🏵✝ **Rottingdean** TQ3702 A pretty place, worth a stop. Enthusiastic local volunteers are responsible for preserving both the handsome Georgian Grange, now a MUSEUM (cl am Sun), and the pleasant 2-acre KIPLING GARDENS, well restored Victorian gardens named after the author who lived here for 5 years from 1897. Burne-Jones was a resident for a while too, designing the windows made by William Morris for the Early English CHURCH.

★✝🏛🏛🛏🏖🎵✈ **Rye** TQ9220 Enchanting, and still relatively unspoilt despite its many charms. Before the wind and sea currents did their work, the little town was virtually surrounded by sea, and as one of the Cinque Ports played an important part in providing men and ships for coastal defence. It's built on a hill crowned by the partly Norman ST MARY'S CHURCH (with a notable churchyard, and very early turret-clock, 2 quarter-jacks by it striking the quarter-hours); up here the largely cobbled streets still follow a 12th/13th-c narrow layout, with most of the houses lining them dating from the 16th c. The views are lovely, and steep Mermaid Street in particular is famously photogenic (the Mermaid itself is a handsome old inn). The HERITAGE CENTRE on Strand Quay is a useful introduction, with a sound-and-light show based around an intricate town model. Shop, disabled access; cl 25 Dec; free, sound and light show £2. LAMB HOUSE (West St) Built in 1723 for a former mayor, James Lamb, and chiefly devoted to mementos of the author Henry James, who lived here from 1898 to 1916; after his death E F Benson, who also became mayor, moved here. Open pm Weds and Sat Apr–Oct; (01892) 890651; *£2.50; NT. RYE CASTLE MUSEUM can be found in the striking 13th-c Ypres Tower (as in Wipers); shop; cl winter wkdys; (01797) 226728; £1.50. The nearby Ypres Castle pub has good food in a nice setting. The town is full of antique shops, book shops and craft shops – mostly good stuff. The HARBOUR, because of the build-up of shingle along this coast, is now a mile or two from the town, though yachts and fishing boats do still come right up the river to the pretty quay. The Inkerman Arms has fine fresh fish (as does the Hope & Anchor up in the town). Tony Easton will take you SEA FISHING for the day; (01797) 252104; from £20. The expanse of shingle stretching around the river mouth is now preserved as a NATURE RESERVE, with hides to watch the shore birds. CAMBER CASTLE is a massive Tudor fort built right on the coast, but now stranded a mile or so inshore by the encroaching shingle (open Sat; £2). Beyond it the Ship on Winchelsea Beach is a welcoming refuge. On the other side of the river CAMBER SANDS TQ9518 is a splendid beach, with plenty of room for walking, and good clean bathing.

Selsey Bill SZ8592 One of the nicest and cleanest BEACHES along the south coast.

🕌 � **Sheffield Park** TQ4124 Wonderful 120-acre garden partly landscaped by Capability Brown, since then imaginatively planted with many varieties of trees unknown to him, especially chosen for their autumn colours. Also marvellous rhododendrons, azaleas and water lilies on the lakes. Snacks, shop, disabled access; cl Mon (exc bank hols), Tues mid-Nov–Dec, all late Dec–Feb, and wkdys in Mar; (01825) 790231; *£4.20; NT. The Griffin at Fletching nearby is good for lunch. Slightly further down the A275, Sheffield Park Station is the start of the BLUEBELL LINE, the earliest preserved steam railway in Britain, and one of the best; 9-mile trips through Horsted Keynes to Kingscote (where there are period bus connections to BR East Grinstead), with splendid stations tricked out with period advertisements and wonderful genuine period carriages. The journey passes woodlands that are a mass of bluebells in late spring, usually at their best in mid-May – hence the name of the line. Part of the station is a museum housing the region's largest railway collection, inc some 30 locomotives. Pullman dining specials, Santa specials, shop, café; trains wknds all year, daily May–Sept and school hols – (01825) 722370 for timetable; £7.20. The Sloop at Scaynes Hill not far off is pleasant for lunch.

🏚🕌✝ **Shoreham-by-Sea** TQ2105 Though not one of England's more famous ports, this is quite a busy one, with several attractive old buildings around the harbour. One such is MARLIPINS on the High St, a Norman building which may once have been a custom house, now a local history museum. Shop; cl 1–2pm, am Sun, Mon, and Oct–Apr; *£1.50. Inland, in Old Shoreham, the early Norman CHURCH is accompanied by some handsome old houses (among them the good 16th-c Red Lion). The airport is England's oldest, with an appealing 1930s art deco terminal; tours available, good-value restaurant with uninterrupted views. It has a MUSEUM OF D-DAY AVIATION, with uniforms, engines, artefacts and a replica Spitfire. Meals, snacks, shop, disabled access; cl wkdys in Mar and Nov, all Dec–Easter; (01374) 971971; £2.50. Not far from here is striking LANCING COLLEGE CHAPEL, begun in 1868, with a soaringly handsome nave, and elaborate stained-glass Rose Window.

⬆↑ **Singleton** SU8713 WEALD AND DOWNLAND OPEN AIR MUSEUM 🎫 Fascinating collection of historic buildings rescued from all over the south east, dismantled and re-erected here. They're arranged to form an authentic-looking village, with outlying farm and agricultural buildings, a Tudor market hall, blacksmith's forge, tollhouse and Victorian schoolroom. You can buy flour from the medieval farmstead's working watermill. Well organised children's activities might include brick-laying or basket-making. Snacks, shop; cl Nov–Feb exc wknds and Weds; (01243) 811348; £4.90. The handy Fox & Hounds is a friendly stop.

🏚🕌 **South Harting** SU7819 A pretty Downland village, with good-value food in the nicely set Ship; the roads round here give attractive drives – the B2141 and B2146 S, the Walderton–E Mardon back road between them, and the Downs-foot road through East Harting, Elsted, Treyford and Cocking. UPPARK (on the B2146 S) Splendid 17th-c house, extensively restored after a disastrous fire in 1989. Incredibly, most of the houses's public treasures were rescued, even the wallpaper, but behind the scenes it's a different story: the family that lives here lost almost everything, and one wonders how they feel about the way the Trust has left a few charred floorboards in place – and recycled others into fruit bowls sold in the shop. The grounds, designed by Humphrey Repton, have a woodland walk and fine views towards the Solent. Meals, snacks, shop, disabled access; open pm Sun–Thurs Apr–Oct; (01730) 825857; £5; NT. Entrance is by timed ticket, a few of which can be booked in advance – otherwise get there between 11.30am and 1.30pm.

✈ **Tangmere** SU9006 MILITARY AVIATION MUSEUM (off the A27) Good collection of flying memorabilia based around the former RAF base where H E Bates finished writing *Fair Stood the Wind for France*. Meals, snacks, shop, disabled access; cl Dec–Jan; (01243) 775223; £3. The nearby Bader Arms has more memorabilia; and there's good food at the Anglesey Arms at Halnaker (with the shell of an 18th-c windmill nearby).

🏰 **Ticehurst** TQ6930 PASHLEY MANOR (on the B2099) 8 acres of beautifully restored, mainly Victorian formal gardens around a handsome house once owned by the Boleyn family. Magnificent old trees, delightfully placed moat and walled garden, views, folly, fine shrubs, roses, herbaceous beds, and clever focal points; very relaxed, charming and peaceful. Tulip festival in May, and a festival of old-fashioned roses in Jun. Snacks, plant sales, limited disabled access; open Tues–Thurs, Sat and bank hols, Easter–Sept; (01580) 200692; £3. The village is attractive; up a side road at Three Legged Cross, Maynards has good PICK-YOUR-OWN and the Bull is pleasant for lunch.

🐖 **Tillington** SU9421 NOAH'S FARMYARD (Grittenham Farm, on the A272) Lambs, calves, goats, rabbits, etc. for children to pet and feed, along with barn owls, short nature trail, and riverside picnic area. Snacks, shop; cl early Sept–Mar; (01798) 861264; *£3. The Horse Guards is a stylish dining pub, and the village is pretty.

🏰 ✝ ⚘ **Upper Dicker** TQ5509 MICHELHAM PRIORY Charming 16th-c house based around a 13th-c Augustinian priory, with a 15th-c gatehouse by the moat (which has plenty of waterfowl). Interesting furniture, tapestries and local ironwork, as well as crafts, working watermill, and ropemaking museum. Meals, snacks, shop, disabled access to ground floor only; open Weds–Sun and bank hols mid Mar–Oct, daily Aug; (01323) 844224; *£4. The Plough is useful for lunch.

🏰 **West Dean** SU8512 WEST DEAN GARDENS Old roses, 100-yard pergola, wild garden, walled kitchen garden and interesting collection of stately mature conifers in park and arboretum; a splendid downland setting, notably peaceful and relaxed. Meals, snacks, shop, some disabled access, plant sales; cl 25 Oct–7 Mar; (01243) 811303; *£3.50. The smart White Horse at Chilgrove or Royal Oak a little further N would be our choice for lunch.

★ ❀ ☺ **West Hoathly** TQ3632 Attractive village tucked quietly away from the road, with tremendous views from the lane downhill past the ancient Cat pub. On a clear day you can see the whole sweep of the South Downs between Chanctonbury Ring and the Long Man of Wilmington. Nr the 13th-c church, the 15th-c timbered PRIEST HOUSE is now a folk museum with a little cottage garden. Shop; cl am Sun, Nov–Feb; (01342) 810479; £2. They can arrange guided tours of the village.

🏛 **Wilmington** TQ5403 Famous for its LONG MAN, a gigantic chalk-cut figure so far impossible to date – guesses hover anywhere between the early 18th c and the Bronze Age. The Giant's Rest has good home cooking.

★ ♪ ✝ **Winchelsea** TQ9017 Storms and French raids pretty much put paid to this once-flourishing port's importance; today it's a quiet and pleasant little place, dwarfed by the distances between the 3 surviving town gates around it. The ROYAL MILITARY CANAL runs from here to

Hythe in Kent, a never-used Napoleonic defence that was meant as a sort of glorified coastal moat – now a peaceful spot for coarse fishermen. The New Inn is popular for lunch, and the tranquil CHURCH of St Thomas is elaborately decorated, with some fine old stained glass and medieval tombs. The Fairlight road has clifftop views.

🐏 **Wisborough Green** TQ0526 FISHERS FARM PARK 🖻 Friendly farm, well equipped for families, with animal show and petting areas, good indoor and outdoor play areas and a go-kart track. Meals, snacks, shop, disabled access; cl 25–26 Dec; (01403) 700063; £3.75; also holiday cottages and campsite. The Three Crowns, with well priced food, has a more solidly adult appeal.

🌢🖻 **Worthing** TQ1402 Restrained but rather charming town, with a pleasant seafront; in the same mould as Brighton but altogether quieter and less gaudy. There's an excellent HERB SHOP on Field Row, opposite M&S. The MUSEUM AND ART GALLERY (Chapel Rd) has an extremely rich archaeological collection, and a sculpture garden. Shop, disabled access; cl Sun; (01903) 239999; free. The formerly separate village of West Tarring has a 250-year-old fig garden by the 14th-c parish hall, a folklore museum in a row of 15th-c cottages, and a welcoming old pub, the Vine.

🐏 **Wych Cross** TQ4231 ASHDOWN LLAMA FARM 🖻 Unusual working llama farm, with big breeding herds of alpacas; sheep and goats too. Snacks, shop, disabled access (but no facilities); cl Mon (exc bank hols), Oct–Mar; (01825) 712040; £2.25. The same people run Barnsgate Manor Vineyard a few miles down the road at Herons Ghyll TQ4828, which has great views from its attractive restaurant.

🐏 Several other flourishing **vineyards** do tours or vineyard trails and tastings, notably ST GEORGES at Waldron TQ5419, well laid out for visitors, with changing art and craft exhibitions in a 11th-c tithe barn (usually cl Mon and Tues, wkdys in Nov, and all Jan and Feb, but up for

sale as we went to press so this may change; free, tours £1.50); BARKHAM MANOR nr Newick TQ4321, appealingly set around a striking manor house with B & B (cl Mon exc bank hols, and Dec–Mar; £1.50); and CARR TAYLOR at Westfield TQ8115, one of England's most successful commercial vineyards, producing sparkling wine as well as still; cl 25 Dec–3 Jan, and Suns Jan–Feb; trails *£1.50.

★ **Attractive villages**, all with civilised pubs doing decent food, include Barns Green TQ1227, Brightling TQ6921 (though Jack Fullers on Oxleys Green is now more restaurant than pub), Burpham TQ0308 (great views; maybe even bison), Byworth SU9820, Chiddingly TQ5414, Eartham SU9409 (small but charming church), Easebourne SU8922, East Dean SU9013 (not the one mentioned in To see and do section above), Elsted SU8119, Findon TQ1208, Fittleworth TQ0118, Fletching TQ4223 (Sussex's Best-Kept Village for the second year running), Frant TQ5835 (ancient church, handsome green), Funtington SU7908, Hartfield TQ4735 (the well stocked shop at Pooh Corner reflects the fact that surrounding Ashdown Forest was the inspiration for A A Milne's tales of Winnie the Pooh), Hellingly TQ5812, Henley SU8925, Icklesham TQ8716 (Norman church, country walks), Kirdford TQ0126, Mayfield TQ5827, Old Heathfield TQ5920, Robertsbridge TQ7323, Rotherfield TQ5529, Rudgwick TQ0833, Rushlake Green TQ6218, Salehurst TQ7424 (14th-c church), Sedlescombe TQ7718 (where there's an unusual organic vineyard), Slaugham TQ2528, Stopham TQ0218, Sutton SU9715, Waldron TQ5419 (ancient church) and Warbleton TQ6018 (more pre-1750 Sussex barns here than anywhere else in the county).

† **Interesting churches** at Etchingham TQ7126 (with station built to match), and West Chiltington TQ0818 (beautiful building in lovely countryside). Now the parish church,

Days Out

A trio of Cinque Ports
Rye; lunch at the Flushing, there; Camber Sands or Camber Castle; Winchelsea; walk from Hastings Old Town on to the cliffs towards Fairlight Cove.

1066 and all that
Pevensey Castle; lunch at the Castle Cottage there; Battle Abbey and battlefield.

The South Downs' dramatic finale
Drusillas, Alfriston, and the village; Litlington church; lunch at Litlington Tea Gardens, or the Star or the George, Alfriston; stroll through Seven Sisters country park to Cuckmere Haven and on to the cliffs; drive past Birling Gap to the clifftop of Beachy Head; view Long Man of Wilmington.

Bloomsbury Group mementos
Berwick church paintings; Charleston Farmhouse and Middle Farm, Firle; lunch at the Ram, Firle; Monks House, Rodmell (limited opening); Lewes.

Pooh and his friends
Ashdown Forest via the B2026 (seek out Milne's memorial and Poohsticks Bridge); picnic at the top of Ashdown Forest, or treat yourself at the Griffin, Fletching; Ashdown Llama Farm, Wych Cross, or the Bluebell Line to and from Sheffield Park.

Brighton Rock
Browse the alternative/junk/secondhand shops of the North Laine area near the railway station; The Lanes; lunch at Il Bistro, Market St (or Il Teatro, Mock Turtle or One Paston Pl – all cl Sun); Royal Pavilion; Museum and Art Gallery; sea front, inc antique slot machines nr the pier, Kemp Town's Regency façades, Sea Life Centre.

Thatched idyll by the watermeadows
Bignor Roman villa; drive up Bignor Hill for the view, and maybe stroll along Stane Street (Roman road); picnic on Bignor Hill, or lunch at the George & Dragon, Houghton; Amberley village and museum.

Vernacular spectacular and the great yew forest
West Dean gardens; lunch at the Horse & Groom, Singleton; Weald and Downland Museum there; walk along the nature trail through Kingley Vale to the top of the South Downs.

Chagall glass and Roman mosaic
Chichester; Fishbourne Roman palace; explore Chichester Harbour by boat from Itchenor, or on foot from East Head, Chidham or Bosham.

A Wealden cross-section
Mayfield; lunch at the Middle House or the Rose & Crown there; Burwash, and Batemans; Bodiam castle or Great Dixter, Northiam.

Great gardens and an Arts and Crafts rarity
Leonardslee, Lower Beeding, or Wakehurst Place, Ardingly or Nymans, Handcross; lunch at the Crabtree, Lower Beeding, Gardeners Arms, Ardingly or the Cat, West Hoathly; Standen, East Grinstead.

12th-c Boxgrove Priory SU9007 is one of the most outstanding Early English churches in the region, with a surprising 16th-c painted ceiling, free-standing chantry chapel, and the atmospheric remains of various monastic buildings outside.

✕ **Well preserved windmills** can be seen at High Salvington TQ1206 (an 18th-c post mill; open pm 1st and 3rd Sun Apr–Sept, 50p), Nutley TQ4427 (17th-c mill saved by enthusiastic locals before such action became more common; open pm last Sun of month Apr–Sept; *60p), and Shipley TQ1422 (smock mill built in 1879 and once owned by Hilaire Belloc; open pm 1st and 3rd Sun Apr–Oct; £1.50).

! The British School of Ballooning at Ebernoe, just N of Petworth SU9721, organises champagne **balloon trips** over the countryside; (01428) 707307; *£125.

Walks

The chalk South Downs dominate the southern part of the county, and have the best of its walks. The South Downs Way makes for quick progress along their crest. **Harting Downs** SU7918 ⌂-1 involve no more than a level stroll from the road nr South Harting SU7819 (the Coach & Horses at Compton SU7714 is a good base for walks in this area). **Kingley Vale** SU8210 ⌂-2 needs much more stamina, whether you approach via the nature trail on the S side or from Stoughton SU8011 to the N (the Hare & Hounds will fuel you well). This nature reserve is Europe's largest yew forest, a magical place where the trees create some eerie pools of darkness on the S slopes of the Downs; above, you can look over Chichester Harbour from a prehistoric burial mound. At **Bignor Hill** SU9813 ⌂-3 the trees that obscure views for much of the way hereabouts give way to open ground; Stane St, a Roman road here relegated to a path, takes a strikingly straight course SW over a woodland and pasture landscape.

At **Arundel** TQ0107 ⌂-4 you can walk along the canalised River Arun and into Arundel Park, with its lakes and woodlands beneath the slopes of the Downs. **Amberley Wild Brooks** TQ0314 ⌂-5, reached from Amberley, is a large expanse of watermeadows which form an important habitat for wetland plants and birds; there's also a way up to the Downs here.

N of Worthing TQ1402 are two of the great landmarks of the Downs, both of them ancient hill forts. **Chanctonbury Ring** TQ1312 ⌂-6 is reached from Steyning TQ1711 or Washington TQ1212. **Cissbury Ring** TQ1308 ⌂-7 is a huge ramparted site quite close to Findon TQ1208 (where the Gun and Village House are both good lunch places). The **Brighton Downs** ⌂-8 above Brighton are open; arable farming and the presence of pylons rather distract from the pleasure of walking, but the steep N slopes are still impressive, as at Devil's Dyke TQ2611 (with its tremendous view over Brighton, even more startling at night than by day), Wolstonbury Hill TQ2813 and the Jack and Jill windmills nr Clayton TQ3014.

Further E, fine stretches of the South Downs Way have distant views over **Ditchling Beacon** TQ3313 ⌂-9 (easy access from the road) and **Firle Beacon** TQ4805 ⌂-10, a lovely walk above Firle, E of Lewes. **Lewes** TQ4110 ⌂-11 has more public paths than the OS map suggests; from the town centre you can walk up Chapel Hill, through the golf course and on via an unspoilt dry valley to Mount Caburn TQ4408, rather grandiosely named for its size but capped by an Iron Age fort with views towards the coast; it's also popular with paragliders. A fine 3-mile circuit from Lewes is made by following the Ouse N, then heading under the railway line, through the woods to cross the A275 at Offham TQ4012, then keeping left to follow a path (not on the OS map) above some spectacularly deep chalk pits; another unmapped path leads along a downland crest past the site of the Battle of Lewes and past the prison to re-enter the town. There are riverside walks (or boat trips) from the Anchor at Barcombe TQ4114.

The **Seven Sisters** TV5396 ⌂-12 are a series of chalk cliffs which, together with Beachy Head, form the spectacular finale of the South Downs; the Way leads up over them past the sea at Cuckmere Haven TV5198. For an interesting circular route you can head inland by Friston Forest TV5499, Westdean TV5299 and East Dean TV5597. **Beachy Head** TV5995 ⌂-13, the giant of these cliffs, has a lighthouse far below, and is within close reach of Eastbourne TV6199.

Lullington Heath TQ5401 ⌂-14 is reached by an inland fork of the Way, which splits off at Alfriston TQ5103, bound for Jevington TQ5601 and Eastbourne. The Heath is a rare survival of downland untouched by modern farming practices, and managed as a National Nature Reserve for its chalkland and heathland flora; a diversion to Wilmington TQ5403 gives a view of the enigmatic chalk figure, the Long Man of Wilmington.

The **Ashdown Forest** ⌂-15 is a major inland attraction, part forest, part heathland – sandy tracks, clumps of Scots pines, secretive glades and exhilarating views. Traffic restrictions introduced in 1997 are already making it even more peaceful. Don't be put off by the OS map: there are far more walking routes than it suggests (there's a useful 1:30,000 scale walkers' map issued by the Ashdown Forest Centre showing all the paths and rides as well as naming the car parks – an extremely useful idea given the Forest's lack of other landmarks. The Forest still looks just like the E H Sheppard drawings for A A Milne's Winnie the Pooh stories, which were set here. Five Hundred Acre Wood TQ4832 is the Hundred Acre Wood of Pooh's world, and with a little searching you can find, SE of Hartfield TQ4735, the Poohsticks Bridge and, by the B2026, Gills Lap TQ4631 (the 'enchanted place' at the top of the Forest, nr Piglet's house), where a memorial to Milne has been placed nr the triangulation point. Camp Hill TQ0311, nr Nutley Windmill, is one of the best walking areas in the Forest. Handy pubs for Forest walks include the Foresters Arms at Fairwarp TQ4646, Half Moon at Lye Green TQ5134 and Hatch at Colemans Hatch TQ4533.

Fernhurst SU8928 ⌂-16 up in the NW of the county has nicely varied countryside nearby; much is densely wooded, but there are some chances to get out on to the open hillsides as on Woolbeding Common SU8625 and the S tip of Black Down SU9129.

Ardingly Reservoir TQ3229 ⌂-17 offers pleasant strolls by its shores, or you can plan a longer walk around the elevated farmland and woodlands surrounding Wakehurst Place TQ3331 and Balcombe TQ3130. **Weir Wood Reservoir** TQ3934 ⌂-18 gives another waterside walk, along its N shore, with paths leading up to Standen House TQ3835. Bewl Water, shared with Kent, is described in that chapter.

Mayfield TQ5827 ⌂-19 has pleasant hilly terrain around it, with a reasonable network of paths, inc a short waymarked circular walk. From **Windmill Hill** TQ6412 ⌂-20 you can follow paths and tracks for an absorbing walk of about 4 miles past Herstmonceux Castle and the former observatory (now the Science Centre).

Around Chichester Harbour, a shoreside path skirts the quiet peninsulas of **Thorney Island** SU7503 ⌂-21 and Chidham SU7903. **East Head** SZ7694 ⌂-22, a National Trust-owned promontory on the E entrance of the harbour, is a sandy spit with dunes overlooking the marshes and mudflats of the estuary. **Climping Beach** SU9902 ⌂-23 allows an attractive few miles' walk; this bit of coast between Middleton-on-Sea SU9700 and Littlehampton TQ0202 is the only other appreciable undeveloped stretch in W Sussex.

Fairlight Cove TQ8711 ⌂-24 in E Sussex is a good destination from Hastings Old Town TQ8209, by a path climbing on to the sandstone cliffs for a rugged couple of miles. The tumbled appearance of the coast here bears witness to the occasional cliff-falls.

S of Horsham, popular bases for local walks include the Bridge at Copsale TQ1725 and Black Horse at Nuthurst TQ1926 (bluebell woods).

Where to eat

Alciston TQ5005 ROSE COTTAGE (01323) 870377 In the same family for over 30 years, this charming wisteria-covered cottage is small and cosy and full of harness, traps, ironware and various bric-à-brac, as well as Jasper the talking parrot (mornings only); very good promptly served food (especially the simply cooked fresh fish), well kept real ales, decent wines, small, no smoking evening restaurant, and seats outside; cl 25–26 Dec; children over 6 in evening. £19|£6.50.

Alfriston TQ5103 MOONRAKERS (01323) 870472 Reliably enjoyable evening food (they offer Sun lunch, too) in this cosy little cottage with a log fire, good wine list, and friendly staff; cl pm Sun, 2 wks early Jan; children over 8. £18 set 3-course meal.

Brightling TQ6821 JACK FULLERS Oxleys Green (01424) 838212 Cosy and softly lit dining pub with enjoyable pies and steamed puddings, good side dishes, and some vegetarian choices – all in big helpings; excellent wines (English ones, too), pleasant service, and seats in the pretty flower-filled garden with fine views; cl Mon, Tues; disabled access. £18.50|£5.95.

Brighton TQ3104 IL TEATRO 7 New Rd (01273) 202158 Friendly and enjoyable Italian restaurant next to the Theatre Royal; cl Sun, Mon; reasonable disabled access. £17.

Brighton TQ3103 MOCK TURTLE 4 Pool Valley (01273) 327380 Delightful, no smoking, traditional English teashop with enjoyable snacks and light lunches (local fish and local sausages), lovely home-made cakes, bread and so forth, and popular cream teas; cl Sun, Mon, Good Fri, 2 wks spring, a few days over Christmas. £6.60|£3.10.

Brighton TQ3203 ONE PASTON PLACE 1 Paston Pl (01273) 606933 Just off the seafront, this enjoyable restaurant, with a big mural on one wall, offers very good modern British food inc super fish and game dishes, and nice puddings; decent house wines, and a friendly atmosphere; cl Sun, Mon, 1st 2 weeks Jan, 1st 2 wks Aug; no children pm. £28.

Brighton TQ3104 WAIKIKAMOOKAU 11a Kensington Gdns (01273) 671117 Easy going and chatty lunchtime restaurant (they do breakfast, too), with interesting, contemporary furnishings in the long L-shaped room; particularly good, very cheap vegetarian (and vegan) food with Thai influences, an unusual list of juices, and fresh fruit milk shakes. |£3.95.

Brighton TQ3004 WHYTES 33 Western St (01273) 776618 Popular and attractive cottagey restaurant just off the sea front, with a relaxed, friendly atmosphere; enjoyable food using fresh local produce, and a decent wine list; cl Sun, Mon, end Feb–early Mar. £23.85.

Broad Oak TQ8220 RAINBOW TROUT Chitcombe Rd (01424) 882436 Pleasant pub with an attractive bustling old bar, and a big restaurant extension; wide range of well cooked food (especially fish) served by friendly waitresses, and well kept real ales; cl 25 Dec, pm 26 Dec; disabled access. £18|£4.95.

Burpham TQ0308 GEORGE & DRAGON (01903) 883131 Smartly comfortable dining pub with splendid views down to Arundel Castle and the river; good promptly served food with unusual specials inc good vegetarian dishes; elegant restaurant – worth booking; cl pm Sun in winter, 25 Dec. £18.75|£6.50.

Chichester SU8605 COMME ÇA 67 Broyle Rd (01243) 788724 Busy little restaurant close to the Festival Theatre; good, classic French cooking, popular Sun lunches and children's menu; cl pm Sun, Mon; disabled access. £22|£9.95.

Chichester SU8605 ST MARTIN'S TEA ROOMS 3 St Martin's St (01243) 786715

Handsome, brick Georgian-fronted house with pretty garden for summer eating, good lunchtime snacks and meals (mainly vegetarian but with some fish dishes) and afternoon teas using organic produce; cl Sun, Good Fri, some bank hols, 2 days Christmas; disabled access. l£4.20.

Chilgrove SU8214 WHITE HORSE (01243) 535219 Smart 18th-c pub/restaurant in a charming South Downs setting; very good, generously served wholesome food, superb wine list, welcoming landlord, and a lovely big garden; cl pm Sun, Mon, Feb; children in restaurant only. £28.50l£7.50

Duncton SU9617 CRICKETERS (01798) 342473 Pretty little white house with welcoming staff and jovial landlord; an inglenook fireplace, standing timbers and a few country tables and chairs in the small bar, and a dining room decorated with farming implements; good popular food, and well kept real ales, also a charming back garden with proper barbecue; skittle alley; no food pm Sun/Mon; no children. £18.95l£5.95.

Eastbourne TV6099 DOWNLAND 37 Lewes Rd (01323) 732689 Pretty, candlelit evening restaurant in a well run small hotel; carefully prepared, innovative food, good vegetables and lovely puddings, a relaxed atmosphere, and friendly service; bedrms; cl 26–30 Dec; children over 10; disabled access. £30.

Edburton TQ2311 TOTTINGTON MANOR (01903) 815757 Cosy country house with particularly good food using fresh seasonal produce in both the bar and restaurant; winter log fires, friendly service and a relaxed atmosphere; bdrms; cl pm Sun; children over 5. £25l£6.

Elsted SU8320 ELSTED INN (01730) 813662 Unprepossessing Victorian roadside pub with a warm and friendly welcome; unpretentious bars with open log fires, lots of original wood, and a candlelit dining room; extremely good, interesting cooking using fresh local ingredients, and very well kept real ales; 2 dogs, and a large garden (with dog-free zone); disabled access. £18l£4.50.

Elsted SU8119 THREE HORSESHOES (01730) 825746 Cosy Tudor pub in lovely setting, with fine views of the South Downs from the garden (and good walks); snug, rustic rooms with huge log fires, ancient beams and venerable furnishings; very good English country cooking inc lovely puddings, well kept real ales, and decent wines by the glass; cl pm Sun Oct–May; well behaved children welcome. £20l£5.50.

Fletching TQ4223 GRIFFIN (01825) 722890 Civilised old country inn with blazing log fires in the quaintly panelled rooms, old photos and hunting prints; very good, innovative food, well kept beers, a good wine list with 10 (inc champagne) by the glass, a relaxed and friendly atmosphere, and a lovely garden; bdrms; cl 25 Dec; disabled access. £25l£6.50.

Hartfield TQ4735 ANCHOR Church St (01892) 770424 Relaxed and friendly pub on the edge of Ashdown Forest, with good bar food, quick service, a chatty, heavily beamed bar, dining area, well kept real ales, and a popular front verandah; cl pm 25 Dec. £20l£4.

Hastings TQ8109 HARRIS 58 High St (01424) 437221 Relaxed, informal and chatty, reasonably priced, mainly Spanish food (enjoyable tapas), friendly staff in long white aprons, and decent wine; cl am Oct–Mar, Sun (exc July–Oct). £17.50l£4.

Hastings TQ8109 ROSER'S 64 Eversfield Pl, St Leonards (01424) 712218 Extremely rewarding and generous, imaginative food using top quality produce inc home-cured, smoked and pickled ingredients in a straightforward-looking little restaurant opposite pier; fine wines, too; cl am Sat, Sun, Mon, early Jan and June; disabled access. £40.

Herstmonceux TQ6312 SUNDIAL (01323) 832217 Pretty and plush 17th-c cottage with excellent, carefully cooked food inc lovely vegetables and delicious puddings; a praiseworthy wine list, relaxed atmosphere, formal but warm and friendly service, and a terrace and garden for summer eating; cl pm Sun, Mon; disabled access. £33.75l£10.50.

Horsham TQ1730 BLACK JUG 31 North Street (01403) 253526 Most attractively refurbished Edwardian town pub with a relaxed atmosphere, a big airy bar running around the central servery, lots of old prints and photographs, and a plant-filled conservatory; very popular, interesting bar food, 9 chilled vodkas, well kept real ales, decent wines, and a small back terrace; no children; cl pm Sun, 26 Dec. £18|£3.75.

Jevington TQ5601 HUNGRY MONK The Street (01323) 482178 Long-standing, popular candlelit evening restaurant (they also do Sun lunch) with 3 beamed sitting rooms, bar, a little dining room, and open fires; a friendly, dinner-partyish atmosphere, and good, interesting food; cl am Mon–Sat, bank hols, Christmas; children over 5. £30.50.

Kirdford TQ0126 HALF MOON (01403) 820223 Family-run inn with marvellous fresh fish (the family have had Billingsgate links for 130 years) inc some really unusual ones, well kept real ales, local wine and cider; friendly service, simple neat bars, and a big garden; cl 25 Dec pm; disabled access. £25|£5.50.

Litlington TQ5201 LITLINGTON TEA GARDENS (01323) 870222 Established 150 years ago, these tearooms still keep their quaint Victorian elegance, with seating on an attractive, sheltered lawn under a copper beech or ginkgo, in renovated beach huts with open fronts, or the tearoom/restaurant; colourful hanging baskets and flowering tubs, and quick efficient service; morning coffee, light lunches, and cream teas; handy for Alfriston; cl Oct–Apr. |£2.55.

Lodsworth SU9223 HALFWAY BRIDGE (01798) 861281 Stylish and civilised, warm and friendly, family-run pub, with big helpings of delicious inventive home cooking in the no smoking restaurant or attractively decorated, comfortable bar rooms; log fires, well kept real ales, ciders and wines; cl pm Sun in winter; children welcome over 10. £21.50|£5.95.

Lower Beeding TQ2227 CRABTREE (01403) 891257 Very popular dining pub, with civilised but simply furnished, cosy beamed bars, a no smoking restaurant with plenty of character, and very imaginative carefully prepared food; good wines, well kept real ales, and prompt friendly service; also a pleasant garden; disabled access. £25|£9.50.

Nuthurst TQ1926 BLACK HORSE (01403) 891272 Warmly welcoming black-beamed pub in lovely walking country; with a log fire in the inglenook fireplace, good, promptly served bar food, very well kept real ales and country wines, friendly service; disabled access. £17.50|£4.

Nyetimber SZ8998 INGLENOOK 255 Pagham Rd (01243) 262495 Extended 16th-c hotel, with enjoyable food in the attractive rustic-style restaurant; beamed bars, a comfortable lounge, open fires, real ales, and a garden for light snacks; disabled access. £22.50|£5.50.

Playden TQ9121 PEACE & PLENTY (01797) 280342 Cottagey dining pub with lots of little pictures, china and lamps and a big inglenook with comfortable armchairs on either side in the cosy bar; 2 intimate dining areas, very well prepared, traditional food, well kept ales, and a pretty garden. £17|£5.95.

Ringmer TQ4515 COCK (01273) 812040 Civilised, heavily beamed country pub with a log fire in the big inglenook, a fine range of good food, decent wines, 2 lounges (one no smoking), and seats on the terrace and in the attractive fairy-lit garden; cl 25 Dec. £18|£5.

Rye TQ9220 FLUSHING 4 Market St (01797) 223292 Run by the same family for 37 years, this fine old, timber-framed inn serves particularly good local fish and seafood (local meat dishes, too) and holds various gastronomic occasions; note the fine 16th-c wall painting; bdrms; cl pm Mon, Tues, first 2 wks Jan. £30.80 dinner, £19.80 lunch|£7.

Rye TQ9220 YPRES CASTLE (01797) 223248 Popular, straightforward pub in a fine setting near the 13th-c Ypres Tower; a fairly spartan decor but a particularly warm and friendly atmosphere; enjoyable, interesting food inc fresh local fish and seafood, daily specials, good fresh vegetables, well kept changing real ales, good-value wine with 20 by the glass, and seats on a sizeable lawn with fine views over the River Rother. £18.75.

Scayne's Hill TQ3623 SLOOP Freshfield Lock (01444) 831219 Country pub tucked away in this lovely spot with a sheltered garden and near the Bluebell line steam railway; long saloon bar with pine furniture and comfy old seats, a simple public bar, good bar food (especially the daily specials), well kept real ales, and decent wines. £20|£7.95.

Seaford TV5199 GOLDEN GALLEON Exceat Bridge (01323) 892247 Cheerfully bustling, popular pub with high, trussed and pitched rafters in the airy bar and dining area, an open fire in a nice little side area, and a conservatory; up to a dozen real ales inc 6 from their own micro-brewery, excellent food inc lots of Italian dishes (the chatty landlord is from Italy), and good views from the tables in the sloping garden; bdrms; cl pm Sun Sept–May. £18|£4.

Slindon Common SU9608 SPUR London Rd (01243) 814216 Attractive little 17th-c pub with 2 big log fires, a good choice of daily changing food, a sizeable restaurant, well kept ales, friendly dogs, and a pleasant garden.£20|£6.

Stopham TQ0218 WHITE HART (01798) 873321 Peaceful place with 3 relaxing, comfortable beamed rooms, super fresh fish (and other food), well kept real ales, and decent wines; also a beamed, candlelit restaurant, and tables on the lawn across the road; fine early 14th-c bridge and tree-lined river walks; cl pm Sun Sept–May; partial disabled access. £24.25|£4.75.

Storrington TQ0814 OLD FORGE 6a Church St (01903) 743402 Good, imaginative food in 500-year-old, converted beamed forge; an excellent choice of sweet wines to go with the rich puddings and home-made ice-creams; cl am Sat, pm Sun, Mon, am Tues, 3 wks spring, 2 wks autumn; well behaved children welcome; £27.

Special thanks to C Southwood, Elizabeth Allen, Jenny and Michael Back, R Kingsmill, B and K Hypher, Paul Kennedy, Mrs Rowan Edwards, E G Parish, G A Martin, E Robinson, J Oldham, N J Bennett.

We welcome reports from readers . . .

This *Guide* depends on readers' reports. Do help us if you can – in return, we offer a discount on the next edition to people who've helped us with reports for it. Tell us what you think about places already in it, and anything extra you think we should say about them. And send us your ideas for inclusion in the next edition: places to visit, eat at or stay in, attractive drives or walks, maybe even unusual interesting shops you know of. Use the card in the middle, the report forms at the end, or just write – no stamp needed: *The Good Guide to Britain*, FREEPOST TN1569, Wadhurst, E Sussex TN5 7BR.

Sussex Calendar

Some of these dates were provisional as we went to press. Please check information with the numbers provided.

FEBRUARY

2 **Ardingly** Antiques Fair: up to 4,000 stands at the South of England Showground – *till Tues 3* (01636) 702326

19 **Hove** Sussex Real Ale and Cider Festival at the Town Hall – *till Sat 21* (01903) 692370

20 **Brighton** Model Festival at Brighton Centre – *till Sun 22* (01273) 202881

21 **Brighton** Sussex Artists Exhibition at Brighton Museum and Art Gallery – *till 22 March* (01273) 290900

MARCH

14 **Amberley** Family Activities for Science Weekend at the Amberley Museum – *till Sun 22* (01798) 831370

15 **Upper Dicker** Outdoor Sculpture at Michelham Priory – *till 13 Sept* (01323) 844224

APRIL

4 **Alfriston** Easter at Drusillas – *till Sun 12* (01323) 870656

5 **Ardingly** Food and Drink Show at the South of England Showground (01444) 892048

6 **Ardingly** Antiques Fair – *till Tues 7* (see 2 Feb for details)

10 **Tinsley Green** Marble Championships at the Greyhound (01403) 211661

11 **Upper Dicker** Medieval Re-enactments and Archery at Michelham Priory – *till Mon 13* (01323) 844224

12 **Singleton** Traditional Food Fair at the Weald and Downland Open Air Museum – *till Mon 13* (01243) 811348

13 **Herstmonceux** Easter Bonnet Celebrations and Egg Hunt at the Castle (01323) 834444

14 **Hastings** Old Town Conducted Walks: free – *till 15 Sept* (01424) 721249

18 **Haywards Heath** Garden Festival at Borde Hill Garden – *till Sun 19* (01444) 450326

26 **Amberley** Veteran Cycle Day at the Amberley Museum (01798) 831370; **Haywards Heath** Children's Animal Fair at Borde Hill Garden (01444) 450326

MAY

1 **Brighton** Horse Driving Trials at Stanmer Park – *till Sun 3* (01323) 841641; **Hastings** Jack in the Green Morris Dance Festival: procession, concerts, street entertainment – *till Mon 4* (01424) 712574

2 **Brighton** Festival: over 450 events – *till Sun 24* (01273) 713875; **Eastbourne** International Folk Festival – *till Mon 4* (01323) 415442

3 **Ardingly** Garden Show at the South of England Showground – *till Mon 4* (01444) 892048; **Bexhill** Festival of Motoring – *till Mon 4* (01424) 730564; **Brighton** London to Brighton Classic Commerical Vehicle Run (01580) 893227

4 **Upper Dicker** May Day Festival at Michelham Priory (01323) 844224

16 **Hastings** International Young Peoples Festival – *till Sun 31* (01424) 718837

Sussex Calendar

MAY cont

17 **Amberley** Stationary Engine Working Day at the Amberley Museum (01798) 831370

21 **Battle** Festival – *till 6 June* (01424) 775275; **Firle** Charleston Festival at Charleston Farmhouse – *till Mon 25* (01323) 811626

22 **Brighton** Old Ship Royal Escape Race: yacht race from beach in front of the Old Ship, Kings Rd (01273) 329001; **Upper Dicker** Crafts: sale, demonstrations, workshops at Michelham Priory – *till Mon 25* (01323) 844224

23 **Broad Oak** Heathfield Agricultural Show (01825) 713369

25 **Upper Dicker** Teddy Bears Picnic at Michelham Priory (01323) 844224

30 **Hadlow Down** Traction Engine Rally – *till Sun 31*

JUNE

1 **Ardingly** Antiques Fair – *till Tues 2* (see 2 Feb for details)

7 **Singleton** Heavy Horses at the Weald and Downland Open Air Museum (01243) 811348

10 **Arundel** Corpus Christi Carpet of Flowers and Floral Festival at the Cathedral – *till Thurs 11* (01903) 882297; **Boxgrove** Classical Concerts at Boxgrove Priory – *till Sat 13* (01734) 813190

11 **Ardingly** South of England Show – *till Sat 13* (01444) 892048

13 **Eastbourne** International Ladies Tennis Championship – *till Sat 20* (01323) 415442; **Pulborough** Parham Park Steam Rally – *till Sun 14* (01903) 744888

16 **Litlington** Festival at Charleston Manor – *till Sun 21* (01323) 639548

19 **Goodwood** Festival of Speed at Goodwood House: historic motor sport event – *till Sun 21* (01243) 774107

26 **Petworth** Open Air Concerts at Petworth Park – *till Sun 28* (01372) 453401

27 **Crawley** Folk Festival at the Hawth (01293) 552941; **Lower Beeding** Country Craft Fair at Leonardslee Gardens – *till Sun 28* (01403) 891212

28 **Chichester** Festival of the Arts – *till 13 July* (01243) 785718

JULY

1 **West Dean** Open Air Theatre Season at West Dean Gardens – *till Tues 14* (01243) 785718

3 **Crawley** Fireworks Concert at Tilgate Park – *till Sat 4* (01293) 552941; **Lewes** Real Ale and Cider Festival: 45 real ales – *till Sat 4* (01273) 462093

4 **Ardingly** Smallholders Show at the South of England Showground – *till Sun 5* (01444) 892048; **Haywards Heath** Horse Trials at Borde Hill Garden – *till Sun 5* (01444) 450326

10 **Upper Dicker** Open Air Shakespeare: *As You Like It* at Michelham Priory (01323) 844224

11 **Amberley** Railway Gala Weekend at the Amberley Museum – *till Sun 12* (01798) 831370; **Ardingly** Vehicle Rally at the South of England Showground – *till Sun 12* (01444) 892048; **Eastbourne** Emergency Services Display at Western Lawns – *till Sun 12* (01323) 415442; **Haywards Heath** Fuchsia Society at Borde Hill Garden – *till Sun 12* (01444) 450326; **Horsham** Carnival and Festival – *till Sun 12* (01293) 851760

SUSSEX CALENDAR

JULY cont

18 **Pulborough** Parham House Garden Weekend – *till Sun 19* (01903) 742021

19 **Singleton** Rare and Traditional Breeds at the Weald and Downland Open Air Museum (01243) 811348

20 **Eastbourne** County Cup Tennis at Devonshire Park – *till Fri 24* (01323) 415442

28 **Goodwood** Glorious Goodwood – *till 1 Aug* (01243) 779922

24 **Worthing** Seafront Fair: procession, gaslit market – *till Sun 26* (01903) 239999

AUGUST

1 **Crawley** International Festival: free music, dance and drama – *till Sun 2* (01293) 552941; **Hartfield** Summer Flower Show (01342) 822372; **Rye** Medieval Festival: battle re-enactment, procession, street theatre – *till Sun 2* (01797) 223404

3 **Eastbourne** Family Festival of Tennis at Devonshire Park – *till Sat 8* (01323) 415442

8 **Burwash** Open Air Concert at Batemans – *till Sun 9* (01892) 891001; **Eastbourne** Horse Show at Gildredge Park – *till Sun 9* (01323) 415442; **Hastings** Old Town Week: open houses, displays, concerts, street party, carnival – *till Sun 16* with Carnival on *Wed 12* (01424) 433142

10 **Ardingly** Antiques Fair – *till Tues 11* (see 2 Feb for details)

13 **Upper Dicker** Guild of Sussex Craftsmen in Action at Michelham Priory – *till Sun 16* (01273) 890088

15 **Singleton** Children's Activities at the Weald and Downland Open Air Museum – *till Sun 16* (01243) 811348

20 **Eastbourne** Airbourne '98 and Birdman Competition – *till Sun 23* (01323) 410044

24 **Eastbourne** South of England Tennis Championship at Devonshire Park – *till Sat 29* (01323) 415442

28 **Worthing** Seafront Fair: procession, gaslit market – *till 6 Sept* (01903) 239999; **Eastbourne** English Wine and Regional Food Festival at the Winter Gardens *till Sun 30* (01323) 415442

29 **Hellingly** Festival of Transport at Broad Farm – *till Mon 31* (01323) 484926; **Herstmonceux** Medieval Fair at the Castle – *till Mon 31* (01323) 834444; **Rotherfield** Torchlight Procession (01273) 515451

31 **Worthing** Fair and Carnival (01903) 239999

SEPTEMBER

5 **Shoreham** RAFA Air Show – *till Sun 6* (01903) 239999; **Uckfield** Torchlight Procession and Fireworks (01273) 515451

6 **Eastbourne** MG Rally at Western Lawns: over 300 vehicles (01323) 415442; **Eastbourne** Historic Bus Rally at Eastbourne Park (01323) 410044; **Upper Dicker** Country Fair at Michelham Priory (01323) 844224

12 **Crowborough** Torchlight Procession and Fireworks (01273) 515451; **Findon** Sheep Fair at Nepcote Farm (01435) 873999

19 **Mayfield** Torchlight Procession and Fireworks (01273) 515451

26 **Amberley** Model Steam Weekend at the Amberley Museum – *till Sun 27* (01798) 831370; **Burgess Hill** Torchlight Procession and Fireworks (01273) 515451

Sussex Calendar

OCTOBER

3 **Hartfield** Autumn Flower Show (01342) 822372
4 **Ardingly** Autumn Show (01444) 892048
5 **Brighton** Festival of Animated Theatre – *till Sat 31* (01273) 608021
10 **Newhaven** Torchlight Procession and Fireworks (01273) 515451
11 **Amberley** Vintage Vehicle Gathering: about 400 vehicles at the Amberley Museum (01798) 831370
19 **Ardingly** Antiques Fair – *till Tues 20* (see 2 Feb for details)
24 **Afriston** Halloween at Drusillas – *till 1 Nov* (01323) 870656; **Singleton** Autumn Countryside Celebration at the Weald and Downland Open Air Museum – *till Sun 25* (01243) 811348
30 **Horsham** Town Centre Festival – *till Sat 31* (01403) 215265
31 **Littlehampton** Torchlight Procession and Fireworks (01273) 515451; **Upper Dicker** Pagan and Christian Halloween Traditions: games, ghost hunt, lantern parade at Michelham Priory (01323) 844224

NOVEMBER

5 **Lewes** Torchlight Procession and Fireworks: best of Britain's bonfire celebrations; town closed to traffic *at 5.30pm*, spectacular celebrations with bands, effigies and burning tar-barrel race (01273) 515451
8 **East Hoathly** Torchlight Procession and Fireworks (01273) 515451
12 **Eastbourne** Motor Show at Western Lawns – *till Sun 15* (01323) 415442
19 **Ardingly** Rural Craft Show at the South of England Showground – *till Sun 22* (01444) 892048
20 **Petworth** Fair at Petworth Park (01798) 342562

DECEMBER

5 **Ardingly** Food and Drink Fair at the South of England Showground – *till Sun 6* (01444) 892048
7 **Ardingly** Antiques Fair – *till Tues 8* (see 2 Feb for details)
12 **Ardingly** Food and Drink Show at the South of England Showground (01444) 892048

We welcome reports from readers . . .

This *Guide* depends on readers' reports. Do help us if you can – in return, we offer a discount on the next edition to people who've helped us with reports for it. Tell us what you think about places already in it, and anything extra you think we should say about them. And send us your ideas for inclusion in the next edition: places to visit, eat at or stay in, attractive drives or walks, maybe even unusual interesting shops you know of. Use the card in the middle, the report forms at the end, or just write – no stamp needed: *The Good Guide to Britain*, FREEPOST TN1569, Wadhurst, E Sussex TN5 7BR.

WARWICKSHIRE

(INCLUDING BIRMINGHAM AND THE WEST MIDLANDS)

Some great day visits for all ages; quietly appealing countryside away from the built-up areas – good scope for an enjoyable short stay.

This area has some excellent family days out. Cadbury World at Bournville fills a most enjoyable half day, and the impressive Sea Life Centre in Birmingham is enthralling. There's a lot to enjoy at the Black Country living museum in Dudley, and Warwick Castle is excellent (though it can be very crowded); the ruins at Kenilworth are perhaps more atmospheric. There are a few good farms, and always a lot going on at the impressive crafts village at Hatton. The Heritage Motor Centre at Gaydon is irresistible to small boys – not to mention their fathers, uncles and grandfathers.

Older people have some striking historic houses to look over, particularly Moseley Old Hall (good guided tours), Arbury Hall, Coughton Court, and Wightwick Manor near Wolverhampton. Birmingham has almost endless scope for day visits – excellent art collections, lively museums, good botanic gardens, and its own (free) period house Aston Hall. Coventry also has quite a lot to see on day visits. The Kingswinford glass museum is quite dazzling, and the Nickelodeon at Ashorne has a fine nostalgic appeal. There's much food for thought at the organic gardening centre at Ryton-on-Dunsmore.

Stratford is the obvious focus for people on the Shakespeare trail, with plenty to interest them (though prices are high here, and others will find more to enjoy elsewhere); there are further Shakespeare connections in the pretty villages nearby, above all at Shottery and Wilmcote.

Warwick has the character and atmosphere to make a short stay enjoyable, coupled as it is with its neighbour Leamington Spa – which still has the gardens, parks and spacious terraces of its heyday as a spa resort. The countryside (which edges into the Cotswolds in the south) is quietly attractive, laced with canals and dotted with charming villages and appealing places to stay in.

Where to stay

Ansty SP3983 ANSTY HALL Ansty, Coventry CV7 9HZ (01203) 612222 **£75w,** plus special breaks; 30 luxurious rms. Handsome 17th-c hotel in 8 acres of grounds; quiet relaxing atmosphere, comfortable and elegantly furnished day rooms, helpful staff, and fine modern English cooking – much produce is grown in the walled garden; cl 24–30 Dec; disabled access.

Avon Dassett SP4150 CRANDON HOUSE Avon Dassett, Leamington Spa CV33 0AA (01295) 770652 *£38, plus winter breaks; 5 rms. Welcoming farmhouse on a small working farm with a variety of livestock; fine views, big garden, comfortable sitting rooms (one with a woodburning stove); nice breakfasts; evening meals by arrangement; cl Christmas; children over 12.

Bishop's Tachbrook SP3262 MALLORY COURT Harbury Lane, Bishop's Tachbrook, Leamington Spa CV33 9QB (01926) 330214 £170, plus special breaks; 10 wonderfully comfortable and luxurious rms. Fine ancient-looking house – actually built around 1910 – with elegant antique and flower-filled day rooms, and attentive staff; excellent food using home-grown produce in the panelled restaurant, and 10 acres of lovely gardens with outdoor swimming pool, tennis, squash, croquet; cl 2–9 Jan; children over 9.

Blackwell SP2443 BLACKWELL GRANGE Blackwell, Shipston on Stour CV36 4PF (01608) 682357 *£52; 3 pretty rms. 17th-c Cotswold farmhouse with a log fire in the comfortable beamed sitting room, and a large inglenook fireplace in the flagstoned dining room; good home cooking using own free-range eggs (evening meal by arrangement; bring your own wine); pretty garden, and nice views of the surrounding fields; cl Jan–Feb; parents with younger children stay in annexe; good disabled access.

Ilmington SP2143 HOWARD ARMS Ilmington, Shipston on Stour CV36 4LT (01608) 682226 *£55; 2 rms. Neatly kept golden stone 17th–18th-c inn opposite the village green, with a pleasant sheltered garden, beamed and flagstoned bar, open fires, and friendly service; very good food, and decent wines.

Leamington Spa SP3165 LANSDOWNE HOUSE Clarendon St, Leamington Spa CV32 4PF (01926) 450505 *£63.90, plus special breaks; 14 rms. Enjoyable Regency town house with particularly good service, very attractive public rooms, and a tranquil atmosphere; good daily-changing dinners, and a fine value wine list; small prize-winning garden; children over 5.

Little Compton SP2630 RED LION Little Compton, Moreton-in-Marsh GL56 0RT (01608) 674397 £36; 3 rms, shared bthrm. Simple but civilised low-beamed Cotswold stone inn with log fires; a separate dining area, big menu with speciality steaks, and an extensive wine list; large, attractive garden; children over 8.

Loxley SP2755 LOXLEY FARM Loxley, Warwick CV35 9JN (01789) 840265 *£50; 2 suites in attractive barn conversion. Not far from Stratford-upon-Avon, this tucked-away thatched, half-timbered, partly 14th-c house has low-beamed ceilings, wonky walls and floors, antiques and dried flowers, and an open fire; a helpful and friendly owner, and good Aga-cooked breakfasts; peaceful garden, and a fine old village church; cl Christmas–New Year.

Sherbourne SP2562 OLD RECTORY Vicarage Lane, Sherbourne, Warwick CV35 8AB (01926) 624562 *£56, plus special breaks; 14 rms, all with antique brass or brass and iron beds, and some in converted stables. Georgian house not far from Warwick, with a cosy sitting room, big log fire, beams, and flagstones; honesty bar, hearty breakfasts and enjoyable evening meals; pretty walled gardens.

Stratford-upon-Avon SP1954 CARLTON 22 Evesham Pl CV37 6HT (01789) 293548 £40; 6 homely rms, most with own bthrm. Neatly kept and very welcoming no smoking Victorian house, close to theatre and restaurants, with helpful owners, very good breakfasts, and a little garden.

Stratford-upon-Avon SP2054 MELITA 37 Shipston Rd, Stratford-upon-Avon CV37 7LN (01789) 292432 *£59; 12 well equipped rms. Friendly, family-run Victorian hotel with pretty, carefully laid-out garden, and a comfortable lounge with open fire; extensive breakfasts, and some provision for non-smokers; close to town centre and theatre; cl 4 days over Christmas; pets by arrangement; disabled access.

Stratford-upon-Avon SP2055 PAYTON 6 John St, Stratford-upon-Avon CV37

6UB (01789) 266442 *£58; 5 charming rms. Quietly set, no smoking Georgian house, handy for theatre; caring owners, and very good breakfasts; cl 24–26 Dec.

Stratford-upon-Avon SP2054 SHAKESPEARE Chapel St, Stratford-upon-Avon CV37 6ER (01789) 294771 £136, plus weekend breaks; 63 comfortable, well equipped rms. Smart hotel, was Forte, based on handsome, lavishly modernised Tudor merchants' houses; comfortable bar, good food, quick and friendly service; tables in back courtyard, and civilised tea or coffee in peaceful chintzy armchairs by blazing log fires; 3 minutes' walk from theatre.

Stratford-upon-Avon SP2054 STRATFORD HOUSE Sheep St, Stratford-upon-Avon CV37 6EF (01789) 268288 £88; 11 comfortable rms. Civilised Georgian house close to theatre, with open fire and lots of flowers in the elegant coffee lounge; fine food in the airy restaurant (pre-theatre dinner, too), friendly, helpful service, and seats and tables in the walled garden.

Stratford-upon-Avon SP2056 WELCOMBE Warwick Rd, Stratford-upon-Avon CV37 0NR (01789) 295252 £160, plus special breaks; 67 rms with antiques and luxurious bthrms. Jacobean-style mansion in parkland estate with an 18-hole golf course and 2 all-weather floodlit tennis courts; deeply comfortable day rooms inc a fine panelled lounge, open fires and fresh flowers, elegant restaurant, and good service; disabled access.

Sutton Coldfield SP1394 NEW HALL Walmley Rd, Sutton Coldfield B76 1QX (0121) 378 2442 £160, plus weekend breaks; 60 lovely rms (the ones in the manor house are the best). The oldest moated manor house in England, in 26 acres of beautiful grounds; luxuriously furnished day rooms, a graceful panelled restaurant with carefully cooked and imaginative food using very fresh (often home-grown) produce, and excellent service; children over 8; disabled access.

Walcote SP1258 WALCOTE FARM Walcote, Alcester B49 6LY (01789) 488264 *£38; 2 rms. Attractive 16th-c oak-beamed farmhouse with log fires in inglenook fireplaces; friendly owners, good breakfasts, a pretty garden, and fine surrounding walks; cl Christmas–New Year.

Warwick SP2864 FORTH HOUSE 44 High St, Warwick CV34 4AX (01926) 401512 *£54; 2 pretty and spacious suites. Attractively decorated, no smoking house with a lovely, surprisingly big garden; good breakfasts (evening meals and supper trays by prior arrangement); self-catering flat.

Willey SP4984 MANOR FARM Willey, Rugby CV23 OSH (01455) 553143 £36; 3 rms, 1 with own bthrm. Tranquil no smoking house with helpful and pleasant owner, and a homely lounge; good filling breakfasts in the relaxed dining room; cl Christmas; no children.

Wilmcote SP1658 PEAR TREE COTTAGE 7 Church Rd, Wilmcote, Stratford-upon-Avon CV37 9UX (01789) 205889 *£46; 7 rms. Charming half-timbered Elizabethan house owned by the same family for 3 generations; with beams, flagstones, country antiques, a cosy atmosphere, good breakfasts, and a sizeable shady garden; self-catering also; cl 24 Dec–1 Jan; children over 3.

To see and do

Birmingham SP0786 Masses of things to see and do here, but best for day visits. It lacks the one thing which a city really needs to make a short or longer stay enjoyable – an attractive town centre. Plans to replace the notorious Bull Ring with a centre more in tune with the city's growing cultural pride seem permanently on hold. However, the formidably efficient traffic system which ploughs through its heart makes it easy to penetrate from outside, particularly at weekends. The city has a long heritage despite its mainly modern centre, and a rich and varied industrial history taking in everything from guns to chocolate buttons. Reputedly, there are more canals here than in Venice, and redevelopment of old canal buildings is bringing quite a lively new focus to the

Gas St/Brindley Pl area. There's a surprising absence of good pubs; a few acceptable ones which do at least some lunchtime food include the new Figure of Eight and Some Place Else (Broad St), Prince of Wales (Cambridge St, behind Symphony Hall), canalside James Brindley (Gas St Basin), Malt House (King Edward's Rd, Brindley Pl) and Square Peg (Temple Ct, Corporation St);

the Bartons Arms (Aston High St) is a classic Edwardian gin palace.

🖼🎨✝CITY MUSEUM AND ART GALLERY (Chamberlain Sq) Perhaps the best collection of Pre-Raphaelite paintings anywhere, plenty still looking as brilliantly, almost shockingly, fresh and detailed as when they were first painted. Other notable paintings too, and lots of coins and archaeology – one of the first two dozen museums to make the Heritage Secretary's new shortlist of excellence and national importance. Meals, snacks, shop, disabled access; cl am Sun, 24–26 Dec, 1 Jan; (0121) 235 2834; free. Local boy Burne-Jones, a leading light in the Pre-Raphaelite movement, was responsible for 4 windows in ST PHILIP'S CHURCH on Colmore Row nearby, since 1905 the city's cathedral.

⚓ NATIONAL SEA LIFE CENTRE (Water's Edge, Brindley Pl) Very much the flagship of the excellent Sea Life Centre chain that we recommend in quite a few resorts around the country. The hi-tech displays are both fun and instructive, with around 3,000 native British marine and freshwater creatures shown off in careful re-creations of their natural habitats. The highlight is a walk-through tube designed to create the impression of walking along the sea bed, with sharks, rays and other creatures swimming above, alongside and beneath you. Sir Norman Foster designed the building. Meals, snacks, shop, disabled access; cl 25 Dec; (0121) 633 4700; £6.50.

⚒ JEWELLERY QUARTER Still Britain's biggest producer of gold jewellery, though Birmingham's importance in the jewellery trade isn't what it was. Around 100 jewellery shops line the streets, so useful for browsing or repairs. The excellent JEWELLERY QUARTER DISCOVERY CENTRE (Vyse St) is built around the perfectly preserved workshops of the Smith & Pepper

company, still much as they were at the start of the century. There's a good overview of the industry, as well as tours of the factory and demonstrations of jewellery-making techniques. Snacks, shop, disabled access; cl Sun; (0121) 554 3598; *£2. The Rosevilla nearby has decent food.

🏛 ASTON HALL (Aston, 2m NE) Strikingly grand Jacobean mansion with panelled long gallery, balustraded staircase and magnificent plaster friezes and ceilings. Snacks, shop, disabled access to ground floor; cl am, and all Nov–Easter; (0121) 327 0062; free (and more satisfying than a good many houses you'd have to pay for).

🖼🎨🏛 BARBER INSTITUTE (University) Excellent collection of paintings and sculptures, well housed in a very attractive gallery; just the right size to be enjoyable without being overwhelming. Quite a lot of Impressionist works as well as European masters. Shop, disabled access; cl am Sun, 25–26 Dec, 1 Jan, Good Fri; (0121) 472 0962; free. The university (marked out by its huge clock tower) is on the outer fringes of Edgbaston, a couple of miles S of the city centre. This area developed as a smart residential part of town, where industry and commerce gave way to parks and greenery, much of which still remains today. The BOTANICAL GARDENS (Westbourne Rd, Edgbaston – closer to centre) are outstanding: 15 acres featuring a tropical house (with lily pool, bananas and cocoa), palm house, orangery, a National Collection of bonsai, cactus house and the gardens themselves, filled with rhododendrons and azaleas and a goodly collection of trees. Bands play on pm summer Suns. Meals, snacks, shop, disabled access; cl 25 Dec; (0121) 454 1860; *£3.90, *£4.30 summer Suns. BIRMINGHAM NATURE CENTRE (Pershore Rd) British and European animals in indoor and outdoor enclosures designed to resemble natural habitats. Snacks, shop, disabled access; cl Nov–Mar exc Sun; (0121) 472 7775; £1.50.

🏠 BLAKESLEY HALL (Yardley, 2m E) Timber-framed 16th-c merchant's house, furnished according to an inventory of 1684. Shop, disabled access to ground floor and garden; cl am, and Nov–Mar; (0121) 783 2193; free.

✗ SAREHOLE MILL (Hall Green, 3m SE) Working 18th-c water mill, with several displays explaining the milling process. Tolkien often came here as a child. Shop; cl am, and Nov–Mar; (0121) 777 6612; free. Other local sites that influenced Tolkien are listed on a leaflet available at information centres.

🚂 BIRMINGHAM RAILWAY MUSEUM (Warwick Rd, Tyseley; 3m SE on the A41) Working railway museum with fully equipped workshop, steam locomotives, and several historic carriages and wagons. Trains run along a short track, but you can ride on them only in summer, usually first Sun of the month. Meals and snacks (wknds only), shop, limited disabled access; cl 25–26 Dec and 1 Jan; (0121) 707 4696; £2.50.

🏰 WEOLEY CASTLE (Alwold Rd, 4m S) Ruins of 13th-c castle with interesting little museum. Shop; open pm Tues–Fri, Apr–Oct; (0121) 427 4270; free.

🐦 ! ♿ Bournville SP0481 (4m S on the A441) A planned village built by the Cadbury family when they moved their factory out of the city centre in 1879. For CADBURY WORLD, attached to the factory, see separate Family Panel on p.678. Part of the Cadbury plans for their garden suburb involved uprooting timber-framed manor houses from elsewhere and re-erecting them here; 2 survive as the SELLY MANOR MUSEUM (Maple Rd), with herb garden, crafts and various exhibitions. Snacks, shop, some disabled access; open Tues–Fri, plus bank hols and Suns Easter–Aug, cl 15 Dec–15 Jan; (0121) 472 0199; *£1.50.

Stratford-upon-Avon SP2054 Visitors who look at the town just as a town can be disappointed, but if you have a grounding in Shakespeare's plays the interesting buildings seem that bit more interesting – and not so outnumbered by the workaday ones, the overpriced antique shops and the gift shops. The gardens by the River Avon make a memorable setting for the Memorial Theatre. If you're looking forward to a good production at the theatre that evening, or, better still, able to run through much of the verse in your head, then you'll love Stratford. But if you've always thought Shakespeare overrated, then you'll think the same about Stratford, too.

The pub with the most theatrical Shakespeare connections is the Mucky Duck, or more properly White Swan (Southern Way) – traditionally where the RSC actors and actresses drink; the Arden Hotel has the closest bar to the Memorial Theatre, with good snacks. Besides **Where to eat** recommendations below, other useful places for lunch include the Brasserie (Henley St), the quaint old Garrick (High St), Vintner Wine Bar (Sheep St) and Slug & Lettuce (Guild St/Union St). Tea in the smart Shakespeare Hotel (Chapel St) is relaxing.

🏠 SHAKESPEARE'S BIRTHPLACE (Henley St) The logical place to start, though despite what they'll tell you, there's no guarantee the playwright really was born here. Even so, there are interesting period features, and good interpretative displays. Shop, disabled access to ground floor only; cl 23–26 Dec; (01789) 204016; *£4.50. If you want to see all the Shakespearian properties it makes sense to buy a joint ticket; this costs £10, and covers the above and the following 4 houses (which all have the same opening hours). You can also buy tickets covering just the 3 in-town sites for £8. A tour bus with commentary links the sites if you don't mind forking out another £7.50; you'll be better off walking, though may need some form of wheels to get to Mary Arden's house (public transport to here is rather sporadic).

🏠 NEW PLACE/NASH'S HOUSE (Chapel St) Shakespeare died here in 1616; the house was destroyed in the 18th c, but the Elizabethan knot garden remains, and the adjacent house, former home of the writer's granddaughter, has a good collection of furniture and local history. Shop, limited disabled access; (01789) 292325; *£3.

🏠 HALLS CROFT (Old Town) Lovely gabled Tudor home of Dr John Hall, who married Shakespeare's daughter; good displays on the medicine of the time, Elizabethan and Jacobean furniture, and a walled garden. Teas, shop, some disabled access; (01789) 292107; *£3.

🏠 ANNE HATHAWAY'S COTTAGE (just W at Shottery SP1854,) A substantial thatched Tudor farmhouse, the home of Anne Hathaway until her marriage to William Shakespeare. Displays of domestic life during the period, and a colourful cottage garden. Snacks, shop; (01789) 292100; £3.50. There's a craft centre next door, and the Bell is handy for something to eat away from the tourists.

🏠 🐦 MARY ARDEN'S HOUSE (Wilmcote SP1658, 3m N) The picturesque home of Shakespeare's mother, with the barns given over to countryside memorabilia. Daily falconry displays, rare breeds. Snacks, some disabled access; (01789) 293455; £3.50. The Swan House, overlooking it, is good for lunch.

✝ Back in town, by the river, 15th-c HOLY TRINITY CHURCH is where Shakespeare was baptised and buried; cl am Sun; *60p to enter the chancel where the grave is.

♄ WORLD OF SHAKESPEARE (Waterside) Not particularly good value, but useful for keeping the interest of children less happy with real history; 25 life-size tableaux re-create Elizabethan life with sound effects and music. Snacks, disabled access; cl 25 Dec; (01789) 269190; £4.

💍 MEMORIAL THEATRE (Waterside) Shakespeare's plays are, of course, still performed here by the Royal Shakespeare Company. You can sometimes book guided tours of their main theatre, and they have a gallery with temporary exhibitions. Meals, snacks, shop, disabled access; cl am Sun, 24–25 Dec; (01789) 296655; *£1.50 for gallery, tours £4. The RSC productions themselves are performed in repertory, so if you're in the area a few days it's quite possible to see several. Advance booking is recommended – (01789) 295623 – though 100 tickets are kept back for each performance and sold on the day from 9.30am; don't leave it much later, they go pretty fast.

The town has a few attractions that have nothing to do with Shakespeare at all, several of them good for children bored with the Bard:

🏠 HARVARD HOUSE (High St) Late 16th-c – no direct connection with Shakespeare, but a striking example of houses of his day; cl mid-Oct–mid-Mar; (01789) 204507; £1.50.

! 👶 NATIONAL TEDDY BEAR MUSEUM 🎟 (special discount offer – 1 free child with 1 full paying adult; Greenhill St) Delightfully displayed, furry friends of all shapes and sizes – mechanical and musical ones, ones that belonged to famous people, and some that are famous themselves. Shop; cl 25–26 Dec; (01789) 293160; *£2.25.

! 🦋 BUTTERFLY FARM AND JUNGLE SAFARI (Tramway Walk) Stratford's quaintly gabled houses here give way to cascading waterfalls and tropical forests, with up to 1,500 exotic butterflies flying free in a re-created jungle habitat. There's an incredible collection of spiders and insects. Snacks, shop, disabled access; cl 25 Dec; (01789) 299288; £3.25.

📺 RAGDOLL (Chapel St) make children's TV programmes like the *Teletubbies* and *Tots TV*; the ground floor of their HQ has a shop, play areas and plenty to amuse small children. Disabled access; cl am Sun, 25 Dec, 1 Jan; free.

🐴 SHIRE HORSE CENTRE AND FARM PARK (Clifford Rd – on the B4632 S) Parades and demonstrations of the huge horses, as well as goats, pigs, rare breeds, owl sanctuary with falconry displays, and an adventure playground. Readers rate this very highly. Good meals and snacks, shop, disabled access (can be a bit bumpy); cl Thurs and Fri Nov–Feb, and 25 Dec; (01789) 415274; £4.50, less winter.

Warwick SP2865 Though many older buildings survived a major fire in 1694, today's centre is dominated by elegant Queen Anne rebuilding. Some of the oldest structures are to be found around Mill St, which is very attractive to stroll along; there are a good few antique shops. The Tilted Wig (Market Pl) has good value food, and the Saxon Mill (Guys Cliffe) is a straightforward family dining pub in very attractive waterside surroundings; the Warwick Arms Hotel does good-value teas.

WARWICK CASTLE (Castle Hill) One of the country's most splendid castles and certainly the most visited. It's a lively place, with plenty for children to enjoy (especially in the summer hols). Several displays show the influence of Madame Tussaud's who own the site, notably the dungeon's gruesome torture chambers, and elaborate re-creations of a Victorian house party and the medieval household's preparations for battle. Purists shouldn't be put off by the gloss – the rooms are excellently preserved, and their fine furnishings and art well worth braving the crowds for. The marvellous grounds were designed by Capability Brown, and the views from the parklands are dramatic, stirring stuff. The only thing that rankles is the price – make sure you allow enough time to get value for money. Meals, snacks, shop, disabled access; cl 25 Dec; (01926) 406600; £8.95 (£9.95 July and Aug). The nearby MILL GARDEN is a delightful series of plantings in a super setting on the river beside the castle – very nice to stroll through, with plenty of old things to look at along the way. Shop, disabled access; open Easter–mid-Oct; (01926) 492877; *£1.

ST MARY'S CHURCH (Old Square) Splendid medieval church on the town's highest point, with a Norman crypt, chapter house and the magnificent 15th-c Beauchamp chapel; in summer you can go up the tower which has excellent views – small admission charge.

LORD LEYCESTER HOSPITAL (High St) Delightfully wonky half-timbered building built in 1383, still used as a home of rest for retired servicemen. Fine old guildhall, candlelit chapel, gatehouse and courtyard, and garden with its Norman arch and a 2,000-yr-old urn from the Nile. Snacks (summer only), shop; cl Mon, Good Fri, 25 Dec; (01926) 491422; *£2.75.

ST JOHN'S HOUSE (St John's) 17th-c house with exhibits from the county museum, and several room reconstructions. Shop, disabled access to ground floor only; cl 12.30–1.30pm, all day Sun (exc pm Apr–Sept), and Mon (exc bank hols); (01926) 410410; free.

DOLL MUSEUM (Castle St) Half-timbered Elizabethan house with comprehensive collection of antique dolls and toys. A fun video shows the exhibits come to life. Shop; cl am Sun, and all Nov–Easter exc Sat; (01926) 410410; *£1.

COUNTY MUSEUM (Market Pl) In the 17th-c Market Hall, with lots of fossils, and a Sheldon tapestry map of the county. Shop; cl Sun exc pm Apr–Sept; (01926) 410410; free.

Please let us know what you think of places in the *Guide*. Use the report forms at the back of the book or simply send a letter.

Other things to see and do

WARWICKSHIRE AND WEST MIDLANDS FAMILY ATRACTION OF THE YEAR

🐦 ! **Bournville** SP0481 CADBURY WORLD Attached to the Cadbury factory, this hugely enjoyable place is ideal for anyone who's ever had a taste for chocolate, with all you could ever want to know about how it's made and marketed. Obviously there's something of a corporate bias (you could be forgiven for thinking nobody else has ever made chocolate apart from the Aztecs and the Cadburys), but the displays and exhibitions have been put together with great verve. It's not a factory tour, though you do visit a production area, with demonstrators hand-making and decorating luxury chocolates, and the Packaging Plant where the more standard bars are wrapped and packed. Children enjoy the alternative view of chocolate-making offered by Mr Cadbury's Parrot at the Fantasy Factory, and in 1997 they added Cadabra, a jolly ride through an imaginative chocolate-themed world in a car shaped like a cocoa bean. Older visitors get nostalgic watching TV adverts for Cadbury's products from the last 40 years (some from overseas), and there's a collection of period wrappers displayed in a 1930s-style sweet shop. Elsewhere cars and climbing frames are disguised as Creme Eggs (and a slide as a box of Roses), and there are plenty of samples to satisfy the cravings created by the sumptuous smells. A typical visit lasts about 2½ hours (most of it under cover), but you'll need to book in advance to be sure of getting in; on popular days tickets can be sold out well in advance. Restaurant and picnic areas, good shop (some bargains and unusual varieties), mostly disabled access; open daily Mar–Oct, and usually wknds and at least a couple of other days Nov–Feb; (0121) 451 4180; £6 (£4.30 children aged 5–15). Family tickets available.

Days Out

Machine aesthetics
Heritage Motor Centre, Gaydon; lunch at the King's Head, Wellesbourne; watermill there (limited opening); Nickelodeon, Ashorne.

Birmingham at work
Birmingham railway museum; Jewellery Quarter Discovery Centre; lunch at Rosevilla (Vyse St); Cadbury World.

Black Country heritage
Broadfield House Glass Museum, Kingswinford; Royal Doulton factory tour (limited opening); lunch at the Crooked House, Himley; Black Country Museum, Dudley.

Canals and country estates
Towpath stroll at the junction of Stratford and Grand Union Canals nr Lapworth; lunch at the Navigation, Lapworth or Fleur de Lys, Lowsonford; Packwood House or Baddesley Clinton House.

Shakespeare's landscapes
Aston Cantlow; Mary Arden's house nr Stratford; lunch at the Blue Boar, Temple Grafton; Wixford; Ragley Hall, Alcester or Coughton Court (both limited opening).

🏠 🏛 🅰 **Alcester** SP0857 RAGLEY HALL (on the A435) Perfectly symmetrical Palladian house in 400 acres of parkland and gardens; excellent baroque plasterwork in the Great Hall, fine paintings (inc some modern art), and adventure playground, maze and woodland walks in the grounds. Good outdoor concerts. Snacks, shop, disabled access; open Thurs–Sun and bank hols, Easter–Sept, plus park open daily in July; (01789) 762090; £4.50, £3.50 grounds only. The village itself is attractive, and the Moat House (on the A435 towards Studley) has good food; the nearby village of Arrow is interesting to stroll around (despite some development) – as is the pretty stream that divides the two. Fruit farming around here is much rarer than it used to be, but you can still find delicious fresh dessert plums for sale in Sept. The county's best drive (partly in Gloucs) circles Alcester, via Walcote, Aston Cantlow, Wilmcote, Temple Grafton, Wixford, Radford, Inkberrow, Holberrow Green, New End and Kings Coughton.

🏠 🏛 👶 ⚘ **Arbury** SP3389 ARBURY HALL (off the B4102 just S of Nuneaton) Splendid-looking place, the original Elizabethan house elaborately spruced up in the 19th c to make it one of the best examples of the Gothic Revival style. The writer George Eliot was born on the estate, and her *Mr Gifgil's Love Story* describes some of the rooms – not unreasonably comparing the dining room to a cathedral. Some work by Wren in the stables (now housing a collection of vintage cycles), and the gardens are a pleasure. Shop, limited disabled access; open pm Sun and bank hols Easter–Sept; (01203) 382804; *£4.50, gardens *£2.50. NUNEATON MUSEUM (Coton Rd, Nuneaton SP3592) A display on the life of George Eliot can be seen at the museum, nicely set in colourful Riversley Park; cl am Sun, all day Mon (exc bank hols); (01203) 350720; free. Good craft centre nearby.

❗ **Ardens Grafton** SP1153 GOLDEN CROSS INN Unusually decorated with over 250 antique dolls, teddies and toys. Small shop, decent food; open licensing hrs (cl 3–6pm).

👶 ❗ 🍴 **Ashorne** SP3057 NICKELODEON 🎹 (Ashorne Hall, off the B4100) Unique collection of mechanically played musical instruments inc self-playing harps, drums and violins, and a vintage theatre, complete with organ rising from the floor. They show silent comedies and 1950s Pathé newsreels, and have various nostalgic tea concerts and events. There's a miniature railway in the grounds (£1.50 extra). Meals, snacks, shop, disabled access; open pm Sun Mar–Nov, plus most Sats, some Fris, and maybe other days too – worth checking; (01926) 651444; *£6.30. The Cottage has good-value food (may cl wkdy lunchtime).

🏠 🏛 ✝ **Baddesley Clinton** SP2070 BADDESLEY CLINTON HOUSE Romantic 13th-c moated manor house, mostly unchanged since the 17th c. Interesting portraits, priests' holes and garden with chapel and pretty walks. The family history is intriguing. Meals, snacks, shop, some disabled access; open pm Weds–Sun and bank hols Mar–Oct (shop and restaurant open till Christmas); (01564) 783294; £4.60 (timed ticket system), grounds only £2.30; NT. The nearby CHURCH has a lovely east window, and the canalside Navigation at Lapworth and prettily set Cock Horse at Rowington do decent food.

🏍 **Bickenhill** SP1882 NATIONAL MOTORCYCLE MUSEUM (Coventry Rd) Handy for the NEC, 5 halls displaying over 650 gleamingly restored motorcycles, all British. Incongruously, they also have the biggest theatre organ in Europe. Meals, snacks, shop, disabled access; cl 24–26 Dec; (01675) 443311; *£4.50. The White Lion at Hampton in Arden has good-value food.

🏛 **Castle Bromwich** SP1489 CASTLE BROMWICH HALL GARDEN (Chester Rd) Carefully restored 18th-c formal gardens, with authentic collection of plants grown here then, inc ancient vegetables as well as herbs and shrubs. Snacks, plant sales, limited

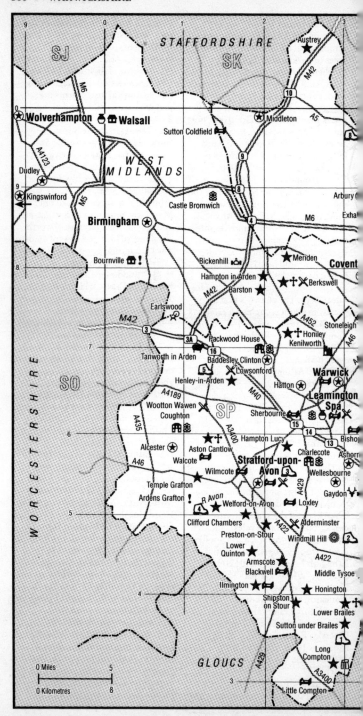

disabled access; cl am, all day Fri, and Oct–Easter; (0121) 749 4100; £2.

⚑ 🏠 **Charlecote** SP2656 CHARLECOTE PARK 250 acres of parkland, full of deer (Shakespeare is said to have poached them from here), along with the descendants of reputedly the country's first flock of Jacob sheep. Well furnished Great Hall and Victorian kitchen, and an impressive Tudor gatehouse. Meals, snacks, shop, disabled access; open Fri–Tues Apr–Oct (cl Good Fri); (01789) 470277; *£4.80; NT. By the park is a charming little 19th-c estate village of timbered cottages, and a show Victorian church. The Boar's Head in pretty Hampton Lucy has decent food.

🏠 ⚑ **Coughton** SP0860 COUGHTON COURT 🖼 (on the A435) Several priests' holes are hidden in this mainly Elizabethan house, renowned for its imposing gatehouse and beautiful courtyard; the Throckmortons have lived here since 1409. Notable furniture and porcelain, and an exhibition on the Gunpowder Plot, with a lake, two churches, pleasant walks, formal gardens and play area in the grounds. Meals, snacks, shop, plant sales, limited disabled access; open pm wknds mid-Mar–mid-Oct, plus pm Mon–Weds May–Sept; (01789) 400777; £5.75, £3.50 grounds only; NT. The Green Dragon on the fine old green at nearby Sambourne and the interesting Old Washford Mill at Studley are good for lunch; a good restaurant, Poppies, has now opened at the Court itself.

✝ 🖼 🏠 🏛 🏠 🏠 ✝ **Coventry** SP3378 Like Birmingham, more a place to dip into than to fix on as your base for a short stay; its most interesting street is Spon St, with one or two ancient buildings that started their lives here and others that have been rescued from elsewhere and rebuilt here (the picturesque Old Windmill does cheap basic lunches). One of the town's most famous inhabitants was Lady Godiva, commemorated best by the Coventry Clock – where she pops out in the pink every hour. CATHEDRAL (Priory Row) Bombed during the war, the old cathedral ruins have been carefully preserved, and parts of it such as the 14th-c tower remain intact. These have been joined by the new cathedral designed by Sir Basil Spence. It is, perhaps quite rightly, in no way an orthodox church building, but is worth a look for unusual modern art (inc windows by John Piper, tapestry by Graham Sutherland, even holograms); the visitor centre (cl Sun) has more, as well as a full history of its development. Meals, snacks, shop, disabled access; cl 4 days in July and Nov for degree ceremonies; £2 suggested donation, £1.25 for visitor centre. TOY MUSEUM (Much Park St) Toys from 1740 to 1990, housed in a 14th-c monastery gatehouse. Shop; cl am, and 25 Dec; (01203) 227560; *£1.50. HERBERT ART GALLERY AND MUSEUM (Jordan Well) Fine silver and furniture, Chinese art, and a lively interactive history of the city. Meals, snacks, shop, disabled access; cl Christmas; (01203) 832381; free. LUNT ROMAN FORT (Coventry Rd) Fun reconstruction of 1st-c Roman fort, interesting to see such a site in all its glory. Good interpretative displays. Shop, disabled access; open wknds and bank hols Apr–Oct, plus daily late July–Aug; (01203) 832381; £2.60. MUSEUM OF BRITISH ROAD TRANSPORT (St Agnes Lane) Big collection of motor cars (developed in Coventry from the already established sewing machine industry), as well as commercial vehicles and bicycles, and a display of die-cast models. Snacks, shop, disabled access; cl 24–26 Dec; (01203) 832425; *£3.30. ST MARY'S GUILDHALL (Bayley Lane) Very well preserved medieval building, with its minstrels' gallery intact, and some Flemish tapestries; it's usually open Easter–Oct (exc Fri and Sat), provided there aren't any civic functions, but best to check; (01203) 832381. The Royal Court Hotel, Greyhound out at Sutton Stop (Aldermans Green/Hawkesbury) and Prince William Henry and William IV (both Foleshill Rd – authentic Indian) are popular for lunch, and Browns

café-bar nr the cathedral (Lower Precinct) serves food all day. Just S of town at the airport, the MIDLAND AIR MUSEUM has displays of civil and military aircraft spanning more than 70 years. Snacks, shop, disabled access; cl 25–26 Dec; (01203) 301033; £3.

⊹⊺ ♨ 🐂 🏰 👄 🖾 **Dudley** SO9490 BLACK COUNTRY MUSEUM (Tipton Rd, 1m N of centre) Well thought-out open-air museum giving a good feel of how things used to be in the Black Country, the heavily industrialised and proudly individual areas on the W part of the Birmingham conurbation. It's an authentically reconstructed turn-of-the-century village, complete with cottages, chapel, chemist, school, baker, pub and old-fashioned fairground, and trips along the canal or even down a mine. All the staff wear period costume, and demonstrations are informative and entertaining. This could easily fill most of a day. Meals, snacks, shop, some disabled access; cl Mon and Tues Nov–Feb, and 25 Dec; (01384) 236275; £6.95. The Dudley Canal Trust do BOAT TRIPS along the Dudley Tunnel, part of a unique network of canal tunnels and limestone mines. Trips Mar–Nov, and some days in Dec – best to ring for times; (01384) 236275; £2.50. DUDLEY ZOO (The Broadway) is based around an impressive RUINED CASTLE, so the animals enjoy rather special views. Meals, snacks, shop, disabled access; cl 25 Dec; (01384) 252401; £5.50. MUSEUM AND ART GALLERY (St James's Rd) Some fine paintings, well displayed geology, and appealing temporary exhibitions. Shop, disabled access; cl Sun; (01384) 818181; free.

🐾 **Earlswood** SP1173 MANOR FARM CRAFT WORKSHOPS (Wood Lane) Ceramics, furniture restoration, stained glass, print-making, needlework, a new vintage car display, and farm shop with home-made ice-cream. Meals, snacks, shop, disabled access; cl Mon, Christmas wk; (01564) 702729; free. The canalside Bluebell and the Red Lion (past the lakes) are useful dining pubs.

🏠 🏵 **Farnborough** SP4349
FARNBOROUGH HALL Palladian villa filled with splendid sculptures, paintings and fine rococo plasterwork; the staircase, hall and 2 main rooms are on show. The 18th-c landscaped gardens have a couple of ornamental temples, and views from the terrace walk – less impressive than they were thanks to the arrival of the M40. Disabled access to ground floor only; open pm Weds and Sat Apr–Sept, terrace also open pm Thurs and Fri; (01295) 690202; £2.80, £1 terrace walk only; NT. The Butchers Arms has good food.

📷 ✿ **Gaydon** SP3654 HERITAGE MOTOR CENTRE (Banbury Rd) Busy centre with the world's biggest collection of historic British cars – 300 in all, starting with an 1895 Wolseley. Also hundreds of drawings, photographs, trophies and models, hi-tech displays and video shows, and a nature reserve. The design of the building is incredible, especially inside. Meals, snacks, shop, disabled access; cl 25–26 Dec; (01926) 641188; £5.50. The Malt Shovel is handy for lunch.

🎡 🚐 🍴 **Hatton** SP2367 COUNTRY WORLD 🏕 (Dark Lane) Britain's biggest crafts village, made up of some three dozen workshops and still growing; demonstrations most wknds. The 100-acre site also includes a rare breeds farm (with some walk-through paddocks), adventure playground, antique and plant centres, and summer PICK-YOUR-OWN soft fruits. Meals, snacks, shop, limited disabled access; (01926) 843411; craft village free, farm £3.50. A nature trail leads to the STAIRWAY TO HEAVEN, an impressive flight of 21 locks on the Grand Union Canal over 2 miles. There's a good farm shop nearby at Windmill House Farm; the Durham Ox at Shrewley is handy for lunch.

🏰 **Kenilworth** SP2871 KENILWORTH CASTLE Dramatic castle transformed by John of Gaunt into a spectacular fortress. These are among the finest castle ruins in the country, with a still impressive keep and several other buildings within the sandstone walls.

Also restored Tudor garden, various re-enactments and open-air plays and operas, and children's activities most summer hol wknds. Shop, disabled access (but no facilities); cl 24 –26 Dec, 1 Jan; (01926) 52078; £2.75. The town itself has a Norman church and some pleasant strolls, especially around the castle area, where the Clarendon House Hotel has good-value food.

🍴 ❗ 🏛 **Kingswinsford** SO8888
BROADFIELD HOUSE GLASS MUSEUM (Barnett Lane) Excellent collection of glass from nearby Stourbridge, displayed to dazzling effect. Clever use of lighting shows off the exhibits quite spectacularly, and even the audio-visual shows create a sense of excitement. One of the area's least expected treasures. Teas, shop, disabled access; cl am exc Sat (when cl 1–2pm for lunch), and all day Mon; (01384) 812745; free. CROOKED HOUSE (off the B4176 E of Himley) SO8791 Extraordinary pub bent by mining subsidence into a three-dimensional optical illusion that'll have you imagining things roll uphill here, instead of down; perhaps surprisingly, it's a good pub too. ROYAL DOULTON (on the A449, Amblecote SO8985) You can tour the factory or visit the factory shop; tours 10am and 11.15am wkdys only (no under 10s), booking recommended; (01384) 552900; shop cl Sun and factory hols; free. The Robin Hood here (Collis St) has good-value food.

🏵 🍴 **Leamington Spa** SP3265
Elegant spa resort popularised by the rich who came to take the waters in the 18th and 19th c. Still many fine Regency buildings, though today the town is better seen as a civilised shopping centre, and perhaps as a base for sallies into the surrounding countryside – or into Warwick, across the River Avon. Beautifully laid-out JEPHSON GARDENS (The Parade) are worth a look, with wild ducks on the lake. The Carpenters Arms (Chandos St) is a decent well restored early Victorian pub.

★ 🏛 **Long Compton** SP2832 This pleasant Cotswoldy village of thatched stone houses has some antique shops; the Red Lion has good food. The ROLLRIGHT STONES, a well preserved stone circle a mile or so to the S, are described under Little Rollright in the Oxon chapter.

🐖 🏠 🐕 **Middleton** SP1798 ASH END HOUSE FARM (off the A4091) Friendly farm set up specifically for children; animals from shire horses to baby chicks and fluffy ducklings, as well as rare breeds of goats, pigs and sheep. A pony ride is included in the price, and there's plenty under cover for wet days. Snacks, shop, disabled access; cl 25–27 Dec, 1 Jan; (0121) 329 3240; £3.60 children (adults half price). MIDDLETON HALL (on the A4091) Varied architecture in the house (still being restored), also nature reserve, walled gardens, orchards and woodland. There's a good craft centre in the stables. Snacks, shop, some disabled access; house open pm Sun and bank hols Apr–Sept, craft centre open all year exc Mon and Tues; (01827) 283095; £1.50. The Green Man is a decent family dining pub.

★ 🌼 🐄 **Napton on the Hill** SP4661 Attractive village on a rounded hill above a curve in the Oxford Canal – perhaps the prettiest canal in this part of the world, with pleasant towpath walks. Great views of 7 counties from the hill. CHURCH LEYES FARM is a friendly 40-acre family-run organic farm with animals, walks and wild-flower conservation headlands by the hedges. Cl Sat, and Jewish holy days; (01926) 812143; *£1.

🏠 🐝 **Packwood House** SP1671 (off the A34) Friendly old house with origins as a 16th-c farmhouse, carefully restored and not at all commercialised; interesting panelling, furniture and needlework, and in the garden unusual yew trees clipped to represent the Sermon on the Mount. Snacks, shop, some disabled access; open pm Weds–Sun and bank hols Apr–Oct; (01564) 782024; £4, garden only £2; NT. The Navigation by the canal at Lapworth has good-value food.

★ **Priors Marston** SP4857 Attractive old houses around the village green, and unusual blue brick paths; the

ancient Holly Bush is a decent pub. There's a walk up Marston Hill behind, and quite a good network of paths around nearby Priors Hardwick taking you down to the Oxford Canal. The old drovers' Welsh Road through here via Southam to Cubbington is a pleasant drive; just before Offchurch it crosses the remarkable Fosse Way, a quiet Roman road running dead straight from Brinklow through Stretton-on-Dunsmore and Princethorpe down to Halford.

🐄 🏠 🚠 **Rugby** SP5075 RUGBY SCHOOL was founded in 1567, moving to its current site nearly 200 years later. A MUSEUM on Little Church St looks at its history and former pupils, such as Rupert Brooke and Lewis Carroll. Shop, disabled access; cl am, all day Sun and Mon, and 2 wks at Christmas; (01788) 574117; £1.50. Guided tours of the school buildings leave here at 2.30pm (not Sun or Mon), and other times by arrangement; £2, or £3 combined ticket with museum. The game the school invented is commemorated at GILBERTS just down the road, the shop that's been making the standard rugby ball since 1842. You can watch them do it, and there are related displays and collections. Shop, some disabled access; cl Sun and a few days over Christmas; (01788) 542426; free. The Three Horseshoes Hotel not far off in Sheep St is useful for lunch.

🐝 **Ryton-on-Dunsmore** SP3874 RYTON GARDENS (off the A45, on Wolston rd) The home of the Henry Doubleday Research Association, the organic farming and gardening organisation, so the grounds are landscaped with thousands of organically grown plants and trees; herb garden, rose garden, garden for the blind, and shrub borders among the displays, as well as some free-range farm animals. Very good meals and snacks in wholefood café, shop, disabled access; cl Christmas wk; (01203) 303517; *£2.50 (usually less in winter).

🐄 **Tanworth in Arden** SP1479 UMBERSLADE CHILDREN'S FARM Friendly family-run farm with

animals to stroke and feed, and play
areas for letting off steam. Also
nature trails and walks, and goat-
milking area. Snacks, shop, disabled
access; cl Nov–Feb and usually some
wkdys Oct and Mar; (01564)
742251; *£2.75.

🏠 🏛 † **Upton House** SP3746 (on the
A422 nr Ratley) The exceptional art
collection is the main draw here, the
enormous range of paintings, inc
works by Bosch, El Greco, Bruegel
and Hogarth, all sensibly arranged
and displayed. Also Brussels
tapestries, Sèvres porcelain, and
woodland and terrace walks. The late
17th-c house was remodelled earlier
this century. Teas, shop, disabled
access; open pm Sat–Weds Apr–Oct;
(01295) 670266; £4.80, garden only
£2.40; NT. There's a timed ticket
system at peak periods. Ratley itself is
a pretty village, with a lovely church
and good home cooking in the Rose
& Crown; and the Castle on Edge
Hill is a very interesting place for
lunch, with terrific views.

👶 🏛 **Walsall** SP0198 LEATHER
MUSEUM (Wisenmore) Well restored
19th-c leather goods factory with
tours of aromatic workshops and
leather-making demonstrations (not
Sun). Meals, snacks, shop (lots of
local leather goods), disabled access;
cl am Sun, all day Mon (exc bank
hols), Easter Sun, 24–26 Dec, 1 Jan;
(01922) 721153; free. 2 other decent
enough museums, both free, are the
JEROME K JEROME BIRTHPLACE MUSEUM
(Bradford St), dedicated to the life
and work of the author of *Three Men
in a Boat*, with a reconstructed 1850s
parlour (cl 1–2pm, pm Sat, all day
Sun and bank hols), and a small
CANAL MUSEUM just N at Top Lock,
Old Birchills, with a replica boat
cabin (open pm Thurs–Sun, and am
Tues and Weds). The Hammakers
Arms (Shaw St/Blue Lane) does good-
value food.

✗ 🦆 👶 **Wellesbourne** SP2855
WELLESBOURNE WATERMILL (on the
B4086) Historic watermill still
producing flour in secluded rural
setting, with striking wooden wheel.
Helpful staff, nature trails,
traditional crafts, and falconry
displays and an owl sanctuary.
Snacks, shop, some disabled access
(there are steep steps); open
Thurs–Sun Easter–Oct (daily exc
Mon in summer hols), plus pm Sun
Oct and Mar; (01789) 470237;
£3.50. WARTIME MUSEUM Housed in
the underground HQ of a former
RAF base, a collection of
aeronautical archaeology and
wartime memorabilia, with a
restored *Vampire* plane. Shop, some
disabled access; open Suns only; *£1.
The King's Head is a decent pub.

👶 🏛 🏵 **Wolverhampton** SO9198 Not
really a town for visitors, though its
MUSEUM (Lichfield Rd) is a good one.
Wightwick Manor and Moseley Old
Hall right out on the outskirts are
splendid. WIGHTWICK MANOR (just off
the A454, 3m W) is only a century
old, but beautifully and unusually
designed by followers of William
Morris, and a fine testimonial to the
enduring qualities of his design
principles. Flamboyant tiles, fittings,
furnishings and glass, and lots of Pre-
Raphaelite art, cannily acquired
while it was unfashionable. Also
period garden with yew hedges and
topiary. Snacks, shop, some disabled
access; open pm Thurs, Sat and bank
hol wknds, Mar–Dec, garden also
open Weds, and other wkdys by
arrangement; (01902) 761108; £5,
£2.40 garden only. MOSELEY OLD
HALL 🏠 (Featherstone, off the
A460/A449, 4m N) Tudor house
famed as a hiding place for Charles II
after the Battle of Worcester. The
façade has altered since, but the
furnishings and atmosphere in its
panelled rooms don't seem to have
changed much, and there's a 17th-c
knot garden. Readers particularly
enjoy the guided tours. Teas, shop,
limited disabled access; open pm
Weds, wknds Apr–May and bank
hols Apr–Oct, plus Tues July and
Aug and after bank hols, and pm Suns
Nov–Christmas; (01902) 782808;
*£3.60; NT.

★ **Attractive villages** include
Armscote SP2444 (picturesque
Cotswold stone); Aston Cantlow
SP1460 (timbered houses and
guildhall, lovely church where

Shakespeare's parents married, fine old pub); Austrey SK2906 (timbered houses and cottages, some thatch); Berkswell SP2479 (pretty Norman church); Bubbenhall SP3672; Clifford Chambers SP1092 (timbered houses and a Tudor rectory which has some claim to being the true birthplace of Shakespeare); Exhall SP3385 (pretty black and white timbering and some pleasant gently hilly walks nearby, despite the proximity of the M6); Henley-in-Arden SP1566 (more small town than village, but a pretty conservation area with good churches); Honiley SP2472 (the village has gone now, and there are only vestiges of the big house, but you can still sense the vanished settlement around the surviving 18th-c church); Honington SP2642 (church on edge of lawn of charming late 17th-c Honington Hall, open pm Weds Jun–Aug); Ilmington SP2143 (path to partly Norman church, lovely inside; pleasant walks on hills above; Howard Arms good for lunch); Lower Brailes SP3139 (lovely slender-spired church, pretty stone houses, good views); Lower Quinton SP1847; Meriden SP2482 (good-value pub, and a cross on the green marks what the village feels is the centre of England – one of the streams rising in the village pond ends up in the Severn and the other over in the Humber); Middle Tysoe SP3344 (with a very traditional cottage bakery); Monks Kirby SP4683; Preston on Stour SP2049; Radway SP3748; Stoneleigh SP3372 (sandstone Norman church, timber-framed houses, and soon to be restored Stoneleigh Abbey; nearby is the showground for the Royal Show); Sutton-under-Brailes SP2937; and Shakespeare's 'Hungry Grafton', now Temple Grafton SP1255 (the Blue Boar is good for lunch). Others, all with decent food in civilised pubs, are Barston SP2078, Easenhall SP4679, Hampton in Arden SP2081, Hampton Lucy SP2557, Lighthorne SP3355, Warmington SP4147 and Welford-on-Avon SP1452. Shipston on Stour SP2540 is a small town with quite a busy shopping centre, but is rewarding to stroll through, with a good church and some handsome old stone buildings, antique shops among them.

Walks

Sutton-under-Brailes SP2937 ⌂-1 has some pleasing Cotswold countryside around it. From **Upper Tysoe** SP3343 ⌂-2 the walk S over Windmill Hill (which does have a windmill) takes you to the church on the edge of Compton Wynyates park, giving views of the attractive Tudor manor – a refreshing bit of brick building, in this Cotswold-edge stone country.

The **River Avon** ⌂-3 offers a pleasant waterside walk from the Ferry, a good dining pub in Alveston SP2356. Another Avon walk is from the Cottage of Content at **Barton** SP1051 ⌂-4, which has day fishing tickets.

Canals give some of the county's best walking opportunities. The **Stratford-upon-Avon Canal** ⌂-5 gives some pleasant towpath walks; the Fleur de Lys at Lowsonford SP1868 is a good start. The **Ashby Canal** ⌂-6 heading off into the Leics countryside from its junction with the Coventry Canal at Marston Junction SP3688 has perhaps the prettiest of the towpath walks. Besides places already mentioned, other useful canalside pubs include the Navigation at Lapworth SP1670, Anchor at Leek Wootton SP2868, Two Boats at Long Itchington SP4164 (the flight of Stockton Locks just E usually has plenty going on), George & Dragon at the Wharf nr Fenny Compton SP4152 (on the A423 – a popular family pub, with aviaries and so forth) and Dog & Doublet at Bodymoor Heath SP2096 (useful for the Kingsbury Water Park too).

Offchurch Bury SP3466 ⌂-7 is attractive riverside parkland, with a pleasant walk winding through from the Stag's Head in Offchurch SP3665.

Hartshill Hayes SP3294 ⌂-8 is a country park with mixed woodland, opening out at the top for broad views towards the Peak District. The Coventry Canal below allows more extended rambles.

Where to eat

Alderminster SP2348 BELL (01789) 450414 Very popular and rather civilised dining pub nr Stratford, with excellent imaginative food using fresh local produce (no fried food at all); several communicating areas with flagstones and wooden floors, fresh flowers, good wines, real ales, obliging service, and no smoking restaurant; disabled access. **£18.95|£5**.

Berkswell SP2479 BEAR (01676) 533202 Pretty timbered 16th-c pub, recently refurbished; traditional relaxed atmosphere, with comfortable, snug, low-beamed areas, nooks and crannies, beams and panelling, and bric-à-brac; well kept ales, decent house wines, and a wide choice of food inc interesting daily specials; seats on the back lawn. **£18.10|£7.15**.

Leamington Spa SP3165 PHOENIX BAR Regent Hotel (01926) 427231 Extremely popular, elegant and comfortable hotel bar with lovely trompe l'oeil murals, open fire, and a relaxed atmosphere; very good food and helpful service; 2 other restaurants also; disabled access. **£22|£7**.

Lowsonford SP1868 FLEUR DE LYS (01564) 782431 Bustling canalside pub with comfortable civilised atmosphere, smart spreading bar with lots of low black beams, and open fires; good food, well kept real ales, and decent wines by the glass; cl 25 Dec; children in dining room only. **£16.90|£6.95**.

Monks Kirby SP4683 BELL Bells Lane (01788) 832352 Busy pub with warmly chatty Spanish landlord, timbered and flagstoned rambling rooms, cheerful locals, marvellous tapas (Spanish hors d'oeuvres) as well as more usual bar food, a very good wine list, well kept real ales, and quite a few whiskies; cl am Mon, 26 Dec, 1 Jan; disabled access. **£25|£4.25**.

Stratford-upon-Avon SP2055 CELLARS 16-17 Warwick Rd (01789) 204109 Renovated and attractive evening cellar restaurant in hotel (separate entrance) with a smoking and a no smoking room, daily-changing, interesting home-cooked mainly Italian food, friendly service, and a reasonably priced wine list; best to book Sat evenings; cl Christmas. **£20|£6.95**.

Stratford-upon-Avon SP2054 RUSSONS 8 Church St (01789) 268822 Cheerful and popular bistro in 17th-c malt house; very good imaginative food and good-value simple wine list; pre-theatre meals, too; cl Sun–Mon; **£21.95|£4.95**.

Stratford-upon-Avon SP2055 SLUG & LETTUCE 38 Guild St (01789) 299700 Cheerfully friendly, popular place, handy for the theatre, with nice food, helpful staff, well kept real ales, decent wine, attractive bar with open fire and newspapers, and a pretty back terrace. **£23|£9**.

Stratford-upon-Avon SP2054 THE OPPOSITION 13 Sheep St (01789) 269980 Small, bustling restaurant with friendly atmosphere, generous helpings of very good interesting food – handy for theatres and open for after-show meals; cl 25–26 Dec. **£20|£5.95**.

Wootton Wawen SP1563 BULLS HEAD (01564) 792511 Charming old black and white timbered building with heavy-beamed bar, low-ceilinged lounge with huge upright timbers, and a handsome restaurant; generous helpings of good often unusual food from a sensibly short menu, notably friendly young staff, several wines by the glass, well kept beer; handy for walks by the Stratford Canal; cl 25 Dec; no children. **£20|£8**.

Special thanks to Suzy Kilgour, Anne Conroy, Peter Harris, Peter Lloyd, Gilbert Hayward, Debby Magee.

WARWICKSHIRE CALENDAR

Some of these dates were provisional as we went to press. Please
check information with the number provided.

JANUARY

1 **Stratford-upon-Avon** *Romeo and Juliet*, *The Merchant of Venice* and
Twelfth Night and others at the Royal Shakespeare Theatre – *till end
Dec* (01789) 295623

FEBRUARY

7 **Ryton-on-Dunsmore** Potato Day: sale, cookery demonstrations at
Ryton Gardens – *till Sun 8* (01203) 303517

11 **Birmingham** BBC *Tomorrow's World* Live at the NEC – *till Sun 15*
(0121) 234 5257

14 **Birmingham** National Boat, Caravan and Leisure Show at the NEC –
till Sun 22 (0121) 234 5257

24 **Atherstone** Shrovetide Football: hundreds of locals gather for the
game in the Main St (01827) 716410

MARCH

5 **Birmingham** Crufts Dog Show at the NEC – *till Sun 8* (0171) 493 7838

21 **Hatton** Horse and Carriage Trials at Country World – *till Sun 22*
(01926) 843411

APRIL

3 **Kenilworth** British Show Pony Society Show at the National
Agricultural Centre (NAC), Stoneleigh Park – *till Sun 5* (01203) 696697

11 **Hatton** Easter Egg Hunt at Country World – *till Mon 13* (01926)
843411

18 **Alcester** Gardeners Weekend at Ragley Hall – *till Sun 19* (01789)
762090

23 **Walsall** Real Ale Festival at the Town Hall – *till Sat 25* (01922) 653141

25 **Stratford-upon-Avon** Shakespeare Birthday Celebrations in the town
centre (01789) 415536

MAY

1 **Leamington Spa** Early Music Festival – *till Tues 5* (01926) 410747

2 **Birmingham** Classic and Sportscar Show at the NEC – *till Mon 4* 0171
402 2555

7 **Perry Barr** National Dog Show at Perry Park Showground – *till Sun 10*
(01536) 791399

9 **Solihull** Festival – *till Fri 15* (0121) 704 6961

10 **West Bromwich** Historic Vehicle Parade and Show (0121) 569 3402

16 **Alcester** Stag Owners' Rally at Ragley Hall (01625) 573477

JUNE

6 **Walsall** Summer Show at Aldridge Airport – *till Sun 7* (01922)
653141

7 **Nuneaton** Transport Spectacular at Arbury Hall (0121) 502 3713

10 **Birmingham** BBC *Gardeners World* at the NEC – *till Sun 14* (0121)
780 4141

21 **Alcester** Outdoor Concert: Themes from the Movies at Ragley Hall
(01625) 573477

27 **Offchurch** British Deer Fair at Cornbury Park – *till Sun 28* (01588)
672708

WARWICKSHIRE CALENDAR

JUNE cont

29 **Birmingham** International Jazz Festival – *till 12 July* (0121) 454 7020

JULY

1 **Warwick and Leamington** Festival – *till Sat 11* (01926) 410747

4 **Kenilworth** Carnival (01926) 56299; **Stratford-upon-Avon** Poetry Festival and *every Sun eve till Aug 30* (01789) 204016; **Warwick** Street Theatre (01926) 410747; **Warwick** Fireworks Concert at the Castle – *till Sun 5* (01926) 410747

5 **Walsall** Classic Car Show at Walsall Arboretum (0121) 502 3713

6 **Kenilworth** The Royal Show at NAC, Stoneleigh Park – *till Thurs 9* (01203) 696969

12 **Alcester** Classic Car and Transport Show at Ragley Hall (01789) 762090

25 **Coughton** Fireworks Concert at Coughton Court (01789) 400777

31 **Walsall** Leather Festival: children's day, horse parade at the Leather Museum – *till Aug 2* (01922) 653141

AUGUST

1 **Alcester** Firework and Laser Concert at Ragley Hall (01625) 573477; **Walsall** Canal Weekend at Birchills Canal Museum – *till Sun 2* (01922) 653141

8 **Alcester** Outdoor Concert at Ragley Hall (01625) 573477

22 **Alcester** Warwicks and West Midlands Game Fair at Ragley Hall – *till Sun 23* (01588) 672708

29 **Kenilworth** Town and Country Festival at NAC, Stoneleigh Park – *till Mon 31* (01203) 696969

30 **Sandwell** Family Show – *till Mon 31* (0121) 569 3402

SEPTEMBER

4 **Alcester** Last Night of the Proms at Ragley Hall (01625) 573477

5 **Hatton** Civil War Re-enactment at Country World – *till Sun 6* (01926) 843411; **Wolverhampton** Festival of Transport at East Park – *till Sun 6* (0121) 502 3713

12 **Alcester** Gardeners Weekend at Ragley Hall – *till Sun 13* (01625) 573477

19 **Walsall** Illuminations at Walsall Arboretum: light and laser show with music, street theatre and live performances – *till 1 Nov* (01922) 653148

20 **Birmingham** International Garden and Leisure Exhibition at the NEC – *till Tues 22* (0121) 780 4141

OCTOBER

17 **Warwick** Hog Roast and Mop Fair – *till Sun 18* (01926) 492212

20 **Birmingham** British International Motor Show at the NEC – *till 1 Nov* (0121) 780 4141

NOVEMBER

14 **Kenilworth** Classic Bike Show at NAC, Stoneleigh Park – *till Sun 15* (01203) 696969

DECEMBER

2 **Birmingham** BBC Good Food, Cooking and Kitchen Show at the NEC – *till Sun 6* (0121) 780 4141

11 **Birmingham** *Clothes Show* Live at the NEC – *till Wed 16* (0121) 780 4141

WILTSHIRE

Plenty of interest and variety for all ages; Salisbury makes a good short break, particularly for older people.

Salisbury is a splendid small city for a short civilised break, with a lovely cathedral precinct and interesting places to visit tucked quite closely around it. Elsewhere, Stourhead's wonderful grounds at Stourton, Wilton House and Lacock Abbey appeal strongly to much the same sort of people as Salisbury itself, as do the recently opened rather exotic gardens at Tollard Royal.

A good range of family outings in the county run from the attractively set Cholderton rare breeds farm (great fun for younger children particularly) to Longleat, which has a great deal to please all ages and tastes.

The two great prehistoric stone circles, Stonehenge and Avebury, are best appreciated at quiet times of day, out of season (with Stonehenge we'd recommend one of the specially authorised Astral tours). The county has a good many other ancient sites to explore, too.

The villages of Castle Combe and Lacock are exceptionally pretty, and there are attractive small towns with a good deal of character: Bradford-on-Avon, Devizes (its museum one of the privileged few to make the Heritage Secretary's new shortlist of excellence and national importance), Marlborough and Malmesbury. Other appealing places include Sheldon Manor at Chippenham, Bowood at Calne, Corsham Court (and the unique underground quarry nearby), Lydiard Park (a real bargain), the intriguing gardens of Hazelbury Manor at Box and the waterside ones at Middle Woodford, the unusual stone-working museum at Great Bedwyn, and the ruins of Old Wardour Castle near Tisbury.

The most attractive countryside is along the valleys of the chalk streams in the south – intimate scenery with stone or flint houses and sparkling rivers. Canal boat trips offer an alternative view of the Wiltshire countryside. The Salisbury Plain is better for driving over than walking – an almost unbroken expanse of rolling high ground, a mixture of pasture and broad unhedged arable fields intersected by tank-training tracks. The A360 gives a good feel of its emptiness. North of here the countryside, though undramatic, has some attractive drives and walks, especially around Marlborough.

Where to stay

Alderton ST8382 MANOR FARM Alderton, Chippenham SN14 6NL (01666) 840271 £50; 3 rms. Warmly friendly 17th-c house on busy working farm with homely lounge and good breakfasts; no children.

Bradford-on-Avon ST8261 BRADFORD OLD WINDMILL 4 Masons Lane, Bradford-on-Avon BA15 1QN (01225) 866842 *£75; 3 rms, one with giant waterbed, another with round bed. Interesting and carefully converted windmill with log fire in attractive circular lounge (former grain store), lots of books, a friendly atmosphere; good evening meals inc vegetarian dishes from Thailand, Nepal, Mexico and so forth, and fine breakfasts eaten around communal refectory table; pretty cottagey garden; no smoking; cl Christmas and New Year; children over 6.

Bradford-on-Avon ST8359 WIDBROOK GRANGE Trowbridge Rd, Bradford-on-Avon BA15 1UH (01225) 864750 £95; 20 rms, many in carefully converted courtyard cottages. Handsome stone former farmhouse in 11 acres, with comfortable drawing rooms, good food in elegant dining room, sunny conservatory, and indoor swimming pool and exercise machines; disabled access.

Bradford-on-Avon ST8361 WOOLLEY GRANGE Woolley Green, Bradford-on-Avon BA15 1TX (01225) 864705 £100, plus winter breaks; 22 rms, with fruit and home-made biscuits. Civilised Jacobean manor house with a relaxed informal atmosphere, lovely flowers, log fires, antiques and comfortable seating in the beautifully decorated day rooms, and a pretty conservatory; delicious food using local (or home-grown) produce, often organic, inc home-baked breads and muffins and home-made jams and marmalades for breakfast; marvellous staff, and very good for children – nursery with full-time nanny, games room, their own sort of food, and outdoor toys; swimming pool, tennis and croquet; limited disabled access.

Burbage SU2361 OLD VICARAGE Burbage, Marlborough SN8 3AG (01672) 810495 £70; 3 rms. Carefully run no smoking Victorian house in 2 acres of lovely grounds, with log fires, books and magazines in very attractive, solidly comfortable drawing room, and good breakfasts (pubs and restaurants nearby for evening meals); croquet and nearby riding; cl Christmas/New Year; no children.

Castle Combe ST8477 MANOR HOUSE Castle Combe, Chippenham SN14 7HR (01249) 782206 *£164, plus special breaks; 45 lovely rms. 26 acres of garden and parkland, inc an Italian garden, around 14th-c manor house with gracious day rooms, panelling, antiques, log fires and fresh flowers; a warm, friendly atmosphere, very good innovative food, and 18-hole golf course; disabled access.

Chicksgrove ST9629 COMPASSES Chicksgrove, Tisbury, Salisbury SP3 6NB (01722) 714318 *£45; 5 rms, showers. Lovely thatched house in delightful hamlet with old bottles and jugs hanging from the beams in the characterful bar, home-made bar food, well kept real ales, and peaceful farm courtyard and garden.

Colerne ST8272 LUCKNAM PARK Colerne, Chippenham SN14 8AZ (01225) 742777 £178, plus special breaks; 42 rms. Noble Georgian house, reached by a long beech-lined drive through extensive grounds, with elegant carefully furnished day rooms, a panelled library, lovely flowers, antiques and paintings, and excellent food and extremely good service in charming restaurant; leisure spa with indoor swimming pool, gym, beauty salon, hairdresser, snooker and floodlit tennis courts; croquet; equestrian centre; children over 12 in evening restaurant; disabled access.

Corsham ST8670 METHUEN ARMS High St, Corsham SN13 0HB (01249) 714867 £50, plus special breaks; 24 rms. Georgian inn (a former nunnery) with mullioned windows and heavy oak beams in 14th-c part, comfortable seats in neatly kept bar, good food, and friendly staff; pretty walled garden and fine skittle alley.

Crockerton ST8642 SPRINGFIELD HOUSE Crockerton, Warminster BA12 8AU (01985) 213696 *£48; 3 rms with garden views. 17th-c house on the edge of Longleat estate, with tennis in the garden, beams, flowers and open fires, dinner by the inglenook fireplace in candlelit dining room, and lots to do nearby; cl 25 Dec.

Devizes SU0061 Bear Market Pl, Devizes SN10 1HS (01380) 722444 *£80, plus special breaks; 24 rms. Very much at the town's heart, this 16th-c inn has an old-fashioned feel, a wide choice of food from snacks to more elaborate meals served in the oak-panelled Lawrence room, 2 more formal restaurants, beams and fresh flowers, and prompt service; cl 25–26 Dec.

Downton SU1721 Warren 15 High St, Downton, Salisbury SP5 3PG (01725) 510263 £44; 6 rms with fresh flowers, some with own bthrm. Friendly 15th-c house with lots of beams and antique furnishings, a lounge with open fire, and enjoyable breakfasts in lovely oak-panelled room with French windows on to big walled garden; cl 20 Oct–6 Jan; children over 5.

Easton Grey ST8987 Whatley Manor Easton Grey, Malmesbury SN16 0RB (01666) 822888 £120, plus special breaks; 29 rms with antique furniture, 18 in main house, 11 in Court House across courtyard (which are cheaper). Lovely Cotswold manor house in quiet gardens with riverside paddocks; spacious and rather fine oak-panelled drawing room, pine-panelled lounge, log fires, a relaxed atmosphere, lots of books in the library/bar, and attractive dining room overlooking garden; tennis court, swimming pool, croquet lawn, putting green, billiards, sauna, solarium and Jacuzzi; partial disabled access.

Ebbesbourne Wake ST9824 Horseshoe Ebbesbourne Wake, Salisbury SP5 5JG (01722) 780474 £40; 2 rms. Particularly welcoming pub with beautifully kept little bar, open fire, fresh flowers and interesting bric-à-brac on beams, popular home-made food in bar or no smoking restaurant, big breakfasts and nice Sunday lunches, well kept real ales, small pretty garden, and pets corner in paddock with goats and a Vietnamese pot-bellied pig; cl 25 Dec.

Ford ST8374 White Hart Ford, Chippenham SN14 8RP (01249) 782213 *£65; 11 rms. Very well run, popular and attractive ivy-covered inn in lovely spot by trout stream, with old-fashioned atmosphere, characterful rooms with heavy black beams, big log-burning stove in ancient fireplace, particularly good imaginative food, well kept real ales, malt whiskies and fine wines, attentive cheerful service, and secluded small swimming pool; disabled access.

Gastard ST8868 Boyds Farm Gastard, Corsham SN13 9PT (01249) 713146 *£36, plus special breaks; 3 rms, shared bthrm. Friendly and handsome 16th-c house on family-run working farm with pedigree herd of Herefords; homely lounge, woodburning stove, and traditional breakfasts; no evening meals.

Heytesbury ST9242 Angel High St, Heytesbury BA12 OED (01985) 840330 *£49; 4 comfortable rms. Beautiful little 16th-c coaching inn with armchairs, sofas, and a good fire in cosy, homely lounge, a long beamed bar with woodburner, quite a few prints, good service from friendly staff, well kept real ales, decent wines, and a wide choice of consistently good food in charming back dining room which opens on to secluded garden; cl 25 Dec.

Hindon ST9132 Lamb High St, Hindon, Salisbury SP3 6DP (01747) 820573 *£65, plus special breaks; 13 rms. Solidly built, welcoming and civilised old inn (once a smugglers' haunt) with log fires in fine old bar, attractive lounges, imaginative food, friendly helpful service, and no smoking restaurant.

Horningsham ST8141 Bath Arms Horningsham, Warminster BA12 2LY (01985) 844308 £42, plus special breaks; 7 well equipped clean rms. By the entrance to Longleat House, this comfortable and carefully modernised old inn has good interesting food, pleasant service, well kept real ales, and attractive gardens.

Lacock ST9167 At the Sign of the Angel Church St, Lacock, Chippenham SN15 2LA (01249) 730230 *£80, plus special breaks; 10 lovely rms. This fine 15th-c house in a lovely National Trust village is full of character, with heavy oak furniture, beams and big fireplaces, a restful oak-panelled lounge, and good English cooking in 2 candlelit restaurants; cl 1 wk Christmas; disabled access.

Malmesbury ST9287 Old Bell Abbey Row, Malmesbury SN16 0AG (01666) 822344 £85, plus special breaks; 31 rms. With some claim to being one of

England's oldest hotels and standing in the shadow of the Norman abbey, this fine wisteria-clad building has traditionally furnished rooms with Edwardian pictures, an early 13th-c hooded stone fireplace, 2 good fires, cheerful helpful service, and attractively old-fashioned garden; very good for families – they have a children's den supervised by nursemaids, and thoughtful food.

Mildenhall SU2069 FISHERMAN'S HOUSE Mildenhall, Marlborough SN8 2LZ (01672) 515390 *£45; 4 lovely rms, most with own bthrm. Extremely pretty house with lawns running down to the River Kennet, fresh flowers and stylish furniture, friendly owners, and good breakfasts in airy conservatory; cl Christmas; children over 8.

Nettleton ST8377 FOSSE FARMHOUSE Nettleton Shrub, Nettleton, Chippenham SN14 7NJ (01249) 782286 *£115, plus special breaks (inc some interesting craft wknds); 5 rms. 18th-c Cotswold stone house extensively restored with decorative French antique furniture and pretty English chintzes; morning coffee, lunch and afternoon cream teas served on the lawns or in very attractive dining room; antique shop with dried flowers and decorative items in former dairy behind the house.

Ogbourne St George SU1973 LAUREL COTTAGE Southend, Ogbourne St George, Marlborough SN8 1SG (01672) 841288 *£50; 3 rms, plus coach house. Charming 16th-c thatched no smoking farm cottage with friendly owners, comfortable lounge, good breakfasts in beamed dining room, packed lunches (popular with walkers), evening meals on request, and neat garden; mountain bikes for hire; cl Nov–March; no children.

Purton SU0887 PEAR TREE Church End, Purton, Swindon SN5 9ED (01793) 772100 *£85; 18 very comfortable, pretty rms. Impeccably run former vicarage with elegant comfortable day rooms, fresh flowers, fine conservatory restaurant with good modern English cooking using home-grown herbs, and 7½ acres of grounds inc a traditional Victorian garden; cl 26–30 Dec; disabled access.

Rowde ST9661 LOWER FOXHANGERS FARM Rowde, Devizes SN10 1SS (01380) 828254 *£40; 3 rms, 1 with own bthrm. 18th-c farmhouse on a 90-acre working farm, with dining room and lounge; boating, fishing and walking on Kennet & Avon canal; mobile homes also; cl Nov–Easter; children over 4.

Salisbury SU1430 FARTHINGS 9 Swaynes Close, Salisbury SP1 3AE (01722) 330749 *£42; 4 rms, some with own bthrm. Spotlessly kept no smoking house with friendly owners, good breakfasts, and pretty garden; close to cathedral; cl Feb; no children.

Salisbury SU1329 OLD MILL Town Path, West Harnham, Salisbury SP2 8EU (01722) 322364 *£75, plus special breaks; 10 comfortably converted rms. Based on a former mill and warehouse – there's been a mill here since 1135 – with terrace out by mill pool, and meadow walks with classic cathedral views; good honest English cooking in evening restaurant and beamed bar.

Salisbury SU1429 RED LION Milford St, Salisbury SP1 2AN (01722) 323334 £108, plus special breaks; 54 individually decorated rms. Handsome, family-run 700-year-old hotel with a mix of antique settles, leather chairs and modern banquettes in small 2-roomed panelled bar, spacious old-fashioned lounge with interesting furnishings inc clock with skeleton bellringers, and medieval restaurant; no pets; disabled access.

Salisbury SU1428 ROSE & CROWN Harnham Rd, Harnham, Salisbury SP2 8JQ (01722) 399955 £140, plus special breaks; 28 rms in the original building or smart, modern extension. It's almost worth a visit just for the view – well nigh identical to that in the most famous Constable painting of Salisbury cathedral; elegantly restored inn with friendly beamed and timbered bar, log fire, good bar and restaurant food, and charming Avonside garden; disabled access.

Salisbury SU1431 STRATFORD LODGE 4 Park Lane, Salisbury SP1 3NP (01722) 325177 *£54, plus special breaks; 8 rms. Warmly friendly and relaxed Victorian house with antique furnishings, fresh flowers, generous helpings of very good carefully prepared evening food, super breakfasts in conservatory, and quiet garden; cl Christmas/New Year; children over 8; limited disabled access.

Sutton Veny ST9041 OLD HOUSE Sutton Veny, Warminster BA12 7AQ (01985) 840344 **£64**; 3 rms. Carefully modernised 17th-c thatched house in 4 acres of quiet grounds; winter log fires, nice food using home-grown vegetables, and good breakfasts; cl Christmas/New Year; no children.

Teffont Evias ST9831 HOWARDS HOUSE Teffont Evias, Salisbury SP3 5RJ (01722) 716392 **£115**; 9 rms. Very well run, welcoming and comfortable little hotel in 2 acres of gardens surrounded by quiet countryside; log fire and lots of fresh flowers from the garden in restful sitting room, delicious food (using their own vegetables and herbs), fine breakfasts, particularly good wines, and extremely good service.

Upper Minety SU0091 FLISTERIDGE COTTAGE Flisteridge Rd, Upper Minety, Malmesbury SN16 9PS (01666) 860343 **£37**; 3 rms, 1 with own bthrm. Warmly welcoming and homely cottage with pretty garden, woodburning stove in sitting room, good breakfasts with home-made preserves (evening meals by arrangement), and friendly helpful owners; children over 11; well behaved pets by arrangement.

Warminster ST8943 BISHOPSTROW HOUSE Bishopstrow, Warminster BA12 9HH (01985) 212312 ***£145**, plus special breaks; 30 sumptuous rms, some with Jacuzzi. Charming ivy-clad Georgian house (carefully refurbished in 1997) in 27 acres with heated indoor and outdoor swimming pools, indoor and outdoor tennis courts, fitness centre, and fishing on own stretch of River Wylye; very relaxed homely atmosphere, log fires, lovely fresh flowers, antiques and fine paintings in elegant day rooms, and really impressive food.

Warminster ST8744 OLD BELL Market Pl, Warminster BA12 9AN (01985) 216611 **£50**, plus special breaks; 16 rms, most with own bthrm. Old-world country-town hotel with traditional bar food, bistro and restaurant, good choice of wines, pretty central courtyard, and friendly service; lots to do nearby.

West Grafton SU2460 ROSEGARTH West Grafton, Marlborough SN8 3BY (01672) 810288 ***£36**; 2 rms. Charming 16th-c thatched and half-timbered cottage in 3-acre garden, with comfortable lounge, good breakfasts, friendly owners, and big garden; no children.

Winsley ST7960 BURGHOPE MANOR Winsley, Bradford-on-Avon BA15 2LA (01225) 723557 ***£70**; 4 rms. Lovely 13th-c manor house in attractive countryside, with carefully preserved old rooms and interesting fireplace engraved with Elizabethan writing; antiques in big drawing room, welcoming caring owners, nice breakfasts, and evening meals by arrangement; handy for Bradford-on-Avon and Bath; wknd self-catering in Dower House in grounds; cl Christmas/New Year; children over 10.

Wootton Bassett SU0783 MARSH FARM HOTEL Wootton Bassett, Swindon SN4 8ER (01793) 848044 **£78**; 32 rms. Handsome Victorian farmhouse in landscaped grounds with particularly warm and friendly atmosphere, comfortable lounge, convivial bar, and enjoyable food in relaxed restaurant; disabled access.

To see and do

Salisbury SU1429 A beautiful and gently relaxed city, with a good many fine old buildings, particularly around the lovely cathedral close. The most extensive close in the country, it's always been a distinct area of town, and the gates to it are still locked each night. The buildings cover a variety of architectural styles from the 13th c to the present, and while of course its great glory is the elegant cathedral itself, you can't help being struck by how impeccably mown the lawns are. Outside the close, there are some interesting antique and other shops, and the broad Market Sq still has a traditional market each Tues and Sat; parking in town can be tricky then. The Haunch of Venison (Minster St) is a delightful old town tavern, while the no smoking New Inn (New St), Red Lion Hotel (Milford St), King's Arms (St John St), and Avon Brewery (Castle St) are all good for lunch, as is the waterside Old Mill out at West Harnham.

✝ CATHEDRAL Begun in 1220 and completed in 1258 – giving a rare uniformity of style. The magnificent spire (added in 1334 along with the tower) is at 123 metres (404 ft) the tallest in the country, and many would say the finest in the world; Christopher Wren discovered it was leaning, and managed to put it right. Also notable are the 14th-c clock (the oldest working mechanical clock in the world), and the tomb of the first Earl of Salisbury, who gave the church one of only 4 surviving copies of the Magna Carta; it's still on display (exc in Dec). The cloisters stand out too. Snacks, shop, disabled access; cl during services, and on Good Fri; (01722) 323273; £2.50 suggested donation. The west front is being restored; while this continues you can don a hard hat, go up in the builder's hoist, and join regular guided tours along the scaffolding, offering a once-in-a-lifetime view of the building's statuary. The guides are entertaining and knowledgeable, on our visit revealing how John the Baptist once again lost his head (it was broken off by local lads following an unduly boisterous night out, but later recovered). There's a good view of the cathedral from outside the 13th-c BISHOP'S PALACE, though the one immortalised by Constable, and still much as then, is from across the meadows by the River Avon over by West Harnham.
🏠 MOMPESSON HOUSE (Cathedral Close) Exquisite Queen Anne building, probably the most interesting in the close, with period furnishings, china and paintings, remarkable collection of 18th-c drinking glasses, and interestingly carved oak staircase. Teas, some disabled access; cl am, all day Thurs and Fri, and Nov–Mar; (01722)

335659; *£3.20; NT. The NT shop is a couple of minutes' walk away on the High St.
♿ SALISBURY AND SOUTH WILTSHIRE MUSEUM (65 The Close) Local history and archaeology in lovely building, with excellent Stonehenge gallery, collections of Wedgwood, costume, lace and embroidery, and some beautiful local watercolours by Turner. Meals, snacks, shop, disabled access to ground floor; cl Sun exc pm July and Aug; (01722) 332151; *£5 – a bit pricey, but the ticket gives unlimited visits all year.
🏠♿🎒✝ Also worth a look in the close are ST ANNE'S GATE, MALMESBURY HOUSE (open Tues, Thurs, Fri and Sat in summer), the regimental museum, and NORTH CANONRY GARDENS, a peaceful place for a stroll near the river – open certain dates in summer, best to check with the very friendly tourist information centre, (01722) 334956. Nearby, ST THOMAS'S CHURCH was built for the cathedral workers, so in part is slightly older than the cathedral itself; it's notable for the unusually expansive medieval painting of Doom.
🏛✳ OLD SARUM SU1332 (off the A345 2m N) This substantial and easily defended Iron Age hill fort continued as a town right through the Roman occupation and Dark Ages into Norman times. In the early 13th c there was a general move to the much more fertile site of the present city, and the fort gradually fell into decline, becoming a quarry for the new centre; consequently there's not much left, but the views are splendid, and the foundations give interesting clues to ancient architecture and styles. Snacks, shop; cl 24–26 Dec, 1 Jan; (01722) 335398; £1.90.

Other things to see and do

WILTSHIRE FAMILY ATTRACTION OF THE YEAR

☛ **Choulderton** SU2242 CHOLDERTON RARE BREEDS FARM ▣ (Amesbury Rd, just off the A338) Plenty of friendly animals at this entertaining farm park, but it's especially good on rabbits: they have nearly 60 breeds on show in spacious pens, and there are always younger rabbits for children to stroke. It's fascinating seeing all the different varieties. Other animals to pet include pygmy goats and sheep, and wandering around you'll come across friendly residents Ebenezer the goat, Hannah the shire horse and Coco the donkey. They have pig racing twice a day at wknds and in school hols (12.30 and 3.30pm), and there are tractor or trailer rides, and pony rides for children. The grounds are attractive, with tranquil carp-filled watergardens, and nature trails through orchards and woodland; on a clear day you can see the spire of Salisbury cathedral 10m away. Plenty of pretty picnic spots. Rare breeds include a herd of Exmoor ponies, and there are a couple of play areas, one aimed at under-7s. Lots under cover (inc the sheep unit), and always plenty going on – families stay here for anything between 2 hours and a whole day. They don't like you to feed the animals with anything other than their own feed; it's on sale in the gift shop. Meals and snacks (good cream teas), shop, disabled access; cl Nov–Mar; (01980) 629438; £3.50 (£2 children 2–14).

🏚 ❋ There are around 4,500 **ancient sites and monuments** in Wiltshire – more than anywhere else in the country. By no means all are dramatic, and at quite a few the non-archaeologist will notice little beyond a few mysterious humps in the ground. The major sites are described individually later, but others worth a look if you're passing are at BARBURY CASTLE SU1677 (splendidly remote and atmospheric), and nr Enford SU1351, Norton Bavant ST9043 and White Sheet Hill ST8034 (its traditionally maintained downland now a nature reserve). WHITE HORSES carved into the chalk hillside are a particular feature of the landscape, with notable examples at Alton Barnes SU0962, Broad Hinton SU1076, Cherhill SU0370, Corston ST9284 and nr Pewsey SU1560.

★ 🏚👹𝄞 **Avebury** SU0969 This spectacular stone circle shares its setting with the pretty village – where Stones does good vegetarian food, and the Red Lion's position within the circle makes it special too. It's the largest stone circle in Europe, the 200 stones enclosed in a massive earthen rampart nearly a mile in circumference. One of Avebury's

main draws has always been the free and open access to the stones, but the number of visitors is beginning to take its toll – it would be a tragedy if this ultimately proved the site's downfall. An interesting MUSEUM has an important collection of archaeological finds from the area. Shop, disabled access; cl 24 –26 Dec, 1 Jan; (01672) 539250; £1.50; NT. GREAT BARN MUSEUM of Wiltshire Life A short stroll from the stone circle, this magnificent 17th-c thatched barn has rural life displays, and craft demonstrations most Suns; as we went to press they weren't sure whether they'd be open in 1998, so best to check on (01672) 539555. There are a good many other prehistoric remains around the village. WEST KENNETT AVENUE Leading away from the circle is this imposing 1½-mile avenue of stones – a good stretch has been restored. WINDMILL HILL ST9623 This is a neolithic enclosure on a slight rise a mile or so N of the stone circle. SILBURY HILL SU1068 This dramatic hill is entirely man-made, the largest such mound in Europe. Purpose unknown, it would have taken 1,000 men about 10 years to build. Don't follow the example of the people you'll see clambering all over it – that's how monuments like this are gradually worn away. WEST KENNETT LONG BARROW SU1067 5,000-year-old chambered tomb and barrow where several dozen people were buried – take a torch if you want to venture in behind the massive entrance stone: the chamber with 2 side chapels runs some 9 metres (30 ft) or more into the barrow. The Waggon & Horses at Beckhampton (of *Pickwick Papers* fame) is quite handy.

★ ☙ † **Box** ST8268 An attractive up-and-down village, its interesting parts hidden down the steep valley below the A4, with cottages and houses using the same stone that's been quarried nearby since Roman times. There's a story that on 9 Apr, Brunel's birthday, the rising sun shines right through the great railway tunnel he quarried through the hill above here (you can see the restored grand entrance from the A4). HAZELBURY MANOR (off the B3109 just E of the centre) Richly varied landscaped gardens, recently restored, with a medieval archery alley, stone and yew circles, fountain, waterfall, pond, large rockery, formal areas and laburnum walk, all laid out as a sort of giant maze. Open by appointment, (01225) 812952; £2.80. In Chapel Plaister ST8367 on the way, look out for the 15th-c CHAPEL for Glastonbury pilgrims on the little hilltop green. The

---

Days Out

Wiltshire superlatives
Salisbury cathedral; lunch at the Haunch of Venison (Minster St) or New Inn (New St); Mompesson House or Old Sarum; Stonehenge.

Marlborough country
Marlborough; lunch at the Royal Oak, Wootton Rivers; Crofton beam engines, and stroll along the Kennet & Avon Canal; Great Bedwyn, for windmill and stone museum.

Prehistoric enigmas
Avebury stone circle and stone avenue; Silbury Hill (view from below); West Kennet Long Barrow; lunch at Stones or the Red Lion, Avebury; Avebury Manor; Great Barn rural museum; walk up on to Fyfield Down to see sarsen stones.

The great canal staircase
Devizes, and Kennet & Avon Canal locks; lunch at the George & Dragon, Rowde; Lacock, or Bowood House

Eye-catchers beneath the downs
A30 SW from Wilton past the Regimental Badges nr Fovant; Ansty's maypole; Old Wardour castle; lunch at the Beckford Arms, Fonthill Gifford, drive through Fonthill park; Farmer Giles Farmstead, Teffont Magna; and/or Wilton House.

Golden stonescape
Castle Combe; lunch at the White Hart, Ford; Corsham's underground quarry; Bradford-on-Avon.

Broad vistas
Walk from Mere on to White Sheet Hill (if open; instead maybe Waterdale House garden, East Knoyle); lunch at the Red Lion, Kilmington; Stourhead, and/or Stourton House garden.

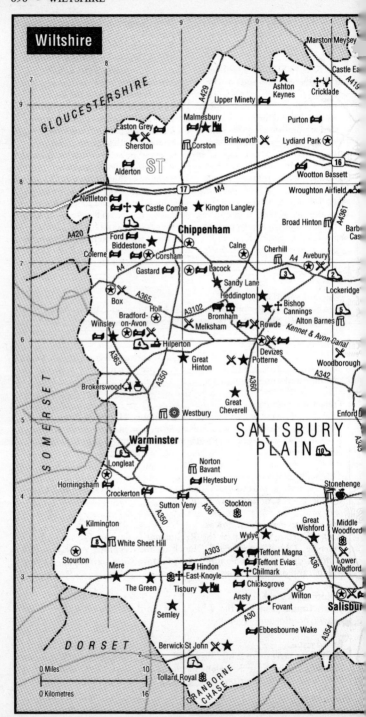

Wiltshire

GLOUCESTERSHIRE

Marston Meysey
Castle Ea
Cricklade
A41
Ashton Keynes
Upper Minety
Purton
Malmesbury
Brinkworth
Lydiard Park
Easton Grey
Sherston
Corston
Alderton
ST
Wootton Bassett
16
Nettleton
Wroughton Airfield
M4
17
Castle Combe
Kington Langley
Broad Hinton
Barb Cas
Chippenham
A4361
Ford
Biddestone
Calne
Cherhill
A4
Avebury
Colerne
Corsham
Gastard
Lacock
3
A4
Box
Sandy Lane
Heddington
Lockeridge
A365
Holt
Bishop Cannings
5
Bradford-on-Avon
Bromham
Alton Barnes
A3102
Rowde
Kennet & Avon Canal
Winsley
Melksham
Hilperton
Devizes
4
Potterne
Woodborough
Great Hinton
A342
Brokerswood
A363
A350
Westbury
Great Cheverell
A360
Enford
SALISBURY PLAIN
Warminster
6
Longleat
Norton Bavant
Heytesbury
Horningsham
Crockerton
Sutton Veny
A36
Stockton
Stonehenge
A343
Kilmington
Wylye
Great Wishford
Middle Woodford
8
Stourton
White Sheet Hill
A303
Teffont Magna
Teffont Evias
Chilmark
Lower Woodford
Mere
Hindon
East Knoyle
Chicksgrove
Wilton
The Green
Tisbury
Ansty
Fovant
Salisbur
Semley
A30
A354
Ebbesbourne Wake
Berwick St John

DORSET

0 Miles 10
0 Kilometres 16

Tollard Royal
CRANBORNE CHASE

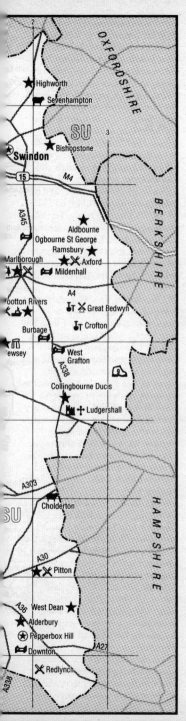

Quarryman's Arms tucked away on Box Hill is good for lunch.

★ † 🏠 ❀ 🐝 **Bradford-on-Avon** ST8261 Attractive hillside town given a distinguished air by the same sort of golden stone as was used in Bath; it's very steep, and has some handsome buildings reflecting its past wealth as a wool town – and quite a few serious antique shops. Near the Norman parish church is a tall narrow late SAXON CHURCH, unusual for having virtually no later additions. The Bunch of Grapes (on picturesque Silver St) is good for lunch. A medieval TITHE BARN can be seen at nearby Barton Farm down by the river and canal, its massive stone-slab roof supported by an impressive network of great beams and rafters. AVONCLIFF ST8059 A short walk along the canal from Bradford, this quite steep gorge is shared by canal, river and railway, the canal disdainfully stepping over the river by way of an aqueduct. The Cross Guns has remarkable views over it, and is a good place for lunch. WESTWOOD MANOR ST8158 (above Avoncliff, just SE of Bradford) Fully furnished 15th-c stone manor house with its original Gothic and Jacobean windows, fine 17th-c plasterwork, and modern topiary garden. Open pm Sun, Tues and Weds Apr–Sept; (01225) 863374; £3.30; NT. The New Inn in Westwood village has decent food, and the CHURCH has some interesting late medieval stained glass. IFORD MANOR ST8058 (just past Westwood) Notable for its stylish Edwardian Italianate riverside terraced garden, with romantic cloisters, colonnade and statues; house not open. Teas wknds and bank hols, May–Aug; open pm Sun and bank hols Apr–Oct, and pm daily (exc Mon and Fri) May–Sept; (01225) 863146; £2.20.

🦆 ♿ **Brokerswood** ST8352 WOODLAND HERITAGE MUSEUM AND WOODLAND PARK 🔲 80 acres of woodland, with lakes, campsites, conservation displays, summer guided walks, adventure playground, and a little railway. Snacks, shop, some disabled access; park open daily, museum cl am term-time; (01373) 823800; £2.50. The Woolpack at Beckington has good food.

🐖 🏭 **Bromham** ST9464 SANDRIDGE FARM They cure bacon and Wiltshire ham using traditional recipes – not pumping them full of slimy water; a viewing window shows the curing process. Also summer nature trail through woodland and pig paddocks (wellies recommended). Shop (good bacon and sausages), disabled access; cl Sun; (01380) 850304; free. The Greyhound in the village has good food, especially fish.

🌼 🏠 🖾 ᵻᶜᵻ **Calne** ST9769 BOWOOD (off the A4) The extensive Capability Brown parkland and colourful pleasure gardens are the glory of Bowood, with their temples, cascades and hermit's cave shielded from the outside world by further miles of partly wooded grounds; in May and Jun a woodland garden is open for rhododendron walks. Much of the main building was demolished in 1955, but there's plenty left, inc the impressive library designed by Robert Adam. Excellent collection of English watercolours, and an outstanding adventure playground. Joseph Priestley discovered oxygen here in 1772. Meals, snacks, shop, garden centre, limited disabled access; cl Nov–Mar; (01249) 812102; £5. The Lansdowne Arms at Derry Hill, near the house, is popular for lunch, and Calne also has a MOTOR MUSEUM.

★ † **Castle Combe** ST8477 For many the prettiest village in Britain, this has a classic group of stone-tiled Cotswoldy cottages by the turreted CHURCH at the bottom of a tree-clad hill running down to a trout stream and its ancient stone bridge. Preservation of the village is taken so seriously that you won't even see television aerials on the houses. Several villagers open their beautifully kept gardens for charity the last wknd of Jun. Best of all during the week out of season; at other times it does get a great many visitors, even though the car park is sited some way up the hill. The Castle Inn (snacks all day, hot meals usual times) is a charming old place.

🏠 🌼 ᷔ **Chippenham** ST8874 SHELDON MANOR (off the A420 W) Charming and particularly welcoming lived-in 13th-c manor house, still with original (and highly unusual) porch, and a 15th-c chapel. The panelled rooms have oak furnishings and collections of glass and porcelain, while the lovely terraced gardens include a mass of old-fashioned roses, and yew trees as old as the house. Good meals and snacks, shop, plant sales, disabled access; open pm Sun, Thurs and bank hols, Easter–Oct; (01249) 653120; £3.50, £2.25 garden only. The White Horse at Biddestone out past here has good-value food. Chippenham itself has a decent local history MUSEUM in the partly timbered 16th-c Guildhall; cl 12.30–2pm, Sun, and Oct–Mar; free.

🐖 **Cholderton** SU2242 *See separate Family Panel on p.696* for CHOLDERTON RARE BREEDS FARM. The thatched Crown is useful for lunch.

🏠 🖾 🌼 † ᷔ **Corsham** ST8770 CORSHAM COURT Fine house and park begun in 1582 but subsequently added to and developed by those busy masters Capability Brown, John Nash, Robert Adam and Humphrey Repton. The paintings are among the best at any stately home in the country, inc works by Caravaggio, Reynolds, Rubens and Van Dyck. In the gardens, the peaceful lake and a Georgian bath-house are patrolled by a number of peacocks – if they haven't decided to wander off into the village. Shop, disabled access; cl am, Mon (exc bank hols), and Nov–Easter (exc pm wknds); (01249) 701610; £4.50. Nearby there are some attractive former weavers' cottages; the CHURCH, on the edge of the park, is largely 12th-c, partly Saxon. UNDERGROUND QUARRY (Park Lane) The only shaft stone mine open to the public anywhere in the world, a fascinating labyrinth of surprisingly spacious tunnels and galleries, from where the gorgeous Bath stone was quarried. Privately owned, it's a refreshingly unspoilt place, and well off the tourist routes so rarely busy.

Wrap up well though – it always stays chilly. There are 159 steps. Shop; open Sun Apr–Oct, and daily exc Fri mid-July–mid-Sept, guided tours 11.30am, 2pm and 3.30pm; (01249) 716288; *£4.10. The town has a surprising number of antique shops, some very fine, and the Methuen Arms is good for lunch.

✝ ✿ **Cricklade** SU1093 Small town quietly separated from the busy A419, with some attractive buildings and a glorious tower crowning the fine parish CHURCH. At the end of the High St, just N of the Thames, a path on the left off the slip road heading back towards the A419 leads to a broad RIVERSIDE MEADOW kept unimproved for decades, and mown only in July after the numerous wild flowers have seeded.

⬇T **Crofton** SU2663 CROFTON BEAM ENGINES Still pumping water into the Kennet & Avon Canal, the oldest working beam engines in the world, an 1812 Boulton & Watt, and an 1845 Harveys of Hayle. Snacks, shop; open Easter–Oct, engines usually static, but in steam bank hols and last wknds of Jun and July; (01672) 870300; static £1.50, steam wknds £3. The Harrow at Little Bedwyn has good food.

⬤ ▣ ✿ **Devizes** SU0061 Lots of grand old buildings in this interesting and friendly town, and a good town trail takes most of them in. The 29 locks of the Kennet & Avon Canal coming up Caen Hill from the W form one of the longest flights of locks in the country. The headquarters of the Canal Trust on the Wharf has a museum and information centre; (01380) 729489; £1. The first-class local history MUSEUM (Long St) is particularly good on finds from the area's ancient sites (the Bronze Age gallery is especially interesting), and has an art gallery with John Piper window. Shop, some disabled access; cl Sun, bank hols, Christmas; (01380) 727369; *£2 (free on Mons). BROADLEAS (Potterne Rd) Rare plants in secluded dell among rhododendrons and other fine flowering shrubs, unusual trees, spring and autumn colour too. Teas

Sun, unusual plant sales; open pm Sun, Weds and Thurs, Apr–Oct; (01380) 722035; £2.50. The Bear Hotel, Elm Tree and Castle, all tied to Wadworths the local brewery, are all good for lunch.

✿ ✝ **East Knoyle** ST8731 WATERDALE HOUSE (Milton) Woodland garden at its best in late spring/early summer, with long-established camellias, rhododendrons and magnolias; also other plants inc watergarden. Teas if fine; open Sun mid-May–mid-July; £1.50. The plasterwork in the chancel of the church was designed by Christopher Wren's father; he was the parish priest. The Fox & Hounds prettily set on a manicured green has good food.

! **Fovant** SU0128 REGIMENTAL BADGES Huge chalk carvings on the escarpment (visible from the road), cut by regiments stationed here in World War I – a sight to rival England's various white horses.

⬇T ✖ **Great Bedwyn** SU2764 BEDWYN STONE MUSEUM Fascinating little open-air museum demonstrating the ancient art of stonemasonry (the nearby church has fine examples of the finished product). Shop, disabled access but a bit bumpy in places; (01672) 870234; free. WILTON WINDMILL SU2661 (off the A338 E of Burbage) The county's only working windmill, built in 1821 after the construction of the Kennet & Avon Canal had diverted the water previously used to power mills. Now restored, it's beautifully floodlit most evenings. Shop (sells flour milled on site); open pm Sun Easter–Sept, plus Sat and Mon bank hol wknds; (01672) 870427; *£1. The little village of Wilton (not to be confused with the larger town nr Salisbury) is attractive; the Swan has decent food.

✿ ♟ ✝ **Holt** ST8661 THE COURTS (B3107) Weavers used to come here to settle their disputes; the 15th-c house isn't open, but there are lovely and extensive formal gardens full of yew hedges, pools and borders, with the other half of the grounds given over to wild flowers among interesting trees. Some disabled access; cl am, Sat, and Nov–Mar;

(01225) 782340; £2.80; NT. The Old Bear at Staverton has good food. GREAT CHALFIELD MANOR ST8663 (N of Holt) Beautiful moated manor house, restored in 1920 and still with its original Great Hall. Open Tues–Thurs Apr–Oct, guided tours only, at 12.15, 2.15, 3, 3.45 and 4.30 pm; (01249) 730141 to book; £3.50; NT. Next door is a small 13th-c CHURCH.

★ † ⌂ ⓣ ❋ ⛪ 🐑 🐸 Lacock ST9168 A favourite village of both visitors and film-makers, its grid of quiet and narrow streets a delightful harmony of mellow brickwork, lichened stone and timber and plaster. The CHURCH is 15th-c, and nothing in the village looks more recent than 18th-c. It's remained so remarkably unspoilt because most of its buildings were owned for centuries by the Talbot family, until they left them to the National Trust in 1944. It gets very busy in summer, but the Trust has preserved it from a surfeit of antique shops (you'll find all you want in the nearby old market town of Melksham ST9063). The village does on the other hand have a splendid collection of pubs – the George is the best. The showpiece is LACOCK ABBEY, a tranquil spread of mellow stone buildings, around a central timber-gabled courtyard, based on the little-altered 13th-c abbey. Tudor additions include a romantic octagonal tower, and there was a successful 18th-c Gothicisation. Surrounded by quiet meadows and trees, this was the setting for Fox Talbot's experiments which in 1835 led to the creation of the world's first photographic negative – a picture of part of the abbey itself. There's a museum devoted to this in a 16th-c barn at the gates, and the gardens are evidence of Fox Talbot's skills in other fields. Limited disabled access; open pm daily Apr–Oct (plus grounds only in Mar), house cl Tues; (01249) 730227; £5.20, £3.50 museum, grounds and cloisters only; NT. The photography museum may also open some winter wknds. LACKHAM COUNTRY ATTRACTIONS 🖼 Plenty of family activities, inc farm museum,

walled garden and glasshouses, rare breeds farm, pleasant woodland and riverside walks, and a children's playground. The 500-acre estate is the home of the Lackham College of Agriculture, and the old roses are worth catching from May to July. Snacks, shop, plant sales, disabled access; cl Nov–Easter; (01249) 443111; £3.

🏠 🚐 ⛲ ! Longleat ST8043 (off the A362, 4m W of Warminster) Easily a full day's activities on this well organised estate, its handsome 16th-c house one of the first lived-in stately homes to open its doors to the public. Children will probably get most excited about the safari park, which as well as the famous lions has rhinos, camels, elephants and a rare white tiger; unusually, there are some parts you can walk through. Among what seem like hundreds of other attractions are displays of parrots, butterflies, and sea lions, a narrow-gauge railway, children's petting zoo, collection of doll's houses, exhibitions based around the worlds of Postman Pat and Doctor Who, a simulator ride, and good play areas. Older visitors may prefer the formal gardens laid out by Capability Brown, and of course the house itself, much restored inside, but still with impressively grand formal rooms, and the individual murals of the colourful current Marquis of Bath. His interest in mazes and labyrinths has led him to commission several such tangled structures around the grounds; one is still Britain's longest, and the latest has a slightly saucy shape that can be appreciated only from the Marquis's private roof terrace. Meals, snacks, shop, disabled access; most attractions, inc safari park, are cl Nov–mid-Mar, but the house is open all year (exc 25 Dec); (01985) 844400; you can get individual tickets to each of the attractions (the house on its own is £4.80, the safari park £5.50, and grounds only £2), but it works out much cheaper to buy the all-in Passport ticket for £12. In 1997 they introduced balloon trips over the grounds, very affordable at £5 (£15 for a family of 4). The Bath Arms at Horningsham at the S entrance to the park, and the White Hart at Corsley on the N side, are good for lunch. One of England's three CENTER PARCS is nearby, a rewarding place to stay with excellent leisure facilities; (01623) 411411.

🏰 ✝ **Ludgershall** SU2650 The ruins of a royal CASTLE and hunting palace, still with some of the original large Norman earthworks, as well as the later flint walling; free. The CHURCH is also Norman. The nearby area is very pretty and unspoilt, the little villages of the Chutes, Tangley and Vernham Dean straddling the Hants border all worth a look (with the pubs over that way worth exploring too).

🏠 🏵 ✝ **Lydiard Park** SU1085 (nr M4 junction 16, or A3102) Painstakingly restored grand Georgian house, with interesting early wallpaper, rare painted glass window, and elegant furnishings much as they would have been when first installed. Extensive lawns, lakes and well wooded parkland, with nature walks and adventure playgrounds. Snacks, shop, disabled access; cl 1–2pm, am Sun, Good Fri, 25–26 Dec; (01793) 770401; car parking £1, house 75p – quite a bargain. The adjacent parish CHURCH has interesting monuments to the St John family, who lived in the house for 500 years.

★ 🏰 **Malmesbury** ST9287 Yet another charming old town, especially around the green facing its serene Norman ABBEY, from the tower of which a medieval monk called Elmer made one of the earliest semi-successful attempts at flight – he covered a couple of hundred yards, but did break both legs when he crash-landed. The picturesque Old Bell is almost as old as the abbey beside it. The B roads radiating from here are all quite pleasant drives.

★ ♣ **Marlborough** SU1868 One of the area's most attractive towns, this has a very pleasing wide High St, scene of the annual autumn Mop Fair which used to be held in most market towns for the hiring of servants, but which has been revived here as a general celebration – there's also a regular market each Weds and Sat. Even the more modern additions don't look obtrusively out of place among the harmonious mix of Georgian and Tudor buildings. The Sun (by St Peter's church where Cardinal Wolsey was inducted as a priest) and Bear are useful for lunch. To the N, the Broad Hinton road gives a good feel of the Downs' great open spaces, as does the Manton–Alton Priors road to the SW, passing one of the area's several white horses cut into the chalk, and leading into a pleasant valley drive through Allington and Horton to Devizes. To the E, the quiet road along the Kennet Valley has some attractive views, with good food stops at the Red Lion in Axford and Bell in Ramsbury, and pleasant walks; there are also walks through the surviving miles of SAVERNAKE FOREST woodland.

🏵 **Middle Woodford** SU1236 HEALE GARDENS 8 acres of lovely formal gardens beside the Avon chalk stream, with lots of varied plants; the watergarden is especially nice in spring and autumn. Specialist plant sales with many rare types propagated from the main gardens, shop, disabled access; cl 25 Dec; (01722) 782504; £2.75. The Wheatsheaf in nearby Lower Woodford is popular for lunch, and this Salisbury road along the Avon's quieter bank is a pretty drive (as is the continuation N of Amesbury, through Fittleworth and East Chisenbury).

❋ ✠ 🏛 **Pepperbox Hill** SU2124, 5m SE of Salisbury, is named after the strangely shaped 17th-c tower on its summit. You can't get into the tower, but the site commands fine views over Salisbury itself, and S as far as Southampton. NE of here beyond East Grimstead is BENTLEY WOOD SU2530, a nature reserve with good walks. The Hook & Glove at Farley has decent food. Another viewpoint over Salisbury is the Iron Age hill fort of FIGSBURY RING SU1833.

🐾 **Sevenhampton** SU2091 ROVES FARM The 8 wk spring lambing season is the time to come to this friendly sheep farm; trailer rides and shearing in summer. Snacks, shop, disabled access; open Weds–Sun Mar–Sept; (01793) 763939; *£3.75. The Saracen's Head in Highworth has good-value food.

❀ Stockton ST9738 LONG HALL Series of meticulous mainly formal gardens laid out along Gertrude Jekyll lines, set against lovely partly medieval hall (not open); also fine trees with a profusion of spring bulbs and hellebores. Teas, plant sales; gardens open only 1st Sat of month Apr–Aug, though nursery open Weds–Sat Mar–Oct; (01985) 850424; gardens *£2. The Bell at Wylye is good for lunch; this is another pretty chalk-stream valley, with a good drive between Great Wishford and Corton, and some pleasant strolls in the valley, with grander walking on the downs above.

🏛 ⛵ Stonehenge SU1142 (off the A344) One of the most famous prehistoric monuments in the world; everyone knows what it looks like, and how they got the stones here has been pretty much sorted out (the larger ones local, the smaller ones all the way from Wales), but no one's really sure exactly what Stonehenge with its careful astronomical alignments was for. Some experts now reckon it could even have been built by the French. In the interests of conservation, you'll have to stand and look from a distance, so if you've come a long way you may end up slightly disappointed. The best views are very early in the morning from the track from Larkhill, on the other side of the A344, or on a cold clear winter evening looking W past the monument towards the sunset; the ancient stones look very impressive silhouetted against the sky. In the crowded light of day the place loses much of its power to inspire awe, and at the best of times is not somewhere to impress young children. The busy main roads nearby detract too, and funding for schemes to solve this problem has so far been refused. Snacks, shop, disabled access; (01980) 624715; cl 24–26 Dec; £3.80 (inc Walkman tour); NT. On a handful of dates through the year you can still wander among the stones by joining one of the coach tours of mysterious sites organised by Astral Travels, (01628) 488413; these cost around £50 for a whole day and currently leave only from London, but it's worth it just for the moment when they set you loose at Stonehenge with dowsing rods.

WOODHENGE SU1543 The scant traces of another prehistoric monument which consisted of 6 rings of timber posts in a ditch; the positions are now marked by concrete posts, and a cairn marks the central spot where the tomb of a little girl ceremoniously axed to death was found. There's good PICK-YOUR-OWN fruit late Jun–late July at Rolleston Manor Farm on the B3086 NW of Stonehenge.

❀ ✿ 🏠 † Stourton ST7734 STOURHEAD (off the B3092) Marvellous 18th-c gardens, gradually laid out in Italian style by the banker Henry Hoare II following his return from an Italian tour; a beautifully harmonious landscape of temples, lakes, bridges and splendid trees and other plants. Remarkable views into Somerset from Alfred's Tower, the very tall 18th-c folly at the far end, though there are 221 steps (cl Mon and Fri). The early Georgian Palladian house has some good Chippendale furniture, and the church in the grounds is in a lovely hillside setting. Meals, snacks, shop, disabled access; garden open all year, house pm daily exc Thurs and Fri, Apr–Oct; (01747) 840348; £7.70 for gardens and house, £4.30 for one or the other (less for gardens Nov–Feb) – if you can do only one, make it the gardens; NT. STOURTON HOUSE GARDEN (A303) An informal garden nearby, profusely planted with interesting and colourful shrubs, trees and other plants, inc unusual daffodils and over 250 varieties of hydrangea. Plant and dried-flower sales, teas, disabled access; open Weds, Thurs, Sun, and bank hols Apr–Nov, and shop open other times too; (01747) 840417; £2. The Red Lion at Kilmington, and Spread Eagle at Stourhead's entrance, are useful for lunch.

❋ ♠ ▣ **Swindon** SU1484 Much older than you might think, this bustling market town and business centre was caught up with a vengeance in the railway age, and in the Railway Village had one of the earliest examples of a planned workers' estate. In the heart of this, the GREAT WESTERN RAILWAY MUSEUM (Faringdon Rd) is excellent, with lots of locomotives and related train memorabilia celebrating this most highly regarded railway. Shop, limited disabled access; cl 1–2pm, am Sun, Good Fri, 24–26 Dec; (01793) 466555; £2.30. Next door, the RAILWAY VILLAGE HOUSE AND MUSEUM (34 Faringdon Rd) is a restored foreman's house furnished in typical turn-of-the-century working-class style; it's included in admission to the main museum, or you can just visit here for 85p. Not far from here, the Garden Restaurant has good Thai dishes among other food; the Gluepot (Emlyn Sq) has decent food in a more down-to-earth atmosphere. MUSEUM AND ART GALLERY (Bath Rd) Includes works by important 20th-c artists such as Moore and Sutherland. Shop, limited disabled access; cl Sun am, bank hols; free. SWINDON & CRICKLADE RAILWAY SU1189 (Blunsdon, off the B4553 N of Swindon) One of the only live steam projects in the area, gradually being restored, with occasional trips through the countryside, and a museum. Snacks, shop, disabled access; trains wknds only, (01793) 721252 for times; £3.

★ ☛ **Teffont Magna** ST9832 Very attractive, full of charming stone-built cottages with neatly banked stone-walled gardens; the Black Horse has good food. FARMER GILES FARMSTEAD ▨ Friendly working dairy farm with 150 cows milked every afternoon; children can feed lambs and other animals, or simply sit and stroke them. Also tractor rides, play areas, old farming equipment, and small vineyard. Meals, snacks, shop, disabled access; cl wkdys Nov–Mar; (01722) 716338; *£3.50.

★ ▙ **Tisbury** ST9429 Charming small town, left behind by the main roads so largely unspoilt, with some fine old buildings, riverside church, and just outside to the E an immensely long medieval tithe barn. The lovely old Crown does decent food. OLD WARDOUR CASTLE (2m S of Tisbury) Remains of a substantial 14th-c lakeside castle. Though badly damaged in the Civil War, its walls still stand to their original 18 metres (60 ft), and you can walk almost to the top. It's a lovely peaceful setting, landscaped in the 18th c (and used for Kevin Costner's *Robin Hood* in the 20th). Disabled access to grounds only; cl 1–2pm, winter Mons and Tues, 25–26 Dec, 1 Jan; (01747) 870487; £1.50.

❋ **Tollard Royal** ST9417 LARMER TREE PLEASURE GROUNDS (off the A354) Attractive Victorian pleasure gardens in the heart of Cranborne Chase. Laid out by General Pitt Rivers, they were the first privately owned gardens open to the public but then closed for almost a century, opening again just a couple of years ago. Pheasants, macaws and peacocks wander merrily about, you can play croquet, and the temples and grottoes are an appealing backdrop to the band concerts they have on Suns at 2.30 and 4pm (50p extra). Teas, disabled access; open Thurs, Sun and bank hols late Apr–Sept, plus Mon–Weds in summer hols; (01725) 516228; £3.

▥ ❊ **Westbury** ST8751 To the E you can see the huge Westbury WHITE HORSE cut into the chalk of the downs; late 18th-c, it was an 'improvement' on an altogether older one which may have been Saxon, and which faced in the opposite direction. Above the white horse is an extensive Iron Age hill fort, with good views right down to the Mendips in Somerset.

♠ ▣ ❋ ✝ ▥ **Wilton** ST0930 WILTON HOUSE One of the most satisfying historic houses we know, well organised and friendly, with lots to see. The original house was damaged by a fire in 1647, and superbly redesigned by John Webb and Inigo Jones, the latter responsible for the magnificent double cube room. There's an outstanding art collection inc works by Rubens, Van Dyck and Brueghel, as well as fine furnishings, Tudor kitchen, Victorian laundry, and the Wareham Bears, a collection of 200 dressed teddies. Outside are 21 acres of landscaped parkland, with water and rose gardens, new cloister garden, woodland walk, and huge adventure playground. Meals, snacks, shop, disabled access; cl Nov–Easter; (01722) 743115; £6.50. The ornately Italianate 19th-c CHURCH incorporates all sorts of more ancient treasures, especially its magnificent medieval Continental stained glass and 2,000-year-old marble pillars. WILTON CARPET FACTORY (King St) Surprisingly interesting demonstrations of how they make Wilton weaves and Axminster carpets. Tours 4 times a day between 10.15am and 3.30pm, best to book, on (01772) 742890; cl 10 days over Christmas; £4. Wiltons (Market Pl) is good for lunch, the Pembroke Arms has a good Sun carvery, and the charming Victoria & Albert in nearby Netherhampton is nicely off the tourist track, with a pleasant riverside walk into Salisbury.

✚ ▮☗▮ **Wroughton Airfield** SU1378 A branch of London's SCIENCE MUSEUM houses national collections of aircraft, rockets, hovercraft, and road transport vehicles. Not really aimed at entertaining the general public, it's usually open around 5 times a year, with lively special events or air displays; (01793) 814466 for 1998 dates.

⚓ **Kennet & Avon Canal** Recently restored, this runs right across the county, and there are pleasant boat trips from several places; Devizes SU0061 or Wootton Rivers SU1963 for example, or the notably friendly hire companies at Hilperton ST8759 and Bradford-on-Avon ST8261. In the canal's restoration, a great deal of attention has been paid to the natural environment, so it's attractive for walks alongside; in winter you may even see a kingfisher flashing along it. For a more sedentary view, try the Barge Inn at Seend Cleeve ST9361 or Bridge Inn at Horton SU0463.

★ **Other attractive villages,** all with decent pubs, include Aldbourne ST2675, Alderbury SU1827, waterside Ashton Keynes SU0494, Axford SU2370, Berwick St John ST9323, Biddestone ST8773, Bishops Cannings SU0364 (outstanding church), Bishopstone SU2483, Castle Eaton SU1495 (by a quiet stretch of the upper Thames, pleasant for strolling), Chilmark ST9632 (with a decent partly 13th-c church), Collingbourne Ducis SU2453, Great Cheverell ST9754, Great Hinton ST9059, Great Wishford SU0735, Heddington ST9966, Highworth SU2092, Kilmington ST7736, Kington Langley ST9277, Lockeridge SU1467, Marston Meysey SU1297, Mere ST8132 (dominated by its 30-metre (100-ft) church tower and with good views from Castle Hill), Pewsey SU1560, Pitton SU2131, Potterne ST9958, Ramsbury ST2771, Sandy Lane ST9668 (the road from here through Bowden Hill is the prettiest approach to Lacock), Semley ST8926 (interesting church), Sherston ST8585, The Green ST8731 (nr East Knoyle), West Dean SU2527, Winsley ST7961, Wootton Rivers SU1963 and Wylye SU0037 (one lane is called Teapot St). Ansty ST9526 has England's tallest maypole. The valley of the Ebble chalk stream winds prettily through a sleepy stream of villages from Odstock SU1526 to Alvediston ST9723 – a delightful drive.

Please let us know what you think of places in the *Guide*. Use the report forms at the back of the book or simply send a letter.

Walks

Castle Combe ST8477 ᐃ-1 has surroundings that are as appealing as the village, and attractive paths along deep peaceful valleys.

Much of the Wiltshire chalklands are unvarying green mono-agricultural expanses, but there are exceptions. The **Marlborough Downs** ᐃ-2 harbour archaeological bounties which you can use to punctuate walks around Avebury SU1069 – for example, to the major prehistoric sites of Silbury Hill SU1068, West Kennet Long Barrow SU1067 and the Neolithic camp on Windmill Hill SU0871. Fyfield Down SU1470 is primeval-feeling and unkempt, scattered with outcrops known as sarsen stones, the raw material of Avebury stone circle and of part of Stonehenge. At the northernmost point of the Marlborough Downs, Barbury Castle SU1476 is an ancient hill fort site with formidable ramparts, on the long-distance Ridgeway Path. There is a car park nearby, but you can also walk up to it from Ogbourne St George SU1974 along Smeathe's Ridge SU1775, a preserved stretch of downland (gorse and all). Further W, **Cherhill Down** SU0469 ᐃ-3 is a large NT area of ancient downland with free access. A range of manmade features of various periods adorn its slopes, inc a figure of a white horse, an Iron Age hill fort (Oldbury Castle), the mid-19th-c Lansdowne Monument, and an assortment of long barrows, tumuli and ancient field systems; the site is rich in chalkland flora such as orchids, and associated butterfly and bird life.

The **Kennet & Avon Canal** ᐃ-4 has a long flight of locks on the W side of Devizes SU0061, and suits a river and canal walk around Barton Farm Country Park at Bradford-on-Avon ST8261. At **Alton Barnes** SU1062 ᐃ-5, the canal lies close enough to Pewsey Down nature reserve for an afternoon's walk to incorporate both features; the spine of the downs here is followed by the Wansdyke, an ancient earthwork which runs across the downs for miles from Morgans Hill SU0267 nr Calne nearly as far as the Savernake Forest. Recommended pubs handy for the canal include the Harrow at Little Bedwyn SU2966, Golden Swan at Wilcot SU1360, Cross Guns at Avoncliff ST8060, Crown at Wootton Rivers SU1963 and Crown at Bishops Cannings SU0364.

Cley Hill ST8345 ᐃ-6 is a steep-sided hill just W of Warminster, involving a short, puffy stroll to the Iron Age hill fort at its summit, looking across Longleat Park. In the S, some of the finest walking is to be found on the Cranborne Chase ST9317, on the Dorset borders, where the county's abundant chalk downland shows at its best. **Ashcombe Bottom** ST9319 ᐃ-7, N of Tollard Royal, is a deep remote valley which plunges into the heart of the Chase. **White Sheet Hill** ST8034 ᐃ-8, easily reached from Mere (via a road bridge over the busy A303) or Stourton, is a lofty chalk downland studded with antiquities – among them a Neolithic causewayed camp and Bronze Age barrows – and a good site for cowslips, orchids and such butterflies as adonis and chalkhill blues.

Haydown Hill SU3156 ᐃ-9, reached from the E by a walk up from Vernham Dean SU3456 (itself in Hants), has the ramparts of a hill fort bounded by steep gradients on its S side; the 3 counties of Berks, Hants and Wilts meet close by at SU3559. There are some pleasant walks around the Cross Keys at Upper Chute SU2954, and the Lamb down on the edge of the New Forest at Nomansland SU2517.

For **Salisbury Plain** ᐃ-10, the County Council has a leaflet mapping out clearly way-marked walks around the edges of the Army's Imber firing range, totalling some 30m for the complete circuit: generally peaceful countryside with large-scale arable farming, but some wide views and maybe the sight of tank and infantry training.

Where to eat

Avebury SU0969 STONES RESTAURANT (01672) 539514 Excellent vegetarian restaurant in converted farm building opposite the stone circle; local, organic and home-grown produce used in the delicious cooking (lovely cakes and soups), afternoon tea, and friendly service; they sell country wines and organic wines; open all day (not evenings) but cl wkdys Nov–March, and all Jan; disabled access. £14.90|£2.95.

Axford SU2370 RED LION (01672) 520271 Welcoming brick and flint pub with fine views over valley from sheltered garden or bustling beamed and pine-panelled bar, good popular food in bar and no smoking restaurant (enjoyable daily specials and fresh fish), decent wines, and well kept real ales; bdrms; disabled access. £24|£4.95.

Berwick St John ST9323 TALBOT (01747) 828222 Well run and friendly village pub with simply furnished heavily beamed bar, huge inglenook fireplace and decent food in bar and restaurant; cl pm Sun; children over 7 in evening. £20.45|£7.95.

Box ST8369 QUARRYMANS ARMS (01225) 743569 Tucked-away unspoilt hillside pub with fine views, 2 small and characterful knocked-together rooms with quarrying memorabilia, wide choice of good home-cooked food, well kept real ales, and very friendly staff; bdrms. £20|£5.50.

Bradford-on-Avon ST8260 BRIDGE TEA ROOMS 24a Bridge St (01225) 865537 Old-fashioned no smoking 17th-c tearooms with a large choice of teas, lots of coffees, sandwiches and snacks, lovely home-made cakes and pastries, cream teas and ice-cream specials served by waitresses in mob caps and aprons; cl 25–26 Dec. |£5.

Brinkworth SU0184 THREE CROWNS The Street (01666) 510366 Friendly atmosphere in villagey pub with imaginative food from a changing menu that covers an entire wall, 10 wines by the glass, well kept real ales, an elegant no smoking conservatory, and a garden looking out towards the church and over rolling country; get there early as they don't take bookings and it is very busy; disabled access. £25|£9.95.

Devizes SU0061 WILTSHIRE KITCHEN 11 St John's St (01380) 724840 Bustling little no smoking self-service place just off the market square and serving breakfast, a fair choice of properly home-made interesting hot and cold lunchtime food, and afternoon tea; disabled access. £12|£4.50.

Lower Woodford SU1235 WHEATSHEAF (01722) 782203 Friendly pub with indoor goldfish pond (crossed by a miniature footbridge), wide choice of popular food, partly no smoking dining room, well kept real ales, helpful staff, and big walled garden; good disabled access. £15|£4.50.

Marlborough SU1869 MUNCHIES 8 The Parade (01672) 512649 Lovely beamed building where you can get a marvellous range of really interesting and delicious sandwiches with daily-changing home-made fillings using the freshest ingredients; cl Sun; disabled access. |£1.75.

Marlborough SU1869 POLLY TEAROOMS 26–27 High St (01672) 512146 In centre of pretty High St, well known for very good cream teas, with home-made bread, scones, jams and cakes; also light lunches and cooked breakfasts; cl evenings, and 25–26 Dec; disabled access. Teas £4.10.

Melksham ST9063 TOXIQUE 187 Woodrow Rd (01225) 702129 Former farmhouse with unusual artwork in colourfully and eccentrically decorated rms, comfortable armchairs in purple lounge, and excellent really adventurous meals, thoughtfully planned and prepared; good atmosphere, popular themed evenings – and booking essential; cl Mon, Tues, am Wed–Sat, pm Sun, bdrms. £35.

Pitton SU2131 SILVER PLOUGH (01722) 712266 Stylish village inn with lots to look at in beamed and comfortable front bar, good bar snacks and more elaborate meals with emphasis on fresh fish and seafood, well kept real ales, country wines, and efficient service. £21.30|£8.95.

Potterne ST9958 GEORGE & DRAGON (01380) 722139 Much-restored 15th-c thatched cottage with a traditional welcoming atmosphere, good food in bar and no smoking dining room, well kept real ales, pleasant service, and unique antique indoor rifle range; bdrms; cl am Mon (exc bank hols). £16|£6.

Redlynch SU2120 LANGLEY WOOD (01794) 390348 Very good innovative food and decent wines in homely creeper-covered restaurant-with-rooms set in its own grounds; cl Mon, Tues, am Sat, pm Sun; children must behave (small helpings but no special menu); disabled access. £26|£6.95.

Rowde ST9762 GEORGE & DRAGON (01380) 723053 Interesting old pub with log fire and plenty of dark wood, a simple dining room, exceptional, imaginative food (especially Cornish fish and lovely puddings), good-value set lunches, a relaxed atmosphere, friendly efficient service, and well kept real ales; no food Sun, cl am Mon, 2 wks Christmas. £22|£8.50.

Salisbury SU1429 NEW INN (01722) 327679 Very attractive pub, no smoking throughout, with ancient heavy beams, timbered walls, an inglenook fire, panelled dining room, an unpretentious and relaxed atmosphere, a good range of well presented home-made food with nice daily specials and good hearty puddings, well kept beer, decent wines, friendly helpful licensees and staff, and a pleasant walled garden looking up to the nearby cathedral. £18.50|£6.75.

Sherston ST8585 RATTLEBONE Church St (01666) 840871 16th-c pub with low beams, country furnishings, big dried flower arrangements, and pleasant relaxed atmosphere in several rambling rooms, wide choice of good interesting food, partly no smoking restaurant, decent wines, well kept real ales, lots of malt whiskies, 20 rums, and pretty little garden; cl pm 25 Dec; disabled access. £18|£3.50.

Woodborough SU1159 SEVEN STARS Bottlesford (01672) 851325 Civilised pub in 7 acres of riverside gardens, with attractively moulded panelling in the main bar, a hot coal fire in a range at one end and a big log fire at the other, a pleasant mix of seats and tables, cosy nooks, retired wine bottles on Delft shelves, an attractive back dining area, exceptionally good, daily-changing Anglo-French cooking (inc marvellous vegetables), an exemplary wine list with a dozen by the glass, and very friendly owners. £20|£6.95.

Wootton Rivers SU1963 ROYAL OAK (01672) 810322 Prettily thatched 16th-c pub with relaxed friendly atmosphere, good food from a huge menu, well kept beer, decent wines, and friendly service; bdrms with help-yourself breakfasts. £18.50|£5.

Special thanks to Mrs May Kelly, John Moss, Mrs L Beint, B Kilcullen, Mrs M Cooper, Janet Pickles, B and K Hypher, Sheila Burgin, Phyl and Jack Street.

WILTSHIRE CALENDAR

Some of these dates were provisional as we went to press. Please check information with the numbers provided.

APRIL

10 Devizes Start of Westminster International Canoe Race (01491) 872042

12 Wilton Easter Egg Treasure Hunt Quiz at Wilton House (01722) 743115; **Warminster** Birds of Prey at Longleat House (01985) 844400

18 Salisbury St George's Spring Festival: traditional medieval events and pageantry – *till Sun 19* (01722) 434300

19 Castle Combe Classic Car Rally at the Race Circuit (01249) 782417

25 Castle Combe Car & Car Conversions Action Day at the Race Circuit (01249) 782417

MAY

3 Amesbury Sarsen Trail Walk and Marathon starting at Avebury (*from 7pm*), crossing Salisbury Plain (normally closed to the public), ends at Stonehenge (01380) 725670

16 Castle Combe Steam & Vintage Rally at the Race Circuit – *till Sun 17* (01249) 782417

22 Chippenham Folk Festival – *till Mon 25* (01249) 657733

23 Salisbury Festival – *till 6 Jun* (01722) 323883; **Wanborough** British Moto Cross Grand Prix at Foxhill Moto Park – *till Sun 24* (01934) 416256

24 Castle Combe Classic Car Run at the Race Circuit (01249) 782417; **Rockley** Marlborough Cup (3m timber horse race) and Country Fair at Barbury Castle Racecourse (01672) 514428

30 Corsham Festival: concerts, open gardens – *till 28 Jun* (01249) 712241; **Warminster** Horse Trials at Longleat House – *till Sun 31* (01985) 844400

JUNE

5 Devizes Festival – *till Sun 28* – (01380) 729408

6 Amesbury Carnival (01980) 622173

7 Warminster Pet, Pig & Goat Show at Longleat House (01985) 844400

20 Chippenham Carnival – *till* procession *on Sat 27* (01249) 660149; **Lacock** Open-air Opera at the Abbey (01249) 730141; **Stourton** Outdoor Concert at Stourhead (01985) 843600; **Whiteparish** Salisbury & South Wiltshire Agricultural Show (01794) 884355

21 Bradford-on-Avon Opera, Concerts and Jazz in the Cloister at Iford Manor – *most Fris and Sats till 16 Aug* (01225) 866233; **Stonehenge** Druid Summer Solstice Ceremony *from midnight of Tues 20*, vigil *till dawn* when service celebrates first rays of sun on altar, Presider crowned *at noon* (01458) 850924

27 Bradford-on-Avon Town Festival – *till 5 July* (01225) 866917; **Wilton** Horse Trials at Wilton House – *till Sun 28* (01722) 743115

28 Teffont Magna Sheep to Jumper: sheep shearing at the Farmer Giles Farmstead (01722) 716338; **Warminster** Amateur Radio Rally at Longleat House (01985) 844400

JULY

4 Heddington Steam Rally at Home Farm: rural crafts and shire horses – *till Sun 5* (01380) 850885; **Warminster** Proms Concert at Longleat House (01985) 844400

WILTSHIRE CALENDAR

JULY cont

6 **Box** Open -air Theatre: Shakespeare at Hazelbury Manor Gardens – *till Sat 11* (01249) 714317

11 **Sherston** Boules: one day competition in the High St (01666) 840871; **Swindon** Old Town Festival – *till Sun 12* (01793) 641033

13 **Marlborough** Festival of Music and Arts inc jazz weekend – *till Tues 28* (01672) 513989

17 **Trowbridge** Village Pump Festival – *till Sun 19* (01373) 830110

23 **Stourton** Fete Champetre: *By the Sea* at Stourhead – *till Sat 25* (01985) 843600

25 **Warminster** Balloon Festival at Longleat House – *till Sun 26* (01985) 844400

AUGUST

1 **Castle Combe** VW Golf Action Day at the Race Circuit (01249) 782417

7 **Marlborough** Wiltshire Artists Annual Exhibition at St Peter's Church: about 275 works for sale – *till Sun 16* (01672) 512771

15 **Castle Combe** Classic Car Action Day at the Race Circuit (01249) 782417

22 **Lacock** Open-air Theatre: *Alice in Wonderland* at the Abbey (01249) 730141

30 **Neston** Vintage Rally at Neston Park – *till Mon 31* (01225) 810211

31 **Corsley** Show (01373) 832643; **Lacock** Village Fair (01249) 730320

SEPTEMBER

5 **Bradford-on-Avon** Wharfside Show – *till Sun 6* (01225) 864378; **Castle Combe** Kitcar Action Day at the Race Circuit (01249) 782417; **Trowbridge** Carnival (01225) 777054

12 **Marlborough** Carnival (01672) 513989

19 **Castle Combe** Mini Action Day at the Race Circuit (01249) 782417; **Pewsey** Illuminated Carnival Procession (01672) 563378

20 **Salisbury** Kite & Juggling Festival at Hudson's Field (01722) 410588

21 **Westbury** Medieval Fayre (01373) 827158

OCTOBER

2 **Calne** Music & Arts Festival – *till Sun 11* (01249) 815417

24 **Warminster** Carnival – *till Sun 25* (01985) 218548

We welcome reports from readers ...

This *Guide* depends on readers' reports. Do help us if you can – in return, we offer a discount on the next edition to people who've helped us with reports for it. Tell us what you think about places already in it, and anything extra you think we should say about them. And send us your ideas for inclusion in the next edition: places to visit, eat at or stay in, attractive drives or walks, maybe even unusual interesting shops you know of. Use the card in the middle, the report forms at the end, or just write – no stamp needed: *The Good Guide to Britain*, FREEPOST TN1569, Wadhurst, E Sussex TN5 7BR.

YORKSHIRE

With so much to see and do in this vast county, we have divided it into three parts, each with its own distinct character, and devoted a separate complete section to the city of York itself, which is an excellent holiday city.

Our three areas are the Dales, with which we have included Ripon, the civilised spa town of Harrogate, and their surroundings (virtually all North Yorkshire west of the A19); the Moors and East Yorkshire (North Yorkshire east of the A19 along with the administrative county of East Yorkshire); and the administrative counties of West and South Yorkshire.

Each of these areas has a rich variety of interesting places to visit – most of all in West Yorkshire. The countryside is at its finest in the Dales and the Moors – memorable for walkers, and very appealing even to people who never leave their cars. There are some dramatic landscapes in West Yorkshire too, but the main draw there is the outstanding range of unusual visitor attractions – many of them free. It has by far the most to entertain families, though there's plenty to keep children amused along the east coast. Yorkshire is one of Britain's friendliest areas, and is very good value for holidays. And it's gaining ground all the time: many superb new places have opened recently or are about to open here, and great imagination (and in some cases pots of money) is going into updating existing attractions. Overall, Yorkshire now stands out as our readers' favourite British holiday area.

YORK

Fascinating for a short break, with masses to see and do in delightful, virtually traffic-free surroundings.

York is full of lovely medieval buildings and twisting alleys, interesting shops and lots of lively cafés, pubs and bars. The whole centre, ringed by strollable 13th-c city walls, is virtually traffic-free – the biggest such area in any similarly-sized European city. The magnificent Minster is one of Britain's great sights, the Castle Museum and National Railway Museum are first class, and the Jorvik Centre is among the country's best heritage centres. There are many other extraordinarily varied things well worth visiting here – suitable for all ages.

It is undeniably a tourist city, with summer queues and crowds at the main attractions; but most people find that all the other visitors actually seem to add to the atmosphere, rather than detracting from it.

A good way to save money is with the York for Less card, which for £3.95 gets two people discounts on some attractions and restaurants for four days; it's available from tourist information centres. Another way to save money – at least in winter – is to come by train; ask for the First Stop York vouchers when you book your ticket, or on arrival at York Station, and you'll usually get half-price entry to most of the city's attractions (and big discounts at some hotels).

York's racecourse is a good one, with monthly meetings; the Ebor Festival in August is the biggest event in the northern racing calendar.

Where to stay

Shipton by Beningbrough SE5458 SIDINGS Shipton by Beningbrough, York YO6 1BS (01904) 470221 *£72, plus special breaks; 8 rms with showers in 2 converted coaches. A railway enthusiast's paradise, based on restored former railway carriages, with good food served at Pullman-style tables, a decent wine list, railway viewing platform, models, videos, paintings and artefacts; disabled access.

York SE5952 ARNOT HOUSE 17 Grosvenor Terrace, York YO3 7AG (01904) 641966 *£45, plus winter breaks; 4 rms with brass beds. Friendly, no smoking, Victorian terraced house with lots of original features, antiques and paintings, good breakfasts in the neat dining room (evening meals on request), and a pleasant, relaxed atmosphere; children over 10.

York SE5849 CURZON LODGE 23 Tadcaster Rd, Dringhouses, York YO2 2QG (01904) 703157 £60, plus special breaks; 10 rms, some in a former old coach house and stables. Charming, early 17th-c house in a marvellous spot just S of the city, overlooking Knavesmire racecourse; with an attractive, comfortable drawing room, a sunny farmhouse dining room (good breakfasts), and a secluded walled garden; cl Christmas.

York SE5952 DEAN COURT Duncombe Pl, York YO1 2EF (01904) 625082 £125 incl dinner, plus special breaks; 40 rms. Next to the Minster, this recently refurbished hotel has fresh flowers and plants in the airy rooms, very helpful, efficient staff, and fine food in the elegant restaurant; good for families, with thoughtful extras; children over 5 in evening restaurant; partial disabled access.

York SE5951 18 ST PAUL'S SQUARE 18 St Paul's Sq, York YO2 4BD (01904) 629884 *£60; 3 rms. Charming, no smoking, Victorian house overlooking a quiet garden square; with a relaxing and friendly atmosphere, comfortable lounge, enjoyable breakfasts, and a garden.

York SE5951 4 SOUTH PARADE York YO2 2BA (01904) 628229 £83, plus special breaks; 3 lovely rms with Edwardian-style furnishings, original fireplaces and fresh flowers. Beautifully decorated house in a small, elegant, Georgian terrace on a private cobbled street, 15 minutes from the Minster and 5 minutes from the station; pretty drawing room, very helpful owners, good breakfasts and candlelit suppers by arrangement in the delightful dining room; no smoking; cl Christmas; no children.

York SE5952 GRANGE Clifton, York YO3 6AA (01904) 644744 £108, plus special breaks; 30 individually decorated rms with antiques and chintz. Close to the Minster, this Regency town house has elegant public rooms, an open fire, newspapers, good breakfasts, excellent restaurant food (there's also a brasserie), and warm, friendly staff; car park; disabled access.

York SE6052 HAZLEWOOD 24–25 Portland St, Gillygate, York YO3 7EH (01904) 626548 £52, plus special breaks; 13 rms. Just 4 minutes from the Minster, this no smoking, neatly kept Victorian house has quite a few original features; cosy lounge, an attractive dining room, helpful owners, and a pretty little garden; off-street parking; children over 6; disabled access.

York SE5951 HOLMWOOD HOUSE 114 Holgate Rd, York YO2 4BB (01904) 626183 £55, plus special breaks; 11 pretty rms. Built as 2 19th-c houses, this no smoking hotel is 5 minutes away from the city walls; a comfortable sitting room with books, and very good breakfasts; children over 8.

York SE5948 MIDDLETHORPE HALL Bishopthorpe Rd, Middlethorpe, York YO2 1QB (01904) 641241 **£154,** plus special breaks; 30 elegant rms, most in the converted stables. Lovely, immaculately restored William III country house just S of the city, with fine gardens and parkland; antiques, paintings and fresh flowers in the comfortable quiet day rooms, and excellent food and service; children over 8.

York SE6052 PALM COURT 17 Huntington Rd, York YO3 7RB (01904) 639387 *£42; 8 rms. Quiet and spotlessly kept Victorian house only 5 minutes from the Minster, with a pleasant sitting room, very good breakfasts, particularly helpful, friendly owners, and evening meals on request; cl Christmas.

To see and do

✝☖❁♿ MINSTER A glorious example of Gothic architecture, in soft-coloured York stone, this is Britain's largest medieval building, begun in 1220 and taking a staggering 250 years to build. The richly detailed interior contains more original medieval glass than any other church in England – and indeed is reckoned to house half of all that's known in the country. Look out for the great east window which shows Genesis and Revelations in 27 panels, the splendid 5 sisters window in the north transept, and the beautiful ceilings of the central tower and chapter house. The choir screen has 15 niches containing statues of the kings of England from William the Conqueror to Henry VI. There's a display on the church's turbulent history in the Foundations Museum and treasury. Shop, disabled access; cl am Sun, and occasionally for major services; £1.80 for museum and treasury, also small charges for chapter house and crypt. You can climb the tower for good views of the city (£2); the Minster's glorious west front was, as we went to press, hidden behind scaffolding. Largely traffic-free, the Close outside is fairly quiet, but not enclosed, and without the tranquil serenity of say Exeter, Salisbury or Winchester. Evening walking tours start from various points around it; our favourite is the ghostly tour that meets at the Minster's front entrance every night at 7.30 pm (£3). 15th-c ST WILLIAM'S COLLEGE opposite has an exhibition, as well as a decent restaurant and 3

finely timbered rooms. Shop; cl 25–26 Dec, Good Fri; (01904) 637134; *60p. Another useful nearby food stop is Peels in High Petergate. ✝☖ The city has quite a few other handsome medieval CHURCHES, though many are no longer used for services. Most were built during the prosperous 15th and 16th centuries, and among the finest are Holy Trinity (Goodramgate, which also contains in Our Lady's Row the oldest houses in the city) and St Helen's (St Helen's Sq). All Saints (North St) has some fascinating windows illustrating the last 15 days of the world. The spire of 15th-c St Mary's is York's tallest (at 152 ft); the church also has good exhibitions on the city's history in the YORK STORY, reorganised this year. ⓗ JORVIK VIKING CENTRE (below Coppergate Shopping Centre) The first place in the country to utilise the sights, sounds and smells technology that's gradually revolutionised the heritage industry, and still one of the best. Time-cars whisk you through an exact reconstruction of the Viking street, market and quayside that used to stand here, with quite astonishing detail: some of the faces were painstakingly constructed from actual Viking skulls. At the end are excavated finds from the site. Queues can be horrifically long, but almost everyone finds the wait well worthwhile. Shop, disabled access; cl 25 Dec; (01904) 653000; £4.95. ☖▥!✝♿ ARC (St Saviourgate) Refreshingly accessible archaeology centre; with the help of hands-on, interactive displays you can decipher

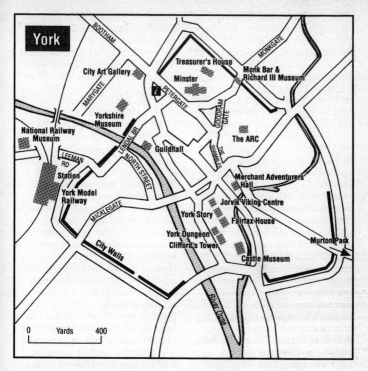

York

BOOTHAM
City Art Gallery
Treasurer's House
Minster
Monk Bar &
Richard III Museum
MONKGATE
MARYGATE
PETERGATE
Yorkshire
Museum
GOODRAMGATE
National Railway
Museum
The ARC
LEEMAN RD
Guildhall
THE SHAMBLES
Station
NORTH STREET
LENDAL BR.
Merchant Adventurers'
Hall
York Model
Railway
Jorvik Viking Centre
MICKLEGATE
York Story
Fairfax House
York Dungeon
Clifford's Tower
Murton Park
City Walls
Castle Museum
RIVER OUSE

0   Yards   400

Viking-age writing or learn to make a
Roman shoe, all with professional
archaeologists on hand to give advice.
During the summer you may even be
able to watch a dig on Walmgate.
Very much on the school-trips circuit,
so best out of term-time. It's set in a
beautifully restored medieval church,
with an interesting, old-fashioned
garden. Shop, disabled access; cl am
Sat, Sun, Good Fri, Christmas wk;
(01904) 654324; £3.50. The
Archaeological Trust that runs the
ARC (and the Jorvik Centre) has
almost finished its restoration of
BARLEY HALL, a medieval family
home, off Stonegate. Snacks, shop,
disabled access; open Mon–Sat July
and Aug; (01904) 643211; £3.50.
The nearby Punch Bowl has good-
value food.
🍽 🛏 ✕ ❋ CASTLE MUSEUM (Tower St)
Housed in 18th-c prison buildings on
the site of the former castle (part of
the outer wall still stands), this is one
of the best museums in the country,
with a huge range of everyday objects
from the past 4 centuries shown in
convincingly reconstructed, real-life
settings. There's even a watermill, by
the river outside. They have one of
only 3 Anglo-Saxon helmets in the
world, found here in York in the
1980s. Again, best out of term-time.
Shop, disabled access to ground floor
only; cl 25–26 Dec; (01904) 653611;
£4.50. The former castle keep nearby,
now known as CLIFFORD'S TOWER, is
perhaps York's most interesting
building after the Minster. You can
walk around the top of the walls,
which enclose a garden, and there are
good views of the city. It gets its name
from Roger Clifford, who was
hanged from the tower in chains.
There's an unusual Lowry painting of
the tower in the City Art Gallery (see
entry below). Shop; cl 24–26 Dec;
(01904) 646940; £1.60. The Tudor
Masons Arms is a handy stop.
🏠 ♿ FAIRFAX HOUSE (Castlegate)
Magnificently restored mid-18th-c
town house, probably one of the
finest in England, its richly decorated

rooms fully furnished in period style. Much of the impressive collection of paintings, pottery, clocks and Georgian furniture was donated by the great-grandson of the confectionery baron Joseph Terry, and there's a re-created mid-18th-c meal. Shop, some disabled access by arrangement (steps at front); cl all Fri (exc Aug and Sept), and Twelfth Night–mid-Feb; (01904) 655543; *£3.50.

🏠 THE SHAMBLES Jettied medieval buildings lean towards each other across these alleys, perked up by witty details such as the red figure of the printer's devil almost opposite the courtyard entry to the Olde Starre (a touristy pub, but genuinely old, with a view of the Minster from seats in its yard). This area has some of the city's most interesting shops, inc good bookshops, all sorts of unusual specialist shops, and, especially in Stonegate, nearer the Minster, and in elegant Micklegate, some serious silver and antique shops.

🏠👁🏠 MONK BAR The most striking and best preserved of York's 4 turreted medieval gateways. It now houses the RICHARD III MUSEUM, where displays on the much-maligned monarch (or evil hunchbacked murderer, depending on your point of view) are themed as if he were on trial – you put your verdict in the appropriate Guilty or Innocent book on the way out. Shop; cl 25–26 Dec; (01904) 634191; *£1. Another gateway, Micklegate, has social history displays (cl wkdys Nov–Mar; *£1.50), while behind it on Toft Green the YORK BREWERY has tours and tastings (not am Sun; £3.50 – includes a pint of their beer). Just along the road from here, the BAR

CONVENT has a museum looking at early Christianity (and decent accommodation).

🔳 CITY ART GALLERY (Exhibition Sq) Well displayed collections running from old masters to the lusciously romantic nudes of William Etty, with some very handsome stoneware pottery. Shop, disabled access; cl am Sun, 25–26 Dec, 1 Jan, Good Fri, maybe other dates for civic events; (01904) 551861; free. They usually have guided tours on Weds Jun–Sept at 12.30pm.

🏠 MERCHANT ADVENTURERS' HALL (Piccadilly) The largest timber-framed building in the city, and one of the finest in Europe. Built for the powerful Merchant Adventurers' Company in the 1350s and hung with banners of medieval guilds, it has a chapel and undercroft as well as the great hall itself. Disabled access; cl Sun Nov–Mar, and Christmas wk; (01904) 654818; *£1.90.

🏠 TREASURER'S HOUSE (Chapter House St, next to the Minster) There's been a house here since Roman times – this one dates from the 17th c, and the basement has an exhibition on its history. The timbered hall is very fine, as is the period furniture. Snacks; cl Fri, all Nov–Mar; (01904) 624247; *£3.50; NT.

🏠 GUILDHALL (St Helen's Sq) Exact replica of the original building of 1446, destroyed in a 1940 air raid. The stone walls of the earlier building form the framework of the new one. Disabled access; cl winter wknds (and am Sun in summer), and bank hols; (01904) 613161; free.

👁🏠🏠🏠 YORKSHIRE MUSEUM (Museum Gardens) A real treasure-trove, crammed with myriad archaeological finds and riches from

A Day Out in York

Clifford's Tower and Castle Museum; Merchant Adventurers' Hall; continue along The Shambles and High Petergate to the Minster; lunch at St William's College Restaurant (College St); Treasurer's House; join the city wall at Monk Bar and follow to Marygate; pass Yorkshire Museum in Museum Gardens; cross Lendal Bridge and follow the city wall back to the beginning; visit Jorvik Viking Centre at the start or end of the day when queues are shorter.

Roman, Anglo-Saxon, Viking and medieval times, inc the fabulous medieval Middleham Jewel. All set out very sensibly, with the displays effectively put into context. Shop, disabled access; cl 25–26 Dec, and am Sun Nov–Mar; (01904) 629745; £3.50, less in winter. Outside are 10 acres of botanical gardens by the wall: peaceful and attractive, around a shapely group of ruins inc the Benedictine St Mary's abbey and the Multangular Tower (medieval, on a Roman base), as well as a working observatory.

! YORK DUNGEON (Clifford St) Carefully researched exploration of superstition, torture and various forms of death, full of grue and gore. There's an extensive Guy Fawkes Experience. Shop, some disabled access; cl 25 Dec; (01904) 632599; £4.45.

NATIONAL RAILWAY MUSEUM (Leeman Rd) The great railway age is celebrated here with lots of panache and flair. The centrepiece is the great hall in which 2 sets of tracks and platforms radiate from central turntables, one with a changing display of two dozen great locomotives from the museum's huge collection, the other with all sorts of carriages and waggons, from the humblest and most utilitarian to Queen Victoria's sumptuous royal coach; you can go inside most of them. In the background is a well reproduced soundtrack of recorded station noises from the steam era; alongside, a mass of material vividly illustrates the history of rail and how it changed the world. Timetabled working demonstrations and rides – one place where the trains are always on time. Meals, snacks, shop, disabled access; cl 24–26 Dec; (01904) 621261; £4.80. The nearby Maltings (Wellington Row) has generous food.

YORK MODEL RAILWAY (York BR Station, Tearoom Sq) Painstakingly re-created miniature town and country landscape, running as many as 20 trains at a time; a second much smaller model shows a typical German town at night. Shop, disabled access; cl 25–26 Dec; (01904) 630169; £2.70.

MURTON PARK (just E of town, at Murton SE6552) Busy 8-acre park best known for its MUSEUM OF FARMING, with exhibitions of agricultural equipment, some animals and a Land Army display. There's also the DERWENT VALLEY LIGHT RAILWAY, which on summer weekends has trips along what was once known as the Blackberry Line, and a reconstructed Dark Age settlement (aimed mostly at children). Meals, snacks, shop, disabled access; open Suns and bank hols Mar–Oct; (01904) 489966; £2.80.

Walks

Within its city walls York is largely pedestrianised and very rewarding indeed to walk through. You can do the circuit of the 13th-c city walls and their many towers in a couple of hours or so, mostly on top. One of the best stretches, with good views of the Minster, is between the Monk Bar and Bootham Bar. If you plan on doing the whole circuit it's well worth using one of the Walkman guides rented by the helpful tourist office (Exhibition Sq).

Where to eat

York SE6051 BETTY'S 6 St Helen's Sq (01904) 659142 Famous tearooms, opened in 1937, with fine teas and coffees (they import their own), good sandwiches and hot dishes, delicious tea breads, scones, and pâtisserie, and an evening pianist; cl 25–26 Dec, 1 Jan. £6.50.

York SE6052 19 GRAPE LANE (01904) 636366 Close to the Minster, this neat timbered restaurant (under new owners) serves a good mix of imaginative and traditional dishes (lovely nursery puddings) in a warm and friendly atmosphere; cl Sun, Mon, last 2 wks Jan, 1st wk Feb, 25–28 Dec; children over 8 in evening. **£26 dinner, £17.50 lunch|£6.**

York SE6050 MELTONS 7 Scarcroft Rd (01904) 634341 Smart little restaurant with very fine, imaginative food, lovely puddings, and a relaxed, friendly atmosphere; cl pm Sun, am Mon, 24 Dec–14 Jan, last wk Aug. **£21.50 lunch|£5.**

York SE6052 ST WILLIAM'S COLLEGE RESTAURANT College St (01904) 634830 Enjoyable and varied food (inc vegetarian) in this pleasant self-service restaurant, in a fine building with an enclosed courtyard for eating outside in summer; cl evenings Oct–Mar. **£12.50|£4.75.**

York SE6052 TREASURER'S HOUSE Minster Yard (01904) 624247 Lovely National Trust property, once home to the medieval treasures of York Minster, with a tearoom in the converted cellars: herbal, fruit and traditional teas, home-baked cakes and scones, savoury dishes and good puddings, all served by friendly staff; no smoking; cl Fri, cl Nov–Mar; limited disabled access. **£12.50|£3.95.**

THE YORKSHIRE DALES, HARROGATE AND RIPON

Plenty of really interesting places to visit – but it's the glorious countryside which tops the list.

The Dales are almost guaranteed to inject a touch of exhilaration into even the most jaded people. Their steep stone-walled pastures, majestic moors, wind-carved limestone crags and rushing streams give drivers and particularly walkers a succession of mouth-watering, quickly varying views. Wharfedale has the most varied countryside, and is the most visited dale. Wensleydale is also attractively varied, with a succession of appealing villages and small towns. Ribblesdale, above Settle, climbs into austerely impressive scenery with challenging walks, though is relatively tame in its lower reaches. Malhamdale, quite small, has some of Yorkshire's most striking landscape features – a magnet for day visitors. The upper reaches of Swaledale in the north are largely unspoilt and relatively austere. Nidderdale has fewer paths than the other dales, but plenty of walking to fill a short stay, and has the advantage of being rather off the tourist track.

Within the Dales themselves, Skipton Castle and Bolton Abbey are very rewarding indeed, and a really enjoyable mix of other places includes an intriguing mechanical music museum at Rufforth, ruined Jervaulx Abbey, Thorpe Perrow garden near Bedale, castle remains at Richmond and Middleham, the delicious cheese creamery in Hawes, lively brewery visits in Masham, and the Ingleton show cave. The train trip over the Pennines from Settle to Carlisle is a wonderful ride on a clear day. There are many charming villages; the larger ones and small towns generally have craft shops and the like, and sometimes interesting bookshops.

Over to the east, Fountains Abbey is a special favourite of many readers. Ripley Castle, Newby Hall and Beningbrough Hall are also memorable, with grand gardens. The most interesting gardens are those at Harlow Carr just outside Harrogate; the newly opened ones at Constable Burton Hall are well worth visiting too. Little known to visitors or even to locals, Markenfield Hall is a gem. The theme park at North Stainley is a great day out for children.

Harrogate is an extremely civilised, former spa resort with some of Yorkshire's smartest shops – well worth a leisurely morning or afternoon, and a very comfortable base for touring. From here you can drive to Grassington (the centre of the Dales) or Helmsley (just below the North York Moors) in about 45 minutes. Ripon, also strategically placed for touring, is an attractive and largely unspoilt market town with one of Britain's largest cathedrals; Richmond is another appealing market town.

All in all, this part of Yorkshire is among the finest places in Britain for adults who enjoy at least a bit of fresh air.

Where to stay

Aldborough SE4066 SHIP Aldborough, Boroughbridge, York YO5 9ER (01423) 322749 £43; 5 rms, showers. Friendly and neatly kept 14th-c pub nr an ancient church and the Roman town; with a coal fire in the stone inglenook fireplace and old-fashioned seats in the heavily beamed bar, ample food, good breakfasts, and well kept real ales; also seats on the spacious lawn.

Arncliffe SD9473 FALCON Arncliffe, Skipton BD23 5QE (01756) 770205 £48; 5 rms, some with own bthrm. Friendly, delightfully basic Georgian inn ideal for walkers; with functional little rooms and a fire, homely front lounge, an airy conservatory, no smoking dining room, and generous, plain lunchtime snacks; no accommodation Nov–Easter; self-catering cottage.

Askrigg SD9591 KINGS ARMS Market Pl, Askrigg, Leyburn DL8 3HQ (01969) 650258 £95, plus special breaks; 11 rms. Smart Georgian manor house with a homely, friendly atmosphere in several bars – one used in the TV series *All Creatures Great and Small*; attractive furnishings, low beams and oak panelling, open fires, imaginative restaurant dishes, excellent bar food, and very good wines; children over 9 in restaurant.

Bainbridge SD9390 ROSE & CROWN Bainbridge, Leyburn DL8 3EE (01969) 650225 *£54, plus special breaks; 12 comfortable rms. 15th-c coaching inn overlooking a lovely village green; with antique settles and other old furniture in the beamed and panelled front bar, open log fires, a cosy residents' lounge, big wine list, and home-made traditional food in both the bar and restaurant; cl 25–26 Dec, 1 Jan; pets welcome by prior arrangement.

Bolton Abbey SE0754 DEVONSHIRE ARMS COUNTRY HOUSE Bolton Abbey, Skipton BD23 6AJ (01756) 710441 £150, plus special breaks; 41 individually furnished rms with thoughtful extras. Close to the priory itself and in lovely countryside, this civilised former coaching inn is owned by the Duke of Devonshire and has been carefully furnished with fine antiques and paintings from Chatsworth; log fires, impeccable service, beautifully presented, imaginative food in the elegant restaurant, super breakfasts; health centre; children over 12 in restaurant; disabled access.

Brafferton SE4370 BRAFFERTON HALL Brafferton, York YO6 2NZ (01423) 360352 *£60; 4 spacious rms. Quietly set in a village by the River Swale, this 18th-c, no smoking, private house has comfortable lounges, welcoming hosts, enjoyable breakfasts, and good evening meals (if ordered in advance) eaten around a candlelit communal table in the dining room; limited disabled access.

Buckden SD9477 BUCK Buckden, Skipton BD23 5JA (01756) 760228 *£72, plus special breaks; 14 comfortable rms. Busy pub surrounded by moorland views (lots of walkers); with a snug original area and a bustling, extended, open-plan bar, popular food served by smartly uniformed staff in the attractive, no smoking dining room, decent wines, and well kept real ales; disabled access.

Burnsall SE0361 RED LION Burnsall, Skipton BD23 6BU (01756) 720204 *£85, plus special breaks; 11 rms. Pretty, 16th-c, family-run ferryman's inn overlooking the river and village green with its tall maypole; an attractively panelled bar, log fires and beams, good food in both the bar and no smoking restaurant, and a decent wine list; also big gardens and a terrace on the river bank; 75 yards of private fishing and permits for a further 7 miles; disabled access.

Carperby SE0189 OLD STABLES Carperby, Leyburn DL8 4DA (01969) 663590

*£45, plus special breaks; 3 rms, showers. Carefully converted stables with warmly welcoming and helpful owners; pleasantly furnished and neatly kept lounge and dining room, log fire in the inglenook fireplace, marvellous breakfasts with home-made marmalade; no smoking and no children or pets; cl Christmas and New Year.

Chapel le Dale SD7477 OLD HILL Chapel le Dale, Carnforth, LA6 3AR (01524) 241256 £35; 3 warm, basic but well furnished rms, also 2 bunk rooms with 8 beds in each; shared bthrms. On the Three Peaks walk, this inn is popular with potholers too, and has stripped stone walls, flagstones, old woodwork, a roaring log fire in the cosy back parlour, popular food inc big breakfasts, and live music Sat nights; camping.

Cray SD9379 WHITE LION Cray, Skipton BD23 5JB (01756) 760262 £50, plus special breaks; 8 comfortable rms in adjoining barn. Welcoming little pub, spectacularly isolated 335 metres (1,100 ft) up, with super views and lots of nearby walks; traditional feel with flagstones, beams and log fires, good bar food, and decent wines.

Danby Wiske SE3499 WHITE SWAN Danby Wiske, Northallerton DL7 0NQ (01609) 770122 *£33; 3 comfortable rms, shared bthrm. Cosy little pub in the middle of nowhere, handy for walkers on the Coast-to-Coast footpath; with very friendly licensees, and a decent choice of good-value food, inc free-range eggs from their chickens.

East Witton SE1586 HOLLY TREE East Witton, Leyburn DL8 4LS (01969) 622383 *£44, plus special breaks; 4 good rms. Very attractively decorated 16th-c house in a peaceful village; with carefully cooked, good food, a homely and welcoming atmosphere, log fire and beams in the sitting room, TV lounge, and a small garden; cl Dec–Feb; children over 10.

Feizor SD7867 SCAR CLOSE FARM Feizor, Austwick, Lancaster LA2 8DF (01729) 823496 £44, plus special breaks; 4 clean, well appointed rms. Friendly converted barn on a working farm, with a large guests' lounge, books, magazines and TV, and big breakfasts and homely evening meals; lovely, quiet surrounding countryside; cl 25–26 Dec, disabled access.

Grassington SE0064 BLACK HORSE Garrs Lane, Grassington, BD23 5AT (01756) 752770 £50, plus special breaks; 15 rms. On the edge of the cobbled square, this is a bustling place with open fires and beams in the comfortable bar, friendly service, and enjoyable food in the attractive little restaurant; sheltered terrace.

Harrogate SE2955 ALEXA HOUSE 26 Ripon Rd, Harrogate HG1 2JJ (01423) 501988 £60, plus special breaks; 13 rms, some in a former stable block. Attractive Georgian house with friendly staff, comfortable lounge, good home cooking in the no smoking dining room, and marvellous breakfasts; good disabled access.

Harrogate SE3055 BALMORAL 16–18 Franklin Mount, Harrogate HG1 5EJ (01423) 508208 £90, plus special breaks; 20 lovely rms, many with four-posters. In lovely gardens but close to the centre, this popular hotel has a restful drawing room, cosy snug, an interesting Oriental bar, fine food in the elegant restaurant, and helpful, friendly staff; disabled access.

Harrogate SE2955 OLD SWAN Ripon Rd HG1 2SR (01423) 500055 £80; 136 rms. Creeper-covered Victorian hotel close to the centre and in quiet gardens; with a friendly atmosphere, attractive day rooms, antiques and fresh flowers, good breakfasts in the splendid dining room, and fine modern cooking in the elegant restaurant.

Hawes SD8789 COCKETTS Market Pl, Hawes DL8 3RD (01969) 667312 *£59, plus special breaks; 8 warm rms. Friendly, hardworking owners make this a most attractive and enjoyable place to stay; a candlelit restaurant, woodburner in the small bar, and a residents' lounge with books; cl Dec and Jan; children over 10; disabled access.

Ingleton SD6972 THORNGARTH HOUSE New Rd, Ingleton, Carnforth LA6 3HN

(01524) 241295 *£50, plus special breaks; 5 comfortable rms. Victorian country house in lovely countryside; with a cosy fire and plenty of books in the sitting room, a small candlelit restaurant with enjoyable, totally home-made food (can take their home-made jam, chutneys, herb oils and vinegars home with you), courteous service, and a tranquil atmosphere; lots to do nearby; no children.

Kilnsey SD9767 TENNANT ARMS Kilnsey, Skipton BD23 5PS (01756) 752301 *£47, plus special breaks; 10 rms. In a nice spot nr the River Wharfe, this spacious, beamed and flagstoned inn has open fires (one fireplace is made from an ornate, carved four-poster), friendly service, good-value food, and views of spectacular overhanging Kilnsey Crag from the restaurant; pets welcome by prior arrangement.

Knaresborough SE3557 DOWER HOUSE Bond End, Knaresborough HG5 9AL (01423) 863302 *£75, plus special breaks; 32 clean, comfortable rms. Creeper-clad former dower house with attractively furnished public rooms of some character; good food in the Terrace Restaurant, super breakfasts, helpful service, and a leisure and health club; disabled access.

Leyburn SE1191 GOLDEN LION Market Pl, Leyburn DL8 5AS (01969) 622161 *£56, plus special breaks; 15 good-value rms. Homely inn with comfortable and quietly friendly, bay-windowed, 2-room bar with light squared panelling; good, home-cooked traditional food in both the bar and evening restaurant, well kept real ales (inc one brewed to their own recipe), and helpful service; self-catering in nearby Hawnby; cl 25–26 Dec; disabled access.

Malham SD8963 MIRESFIELD FARM Malham, Skipton BD23 4DA (01729) 830414 *£46, plus winter breaks; 14 rms. Spacious old farmhouse with good, freshly prepared food, a pleasant conservatory, 2 lounges and a lovely garden by the stream and village green; disabled access.

Markington SE2764 HOB GREEN Markington, Harrogate HG3 3PJ (01423) 770031 £90; 12 well equipped, pretty rms. Lovely gardens and over 800 acres of rolling countryside surround this charming stone hotel; comfortable lounge and garden room, log fires, fresh flowers, relaxed atmosphere, good food and friendly service.

Masham SE2280 KINGS HEAD Market Sq, Masham, Ripon HG4 4EF (01765) 689295 £58; 10 rms. Tall and handsome Georgian stone inn on the market square of this attractive small town; with lovely hanging baskets, 2 opened-up rooms of the neatly kept lounge bar, home-made food from an extensive menu, a separate restaurant, well kept real ales, helpful service, and good breakfasts.

Middleham SE1288 GREYSTONES Market Pl, Middleham DL8 4NR (01969) 622016 *£54, plus special breaks; 4 rms. Friendly, family-run Georgian house with a log fire, books, magazines and TV in the restful lounge, and generous helpings of good home-made food using home-grown vegetables; also home-made bread, cakes and sweet and savoury biscuits, and enjoyable breakfasts; cl Dec–Jan exc New Year.

Middleham SE1288 MILLERS HOUSE Market Pl, Middleham DL8 4NR (01969) 622630 £74, plus special breaks; 7 pretty rms; Neatly furnished Georgian house with fine views, an open fire in the pleasant lounge, attractive restaurant with good, interesting, home-cooked food using vegetables and herbs grown in their garden, lunchtime picnic hampers, and helpful service; cl Jan; children over 10.

Ramsgill SE1171 YORKE ARMS Ramsgill, Harrogate HG3 5RL (01423) 755243 £70, plus special breaks; 13 attractive rms. Enjoyable small hotel (under new owners) with antique furnishings, log fires, particularly good, imaginative cooking, smart dress in the no smoking evening restaurant, and lovely surrounding walks; open all day for tea and coffee.

Reeth SE0499 ARKLESIDE Village Green, Reeth, Richmond DL11 6SG (01748) 884200 £59; 9 pretty rms. Charming, small Swaledale hotel with warm and friendly, caring owners; attractively furnished lounge, an airy conservatory bar overlooking the gardens, a relaxing atmosphere, and good Yorkshire cooking in candlelit restaurant; cl Jan–early Feb; children over 10.

Richmond NZ1701 OLD BREWERY 29 The Green, Richmond DL10 4RG (01748) 822460 *£39; 5 rms. In a pretty corner overlooking the village green and castle ruins is this delightful old inn with Victorian-style renovations and furnishings, a hospitable atmosphere, and a nice garden; dinner by arrangement; cl Dec/Jan; children over 8.

Richmond NZ1404 WHASHTON SPRINGS FARM Whashton Springs, Richmond DL11 7JS (01748) 822884 *£42; 8 comfortable rms. Attractive, stonebuilt Georgian farmhouse on a 600-acre working mixed farm; with a log fire in the comfortable sitting room, good country breakfasts in attractive dining room (no evening meals), and lovely surrounding countryside; cl Christmas/Jan; children over 5; partial disabled access.

Ripley SE2860 BOARS HEAD Ripley, Harrogate HG3 1AY (01423) 771888 £98; 25 charmingly decorated rms. Fine old coaching inn with comfortable sofas in the attractively decorated lounges, a long flagstoned bar, notable wines by the glass, good food in both the bar and restful dining room, and unobtrusive service; disabled access.

Ripon SE3171 RIPON SPA Park St HG4 2BU (01765) 602172 *£75, plus special breaks; 40 rms. Neatly kept, friendly and comfortable Edwardian hotel with 7 acres of prize-winning gardens, yet only a short walk from the centre; attractive public rooms, and good food in both the bar and restaurant; disabled access.

Sedbusk SD8891 STONE HOUSE Sedbusk, Hawes DL8 3PT (01969) 667571 *£68, plus special breaks; 22 rms, 2 with own conservatories. Small, warm and friendly Edwardian hotel with a country-house feel and appropriate furnishings, and a stunning setting with magnificent views; attractive, oak-panelled drawing room, billiard room, log fires, exemplary service, good local information; pleasant, newly extended dining room with excellent, wholesome food (special needs catered for) inc super breakfasts, and a reasonable choice of wines; tennis lawn in the grounds, wonderful walks; P G Wodehouse stayed here as a guest of the original owner who employed a butler called Jeeves – it was on him that Wodehouse based his famous character; cl Jan; dogs welcome; good disabled access.

Settle SD8162 FALCON MANOR Skipton Rd, Settle, BD24 9BD (01729) 823814 *£80, plus special breaks; 19 rms. Quietly set, imposing Victorian hotel in its own grounds, with original features in the spacious public rooms, log fires, fine food and lovely views in the elegant restaurant, and obliging service; a well placed touring base; disabled access.

Simonstone SD8791 SIMONSTONE HALL Simonstone, Hawes DL8 3LY (01969) 667255 £90; 18 pretty rms. Carefully restored, warmly welcoming country house in beautiful countryside with fine views; spacious, panelled drawing rooms with antiques, paintings and old maps of the area, and good, carefully cooked food and interesting wines; dogs welcome.

Starbotton SD9574 FOX & HOUNDS Starbotton, Skipton BD23 5HY (01756) 760269 £50; 2 rms with showers. Prettily placed and rather smart little Upper Wharfedale village inn, with a warmly welcoming atmosphere, flagstones, beams, and a big log fire; imaginative food, and well kept real ales; cl Jan–mid-Feb.

Studley Roger SE2970 LAWRENCE HOUSE Studley Roger, Ripon HG4 3AY (01765) 600947 £76; 2 spacious, lovely rms. Attractive Georgian house with 2 acres of garden on the edge of Studley Royal deer park and Fountains Abbey; lovely antiques and fine pictures, log fires, good breakfasts, and delicious evening meals; cl Christmas and New Year; children by arrangement.

Thoralby SE0086 SCARR HOUSE Thoralby, Leyburn DL8 3SU (01969) 663654 £53; 3 rms with showers. Relaxed and friendly, no smoking, 18th-c former farmhouse with lovely views; lots of books (no TV), comfortable lounge in a converted hayloft with beams, exposed stonework and an open fire; carefully cooked food (bring your own wine) at candlelit tables, and nice breakfasts; no children.

Thornton Watlass SE2486 BUCK Thornton Watlass, Ripon HG4 4AH (01677) 422461 £52; 7 rms, most with own bthrm. Warm and friendly country pub overlooking the cricket green in a very attractive village; interesting beamed and panelled rooms, open fire, live music on weekends in the function room, excellent food inc summer barbecues, and lots of nearby walks (the arboretum is very popular); the inn offers guided walking holidays; cl pm 25 Dec.

Wath in Nidderdale SE1467 SPORTSMANS ARMS Wath in Nidderdale, Harrogate HG3 5PP (01423) 711306 £60; 7 simple rms, some with own bthrm. Friendly, quietly placed, 17th-c hotel with lovely views; an elegant bar, a decent range of wines, excellent food (especially fish) in the no smoking evening restaurant, super lunchtime bar food, and attentive service; particularly good Sunday lunch, and lots of fine cheeses; cl 25 Dec.

West Burton SE0186 FOX & HOUNDS West Burton, Leyburn DL8 4JY (01969) 663279 £52, plus special breaks; 8 good modern rms in a cobbled courtyard. Unspoilt, simple local in an idyllic Dales village around a long green, with a homely and welcoming atmosphere; small bar with extension, generous, wholesome, home-cooked food in both the residents' dining room and the bar, and good service from friendly staff; no children; disabled access.

West Witton SE0688 WENSLEYDALE HEIFER West Witton, Leyburn DL8 4LS (01969) 622322 *£70, plus special breaks; 15 rms in 2 adjacent old buildings. Friendly, 17th-c stone coaching inn with comfortable furnishings and log fires in the oak-beamed rooms, and a cosy bar; good local game and fresh seafood in the bistro or spacious restaurant; well behaved dogs allowed.

Wigglesworth SD8157 PLOUGH Wigglesworth, Skipton BD23 4RJ (01729) 840243 £50, plus special breaks; 12 well equipped rms. Friendly and well run country inn with popular food in the barn/conservatory restaurant and bar; lots of little rooms surrounding the bar area, some smart and plush, others more spartan yet still cosy; friendly service, big breakfasts, packed lunches, and views of the Three Peaks; disabled access.

To see and do

🏛☗★✝**Aldborough** SE4066 ROMAN TOWN The northernmost civilian Roman town was on this site, its houses, courts, forum and temple surrounded by a massive 6-metre (9-ft) wall. All that remain are 2 pavements, the position of the wall and, in the museum, some finds from the site. Shop; open pm Apr–Oct; £1.40. It's a pleasant village with an impressive church (check out the sundial); the Ship opposite is good for lunch.

☗꙳**Aysgarth** SE0088 WATERFALLS The Lower Fall is the most spectacular of this famously romantic series of waterfalls, via a path over the road from the car park. The falls do get crowded, particularly through Aug (when even parking can be a problem here). They're better in late spring or early autumn, when there tends to be more water in the river and therefore a better show. In severely cold weather they can be stunning, with wonderful ice sculptures building up. There's generally a small charge to see the Upper Fall (it's on private land), but you can see it almost as well without paying, from the bridge on the road. The main car park (around £1 for 3 hours) has a NATIONAL PARK CENTRE, with displays on the Dales, and useful walks, maps, and guides. Café, shop, disabled facilities; cl wkdys Nov–Mar; (01969) 663424; free. YORKSHIRE CARRIAGE MUSEUM (Yore Mill) A collection of Victorian coaches and carriages, and a decent craft and pottery shop. Meals, snacks; cl Christmas; (01969)

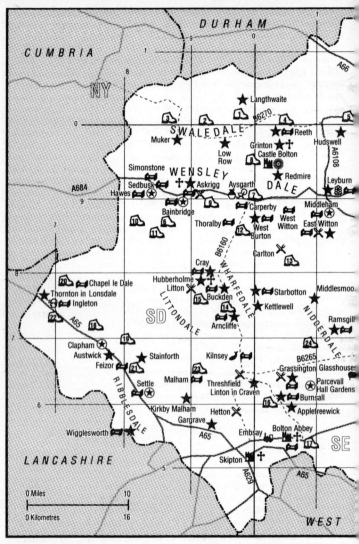

663399; *£2. The George & Dragon is a handy place for lunch.

★ ✗ 🕿 **Bainbridge** SD9390
Delightful, its broad sloping green still with the village stocks, and still ringing with the blowing of a buffalo-horn to guide shepherds down through the mists each night at 9pm from the end of Sept till late Feb, as it has done for centuries. There's a restored 18th-c CORN MILL, with a collection of fully furnished, hand-made dolls' houses, all produced on the premises. Good shop (sells plans to make your own). Open pm Weds July–mid-Sept, maybe bank hols, and by appointment; (01965) 650416; *75p.

🐝 🍃 🐦 **Bedale** SE2685 THORPE PERROW (off the B6268, S of Bedale) Well laid out, 60-acre, landscaped lakeside collection of rare trees and shrubs among some splendid mature specimens that have been growing

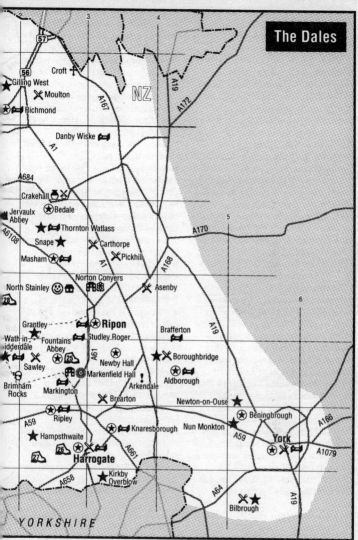

The Dales

here for over 400 years. Particularly strong on oaks, ornamental cherries, willows and hazels, and lovely in spring when the bulbs are out. Snacks, shop, disabled access; (01677) 425323; £3. In the town, the convivial Olde Black Swan does good-value lunches. BIG SHEEP AND LITTLE COW FARM (Aiskew) SE2889 Small-scale dairy farm, with friendly sheep and dexter cows (Britain's smallest), pigs and chicks –

the family in charge love talking to visitors. Don't come when it's wet. Shop, snacks, some disabled access; cl Sept–Mar; (01677) 422125; £2.50. Beningbrough SE5158 BENINGBROUGH HALL Stately, early 18th-c baroque mansion, with a good collection from the National Portrait Gallery, also a marvellous staircase with balusters carved in imitation of wrought iron, fine carvings, and a big, restored Victorian dairy. Regular events for families, and lovely formal gardens. Meals, snacks, shop, disabled access; cl Thurs, Fri (exc July/Aug), and Nov–Feb; (01904) 470666; £4.50, garden only £3; NT. The riverside Dawnay Arms, at Newton-on-Ouse is useful for lunch.

☙ † Bolton Abbey SE0754 Beautiful spot in lovely, rolling wooded parkland on a knoll above the River Wharfe. Most of the priory buildings, dating from the 12th to the 16th centuries, are in ruins, but the central core of the main church is still used for Sunday services. 19th-c additions such as stained glass (some by Pugin) and murals oddly don't strike a false note. The car park gets rather full in summer. Attractive walks lead off in most directions, and the Devonshire Arms is very fine for lunch.

☙ Brimham Rocks SE2164 (off the B6265) Spectacular and extraordinarily weathered gritstone pinnacles, tors and boulders facing the winds at a height of 290 metres (950 ft), conjuring up people, animal heads and other strange figures – a Victorian guidebook declared that they were 'grim and hideous forms defying all description and definition'. Children like them a lot – Henry Moore said that when he was a boy they strongly influenced his imagination. Information centre, shop and tearoom open wknds and bank hols Easter–Oct, daily Jun–Sept and school hols – weather permitting, the site is open all year; (01423) 780688; parking *£2; NT. The Half Moon on the B6265 is handy for food.

☙ ❀ Castle Bolton SE0392 14th-c BOLTON CASTLE (off the A684) A massive structure towering over the tiny, single-street village built for it. Considering it was partly dismantled in 1645 and has been empty ever since, it's still in fine shape; great views from the 100-ft towers. Meals, snacks, shop; cl Nov–Feb; (01969) 623981; *£3. The King's Arms at Redmire has decent food.

★ ☙ ♖ Clapham SD7569 Attractive village that has turned walking and caving into something of an industry. It has a good NATIONAL PARK CENTRE

with an audio-visual show and useful local information; best to check winter opening, usually wknds only; (01524) 251419; parking 80p for 3 hours. The riverside New Inn is useful for lunch (and a nice place for walkers to stay in). The OUTDOORS CENTRE of Ingleborough Hall was formerly the family home of the great plantsman Reginald Farrer, who in his short life introduced and eulogised many notable plants from the Himalayas and China.

INGLEBOROUGH CAVE One of the most easily visited of the vast network of caverns plunging into the limestone hills around here – and probably the only one that wheelchairs can go all the way through. A NATURE TRAIL leads past Farrer's woods and a small lake to its entrance; unusually, it's a place that looks better in wet weather. Snacks, shop; cl wkdys Nov–Feb; (015242) 51242; *£3.50.

❌ ♨ Crakehall SE2490 CRAKEHALL WATERMILL 17th-c, on the site of a still earlier one; restored in 1980, it now produces flour again. Even when they're not milling, the wheel should still be turning. Snacks, shop; cl Mon, Fri and Oct–Easter; (01677) 423240; £1. Nearby is a little MUSEUM OF BADGES AND BATTLEDRESS; cl am wknds, Mon (exc bank hols), and Oct–Easter; (01677) 424444; *£1.50. The Bay Horse, in a nice spot on Little Crakehall green, has good value food.

† Croft NZ2909 Right on the border with County Durham is a pleasant CHURCH, where Lewis Carroll's father was parson; there's a plaque in memory of the writer, complete with an enamelled White Rabbit, and an unusual family pew reached by a staircase. If the church is closed, the key is kept at the hotel across the road. Nice river views.

☙ Embsay SE0053 EMBSAY STEAM RAILWAY ▣ Steam trips along a couple of miles of railway, prettily set beneath limestone crags. There's a ticket office originally at Ilkley, and a collection of old locomotives and carriages. They hope this year to extend the track to Bolton Abbey. Snacks, shop (remarkable range of books), disabled access (notice preferred); usually open Sun all year, daily in Aug (exc Mon and Fri), plus Sat in Jun and Sept, and Tues in July – best to ring (01756) 795189 for timetable; £4. The well run Elm Tree has decent food, and the Wayside Café, in nearby Draughton, does good scones.

🏛 🕃 ✚† **Fountains Abbey** SE2768 FOUNTAINS ABBEY AND STUDLEY ROYAL WATERGARDEN (off the B6265) The largest monastic ruin in the country, this romantic place was founded in 1132 by Cistercian monks, in a delightful riverside setting. Said to be haunted by a full choir of ghostly monks, most of the remains are 12th-c, but the proud main tower is 15th-c. Opposite are the lovely landscaped gardens begun by William Aislabie in 1768, which include ornamental temples and follies, formal watergardens, lakes aflutter with waterfowl, and 400 acres of deer park. The most beautiful approach is through the extraordinarily ornate Victorian church at the far end (open pm May–Sept only), and this 'back-door' entrance is the most tranquil too. A modern visitor centre has been skilfully constructed so that it blends in and doesn't spoil the view. Free guided tours 2.30pm Mar–Oct, plus 11am May–Sept. Meals, snacks, shop, good disabled access; cl Fri Nov–Jan, and 24–25 Dec; (01765) 608888; *£4.20, deer park free; NT. The very civilised Sawley Arms, in Sawley just W, does good food.

🍴 **Glasshouses** SE1764 YORKSHIRE COUNTRY WINES (The Mill) Traditional country wines produced in a 19th-c flax mill, with free tastings, antiques, and tearoom overlooking the River Nidd. Cl Mon and Tues, winery tours (*£2.50) Fri and Sat at 11.45am; (01423) 711947.

★ **Grassington** SE0064 Pleasant small town or large village around a sloping cobbled square, depending a lot on walkers and other visitors, with some attractive shops and a few interesting old buildings; there's a National Park information centre. The Black Horse has decent food and comfortable bedrooms. The B6160

gives lovely Wharfedale views, and the B6265 to Pateley Bridge also has memorable views (and passes the colourfully lit, underground Stump Cross Caverns SE0863, well worth a look if you're passing).

★ 🕃 🏠 🔲 🕃 **Harrogate** SE2955 This elegant and self-confident inland resort has kept its Victorian spa-town atmosphere despite now filling many of its handsome hotels with business conferences and so forth. The layout of the town is very gracious, and you couldn't ask for better shops (interesting antiques and some top-notch specialist shops). Almost every available space is filled with colourful plant displays, as if to shake off the gloom of the dark stone buildings. The first thing a visitor notices is the great swathe of The Stray, open parkland which runs right along and through the S side of the centre. The elegant buildings of the compact central area sweep down from here to the pleasantly laid out Valley Gardens, very Victorian, their curlicued central tea house run by a friendly Italian family. The relaxed tempo of the place, and the clean bracing climate (it's quite high on the moors), have made it a popular retirement area. ROYAL PUMP ROOM MUSEUM (Royal Parade) The central sulphur wells (there are other outlets all over the town) are housed here, enclosed by glass to contain the reek. You can still order a free glass of the water at the original spa counter, now the ticket counter for the museum. The octagonal pump room building contains displays of 19th-c fine china and jewellery, as well as bath chairs and other impedimenta of the golden spa days. Shop, disabled access; cl Oct–Mar; (01423) 503340; £1.75. Next door the elegant ASSEMBLY ROOMS are kept much as they were, very genteel and palm-courtish; you can stroll around, sit down for musical coffee and cakes, or plunge into a (non-sulphurous) Turkish bath. The very first sulphur well was discovered in the 16th c and named the TEWIT WELL, after the local word for the lapwings which led a local sporting gent to ride into what was then a smelly bog. It's up on The Stray, grandly encased in what looks like an Italianate mausoleum. Another early spa building on Swan Rd is now the MERCER ART GALLERY, with an excellent collection of antiquities (cl am Sun, and Mon; free).

Besides the places mentioned in the **Where to eat** section below, the Drum & Monkey (fish restaurant/wine bar, Montpellier Gardens), Hedleys (wine bar, Montpellier Parade) and the Regency (off East Parade) are all good for lunch or a snack; the café of the Theatre Royal is also pleasant, as is the Lascelles Arms out in Follifoot SE3452.

HARLOW CARR BOTANICAL GARDENS (Crag Lane, on W edge of town, off the B6162) Ornamental and woodland gardens spread over 68 acres, with streams, pools, rockeries, rhododendrons, spring bulbs and many interesting plants. Also a museum of gardening, model village, scented garden, and a developing rose garden. A place of real peace and fresh moorland air, virtually deserted out of season, when the excellent collection of heathers comes into its own. Meals, snacks, plant centre, disabled access; (01423) 565418; £3.40. The adjacent Harrogate Arms has good-value food.

★ ☺ 🍴 🐾 🏠 **Hawes** SD8789 Busy in summer with hikers and coach parties, but pretty, and a proper market town, its Tuesday mart alive with sheep in late summer (cattle too, in normal years less overshadowed by BSE). WENSLEYDALE CREAMERY (Gayle Lane) Saved from closure by a timely management buy-out a few years ago, this has developed a fascinating visitor centre, with a well set out dairying/cheese museum; you can watch the cheese being made by the traditional method, all by hand. The shop (busy in summer) has samples of their variously flavoured cheeses – our favourite was the one with blueberries. Very good café, disabled facilities; cl 25 Dec; (01969) 667644; *£2.50. DALES COUNTRYSIDE MUSEUM AND NATIONAL PARK CENTRE (Station Yard) Developing centre with

interesting displays of local crafts and domestic and industrial life. Shop, disabled access; limited winter opening – best to check; (01969) 667450; *£2. OUTHWAITES ROPEMAKERS (Town Foot) They've been making rope for 200 years – see how it's done. Shop (not just great hawsers, useful things too like dog-leads), disabled access; cl wknds (exc summer Sats, Easter and spring bank hol), 10 days over Christmas; (01969) 667487; free. The Crown and White Hart are useful for lunch. HARDRAW FORCE SD8691 (just N of Hawes) England's tallest waterfall cascading over a 30-metre (100-ft) lip; it's best after rain (though the paths can be muddy then), and at dry times you may see barely a trickle; small fee at Green Dragon pub. The valley above the falls is attractive, and this can be a start for the long day's walk to Great Shunner Fell. The B6255 up to Ribblehead gives fine mountain views, and the Buttertubs Pass over into Swaledale is a spectacular drive (the Buttertubs are deep ferny holes nr the summit where carriers used to cool their butter in hot weather).

★ † **Hubberholme** SD9178 Beautifully placed dales hamlet with a good 13th-c CHURCH, built on an ancient burial site, with a Norman tower, an unusual rood loft and pews by Thompson of Kilburn – with their little carved mouse trademark. The charmingly set George, J B Priestley's favourite pub, has decent food and bedrooms.

🍴 **Ingleton** SD7174 WHITE SCAR CAVE 🏠 (B6255 towards Hawes) The country's biggest show cavern and one of the most spectacular, with underground waterfalls and streams, and an Ice Age cavern. Some amazing sights and atmospheric formations, and stunning stalactites and stalagmites that have been here for 100,000 years. Wrap up well – the guided tour takes about 80 minutes so it gets chilly. Snacks, shop, disabled access by arrangement; cl 25 Dec (and sometimes after heavy rain); (015242) 41244; £5.95. The Three Horse Shoes, Wheatsheaf and Bridge are all useful pubs, and the B6255/B6479 is a very scenic long way round to Settle.

🏛 **Jervaulx Abbey** SE1785 Less imposing than Fountains, Rievaulx and Bolton, but in some ways even more appealing – perhaps because the rough-cropped grass and wild flowers around the shattered walls emphasise the slightly melancholy atmosphere of a place of great worldly wealth and power that's come to nothing. Teas, shop, disabled access; cl am Nov–Dec, and all Jan–Feb; (01677) 460391; £1.50. The Blue Lion at East Witton nearby has superb food.

🎣 **Kilnsey** SD9767 KILNSEY PARK TROUT FARM (B6160) 2 lakes for fly-fishing, plus a fun-fishing area for children, an adventure playground, and a good estate shop with fish, oven-ready game and other local produce. There's an aquarium in the visitor centre, and a sizeable collection of orchids. Good meals and snacks (tasty trout, and local cheeses), disabled access; cl 25 Dec; (01756) 752150; *£1.50 for visitor centre, *£3.75 for children's fishery, and proper fishing from *£11.50 per half-day. The Tennant Arms has decent food.

🍷🍺❗🍴★🏛🕌 **Knaresborough** SE3557 In the 19th c quite a little tourist industry was concocted for the toffs from Harrogate around the alleged 16th-c prophecies of Mother Shipton. The cave she lived in is pleasantly set in 12 acres of riverside parkland, along with a limestone spring, the PETRIFYING WELL, which quickly coats teddy bears and other unlikely objects in rock so that they can be sold as souvenirs. There are guided tours, and a local history museum, but admission to the site is £3.95 and not everyone comes away feeling it was worth it. Snacks, shop, some disabled access; (01423) 864600; cl 25 Dec. You'll be better off following the riverside paths and walks in the area that you don't have to pay for: from Abbey Rd for example you should be able to see the intriguing HOUSE IN THE ROCK (currently closed for renovation), and

a 15-minute walk down here brings you to St Robert's Cave, the riverside home of a 12th-c hermit. The little town itself above the steeply picturesque river gorge, with its spectacular railway viaduct, is pleasant and colourful (especially on Weds market day), with some attractive buildings. All that remains of the 14th-c CASTLE are the keep (with museum and suitably dank dungeon), gatehouse and some of the curtain wall, but it's easy to imagine what an imposing sight it must have made, glowering over the gorge of the River Nidd – a suitable spot for Thomas à Becket's murderers to hide in. Shop; open Easter wknd, then daily May–Sept; (01423) 503340; £1.75, also inc entrance to the 14th-c OLD COURT, now a local history museum. The chemist's shop on the square is said to be the oldest in the country; established in 1720, it still has all its original fittings. You can hire ROWING BOATS down on the river. The Mother Shipton and Yorkshire Lass both have good-value food.

★ 🏛 **Leyburn** SE1190 Bustling little agricultural town with a proper country atmosphere and a lively Fri market: the Sandpiper's the nicest pub, and Tennants is Europe's largest AUCTION ROOM for house clearances and antiques. CONSTABLE BURTON HALL GARDENS (A684, E of Leyburn) A series of fine terraced gardens around a handsome Georgian house (not open); the cyclamen at the end of the short lime avenue flower beautifully in early Aug. Some disabled access; cl Nov–late Mar; (01677) 450428; *£2. Off the A684 W there are fine drives: up Coverdale to Kettlewell; up Bishopdale on the B6160 and on down past Cray into Wharfedale; up into the Eden Valley's Cumbrian headwaters on the B6269; and the Carperby–Castle Bolton–Reeth road.

🏚 ❀ **Markenfield Hall** SE2967 A hidden treasure, reached by a longish walk along a riverside track S from Ripon, or its main drive, another track turning right off the A61 heading S from Ripon, just past the drive to Hollin Hall on the left. It's a secluded, fortified and moated medieval manor house around a charming courtyard, with 3 lovely original rooms and splendid views from the battlements. Open Mon Apr–Oct, cl 12.30–2.15pm; £2.

★ † 🏠 ♖ **Masham** SE2280 (pronounced Mazzum) Civilised small market town, with an interesting church, and dignified Georgian houses around its broad market square – which comes to life on Weds. THEAKSTON BREWERY VISITOR CENTRE Next to the brewery, this explains the brewing process behind Theakstons beer, inc their Old Peculier. Shop, disabled access; cl Tues Easter-Oct, and all wkdys (exc Weds) Nov–Dec; £1. Enthusiastic tours of the brewery itself (£2.50) should be booked in advance on (01765) 689544; you see more in the mornings; no under 10s. You can also visit the BLACK SHEEP BREWERY, set up by a breakaway member of the Theakston family a few years back (its beers since proving very popular). Again, best to book, tel (01765) 689227 – evening tours are best, with more time to enjoy samples at the end. UREDALE GLASS (42 Market Pl) Hand-made glassware, with glass-blowing demonstrations (not Sun or Mon); cl Christmas wk; (01765) 689780; free. The King's Head does good food.

★ 🏰 ❀ **Middleham** SE1288 Attractive and civilised, basically Georgian, stonebuilt village, still with the style that came from its days as the country's top racehorse-training centre in the 18th and early 19th centuries. Even now there are times when it seems to have more horses than people: pick up breeding and gallops gossip in the bar of the good Black Swan. The village is dwarfed by 12th-c MIDDLEHAM CASTLE, for a time the home of young King Richard III. Only the huge keep and some later buildings remain, but there are marvellous views from the top. Snacks, shop, disabled access; cl 1–2pm, winter Mon and Tues, 24–26 Dec; (01969) 623899; £2.20. This is a good area for self-catering accommodation – and fine walking country.

🏠 🏰 🖼 ⛴ **Newby Hall** SE3467 🔲 (off the B6265 E of Ripon) In beautiful formal gardens covering 25 acres, this late 17th-c mansion, redesigned inside and out by Robert Adam, has an important collection of classical sculpture and Gobelins tapestries, as well as a fine range of Chippendale furniture. In the grounds are a miniature railway, children's adventure garden and woodland discovery walk. Meals, snacks, shop, some disabled access; house cl am, all Mon (exc bank hols), and Oct–Mar; (01423) 322583; £5.60, £4 gardens only. The Ship over in Aldborough is the nearest good place for food.

☺ 🏰 **North Stainley** SE2876 LIGHTWATER VALLEY THEME PARK Family fun from the nostalgic pleasure of a steamtrain to the white-knuckle, green-faced thrills of one of the world's biggest roller-coasters; another roller-coaster is entirely under ground. Meals, snacks, shop, disabled access; open wknds and bank hols Easter–Oct, and daily Jun–early Sept; (01765) 635368; £11.95 (Aug-Sept), less at other times. There's an adjacent factory shopping village, open all year. The Staveley Arms does decent food.

🏰 🏠 **Norton Conyers** SE3176 (3½ miles N of Ripon) The same family have lived in this late medieval house for 370 years, and the furniture and pictures reflect the fact that it's still very much a family home. Charlotte Brontë used the building as one of her models for Thornfield Hall. Look out for the hoofprint on the stairs. Attractively planted, 18th-c walled garden. Shop (with unusual plants and, in season, garden fruits), limited disabled access; open pm bank hol Sun and Mons, then pm Sun 7 Jun–mid-Sept, plus pm daily 20–25 July, and maybe other dates too; (01765) 640333; £2.95. The Freemasons Arms at Nosterfield is useful for lunch.

🏰 🏠 ❀ **Parcevall Hall Gardens** SE0661 Surrounding an Elizabethan house, 16 acres of woodland gardens charmingly set on a hillside E of the main Wharfedale Valley; superb views from the cliff walk. Snacks, plant sales; cl Nov–Easter exc by appointment; (01756) 720311; *£2. The Craven Arms at nearby Appletreewick is good for lunch, with lovely views.

★ 🏰🏛♿ **Richmond** NZ1701 A most attractive riverside country town, with steep and pretty streets of old stone buildings, and a splendid broad sloping market square (still cobbled, and perhaps the biggest in the country; market day is Sat). It's dominated by the austere and intricate ruins of RICHMOND CASTLE, which overlook the River Swale from a high rocky outcrop. Snacks, shop; cl 1–2pm in winter, 24–26 Dec; (01748) 822493; £1.80. Scollards Hall, which was built in 1080, is possibly the oldest domestic building in Britain. The THEATRE ROYAL (Victoria Rd) is the country's oldest and most authentic working theatre still in its original form, complete with gallery, boxes and pit. Built in 1788, it doesn't look much from the outside but the immaculately restored interior is really special. Shop; guided tours and museum open Easter–Oct (not am Sun); (01748) 823021; £1.50. The GREEN HOWARDS MUSEUM (Market Sq), in a converted 12th-c church, includes amongst duller regimental history the blood-stained pistol holsters of the Grand Old Duke of York. Shop, some disabled access; cl wknds in Feb, Sun in Mar and Nov, am Sun Apr–Oct, and all Dec–Jan; (01748) 822133; *£2. The army connection with the town is still strong; nearby Catterick Camp is the biggest in the north. The Black Lion in Finkle St is good value for lunch.

🏰 ⊛ ♥ ★ **Ripley** SE2860 RIPLEY CASTLE 🖼 (off the A61) Beautifully picturesque castle, in the same family for an amazing 26 generations. Most of the current building dates from the 16th c, inc the tower housing a collection of Royalist armour. For some the main attraction is the splendid gardens, the setting for a national collection of hyacinths and (under glass) a fine tropical plant collection. Also, a birds of prey centre. Meals, snacks, shop, some

disabled access; open wknds Apr, May and Oct, Thurs–Sun Jun and Sept, daily July and Aug; (01423) 770152; *£4.50, gardens only *£2.75. The attractive village, rebuilt in the 1820s, has a superb delicatessen, and the Boar's Head Hotel is a fine old place for lunch.

★ ✝♿ **Ripon** SE3171 On Thurs, colourful stalls fill the attractive and ancient market square (quite a few stalls too on Sat, inc bric-à-brac); it's largely unspoilt, lined with specialist shops and old inns and hotels. At 9pm each night the Wakeman, a red-coated bugler, blows a buffalo horn here, as one has done for centuries. Going from here down one of the town's engagingly narrow old streets, you're rewarded by a magnificent view of the elegant Early English west front of the CATHEDRAL, spectacularly floodlit at night. It's one of the largest half-dozen in the country, and there is plenty to see, inc very fine carving indeed in both stone and wood, and a 7th-c crypt – the oldest surviving part of any British cathedral building (and probably the oldest surviving crypt outside Italy). Shop, disabled access; £2 suggested donation. There's a nicely chilling little PRISON MUSEUM on St Marygate (cl Nov–Easter; £1). The Golden Lion, just off the market sq, is useful for a bite to eat. Fountains Abbey and Markenfield Hall are within a walk from here, and Newby Hall and Norton Conyers are also quite close.

★ 🏛♥ **Settle** SD8264 Market day (Tues) around The Shambles is particularly attractive; look out to the right of here for the Folly, an extraordinary 17th-c town house. Mary Milnthorpe & Daughter is a good antique jewellery and silver shop, and the Golden Lion has decent food. Just across the Ribble, Giggleswick SD8164 is a peaceful contrast to the hectic little town. SETTLE–CARLISLE RAILWAY A magnificent 70-mile route carved up through Ribblesdale across the wild moors between here and Cumbria, and then dropping down through the lovely Eden Valley; (0345) 484950 for times and fares, £15.30 for day return. All year on Sats and some Suns and Weds there's a programme of walks connecting with the moorland stops; they start quite early, (8.45am Sat), with dates and times listed on the timetable. Aside from the setting, it's an ordinary BR line: steamtrains do run most Sats in summer, but only from cities in the South (01543 419472 for routes and times), resulting in the bizarre situation that you can travel by steam if you're coming from Norwich or London, but not if you're in the immediate vicinity. The B6479 is not quite comparable to the train, but a pleasant drive. YORKSHIRE DALES FALCONRY AND CONSERVATION CENTRE (top of Crows Nest, off the A65 N of Settle) Well organised, with lots of vultures, eagles, hawks, falcons and owls, and regular flying displays (from noon). Meals, snacks, shop, disabled access; cl 25 Dec, maybe

Days Out

Malham's limestone wonders
Walk along the Pennine Way to Janet's Foss waterfall; Gordale Scar; lunch down at the Lister Arms, Malham – or picnic; Malham Cove; explore the limestone valley above the limestone pavement towards Malham Tarn (see **Walks** section below).

Caves and waterfalls
Reginald Farrer Trail from Clapham to Ingleborough Cave; lunch at the New Inn in Clapham; Ingleton Falls walk (best part is the first stage to Thornton Force); White Scar Cave if you have time.

Southern gateway to the Dales
Embsay railway; Skipton castle; lunch at the Royal Shepherd in Skipton, or the Angel, Hetton, or Old Hall at Threshfield; Grassington; walk through Strid Wood (see **Walks** section below); Bolton Abbey.

Drive through Wensleydale and Swaledale
Hawes; Bainbridge; lunch at the King's Arms in Askrigg, or the George & Dragon, Aysgarth; Aysgarth Falls; Castle Bolton; Reeth, Gunnerside (old lead mines in Gunnerside Gill), Muker (optional walk along the Swale to Keld and return on the Pennine Way – see **Walks** section below); cross the Buttertubs Pass to return to Hawes.

Stone curios
Brimham Rocks; lunch at the Sportsmans Arms, Wath in Nidderdale; How Stean Gorge (walk nr Lofthouse), Druids Temple (walk nr Ilton) – see **Walks** section below; Jervaulx Abbey – or Masham (for Theakstons Brewery).

Monastic mementos and Georgian follies
Ripon Cathedral; lunch at the Sawley Arms, Sawley; Fountains Abbey and Studley Royal watergarden.

Market town showpiece above the Swale
Richmond; lunch at the Black Lion (Finkle St); walk along the Swale to Easby Abbey; auction at Leyburn (when taking place); Middleham.

Spa treats at Harrogate
Pump Room; coffee at the Assembly Rooms; Turkish baths; lunch at the Tannin Level wine bar or the William & Victoria; Harlow Carr gardens; tea at Betty's (Parliament St).

other days too in winter; (01729) 825164; £4.50.

🏰 ✝ **Skipton** SD9851 On Sat the main street has a colourful market (at least some stalls here most other days too, exc Sun, Tues and Thurs). A canal runs through the town, and the Royal Shepherd, in an attractive spot, has good-value, quick food. The 12th-c CASTLE is properly romantic, with sturdy round towers, broad stone steps, and a lovely central flagstoned and cobbled courtyard with a seat around its venerable yew tree. One of the best-preserved medieval castles in Europe, it really is remarkable how much is left, interior and all – very few other castles have kept their roofs and stayed habitable. The original Norman arched gateway still stands – the word 'Desormais' carved above it is the motto of the family who lived here 1310–1676. Snacks, shop; cl am Sun, 25 Dec; (01756) 792442; *£3.80. The 14th-c CHURCH nearby has a 16th-c rood screen and interesting stained glass.

★ **Particularly attractive villages** here include Askrigg SD9591 – a delightful collection of elegant stone houses around neat streamside greens, walks to nearby waterfalls, a fine 15th-c church, and a nice pub, the King's Arms; and Reeth SE0499, with another high, wide, sloping green (the King's Arms is a popular dining pub, and the B6270 through Swaledale is a very scenic road). Other pretty villages, all with decent pubs, include Appletreewick SE0560, Arncliffe SD9473 (the road up Littondale is pretty, and that to Langcliffe in Ribblesdale runs through dramatic scenery), Austwick SD7768, Bilbrough SE5346, Boroughbridge SE3967, Buckden SD9477, Burnsall SE0361, Cray SD9379, East Witton SE1586 (ancient houses, long wide green), Gargrave SD9354 (on the Pennine Way), Gilling West NZ1804, Grantley SE2369, riverside Grinton SE0598 (charming church, pleasant walks), Hampsthwaite SE2659, Hudswell NZ1400, Kettlewell SD9772 (exhilarating views from the back roads up into Coverdale, and to Hawes via Hubberholme), Kirkby Malham SD8961, Kirkby Overblow SE3249, Langthwaite NZ0003 (good circular walks from the pub – and the Arkengarthdale road up to the remote but very popular Tan Hill Inn is very fine), Linton in Craven SD9962 (a gem), Low Row SD9897 (popular with potholers), Middlesmoor SE0874, Muker SD9097 (very good woollens shop and well liked tearooms), Newton-on-Ouse SE5160, Nun Monkton SE5058 (broad avenue, meeting of rivers Nidd and Ouse), Ogden SE0730, Ramsgill SE1271, Redmire SE0591, Snape SE2784, Stainforth SD8267, Starbotton SD9574, Thornton in Lonsdale SD6873 (Conan Doyle was married in the charming church), Thornton Watlass SE2486, Wath SE1467, West Burton SE0186, and Wigglesworth SD8157. Past Wath and Ramsgill, there's a splendid moorland drive over to Masham.

❗ You can book BALLOON TRIPS from the Flight Centre at Arkendale SE3961, tel (01423) 340664, £115; they also have an authentic Boeing 737 flight simulator, though you may experience some turbulence paying for the £120 session.

Please let us know what you think of places in the *Guide*. Use the report forms at the back of the book or simply send a letter.

Walks

SWALEDALE is the northernmost of all the dales, and one of the least visited – giving more chance of getting away from it all at even peak times. Its bold hills, abundant stone barns and extreme tranquillity make it a walkers' favourite. It's grandly austere for the most part, though quite heavily wooded as it drops down towards Richmond NZ1701. In the steeper parts there are some fine waterfalls. The upper slopes, especially towards the Durham and Cumbrian borders, are wild and empty, except for the huge scattered flocks of hardy, clean-limbed, Swaledale sheep with their dark faces, grey muzzles, thick fleeces and curly-horned rams. The meadowland down in the valleys of this dale and its broad tributary **Arkengarthdale** NZ0003 ⌂-1 is largely unimproved, with slow-growing natural grasses and lots of wild flowers. Many of the area's 1,200 traditional stone hay barns, which are such a distinctive feature here, have been rehabilitated in the last few years, with generous National Parks grant aid. **Gunnerside** SD9598 ⌂-2 still has around it many of the 'rushes' where lead-miners dammed streams to form torrents that could break up the lead-bearing rock strata below; this whole area was an important lead centre until Victorian times, and other visible mementos are ruined mill buildings, tunnel entrances and spoil heaps.

Between **Muker** SD9097 and **Keld** NY8901 ⌂-3, the Swale enters a deeply cut valley and tumbles over waterfalls; there are paths on both sides of the river, or you can take a more upland route over neighbouring Kisdon SD8999. **Reeth** SE0499 ⌂-4 is a centre for rambles ranging from pottering along the meadows by the Swale to walks over moors into adjacent Arkengarthdale (where the ascent on to Fremington Edge NZ0400 is memorable). **Richmond** NZ1701 ⌂-5 gives attractive riverside walks beneath the towering bulk of its castle – E to Easby Abbey NZ1800, or W through Hudswell Woods NZ1400, with an extension to Whitcliffe Scar NZ1302, a cliff above the Swale with an exciting path along its top.

WENSLEYDALE More expansive in character and not quite as dramatic as Swaledale, but richly picturesque; its unspoilt villages and numerous waterfalls make for pleasurable walking. It used to be one of the richest dales, its broad pastures and countless sheep supporting the wealthy abbeys and castles whose ruins now add so much interest to its scenery. Wensleydale sheep are very distinctive, with long, fleecy, dreadlock curls. **Upper Wensleydale** ⌂-6 around and W of Hawes SD8789 is steep and wild; E of here the valley starts widening out, with richer lower pastures, and more regular farmland below Middleham SE1288. Hardraw Force SD8691 is, as we've said, reached through the Green Dragon at Hardraw, but a longer excursion follows the Pennine Way from Hawes and over the River Ure. **Aysgarth Falls** SE0888 ⌂-7, the National Park's chief visitor honeypot, involve a short amble from the car park; or you can contrive longer routes along the S bank of the Ure from the delightful village of West Burton SE0186. **Apedale Head** SE0095 ⌂-8 is reached by a 3-mile plod up tracks NW of Castle Bolton SE0392; on fine days it feels like the top of the world, with views encompassing both Wensleydale and Swaledale. **Raydale** SD8288 ⌂-9, nr Bainbridge SD9390, is the most interesting of Wensleydale's subsidiary valleys for walkers. Its lower neck is quite narrow, but it broadens out into quite a wide, sheltered bowl of valley, with Semer Water SD9187, a sizeable glacial lake which legend has it was conjured up by a wandering beggar to drown a village which had spurned him. It's Yorkshire's third largest natural lake, and has a path along its half-mile-long S side, but to make up circular routes you have to do some road walking. The walled track (a Roman road), just N, has wide-ranging views as it descends to Bainbridge. **Widdale** SD8288 ⌂-10, with extensive conifer plantations above it, **Sleddale** SD8586 ⌂-11 above Hawes, and the broader **Bishopdale** ⌂-12 SD9885 are steep-sided and dramatic. **Coverdale** SD0582

⌂-13, Wensleydale's major tributary valley, is relatively very quiet; fairly gentle in its lower reaches, climbing high into a wild and untamed-feeling world of lonely sheep farms.

WHARFEDALE, with its tributary valley Littondale and its headwaters up in the steep conifer plantations at the top of Langstrothdale, is one of England's most popular areas for walkers, and very beautiful indeed in parts. The Dales Way follows the River Wharfe for the length of the dale, except between Kettlewell SD9672 and Grassington SE0064. Upper Wharfedale, above Grassington, has a level floor of sheltered, well drained pastures with the river winding through, a few grey stone barns, and steep sides laced with dry-stone walls, gnarled woodland and occasional austere crags, climbing up to high, fairly level tops some 365 metres (1,200 ft) above the valley floor. The smaller villages are delightfully private and unspoilt, their grey or whitewashed stonework blending perfectly with the long scars of the limestone terraces above them. Away from the valley floor, stone-walled grassy tracks are the easiest ways of gaining height. From **Starbotton** SD9574 ⌂-14 a good walk is along the river to Kettlewell, then back up over the high land; or follow less obvious paths W to Arncliffe SD9473 in Littondale – which is very similar to the parent valley, though with a flatter, damper valley floor. From **Hubberholme** SD9178 ⌂-15 a walk not to be missed is up to Scar House SD8998 and along a level turfy terrace, which commands magnificent views down the dale, to Cray SD9379. Both hamlets have good inns, and the walk can be expanded to include Buckden SD9447 – in fact there are worthwhile walks between all the Wharfedale/Littondale places marked on our map, with decent pub food available in each of them.

Below Grassington, there's an extremely pretty stretch where the valley winds more sinuously past **Burnsall** SE0361 ⌂-16, Appletreewick SE0560 and Bolton Abbey SE0754, below which though less grand are more varied in shape, with rather sensitively laid out conifer plantations adding a slightly subalpine feel to some of the views. There's a rewarding walk from Hebden SE0263 up Hebden Beck, with its legacy of old lead-mine workings; the route can be extended to take in Grassington and the path along the River Wharfe.

Around **Bolton Abbey** ⌂-17 the landscape has a lowland beauty: the ruined abbey, the turf banks of the Wharfe and the oaks of the Strid Wood SE0656, where a leaflet detailing nature trails is available. A steep ascent from Howgill SE0659 is rewarded by views from Simon's Seat SE0759, perched on the edge of moors.

RIBBLESDALE climbs above Settle into severe and grand mountain scenery, craggy and remote: this is a major magnet for walkers on the Three Peaks Walk, 24 miles taking in the summits of Ingleborough SD7474, Pen-y-ghent SD8473 and Whernside SD9975. This is a tough undertaking in its entirety, but each of the peaks on its own is a manageable half-day excursion: choose a clear day – not just for the magnificent views but for your own safety.

Ingleborough (721 metres – 2,376 ft) ⌂-18 is best approached from Clapham SD7569, along the Reginald Farrer Trail (see Clapham entry above), past Ingleborough Cave SD7571 (guided visits) and Gaping Gill SD7572 (a vast pothole); the panorama extends far across Lancs and into Cumbria. **Pen-y-ghent** (694 metres – 2,277 ft) ⌂-19, reached from Horton in Ribblesdale SD8072, has a satisfyingly compact summit, the craggiest feature on the Pennine Way, which nr here passes some potholes inc Hull Pot.

Whernside (736 metres – 2,415 ft) ⌂-20, sometimes criticised as the boring one of the three, is Yorkshire's highest point, and has an exhilarating ridge section; start from the magnificent Ribblehead Viaduct SD7779 carrying the Settle–Carlisle railway over the head of the dale (the Station Hotel here is a comfortable halt). Upper Ribblesdale is riddled with impressive potholes, some of them gaping chasms of sensational size that can be admired from the surface, as well as the intricate underground passages that make the area so popular with cavers. Up in the loneliest parts, useful refuges are the cheerful cavers' inn, the Old Hill at Chapel le Dale SD7477, and the isolated Station Inn at Ribblehead SD7779. At **Stainforth** SD8267 ⌂-21 there is a pleasant, gentle, riverside walk from Stainforth Force SD8167 to Langcliffe SD8971. **Ingleton** SD6972 ⌂-22, on the other side of Ingleborough Hill, has a lovely wooded walk up the River Twiss, over the moor and back down the River Doe, past a series of picturesque waterfalls; not too strenuous, very varied scenery, 2 or 3 hours – the admission fee for this Ingleton Glen is amply justified by the delightful gorge and waterfalls. Below Settle SD8264, the valley is less interesting for walkers, and marred by some quarrying. N of Whernside is Dentdale SD7186 (now in Cumbria), which offers walks along a lonely green track above the S side of the dale.

MALHAMDALE is much smaller, its upper stretches cut tortuously and deeply out of the limestone by the River Aîre and its steep tributaries, leaving spectacular cliffs, extensive, bare upland limestone 'pavements', craggy bowls carved out of the overhanging hillsides, and sparkling waterfalls. This area is understandably a magnet for visitors. Walk along the beck from **Malham** SD8963 ⌂-23, where there is a good National Park information centre and the Lister Arms is a pleasant refuge, to Janet's Foss waterfall SD9163 and to the romantic severity of dramatic Gordale Scar SD9164, the dale's most memorable natural feature, where a beck makes a spectacular leap from the rocks. The Pennine Way N of Malham waterfall ascends the side of Malham Cove SD9864, a great cliff, then crosses a natural rock pavement and heads over a landscape of limestone scars, disappearing streams and green turf to Malham Tarn SD8966, a lovely mountain lake skirted on its E side by a nature trail.

NIDDERDALE is a quiet yet beautiful valley with an impressive, solitary grandeur. Just outside the National Park, it and the hills above are less liberally laced with footpaths and open-access moorland than the other dales here, and attract far fewer visitors – but there are plenty of relatively unfrequented walks, often on good paved but untarred tracks. The **Nidderdale Way** ⌂-24 allows a fine, fairly gentle walk of a couple of hours or so, up on to the high pastures (see lambs being born in spring) and moorland at Glasshouses SE1764 and back, with spectacular views almost all the way. It's well signed; start from Dacre Banks SE1962 and take the lane a couple of hundred yards past the church. The stretch between the attractive small town of Pateley Bridge SE1565 and the little village of Lofthouse SE1073 is dominated by the sheltered 2-mile waters of Gouthwaite Reservoir SE1269, serenely set below the hills with some tall trees alongside. From Lofthouse a path runs beside the River Nidd, with picturesque tracks among small woods and ruined farmhouses, to Scar House Reservoir SE0576, quite exposed at the valley head (there's also a toll road up to it); high, exposed routes line the N side of the dale up here. To the W of Lofthouse, **How Stean Gorge** SE0673 is a spectacular ravine pocked with potholes and caverns; a footpath snakes between miniature cliffs, with bridges giving views into the gorge; there's also a visitor centre.

The area E of the Dales really has nothing to compare with the Dales themselves for serious walking, but the grounds of **Studley Royal** SE2768 ⌂-25 are excellent for strolling, as are **Harlow Carr** gardens SE2854 ⌂-26 on the edge of Harrogate SE2955. The moorland W of Harrogate has some possibilities for more stretching walks, for instance on **Stainburn Moor** SE2352 ⌂-27, from the car park by the woods along the side road W from Beckwithshaw SE2653, or on Denton Moor above the reservoirs S of Blubberhouses SE1655. Nr the hamlet of Ilton SE1978 a no-through road leads up to woodlands, where you can walk to the **Druids Temple** ⌂-28, a scaled-down Stonehenge built by a landowner in the 1820s as work for local unemployed people.

Where to eat

Asenby SE3975 CRAB & LOBSTER (01845) 577286 Old, thatched pub/restaurant with a relaxed, informal but civilised atmosphere; interestingly furnished and cosy with lots of bric-à-brac, delicious food, and good wines by the glass; cl pm Sun, 25 Dec. £25.50|£11.

Askrigg SD9591 ROWAN TREE (01969) 650536 Cosy little candlelit stone barn run by an Irish husband and German wife team; 7 or 8 tables so booking advisable, good, imaginative evening meals and a reasonably priced wine list; cl Sun, Mon, Jan–Feb; children over 10. £21 for 5 courses|£8.

Bilbrough SE5346 THREE HARES (01937) 832128 Smartly refurbished dining pub with a welcoming landlord and staff; traditional bar with lots of polished copper and brass, a no smoking restaurant, very good modern cooking using the freshest local produce, an interesting wine list and well kept real ales; children over 8; cl Mon, 25 Dec, pm 26 Dec, pm 1 Jan; disabled access. £20.25|£6.50.

Boroughbridge SE3967 BLACK BULL St James Sq (01432) 322413 Lovely old inn said to date from the 13th c, with a big stone fireplace in the main bar area (service from an old-fashioned hatch), a cosy traditional snug, and an extended dining room; well presented food – the bread, pasta, sorbets and ice-creams are all home-made – fresh daily fish and lovely puddings, well kept real ales, enjoyable wines with 10 by the glass, afternoon teas (not Sun), friendly and attentive service; also a plump ginger cat, and classical piped music; bedrooms. £17.20|£5.95.

Brearton SE3261 MALT SHOVEL (01423) 862929 Unspoilt village pub with hard-working licensees; heavily beamed rooms with open fires and lively hunting prints, very good bar food (super fresh fish and lovely puddings), well kept real ales, and a fine choice of malt whiskies and wines; cl pm Sun, Mon, 1st 2 wks Jan; disabled access. £15|£5.50.

Carlton SE0684 FORESTERS ARMS (01969) 640272 Friendly, carefully restored inn with log fires, low beams and a nice atmosphere; well kept real ales, a decent choice of whiskies, imaginative food in both the bar and restaurant, and friendly, helpful service; good bedrooms; no food Mon or pm Sun; children over 12 in restaurant in evening. £30|£6.50.

Carthorpe SE3083 FOX & HOUNDS (01845) 567433 Pretty little extended village house with an extended bar, 2 log fires and some evocative Victorian photographs of Whitby; attractive, high-raftered, no smoking restaurant with lots of farm and smithy tools, good, imaginative food (fine daily specials and puddings), decent wines, and helpful service; cl Mon, early Jan; disabled access. £15|£7.95.

East Witton SE1586 BLUE LION (01969) 624273 Stylish and civilised dining pub with a log fire, daily papers, bric-à-brac, and rugs on the flagstones in the distinctive old rooms; exceptionally good and imaginative food, nice breakfasts, decent wines, real ales, and a pretty garden; bedrooms. £31.50|£6.95.

Grassington SE0064 DALES KITCHEN TEAROOM & BRASSERIE 51 Main St (01756) 753208 Former apothecary's house (no smoking) with lovely cakes, scones and so forth, very good, imaginative light lunches, delicious puddings, and a children's menu; cl Christmas wk; disabled access. £15|£4.75.

Harrogate SE3055 BETTYS 1 Parliament St (01423) 502746 Famous cake shop run by the same Swiss family that started this small chain in 1919, with special blends of teas and coffees, Alsace wines, wonderful, light, home-cooked meals and traditional afternoon tea; over 75 different delicious cakes and pastries; cl 25–26 Dec, 1 Jan. £18|£5.80

Harrogate SE3055 LA BERGERIE 11–13 Mount Parade (01423) 500089 Delightful, unassuming, French evening restaurant with freshly prepared and interesting food, and very good French staff; cl Sun and bank hols; disabled access. £15.75.

Harrogate SE3055 TANNIN LEVEL 5 Raglan St (01423) 560595 Very nice basement wine bar with brick walls and country dining chairs; good, often French food, lovely puddings, a fine wine list, and early evening tapas; cl Sun, bank hols; children allowed but not encouraged. £21|£6.95.

Harrogate SE2954 WILLIAM & VICTORIA Cold Bath Rd (01423) 521510 Busy wine bar with an upstairs evening restaurant and hearty helpings of decent country cooking; cl Sun, 1st wk Jan; children over 11. £15|£4.95.

Hetton SD9558 ANGEL (01756) 730263 Extremely popular dining pub with old-fashioned, rambling rooms, consistently excellent and imaginative food, very good service from the hard-working, friendly staff, well kept real ales, and over 300 wines; disabled access. £34|£7.50.

Litton SD9074 QUEENS ARMS (01756) 770208 Welcoming quietly placed 17th-c inn with popular food, a big collection of cigarette lighters in the main bar, another room with more of a family atmosphere, and 2 coal fires; no food Mon; pretty bedrooms; cl Jan; limited disabled access. £13|£3.

Moulton NZ2404 BLACK BULL (01325) 377289 Decidedly civilised, well run pub with old-fashioned style and standards of service; memorable bar snacks (excellent smoked salmon), conservatory restaurant or one in the Brighton Belle Pullman dining car, and good wines; cl Sun, 24–28 Dec; children over 7. £15.50|£5.25.

Pickhill SE3483 NAGS HEAD (01845) 567391 Deservedly popular old inn with a nice mix of customers; busy tap room, smarter lounge, a no smoking restaurant, particularly good food inc interesting daily specials and lovely puddings, friendly and efficient staff, a fine wine list and well kept real ales; bedrooms; disabled access; cl pm 25 Dec. £20|£4.25.

Sawley SE2467 SAWLEY ARMS SE2568 (01765) 620642 Rather smart pub with absolutely stunning flowering tubs and baskets; several small rooms with log fires and comfortable furniture, daily papers to read, a no smoking restaurant, good, enjoyable bar food (inc interesting soups), friendly service, and nice house wines; children over 9. £18.25|£6.

Threshfield SD9763 OLD HALL (01756) 752441 Very busy pub handy for Dales walks; with a lively atmosphere in the 3 communicating, simply decorated rooms, a nice mix of customers, good imaginative food relying on seasonal produce, and well kept real ales; cl Mon; disabled access. £20.40|£9.45.

NORTH YORK MOORS AND EAST YORKSHIRE

Expansive countryside, interesting coast, some classic and unusual places to visit.

The North York Moors National Park has fewer visitors than the Dales: rich valley pastures, with red-tiled stone farmhouses, twisting rivers, quiet roads, and few villages. The higher moorland is generally very grand and empty, mile after mile of heather scoured by breath-snatching winds, where the few walkers have for company scatterings of hardy sheep and the occasional harsh cry of a grouse.

South of here are the gentle rather patrician landscapes of the generously wooded Howardian Hills, and east of those more open rolling wolds – sweeping vistas of low chalk downs dissected by riverless valleys; the B1249 and B1252 out of Driffield and the B1253 west of Bridlington give a good sampling.

All this is enjoyable driving country, with relatively little traffic (though summer traffic is building up on the moors – in 1997 the National Park tried an experimental free bus scheme for people reaching the north edge by car). The pace of change in the landscape often suits driving rather than walking speed, but walkers do have a good choice too, and the paths are less heavily trodden than in the Dales. There are quite a few handsome villages (Coxwold is delightful), and some pleasant small towns such as Helmsley and Beverley.

The coast is splendidly cliffy and full of character north of the attractive, traditional seaside resort of Scarborough (lots to see and do here), with some delightful little fishing villages. The other main seaside resort, Bridlington, is also attractive, with a restrained charm and plenty of family amusements. Whitby is a working fishing port of real individuality – an enjoyable place to stay; Hull is a bigger port, but again has a lot to interest visitors.

The ruins of Rievaulx Abbey have a particularly powerful appeal. Castle Howard is one of England's most magnificent houses, and other great houses include Burton Agnes Hall, Sledmere House and, at Sproatley, Burton Constable Hall – all in splendid grounds. Sutton Park, Duncombe Park on the edge of Helmsley, and Nunnington Hall are also well worth a visit. Eden Camp, just outside Malton, is an unusual re-creation of World War II experiences, and the army transport museum in Beverley is much more fun than you'd guess. Altogether gentler, Music in Miniature at Robin Hood's Bay is charming, as is the Hutton-le-Hole folk museum; and for something different you could try llama-trekking in Staintondale.

Where to stay

Ampleforth SE5678 CARR HOUSE FARM Shallowdale, Ampleforth, York YO6 4ED (01347) 868526 *£30; 3 rms. In peaceful undulating farmland and with an acre of garden, this no smoking, 16th-c stone farmhouse has beams and oak panelling, a flagstoned dining room with a woodburning stove in the inglenook fireplace, separate lounge, and good breakfasts using home-made butter and preserves and fresh farm eggs; cl Christmas and New Year; children over 7; no dogs.

Blakey Ridge SE6897 LION Blakey Ridge, Pickering YO6 6LQ (01751) 417320 £53, plus special breaks; 10 clean rms, most with own bthrm. The 4th-highest inn in England, this has spectacular moorland views, characterful rambling bars, blazing fires (a good place to be snowed up in), and generous helpings of decent food served all day; also, good breakfasts and a candlelit restaurant, 8 real ales, and genuinely friendly licensees and staff; fine walking country; disabled access.

Chop Gate SE5699 HILLEND FARM Chop Gate, Bilsdale, Middlesbrough TS9 7JR (01439) 798278 £40; 2 rms. Friendly 17th-c farmhouse with good home cooking, a comfortable lounge and dining room, and fine walks; on the farm is part of one of the last remaining ancient oak forests; cl Nov–Mar.

Coxwold SE5377 FAUCONBERG ARMS Coxwold, York YO6 4AD (01347) 868214 *£55; 4 rms, 2 with own bthrm. Civilised old stone inn in a lovely setting; big log fire, some handsome settles and gleaming copper in the 2 cosy and comfortably furnished rooms of the lounge bar, good food in both the restaurant and bar, an extensive wine list, and decent breakfasts.

Egton Bridge NZ8105 Horse Shoe Egton Bridge, Whitby YO21 1XE (01947) 895245 *£48, plus special breaks; 6 rms, most with own bthrm. Beautifully placed inn by the River Esk (stepping stones big enough for children to sit on), lots of friendly wild birds, and a pleasant, sheltered lawn; open fires, attractive and traditionally furnished bars, well cooked food inc excellent breakfasts in the cottagey dining room, and decent wines; no accommodation 25 Dec.

Great Ayton NZ5611 Ayton Hall Low Green, Great Ayton, Middlesbrough TS9 6BW (01642) 723595 £90w, plus special breaks; 9 rms. Handsome building in 6 acres of parkland, with elegant day rooms, paintings, antiques and a big collection of commemorative plates; cosy restaurant with interesting food and a thoughtful wine list; archery, tennis, croquet and clay-pigeon shooting.

Harome SE6482 Pheasant Harome, Helmsley, YO6 5JG (01439) 771241 *£80, plus special breaks; 12 rms. Family-run hotel with a relaxed, homely lounge and traditional bar with beams, inglenook fireplace and flagstones; good, very popular food, efficient service, and an indoor heated swimming pool; cl Dec–Feb; children over 7; disabled access.

Hartoft End SE7593 Blacksmiths Arms Hartoft End, Rosedale Abbey, Pickering YO18 8EN (01751) 417331 *£70, plus special breaks; 14 rms. Carefully extended and modernised former farmhouse in lovely surroundings at the foot of Rosedale; with a friendly, traditionally furnished bar, open fires in the cosy and comfortable lounges, and imaginative food in the spacious and attractive restaurant; lovely walks all round.

Hawnby SE5690 Laskill Farm Easterside, Hawnby, York YO6 5NB (01439) 798268 *£47; 7 rms, most with own bthrm, and some in a beamy, converted outside building. Attractive and welcoming, creeper-covered stone house on a big sheep and cattle farm nr Rievaulx Abbey; open fire and books in the comfortable lounge, good food using home-grown produce, and their own natural spring water; partial disabled access.

Helmsley SE6183 Black Swan Market Pl, Helmsley YO6 5BJ (01439) 770466 £168, plus special breaks; 44 well equipped and comfortable rms. Striking Georgian house and adjoining Tudor rectory with a beamed and panelled hotel bar, attractive carved oak settles and Windsor armchairs, cosy and comfortable lounges with lots of character, and a charming, sheltered garden; disabled access.

Helmsley SE6183 Feathers Market Pl, Helmsley YO6 5BH (01439) 770275 £60, plus special breaks; 13 rms. Handsome and atmospheric old inn with heavy beams, dark panelling and log fires; good-value, well prepared food in both the restaurant and comfortable lounge bar, lots of wines, well kept beers, and an attractive back garden.

Hovingham SE6675 Worsley Arms Hovingham, York YO6 4LA (01653) 628234 *£80, plus special breaks; 18 individually decorated bedrooms. Stonebuilt Georgian inn with comfortable and pretty sitting rooms, fresh flowers and open fires, and carefully cooked food in the elegant restaurant; also, seats out by the stream; disabled access.

Kilburn SE5179 Forresters Arms Kilburn, York YO6 4AH (01347) 868386 *£58, plus special breaks; 10 clean, bright rms. Friendly old coaching inn opposite the pretty village gardens; with sturdy but elegant furnishings made next door at the Thompson furniture workshop, a big log fire, and decent food in both the restaurant and beamed bar; disabled access.

Kirkbymoorside SE6986 George & Dragon 17 Market Pl, Kirkbymoorside, York YO6 6AA (01751) 433334 *£79, plus special breaks; 19 large luxurious rms in a converted corn mill and ex-rectory behind. Handsome 17th-c coaching inn, very well run, with excellent food using the best local produce in the elegant restaurant, and a particularly fine choice of wines (the owner used to be a wine merchant) and whiskies; pretty, beamed residents' lounge, warm and friendly staff, log fire in the relaxed, beamed bar, well kept real ales, and peaceful gardens; activity breaks, too.

Lastingham SE7391 LASTINGHAM GRANGE Lastingham, York YO6 6TH (01751) 417345 £181, plus special breaks; 11 rms. Attractive, stone-walled country house in 10 acres of neatly kept gardens and fields – with the moors beyond; relaxed and homely atmosphere in the spacious lounge, open fire, fine breakfasts and dinners, extremely helpful service, and marvellous nearby walks; cl Dec–Feb.

Middleton SE7885 COTTAGE LEAS COUNTRY HOTEL Nova Lane, Middleton, Pickering, YO18 8PN (01751) 472129 £70, plus special breaks; 12 comfortable rms. Delightful 18th-c farmhouse with extensive gardens, comfortable and informal rooms, beamed ceilings, an open log fire in cosy lounge, and a snug bar; pets by prior arrangement; disabled access.

Nafferton TA0559 WOLD HOUSE Nafferton, Driffield YO25 0LD (01377) 254242 *£55; 6 rms. Informal and comfortable, early 19th-c country house with panoramic views, friendly service, and traditional English cooking; outdoor pool, putting green and snooker; cl Christmas.

Pickering SE7984 WHITE SWAN Market Pl, Pickering YO18 7AA (01751) 472288 *£70, plus special breaks; 12 comfortable rms. Inviting, small and quiet, plush hotel bar, friendly staff and locals, log fires, and antiques in the comfortable, beamed, residents' lounge; good, traditional bar food, attractive restaurant with fine clarets and daily changing food using the best local produce, and breakfasts with home-made marmalade; pets welcome.

Robin Hood's Bay NZ9504 COBLE Covet Hill, Robin Hood's Bay YO22 4SN (01947) 880042 *£38, plus special breaks; 3 rms, 1 with own shower. 17th-c former coastguard's cottage by the beach with views over the bay from both the lounge and sun terrace; warm, friendly and caring owners, and huge, first-class breakfasts (8 courses); good nearby walks.

Robin Hood's Bay NZ9504 ROUNTON HOUSE Mount Pleasant South, Robin Hood's Bay, Whitby YO22 4PD (01947) 880341 £32; 3 rms, shared bthrm. Big, friendly, family Victorian house with homely rooms, a relaxed atmosphere, good breakfasts served at one big table in the dining room, and a pleasant garden with summerhouse; cl Dec–Jan; well behaved dogs allowed.

Rosedale Abbey SE7395 MILBURN ARMS Rosedale Abbey, Pickering YO18 8RA (01751) 417312 £68, plus special breaks; 11 rms. Friendly, 18th-c inn in a village surrounded by fine steep moorland; with a log fire and books in the comfortable drawing room, traditionally furnished beamed bar, very good English cooking in the attractive restaurant, decent wine list, excellent breakfasts, and helpful staff; cl last 2 wks Jan; pets welcome by prior arrangement.

Rosedale Abbey SE7294 WHITE HORSE FARM HOTEL Rosedale Abbey, Pickering YO18 8SE (01751) 417239 £70, plus special breaks; 15 rms. Friendly country hotel, above the village, in 11 acres, with marvellous views; cosy, beamed bar and a log fire, comfortable lounge, generously served food, and a decent range of wines and malt whiskies; excellent nearby walks; cl 24–25 Dec; dogs by prior arrangement.

Scalby TA0191 WREA HEAD Scalby, Scarborough YO13 0PP (01723) 378211 £115, plus special breaks; 21 individually decorated rms. Victorian country house in 14 acres of parkland and gardens; with friendly staff, a minstrels' gallery in the oak-panelled hall and lounge, open fires, a bow-windowed library, pretty flowers, and good food in the airy restaurant; disabled access.

Wass SE5679 WOMBWELL ARMS Wass, York YO6 4BE (01347) 868280 £49, plus special breaks; 2 individually furnished rms. Attractive, warmly welcoming small inn with a cosy, rambling bar, imaginative food and fine wines, and enjoyable breakfasts; cl 10 days Jan; children over 8.

Wharram le Street SE8666 RED HOUSE Wharram le Street, Malton YO17 9TL

(01944) 768455 *£50, plus special breaks; 3 rms. Spacious and comfortable country house with friendly owners, log fires in the sitting rooms, good home cooking in the dining room (using home-grown produce where possible), and a lovely garden with tennis court; cl Christmas wk; pets welcome.

Willerby TA9028 WILLERBY MANOR Well Lane, Willerby, Hull HU10 6ER (01482) 652616 £60w; 51 rms. Family-owned Victorian house in 3 acres of gardens, with an airy conservatory/dining bar and a more formal restaurant, good food and helpful service; cl 25 Dec.

To see and do

❀ ✦ **Acklam** NZ4917 BOTANIC CENTRE (Ladgate Lane) Thriving environmental demonstration centre, developing all the time, with organic gardens, nature trails, and a number of re-created natural habitats (moorland, wetlands, etc.) under construction. Splendid home-cooked meals and snacks, shop, disabled access; cl 25 Dec; (01642) 594895; £3.

✦ ♣ **Bempton Cliffs** TA2074 The RSPB BIRD RESERVE here has the biggest colony of seabirds in the country, with up to a quarter of a million of them nesting in the cliffs. Best views of puffins Jun–July, but plenty of skuas and shearwaters later in summer, with weekend BOAT TRIPS from Flamborough (North Landing) or Bridlington, though what you'll see depends on the weather. Snacks, disabled access; visitor centre cl all Jan, wknds Dec and Feb; (01262) 851179 – book well ahead for the boats; £1.50 car parking charge. Local fishermen run early summer weekend boats to the cliffs too.

★ ✝ ✚ 🏚 🏮 🛆 🏢 **Beverley** TA0340 An attractive country town, in a way like a small-scale York, with much the same sort of appeal. It's partly pedestrianised, with many fine Georgian buildings, several antique shops and the like, but unlike York is still very much an honest market town rather than a tourist place. Up to 1,000 animals, mainly pigs, are still sold at the Tues and Thurs market, and the racecourse is central to local life. The B1248 N has rolling Wolds views. The MINSTER is a wonderful 12th/14th-c building, with elegant buttressing and elaborately pinnacled towers. The west front is

richly carved yet extraordinarily harmonious. Inside are several delights, inc the intricately carved Percy tomb canopy, the unusual Saxon *fridstol* (one of only two such seats in the country), and the biggest collection of misericords in Britain. Shop, disabled access; guided tours summer only; £2 suggested donation. The former wealth of the town can be guessed at from the magnificence of another subsidiary church not far away, ST MARY'S CHURCH in Hengate; the weather-vane on the south-west turret is said to have been the last design by Pugin, who sketched it on the back of an envelope. Opposite is the White Horse, a quaint, old, gaslit, bare-boarded tavern (for meals, the comfortably traditional Beverley Arms and the cheap Queen's Head are good).

MUSEUM OF ARMY TRANSPORT (Flamingate) Huge hangar with all sorts of military vehicles inc planes, tanks and cars, many displayed in realistic settings – down to farm-building camouflage for the Second World War and scratchy sand for the Gulf War. Children can climb into the jeeps and so on. Some vehicles may be demonstrated on summer Suns. Meals, snacks, shop, disabled access; cl 24–26 Dec; (01482) 860445; £4. You can visit parts of the mostly Georgian GUILDHALL on Register Sq, best on bank hols or Weds May–Sept when more rooms are open and guides are in attendance (cl winter Suns, free), and the ART GALLERY AND MUSEUM (Champney Rd) includes lots of pieces by Fred Elwell the woodcarver, most famous for his work in the Minster (cl 12.30–1.30pm wknds, all Mon and

Tues, 25–26 Dec, 1 Jan; free).

★ ☙ **Blacktoft** SE8424 An attractive Humber-side village; its pub the Hope & Anchor, with tables out by the waterside, is great for birdwatchers, being right by the RSPB marsh reserve.

✝☗❀⚊♪🏠🐎🏛❗🎞🏛🐎☙

Bridlington TA1766 Famous for its bracing image in the heyday of the traditional seaside resort, and the way the country rolls down to the long sands of the shore still gives that feeling. The centre is a quay and small harbour, with the usual summer attractions, but the original core of the town is half a mile in from the sea, with some charming old houses among the more modern ones around the heavily restored PRIORY CHURCH. A 14th-c gateway gives some idea of how imposing the priory must have been before the Dissolution, and now houses a local history museum (open pm Tues–Thurs, Jun–Sept; £1). HARBOUR MUSEUM AND AQUARIUM (Harbour Rd) The best place to find out about the town's seafaring heritage; shop, disabled access; cl winter wkdys; *40p. SEWERBY HALL (NE edge of Bridlington) In spacious parkland right on the coast, with a miniature zoo and aviary (good for children), and a charming garden. The elegant, early 18th-c house includes some Amy Johnson memorabilia – the pioneer aviator lived nearby. Snacks, shop, disabled access (but not to the Hall); grounds open daily all year, house open Mar–mid-Jan, though only Sat–Tues out of season; (01262) 673769; £2.60. There's a good MODEL VILLAGE in Bondville. Disabled access; cl Oct–Apr; (01262) 401736; *£2.50. A walk along the low cliff from here towards Flamborough Head soon brings you to a strip of woodland by a stream; if you follow the lane up from here past the car park and along the wood, you come to Iron Age earthworks which cut right across the head – making it a pretty impressive defensive position. PARK ROSE POTTERY (Carnaby Covert Lane, off the A614 SW of Bridlington) Factory visits and a seconds shop, as well as 12 acres of strollable parkland with play areas, an owl sanctuary and a new bee exhibition. Meals, snacks, shop, disabled access; cl Christmas wk; (01262) 602823; site entry free, £2 owl sanctuary. Also out here you can tour JOHN BULL'S WORLD OF ROCK (Carnaby Industrial Estate), and maybe even personalise your own stick of the seaside favourite. Cl winter wknds, Christmas; (01262) 678525; £1 factory and exhibition. Broadacres (A165) has reliable family food inc a carvery. The coast to the S is generally much flatter.

🖼☗★ **Brompton** SE9683 WORDSWORTH GALLERY (Gallows Hill) The former home of Mary Hutchinson, who married William Wordsworth at Brompton Church in 1802. The medieval barn has an exhibition on the poet and Samuel Coleridge, as well as an exhibition of paintings and prints. Meals, snacks, shop; cl 25–26 Dec, most of Jan; (01723) 863298. The village is pretty, and the Cayley Arms does good food.

🏠🖼🐎✝ **Burton Agnes** TA1063 BURTON AGNES HALL Marvellous, richly decorated Elizabethan house, with a fantastically carved great hall, 16th-c antiques, and some splendid Impressionist paintings. A fine woodland garden has colourful borders, a pets corner and a topiary walk to an orangery. Meals, snacks, shop, disabled access to ground floor only; cl Nov–Mar; (01262) 490324; £4. The earlier Norman manor house stands between here and the church. The attractive CHURCH at nearby Kilham has a memorable Norman door; the 18th-c Bell in Driffield is pleasant for lunch.

🏛 **Byland Abbey** SE5579 The jagged ruins of this abbey, built for the Cistercians, date from the 12th and 13th centuries. Enough detail survives to show how fine it must have been: look out for the well preserved floor tiles and carved stone. Good for picnics. Snacks, shop, some disabled access; cl Nov–Mar; (01347) 868614; £1.40. The nearby Abbey Inn is most enjoyable for lunch. The drive past here from Bagby (SE of Thirsk), Kilburn and Coxwold, and

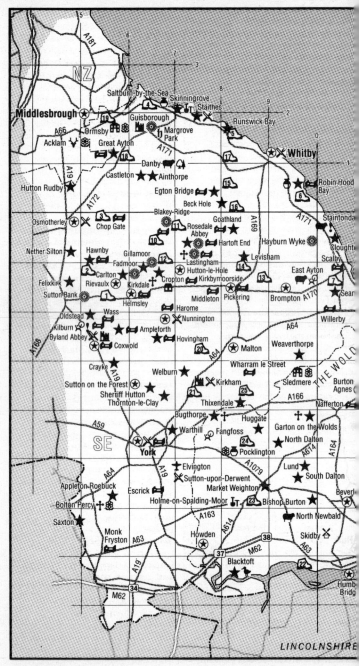

on via Wass and Ampleforth to
Oswaldkirk is very pleasant.

★ 🏛 🎪 † **Coxwold** SE5377 Neat and
very attractive, little stonebuilt

North & East Yorkshire, Humberside & Cleveland

0 Miles 10
0 Kilometres 16

ewlands 2
9
arborough
Filey
Bempton Cliffs
Flamborough
Flamborough Head
Bridlington
14
Foston on
the Wolds
A165
TA
Hornsea
A165
Sproatley
Hull
A1033
Withernsea
Patrington
River Humber
Spurn Head

village, very harmonious. Laurence Sterne's quaint SHANDY HALL has been

well restored, the little study much as it must have been when he wrote *Tristram Shandy* here. Outside is a lovely walled garden. Shop with unusual plant sales; open May–Sept, house pm Weds and Sun, gardens daily exc Sat; (01347) 868465; *£2. Close by is the the handsome 15th-c CHURCH of which Sterne was curate – it still has the box pews it had in his day. The Fauconberg Arms does good food. NEWBURGH PRIORY (just S of Coxwold) Charming old house, partly Norman with Tudor and Georgian additions. One of the family married Oliver Cromwell's daughter, who is supposed to have rescued her father's headless corpse and had it reburied here; the room with the tomb is on the tour. Outside is a 40-acre lakeside and riverside garden with a fine collection of dogwoods, splendid formal borders and lots of unusual plants; also a miniature railway, children's adventure garden, woodland trail and 19th-c statuary walk. Snacks; open pm Weds and Sun Apr–Jun; (01347) 868435; £3.50, grounds only £1.50.

☎ **Cropton** SE7689 The small, family-run CROPTON BREWERY has guided tours on the hour (10–4pm summer, 10–2pm winter), and samples of their robustly flavoured beers, as well as a children's treasure hunt, and a good adjacent pub, the New Inn; disabled access to ground floor; (01751) 417310; *£2.25.

🐖 ♠ **Danby** NZ7008 MOORS CENTRE (Lodge Lane) Helpful National Park information centre, with exhibitions, guided walks and events, and an adventure playground; terraced riverside and woodland grounds. Meals, snacks, shop, disabled access; cl wkdys Oct–Easter; (01287) 660540; free. The Duke of Wellington has good-value food.

🐖 ♠ **East Ayton** TA0085 HONEY FARM ▣ (Betton Farm Centre) Exhaustive exhibition on bees and honey-making, with sales of wax and honey-based products. Also animals, craft shops, farm shop and a play area. Meals, snacks, disabled access; (01723) 864001; *£2.95. The

Londesborough Arms at Seamer has decent food, and the Forge Valley drive to Hackness runs through ancient woodlands.

🏇 **Fangfoss** SE7653 ROCKING HORSE SHOP Splendid collection of antique rocking horses; you can watch replicas being constructed, and buy either a finished horse or plans for doing it yourself. Open by appointment (not Sun), (01759) 368737.

⛱ **Filey** TA1180 Much quieter seaside resort than Scarborough, its neighbour up the coast, with the main road dropping down a steep little valley between the church and the old town (and under a footbridge linking the two) to the beach, where fishermen still haul up their boats. There's a small and attractively homely, summer local MUSEUM in medieval fishermen's cottages (Queen St; cl 1–2pm and am Sat). The rock reef N of the town beyond the sands is interesting; to the S are holiday camps, and the seafront Coble Landing Bar has decent food and great views.

✝ ❀ **Flamborough** TA2270 A blowy place, high on the headland, with some old houses at its core around the 15th-c CHURCH; down below, past the holiday camp, the natural rock harbour is well sheltered, with a lifeboat station, and there are fine views of coast and sea from the point of the headland, by the lighthouse. Flamborough Marine sell a local version of guernseys, weatherproof 'ganseys', hand-knitted in the round. The Seabirds is good for lunch, and the B1259 and B1229 are the most interesting coast roads.

🐗 **Foston on the Wolds** TA1055 CRUCKLEY FARM Friendly working farm, with lots of animals to fuss over – inc some very strange-looking rare breeds. Daily milking displays (usually around 10.45am). Snacks, shop; cl Oct–Apr; (01262) 488337; £2.75. The Trout at Wansford has decent food.

★ **Goathland** NZ8301 In the heart of the moors, the picturesque setting for TV's *Heartbeat*; filming can be rather intrusive, and some villagers have started to wonder how they can cope with the coachloads of tourists, but there are interesting walks from here (see **Walks** section below), and the Mallyan Spout Hotel does popular food.

🏰 ❀ **Guisborough** NZ6115 This market town has attractive corners, and GUISBOROUGH PRIORY, a 14th-c ruined church, one huge window rising dramatically from the rest of the more or less foundation-level ruins. The gatehouse is fairly well preserved, and it's an atmospheric spot for a picnic. Shop; cl Mon Oct–Mar, 24–26 Dec, 1 Jan; 85p. The Fox nearby has decent food, and out at Newton (on the A173) the King's Head is a popular dining pub by Roseberry Topping viewpoint (see **Walks** section below).

❀ **Hayburn Wyke** TA0097 From the very well sited hotel here (good-value Sun carvery), steep Victorian woodland paths wind down to the cliff-sheltered cove; a clifftop path to the S gives fine views.

★ 🏰 🐾 ✙ **Helmsley** SE6183 Lanes run straight up on to the moors from this attractive small market town (the B1257 is one of the best moorland roads). There's a large cobbled square (busy Fri market), and enough antique shops and craft shops to please a visitor without seeming too touristy. A lively and bustling place, with a lot of class. It's dominated by the 12th-c CASTLE, ruined in 1644, and standing within enormous earthworks; good for picnics. Shop; cl 1–2pm, winter Mon and Tues; (01439) 770442; £2. DUNCOMBE PARK Beautifully restored, early 18th-c house, rebuilt after a fire at the turn of this century. The landscaped gardens, with grand terracing, are magnificent, covering around a tenth of the 300 acres of memorable parkland. Meals, snacks, shop, some disabled access; cl Thurs/Fri Apr and Oct, and all Nov–Mar; (01439) 770213; *£4.95, gardens only *£2.75. You can wander through the estate (recently granted nature reserve status) for £1. Besides the other hotels and inns we recommend, the courtyard café outside the

Edinburgh Woollen Mill does imaginative light lunches. A rewarding and very varied drive is past Rievaulx Abbey, Old Byland and Cold Kirby to Sutton Bank, left along the A170, then next right turn to Kilburn, Coxwold, Byland Abbey and back via Ampleforth and Oswaldkirk.

⊹† Holme upon Spalding Moor
SE8138 MAJOR BRIDGE PARK (Selby Rd) Private collection of working rural equipment and vintage fairground rides (you can go on these), with nature trails through the surrounding countryside. Snacks, shop, disabled access; open Thurs and Sun May–Sept, daily (exc Sat) in Aug; (01430) 860992; *£1. The Red Lion has good food.

🏠 🦋 ☺ 🐾 ☺ 🐦 Hornsea TA1947
Sizeable east coast resort, home to one of the area's most visited attractions, the HORNSEA FREEPORT 🖼 (Rolston Rd), a developing leisure centre based around a factory shopping village. Several well known brands and stores (some good bargains), and family-orientated features such as butterflies, vintage cars, a model village, small children's zoo, and an adventure playground. Meals, snacks, shop, disabled access; cl 25–26 Dec; (01964) 534211; *£5 for everything, though you can buy individual tickets for each attraction. Next door is a well established working POTTERY. The enthusiastic MUSEUM (Newbegin) has regular craft demonstrations; cl Nov–Easter; (01964) 533443; £2. Behind the town, Hornsea Mere, 2 miles long, is the biggest natural lake in this region, with herons and other birds.

★ † 🏛 Howden SE7528
Unpretentiously attractive place, with cobbled alleys, a fine market hall, a majestic MINSTER with a tall tower, the ruins of a charming medieval chapter house, and a small marshland country park, down the lane opposite the Minster, with ponds and raised walkways. The White Horse is useful for lunch.

🏠 ☸ ☂ 🖼 🏰 ⊹† Hull TA0928
Kingston-upon-Hull is the full name of this big port, surprisingly pleasant for visitors now that the former docks have been so well tidied up. The landing stage for the former Humber ferry has become an attractive pedestrian enclave with some solid, well restored Georgian buildings, and nice Humber views from the waterfront Minerva (which brews its own beer). Nearby, the original dock has become a yacht marina, with quite cheerfully buoyant modern buildings around it. Away from the water, some of the most ancient buildings in the narrow streets of the old town have survived, notably on the High St. One of the most delightful old buildings is the Olde Whyte Harte just off Silver St; it was in its heavily panelled upper room that the town's governor made the fateful decision to lock the town's gate against King Charles in 1642, depriving him of the arsenal that might otherwise have swung the Civil War in his favour. These 2 enclaves, the old town and former docks, are separated from each other by good main roads through to the modern container and ferry docks; the traffic just sweeps by, leaving them as self-contained islands – very quiet at weekends.

Hull's clutch of museums are mostly concentrated in the old town, so it's easy to walk from one to another. It's impossible to miss the TOWN DOCKS MUSEUM (Queen Victoria Sq), a massive yet solidly stylish 3-domed Victorian building, with good displays on Hull's maritime history. There's a long-established section on whales and whaling, and the huge skeletons on display were mentioned in *Moby Dick*. Shop, disabled access; cl Christmas wk; (01482) 613902; £1. The next 6 exhibitions share the same opening times, telephone number, and price. WILBERFORCE HOUSE (High St) William Wilberforce was born in this 17th-c house, and its Jacobean and Georgian rooms have an interesting exploration of the horrors of the slave trade and the struggle for its abolition; also a notable collection of dolls. The Olde Black Boy nearby was the site of slave auctions. FERENS

ART GALLERY (Queen Victoria Sq) Enterprisingly run general collection, with lots of maritime paintings and Dutch old masters; particularly strong on Frank Brangwyn. MUSEUM OF TRANSPORT (High St) Recently doubled in size, this expanding collection is devoted mainly to local public transport and bicycles, some weird and wonderful, with a few interactive displays. The HULL AND EAST RIDING MUSEUM on the High St has re-opened after refurbishment, and contains some fine mosaics, and the OLD GRAMMAR SCHOOL (South Church Side) has a rapidly expanding social history collection. SPURN LIGHTSHIP (Princes Dock) Operating from the 1920s to the 1970s, and now moored in Hull Marina – interesting to go below decks and imagine being confined to this for weeks at a time, not going anywhere, tossed about in storms or blanketed in fog.

MAISTER HOUSE (High St) Only the staircase and entrance hall are open in this mid-18th-c building (the rest is still used as offices), but the Palladian staircase is splendid, and the doors ornate and finely carved. Cl wknds and public hols; 80p; NT. WATER MUSEUM (Springhead Ave) Its main feature is a beam engine that in its day could raise about a million litres of water an hour from the well below. Shop, limited disabled access; open pm Fri–Sun, cl Dec; (01482) 652283; free.

❋ 🐝 🐟 **Humber Bridge** TA0224 The longest single-span suspension bridge in the world, nearly a mile between the towers, and a very impressive sweep of engineering (there's a footway across as well as the road). At the N end is the HUMBER BRIDGE COUNTRY PARK, with plenty of woodland and clifftop walks, and an old mill. Meals, snacks, shop, good disabled access; (01482) 884883.

★ ☷ ⬇️ **Hutton-le-Hole** SE7090 Neat and pretty streamside village at the mouth of Farndale; sheep wander the streets – though they won't be alone in the summer months. Its excellent FOLK MUSEUM is practically a village itself, made up of various old buildings from the area re-erected in the 2-acre grounds, inc an Elizabethan manor house, gypsy caravan, and an Edwardian photographic studio. Shop, disabled access; cl Nov–Mar; (01751) 417367; £3. The Crown here is useful for lunch, and the Blakey Ridge road to Castleton is a great drive.

❦ ! **Kilburn** SE5179 This quiet village is almost a place of pilgrimage to the Robert Thompson FURNITURE WORKSHOP, famous for the unobtrusive little mouse carved as a trademark that you'll see all over North Yorks, on church pews and in the better inns and pubs. A visitor centre traces the company's history, and you can watch the craftsmen at work. Shop; cl Mon (exc bank hols and Jun–Sept), and Nov–Mar; (01347) 868218; £1.50. They make lovely, simple furniture – though not cheap (for a wider choice you might try the Old Mill at nearby Balk SE4881, where the craftsmen include an ex-Thompson employee and prices seem lower). The oak they use can be seen all around. Nr the church (with a memorial to Thompson carved by his own craftsmen), the Singing Bird does refreshments, as does the Forresters Arms – full of Thompson work. Up above the village, on Roulston Scar, is a WHITE HORSE cut in the turf in 1857 and unique in this part of the country.

🏛️ **Kirkham** SE7365 KIRKHAM PRIORY Remains of an Augustinian priory in an attractive, quiet spot by the River Derwent; finely sculpted lavatorium, graceful arcaded cloister, and a handsome, 13th-c gatehouse with some neatly carved sculptures and shields. Shop, disabled access; open pm Apr–Sept; (01653) 618768; £1.40. The Stone Trough overlooking the ruins is good for lunch.

🏠 ▣ 🐝 ☷ ! 🚌 **Malton** SE7871 CASTLE HOWARD (off the A64 W of Malton) Quite magnificent 18th-c palace designed by Sir John Vanbrugh, who up to then had no architectural experience whatsoever, but went on to create Blenheim Palace. The striking 90-metre (300-ft) long façade is topped with a marvellous painted and gilded dome, an unforgettable sight beyond the lake as you approach from the N. Splendid apartments, sculpture gallery and long gallery (192 ft to be exact), a glorious chapel with stained glass by Burne-Jones, and beautiful paintings inc a Holbein portrait of Henry VIII. The grounds are impressive but inviting, inc the domed Temple of the Four Winds by Vanbrugh, a lovely rose garden and the family mausoleum designed by Hawksmoor. Also a fantastic collection of period costume, and a good, unobtrusive adventure playground. Meals, snacks, shop, disabled access; cl Nov–mid-Mar; (01653) 648333; £6.50. A grand public road runs through the grounds, from Slingsby on the B1257.

EDEN CAMP (A64/A169 N of Malton) Elaborately re-created wartime scenes in the buildings of a former prisoner-of-war camp, very well done with sound, smells and even smoke effects. Covers a wide range of World War II experiences, from the rise of the Nazis to the Blitz and Bomber Command ops room. There's a children's commando assault course, but it's perhaps the wartime generation that will get most out of the place. Meals and snacks in NAAFI, shop, disabled access; cl 24 Dec–12 Jan; (01653) 697777; £3.50.

EDEN FARM (Old Malton) Working farm with animals, trails, a working gin wheel and combine harvester, and daily dog, duck and parrot shows. Snacks, shop, disabled access; cl Sat, and Nov–Mar; (01653) 692093; *£2.50.

Malton itself is a comfortable market town with some interesting side streets, in prosperous farming and racehorse-training country. Sat is a busy market day (the lively livestock mart is on Tues and Fri). The Cornucopia (Commercial St, Norton) is a well run dining pub, and the Royal Oak and King's Head do good, generous food; handier for Castle Howard is the decent food at the Bay Horse at Terrington SE6571. A scenic road towards York is the old coach road parallel to the A64, from Norton to Buttercrambe and Gate Helmsley.

ꔛ **Margrove Park** NZ6516 SOUTH CLEVELAND HERITAGE CENTRE Right on the edge of the moors, with natural history and wildlife exhibitions, and can organise walks and nature trails. Meals, snacks, shop, disabled access; cl am Sun, all Fri and Sat, and every am in winter; (01287) 610368; free.

★ **Market Weighton** SE8742 Neat and pleasant old market town with one or two useful antique shops; the Londesborough Arms has interesting food (and comfortable bedrooms).

ꔛ 🐾 **Middlesbrough** NZ4920 Not a particular attraction for visitors, but it does have good places to visit nearby. Its TRANSPORTER BRIDGE (A178) across the Tees is unique, with the central section serving as a ferry, every 15 minutes shuttling cars and pedestrians across the river; cl am Sun. DORMAN MUSEUM (Linthorpe Rd) Summer activities for children, as well as interesting, changing exhibitions. Shop, disabled access to ground floor; cl am Sun and all Mon (exc bank hols); (01642) 813781; free. CAPTAIN COOK BIRTHPLACE MUSEUM (Stewart Park, Marton, 3m S of Middlesbrough) The sound of a creaking ship's timbers accompanies some of the displays here, and the impressive grounds have a conservatory with tropical plants, animals and birds. Meals, snacks, shop, disabled access; cl Mon exc bank hols; (01642) 311211; *£2. NEWHAM GRANGE LEISURE FARM (Coulby Newham, off the A174) Rare breeds and other animals and poultry, an agricultural museum, and a reconstructed vet's surgery and merchant's shop. Snacks, shop, disabled access; cl wkdys Nov–Mar; (01642) 300202; £1.50.

🐾 **North Newbald** SE9136 NORTHERN SHIRE HORSE CENTRE (Flower Hill Farm) Busy working farm with pedigree shire horse stud. Also farming bygones, decent walks, and plenty of animals inc rare sheep and cattle. Snacks, shop, disabled access; cl Fri, Sat, and Oct–Easter (though you can usually see at least some animals on Suns then); (01430)

827270; £2.75.

🏠 ★ † **Nunnington** SE6679
NUNNINGTON HALL Big 16th/17th-c
house, nicely set on the banks of the
River Rye, with fine panelling and a
magnificent staircase. A family home
for nearly 400 years, with the
intriguing Carlisle Collection of
miniature rooms, each of them ⅛th
life-size. Snacks, shop, limited
disabled access; cl am, all Mon (exc
bank hols) and Tues (exc Jun–Aug),
and Nov–Mar; (01439) 748283;
*£3.80, garden only £1; NT. In the
attractive village, the Royal Oak is
good for lunch, and the church has a
fine effigy of a knight said to have rid
the district of a Loathly Worm.

🏠 🏵 **Ormesby** NZ5416 ORMESBY
HALL Elegant 18th-c house with
elaborate plasterwork, Victorian
laundry and kitchen, a model
railway, and pleasant gardens and
grounds. Monthly family fun days
(usually 1st Sun of month). Snacks,
shop, disabled access to ground floor
only; cl am, all Mon (exc bank hols),
Fri, Sat, and Nov–Mar; (01642)
324188; £3.50; NT.

★ 🏔 🏠 ! **Osmotherley** SE4598
Perhaps more a small town than a
village, but quietly attractive; the
Three Tuns has good food (and
comfortable bedrooms). MOUNT
GRACE PRIORY (A19, NW) Carthusian
monks not only took a vow of silence
but rarely emerged from their own
individual cells. One of those cells at
this ruined 14th-c priory has been
fully restored, giving a good
illustration of how the monks must
have worked and lived. The ruins are
better preserved than those of any
other Carthusian establishment in
England, and in spring an impressive
display of daffodils makes it
especially attractive. An adjacent
17th-c manor house has an
exhibition, and interesting Arts and
Crafts connections. Snacks, shop; cl
winter Mon and Tues; (01609)
883494; £2.50. Just up the road at
Ingleby Cross NZ4501, the
ADVENTURE CENTRE can organise
climbing, caving and canoeing,
(01609) 882571.

★ † 🏔 🏔 ❄ ♨ **Pickering** SE7984

Another attractive small town,
usually very quiet (busier Mon
market day), with vividly restored,
medieval murals in the splendid, tall-
spired CHURCH. NORTH YORKSHIRE
MOORS RAILWAY (Pickering Station)
Steamtrain trips through some lovely
countryside and nostalgically
restored stations, a distance of 18
miles; the line was originally built by
George Stephenson. The Grosmont
end has various locomotives and
antique carriages, and you can stop
off at Goathland (see entry above).
Meals, snacks, shop, disabled access;
cl Nov–Mar (exc Dec wknds);
(01751) 472508 for timetable; £8.50
full return journey. PICKERING CASTLE
Ruins of a 12th-c keep and later
curtain walls and towers, with fine
views from its imposing castle mound
above the town. Snacks, shop, some
disabled access; cl winter Mon and
Tues; (01751) 474989; £2. BECK ISLE
MUSEUM Charmingly set, 17th-c
riverside house with a wonderful
collection of local bygones and period
shops. Shop, limited disabled access;
cl Nov–Mar; (01751) 473653; £2.
The White Swan, Black Swan, Bay
Horse and Forest & Vale do decent
food; the A169 N has sweeping
moorland views (up there the
Saltergate Inn is a good stop).

🏵 ♨ **Pocklington** SE8048 An open-
faced market town below the Wolds,
with quite a few handsome buildings;
the Feathers is popular for lunch (and
has decent bedrooms). BURNBY HALL
GARDENS (B1247, S) Famous for their
waterlilies, with dozens of varieties in
2 lakes; also a splendid rose garden,
and an intriguing collection of all
sorts of ethnic material and sporting
trophies from across the world.
Snacks, shop, disabled access; cl
Oct–Mar; (01759) 302068; £2.20.
From out here it's not far to the
Plough at Allerthorpe (good for
lunch); the B1246 Driffield road runs
through some quite picturesque hills.

🏔 ❄ 🏠 **Rievaulx** SE5785 RIEVAULX
ABBEY Superbly atmospheric ruins of
a magnificent and once highly
prosperous abbey, among the
wooded hills of Rye Dale. The nave,
dating from 1135, is one of the

earliest built in England. Also among the spectacular 3-tiered remains is a fine 13th-c choir, and there's a visitor centre with displays on monastic life. The graceful colonnades, arches and lancet windows are especially evocative if you get there early or late on a weekday out of season (if they're not shrouded in scaffolding). Snacks, shop, some disabled access; cl 25–26 Dec, 1 Jan; (01439) 798228; £2.90. Dramatic views of the abbey from RIEVAULX TERRACE, a half-mile-long, grass-covered 18th-c terrace overlooking it. Each end is adorned with a classical temple; one a small Tuscan rotunda built to while away the hours in peaceful contemplation, the other, an elaborate Ionic creation, for hunting parties. An ideal spot for a picnic, with good frescoes and an exhibition on landscape design. Snacks, shop, disabled access; cl Nov–Apr; (01439) 798340; £2.80; NT. Besides the many places in Helmsley not far off, the Hare over in Scawton (a pleasant drive) is useful for lunch.

★ ☺ **Robin Hood's Bay** NZ9504 Picturesque fishing village, once popular with smugglers and still largely unspoilt (though there are quite a few shops and cafés for visitors now), its cottages clustered steeply above the rocky shore – a rich hunting-ground for pottering at low tide, when a surprising expanse of sand is exposed, too. MUSIC IN MINIATURE (Albion Rd, church hall) Charming collection of painstakingly created models illustrating English musical history; among the 50 or so dolls' house-sized scenes are medieval minstrels, Victorian carol singers, and a 1920s palm court orchestra, all imaginatively put together by one dedicated woman. Shop, disabled access; cl Nov–Easter; (01947) 880512; *£1. There's a BIKE HIRE centre on Station Rd; (01947) 880488. The Laurel and Olde Dolphin have enjoyable food. The village car park is up at the top – quite a climb.

☺ **Saltburn-by-the-Sea** NZ6722 Originally a superior Victorian seaside resort, with traces of those days still in the Italianate valley garden and the water-operated sloping tramway by the pier. The Ship Inn, a good pub right by the boats pulled up on the beach, is probably the most ancient building. The old cottages alongside it house the SMUGGLERS' EXPERIENCE, a vivid, interactive exhibition on the town's smuggling heritage. Cl wkdys Oct–Easter; (01287) 625252; *£1.60. The beach is sheltered by the great headland of Warsett Hill to the S.

★ 🏰 ☀ ⌂ ☺ ▣ ♄ ✝ ✦ ! **Scarborough** TA0388 All the usual seaside attractions in a place of some style, its 2 great curves of firm sandy beach separated by the small harbour below a high, narrow headland. It gained unwelcome publicity last year when former local darling Alan Ayckbourn was quoted as claiming there was nothing to do in the town apart from get drunk or buy shoes. His comments came as the council tried to decide whether to grant his theatre extra funding; in the end they did so, disappointing the national press, who'd whipped up a controversy about whether the town could fund both a theatre and more everyday conveniences (luvvies or lavvies they called it).

Looking down over the town from the headland, the once impressive CASTLE stands on the site of British and Roman encampments. It was a royal palace of some importance until the reign of James I. Remains include the 13th-c barbican, medieval chapels and house, and the shell of the original 12th-c keep; great coastal views from the walls. Shop, disabled access; cl winter Mon and Tues, 24–26 Dec; (01723) 372451; *£1.80. Between castle and cliff are the remains of a Roman signal station, one of 5 such structures built in the 4th c to warn of approaching raiders. To the S is the older part of the resort, with antique tracked cliff lifts between the promenade and the pleasant streets of the upper town; a house associated with Richard III is here (it now looks a little dilapidated), and there's a small craft centre in a former 14th-c inn. The train station has one of the longest benches in the world; 456 ft (139 metres) long, it can seat 228 people. ROTUNDA MUSEUM (Vernon Rd) Georgian local history museum, with a Bronze Age skeleton and displays on the resort's Victorian heyday. Shop; cl Mon, and also cl Tues–Thurs Nov–May; (01723) 374839; free. WOOD END (The Crescent) The Sitwells lived here for 60 years from 1870 (Edith was born here), and there are displays of their work and associated memorabilia. Also lots of fossils, and a Victorian conservatory with tropical plants – though not the free-flying birds that once mingled with party-goers. Some disabled access. Open as Rotunda Museum above, and the same for the ART GALLERY next door, a striking Italianate villa with good temporary exhibitions. MILLENIUM ⬛ Down by the harbour, a vivid journey across 1,000 years of the town's history, through Vikings, Normans and the Civil War to the early days of rail and Victorian sea-bathing – very entertainingly done. Shop, limited disabled access; cl 25 Dec; (01723) 501000; £4.50. Nearby the *Hatherleigh* is a deep-sea trawler converted into a little museum; free. Interesting CHURCHES include medieval St Mary's, where Anne Brontë is buried, and 19th-c St Martin's with elaborate work by Burne-Jones, William Morris and other Pre-Raphaelite artists. SEA LIFE CENTRE ⬛ (Scalby Mills) The same lively mixture we've described in several other resorts. Meals, snacks, shop, disabled access; cl 25 Dec; (01723) 376125; £4.75.

One unique and entertainingly quaint tradition is the summer staging of miniaturised sea battles, with all sorts of special effects among the ducks on the lake of Peasholm Park, in the more seasidey north part of the town; 3.30pm Mon and Thurs, May–early Sept. Good views of the bay from the top of Olivers Mount (and harbour views from the Golden Ball on the front).

✴ **Skidby** TA0133 Has a WORKING WINDMILL (cl Mon and Tues; £1.50), and

gentle country walks nearby; the Half Moon is useful for something to eat.

⬛⬛ ★ **Skinningrove** NZ7119 An industrial village with a steel-rolling mill – far from picturesque, but it has strong local colour. TOM LEONARD MINING MUSEUM Good mining museum, well demonstrating the reality of work underground. You can see how the stone is drilled, charged with explosives and fired. Snacks, shop; cl am, and all Nov–Mar; (01287) 642877; £2. The monumental Boulby Cliff is fairly near, and a bit further on, the very pretty seaside village of Staithes has several decent pubs.

⬛⬛ **Sledmere** SE9365 SLEDMERE HOUSE ⬛ Grand 18th-c mansion decorated and furnished in the style of the period, with one showpiece room done in Turkish tiling and a library bigger than many public ones. The extensive park was landscaped by Capability Brown. They usually play their pipe organ pm Weds, Fri and Sun. Cl am, all Mon (exc bank hols), Sat, and Sept–Easter; (01377) 236637; *£4.50. The Triton nearby is useful for lunch.

⬛⬛ **Sproatley** TA1934 BURTON CONSTABLE HALL The wonderful exterior gives away this delightful house's Elizabethan origins, but the inside was extravagantly remodelled in the 18th c. Around 30 beautifully preserved rooms to see, with a sweeping long gallery and some intriguing collections. Capability Brown landscaped the 200 acres here too, and there's a riding centre in the stables. Teas, shop, disabled access to ground floor only; cl am, all Fri, Sat (exc July and Aug), and Oct–Easter; (01964) 562400; £4. Camping, caravanning and seasonal fishing are available. The Cock & Bell down at Preston does good-value lunches.

❗⬛ **Staintondale** SE9998 Bruce Wright organises LLAMA-TREKKING across the moors or along the coast; the llamas hump your bags while you walk beside them. They can do specialist treks with forest rangers or experts on wild flowers or archaeology. All treks include home-made food; (01723) 871234; from

£10 for 2 hours. SHIRE HORSE FARM 🔲
Friendly little farm with good
demonstrations and talks; as well as
horses there are various rabbits, small
animals and poultry, nature trails,
and bracing clifftop walks along part
of the Cleveland Way. Snacks, shop,
disabled access; open Sun, Tues,
Weds, Fri and bank hols Easter–Sept;
(01723) 870458; *£3. The
Bryherstones Hotel, off the
Cloughton road, has good-value
food.

★ **Staithes** NZ7818 Steep fishing
village, unspoilt down by the shore,
where little cottages and the storm-
battered Cod & Lobster pose
fetchingly against the staggering
background of a great red sandstone
headland, a striking colour picture as
the sun comes up.

🏘 🐝 ★ **Sutton on the Forest** SE5864
SUTTON PARK The friendly 1730s
manor house itself is now open only
the last Sun in July (for the Sutton
Show), but the delightful grounds are
open pm daily Mar–Sept, with
terraced gardens, a Georgian ice
house, lily-pond, and pleasant
woodland walks and nature trails.
Snacks, shop, disabled access; house
open pm bank hols, gardens open
Easter–Sept; (01347) 810249; £4, £2
gardens only. The village with its
broad street is pretty, and the smart
Rose & Crown has good food.

★ ✝ 🏰 🐾 🍽 ! **Whitby** NZ8910
Famous as the port at which Count
Dracula came ashore; Bram Stoker
got the idea for the book in the
fishermen's graveyard of the partly
Norman CHURCH, 199 steps up from
the harbour, with lovely woodwork.
A famous scene in the novel takes
place at WHITBY ABBEY, an impressive
set of 13th-c ruins dramatically
overlooking the harbour from their
windswept clifftop setting. You can
see the skeletal remains of the
magnificent 3-tiered choir and the
north transept, and it's an evocative
spot for a picnic. An earlier building
had been the site of the Synod of
Whitby, where the dating of Easter
was thrashed out in 664. Snacks,
shop; cl 24–26 Dec; (01947) 603568;
*£1.60. Not too far from the abbey
on Church Rd is a small but
interesting workshop where you can
watch jet being crafted into jewellery.

Away from the bright waterfront,
the town is steep and quite attractive,
with picturesque old buildings (now
often rather smart shops) and some
quaint cobbled alleys at its original
core east of the busy harbour, where
excellent fresh fish is sold straight
from the catch. The town's
delightfully old-fashioned and
crowded MUSEUM (Pannett Park)
includes the only surviving part of
Captain Cook's original journal,
Queen Victoria's nightdress, and the
hand of a murderer used as a candle-
holder by superstitious burglars.
Shop, some disabled access; cl am
Sun, and in winter cl pm Tues and all
Mon; (01947) 602908; £1.50. The
CAPTAIN COOK MEMORIAL MUSEUM
(Grape Lane) is housed in the
building where the great explorer
lived as an apprentice in the shipping
trade from 1746; rooms are furnished
in period style with models, letters

We welcome reports from readers . . .

This *Guide* depends on readers' reports. Do help us if you can – in return,
we offer a discount on the next edition to people who've helped us with
reports for it. Tell us what you think about places already in it, and anything extra you think we should say about them. And send us your ideas
for inclusion in the next edition: places to visit, eat at or stay in, attractive
drives or walks, maybe even unusual interesting shops you know of.
Use the card in the middle, the report forms at the end, or just write –
no stamp needed: *The Good Guide to Britain*, FREEPOST TN1569,
Wadhurst, E Sussex TN5 7BR.

and drawings from Cook's later voyages. Shop; cl Nov–Mar; (01947) 601900; £2.20. Children probably won't be satisfied until they've visited the spooky DRACULA EXPERIENCE 🎫 (Marine Parade), which vividly re-creates scenes from the classic tale. Shop; cl winter wkdys; (01947) 601923; *£1.95.

Besides excellent fish and chips from the Magpie café, the Duke of York (Church St, at the bottom of the 199 steps) does decent food all day. In the 2 weeks around the summer solstice, the sun both rises and sets above the sea.

❋ **Withernsea** TA3427 LIGHTHOUSE Towering above the houses of this little resort, with fantastic views for those keen enough to climb the 144 steps. Teas, shop, disabled access to ground floor only; open pm wknds and bank hols Mar–Oct, daily mid-Jun–mid-Sept; (01964) 614834; £1.50. The Commercial Hotel has very low-priced food.

❋ **Classic views** of the interlocking moor and valley landscapes are to be had from the graveyard of Gillamoor church SE6890; the lane at SE6188, a bit more than a mile N of Carlton, itself N of Helmsley; the hillside just S

Days Out

Rye Dale's graceful ruins
Helmsley – lunch at the Feathers; Rievaulx Abbey; Rievaulx Terrace.

Captain Cook's coast
Robin Hoods Bay; Whitby – lunch at the Magpie Café, Duke of York or Trenchers there; Staithes (can walk along the coast from Runswick Bay); Skinningrove mining museum.

Crossing the primeval moor
Walk the historic rail trail from Grosmont to Goathland; lunch at the Mallyan Spout Hotel there; walk down to Mallyan Spout (waterfall) and if there is time continue via West Beck gorge to Wade's Causeway Roman road on Wheeldale Moor (see **Walks** section below); return from Goathland to Grosmont by North Yorkshire Moors Railway.

Windows on times past
Pickering; drive on to the high moors via Ralph Cross; lunch at the Lion, Blakey Ridge; Lastingham church crypt; Hutton-le-Hole and folk museum.

Seabirds' citadel
Cliff stroll at Flamborough Head; lunch at the Seabirds in Flamborough; boat trip or walk to see Bempton Cliffs.

Backroads of the Wolds
Burnby Hall waterlily gardens; Londesborough, with a stroll into parkland on the Wolds Way (see **Walks** section below); South Dalton and Lund villages; lunch at the Star, North Dalton; Sledmere House (limited opening); Wharram Percy medieval village site.

The giant Humber span
Beverley – lunch at the Beverley Arms or Queen's Head there; Skidby windmill (limited opening); Humber Bridge country park.

Where Yorkshire ends
Patrington church; Withernsea lighthouse; lunch at the Commercial Hotel, Withernsea; Spurn Head (see **Walks** section below).

of Lastingham SE7290; the hillside at the top of the dreadfully steep Rosedale Chimney road SE7294, heading S over Spaunton Moor from Rosedale Abbey; and the road on either side of Blakey Ridge SE6899. Sutton Bank SE5182 is a classic viewpoint for motorists.

✝ **Interesting churches**, often in very pretty settings, at Bugthorpe SE7758 (the village is especially nice in spring), Garton-on-the-Wolds SE9859 (12th-c, and very High Church inside, with 19th-c mosaics and frescoes), Kirkdale SE6886 (Saxon, with a unique sundial, and 7th-c Celtic crosses and carved stones), Lastingham SE7391 (a former monastery, once one of the area's most sacred spots of pilgrimage, with an outstanding 11th-c crypt), Patrington TA3122 (a glorious church, with lovely carving inside – its graceful spire beckoning you from a long way off).

★ **Other attractive villages** here, all with decent pubs, include Ainthorpe NZ7008, Ampleforth SE5878 (with its famous school and partly wooded moors), Beck Hole NZ8202 (Birch Hall is a unique cross between country tavern and village store; ideally visited along the former railway track – see **Walks** section below), Bishop Burton SE9939, Castleton NZ6908 high above the Esk Valley, Carlton in Coverdale SE6084, Cloughton Newlands TA0196, Crayke SE5670, Egton Bridge NZ8105 (pleasantly eccentric, twinned with a fictional French village; lovely Esk views), Fadmoor SE6789 (charming drive from Kirkbymoorside, on over Rudland Slack and past Cockayne to Helmsley), Felixkirk SE4785 (good drive to Kepwith and Nether Silton), Great Ayton NZ5611, Hawnby SE5489 (on the very scenic Rievaulx Abbey–Osmotherley road), Hovingham SE6675 (good drive S to Sheriff Hutton and Flaxton), Huggate SE8855 (easy walks nearby), Hutton Rudby NZ4706, Levisham SE8390, Lund SE9748, Nether Silton SE4692, North Dalton SE9352, Oldstead SE5380, Rosedale Abbey SE7395, Runswick Bay NZ8217 (a very pretty, harbourless fishing village), Seamer TA0183, Sheriff Hutton SE6566 (castle and 12th-c church), South Dalton SE9645, Thixendale SE8461, Thornton-le-Clay SE6865, Weaverthorpe SE9670, and Welburn SE7268. Thornton Dale SE8383 is delightful, but we've had no pub recommendation there. Wharram Percy SE8564 doesn't even have houses – the most famous of the medieval abandoned villages of the Wolds, with lots of grassy humps and an evocative ruined church; English Heritage site, free access.

This area has decent **horse riding** centres, good for experts and beginners alike; the Moors Centre at Danby (see entry above), has the full list, and can also provide numbers for the various **cycle hire** centres dotted about the region.

Walks

The Cleveland Way, meticulously waymarked and signposted, is a great help to there-and-back walks in this area, following the W, N and E margins of the North York Moors National Park. Starting from Helmsley SE6183, it passes Rievaulx Abbey SE5785 (itself more dramatically viewed from approach routes down Rye Dale from the N). **Sutton Bank** SE5182 ⌂-1 is a steep escarpment with an enthralling view, and the most popular section of the Way here is S from the A170, along the level clifftop to the white horse cut into the hill at SE5181. Immediately N of the A170, you can combine the path along the top of the slope with a venture down the nature trail into Garbutt Wood SE5374, a nature reserve abutting Gormire Lake SE5083, the only natural lake in the National Park. There's a lonely stretch with some road access over the **Hambleton Hills** SE5187 ⌂-2 to Osmotherley SE4597. N of **Chop Gate** SE5699 ⌂-3 (where the Buck does good food) is a fine section off the B1257, where the path westwards on the N slopes of the moors takes in rocky outcrops.

Along the coast the Cleveland Way is consistently interesting – and so much more rewarding than the immediate hinterland, that there-and-back walks keeping to the Way itself are more fun than trying to work out circular walks heading inland. **Saltburn-by-the-Sea** NZ6722 ⌂-4 starts a grand section, passing Skinningrove NZ7119 (an odd shantytown of pigeon-fanciers' sheds spreads over the cliff) to ascend Boulby Cliff NZ7619, the highest point on the E coast, before re-entering the National Park. The village of **Runswick Bay** NZ8217 ⌂-5 makes a pretty starting-point for the path to Staithes NZ7818, or you can begin closer from tiny Port Mulgrave NZ7197. A bus service is useful for the section linking Whitby NZ8910, Robin Hood's Bay NZ9505 and Scarborough TA0388. At the famous village of **Robin Hood's Bay** ⌂-6 the foreshore is a fascinating place for rock-pools, except at high tide; or you can walk along a fine section of cliffs to Ravenscar NZ9801, where a geological trail takes in old alum quarries; an abandoned railway provides an easy walkway back. S of **Scarborough** ⌂-7 to Filey TA1180 is an agreeable few hours' walk, though of less scenic significance than the cliffs further N. Oddly, the Way stops just short of Filey, at the headland of Filey Brigg TA1381, although there is nothing to prevent you from walking on into town.

Further S, **Flamborough Head** TA2670 ⌂-8 has some quite exciting walking, particularly around its N side, with the cacophony of thousands of kittiwakes sounding within the inlets; puffins can sometimes be seen on rock ledges. A level mile and a half from the lighthouse along clifftops leads to North Landing TA2273 (café and car park). A longer walk making the Head the midway point starts from Flamborough village TA2270, skirting fields to join the coastal path; to avoid anticlimax, walk the southern cliffs first and keep the real drama for later on. To the N, the path follows the coast closely nearly all the way, and hilly country coming right to the coast makes for interest.

The area between the Wolds, Humber and coast, known as Holderness, is flat: rich farming country with huge fields and not many buildings, though the fine village churches, often with soaring towers or spires, reflect the wealth that this fertile land has put into them in the past. The long southern stretch of coast is flat country too, without a great deal of appeal for walkers – except for long, lonely, off-season walks by the edge of the North Sea.

Spurn Head TA4011 ⌂-9, the spit which curls like a claw round the mouth of the Humber estuary, has a rough track open to cars almost to its end: a bleak place to some but a paradise for birdwatchers, who often wait here in spring and autumn for glimpses of rare migrant species. Thanks to the vagaries of nature the peninsula is gradually becoming an island, so best to check tide times carefully. The estuary itself is usually grey, solemn and grim.

Inland, Farndale and Rosedale have characteristic North York Moors scenery – lush green fields and red-roofed, yellow-stone houses beneath the brooding moorland plateau. **Farndale** ⌂-10, the largest dale, is famous for its miles of wild daffodils in Apr, introduced and naturalised here many centuries ago. They're at their best around Low Mill SE6795, and any walk to enjoy them gives the chance of coming back down the ancient green lane of Rudland Rigg, for spectacular views. The friendly Feversham Arms at Church Houses SE6697, right next to the daffodil reserve, does very good-value food. **Rosedale** ⌂-11 now seems to typify the quiet pastoral countryside of the area, though until 60 or 70 years ago it was a busy iron-working site. The old railway track that once served the quarries loops around the moor above, and makes an easily followed stroll. **Hutton-le-Hole** SE7090 ⌂-12 and Lastingham SE7391 are 2 charming villages, an hour or so apart on foot.

The eastern part of the National Park has large forest plantations; **Dalby Forest** SE8788 ⌂-13 has colour-coded trails. **Levisham** SE8390 ⌂-14 has open scenery around it, with a track across the blustery moors, and an attractive valley giving separate routes to and from the Hole of Horcum, just below the A169. From **Grosmont** NZ8205 ⌂-15 you can walk an historic rail trail via Beck Hole along the abandoned line that preceded the current North Yorkshire Moors Railway route to Goathland NZ8301. **Goathland** ⌂-16 has a short popular walk from opposite the church to Mallyan Spout, a waterfall which tumbles into the side of a fine, wooded, smooth-rocked gorge. **Wade's Causeway** NZ8312 ⌂-17 is a rather longer walk S from Goathland, or reached direct by the narrow moorland lane S from Egton Bridge NZ8105; also known as Wheeldale Roman road, this is a mile-long stretch of broad, paved, Roman road up over the moors, well restored and maintained (open to walkers only). **Roseberry Topping** NZ5712 ⌂-18 is a memorable viewpoint on the extreme northern edge of the moors, reached by a moorland walk from Gribdale Gate car park E of Great Ayton NZ5611; a popular circuit goes by way of Airy Home Farm, the childhood home of Captain Cook. **Eston Nab** NZ5618 ⌂-19, outside the National Park, has a massive view over industrial Teesside.

S of the moors, the gentle **Howardian Hills** ⌂-20 have a path along their N flanks giving intermittent views across the plain to the North York Moors. Castle Howard SE7170 is, of course, the principal feature of the area, its vast estate threaded by a few public footpaths which gain glimpses of the great house and the landscaped parts of its grounds. From **Kirkham** SE7365 ⌂-21 a pleasant path meanders S by a placid stretch of the River Derwent, to Howsham Bridge SE7362 and beyond.

The Yorkshire Wolds are quiet, agricultural chalk country dissected by dry valleys, with extensive views over huge corn fields. The bulk of the off-road walking is found on the well signposted, 79-mile Wolds Way from Hessle Haven TA0325 down on the Humber to Filey Brigg TA1381 on the coast, where it meets the Cleveland Way; some of the lesser roads are a delight to walk on, with wide verges, good views and virtually no traffic. Worthwhile areas for round walks based on the Wolds Way include **Welton** SE9627 ⌂-22, with fine views over the Humber in places; **Market Weighton** SE8741 ⌂-23, where the Way briefly divides in two, allowing a circuit taking in the old railway line, now the Hudson Way, and the villages of Goodmanham SE8843 and Londesborough SE8645, with its pleasant parkland; **Millington** SE8351 ⌂-24 where the landscape rolls most attractively; and **Thixendale** SE8461 ⌂-25, passing within sight of the abandoned medieval village of Wharram Percy SE8564 and taking in a stretch of classic dry valley.

Where to eat

Byland Abbey SE5579 ABBEY (01347) 868204 Beautifully placed dining pub opposite the abbey ruins, with friendly new owners (they have kept the same chef), good food, decent wines and well kept beers; an interesting series of rambling old rooms, and a big garden; cl pm Sun and Mon; disabled access. £20|£7.50.

Flamborough TA2270 SEABIRDS (01262) 850242 Friendly old pub full of shipping memorabilia, with excellent fresh fish and other home-made dishes, lots of wines, and cheerful, hard-working staff; cl pm Mon in winter; partial disabled access. £18|£3.95.

Kirkham Abbey SE7466 STONE TROUGH (01653) 618713 Quaint, beamed inn with small, cosy and interesting bars with log fires, good lunchtime bar food, an old-fashioned restaurant with a farmhouse atmosphere, seats outside with valley views; £16.95|£5.95.

Nunnington SE6779 ROYAL OAK (01439) 788271 Attractive little dining pub nr Nunnington Hall; log fires, beams hung with copper jugs, antique keys and earthenware flagons, carefully chosen furniture, and generous helpings of enjoyable, home-made bar food – super daily specials; cl Mon; children over 8. £18.25|£7.50.

Osmotherley SE4597 THREE TUNS (01609) 883301 The front part of this pub is unassuming and popular with walkers and visitors enjoying this lovely village; there's a comfortable and stylish back restaurant with a particular emphasis on fish, good bar food inc interesting daily specials, well kept real ales, and courteous service; also, tables in the garden with lovely views; bedrooms. £18|£6.95.

Staithes NZ7818 ENDEAVOUR 1 High St (01947) 840825 Popular little quayside restaurant at the bottom of a steep hill; lovely, fresh local fish dishes (delicious meat and game, and vegetarian dishes, too), super puddings, decent, good-value wine list, and friendly service; bedrooms; cl winter Sun (except over bank hols), 25–26 Dec, wkdys during Jan and Feb; well behaved children only. £23.

Sutton-upon-Derwent SE7047 ST VINCENT ARMS (01904) 608349 Relaxed atmosphere in the traditional, panelled front parlour with an open fire, high-backed old settles, good, solid, home-cooked food in the spacious dining room, friendly staff, well kept beers and a decent choice of wines; big garden. £16.70|£6.50.

Whitby NZ8910 DUKE OF YORK Church St (01947) 600324 Bustling, welcoming pub, with a nice outlook over the harbour entrance and western cliff from the comfortable beamed bar (lots of fishing memorabilia); a wide choice of good-value, fresh local fish as well as other things, well kept real ales, fine wines, and quick, pleasant service; bedrooms. £14|£5.

Whitby NZ8910 MAGPIE CAFE Pier Rd (01947) 602058 Overlooks the town and river, with lots of wonderfully evocative sepia photographs on the walls, and much liked for its wonderful fresh haddock served by cheerful staff; cl Jan, 24–25 Dec. £11.95|£5.

Whitby NZ9011 TRENCHERS Newquay Rd (01947) 603212 Neatly kept, big busy diner by the harbour, with delicious fresh fish (and other food), friendly and helpful staff, and a good wine list; cl 1 Nov–1 Mar; disabled access. £15.90|£3.95.

WEST AND SOUTH YORKSHIRE

Packed with fascinating places to visit – many of them free, and many especially good for children; lively towns and cities, and some striking scenery in the west.

Leeds has become a really rewarding place to visit, with something for all ages: its Royal Armouries Museum makes an outstanding family day out, Tropical World is very enjoyable (and free), and there's plenty more to fill a short stay.

Elsewhere, stately Harewood House (letting its hair down a little these days) is a favourite of many readers. The Earth Centre at Denaby Main opens the first stage of its intriguing and colossally expensive redevelopment this year. Other fine places include Brodsworth Hall, the National Coal Mining Museum at Middlestown, Bramham Park, Conisbrough Castle, the pioneering industrial village of Saltaire, Nostell Priory, the Bagshaw Museum in Batley, the Colne Valley Museum at Golcar and (out of season) the Brontës' parsonage in Haworth – where the picturesque Keighley & Worth Valley Railway is fun for family outings. Another good spot for children is the open farm at Cawthorne.

Halifax is an appealing, cleaned-up mill town with lots to see: its Eureka! centre is riveting for 5–12 year-olds. The sprawling city of Sheffield has a lot of things worth tracking down – and its new pop music museum looks very promising. Bradford, too, has unexpected riches for the visitor, particularly its entertaining new transport museum. Ilkley is an attractive, moors-edge spa town, and Hebden Bridge, interesting in itself, is a good base for both Bradford and Halifax – there's an incredibly good-value subsidised train, with links also to Saltaire and Huddersfield (the Halifax–Huddersfield journey is fascinating for those who like trouble-up-mill scenery).

The west of the area has a real Yorkshire mix of steep stone cottage terraces, remarkable mill buildings and some dramatic moorland coming right up to the towns, with plenty of exhilarating walking.

With the present counties of South and West Yorkshire, we have included the bottom corner of North Yorkshire, below York itself and the A64.

Where to stay

Bradford SE1633 VICTORIA Bridge St, Bradford BD1 1JX (01274) 728706 *£89, plus wknd breaks; 60 well equipped rms with CD- and video-player (they have a library). Carefully renovated Victorian station hotel with many original features and lots of stylish character; a bustling bar, popular and informal brasserie serving good modern food, and marvellous breakfasts; disabled access.
Escrick SE6343 CHURCH COTTAGE Escrick, York YO4 6EX (01904) 728462 *£55; 8 rms. Family-run guesthouse set next to the church, in 2 acres of lawn and woodland; with friendly owners, most attractively decorated rooms, and

good breakfasts; cl Jan; disabled access.

Firbeck SK5688 Yews Farm Firbeck, Worksop S81 8JW (01909) 731458 *£52; 2 rms. Charming, carefully furnished, 18th-c country home in an attractive village, with views over woodland and fields; tasty home cooking; cl Nov–Feb.

Grenoside SK3393 Whitley Hall Elliott Lane, Grenoside, Sheffield S30 3NR (0114) 245 4444 £83; 18 rms. 16th-c creeper-clad hotel, in 30 acres; with a relaxed beamed bar, good, popular food in the spacious restaurant, and friendly, helpful service; cl 25–26 Dec.

Halifax SE0828 Holdsworth House Holdsworth, Halifax HX2 9TG (01422) 240024 £90, plus wknd breaks; 40 pretty, individually decorated rms. Lovely 17th-c house a few miles outside Halifax; with antiques, fresh flowers and open fires in the comfortable lounges, friendly, helpful staff, a very fine, oak-panelled dining room with imaginative food and carefully chosen wines, and a garden; dogs welcome by prior arrangement; cl 1st wk Jan; disabled access.

Haworth SE0337 Old White Lion Haworth, Keighley BD22 8DU (01535) 642313 £55, plus special breaks; 14 rms. Friendly, warm and comfortable, 300-year-old inn with 3 bars, a cosy restaurant with enjoyable food, and an oak-panelled residents' lounge; close to Brontë Museum, parsonage and church, and the Keighley & Worth Valley steam railway.

Leeds SE3033 42 The Calls 42 The Calls, Leeds LS2 7EW (0113) 244 0099 £98w, plus special breaks; 41 extremely attractive rms with original features, and lots of extras – CD stereo with disc library, satellite TV, and good views. Stylish modern hotel in a converted riverside grain mill, with genuinely friendly staff, marvellous food in both the restaurant and next-door Brasserie Fourty-Four, and fine breakfasts; cl 5 days over Christmas; limited disabled access.

Linton SE3946 Wood Hall Trip Lane, Linton, Wetherby LS22 4JA (01937) 587271 £118, plus special breaks; 43 spacious, well furnished rms. Grand Georgian mansion set in over 100 acres of parkland overlooking the River Wharfe; comfortable reception rooms, log fire, antiques and fresh flowers, and imaginative cooking in the no smoking restaurant; indoor swimming pool and health centre; disabled access.

Monk Fryston SE5029 Monk Fryston Hall Monk Fryston, Leeds LS25 5DU (01977) 682369 £98, plus special breaks; 28 comfortable rms. Grand manor house in attractive grounds; with antiques, log fires and fresh flowers in the oak-panelled bar and lounge, friendly staff, and good food in the original manor house dining room; disabled access.

Otley SE2143 Chevin Lodge Yorkgate, Otley LS21 3NU (01943) 467818 £89w, plus special breaks; 50 rms. Built of Finnish logs; lots of walks through the 50 private acres of birchwood (free mountain bikes too), and good restaurant food; tennis, fishing, and free membership of the nearby leisure club: indoor swimming pool, gym and supervised creche; disabled access.

Roydhouse SE2112 Three Acres Roydhouse, Shelley, Huddersfield HD8 8LR (01484) 602606 £60, plus special breaks; 20 refurbished, pretty rms. In lovely countryside, this extended 18th-c hotel has a welcoming atmosphere in its traditional bars, good wines and well kept real ales, and excellent food in the 2 restaurants (one with an occasional pianist), using fresh local produce; cl 25 Dec.

Sheffield SK3485 Charnwood 10 Sharrow Lane, Sheffield S11 8AA 0114 258 9411 £90, plus special breaks; 22 comfortable, well equipped rms. Friendly, extended Georgian house with peaceful lounges, a conservatory, and very good food in both the Brasserie and elegant little Henfrey's restaurant; cl 24–29 Dec; disabled access.

Wentbridge SE4817 Wentbridge House Old Great North Rd, Wentbridge, Pontefract, N Yorks WF8 3JJ (01977) 620444 £62w; 20 rms. Fine hotel dating from 1700 and set in 20 acres of beautiful grounds; with attractive public rooms, a relaxed bar, and enjoyable food in the pretty restaurant; cl pm 25 Dec; disabled access.

To see and do

YORKSHIRE FAMILY ATTRACTION OF THE YEAR

♨ ! **Leeds** SE3034 ROYAL ARMOURIES MUSEUM (Clarence Dock, Waterfront) Probably the most ambitious and certainly the most expensive museum to open in Britain in recent years, this £42.5 million complex houses the National Museum of Arms and Armour, previously displayed at the Tower of London, but shown off here in a radically different way. It's almost completely interactive, with hi-tech effects and push-button displays, and plenty of costumed demonstrations showing not just how weapons were made and used, but how they affected everyday life. Keeping the interest of families has clearly been their top priority: children can try on costumes and helmets, or even test their aim with a crossbow. The building's design is stunning (don't miss the breathtaking Hall of Steel, with 3,000 pieces of gleaming arms and armour on the walls), but the most spectacular feature is outside: the country's only full-size, authentically re-created tiltyard, with dramatic exhibitions of jousting, fencing and duelling, as well as hunting dogs and birds of prey. They don't do all of these every day (and in winter it all depends on the weather), so check first if there's something you particularly want to see. An inside display area often has martial arts displays, and there are demonstrations of traditional skills in the Craft Court. The 5 main galleries are themed around subjects like war, tournaments, self-defence and hunting, all with elaborate room settings and state-of-the-art computer displays; it's a long way from your average military museum. A visit should keep all members of the family entertained for most of the day, and at the very least you'll need 4 hours even to begin to see it all. Meals and snacks, shop, good disabled access; cl winter Mons, 25–26 Dec, 1 Jan; (0990) 106666; £7.95 (£4.95 children 4–15). A family ticket admitting either 1 adult and 4 children, or 2 adults and 3 children, is £22.95. You'll have to pay a bit extra for parking.

🎠♨🏵 **Batley** SE2424 BAGSHAW MUSEUM (Wilton Park) Beautiful Victorian Gothic mansion in a pleasant lakeside park, with one of those excellent miscellaneous collections based on the curio-hunting of an individual enthusiast. Shop, some disabled access; cl am wknds, Good Fri, 25–26 Dec, 1 Jan; (01924) 472514; free. The Old Hall at Heckmondwike (B6117), once Joseph Priestley's home, is interesting for lunch.

† 🏵 **Bolton Percy** SE5341 Behind its medieval gatehouse the 15th-c church has perhaps the most unusual CHURCHYARD in the country. 15 years ago local lecturer Roger Brook set about tackling its profusion of weeds, and since then has transformed it into a splendidly colourful garden, with more than a thousand different types

of plant creeping around and over the headstones. Rather like a semi-wild cottage garden, it houses part of the National Collection of dicentra. Open all the time, with regular open days to find out more; (01904) 744213 for dates. The Crown has generous, simple food (not Mon or Tues).

🎠♨🚻🖼🛆! **Bradford** SE1633 Though horribly knocked about by heavy-handed civic designers in the 1960s and 1970s, many buildings survive from what was one of Britain's finest Victorian cities. These, in a solidly unifying northern stone, are a staggering monument to the days when its wools, woollens and worsteds ruled the world: gigantic and confidently Renaissance-style woollen and velvet mills, the imposing Wool Exchange, the

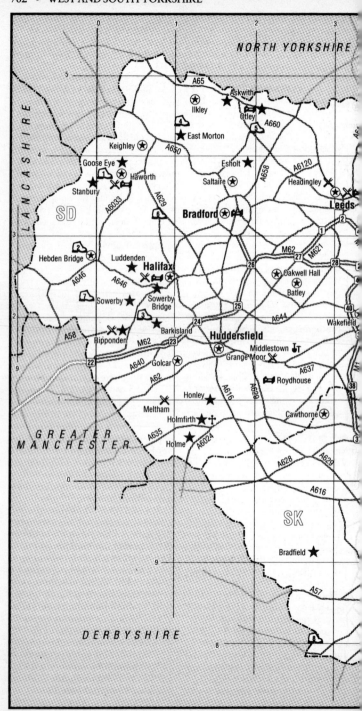

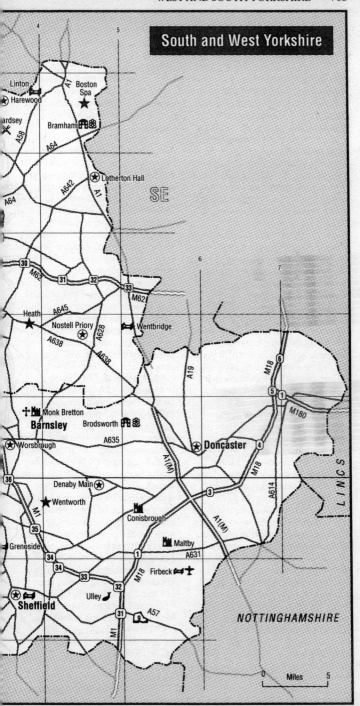

South and West Yorkshire

Linton
Harewood
Boston Spa
ardsey
Bramham
Lotherton Hall
SE
Heath
Nostell Priory
Wentbridge
Monk Bretton
Barnsley
Brodsworth
Worsbrough
Doncaster
Denaby Main
Wentworth
Conisbrough
Maltby
Grenoside
Firbeck
Ulley
Sheffield
NOTTINGHAMSHIRE
LINCS

Miles

opulent city-centre cliffs of heavily ornate merchants' warehouses in Little Germany behind the mostly 15th-c cathedral, and the florid exuberance of the municipal buildings such as the Gothic city hall, the neo-classical St George's concert hall, even the great Undercliffe cemetery with its sumptuous Victorian memorials (and sweeping Pennine views) – it's been called the most spectacular graveyard in Britain. The city's Asian immigrants have brought a vivid and visible dash of cultural diversity, and there's a feeling of underlying vigour and zest which makes it exciting to visit.

The NATIONAL MUSEUM OF PHOTOGRAPHY, FILM AND TELEVISION (Princes View) is one of the best liked museums in the entire country, but will be closed most of the year for major redevelopment, re-opening hopefully in December; (01274) 727488 for latest news. In the meantime the huge IMAX cinema should still be open, and they'll have temporary exhibitions at the Business, Arts and Media Mill in the city centre. INDUSTRIAL MUSEUM 🖬 (Moorside Rd, Eccleshill) Former spinning mill, well illustrating the growth of the woollen and worsted textile industry. A tramway carries you up and down the Victorian street, which is complete with workers' cottages and working Victorian stables with shire horses. Meals, snacks, shop, disabled access; cl am Sun, and all Mon (exc bank hols), 25–26 Dec, Good Fri; (01274) 631756; *£2. COLOUR MUSEUM (Grattan Rd) Imaginative exhibition on the use and perception of colour, with interactive displays on the effects of light and colour in general, and particularly the story of dyeing and textile printing. Shop, disabled access; cl am (exc Sat), all Mon and Sun, Christmas; (01274) 725138; £1.50. CARTWRIGHT HALL ART GALLERY (Lister Park) Dramatic, baroque-style building in an attractive floral park, housing the *Brown Boy* by Reynolds and a good representative selection of late 19th- and early 20th-c paintings. Snacks,

shop, disabled access by prior arrangement; (01274) 493313; cl am Sun, and all Mon (exc bank hols); (01274) 493313; free. BOLLING HALL (off Brompton Ave, S) Classic, mainly 17th-c Yorkshire manor house, now home to the city's collection of local furniture and pictures. Shop; cl Mon (exc bank hols) and Tues; (01274) 723057; free.

A couple of miles S at Low Moor, TRANSPERIENCE 🖬 (Oakenshaw, S) Splendidly enjoyable new transport museum, excellent for families, and all under cover so good in any weather. Well put together displays include hi-tech simulators, period reconstructions, entertaining multimedia shows, and, of course, some well restored vehicles – some of which can take you round the 15-acre park. Also a timely exhibition on transport and the environment, and excellent play areas. The historical bent is put firmly into a contemporary context, helping to make this the most accessible and generally appealing transport museum we know of. Meals, snacks, shop, disabled access; cl 25–26 Dec; (01274) 690909; *£4.95.

Useful places for a pub lunch include the Fountain (Heaton Rd), Office (off City St) and Ram's Revenge (Kirkgate), but you might prefer one of the multitude of Indian, Pakistani or Bangladeshi restaurants. 🕸 🏠 **Bramham** SE4141 BRAMHAM PARK The garden here is really quite beautiful, very much in the grand style – Versailles comes to Yorkshire. Long prospects of ornamental lakes, cascades, temples, statuary, grand hedges and stately trees and avenues surround this classical Queen Mary house of great distinction, with lovely period furnishings and paintings. Disabled access to grounds; open pm Sun and Tues–Thurs mid-Jun– 6 Sept, and gardens also open Easter, May and spring bank hol wknds; (01937) 844265; £4, grounds and gardens only £2.50. The Red Lion has decent food.

🏠 🕸 **Brodsworth** SE5007 BRODSWORTH HALL Grand house vividly illustrating life in Victorian times; the family that lived here closed off parts of the house as their fortunes waned, inadvertently preserving the contents and décor exactly as they were (right down to the billiard score-book). Richly furnished rooms, lots of marble statues, and a busily cluttered servants' wing. Also marvellous formal gardens and parkland gradually being restored. Snacks, shop, some disabled access; cl Mon (exc bank hols), and all Oct–Mar; (01302) 722598; *£4.50.

🐖 ⛩ ★ **Cawthorne** SE2808 CANNON HALL OPEN FARM Unusual animals like wallabies and llamas among the residents at this busy working farm; also baby animals throughout the year, with piglets born every 2 weeks. Good play areas, and mostly concreted so doesn't get muddy. Meals, snacks, shop, disabled access; cl 25 Dec; (01226) 790427; £1.75. There's a country park nearby, and the village is attractive.

🏰 **Conisbrough** SK5098 CONISBROUGH CASTLE (Castle Hill) Mightily impressive 12th-c castle with a uniquely designed 27-metre (90-ft) keep – circular, with 6 buttresses and a curtain wall with solid round towers. They've added a roof and floors to re-create something of the original feel, and there's a good audio-visual show. Snacks, developing craft shop, some disabled access; cl 24–25 Dec, 1 Jan; (01709) 863329; *£2.50. Sir Walter Scott set much of *Ivanhoe* here, writing the novel while staying at the Boat at Sprotbrough nearby; then a riverside farm, it's now a popular dining pub.

! ⇃⇂ ⛩ **Denaby Main** SK4999 The first stage of the redevelopment of the excellent EARTH CENTRE should be complete by May. Spread over 400 acres, this environmental centre was awarded one of the Millennium Commission's biggest grants, and by the time it's finished at the start of the century, it will have cost around £100 million. The green message will be obvious as soon as you enter the main building under a huge array of solar panels (35 per cent of the centre's energy will come from the sun), but it won't be too preachy: the aim is to promote environmental issues in an enjoyable way, so children's activities in the landscaped gardens will include building dens, grottoes and pond-dipping, as well as trails and play areas. They're constructing all sorts of exhibitions and displays on 21st century life, and it sounds as if there'll be lots going on. Meals, snacks, shop, disabled access; (01709) 512000 for exact opening date; *£8.95 (less if you come by public transport). In an ironic twist, the centre has been accused by local naturalists of damaging the environment and habitats in the immediate vicinity.

⛤ 🖼 🏛 **Doncaster** SE5803 Not really a great deal to attract visitors apart from its race meetings, but there is some fine architecture, especially around the High St and Market Pl, and a good antiques and junk market on Weds. The MUSEUM AND ART GALLERY on Chequer Rd has quite a number of natural history exhibits (cl am Sun; free). CUSWORTH HALL (Cusworth Lane, Cusworth; just W) SE5403 Excellent museum of South Yorkshire life, in an elegant 18th-c house. Displays on mining, transport, costume and entertainment, and an especially popular gallery of toys and childhood. Snacks, shop, disabled access; cl am Sun, 25–27 Dec; (01302) 782342; free. The Boat at Sprotbrough is a fairly handy waterside dining pub.

✠ **Elvington** SE7047 YORKSHIRE AIR MUSEUM Part of a World War II airfield and base preserved as it was then, with fine aircraft, an old control tower and plenty of other memorabilia inc engines, models and photographs. Meals, snacks, shop, disabled access; cl 25–26 Dec and 1 Jan; (01904) 608595; *£3.50. The St Vincent Arms, at Sutton-upon-Derwent, is good for lunch.

✠ ★ **Firbeck** SK5688 SOUTH YORKS AIRCRAFT MUSEUM (Home Farm) More aviation history, in a former RAF Officers' Mess. Relics from crashes, 20 aero engines, uniforms, a changing collection of planes and a couple of helicopters. Snacks, shop, some disabled access; open Sun and bank hols, or by appointment; (01709) 812168; £1 suggested donation. In the attractive village, the Black Lion has generous food.

🔥 ⚘ ♿ **Golcar** SE0915 COLNE VALLEY MUSEUM (Cliff Ash) Enthusiastic museum spread over 3 weavers' cottages, with hand-weaving, spinning and clog-making in gaslit surroundings, and a re-created 1850s living room. Snacks, shop, occasional craft festivals, some disabled access; open pm wknds and bank hols; (01484) 659762; £1. The Sands House, up on Crosland Moor, is a good dining pub. There's a pleasant, year-round walk along the Huddersfield Canal's restored towpath between here and Marsden SE0412 in *Last of the Summer Wine* country, where a small TUNNEL END CANAL AND COUNTRY CENTRE has canalia, café and summer BOAT TRIPS; (01484) 846062. The Tunnel End pub here is useful for food, as are the Carriage House and Olive Branch a little further off.

❗🔥🍴⚓♿✝📷🚲☀ **Halifax** SE0925 Another town with an impressive show of former textiles wealth, interesting to drive through when it's quiet on a summer evening or a Sun, and surrounded by a splendid ring of moorland. The centre's been cleaned up and partly pedestrianised, which makes it pleasant to potter through, and there are a number of first-class attractions, with the town now going through something of an artistic renaissance. EUREKA! 🔤 (Discovery Rd) Remarkable hands-on museum designed exclusively for children; few places are as likely to spellbind anyone aged between 5 and 12. Each of the 4 main galleries ostensibly explores one subject, but in fact covers a multitude of topics and ideas. Particular highlights are the broad-based Things Gallery, full of bright colours and images, the Communications Gallery (you can put your picture on a front page, save a yacht in distress, or read the TV news), and Living and Working Together, where children try their hand at grown-up activities like filling a car with petrol at the garage,

working in a shop or bank, or making a meal in the kitchen. Easy to see why in the 5 years it's been open Eureka! has won just about every award going, from Most Parent Friendly and Best Customer Care to several for Loo of the Year. Meals, snacks, shop, disabled access; cl 24–26 Dec; (01426) 983191; £4.95.PIECE HALL (city centre) Magnificent, Renaissance-looking, galleried and arcaded building put up in 1775 by the merchants of Halifax as a market for their cloth. Now it's filled with specialist shops selling books, antiques and bric-à-brac, as well as an art gallery (cl Mon) and other exhibitions. Meals, snacks, shop, disabled access; cl 25–26 Dec; free. The Italianate courtyard comes to life on Fri and Sat when there are 160 bustling stalls; a good few on Thurs too. CALDERDALE INDUSTRIAL MUSEUM (Central Works, Square Rd) re-creates the sights, sounds and smells of the 1850s in reconstructed street scenes, shops, pubs and basement dwellings. Meals, snacks, shop, disabled access; cl am Sun, all Mon (exc bank hols); (01422) 358087; £1.60. Close by, the medieval CHURCH has an extremely grand spire and fine carving. Look out for Old Tristram, the life-size painted carving of a beggar which was used to collect alms. DEAN CLOUGH Enormous carpet mill, faced with demolition when it closed down some years ago, but now well restored and home to a thriving complex of galleries and small businesses; best are the Crossley Gallery and Henry Moore Studio, the latter a good showcase for contemporary sculpture (cl am and all day Mon). SHIBDEN HALL AND FOLK MUSEUM (Godley Lane, off the A58, just E) Excellently refurbished 15th-c house in a 90-acre park, each room illustrating a different period from its history. In the barn, a folk museum has an interesting collection of horse-drawn vehicles, while around it is a reconstructed 19th-c village, with workshops, cottage and even a pub. For many this is a real Halifax highlight. Snacks, shop, limited disabled access; cl am Sun, and all

Dec–Feb (exc pm Sun in Feb); (01422) 352246; £1.60. BANKFIELD MUSEUM (Ackroyd Park, Boothtown Rd) Collection of textiles and costume, as well as a regimental museum and a display of toys. Shop; cl am Sun, all Mon (exc bank hols), 25–26 Dec, 1 Jan; (01422) 354823; free. The 75-metre (250-ft) folly of WAINHOUSE TOWER (off the A646, just W) offers good views if you can manage all those steps; usually open only bank hols and a couple of other dates – best to check with Calderdale Industrial Museum (see above); 65p. The Shears (Paris Gates, Boys Lane), down steep lanes among the mill buildings, is a pub that embraces much of Halifax's past and atmosphere; the Sportsman (Lee Lane, Shibden – off the A647) has a good-value carvery and impressive views.

🏠🖼️🐷🌱✝️🎣 **Harewood** SE3144 HAREWOOD HOUSE (A61) The area's most magnificent stately home, inside and out. The 18th-c exterior is splendidly palatial, while recent restoration work inside has left the glorious Robert Adam plasterwork looking better than it has done for probably 150 years. Fine Chippendale furnishings, exquisite Sèvres and Chinese porcelain, and paintings by Turner, El Greco, Bellini, Titian, and Gainsborough. Capability Brown designed the thousand-acre grounds, which have very pleasing lakeside and woodland walks, an outstanding collection of rhododendron species, and the famous landscaped bird gardens (you could spend half a day in just this part). Charles Berry's Terrace has an excellent gallery with contemporary art and crafts. Try to visit the 15th-c CHURCH, with a splendid array of tombs, and a curious tunnel under the wall of the churchyard, so that servants could arrive unseen by sensitive souls. There's also a first-class adventure playground. Meals, snacks, shop, helpful disabled access; cl Dec–mid-Mar; (0113) 288 6331; £6.50 everything, £5.25 bird garden and grounds only, £4 grounds and terrace gallery only. TV's *Emmerdale*

is now filmed on a purpose-built set on the Harewood estate. Just N, Wharfedale Grange has PICK YOUR OWN fruit. The Bingley Arms at Bardsey and the Windmill at Linton are good, civilised, nearish places for food.

👶🏠❄️🦮 **Haworth** SE0337 A touristy village with plenty of craft shops, antique shops and tea shoppes catering for all the people drawn here by the Brontës (spelt Brunty before father Patrick went posh). A visit out of season catches it at its best, though at any time the steep cobbled main street has quieter, more atmospheric side alleys. The Brontës' former home, the PARSONAGE MUSEUM, has some 120,000 visitors a year (it was something of a tourist attraction even while Charlotte still lived here). The house is very carefully preserved, with period furnishings, very good changing exhibitions, and displays of the siblings' books, manuscripts and possessions. Several relics made a high-profile return last year, inc the original ink-stained manuscript of *Jane Eyre*, and the sisters' writing table. Shop; cl 12 Jan–6 Feb, 24–27 Dec; (01535) 642323; £3.80. Most of the family are buried in the nearby churchyard, except Anne, interred in Scarborough. For the most evocative views and atmosphere go up to the moors above town, very grand and not much different from when the Brontës knew them – despite the Japanese footpath signs. The KEIGHLEY & WORTH VALLEY RAILWAY actually begins just N at Keighley (where you can connect with BR trains) but is based here. Run by enthusiastic volunteers, the line was built to serve the valley's mills, and passes through the heart of Brontë country. The Oxenhope terminus has a museum, but the prettiest station is Oakworth (familiar to many from the film *The Railway Children*). Snacks, shop, some disabled access; open wknds all year, daily Jun–early Sept, and most school hols; (01535) 647777 for timetable; £6.50 Day Rover ticket. The Fleece and Old White Lion are useful for lunch; and see also **Where to eat** section below.

The A6033 is an interesting drive to our next entry, and there's a fine old moors road via Stanbury over to the Colne Valley in Lancs.

★ ⏣ 🏠 🍺 🅿 ♿ **Hebden Bridge** SD9927 Engaging small town deep in a valley below the moors, and stepped very steeply up the hillsides, with quite a lively subculture of art and craft shops. Sylvia Plath is buried in the churchyard in the ancient village of Heptonstall SD9728, a crippling climb above the town, leading on to an exhilarating old high road to Widdop and beyond, and another via Colden and Blackshaw Head. Down in the main town is a small museum; the Robin Hood (A6033 towards Keighley) has good-value food. MAUDE-WALKLEYS CLOG MILL (A646) Makes an enormous number of different kinds of clog, from heavy-duty, steel-toed industrial numbers to more fashionable frippery; you can watch them being made. Also craft and specialist shops, a small farm and adventure playground. Meals, snacks, shop, disabled access; cl 25–26 Dec; (01422) 842061; £1. WORLD OF THE HONEY BEE 🖼 (now on the same site) Bees at close quarters, with working hives, and free samples of over 30 different types of honey. Weekend snacks, shop, limited disabled access; cl Jan–Feb; (01422) 846976; adults free, children 50p. The attractively placed, nearby Tythe Barn does decent food. At Hebble End are several working craftsmen, with demonstrations of skills inc glass-making, and in summer there are horse-drawn barge trips along the canal basin; tel (01422) 845557. The hold of one barge in the marina has been converted into a VISITOR CENTRE with a traditional boatman's cabin (cl Jan–Easter; free). HARDCASTLE CRAGS SD9630 A pretty spot above the wooded river valley, ideal for walks or a picnic; parking £2, less mid-week. The Nutclough House on the way up also has reasonable food.

★ ✝ **Holmfirth** SE1408 Instantly recognisable as the setting for TV's *Last of the Summer Wine*, with evocative little alleys, several good pubs, and a handsome Georgian CHURCH.

❋ 🅿 ⏣ 🍴 **Huddersfield** SE1416 There's a great sense of style in many of its buildings, especially around the station and central square, and much of the centre is now closed to traffic. 275-metre (900-ft) CASTLE HILL (Almondbury) Unrivalled views of the surrounding moors and towards the Pennines and Peak District, best from the top of the 165 steps of the Victoria Tower (open pm May–Sept, plus most bank hols; £1.20). The Castle Hill Inn is another good place to take in the panorama. Also up here is an ART GALLERY with a range of 19th-c English paintings. Cl Sun, bank hols, Christmas; (01484) 221964; free. The myths and legends asssociated with the hill are outlined at the TOLSON MEMORIAL MUSEUM (Ravensknowle Park), housed in a former wool baron's mansion, which also has a look at the cloth industry, and a collection of horse-drawn vehicles. Shop, disabled access; cl am wknds, 24–26 Dec, 1 Jan, Good Fri; (01484) 223830; free. There's a decent TRANSPORT MUSEUM on Leeds Rd; cl am Sun; (01484) 559086; *£2. The A640 W is a nice moorland drive.

★ ⏣ 🏠 ✝ 🏛 **Ilkley** SE1147 Owes its Victorian and Edwardian spaciousness and style to the mid-19th-c and later craze for hydropathic 'cures', which produced quite a rash of luxurious hydros using the town's pure moorland spring water. Their forerunner was the simple little bath-house built in the mid-18th c around the ice-cold spring up on the moor, just S at WHITE WELLS – you can still follow the paths the infirm took by donkey. The group of quaintly shaped rocks known as the Cow & Calf up here also makes a pleasant short walk above the town. MANOR HOUSE GALLERY AND MUSEUM (Castle Yard) One of the few buildings in town to predate the 19th c, an Elizabethan manor house built on the site of a Roman fort, with local history displays. Shop; cl am Sun, all Mon (exc bank hols) and Tues, Christmas, Good Fri; (01943) 600066; free. The CHURCH has 3 lovely Saxon crosses, and just beside it are more traces of the Roman fort. There are quite a few prehistoric remains around the town, the best known of which is the Bronze Age SWASTIKA STONE, a symbol of eternity carved on a flat rock by a moorland path SE of the town, above wooded Heber's Ghyll; the stone is marked on the Ordnance Survey 1:50,000 map, at SE095469. Heber's Ghyll itself is a picturesque area of steep Victorian walkways, and the town with its attractive gardens and interesting shops (you can see chocolate being made at Humphreys) makes a nice stop. Useful places for lunch include the Ilkley Moor Vaults (Stockel Rd/Stourton Rd) and the Wheatley Arms (Ben Rhydding).

🏠👹 **Keighley** SE0641 (pronounced 'Keithly') A busy working town with a pleasant centre. The Grinning Rat nr the 16th-c church is useful for lunch. CLIFFE CASTLE MUSEUM AND GALLERY (Spring Gardens Lane) 19th-c mansion with French furniture from the Victoria & Albert Museum, as well as various local ephemera. Though quite close to the centre, it's set in a park well above the main road, with an aviary and greenhouses. Shop, disabled access to ground floor only; cl am Sun, all Mon (exc bank hols), 25–26 Dec, Good Fri; (01535) 618238; free. EAST RIDDLESDEN HALL (Bradford Rd, just NE) Interesting, early 17th-c, oak-panelled, stone manor house with attractive plasterwork, period textiles and furniture, and a formal walled garden. There's a medieval monastic fishpond, and a huge medieval tithe barn. Meals, snacks, shop, limited disabled access; open pm Sat–Weds Mar–Oct, plus Thurs July and Aug; (01535) 607075; £3; NT.

🏠👹❗️📷⏳♿🚗 🏛🔭🐎⚓ **Leeds** SE3034 A great deal of effort has gone into developing a 24-hour café culture here, and behind the hype there really is a surprisingly cosmopolitan city, its compact centre increasingly popular with young people in the evenings (lots of bars and clubs), and ideal for exploring

during the day – it's largely free of traffic. There are lots of splendid covered arcades (Victorian, Edwardian and modern), and all sorts of interesting and engaging Victorian architectural details to spot. Shoppers and theatre-goers are well catered for – the former in the exuberantly Venetian/Oriental glass-roofed MARKET, the biggest in Yorkshire, and the latter by the West Yorkshire Playhouse (a useful meeting-place with fine city views from its good café/bar) and The Grand (home of Opera North). The impressive 1860s CORN EXCHANGE is now filled with neat little specialist and designer shops, and has plenty of places for tea, coffee and so forth, as well as an excellent, fresh, continental bread stall; there's a stamp market here on Sun, and often a small jazz group at teatime. The imposing TOWN HALL is perhaps the high point of Leeds's essentially Victorian centre; and there are pleasant gardens and open spaces. Whitelocks (Turk's Head Yard, off Briggate) is a marvellous old city tavern, very much a Leeds institution.

The historic Waterfront area has been well developed for visitors in recent years; for the ROYAL ARMOURIES MUSEUM here *see separate Family Panel on p.761*. TETLEY BREWERY WHARF (Waterfront) Lively centre exploring the history of the English pub, from a 14th-c monastic brewhouse to the Star & Crater, a bizarre prediction of what a pub might be like in the next century. Also period costumed characters, an interesting look at pub games and traditions, various crafts, shire horses, and an optional tour of the Tetley brewery itself (booking recommended – or at least reserve a place as soon as you arrive). Indoor and outdoor play areas for children. Meals, snacks, shop, disabled access (exc to brewery); (0113) 242 0666; £4.95. Granary Wharf, nr here on Nevill St, has plenty of interesting shops and weekend events, festivals and entertainment. CITY ART GALLERY (The Headrow) Excellent collection of 20th-c British art, as well as English watercolours and sculpture gallery, inc carefully chosen works by Henry Moore (he had his first exhibition here in 1941). Meals, snacks, shop, limited disabled access; cl am Sun, bank hols, Christmas, 1 Jan; (0113) 247 8248; free. Over a footbridge is the delightful HENRY MOORE INSTITUTE, with temporary exhibitions of sculpture from Roman times to the present, displayed in quite an unusual building (they don't actually show anything by Henry Moore). Shop, disabled access; cl bank hols; (0113) 234 3158; free. Both these galleries open late on Weds. THACKRAY MEDICAL MUSEUM (Becket St) Dynamic new museum at St James's Hospital, well known from the TV series *Jimmy's*. Interactive displays on how the body works, and good reconstructions showing the progress of medical care in Britain, inc some deliciously gruesome parts on surgery before the development of anaesthetics. Snacks, shop, disabled access; cl Mon (exc bank hols), 25–26 Dec, 1 Jan; (0113) 244 4343; *£3.95. ARMLEY MILLS MUSEUM (Canal Rd) Once the largest woollen mill in the world, now a huge working museum, its floors given over to a massive display of textile machinery. Also reconstructions of a turn-of-the-century tailor's shop, buying room and clothing factory, and demonstrations of static engines, steam locomotives and underground haulage. Snacks, shop, disabled access; cl am Sun, Mon (exc bank hols), 25–26 Dec; (0113) 263 7861; £2. CITY MUSEUM (Claverley St) Deservedly on the Heritage Secretary's new shortlist of excellent museums, of national importance. Cl Sun, Mon and bank hols; (0113) 247 8275; free. MUSEUM OF THE HISTORY OF EDUCATION (University) Small but interesting, inc text and exercise books going back to the 17th c – it's usually best to book with Dr Foster. Cl pm, all Fri; (0113) 233 4665 free. MIDDLETON COLLIERY RAILWAY, running from Turnstall Rd roundabout to Middleton Park, is the oldest running railway in the world and was the first to be authorised by Parliament. Later it was the first to

succeed with steam locomotives, and in 1960 became the first standard-gauge line to be operated by enthusiasts. With a picnic area, fishing, nature trail and playgrounds as well as the trains, there's plenty for families here. Snacks, shop, disabled access; diesel trains pm Sat Apr–Sept, steam trains pm Sun Apr–Dec, bank hols, and Dec Sats; (0113) 271 0320; £2. THWAITE MILLS (Stourton, 2 miles S of the city centre) This water-powered mill was the focus of a tiny island community perched between the River Calder – which drives the mill wheels – and the Aire & Calder Navigation. The Georgian mill-owner's house has been restored and has displays on the site's history. Snacks, shop, disabled access; cl am, all Mon (exc bank hols), and Nov–Mar; (0113) 249 6453; £2.

ROUNDHAY PARK (off the A58 N) 700 acres of rolling parkland, well known for concerts and events. On Princes Ave here the CANAL GARDENS are a very pleasant and peaceful corner of the city, with several national flower collections (inc dahlias and violas), lots of roses, and ornamental wildfowl; free. The huge conservatory next door is TROPICAL WORLD, housing the biggest collection of tropical plants outside Kew, along with all sorts of exotic trees, reptiles, fish, birds, and butterflies, in careful re-creations of their natural settings. Meals, snacks, shop, disabled access; cl 25 Dec; (0113) 266 1850; free. KIRKSTALL ABBEY (A65 towards Ilkley) The most complete example of a Cistercian abbey in the country, the ruins now standing among trees in a quiet suburban park. The massive arches of the Norman nave are impressive, and you can wander through several of the quite well preserved ancillary buildings. The 15th-c gatehouse has social history displays. Snacks, shop, disabled access to ground floor only; cl am Sun, Mon (exc bank hols), 25–26 Dec, 1 Jan; (0113) 275 5821; £2. The riverside Old Bridge (nearby, towards Headingley) has good-value food. MEANWOOD VALLEY URBAN FARM (Meanwood) Small working farm on regenerated waste land N of the city centre, with rare breeds, an organic garden, and a new environment centre. Meals and snacks (not Mon), shop, good disabled access; (0113) 262 9759; *50p. TEMPLE NEWSAM HOUSE (5m E, S of the A63) That trusty old faithful Capability Brown designed the wonderful 1,200 acres of landscaped parkland and gardens in which this house stands, an extraordinary asset for any city. The house itself dates from Tudor and Jacobean times, and contains the city's very good collections of decorative and fine art, as well as an exceptional assemblage of Chippendale furniture. Rare breeds in the grounds. Snacks, shop, disabled access to ground floor only; cl Mon, and Jan–Feb; (0113) 264 7321; *£2.

🏛 🖻 🏵 🐦 **Lotherton Hall** SE4436 (B1217 Garforth–Tadcaster road) Edwardian house with displays ranging from Oriental art to British fashion, as well as collections of paintings, silver and ceramics and some lovely furnishings. The grounds are being restored, and there's a bird garden. Meals, snacks, shop, some disabled access; cl Mon (exc bank hols), and Christmas–Feb; (0113) 281 3259; £2 house, grounds free. The Swan at nearby Aberford is very popular for lunch.

🏚 **Maltby** SK5489 ROCHE ABBEY (off the A634 SE) A fine gatehouse to the NW and the still-standing walls of the south and north transepts are all that's left of this 12th-c Cistercian abbey, but they make an impressive sight. Snacks, shop, disabled access; cl am, all Nov–Mar; (01709) 812739; £1.40.

↓T **Middlestown** SE2617 NATIONAL COAL MINING MUSEUM (Caphouse Colliery, New Rd) Well deserves its many awards for its exploration of life as a coal miner. No simple reconstruction this – they take you 140 metres (450 ft) underground, down one of Britain's oldest working mine shafts, where models and machinery have been set up to show the methods and working conditions of miners from the 1800s to the present. For the faint-hearted (and under 5s), on the surface there are pit ponies, 'paddy train' rides, steam winder, nature trail and an adventure playground. Dress sensibly if you're going underground. Meals, snacks, shop, disabled access and excellent facilities – helpful to arrange it in advance; cl 24–26 Dec, 1 Jan; (01924) 848806; £5.75. The Kaye Arms at Grange Moor is a good, smart dining pub.

🏚 † **Monk Bretton** SE3607 The red sandstone remains of an important 12th-c PRIORY, with gatehouse, church and other buildings, as well as some unusually well preserved drains. The ancient Mill of the Black Monks is pleasant at lunchtime (live music for young people most nights).

🏛 🏵 🎵 † ⚘ **Nostell Priory** SE4017 (off the A638) Sumptuous Palladian mansion, with an additional wing built by Adam in 1766. It has perhaps the best collection of Chippendale furniture anywhere, all designed for this house, and other highlights include the tapestry room, charming saloon, and a remarkably intricate 18th-c doll's house, also said to have been furnished by Chippendale. The grounds are most attractive, with woodland walks, and a lovely rose garden; you can arrange coarse fishing on the lakes. There's an interesting MEDIEVAL CHURCH nr the entrance, and a craft centre in the stables. Meals, snacks, shop, disabled access; open pm wknds and bank hols Mar–Oct, plus pm Mon–Thurs July–early Sept; (01924) 863892; £3.80 house and grounds, £2.50 grounds only; NT. The Spread Eagle has decent food.

🏛 🏵 👂 **Oakwell Hall** SE2127 🖼 (signed off the A651/A652 S of Birkenshaw) Moated Elizabethan manor house, altered in the 17th c, and still furnished to give something of the atmosphere then; look out for the unusual dog gates at the foot of the staircase. Also period formal gardens, an extensive country park with adventure playground, and weekend events throughout the year. Snacks, shop, limited disabled access; cl am wknds, Christmas wk, 1 Jan;

(01924) 326240; £1.20. The Black Bull, opposite the ancient Norman church in nearby Birstall, has good-value home cooking. A couple of miles away at Gomershal SE2026, the RED HOUSE MUSEUM on Oxford Rd vividly re-creates the 1830s in its 9 carefully furnished period rooms. Charlotte Brontë often stayed at the house (which stands out from its stone neighbours for its unusual red brick), and used it as the basis for Briarmains in her novel *Shirley*. New galleries this year. Cl am wknds, Christmas, Good Fri; (01274) 335100; free.

★ 🏨🅿️♿⚠️! **Saltaire** SE1437 The pioneering industrial village Titus Salt developed in Shipley in the 1850s. Salt's beautifully thought out, classically designed village was so successful that even now it's a favoured place to live. It's well worth looking around, and you might want to try the antique CABLE RAILWAY. The 1853 GALLERY, named from the date when the magnificent mill it's housed in was built, is probably one of the largest private collections of art in the country, and includes around 300 works by David Hockney, inc some of his intriguing experiments with photography. Huge bookshop, disabled access; (01274) 531163; cl 25–26 Dec; free. Some good smart shops in the building too (inc one selling clothes made in the mill). Just up the road, the unique REED ORGAN AND HARMONIUM MUSEUM (Victoria Hall, Victoria Rd) has some eye-opening exhibits, inc one organ no bigger than a family bible. If you're an organ-player you may get the chance to try some of those on display. Limited disabled access; cl Fri, Sat, 2 wks at Christmas; (01274) 585601; £1.50. FUREVER FELINE (Windmill Manor, Leeds Rd) Animatronic cats stroll through pine-scented woodland scenes and talk in broad Yorkshire accents; useful for young children. Meals, snacks, shop, disabled access; cl 25 Dec; (01274) 531122; *£1.50. There's a splendid flight of locks on the Leeds–Liverpool Canal here.

♿🍴🏛️🏢⚠️ **Sheffield** SK3587 A vast industrial city, redeveloped extensively in post-war years – you really have to be a local to tap into the increasingly thriving and enjoyable cultural life of the place, but several places are rewarding to visit – though needing a street map and quite a bit of journeying. Best to use the tram to get about; it runs out to the giant indoor shopping mall at Meadowhall. Sheffield is likely to be put more firmly on the tourist map when the NATIONAL CENTRE FOR POPULAR MUSIC opens in the city centre later this year. Costing £15 million and set in a distinctive building shaped like a pair of drums, exhibitions will look at the development of popular music from classical to hip-hop, with an emphasis on post-1945 sounds, and a look at how they're made and played. It's expected to be open by Aug, but best to ring (0114) 279 8941 for the latest news. KELHAM ISLAND MUSEUM (around Alma St; and signed from the city centre) Lively exploration of Sheffield's industrial development, with all sorts of buildings, workshops and machinery collections (inc formidable working engines), and traditional cutlery craftsmen at work. Snacks, shop, disabled access; cl Fri, Sat; (0114) 272 2106; £2.80. The Fat Cat here has good food. Some fine cutlery at the CITY MUSEUM AND MAPPIN ART GALLERY (Weston Park), firmly traditional in its approach, but with some interesting collections, inc a splendid display of antique Sheffield plate. The excellent gallery features works by Renoir, Cézanne, Turner and even Walt Disney. Meals, snacks, disabled access; cl Mon (exc bank hols), Tues, 25 Dec, 1 Jan; (0114) 276 8588; free. Two other notable galleries in town are the GRAVES (Surrey St) with some fine decorative art, and the RUSKIN (Norfolk St), containing the collection of Victorian artist and writer John Ruskin, with an adjacent craft gallery; both cl Sun; free. BISHOP'S HOUSE (Meersbrook Park, S of the city centre) Striking 15th- and 16th-c yeoman's house, now a good museum of social history. Shop; cl Mon (exc bank hols), Tues; (0114) 255 7701; £1. N of the centre at Tinsley the SHEFFIELD BUS MUSEUM has a diverse collection of buses and even pre-war milk floats, with related memorabilia and a big model railway. Shop, snacks, some disabled access; open pm wknds for restoration work, with special open days every couple of months when the displays are more lively; (0114) 255 3010; £1. Sheffield's botanic gardens are to be restored, thanks to a hefty lottery grant.

⚓ Ulley SK4687 Pleasant walks around a reservoir, also good for fishing and watersports; the Royal Oak is in a lovely setting by the church.

✝ 🏠 ▣ ☕ 🕸 Wakefield SE3320 A number of handsome buildings, inc its CATHEDRAL, much restored in Victorian times but with some fine 15th-c masonry and carvings (and a marvellous spire – the tallest in Yorkshire), its rare 14th-c BRIDGE CHAPEL over the River Calder, some Georgian and Regency houses most notably around Wood St and St John's Sq, and its imposing civic buildings. ART GALLERY (Wentworth Terrace) Good collection of 20th-c painting and sculpture, internationally famous for its galleries devoted to 2 famous local sculptors – Barbara Hepworth and Henry Moore. Shop; cl am Sun, all Mon, 25–26 Dec, 1 Jan; (01924) 305796;

Days Out

Sheffield steel
Kelham Island Museum; lunch at the Fat Cat (Alma St); Sheffield City Museum; when it opens, National Centre for Popular Music.

Bradford bounce
Transperience, S of Bradford; Bradford's industrial museum; stroll through Little Germany, behind the cathedral; lunch at one of the city's Indian restaurants; Saltaire (easiest by train).

Craggy heights above Calderdale
(Drive, or long day's walk on good paths and tracks.)
Hebden Bridge; Hardcastle Crags, and on through Hebden Dale; lunch at the Pack Horse, Widdop; Heptonstall and Heptonstall Crags; Rochdale Canal towpath back to Hebden Bridge (see **Walks** section below); if there's time, Halifax – to see Piece Hall.

The railway children and the literary sisters
Keighley & Worth Valley Railway from Keighley to Oxenhope and back to Haworth – have a snack in the antique buffet car, or lunch at the Old White Lion there; walk to Brontë waterfalls and Top Withins (Wuthering Heights) if there's time – see **Walks** section below; back to Keighley by train

Last of the Summer Wine
Holmfirth; lunch at Will's o' Nat's in Meltham; Colne Valley Museum, Golcar; stroll along Huddersfield Canal towpath.

Leading Leeds
Royal Armouries Museum; lunch at the Brasserie Forty-Four (The Calls); Temple Newsam House.

... and Leeds for free
Walk past arcades, market and town hall; City Museum; City Art Gallery and Henry Moore Institute; lunch at Whitelocks (off Briggate); Roundhay Park.

free. The MUSEUM (Wood St) has a unique collection of preserved animals and exotic birds, and an exhibition of 1940s women's costume. Shop; cl am Sun; (01924) 305351; free. YORKSHIRE SCULPTURE PARK (Bretton Hall College, West Bretton; A637 SE of Wakefield) SE2813 Carefully and imaginatively displayed series of major contemporary sculpture set in fine, 18th-c, landscaped parkland. There are 16 works by Henry Moore in the adjacent country park, often surrounded by grazing sheep. Shop; cl 25 and 31 Dec; (01924) 830579; free (though £1.50 car parking charge). Up at Heath, there's an extraordinarily old-fashioned common with gypsy ponies alongside 18th-c mansions; the gaslit King's Arms here is good.

🦡 ☕ ✗ 🐾 **Worsbrough** SE3503 COUNTRY PARK, FARM AND MILL MUSEUM (A61) Hard to believe this peaceful country park was once a busy industrial area; the only sign of those days is the working corn mill, now a museum but still producing stoneground flour. The 200 acres also include nature trails, traditional and rare breeds, and several beehives; lots of events throughout the year, especially on bank hols. Snacks, shop, some disabled access; cl Mon (exc bank hols), Tues, and Christmas wk; (01226) 774527; *50p.

★ **Attractive or attractively placed villages** with decent pubs include Appleton Roebuck SE5542, Askwith SD1648, Barkisland SE0420, Bradfield SK2692 (interesting church, good walks in great scenery), Boston Spa SE4345, East Morton SE1042, Esholt SE1840, Goose Eye SE0340 (nice drives around here), Heath SE3519, Holme SE1006, Honley SE1312, Luddenden SE0426 (the enormous Oats Royd Mill in the valley is a remarkable sight), Ripponden SE0419 (medieval packhorse bridge; the B6113 and B6114 above here are interesting moors roads), Saxton SE4736 (where Lord Dacre is buried sitting on his war horse), Sowerby SE0423, Sowerby Bridge SE0623 (the canal basin here

always has a lot going on), Stanbury SE0037, Warthill SE6755 and Wentworth SK3898 (reckoned by some readers to be the prettiest village they've ever seen). Otley SE2045 is a market town rather than a village, but an attractive one.

Other useful **pubs in fine positions** or with good views include Dick Hudsons on the Otley Rd at High Eldwick SE1240 above Bingley, the Castle overlooking the reservoirs nr Bolsterstone SK2796, the Brown Cow by the open-access woods at Ireland Bridge (on the B6429) nearer Bingley SE1039, the Strines nr Strines Reservoir above Bradfield SK2692, the Stanhope Arms on Windle Edge Lane, nr Winscar Reservoir by Dunford Bridge SE1502, the New Inn at Eccup SE2842, the Scapehouse on Scapegoat Hill above Golcar SE0915, the Cow & Calf up Skew Hill Lane, at Grenoside SK3393 above Sheffield, the Malt Shovel at Harden SE0838, the Robin Hood at Pecket Well SD9928 outside Hebden Bridge, the Cherry Tree on Bank End Lane at High Hoyland SE2710, the Fleece at Holme SE1006, the Buckstones on the A640 towards Denshaw, high above Huddersfield SE1416, the Blacksmith's Arms on Heaton Moor Rd at Kirkheaton SE1818, the Shepherd's Rest on Mankinholes Rd at Lumbutts SD9523, the Mount Skip nr Midgley SE0027, perched high over Hebden Bridge, (on the Calderdale Way footpath), the Hinchcliffe Arms at Cragg Vale, Mytholmroyd SE0126 (the B6188 S is a good moors road), the Hobbit up Hob Lane, Norland SE0723, the Grouse on Harehills Lane, Oldfield, nr Oakworth SE0038, the Causeway Foot on the Keighley rd by Ogden Reservoir SE0631, the Waggon & Horses (on the A6033) and Dog & Gun (off the B6141 towards Denholme) both nr Oxenhope SE0335, the Pineberry on the A644 Keighley rd out of Queensbury SE1030, the Brown Cow (on the A672) dramatically overlooking Scammonden Reservoir SE0215, the Clothiers Arms in Station Rd, Stocksmoor, nr Shepley SE1810, the

White House (on the B6107) at Slaithwaite SE0813, the Blue Ball nr Soyland SE0120, the Sportsman's Arms at Hawks Stones, Kebcote on Stansfield Moor SD9227, the Ring o' Bells on Hill Top Rd at Thornton SE0933, the Freemason's Arms on Hopton Hall Lane at Upper Hopton SE1918, the Delvers on Cold Edge Rd and Withens on Warley Moor Rd at Wainstalls SE0428 and the Pack Horse at Widdop SD9333.

Walks

The best walking in this part of Yorkshire is in the west, particularly on the Pennine moors. The **Brontë country** ⌂-1 around Haworth SE0337 is a favourite stamping-ground, with a good walk W through Penistone Hill Country Park SE2403 to the much-visited Brontë Waterfalls SD9935, and on through a remote valley to Top Withins SD9835, the original Wuthering Heights. There are plenty of paths, though finding the way across fields frequently entails searching for unprominent stone stiles over the dry-stone walls.

From **Hebden Bridge** SD9927 ⌂-2, a fearsomely steep cobbled lane up to Heptonstall SE9278 (you can get up there by car) leads to a rewarding scenic path along Heptonstall Crags (the cliffs above the wooded valley of Colden Water) SD9429. Hardcastle Crags SD9630, a beauty-spot to the N of Hebden Bridge, protrude above the trees that shelter Hebden Water. **Norland Moor** SE0621 ⌂-3, S of Sowerby Bridge SD0623, gives views from the Calderdale Way into adjacent Calderdale, with the Rochdale Canal along its foot.

Ilkley Moor ⌂-4 S of Ilkley SE1147 has potential for satisfying high-level walks, while closer to Ilkley the Swastika Stone makes an interesting objective beyond the pretty ravine of Heber's Ghyll SE0947. **The Chevin** SE2044 ⌂-5 behind Otley SE2045, though not a high hill, gives a grand view of Wharfedale.

Numerous reservoirs on the moors are served by footpaths, inc **Ogden Reservoir** SE0630 ⌂-6 N of Halifax, and **Withens Clough Reservoir** SD9822 ⌂-7 S of Hebden Bridge, from which you can climb up to the prominent monument on Stoodley Pike.

South Yorkshire does not have much good walking country, though the moors and reservoirs of the Pennines W of Sheffield have a certain rugged austerity. The high lands just touch the Peak District National Park: **Carl Wark** SK2561 ⌂-8 is a hill fort set handsomely in a great bowl fringed by gritstone outcrops. The **Anston Brook** ⌂-9, accessible on foot from South Anston SK5183, flows through a wooded valley that interrupts the monotony of the flat farmlands SE of Rotherham and can be combined with a walk along the towpath of the derelict Chesterfield Canal.

Where to eat

Bardsey SE3642 BINGLEY ARMS Church St (01937) 572462 Ancient pub and decorated in keeping, full of interest and atmosphere, with a big fireplace in the spacious lounge (split into intimate areas), a smaller public bar, and an upstairs brasserie; warm and friendly atmosphere, a wide range of fair-value food inc good daily specials, well kept real ales, nice wines, and a charming terrace. £15.50|£5.

Grange Moor SE2215 KAYE ARMS (01924) 848385 Civilised and busy, family-run dining pub with a smart dining lounge; particularly good, imaginative food, exceptional-value house wines from a fine list, decent malt whiskies, and helpful, courteous service. £22|£9.50.

Halifax SE0925 DESIGN HOUSE Dean Clough (01422) 383242 Stylish modern restaurant in this thriving, carefully restored carpet mill complex, with enjoyable cooking to match; relaxed and friendly atmosphere, good service, and a thoughtful wine list; disabled access. **£25 dinner, £17.50 lunch**|£5.

Haworth SE0337 WEAVERS 15 West Lane (01535) 643822 Charming evening restaurant made up of weavers' cottages, with most enjoyable, hearty (not heavy) food, cheerful service, and lovely puddings; bedrooms; cl Sun, Mon, 1 wk Jun, 1 wk Christmas. **£25**.

Headingley SE2836 SALVOS 115 Otley Rd (0113) 275 5017 Welcoming, family-run Italian restaurant with good modern food and cheerful service; cl Sun, 24–26 Dec, 31 Dec–1 Jan; disabled access. **£17.50**|£5.75.

Leeds SE3033 BRASSERIE FORTY-FOUR 44 The Calls (0113) 234 3232 Originally a grain mill (and set under 42 The Calls, see **Where to stay** section above), this riverside restaurant is simply furnished with modern designs, and serves enjoyable British and Mediterranean food, and a good-value wine list; cl am Sat, Sun, bank hols. **£27**|£5.

Leeds SE3033 LEODIS Victoria Mill, Sovereign St (0113) 242 1010 Stylish modern restaurant on the ground floor of a former Victorian mill, with carefully cooked, popular brasserie food, decent wines, and a bustling buoyant atmosphere; cl Sun, am Sat, am bank hols, 25–26 Dec, 1 Jan; disabled access. **£25**.

Leeds SE2933 SOUS LE NEZ EN VILLE The Basement, Quebec House, Quebec St (0113) 244 0108 Imaginative and popular food in this fashionable basement restaurant with tiled floors and exposed brick walls; very good wine list, and efficient service; cl Sun, bank hols. **£14.95**|£4.50.

Meltham SE0910 WILL'S O' NAT'S Blackmoorfoot Rd (01484) 850078 Well run pub, alone in a fine moorland spot; with comfortable seating and lots of interesting old photographs and drawings of the area on the walls of the spacious bar, nice views from the raised, partly no smoking dining extension, a wide choice of popular, good-value food, well kept real ales, and a big collection of malt whiskies; cl pm 25 and 26 Dec; limited disabled access. **£14.50**|£4.60.

Ripponden SE0419 OLD BRIDGE (01422) 822595/823722 Well kept medieval inn by a pretty bridge over the River Ryburn; with interesting rooms, good wines and real ales, and very popular cold buffet on weekday lunchtimes (best to book); charming evening restaurant just over the bridge; no bar food Sat, pm Sun; no children; disabled access. **£25 for 4 courses in restaurant**|£3.75.

Special help from A Cartlidge, Lisa Grey, Lisetta Tripodi, Bill Jupp, E G Parish, Miss L Jones, M and J Back, Peter and Ann Mumford, Heather Martin, Bob and Maggie Atherton, Melinda Simmons, Derek and Sylvia Stephenson, J Palmer, Kevin Green, Mrs Julie Robinson, Paul Kennedy, Roger Bellingham, Victoria Marcott, Andrew Elton, B Speight, R T Colley.

YORKSHIRE CALENDAR

Some of these dates were provisional as we went to press. Please check information with the numbers provided.

JANUARY

1 **Embsay** Family Day at Embsay Steam Railway (01756) 794727; **York** Anne Frank Exhibition at the Merchant Adventurers' Hall – *till Sat 31* (01904) 554433

5 **Hubberholme** Land Letting at the George pub, *at 8pm* – ancient auction for church lands grazing (01756) 760223

17 **Goathland** Day of Dance: ancient long sword dance (Norse origin) around the village *from 9am* (01904) 770318

FEBRUARY

14 **York** Viking Festival: warriors' procession and combat, torchlit procession, boat burning and fireworks – *till Sun 15* and *Sat 21–Sun 22* (01904) 643211; **York** Thomas the Tank Engine Week at the National Railway Museum – *till Sun 22* (01904) 554433

24 **Scarborough** Shrovetide Skipping Festival *at noon*: ¾ mile of Foreshore Rd closed to traffic *till 5pm* (01723) 373333

MARCH

1 **Harrogate** Northern Classic Car Restoration Show at the Great Yorkshire Showground (01484) 660622

7 **Eskdale** Festival of Arts – *till Sat 14* (01947) 602674

8 **Harrogate** National Classic Bike Show at the Great Yorkshire Showground (01484) 660622

16 **Skipton** Music Festival – *till Sat 21* (01756) 793195

22 **York** City of York European Week – *till Sun 29* (01904) 554433

28 **Leeds** Doll and Teddy Bear Fair at the Civic Hall (01914) 240400

31 **Bainbridge** Lambing Open Days at High Force Farm – *till 19 Apr* (01969) 650379

APRIL

1 **Nunnington** Photographic Exhibition: National Trust Countryside in Yorkshire at Nunnington Hall – *till Weds 29* (01439) 748283

9 **Doncaster** Easter Egg Rolling at Cusworth Hall Museum of South Yorkshire Life (01302) 782342

10 **Hebden Bridge** Pace Egg Plays (01422) 843831; **Harrogate** International Youth Festival – *till Sun 12* (01306) 744360; **Keighley** Easter Events at East Riddlesden Hall – *till Tues 14* (01535) 607075; **Middleham** Trainers Open Day at Middleham Stables (01969) 623350

11 **Cawthorne** Easter Activities at Cannon Hall – *till Mon 13* (01226) 790270; **Kingston-upon-Hull** Easter Organ Festival in the city centre (01432) 610610; **Murton** Easter Celebrations at Murton Park – *till Mon 13* (01904) 489966; **North Stainley** Easter Egg Hunt at Lightwater Valley Theme Park (01765) 635321; **Overton** Easter Celebrations at the National Coal Mining Museum – *till Sun 12* (01924) 843306; **York** Model Railways: about 30 layouts – *till Tues 14* (01653) 694319

12 **Beningbrough** Easter Bunny Hunt at Beningbrough Hall – *till Mon 13* (01904) 470666; **Nunnington** Easter Egg Hunt at Nunnington Hall (01439) 748283

YORKSHIRE CALENDAR

APRIL cont

13 **Elsecar** Easter Country Fayre at Elsecar Workshops (01226) 740203;
Ossett World Coal-carrying Championship (01924) 295000

18 **Harrogate** Spring Flower Show – *till Sun 26* (01423) 561049

24 **Halifax** National Young Musicians' Chamber Music Festival – *till 2
May* (01706) 817633; **Whitby** Gothic Convention – *till Sun 26* (0115)
949 7659

26 **Horton in Ribblesdale** Three Peaks Race (01423) 712000

MAY

 1 **Cleethorpes** Beer Festival at the Winter Gardens: over 40 real ales – *till
Sun 3* (01472) 692925

 2 **Marsden** Cuckoo Day at Marsden Mechanics Hall (01484) 847016;
Sowerby Bridge Town and Canal Festival at Tuel Lane Lock – *till Mon
4* (01422) 831627

 3 **Scorton** Vintage Vehicle and Machinery Event at Kiplin Hall (01429)
268760

10 **Scarborough** Brass Band Contest at the Spa Complex (01430) 423451

15 **Whitby** Folk Festival – *till Sun 17* (01947) 820408

17 **Mytholmroyd** World Dock Pudding Championships (01422)
883023; **Nunnington** Plant Sale at Nunnington Hall (01439) 748283

19 **Sheffield** Chamber Music Festival – *till Sun 24* (0114) 273 4671

20 **Whitby** Planting of the Penny Hedge (corruption of penance hedge): a
tradition since 1159 (01947) 602674

21 **Beverley** and **East Riding** Early Music Festival – *till Sun 24* (01482)
867430

23 **York** Busking Festival (01904) 551677

24 **Nunnington** Rye Dale Spring Fair at Nunnington Hall (01439) 748283

27 **Hebtonstall** Pennine Spring Music Festival – *till Sat 30* (01422)
843831

28 **Keld** Tan Hill Show at Tan Hill Inn (01833) 628246

30 **Kirby Wiske** Vintage Vehicle and Machinery Event at Sion Hill Hall –
till Sun 31 (01429) 268760

JUNE

 7 **York** Lord Mayor's Parade (01904) 554433

11 **Bramham** International Horse Trials and Country Fair at Bramham
Park – *till Sun 14* (01937) 844265

13 **Hebden Bridge** Arts Festival – *till 12 July* (01422) 843831; **Kingston-
upon-Hull** International Festival – *till 31 July* (01482) 223559; **York**
Outdoor Chess Festival – *till Sun 14* (01904) 554433

14 **Beningbrough** Fun and Games in the Garden at Beningbrough Hall
(01904) 470666; **Rievaulx** York Concert Band at Rievaulx Terrace
(01439) 798340

20 **Nunnington** *Pirates of Penzance* Outdoors at Nunnington Hall
(01439) 748283; **Otley** Carnival (01943) 464204

21 **Walkington** Hay Ride to Bishop Burton (01482) 866694

26 **Bradford** Festival: street theatre, music, dance and Asian Mela – *till 12
July* (01274) 752000

27 **Malton** Concert at Castle Howard (01904) 554433; **South
Otterington** North Yorkshire County Agricultural Show at
Otterington Hall (01609) 773429; **Thirsk** North Yorkshire County
Show at Ryebeck Farm (01609) 773429

YORKSHIRE CALENDAR

JULY

1 **Whitby** Angling Festival – *till Fri 10* (01947) 602674
3 **York** Early Music Festival – *till Sun 12* (01904) 658338
4 **Helmsley** Traction Engine Steam Fair and Rally at Duncombe Park – *till Sun 5* (01439) 770213; **York** Street Art Festival *till Sun 5* (01904) 554433
5 **Halifax** Irish Festival at Piece Hall (01422) 358087; **Oxenhope** Straw Races: teams in fancy dress race through the village carrying a bale of straw and drinking at 5 pubs (01535) 644298
11 **Huddersfield** Carnival at Greenhead Park (01484) 539552
12 **Rievaulx** Medieval Music at Rievaulx Terrace (01439) 798340; **York** Mystery Plays (01904) 621756
14 **Harrogate** Great Yorkshire Show – *till Thurs 16* (01423) 561536
17 **Rye Dale** Festival – *till 1 Aug* (01439) 771518
18 **Malton** Concert at Castle Howard (01904) 554433
19 **Beningbrough** Teddy Bears Picnic at Beningbrough Hall (01904) 470666; **Nunnington** York Concert Band at Nunnington Hall (01439) 748283
24 **Harrogate** International Festival – *till 8 Aug* (01423) 562303
25 **Middlesbrough** Cleveland County Show (01642) 327583; **York** Celebration of Band Music in the city centre (01904) 551677
26 **Robin Hood's Bay** Sports, Gymkhana and Working Hunter Show (01947) 880441; **Rievaulx** Children's Workshop at Rievaulx Terrace (01439) 748283
28 **Rye Dale** Show (01653) 697820
29 **Whitby** Sneaton and Hawsker Agricultural Show at Russel Hall Farm (01947) 602674

AUGUST

1 **Hebden Bridge** Vintage Transport Rally at Calder Holmes Park – *till Sun 2* (01484) 559086; **Nunnington** Outdoor Concert at Nunnington Hall (01439) 748283; **Ripon** St Wilfrid's Procession (01765) 604579; **York** Yorkshire Day (01904) 554433
4 **Egton Bridge** Old Gooseberry Show at St Heddas School: since 1800, tastings *from 5pm*, also local bands in the Postgate and Horse Shoe pubs (01924) 384714; **Littlebeck** Garden Fête and Rose Queen Ceremony (01947) 810720
5 **Kingston-upon-Hull** Jazz Festival – *till Sun 9* (01482) 615624
7 **Filey** Flower Festival at St Oswald's Parish Church – *till Sun 9* (01723) 513264
8 **Halifax** Agricultural Show at Savile Park (01422) 355056; **Whitby** Regatta and Carnival – *till Mon 10* (01947) 602674
16 **Beningbrough** Photographic Exhibition: Aspects of Yorkshire at Beningbrough Hall – *till 15 Sept* (01904) 470666
22 **West Witton** Burning of the Bartle: effigy of legendary outlaw, and fun day – *till Sun 23* (01969) 622034; **Whitby** Lifeboat Day (01947) 602674; **Whitby** Folk Festival – *till Fri 28* (01947) 602674
23 **Nunnington** Children's Day at Nunnington Hall (01439) 748283
26 **Egton** Horse and Agricultural Show (01947) 895281
29 **Elvington** Air Spectacular at the Airbase – *till Mon 31* (01904) 554433; **Harrogate** Fuchsia Festival at Harlow Carr Botanical Gardens – *till Mon 31* (01423) 565418; **Leyburn** Wensleydale Agricultural Show (01969) 663658; **York** Peace Festival: free family day at Rowntree Park (01904) 553380

YORKSHIRE CALENDAR

AUGUST cont

30 **Beningbrough** Treasure Hunt at Beningbrough Hall – *till Mon 31* (01904) 470666

31 **Burniston** Horticultural and Agricultural Show (01723) 882271; **Epworth** Show (01427) 873865

SEPTEMBER

3 **Nunnington** Yorkshire Watercolour Society at Nunnington Hall (01439) 748283

5 **Keighley** and District Agricultural Show (01535) 643206; **Lealholm** Show (01947) 602674; **Malton** Concert at Castle Howard (01904) 554433; **Sowerby Bridge** Rushbearing Festival – *till Sun 6* (01422) 831896; **York** Festival of Traditional Dance in the city centre – *till Sun 6* (01904) 551677

6 **Rievaulx** York Concert Band at Rievaulx Terrace (01439) 798340

10 **Kingston-upon-Hull** International Sea Shanty Festival: music, hornpipe dancing and North Sea classic boat regatta – *till Sun 13* (01482) 615682

12 **Castleton** and **Danby** Floral and Horticultural Show (01287) 660409; **Whitby** Heritage Week – *till Sun 20* (01947) 602674

13 **Beningbrough** Plant Fair: rare and unusual plants at Beningbrough Hall (01904) 470666; **Hardraw Scar** Brass Band Competition at the Green Dragon Inn (01904) 412383; **Nunnington** Popular Music and Dance from the English Civil War at Nunnington Hall (01439) 748283; **Sheffield** Transport Rally at Meadowhall Centre (01742) 489166

18 **York** Book Fair at the Barbican Centre – *till Sat 19* (01904) 656688

19 **Scarborough** Angling Festival – *till Sat 26* (01723) 859480; **Stokesley** Show at the Showground (01642) 713209; **York** Festival of Food and Drink – *till Sun 27* (01904) 653655

OCTOBER

9 **Kingston-upon-Hull** Fair – *till Sat 17* (01482) 615624; **Middlesbrough** Writearound Festival – *till Sun 18* (01642) 264341

17 **Whitby** Captain Cook Festival Week – *till Sun 25* (01947) 602674

19 **Beningbrough** Apple Week at Beningbrough Hall – *till Sun 25* (01904) 470666

29 **York** Halloween in the city centre – *till Sat 31* (01904) 554433

31 **Beningbrough** Halloween at Beningbrough Hall (01904) 470666

NOVEMBER

5 **York** Guy Fawkes Weekend – *till Sun 8* (01904) 554488

11 **Kingston-upon-Hull** Literature Festival – *till Sun 22* (01482) 615624

14 **Nunnington** Concert at Nunnington Hall (01439) 748283

18 **Huddersfield** Contemporary Music Festival – *till Sun 29* (01484) 430528

26 **York** St Nicholas Fair: crafts, choirs – *till Sun 29* (01904) 632257

DECEMBER

6 **Knaresborough** Edwardian Sunday (01709) 862914

20 **Haworth** Torchlight Procession and Carol Service (01535) 642329

24 **Dewsbury** Old Custom: tolling the Devil's knell (01484) 223200

LONDON

Exciting new openings, lots of change to existing places; bargains as well as high prices, and an unsurpassed range of things to look at, do, eat and buy.

With the Millennium coming, there is more to see than ever before. One of the great things about London is that almost everything worth visiting or looking at is concentrated in the relatively small centre, and it seems likely that in the next year or two more of the central tourist places will be closed to most traffic.

We have divided the centre into a few general areas which are easy for most people to walk across, so that the places we describe in each of these are close enough to walk between (and so that we can give a thumb-nail sketch of the character of that area). The only parts of outer London which we have included are those which would really add something significant to a stay in the centre.

With London prices so high, it's important to note that some of the most outstanding places to visit are free: the National Gallery, National Portrait Gallery and Wallace Collection (West End), the Tate Gallery (Westminster), Leighton House (Kensington), the Geffrye Museum, Museum of Childhood and Guildhall (City), the British Museum (despite pressure on it to introduce charges), and the extraordinary Sir John Soane's Museum (Bloomsbury), Kenwood (Hampstead) and the Horniman Museum (Forest Hill). The new British Library is free, too. And there's often free entertainment in several places – most notably, Covent Garden, the Barbican Centre and the South Bank.

Among places that do charge admission, you get a real feeling of value for money at the Natural History Museum (Kensington), the Museum of the Moving Image (MOMI), Britain at War, and the Imperial War Museum (south of the River; the War Museum's free after 4.30pm), and the toy and model museum at Lancaster Gate (West End). The remarkable new London Aquarium in the former County Hall (south of the River) is a great family outing, and the BBC's new broadcasting show (West End) is quite something. The Rugby Experience out at Twickenham is immensely popular with people hooked by the game. And a fine antidote to the richness and sense of history in the great central collections is the National Trust's new Modernist property at 2 Willow Road up in Hampstead. The excellent Museum of London (City) always seems to have something new – and its admission ticket is valid for 3 months.

There are plenty of ways to save money on attractions: one of the best is the London White Card, which covers entry to 15 of the top museums (including the Science Museum, MOMI, and the V&A) for £15, provided you can squeeze them all into 3 days. The London for

Less scheme gives discounts on some attractions (including the appallingly expensive Madame Tussaud's), restaurants, theatres and hotels: quite a bargain, it covers 4 people for 8 days for £12.95, and is on sale at the tourist information centre at Victoria.

London's Tube, the underground railway, is the most straightforward way of getting around, and easy even for first-time visitors. Around rush hour and late at night, though, the underground becomes rather unpleasant, with infrequent trains and overcrowded carriages. Buses have the advantage of letting you sightsee as you go (there are also several hop-on hop-off tour buses, day or night, with commentaries). Pocket tube and London Transport bus route maps are free from ticket offices. In the text, we have grouped things to see and do under the heading of the most convenient tube station, using the ⊖ symbol – or the ⇌ symbol if it's surface rail instead.

A one-day Travelcard is an excellent investment for the visitor; you can even buy them in advance from newsagents. It's valid on buses, tube and rail trains, for as many journeys as you want to make during the day (not the morning rush hour). For only slightly more, you can get a travelcard for the whole weekend, or a book of 10 individual tickets. If you're coming up to London by train, you can add a one-day Travelcard to the rail fare at a big discount. Tickets on some rail routes allow discounts at a few London attractions.

If you're going to be wandering around, you should have an A–Z street guide; even people who've lived here for years carry one almost wherever they go.

A point to note is that food in London pubs (as opposed to the better ones elsewhere) tends to be very ordinary indeed; few, apart from those we mention, are worth considering for a decent bite to eat.

All the places to stay that we include are within reasonably easy reach of the centre, and many of them are actually part of it.

Where to stay

22 JERMYN STREET 22 Jermyn St SW1Y 6HL (0171) 734 2353 *£230; 5 rms and 13 suites – spacious with deeply comfortable seats and sofas, flowers, plants, and antiques. Stylish little hotel owned by the same family for 80 years and much loved by customers; no public rooms, wonderful 24-hour service, helpful notes and suggestions from the friendly owners, in-room light meals, and a warm welcome for children; disabled access.

BASIL STREET HOTEL 8 Basil St SW3 1AH (0171) 581 3311 £199.75, plus special breaks; 91 pleasant, decent-sized rms, most with own bthrm. Handy for Harrods and Hyde Park, this very civilised, privately owned Edwardian hotel has a relaxed atmosphere, antiques, fine carpets and paintings in the public rooms, a panelled restaurant with reliably good food, cellar wine bar, afternoon teas in the lounge, and ladies' club (named after a parrot who had to go when his language became inappropriate); helpful, courteous service – many of the staff have been here for years, the manager for over 40; children free in parents' rm.

CHESTERFIELD 35 Charles St W1X 8LX (0171) 491 2622 £243.50w; 110 well equipped, pretty rms. Charming hotel with particularly courteous and helpful staff; afternoon tea in the panelled library, a relaxed club-style bar with resident pianist, and fine food in attractive restaurant or light and airy Terrace Room.

CLARIDGES Brook St W1A 2JQ (0171) 629 8860 £260w inc champagne and chocolates; 190 excellent rms. Grand hotel long used by Royalty and heads of state, with liveried footmen, lift attendants and valets, elegant and comfortable day rooms, civilised colonnaded foyer where the Hungarian Quartet plays; lovely formal restaurant with mirrored mural and terrace, and a more intimate smaller restaurant called the Causerie; dinner-dance pm Fri–Sat; free golf at Wentworth (and tennis at the Vanderbilt Racquet Club); disabled access.

CLAVERLEY 13–14 Beaufort Gdns SW3 (0171) 589 8541 £120; 30 individually decorated rms. Friendly, privately owned Edwardian house with a comfortable lounge, panelled reading room, and good breakfasts in the cheerful dining room; disabled access.

CONNAUGHT Carlos Pl W1Y 6AL (0171) 499 7070; 90 lovely, individually decorated rms inc 24 suites. A very special place with fine old-fashioned dignified values – there's no brochure, no price list; elegant, restful day rooms filled with lovely flowers and antiques, fine panelling, exemplary service, and outstanding food in the 2 formal restaurants; disabled access.

CONRAD Chelsea Harbour SW10 0XG (0171) 823 3000 £175w; 159 suites with a light and spacious living-room area (many have sofa-beds so 2 small children could stay with parents at no extra cost). American-owned, Europe's first purpose-built luxury 'suite hotel' is tucked away in the quiet modern enclave of the Chelsea Harbour development and overlooks its small marina; good food in the Brasserie (marina views) or the Long Gallery, friendly service, evening pianist, and health club; disabled access.

CUMBERLAND Marble Arch W1A 4RF (0171) 262 1234 £182; 903 comfortable, well equipped rms. Very well run and popular hotel with a fine choice of food in several cafés and restaurants, lots of comfortable public rooms, a shopping arcade, and very good service.

DURRANTS George St W1H 6BJ (0171) 935 8131 £136.50; 92 well equipped rms, with own bthrms; the quietest are at the back. Managed by the same family for over 70 years, this surprisingly quiet central hotel is set behind a delightful Georgian façade, and has fine paintings and antiques, a clubby bar, and relaxing lounges; cosy panelled restaurant with essentially English cooking, and helpful, pleasant staff; disabled access.

FIELDING 4 Broad Court WC2B 5QZ (0171) 836 8305 £95; 24 rms, all with showers. Carefully renovated and well run small 18th-c hotel opposite the Royal Opera House site and charmingly lit at night by the preserved 19th-c gas lamps; residents' bar (watched over by Smokey the African grey parrot), and good breakfasts; cl 1 wk over Christmas; children over 12.

FIVE SUMNER PLACE 5 Sumner Pl SW7 3EE (0171) 584 7586 *£126; 13 well equipped rms. Friendly Victorian terraced house with good breakfasts in an attractive conservatory, and comfortable lounges.

GORING 15 Beeston Pl, Grosvenor Gardens, SW1W OJW (0171) 396 9000 £220.75, plus special breaks; 76 individually decorated rms, some with balconies overlooking a pretty garden. Built in 1910 by the grandfather of the present Mr Goring, this family-run, impeccably kept and very English hotel has a particularly welcoming atmosphere (many of the staff have been there for years); very good enjoyable cooking in the elegant restaurant, a super wine list, comfortable lounge for afternoon tea, airy cocktail bar, and staunchly loyal customers; disabled access.

HALKIN 5 Halkin St SW1X 7DJ (0171) 333 1000 *£260, plus special breaks; 41 stylish, well equipped rms, with wonderful marble bthrms. Despite its Georgian exterior, the décor and furnishings here are ultra-modern but enjoyable; there's a particularly good Milanese restaurant overlooking the garden, fine breakfasts, and really charming staff; much liked by the business community, too – lots of facilities for them; cl 25 Dec; disabled access.

HAZLITTS 6 Frith St W1V 5TZ (0171) 434 1771 £174; 23 rms with 18th- or 19th-c beds and free-standing Victorian baths with early brass shower-mixer units. Behind a typically Soho façade of listed early Georgian houses, this is a well kept and comfortably laid-out little hotel which could scarcely be handier for the West End; good continental breakfasts served in your bedroom, snacks in the sitting room, lots of restaurants all around; kind, helpful service; cl Christmas; disabled access.

KNIGHTSBRIDGE GREEN 159 Knightsbridge SW1X 7PD (0171) 584 6274 £137, plus special breaks; 27 rms, most suites with sitting room. Friendly, family-owned hotel, carefully refurbished and neatly kept; very good in-room breakfasts (no restaurant), bar service, free coffee and tea in the lounge, and helpful, efficient staff; limited disabled access.

L'HOTEL 28 Basil St SW3 1AS (0171) 589 6286 *£146.88; 12 well equipped rms. Small, family-owned, French-style city hotel, close to Harrods and above the neatly kept, well run Metro wine bar where English and continental breakfasts are served, as well as good modern French café food; friendly staff; disabled access.

LE MERIDIEN PICCADILLY 21 Piccadilly W1V 0BH (0171) 734 8000 £332.62, plus special breaks; 266 comfortable, well equipped rms. The very best in modern French hotel-keeping; attractive, quiet public rooms with professional and friendly service, popular afternoon tea, fine restaurant food, and free membership of the good health club downstairs; one child under 12 free in parents' room; disabled access.

LINCOLN HOUSE 33 Gloucester Pl W1P 3PD (0171) 486 7630 £79; 22 rms, most with own bthrm. Good-value Georgian hotel in the West End; with decent English breakfasts in the pleasant dining room, and friendly staff.

NUMBER SIXTEEN 14–17 Sumner Pl SW7 3EG (0171) 589 5232 *£150; 36 individually decorated pretty rms, most with own bthrm. Attractive terrace of early Victorian town houses with pretty flower tubs outside; particularly friendly and helpful staff; antiques, a restful atmosphere, fresh flowers and an open fire in the drawing room, cosy library with an honesty bar, and a conservatory opening onto a secluded walled garden; in-room continental breakfast; children over 12.

RUBENS 39–41 Buckingham Palace Rd SW1W OPS (0171) 834 6600 £146, plus special breaks; 180 well equipped rms. Opposite Buckingham Palace and nr Victoria Station, this attractive hotel has comfortable day rooms inc an airy lounge with views of the Royal Mews, a restful library, an open fire in the bar, and attractive split-level restaurant with good food.

ST GEORGE'S Langham Pl W1N 8QS (0171) 580 0111 £185.90; 86 light rms with marvellous views over London. Popular modern hotel, a stone's throw from Oxford Circus; afternoon tea in the bar and lounge, a fine rooftop restaurant and dinner-dance every Fri and Sat.

STAKIS ST ERMIN'S 2 Caxton St SW1H OQW (0171) 222 7888 £193.90; 290 rms. Opulent Edwardian hotel with fine staircase, ornate plasterwork, antiques and elegant furniture in the luxurious day rooms; fine food in 2 restaurants, and helpful staff.

SWISS HOUSE 171 Old Brompton Rd SW5 0AN (0171) 373 2769 *£75; 16 rms. Festooned with ivy and flower boxes, this is a warmly friendly and good-value, family-run hotel, relaxed and tidy inside, with very good buffet continental breakfasts.

TOPHAMS BELGRAVIA 28 Ebury St SW1W 0LU (0171) 730 8147 *£115; 40 cosy rms, most with own bthrm. Small, charmingly old-fashioned hotel, made up of several town houses, with a friendly country-house atmosphere, downstairs bar, attractive lounges, good food in the elegant restaurant, and decent wines; cl Christmas.

TOWER THISTLE St Katharine's Way E1 9LD (0171) 481 2575 **£183.50,** plus special breaks; 802 rms (ask for one with a view). In a marvellous location next to Tower Bridge and the Tower of London, this busy modern hotel has stylish public rooms and several eating areas with fine river views, and a café that transforms into an evening nightclub; disabled access.

WILBRAHAM Wilbraham Pl, Sloane St SW1 9AE (0171) 730 8296 **£102.23;** 45 simply furnished rms. Privately owned, old-fashioned hotel with pleasant public rooms, good in-room breakfasts, and decent food in the bar-cum-buttery.

WINDERMERE 142-144 Warwick Way SW1V 4JE (0171) 834 5163 **£78;** 23 attractive modern rms, 19 with own bthrm. Small private hotel with a cosy lounge; decent breakfasts and evening meals in the attractive, no smoking dining room, and a friendly informal atmosphere.

THE WEST END

This area is world-famous for its shopping and window-shopping, from the daunting bustle of Oxford St, through the bookshops around Charing Cross Rd, the specialist food and cookery shops of Soho, and the elegant stores of Regent St and Piccadilly, to the ultra-smart clothes shops of South Molton St and Bond St. There are great opportunities for window-shopping in the auction houses and fine art galleries.

The West End is synonymous with theatre; it's worth knowing that on Leicester Sq a half-price ticket booth sells off surplus tickets for that day's performances: open around 12–2pm for matinée tickets, then from about 2.30pm for evenings – there's usually a queue so it's worth getting there earlier.

Highlights here include the National Gallery and Trafalgar Square, Piccadilly with the Royal Academy, and Covent Garden. The new BBC Experience up by Oxford Circus is great for anyone interested in what goes into TV or radio, not just what comes out. Quieter places such as the toy and model museum out at Lancaster Gate are well worth tracking down. Chinatown is a vivid enclave; Neal St is a focus for vegetarian restaurants and rather alternative shops; and there are staunchly old-fashioned institutions of Englishness and English cooking like Rules or Simpson's – among an extraordinarily eclectic flood of other places to eat.

To see and do

Charing Cross The tube station here is tucked away under TRAFALGAR SQUARE, which many people think of as the heart of central London (distances to and from central London used to be measured from the Cross on the Strand). Named for the great naval victory of 1805, it was designed by Nash and completed in 1841; the fountains were added a century later. The centrepiece, NELSON'S COLUMN, stretches up 56 metres (185 ft), its base guarded by 4 huge identical lions. Look out for the gifted roller-skaters who perform in the evenings around the base – and, of course, for the innumerable pigeons; Nelson has a special coating to protect him from their droppings.

▣ NATIONAL GALLERY This magnificent building right on the square houses the national collection of Western European painting, with around 2,000 pictures dating from the 13th c to the end of the 19th (some 20th-c works were recently swapped with the Tate, after a decision that 1900 is the date when modern art begins). You'll enjoy it most if you're firm and restrict yourself to just a few of the galleries, rather than trying to see everything. It's hard to pick out highlights (the whole collection is worth studying), but don't miss the Sainsbury Wing, which gives perfect lighting and viewing conditions for its treasure-trove of early Renaissance works. The gallery gets very busy, especially on a Sat, or at any time around the Impressionist works. The hi-tech audio tour, with a CD rather than a cassette (so you can skip to whichever bit you want), is well worth the cost, with a commentary on every single picture in the main gallery. This year's exhibitions include a collection of 17th-c Dutch works (6 May–2 Aug), and a look at reflections and mirrors in paintings (16 Sept–13 Dec). Meals, snacks, shop, disabled access; cl am Sun, 24–26 Dec, 1 Jan, Good Fri; (0171) 839 3321; free, charges for some special exhibitions.

▣ NATIONAL PORTRAIT GALLERY (St Martin's Pl, just round the corner) Grandly illustrates British history, with paintings of kings, queens and other notable characters arranged in chronological order from the top floor (medieval) to the present. Recent extensions have greatly broadened the gallery's appeal (creating space for some delightfully varied temporary exhibitions), and there are more on the way. Shop, disabled access; cl am Sun, 24–26 Dec, 1 Jan, Good Fri, May Day bank hol; (0171) 306 0055; free, charge for some special exhibitions.

▥ Plenty of theatres nr here, with a group based around this end of the Charing Cross Rd, and another up along the Strand. Marked out by the globe on top of the building, the Coliseum (St Martin's Lane) is the home of the English National Opera, though they plan to move elsewhere early next century; in the meantime, you can usually get decently priced seats on the day, from 10am. (London's more famous Covent Garden Opera House is currently closed for restoration and extension.) Almost next door to the Coliseum, the Chandos is a good pub with food all day (upstairs is best), down past the Post Office the underground Tappit Hen is an atmospheric wine bar, and there's no end of smart little coffee shops and cafés nearby – Gabys (30 Charing Cross Rd) does perfect hot salt beef sandwiches.

✝ ▣ ✗ ST MARTIN-IN-THE-FIELDS This elegant church has frequent lunchtime and evening concerts; (0171) 930 0089 for programme. Unmistakable for its blue clock-dial – the only clock in this part of London that seems always to keep the right time – the church has a busy coffee bar in its crypt, with frequent art exhibitions; also brass-rubbing centre, shop (inc all the Academy of St Martin-in-the-Fields CDs) and good afternoon craft market, useful for bargains. Every night the church is used as a shelter for the homeless, but even so as you make your way home from the theatre you're likely to see plenty of bodies huddled in shop doorways in these streets – a sadly common sight all over London but especially obvious around here.

⊖ 🏛 ♔ **Covent Garden** Partly pedestrianised, the former vegetable, fruit and flower market with its elegant buildings is now made over to smart café-bars, boutiques and stalls, such as those in the covered piazza, selling good but expensive handmade clothes and craft items. There's also the Jubilee Market which specialises in different wares on different days. The many bars and restaurants are always lively at night, but again they're not cheap.

♿! LONDON TRANSPORT MUSEUM (The Piazza) On the site of Covent Garden's former flower market, this is more than just a collection of vehicles: you don't just see the buses and trams, you hear and smell them, and can even try your hand at driving a computerised Tube train (the knack is to close the doors just as you see people trying to get on). Plenty of touch-screen exhibits, as well as a good range of the splendid posters used by London Transport over the last century. Costumed actors tell nostalgic transport tales, and there are children's activities in the summer hols. Snacks, interesting shop, disabled access; cl 24–26 Dec; (0171) 836 8557; £4.50.

♿! CABARET MECHANICAL THEATRE Tucked away in the heart of the former market buildings, an appealing collection of unique hand-made working automata, operated by the touch of a button or by inserting a coin. Great fun – though several exhibits are quite bizarre, notably the incredible *Last Judgement* by Paul Spooner. Shop, some disabled access; cl 25–26 Dec; (0171) 379 7961; *£1.95.

♿ THEATRE MUSEUM (Tavistock St) Exhaustive look at events and personalities on the stage over the last few hundred years. Posters, puppets and props are among the permanent collection, which although astonishingly comprehensive is arranged a little confusingly; it's easy to find yourself going round

backwards. The very good temporary displays leave the deepest impression: they sometimes have free stage make-up demonstrations. Shop, disabled access; cl Mon, 25–26 Dec; (0171) 836 7891; *£3.50.

🏛 THEATRE ROYAL (Drury Lane) The oldest working theatre in the world, first opened in 1663 (Nell Gwynn was one of its earliest performers), but rebuilt several times over the next few centuries. Tours show backstage features inc the intriguing hydraulic lift beneath the stage, still in use. Meals, snacks, shop, disabled access; 4 tours a day (exc on Weds and Sat when only 2 because of matinée), 10.30am, 1pm (12.30pm Weds and Sat), 2.30pm and 5.30pm, best to check Sun times (though usually 12, 2 and 3.30pm); (0171) 494 5091; *£4.

✝! ST PAUL'S CHURCH The actors' church, full of interesting memorials to performers. Pepys watched the first-ever Punch and Judy show here in 1662. Outside its back gate, facing the covered market, the theatrical tradition continues, with jugglers, clowns, mountebanks and unusual musicians performing on the cobbles.

One of the delights of this area is its range of unusual or specialist SHOPS. In the streets around the Piazza, Knutz (Russell St) has everything for the practical joker, and Penhaligons (Wellington St) sell lovely old-fashioned toiletries. On the other side of the market, N of the tube station, interesting and unusual shops are set in a labyrinthine network of attractively rejuvenated alleys and streets; you will get lost, but wandering around is great fun, and they all lead back to roughly the same area. Neal St is rewarding for its small craft and specialist shops, and Neal's Yard is full of healthy living – delightful in summer with its fresh paint and tubs of flowers. Floral St has elegant and expensive clothes and shoe shops (plus the Tintin shop – paradise for the Tintin fan). The Africa Centre on King St may have exhibitions of African art and culture. No shortage of places to eat around here, but useful pubs for lunch or refreshment include the Marquess of

Anglesey on Bow Street, with a good-value upstairs restaurant, and the Lamb & Flag on Rose St, an attractive 300-year-old pub with decent snacks, its back room still much as Dickens described it.

✆ **Leicester Sq** All central London's attractions are within easy walking distance of here, with several of the more interesting theatres little more than 5 minutes' stroll. The tube station's various exits are a favourite with Londoners stuck for a place to meet; hordes of them mill around, anxiously looking for the friends they finally discover they've been standing next to for half an hour. Around the bustling edges of the pedestrian square, attractively cleaned up in recent years, are several huge cinemas, pricy but with excellent sound; you can see films more cheaply at the Prince Charles in Leicester Pl, leading off the square (where Notre Dame de France has an impressive Jean Cocteau mural). The Swiss Centre on the far corner of the square sells exquisite chocolates and Swiss groceries; the well run Moon Under Water is much more reasonably priced than most pubs around here. Marked out by its dramatic ornamental gate, CHINATOWN has developed its own character, inviting despite the locals' cool indifference to outsiders; the supermarkets and shops along pedestrianised Gerrard St and in neighbouring streets are fascinating, with their weird and wonderful vegetables, strange squidgy things in little cellophane packets, and odd-smelling dried meats and fish. Plenty of authentic Chinese restaurants, as well as less convincingly adapted telephone boxes.

Back by the tube station, this stretch of the Charing Cross Rd is justifiably famous for its BOOKSHOPS, specialist and general, new and secondhand. Foyles is the biggest city bookstore, but trying to find what you want is time-consuming; Waterstones is very friendly and relaxed, with informed staff. The side alleys between here and St Martin's Lane have good secondhand bookshops, several with specialisations such as the occult, antique children's books, or the theatre; Cecil Court is perhaps the best. Two distinctively designed pubs round here are the good-value Moon Under Water opposite Blackwells on the Charing Cross Rd, and the Salisbury on St Martin's Lane, a splendid Victorian pub, all velvet and cut glass. Not far away on Long Acre is Stanfords, the best map and guidebook shop in Britain, with helpful knowledgeable staff, and books and maps covering all corners of the globe. Leicester Sq is very handy for Soho, described below under Tottenham Court Rd.

✆ **Piccadilly Circus** Another lively hub of London life, with famous streets radiating off in every direction, each quite different in character; handsome Piccadilly roughly to the W, the theatres of bustling Shaftesbury Avenue to the E, with smarter ones on Haymarket to the S, Regent St coolly curving N towards Oxford Circus – and, of course, the famous statue of Eros, where all the foreign students sit to be photographed.

🏛 🖼 ROYAL ACADEMY OF ARTS (Burlington House, Piccadilly) Splendid building with excellent changing exhibitions for most of the year, then from 7 Jun–16 Aug its famous (often notorious) Summer Exhibition of works by living artists great and small. An exhibition of art from England's regional museums, inc works by Canaletto, Hogarth, Turner and Bacon, runs from 22 Jan–13 Apr. Meals, snacks, shop, disabled access; cl 24–26 Dec, Good Fri; (0171) 439 7438; admission charge varies – usually between £5 and £7.

❗👍☺ Rock Circus 🚇 (London Pavilion, Piccadilly Circus) Exuberant romp through the history of rock and roll, more fun than its stablemate Madame Tussaud's, but still alarmingly high-priced considering its comparitive brevity. Wax figures from Elvis to Bono, some interesting archive film, and a finale with moving animatronic models.

The headsets that provide musical accompaniment are ingeniously designed, though they don't always work properly. Snacks, shop, disabled access; cl 25 Dec – it's open most nights till 9 or even 10pm; (0171) 734 8025; £7.95. The neighbouring Trocadero is a vast preserved building, redeveloped for mammoth SEGAWORLD, which hasn't quite lived up to its promise, thanks mainly to a change in pricing policy; you now pay individually for all the rides and games, and though they insist the original cover-all charge had to go because it led to queues and overcrowding, the result is that this now seems little more than a glorified amusement arcade, which is a real shame. The best ride, Aqua Planet, has remarkable 3-D graphics. Several other fairground-style attractions have sprung up around it: the Giant Drop is the first indoor free-fall ride in the world – you fall through 38 metres (125 ft) of flashing lights and screeching noises. Though touristy, the Glassblower in Glasshouse St is handy for a bite to eat.

The streets around here are excellent for SHOPPING. On opposite sides of the traffic islands in Piccadilly Circus are Tower Records, 3 floors of pop, classical and jazz (open till midnight), and Lillywhites, the long-established sports clothes and equipment store. On Piccadilly, Simpson's has several floors of good classic British clothes, for men and women (as well as unusual anti-reflection curved windows, famous for their inventive Christmas displays), while friendly Hatchards is a nicely old-fashioned bookshop where the staff can still sometimes turn vague requests into actual books. Almost next door, Fortnum's (Fortnum & Mason) has superior if expensive clothes, as well as the foods for which they're world-famous. Nearby, the Burlington Arcade is an elegant Regency covered arcade of expensive but good shops (excellent cashmere and knife/scissors shops, for instance), with a delightful set of rules, still enforced, that stop people whistling, singing or running in its

confines. The Ritz hotel is gorgeously flamboyant inside: well worth the high price of having a frogged and liveried waiter bring you a cup of tea or a perfectly mixed whisky sour. Behind Piccadilly's S side is Jermyn St, where among other splendid but top-of-the-range shops you can buy fine cheeses at Paxton & Whitfields, briar pipes at Astleys, hand-made shoes at Trickers, hand-made shirts from Turnbull & Asser, flat hats at Bates, and old-fashioned toiletries at Floris. The Red Lion in Duke of York St just off here is a little gem of a pub, with decent snacks (but very busy on weekday lunchtimes). A landmark on Haymarket is one of the two branches of Burberrys the mac-makers (the other's in Regent St).

⊖ Tottenham Court Rd is the handiest station for the most fashionable parts of SOHO, its coffee bars and cafés swarming with colourful young people in the evenings. Many of Soho's Georgian terraces are rather run-down, with peepshows and naughty video shops stuffed into basements and ground floors. But there are parts that have had much of their original quiet charm restored, like Soho Sq and Meard St, and it's still good for restaurants, and for shops connected with food or cooking. Old Compton St, central London's gayest street, has a good few interesting shops – Italian delicatessens (I Camisa is the best, with fabulous salamis), the Algerian Coffee Store which also sells lots of fruit teas, and 2 cheap but good wine and spirits shops. Milroys in Greek St has a wonderful collection of hundreds of different malt whiskies. Berwick St has a daily fruit and vegetable market – the lower half is more expensive but has better produce; at Simply Sausages down here you can watch them making some of their 43 different varieties of sausage, which include vegetarian and seafood flavours. The little Dog & Duck in Frith St and Coach & Horses in Poland St (the *Private Eye* pub) are 2 of the nicest Soho locals; in Romilly St another Coach & Horses is also on the well known Soho characters' circuit, and Kettners, now part of the Pizza Express chain, is a very entertaining old building. The area as a whole forms a sort of square, with the tube stations at Leicester Sq, Piccadilly Circus and even Oxford Circus all just as handy. **⊖ Oxford Circus** is at the heart of the city's busiest shopping areas, busy and noisy Oxford St to the left and right, and altogether nicer Regent St to the S. OXFORD ST doesn't have a lot of character, but is full of good stores such as Selfridges, John Lewis (the self-service restaurant is good for lunch), Marks & Spencer (2 major outlets), the 2 giant music shops HMV and Virgin Megastore, and the usual high street chains. South Molton St and St Christopher's Pl on either side of Oxford St are full of designer clothes shops and smart cafés; St Christopher's Pl also has quite an interesting antiques market. REGENT ST is one of the grandest streets in the whole area, with a splendid curve as it reaches Piccadilly Circus. A harmonious street of considerable character, with the fine shops definitely enhancing its appeal, even if all you want to do is browse. Liberty's is a splendid art nouveau timbered building, full of gorgeous soft furnishings and clothes, Oriental and leather goods, jewellery and a good gift department. Other high points include Mappin & Webb for fine china, glass, and jewellery; Hamleys, a marvellous toy shop (not cheap, though); Aquascutum, great for expensive English classic clothes; Garrard's the Royal jewellers; and Waterford/Wedgwood, for lovely china and glass in quite a wide range of prices. The Old Coffee House in Beak St around the corner from here, and the Red Lion in Kingly St, are useful for lunch. Carnaby St, tucked away behind, has some rather florid men's shops and good street-fashion houses, but is mainly full of small boutiques with trendy accessories, leather goods and tacky souvenirs; not really worth seeking out, though it recently changed hands so could well revive.

☺! BBC EXPERIENCE Below the imposing yet rather bullying bulk of Broadcasting House, this excellent new visitor centre celebrates the work and programmes of the BBC over the last 75 years, with a mixture of multi-media exhibitions and hands-on displays. You can try your hand at directing *East Enders*, or presenting the TV weather or sport, while the radio sections offer an interactive *Desert Island Discs*, and the chance to make a 3-minute play. Plenty for families, but also a great deal to please nostalgic-minded adults, and you'll come out with a much better idea of how programmes are put together. Snacks, big shop, disabled access; (0870) 603 0304; *£5.75.

⊖ 回 Bond St MAYFAIR, W of Regent St and N of Piccadilly (and only the shortest of strolls from them; Green Park tube station nr the S end of Bond St is also handy), is mostly a quietly discreet area of elegant town houses, smart well established hotels, and richly unobtrusive offices. Despite their famous names, Berkeley Sq and Grosvenor Sq don't have any special appeal for visitors – though you might want to stroll down Brook St to see the neighbouring blue plaques commemorating Handel and Jimi Hendrix living there (Handel House is being restored as a museum). Bond St with its continuation New Bond St is the area's main street for SHOPPING, though unless you want to spend a great deal of money on top-notch designer clothes and shoes, jewellery or Oriental rugs this is likely to be confined to the window. Plenty of art and antique galleries, and a good indoor antique market (124 New Bond St). Asprey's is a remarkable place, famous for its opulent luxury goods and glittering with an awesome tonnage of gems and precious metals. Sotheby's auction rooms are fascinating to wander around. Other small and prestigious art galleries are dotted throughout Mayfair, particularly in nearby Dover St and Cork St; Grays antique market, off 58 Davies St, has hundreds of indoor stalls. South Audley St has Hobbs of Mayfair, a delicious smart delicatessen, and Goodes, a magnificent glass and china shop. Higgins in Duke St is the Queen's coffee-man. The best Mayfair pub is the Red Lion in Waverton St.

🔲🏛 WALLACE COLLECTION (Hertford House, Manchester Sq – across Oxford St) Excellent art collection beautifully displayed in an elegant 18th-c house. It's visually very seductive, with probably the best collection of 18th-c French paintings in the world, inc luscious offerings from Watteau, Boucher and Fragonard. Also great Canalettos, fine works by Rembrandt, Rubens and Van Dyck, works by British painters, furniture (mostly 18th-c French), a notable assemblage of Sèvres porcelain, and an amazing array of arms and armour, both Oriental and European. It's rarely busy, and in places feels more like an historic home than a museum. Shop, disabled access with prior warning; cl am Sun, 24–26 Dec, Good Fri, 1 Jan, May Day bank hol; (0171) 935 0687; free.

! 🔲 ⊖ **Marble Arch** is striking in itself; originally a grand entrance for Buckingham Palace, moved here decades ago, and gleaming after its recent restoration. Over the road SPEAKERS CORNER on the edge of Hyde Park is where every Sun morning you can still hear impassioned diatribes on all sorts of causes. Traditional debating methods have practically disappeared, and disputes between rival fundamentalist groups have been known to become extremely heated, with the result that extra police armed with hidden cameras now patrol this famous bastion of free speech. Also on Sun you can see what's probably the longest, free open-air art exhibition in the world, with the work of 300 artists and craftsmen laid out along the park railings on Bayswater Rd; the Swan opposite gives a pleasant break. The HYDE PARK RIDING STABLES (Bathurst Mews) can organise horse-riding in the park; (0171) 262 3791; £25 an hour. The tube station – with so many exits it's a real initiative test finding your way out – is also handy for Oxford St.

♨ ⊖ **Lancaster Gate** LONDON TOY AND MODEL MUSEUM (Craven Hill) Particularly fine collection of toys, dolls, models and trains spread over 20 themed galleries, from Roman dolls to the latest from Japan. Much appeals to adults more than children, but they've put a lot of effort into making it fun for younger visitors – some interactive displays, for instance, and a carousel in the walled garden. Many exhibits are working; hang around a bit if they're not moving when you first go past. A collection of working Victorian slot-machines downstairs is one of the most popular features, and there's an amazing miniature town. Good activities and events in school hols. Snacks, shop; cl 25 Dec, 1 Jan; (0171) 402 5222; £4.95.

WESTMINSTER

This centre of Court and Government is a pleasant area to walk around, much of it with only light traffic, and with few shops to add extra people to the wide pavements. The Abbey's new admission charge should bring back some space and tranquillity to its chapels and cloisters. London's other great centrepiece, Buckingham Palace, is just the other side of St James's Park – a fine walk between the two. The Tate Gallery, Westminster Cathedral and the RHS flower shows are also highlights here.

To see and do

🏠🖼️↔ **St James's Park** BUCKINGHAM PALACE Now firmly established as one of London's most visited attractions, usually drawing around 400,000 visitors in the 8 weeks it's open. The main appeal is that this is where the Queen actually lives – her official London residence, and where she meets other Heads of State; the Royal Standard flies above it when she's home. But beyond that, while perhaps not the most satisfying of the Royal Palaces, it does pile a magnificent series of opulent sights into your walk through the state rooms. Highlights include the beautiful Picture Gallery, 46-metres (150-ft) long and filled with paintings from the Royal collection, the spectacular Grand Staircase, and the throne room with its predominant impression of gold, red and splendour. Tours are unguided, and there aren't many clues to help you, so it's definitely worth buying the guide book. Theoretically, you see everything at your own pace, but in practice you're likely to be carried along in the stream of other people, and you won't get much of a chance to linger. Tickets are sold from a little booth opposite the palace by the entrance to Green Park, though you can book in advance, on (0171) 839 1377 – ask for the Visitor Office. Busy shop, disabled access (with notice); open Aug–Sept; £9. The former chapel is now the QUEEN'S GALLERY, showing further magnificent paintings from the Royal collection. Shop; cl between exhibitions; £3.50. The ROYAL MEWS contains the State Coaches, private driving carriages and even sleighs of the Royal Family, as well as the immaculately turned out Windsor greys and Cleveland bay carriage horses. The longest painting in the Royal Collection is here too, a 36-metre (120-ft) canvas depicting William IV's Coronation procession. Shop, disabled access; open pm Weds all year, plus pm Tues and Thurs Apr–Aug, and pm Mon–Thurs Aug–Sept; (0171) 839 1377; £3.70 (a joint ticket with the Gallery is £6.20). At the grand front palace gates, the guards still keep their unflinchingly solemn positions: you can watch the CHANGING OF THE GUARD every day Apr–Aug (every other day in winter) at 11.30am; the ceremony may be late or even cancelled in exceptionally wet weather.

🖼️ St JAMES'S PARK This is the best approach to the Palace (you can get there more quickly, though less attractively, from Victoria). The oldest of London's Royal Parks, it was drained and converted into a deer park for Henry VIII, redesigned in the style of Versailles by order of Charles II (who often went for walks through it), and then re-created by Nash for George IV – this is the park which we see today, its relaxing lakeside environment particularly enjoyed by lunch-breaking office workers (and by hundreds of more or less exotic waterfowl), with a brass band in summer. It's beautifully floodlit at night, and on Sun traffic is barred from its roads. THE MALL Running all the way along the top of the park, this 1,040-metre (3,412-ft) long ceremonial route was laid out from 1660 for Charles II, with the Palace at one end and the magnificent Admiralty Arch at the other. In between, as well as various grand buildings and government departments, are a couple of good contemporary art galleries, with various changing exhibitions at the MALL GALLERIES (cl Christmas–New Yr, (0171) 930 6844 for exhibition info; *£2), and a wonderfully informal little restaurant and bar at the ICA, which, with exhibitions and cinemas too, is an excellent place to spend an afternoon – and possibly the evening as well (cl am; (0171) 930 0493; £1.50 day membership).

↔ **Green Park** The park itself is the smallest of the parks in Central London. It's not a formal garden but, watered by the Tyburn stream which runs below the park, stays genuinely green even in hot summers when London's other grassy spaces are dry and dusty. It's a short stroll to SHEPHERD MARKET, a colourful place where Mayfair lets its hair down, no longer a market but busy with cafés, good wine bars and pubs (the Bunch of Grapes and King's Arms), and little lanes to wander down; Sofra do very good Middle Eastern food.

🍴 Overlooking the park from the end of St James's Pl, SPENCER HOUSE is a gleaming, gilt-filled town house built for the first Lord Spencer in the mid-18th c. Its sumptuous rooms, restored to their full glory, were among the first neo-classical interiors in Europe. Disabled access; open for guided tours every Sun (exc Jan and Aug), may be best to book on (0171) 499 8620; £6. Nearby ST JAMES'S PALACE, one of the focal points of public grief after the death of Diana Princess of Wales, is comparatively domestic-looking but exceptionally harmonious. It's not open to the public (its apartments are used by members of the Royal Family and their officials), but does provide another good spot for the CHANGING OF THE GUARD, with guardsmen leaving here at 11.15am to go the Palace, and coming back at around 12.10pm.

The area around St James's St and Pall Mall seems to have more gentlemen's clubs than anything else, but there is a good number of interesting upmarket SHOPS too: hand-made shoes at Lobb's, hats at Lock's, wonderful antiques and antiquities at Spink's, fishing equipment at Hardy's, and fine wines at Berry's, or Berry Bros & Rudd to give it its full name. This last is the only shop in London still to look both inside and out just as it did in the early 19th c (they've only just taken down the full-screen shutters), and they are very helpful even if you want just one humble bottle. Farlow's on Pall Mall have everything you might need for that expedition up the Limpopo or into the Gobi Desert. Christie's auction galleries are on King St (the friendly Red Lion off here in Crown Passage is useful for a snack), and there are some other top-of-the-market antique and bookshops

nearby, especially up Duke St.

✝ ♨ ⊖ Westminster WESTMINSTER ABBEY Surely one of the most impressive pieces of architecture to survive from the Middle Ages: Edward the Confessor transformed it into the crowning place of English kings, and his body now lies in the great shrine of the present building, erected in the 13th c on the site of his original. Recent restoration work has left the exterior looking almost as good as new (in fact, some bits *are* new), and a quite different colour from the one visitors had become used to, with monthly hawk patrols now deterring pigeon nesting. Pretty much every king and queen up to George II is buried here; Henry VII's chapel is particularly impressive, and there are splendid tombs erected by James I for his mother Mary, Queen of Scots, and his predecessor Elizabeth I, under whose orders Mary was executed. Perhaps it's in revenge for this that Elizabeth was lumped in with her sister Mary I, with whom she never got on. The loosely named Poets Corner takes in a wide range of cultural figures. There's a brass-rubbing centre and a small medieval garden in the charming, tranquil cloisters. Shop, disabled access (but not to Henry VII chapel); Royal chapels cl Sun, and between 2.45 and 3.45pm Sat. From Easter the £4 charge for the Royal chapels will be increased to £5 and extended to cover the church and cloisters as well; you won't be able just to walk in unless you can convince the stewards all you want to do is pray. The Abbey isn't short of money; admission charges are being introduced to help with crowd control. If you like history the MUSEUM in the Norman undercroft shouldn't be missed – it has effigies of many ancestors of the Royal Family made from their death masks, and often wearing their own clothes; *£2.50 (which also includes entry to the Chapter House and Pyx Chamber). Adjacent ST MARGARET'S CHURCH is worth a look too; the official church of the House of Commons, it has some exceptional 16th-c Dutch stained glass, and Sir

Walter Raleigh is buried here.

🏠⛪ HOUSES OF PARLIAMENT Across the road from St Margaret's, these buildings are now, of course, the main seat of British government, but until Henry VIII moved to Whitehall Palace in 1529, the site was the main residence of the monarch – when they answer the phone today they still call it the Palace of Westminster. The present 19th-c building was designed by Charles Barry, though the Gothic detail which has given so much life to what would otherwise be rather a tiresomely deadpan, classical façade is by Pugin. One end of the extraordinary 286-metre (940-ft) structure finishes in a lofty Victorian tower (which flies the Union Jack when Parliament is in session), and the other in the clock tower which contains BIG BEN, the 3½-ton bell whose sonorous hourly rings are one of the best known sounds in the world. Inside, over 2 miles of passages link the central hall and 2 chambers – the Houses of Lords and Commons to the N and S of the building respectively. The Commons sits from 2.30pm Mon–Thurs, and from 9.30am on Fri; to gain entrance to the Strangers' Galleries, you'll need to queue by St Stephen's Gate (on the left for the Commons, and on the right for the Lords – rather appropriate in a way) – or arrange it first with your MP. A letter from your MP can also give access to what's called the Line of Route, going through both Houses and the Members' Lobby and Divisions Lobby, to Westminster Hall, from 1224–1882 the chief law court of the country. It witnessed trials such as those of Sir Thomas More and Charles I, and organising admission is worth the trouble even just to admire the magnificent hammer-beam roof, the earliest surviving example of its kind. Across the road from the statue of Oliver Cromwell (whose attitude towards Parliament when he was Lord Protector was not unlike that of Charles I – it was more trouble than it was worth), there's an exhibition on Parliament's history in the 14th-c JEWEL TOWER, formerly a huge treasure chest for Edward III. Cl 24–26 Dec, 1 Jan; (0171) 222 2219; £1.50. The Westminster Arms in Storeys Gate across the square is a good pub, and you're likely to see politicians in the imposing Albert on Victoria St.

⛪🏠 CABINET WAR ROOMS 🎧 (King Charles St, just off Whitehall) An intriguing series of 21 rooms built to provide Sir Winston Churchill, the War Cabinet and his Chiefs of Staff with a safe place from which to plan their strategies during World War II. The Cabinet Room, Map Room and Prime Minister's Room were preserved intact from the end of the war, and the other rooms have been authentically restored since. Quite basic, they're very evocative, with sound effects adding to the atmosphere. Shop, disabled access; cl 24–26 Dec; (0171) 930 6961; £4.40. In the middle of Whitehall, the CENOTAPH, designed by Lutyens, is a more sombre reminder of this century's two world wars. Just along from here is DOWNING ST, with the Prime Minister at No 10 and the Chancellor of the Exchequer at No 11. You can't get past the gates, but you can at least have a passing look at its surprisingly modest buildings.

🏠🎧 BANQUETING HOUSE (Whitehall) The only surviving part of the Palace of Whitehall, designed by Inigo Jones and built in 1619; it was a Royal residence until late that century. The severely classical hall is pretty much all there is to see, but an entertaining Walkman tour and good audio-visual exhibition keep up your interest for quite some time. The highlight is the wonderful ceiling painted by Rubens, commissioned by Charles I to glorify the Stuart monarchy. They've put mirrored tables underneath so you can study the detail without straining your neck; don't lean on these though – they're on wheels and liable to speed off like errant supermarket-trolleys. Snacks, shop; cl Sun, 24–26 Dec, 1 Jan, Good Fri, bank hols, and for some government functions; (0171) 839 7569; *£3.30. Charles I was executed here, and it was also the site of his son's restoration. A survival of the kind of Royal pageantry this area was once full of can be seen in the daily MOUNTING THE GUARD ceremony at Horse Guards Parade opposite, 11am Mon–Sat and 10am Sun. The partly 13th-c Silver Cross is an interesting old pub, and the huge and very ornate Lord Moon of the Mall is another good refuge.

Westminster tube station is also handy for several attractions on the other side of the bridge; see our **South of the River** section on p.808.

✝ ✿ ⊖ **Victoria** Not much to detain the visitor around here, but it is worth taking a detour from the glassy governmental cliffs of Victoria St to the Byzantine splendour of the Roman Catholic WESTMINSTER CATHEDRAL, which offers the best views over Central London from its tall tower (lift; £2). Built in 1903, the red-brick building is an astonishing structure, very un-English, with handsome mosaics and marble work in its richly ornamental interior. Behind here, in Vincent Sq, the Royal Horticultural Society has regular flower shows, filled with beautifully arranged displays by specialist nurserymen; (0171) 828 1744 for information.

🏠 ▣ ⊖ **Pimlico** TATE GALLERY (Millbank) Designed in classical style to house the collection of Sir Henry Tate, the sugar refiner, and now containing the national collection of British art. It covers all important British artists for the past 450 years, with a large number of works by Turner and Constable, and plenty of contemporary sculpture. A hi-tech audio guide looks rather like a mobile phone, and at the push of a button murmurs comments on what you're looking at. Major exhibitions this year include works by Bonnard (12 Feb–17 May), Patrick Heron (18 Jun–6 Sept) and John Singer Sargent (from 15 Oct). Meals, snacks, shop, disabled access; cl 24–26 Dec; (0171) 887 8000; free (exc for special exhibitions). If you've not been for a while, note that it's now open Sun mornings. Though the Tate Gallery restaurant is a particularly good one, you might find the Morpeth Arms nearby useful, with its views of the glossy MI6 ziggurat across the river.

KNIGHTSBRIDGE, CHELSEA AND KENSINGTON

The 3 great South Kensington museums between them have something for everyone: the visually spectacular collections of the Victoria & Albert; and the lively Natural History and Science Museums, both favourites for children. The new Commonwealth Experience is good (with plenty for younger children) and there's grandeur in Kensington Palace, the less visited but free Leighton House and, across Hyde Park, the excellent Apsley House. Harrods seems irresistible to most visitors. Down towards the Thames, the Chelsea Physic Garden and the nearby free National Army Museum are both rather special.

A placid grid of clean-cut, subdued Georgian terraced houses contrasts with the ostentatious bustle of the King's Rd in the S and the hubbub of the Portobello Rd market in the N.

Please let us know what you think of places in the *Guide*. Use the report forms at the back of the book or simply send a letter.

To see and do

🏠 �transport ✚ **High St Kensington**

KENSINGTON PALACE (Kensington Gardens) Once-humble town house remodelled by Sir Christopher Wren and then enlarged by William Kent, the birthplace of Queen Victoria, and principal private Royal residence until the death of George II. Diana Princess of Wales lived here until her death last year; it's still the home of Princess Margaret and Prince and Princess Michael of Kent. Some of the rooms are quite magnificent, with elaborate furnishings and décor, while others are interesting for their comparatively restrained understatement; a couple of the older ones could even be described as downright poky. Make sure you look up at the ceilings: some are exquisitely painted, inc an effective trompe-l'oeil dome (a couple of the patterns transfer very nicely to stationery in the gift shop). Also pictures and furniture from the Royal collection, and a court dress collection. Snacks, shop, disabled access to ground floor only; open for guided tours May–Sept; (0171) 937 9561; £6. Surrounding the Palace, KENSINGTON GARDENS are well worth a wander, though they are less lush than neighbouring Hyde Park. There's a toy boats' lake, playground, a fetching statue of Peter Pan, and a tree trunk carved with all sorts of little painted animals. On a sunny day you could be forgiven for thinking you'd stumbled on a beach club, as the grass is covered with prone bodies soaking up the radiation.

✚ ✸ COMMONWEALTH EXPERIENCE (Kensington High St) A massively hyped helicopter simulator ride is the first stage in the Commonwealth Institute's campaign to shake off its dated image, and though there's still a way to go they're definitely moving in the right direction. The well filmed flight is over Malaysia and Kuala Lumpur, though it's a little short, and the soundtrack isn't always easy to understand. Small children were thoroughly enjoying a new interactive area on our visit (it's a

little basic for anyone older). The displays on each of the Commonwealth countries are shortly to be overhauled, and if things go well they hope to add a multi-media ride by the end of the century. Snacks, shop; cl 18–25 Dec; (0171) 371 3530; £4.45. Behind it, down Holland Walk, HOLLAND PARK is one of London's lesser-known open spaces, a wooded park with peacocks, summer open-air theatre and an airy restaurant.

🏠 ◻ LEIGHTON HOUSE (12 Holland Park Rd) This splendid 19th-c house is a uniquely opulent monument to high Victorian art, its lavish décor and collections assembled by the first owner, Lord Leighton, former President of the Royal Academy. The centrepiece Arab Hall has a fountain and an almost dazzling assemblage of Islamic tiles, and there's a fine collection of paintings by Millais, Burne-Jones, and Leighton himself. Cl Sun and bank hols; (0171) 602 3316; free. Another interesting period house nearby is LINLEY SAMBOURNE HOUSE (18 Stafford Terrace), the 19th-c home of the celebrated *Punch* cartoonist. Unchanged since then, it's a fascinating example of a Victorian town house, with a fine collection of his work. Shop; open Weds and pm Sun, Mar–Oct; (0181) 994 1019; £3.

Kensington is a good area for SHOPPING, especially if you consider yourself young and fashionable. An unusual haven from the crowds is the ROOF GARDENS above BHS on the High St; these extraordinary gardens are usually open every day, but are often closed for private functions, so you'll need to check first on (0171) 937 7994; free. Besides the outstanding Ladbroke Arms (Ladbroke Rd, see **Where to Eat** section below), good food pubs in this area include the Windsor Castle (Campden Hill Rd; excellent courtyard garden) and (a walk up Kensington Church St, which has some interesting antique shops) the Churchill Arms – surprisingly good Thai food.

🛇🖼†🕸 ⊖ **South Kensington**

VICTORIA & ALBERT MUSEUM (Cromwell Rd) Britain's national museum of art and design is one of the finest in the world; it was founded in 1851 by Prince Albert, and houses all manner of decorative arts, from all ages and countries. The galleries run to over 7 miles, inc a spectacular glass gallery (with touch-screen computer displays), a dazzling silver gallery, and the world's greatest collection of Constables. This year's major exhibitions are devoted to *The Power of the Poster* (9 Apr–26 July), and Grinling Gibbons, the great decorative woodcarver (autumn). They have ambitious plans for extensions and improvements, though haven't had much luck bidding for Lottery funds. Meals and snacks (they do a good Sunday brunch with jazz), shop, disabled access; cl am Mon, 24–26 Dec; (0171) 938 8500; *£5 though free after 4.30pm, and any time for the unwaged. Nearby, the Roman Catholic BROMPTON ORATORY has a heavy magnificence, sombre despite the pallor of its marble. Beside it the gardens of HOLY TRINITY BROMPTON – London's most fashionable and perhaps most lively church – lead you into a very peaceful corner of residential London, with a decent pub in Ennismore Mews (the Ennismore Arms, which does Sun lunches).

🛇📣 NATURAL HISTORY MUSEUM (Cromwell Rd) This elaborate Romanesque building is a vast place covering 4 acres, with a huge range of informative and entertaining displays and activities. It's been very successfully jazzed up in recent years; museum purists may feel some of the grandeur of the place has been lost, but families will find plenty to keep them busy for a good chunk of the day. It's long been a place where people have come to see the dinosaurs, but while that used to mean fossils and skeletons, it now involves a high-tech exhibition that even has robotic versions of the monsters. The revamped Earth Galleries are a current highlight – an escalator whisks you up towards a revolving metal globe, and there's an earthquake simulator. Meals, snacks, shops, disabled access; cl 23–26 Dec; (0171) 938 9123; £6.

🛇 SCIENCE MUSEUM (Exhibition Rd) No problems getting children interested in this amazing place: over 600 working exhibits whizz you through all aspects of science and industry, with the highlight perhaps the very successful Launch Pad, a high-tech interactive gallery where you can have great fun carrying out your own experiments. Exhibits elsewhere range from Stephenson's Rocket to the Apollo 10 space capsule, with lively displays on food, flight and pharmaceuticals. Various temporary exhibitions, and special events like their all-night camp-ins – which enthrall children. A major exhibition on Science and Sport will run until Oct. Meals, snacks, shop, disabled access; cl 24–26 Dec; (0171) 938 8080; £5.95.

📣 ROYAL ALBERT HALL (Kensington Gore) The home of the summer Promenade Concerts and many other concerts throughout the year; completed in 1871, this huge oval arena was built in honour of Prince Albert. Below its massive metal and glass dome a terracotta frieze shows the progress of Man in the arts and sciences throughout the ages. Before modern technology got to grips with its acoustics, the hall used to be famous for its echo – it was said that this was the only hall where you could hear the works of modern composers twice. Across the road is the ALBERT MEMORIAL, still swathed in scaffolding as we went to press, but due to start emerging later this year, with restoration work finished by summer 1999. Many Londoners had given up hope of ever seeing this remarkable monument again, it's been under wraps for so long. There's an adjacent visitor centre.

⊖ **Knightsbridge** HARRODS is a wonderful place to browse, and has most things anyone could want – there's even a personal shopper available to help you choose. But it's the food halls that visitors to London really enjoy; they're divided into fruit and vegetables, an interesting delicatessen, grocery, meat, poultry, fish (the display of fresh fish at the end of the room is legendary), bread and cakes, flowers, and wines – and the downstairs pantry is not as expensive as you might think. The Scotch House, almost opposite, is not cheap but does have lovely cashmeres, fine woollens, kilts and so forth. Harvey Nichols is a long-standing fashion store now split into numerous famous-brand boutiques; its 5th-floor food store is superb, alongside a very good bar/restaurant. Sloane St stretching down from here has had something of a renaissance recently, with international designers jostling to open very expensive new stores. In the handsome terraces beyond Sloane St can be found the charming Grenadier (Wilton Row; no food in the bar, but a snug little restaurant) and the surprisingly countryish Nag's Head (Kinnerton St).

🎯 🔳 ♨ 🏛 ⊖ **Hyde Park Corner** 340-acre HYDE PARK used to be a Royal hunting park, and in 1851 was the site of the Great Exhibition. In the grounds of the park nr the boating lake is the SERPENTINE GALLERY, often with interesting exhibitions concentrating on younger contemporary artists; (0171) 823 9727 for what's on. You can hire boats on the lake (around £6 an hour), or even swim in parts of it. At its bottom corner is the relentless torrent of traffic around Hyde Park Corner; the subway can bring you up nr the glittering neo-baroque gates erected in honour of the Queen Mother, or at the Duke of Wellington's elegant former home APSLEY HOUSE. Designed by Robert Adam, this soon became known as Number One London, as it was the first house beyond a toll gate at the top of Knightsbridge. The magnificent building has been painstakingly restored; everything gleams and looks as good as new, and works by Correggio, Rubens and Velasquez amassed by Wellington as the spoils of war are back in their original positions (not always to their

best advantage). Sumptuous furnishings, décor and sculpture – inc a statue of Napoleon by Canova that has him looking quite different from the usual image. Shop; cl Mon (exc bank hols), 1 Jan, Good Fri, May Day bank hol, 24–26 Dec; (0171) 499 5676; *£4.

⊖ **Sloane Sq** The heart of Chelsea, with Peter Jones, the mecca of Sloanes, on the square itself (a sister department store of John Lewis, it's good-value for money). Just around the corner, the Antelope in Eaton Terrace is a useful lunch stop. The bottom end of Sloane St has 2 interesting though expensive shops: Partridges, a fancy food shop, and the General Trading Company, with a fine collection of oddities, besides stylish kitchenware, soft furnishings, antiques, glass and so forth. Sloane Sq's most famous offshoot is the KING'S RD: not what it used to be in the '60s and '70s, but you can still find some really individual clothes and shoe shops, and 3 good antique markets (the Chenil Galleries have some fine specialist stalls; the other 2 go further down the price range but have interesting stuff). On your way along, refresh yourself at Henry J Beans (197 King's Rd; a rather stylish American-style bar with good, quick snacks), La Bersagliera (a pleasantly clattery, matriarchal pizza house, just past Beaufort St) or the Sporting Page (Camera Pl/Limerston St). S from here, it's quite a short-cut through to the Thames.

🏛 CARLYLE'S HOUSE (Cheyne Row) The home of the writer from 1834 till his death, with lots of letters and personal possessions, and an early piano played by Chopin. There's a charming little Victorian walled garden. Open Weds–Sun and bank hols Apr–Oct; (0171) 352 7087; £3; NT. The nearby King's Head & Eight Bells, across a green and a busy road from the Thames, is almost villagey.

🏛 🎯 THE ROYAL HOSPITAL (Royal Hospital Rd) Christopher Wren's most glorious secular building, which still houses some 400 Chelsea Pensioners. Cl 12–2pm, am Sun (though you can go to the full dress service in the chapel at 11am on Sun); free. The spacious and calm adjacent riverside Ranelagh Gardens are the site of the Chelsea Flower Show.

⚘ NATIONAL ARMY MUSEUM (Royal Hospital Rd) Surprisingly little visited but well and honestly presented – the history of the men of the British, Indian and Colonial armies from 1485, told with photographs, models, uniforms, prints and other mementos, and portraits by Gainsborough and Reynolds. Also the collections of the former Museum of the Women's Royal Army Corps. Snacks, shop, disabled access; cl 24–26 Dec, 1 Jan, Good Fri, May Day bank hol; (0171) 730 0717; free.

🏵 CHELSEA PHYSIC GARDEN (Royal Hospital Rd) If you're tired of the braying crowds of Chelsea, take refuge here. A real haven of peace, it was started in 1673 to study the plants used in medicine by the Society of Apothecaries. It's still used for botanical and medicinal research (there's a unique garden of medicinal plants), but is also full of lovely and unusual plants which thrive here in Thames-side London's warm microclimate. Snacks, shop, disabled access; open pm Weds and Sun Apr–Oct; (0171) 352 5646; £3.50. Where the road joins the river embankment, Old Church St past the elegant Chelsea Old Church takes you quickly to a good food pub, the Front Page.

The Pimlico Rd has an interesting collection of antique and other small SHOPS (and Peter's Restaurant, a very good-value all-day Italian-run café which has been a taxi-drivers' haunt for more than 25 years). The Orange Brewery here is a pub brewing its own beers, with decent food. Keep on along to Ebury Bridge for a classic photographic view of the partly dismantled Battersea Power Station, beyond a sinuous network of railway lines; work is just starting on its promised eventual rebirth as a leisure and entertainment centre.

⊖ Fulham Broadway is the best station for the clutch of good-value ANTIQUE SHOPS towards the bottom end of the Fulham Rd. You can quickly cut through to the interesting series of more specialised antique shops on the New Kings Rd, some of which yield unexpected treasures: lovely old clocks, imposing model ships, garden furniture, and ornaments going back to the 16th c. Two shops specialise expensively but magnificently in mirrors, and there's also Christopher Wray's enormous lighting shop which largely fuelled the vogue in Tiffany-style lamps and has almost any sort of lamp fitting you could possibly want. Not far from here CHELSEA HARBOUR has a striking modern covered mall (mainly luxurious soft furnishings specialists), with popular Deals Restaurant and the stylish Canteen (see **Where to Eat** section, p.820), the smart but relaxed Matts café, and an adjacent marina. Children like the glass-sided lifts which swoop up into the big dome, and on pm Sun they often have jazz by the marina. The tube station is also handy for Chelsea Football Club, and the unfrequented, rather melancholy tranquillity of the somewhat overgrown BROMPTON CEMETERY. Nr here the countrified Fox & Pheasant in Billing St makes a pleasant break.

⊖ **Notting Hill Gate** Not really an area for visitors, despite good bars and restaurants, but the best stop for the market at Portobello Rd – fruit and vegetables during the week, antiques on Sat from 6am; with well over a thousand dealers, you can still pick up a bargain. The quality and prices are higher at the Notting Hill end; it's more bric-à-brac as you go towards Ladbroke Grove.

Please let us know what you think of places in the *Guide*. Use the report forms at the back of the book or simply send a letter.

THE CITY AND EAST END

The City's most typical financial buildings are mainly Victorian and Edwardian, and its landmark churches are mostly elegant classical designs, but the ground-plan follows the narrow twisting streets and alleys of medieval times – though because of the Great Fire of 1666 only a handful of buildings are medieval or Tudor. Around St Paul's and the Tower of London (a winner with children), the layout is more open – and far less affected by the City's human tides: most of the rest of the area is packed with worried financial workers during weekdays, then when they leave goes into a catatonic trance in the evening and at weekends. For every person who actually lives in the City, another 60 or 70 flood in each day to work there, then flood out again at night.

Besides the Tower, St Paul's and the host of glorious churches, highlights here include the Museum of London, Geffrye Museum and Museum of Childhood, and the highly individualistic 18 Folgate Street. The newly opened Lothbury Gallery has a good art collection, and the Tower Bridge Experience is something a little different.

Originally, particular streets came to be associated with particular crafts and trades, and this is reflected in street names throughout the City – Carter Lane, Hosier Lane, Cloth Fair, Ropemaker St, Milk St, Silk St, Coopers Lane and so forth. The great City Livery Companies representing the various trades have effectively run local government in the City for 800 years or more, and it's only now that the franchise is to be widened to allow more modern financial institutions a share in local government here. Many guilds have only a tenuous connection with the original crafts involved in their trades. But in Billingsgate Market, still controlled by the ancient Fishmongers Company, you can still see the fish trade being carried on in much the same way as ever (West India Dock Rd, early morning Tues–Sat).

Though the halls of the City Livery Companies may have been rebuilt since they were first established in the Middle Ages, they still house some remarkable treasures. Some are open to visit, but only by prior arrangement: you'll have to book well ahead, through the City of London Information Centre, St Paul's Churchyard, EC4; (0171) 332 1456.

The liveliest glimpse of East End life nowadays is to be had on Sunday mornings in Brick Lane market.

To see and do

🏛 👁 ⊕ **Tower Hill** TOWER OF LONDON Picturesque classic castle, the most notable building to survive the Great Fire of London. A lot of fun to look at even superficially, it dates back to the late 11th c, though the site had been used as a defensive position by the

Romans much earlier. Almost every period of English history has witnessed gruesome goings-on here, with not even the highest or mightiest safe from imprisonment or execution: Walter Raleigh, Lady Jane Grey and 2 of Henry VIII's wives spent their last days in the Tower. There's a mass of things to see, inc enough armour and medieval weaponry to glut the most bloodthirsty small boy's appetite, the Crown Jewels, the Beefeaters and the ravens. You can also walk along the elevated battlements. The Jewel House shows off the Crown Jewels to dazzling effect; on the busiest days those tempted to linger are gently drawn along by moving floorways. Two towers that were part of Edward I's medieval palace are furnished in period style, and peopled with appropriately costumed helpful guides; one room in this part has been left untouched to show what a difficult job the restoration was. A reorganisation of the oldest part, the White Tower, has revealed that the inside of the fortress when built was much less imposing than was suggested by the formidable exterior – they were clearly just trying to intimidate the locals. You need a fair bit of time to see everything properly. Shop, some disabled access; cl 24–26 Dec, 1 Jan; (0171) 709 0765; £8.50.

🏠 ❄ ⚙ TOWER BRIDGE EXPERIENCE Inside the landmark bridge, there are wonderful views from its glass-covered walkways, 43 metres (142 ft) above the Thames; animatronic characters and hi-tech displays present the view at various other dates in the bridge's history, with lively multi-media shows designed to leave you feeling proud to be British. The bridge is unusual not just for its design, but because it's still fully operational, raising the roadway from each side drawbridge-style to allow ships to pass; you can see some of the Victorian machinery that does the work. Snacks, shop, disabled access; cl 24–26 Dec, 1 Jan, 28 Jan; (0171) 403 3761; £5.70.

♭ ! TOWER HILL PAGEANT (Tower Hill Terrace) Entertaining dark ride through centuries of London's history, from the Romans right through to Docklands. There's more to see than in similar places (just as well, given the price), and the cars are quite ingeniously designed. At the end is an exhibition of excavated finds from nearby, and they have a display of huge hi-tech holograms. Snacks, shop, disabled access; cl 25 Dec; (0171) 709 0081; £6.95. Tower Hill is also the best tube station for visiting St Katharine's Dock (see Docklands entry, p.804).

✝ ⊖ St Paul's ST PAUL'S CATHEDRAL looms out at you suddenly from among the crowded streets, despite the attempts of brasher, taller modern buildings to take over. Its huge dome is a pleasing shape after the stolid self-satisfaction of the Victorian and Edwardian masonry which still dominates this area. Originally the cathedral was Gothic in style, with a towering 150-metre (500-ft) spire. It fell into disrepair and Wren was assigned to work on its renovation. He didn't relish the job, and no doubt was delighted when the Great Fire of London swept the old church away, allowing him to construct something entirely new. His mainly classical design is unlike any other cathedral in Britain, and took just 35 years to build. The setting for various state occasions, it's full of interesting monuments – the one to John Donne was the only complete figure to be salvaged from the Great Fire. Look out for the wonderful carving on the exterior – some of which is by Grinling Gibbons, who also did the choir stalls. Other highlights include the dizzying Whispering Gallery, the panoramic views from the top (quite a walk), and the crypt, full of tombs and memorials to notable figures from British history. Snacks, shop, disabled access; cl most of Sun; (0171) 236 4128; £3.50 (more to climb the dome). The City Pipe by the tube station is an enjoyable weekday wine bar.

🏠 ⚙ The 15th-c GUILDHALL (off Gresham St) is where the Court of Common Council, over which the Lord Mayor presides, administers the City of London. The Lord Mayor's Banquet is held in the Great Hall, hung with the banners and shields of the City's 90-odd livery companies. Underneath is the largest 15th-c crypt in the City, and there's also a clock museum, and library with an unrivalled collection of City-related manuscripts and books. Disabled access; cl Sun Oct–Apr, and for civic occasions; guided tours, must book, (0171) 332 1460; free.

🏛 ✳ ✛ **Monument** The MONUMENT (Monument St) is a fluted Doric column designed by Wren and Hooke at an exact height of 202 ft (62 metres) to mark the spot where the Great Fire of London began – in Pudding Lane 202 ft from its base. The views of the city from the top are tremendous, though there are 311 spiral steps up. The viewpoint was designed as a cage to prevent people jumping off. Cl am wknds (and all day winter Suns), some bank hols, and occasional other dates; (0171) 626 2717; *£1.

🏛 🍴 🎫 ✛ **Bank** Some of the City's finest buildings are around here, though with most you'll have to content yourself with looking at just the outside. The neo-classical fortress that's the BANK OF ENGLAND (Bartholomew Lane) does still contain oodles of gold – though you can't see it, let alone get your hands on it. There's a small but interesting MUSEUM, which even shows how computerised currency speculators work. Disabled access; cl wknds and bank hols; (0171) 601 5545; free. Behind here on Lothbury, the NatWest Bank has opened up its excellent collection of 17th- to 20th-c paintings as the LOTHBURY GALLERY, and is well worth tracking down (open wkdys only, free). Other handsome or interesting buildings include the neo-classical Custom House on Lower Thames St, Lloyds of London on Lime St, and the Renaissance-style Royal Exchange on Cornhill, with several proud columns in front. If you apply in writing in advance, you should be able to see inside the MANSION HOUSE (Bank), the official residence of the Lord Mayor. There's a suite of sumptuous 18th-c rooms inc the fabulous Egyptian Hall. More vibrant is LEADENHALL MARKET (Whittington Ave, off Gracechurch St), a Victorian iron and glass covered market, alive with Cockney humour yet quite smart, and

filled with seafood, game, vegetables and fruit; cl afternoonish, and wknds. The Lamb's top-floor dining bar gives good views of the market activity.

🎫 🍴 ✛ **Barbican** MUSEUM OF LONDON 🚇 (London Wall) No other city museum in the world is quite as comprehensive as this; anyone with just a passing interest in history will find it compelling. London's development is told through chronological reconstructions and period clothes, music and various remains, from a medieval hen's egg to an early (and quite different) tube map – ever heard of the station called Post Office? – while the 18th-, 19th- and 20th-c sections have almost too much to take in. They're in the early part of a 7-year redevelopment programme, and are tackling each gallery in turn: first to be completed was the excellent new Roman gallery (the building adjoins a stretch of original Roman wall). Meals, snacks, shop, disabled access; cl am Sun, all day Mon (exc bank hols), 24–26 Dec; (0171) 600 0807; £4 – ticket valid for 3 months, and it certainly is the sort of place you want to come back to.

🎫 NATIONAL POSTAL MUSEUM (King Edward St) Guaranteed to tickle any philatelist's fancy, with practically every stamp issued anywhere since 1840. A history of the postal system includes an exhibition devoted to the letter box, a useful device introduced to Britain by Post Office surveyor (and novelist) Anthony Trollope. Shop; cl wknds and bank hols; (0171) 239 5420; free.

The Barbican could be called the North Bank's equivalent to the South Bank Centre – certainly its aesthetic equal. This complex includes theatres, exhibition halls, galleries, and what some would say is the city's most comfortable cinema. There's often free entertainment in the foyers.

🏛 ❗ **Liverpool St** You can visit a quite remarkable house at 18 FOLGATE ST – but be warned, this is no ordinary guided tour. It doesn't do the place justice to say that it's been furnished and decorated in period style – to all intents and purposes you really are back in the 18th c, with candles and firelight flickering away, food and drink laid out on the table, even urine in the chamber-pots. Dennis Severs the owner, who lives here, spends hours getting everything ready, and goes to extreme lengths to immerse people in the experience – it's not unusual to be locked in a cold dark cellar, and he's been known to throw people out if he doesn't like them. Open 2–5pm the first Sun of each month; (0171) 247 4013; £5. Elaborate candlelit tours the first Mon evening of the month, £10. In Liverpool St Station, Hamilton Hall is an extraordinarily grand ex-ballroom pub.

♿♨✝⊖ **Old St** GEFFRYE MUSEUM (Kingsland Rd) One of London's most friendly and interesting museums, yet least known; 18th-c almshouses converted to show the changing style of the English domestic interior – a sort of historical *Through the Keyhole*. Displays go from lovely 17th-c oak panelling and furniture through elegant Georgian reconstructions and Victorian parlours to art deco fashions, though not all is as it seems – out of sight, inside the shell of a vintage radio for example, there's actually a distinctly modern CD player. There is a notable herb garden, and they have an excellent programme of special events, talks and activities. Well worth tracking down. New galleries open this autumn. Snacks, shop, disabled access; cl am Sun, all day Mon (exc pm bank hols), 24–26 Dec, 1 Jan, Good Fri; (0171) 739 9893; free. WESLEY'S HOUSE (49 City Rd) The father of Methodism had his house and chapel built here in 1778, and they're still much as they were then, with plenty of his personal possessions. You can see Wesley's tomb in the chapel, and the crypt has a museum on the history of Methodism. Shop, disabled access – limited in house, but good in museum; cl bank hols, and limited opening Sun (when services); (0171) 253 2262; *£4.

♨⊖✝⊖ **Farringdon** MUSEUM OF THE ORDER OF ST JOHN (St John's Lane) Housed in a 16th-c gatehouse and 12th-c crypt, silver, paintings and furniture belonging to the medieval Order, and displays relating to the history and work of its more modern offshoot, the St John's Ambulance Brigade. Shop, some disabled access; cl Sun, Christmas, Easter, bank hol wknds; (0171) 253 6644; free, £3.50 guided tours of the gatehouse and priory church on Tues, Fri and Sat at 11am and 2.30pm. The Eagle in Farringdon Rd/Bakers Row has outstanding food.

! ⊖ **Aldgate East** Once the terror-stricken haunt of Jack the Ripper, Whitechapel is still one of London's poorest areas. BRICK LANE MARKET is London's biggest and most atmospheric street Market, a riot of colour, smells and sound, inc some very entertaining market patter. There are plenty of bargains for early risers (and things to avoid – we've even seen someone specialising in secondhand felt-tip pens). The community is largely Asian, so much of the food and other wares are quite exotic; Sun 5am–2pm. COLUMBIA ST MARKET a few streets N, is entirely devoted to garden and house plants, and has bargains as it closes around 1pm on Sun.

! ⊖ **Bethnal Green** MUSEUM OF CHILDHOOD (Cambridge Heath Rd) This very special little museum houses the V&A's collection of toys, dolls, dolls' houses, games, puppets and children's costumes. Excellent programme of events, theatre shows, and children's activities (most Sats and several school hols) – most completely free. Snacks, shop, disabled access with prior notice; cl am Sun, all day Fri, 24–26 Dec, 1 Jan, May Day bank hol; (0181) 980 2415; free.

✝ The City is full of striking CHURCHES, many of which have good lunchtime or evening concerts; among the more interesting ones are St Anne and St Agnes (Gresham St), particularly worth knowing for the Bach cantatas that may grace its Lutheran Sun services; (0171) 606 4986 for programme; St Bartholomew the Great (West Smithfield), partly Norman, with a

13th-c gateway into the market precincts, lunchtime recitals and choral evenings; (0171) 606 5171 for details; and St Mary le Bow (Cheapside), with the famous Bow Bells and Thurs lunchtime early-music concerts; (0171) 248 5139.

🏠 🛥 **Docklands** Once the heartland of Britain's trade-based Empire, these 8½ square miles over the last decade became the largest redevelopment site in Europe, the old warehouses imaginatively converted into smart apartments and office blocks. 244-metre (800-ft) Canary Wharf is an all-too-obvious landmark, though as most of its floors are filled with offices the ground-level shops are the only parts you can visit inside. Many of the buildings around it were designed to give a taste of the 21st c. While they're undoubtedly striking, there's sometimes a soullessness about the place that's positively eerie; on a wknd or holiday Docklands seems even more deserted than the rest of the City. It's reached and seen best by the DOCKLANDS LIGHT RAILWAY; the best bit is between West India Quay and Island Gardens, where you can get off and walk through the foot tunnel under the Thames to Greenwich (see **Further Afield** section, p.812). The LONDON DOCKLANDS VISITOR CENTRE, 3 Limeharbour, E14, (0171) 512 1111, offers information, free maps and an audio-visual show. The earliest docks to be redeveloped are the most visitor-friendly: St Katharine's Dock (not far from Tower Hill), which has a lively marina, a quite cheerful pastiche of a Victorian pub, and lots going on, and Tobacco Dock, with an American-style factory shopping centre. Further E down the river is the gigantic, closeable THAMES FLOOD BARRIER, built to protect the city from freak tides; a Visitor Centre is on Unity Way, Woolwich SE18, (0181) 854 1373 (£3.40). You can get boats down here from Westminster Pier; (0171) 930 3373; £6.50 return, and these now stop at Canary Wharf too.

BLOOMSBURY/HOLBORN/ REGENT'S PARK

The British Museum is the outstanding attraction in Bloomsbury and Holborn, a civilised and genteel if slightly faded area of Georgian squares, gardens and courts between the City and Westminster – legal and academic London. Much less well known, the Sir John Soane's Museum is also not to be missed, and the new British Library is at last ready.

We have included with this area the part over towards Marylebone (inc Madame Tussaud's), with smart Regent's Park (and the Zoo) on its northern border; away from the shopping streets of Marylebone High St and Baker St this is largely residential, and the capital of private medicine and dentistry.

Bloomsbury does have a large number of hotels, especially for the more budget-conscious visitor, though many are on the tawdry side. Ones which can be recommended include the Academy (17 Gower St WC1E 6HG (0171) 631 4115), the Morgan (24 Bloomsbury St WC1B 3QJ (0171) 636 3735) – both handy for the British Museum – and the George (60 Cartwright Gardens WC1H 9EL (0171) 387 6789).

To see and do

☗ ⊖ **Russell Sq** BRITISH MUSEUM (Great Russell St) Monumental 19th-c building housing spectacular collections of priceless man-made objects from all over the world, some of them over 3,000 years old. The range is staggering, in which just a few highlights are the Elgin Marbles, the log-book of Nelson's *Victory*, the wonderful and intriguing Egyptian galleries, the comprehensive galleries of Greek vases, the Oriental antiquities, and the Amaravati sculpture. Their book displays are moving to the new British Library this year, but to more than make up they are recovering the fascinating collections of non-Western art and culture that have been in the Museum of Mankind for the last few years. Don't try to take it in all at once – decide what interests you most and stick to that, or your head will start reeling with the extent of this treasure-house before you've got even a tenth of the way through. Ambitious redevelopment is planned over the next few years, inc the transformation of the museum's currently hidden centre courtyard into a covered public square. Meals, snacks, shop, disabled access; cl am Sun, 24–26 Dec, 1 Jan, May Day bank hol, 10 Apr; (0171) 636 1555; free exc for special exhibitions. Just up Gower St, Dillons is a first-class serious bookshop, and in Museum St the Museum Tavern does decent food all day.

🏠 ☗ DICKENS' HOUSE Dickens lived at 48 Doughty St during his 20s, and during that period wrote the *Pickwick Papers*, *Oliver Twist* and *Nicholas Nickleby*. The drawing room has been reconstructed to appear as it was then, and there are original manuscripts and first editions, pictures and personal possessions. His wife's sister died here in 1837, an event which the writer later used as the model for the death of Little Nell in *The Old Curiosity Shop*. Shop; cl Sun and some public hols; (0171) 405 2127; £3.50.

☗ ⊖ **Goodge St** POLLOCK'S TOY MUSEUM ▦ (1 Scala St) Housed in a rather charming setting, a wide range of playthings from all over the world and from all periods, almost as if lots of enthusiastic children had just left them scattered through these little rooms. Mechanical and optical toys, teddy bears, furniture, board games and model theatres, and a proper toy shop downstairs. Disabled access to ground floor only; cl Sun and bank hols; (0171) 636 3452; £2.50.

⚇ 🏠 ☗ ⊖ **Holborn** LINCOLN'S INN FIELDS A perfect example of the tranquil architecture of this area – a large open space with trees and lawns surrounded by handsome houses, also tennis courts and summer band concerts; it's a pleasant place to spend a summer afternoon. One of London's hidden highlights, SIR JOHN SOANE'S MUSEUM (13 Lincoln's Inn Fields) was built by the architect for his splendid collection of pictures, books and antiquities. It's most eccentric, full of architectural tricks and mirrors, which form a complex natural-lighting system for the antiquities covering most of the walls. There's a lovely picture by Turner and an Egyptian sarcophagus, but the highlight is Hogarth's acid series on *The Rake's Progress* and *The Election*. When you've seen them the guide swings open the hinged 'walls' and further treasures emerge, inc choice Piranesi drawings and a scale model of the Bank of England. The house is built around a central courtyard monument to his dog ('Alas, poor Fanny!'); you ring the bell to get in, and sign a visitors' book. The guides are very friendly and helpful, and the guidebook is well worthwhile. Shop; cl Sun, Mon and Christmas; (0171) 405 2107; free (donations welcome). The breakfast room of Soane's first house, No 12 next door, can also be visited.

Nearby, the Gothic ROYAL COURTS OF JUSTICE are impressive, and you can also stroll through the gardens of GRAY'S INN, said to have been laid out by Francis Bacon around 1600. This area really is legal London, and you'll usually find a good number of lawyers in the splendid Cittie of York (22 High Holborn), an enormous and very atmospheric basement pub with little private booths down one side. Other fine pubs in this area are the opulent Victorian gin palace, the Princess Louise (208 High Holborn; good Thai food upstairs, not weekends); and the classic Lamb in Lamb's Conduit St. Dom Vitos Sandwich Bar on Kingsway has superb sandwiches.

⊞ ⊖ Temple COURTAULD INSTITUTE GALLERIES (Somerset House, Strand) Outstanding collection of Impressionist and Post-Impressionist paintings inc works by Monet, Renoir, Degas and Cezanne, also Michelangelo, Rubens, Goya and other masters. It's closed until autumn for major restoration work; best to ring (0171) 873 2526 for reopening date. Other parts of Somerset House are set be opened up to visitors over the next few years.

⊞ † TEMPLE Of all the Inns of Court, this is perhaps the most impressive, and it boasts many famous literary figures among its former members. Most of the buildings date from after the reign of Elizabeth I or the Great Fire, but the name points to an older history: the land was owned by the Knights Templar from about 1160. MIDDLE TEMPLE HALL is a fine example of Tudor architecture, with a double hammerbeam roof and beautiful stained glass. There is a table made from timber from Sir Francis Drake's ship the *Golden Hind* – he was a member of the Middle Temple – while a single oak tree from Windsor Forest supplied the wood for the 9-metre (29-ft) long High Table. Open 10am–noon and 3–4pm Mon–Fri exc bank hols, during Aug, and over some vacations – best to check first, (0171) 427 4800; free. The Inner Temple has an unusual round church.

⊞ DR JOHNSON'S HOUSE (17 Gough Sq) A perfect example of early 18th-c architecture, just as Dr Johnson himself was a perfect example of 18th-c barbed, slightly flawed gentility. Between 1749 and 1759 he wrote his great *English Dictionary* here, and a first edition of this is on display, along with various memorabilia from his learned life. Shop; cl Sun and bank hols; (0171) 353 3745; £3. The passages and walkways around here are a good reminder of how London's streets used to be laid out; the 17th-c Olde Cheshire Cheese nearby is a splendid old tavern.

† ⊙ ⊞ ST BRIDE'S CHURCH (Fleet St) A Wren masterpiece, its splendid steeple the influence for today's traditional 3-tiered wedding cake; good Sun choir and frequent short lunchtime recitals; (0171) 353 1301 for programme. There's an interesting MUSEUM in the partly Roman crypt (cl bank hols; free). Caxton set up his first printing press alongside, and ever since St Bride's has been the parish church for anyone involved in the press. This was useful in the days when adjoining Fleet St was the hub of newspaperland; today, it's really just a passage between the law courts and the City – but look out for relics of the newspaper kingdoms such as the black-glass former Daily Express Building. The opulent Old Bank of England is now a magnificent pub.

⊙ ! ⊖ Baker St MADAME TUSSAUD'S (Marylebone Rd) Almost half of overseas visitors place this famous waxworks museum at the top of their list of things to do in London, which explains why the queues can be so long and slow-moving (and perhaps why German TV presenters and Japanese sumo wrestlers now crop up among more familiar simulacrums). Some of the models are uncannily realistic, others rather less so (several members of the Royal Family spring to mind). They've successfully reworked the famous Chamber of Horrors (it no longer has that rather unpleasant emphasis on real-life crime), and the Spirit of London finale is entertaining – you sit in a black cab and are whisked through a cheery interpretation of the city's history. This part is excellently put together, and in places rather witty, but is over a little quickly – like the waxworks as a whole. As you can be in and out of the museum in little over an hour, you're paying more per minute here than practically anywhere else in Britain. Meals, snacks, shop, disabled access; cl 25 Dec; (0171) 935 6861; £8.95. The LONDON PLANETARIUM next door is rather more satisfying, showing off one of the most advanced star projectors in the world. Surround-sound gives its enjoyable presentations an added sense of realism. Make sure you get to each show on time – stragglers barely have a moment to find a seat before the lights are dimmed. Plenty of interactive displays too – you can even see how much you'd weigh on another planet. Meals, snacks, shop, disabled access; cl 25 Dec; £5.65 (joint ticket with Madame Tussaud's available). Opposite, the café of St Marylebone Church has good-value simple vegetarian meals.

To many people the world over, Baker St calls to mind only one thing – Conan Doyle's great detective. The famous address of 221b has a SHERLOCK HOLMES MUSEUM, with various Holmes paraphernalia, and something of the atmosphere of the books re-created – though 'The Case of Why They Charge So Much To See It' might have baffled even brother Mycroft. Shop; cl 25 Dec; (0171) 935 8866; £5.

King's Cross British Library (Euston Rd) Open to visitors from spring 1998, this vast new library has good exhibition space for its national treasures, such as the Lindisfarne Gospels and Magna Carta, and will change its displays frequently, as well as mounting special exhibitions; the entrance courtyard has a gigantic bronze of a crouching Sir Isaac Newton, by Paolozzi after William Blake. Opening details still undecided as we went to press – best to check (0171) 412 7111; free, exc for special exhibitions.

Great Portland St REGENT'S PARK Covering over 400 acres, this is the culmination of a glorious swathe of Regency terraces designed by John Nash, which can be seen almost all around it; the buildings of Park Crescent are among the finest. The park was originally intended to be the setting for a palace for the Prince Regent, after whom it was named: now it contains an open-air theatre where Shakespeare and other plays are performed in the summer, the lovely Queen Mary's Rose Garden, the spectacular Avenue Garden (now restored to its 1864 glory), a boating lake, bandstand concerts on summer Suns, and plenty of paths to stroll along. LONDON ZOO (easily reached also from Regent's Park or Camden Town tubes) In the N corner of the Park, the zoo last year opened the listed Mappin Terraces as a sort of animal playground shared by deer, peacocks, monkeys and bears. Sadly, other areas show only too well that the last few years haven't been the zoo's easiest, and despite the presence of lions and rhinos, it's with the smaller creatures that the zoo currently excels: there's a fascinating insect house, and other highlights are the irresistible children's zoo, where you can get right up to the animals (and maybe help feed the pigs at lunchtime), the biggest reptile house of any British zoo, and the spellbinding Moonlight World, where day and night are reversed so that you can watch nocturnal creatures such as vampire bats. Meals, snacks, shop, disabled access; cl 25 Dec; (0171) 722 3333; £8. The London Waterbus Company – one of several companies who now run CANAL BOAT TRIPS along the stretch of Regent's Canal between Little Venice and Camden Lock – make a stop for passengers who want to get off at the zoo; (0171) 482 2550 for timetable.

Please let us know what you think of places in the *Guide*. Use the report forms at the back of the book or simply send a letter.

SOUTH OF THE RIVER

South of the river, the magnificent new London Aquarium, splendid Museum of the Moving Image (MOMI), the Imperial War Museum, Britain at War and perhaps the Design Museum are strong draws: children particularly like MOMI, and the expensive London Dungeon (with an enjoyable new water-ride this year). Though small, the Old Operating Theatre is eye-opening.

The buildings of the South Bank arts centre have been largely humanised inside, with pleasant bars and so forth, and there is usually something going on in their foyers – inc free entertainment. The magnificent reconstruction of Shakespeare's Globe Theatre had its first full season last summer, and other new projects are livening up other parts of the South Bank. A stroll along its walkways give marvellous views across the river – the best views of the Houses of Parliament are from the quiet riverside walk between Westminster Bridge and the ancient palace of the Archbishop of Canterbury by Lambeth Bridge.

To see and do

LONDON FAMILY ATTRACTION OF THE YEAR

♪ ! ⊖ **Westminster** LONDON AQUARIUM (County Hall, a pleasant walk across Westminster Bridge) The first of several new attractions in the elegant home of the former Greater London Council, this £25 million exhibition is one of Europe's biggest collections of underwater life, housed in around 2 million litres of water. Most new aquariums tend to go for the show-stopping, walk-through tunnel experience, but what they've done here is actually more spectacular: the main Atlantic and Pacific tanks go right through all 3 display levels of the building, with huge windows at every stage giving great views of the sharks, stingrays and conger eels swimming round the Easter-Island-style giant heads. So not only do the creatures (and occasional divers) have plenty of room to swim about, but if you come at a sensible time there isn't much congestion around these more popular exhibits – everyone gets several chances to stare at the sharks close-up. Even though you know they can't get at you, the downright mean-looking expressions on their faces still pack quite a punch.

The rest of the displays – arranged in different themed areas representing rivers, coral reefs and rainforests – are a more conventional size, so you may have to wait a couple of minutes to get right up to them (for example, on our summer holiday visit no-one left the seahorse tank until one of the shy little creatures had finally appeared). Some areas are fairly imaginative, making good use of sound and light effects, and, of course, the fish and sea life are quite spectacular, with breath-taking colours and patterns; some species haven't been seen in Britain before. Well sized touch-tanks let you stroke a ray or gingerly handle a crab, but they do need to be slightly better supervised: despite the signs, we saw quite a few people cheerfully examining the crabs out of the water. A few extra staff would be helpful in other areas too, both to answer questions and to stop younger visiters enthusiastically climbing where they shouldn't. Children love it, and you can spend a couple of hours here without any trouble at all. To avoid the crowds at weekends and school holidays, try to come early or late in the day (its open till 7.30pm in summer), otherwise you may end up having to queue. Meals, snacks, big shop, disabled access; cl 25 Dec; (0171) 967 8000; £6.50 (£4.50 children aged 3–14). A family ticket for 2 adults and 2 children is £20. Great views of the Houses of Parliament and river from outside.

🖼🚻⚠🏧♿🚆 **Waterloo** SOUTH BANK CENTRE These theatres, cinemas and galleries contain multifarious cultural treasures – not for nothing do they boast that it's the biggest arts complex in the world. Externally, it's not appealing. Exciting plans to float a spectacular 'crystal wave' over the complex to bring some charm and warmth to the uninviting space around these rather dismal blocks of stained concrete have been delayed, if not scuppered, by the recent diversion of Lottery money into non-arts projects. In the meantime occasional open-air festivals, with stalls of books, clothes and jewellery going down to the river, are a well meaning substitute and can be pleasant on a sunny day. But generally it's best to get inside as quickly as you can – a different, altogether more joyful world, with frequent free performances and interesting small exhibitions in the foyers of the various halls.

The National Theatre, as well as the excellent productions in its 3 different-sized auditoria, has interesting artistic exhibitions, guided tours behind the scenes, and good places to eat – often accompanied by live music in the foyer of the Olivier Theatre; (0171) 633 0880 to book a tour (£3.50; not on Sun). The National Film Theatre has good themed screenings and events, and was building a new riverside café as we went to press. The Hayward Gallery specialises in world-class art exhibitions; exhibitions this year will include works by Francis Bacon (5 Feb–5 Apr) and Anish Kapoor (30 Apr–21 Jun). The Royal Festival Hall has a full programme of music and dance; its People's Palace is a good modern restaurant and bar. The MUSEUM OF THE MOVING IMAGE 🎬, or MOMI as it's usually called, is also here, providing a romp through cinematic history which everyone really enjoys. Lively displays trace moving pictures from magic lanterns to today's hi-tech special effects, taking in clips from favourite films, TV shows and cartoons along the way. You can learn how to operate a television studio, read the news or fly like Superman, while older visitors find the montage of old Pathé newsreels particularly nostalgic. The costumed actors work really hard with their performances, and there are temporary themed exhibitions (one on the Hammer House of Horror runs until May). MOMI is one of London's best attractions, and a visit can easily last several hours. Meals, snacks, shop, disabled access – contact reception when you get there; cl 24–26 Dec; (0171) 401 2636; *£5.95.

Quite a few projects have brightened up the area in recent years: relaxed GABRIEL'S WHARF on Upper Ground has a number of cheery designer and craft workshops, along with cafés, events, and a Fri craft market, and the new OXO TOWER WHARF offers great views over the city from the top of the lavishly restored art deco tower with its landmark logo. Though the South Bank and its attractions are well signposted from Waterloo, if you have time to spare the walk is more pleasant over Blackfriars Bridge, or from Westminster (see below); it's a short walk from the South Bank Centre to the London Aquarium. Nr the Old Vic, just S of Waterloo, La Barca (Lower Marsh St) is an enjoyably theatrical Italian restaurant, and Livebait (The Cut) is renowned for its fish. The café of the Young Vic (The Cut) does very good-value light lunches, but you'll feel centuries old if you're out of your 20s.

✪ **Westminster** is north of the river, but is the closest stop to the London Aquarium (*see separate Family Panel on p.808*) across Wesminster Bridge at County Hall, and handy for the places listed under Waterloo. County Hall also has simulator rides, video games and ten-pin bowling, and a couple of new hotels will open this spring (one with budget prices). This is also where the huge Ferris wheel to mark the Millennium will be, designed as a 'working sculpture' rather than a fairground attraction. It's scheduled for completion by the end of this year, though work had yet to begin as we went to press. You can get to the Imperial War Museum from here too (see Lambeth North entry, p.811).

❋ 🏠 ! ✪ **London Bridge** The area around Bankside is very much on the up at the moment; there's quite a bit of redevelopment going on in the old buildings, and plenty more to come (the Tate are to open a £106 million modern art gallery in the old Bankside power station). Riverside promenades offer good Thames and City views – Wren is said to have watched the building of St Paul's from here, and Pepys certainly did watch London burning down in the Great Fire, from nr the interesting old Anchor tavern. One of the best cross-river views of St Paul's is from the modern Founders Arms. For centuries this was London's entertainment centre, full of theatres, bars and licensed brothels. The most famous of the theatres, Shakespeare's GLOBE THEATRE, has been reconstructed on its original site, where it was open from 1599 to 1642 (when the Puritans closed it down). The late Sam Wanamaker's ambitious project was derided when first mooted, but the theatre has now enjoyed a very well received first season. It couldn't be more different from the West End: shaped like an O, the 3-tiered, open-topped theatre is 30 metres (100 ft) in diameter, seating audiences of 1,500 with a further 500 promenaders. Shakespeare's works are performed almost the way they were in the early 1600s – no spotlights, canned music or elaborate sets. Anyone who tells you the seats are uncomfortable has rather missed the point. You can tour the site during the day, and there's an exhibition on the Globes old and new. Shop, disabled access; cl 24–25 Dec; (0171) 928 6406; tours £5. The 17th-c galleried George in Borough High St, back past London Bridge station, gives another idea of how the area's buildings used to look back then; NT.

👿 ✝ CLINK EXHIBITION (Clink St) A look at the less salubrious side of the area's history: the displays are very traditional in their approach, with lots to read and look at rather than to poke and push, but quite fascinating. Snacks, shop; cl 25–26 Dec; (0171) 403 6515; £3.50. Next door are the medieval remains of the Bishop of Winchester's palace, once said to be the biggest building in Europe but now reduced to a single wall and an atmospheric rose window. A full-size replica of Francis Drake's *Golden Hind* is moored nearby.

✝ 👿 SOUTHWARK CATHEDRAL Quite a contast to the buildings cluttered all around it, and well worth a passing look, with parts over 600 years older than the present late 19th-c nave; interesting memorials to William Shakespeare (whose brother is buried here) and John Harvard, the founder of the American university. They generally have free recitals Mon lunchtime, and sometimes Tues too. Across the busy main road, the church of St Thomas (St Thomas St) has a unique reconstructed OLD OPERATING THEATRE in its roof, and a developing museum looking at the history of surgery and herbal medicine. Shop, cl 25 Dec; £2.50.

! 👿 👿 LONDON DUNGEON (Tooley St) A more sensationalised look at London's seamy underside than you'll find at the Clink (see entry above), so it's better for unsqueamish children, with witchcraft, torture, black magic and death all presented in ghoulishly life-like waxwork scenes. The Jack the Ripper Experience has a computer-controlled fireball blasting towards visitors as its climax, and there's an entertaining new water-ride, Judgement Day. The whole place is very atmospheric, and genuinely historical in its own way, though families may find the scariest thing about it is the rather high price. Snacks, shop, disabled access; cl 25 Dec; (0171) 403 0606; £8.95. Down the road, BRITAIN AT WAR ⚅ is a splendidly put together re-creation of Blitz-hit London, from reconstructed streets and air-raid shelters to a BBC radio station and GI club. The special effects are suitably dramatic, with lots of smoke, smells and noise. Also authentic period newsreels and front pages, a fully stocked shop and pub, and lots of fascinating little details. Shop, disabled access; cl 24–26 Dec; (0171) 403 3171; *£5.95. Off Tooley St, HAYS GALLERIA is an old dock attractively converted into a shopping arcade, with several places to eat inc a good river-view pub, and a fascinating, whimsical pirate-ship working sculpture by David Kemp. ✹ HMS BELFAST On the E side of the bridge, docked permanently in the pool of London, is the largest preserved cruiser ever built for the Royal Navy. Its 7 decks are now a floating naval museum, with sound and light displays and various exhibitions. Anyone with even a passing interest in naval life and history should get a lot out of this, and there's plenty to see, from the ship's gun decks to its dental surgery. Meals, snacks, shop, limited disabled access; cl 24–26 Dec; (0171) 407 6434; £4.40. ᕗ DESIGN MUSEUM (Butlers Wharf) Intriguing museum showing how design is used in the mass production of everyday objects, from cars and furniture to graphics and ceramics. A look at Porsche's contribution to vehicle design runs from 9 Apr–31 Aug. Meals, snacks, shop, disabled access; cl am wknds, 25-6 Dec; (0171) 403 6933; £5. Close by, the almost scholarly BRAMAH TEA AND COFFEE MUSEUM (Clove Building) charts the history of these 2 favourite commodities, with around 1,000

teapots, and lots of ceramics, silver and prints. Teas (good stuff – they're not fans of the tea bag), Snacks, shop, disabled access; cl 25–26 Dec; (0171) 378 0222; £3.50. Nearby, the Anchor Tap (just off Shad Thames) is a handy refreshment stop.

ᕗ ⊖ **Lambeth North** (or Westminster on the other side of the river) IMPERIAL WAR MUSEUM (Lambeth Rd) This top-notch museum uses very up-to-date presentation techniques to give a vibrant and sometimes even nerve-racking exploration of aspects of all wars involving Britain and the Commonwealth since 1914. The Blitz Experience vividly re-creates London's darkest days, and a Trench Experience gives World War I the same treatment. Small boys of all ages love it, though the tone isn't all gung-ho: the interesting archive recordings of people's experiences of war can leave a deep impression, as do some of the harrowing paintings by official war artists. Meals, snacks, shop, disabled access; cl 24–26 Dec; (0171) 416 5000; £4.90, free after 4.30pm. It's housed in the former lunatic asylum known as Bedlam, the name a corruption of Bethlehem: the site was originally a hostel set up in the 13th c by the bishop of that town. There's a clutch of useful tapas bars and the like up past here, around the junction of Kennington Rd and Kennington Lane, and on Waterloo Rd the Fire Station does good food.

🏛 † ᕗ LAMBETH PALACE (S end of Lambeth Bridge) The official residence of the Archbishop of Canterbury, with a charming late 15th-c red-brick exterior; though there are twice-weekly tours of the partly early medieval interior, they're fully booked for the whole of this year – and well into next. The adjacent CHURCH OF ST MARY has the tombs of several archbishops, and Captain Bligh of the *Bounty* is buried here too. Just by the south gateway is a little MUSEUM OF GARDEN HISTORY founded in memory of John Tradescant, Charles I's gardener (also buried in the church), with a small area planted with plants grown in his time. Snacks, shop, some disabled access; cl Sat, and early Dec–early Mar; (0171) 401 8865; free.

♨ FLORENCE NIGHTINGALE MUSEUM (St Thomas's Hospital, Lambeth Palace Rd) On the site of the first School of Nursing, a re-created hospital ward in the Crimea, and various artefacts and possessions of the Lady with the Lamp. Shop, disabled access; cl Mon (exc bank hols); (0171) 620 0374; *£3.50.

! ⊖ ELEPHANT & CASTLE Get up very early on Fri for the bargains at BERMONDSEY MARKET (Bermondsey St/Long Lane): when the antique-dealers start arriving around 5am, other dealers literally pounce on the choice items while they're being set out, and by 8 or 9am things are more ordinary. It's probably the biggest primary source of antiques and bric-à-brac in London, and can be the most exciting. Take a torch in winter.

FURTHER AFIELD

We include here only those places which, despite being away from the centre, appeal so much at least to some people that, for them, even a short stay in London would be incomplete without them. The most generally appealing of these places are Greenwich and Kew; elsewhere the lively RAF Museum in Colindale is excellent, Kenwood is a Hampstead highlight, and the unusual Horniman Museum makes Forest Hill well worth a family expedition.

Other parts of London do have many treasures tucked away, and though we don't list them, they are worth Londoners themselves tracking down: prime among them the Whitechapel Gallery in Whitechapel High St, E of the City, and, out in west London, Osterley Park, Sion House, Chiswick Mall (18th-c Thames-side village), Chiswick Park (the first true example of English naturalistic landscaping, with Chiswick House, an early 18th-c partying pavilion), and perhaps Hogarth's House.

♟!♨⊖ **Camden Town** A bohemian's idyll, with a very wide variety of unusual shops from radical bookshops to fashion workshops, from comic shops to one of London's best brassware and ironmongery shops. Lots of restaurants and cafés too, and good delis serving the area's Italian and Greek communities; try the Parkway Deli for Italian, and Chris Milia (Pratt St) for Greek. The area's biggest draw is its weekend series of lively MARKETS, particularly the interesting craft, hand-made fashion and other stalls around the attractively converted former warehouses of Camden Lock. There's also a covered market on Camden High St, the Inverness St Market for fruit and vegetables, and the Stables, where the best food stalls are to be found. Go and browse, but be warned that you may never again see such huge crowds – the markets here draw 200,000 people every weekend. JEWISH MUSEUM (129 Albert St) Excellent look at Jewish life, history and religion, with a particularly fine collection of ceremonial art, portraits and antiques, and various audio-visual displays. Shop, disabled access; cl Fri, Sat, all bank and Jewish hols; (0171) 388 4525; £3. The Princess of Wales up towards Primrose Hill (Chalcot Rd/Regent's Pk Rd) does good bistro food.

♟🏠❀🐘☀♨!♨≷ **Greenwich** The sort of place you can come back to time and time again; some of our contributors rate Greenwich more highly than anywhere else in the country. Once a favoured residence of the Royal Family, Greenwich has a long and illustrious maritime heritage, still reflected in the museums, boats and grand old ships you can visit. A weekend market has some excellent antiques, junk and secondhand books, and also arts and crafts. The almost constantly controversial Millennium Exhibition, with its centrepiece riverside Dome, is to be staged here, the projected cost climbing towards an uncomfortably millenary £1,000 million. Three of the best attractions, the Queen's House, National Maritime Museum and Royal Observatory, can be visited on a joint ticket for a bargain £5.50. You'll still pay this even if you can visit only one of them, but you don't have to do them all on the same day.

The QUEEN'S HOUSE (Romney Rd) stands on the site of the original magnificent Royal palace; all that's left of that is the vaulted crypt beneath what's now called Queen Anne's Block. The new building was designed in the early 17th c by Inigo Jones for Anne of Denmark, and was finished for the wife of Charles I, Queen Henrietta Maria. The first Palladian-style villa in the country, it's been grandly refurbished to show how it was when first built. Sumptuous silks and furnishings, as well as a collection of Dutch seascapes; good Walkman commentary. Shop, disabled access (with notice); cl 24–26 Dec; (0181) 858 4422; £5.50, though see above. It's the focal point of the glorious group of buildings that make up the ROYAL NAVAL COLLEGE, designed initially by Webb in the late 17th c, then augmented in succession by Wren, Vanbrugh, Hawksmoor and Ripley. It's a magnificently preserved part of old London. Visitors can see an interesting chapel and a notable painted hall. Shop; cl am, Good Fri, 25 Dec; (0181) 858 2154; free. The view from across the river (there's a pedestrian tunnel under the Thames here) looks like an 18th-c print come to life. NATIONAL MARITIME MUSEUM 🖼 (Romney Rd) Good fun, telling the story of Britain and the sea, with

plenty of boats, details of past Royal fleets and vessels, and great masterpieces of naval battles. Much of the museum is closed during 1998 for restoration work, although the impressive exhibition on Nelson, scheduled to run for the next decade, will still be open; details as Queen's House.

GREENWICH PARK Wonderful views from this carefully landscaped park sloping down towards the river. A herd of deer graze in a smallish area of woodland and wild flowers known as the Wilderness, and there's the largest children's playground in any Royal Park (as well as the preserved trunk of a tree in which the young Elizabeth I is said to have played). The park's chiefly famous for the ROYAL OBSERVATORY, the original home of Greenwich Mean Time – standing as it does on zero meridian longitude. The brass line marking the meridian is still there set in the ground: standing over it with one foot in the western hemisphere and one in the eastern is almost irresistible. As you do so you can check your watch against the big new clock counting down the days to the Millennium. The Wren-built observatory was founded by Charles II in 1675, and now houses a comprehensive collection of historic instruments for time-keeping, navigation and astronomy. Good views from the top. The Time Ball is rather confusing – it can go down and up so fast you barely notice it. Meals, snacks, shop; details as Queen's House. The park is a great place for a picnic.

CUTTY SARK Moored not far from Greenwich Pier, this clipper built in 1896 was the fastest of her time – she once sailed 363 nautical miles in a single day. On board, you can watch a video telling her story, and there's an impressive collection of ships' figureheads. Shop; cl am Sun, 24–26 Dec; (0181) 858 3445; £3.50. You should be able to get boat trips from here up to Westminster (around £5). Nearby College Approach has a good weekend covered craft market. The pub named after the Cutty Sark, nearby in Lassell St, is an attractive old place for lunch; other reliable Thames-view pubs here are the Trafalgar (Park Row) and Yacht (Crane St).

FAN MUSEUM (12 Crooms Hill) Unique collection of around 3,000 fans and related items from all over the world. They even do fan-making classes. Shop, disabled access (with notice); cl am Sun, and all day Mon; (0181) 858 7879; £3. It's not far from here to Blackheath, a civilised place and good for a pleasant stroll, with the RANGER'S HOUSE (Chesterfield Walk), a lovely stately home with fine furnishings, portraits and a collection of musical instruments. In the 19th c it was the official residence of the Greenwich Park ranger. Cl winter Mon and Tues, 24–26 Dec; (0181) 853 0035; £2.50.

🏠♿🎱❄✳🖼❤ **Hampstead** prides itself on its villagey atmosphere, and off the main streets its maze of twisting lanes is very picturesque and seductively charming. It's home to artistes of all kinds, and well heeled bohemians in general; in some streets a commemorative blue plaque on the front of the house is almost compulsory. Down in Keats Grove (past the little Downshire Hill church, which has lovely candlelit Christmas carol services), Keats and his lover and nurse Fanny Brawne lived in 2 fine Regency houses; KEATS HOUSE now has interesting displays relating to his life, with manuscripts, letters and personal mementos (and a recorded nightingale out in the garden on summer nights). Shop; cl 1–2pm, am Sun, winter wkdys and am bank hols, 24–26 Dec, 1 Jan, Good Fri, May bank hol; (0171) 435 2062; free. SIGMUND FREUD'S HOUSE (20 Maresfield Gdns) Extraordinary collection of antiques from various ancient cultures, as well as Freud's library, papers and indeed his desk and couch. Shop, some disabled access; open pm Weds–Sun; (0171) 435 2002; *£3. The monumental seated statue of Freud by Oscar Nemon can now be seen outside the Tavistock Clinic on nearby Belsize Lane. FENTON HOUSE (Windmill Hill)

Fine William and Mary merchant's mansion, set in a walled garden, with Oriental, English and European china and an exceptional collection of early keyboard instruments. Their period-music concerts on some summer Weds evenings are well worth catching. Open pm Weds–Sun Apr–Oct, plus pm wknds in Mar; (0171) 435 3471; £3.60; NT. The gaslit Holly Bush, prettily tucked away up Holly Mount, is a good pub, as is the Flask in Flask Walk (a long-standing favourite of local actors). 2 WILLOW RD The first Modern Movement house acquired by the National Trust. Designed and built by the architect Erno Goldfinger, it has a good range of work by the artists and intellectuals who lived around Hampstead in the 1930s – as well as the only working TV on show in any NT property. Guided tours from noon Thurs–Sat mid-Apr–Oct; (0171) 435 6166; £4; NT. Other particularly attractive areas in the area include the early Georgian Church Row, and Squires Mount (where the Regency-looking house at the end on the left, in fact built in the 1950s, belonged to Richard Burton and Elizabeth Taylor). Across the road from here is HAMPSTEAD HEATH, north London's best open space, with lakes, hilly prospects, and some wonderful views of the city skyline – Parliament Hill has a direction-finder pointing out various landmarks. Across the heath, KENWOOD achieved its present splendid proportions in the 18th c at the hands of Robert Adam. The house contains a fine collection of paintings, inc old masters and 18th- and 19th-c portraits by Reynolds and Gainsborough, and efforts are being made to reacquire its original contents. The grounds are lovely, and in summer there are concerts out here, idyllic when it's fine, with the music drifting across the lake with its Japanese bridge, and sometimes a fireworks finale (virtually impossible to park anywhere near – but a free shuttle bus runs from East Finchley tube from 5pm then). Meals, snacks, shop, disabled access; cl 24–25 Dec;

(0181) 348 1286; free. Nearby the ancient Spaniard's Inn is still as good as when Dickens made it famous in his *Pickwick Papers*.

🏠🏛♿⚓�∿**Hampton Court** HAMPTON COURT An amazing place, just as a Royal palace should be. Begun by Cardinal Wolsey in the early 16th c, the house's splendour soon so pricked Henry VIII's jealousy that Wolsey felt compelled to present it to his king in an attempt to appease him. Successive monarchs have left their architectural marks: the hammerbeamed hall and kitchens were Henry's addition, the Fountain Court was designed by Wren for William and Mary, and much comes from the work of the Victorians (the chimneys mostly date from then). The rooms have managed to keep their distinctive styles, from the starkly imposing Tudor kitchens (themselves taking up 50 rooms) to the elaborate grandeur of the Georgian chambers. The King's Staircase is wonderfully over the top, and the Picture Gallery has the finest Renaissance works from the Royal collection, inc Brueghel the Elder's fascinating *Massacre of the Innocents*. Look out too for the carvings by Grinling Gibbons and the cartoons by Mantegna in the Lower Orangery. There are several audio guides you can pick up and listen to as you go along, with no extra charge. Meals, snacks, shops, disabled access; cl 24–26 Dec; (0181) 781 9500; £8.50. HAMPTON COURT GARDENS are worth a visit in their own right, especially since the restoration of William III's Privy Garden, damaged in the Palace's 1986 fire. The last time these gardens looked as they do now was in 1702. The elaborately landscaped grounds also include the famous maze, and the annual flower show here is one of the world's biggest. Open as for the palace; £2 gardens only. The King's Arms, next to the Lion Gate, is useful for something to eat. BUSHY PARK nearby is another Royal Park, formerly reserved for hunting. Wren laid out its famous double chestnut avenue, which runs from the great house to the

Teddington Gate. There are pleasant Thames-side walks around Hampton Court, and summer cruise boats from here back down to Westminster, (0171) 930 4721; £8.

🏠❗⊖**Highgate**, an easy walk across the Heath from Hampstead, dates largely from the Victorian period and still keeps a villagey atmosphere, centred as it is around the High St. The village is dominated by Highgate School (which Betjeman attended and where T S Eliot taught). There are lots of pubs in this area, and some smart little cafés. The Grove, a row of very elegant Victorian houses, is home to such diverse musicians as Yehudi Menuhin and Sting. HIGHGATE CEMETERY (Swains Lane) The most impressive of a series of landscaped and formal cemeteries started in the early decades of Victoria's reign on the outskirts of the city, very well restored over the last 20 years, and still in use. You'll find it hard to miss the tomb of Karl Marx – a monstrous head, frequently daubed with paint and slogans. It's more difficult to search out the graves of Christina Rossetti and George Eliot in the wonderfully atmospheric tangle of trees, shrubs and crumbling, ivy-covered monuments. The east cemetery is open all year (exc 25–26 Dec), the west by guided tour only (not wkdys Dec–Feb), (0181) 340 1834 for times; east cemetery £1, west cemetery £3.

🅿♿🏠🚻⛵♿⊖**Kew** KEW GARDENS were started here in 1759 by George III's mother, and consisted of 9 acres landscaped by Capability Brown. By 1904, they had grown to cover 300 acres, with the foundations of the present wonderful collection firmly laid. The glasshouses include the magnificent modern Princess of Wales range and the remarkable restored Victorian Palm House, as well as an Evolution House displaying plants from up to 400 million years ago. The gardens nr the entrance are largely formally arranged, and drift into attractively landscaped woodland, glades and tree collections further out. There's also a gallery, and on some summer evenings jazz concerts with fireworks. A wonderful place you can come back to time and time again – always discovering something new. Meals, snacks, shop, disabled access; cl 25 Dec, 1 Jan; (0181) 332 5622; £4.50. In the grounds too is KEW PALACE, built in 1631 and used by members of the Royal Family until Queen Charlotte's death in 1818. It's a Dutch-style brick building that seems remarkably unroyal, and remains much as it was during George III's reign, with family paintings, furniture and tapestries. It was closed as we went to press, but should open again this year; (0181) 781 9500 to check. The garden has been planted to appear as it would have done in the 18th c. Kew was at that time one of the Royal Family's favourite residences, somewhere they could enjoy quiet times as a family. In the gardens they built a rusticated summerhouse, QUEEN CHARLOTTE'S COTTAGE, its interior designed to look like a tent; it's usually open wknds and bank hols Apr–Sept. The Flower & Firkin at Kew BR station does decent, simple food. KEW BRIDGE STEAM MUSEUM (Green Dragon Lane) Over the bridge from the gardens, by the tube station, this is a splendid old pumping station housing 5 Cornish beam engines – one of which you can walk through while it's working. Also a miniature railway, and a surprisingly interesting exhibition on the development of London's water supply: there are peepholes into the sewers. It won't appeal unless you've at least some interest in the subject – in which case you'll find the engines prime examples of their type. Wknd snacks, shop, some disabled access; cl Christmas, Good Fri; (0181) 568 4757; £3.25 wknds (when engines in

steam), £2 wkdys. MUSICAL MUSEUM (368 Brentford High St, just W of Kew Bridge) Worth a look if you have the time, with a fascinating collection of continuously playing automatic musical instruments. Shop, disabled access; open pm wknds Apr–Oct, plus pm Weds July and Aug; (0181) 560 8108; *£3.20. In summer you can come to Kew by cruise boat from Westminster – see the tel numbers we give for Hampton Court above and Richmond below.

♨ ⚛ ♥ 🏠 ➤ **Richmond** is an agreeable if much extended Thames village, with lots of fine 18th-c houses especially around the Green and up Richmond Hill. There are quite a few good dining pubs, inc the riverside White Cross, and the White Swan (Old Palace Lane), Orange Tree (Kew Rd) and Rose of York (Petersham Rd). The river here is really attractive for strolls, and there are summer cruise boats from here back down to Westminster, stopping at Kew and Putney (more fine riverside walks) on the way; (0171) 930 2062. RICHMOND PARK The most country-like of all London's parks, with great rolling spaces and wildlife (inc herds of deer), model boats on Adam's Pond, and fishing in the 18-acre Pen Ponds. There's a good formal garden at Pembroke Lodge, and the Isabella Plantation's rhododendrons and azaleas are a must-see in season. It's a pleasant 2-mile walk W along the river to HAM HOUSE in Petersham, an outstanding Stuart mansion, recently wonderfully restored. Meals, snacks, shop, disabled access; open pm Sat–Weds Apr–Oct; (0181) 940 1950; £4.50; NT. The garden (still being restored) is free. If you happen to be in Twickenham you can get a ferry across.

MORE SPECIALISED EXPEDITIONS

✆ **Angel** Camden Passage and the surrounding streets have a great collection of ANTIQUE SHOPS, well worth the expedition if that interests you. The nearby Island Queen (Noel Rd) does good food in its bar and upstairs restaurant.

✆ ⇌ **Chislehurst** CHISLEHURST CAVES (entrance off Caveside Close nr the Bickley Arms, on the B264; nr BR station) Atmospheric 45-minute lamplit tours of labyrinthine tunnels and passageways carved out of the rock over 8,000 years. They've been used by druids, flint-knappers, and as an air-raid shelter during the war. Longer more adventurous tours on Suns and bank hols at 1.30pm. Snacks (wknds and school hols), shop; cl Mon and Tues (exc school hols); (0181) 467 3264; *£3 (£5 longer tour).

✝ ✆ **Colindale** RAF MUSEUM (Grahame Park Way) The story of flight from early times, with 70 full-size aeroplanes, dramatic simulators, films and hands-on exhibits (you can have a go at the controls of a modern jet trainer), lively Battle of Britain Experience, and an interesting examination of the impact of flight on history and politics. Excellent for enthusiasts and flying-minded children, and warmly recommended by several of our contributors. Meals, snacks, shop, disabled access; cl 24–26 Dec, 1 Jan; (0181) 205 9191; £5.85 (includes free return visit within 6 months).

✆ ♪ ⇌ **Forest Hill** HORNIMAN MUSEUM (London Rd) Art nouveau building with eclectic, mainly ethnographic collections inc a fine group of mummies, religious artefacts, and exotic folk art; also a remarkable musical instrument collection, stuffed animals, and a very well laid out aquarium/ecosystem; children love it, despite the old-fashioned feel. Snacks, shop, disabled access; cl am Sun, 24–26 Dec; free wknd talks/concerts; (0181) 699 1872; free.

✆ 🎴 ✿ ✆ **St John's Wood** LORD'S CRICKET GROUND (St John's Wood Rd) Tours of the famous club and grounds, and the excellent MCC Museum, with an exhaustive collection of cricket memorabilia, inc the Ashes urn and 18th-c paintings of the game. As this is a private club, visits are by appointment only; (0171) 266 3825 (usually at 12 and 2pm), though you can also see the museum if you're watching a cricket match during the season. Shop, disabled access by prior arrangement; £2. Down in Aberdeen Pl, Crockers is a remarkably opulent Victorian pub with decent food. On the far side of this sober residential area, take a stroll through PRIMROSE HILL, which was once part of the same hunting park as Regent's Park. From the summit there are eye-opening views of the city.

✆ ✗ ✆ ✗ **Southfields** WIMBLEDON LAWN TENNIS MUSEUM ♿ (Church Rd) The only museum of its type, with trophies, pictures and other tennis memorabilia tracing the development of the game throughout this century. Also highlights of past Wimbledon Championships, and an interesting display on the changes in tennis fashions. You can see the famous Centre Court outside. Snacks, shop, disabled access; cl am Sun, all day Mon, and every day during the Championship fortnight (unless you've gone to watch the tennis); (0181) 946 6131; *£2.50. If you're in London during the Wimbledon fortnight it's always worth popping along to the club in the early evening around 5.30 or 6pm – lots of people leave then and their seats are resold cheaply. Wimbledon itself has an attractive old core around the common, and a striking WINDMILL on Windmill Rd (open pm wknds and bank hols Easter–Oct; *£1).

✆ ! ⇌ **Twickenham** TWICKENHAM EXPERIENCE ♿ (Rugby Rd) Combines tours of the 75,000-seat home of rugby union with an excellent museum of related memorabilia under the East Stand; interactive displays and period reconstructions illustrate the game's history, and there's plenty of footage from classic matches. Snacks, shop, disabled access; cl Mon (exc bank hols), 24–26 Dec, Good Fri, and 2 days before and after matches; 4 tours a day (only two on Sun); best to book on (0181) 892 2000; £4, £2.50 for either the museum or tour only.

🅿 ⛟ ♿ **Walthamstow Central** WILLIAM MORRIS GALLERY (Lloyd Park, Forest Rd) William Morris lived here 1846–58, and the house has an excellent collection of his work: fabrics, furnishings and wallpaper, much of it still fashionable today. Pre-Raphaelite works upstairs include pictures by Burne-Jones and Rossetti. The attractive grounds are ideal for picnics. Shop, disabled access to ground floor only – though this is where the main exhibition is; cl 1–2pm, all day Mon, and Sun (exc 1st Sun in month); (0181) 527 3782; free.

! ♿ **Wembley Central** WEMBLEY STADIUM 🚆 (Empire Way) Tours of the most famous football stadium in the land, going from the dressing rooms through the players' tunnel and on to the pitch itself, with an audio-visual show and displays of trophies and related memorabilia. You can receive the cup or sit in the Royal Box. Snacks, shop, some disabled access (with notice); cl 25–26 Dec, and during occasional special events; (0181) 902 8833; *£6.95.

🅿 ⛟ ⇌ **West Dulwich** DULWICH PICTURE GALLERY (College Rd) The country's oldest public picture gallery, and though not large one of the best; a good range of European Old Masters with works by Poussin, Van Dyck, Gainsborough and Rembrandt. Guided tours 3pm wknds. The building itself is impressive, surrounded by parks and fields. Summer teas, shop, disabled access; cl Mon (exc bank hols); (0181) 693 5254; *£3, free on Fri. The village is still villagey, with imposing 18th-c houses, duckpond and a good pub, the Crown & Greyhound.

London Walks

Central London is fun to explore on foot, though the traffic and stop-start rhythm can be wearying. There is no end of potential walks concentrating on particular interests – architecture, history, royalty or whatever. One of the best overviews of the capital is had by walking along the south bank of the Thames from Lambeth Bridge to Tower Bridge, giving mostly traffic-free panoramic views of the West End, St Paul's Cathedral, the City, the Tower of London and, finally, Docklands. Quite a number of people lead guided walks. We have found Original London Walks, (0171) 624 3978, consistently good over the last few years, with a choice of 9 or 10 walks a day. Walks last about 2 hours, usually starting from a tube station; you don't need to book, and the cost is around £4.50.

Out of the centre, London has idyllic verdant stretches around Kew and Richmond; the old villages along the riverside have considerable charm and some good pubs. The Thames towpath can be combined with a walk in Richmond Park and to Ham House. The towpath between Putney and Kew Bridge (you have to cross the river a few times) has train stations at either end, and you can take in Chiswick Mall, Chiswick Park (a necessary diversion from the river at a point where there is no towpath on the N bank), and Strand on the Green, as well as Kew Gardens.

Hampstead Heath is the airy escape for north Londoners, with lots of paths, ponds, glades and hollows, and views of central London from Parliament Hill. The Regent's Canal offers an excellent walk from Little Venice to Camden Lock, passing by Regent's Park and Primrose Hill (another good viewpoint);

boat cruises also operate along here – one-way tickets available.

In south London, numerous commons and parks provide pleasant strolling grounds, such as Wimbledon Common with its ponds and windmill. A notable semi-rural enclave is in the Dulwich area where you can walk through the still villagey Dulwich Village, through Dulwich Park (best in rhododendron time) and through Dulwich Wood to adjacent Sydenham Hill Wood – the largest fragment of ancient woodland in inner London, and a most surprising place (just big enough to lose your way in), with woodpeckers among the oak and hornbeam trees. The best of the wood is a nature reserve, jealously guarded against developers by the London Wildlife Trust; a trail starts from the Crescent Wood Rd entrance on the Sydenham side.

The SE fringes of London give way to surprisingly rural North Downs countryside, still within the London borough of Bromley, around Knockholt, High Elms and Downe; paths are plentiful and well maintained. Only the view over S London from behind Knockholt church shows how close you are to the capital.

Where to eat

ALFRED 245 Shaftesbury Ave WC2 (0171) 240 2566 Easy-going café with very simple furnishings, lots of real ales, a good wine list inc English wines, and good, enjoyable British food; cl 24 Dec–2 Jan; limited disabled access. £30.50|£8.75.

APPRENTICE Butlers Wharf Chef School, Cardamon Building, 31 Shad Thames SE1 (0171) 234 0254 The school is a charitable organisation for hopeful chefs and front-of-house personnel; long, simple restaurant and good-value modern meals in an enjoyable atmosphere; weekend courses; cl 2 wks Christmas, weekends, bank hols; disabled access. £21|£9.50 for 2 courses.

AUBERGINE 11 Park Walk SW10 (0171) 352 3449 Exceptionally popular, smart and warmly decorated restaurant (have to book well in advance for evening meals but lunchtimes are easier); outstanding sophisticated Mediterranean cooking, a good wine list, and French service; cl am Sat, Sun, 2 wks Aug, bank hols. £52.50 dinner, £31.50 lunch.

BIBENDUM 81 Fulham Rd SW3 (0171) 581 5817 Magnificent art deco Michelin building housing a light and spacious restaurant; good French-style cooking (more elaborate in the evening), and an exceptional wine list; the downstairs oyster bar is popular too; cl 25–27 Dec; disabled access. £28 set lunch.

BILL BENTLEY'S Beauchamp Pl SW3 (0171) 589 5080 Though there's a decent upstairs fish restaurant, the nicest place is the crowded little bar, very popular with well-off local residents for good wine, highly individual service and choice nibbles such as fresh ham or oysters; cl Sun, bank hols. £32|£6.50.

BLOOMS 130 Golders Green Road NW11 (0181) 455 3033 Strictly kosher Jewish restaurant with enjoyable food – most fun on Sun lunchtime when it's packed with Jewish families; cl Fri evening, all Sat and on Jewish hols; disabled access. £20|£6.50.

BLUE ELEPHANT 4-6 Fulham Broadway SW6 (0171) 385 6595 Luxurious Thai food eaten among waterfalls and exotic jungle greenery, with produce flown in weekly from Thailand; the set meals are better value; cl am Sat, 24–26 Dec; disabled access. £40|£12.

BOMBAY BRASSERIE Courtfield Cl, Courtfield Rd SW7 (0171) 370 4040 Grand colonial-style furnishings in big restaurant and conservatory; very good Indian food using recipes from all over India (lots of vegetarian dishes), and courteous, helpful staff; it's cheaper at lunchtime when there's a buffet; cl 25–26 Dec; children over 10; disabled access. £35|£15.95 buffet lunch.

CAFÉ FISH 39 Panton St SW1 (0171) 930 3999 Bustling, well run fish restaurant (popular with theatre-goers), with nice fresh produce, a downstairs wine bar for lighter meals, and a fair wine list; cl am Sat (wine bar open then), Sun. £23|£9.

Café in the Crypt St Martin-in-the-Fields, Trafalgar Sq WC2 (0171) 930 0089 Popular place under the lovely arches of the church with good, freshly prepared food. £13|£5.

Canteen Chelsea Harbour SW10 (0171) 351 7330 Some tables overlook the marina in this smart modern restaurant with its pack-of-cards theme; excellent European food, and French-speaking service; cl am Sat, pm Sun, Christmas and bank hols; disabled access. £34|£15.50 2-course lunch.

Chez Nico at Ninety Park Lane 90 Park Lane W1 (0171) 409 1290 Comfortable, elegant restaurant run by Nico Ladenis, one of the country's best-known chefs, serving impeccable food (the set lunch is marvellous value) and fine wines (at a price); cl am Sat, Sun, 23 Dec–2 Jan, Easter and bank hols; children over 6; disabled access. £65 dinner not inc wine, lunch £35 for 3-courses. There's also Nico Central 35 Great Portland St W1 (0171) 436 8846, Simply Nico 48a Rochester Row SW1 (0171) 630 8061, and Café Nico, Grosvenor House, Park Lane W1 (0171) 495 2275.

Chutney Mary 535 King's Rd SW10 (0171) 351 3113 Interesting Anglo-Indian food in light conservatory and 2 dining rooms, plus a verandah bar; buffet only Sun, cl pm 25 Dec, 26 Dec; some disabled access. £30 dinner, £20 lunch|£10 2-course lunch.

Coast 26b Albemarle St W1 (0171) 495 5999 Light and airy, rather smart restaurant with a huge window overlooking the street, stylish simple furnishings, very friendly service, delicious modern cooking, and a good wine list. £37.

Cork & Bottle 44-46 Cranbourn St WC2 (0171) 734 7807 Popular basement wine bar that recently celebrated its 25th year, nr West End theatres; good food inc interesting salads, cold buffet and unusual hot dishes, excellent wines, and cheerful service; cl 25–26 Dec, 1 Jan. £18|£6.95.

Deals Chelsea Harbour SW10 (0171) 795 1001 Bustling café-restaurant with good food ranging from hamburgers to sizzle platters, generous glasses of decent house wine, good cocktails and very friendly service; best at lunchtime when it's less frenetic; good for children on Sun lunchtime (must book); cl 25–27 Dec, 1 Jan; disabled access; other branches. £20|£7.

Eagle 159 Farringdon Rd EC1 (0171) 837 1353 Particularly good Mediterranean-style food in this popular, stylish pub where the open kitchen forms part of the bar; well kept real ales, lots of wine by the glass, properly made cocktails, a lively and chatty atmosphere (lots of young media folk), and simple furnishings. £21|£8.50.

Ebury Wine Bar 139 Ebury St SW1 (0171) 730 8206 Said to be London's first wine bar (established in 1959) with a loyal following, an excellent list of wines by the glass, and very good modern cooking; weekend discounts; cl 3 days at Christmas; children over 5. £29.50|£6.50.

Food for Thought 31 Neal St WC2 (0171) 836 9072 Long-established and consistently good, unlicensed vegetarian restaurant, with a take-away service upstairs and communal eating at long tables downstairs – you can also eat at tables outside; no corkage; cl pm Sun, 24 Dec–2 Jan and Easter Sun. £7.90|£3.50.

Footstool St John's, Smith Sq SW1 (0171) 222 2779 Partly no smoking restaurant in the church crypt below the concert hall, with plants, pictures and stripped brick, and good food from a monthly-changing menu; lighter lunchtime buffet; cl am Sat–Sun. £25|£7.50.

Fortnum & Mason 181 Piccadilly W1 (0171) 734 8040 Famous store with lively fourth-floor St James's Restaurant (must book), Fountain Restaurant (lower ground floor), and Patio Restaurant (on the mezzanine) offering good breakfasts, lunches and fine afternoon tea; cl Sun, bank hols, 25–26 Dec and Easter; disabled access. £12|£7.50

Gay Hussar 2 Greek St W1 (0171) 437 0973 Long-standing Hungarian restaurant with bags of atmosphere (downstairs has the most); generous helpings of good and authentic food, and friendly service; cl Sun, bank hols. £25.

HANOVER SQUARE WINE BAR 25 Hanover Sq (0171) 408 0935 Under the same enthusiastic ownership as the popular long-standing Cork & Bottle in Leicester Sq, this bustling wine bar offers a constantly changing cold buffet plus daily hot dishes and charcoal grills, and a particularly interesting wine list; cl Sat, Sun, bank hols. £25|£6.95.

KALAMARES MICRO 66 Inverness Mews W2 (0171) 727 5082 (Not to be confused with its larger sister restaurant at No 76). Tiny, close-packed, authentically Greek restaurant with very good cheap food and friendly service; unlicensed, take your own wine; cl Sun, am, and bank hols; £17|£6.50.

LADBROKE ARMS 54 Ladbroke Rd W11 (0171) 727 6648 Stylish pub with imaginative home-made food, friendly staff, real ales and quite a few malt whiskies; immaculate bar with flowers, newspapers, and a smart and chatty atmosphere. cl 25 Dec; limited disabled access. £20|£8.

MON PLAISIR 21 Monmouth St WC2 (0171) 836 7243 Bustling French bistro with super atmosphere, good-value, well prepared food, decent wines, and friendly staff; popular for pre-theatre meals; cl am Sat, all day Sun, bank hols, Christmas, New Year and Easter; disabled access. £32|£13.95 3-course pre-theatre meal.

ODETTES 130 Regents Park Rd NW1 (0171) 586 5486 Smart front dining room with lots of gilded mirrors, an airy back conservatory, and slightly cheaper downstairs wine bar offering good modern English and more unusual dishes; friendly service, and thoughtful wine list; cl am Sat, pm Sun, 1 wk Christmas; limited disabled access. £33|£10 3-course set menu.

OLDE WINE SHADES 6 Martin Lane EC4 (0171) 626 6303 One of the few buildings to have escaped the Great Fire of 1666, and much as it was when Dickens used it as a tavern – heavy black beams, dignified alcoves, dark panelling and old-fashioned, high-backed settles; good wine and good-value traditional lunchtime snacks; packed with smart City types; cl wknds and bank hols; no children. £19|£7.50.

L'ORANGER 5 St James's St SW1 (0171) 839 3774 Comfortable, two-part dining room and small outside area for summer evenings, this is under the same ownership as the popular Aubergine (see entry above); wonderful, carefully, cooked food inc lovely fish dishes and super puddings, a good, mainly French wine list, and careful service; cl am Sun. £41.50 dinner, £34 lunch.

OXO TOWER Barge House St SE1 (0171) 803 3888 Briskly modern brasserie and restaurant on the 8th floor of this South Bank redevelopment; light and airy, with a busy open kitchen, lots of functional tables and chairs, and promptly served, modern English food; what stands out, of course, is the panoramic view over the Thames and City – best in summer from tables on the outside terrace; restaurant cl am Sat. £35.

POONS 27 Lisle St WC2 (0171) 437 4549 WC2 Atmospheric unlicensed and unmodernised Chinese restaurant with extremely good-value tasty barbecued and wind-dried food; cl Good Fri, 24–26 Dec. £14|£5.75. Other branches (more modern and expensive) at 4 Leicester St WC2 (0171) 437 1528, 50 Woburn Place, Russell Square WC1 (0171) 580 1188, and 2 Minster Ct, Mincing Lane EC3 (0171) 626 0126.

QUAGLINOS 16 Bury St SW1 (0171) 930 6767 Very fashionable restaurant with a big stone staircase to the antipasti bar overlooking the huge dining room with its flamboyantly painted pillars, fine flowers, highly modern attractive furnishings, and buoyant buzzing atmosphere; lovely fresh fish and other modern cooking, good wine list, and efficient service; cl 25 Dec; children over 12; disabled access. £30|£13.

REBATO'S 169 South Lambeth Rd SW8 (0171) 735 6388 Busy, high-ceilinged tapas bar with friendly barman and waiters, good choice of tapas, and lots of

Spanish wines; also Spanish restaurant; cl Sun, am Sat, bank hols. £19.20|£3.95.

RSJ 13a Coin St SE1 (0171) 928 4554 Handy for the South Bank, this relaxed and friendly restaurant serves fine modern British and Mediterranean cooking and exceptional Loire wines in simple surroundings; handy for the South Bank; cl am Sat, Sun. £25.

RULES 35 Maiden Lane WC2 (0171) 836 5314 One of the oldest restaurants in London, this smart and very British place serves good English food inc fine game and oysters in season; interesting history; cl 4 days over Christmas; some disabled access. £38.25|£13.95.

SAN FREDIANO 62 Fulham Rd SW3 (0171) 584 8375 Consistently good (and very popular), long-standing Italian restaurant with lots of interesting daily specials and decent wines; disabled access. £30|£9.

SIMPSONS IN THE STRAND 100 Strand WC2 (0171) 836 9112 Marvellously old-fashioned place with traditional English cooking inc nursery puddings, and roasts carved as you want them at your table on silver-domed trolleys; all very decorous – the surroundings and atmosphere are more memorable than the food; cl 25–26 Dec, 1 Jan, Good Fri; disabled access, children over 2. £37|£12.50 for 2 courses.

TANTE CLAIRE 68 Royal Hospital Rd SW3 (0171) 352 6045 Exceptional, beautifully presented French cooking in Pierre Koffmann's elegant restaurant – more relaxed at lunchtime when the set menu is very good-value; courteous service, and some good-value French country wines; jacket and tie required; cl wknds, Easter, most of Aug, Christmas. £80, 3-course set lunch £27.

TAPPIT HEN 5 William IV St WC2 (0171) 836 9839 Cosy and atmospheric little wine bar, very old-fashioned feeling, with good snacks and good-value wines – more for lunchtimes (when the smoked salmon sandwiches are lovely), though you can book for upstairs in the evening; cl Sat, Sun, bank hols. £19|£7.50.

WAGAMAMA 4 Streatham St WC1 (0171) 580 9365 You will have to queue to get into this trendy, simply furnished Japanese basement restaurant with its long tables and benches for communal eating; very friendly, cheerful service, and a noisy and informal atmosphere; good healthy food – raw salads, ramens (huge bowls of noodles with meat, vegetables and Japanese additions), rice dishes, sake, grape and plum wines, beer, and free green tea; exceptionally good value; cl Christmas; another branch is in Lexington St. £7.50 set meal with Japanese beer|£5.

Special thanks to E G Parish, Ian Donaldson, Mr and Mrs A Barclay, Mary Ellen McSweeney, Nicki and Terry Pursey.

LONDON CALENDAR

Some of these dates were provisional as we went to press. Please check information with numbers provided.

JANUARY

1 **Westminster Bridge to Berkeley Square** London Parade *from 12am*: Lord Mayor, marching bands from over 40 countries, vintage cars (0181) 744 1750

9 **Earls Court** International Boat Show – *till Sun 18* (01784) 473377

22 **Kensington Town Hall** Antiques Fair – *till Sun 25* (01444) 482514

25 **Trafalgar Square** Charles I Commemoration Ceremony: procession of members of the Society of King Charles and Royal Stuart Society in 17th-c costume (0171) 730 3450

29 **Alexandra Palace** Road Racing and Superbike Show – *till 1 Feb* (01440) 707055

FEBRUARY

1 **Soho** Chinese New Year Celebrations: Lion Dances (0171) 734 5161

21 **Twickenham** Five Nations; England v Wales Rugby International (0181) 892 8161

22 **Kensington Old Town Hall** Beer Festival (01273) 697974

24 **Olympia** Fine Art and Antiques Fair (0171) 370 3188

26 **Olympia** Holiday Show – *till 1 March* (0171) 385 1200

MARCH

6 **Olympia** House Buyers' Show – *till Sun 8* (0171) 385 1200

7 **Alexandra Palace** Sailboat '98 – *till Sun 8* (01703) 650885

11 **Alexandra Palace** Creative Arts and Crafts: over 150 craftsmen – *till Fri 13* (0181) 366 3153

12 **Olympia** Bicycle Show – *till Sun 15* (01225) 442244

19 **Chelsea Old Town Hall** Antiques Fair – *till Sun 29* (01444) 482514; **Earls Court** Ideal Home Exhibition – *till 13 April* (01895) 677677

21 **Alexandra Palace** Classic Motor Show – *till Sun 22* (01296) 631181; **Mortlake to Putney** Head of the River Race on the Thames (01932) 220 401

22 **Olympia** London International Book Fair – *till Tues 24* (0171) 371 2600

28 **Olympia** International Dive Show – *till Sun 29* (0181) 943 4288; **Putney to Mortlake** Oxford v Cambridge Boat Race (0171) 379 3234

APRIL

2 **Olympia** BBC Good Food Show – *till Sun 5* (0181) 948 1666

4 **Twickenham** Five Nations; England v Ireland Rugby International (0181) 892 8161

12 **Tower of London** State Parade and Church Service (0171) 709 0765

13 **Battersea Park** Harness Horse Parade: extensive display of horse-drawn vehicles (01733) 234451

23 **Chelsea Old Town Hall** Arts Fair – *till Sun 26* (01444) 482514; **St Pancras** World Book Day at the British Library; **London** Friends of City Churches Open Day: over 40 city churches open inc several not usually open – *till Fri 24* (0171) 228 3336

26 **Greenwich to the Mall** London Marathon (0171) 620 4117

MAY

2 **Wembley** Rugby League Challenge Cup Final (0113) 262 9991

LONDON CALENDAR

MAY cont

9 **Wembley** Rugby Union Cup Final (0181) 892 8161

10 **Kensington Old Town Hall** Beer Festival (01273) 697974

16 **Wembley** FA Cup Final (0171) 262 4542

19 **Chelsea Royal Hospital** Flower Show – *till Fri 22*, members only *19 and 20* (0171) 344 4343; **Tower of London** Anne Boleyn's Memorial (0171) 709 0765

23 **Westminster** Mind-Body-Spirit Festival at RHS Halls – *till Sun 31* (0171) 938 3788

24 **Colindale** Emergency Services Weekend at RAF Museum – *till Mon 25* (0181) 205 2266

30 **Horse Guards Parade** First Rehearsal: Trooping the Colour (0171) 839 5323

31 **Southbank** Coin Street Festival: free events and music at Gabriel's Wharf, Bernie Spain Gardens and Oxo Tower Wharf – *till 13 Sept* (0171) 401 3610

JUNE

3 **Horse Guards Parade** Beating Retreat: Massed Guards of the Household Division – *till Thurs 4* (0171) 839 5323; **Spitalfields** Festival – *till Wed 24* (0171) 247 4667

4 **Olympia** Fine Art and Antiques Fair – *till Sun 14* (0171) 370 8188

5 **Piccadilly** Festival of Baroque Music at St James's Church – *till Sun 21* (0171) 437 5053

6 **Horse Guards Parade** Second Rehearsal: Trooping the Colour (0171) 839 5323

7 **Piccadilly** Royal Academy Summer Exhibition: large open contemporary art exhibition – *till 16 Aug* (0171) 300 5615; **Syon Park and Crystal Palace Park** London to Brighton Classic Car Run (01296) 631181

8 **Hampton Court Palace** Music Festival – *till Sun 21* (0181) 233 5800; **West Kensington** Tennis Championships at Queen's Club – *till Sun 14* (0171) 225 3733

11 **Grosvenor House Hotel** Antiques Fair – *till Sat 20* (0171) 499 6363

13 **Horse Guards Parade** Queen's Birthday Parade: Trooping the Colour (tickets in advance only) (0171) 414 2497; **Islington** International Festival – *till Sat 27* (0171) 247 4667

21 **Covent Garden** Flower Festival – *till Sun 28* (0171) 379 7020

22 **Chelsea** Festival – *till Tues 30* (0171) 247 4667; **Wimbledon** Lawn Tennis Championships – *till 5 July* (0181) 946 2244

23 **City of London** Festival – *till 16 July* (0171) 247 4667

JULY

5 **Catford** Arts Festival – *till Tues 7* (0171) 247 4667

7 **Hampton Court Palace** – Flower Show – *till Sun 12* (0171) 834 4333

10 **Greenwich and Docklands** Festival – *till Sun 19* (0171) 247 4667

17 **Royal Albert Hall** Henry Wood Promenade Concerts – *till 12 Sept* (0171) 765 4296

21 **Earls Court** Royal Tournament – *till 2 Aug* (0171) 370 8202

AUGUST

2 **Hyde Park** London Riding Horse Guard Parade (0181) 851 1158

4 **Olympia** Great British Beer Festival at Grand Hall – *till Sat 8* (01727) 867201

LONDON CALENDAR

AUGUST cont

20 **Kensington Town Hall** Antiques Fair – *till Mon 24* (01444) 482514
30 **Kensington Old Town Hall** Beer Festival (01273) 697974; **Notting Hill** Carnival – *till Mon 31* (0181) 964 0544

SEPTEMBER

4 **Kensington** International Exhibition of Early Music at the Royal College of Music – *till Sun 6* (01274) 393753
10 **Chelsea Old Town Hall** Antiques Fair – *till Sun 20* (01444) 482514
11 **River Thames** Thames Festival between Westminster Bridge and Southwark Canal – *till Sun 13* (0171) 620 0544
15 **City** Flower Show at the Guildhall – *till Wed 16* (0181) 472 3584
24 **Soho** Jazz Festival – *till 4 Oct* (0171) 437 6437
30 **Wembley** Horse of the Year Show – *till 4 Oct* (01203) 693088

OCTOBER

4 **Trafalgar Square** Pearly Kings' and Queens' Service at St Martin-in-the-Fields: since the 19th-c, best occasion to see Kings and Queens in traditional button-covered costumes (0171) 930 0089
18 **Trafalgar Square** Trafalgar Day Parade: naval parade in memory of the Battle of Trafalgar (0171) 928 8978
21 **London** Dance Umbrella – *till 15 Nov* (0171) 247 4667
29 **Kensington Town Hall** Fine Art and Antiques Fair – *till 1 Nov* (01444) 482514

NOVEMBER

1 **Hyde Park** London to Brighton Veteran Car Run (01753) 681736
8 **Whitehall** Remembrance Day Service and Parade at the Cenotaph (0171) 414 2357
14 **City** Lord Mayor's Show: from Guildhall to the Royal Courts of Justice (0171) 606 3030
29 **Kensington Old Town Hall** Beer Festival (01273) 697974

DECEMBER

16 **Trafalgar Square** Christmas Tree and Carol Singing – *till 6 Jan* (0171) 211 6393
17 **Olympia** International Showjumping Championships – *till Mon 21* (0171) 370 8399
20 **Tower of London** State Parade and Church Service (0171) 709 0765
31 **Trafalgar Square** New Year's Eve Celebrations

We welcome reports from readers . . .

This *Guide* depends on readers' reports. Do help us if you can – in return, we offer a discount on the next edition to people who've helped us with reports for it. Tell us what you think about places already in it, and anything extra you think we should say about them. And send us your ideas for inclusion in the next edition: places to visit, eat at or stay in, attractive drives or walks, maybe even unusual interesting shops you know of. Use the card in the middle, the report forms at the end, or just write – no stamp needed: *The Good Guide to Britain*, FREEPOST TN1569, Wadhurst, E Sussex TN5 7BR.

SCOTLAND

We have divided Scotland into four areas. South Scotland includes Edinburgh (very rewarding for a short break), Glasgow (lots to see here, too) and many of the most enjoyable places to visit, as well as quietly charming countryside towards the Borders and the south-west corner. Our East Scotland is the area north of the Forth, right up to Inverness at the north-east end of the Great Glen. This area has plenty of interesting places to visit, and scenery to suit most tastes: from Highland grandeur to placid lochs and rich valleys, from intimate fishing villages and sandy beaches to rugged cliffs. What we have called West Scotland is the glorious series of mountain and coastal landscapes north of the Clyde and south of the Great Glen, with Loch Lomond marking its eastern edge. This part has magnificent gardens, at their best in May and June. North Scotland – everything north of the Great Glen – has fewer places to visit (and fewer visitors); there is magnificent scenery on the west coast and on Skye, a quieter sandy east coast, and some wild and desolate places in the north.

Outside Edinburgh, Glasgow and areas within easy reach of them, many places to visit close for the winter – and others change to shorter winter opening hours in September, rather than October (the usual month for a change in England). For the scenery, the best time to visit is May and June, when the days are very long, the weather is generally at least as fine as in high summer, the roads are not yet clogged by summer crowds, and (as the **Calendar** shows) there's lots going on.

The Scottish Tourist Board are working hard to attract visitors in the autumn – they've introduced a card that will save money then on flights, trains, accommodation and attractions, as well as securing two-for-one entry to the properties of the National Trust for Scotland and Historic Scotland.

The latter organisation looks after most of the castles and abbeys we list. A good-value Explorer ticket admits you free to all their properties, for £12 (one week) or £17 (two weeks); from tourist information centres, or in advance (0131) 668 8600. Generally, admission prices have held very steady here this year.

For most adults, the long drive to this or that castle is in Scotland part of the pleasure, thanks to the scenery. Of course that's not the case for children. So unless you pick a place within fairly easy reach of obvious family visitor attractions – which means almost certainly in South or East Scotland – the best family holidays here will be of the amuse-yourself variety.

A three-hour drive will get anyone living north of Manchester or York well into the southern parts of Scotland. Beyond that, you need a longer stay to make the driving worth while. Rail and air, of course, bring Scotland much closer. The fastest trains do the London–Edinburgh run in around four hours; there are good services up both sides of Britain. Direct flights connect London and some regional airports with Edinburgh, Glasgow, Inverness and Aberdeen, with some local connections from there.

Golfers will find plenty of courses to impress; some local tourist boards sell passes covering a round at that area's finest – such as the Freedom of the Fairways passport available in the Borders.

SOUTH SCOTLAND

Very rewarding sightseeing, with Edinburgh excellent for short city breaks; the extreme south is very quiet and relaxing.

Edinburgh is a city of great visual appeal, with lots of interesting places within a pleasant walk of each other; the Festival is in August (when to go if that appeals, a time to avoid otherwise). There are some great things to visit in Glasgow, too – almost all free.

This part of Scotland has an abundance of ancient and evocative castles, romantic ruined abbeys, and some glorious gardens and grand houses such as Culzean Castle, Traquair, Manderston at Duns and Mount Stuart on Bute. There are plenty of enjoyable family outings, most notably at New Lanark and in Dalkeith and Largs; Edinburgh Zoo is a great favourite.

The Borders countryside, grand without being austere, includes some of Scotland's best walking, and the gentler south-west corner is one of Britain's friendliest areas; there aren't too many tourists.

Where to stay

Auchencairn NX7951 BALCARY BAY Auchencairn, Castle Douglas, Kirkcudbrightshire DG7 1QZ (01556) 640217 *£94, plus special breaks; 17 rms with fine views. Once a smugglers' haunt, this charming and much-liked hotel has wonderful views over the bay, neat grounds running down to the water, comfortable public rooms (one with log fire), a relaxed, friendly atmosphere, good, enjoyable food inc super breakfasts, and lots of walks; cl mid-Nov–Feb.

Beattock NT0905 AUCHEN CASTLE Auchen, Beattock, Moffat, Dumfriesshire DG10 9SH (01683) 300407 *£60, plus special breaks; 26 pleasantly decorated rms, some in lodge. Smart but friendly country-house hotel in lovely quiet spot with a trout loch and spectacular hill views, good food, and peaceful comfortable bar; disabled access.

Bonnyrigg NT3065 DALHOUSIE CASTLE Bonnyrigg, Midlothian EH19 3JB (01875) 820153 *£135, plus special breaks; 28 rms, some of great character. Turreted red sandstone castle with some fine historic features such as the dungeon restaurant and oak-panelled library bar; children under 12 free if in parents' room and meals half-price; cl 2 wks Jan; disabled access by arrangement.

Brodick NS0136 AUCHRANNIE COUNTRY HOUSE Brodick, Isle of Arran KA27 8BZ (01770) 302234 £109, plus special breaks; 28 attractive rms. Victorian country-house hotel in 6 acres of grounds with indoor leisure complex (adults' and children's swimming pools, too), several lounges, carefully prepared food in conservatory restaurant and more informal bistro, and a relaxed friendly atmosphere; self-catering lodges; disabled access.

Canonbie NY3976 RIVERSIDE Canonbie, Dumfriesshire DG14 OUX (01387) 371512/371295 £75; 7 chintzy rms, 2 in cottage. Civilised little inn with friendly owners, comfortable communicating bar rooms, open fire, attractive furnishings, good imaginative food with home-made breads and preserves and using top-quality produce, a fine wine list, and marvellous breakfasts.

Clarencefield NY0968 COMLONGON CASTLE Clarencefield, Dumfries DG1 4NA (01387) 870283 *£85; 11 rms. 15th-c castle keep with 18th-c mansion house adjoining – suits of armour and a huge fireplace in oak-panelled great hall, good food in Jacobean dining room, and a relaxing drawing room; also, dungeons, lofty battlements, archers' quarters and haunted long gallery – candlelit tour before dinner if you like; disabled access.

Edinburgh NT2573 BALMORAL Princes St, Edinburgh EH2 2EQ (0131) 556 2414 £180, plus special breaks; 186 luxurious rms. Splendid Victorian hotel with wonderfully opulent entrance hall, elegant day rooms, lovely flowers, particularly friendly helpful staff, and very good food in several restaurants; excellent leisure facilities; good disabled access.

Edinburgh NT2374 CHANNINGS South Learmonth Gardens, Edinburgh EH4 1EZ (0131) 315 2226 *£150; 48 pretty rms. Privately owned hotel carefully converted from 5 Edwardian townhouses, with a cosy atmosphere, lots of original features, antiques and open fires in the peaceful lounges, good food in downstairs brasserie, and friendly service; cl 24–28 Dec.

Edinburgh NT2574 DRUMMOND HOUSE 17 Drummond Pl, Edinburgh EH3 6PL (0131) 557 9189 *£90; 4 charming rms. Georgian town house in handsome square with antiques and fine rugs in elegant rooms, a warmly welcoming atmosphere, and good Scottish breakfasts; cl Christmas; children over 12.

Edinburgh NT2572 ELMVIEW 15 Glengyle Terrace, Edinburgh EH3 9LN (0131) 228 1973 *£70; 3 large rms. Quietly placed in fine Victorian terrace 15 minutes' walk from the castle and city centre overlooking a park; elegantly furnished, good breakfast and welcome; no children

Edinburgh NT2674 GREENSIDE 9 Royal Terrace, Edinburgh EH7 5AB (0131) 557 0022 *£65; 14 individually decorated rms. Family-run hotel in Georgian terrace with friendly atmosphere, big lounge, hearty breakfasts, and quiet terraced garden.

Edinburgh NT2574 HOWARD 34 Great King St, Edinburgh EH3 6QH (0131) 557 3500 *£195; 15 luxurious rms. Fine civilised 18th-c hotel with comfortable, elegant public rooms, courteous efficient service and good food; cl 24–28 Dec.

Edinburgh NT2776 MALMAISON 1 Tower Pl, Edinburgh EH6 7DB (0131) 555 6868 *£97.50; 59 stylish rms with CD players and satellite TV. Converted baronial-style seamen's mission in the fashionable docks area of Leith with very good food in the downstairs French brasserie, a cheerful café/bar, and friendly service; free parking; pets by arrangement; disabled access.

Edinburgh NT2574 SIBBET HOUSE 26 Northumberland St, Edinburgh EH3 6LS (0131) 556 1078 *£90; 5 good rms. Lovely little Georgian house with warmly friendly owners, comfortable public rooms filled with antiques, delicious breakfasts, and suppers on request; self-catering flat also; partial disabled access.

Ettrick Valley NT3018 TUSHIELAW Ettrick Valley, Selkirk TD7 5HT (01750) 62205 *£42, plus special breaks; 3 small but well furnished rms. Friendly little inn in lovely spot on Ettrick Water, with good imaginative restaurant food, intimate bar, fine views, own loch, and shooting and fishing (as well as birdwatching and walking); cl 25 Dec.

Gatehouse of Fleet NX6056 CALLY PALACE Gatehouse of Fleet, Castle Douglas, Kirkcudbrightshire DG7 2DL (01557) 814341 £56, plus special breaks; 56 rms. 18th-c country mansion with marble fireplaces and ornate ceilings in the public rooms, a relaxed cocktail bar, enjoyable food in elegant dining room (smart dress required), evening pianist and Saturday dinner dance, helpful, friendly staff, an 18-hole golf course, croquet and tennis, an indoor leisure complex with heated swimming pool, and a private fishing/boating loch; cl Jan/Feb; disabled access.

Gifford NT5368 TWEEDDALE ARMS Gifford, Haddington, East Lothian EH41 4QU (01620) 810240 *£65, plus special breaks; 16 rms. Civilised old inn in quiet village with comfortable sofas and chairs in tranquil lounge, gracious dining room, wide choice of good daily-changing food, and charming service; disabled access.

Glasgow NS5965 BABBITY BOWSTER 16–18 Blackfriars St, Glasgow G1 1PE (0141) 552 5055 £65; 6 clean simple rms, showers. Warmly welcoming, rather continental place with decent breakfasts (served till late), attractively decorated airy bar, and a cheery first-floor restaurant which hosts a gallery as well as a programme of musical and theatrical events; cl 25 Dec–1 Jan.

Glasgow NS5865 MALMAISON 278 West George St, Glasgow G2 4LL (0141) 221 6400 *£95; 21 smart rms. Stylishly converted Nonconformist church with striking central wrought-iron staircase, friendly young staff, enjoyable food in the basement brasserie, café/bar with all-day snacks, and a relaxed no-frills atmosphere; disabled access.

Glasgow NS5567 ONE DEVONSHIRE GARDENS Glasgow G12 0UX (0141) 339 2001 £154w; 27 huge, opulent rms. Elegant cosseting hotel a little way out from the centre, with luxurious Victorian furnishings, fresh flowers, exemplary staff, and fine modern cooking in the stylish restaurant; disabled access.

Glasgow NS5965 RAB HA'S 83 Hutcheson St, Glasgow G1 1SH (0141) 552 2206 £69.90; 4 elegant rms. Sensitively converted and warmly friendly Georgian town house with delightfully informal ground-floor bar, popular restaurant, and good service; cl 25 Dec/1 Jan.

Gullane NT4882 GREYWALLS Duncar Rd, Gullane, East Lothian EH31 2EG (01620) 842144 £185, plus special breaks; 22 individually decorated rms. Overlooking Muirfield golf course, this beautiful family-run Lutyens house has antiques, open fires and flowers in its comfortable lounges and panelled library, very good food and fine wines in the restaurant, impeccable service, and a lovely garden; cl Nov–Mar; disabled access.

Innerleithen NT3336 TRAQUAIR ARMS Innerleithen, Peeblesshire EH44 6PD (01896) 830229 £64, plus special breaks; 10 comfortable rms. Very friendly pub with interesting choice of good food in attractive dining room, cosy lounge bar, friendly service, the superb local Traquair ale on handpump, and nice breakfasts; cl 25–26 Dec, 1–2 Jan.

Lockerbie NY1381 DRYFESDALE HOTEL Lockerbie, Dumfriesshire DG11 2SF (01576) 202427 £84; 15 rms, 6 at ground-floor level. Relaxed and comfortable former manse with 5 acres of grounds, open fire in homely lounge, good food in pleasant restaurant, and lovely surrounding countryside; good disabled access.

Maybole NS3103 LADYBURN Kilkerran, Maybole, Ayrshire KA19 7SG (01655) 740585 £140, plus special breaks; 6 rms. Quietly set family home in lovely wooded countryside with antiques, books and open fires in comfortable day rooms, and friendly staff; shooting and fishing can be arranged; self-catering flat also; cl 2 wks Nov–Dec, 4 wks Jan–Mar; no children.

Melrose NT5434 BURTS HOTEL Melrose, Roxburghshire TD6 9PN (01896) 822285 *£82, plus special breaks; 20 rms. Welcoming 18th-c inn in delightfully quiet village, close to abbey ruins; coal fire in bustling bar, residents' lounge, consistently popular imaginative food, exceptional breakfasts, and a decent wine list; cl for accommodation 24–26 Dec.

Melrose NT5434 DUNFERMLINE HOUSE Buccleuch St, Melrose, Roxburghshire TD6 9LB (01896) 822148 *£44; 5 rms. Neatly kept Victorian terraced house close to abbey ruins, with good breakfasts and friendly owners.

Minnigaff NX4166 CREEBRIDGE HOUSE Minnigaff, Newton Stewart, Wigtownshire DG8 6NP (01671) 402121 *£84, plus special breaks; 19 rms. Attractive country-house hotel in 3 acres of gardens with relaxed, friendly atmosphere, open fire in comfortable drawing room, cheerful bar, and big choice of delicious food inc fine local fish and seafood.

Nenthorn NT6938 WHITEHILL FARM Nenthorn, Kelso, Roxburghshire TD5 7RZ (01573) 470203 *£38; 4 rms, 3 with shared bthrm. Comfortable farmhouse on mixed farm with fine views, big garden, log fire in sitting room, and good home cooking; cl Christmas/New Year.

Peebles NT2344 CRINGLETIE HOUSE Cringletie, Peebles EH45 8PL (01721) 730233 *£120, plus special breaks; 13 pretty rms. Surrounded by 28 acres of garden and woodland and with fine views, this turreted baronial mansion, run by the same couple for over 20 years, is very welcoming and quiet, with delicious food using home-grown vegetables, extensive Scottish breakfasts, and excellent service; cl Jan–Feb.

Portpatrick NX0154 CROWN Portpatrick, Stranraer, Wigtownshire DG9 8SX (01776) 810261 £72; 12 attractive rms. Atmospheric harbourside inn with rambling and interestingly furnished old-fashioned bar, airy art deco dining room, good food with an emphasis on local seafood, excellent breakfasts, and carefully chosen wines.

Portpatrick NX0252 KNOCKINAAM LODGE Portpatrick, Stranraer, Wigtownshire DG9 9AD (01776) 810471 £190 incl dinner, plus special breaks; 10 individual rms. Lovely, very neatly kept little hotel with comfortable, pretty rooms, open fires, wonderful food, and friendly caring service; the surroundings are dramatic, with lots of fine cliff walks; children over 12 in evening restaurant (high tea at 6pm); disabled access to restaurant only.

Quothquan NS9939 SHIELDHILL Quothquan, Biggar, Lanarkshire ML12 6NA (01899) 220035 *£104, plus special breaks; 12 pretty rms. Partly 13th-c hotel in a fine setting with comfortable oak-panelled lounge, open fires, library, particularly good food in the no smoking restaurant, and warm, friendly service; children over 11.

Selkirk NT4429 PHILIPBURN HOUSE Selkirk TD7 5LS (01750) 20747 £100; 16 pretty rms. Extended and charming 18th-c house run by the same family for over 25 years, with fine surrounding walks, flower-filled gardens, prettily decorated public rooms, a relaxed and friendly atmosphere, very good imaginative food, and an interesting wine list; swimming pool, badminton, children's playground (leisure centre planned); disabled access.

Swinton NT8448 WHEATSHEAF Swinton, Duns, Berwickshire TD11 3JJ (01890) 860257 *£69.50, plus special breaks; 6 rms, most with own shower. Warmly friendly inn with exceptionally good food, a pleasantly decorated and relaxed main lounge plus small pubby area, separate locals' bar, and no smoking front conservatory; garden play area for children; cl last wk Feb, last wk Oct.

Turnberry NS2005 TURNBERRY Turnberry, Ayrshire KA26 9LT (01655) 331000 £255, plus special breaks; 132 stylish and comfortable rms. Grand Edwardian country house in spectacular 360-acre coastal setting with 2 championship golf courses that are ranked among the best in the world. Elegant reception rooms, quite a choice of places to eat including a very good restaurant using top quality local produce – and plenty of sporting activities: 12-hole pitch and putt (plus the 2 18-hole golf courses), indoor swimming pool, health spa, gym, sauna, solarium, squash, and tennis courts; disabled access.

Tweedsmuir NT0924 CROOK INN Tweedsmuir, Biggar, Lanarkshire ML12 6QN (01899) 880272 £52; 7 rms. Old drovers' inn on lonely road through grand hills with large airy 1920s lounge, simply furnished back bar, sun lounge, various art deco features, good food and friendly service; attractive garden across the road, pétanque and putting in adjoining field, and glass-blowing centre and heritage centre in old stable block (open daily); fishing permits.

Uphall NT0571 HOUSTOUN HOUSE Uphall, Broxburn, West Lothian EH52 6JS (01506) 853831 *£160; 73 comfortable rms, 26 in new extension. 17th-c house divided into 3 distinct buildings: fine food in 3 wood-panelled dining rooms, vaulted bars (one with a fire that burns nearly all year), a quiet lounge, lovely grounds, and a newly opened leisure complex with swimming pool, sauna, gym, tennis courts and bistro; disabled access.

To see and do

Edinburgh NT2573 One of Britain's most rewarding cities for visitors, whether you've been dozens of times before or are popping in for the first time. It's dominated by the ancient silhouettes of Edinburgh Castle on its castle cliff and of the long erratic line of tall, narrow Old Town buildings stretched along beside it. Up here narrow streets and alleys with steep steps between them and courtyard closes leading off have a real flavour of the distant past, with a good many interesting ancient buildings (and a lot of the city's antiquarian bookshops and other interesting specialist shops). When the authorities decided to redevelop the city in the 18th c, they did it not by knocking down the medieval buildings, but instead by creating an entirely new part of the city, working from scratch. The resulting New Town is a masterpiece of spacious Georgian town planning, stretching out handsomely below the steep crag of Castle Rock and its medieval skyline.

As in most cities, there's a hop-on hop-off tour bus, and the ticket gives discounts to some of the places to visit. Walking tours in the evenings are often led by students. The regular bus services have good-value daily and weekly passes, and it is worth getting used to the public transport: the city council has come up with a radical road-pricing scheme to ease congestion and cut pollution, which they hope will be running by 2000. You can save money with the Edinburgh for Less card, which for £3.95 gets 2 people discounts at some restaurants and attractions (inc the castle) for up to 4 days; it's on sale in information centres. Edinburgh does put on its best clothes and best events for its Festival; it's easier to see, and truer to itself, at other times of year. If you do visit the Festival, make sure you've got accommodation sorted out well in advance.

Edinburgh's pubs and bars are a special delight, chatty places often of great character. Among the best for atmosphere are the Bow Bar (Victoria St), Bannerman's Bar (Cowgate), Bennet's Bar (Leven St), Café Royal and Guildford Arms (both West Register St), Cumberland (Cumberland St), Athletic Arms (Angle Park Terrace/Kilmarnock Rd), Kays Bar (Jamaica St W) and Jolly Judge (James Court, off Lawnmarket); for food too, the Abbotsford, Kenilworth and Milnes (all Rose St), Starbank (Laverockbank Rd), Golf Tavern (Wright's Houses), Braidwoods (West Port) and Ship on the Shore (The Shore, Leith). The corner lobby bar of the Balmoral (see **Where to stay** section above) is a relaxing spot at the hub of the town. For a fuller meal, the city has a remarkable number of good-value bistro-style restaurants (as well as the places we mention in the **Where to eat** section below).

There are lots of good shops dotted around town, especially on or near PRINCES ST – its tall, mainly Georgian buildings lining just the one side, giving an expansive view across the sunken gardens to the castle. Parallel is GEORGE ST, with some superior shops, while Rose St, an alley between the two, has plenty of pubs and cafés. More bars around the GRASSMARKET and LAWNMARKET, a lively area of the Old Town; Victoria St here has interesting shops, notably that of Ian Mellis, who specialises in Scottish, Irish and English farm cheeses. Valvona & Crolla on Elm Row is a dazzling delicatessen.

🖼✝⛰❀ EDINBURGH CASTLE Perched on its hill above the city, this is a place of great magnetism; it's been a fortress since at least the 7th c, and excavations show there's been a settlement here for 4,000 years. The oldest building today is the beautiful St Margaret's Chapel, thought to have been built in the 12th c and little changed since. Other highlights include the apartments of Mary, Queen of Scots, Mons Meg (the 15th-c Belgian cannon with which James II cowed the Black Douglases), the Scottish Crown Jewels (centuries older than the English ones), and for romantics the Stone of Destiny or Scottish coronation stone, now returned by England which had seized it 700 years ago. Glorious views from the battlements, over the Firth of Forth to Fife beyond. You can wander around on your own, but the official guides are a great bonus – they leave from the drawbridge, several times a day. Meals, snacks, shop, disabled access; cl 25–26 Dec; (0131) 225 9846; *£5.50. If you're around at lunchtime, look (and listen) for the firing of the One o'Clock Gun from the parapet.

🏠▣🐾 PALACE OF HOLYROODHOUSE (Canongate) Imposing yet human-scale palace with its origins in the Abbey of Holyrood, founded by David I. Later the court of Mary, Queen of Scots, it was used by Bonnie Prince Charlie during his occupation of Edinburgh, and is still a royal residence for part of the year. The oldest surviving part is James IV's tower, with Queen Mary's rooms on the second floor, where a plaque on the floor marks where her secretary Rizzio was murdered in front of her. The throne room and state rooms have period furniture, tapestries and paintings from the Royal Collection. Much more inviting than many English palaces, and in the last few years they've really improved visitor facilities. The palace gardens are open Apr–Oct. Shop, limited disabled access by prior arrangement; cl Good Fri, 25–26 Dec, and occasional other dates (if the Queen is in residence, for example) – best to check first on (0131) 556 1096; *£5.30.

❗❀♄🏠⛰✝ ROYAL MILE Between the Castle and the Palace (for most people the 2 must-sees) is this largely medieval street, around which you'll find all sorts of interesting or historic houses and features, and quaint lanes leading off in all directions. Usefully, it's punctuated with cafés and bars in which to stop and work out your next move, starting with the old-world Ensign Ewart on the left as you leave the Castle. We list the pick of the attractions as you'll find them heading down. Up at the top, the revolving lenses and mirrors of the 19th-c CAMERA OBSCURA 🔳 (Castlehill) create unique panoramas of the city as soon as the lights go down, with a good commentary; best on a sunny day. Shop; cl 25 Dec; (0131) 226 3709; *£3.50. Across the road, the SCOTCH WHISKY HERITAGE CENTRE entertainingly illustrates the story of the national drink, starting off with a shortish journey in a barrel-shaped car through well put together sets and tableaux. The full tour is a useful introduction to the distilling process; if you haven't been to a real distillery it's a good substitute, and there's a decent sample and well stocked shop at the end. Snacks, disabled access; cl 25 Dec; (0131) 220 0441; *£4.20. GLADSTONE'S LAND (Lawnmarket) 6-storeyed early 17th-c building, still with its arcaded front, and refurnished in period style. The walls and ceilings have remarkable tempera paintings. Shop; cl am Sun, and Nov–Mar; (0131) 226 5856; £2.80; NTS. Named after its 18th-c occupant, 17th-c LADY STAIR'S HOUSE (just off the Royal Mile, on Lady Stair's Close) is home to the Writers Museum, a collection of manuscripts and objects associated with Robert Burns, Walter Scott and R L Stevenson. Shop; cl Sun exc during Festival, 25–26 Dec, 1–3 Jan; (0131) 529 4901; free. The street widens out briefly around Scotland's High Kirk, ST GILES' CATHEDRAL (High St), the city's most impressive ecclesiastical building, mainly 15th-c, but dating from around 1120. Topped with an ornate crown-like tower, it has monuments to famous Scots from Knox (minister here until his death) to R L Stevenson. Just behind here in Parliament Sq, PARLIAMENT HOUSE was the seat of Scottish government until the Union of 1707, and now houses the supreme law courts of Scotland. Don't miss the fine hammerbeam roof in the Hall. Limited disabled access; cl 1–2pm and wknds; (0131) 225 2595; free. The oldest house on the Royal Mile is JOHN KNOX HOUSE where the great reformer is supposed to have died. Now looking every bit of its 500 years, it still has its original timber galleries, oak panelling and splendid painted ceiling. Snacks, shop, disabled access to ground floor only; cl Sun, 25–28 Dec, 1–3 Jan, 5 May and 15 Sept; (0131) 556 9579; *£1.75. The MUSEUM OF CHILDHOOD opposite, the first of its type, is still one of the best, an outstanding collection of games, toys and dolls from all over the globe. Shop, some disabled access; cl Sun exc pm during Festival, Christmas and New Year; (0131) 529 4142; free. The elaborate CANONGATE TOLBOOTH houses an excellent social history exhibition, the People's Story, with reconstructions built very much around firsthand accounts of Edinburgh life. Shop, disabled access; cl Sun exc pm during Festival; (0131) 200 2000; free. Across the road, 16th-c HUNTLY HOUSE (Canongate) is the city's main local history museum, with all the exhibits thoughtfully – even artistically – arranged. Shop; cl Sun exc pm during Festival; (0131) 529 4143; free.

🐾 ROYAL MUSEUM OF SCOTLAND (Chambers St) A tremendous variety of collections, covering virtually anything you might care to poke around in. Children enjoy its intricate working scale models of early engines, but it has something for everyone – in a gloriously light and spacious Victorian building. Meals; snacks, shop, disabled access; cl Sun, 25 Dec; (0131) 225 7534; free.

🏛 🎇 NATIONAL GALLERY OF SCOTLAND (The Mound) Fine neo-classical building with particularly good examples of most European schools and periods. Plenty of Scottish paintings too, with many great works by Ramsay, Raeburn, Wilkie and McTaggart. Some art critics have objected to changes in the look of the gallery under its current director, but few would dispute that it's undoubtedly still one of Britain's best. Shop, disabled access; cl am Sun, 25–26 Dec, 1–2 Jan; (0131) 624 6200; free (exc for major exhibitions). The ROYAL SCOTTISH ACADEMY, founded in 1826, is in a second neo-classical temple alongside, with good changing exhibitions. Shop, disabled access; cl am Sun, and between exhibitions; (0131) 225 6671 for what's on; £1.50 for annual exhibition Apr–July. On either side, like a broad moat for the castle (this was a loch before the New Town was built), are well tended gardens.

🏛 🐾 SCOTTISH NATIONAL PORTRAIT GALLERY (Queen St) The history of Scotland through a huge collection of portraits in a variety of media. Meals, snacks, shop, disabled access; cl am Sun, 25–26 Dec, 1–3 Jan; (0131) 624 6200; free. It shares a building with the antiquities branch of the ROYAL MUSEUM OF SCOTLAND, where old-fashioned displays show a very rich collection of artefacts, jewellery and so forth from the Stone Age to the present; there's also a presentation on Stuart rule in Scotland. Snacks, shop, disabled access; cl am Sun, 25–26 Dec, 1–2 Jan; (0131) 624 6200; free.

🏛 SCOTTISH NATIONAL GALLERY OF MODERN ART (Belford Rd) Breathtaking collection inc outstanding recently acquired range of Surrealist works, and great works by Picasso, Barbara Hepworth and Lichtenstein. Meals, snacks, shop, disabled access; cl am Sun, 25–26 Dec, 1–2 Jan; (0131) 624 6200; free, maybe charges for temporary exhibitions.

🏠 🏠 GEORGIAN HOUSE Archetypal period house, part of Robert Adam's magnificent terrace along the N side of Charlotte Sq. The rooms and servants' quarters have been refurbished in the style of 1800.

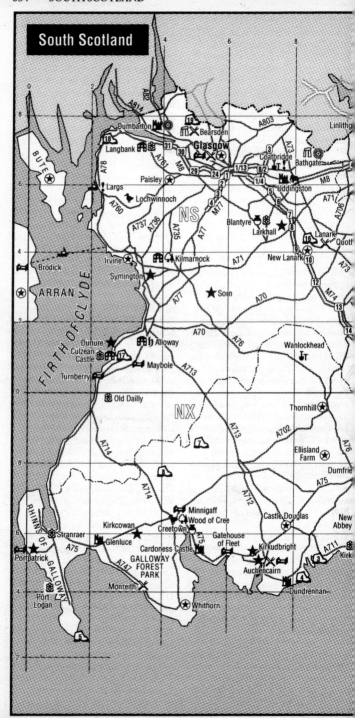

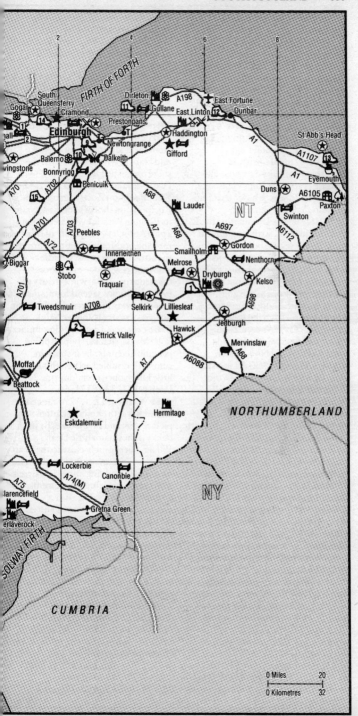

Shop, disabled access to ground floor only; cl am Sun, and Nov–Easter; (0131) 225 2160; *£4.20; NTS. Close by, nr Queen St, beyond a further strip of gardens, is another Georgian area with some interesting shops. Hoggs in the alley behind stately Great King St has a wide choice of malt whiskies at low prices.

🏛 SCOTT MEMORIAL (Princes St) After the castle, probably Edinburgh's most memorable building: remarkably ornate, with its handsome if mucky exterior. The historic crypt of St John's episcopal church on Princes St has interesting vegetarian and vegan food.

※ ! CALTON HILL Dominating the E end of Princes St, with magnificent views over the city, best of all from the top of the 31-metre (102-ft) NELSON MONUMENT – if you can face the climb. Every day at 1pm (exc Sun) the time ball drops as the gun at the castle goes off. Shop; cl am Mon; £2. An observatory nearby houses the EDINBURGH EXPERIENCE, a 20min 3-D history of the city (they provide special glasses); cl Nov–Easter; (0131) 556 4365; *£2. An unusual sight up here is a romantic Doric colonnade, intended to be a full replica of the Parthenon (until the money ran out).

🌳 ROYAL BOTANIC GARDEN (Inverleith Row) Founded as a physic garden in 1670 at Holyrood and then transplanted here (just N of the centre) in the early 19th c. Covering 72 acres, it has various splendid themed areas, with a woodland garden, peat garden, arboretum and the Glasshouse Experience, inc palm houses, fern house and aquatic house. They keep the most comprehensive rhododendron collection in Britain, and grow many other rare Asiatic plants to perfection – particularly primulas and lilies and their more awkward relatives. Guided tours leave from inside the West Gate at 11am and 2pm Apr–Sept. Meals, snacks, shop, disabled access; cl 25 Dec, 1 Jan; (0131) 552 7171; free.

! ※ ROYAL OBSERVATORY VISITOR CENTRE (Blackford Hill) Good range of often lively astronomy displays, inc videos, computer games, and the biggest telescope in Scotland. Glorious views down over the city, and even as far as the Braid Hills. Shop, limited disabled access; cl am Sun, 25 Dec–3 Jan; (0131) 668 8405; £2.50. In winter some telescopes are open till 9pm.

! EDINBURGH DUNGEON (Shandwick Pl) All too realistic scenes recalling the darker moments in Scottish history, from the body-snatching of Burke and Hare to witches burned at the stake on Castle Hill. Shop; cl 24–26 Dec, 1–2 Jan; (0131) 225 1331; *£4.

🐘 ! EDINBURGH ZOO (Corstorphine Rd, 3m W on the A8) Best known for its Penguin Parade every afternoon at 2pm (Apr–Oct), but plenty of other rare and odd-looking animals around the attractive grounds. Children enjoy the yew-hedge maze loosely themed around Darwin's theory of evolution; it has several fountains along the way that periodically shoot out jets of water (summer only). Extra events and activities in summer hols. Meals, snacks, shops (special penguin and polar bear shops in summer), disabled access (though a little hilly); open every day (inc 25 Dec); (0131) 334 9171; £6.

★ 🏰 WATER OF LEITH W of the centre and well worth exploring, often very picturesque and ravine-like. By its banks is the quaint little Dean Village, surprisingly close to the heart of the city, yet unaffected by all the New Town building above it. There's a fine series of Georgian crescents around Moray Pl. The river eventually winds down to Leith itself (a once prosperous and separate dockland area now swallowed up by the city, its waterfront reviving again with trendy bars). The Scottish Malt Whisky Society (Giles St), dedicated to cask strength top-quality malt whiskies, has a downstairs bar/restaurant. CLAN TARTAN CENTRE (Leith Mills, Bangor Rd) Displays of various clans and their costume, and a factory shop with good-value Pringle knitwear and tweeds. Meals, snacks, shop, disabled access; cl 25 Dec; (0131) 553 5161; free.

※ 🏛 ARTHUR'S SEAT Out beyond

Holyrood in Holyrood Park is this great saddleback hill, a pleasant place for wandering, with a hill fort on top and the largely unspoilt Duddingston village below it (the Sheep Heid here is a good pub).

Glasgow NS5965 There's a real zing and vitality about this proud city, which is making great strides in its efforts to shake off its rather rough image. Or at least it is in the centre, where smart shops and galleries seem to be springing up all the time. Besides the excellent art galleries and interesting museums, which the local director of museums has fought hard to keep free, it houses the Royal Scottish Orchestra (with a fine-sounding concert hall), the Scottish Opera and the Scottish Ballet. Another cultural highlight is the annual Mayfest, which, like the Edinburgh Festival, has unorthodox fringes; other festivals take you virtually right through the year. Though there are many places to see and visit, a snag for visitors is that they are scattered around this sprawling city: the Burrell Collection, the most interesting place of all, is out in the suburbs. It's worth investing in a Day Tripper ticket, which allows virtually unlimited bus and train travel not just in the city but as far out as Ayr and Lanark. Besides the restaurants and bars mentioned in the **Where to eat** section below, Glasgow is full of places to eat out in, formal and informal; interesting and undaunting pubs and bars include the Bon Accord (North St), Brewery Tap (Sauchiehall St), Cask & Still (Hope St) and Church on the Hill (Algie St).

🖼🏠 ! The MERCHANT CITY area around George Sq and Buchanan St was built on a grid plan in the 19th c, and visually has something in common with New York City – Americans are said to feel at home here. With its proud Victorian buildings cleaned back to their warm sandstone, this smart shopping quarter is the city's most comfortable area to stroll around. The City Chambers (George Sq) is a spectacular monument to 1880s civic pride, marble everywhere; free tours. The Counting House is a splendid new pub in an opulent converted bank nearby. Just round the corner is Glasgow's latest big gallery, the GALLERY OF MODERN ART (Queen St), concentrating on art by living British artists – not just Scottish. Lively café/bar (open some evenings too), shop, good disabled access; cl am Sun, all day Tues; (0141) 229 1996; free. There are café/bars and bistros off Princes Sq, and antique stalls in Victorian Village (West Regent St). The TENEMENT HOUSE (145 Buccleuch St) is a one-floor late 19th-c flat giving a vivid impression of life for many Glaswegians at the turn of the century. The same woman lived here from 1911 to 1965 and in that time scarcely changed a thing; its time-

capsule quality was preserved by a subsequent owner, and then the flat, still with its original furnishings and fittings, was left to the National Trust for Scotland. Open pm Mar–Oct; (0141) 333 0183; £2.80; NTS. On the SE edge of this area, between Gallowgate and London Rd past the Tolbooth, the BARRAS (barrows) is an entertaining weekend flea-market. With around 800 stalls it's one of the biggest covered markets in the world, great for bargains or just passing time; try the plump fresh clappie doos (mussels).

✝☕🎨🏠 CATHEDRAL AREA Just NE of the centre, this is the oldest area, though not the most interesting. The 12th-c CATHEDRAL is dedicated to St Mungo, the founder of the city. It's very well preserved, though most fittings date from the 19th c; best parts are the crypt, a gracefully vaulted affair built in the mid-13th c, and the Blackadder aisle. The spectacular Necropolis graveyard is closed for restoration, but there's a fine overview from the cathedral. ST MUNGO MUSEUM OF RELIGIOUS LIFE AND ART (Cathedral Precinct) Unique collection of art from all the world's major religions – and some rather obscure ones too. Everything from an Egyptian mummy mask to Dali's

Christ of St John of the Cross, and in the grounds Britain's only permanent Zen garden. Meals, snacks, shop, disabled access; cl Tues, 25 Dec, 1 Jan; (0141) 553 2557; free. Opposite on Castle St is Glasgow's oldest house, PROVAN'S LORDSHIP, used by the Prebend of Provan – a canon of the cathedral. Dating from 1471, it's been carefully restored and furnished according to several period styles. Shop; cl 25 Dec, 1 Jan; (0141) 552 8819; free.

♿ 🏛 PEOPLE'S PALACE (Glasgow Green) Very enjoyable social history museum looking at Glaswegians over the centuries, set in a park just SE of the centre; it's closed until May 1998 for restoration – best to ring (0141) 554 0223 for full details; free. The museum's café is in the adjacent WINTER GARDENS, a massive conservatory with huge tropical plants.

♿ 🏛 🏚 🏛 🏠 NW of the centre, the West End, Kelvingrove and the university quarter have some elegant streets, the main concentration of museums, and the botanic gardens. Scotland's oldest museum, the HUNTERIAN MUSEUM (Hillhead St), houses the university collections of ethnographic, palaeontological and anthropological material, along with lots of archaeology, and a new coin display. Some disabled access, shop; cl Sun and public hols (exc in May); (0141) 330 4221; free. The exhibitions were founded by Dr William Hunter, the 18th-c physician, who also bequeathed the core of fine paintings which form the basis of the beautifully hung collection in the adjacent HUNTERIAN ART GALLERY. A grand range of works by Whistler, interesting and well chosen contemporary British art and sculpture, and an amazing re-creation of the home of Charles Rennie Mackintosh, the designer/architect whose exuberant yet very disciplined and clean-lined art nouveau buildings stand out among the more traditional solidity of much of Glasgow. Shop, disabled access with prior notice; cl Sun, public hols; (0141) 330 5431; free. GLASGOW ART GALLERY AND MUSEUM (Kelvingrove Park) Huge Victorian building with remarkably rich collection of paintings, especially strong in works by the French Impressionists, Post-Impressionists, and Scottish artists from the 17th c. Also sculpture, silver, porcelain, armour, ethnography and natural history, and May–Aug 1998 will have an exhibition of the Dead Sea Scrolls (only their second trip ever to Europe). Meals, snacks, shop, disabled access; cl 25–26 Dec, 1–2 Jan; (0141) 287 2699; free. MUSEUM OF TRANSPORT (Kelvin Hall, Bunhouse Rd) Comprehensive collection of vehicles, from trams to ships, very well displayed; the walk-through car showroom is arranged as if some were for sale, with original prices displayed on the windscreens. Meals, snacks, shop, disabled access; cl Tues, 25 Dec, 1 Jan; (0141) 287 2720; free. UNIVERSITY OF GLASGOW VISITOR CENTRE (University Ave) Interactive displays on the history and life of the university (founded in 1451), with tours around some of its grander features, such as the Lion and Unicorn Staircase, Bute and Randolph Halls and Memorial Chapel. Snacks, shop, disabled access; cl Sun, Oct–Apr, 25–26 Dec, 1–2 Jan; (0141) 330 5511; visitor centre free, tours (11am and 2pm Weds, Fri and Sat May–Sept, Oct–Apr just 2pm Weds) £1.50. You can stay in some of the university buildings during vacations. BOTANIC GARDENS (730 Great Western Rd) Sloping gently down to the River Kibble, these are famous for their fantastic glasshouses, particularly the ½-acre Kibble Palace, with its soaring tree ferns interspersed with Victorian sculpture. Disabled access; main glasshouse cl am wknds; (0141) 334 2422; free. Sauchiehall St, one link between this area and the centre, is an ordinary shopping street, but well worth the walk for Mackintosh's most famous building the GLASGOW SCHOOL OF ART (Renfrew St, just off; the tours are highly recommended, (0141) 332 9797), and the decoratively mirrored WILLOW TEA ROOM (open till 5pm), furnished to his designs, too. (As well as other places we mention with Mackintosh connections, you can buy works after him at the Glasgow Style Gallery on Great Western Rd). The spacious and well lit MCLELLAN GALLERIES (Sauchiehall St) have good changing art exhibitions; shop, disabled access; cl between shows; (0141) 331 1854; charge varies according to exhibitions.

🕭 🅿 🏛 BURRELL COLLECTION (Pollok Country Park, SW) A couple of miles out in the suburbs, but not to be missed – and rarely gets too crowded. Splendidly and imaginatively housed in a modern building created to show its different parts to perfection, the huge collection – far too much to see at one go – includes Egyptian alabaster, Chinese jade, oriental rugs, remarkable tapestries, medieval metalwork and stained glass, even medieval doorways and windows set into the walls, as well as paintings by Degas, Manet and Rembrandt among others. Good meals and snacks, shop, disabled access; cl Tues, 25–6 Dec, 1–2 Jan; (0141) 649 7151; free, though you may have to pay for parking. The treasures of nearby POLLOK HOUSE include silver, ceramics and porcelain, but it's the paintings that stand out, with a collection of Spanish masters such as Goya and El Greco cannily acquired in the days when they were greatly undervalued. Snacks, shop; cl Apr–Oct; (0141) 649 7151; free. Both of these are set in 361-acre POLLOK COUNTRY PARK, one of the best of the several parks and gardens you'll find around the centre, with waterside and woodland trails, guided Sun afternoon walks, rose garden, shire horses, and a herd of highland cattle.

🏛 🏛 PROVAN HALL (Auchinlea Park, 4m E of centre on the B806) Mansion house virtually unchanged since the 16th c, in a pleasant park with a variety of formal and informal gardens inc a herb garden. Disabled access; cl wknds and public hols; (0141) 771 4399; free; NTS.

🏛 🏛 BELLAHOUSTON PARK (3m SW) The Empire Exhibition of 1938 was held on these 171 acres, which now comprise a walled garden, sunken garden and sweeping lawns. An additional attraction is the Charles Rennie Mackintosh-designed house built here. Disabled access; free.

🏛 Other good parks out towards the fringes of town include ROUKEN GLEN PARK (Thornliebank, some miles SW), a place of great tranquil beauty, with a walled garden, gorgeous lawns, and woodland walks to a waterfall at the head of the glen, and tree-lined VICTORIA PARK (Victoria Park Drive N, NW of centre) where the fossil remains in the Fossil Grove, some of them 230 million years old, were discovered by workmen digging a path in the late 19th c. Lots to do in LINN PARK (Cathcart/Castlemilk, some miles S) – riverside walks, nature trails, children's zoo, golf course, and collections of British ponies and highland cattle, as well as a ruined 14th-c castle, and an adventure playground for the disabled (prior arrangement preferred). Visitor centre open pm wknds only; (0141) 637 1147; free.

🏛 GREENBANK GARDEN (Flenders Rd, Clarkston; 6m S off the A726) Aims to encourage and help owners of small gardens, so has lots of different shrubs and flowers to spark ideas. Also garden and greenhouse designed to meet the needs of disabled gardeners, with advice on specially designed tools. Croquet tuition 2.30pm the last Sun of the month, May–Sept. Tearoom and shop, disabled access; (0141) 639 3281; £2.80; NTS.

⚓ A walkway tracks along the Clyde now, its waterfront cleaned up. The veteran pleasure steamer *Waverley* makes some runs from here Jun–Aug – (0141) 221 8152 for times and prices.

Please let us know what you think of places in the *Guide*. Use the report forms at the back of the book or simply send a letter.

Other things to see and do

♫ 🏛 **Alloway** NS3318 A key stop on the Burns Trail: the poet was born here in 1759. The associated local sites are grouped together under the name BURNS NATIONAL HERITAGE PARK 💷, and the introductory visitor centre at Murdochs Lane has been brightly revamped. Rechristened the TAM O' SHANTER EXPERIENCE, its main feature is a multi-media show bringing Burns's famous poem vividly to life. Up the road you can explore the tiny rooms of the poet's birthplace, the thatched BURNS COTTAGE, and there's an adjacent museum of his life, with a good collection of manuscripts and letters. In the other direction, S of the centre, the BURNS MONUMENT was built in 1823 to a fine design by Thomas Hamilton Jr, and is adorned with characters from Burns's poems sculpted by James Thorn. Snacks, shop, disabled access; cl 25 Dec, 1 Jan; (01292) 443700; £4.25 for all 3 sites, £2.50 for the monument plus either of the other 2.

⚓🏰🧺👕🏛 **Arran** This island is just under an hour by ferry from Ardrossan NS2342 (2 ferries a day in winter, more in season; a popular public-transport day trip from Glasgow, though vulnerable to strikes on the state-owned ferry company – as the summer of 1997 showed), with summer ferries from Claonaig on Kintyre too; (01475) 650100 for ferry enquiries. It has a marvellous variety of scenery from subtropical gardens to mountain deer forest – and highly regarded (and beautifully set) golf courses. The main settlement Brodick NS0136 is distinguished by its fine old CASTLE, in lovely surroundings between the sea, hills and majestic mountain of Goatfell. Partly 13th-c, and extended in 1652 and 1844, it's very fierce-looking from the outside, but comfortably grand inside – even a little homely in places. There are almost a hundred antlered heads on the walls of the main staircase. It's surrounded by magnificent formal gardens, with the highlight the woodland garden started in 1923 by the Duchess of Montrose, inc many lovely rare and tender rhododendrons. Meals, snacks, shop, disabled access; castle cl Nov–Mar, garden and country park open all year; (01770) 302202; £4.50, £2.30 garden and country park only; NTS. The Kingsley on the esplanade has decent home cooking, and the Ormidale Hotel has good-value food. Well presented local history at the nearby HERITAGE MUSEUM, in an 18th-c croft farm. Meals, snacks, shop, disabled access; cl Nov–Mar; (01770) 302636; £1.50. On the opposite side of the island near Machrie NR8834 are several intriguing Bronze Age stone circles. Arran has a good circular walk up and down Goatfell, prominent for miles around, and you can follow the shore right around the N tip, the Cock of Arran. Up near here the waterside Catacol Hotel has decent food. Brodick has several places to hire bikes.

🌸 **Balerno** NT1666 MALLENY HOUSE GARDEN (off the A70) Charming gardens that are home to a national collection of 19th-c shrub roses (best in late Jun), as well as 4 clipped old yew trees – the survivors of a dozen planted in 1603. Limited disabled access; open all year; (0131) 226 5922; £1; NTS. The handsome Johnsburn House Hotel does good lunches.

🏛 ❊ **Bathgate** NS9871 CAIRNPAPPLE HILL (just E of Torpichen, off the B792) One of the most important prehistoric sites in Britain, a stone circle and series of successive burial cairns that seems to have been used for around 3,000 years from Neolithic times to the first century BC, and especially during the second millennium BC. Extraordinary views from this raw and atmospheric hilltop site, known locally as 'windy ways'.

🏛 **Bearsden** NS5471 ROMAN BATH HOUSE (Roman Rd) Probably the best surviving visible Roman building in Scotland, built in the 2nd c for the garrison at Bearsden Fort, part of the

Days Out

Edinburgh's New Town
National Gallery of Scotland; Scott Memorial; lunch at the Café Royal Circle Bar or Guildford Arms (West Register St); Calton Hill, for the view, and Edinburgh Experience; walk along George St to the Georgian House; walk through Moray Pl and Ainslie Pl, then along the Water of Leith; if time, the Royal Botanic Garden.

Edinburgh's Old Town
From Edinburgh Castle, walk down the Royal Mile past the Camera Obscura and Gladstone's Land; walk along Victoria St, Grassmarket and Candlemaker Row; lunch at Pierre Victoire (Grassmarket) or Bannerman's Bar (Cowgate); Royal Museum of Scotland; rejoin the Royal Mile, and continue past John Knox's House and Canongate Tolbooth to Holyrood Palace; Arthur's Seat.

Glasgow's Merchant City and the Clyde
City Chambers, and the Gallery of Modern Art; walk along Buchanan St; lunch at the Horseshoe (Drury St) or Counting House (George Sq); walk along Jamaica St and the Clyde walkway; People's Palace; the cathedral and Provan's Lordship.

Two Glaswegians: Rennie Mackintosh and Agnes Toward
Tour of Glasgow School of Art; lunch at Willow Tea Rooms (Sauchiehall St); Tenement House.

Glasgow's West End
Kelvin Bridge Underground Station; walk via Park Circus and Woodlands Terrace to Kelvingrove Park; Glasgow Art Gallery and Museum, or Museum of Transport; lunch at the Ubiquitous Chip (Ashton Lane/Byres Rd); Mackintosh Wing of Hunterian Gallery; walk down Hillhead St, go through the Botanic Garden and return to the start via the River Kelvin walkway.

Adam's masterpiece in Burns country
Alloway; lunch in Culzean country park (picnic or restaurant); stroll in the park, visit the castle.

A cycle ride on Arran
Ferry to Brodick; Brodick Castle; lunch at the Kingsley, Brodick; hire a cycle and take the B880 to the W coast to see stone circles; same way back, or the coast road.

The hammerhead peninsula
Glenluce Abbey; lunch at the Crown, Portpatrick; Logan Botanic Garden; Mull of Galloway for a stroll and birdwatching.

By the sands of the Solway Firth
Kirkcudbright; lunch at the Smugglers, Auchencairn; coastal stroll from Rockcliffe to Castle Hill Point; Threave Garden, Castle Douglas.

An industrialist's Utopia
New Lanark; walk past the Falls of Clyde, if there's time; lunch at the East India Company, La Vigna or Crown, all in Lanark; Biggar.

Estuarine exploration
Forth bridges and visitor centre; lunch at Hawes, South Queensferry; boat to Inchcolm Abbey; Hopetoun House, South Queensferry.

Scott's landscapes
Scott's View from the B6356 N of Dryburgh; Dryburgh Abbey; lunch at the Burts Hotel, Melrose; Melrose Abbey and town; walk up the Eildon Hills, or visit Smailholm tower house or Mellerstain.

Abbey towns of the Borders
Floors Castle; Kelso; lunch at Cobbles or the Queen's Head there; Jedburgh Abbey and town.

East of Edinburgh
Haddington; Hailes Castle; lunch at the Drovers, East Linton; Museum of Flight, East Fortune; Dirleton Castle.

Antonine Wall defences; free. The appropriately named Fifty-Five BC (Drymen Rd) has decent food, as does the Beefeater (Station Rd).

⚭🏠♨⬆! **Biggar** NT0438 Several good museums here: the GLADSTONE COURT MUSEUM (North Back Rd) houses an entire reconstructed village street (cl 12.30–2pm, am Sun, and all Nov–Mar; £1.80), while the adjacent GREENHILLS COVENANTERS HOUSE is a 17th-c farmhouse originally at Wiston but moved piece by piece and reassembled here, with rare breeds of sheep and poultry (cl am, and all Nov–Mar; £1). You can get a joint ticket that also includes the local history collections at the MOAT PARK HERITAGE CENTRE (cl am Sun, and all Nov–Mar; £2.40 on its own). The striking old GASWORKS building (Gasworks Rd) is now a museum on the coal-gas industry (open pm Jun–Sept; £1). There's a very jolly PUPPET THEATRE just off the A702; when they're not doing shows they sometimes do backstage tours. Teas, shop, disabled access (tel first – they have to remove some seats in the theatre); cl 25 Dec, 1 Jan, and maybe winter Suns; (01899) 220631; shows £4.40.

⚭🏵 **Blantyre** NS6857 DAVID LIVINGSTONE CENTRE (Station Rd, off the A724) The birthplace of the famous explorer, with a museum on his life and work. An African pavilion looks at the continent today, with contemporary crafts, and there's an adventure playground in the landscaped grounds. Meals, snacks, shop, some disabled access; cl am Sun, and limited opening Nov–Mar – best to check first then; (01698) 823140; £2.95. The Cricklewood at Bothwell (B7071) is a good dining pub.

⛵🏠🏵♫🏊⚭ **Bute** This popular Glasgow holiday island is a ½hr ferry trip from Wemyss Bay/Skelmorlie NS1967; it has a mix of fresh air and ebullient summer entertainments. There's lovely open country in the N, and its S tip has the remote windswept ruin of the MONASTERY OF ST BLANE, with a ruined Norman chapel in a delightful spot, a short

way uphill from the road – just sheep and the occasional walker. Amidst this bracingly bleak landscape the spectacular Victorian 'gothick' of MOUNT STUART HOUSE AND GARDENS (off the A844, just E of Upper Scoulag) is quite a shock; the elaborate rooms are splendidly over the top too. The 300 acres of landscaped grounds and woodland include several pretty gardens, as well as a pinetum of mature conifers and a nicely isolated stretch of sandy beach, reached via a lime tree avenue. Meals, snacks, shop, disabled access; cl am, all day Tues and Thur, and Oct–Apr; (01700) 503877; £5.50, £3 garden only. The island's main town Rothesay NS0864 has a 13th-c CASTLE (cl am Sun, and in winter pm Thurs and all day Fri; £1.50), and a decent museum on Stuart St (cl Sun exc summer pms, and Mon Oct–Mar; £1). The seafront Black Bull has good food. There are lovely sea views from the Kames Inn NR9671, which has food all day.

🏛🦆 **Caerlaverock** NX9968 13th-c CAERLAVEROCK CASTLE Protected not just by its moat but by the wild swampy marsh around it, it has an unusual triangular inner courtyard, and elaborate projecting tops for dropping missiles on assailants. Snacks, shop, disabled access; cl am Sun, 1–2pm Nov–Mar; (01387) 770244; £2.30. The surrounding salt marshes are a reserve of the WILDFOWL AND WETLANDS TRUST, with outstanding hide facilities and observation towers. Countless wildfowl flock here, especially barnacle geese; between Oct and Apr there are generally around 13,000 of them, very dramatic when they're all in flight. Snacks, shop, some disabled access; cl 25 Dec; (01387) 770200; £3 – discounts if you turn up by bike, foot or public transport. The Nith at Glencaple has good-value food.

🏛 **Cardoness Castle** NX5956 (A75) Well preserved 15th-c 4-storey tower house, overlooking the Water of Fleet; interesting fireplaces. Shop; cl occasional lunchtimes, am Sun, and all winter wkdys; (01557) 814427; *£1.50. A mile NE, Gatehouse of

Fleet has places to eat.

🟦 ⛺ ♿ **Castle Douglas** NX7560 THREAVE GARDEN (1m W off the A75) The National Trust for Scotland's horticulture school, with plenty to see throughout the year in its walled garden and glasshouses. If you're there in spring, don't miss the massed display of over 200 varieties of daffodil. Meals, snacks, shop, disabled access; visitor centre cl Nov–Mar; (01556) 502575; £3.70; NTS. The Black Douglas, Archibald the Grim, built THREAVE CASTLE in the 14th c; 4 storeys high, it stands on an islet in the River Dee and you have to get a ferry across (ring the bell and the custodian will come to get you). Shop; cl am Sun, and Oct–Mar (exc maybe pm Sun in Oct); (01831) 168512; £1.50, inc ferry. The Royal Hotel has good-value food.

⛺ **Clarencefield** NY0968 15th-c COMLONGON CASTLE 🖼 (B725) Unusually well preserved, with interesting original features inc dungeons, kitchen, great hall and even privies. Meals; cl Christmas; (01387) 870283; *£3. See also the **Where to stay** section, page 828 above (non-residents may be able to join their candlelit pre-dinner tours); it's a popular spot for weddings.

↓⊤ ! **Coatbridge** NS7265 SUMMERLEE HERITAGE TRUST (West Canal St) Ambitious centre looking at the local iron, steel and engineering industries. Lots going on, spread over 25 acres of a former iron works; the din from the working machines creates a real feeling of authenticity. Meals, snacks, shop, limited disabled access; cl 25–26 Dec and 1–2 Jan; (01236) 431261; free. The TIME CAPSULE on Buchanan St is fun – swimming pools and leisure centre with a loose historic theme: water chutes whizz you through the origins of man, and a woolly mammoth holds court in the centre of the ice rink.

♂ **Creetown** NX4758 GEM ROCK MUSEUM (Chain Rd) Enormous private collection of gemstones and minerals, some displayed in an atmospheric crystal cave. Also an unusual fossilised dinosaur egg. Snacks, shop, disabled access; cl

wkdys in Jan and Feb, plus 23 Dec–7 Jan; (01671) 820357; £2.50.

🏚 🟦 **Culzean Castle** NS3309 (pronounced 'Cullane') CULZEAN CASTLE AND COUNTRY PARK A day here is one of the most popular outings in the region. The 18th-c mansion is one of great presence and brilliance, and the 563 acres of grounds are among the finest in Britain, lushly planted and richly ornamental, with bracing clifftop and shoreline walks, and an 18th-c walled garden. The house was splendidly refashioned by Robert Adam, and has been well restored to show off his work to full effect. Meals, snacks, shop, disabled access; house open Easter–Oct, park all year; (01655) 760274; £6 park and castle, £3 park only; NTS. You can stay in rather smart self-contained apartments on the top floor; the harbourside Anchorage in the pleasant village of Dunure (off the A719 N) does decent lunches.

🦋 **Dalkeith** NT3367 EDINBURGH BUTTERFLY AND INSECT WORLD 🖼 (Dobbies Nursery, off the A720 at Gilmerton junction) Gloriously coloured exotic butterflies, as well as scorpions and tarantulas, bee garden, and rainforest frogs. Meals, snacks, shop, disabled access; cl 25–26 Dec, 1 Jan; (0131) 663 4932; *£3.75. The Sun at Lothianbridge (A7 S) has good-value food.

⛺ 🟦 **Dirleton** NT5184 DIRLETON CASTLE (A198) Grandly rebuilt after a siege in 1298, only to be destroyed again in 1650. It has a charming garden planted in the 16th c, with ancient yews and hedges around a bowling green; cl am Sun, 25–26 Dec, 1–2 Jan; (01620) 850330; £2. The Castle Hotel and Open Arms in this pleasant golfing village are both good for lunch.

⛺ ❄ **Dryburgh** NT5932 DRYBURGH ABBEY Remarkably complete ruins of one of David I's monasteries, in a lovely setting among old cedars by the River Tweed – its graceful cloisters are very peaceful. Walter Scott is buried here (and on the B6356 N SCOTT'S VIEW is idyllic). Shop, some disabled access; cl am Sun, 25–26 Dec, 1–2 Jan; (01835) 822381;

*£2.30. The Buccleuch Arms at St Boswells is a civilised place for something to eat.

☫❋ Dumbarton NS4075
DUMBARTON CASTLE (A82) Perched on a rock 73 metres (240 ft) above the River Clyde, with dramatic views of the surrounding countryside. Most of what can be seen dates from the 18th and 19th c, though there are some earlier remains. Snacks, shop; cl am Sun, and in winter 12.30–1.30pm, plus pm Thurs and all day Fri, 25–26 Dec, 1–2 Jan; (01389) 732167; £1.50. The Ettrick in the picturesque Clydeside village of Old Kilpatrick has good-value food.

☖🏛! Dumfries NX9776 Another place with close Burns connections (you can get a ticket that covers all the related attractions). The ROBERT BURNS CENTRE (Mill Rd) has an exhibition and audio-visual display, as well as an interesting scale model of the town at the time he wrote. Snacks, shop, disabled access; cl 1–2pm in winter, am Sun (all day in winter), and winter Mons; (01387) 264808; £1.20 for audio-visual exhibition. BURNS HOUSE (Burns St) is where he lived for the 3 years before his death, and has original letters and manuscripts along with the chair in which he wrote his last poems and songs. Shop; open as Burns Centre; (01387) 255297; free. The GLOBE TAVERN (off High St) has 2 rooms still very much as they were when this was his regular haunt (Anna Park, the barmaid, bore his child). Neatly rounding off the tale is the BURNS MAUSOLEUM in St Michael's churchyard, containing the tombs of Robert Burns, his on-and-off wife Jean Armour, and their 5 sons; you can usually make an appointment to visit at the Burns House. The town MUSEUM, in the tower of an 18th-c windmill, has a CAMERA OBSCURA. Shop; cl winter Sun and Mon; (01387) 253374; museum free, camera obscura £1.20.

Dunbar NT6778 The harbour here is pretty, with some picturesque fragments of the medieval castle, and pleasant walks nearby; the Eagle is good value. Quite a few decent clean beaches near here, notably Belhaven, nearby Whitesands Bay, and the one at Thorntonloch NT7574 a few miles down the coast.

☫ Dundrennan NX7447
DUNDRENNAN ABBEY (A711) Ruined Cistercian abbey famous as the place Mary, Queen of Scots is thought to have spent her last night in Scotland; cl am Sun, wkdys in winter; (01557) 500262; *£1.50.

🏛❋☖♥ Duns NT8154
MANDERSTON (2m E off the A6105) Splendidly lavish house built for the plutocrat racecourse owner Sir James Miller; he told the architect to spare no expense, so ended up with the world's only silver staircase. Other gloriously extravagant parts are the painted ceilings, and a ballroom decorated in Miller's racing colours. Also fine formal gardens, and an unusual biscuit-tin museum. Teas, shop, limited disabled access; open pm Thurs and Sun May–Sept, plus English bank hols in May and Aug; (01361) 883450; £5, £2.50 grounds only. Just across the road, children enjoy the CRUMSTANE FARM PARK; cl Tues and all Oct–Easter; (01361) 883268; *£2. The Wheatsheaf at Swinton isn't far, for a very good meal.

✝ East Fortune NT5579 MUSEUM OF FLIGHT ⊞ (East Fortune Airfield, B1347) Good range of aircraft, with 35 aeroplanes from a Spitfire to a Vulcan bomber, and displays on famous flyers and air traffic control. Snacks, shop, disabled access; cl wknds Nov–Mar; (01620) 880308; £2.

☫✗ East Linton NT5977 HAILES CASTLE Another brief stopping point for Mary, Queen of Scots, now in ruins, but lovely in spring, with wild flowers along the stream; free. PRESTON MILL One of the oldest working water-driven oatmeal mills surviving in Scotland. It's a pretty spot, with an old dovecot nearby. Snacks, shop, limited disabled access; cl 1–2pm, am Sun, wkdys in Oct, and all Nov–Apr; (01620) 860426; £1.80; NTS. The Drovers Inn has good food.

🏛☖♥ Ellisland Farm NX9283 ⊞

(off the A76) Robert Burns lived here from 1788 to 1791, trying unsuccessfully to introduce new farming methods. There are displays of material associated with the poet (who wrote *Tam o' Shanter* and *Auld Lang Syne* while living here), and cattle and sheep wander around much as they must have done then. Some disabled access; cl 1–2pm, am Sun, and in winter all day Sun and Mon; (01387) 740426; £1.50.

🕭 **Eyemouth** NT9564 Understated family holiday seaside town around busy but pretty fishing harbour, with a decent beach, and a good local history MUSEUM (cl am Sun and pm too in Oct, all Nov–Easter; £1.50). The Ship overlooking the harbour has reasonable food.

🝔 🌼 🗣 🎣 **Galloway Forest Park** Attractive and easily accessible, taking in around 100 lochs, 300 miles of river, great views, and thousands of hectares of forest, mountain and moorland. Many of the trees are fairly recent replantings, the original woodland having from the 15th c onwards rapidly fallen victim to the demand for timber; one of the best surviving stretches of ancient forest is at WOOD OF CREE NX4165, which has an RSPB reserve among its trees and marshes. Many of the lochs are ringed by waymarked walks and trails, and there are plenty of scenic drives and cycle routes. Visitor centres (open Apr–Sept only) at Kirroughtree NX4571, Glen Trool NX3578 and Clatteringshaws NX5477 all have exhibitions and information to help you make the most of the forests, inc details of where you can camp or fish, and the best places to spot wildlife. Stones beside Loch Trool and Clatteringshaws Loch commemorate battles between Robert the Bruce and the armies of Edward I in 1307, and elsewhere others recall the 1680s Killing Time, when Scottish covenanters were hunted down and killed in the government's attempts to impose bishops on the Scottish church.

🏚 **Glenluce** NX1858 GLENLUCE ABBEY Ruined Cistercian abbey founded in the late 12th c, in beautiful surroundings. Limited disabled access; cl am Sun, and usually wkdys Oct–Mar; (01581) 300541; £1.50.

🎱 **Gogar** NT1672 SUNTRAP GARDEN AND ADVICE CENTRE (off the A8 nr Edinburgh Airport) Splendidly informative as well as sumptuous to look at, with several different gardens (Italian, Japanese, rock, peat, herbaceous and woodland), and free advice and tips. Plant sales (wkdys only); cl wknds Oct–Mar; (0131) 339 7283; *£1; NTS. The Bridge at Ratho is a good canalside family dining pub.

🏚 🖼 🎱 🌼 **Gordon** NT6439 MELLERSTAIN HOUSE (just W, off the A6089) William and Robert Adam both worked on this striking Georgian house, which has impressive plasterwork and furnishings, and paintings by Van Dyck and Gainsborough. Every house in Scotland seems to have something that belonged to Bonnie Prince Charlie – this one has his bagpipes. Very pleasant terraced gardens and parkland, with fine views towards the distant hills. Meals, snacks, shop; cl am, all day Sat, and Oct–Apr; (01573) 410225; £4.50. The Gordon Arms has decent food.

! **Gretna Green** NY3268 It's now tourists rather than runaway couples that flock to the Old Blacksmith's Shop in this little Borders village. More people come here than to just about any other Scottish attraction outside Edinburgh, despite the fact that there's really very little to see. An exhibition centre looks at the once thriving marriage business; cl 25 Dec, 1 Jan; (01461) 338224; £1.

★ 🏚 🎱 **Haddington** NT5174 A pretty market town; the comfortable George and Maitlandfield House hotels, and the aptly named Waterside Inn, all have above-average food. LENNOXLOVE (1m S on the B6369) The Duchess of Lennox (La Belle Stuart) gave this old house its unusual name in memory of her dead husband. Among reminders of other members of her family are the casket and death mask of Mary, Queen of Scots. In the grounds the

Cadzow herd of white park cattle are said to be descended from the sacrificial cattle of the Druids. Meals, snacks; open pm Wed, Sat and Sun Easter–Oct; (01620) 823720; £3.25.

🏰 ♨ 🎡 Hawick NT5014 DRUMLANRIG'S TOWER ⌷ (Towerknowe) Fearsome-looking 16th-c tower with state-of-the-art displays of Borders history, some quite gripping. Shop, disabled access; cl Nov–Mar; (01450) 377615; £2.50. Hawick's MUSEUM (Wilton Lodge Park) is made considerably more appealing by its setting, a park with riverside walks and gardens; cl 12–1pm, am Sun, and all day winter Sats; (01450) 373457; £1.25.

🏰 Hermitage NY5094 HERMITAGE CASTLE Almost perfect from the outside, the well restored but very forbidding remains of a 14th-c Borders stronghold reeking of dire deeds. Shop; cl am Sun, all day Thurs and Fri in winter; (01387) 376222; *£1.50.

🎪 Innerleithen NT3336 ROBERT SMAIL'S PRINTING WORKS (High St) Fully restored Victorian printer's shop, with water-powered press; you can try your hand at metal typesetting and hand-print your own bookmark. Shop, limited disabled access; cl 1–2pm, am Sun, and all Oct–Apr (exc Oct wknds); (01896) 830206; £2.30; NTS. The Traquair Arms is the place to eat.

🎦 ♨ ❀ Irvine NS3239 GLASGOW VENNEL MUSEUM and Burns Heckling Shop Art gallery and museum, and behind, a reconstruction of the Heckling Shop where, as a young man, an unwilling Burns tried to learn the filthy trade of flax dressing. Happily for him, during a New Year's Eve party his aunt knocked over a candle and burnt the building to ashes. Disabled access; cl 1–2pm, am Sun, all day Weds, and in winter all day pm Sun and Mon too; (01294) 275059; free. Down by the harbour, the SCOTTISH MARITIME MUSEUM (Gottries Rd) is very much a working museum, with lots of restoration work on the good range of historic vessels. Snacks, shop, some disabled access (not to boats); cl Nov–Mar;

(01294) 278283; £2. The nearby Keys has decent food (all day wknds).

🏰 🏠 ♨ Jedburgh NT6521 12th-c JEDBURGH ABBEY The most complete of the ruined Borders monasteries founded by David I, and an impressive sight, despite its town setting. Imposing 26-metre (86-ft) tower, splendid west door, and audio-visual show in visitor centre. Snacks, shops, disabled access; cl am Sun, 25–26 Dec, 1–2 Jan; (01835) 863925; £2.80. MARY QUEEN OF SCOTS HOUSE (Queen St) Charming 16th-c fortified dwelling where Mary had to prolong her 1566 stay because of a near-mortal fever (she was later to say she wished she'd died here). There's a good interpretation of her life. Shop; cl Nov–mid-Mar; (01835) 863331; £2. The former CASTLE JAIL (Castlegate) is now a local history museum (cl am Sun, Nov–Feb; £1.25). The Pheasant has good food (and makes a point of having good-value pheasant in season). Just off the A68 S of town are the ruins of FERNIEHURST CASTLE.

★ 🏰 ♨ 🏠 🎡 Kelso NT7334 KELSO ABBEY was the greatest and wealthiest of the 4 famous Borders abbeys, though today not much of the building remains. A nearby MUSEUM (Turret House, Abbey Court) explains its history, and also has a reconstructed 19th-c market place; cl 12–1pm, am Sun, all day Mon, and Oct-Easter; (01573) 225470; £1.25. The town is attractive to wander round, and its Sept ram sales are altogether more fun than you could imagine they'd be. The Cobbles (Beaumont St) and Queen's Head (Bridge St) both have good food. FLOORS CASTLE ⌷ (1m N) Magnificent building designed by William Adam in 1721, much embellished in the next century. It's reputed to be Scotland's biggest inhabited house, with a window for every day of the year. Splendid collection of tapestries and French furniture, and wonderful walled garden (best July–Sept). Good home-made meals and snacks, shop, disabled access; cl Oct–Easter (exc Sun and Weds in Oct); (01573) 223333; £4.50.

🏚 🦢 **Kilmarnock** NS4337 DEAN CASTLE (off the Glasgow Rd) Very well restored family home, housing a wonderful collection of medieval arms and armour, musical instruments, tapestries, and a display of Burns's manuscripts. It's surrounded by 200 acres of woodland, with nature trails, deer park, riding and other activities. Snacks, shop; cl am, 25–26 Dec, 1–2 Jan; (01563) 522702; £2.50. The 18th-c Wheatsheaf in the pretty village of Symington on the other side of town has good original food.

🐝 👌 **Kirkbean** NX9857 ARBIGLAND GARDENS (off the A710) Extensive woodland, formal and water gardens based around a lovely sandy bay. The US Admiral John Paul Jones worked here as a boy (his father was the gardener), and his birthplace nearby has been turned into a little museum. Snacks, shop, some disabled access; cl am, all day Mon exc bank hols, and all Oct–Apr; (01387) 880283; *£2.50. The Steamboat at Carsethorne has good home cooking and sea views.

🏚 🐝 **Langbank** NS3673 FINLAYSTONE (1m W on the A8) Some say the garden here is the finest in Scotland – formal and walled, with woodland walks and adventure playgrounds. The house has connections with Robert Burns and John Knox (unlikely partners), as well as displays of dolls, Victorian flower books and Celtic art. Snacks (not winter wkdys), shop, disabled access; gardens open all year, house pm Sun Apr–Aug, or by arrangement; (01475) 540505; *£2.50, house £1.20 extra. The modern Langbank Lodge nearby has sensibly priced food (inc afternoon tea and scones) and incredible Clyde views.

🛥 ! **Largs** NX6755 The pick of the traditional Clydeside resorts, with boats across the narrow strip of water to the island of Great Cumbrae. VIKINGR! 🔲 (Barrfields Centre, Greenock Rd) Lively look at the Vikings in Scotland, from their arrival in Scotland to their defeat at the Battle of Largs. Very much an 'experience', with lots of interactive displays, and a

multi-media show as the centrepiece. Meals, snacks, shop, disabled access; cl 25–26 Dec, 1–2 Jan; (01475) 689777; £3.50. The pleasure steamer *Waverley* calls here in summer, and Nardinis (Esplanade) is a vintage tearoom – or rather tea palace, with acres of immaculate tables and smartly aproned motherly waitresses.

🏰 **Lauder** NT5347 THIRLESTANE CASTLE 🔲 (off the A697) Charming old castle with recently restored assemblage of pictures, interesting collection of old toys (some of which children can touch), and some outstanding plasterwork in the 17th-c state rooms. Snacks, shop; open pm Easter wk, then pm Weds, Thurs, Sun and Mon May–Sept, and pm daily (exc Sat) July and Aug; (01578) 722430; *£4, *£1 grounds only. The Eagle and Lauderdale Hotel are useful for lunch.

🏰 🏚 **Linlithgow** NS9976 LINLITHGOW PALACE The birthplace of Mary, Queen of Scots, a magnificently sombre lochside ruin. You can still see the chapel, great hall and a quadrangle with fountain. Shop, limited disabled access; (01506) 842896; £2.30. In the town a pleasant old tavern, the Four Marys, is named for her maids-in-waiting Mary Livingstone, Mary Fleming, Mary Beaton and Mary Seton, with relevant memorabilia. HOUSE OF THE BINNS (3m E, off the A904) The home of the Dalyell family since the 17th c, with some splendid plaster ceilings and a varied collection of furniture and porcelain. Limited disabled access; cl am, all day Fri, and mid-Oct–Apr; (01506) 834255; £3.50; NTS.

♭ 🍖 ✕ 🔲 **Livingston** NT0367 ALMOND VALLEY HERITAGE CENTRE 🔲 (off the A705) Friendly 16-acre museum, with lots to see inc working farm, watermill, and underground shale mine. Also trailer rides, adventure playground, and demonstrations of milking and other seasonal activities. Meals, snacks, shop, disabled access; cl 25–26 Dec, 1–2 Jan; (01506) 414957; £2.20.

🦅 **Lochwinnoch** NS3559 RSPB NATURE CENTRE (Largs Rd) Bird

reserve with fine views, good woodland and marsh nature trails, and several observation hides – one specially for disabled visitors. Wknd snacks (wkdys too July and Aug), shop, disabled access; cl Christmas and New Year; (01505) 842663; *£1. The Mossend is a useful dining pub.

🏨 ⊛ ! 🏨 **Melrose** NT5434 The ruins of MELROSE ABBEY are among the finest in Britain – best in moonlight, as Scott says (though he admitted he never saw them thus himself). Look out for the wonderful stonework on the 14th-c nave (and the pig playing the bagpipes). Archaeological investigations now leave little doubt that this was the burial place of Robert the Bruce's heart. Shop; limited disabled access; cl am Sun, 25–26 Dec, 1–2 Jan; (01896) 822562; £2.80. PRIORWOOD GARDEN (Abbey St) Specialises in flowers suitable for drying, with a herb garden and display orchard illustrating apples through the ages. Shop, disabled access; cl am Sun, and 24 Dec–Easter; (01896) 822493; *£1; NTS. TEDDY MELROSE 📼 (The Wynd) Unusually comprehensive and informative teddy bear museum, with resident bear-maker on site and bear fairs in May, Aug and Nov. Snacks (inc award-winning coffee), shop, disabled access; cl 25–26 Dec; (01896) 822464; *£1.50. Besides the Burts Hotel, the King's Arms is useful for lunch. ABBOTSFORD HOUSE (3m W on the B6360) Set grandly on the River Tweed, this was the home of Walter Scott until his death in 1832. You can still see his mammoth 9,000-volume library, and several of the historical oddities he liked to collect, like Rob Roy's sporran. Snacks, shop, disabled access; cl am Sun (Mar–May and Oct), plus all Nov–mid-Mar; (01896) 752043; £3.40.

🐾 **Mervinslaw** NT6713 JEDFOREST DEER AND FARM PARK (A68) Working hill farm with deer as well as other animals, and several rare breeds. Good for children, and peaceful walks and trails nearby. Snacks, shop, some disabled access; cl Nov–Apr; (01835) 840364; £3.

🐾 **Moffat** NT0805 TWEEDHOPE

SHEEPDOG CENTRE (Hamerlands Farm, Selkirk Rd) Friendly place with demonstrations of working sheep dogs (11am and 3pm), and an exhibition. Shop, some disabled access; open wkdys Apr–Oct (wknds by appointment); (01683) 221471; £2.50. The small town still has some of the poise of its former days as a spa; the Black Bull, Star (Britain's narrowest hotel) and Moffat House Hotel all do decent food.

🏨 ⊙ ✗ **New Abbey** NX9666 SWEETHEART ABBEY (A710) One of the most romantic ruins in the area, with a lofty arched nave open to the sky, and a touching story attached. Shop; best to check winter opening; (01387) 850397; £1. SHAMBELLIE HOUSE OF COSTUME (A710) Much extended in recent years, often dazzling displays of costume, thoughtfully arranged in appropriately furnished rooms. Shop; cl Nov–Mar; (01387) 850375; £2.50. The pretty village also has a restored 18th-c CORN MILL; cl am Sun, pm Thurs and all day Fri in winter; (01387) 850260; *£2.30.

🎵 ✗ ✗ 🏨 🛏 🌊 **New Lanark** 📼 NS8842 (off the A73) Founded in 1785 and now the subject of a major conservation programme, this is Scotland's best example of an industrial village, with plenty to keep families amused for a good chunk of the day. Many of the old millworkers' buildings have been interestingly converted to modern accommodation, so it's very much a living village rather than a museum. The award-winning VISITOR CENTRE has a dark ride looking at life here in the 1820s (lots of special effects), as well as various other displays and working machinery. Snacks, shop, disabled access; cl 25 Dec, 1–2 Jan; (01555) 661345; £3.75. Included in the visitor centre ticket are a nature reserve, craft workshops, and period shop and house; a little extra gets you a classic car collection, and Scotland's biggest model railway. The village can be busy at wknds; try to visit during the week if you can. The surrounding countryside is spectacular, with a short walk through a verdant gorge to the Falls of Clyde that used to power the mill; a visitor centre here has lots of information on badgers (open pm wknds Nov–Easter, then daily till Oct; cl all Jan). The Crown (Hope St, Lanark) has a decent restaurant.

⛏ **Newtongrange** NT3364 SCOTTISH MINING MUSEUM ▨ (Lady Victoria Colliery, A7) Vivid re-creation of mining days, both at the well restored pithead and back home, even in the tearooms. Home-baked snacks, shop, limited disabled access; cl Nov–Mar; (0131) 663 7519; £3.

🕸 **Old Dailly** NS2400 BARGANY GARDENS Fine ornamental trees, woodland walks winding through springtime glades of snowdrops, bluebells and daffodils, and a lily pond enveloped by azaleas and rhododendrons. Disabled access; cl Nov–Feb; (01465) 871249; donations.

♨◨! **Paisley** NS4864 Not just a place but a pattern, as well as a very wide range of 19th-c art, the appealing MUSEUM AND ART GALLERY (High St) has a marvellous collection of antique and more modern Paisley shawls, along with the looms on which they were made. Shop, some disabled access; cl Sun and bank hols; (0141) 889 3151; free. Next door the COATS OBSERVATORY has displays on astronomy, meteorology and space flight. Shop, cl am Mon, Tues, and Thurs (open till 7.45pm these days), and all day Sun and bank hols; (0141) 889 2013; free. The Anchor (Glasgow Rd) does decent lunches.

🏚 ♺ **Paxton** NT9352 PAXTON HOUSE ▨ (B6461) Built in 1758 by the lovestruck Patrick Billie, who hoped to marry a daughter of Frederick the Great; the marriage never took place, but the result was a splendid neo-Palladian mansion, designed and later embellished by the Adam family, and furnished by the Chippendales. Also woodland and riverside walks, huge herd of highland cattle, and adventure playground designed by the Territorial Army. Meals, snacks, shop, disabled access; cl Nov–Mar, plus house cl am; (01289) 386291; £4, £2 gardens only.

★ ⛏♨✿ 🕸 ◨ **Peebles** NT2540 Attractive if sedate Borders town, with quite a lot for visitors; the old-fashioned Tontine Hotel has reliable food. NEIDPATH CASTLE ▨ (just W off the A7) Spectacularly set, converted from the original 14th-c tower in the late 16th and early 17th c. There's a rock-hewn well, small museum (children like the mummified rat), period kitchen, and a pit prison – not much chance of escape, as some of the walls are 3½ metres (11 ft) thick. Super views from the parapets. Shop, ltd disabled access; cl am Sun, and Oct–Easter; (01721) 720333; *£2.50 KAILZIE (2m SE on the B7062) Extensive grounds with lovely old trees flanked by azaleas and rhododendrons, formal rose garden, walled garden, and small art gallery. Meals, snacks, shop, disabled access; restaurant and gallery cl Nov–Easter; (01721) 720007; £2 (less in winter).

☎ **Penicuik** NT2360 EDINBURGH CRYSTAL VISITOR CENTRE (Eastfield) Demonstrations of glass-blowing, cutting and engraving, with an exhibition on the crystal's history. Meals, snacks, shop, disabled access; tours Mon–Fri all year and wknds Apr–Sept (last wknd tour 2.30pm), cl 25–26 Dec, 1–2 Jan; (01968) 675128; £2. They run a free minibus service from Waverley Bridge in Edinburgh (on the hour, Apr–Sept only). The Horseshoe out on the Peebles road is a civilised dining pub.

🕸 **Port Logan** NX0942 LOGAN BOTANIC GARDEN (off the B7065) A specialist garden of the Royal Botanic Garden of Edinburgh, containing a wide range of plants from the warm temperate regions of the southern hemisphere. Snacks, shop, disabled access; cl Nov–mid-Mar; (01776) 860231; £2. The village itself has a natural sea pool where fat fish will eat from your fingers; the Inn does good food.

⛏ **Prestonpans** NT3773 The setting for Bonnie Prince Charlie's 1745 rout of the Hanoverians. The INDUSTRIAL HERITAGE MUSEUM at nearby Prestongrange (B1348) is based around the oldest documented coal mining site in Britain. Reconstructed coalface and colliery workshop, as well as displays on other local industries, from brick and pipe making to brewing and weaving. Lots going on, especially at wknds. Snacks, shop, disabled access; cl Nov–Mar; (0131) 653 2904; free. The **Rhinns of Galloway** – the hammerhead of land in the extreme W of the area – is largely empty even in high summer, a very peaceful place, with cliffs (especially on the S point), rocks and small coves.

★ 🐦 🏠 **St Abbs** NT9167 A steep and pretty little seaside village on the E coast, with a sandy beach and old fishing harbour, little used now. The cliffs of St Abb's Head are noisily crowded with breeding seabirds in late spring, with high breezy walks, and a LIGHTHOUSE often open for visits.

🏠 🏠 🖼 🌺 **Selkirk** NT4728 A decorous town, good for bargain-hunting for the tweeds, woollens and cashmeres which are woven and knitted here; the Queen's Head has freshly cooked food. There's an exhibition on Walter Scott in the former courtroom where, as sheriff, he dispensed justice to the people of Selkirk (cl am Sun, £1); not that gripping, but easily combined with Abbotsford (see Melrose entry above). You can watch demonstrations of paperweight-making at SELKIRK GLASS (just N, off the A7). Snacks, factory shop; cl am Sun, no glass-making wknds; (01750) 20954; free. BOWHILL HOUSE 🏛 (3m W, off the A708) Outstanding collection of paintings, inc works by Canaletto, Van Dyck, Gainsborough and Claude, as well as impressive furnishings and porcelain, and memorabilia relating to Scott and Queen Victoria. Also restored Victorian kitchen, adventure playground, very active little theatre, and surrounding country park. Snacks, shop, disabled access; grounds open pm May–Aug (exc Fri), house pm in July only; (01750) 22204; *£4.50, *£1 park only.
🏠 **Smailholm** NT6435 BORDER TOWER HOUSE (just S, signed off the B6404 NE of St Boswells) Classic 15th-c Borders tower house, very well

preserved – all 17 metres (57 ft) of it. Display based on Walter Scott's book *Minstrels of the Borders*, and an exhibition of dolls. Shop; cl am Sun, and all Oct–Mar; (01573) 460365; *£1.50.

🌺 🏠 🖼 🌺 ⛵ 🏔 **South Queensferry** NT1477 Notable for its views of the two great Forth bridges on either side, with piers to potter on; the Hawes Inn, famous from *Kidnapped*, is still going strong. HOPETOUN HOUSE (2m W, off the B904) This huge place is probably Scotland's best example of the work of William and Robert Adam. The magnificent reception rooms have a wonderful art collection with works by Canaletto and Gainsborough, while the superb grounds include a deer park and a flock of rare sheep. You can play croquet on the lawn, or climb to the rooftop for wonderful views. Meals, snacks, shop, some disabled access; cl Oct–Easter; (0131) 331 2451; £4.50, £2.50 grounds only. DALMENY HOUSE (3m E on the B924) Despite its Tudor Gothic appearance, this splendidly placed house dates only from the 19th c – there's a superb hammerbeamed roof, as well as fine furnishings, porcelain and portraits. Good walks in the grounds and on the shore. Snacks, disabled access; open pm Sun, Mon and Tues July–Aug, or by appointment; (0131) 331 1888; £3.60. INCHCOLM ABBEY Out in the Forth (a lovely ½hr seal-spotting ferry trip), this Augustinian abbey founded by Alexander I is better preserved than any other in Scotland, with a fine 13th-c octagonal chapter house and a wall painting from the same period. Ferries usually 11am, 1pm and 3pm, summer only, but best to check on (0131) 331 4857; £6.75 inc ferry.
🌺 ⚘ **Stobo** NT1635 DAWYCK BOTANIC GARDEN (B712) Another specialist garden of the Royal Botanic Garden, particularly noted for its arboretum rich in mature conifers (inc a larch believed to have been planted in 1725), with notable Asiatic silver firs and many rarities. Snacks, shop, limited disabled access; cl late Oct–mid-Mar; (01721) 760254; £2.

⚅ **Stranraer** NX1059 CASTLE KENNEDY GARDENS (4m E on the A75) Prettily set between 2 lochs (with lots of good walks around), these gardens were first laid out in the early 18th c, then after years of neglect were restored and developed in the 19th. They're particularly admired for their walled garden and flowering shrubs. Snacks, shop, limited disabled access; cl Oct–Mar; (01776) 702024; £2.

⚔🎦✿➤ۑ **Thornhill** NX8599 DRUMLANRIG CASTLE 🎦 (off the A76) Spectacular and rather unusual pink sandstone castle built in the late 17th c, with a glory of fine panelling and furnishings (mainly Louis XIV), and splendid paintings by Leonardo, Holbein, Rembrandt and Murillo; you can see what's said to be Bonnie Prince Charlie's campaign kettle. Also craft workshops, peacocks wandering over the lawn, birds of prey, and extensive woodland walks. You can hire bikes. Snacks, shop, disabled access; cl Thurs, and Sept–Apr; (01848) 330248; £4.

🏰⚅!🎦✿ **Traquair** NT3235 TRAQUAIR HOUSE (B709) One of the longest-inhabited and most romantic houses in Britain; no less than 27 English and Scottish kings have stayed here. The Bear Gates have remained closed since 1745 when Bonnie Prince Charlie passed through them for the last time – they won't open again unless the Stuarts regain their place on the throne. An 18th-c brewery still produces tasty beers; you can try them between 3 and 4pm on Fri Jun–Sept. Traquair is particularly popular with our contributors, and with a maze, art gallery, and antique and craft shops (best on Weds and Thurs) as well as the house and gardens, there's plenty to see. Meals, snacks, shop, some disabled access; cl am (exc Jun–Aug), and all Oct–Apr (exc pm Fri–Sun in Oct); (01896) 830323; *£4.50, £2 grounds only. The Traquair Arms is good.

🐾⚔ **Uddingston** NS6960 GLASGOW ZOO (Calderpark) Growing open-plan zoo, specialising in cats and reptiles (snake-handling every day), with other rare mammals and birds,

children's farm, wildlife garden, and wknd car boot sales. Snacks, shop, disabled access; cl 25 Dec; (0141) 771 1185; £4.40 (less in winter). Nearby is picturesquely set BOTHWELL CASTLE, now ruined, but once the finest stone castle in Britain; in winter cl pm Thurs and all day Fri; £1.50.

⬇ᴛ **Wanlockhead** NS8713 MUSEUM OF LEAD MINING (B797) Guided tours of an 18th-c lead mine, and miners' cottages furnished in the styles of 1740 and 1890. You can have a go at panning for gold. Meals, snacks, shop, limited disabled access; cl Nov–Easter; (01659) 74387; £3.50. This remote village is Scotland's highest.

⚔🎦☕⚓ **Whithorn** NX4440 Scotland's first-recorded Christian settlement was established here by St Ninian 1,500 years ago. There have been several churches on the site since, the last of the line the ruined 13th-c priory you can see today. Archaeologists have been hard at work here for some time, and you can generally watch the dig's progress during the summer. An excellent visitor centre and museum have plenty of the finds, with some fine Celtic crosses. Shop, disabled access; museum and visitor centre cl Oct–Easter (though you may still be able to wander round the priory ruins then); (01988) 500508; *£2.70. Down on the coast the Isle of Whithorn is a picturesque harbour with BOAT TRIPS and lots of yachtsmen: the Steam Packet has good local fish. **The coasts** have some fine stretches, with some attractive villages. On the W coast, Portpatrick NW9954 is an attractive harbour town, usually with something going on down by the water, and Kippford NX8354 and Rockcliffe NX8453 are charming yachting places; there's a vast stretch of tidal sands backed by dunes just around the headland from Rockcliffe. All have useful pubs serving food.

★ **Other attractive villages** with decent pubs in the area include Auchencairn NX7951 (don't miss the lane down to Balcary Bay), Cramond NT1876 (Lauriston Castle here is interesting, with mostly Edwardian décor and antiques; cl Fri, and wkdys Nov–Mar; £3.50), Dunure NS2515, Eskdalemuir NY2597 (it also has an unexpected Tibetan Buddhist temple and monastery), Gifford NT5368, Kirkcowan NX3260, Kirkcudbright NX6851 (particularly enjoyable), Larkhall NS7651, Lilliesleaf NT5325, Sorn NS5526 and Symington NS3831. Some Clydeside pubs with decent food and good sea views include the Cardwell at Cardwell Bay in Gourock NS2477 and the Spinnaker there, and the Lookout in Troon Marina NS3230. Besides those we've mentioned as places to eat at or stay in, inns where you can get a decent bite to eat and which are particularly well placed for walkers, drivers or just strollers in these parts include the Murray Arms, Masons Arms and Angel at Gatehouse of Fleet NX5956, Golf Hotel at Gullane NT4882, Breadalbane Hotel at Kildonan NS0231, Swan at Kingholm Quay NX9773, Border at Kirk Yetholm NT8328, Selkirk Arms at Kirkcudbright NX6851 and Buccleuch Arms at St Boswells NT5931.

Walks

The Borders hills have plentiful solitary hill-walking. The Southern Upland Way (which makes a 212-mile coast-to-coast journey over the hills from Portpatrick to Cockburnspath) is a good basis for day walks, though large distances between places often make it hard to find focal points for walks. The **Eildon Hills** ⌂-1 above Melrose NT5434 are splendidly compact, giving a very pleasing ridge walk along the top. **St Mary's Loch** NT2422 ⌂-2 is tracked by the Southern Upland Way along its E shore; the Tibbie Shiels Inn is a handy stop here. A short drive to the S is a car park and starting point for a pretty walk up a narrow glen to the spectacular Grey Mare's Tail waterfalls NY0195. You can continue beyond them along Tail Burn to Loch Skeen NT1716.

The Dumfries and Galloway coast is long and unspoilt. Good peaceful walks include from Rockcliffe NX8453 E to **Castle Hill Point** NY9169 ⌂-3 and beyond; or to **Balcary Point** NX8249 ⌂-4 on the W side of Auchencairn Bay; or around the **Mull of Galloway** NX1530 ⌂-5, Scotland's SW toe. **Criffel** NX9562 ⌂-6, S of Dumfries, gives from its summit an astonishing view of the English Lake District over the Solway Firth; the best access point is New Abbey NX9666. The **Rhinns of Kells** ridge ⌂-7 has energetic hill walking from Forrest Lodge NX5586 NW of New Galloway. Galloway Forest Park has attractive trails around **Loch Trool** NX4179 ⌂-8, and a walk up Merrick NX0054, the highest point in SW Scotland.

There is excellent walking close to Edinburgh. **Arthur's Seat** ⌂-9 in Holyrood Park is a mountain virtually in the city centre – a great volcanic mass giving a wonderful panorama over the city, and just S **Blackford Hill** ⌂-10 has more of the same.

The **Firth of Forth** ⌂-11 has excellent shoreside walks along the sands from Aberlady NT4679 to North Berwick NT5485, with stop-off possibilities at Dirleton NT5184 and Gullane NT4882; a good bus service connects the shoreside villages between North Berwick and Edinburgh, though the hinterland is dull. At **Dunbar** NT6778 ⌂-12, the John Muir Country Park includes the jagged ruins of Dunbar Castle, and a section of coast with clifftop walks and the marshy inlets of Belhaven Bay. **St Abb's Head** NT9169 ⌂-13 has the best of the E coast scenery around it; walk from Eyemouth or St Abbs, with a good path along the cliffs.

W of Edinburgh, from the Cramond Brig Hotel on the A90, you can walk along the wooded **River Almond** ⌂-14 to Cramond NT1876, cross the Almond by ferry, then go along the shore past Dalmeny House, and finish below the Forth Bridge at South Queensferry NT1477. There are frequent buses back to the start, and to Edinburgh. The **Pentland Hills** NT1358 ⌂-15, within easy reach of Edinburgh, are genuine uplands with some good high-level walks and attractive reservoirs.

The **Falls of Clyde** NS8841 ⌂-16 just outside Lanark are dramatic when the hydro-electric station upriver opens the sluices; a path snakes around river cliffs from New Lanark NS8842. The **Culzean Castle** estate NS3309 ⌂-17 nr Ayr is a country park with an abundance of paths; woods, landscaped grounds, a lake, and the adjacent coast add up to a worthwhile outing. The **Greenock Cut** NS2474 ⌂-18 (part of an elaborate abandoned water scheme for Greenock below) allows a level walk meandering around a hillside terrace giving views into the Highlands. The country parks around Glasgow have lots of short walks: the one by **Mugdock** NS5576 ⌂-19, N of the city, has 2 castle ruins, a view over Glasgow, and an attractive loch. Level walks can take in the early stages of the West Highland Way, which starts at Milngavie NS5574 and takes glen routes to Fort William (up in the area we discuss next), the scenery getting better all the way.

Where to eat

Auchencairn NX7951 SMUGGLERS Main St (01556) 640331 18th-c inn with clean, fresh and comfortable lounge bar and eating area serving good food inc outstanding puddings and cakes. **£20|£4.50.**

Bearsden NS5471 FIFTY-FIVE BC 128 Drymen Rd (0141) 942 7272 Friendly little place with reliably good honest cooking, and pleasant staff; cl 1st Jan; disabled access. **£30|£5.**

East Linton NT5977 DROVERS (01620) 860298 18th-c pub with attractively furnished bar, fresh interesting food inc local fish in upstairs restaurant, and young enthusiastic staff; disabled access. **£20|£6.**

Edinburgh NT2473 ATRIUM 10 Cambridge St (0131) 228 8882 Next to Usher Hall and Traverse Theatre, this unusually modern restaurant has wire sculptures, railway sleepers, and dim lighting from glass torches, cheerful, friendly staff, a varied, interesting wine list, and extremely good, imaginative modern Scottish food – lunchtime snack menu, too; cl am Sat, Sun, 1 wk Christmas/New Year; disabled access. **£30 dinner, £22.50 lunch|£5.50.**

Edinburgh NT2672 KALPNA 2–3 St Patrick Sq (0131) 667 9890 Extremely good Indian restaurant with carefully cooked very fresh Gujerati vegetarian food (super lunchtime buffets) and efficient service; cl Sun and Christmas/New Year; disabled access. **£14.50|£4.50.**

Edinburgh NT2573 PIERRE VICTOIRE 38–40 Grassmarket (0131) 226 2442 Bustling French restaurant with cheerful atmosphere, very good-value food (especially at lunchtime), and decent little wine list; cl 25 Dec, 1 Jan. **£16|£5.**

Glasgow NS5667 DI MAGGIOS 61 Ruthven Lane (0141) 334 8560 A Glasgow institution with good Italian and other food, and a cheerful atmosphere; disabled access. **£12.50|£3.95.**

Glasgow NS5865 HORSESHOE BAR 17 Drury St (0141) 221 3051 Good unspoilt Victorian pub with horseshoe motif throughout, popular with lawyers and journalists, and amazingly cheap food; karaoke every night; no bar food Sun; **£2.40 3-course lunch.**

Glasgow NS5965 ROGANO 11 Exchange Place (0141) 248 4055 Long-standing restaurant in splendid 1930s ocean liner style with quite an emphasis on fish – vegetarian and meaty dishes, too; Café Rogano (downstairs) is open all day for lighter meals. **£35.50 in restaurant, £22 in café|£6.95.**

Glasgow NS5667 UBIQUITOUS CHIP 12 Ashton Lane, Byres Rd (0141) 334 5007 Friendly and informal restaurant (no chips, hence the name) in Victorian coach house with interesting modern Scottish cooking, outstanding wines, and no smoking areas; disabled access; cl 25 Dec, 31 Dec, 1 Jan. **£28.60 lunch,**

£36.60 dinner|£4.95. Upstairs is similar but less expensive.

Glasgow NS5865 WILLOW TEA ROOM 217 Sauchiehall St (0141) 332 0521 Beautifully restored from the 1903 art deco original with careful reproductions of the stylish furniture, this tearoom (and the newly opened downstairs Gallery) offers pastries and cakes, good sandwiches, toasties, filled croissants and bagels, salads, teas (herbal, fruit and loose), quite a choice of coffees, and milk shakes. |£3.95.

Lanark NS8843 EAST INDIA COMPANY 32 Wellgate (01555) 663827 Simply but attractively decorated Indian restaurant with exceptionally good, carefully prepared food, and helpful friendly service; disabled access. £15|£4.50.

Lanark NS8843 LA VIGNA 40 Wellgate (01555) 664320 Imaginative Italian menu with good basics, more imaginative dishes and lots of fresh fish; cl am Sun; disabled access. £25.50|£8.25.

Linlithgow NS9977 CHAMPANY (01506) 834532 Wonderful Aberdeen Angus beef as well as lovely fresh fish (they also have their own smoke-house), home-made ice-creams, and good wines; cheaper bistro-style meals in their Chop & Ale House next door; restaurant cl am Sat, Sun 25 Dec, 1 Jan; children over 8 in restaurant; disabled access. £50|£15.75.

Monreith NX3541 GLEN ROY (01988) 700466 Friendly restaurant with good home cooking using fresh local produce – lovely fish; cl Mon, last 2 wks Nov; disabled access. £20|£5.95.

EAST SCOTLAND

Picturesque scenery – mountain, valley and coast; plenty to see and do, with memorable outings.

The best scenery here is in the north: both Highland, and the picturesque valleys – the well known Spey, Dee and Don, and lesser-known places such as the Angus glens of Glen Clova, Glen Esk and Glen Isla. Further south, the Trossachs are a sort of Highlands in miniature, with lovely if small-scale landscapes of loch, river, forest, moor and mountain, but not the grandeur of the true Highlands. The coast is attractive, with appealing fishing villages in Fife, and a little-known but charming stretch from Nairn to Aberdeen, with good sands, quaint little coves and awesome cliffy crags such as Slains Castle and the nearby Bullers of Buchan.

There are plenty of rewarding days out, from the distinctive towns and cities to glorious castles, palaces and great houses. The Kincraig wildlife park is an excellent-value family outing, and other good varied family attractions include the deep-sea centre at North Queensferry, Landmark Park at Carrbridge, the lively science and technology centre in Aberdeen, the unique collection of great land birds and other creatures at Collessie, and (for some children at least) the Fraserburgh lighthouse museum.

The relatively few roads through the best parts do tend to make them feel crowded in high summer; to get a feeling of peace, June (when it's still light as midnight approaches) is much better.

Where to stay

Aberdeen NJ9305 Ferryhill House 169 Bon Accord St, Aberdeen AB11 6UA (01224) 590867 **£63**; 9 rms. Well run small hotel with comfortable and spacious communicating bar areas, well over 100 malt whiskies, real ales, friendly staff, a wide choice of food in bar and restaurant and lots of tables on the neat, well sheltered lawns; cl 25 Dec–1 Jan.

Aberfeldy NN8249 Farleyer House Aberfeldy, Perthshire PH15 2JE (01887) 820332 *£150, plus winter breaks; 19 pretty rms. Charming country house with fine Tay Valley views, log fires, antiques and flowers in library and drawing room, excellent food in airy and elegant restaurant and Scottish bistro; use of nearby leisure club; disabled access.

Alloa NS8794 Gean House Gean Park, Tullibody Rd, Alloa, Clackmannanshire FK10 2HS (01259) 219275 *£120, plus special breaks; 7 luxury rms. Carefully restored mansion house in mature parkland with views of the Ochil Hills; elegant drawing room with inglenook fireplace, minstrels' gallery and marvellous windows, cosy library, and very good food in no smoking walnut-panelled dining room overlooking the rose garden.

Ardeonaig NN6635 Ardeonaig Ardeonaig, Killin, Perthshire FK21 8SU (01567) 820400 *£87, plus special breaks; 14 rms. Extended 17th-c farmhouse on the S shore of Loch Tay with log fire in snug and lounge, a library with fine views, and good food using plenty of fish and game; salmon fishing rights on the loch – as well as fishing for trout and char – a drying and rod room, and boats and outboards; shooting and stalking can be arranged, lots of surrounding walks, and pony trekking; cl Nov–Mar.

Auchterarder NN9211 Gleneagles Auchterarder, Perthshire PH3 1NF (01764) 662231 **£305**; 234 individually decorated rms. Grand hotel in lovely surroundings with attractive gardens and outstanding leisure facilities: golf courses (inc a championship one designed by Jack Nicklaus), shooting, riding, fishing, a health spa, tennis, squash, bowling green, croquet and even falconry; comfortable, elegant high-ceilinged day rooms, a fine new bar, exceptional service, pianists, good food using local produce (much is home-grown) in 4 restaurants; disabled access.

Ballater NO3695 Auld Kirk Royal Deeside, Ballater, Aberdeenshire AB35 5RQ (013397) 55762 *£44, plus winter breaks; 6 attractive rms. 19th-c church, converted to a hotel in 1990, still with bell tower (the bell is in the main entrance), stained glass and exposed rafters; lacy dining room has original pillared pine ceiling, homely decor in public rooms with lots of knick-knacks, home cooking; cl 25 Dec–1 Jan.

Ballater NO3695 Balgonie Country House Braemar Place, Ballater, Aberdeenshire AB35 5NQ (013397) 55482 *£100, plus special breaks. 9 pretty rms. Quietly set and spotlessly kept Edwardian house with fine views from 4 acres of mature gardens, particularly helpful friendly owners, fresh flowers, games and books in lounges, and most enjoyable food using the best local produce in charming dining room; cl Jan–Feb; children over 5; dogs by arrangement (away from public rooms).

Ballater NO3695 Green Inn 9 Victoria Rd, Ballater, Aberdeenshire AB35 5QQ (013397) 55701 *£49.50 inc dinner, plus special breaks; 3 pleasing rms. Friendly and attractively decorated restaurant with rooms, delicious food using the best local produce and inc interesting Scottish cheeses, fine breakfasts; cl 2 wks Nov.

Balquhidder NN4318 Monachyle Mhor Balquhidder, Lochearnhead, Perthshire FK19 8PQ (01877) 384622 *£60; 10 rms with fine views overlooking Voil and Doine lochs. Remote 18th-c farmhouse/hotel several miles W of Balquhidder on 2,000-acre estate with prettily furnished rooms and good food using own game and herbs; private fishing and stalking for guests; cl last 2 wks Jan; no children.

Blairgowrie NO1244 KINLOCH HOUSE, Blairgowrie, Perthshire PH10 6SG (01250) 884237 *£183 **full board,** plus special breaks; 21 individually decorated rms. Creeper-covered 19th-c country house in 25 acres of parkland with highland cattle and fine views; relaxed lounges, comfortable bar, pretty conservatory with lots of plants, and fine choice of carefully prepared food in an elegant dining room; popular sportsmen's room with own entrance, drying facilities, gun cupboard, freezer, game larder and so forth; cl 20–30 Dec; no children under 7 in dining room; disabled access.

Bridge of Cally NO1451 BRIDGE OF CALLY Bridge of Cally, Blairgowrie, Perthshire PH10 7JJ (01250) 886231 *£59, plus special breaks; 9 rms. In an acre of grounds along the River Ardle, this former drovers' inn is a friendly family-run place with good-value home-made food using seasonal game in restaurant and comfortable bar; cl 25–26 Dec.

Bridge of Marnoch NJ5950 OLD MANSE OF MARNOCH Bridge of Marnoch, Huntly, Aberdeenshire AB54 7RS (01466) 780873 *£90, plus special breaks; 5 light, well equipped rms. Neat Georgian country house in 3 acres of gardens on the banks of the River Deveron, with antiques in comfortable sitting room, a friendly and informal atmosphere, imaginative 4-course set dinner in elegant dining room, a carefully chosen wine list, and superb breakfasts; liked by fishing people; cl 2 wks Oct; children over 12.

Callander NN6208 POPPIES Leny Rd, Callander, Perthshire FK17 8AL (01877) 330329 *£50, plus special breaks; 8 rms. Small private hotel with excellent food in popular and attractive candlelit dining room, convivial bar with RAF theme, comfortable lounge, helpful friendly owners, and seats in the garden; cl 1 Oct–1 Apr; disabled access.

Carronbridge NS7585 LOCHEND FARM Carronbridge, Denny Stirlingshire FK6 5JJ (01324) 822778 £34; 2 rms, shared bthrm. 18th-c farmhouse in lovely position beside Loch Coulter on 750-acre upland sheep farm, with sitting room, dining room and carefully prepared farmhouse cooking using own and local farm produce; cl Nov–Easter; no children.

Crianlarich NN3726 ALLT-CHAORAIN COUNTRY HOUSE Crianlarich, Perthshire FK20 8RU (01838) 300283 *£74, plus special breaks; 7 rms. Comfortable small hotel with homely atmosphere, log fire in lounge, honesty bar, sunroom with marvellous views, and good home-cooked food in panelled dining room; lots of fishing, golf and walks nearby; cl 1 Nov–Easter; children over 7; disabled access.

Dalcross NH7451 EASTER DALZIEL FARM Dalcross, Inverness IV1 2JL (01667) 462213 *£38, plus special breaks; 3 rms with shared bthrm. Early Victorian farmhouse on 210 acres of family-run mixed farm (beef cattle and grain) with friendly helpful owners, log fire in lounge, good Scottish breakfasts in big dining room and – when farm commitments allow – evening meal using own beef, lamb and vegetables; holiday cottages, too; cl Christmas/New Year.

Dunblane NN7606 CROMLIX HOUSE Kinbuck, Dunblane, Perthshire FK15 9JT (01786) 822125 *£175, plus special breaks; 14 rms inc 8 spacious suites. Walking, loch and river fishing or shooting are available on the 3,000 acres around this rather gracious country house; relaxing day rooms with fine antiques and family portaits, an informal atmosphere, very good food using estate game and local meats and fish in 2 dining rooms, and courteous service; cl 2–28 Jan.

Dunkeld NN9849 KINNAIRD HOUSE Kinnaird Estate, Dunkeld, Perthshire PH8 0LB (01796) 482440 £230, plus special breaks; 9 spacious, individually decorated rms. 18th-c country-house hotel on 9,000-acre estate with very restful civilised atmosphere in deeply comfortable antiques-filled rooms, lovely flowers, family mementos and pictures, log fires, good creative food in no smoking dining room with early 19th-c hand-painted frescoes, and a fine wine list; excellent fishing on River Tay and 3 hill lochs, and shooting; cl Mon and Tues during Jan/Feb; children over 12.

East Haugh NN9656 EAST HAUGH HOUSE East Haugh, Pitlochry, Perthshire PH16 5JS (01796) 473121 *£58, plus special breaks; 12 rms, 4 in converted bothy. Turreted stone house with lots of character, a delightful conservatory bar, house-party atmosphere, helpful cheerful owners, and very good popular food inc local seafood and game in season; excellent shooting, stalking and salmon and trout fishing on surrounding local estates; cl Feb.

Elgin NJ2162 MANSION HOUSE The Haugh, Elgin, Moray IV30 1AW (01343) 548811 £120, plus special breaks; 23 rms. Relaxed and friendly Scottish baronial mansion with prettily furnished public rooms, fresh flowers, lovely food inc fine breakfasts, and good wine list; country club facilities; disabled access.

Fintry NS6287 CULCREUCH CASTLE Fintry, Glasgow G63 0LW (01360) 860228 *£106, plus special breaks; 8 individually decorated rms with lovely views. Scotland's oldest inhabited castle, nearly 700 years old, in beautiful 1,600-acre parkland and surrounding hills and moors, with log fires and antiques in the public rooms, good freshly prepared food in candlelit panelled dining room, and a friendly relaxed atmosphere; 8 modern Scandinavian holiday lodges, too.

Glendevon NN9904 TORMAUKIN Glendevon, Dollar, Clackmannanshire FK14 7JY (01259) 781252 £72, plus special breaks; 10 rms, some in converted stable block. Comfortable neatly kept inn in good walking country, with loch and river fishing, lots of golf courses within reach, a beamed dining room and softly lit bar, very good food (soup and coffee all day), and fine breakfasts; cl 2 wks mid-Jan; limited disabled access.

Glenrothes NO2803 BALBIRNIE HOUSE Balbirnie Park, Markinch, Glenrothes, Fife KY7 6NE (01592) 610066 £160, plus special breaks; 30 rms. Fine Georgian country house in 416-acre park landscaped in Capability Brown style, with fresh flowers, open fires and antiques in gracious public rooms, extremely good inventive food, and a big wine list; disabled access.

Grantown-on-Spey NJ0328 CULDEARN HOUSE Woodlands Terrace, Grantown-on-Spey, Moray PH26 3JU (01479) 872106 *£120 full board, plus special breaks; 9 rms. Victorian granite stone house with homely decor and local watercolours, a friendly chatty atmosphere, and enjoyable Scottish food; packed lunches on request; cl 1 Nov–28 Feb; children over 10.

Inverness NH6245 BUNCHREW HOUSE Bunchrew, Inverness IV3 6TA (01463) 234917 £110, plus special breaks; 15 individually decorated rms. Warmly friendly 17th-c mansion on the shore of Beauly Firth with fine views and landscaped gardens, log fire in the elegant panelled drawing room, and traditional cooking using local produce and local game and venison.

Kirkton of Glenisla NO2160 GLENISLA Kirkton of Glenisla, Blairgowrie, Perthshire PH11 8PH (01575) 582223 *£80, plus special breaks; 6 rms. Attractively placed, peaceful 17th-c coaching inn, prettily restored with natural unpainted wood throughout, happily unmatched furniture, bar with open fire and 2 real ales, good food, very attentive owners and a cheerful, warm atmosphere; nice garden; cl 20–27 Dec; dogs welcome.

Monymusk NJ6815 GRANT ARMS Monymusk, Inverurie, Aberdeenshire AB51 7HJ (01467) 651226 £62; 17 rms, some with own bthrm. Smart old inn with dark-panelled lounge bar divided into 2 areas by a log fire in the stub wall, simpler public bar, and exclusive right to 15 miles of good trout and salmon fishing on the River Don; ghillie available; disabled access.

Nairn NH8856 CLIFTON HOUSE Viewfield St, Nairn IV12 4HW (01667) 453119 £96, plus special breaks; 12 individually decorated comfortable rms. Lovely, civilised, flower-filled old family hotel (the present owner has lived in this elegant Victorian house all his life and has been running it as a hotel since 1952), individually furnished with antiques, paintings and sculptures; extremely good food using local eggs, fish, meat and game, fine breakfasts with home-made jams, bread, and oatcakes, and an exceptional wine list;

during the winter they stage some 20 concerts, plays and recitals; cl Dec/Jan; pets welcome.

Peat Inn NO4509 PEAT INN Peat Inn, Cupar, Fife KY15 5LH (01334) 840206 *£135, plus special breaks; 8 luxurious rms. Famous restaurant with rooms: beams and white plaster walls, log fires and comfortable sofas, friendly service, fine interesting food using the best local produce inc plenty of game and seafood, and an excellent wine list; cl Sun, Mon; disabled access.

Pitlochry NN9162 KILLIECRANKIE Pitlochry, Perthshire PH16 5LG (01796) 473220 £100 inc dinner, plus special breaks; 10 spotless rms. Comfortable country hotel in spacious grounds with putting course and croquet lawn, splendid mountain views, mahogany-panelled bar with stuffed animals and fine wildlife paintings, spacious sitting room with books and games, a relaxed atmosphere, very friendly owners and helpful staff, and excellent, well presented food in elegant restaurant; cl 1 wk mid-Dec, Jan–Feb.

Scone NO1526 MURRAYSHALL HOUSE Scone, Perth PH2 7PH (01738) 551171 *£120, plus special breaks; 26 rms, plus lodge which sleeps 6. Handsome mansion in 300 acres of parkland, very popular with golfers (it has its own course): comfortable, elegant public rooms, warm friendly staff, a relaxed atmosphere, imaginative food, good wines; dogs welcome; disabled access.

Spean Bridge NN2491 LETTERFINLAY LODGE Spean Bridge, – Inverness-shire PH34 4DZ (01397) 712622 £76, plus special breaks; 13 rms, 9 with own bthrm. Secluded and genteel family-run country house with picture window in extensive modern bar overlooking loch; elegantly panelled small cocktail bar, good popular food, friendly attentive service; grounds run down through rhododendrons to the jetty and Loch Lochy; fishing can be arranged; cl Nov–Apr.

To see and do

SCOTLAND FAMILY ATTRACTION OF THE YEAR

🐾 **Kincraig** NH8305 HIGHLAND WILDLIFE PARK (B9152) Owned by the same charity as Edinburgh Zoo, this 260-acre wildlife park somehow manages to seem a bit wilder than most animal attractions; perhaps it's because they specialise in species once native to the area, so you really get a feeling that the animals could have wandered out of the surrounding woods and mountains. You drive safari-style around enclosures of reindeer, bears, wildcats and enormous bison, and it's better value the more people you have in your car. A guidebook is included in the entrance price (as we've said before, something more places should do), as is children's face-painting at wknds (perhaps not such a universal necessity, but very welcome here). The most exciting feature at the moment is the new wolf territory, where a walkway takes you to a safe vantage point right in the heart of the enclosure. Plenty of rare breeds – including the wild Przewalksi's horses, one of the world's rarest mammals – and you may see red squirrels feeding in the forest. You can wander round smaller themed habitats for foxes, badgers, otters and lynx, and there are trails for children. Every afternoon the warden leads feeding tours, and at wknds there's an afternoon talk on a particular animal. They have sheepdog demonstrations behind the picnic area at 2pm on Tues, Thurs and Sun. Easily good for a couple of hours on a dry day – longer on Sunday afternoons when there's more going on. They don't open in winter if the weather is bad, so best to ring before setting out then. The visitor centre usually closes slightly earlier than the park as a whole. Snacks and shop in visitor centre (cl in winter), disabled access; cl Nov–Mar in bad weather; (01540) 651270; admission depends on how many there are in your car, from £6 for a car with 1 passenger to £17 for one with 5 (less in winter).

★ ! ✿ 🏢 ♨ 🏛 † 🕸 **Aberdeen** NJ9305
Scotland's third-largest city, with a
large and interesting HARBOUR, well
worth pottering around (especially its
early morning Fishmarket). The
granite centre has wide, orderly
streets not unlike Edinburgh's New
Town in places, and parks.
SATROSPHERE 🎫 (Justice Mill Lane)
Lively hands-on science and
technology centre – everything is
there to be touched, and they have
lots of changing displays and
exhibitions. Great fun. Snacks, shop,
disabled access; cl 25–26 Dec, 1–2
Jan; (01224) 213232; £3.50.
MARITIME MUSEUM (Provost Ross's
House, Shiprow) In the town's third-
oldest building (very striking), with
very good displays on the city's
nautical heritage. Meals, snacks,
shop, disabled access; cl 25–26 Dec,
1–2 Jan; (01224) 337700; free.
PROVOST SKENE'S HOUSE (Guestrow)
Named after its most famous
resident, a stately well restored 16th-c
house with refurbished period rooms,
and remarkable painted ceilings.
Meals, snacks; cl Sun, 25–26 Dec,
1–2 Jan; (01224) 641086; free. Other
good museums include the civic
history collection in the 17th-c
TOLBOOTH on Castle St (cl Mon,
Nov–Mar; free), and the ART GALLERY
on Schoolhill, with a first-class
collection of Scottish and English
painting since the 16th c, especially
strong on contemporary works (cl am
Sun, 25–26 Dec, 1–2 Jan; free).
MARISCHAL COLLEGE (Broad St) The
later Protestant rival to King's (see
below), though the two were joined
to form Aberdeen University in the
last century. A splendid neo-Gothic
structure, it has a decent MUSEUM; cl
Sat, am Sun; (01224) 273131; free.
The Ferryhill House Hotel (Bon
Accord St), Royal Hotel (Bath St) and
Athol (King's Gate, W of centre) are
useful for lunch, and the Prince of
Wales (St Nicholas Lane) is the best
proper pub in this part of Scotland.

N of the centre, really too far to
walk, the OLD TOWN above the River
Don seems quite separate. It has some
charming old streets to explore, and
attractive buildings; its
pedestrianised villagey High St is
dominated by the university,
especially the very Oxbridge-like
King's College, founded in 1495. A
VISITOR CENTRE outlines its history.
Meals, snacks (in barrel-vaulted
former library), shop, disabled
access; cl am Sun; (01224) 273702;
free. Its CHAPEL is one of the most
complete examples of a medieval
collegiate church in Britain. ST
MACHAR'S CATHEDRAL is an austere
mainly 15th-c church notable for its
painted wooden heraldic ceiling. It's
the only granite cathedral in the
world. Just along from here the 19th-
c CRUICKSHANK BOTANIC GARDEN (St
Machar Drive) covers 11 acres with
various smaller gardens – rock,
water, rose and herbaceous – as well
as trees and shrubs and a small
terrace garden; cl winter wknds;
(01224) 272704; free. Leafy Seaton
Park is famous for its 14th-c Brig (or
bridge) o' Balgownie.

★ ✘ **Aberfeldy** NN8549 This quiet
and pleasant small Highland
shopping town has a fine 18th-c stone
bridge designed by William Adam.
There's a well restored WATERMILL on
Mill St (still mills oatmeal; all parts
open to visit), and just S of town the
delightful 1½-mile walk along to the
oak-lined Den and Falls of Moness
inspired Burns's song *The Birks of
Aberfeldy*. Weem, for a good lunch at
the Ailean Chraggan, is close by.

🍺 ⚡ **Aberfoyle** NN5201 Lots of
woollen shops, and in the heart of
Queen Elizabeth Forest Park, so
lovely scenery around; you can hire
bikes. SCOTTISH WOOL CENTRE 🎫 The
story of Scottish wool from sheep to
shop, entertainingly told by a live
sheep show in the amphitheatre. They
have demonstrations of spinning and
weaving. Meals, snacks, good shop,
disabled access; cl 25 Dec, 1 Jan;
(01877) 382850; £2.50.
🏰 🕊 **Alford** NJ5716 GRAMPIAN
TRANSPORT MUSEUM 🎫 (A944) Big
collection of vintage vehicles, from
horse-drawn sledges and carriages to
motorcycles, cars and steamers;
always plenty going on. Snacks, shop,
disabled access; cl Nov–Mar;
(019755) 62292; £2.75. More

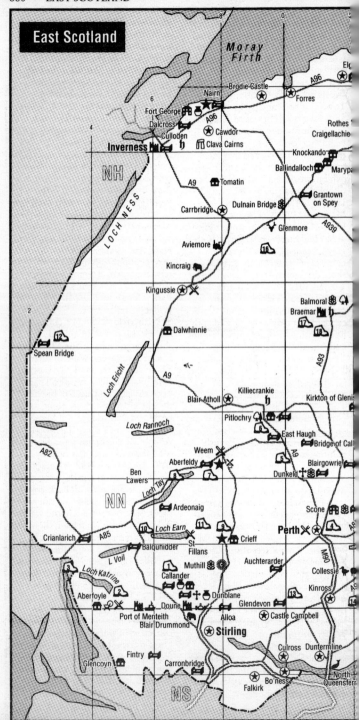

East Scotland

Moray Firth

Elg
A96
Brodie-Castle
Nairn ★ ⚑ Forres
Fort George ⚑ 6 A96
Dalcross Rothes
Culloden ★ Cawdor Craigellachie
Inverness Clava Cairns Knockando
Ballindalloch Maryp
NH
A9 Tomatin Grantown
Carrbridge ★ Dulnain Bridge on Spey
A939
Glenmore
Aviemore
16
Kincraig
Kingussie ★ Balmoral
Braemar
Dalwhinnie 17
18
NH
Spean Bridge 12
Loch Ericht
A9
Killiecrankie
Blair Atholl ★ Kirkton of Glenis
Pitlochry
Loch Rannoch East Haugh
Bridge of Call
A82
Weem
Aberfeldy Blairgowrie
Ben Dunkeld
Lawers 15
Loch Tay
NN
Ardeonaig Scone
10 Loch Earn 11
Crianlarich A85 St Perth ✕
Balquhidder Fillans ★ Crieff
L Voil
Muthill Auchterarder
Callander Collessie
Aberfoyle M90 Kinross
Doune 13
Port of Menteith Dunblane Glendevon 14
Blair Drummond Alloa
Stirling Castle Campbell
Culross Dunfermline
Fintry Bo'ness North
Glencoyn Carronbridge Queensferr
Falkirk
NS

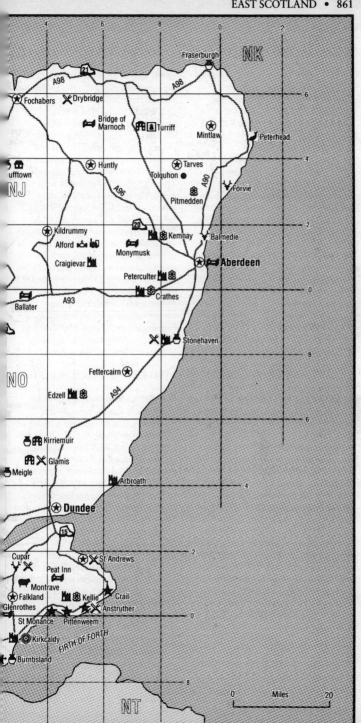

historic transport at the ALFORD
VALLEY RAILWAY next door, a narrow-
gauge passenger railway with trips in
2 one-mile sections, and a good static
display at the station. Shop, disabled
access; trains in steam wknds
Apr–Oct and pm daily Jun–Aug;
(019755) 62326; *£1.50. There's a
dry ski slope on Greystone Rd, and
the Forbes Arms at Bridge of Alford
has decent home cooking.

🏛 **Arbroath** NO6340 ARBROATH
ABBEY Substantial remains of 12th-c
abbey, connected with Thomas à
Becket and Robert the Bruce. Shop,
disabled access to ground floor only;
cl 12.30–1.30pm in winter, am Sun,
25–26 Dec, 1–2 Jan; (01241)
878756; £1.50.

🚂 **Aviemore** NH8912
Uncompromisingly modern ski-
resort village; the STRATHSPEY STEAM
RAILWAY covers 5 miles of great
scenery between here and the Boat of
Garten. Meals, snacks, shop, limited
disabled access; usually open daily
Jun–Sept, plus other dates and wknds
– best to ring for timetable; (01479)
810725; *£5. There are plenty of
places to get something to eat in this
sizeable tourist development (the
Olde Bridge is our current
recommendation); it's a useful
springboard for the Cairngorms and
Glen More.

♈ **Balmedie** NJ9618 COUNTRY PARK
Along a constantly shifting stretch of
coast, this is splendidly bleak-feeling
despite the closeness of Aberdeen.
The beaches are clean and safe.

🎱 ♈ **Balmoral Castle** NO2588 (off
the A93) The royal family's Highland
residence. Prince Albert bought the
property 4 years after he and Queen
Victoria had first rented it in 1848,
and had a new castle built here by
1855. You can't go inside, but you
can explore the wonderful gardens
and woodlands, and there are various
exhibitions in the ballroom. Snacks,
shop, disabled access; cl Sun
Easter–July, and all Aug–Easter;
(013397) 42334; *£3.50.

🏰 🎱 ! 🛇 **Blair Atholl** NN8666 BLAIR
CASTLE ▦ (off the A9) Nestling
among forests and heather-clad hills,
this is Scotland's most visited

privately owned house, dating back
to the 13th c, though largely
renovated in the 18th. You can see 32
of the rooms, and they recently
opened an 18th-c walled garden. A
piper outside every day in summer
adds to the atmosphere. Meals,
snacks, shop, disabled access to
ground floor only; cl Nov–Mar;
(01796) 481207; £5.50, plus grounds
charge of £2 per car. The Duke of
Atholl's unique private army turns
out here for its annual parade in May.
There's a friendly little FOLK MUSEUM
beside the turn-in for the White
Horse; cl am May–Oct (exc wkdys
July–Sept and all Nov–Apr); *£2.

🐾 **Blair Drummond** NS7399 SAFARI
AND LEISURE PARK (A84) Wild animals
in natural surroundings, with an
unusual aerial walkway above the big
cats' reserve and a boat trip round the
chimps' island. Very much a family
day out, with gentle rides, pets
corner, arcade, and playgrounds.
Feeding times of lions, sea lions, and
penguins are posted up near the
entrance. Meals, snacks, shops,
disabled access; cl Oct–Apr; (01786)
841456; £7. The Lion & Unicorn at
Thornhill does good family lunches.

🏛🎱🏰🛇♈🛇⬆T **Bo'ness** NS9880
The KINNEIL ESTATE includes the
interesting if not extensive remains of
a Roman fortlet, as well as a few later
ruins and remains. The converted
stables of adjacent Kinneil House
have a museum on the site's history,
with lots of local pottery. You can
still see the workshop where James
Watt developed the steam engine, and
there are pleasant woodland walks.
Shop, disabled access; cl 12.30–1.30
pm, and all Oct–Mar exc Sat;
(01506) 778530; free. BO'NESS &
KINNEIL RAILWAY Re-creation of the
days of steam complete with
relocated railway buildings and
Scotland's largest collection of
locomotives and rolling stock. The
round trip is 7m long, and takes
passengers to the woodlands of the
Avon Gorge at Birkhill, where there
are tours of an old clay mine. Snacks,
shop, disabled access to railway only;
trains usually run wknds Apr–mid-
Oct, and daily (exc Mon) July and

Aug, though you can see the locomotives all year; (01506) 822298; £6 mine and railway, £3.60 train only.

ⓗ 🚂 **Braemar** NO1491 One of the best-known Highland villages, with a good HERITAGE CENTRE (Mar Rd) showing useful films on the area's history and scenery (inc an interesting look at the building of Balmoral Castle), and on Braemar's famous Highland Gathering. Shops, disabled access; (013397) 41944; free. Slightly NE on the A93, BRAEMAR CASTLE has a highly unusual and charming exterior. Shop; cl Fri, and all Nov–Easter; (013397) 41219; £2. The Fife Arms (very much on the coach routes) is good for lunch.

🏰 🏛 ♿ **Brodie Castle** NH9757 (off the A96) Handsome gabled castle with extensive art collection featuring 17th-c paintings of the Dutch school, English watercolours and French Impressionists. Before the National Trust for Scotland took it over in 1980 it had been the seat of the same family since 1160. Outside are woodland walks and wildlife observation hides, and beautiful daffodils in spring. Snacks, shop, disabled access; cl am, and all Nov–Mar; (01309) 641371; £4; NTS. Their occasional evenings of traditional Scottish music are enjoyed by readers. The nearest really good place for a meal is the Clifton Hotel in Nairn.

✝ 👓 **Burntisland** NT2386 Once famous for shipbuilding (and shipbreaking), now a popular little resort, with an unusual octagonal CHURCH where the decision was made to produce the Authorised Version of the Bible in 1601. EDWARDIAN FAIR MUSEUM (High St, above library) Quirky museum re-creating the sights and sounds of the town fair, with rides, stalls and sideshows all modelled on those in a painting of the scene by a local artist; cl 1–2pm, all day Sun and bank hols; (01592) 260732; free.

👓 🏰 **Callander** NN6208 Quite a busy tourist town, popular in Victorian times thanks to the works of Walter Scott, and later this century for its

appearances in the original *Dr Finlay's Casebook*. ROB ROY AND TROSSACHS VISITOR CENTRE (Ancaster Sq) The story of Scotland's most whitewashed rascal (or brave supporter of the downtrodden, depending on your point of view), well told with hi-tech displays. Also information on the beautiful surrounding countryside. Shop, disabled access; cl wkdys Jan–Feb; (01877) 330342; *£2.50. KILMAHOG WOOLLEN MILL (just N) Restored watermill with 250-year-old working wheel, selling tweeds, tartans and other woollen gifts. Meals, snacks, shop, some disabled access; cl 25 Dec, 1 Jan; (01877) 330268; free. The Lade Inn out here and the Byre at Brig o' Turk out in the Trossachs are both good food places.

☺ ♿ 🌼 **Carrbridge** NH9022 LANDMARK HIGHLAND HERITAGE & ADVENTURE PARK Good family day out, with films on Highland life (inc one in 3-D), well signposted forest trails (one through the tree-tops), an elaborate adventure playground, and Forestry Heritage Park with fully operational steam-powered sawmill (Apr–Oct). You can sometimes have a go at log-cutting or bark-stripping. Great views from the top of the viewing tower. Meals, snacks, shop, disabled access; cl 25 Dec; (01479) 841614; *£5.80, less in winter. The Dalrachney Lodge Hotel does good lunches.

🚂 🌼 ♿ **Castle Campbell** NS9698 Once known as Castle Gloom, this late 15th-c castle was burned by Cromwell's troops in the 1650s, but still has its courtyard, great hall and barrel roof, as well as splendid views from the tower. Meals, snacks, shop; cl am Sun, 25–26 Dec, 1–2 Jan, and in winter pm Thurs and all day Fri; (01259) 742408; *£2.30. The most attractive approach is through the spectacular DOLLAR GLEN, 60 acres of Arthur Rackham-esque woodland; take care, some paths are steep and narrow, and can be dangerous after rain. The King's Seat in Dollar has good home-made food.

🏰 🎇 ⚘ **Cawdor** NH8450 CAWDOR CASTLE (B9090) Home of the Thanes of Cawdor since the 14th c, this splendid old house is one of the most entertaining as well as interesting places to visit in the whole area. Look out especially for the tree inside a tower and the freshwater well inside the house, as well as the more usual fine tapestries, furnishings and paintings (inc Dali's odd interpretation of the Macbeth tale). The busy grounds have several pretty gardens, craft and wool shops, nature trails, and a little pitch-and-putt course. Meals, snacks, shop, disabled access; cl Oct–Apr; (01667) 404615; £5, £2.50 grounds only. The nearby Cawdor Tavern is good for lunch.

🏛 **Clava Cairns** NH7748 A group of circular burial cairns from around 1600 BC surrounded by 3 concentric rings of great stones, on the banks of the River Nairn.

🐦 🐖 **Collessie** NO2813 OSTRICH KINGDOM (B937) Unique collection of ostriches, emus and rheas – they have birds of all ages (inc maybe newly hatched ones in the incubator house), as well as videos, play area, and animals like lambs, pigs, and wallabies. Meals, snacks, shop, good disabled access; (01337) 831830; *£3.85.

🏛 **Craigellachie** NJ2945 SPEYSIDE COOPERAGE CENTRE (Dufftown Rd) Working cooperage and visitor centre, with a viewing area to watch the craftsmen at work. There's a reconstructed Victorian cooperage where life-size models speak in the local dialect. Shop (wide range of wood goods), disabled access to exhibition only; cl Sun, winter Sats, 2 wks Christmas; (01340) 871108; £2. The little Fiddichside Inn (Keith Rd) is a charmingly old-fashioned fishing pub.

🏰 **Craigievar** NJ5509 CRAIGIEVAR CASTLE (A980) Perhaps the most fairytale-romantic of the area's castles, this picturesque early 17th-c multiple tower dotted with erratically shaped windows soars to a mushrooming of corbels, turrets and crow-stepped gables. Inside, a warren of narrow staircases climbs through a rich series of ornately beamed and plastered rooms. The National Trust for Scotland are worried that too many people come here, so if you do decide to visit (and it is worthwhile), try to avoid busy times – it's not a place to absorb coach parties comfortably. Castle cl am May–Sept and all Oct–Apr, grounds open all year; (013398) 83635; *£5.80; NTS.

🏛 🏰 **Crathes** NO7596 CRATHES CASTLE (A93) Beautiful 16th-c tower house with wonderful interiors – especially its ceiling paintings, filled with wise old sayings in a mixture of Scots and English. Best of all are the surrounding gardens, inc a 4-acre walled garden with a remarkable series of carefully toned colour borders. Meals, snacks, shop, some disabled access; cl Nov–Mar; (01330) 844525; *£4.50, garden only ticket available; NTS.

★ 🏰 **Crieff** NN8621 A pleasant airy town, perched on the edge of the Highlands. GLENTURRET DISTILLERY (A85) Scotland's oldest distillery, dating from 1775 and using the pure water of the Turret Burn. There's a statue of the distillery cat Towser, who died in 1987 but is still in the *Guinness Book of Records* as World Mousing Champion – challengers have 28,899 to beat. Good meals and snacks, shop, some disabled access; cl am Sun, all wknd Jan, 25–26 Dec, 1–2 Jan; (01764) 656565; *£2.90. Nearby a modern visitor centre has a pottery, plant centre and demonstrations of paperweight-making, and there's a Stuart Crystal factory shop on Muthill Rd.

🏵 **Culloden** NH7345 (B9006) The bleak site of the gruesome massacre in which the 25-year-old Duke of Cumberland destroyed the Highland army of Bonnie Prince Charlie. On the moor a cairn marks this last bloody battle fought on mainland Britain. You can see the Graves of the Clans and the Wells of the Dead, as well as the Old Leanach Cottage around which the battle was fought, now refurbished in period style. Meals, snacks, shop, disabled access; visitor centre cl Jan; (01463) 790607; £2.80; NTS. The Coach House (Stoneyfield, A96) does food.

★ 🏛 🏰 **Culross** NO3714 (off the

A985) Fascinating small town on the Forth, virtually unchanged since the 16th and 17th c. Until the 1930s this was because no one could afford any improvements, and since then its red pantiled-roofed houses have been carefully restored and preserved by the National Trust for Scotland (they are still lived in). The laird's PALACE, the first building the Trust purchased here, is fully furnished in 17th-c style, and they're creating a period garden. Guides are good at pointing out those small but fascinating details that make the difference between just another building and a real experience. Snacks, shop; cl wkdys in Oct, and all Nov–Mar; (01383) 880359; £4; NTS. The price includes admission to the Trust's 2 other main properties here, the TOWN HOUSE (a good visitor centre), and the STUDY, with a Norwegian painted ceiling in the drawing room. There are also the remains of a 13th-c abbey.

✣ Cupar NO3212 SCOTTISH DEER CENTRE (Bow of Fife, just W on the A91) You can stroke the deer and feed the young fawns at this friendly place, and there are also nature and heritage trails, aerial walkways and observation platforms, and an adventure playground. Snacks, shop, disabled access; (01337) 810391; £2.50.

▦ ⚘ Doune NN7201 DOUNE CASTLE (A84) A 14th-c stronghold with 2 fine restored towers, on the banks of the River Teith. Strong associations with Bonnie Prince Charlie and Walter Scott. Shop; in winter cl pm Thurs and all day Fri; (01786) 841742; *£2.30. Close by, the DOUNE MOTOR MUSEUM has around 50 cars on display. Meals, snacks, shop, disabled access; cl Dec–Mar; (01786) 841203; *£3. The village's bridge is said to have been built out of spite by James IV's tailor when the ferryman refused him passage.

☎ ⚘ Dufftown NJ3240 GLENFIDDICH DISTILLERY (slightly N on the A491) The only Highland distillery where you can follow the entire whisky production process from barley to bottle; most other distilleries bottle elsewhere. Tastings, shop, disabled

access; cl winter wknds, Christmas; (01340) 820373; free. Dufftown also has a useful museum.

❀ Dulnain Bridge NH9925 SPEYSIDE HEATHER (Skye of Curr, off the A95) Over 300 different types of heather growing in ornamental landscaped garden, along with exhibition on its various uses, and shop with wide range of heather-based goods. Home-made meals and snacks, garden centre, disabled access; cl Jan (exc by appointment); (01479) 851359; *75p exhibition.

✝ ⚘ Dunblane NN7801 A small town of ancient origin, its name now tragically familiar all over the world. Plenty of old buildings in its narrow streets, especially around the close of its elegant 13th-c CATHEDRAL. This incorporates a much older tower, and has a beautiful oval window that you can see only from outside. There's a MUSEUM nearby (cl 12.30–2pm, all day Sun, some Sats, and Oct–May; free) and the Stirling Arms has good food.

✿ ⚘ ▣ ! ❀ ✣ Dundee NO4030 Beneath the straightforward modern wrappings of this bustling city, you can uncover signs of its distinguished heritage in a number of museums. DISCOVERY POINT (Docks) ▦ Excellent lively visitor centre with hi-tech displays on the Royal Research Ship *Discovery*, moored here, which was the first British purpose-built research vessel, commissioned for Scott's ill-fated expedition to the Antarctic; displays too on him and others who used the ship. Snacks, shop, disabled access; cl 25 Dec, 1–2 Jan; (01382) 201245; £4.50. Nearby at Victoria Dock, the 1824 frigate UNICORN is the oldest British-built warship still afloat, now with a museum of naval life in her days in commission. Snacks, shop, limited disabled access; cl wknds Nov–Mar; (01382) 200900; *£3. Other museums worth a look include the MCMANUS GALLERIES (Albert Sq), with important works by 19th-c Scottish and English artists, and a splendid hall with vaulted ceiling and stained glass, and the BARRACK NATURAL HISTORY MUSEUM; both cl

Sun, 25–26 Dec, 1–2 Jan; free. MILLS OBSERVATORY (Balgay Park) Exhibits on space research and astronomy, as well as a small planetarium (by prior arrangement only), and splendid 10in refracting telescope. Shop; best to ring for opening times, which vary depending on when the sun sets – in autumn and winter for example they're open 4–10pm (not wknds or Mon); (01382) 435846; free. CAMPERDOWN COUNTRY PARK (off the A90) 400 acres of fine parkland with golf course, nature trails, woodland footpaths, and wildlife centre with indigenous animals from wolves to wildcats. Also adventure play area themed around the defeat of the Dutch at the 1797 Battle of Camperdown. Snacks, shop, disabled access; (01382) 432689; free, *£1.50 wildlife centre. BROUGHTY CASTLE MUSEUM (Broughty Ferry, 4m E off the A930) 15th-c seaside castle rebuilt in the 19th c to defend the estuary, now a maritime museum. Plenty of harpoons and whaling exhibits – whaling used to be one of Dundee's major industries. Shop; cl 1–2pm, all day Sun (exc pm summer) and Fri, 25–26 Dec, 1–2 Jan; (01382) 776121; free. The Number 10 (South Tay St), Royal Oak (Brook St), Mercantile (Commercial St) and Number 1 (Constitution Rd) all do good-value food, and in Broughty Ferry the Fisherman's Tavern and Ship (fantastic view upstairs) are good.

🏰 ✝ 🌳 ⊕ **Dunfermline** NT0987 Quite a prosperous light-industry town with a distinguished distant past; the remains of a Benedictine ABBEY and later church buildings are pleasantly set in quiet precincts away from the busy centre. The foundations of the original 11th-c church are still under the more elaborate Norman nave, and the grave of King Robert the Bruce is marked by a modern brass in the choir stalls. The monastery guest house was the birthplace of Charles I. Shop, mostly disabled access; cl am Sun, plus in winter pm Thurs and all day Fri; (01383) 739026; *£1.50. One of the major figures in Dunfermline's history is St Margaret

of Scotland, whose shrine is outside the abbey nr the East Gate. There's an exhibition on her life in ABBOT HOUSE on Maygate (cl 25 Dec, 1 Jan; (01383) 733266; £3), and the cave she used to pray in is 84 steps below the Glen Bridge car park (cl Oct–Easter; free). Other museums include the DISTRICT MUSEUM (Viewfield Terrace), looking at the local manufacture of damask linen (cl Sun; free), the PITTENCRIEFF HOUSE MUSEUM (Pittencrieff Park), a fine 17th-c mansion in a lovely rugged glen, with costume displays (cl Tues, and Nov–Apr; free), and the ANDREW CARNEGIE MUSEUM (Moodie St) focusing on the man who from humble origins here made a fortune in Pittsburgh steel, then gave away over $350 million – all the while claiming he didn't believe in charity (cl am Sun, am daily in winter; *£1.50). This last museum has handloom weaving demonstrations the first Fri of each month, May–Oct.

✝ 🏛 **Dunkeld** NO0243 and nearby Birnam are 2 pleasant tiny towns either side of the River Tay, a 15min walk between them. Dunkeld's CATHEDRAL has the tomb of the notorious Wolf of Badenoch, Alexander Stewart (the illegitimate son of English king Richard II), pretty preserved cottages (NTS), and walks through National Trust land around the waterfalls nr THE HERMITAGE, an 18th-c folly; there may be bat tours and other ranger-led walks in summer. Over in Birnam, a small garden next to the Birnam Institute recreates the house of Mrs Tiggywinkle and Peter Rabbit's burrow (summer only; free); Beatrix Potter spent holidays here. Birnam Wood (of *Macbeth* fame) has a venerable oak, and there's plenty of stirring walking country around.

🏰 🏛 **Edzell** NO5969 EDZELL CASTLE (B966) Some unique features at this pretty old place – the walled garden planted here in 1604, and the charming series of heraldic and mythical sculptures that decorate the walls around it; these alternate with recesses for flowers and nests for birds. They claim to have captured on camera the castle's rather active ghost. Shop, disabled access; in winter cl am Thurs and all day Fri; (01356) 648631; *£2.30. The Ramsay Arms in Fettercairn has decent food, and just N there's a lovely drive up Glen Esk, passing a wayside folk museum.

🎭 ⚲ 🏠 🏛 ⚘ ✝ **Elgin** NJ2162 is a shopping town of some poise, with some handsome ancient buildings and handy for the coast; Thunderton House has decent food. There's still quite a lot to see of the ruined CATHEDRAL, founded in 1224, and known as the Lantern of the North and the Glory of the Kingdom because of its extraordinary beauty and fine-traceried windows. The 15th-c nave has some ancient Celtic cross slabs with Pictish symbols, and you can go inside the spires. Snacks, shop, some disabled access; cl am Sun, plus in winter pm Thurs and all day Fri; (01343) 547171; £1.50. The MUSEUM in the High St has a world-famous fossil collection (cl am Sun, all Nov–Mar; £1.50), and there's a decent little MOTOR MUSEUM in a converted mill on Bridge St (cl Oct–Mar; £2). SPYNIE PALACE (2m N on the A941) Former residence of the Bishops of Moray, the biggest tower house in Scotland, with good views over Spynie Loch. Shop, disabled access; cl Oct–Mar; (01343) 546358; £1.50. PLUSCARDEN ABBEY (nr Barnhill, 5m SW) Fascinating; built in the 13th c, it gradually fell to ruin, but was rebuilt this century by monks from Priknash Abbey in Gloucs – they now sing a recently rediscovered chant which may well have been sung by St Columba himself; cl wk of annual retreat, usually in Nov; (01343) 890257; free.

⚘ ⚲ 🏠 🏛 **Falkirk** NS8880 CALLENDER PARK (just E on the A803) This huge park, with woodland walks and lots of summer activities, includes CALLENDER HOUSE, a striking old house used briefly as a headquarters by Oliver Cromwell. Remodelled in the last century to look like a French château, it's now a museum, with costumed guides interpreting its history. Part of the Antonine Wall, the Roman Empire's farthest frontier, runs through the grounds. Meals, snacks, shop, disabled access; house cl winter Suns; (01324) 503770; house *£1.80, park free. ROUGH CASTLE (6m W) One of the best preserved sections of the Antonine Wall; not too much is left of the Roman fort that once stood here, but you can still see the ramparts and ditches; free.

★ 🏛 ⚘ **Falkland** NO2507 FALKLAND PALACE Lovely Renaissance palace of the Stuart kings and queens, set below the Lomond Hills on the main street. Not all is as old as it looks, but it doesn't really matter – accurate restoration work has created a comfortably cosy and genuinely lived-in feel. Pleasant gardens and grounds, with the 1539 tennis courts said to be the oldest in Britain. Shop; cl am Sun, and Nov–Mar; (01337) 857397; £4.50, £2.30 garden only; NTS. Parts of the village are delightful and were Scotland's first conservation area – the Stag prettily set on the green is useful for lunch.

🏛 🏠 ⚘ **Fettercairn** NO6475 FASQUE (just N) still belongs to the Gladstones, and the Prime Minister lived here 1830–51. The main rooms look as if they've scarcely been changed (let alone modernised) since he moved to Wales, and it's quite cluttered with homely odds and ends. In summer 1997 a parcel of shooting targets turned up behind a chair posted from London in the 1920s and covered with 'Urgent' stickers – but not yet even opened. There's a touching gallery of servants' portraits. Snacks, shop, disabled access; cl Oct–Apr; (01561) 340569; *£3.50. FETTERCAIRN DISTILLERY (Distillery Rd) One of Scotland's oldest licensed distilleries, with tours, tastings, and good audio-visual show. Shop, disabled access to visitor centre only; cl Sun, and Oct–Apr; (01561) 340205; free. Fettercairn's square has a magnificent archway erected to commemorate a visit by Queen Victoria, and the Ramsay Arms has decent food. The drive along the twisting and climbing B974 Fettercairn–Banchory is good, with spectacular views from CAIRN O' MOUNT at the top – and when the water's high enough salmon jumping nr the Dee bridge as you enter Banchory.

☗ 🏠 🏚 🐟 **Fochabers** NJ3458 The small town has a very good FOLK MUSEUM on the High St (cl 1–2pm, free), and the Gordon Arms is a reliable food stop. BAXTERS VISITOR CENTRE (just W on the A96) Explores how the grocery shop set up by George and Margaret Baxter grew into a company whose food is now sold all over the world. Tours (not wknds), landcaped gardens and woodland walk. Meals, snacks, good shops, some disabled access; cl 25–26 Dec, 1–2 Jan; (01343) 820393; free.

🏛☗❋ **Forres** NJ4265 At the E end of town the SUENOS STONE is a mysterious 9th- or 10th-c stone that may have been erected to commemorate a forgotten battle. It's 6 metres (20 ft) high, carved with a cross on one side and groups of warriors on the other. The FALCONER MUSEUM (Tolbooth St) has a good fossil collection; cl wknds Oct–Apr, Sun all year; free. In summer you can usually climb the Nelson Tower in Grant Park for good views of the Moray Firth; free. DALLAS DHU (2m S) Perfectly preserved Victorian distillery, which you can wander around on your own. Animatronic models explain what's happening. Shop (nearly 200 different types of whisky), disabled access; cl am Sun, plus in winter pm Thurs and all day Fri; (01309) 676548; £2.30.

🏛☗ **Fort George** NH7657 One of the finest examples of an 18th-c artillery building, one of 3 fortresses built after 1745, when the Hanoverians were taking no risks in keeping this area firmly under their thumb. Very big, with quite a bit to see. Snacks, shop, disabled access; cl Christmas and New Year, museum cl Sat; (01667) 462777; £2.50. Just off from the fort in the Moray Firth you may be lucky enough to see one of the very few inshore schools of dolphins around the British coast.

🐟 **Forvie** NK0228 FORVIE NATURE RESERVE The fifth-largest sand dune system in Britain – and the one least disturbed by people, so lots of wildlife. From Apr to Aug you have to stick to the footpaths so as not to disturb the birds, but the rest of the year you can go where you like. Disabled access; visitor centre cl winter wknds; (01358) 751330; free.

☗ **Fraserburgh** NJ9966 SCOTTISH NATIONAL LIGHTHOUSE MUSEUM (Quarry Rd) Based around a lighthouse working up to 1991; guided tours take you to the top and demonstrate how everything works. Snacks, shop, limited disabled access; cl 25–26 Dec, and 1–2 Jan; (01346) 511022; *£2.50.

🏯 **Glamis** NO3848 GLAMIS CASTLE (A94) The family home of the Earls of Strathmore, and the childhood home of the Queen Mother; a splendid creation, utterly suitable as the setting for Shakespeare's murder of Duncan in *Macbeth*. Notable features include the chapel with its painted panels and ceiling, and of course there are those stories about what's locked away in one of the towers. Meals, snacks, shop, limited disabled access; cl Nov–Mar; (01307) 840393; *£5.20. The Strathmore Arms is good for lunch.

🦌 **Glenmore** NH9808 CAIRNGORM REINDEER CENTRE (A951) Mingle with free-ranging reindeer in their natural surroundings, a pretty stretch of the Cairngorms; you can feed and stroke them too. Guided walks leave the visitor centre every day at 11am (maybe 2.30pm too in summer). Shop, disabled access to visitor centre only (though usually reindeer down here too); (01479) 861228; £3.50.

🏰☗🦅 **Huntly** NJ5240 CASTLE The original medieval castle here was destroyed and rebuilt several times, once by Mary, Queen of Scots. Reconstructed for the last time in 1602, the ruins are worth a look for their ornate heraldic decorations. Shop; in winter cl pm Thurs and all day Fri; (01466) 793191; *£2.30. In the square is a little local history museum, and a ski centre can teach you how to cross-country ski through the local forest. NORTH EAST FALCONRY CENTRE (Cairnie, off the

A96 N) 4 flying displays a day in a richly meadowed glade, as well as herd of red deer. Snacks, shop, disabled access; cl Nov–Feb; (01466) 760328; £3.75.

Inverness NH6645 The biggest town up here, and the main shopping town for the whole of the N of Scotland (Melvens is a good bookshop). It has an attractive riverside setting and is a handy centre without being at all touristy. Nicky Tams (Ness Bank Rd) has decent food, and the Blackfriars (Academy St) is good for local colour. CASTLE STUART Looking over the Moray Firth a few miles E of Inverness, this was built for the Earl of Moray in 1621 when his family, the Stuarts, ruled Great Britain; it was soon abandoned for nigh on 3 centuries, but has been restored to reflect its days of glory. So much celebration of Bonnie Prince Charlie is quite poignant just 3m from the scene of his final downfall. You can stay here by appointment. Shop; open all year (01463) 792604; *£4.

Kellie NO5105 KELLIE CASTLE (B9171) Fine example of 16th- and 17th-c domestic architecture, though parts date from the 14th c, with good collections of plasterwork, panelling and furniture. Also 4 acres of gardens inc a Victorian walled garden. Snacks, shop; house cl am, wkdys in Oct, and all Nov–Apr (exc Easter), grounds open all year; (01333) 720271; £3.50, £1 garden only; NTS. This is very handy for the seaside villages of Fife's East Neuk.

Kemnay NJ7212 CASTLE FRASER (off the A944) Once one of the grandest castles of Mar, the z-shaped building incorporates the remains of an earlier one, and there are excellent formal gardens. Snacks, shop; castle cl wkdys in Oct, and all Nov–Apr (exc Easter), grounds open all year; (01330) 833463; £4; NTS.

Kildrummy NJ4516 KILDRUMMY CASTLE Now in ruins, though still with its original 13th-c round towers, hall and chapel, as well as some later remains; cl am Sun, plus pm Thurs and all day Fri when quiet, and all Oct–Mar; (01975) 571331;

*£1.50. It provides a spectacular backdrop to the GARDENS (A97), which are very beautiful indeed and of some botanical interest. There's an alpine garden in an old quarry, a watergarden, walks in the woods and a video showing the changes through the seasons. Shop, disabled access; cl Nov–Mar; (01975) 571203; £2.

Killiecrankie NN9162 Queen Victoria was just one of the people to have found this romantic spot beguiling, but it wasn't always so serene. In 1689 it was the site of a fierce battle when the Highlanders routed the troops of William IV, and a VISITOR CENTRE tells the tale. Snacks, shop, disabled access; cl Nov–Mar; (01796) 473233; *£1; NTS. The Killiecrankie Hotel, with good food, is an attractive place.

Kincraig NH8305 *See separate Family Panel on p.858 for HIGHLAND WILDLIFE PARK).*

Kingussie NH7501 (pronounced Kinoossie) HIGHLAND FOLK MUSEUM (Duke St) The first folk museum in Britain, originally opened on Iona in the 1930s. Still a good range of exhibits, inc craft demonstrations and a reconstructed mill. Shop, disabled access; cl am Sun, and all Nov–Mar; (01540) 661307; *£3. The Royal is useful for lunch. HIGHLAND FOLK PARK (nr Newtonmore, A86 SW) Demonstrates the life and work of crofters at the turn of the century; you may be able to help with some of the farming activities. Also a Museum of Highland Sport, which explains why so many of the area's golfers are left-handed. Usually open wkdys Jun–Sept; (01540) 673551; £3.

Kinross NO1102 LOCH LEVEN CASTLE Reached by ferry from the jetty, the island fortress where Mary, Queen of Scots was imprisoned for a while; she was rowed to freedom by a page boy, but only after she had been persuaded to abdicate in favour of her infant son. Shop; limited disabled access; cl am Sun, and all Oct–Mar; (0131) 668 8800; *£2.80 (inc ferry). The loch itself is rather undramatic, but in the winter the evening flights and sounds of the thousands of ducks and geese here seem a mournful echo of those days. An RSPB RESERVE at the S end of the lake has good facilities for watching the birds; cl Christmas and New Year; (01577) 862355; £2. KINROSS HOUSE GARDENS Rather fine and formal, with yew trees, roses and herbaceous borders. Disabled access; cl Oct–Apr; (01577) 863467; *£2. The Muirs has good-value food, as does the Lomond Hotel with its lovely views over Loch Leven from Kinnesswood.

🏛 ❀ **Kirkcaldy** NT2791 (locally pronounced 'Kirkawdy' by Blairites, 'Kirkuddy' by the left wing) This busy resort and shopping town is not too interesting to visitors, but has some charming old wynds and houses in the eastern suburb of Dysart, which has its own picturesque little harbour. Between here and the main town is 15th-c RAVENSCRAIG CASTLE, perhaps most notable for its symmetrical shape. Great views over the Firth of Forth. Snacks, limited disabled access; open all year; free.

🏚👶 **Kirriemuir** NO3954 BARRIE'S BIRTHPLACE (Brechin Rd) The birthplace of the writer of *Peter Pan* in 1860: the upper floors are furnished in the style of the period, and next door are displays relating to his work, both literary and theatrical. Teas, shop, disabled access; cl wkdys in Oct, all Nov–Apr (exc Easter); (01575) 572646; £1.80; NTS.

👶 **Meigle** ND2844 MUSEUM Outstanding collection of Celtic Christian SCULPTURED STONES, all found in or around the churchyard. Shop, disabled access; cl 12.30–1.30pm, am Sun, and all Nov–Apr; (01828) 640612; £1.50.

❀ 🐸👶 **Mintlaw** NJ9847 ADEN COUNTRY PARK More than 200 acres of lovely woodland and farmland, criss-crossed with nature trails and with plenty of wildlife. The ABERDEENSHIRE FARMING MUSEUM here illustrates 2 centuries of farming history, with seasonal open-air demonstrations and tours. Meals, snacks, shop, disabled access; museum cl Nov–Mar, park open all year; (01771) 622906; free.

🦌 **Montrave** NO3806 PRAYTIS FARM PARK (A916) An indoor putting green and crazy golf in addition to the usual farm animals and walks; also deer park, play areas, and big farm shop with venison and smoked salmon. Home-made meals and snacks, some disabled access; cl 25–26 Dec, Jan–Mar; (01333) 350209; £4.

❀ ❀ **Muthill** NN8418 (pronounced 'mewtle') DRUMMOND CASTLE GARDENS (A822) Majestic formal gardens originally laid out in 1630 by the 2nd Earl of Perth. Lovely views from the upper terrace, splendid early Victorian parterre, and centrepiece sundial designed and built by the master mason of King Charles I. Some disabled access; cl am Jun–Oct, and all Nov–May; (01764) 681257; *£3.

★ **Nairn** NH8856 A quiet, relaxed and rather discreet old-fashioned resort, with good clean sheltered beaches.

🐟 **North Queensferry** NT1380 DEEP-SEA WORLD One of the most elaborate aquariums we know; moving walkways take you through an incredible transparent viewing tunnel as long as a football pitch, surrounded by a million gallons of water and sharks and exotic fish from all around the world. You can go round and round as often as you like. Meals, snacks, shop, disabled access; cl 25 Dec; (01383) 411411; £6. The Ferrybridge Hotel has good-value food.

❀ 👶📷🏠🏛 **Perth** NO1123 Spaciously laid out along the broad River Tay; with an excellent specialist rhododendron nursery at Glendoick Gardens (A85). There are a couple of decent museums and galleries, and the Greyfriars and Timothy's are popular for lunch. BRANKLYN GARDEN (116 Dundee Rd) Only about 2 acres but seems much bigger, thanks to a remarkable planting of interesting rhododendrons, small trees, Asiatic primulas, meconopsis, lilies and the like. Shop, disabled access; cl Nov–Feb; (01738) 625535; £2.30; NTS. CAITHNESS GLASS (Inveralmond Industrial Estate, N edge of town) Displays of paperweight-making, with new audio-visual theatre, collectors' museum and factory shop. Meals, snacks, disabled access; cl am Sun Nov–Mar, 25–26 Dec, 1–2 Jan, no glass-making wknds (exc July and Aug); (01738) 637373; free. HUNTINGTOWER CASTLE (just W) The main thing to see is its interesting painted ceiling; in winter cl pm Thurs and all day Fri; £1.50.

Peterculter NJ7900 DRUM CASTLE (off the A93) still looks out over what's left of the medieval forest granted to the family by Robert the Bruce. Mainly a much-altered Jacobean mansion, the house is based around a 13th-c keep, one of the 3 oldest tower houses in Scotland. There's a historic rose garden in the grounds. Snacks, shop, limited disabled access; cl Nov–Mar; (01330) 811454; £4; NTS. The Lairhillock Inn at Netherley a few miles S is good for lunch.

Peterhead NK1246 One of Europe's busiest fishing ports, with a bustling market and smartened up marina. The ancient UGIE FISH HOUSE sells a good range of salmon and trout, caught from the adjacent river in season; cl pm Sat, all day Sun; (01779) 476209; free.

Pitlochry NN9458 An inland resort town for a good long time, beautifully set in fine countryside; a happy sort of place, with a comfortable feel. The Westlands and the Moulin Inn (which brews its own beer) have decent food. EDRADOUR (A924 E) Scotland's smallest distillery, founded in 1825 and virtually unchanged since Victorian times. Guided tours, tastings, shop, some disabled access; cl am Sun, all Nov–Mar (exc shop); (01796) 472095; free. Lovely woodland on the banks of man-made Loch Faskally, with walks and nature trails.

Pitmedden NJ8828 PITMEDDEN GARDEN (A920) Originally planted in the 17th c and pretty much unchanged since, with sundials, fountains and pavilions among the elaborate formal gardens. Meals, snacks, shop, limited disabled access; cl Oct–Apr; (01651) 842352; *£3.50;

NTS. The Redgarth Hotel over at Oldmeldrum has decent food (and good bedrooms).

Port of Menteith NN5700 INCHMAHOME PRIORY Famous as the refuge of the infant Mary, Queen of Scots in 1543, this Augustinian priory was founded in 1238 on an island in the middle of the lake, and in spring and summer you can get a boat across. Robert the Bruce prayed here before the Battle of Bannockburn. Snacks, shop; cl Oct–Mar; (01877) 385294; £2.80 inc ferry.

Rothes NJ2749 GLEN GRANT DISTILLERY Founded in 1840 by the brothers Grant, whose malt whisky was one of the first to be bottled and sold as a single malt. Guided tours, tastings, shop, some disabled access; cl am Sun, all Nov–Mar; (01542) 783318; *£2.50.

★ **St Andrews** NO5116 This civilised university town doubles as a rather dignified seaside resort, with clean, safe beaches. It's outstanding for golfers, though to play on the hallowed greens of the Old Course, you'll need to ring the St Andrews Links Trust on (01334) 466666 before 2pm the day before you want to go, and you'll be entered into a daily ballot; after that you'll have to tee up £70. The 13th-c CASTLE was the scene of Bishop Beaton's murder during a wave of anti-Catholic feeling in 1546. It was largely demolished in the 17th c, but some substantial ruins remain. Shop, disabled access; cl am Sun, 25–26 Dec, 1–2 Jan; (01334) 477196; £2.30. The twin-towered remains of the Norman CATHEDRAL are impressive. In its time this was the largest cathedral in Scotland, but angry locals sacked it in the 16th c. Shop, disabled access; cl 25–26 Dec, 1–2 Jan; (01334) 472563; £1.50. You can get a joint ticket with the castle. Beside it the very tall and narrow Romanesque ST RULES TOWER is part of the older church the cathedral was built to replace (perhaps pre-Conquest), and if you can face over 150 steps gives wonderful views from the top. There are a few interesting MUSEUMS on the city's history, some quite lively, and a number of fine buildings belonging to Scotland's oldest university – especially St Leonard's and St Mary's colleges. South St is worth strolling along: attractive riggs or small courts and alleys off, the ancient West Port gateway at the end, and Holy Trinity Church where John Knox preached his first sermon in 1547. The GOLF MUSEUM (Bruce Embankment) fascinates anyone keen on the game, with interactive and audio-visual displays going right through its 500-year history. Assorted memorabilia include lots of glamorous golfing gear, and the technology is some of the most up-to-date you'll find in any museum. Shop, disabled access; cl Tues and Weds Nov–Apr, 25 Dec–1 Jan; (01334) 478880; £3.75. SEA LIFE CENTRE (The Scores) 3 resident seals, and lots of other examples of British native marine life, well displayed in realistic re-creations of the sea bed. Meals, snacks, shop, limited disabled access; cl 25–26 Dec, 1 Jan; (01334) 474786; £4.25. Just off Canongate, the BOTANIC GARDEN has around 18 pleasantly landscaped acres, with a good range of trees and shrubs, and several glasshouses. Disabled access; (01334) 477178; £1.50. You can arrange fishing trips with Mr Thomas on (01334) 870960; rod and tackle provided. The Vine Leaf, Ma Bells (pleasant seafront views outside), the St Andrews Wine Bar and (1m S) the Grange are all good eating places.

🏠 🦞 **Scone** NO1126 (pronounced 'Scoon') SCONE PALACE (off the A93) The seat of government in Scotland from Pictish times, though the current building is largely 16th-c behind an 18th-c castellated façade. It was the site of the Stone of Destiny – the famous coronation stone – until it was seized by the English in 1296 (it's at last returned to Scotland, though to Edinburgh Castle). Good displays of porcelain, furniture, clocks and needlework, and the grounds are pleasant. Meals, snacks, shop, some disabled access; cl mid-Oct–Good Fri; (01738) 552300; £5.20.

★ 🏰 ❄ † 🖼 🏠 🎶 **Stirling** NS7993 Strategically placed on the Firth of Forth, this is a very unstuffy place, with the university students putting quite a bit of buzz into the atmosphere. Currently undergoing extensive restoration, STIRLING CASTLE provides magnificent views from its lofty hilltop site. It became very popular with the royal family in the 15th and 16th c, and most of the buildings date from that period. The finest features are the Chapel Royal built by James VI (and I of England), and the Renaissance palace built by James V. Snacks, shop; cl 25–26 Dec, 1–2 Jan; (01786) 450000; £4. There's a good visitor centre in a restored building next door; cl 25–26 Dec, 1–2 Jan; free. Whistlebinkies (St Mary's Wynd), formerly part of the ancient castle stables, has decent food. Dropping down the steep hill on which the castle stands is an attractive and interesting network of old streets, with a lot of character in their old-to-ancient buildings; ARGYLE LODGINGS is an interesting ruined Renaissance-style mansion, and the CHURCH OF HOLY ROOD was where Mary, Queen of Scots and James VI were crowned as babies. The SMITH ART GALLERY on Dumbarton Rd has good changing exhibitions; cl am Sun, all day Mon; (01786) 471917; free. WALLACE MONUMENT 📺 (on top of Abbey Craig, just NE) Perhaps Stirling's most satisfying attraction, a huge 67-metre (220-ft) Victorian tower with dramatic views from the top of its 246 spiralling steps. Each floor has lively audio-visual displays, one looking at Sir William Wallace, another examining other Scottish heroes. Snacks, shop; cl wkdys Jan–Feb and 25–26 Dec; (01786) 472140; *£2.50. BANNOCKBURN HERITAGE CENTRE (A872 S) Plenty of information on Robert the Bruce's finest hour, inc an audio-visual show on the battle itself. Shop, disabled access; cl Jan and Feb; (01786) 472140; £2.30.

🍴 🏰 **Stonehaven** NO8786 An old fishing town, with its more seasidey but discreet Victorian streets in the upper part; the harbourside Marine has good, reasonably priced food. There's a decent local history

museum in the old TOLBOOTH on the quay; cl 12–2pm, Tues, am Weds, and Oct–May; (01779) 477778; free.
DUNNOTTAR CASTLE (just S of Stonehaven) On a precipitous sea-girt crag stands this the bleak and battered but still extensive and well preserved 14th-c ruin. It sheltered the Scottish Crown Jewels during the Civil War, but has seen much darker episodes in its time. Shop; cl am Sun, 25–26 Dec, 1 Jan; (01569) 762173; £3.

🏠 🏤 🖼 Tarves NJ8634 HADDO HOUSE (off the B999) Wonderfully grand yet still very much a family home; designed by William Adam, and refurbished in the 1880s in the Adam Revival style. The chapel has stained glass by Burne-Jones. Its choral society is renowned, holding concerts and operas in the adjacent hall; (01651) 851770 for what's on. Meals, snacks, shop, disabled access; house cl am May–Sept, wkdys in Oct, and all Nov–Apr (exc Easter), gardens open all year; (01651) 851440; £4; NTS. Surrounding the house is a 150-acre country park, with wildlife exhibition and guided walks, and a shop selling produce from the estate, and local salmon, venison, whisky and crafts. There's an interesting medieval tomb in Tarves churchyard. TOLQUHON Nearby village with a decidely unstuffy little GALLERY of contemporary Scottish art and crafts (cl am Sun, all day Thurs, and wknds Jan and Feb; free), and the impressive remains of a 15th-c CASTLE (cl winter wkdys, *£1.50).

🏠 🖼 Turriff NJ7639 FYVIE CASTLE (off the A947) Each of the 5 towers of this magnificent palace was built in a different century by the family that lived here throughout; the oldest parts date back to the 13th c, and the whole building is one of the most fantastic examples of Scottish baronial architecture. Collections of armour and tapestry, and paintings by Romney and Gainsborough. Snacks, shop, limited disabled access; cl am (exc July and Aug), wkdys in Oct, and Nov–Easter; (01651) 891266; *£4; NTS. The Towie

Tavern does good food.
★ The EAST NEUK or E coast has pretty **fishing villages**, especially Crail NO6108, and Pittenweem NO5403, which has some attractive crow-gabled houses (the gables in steps which seagulls rather than crows sit on here). The beach at Elie NO4900 is notably clean and safe (and has a good pub, the Ship), while St Monance NO5202 has an unusual fisherman's church and a restored 18th-c windmill (the Cabin has good seafood and sea views). Anstruther NO5704 is pretty, with the nicely evocative SCOTTISH FISHERIES MUSEUM in a little cobbled courtyard by the harbour (cl am Sun; £2.50). From May–Sept (weather permitting) you can get BOAT TRIPS out to the nature reserve of the Isle of May (home to countless puffins and seals in summer), while a few miles inland up the B940, beneath an innocuous-looking farmhouse, SCOTLAND'S SECRET BUNKER is a network of underground rooms and corridors from where the government would have run the country in the event of a nuclear attack (cl Oct–Easter; *£4.95).

Of the area's abundance of lochs, **Loch Rannoch** NN6580 is among the quieter and more beautiful ones. **Loch Tay** NN6838 seems to change moment by moment as the clouds flit across the sky, and has a quiet road along its S side; **Ben Lawers** NN6340 is an interesting spot, with alpine wild flowers not found elsewhere in Britain and a quite different feel from other Highland mountains; a steep road leads up the side. **Loch Ericht** NN5574 is very peaceful but does involve foot-slogging to make the most of it. **Loch Katrine** NN4510 is a lovely stretch of water that inspired Scott's *Lady of the Lake*, and has a Victorian steamer in summer. **Loch Voil** NN5020 further N is, like Loch Katrine, served by just a narrow back road, so fairly peaceful even in summer; it's famous for having Rob Roy's grave at Balquhidder NN5320. LOCH EARN NN6523 with a trunk road alongside is largely given over to water-skiing and that sort of thing.

Days Out

From the Forth to the Ochils
Deep-Sea World, North Queensferry; lunch at the Ferrybridge Hotel there; Culross, or Castle Campbell/walk in Dollar Glen.

Villages of the East Neuk
St Andrews; Crail; lunch at the Cellar, Anstruther; Pittenweem; Kellie Castle.

The heart of the Trossachs
Scottish Wool Centre, Aberfoyle; drive along the A821 past the Trossachs Viewpoint, detour to Loch Katrine; detour along the A84 to the Falls of Leny; lunch at the Lade Inn, Kilmahog nr Callander; look at woollen mill or walk up to Callander Crags; boat to Inchmahome Priory.

Perthshire heights
Dunkeld, for walk up Birnam Hill or along river to the Hermitage; Pitlochry; lunch at the Moulin there (Kirkmichael Rd), or the Killiecrankie Hotel (just N); Killiecrankie Visitor Centre; Blair Castle.

Lochs and glens
Stroll through the Birks of Aberfeldy; drive up Glen Lyon, if there's time; lunch at the Ailean Chraggan, Weem; Kenmore and Loch Tay; Loch Earn, passing Comrie (for walk to Deil's Cauldron, see **Walks ⌂-11**).

Cairngorm encounter
Strathspey Steam Railway, Aviemore; lunch at the Olde Bridge there; Highland Wildlife Park, Kincraig – or take the chairlift up to Cairngorm summit, and/or walk round Loch an Eilein.

Bonnie Prince Charlie's downfall
Cawdor Castle; lunch at the Cawdor Tavern there; Culloden battlefield; Clava Cairns.

Shrines to Peter Pan and Macbeth
Barrie's Birthplace, Kirriemuir; lunch at the Strathmore Arms, Glamis; Glamis Castle; Meigle museum (Celtic stones).

Castles of Royal Deeside
Braemar Castle; lunch at the Fife Arms, Braemar; drive past Balmoral, then up Glen Muick for a walk round Loch Muick; Crathes Castle or Craigievar Castle.

Mr Gladstone at home
Edzell Castle (or drive up Glen Esk, off the B966 just N of Edzell); lunch at the Ramsay Arms, Fettercairn; Fasque; drive up the B974 to the top of the pass.

Palatial contrasts
Fyvie Castle (limited opening); lunch at Towie Tavern, Turriff, or picnic in Haddo country park, Tarves; Haddo House, stroll in the country park.

A day in Aberdeen
King's College chapel; St Machar's cathedral; Cruickshank botanic gardens and Seaton Park; lunch at the Prince of Wales (St Nicholas Lane) or Ferryhill House Hotel (Bon Accord St); Maritime Museum; Provost Skene's House; Satrosphere.

Loch Ness NH5023 (see also Drumnadrochit entry in **North Scotland** section of this chapter, below) is of course the granddaddy of them all, and a place of great beauty; the calmest drive along it is the B862, though it leaves the loch shore more than the trunk road on the other side.
☎ As well as those mentioned above, **working distilleries** open for tours and tastings include those at Glencoyne (on the A81 nr Killearn NS5285), Tomatin NH8029 (not wknds exc summer Sats), and Dalwhinnie NN6384 (Scotland's highest distillery; cl wknds), the Cardhu Distillery on the B9102 nr Knockando NJ1842 (cl wknds exc July–Sept; £2), and the Glenfarclas Distillery at Marypark NJ1938 (cl wknds exc Jun–Sept; £2.50). The Glenlivet Distillery at Ballindalloch NJ1636 was the first Highland distillery to be licensed; (01542) 783220 for opening times; free. Besides those we've mentioned as places to eat at or stay in, inns where you can get a decent bite to eat and which are particularly well placed for walkers, drivers or just strollers in these parts include the lochside Achray at St Fillans NN6924, seaview Creel at Catterline NO8778, Loch Ericht Hotel at Dalwhinnie NN6384, Dores Hotel at Dores by Loch Ness NH5930, Anchor at Dunipace NS8083, Hungry Monk at Gartocharn NS4286, Clova Hotel in Glen Clova NO3373, Old Mill at Killearn NS5285, Cross Keys at Kippen NS6594 (pretty village), Trossachs Hotel nr Loch Achray NN5106, Corriegour Lodge nr Altrua on Loch Lochy NN2390, Loch Tummel Hotel above Loch Tummel NN8460, Meikleour Inn at Meikleour NO1539 (handy for the 30-metre (100-ft) high beech hedge planted in 1746), Pennan Inn in the pretty seaside *Local Hero* village of Pennan NJ8465, Potarch Hotel at Potarch NO6097, Sheriffmuir Inn on wild Sheriff Muir NN8202 and Tomdoun Hotel at Tomdoun NH1501.

Walks

For non-mountaineers the Highlands can be tantalising but problematic: compared to the uplands of England and Wales there are few obvious walking routes (OS maps show hardly any), and the scale of the scenery is often so vast that you need to walk for hours before the views change. The high peaks are mostly for the dedicated (and fit) enthusiast. There is an informal tradition of allowing general access to the mountains, but there are few rights of way, and areas are often closed for at least part of the grouse-shooting season (12 Aug–10 Dec), particularly its first few weeks, or the deer-stalking season (1 July–20 Oct for stags, 21 Oct–15 Feb for hinds).

Although not quite as consistently spectacular as the W coast, this area does have plenty of well above average walking.

The Trossachs NN5007, famously popular for their dense conifer forests, steep glens and beautifully framed lochs, are not brilliant for low-level walks unless you like forests; the route on to **Callander Crags** NN6308 ☖-1 from Callander NN6307 is one of the best. However, this area allows some good mountain walks comparable in difficulty to some of the fells of the English Lake District: **Ben Venue** NN4706 ☖-2 and **Ben Vorlich** NN2912 ☖-3 are among the finest.

Kinnoull Hill NO1322 ☖-4, just outside Perth, has forest tracks and paths, and two folly 'castles' above the River Tay. The Perthshire uplands have numerous forest trails and hill walks. **Dunkeld** NO0242 ☖-5 makes a starting point for the ascent of Birnam Hill NO0340 or a riverside walk past the Falls of the Braan through the forest to the Hermitage NO0041 and so-called Ossian's Cave. From **Pitlochry** NN9458 ☖-6 you can follow the shores of Loch Faskally. **Aberfeldy** NN8549 ☖-7 offers a verdant ascent through the

Birks of Aberfeldy to the Falls of Moness. **Loch Tay** NN6838 ⌂-8 is dominated by the towering bulk of Ben Lawers NN6341, well over 1,200 metres (nearly 4,000 ft) but with a good track up. There are easier walks at the E end of the loch, from the attractive estate village of Kenmore NN7745 along the banks of the River Tay, or into the adjacent forest to a viewpoint over the loch. The **Knock of Crieff** NN8622 ⌂-9 is a wooded hill just above Crieff with a good viewpoint. **Lochearnhead** NN5823 ⌂-10 has a round walk along a nature trail into Glen Ogle and back via the trackbed of an abandoned railway. The **Deil's Cauldron** NN7623 ⌂-11 is reached by a signposted circular walk through Glen Lednock from Comrie NN7722 (the Earthquake House at Comrie records tremors).

Glen Roy NN2985 ⌂-12 and its curious Parallel Roads (not actually roads but the tubmarks of a former glacier) can be seen from an easy track along its bottom, a spectacular 4-mile route from Brae Roy Lodge NN3392 (return the same way).

The **Ochil Hills** NO0409 ⌂-13 are a range of green mountains which rise without preamble from the lowland plain – a striking textbook example of the Highland Fault. A path from Tillicoultry NS9197 up Mill Glen NS9198 takes you to Ben Cleuch NN9000, the highest point of the range. Don't miss the amazing short path around the base of Castle Campbell NS9699 above Dollar NS9698 – catwalks, rock overhangs, jungle-thick vegetation, and a swirling stream below.

Fife has some pleasant rambles on the **Lomond Hills** NO2206 ⌂-14, a level walk from the car park by the road above Falkland NO2507 – not to be confused with Loch Lomond, this upland gives views over most of SE Scotland. The **Tentsmuir Sands** ⌂-15 on the Fife coast give 5 miles of shore walking from Kinshaldy car park NO5024; you may see common and grey seals on the sandbanks, and there are good clean beaches – shorter routes back through the forest.

The **Cairngorms** ⌂-16 have an easy way up to the summits – a ski-lift from Glen More NH9807 above Aviemore; there are manageable paths down. Loch an Eilein NH8907 nestles beneath the mountains on the Aviemore side; a forest track encircles this delightful little loch, with its castle romantically placed on an isle – great echoes here.

The **Linn of Dee** NO0689 ⌂-17 not far from Braemar has long glen walks into the Cairngorms along Glen Dee and the Lairig Ghru. From Braemar itself NO1491 you can follow a steep path up **Morrone** NO1388 ⌂-18, along a route used for a race in the Highland Gathering. **Loch Muick** NO3085 ⌂-19 nestles beneath the summit of Lochnagar and has paths around its shores, with a car park at the end of the Glen Muick road from Ballater. **Bennachie** NJ6522 ⌂-20 on the E edge of the Grampians, nr Inverurie NJ7721, is not that high but has tremendous views over lowland Aberdeenshire; the gently rolling moorland top has several colour-coded Forestry Commission trails (the lower slopes are forested).

The coast around **Banff** NJ6864 ⌂-21 can be followed for some stretches (a bus service along the main road is a useful method of return), for instance from Portsoy NJ5866 to Findlater Castle NJ5467, a windswept ruin on the cliff-edge.

Where to eat

Many places in the **Where to stay** section, above, also have very good food.
Aberfoyle NN5200 Braeval (01877) 382711 TV chef Nick Nairn's small country restaurant is in a converted mill with stone walls and flagstones, fresh flowers and a woodburning stove, and serves particularly good imaginative modern cooking from a daily-changing set menu, fine French cheeses, good-value wine list, and helpful friendly staff; cl pm sun, Mon, Tues, 1 wk

Feb/June/Nov; children over 10; disabled access. **£30 dinner**.

Anstruther NO5603 CELLAR 24 East Green (01333) 310378 Close to the harbour, this characterful restaurant has beams, stone walls, and peat fires and is set off a little courtyard; wonderful fresh fish, good wines; cl Sun, am Mon, am Tues, 25 Dec, 1 Jan. **£35|£8.50.**

Cupar NO3714 OSTLERS CLOSE 25 Bonnygate (01334) 655574 Cosy, unpretentious restaurant with lovely food using local fresh produce, game and fish; good puddings and decent wines; cl Sun, Mon, 2 wks June; well behaved children over 6 at lunch, no children at dinner. **£33 dinner, £23 lunch|£9.50.**

Drybridge NJ4362 OLD MONASTERY (01542) 832660 Lovely views from this former monastery – as well as very good fish, game and Abderdeen Angus beef, reasonably priced wines and friendly service, cl Sun, Mon, 2 wks Nov, 3 wks Jan; children over 8. **£28|£9.**

Glamis NO3846 STRATHMORE ARMS (01307) 840248 Picturesque unspoilt village with simply decorated old inn, well presented delicious food inc wonderful puddings, roaring log fire in lounge, and good caring service; disabled access. **£19|£7.**

Kingussie NH7500 THE CROSS (01540) 661166 No smoking, friendly tweed mill beside a stream offering fine Scottish cooking based on the best local produce, an excellent wine list (popular wine weekends), and super breakfasts; bdrms; cl pm Tues, 1–26 Dec, 8 Jan–28 Feb; children over 12; disabled access. **£40 for 5 courses.**

Perth NO1123 NUMBER THIRTY THREE 33 George St (01738) 633771 Seafood restaurant (useful for the theatre) with lighter meals in the Oyster Bar and main meals in the restaurant beyond – good puddings, too; cl Sun, Mon, 3 wks end Jan/Feb; children over 5. **£26|£5.50.**

Perth NO1123 PATRICKS WINE BAR 1 Speygate (01738) 620539 Popular wine bar and bistro with good-value, imaginative home-cooked meals; cl 25 Dec. **£19|£7.95.**

St Andrews NO5116 VINE LEAF 131 South St (01334) 477497 Warm welcome; attractively laid out dining room overlooking walled herb garden, very good food, unobtrusive service and decent wines; evenings only; cl Sun, Mon and 1st wk Jan; disabled access. **£25.**

St Fillans NN6924 FOUR SEASONS (01764) 685333 Long white family-run hotel with wonderful Loch Earn views, generous helpings of very good Scottish food inc super fish and game dishes; lunchtime snacks, too; you can eat in Tarken Bar, on terrace or in smarter restaurant; comfortable bdrms and chalets; cl Nov–Mar. **£29 for 4 courses|£7.**

Stonehaven NO8786 LAIRHILLOCK (01569) 730001 Relaxed and friendly extended 18th-c country pub with a wide choice of good, popular and imaginative food, well kept real ales, lots of malt whiskies and wines, nice views from the cheerfully atmospheric beamed bar, central fire in spacious lounge, and airy conservatory; disabled access. **£33.95 dinner, £18 lunch|£4.75.**

Weem NN8449 AILEAN CHRAGGAN (01887) 820346 Emphasis on well presented fish dishes in friendly inn with lovely views; comfortable bdrms; cl Christmas/New Year. **£15.50|£2.25.**

WEST SCOTLAND

Mainland Scotland's finest scenery, especially on the coast.

Roads threading along the mountainous coast make driving here a succession of glorious views. Inland too has its delights: Loch Lomond, with the Trossachs nearby in East Scotland, is to become

Scotland's first National Park, early in the new millennium. Places to visit are mostly low-key, suiting the relaxed pace of life here – the great gardens are the high point for most people, and are at their peak in May and June. That's anyway the best time to visit this part, with very long days and lots of wild flowers. In high summer the traffic on the intricately twisting roads in the most scenic parts can make driving painfully slow, and the midges become a menace. In autumn the Highland heather's still glorious and the weather can be very kind, but the days are shortening dramatically. In winter most hotels here do remain open, and the coast stays very mild, but the days are too short to make much of – and most of the attractions close; a time to do some brisk walking, then cosset yourself indoors in one of the particularly comfortable places to stay.

Oban is quite lively, Inveraray is interesting, and Dunoon has all you'd expect of a long-standing summer resort; all three have things to keep children entertained, as does Glencoe. You can find excellent fresh seafood.

Where to stay

Ardrishaig NR8485 ALLT-NA-CRAIG Tarbert Rd, Ardrishaig, Lochgilphead, Argyll PA30 8EP (01546) 603245 *£64, plus special breaks; 6 rms. Victorian mansion overlooking Loch Fyne with big lounge and dining area (fine views), log fire, big breakfasts, and evening meals by request; self-catering also; cl Christmas/New Year.

Arduaine NM7910 LOCH MELFORT Arduaine, Oban, Argyll PA34 4XG (01852) 200233 £99; 27 rms, gorgeous sea views. Comfortable hotel popular in summer with passing yachtsmen (hotel's own moorings), nautical charts and marine glasses in airy modern bar, own lobster pots and nets so emphasis on seafood; pleasant foreshore walks, outstanding springtime woodland gardens; cl mid-Jan–mid-Feb; disabled access.

Ballachulish NN0757 BALLACHULISH HOUSE Ballachulish, Argyll PA39 4JX (01855) 811266 £79 inc dinner; 8 rms with views. Remote 18th-c house with a friendly atmosphere, spacious antique-furnished elegant rooms, log fires, an honesty bar, hearty helpings of good food using local fish and beef, and a billiard room; cl Nov–Feb; children over 3.

Crinan NR7894 CRINAN HOTEL Crinan, Lochgilphead, Argyll PA31 8SR (01546) 830261 £200 inc dinner, plus special breaks; 20 rms. Rather smart hotel by start of coast-to-coast canal, marvellous views from stylish formal top-floor restaurant, nautical decorations in lounge bar, lots of local fish and large wine list; disabled access.

Dervaig NM4749 DRUIMARD COUNTRY HOUSE Dervaig, Tobermory, Island of Mull PA75 6QW (01688) 400345 £75, plus special breaks; 6 rms. Peaceful Victorian country house with wonderful views across the glen and River Bellart, friendly helpful owners, a comfortable lounge and conservatory with lots of pictures, books and magazines, good breakfasts, and excellent food using the best local produce; the Mull Little Theatre is in the grounds; cl Nov–March; dogs welcome.

Duror NM9854 STEWART Duror, Appin, Argyll PA38 4BW (01631) 740268 *£87; 26 rms in modern wing. Family-run Victorian country house with splendid views towards Loch Linnhe, 5 acres of splendid gardens (lovely in May/June), comfortable lounge with open fire, and good food using local fish and game; own boat moorings and 31ft sloop; cl 30 Oct–1 Apr.

Ellanbeich NM7417 Inshaig Park Ellanbeich, Easdale, Oban, Argyll PA34 4RF (01852) 300256 *£68; 6 rms. Solid family-run stone building on Seil island (bridge to mainland), a hotel since Victorian times, with stunning sea views, good food inc fresh local seafood, a friendly bar, and a warm welcome; cl mid-Oct–Easter.

Eriska NM9037 Isle of Eriska Hotel Ledaig, Eriska, Oban, Argyll PA37 1SD (01631) 720371 £185, plus winter breaks; 17 rms. In a wonderful position on a tiny island linked to the mainland by a bridge, this impressive baronial hotel has a very relaxed country house atmosphere, log fires and a pretty drawing room, excellent, really enjoyable food, exemplary service, and a comprehensive wine list; leisure complex with indoor swimming pool, sauna, gym and so forth, lovely surrounding walks, and 9-hole golf course, windsurfing or water-skiing, clay pigeon shooting, pony-trekking, and golf – and plenty of wildlife including the tame badgers who come nightly to the library door for their bread and milk; cl Jan; children over 5 in evening restaurant (high tea provided) and pool; disabled access.

Fort William NN1074 Grange Grange Rd, Fort William, Inverness-shire PH33 6JF (01397) 705516 *£66; 3 rms. Charming Victorian house in quiet landscaped gardens with log fire in comfortable lounge, fine breakfasts in dining room overlooking Loch Linnhe, and helpful hard-working owners; cl Dec–Feb; children over 12.

Gigha Island NR6449 Gigha Island Hotel Gigha Island, Argyll PA41 7AD (01583) 505254 £76, plus special breaks; 13 rms, most with own bthrm. Attractive traditional family-run small hotel with lots of charm, a bustling bar (popular with yachtsmen and locals), neatly kept and comfortable residents' lounge, and local seafood in restaurant; cottages also; cl end Oct–mid-Mar.

Kilberry NR7164 Kilberry Inn Kilberry, Tarbert, Argyll PA29 6YD (01880) 770223 *£63; 3 ground-floor, no smoking rms. Homely and warmly welcoming inn on W coast of Knapdale with fine sea views, old-fashioned character, entertaining owner, and outstanding country cooking – everything home-made, from soups and breads to chutney and marmalade; cl Oct–Easter; well behaved children over 8.

Kilchrenan NN0222 Taychreggan Kilchrenan, Taynuilt, Argyll PA35 1HQ (01866) 833211 £94; 20 rms. Civilised and extensively refurbished hotel with fine garden running down to Loch Awe, comfortable airy bar with stuffed birds and fish, attractively served lunchtime bar food, polite efficient staff, good, freshly prepared food in no smoking dining room, careful wine list, dozens of malt whiskies, and pretty inner courtyard; no children.

Kilfinan NR9379 Kilfinan Hotel Kilfinan, Tighnabruaich, Argyll PA21 2EP (01700) 821201 *£75, plus special breaks; 11 rms. Friendly former coaching inn, popular locally, in fine scenery with sporting activities such as shooting, fishing and stalking; very good restaurant food, decent bar food, and log fires; cl Feb; children over 12.

Kilninver NM8523 Knipoch Kilninver, Oban, Argyll PA34 4QT (01852) 316251 £150; 16 rms. Elegant and very well kept Georgian hotel in lovely countryside overlooking Loch Feochan; fine family portraits, log fires, fresh flowers and polished furniture in comfortable lounges and bars, carefully chosen wines and malt whiskies, and marvellous food inc their own smoked salmon; cl mid-Nov–mid-Feb.

Oban NM8630 Dungallan House Hotel Gallanach Rd, Oban, Argyll PA34 4PD (01631) 563799 £68; 13 rms, most with own bthrm. Victorian house in neat grounds with fine views over the bay to the islands of Mull and Lismore; marvellous food in elegant no smoking dining room, relaxed lounge bar and reading room, warm coal fires, and helpful friendly owners and staff; cl Nov and Feb; limited disabled access.

Onich NN0261 Allt-Nan-Ros Onich, Fort William, Inverness-shire PH33 6RY (01855) 821210 £80, plus special breaks; 20 rms. Victorian shooting lodge with fine Scottish food, a friendly atmosphere, bright airy rooms, and magnificent views across Loch Linnhe and the gardens; cl mid-Nov–New Year; disabled access.

Pennyghael NM5226 PENNYGHAEL Pennyghael, Island of Mull, Argyll PA70 6HB (01681) 704288 **£105 inc dinner**; 6 rms. Beautifully placed converted byre on the edge of Loch Scridain with comfortable little lounge, generous breakfasts, lovely (if limited in choice) evening food using local fish and venison, and really friendly owners and staff; disabled access.

Port Appin NM9045 AIRDS HOTEL Port Appin, Appin, Argyll PA38 4DF (01631) 730236 **£165 inc dinner**, plus winter breaks; 12 rms. Instantly relaxing 18th-c inn with lovely views of Loch Linnhe and the island of Lismore, blissfully comfortable day rooms, friendly helpful service, and charming owners; the food is exceptional (as is the wine list) and there are lots of surrounding walks, with more on Lismore (small boat every 2 hours); cl 10–31 Jan; dogs by arrangement.

Strachur NN0901 CREGGANS Strachur, Cairndow, Argyll PA27 8BX (01369) 860279 *****£90**; 19 rms. Smart inn in extensive grounds overlooking sea loch and hills (deer-stalking, fishing and pony-trekking arranged), with attractive lounge, conservatory and cocktail bar, lively locals' bar, particularly fine cooking and carefully chosen wines; coffee bar and gift shop.

Tarbert NR8668 STONEFIELD CASTLE Tarbert, Argyll PA29 6YJ (01880) 820836 **£90**, plus special breaks; 33 rms. With wonderful views and surrounding wooded grounds, this Scottish baronial mansion has comfortable public rooms and decent restaurant food; snooker room, sauna and solarium; heated swimming pool open in summer only; disabled access.

To see and do

🦌 **Arduaine** NM8010 (A816) The seaside GARDENS here, a very sheltered spot with lovely views of the islets and islands, are almost subtropical, with many rarities beside the rhododendrons, camellias and magnolias which flourish so in this part of the world. Open all year; (01852) 200366; *£2.30; NTS. The comfortable Loch Melfort Hotel, with great sea views, does good bar lunches.

🦌 **Auchindrain** NN0303 AUCHINDRAIN TOWNSHIP OPEN-AIR MUSEUM (A83) The only communal tenancy township to have remained on its ancient site much in its original form. All the buildings have been excellently restored and simply furnished in period style, so you get a real feeling of stepping back into the past. Snacks, shop; cl Oct–Mar; (01499) 500235; £3.

🦌 **Barcaldine** NM9642 SEA LIFE CENTRE (A828) Lively underwater centre (part of a chain with several in England and one in St Andrews), with hi-tech face-to-fish-face displays of native marine life, and playful seal

puppies. Also nature trails and woodland adventure playground. Meals, snacks, shop, limited disabled access; cl wkdys Jan and Feb, 25 Dec; (01631) 720386; *£5.50. The Lochnell Arms and Falls of Lora down at Connel are reliable lunch stops.

🦌 **Benmore** NS1385 YOUNGER BOTANIC GARDEN (A815) An outstation of the Royal Botanic Garden in Edinburgh, with attractive woodland and glorious rhododendrons. Some enormously tall and magnificent conifers here, and a good many rarities. Nice views too. Meals, snacks, shop, disabled access; cl Nov–mid-Mar; (01369) 706261; £2.

🦌 **Cairndow** NN1810 ARDKINGLAS WOODLAND GARDEN (off the A83) On a hillside overlooking Loch Fyne, the pinetum here includes the tallest tree in Britain, a grand fir well over 61 metres (200 ft) and still shooting upwards. Also rhododendrons, azaleas and other exotic plants, and daffodils in spring. Disabled access; open all year;

*£1.50. The same people run the TREE SHOP (about 2m N at the top of the loch), which specialises in specimen trees, indigenous Highland trees, and shrubs. Also lots of well crafted woodware (inc some lovely toys and puzzles); cl Jan; (01499) 600263. Next door the Loch Fyne Oyster Bar is renowned for its fresh shellfish, which you can eat in the restaurant or buy in the shop; the Cairndow Hotel with a waterside garden is also good.

★ ❀ **Colintraive** NS0374 This attractive village spreads along the shore of the sea loch, with lovely views (for example from the well run Colintraive Hotel) across the narrow Kyles of Bute. There's a short ferry crossing to Rhubodach on Bute.

� **Corpach** NN0977 TREASURES OF THE EARTH (Mallaig Rd) Award-winning collection of gemstones, crystals and minerals, imaginatively displayed in carefully lit rock cavities and caverns. Shop, disabled access; cl 25–26 Dec, 3–31 Jan; (01397) 772283; *£3.

★ **Crinan Canal** NR8390 Cut through the 9m at the top of the Kintyre peninsula at the end of the 18th c, to save coastal sailors many miles of dangerous waters; the end at Crinan is attractive, usually with one or two yachts or even a rare fishing boat waiting to enter the first lock, and the Crinan Hotel is a comfortable lunch stop.

❀ **Dunoon** NS1776 Brought in easy reach of Glasgow by frequent ferries from Gourock, this late Victorian resort has pleasant views from its fine long promenade; very busy in Aug.

☘⚓🏰 **Fort William** NN1174 A largely Victorian town that manages to combine its role as a regional centre with its other life as a holiday base, particularly for solid Ben Nevis which rises above it, and for the Caledonian Canal which leads on up into the Great Glen and across eventually to the North Sea. The recently refurbished WEST HIGHLAND MUSEUM (Cameron Sq) is especially good on Jacobite relics: a secret portrait of Prince Charlie requires a curved mirror to decode it. Best to ring for opening times, (01397)

702169; £2. The Alexandra and Nevis Bank hotels are useful for food, as is the upstairs part of the Grog & Girvel pub; the Nevisport is the place for walking and climbing chat. In summer you can take steamtrain journeys on the WEST HIGHLAND LINE from here – it goes right up into the Highlands and the views are quite superb. On the NE edge of town (usually under scaffolding) are the ruins of partly 13th-c INVERLOCHY CASTLE, site of the 1645 battle between Montrose and the Campbells; free.

⛳🎱🎣 **Gigha** NR6449 3m offshore, linked by frequent ferries from Tayinloan on the A83 down the W coast of Kintyre; the island is a perfect place for really getting away from it all. Apart from the small hotel, there are rooms at the post office and other places, and you can hire bicycles to explore it properly. The island was bought in 1944 by Sir James Horlick, who created ACHAMORE GARDENS, a garden of woodlands filled with rhododendrons and azaleas, bringing over many of the plants from his home in Berkshire in laundry baskets. Lots of subtropical plants – the climate and soil are perfect for them. Meals, snacks, shop, limited disabled access; open all year; £2. Try to see the strange old stones, some of which are supposed to have mysterious powers. Tel (01583) 505254 for ferry times.

❣! **Glencoe** NN1058 The scenery around here is some of Scotland's most beautiful and wild. It's understandably popular with walkers and climbers, who share it with deer, wildcats and golden eagles. The area is most famous for the massacre of 1692 when billeted troops tried to murder all their MacDonald hosts. The GLENCOE VISITOR CENTRE (A82) has the whole story, as well as useful local information. Snacks, shop, disabled access; cl Nov–Mar; (01855) 811307; 50p, free parking all day; NTS. You can get fishing permits from here too. Children enjoy the spooky local myths and legends at the HIGHLAND MYSTERYWORLD, which in 1997 added an outdoor theatre to its

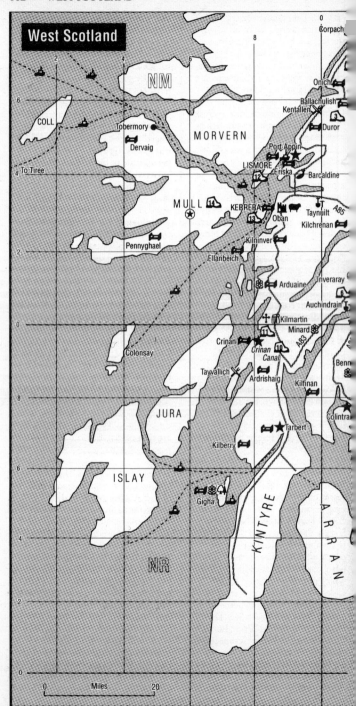

West Scotland

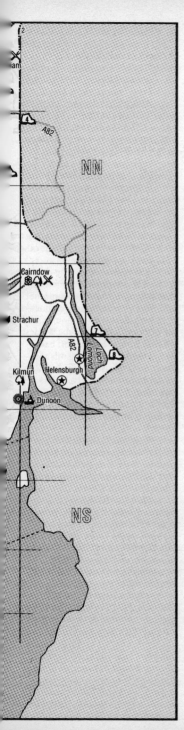

entertaining mix of bogles, kelpies and haunted lochs. Meals, snacks, shop, disabled access; cl Nov–mid-Mar; (01855) 811660; £4.95. The Clachaig and King's House do food.

🏚🏵❋ **Helensburgh** NS2982 THE HILL HOUSE (Upper Colquhoun St) In an area short of many great houses, this is a wonderful example of the work of Charles Rennie Mackintosh; there's an exhibition on his life, and the gardens are being restored. Snacks, shop; cl am Apr–Oct, and all Nov–Mar; (01436) 673900; £4.50; NTS – it's one of their busier properties, with more visitors than they'd really like. The dignified resort town, attractively placed on the Clyde, has some good views from its broad streets.

★ † 🏚 ♨ 🏛 **Inveraray** NN0908 Beautifully placed and rather self-consciously elegant, this was built as an estate village in the 18th c. The bell tower of ALL SAINTS CHURCH has the world's second-heaviest ring of 10 bells, installed in 1931. Even if there's no one ringing them you should be able to hear a recording; cl 1–2pm, am Sun, all Oct–Apr; (01499) 302259; £1.50 for tower, exhibition free. The CASTLE was built in 1743, long before the town became a magnet for visitors. Still the home of the Duke and Duchess of Argyll, it has particularly impressive state rooms, and a striking hall. Snacks, shop, disabled access to ground floor only; cl 1–2pm (exc July and Aug), am Sun, all day Fri (exc July and Aug), and Nov–Mar; (01499) 302203; £4. INVERARAY JAIL 🎫 (Church Sq) Excellent prison museum, with costumed guides really bringing the place to life. You can watch a trial, try your hand at hard labour, and even experience being locked up in one of the sparse little cells. Shop; cl 25 Dec, 1 Jan; (01499) 302381; £4.20. The Loch Fyne Hotel is pleasant for lunch, with stunning views; the George is popular too. ARGYLL WILDLIFE PARK 🎫 (Dalchenna) A collection of local or once-local animals, from wild boars to wildcats – with some eminently tame wild creatures wandering around. Snacks, shop, disabled access; cl Jan–Feb; (01499) 302264; £3.50.

✝ 🏚 **Kilmartin** NR8393 CHURCH Plain and Victorian, but it has a stunning 10th-c cross; the graveyard has interesting carved medieval tombstones. A short walk away are the well signed North, Mid and South Cairns (impressive prehistoric monuments – you can climb into the North one via trapdoor and ladder, to see cup-and-ring carvings), and the Templewood stone circles. The simple Kilmartin Hotel is useful for lunch. DUNADD (3m S) This prehistoric hill fort was one of the ancient capitals of Dalriada from which the Celtic kingdom of Scotland was formed. Look out for the carvings nearby of a boar and a footprint, which probably mark the spot where early kings were invested with royal power.

🌂 **Kilmun** NS1781 Wonderful FOREST WALKS among rare conifers, an arboretum of great beauty, and some striking gum trees.

❋ 🕸 🐾 🌂 **Loch Lomond** NS3957 In spite of being so close to Glasgow and on every coach company's hit list, it does have a serene beauty that seems unspoilt by the visitors. Wee birdies sing and wild flowers spring – and the water is often calm enough to reflect the mountains. The best views are from the narrower N end, the quietest spots along the E shore. BALLOCH CASTLE COUNTRY PARK A useful introduction to Loch Lomond, with a visitor centre, woodland and meadow trails, walled garden, and fine views. Snacks, shop, disabled access; cl 1–2pm, late Oct–Apr; (01389) 758216; free. 8m up the A82 is the jolly little THISTLE BAGPIPE WORKS, which sometimes has demonstrations of bagpipe-making; cl 25 Dec, 1 Jan; (01436) 860250; free. Cruises round the lake leave from Balloch, as well as from the pretty village of Luss, a good place to hire a boat for pottering about on the water (there's a visitor centre here too). Past the N end of the loch, the Inverarnan Drovers Inn is an entertaining and very idiosyncratic stop.

🕸 **Minard** NR9897 CRARAE GARDENS (A83) Lovely gardens noted for their rare ornamental shrubs and rhododendrons, azaleas and conifers, set in a beautiful gorge overlooking Loch Fyne. Snacks, shop, and interesting plant sales (all summer only), limited disabled access; visitor centre cl Oct–Easter; (01546) 886614; £2.50.

🐾 🏚 🐌 **Mull** NM5834 For most people this island takes a bit of getting to, but if you are within reach its unspoilt coasts are certainly a dramatic lure. There's a good ferry service from Oban and Lochaline (and in summer from Kilchoan). A couple of castellated mansions, one going back to the 13th c and the other 19th-c, and a small museum in Tobermory, give some rainy-day scope. The interior is less interesting than the coast, with brackeny moors and conifer plantations over much of it, though there is some mountainous hill walking in the S. On the W coast the Keel Row at Fionnphort has decent food, overlooking offshore IONA, a is lovely island filled with a sense of spirituality as well as its tangible remains of ancient shrines; Scotland's first kings were buried here (as is former Labour leader John Smith).

🐾 🏚 🚂 **Oban** NM8630 This bustling coastal town is a busy ferry port and a popular place for holidaymakers, with a good cheerful atmosphere; the Oban Inn is fun, and the Lorne has decent food inc fresh local fish. Besides the main ferries, there are boats to Lismore and (just a hop really) Kerrera. DUNSTAFFNAGE CASTLE (4m N, off the A485) Beautifully set, this was once the prison of Flora MacDonald. It's now in ruins, but you can still see its gatehouse, round towers and masively thick walls. Shop, disabled access to visitor centre only; cl Oct–Mar; (01631) 562465; £1.50. A little way S at Cologin, the countrified Barn is useful for lunch, and often has evening folk music. Slightly further S towards Kilmore, the OBAN RARE BREEDS FARM has a collection of very visitor-friendly animals. Teas, shop, some disabled access; cl Nov–Easter; (01631) 770608; £4.

★ **Port Appin** NM9045 An attractive little settlement, very peaceful, where you can pick wild blueberries by the roadside, catch a boat across to Lismore, or just sit by the water keeping your eyes open for the seals that are so common around here. This is *Kidnapped* country, with the scene of the Appin Murder not far off, and a monument marking where James of the Glens was wrongly hanged at Ballachulish to the N (the Ballachulish Hotel has decent food and wide views).

★ **Tarbert** NR8668 Pleasant and quite picturesque small harbourside town; the West Loch Hotel (A83 W) does good local seafood.

⛴ **Taynuilt** NN0131 BONAWE IRON FURNACE (off the A85) The most complete remaining charcoal-fired ironworks in Britain, worked until 1876. Iron produced here was used for the cannonballs for Nelson's ships. Shop; cl Oct–Mar; (01866) 822432; £2.30. The Polfearn Hotel on the lochside does good food.

Besides those we've mentioned in the text above, or as places to eat at or stay in, inns where you can get a decent bite to eat and which are particularly well placed for walkers, drivers or just strollers in these parts include the Ardentinny Hotel by Loch Long at Ardentinny NS1887, Galley of Lorne at Ardfern NM8004, Village Inn at Arrochar NN2904, Tigh an Truish at Clachan Seil nr the bridge linking the little island of Seil NM7718 to the mainland (pleasant walk over to anchorage looking out to Jura), Kilchrenan Inn at Kilchrenan by Loch Awe NN0222, Portsonachan Hotel on the opposite side of that loch NN1227, Inverbeg Inn at Luss on Loch Lomond NS3593, Whistlefield Hotel by Loch Eck NS1493 and Loch Gair Hotel on Loch Gair NR9190.

Days Out

On the shores of Loch Fyne
Inveraray Jail and village; lunch at the Loch Fyne Hotel there; Inveraray Castle, or walk up to All Saints Church Bell Tower; Auchindrain Township, or Crarae garden.

Mementos of early settlers
Stroll along the towpath of the Crinan Canal; lunch at the Crinan Hotel, Crinan; Kilmartin's church, prehistoric cairns and Dunadd.

Island walkabout
Dunstaffnage castle; lunch at the Oban Inn, Oban (North Pier); take a boat to Kerrera, or visit Oban Rare Breeds Farm.

Underwater views and an industrial time warp
Sea Life Centre, Barcaldine; lunch at the Lochnell Arms or Falls of Lora, Connel; Bonawe furnace, Taynuilt.

The grandeur of the glens
Stroll in Glen Nevis, or along the Caledonian Canal at Neptune's Staircase; Glencoe Visitor Centre; lunch at the Clachaig there; drive on the A82 through Glencoe to Rannoch Moor, with a walk up to the Lost Valley or up the Devil's Staircase.

Walks

For general remarks about walking in the Highlands, see the Walks section of the **East Scotland** section of this chapter, above.

There are attractive walks along many inland lochs, and around the complex coast and sea lochs. The area has a fair number of forestry walks, sometimes taking in viewpoints and waterfalls. Many of the glens (valleys) give good scope for walking: the **River Leven** ⌂-1 has a fine walk through semi-wooded terrain along its glen, from Kinlochleven NN1861 to the dam of the gigantic Blackwater Reservoir NN3059 – with an awesomely bleak view of empty hills ahead.

Glen Nevis NN1570 ⌂-2 nr Fort William NN1174 is probably the best-known valley, with splendid gorge scenery for an easy long mile to Steall Falls. Nearby Ben Nevis NN1671, though Britain's highest mountain, is one of the more easily managed summits, with a long, safe path up: expect big crowds in season. Munro-baggers say it's far from being the best viewpoint mountain, though. (A 'Munro' is any 3,000ft peak (914 metres), named for Sir Hugh Munro, who first tabulated them; in 1997 climbers relaxing after a lifetime of gaining them all were shocked by the publication of a new list adding several more.) The Pap of Glencoe NN1259 and the succession of peaks in the largely unwooded Mamore Forest NN1565 (access also from Glen Nevis) are more interesting; they don't need rock-climbing expertise, just reasonable fitness and plenty of time.

Glencoe NN1556 ⌂-3 has a forest walk from the hospital by Glencoe village NN1058 past a lochan (small loch) above Loch Leven. Further into the glen you can discover the Lost Valley, a secret pasture-ground used by the MacDonalds for stolen cattle in times of clan warfare; it involves an ascent from the Meeting of the Three Waters NN1756. From **Altnafeadh** NN2256 ⌂-4 at the top of the glen, the West Highland Way takes a zigzag route N up the Devil's Staircase and through the mountains to Kinlochleven; another hill walk from Altnafeadh heads E up Beinn a' Chrôlaiste NN2456, one of Glencoe's more manageable peaks. **Glen Etive** NN1650 ⌂-5 is reached from Glencoe by a squelchy walk along glens, with close-ups of mighty peaks for reward.

Around **Inveraray Castle** NN0908 ⌂-6 woodland trails include a view over Loch Fyne from Dunchuach Tower.

Loch Lomond, surprisingly, hasn't a lot of paths: the shoreline track, partly metalled, on the quieter E side comes closest to the water. **Ben Lomond** NN3602 ⌂-7, the southernmost Munro, has a good ascent from Rowardennan NS3699 on this E side. **Conic Hill** NS4392 ⌂-8 is less than half Ben Lomond's height but more accessible, a straightforward but rewarding climb at the loch's SE corner from Balmaha NS4290.

The **Caledonian Canal** ⌂-9, leading NE from Corpach NN0976 and up a flight of locks known as Neptune's Staircase, has straightforward towpath walks with mountain backdrops. There's good access to the locks from the Moorings Hotel (good-value basement wine bar) at Banavie NN1177. The **Crinan Canal** ⌂-10 between Crinan NR7894 and Lochgilphead NR8687 provides a gentle stroll. Just N nr **Kilmartin** NR8398 ⌂-11, tracks link a succession of ancient burial mounds.

Islands within reach of Oban have a few shoreside walks and the odd castle, e.g. Lismore ⌂-12 (also ferry from Port Appin) and **Kerrera** ⌂-13. There are a few good walks on **Mull** ⌂-14, though as usual not many defined paths.

Where to eat

Cairndow NN1810 Loch Fyne Oyster Bar Clachan Farm (01499) 600264 Relaxed restaurant in converted farm buildings by Loch Fyne and serving high-quality seafood and smoked fish (they have their own smokehouse); reasonably priced wine list and a warm welcome; cl 25 Dec, 1 Jan; disabled access. £17|£5.95.

Fort William NN1074 ALEXANDRA The Parade (01397) 702241 Popular hotel in town square with meals and snacks in the Great Food Stop (open all day) and evening restaurant; disabled access. £18 in restaurant|£5.

Kentallen NN0057 ARDSHEAL HOUSE (01631) 740227 Particularly good food in attractive conservatory dining room of fine hotel set in 900 acres; very comfortable rooms, antiques, and relaxed atmosphere; lovely bdrms; cl Dec–Feb; disabled access in dining room (not bdrms). £23 4-course dinner.

Kentallen NN0057 HOLLY TREE (01631) 740292 Super food in carefully converted railway station, cosy public rooms, lovely shoreside setting (best to book in winter); bdrms; cl Nov; disabled access. £33|£5.50.

Tayvallich NR7386 TAYVALLICH INN (01546) 870282 Simply refurbished pub overlooking yacht anchorage with quite superb local seafood (other decent dishes too), dining conservatory (no smoking), and friendly service; cl Mon Nov–Mar; limited disabled access. £28.

NORTH SCOTLAND

Sensational scenery in the west and on Skye, solitude in the north, good golf and empty beaches on the east coast.

There are a few interesting places to visit scattered through the area, but its main draw is unquestionably the scenery, and the feeling of getting away from it all. The west coast has glorious vistas of sea, mountains and islands. Long empty sandy beaches (and good golf courses) make the east coast suit a quiet summer holiday. The north coast is relatively wild and empty: addictive to some people, harsh and inhospitable to others. Skye is idyllic in good weather – and fears that the new toll bridge would flood it with too many tourists have proved unfounded.

The area is usually at its best between late May and early July, while the days are very long and before the midges have really got into their stride.

Where to stay

Achiltibuie NC0208 SUMMER ISLES Achiltibuie, Ullapool, Ross-shire IV26 2YG (01854) 622282 *£88; 12 comfortable rms. Beautifully placed above the sea towards the end of a very long and lonely road, this warm, friendly and well furnished hotel has delicious set menus using fresh ingredients (in which it's largely self-sufficient), a choice of superb puddings and an excellent array of uncommon cheeses; pretty watercolours and flowers; cl mid-Oct–Easter; children over 6.

Applecross NG7144 APPLECROSS Applecross, Strathcarron, Ross-shire IV54 8LR (01520) 744262 *£50; 5 rms with breathtaking sea views over Sound of Raasay, shared bthrms. Gloriously placed informal inn with beer garden on the shore, simple, comfortable and friendly bar, log or peat fire in lounge, lively landlord, small restaurant with excellent fresh fish and seafood; cl 23 Dec–5 Jan.

Ardvasar NG6203 ARDVASAR Ardvasar, Island of Skye IV48 8RS (01471) 844223 *£70, plus special breaks; 9 rms. Comfortably modernised 18th-c inn with spectacular views and friendly owners; nice residents' lounge and cocktail bar, popular locals' bar, open fire, enjoyable food inc local fish and shellfish, and very good breakfasts; cl Nov–Feb.

Arisaig NM6586 ARISAIG HOUSE Beasdale, Arisaig, Inverness-shire PH39 4NR (01687) 450622 *£168, plus special breaks; 14 most attractive rms with wonderful views, and 2 suites. Beautifully furnished extremely comfortable hotel in attractive wooded and terraced grounds close to the shore; elegant drawing room, cosy morning room, lovely flowers, and very good, imaginative food using fresh local produce; billiards room, croquet; cl Nov–Apr; children over 10.

Cromarty NH7867 ROYAL Marine Terrace, Cromarty, Ross-shire IV11 8YN (01381) 600217 *£55, plus special breaks; 10 rms. Traditional hotel by the waterfront with friendly owners and staff, attractive lounges, bars and sun lounge, and Scottish dishes in dining room; becomes particularly busy in the summer.

Drumnadrochit NH5029 BORLUM FARMHOUSE Drumnadrochit, Inverness IV3 6XN (01456) 450358 £54; 6 rms. Traditional stone farmhouse with marvellous views over Loch Ness, warm comfortably furnished sitting room with log fire, summer conservatory sitting room, friendly atmosphere, and good Scottish breakfasts; BHS-approved riding centre, and you can help with animals on the farm; good provision for families; self-catering and caravan/camping also.

Drumnadrochit NH5029 POLMAILY HOUSE Drumnadrochit, Inverness IV3 6XT (01456) 450343 *£117, plus special breaks; 11 light, pretty rms. Very relaxing and homely hotel in 18 acres of grounds, with comfortable drawing room and library, open fires, and excellent food in the no smoking restaurant (wonderful packed lunches too); a happy place for families, with swimming pool, tennis, croquet, ponies and pets; disabled access.

Garve NH3969 INCHBAE LODGE Inchbae, Garve, Ross-shire IV23 2PH (01997) 455269 £66, plus special breaks; 12 rms, 6 in chalet. Friendly former hunting lodge in lovely Highland setting with comfortable, homely lounges, winter log fires, small bar (liked by locals), and good fixed-price 4-course evening meals using fresh local produce; lots of wildlife, marvellous walks; cl 25–29 Dec; pets welcome by prior arrangement.

Glenelg NG8119 GLENELG Glenelg, Kyle, Ross-shire IV40 8JR (01599) 522273 £98 inc dinner, plus special breaks; 6 individually decorated and comfortable rms, all with fine views. Overlooking Skye across its own beach, this carefully refurbished, homely hotel has a relaxed bar, comfortable sofas and blazing fires, friendly staff and locals, good food using local venison, local hill-bred lamb and lots of wonderfully fresh fish and seafood, and quite a few whiskies; the drive to the inn involves spectacular views from the steep road; cl Nov–Feb; disabled access.

Harlosh NG2842 HARLOSH HOUSE Harlosh, Dunvegan, Island of Skye IV55 8ZG (01470) 521367 £95; 6 rms, 5 with own bthrm, and most with lovely views. One of the oldest buildings on NW Skye, this 18th-c house is on a small peninsula jutting into Loch Bracadale; lochside gardens and lots of wildlife, a wonderfully quiet, homely lounge, home-made breads, imaginative cooking using fresh local produce in evening restaurant, and fine breakfasts; cl late Oct–Easter.

Isle Ornsay NG6912 KINLOCH LODGE Isle Ornsay, Island of Skye IV43 8QY (01471) 833214 £122, plus special breaks; 10 rms. Surrounded by rugged mountain scenery at the head of Loch Na Dal, this charming little white stone hotel has a relaxed atmosphere in its comfortable and attractive drawing rooms, antiques, portraits, flowers, log fires, and good imaginative food; cookery demonstrations; cl Christmas and New Year; children by arrangement.

Isle Ornsay NG6912 TIGH OSDA EILEAN IARMAIN Isle Ornsay, Island of Skye

IV43 8QR (01471) 833332 *£95, plus special breaks; 12 individual rms (best in main hotel), all with fine views. Sparkling white hotel with Gaelic-speaking staff and locals, big cheerfully busy bar, pretty dining room with lovely sea views, and very good food.

Kilchoan NM4863 MEALL MO CHRIDHE COUNTRY HOUSE Kilchoan, Acharacle, Argyll PH36 4LH (01972) 510238 *£78, plus special breaks; 3 warmly comfortable rms. Attractive 18th-c former manse in 45 acres with really lovely views over the Sound of Mull; log fire and sea views in homely lounge, very good food at candlelit dining table using fresh local and home-grown produce, their own free-range eggs, and home-made bread, scones and preserves (which they also sell in their small farm shop), and very friendly owners; take your own wine; handy summer car ferry Kilchoan–Tobermory; cl Nov–end Mar; children over 12.

Kylesku NC2333 UNAPOOL HOUSE (A894 just S) Unapool, Kylesku, Sutherland IV27 4HW (01971) 502344 *£35; 1 rm. Traditional late 18th-c W Highland cottage on the edge of Loch Glencoul and surrounded by magnificent scenery; cosy lounge with open fire, very good home-cooked meals by prior arrangement, and boat hire; self-catering cottages; cl Nov–Apr.

Lybster ND2436 PORTLAND ARMS Lybster, Caithness KW3 6BS (01593) 721208 £68; 23 comfortable rms. Staunch old granite hotel with really friendly staff, attractive dining room, generous helpings of good fresh food and fine breakfasts, small cosy panelled lounge bar, and informal locals' bar; shooting/fishing can be arranged; disabled access.

Melvich NC8765 MELVICH HOTEL Melvich, Thurso, Caithness KW14 7YJ (01641) 531206 *£65, plus special breaks; 14 rms with showers (4 bthrms in addition). Small traditional hotel in lovely spot with homely furniture and peat fires in the civilised lounge, cosy bar, very relaxing atmosphere, friendly owners and staff, good food (especially local seafood and wild salmon), and fine views over Melvich Bay.

Mey ND2873 CASTLE ARMS Mey, Thurso, Caithness KW14 8XH (01847) 851244 *£58; 8 good-value rms. Warm friendly village inn in wide open countryside with marvellous restaurant food, wide range of good bar food, interesting whiskies, and welcoming staff; disabled access.

Plockton NG8033 PLOCKTON 41 Harbour St, Plockton, Ross-shire IV52 8TN (01599) 544274 £55; 8 rms, 4 in cottage. Small notably friendly hotel in a row of elegant houses by a shore lined with palm trees and flowering shrubs, looking over the sheltered anchorage to rugged mountains, with comfortably furnished, lively lounge bar, separate public bar, enjoyable food in little no smoking restaurant, good breakfasts, a good choice of whiskies, and attentive owners; disabled access to cottage.

Portree NG4843 CRAIGLOCKHART Beaumont Crescent, Portree, Island of Skye IV51 9DF (01478) 612233 *£44; 9 rms, 3 with own bthrm. Small family-run guesthouse overlooking harbour, with fine views through picture windows in lounge and dining room and good breakfasts.

Portree NG4843 ROSEDALE Beaumont Rd, Portree, Island of Skye IV51 9DF (01478) 613131 £80, plus special breaks; 23 rms, many with harbour views. Built from 3 fishermen's cottages with lots of passages and stairs, this waterfront hotel has 2 traditional lounges, small first-floor restaurant with freshly cooked popular food, lots of whiskies in the cocktail bar, helpful staff, harbourside garden and marvellous views; cl Oct–Apr.

Raasay NG5641 (off Skye) ISLE OF RAASAY Raasay, Kyle of Lochalsh, Ross-shire IV40 8PB (01478) 660222 *£50, plus special breaks; 12 rms. Victorian hotel with marvellous views over the Sound of Raasay to Skye, popular with walkers and birdwatchers; no petrol on the island; disabled access.

Scarista NG0996 SCARISTA HOUSE Scarista, Harris, Western Isles HS3 3HX (01859) 550238 £100; 5 rms, some in annexe. Marvellously wild countryside and empty beaches surround this isolated small hotel with its homely rooms, warm, friendly atmosphere, plenty of books and records (no radio, T-V or newspapers), and good food in candlelit dining room using home-grown vegetables and herbs, hand-made cheeses, their own eggs, home-made bread, cakes, biscuits, yoghurt and marmalade, and lots of fish and shellfish; excellent for wildlife, walks and fishing; cl Oct–April; children over 8; dogs allowed.

Scourie NC1544 EDDRACHILLES Badcall Bay, Scourie, Lairg, Sutherland IV27 4TH (01971) 502080 *£79, plus special breaks; 11 comfortable rms. Well run hotel in its own 320 acres and overlooking Badcall Bay with wonderful island views; popular with nature-lovers – bird sanctuary nearby, seals, fishing and walking; cl Nov–Feb; children over 3.

Shiel Bridge NG9318 KINTAIL LODGE Shiel Bridge, Kyle of Lochalsh, Ross-shire IV40 8HL (01599) 511275 £75, plus special breaks; 12 good-value big rms, most with own bthrm. Pleasantly informal and fairly simple former shooting lodge on the shores of Loch Duich, with magnificent views, 4 acres of walled gardens, residents' lounge bar and comfortable sitting room, good, well prepared food inc wild salmon, and fine collection of malt whiskies.

Shieldaig NG8154 TIGH AN EILEAN Shieldaig, Strathcarron, Ross-shire IV54 8XN (01520) 755251 *£100.50; 11 rms. Attractive hotel in outstanding position with lovely views of pine-covered island and sea, and within easy reach of NTS Torridon Estate and Beinn Eighe nature reserve; pretty, comfortable residents' lounge with well stocked honesty bar, modern dining room with delicious, excellent quality food, and warmly friendly owner; private fishing and sea fishing arranged; cl end Oct–Apr.

Skeabost NG4148 SKEABOST HOUSE Skeabost, Portree, Island of Skye IV51 9NP (01470) 532202 £90, plus special breaks; 26 rms, 5 in annexe in Garden House. Smart, friendly little hotel with lawn that runs down to Loch Snizort (good salmon fishing), spacious no smoking lounge (marvellous buffet table), Victorian-style dining conservatory, lovely afternoon tea, log fires, high-ceilinged bar off stately hall, and billiards room; bog-and-water garden, 9-hole golf course; cl Jan/Feb.

Strontian NM8161 KILCAMB LODGE HOTEL Strontian, Acharacle, Argyll PH36 4HY (01967) 402257 £139 inc dinner; plus special breaks; 11 rms. Warmly friendly little hotel in 30 acres by Loch Sunart, with log fires in 2 lounges, carefully cooked food using fresh local ingredients, fine choice of malt whiskies in small bar, and a relaxed atmosphere; cl Dec–Feb; children over 8 in dining room; disabled access.

Torridon NG8956 LOCH TORRIDON Torridon, Ashnasheen, Ross-shire IV22 2EY (01445) 791242 £110, plus special breaks; 21 comfortable rms. Built in 1887 as a shooting lodge in 58 acres at the foot of Ben Damph on the shores of Upper Loch Torridon, this turreted stone house has unusual ornate ceilings and panelling, log fires and innovative cooking; disabled access.

Ullapool NH1294 ALTNAHARRIE Ullapool, Ross-shire IV26 2SS (01854) 633230 *£330 inc dinner; 8 rms. On the shores of Loch Broom and reached by a 10min boat journey, this carefully restored house was originally built for drovers: 2 lounges with lots of books, an open fire, a mix of Scandinavian and English furnishings, marvellously quiet relaxing atmosphere, room service (they think tea-making facilities in rooms are a sign of neglect), perhaps the best food in Scotland – 5 set courses with much of the food home-grown or caught locally – and very good wine list; no smoking; cl Nov–Easter; children over 8.

Ullapool NH1294 CEILIDH PLACE Ullapool, Ross-shire IV26 2GY (01854) 612103 £110, plus special breaks; 13 rms, most with own bthrm, plus 10 in annexe across the road. White-painted hotel in quiet side street with attractive conservatory dining room, stylish café/bar with attractive modern prints and plants, good food, decent wines and cognacs, and a relaxed friendly atmosphere; cl 2 wks mid-Jan.

To see and do

⊛ **Achiltibuie** NC0208
HYDROPONICUM Bizarre indoor garden of the future – without any soil. Fascinating guided tours show how plants such as figs, lemons and bananas grow quite happily using the nutrients from the soil, but not the soil itself. Good home-made meals and snacks, shop; hourly tours Easter–Sept; (01854) 622202; £4.

♂ **Auckengill** ND3664 NORTHLANDS VIKING CENTRE (Old School) Interesting displays on how the Norsemen came from Scandinavia to Shetland, Orkney and Caithness, with a Viking longship and other relics. Shop, disabled access; cl early Sept–May; (01955) 607771; £1.20.

★ ❀ ⊛ ♤ **Balmacara** NG8127 (A67) Huge crofting estate surrounding the Kyle of Lochalsh, with walks through breathtaking scenery; you can still see traditional crofting at Drumbuie and Duirnish. The landscape is interspersed with lochs and impressive landmarks like the Five Sisters of Kintail and Beinn Fhada. LOCHALSH HOUSE (3m E of Kyle of Lochalsh on the A87) Wonderful woodland gardens, with peaceful walks, collections of rhododendrons, hydrangeas, fuchsias and other plants, and views towards Skye. Open all year, guided walks Jun–Aug; (01599) 566325; £1; NTS. PLOCKTON This nearby waterside village is idyllic, with palm trees along the village street; the TV series *Hamish Macbeth* was filmed here. The Plockton Hotel has good generous food.

⚘ **Balnakiel** NC3969 The most NW part of mainland Britain, a wild and remote spot with spectacular scenery, and a little CRAFT VILLAGE (some bits cl Sun, and limited opening in winter; (01971) 511277; free).

♂ ✙ **Bettyhill** NC7062 STRATHNAVER MUSEUM A good informative memorial to the notorious Clearances of the Highlands (cl winter Mons and wknds; £1.50), with a finely carved 9th-c Celtic stone in the churchyard outside. The Bettyhill Hotel does decent food. Just S is a wonderful NATURE RESERVE, and the beach nearby is attractive.

⚓ ♋ **Cape Wrath** NC2575 This stormy tip of coast is guarded by a lonely lighthouse. In summer you can make an adventurous expedition here from Durness nr the beautiful sea loch of Eriboll, by boat across the Kyle of Durness and then along a very long rough track to the lighthouse itself. Durness also has atmospheric boat tours of the Smoo Cave and its underground waterfall; cl Nov–May; (01971) 511259; £2.50.

⚓ **Cromarty** NH7867 DOLPHIN ECOSSE (Bank House) Boat trips out to see the local bottlenose dolphins: they can't guarantee sightings, but nine out of ten of their trips do come across dolphins, and they point out various seabirds and local landmarks along the way. Very friendly and informal, and rated very highly by readers. Whale-watching trips too in Aug and Sept – best to book on (01381) 600323; *£15. The friendly Royal Hotel has good-value food and lovely views.

🏛 **Dornie** NG8825 EILEAN DONAN CASTLE (off the A87) Connected to the mainland by a causeway, and unforgettably beautiful. First built in 1220, destroyed in 1719, and then restored at the beginning of this century, it's perfectly positioned at the meeting point of Lochs Long, Duich and Alsh; cl Nov–Mar; (01599) 555202; £3.

! ⚓ 🏛 **Drumnadrochit** NH5029 The best place to begin exploring LOCH NESS, a striking 24-mile loch with the largest volume of fresh water of any lake in the British Isles; up to 215 metres (700 ft) deep in places, so it's not hard to see why stories sprang up of what was hidden in its waters. The OFFICIAL LOCH NESS MONSTER EXHIBITION (Drumnadrochit Hotel) is a walk-through multi-media experience tracing the legend from its beginnings in Highland folklore to the scientific investigations of recent years. There's a kilt-maker on site. Meals, snacks, shop, disabled access; cl 25–26 Dec; (01456) 450218;

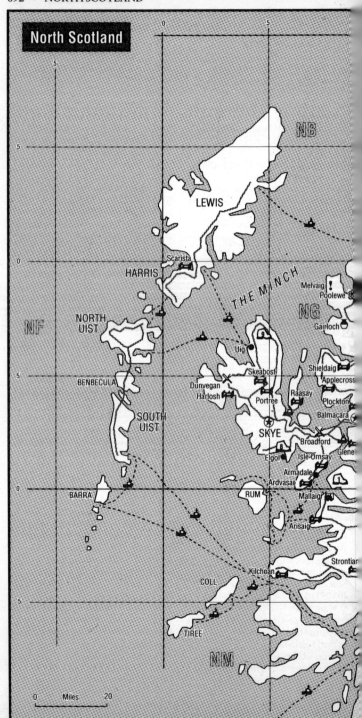

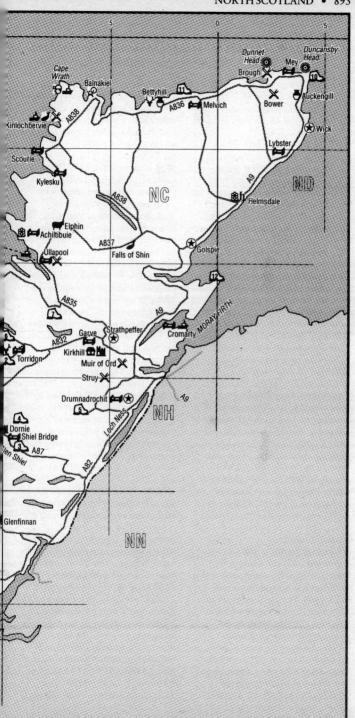

£4.50. You can generally take BOAT TRIPS on the lake, some of them equipped with sonar for monster-spotting. Just SE of town on the western shore are the remains of 14th-c URQUHART CASTLE, once the biggest castle in Scotland. A piper plays here every day Jun–Sept. Snacks, shop; cl 25–26 Dec, 1–2 Jan; (01456) 450551; £3.20.

❈ **Duncansby Head** ND4073 A grand spot on a fine day, with cliff walks giving a good view of the spectacular Duncansby Stacks offshore. It's nr John o' Groats, where the hotel on the harbour looking across to the Orkneys has decent food, and which gets its share of visitors under the mistaken impression that it's the most northerly point on mainland Britain – see next entry.

❈ **Dunnet Head** ND2076 Mainland Britain's furthest point N, with views to Orkney. A lovely spot on a clear early summer's day, with spring flowers in the close turf, and puffins pottering around – but wild and unforgiving when the weather changes.

🐗 **Elphin** NC2112 HIGHLAND AND RARE BREEDS FARM 🔲 (A835) Traditional Scottish farm animals close up, on a family-worked croft in attractive setting. They sell fleeces and hand-spun wool. Snacks, shop, some disabled access; cl Oct–mid-May; (01854) 666204; £2.95.

🐟 **Falls of Shin** NC5806 (B864 S of Lairg) There's a good chance of seeing SALMON LEAPING here in Jun or early July, especially if there's been a dry spell followed by rain so that the river is in spate.

🐚 **Gairloch** NG8076 The enthusiastically run GAIRLOCH HERITAGE MUSEUM is perhaps the best of the several heritage museums in the Highlands. There's a secret portrait of Bonnie Prince Charlie which at first looks like the meaningless daubings of a child, but when revolved at speed in a metal cylinder reveals his likeness. Meals, snacks, shop, disabled access; cl Sun, and all Oct–Mar exc by arrangement; (01445) 712449; £1.50. The Old Inn

here is a useful stop, and Gairloch is a useful base for hikers.

🏛 **Glenfinnan** NM8980 JACOBITE MONUMENT (A830) Built in 1815 to commemorate the Highlanders who fought and died for Bonnie Prince Charlie, in a commanding position at the head of Loch Shiel. A visitor centre has exhibitions on the prince. Good snacks, shop, limited disabled access; cl Oct–Easter; *£1.50; (01397) 722250; NTS.

🏰 ❀ 🔳 **Golspie** NC8500 DUNROBIN CASTLE (A9) Splendid castle – a gleaming turreted structure with views out to sea and gardens modelled on those at Versailles. The family home of the Earls and Dukes of Sutherland for longer than anyone can remember, the site was named after Earl Robin in the 13th c; he was responsible for the original square keep. Drastically renovated in the 19th c, it has fine collections of furnishings and art, inc several Canalettos, and a unique collection of Pictish stones. Snacks, shop; house cl am Sun, and mid-Oct–Easter, gardens open all year; (01408) 633177; *£5 (gardens free when castle closed).

🎋 ❀ **Helmsdale** ND0315 TIMESPAN VISITOR CENTRE 🔲 (Dunrobin St) Reconstructions of scenes in Highland history (with sound effects), and interesting herb garden. Teas, shop, disabled access; cl am Sun, mid-Oct–Easter; (01431) 821327; £2.75.

🐟 **Kinlochbervie** NC2156 A friendly village with decent beaches, mountains and scenery around; it's most lively around 6pm on Mon–Thurs (2pm Fri), when the fishing boats return to the pier and auction their catch. There may be boat trips round the harbour.

🎋 ☕ **Kirkhill** NH5543 MONIACK CASTLE (A862) Former fortress of the Lovat chiefs, now producing traditional country wines – also meat and game preserves, and an interesting apricot, almond and banana jam. Meals, snacks, shop; cl Sun, 25 Dec; (01463) 831283; free.

! **Melvaig** NG7391 RUBHA REIGH LIGHTHOUSE Remote outpost several miles along a track N of Melvaig; they organise enjoyable activity holidays in the splendidly wild countryside around, from walking and abseiling to rolling in mud pools; B & B or hostel-style rooms – don't worry about the colour of the water, it's just peaty; (01445) 771263.

⊛ Poolewe NG8580 INVEREWE (A832) Unmissable beautiful gardens full of rare and subtropical plants, with a magnificent background of mountain scenery. The Atlantic Drift is responsible for the special microclimate which lets these unusual plants flourish even though this is further N than Moscow. Guided walks wkdys at 1.30pm, Apr–mid-Oct. Meals, snacks, shop, disabled access; visitor centre and restaurant cl Nov–mid-Mar; (01445) 781200; £4.50; NTS. Choppys has good well priced food.

🏔 👒 ⊛ 🏌 ⛵ Island of Skye NG4432 After Lewis, the biggest of the islands off the Scottish coast, now linked to the mainland by a bridge: islanders who'd campaigned for the bridge didn't expect the high tolls (which were later reduced), and others were initially unnerved by the prospect of easier access bringing floods of visitors and the end of the island's unique air of romance – so far neither has happened. The closing of the Kyle of Lochalsh ferry is lamented (though you can still emulate Bonnie Prince Charlie and Flora MacDonald on one from Mallaig, or the tiny summer one to Kylerhea NG7825 from past Glenelg NG8119). CLAN DONALD CENTRE (Armadale) The castle was built for Lord Macdonald in 1815; it now houses an excellent visitor centre looking at the history of the clan, and the surrounding 40 acres offer beautiful walks among gardens and woodlands. Sleat, this southern peninsula, is known as the Garden of Skye. Very good restaurant, shop, disabled access; cl Nov–Mar; (01471) 844305; £3.40. DUNVEGAN CASTLE Dramatically set on the sea loch of Dunvegan, this has been the home of the Chief of Macleod for 800 years; no other Scottish castle has been inhabited by the same family for so long. Among its relics is a lock of Bonnie Prince Charlie's hair. Staying here inspired Walter Scott's *Lord of the Isles*. Meals, snacks, shop, limited disabled access; cl am Sun, and usually Nov–Mar (though worth giving them a ring if you're here then); (01470) 521206; £4.80. There are several good self-catering cottages in the attractive grounds, and BOAT TRIPS go from the jetty to a nearby colony of brown and great grey Atlantic seals (Easter–Oct). Nearby Kilmuir has a MUSEUM OF ISLAND LIFE; cl Sun, and Nov–Mar; £1.50. The coasts of Skye have plenty of opportunities for gentle pottering, and for finding quiet coves and bays, especially on the W coast, where for instance Tarskavaig NG5810 or Elgol NG5114 in the S, or Stein NG2556 in the N, are lovely spots to watch the sun go down. There may be summer boat trips to the lonely and dramatic inlet of Loch Coruisk from Elgol: (01471) 866230 for times. The TROTTERNISH PENINSULA in the NE has some quite extraordinary rock scenery; the Glenview Hotel at Culnaknock up here has good food, and in season the Flodigarry Hotel serves food all day. The jagged teeth of the Cuillin mountain range to the SE of the centre are unforgettable. Portree NG4843, the busiest harbour, is attractive and quite picturesque, though in summer tends to swarm with visitors; the harbourside Pier Hotel is right in the thick of the action, the quieter Cuillins View on the outskirts has good-value food in its conservatory. Besides places mentioned in the **Where to stay** and **Where to eat** sections, the Misty Isle at Dunvegan, Sligachan Inn at the junction of the A850 and A863 in the middle of the island, Struan Grill at Struan and the waterside Old Inn at Carbost (handy for the Talisker distillery, which can be visited) all do decent food. Offshore, Raasay is very peaceful, an ideal place for gentle pottering without lots of competition from other visitors – and for some quite stiff hill walks if that's what you prefer.

★ ☼ ♘ **Strathpeffer** NH4858
Originally a fashionable 19th-c spa
resort, this has quite a different feel
from the rest of the area, with its
rather continental appearance of
dignified hotels and villas stepped up
among its wooded slopes; some call it
the Harrogate of the North. The
restored Victorian railway station
houses a MUSEUM OF CHILDHOOD, with
several craft workshops in summer.
Snacks, shop; disabled access; cl am
Sun, and Nov–Feb (exc by
appointment); (01997) 421031;
*£1.50.

✟ **Torridon** NG8956 COUNTRYSIDE
CENTRE (junction of the A896 and the
Diabaig road) This is the gateway to a
huge area of nature reserve in
stunning mountain scenery – some
say the best in Scotland. It has
displays on the scenery and wildlife,
as well as a deer park and deer
museum. Visitor centre cl am Sun,
and all Oct–Apr; (01445) 791221;
£1; NTS. Nearby at the Mains there
are herds of red deer. The Kinlochewe
Hotel (A896 E) has decent food; to
reach anywhere N of here by car from
the S, incidentally, it's much quicker
to go by Inverness than to make your
way all the way up the W coast.

⚓ **Ullapool** NH1294 A good centre,
with quite a busy harbour, a lot going
on for a small place – and good eating

(besides the places we've picked out
in the **Where to stay** and **Where to eat**
sections, the fish and chip restaurant
is very good, with surprisingly
presentable white wines, and the
Ferry Boat is useful). You can get a
ferry out to the Summer Isles.

♌ 🏠 🏔 **Wick** ND3551 The history of
the town is well presented at the very
good WICK HERITAGE CENTRE, in 8
buildings by the harbour; cl Sun, all
Oct–May; (01955) 605393; £2. You
can buy factory seconds at the
CAITHNESS GLASS FACTORY (Airport
industrial estate) and watch glass-
making demonstrations (not wknds).
Meals, snacks, shop, disabled access;
cl Sun Jan–Mar; (01955) 602286;
free. Just S of town, the CASTLE OF OLD
WICK is a ruined 4-storey square tower,
probably dating from the 12th c.

🚂 ❀ A good way of seeing the
scenery of the Highlands is by train:
the WEST HIGHLAND LINE runs
steamtrains in summer between Fort
William and Mallaig, and year-round
normal trains. The views are terrific.
Another good train service is the
cross-Highland line from Inverness to
Kyle of Lochalsh, in 2½ hours – the
last minutes of which are much the
best.

This is a part of the world where
inns doing a decent bite to eat are very
much at a premium, and a welcome

Days Out

Highland drama
Beinn Eighe nature reserve/mountain trail; lunch at the Kinlochewe Hotel;
Torridon Countryside Centre; drive to Applecross.

Sea lochs of the far north-west
Ullapool; lunch at Morefield Motel there; drive SE on the A835 to the Falls
of Measach; take the A832 to Inverewe garden, Poolewe; Gairloch
Heritage Museum.

Monsters
Drive into Glen Affric (see **Walks** ⌂-5) for a stroll; lunch at the Struy Inn,
Struy; Loch Ness Monster show, Drumnadrochit; Urquhart Castle; Loch
Ness boat trip.

Skye's changing moods
Portree; drive round the Trotternish peninsula, past the Old Man of Storr
and the Quiraing; lunch at Skeabost House, Skeabost; Dunvegan Castle,
Armadale; boat trip to spot seals, or Museum of Island Life (cl Sun).

sight indeed after miles of empty road. Besides those listed elsewhere, ones we can recommend for their positions include the Aultbea Inn at Aultbea NG8689, Aultguish Hotel NH3570 on the A835 nr Loch Glascarnoch, Badachro Inn at Badachro NG7773, Northern Sands at Dunnet ND2170, Lock at Fort Augustus NH3709, Cluanie by the loch (walks and maybe eagles) in Glen Shiel NH0711, Garvault Inn extraordinarily isolated on the B871 N of Kinbrace NC8732, Kylesku Hotel at Kylesku NC2234 (the boatman here has taken readers for fascinating 4 hr boat tours), Lewiston Arms at Lewiston NH5029, Loch Carron Hotel on Loch Carron NG9039, Glenuig Hotel at Lochailort NM7682, Inver Lodge Hotel overlooking Lochinver harbour NC0923 and Scrabster Inn at Scrabster ND0970. Almost all have bedrooms.

Walks

The Highlands offer ultra-tough mountain walking, but relatively few easier routes on defined paths (see general remarks in the **Walks** section of the **East Scotland** section of this chapter); shorter circular walks are few and far between. **Knoydart** NG8000 ⌂-1 is a real Highland wilderness on the W coast, glorious roadless country that's irresistible – given good weather, full equipment and strong legs. On this coast the areas of **Torridon** NG8956 ⌂-2 and **Kintail** NG9917 ⌂-3, inc the Five Sisters of Kintail, are also wonderful for challenging walks, and there are a few outstanding easier ones, based, for example, on Loch Torridon's shores. The **Falls of Glomach** NH0125 ⌂-4 on Kintail are a tremendous waterfall in a wilderness setting.

Glen Affric NH1922 ⌂-5 is one of the most majestic inland glens, with a walking route along its floor. **Beinn Eighe** NG9660 ⌂-6 is one of the easier mountain ascents, with a well marked mountain trail making a circular route above Loch Maree. The **Falls of Measach** NH2078 ⌂-7, with a mighty 60-metre (200-ft) – drop, are the highlight of the mile-long, sheer-sided Corrieshalloch Gorge, owned by the National Trust for Scotland and equipped with a viewing platform. Skye has lovely shoreside walks, such as from **Elgol** NG5213 ⌂-8 to Loch na Creitheach NG5120 at the heart of the formidable Cuillin, a mecca for rock-climbers. The **Quiraing** NG4569 ⌂-9 in the NE is a fascinating tumbled mass, with a surprisingly manageable path through it.

The E coast lacks the Highland drama but is blessed with a much drier climate: it's often nice to escape here from the W when the rain gets you down. **Duncansby Head** ND4073 ⌂-10, the NE tip of Britain, offers an absorbing coastal walk S to see the 60-metres (200-ft) high Stacks of Duncansby, rock pinnacles now detached from the land. **Strathy Point** NC8269 ⌂-11 W of Thurso, with a lighthouse at the end of a narrow peninsula, is a pleasant stroll along the little road from its car park. **Tarbat Ness** NH9487 ⌂-12 juts out from the S side of Dornoch Firth; rather isolated, but worth the journey. You can walk around the peninsula here, from Portmahomack NH9184, past the lighthouse, and then along the S coast past a ruined castle to reach Rockfield NH9283.

Where to eat

Bower ND2363 Bower 1½m S of the B876 (01955) 661292 Small, fairly simple country inn with good-value food, dining room, low ceilings, open fires, warship and submarine memorabilia, and friendly informal service; high chairs available; disabled access; £18.50|£5.

Broadford NG6423 FIG TREE (01471) 822616 Enjoyable home-made food inc fresh fish and vegetarian choices in friendly little place on the Island of Skye; cl end Nov–1st Mar; disabled access. £17.95|£4.

Brough ND2274 DUNNET HEAD TEAROOM/RESTAURANT (01847) 851774 Small, traditional, unpretentious cottage with good, reasonably priced food and snacks served by warmly friendly owners – fair choice of vegetarian dishes, fresh salmon, local seafood, and local beef; take your own wine; bdrms; open 3–8pm (last orders then), tearoom cl Oct–Easter; children must be well behaved. |£6.

Dunvegan NG1757 MACLEOD'S TABLE (01470) 521310 Decorated with pine throughout, this popular family restaurant in Dunvegan Castle on the Island of Skye serves very reasonably priced, generous helpings of all-day breakfasts, morning coffee, snacks and full meals, and afternoon teas; friendly, helpful staff; loch cruises, sea colony, castle gardens and craft shops; cl 31 Oct–2 wks before Easter; disabled access. £15|£5.

Kinlochbervie NC2156 OLD SCHOOL HOUSE (01971) 521383 Very good food in old school building with school-related items like photographs, maps, notebooks on tables; home-grown vegetables, local fish and venison, enjoyable puddings, and very good service; bdrms in newish building; disabled access; cl 25 Dec/1 Jan. £16|£3.50.

Muir of Ord NH5250 DOWER HOUSE (01463) 870090 Very good modern cooking in attractive hotel restaurant, fine wines, and friendly service; lovely gardens; bdrms; children over 5 in restaurant; disabled access. £31.50|£2.80.

Struy NH3939 STRUY INN (01463) 761219 Clean, pleasant and friendly small inn with very good, fairly priced food, and good range of malt whiskies; bdrms; cl Mon–Thurs Nov–March. £20|£6.25.

Ullapool NH1294 MOREFIELD MOTEL (01854) 612161 Large helpings of exceptionally fresh fish and seafood (owners are ex-fishermen and divers), cooked enterprisingly, Aberdeen Angus steaks and roast beef, and vegetarian dishes in smart restaurant of basic hotel, also bar food; restaurant cl 25–26 Dec, 1–2 Jan; disabled access. £16.50|£6.50.

Special thanks to Tom and Joan Thirlaway, Mrs L Weare, Bob and Maggie Atherton.

We welcome reports from readers . . .

This *Guide* depends on readers' reports. Do help us if you can – in return, we offer a discount on the next edition to people who've helped us with reports for it. Tell us what you think about places already in it, and any-thing extra you think we should say about them. And send us your ideas for inclusion in the next edition: places to visit, eat at or stay in, attractive drives or walks, maybe even unusual interesting shops you know of. Use the card in the middle, the report forms at the end, or just write – no stamp needed: *The Good Guide to Britain*, FREEPOST TN1569, Wadhurst, E Sussex TN5 7BR.

Scotland Calendar

Some of these dates were provisional as we went to press. Please check information with the telephone numbers provided.

Highland Games take place all over Scotland and include ancient traditional sports: putting the stone, throwing the hammer and tossing the caber, as well as athletics, Highland dancing, piping and carnival entertainments.

JANUARY

1 **Edinburgh** *Turner Watercolours* at the National Gallery of Scotland – *till Sat 31* (0131) 556 8921; **Kirkwall** Boys' and Men's Ba' Games: 200-year-old mass football game with tussles lasting up to 6 hours (01856) 872961

9 **Scalloway** Fire Festival: torch procession and burning galley – *till Sat 10* (01595) 880345

10 **Burghead** Burning of the Clavie: old Scottish New Year, when a burning tar barrel is carried at the head of a procession (01343) 835773

15 **Glasgow** Celtic Festival at the Glasgow Concert Hall – *till 1 Feb* (0141) 353 4137

24 **Aviemore** Sled Dog-racing in Glenmore Forest – *till Sun 25* (01604) 686281

27 **Lerwick** Up-Helly-Aa: traditional Viking Fire Festival (01595) 693782

FEBRUARY

4 **Glasgow** Leisure Show at Scottish Exhibition Centre – *till Sun 8* (0141) 204 0123

14 **Aviemore** St Valentine Day Ski Race (01479) 861261

21 **Edinburgh** Rugby International: Scotland v France (0131) 346 5000; **Inverness** Music Festival – *till Fri 27* (01463) 233902

28 **Aviemore** Try a Snow-Sport – *till 1 Mar* (01479) 861261

MARCH

2 **Glenshee** Snow Fun Week – *till Fri 6* (01575) 582213

8 **Aviemore** Alpine Skiing European Cup Finals – *till Sat 14* (01506) 884343

20 **Aviemore** Cairngorm Snow Festival – *till Sun 22* (01479) 861261

22 **Edinburgh** Rugby International: Scotland v England (0131) 346 5000

27 **Gatehouse of Fleet** Festival of Music, Arts and Crafts – *till Sun 29* (01557) 814030

APRIL

2 **Lerwick** Shetland Folk Festival – *till Mon 6* (01595) 694757

3 **Auchterarder** Gleneagles Spring Show-jumping Festival – *till Sun 5* (01764) 665307; **Edinburgh** Folk Festival – *till Sun 12* (0131) 554 3092

4 **Edinburgh** Science Festival – *till Sun 19* (0131) 220 3977

8 **Isle of Arran** Folk Festival – *till Tues 14* (01770) 302144

12 **Innerleithen** Easter at Traquair House (01896) 830323

18 **Ayr** Scottish Grand National at the Racecourse (01292) 264179

24 **Tobermory** Island of Mull Music Festival – *till Sun 26* (01688) 302383

25 **Fairlie** Woodcraft and Forestry Fair – *till Sun 26* (01475) 568685; **Oban** Fiddlers Rally (01631) 710488

26 **Aberdeen** Highland Dancing Festival at the Music Hall (01358) 789492

SCOTLAND CALENDAR

APRIL cont

30 **Isle of Bute** Jazz Festival – *till May 4* (01700) 841283

MAY

1 **Pitlochry** Festival Theatre: plays, concerts and fringe – *till 10 Oct* (01796) 472680

4 **Fort William** International Motorcycle Trials: oldest, biggest trial of its type – *till Sat 9* (01382) 562500

18 **Edinburgh** Children's Festival – *till Sun 24* (0131) 553 7700

21 **Orkney** Traditional Folk Festival – *till Sun 24* (01856) 872856

22 **Dumfries & Galloway** Arts Festival – *till Sun 31* (01387) 260447; **Highlands & Islands** Festival – *till 6 Jun* (01463) 711112; **Jedburgh** Borders Food Fair: local products – *till Sun 24* (01450) 870786; **Perth** Festival of the Arts – *till Sun 31* (01738) 475295

23 **Armadale** Garden and Craft Fair at Clan Donald Visitor Centre – *till Mon 25* (01471) 844227; **Fairlie** Festival of Flight at the Kelburn Country Centre – *till Mon 25* (01475) 568685; **Innerleithen** Beer Festival – *till Sun 24* (01896) 830323; **Isle of Islay** Festival of Traditional and Contemporary Music – *till Sun 31* (01496) 302413; **Loch Fyne** Seafood Fair – *till Sun 24* (01499) 600217

24 **Blair Atholl** Atholl Highland Parade (01796) 481355

25 **Isle of Skye** Story-telling Festival – *till Sat 30* (01470) 511340

29 **Motherwell** National Gardening Show at Strathclyde Country Park – *till Sun 31* (01698) 252565

30 **Bathgate** and **West Lothian** Highland Games (01506) 654507; **Blackford** Highland Games (01764) 682314

31 **Blair Atholl** Highland Games (01796) 481355

JUNE

1 **Dundee** Jazz Festival – *till Sun 7* (0131) 553 4000

4 **Dumfries** International Motor Rally – *till Sat 6* (0141) 204 4999

6 **Cunningham** Festival – *till Mon 15* (01294) 274166; **Galston** and **Loudon** Agricultural Show at Loudon Castle (01560) 320375; **Hawick** Common Riding: horse-racing and athletics – *till Sun 7* (01450) 378853; **Strathmiglo** Highland Games (01337) 860467

11 **Lanark** Lanimer Day Celebrations: street tableaux, beating the retreat, checking of old burgh boundaries (01555) 663251

12 **Aberfeldy** Perthshire and Angus Provincial Mod: Gaelic competitions, prose, piping and choirs – *till Sat 13* (01567) 820435; **Bowmore** Islay Mod: Gaelic singing and recitation – *till Sat 13* (01496) 810509; **Keith** Festival of Traditional Music and Song – *till Sun 14* (01542) 810222; **Selkirk** Common Riding – *till Sat 13* (01750) 21344

12 **Aberdeen** *La Traviata* at His Majesty's Theatre – *till Sat 13* (01224) 641122; **Dumfries** Festival Week – *till Sun 21* (01387) 254805

13 **Eyemouth** Seafood Festival – *till Sun 14* (01890) 750618; **Strathpeffer** Victorian Street Market, musical entertainment and flower festival – *till Sun 14* (01997) 421214

14 **Peebles** March Riding and Beltane Queen Festival: riding of the town boundaries – *till Sat 20* (01721) 729559; **Turriff** Pipe Band Contest at the Haughs (01888) 562401

27 **Aberdeen** Arts Carnival – *till 16 Aug* (01224) 635208; **Rothesay** Scottish Pipe Band Championships (0141) 221 5414

SCOTLAND CALENDAR

JUNE cont

19 **Armadale** Piping Contest at Clan Donald Visitor Centre (01471) 844227; **Killin** Traditional Scottish Music and Dance Festival – *till Sun 21* (01567) 820224; **Orkney** St Magnus Festival – *till Weds 24* (01856) 872856

21 **Aberdeen** Highland Games in Hazelhead Park (01224) 522190; **Ratho** Canal-jumping Competition (0131) 333 1320

25 **Edinburgh** Royal Highland Show at Ingliston Showground – *till Sun 28* (0131) 333 2444

26 **Dingwall** Highland Traditional Music Festival – *till Sun 28* (01349) 877434; **Glasgow** International Jazz Festival – *till 5 July* (0141) 552 3552; **Portsoy** Scottish Traditional Boat Festival: racing, music and drama – *till Sun 28* (01261) 813218

27 **Helensburgh** Faslane Fair: helicopters, ships, dancing (01436) 674321

28 **Perth** Re-enactment of James IV's coronation at Scone Palace (01738) 552300

JULY

4 **Perth** Scottish Game Conservancy Fair at Scone Palace – *till Sun 5* (01620) 850577

8 **Luss** Loch Lomond World Invitational Golf Championship – *till Sat 11* (0131) 317 7773

10 **Stonehaven** Folk Festival – *till Sun 12* (01569) 763519

11 **Glamis** Transport Rally at Glamis Castle – *till Sun 12* (01307) 462496

17 **Callander, Aberfoyle** and **Brig o' Turk** Highland Festival – *till Sun 26* (01877) 376238

18 **Elgin** Highland Games (01343) 870560; **Lochearnhead** Highland Gathering (01567) 830229

19 **Alford** Cavalcade: arena events, over 200 exhibits at Grampian Transport Museum (019755) 62292; **Stonehaven** Highland Games (01569) 768354

21 **Inveraray** Highland Games at the Castle (01499) 302203

25 **Dufftown** Highland Games (01340) 820487; **Eyemouth** Herring Queen Festival: parade of fishing fleet, and a torchlight procession – *till Mon 27* (01890) 751793; **Forfar** Grand Scottish Prom at Glamis Castle (01307) 840393

26 **St Andrews** Highland Games (01334) 476305

30 **Braco** National Sheepdog Trials – *till 1 Aug* (01234) 352672

31 **Crinan, Oban, Tobermory** West Highland Yachting Week – *till 7 Aug* (01631) 563309; **Langholm** Common Riding: ceremonial procession, Highland dancing and sports (01387) 380428

AUGUST

1 **Innerleithen** Arts and Crafts Fair: theatre, street entertainment – *till Sun 2* (01896) 830323; **Edinburgh** International Jazz Festival – *till Fri 7* (0131) 557 1642

2 **Maybole** Classic Vehicle Show at Culzean Castle (01655) 760269; **Parton** Scottish Alternative Games (01557) 814030

3 **Auchterarder** WPGA Golf Tournament at Gleneagles – *till Sun 9* (01764) 698884

5 **Aberdeen** International Youth Festival – *till Sat 15* (0181) 946 2995

7 **Edinburgh** Military Tattoo at Edinburgh Castle: massed piped bands, display teams and dancers – *till Sat 29* (0131) 225 1188; **St Andrews** Lammas Street Fair – *till Tues 11* (01334) 412200

SCOTLAND CALENDAR

AUGUST cont

9 **Edinburgh** Festival Fringe – *till Mon 31* (0131) 226 5257

15 **Edinburgh** Book Festival – *till Mon 31* (0131) 228 5444; **Glasgow** World Pipe Band Championships (0141) 221 5414; **Lauder** Scottish Championship Horse Trials at Thirlestane Castle – *till Sun 16* (01896) 860242

16 **Edinburgh** International Festival – *till 5 Sept* (0131) 473 2001; **Edinburgh** International Film Festival – *till Sun 30* (0131) 228 4051

26 **Oban** Argyllshire Gathering and Highland Games – *till Thurs 27* (01546) 602615

28 **Dunoon** Cowal Highland Gathering: world's largest Highland Games – *till Sat 29* (01369) 703206

29 **Largs** Viking Festival: fireworks, battle re-enactments, crafts and theatre – *till 6 Sept* (01475) 674521

SEPTEMBER

4 **Dundee** Flower Show: over 500 exhibitors at Camperdown Country Park – *till Sun 6* (01382) 433815

5 **Braemar** Royal Highland Gathering (01339) 755377; **Dumfries** British Pipe Band Championships (0141) 221 5414

10 **Biggar** International Sheepdog Trials – *till Sat 12* (01234) 352672

11 **Hawick** Borders Festival of Jazz and Blues – *till Sun 13* (01450) 377278

12 **Leuchars** RAF Battle of Britain Airshow: over 100 aircraft (01334) 839000; **Pitlochry** Highland Games (01796) 472960

16 **Ayr** Gold Cup – *till Fri 18* (01292) 264179

18 **Loch Fyne** Tarbert Music Festival: open-air concerts, fishing-boat trips with music – *till Sun 20* (01880) 82034

OCTOBER

3 **Gatehouse of Fleet** Beer Festival at Cardoness Castle (01557) 814030

8 **Aberdeen** Alternative Festival: music, dance, comedy, theatre, and children's events – *till Sat 17* (01224) 635822

9 **Tobermory** Island of Mull Car Rally – *till Sun 11* (01254) 826564; **Skye** and **Lochalsh** Royal National Mod – *till Fri 16* (01463) 231226

26 **Edinburgh** and **Speyside** International Scotch Whisky Festival – *till 1 Nov* (0131) 556 7441; **Edinburgh** and **Lothians** International Story-telling Festival at Netherbow Arts Centre – *till 8 Nov* (0131) 556 9579

NOVEMBER

7 **Isle of Skye** Fireworks: pipe band and torchlit procession at Dunvegan Castle (01470) 521206

29 **Inverness** Hogmanay and Winter Festival – *till 1 Jan* (01463) 234353

DECEMBER

25 **Kirkwall** Boys' and Men's Ba' Games (see *1 Jan* for details)

26 **Ayr** Boxing Day Meet at the Racecourse (01292) 264179

28 **Edinburgh** Hogmanay – *till 1 Jan* (0131) 557 3990

30 **Edinburgh** *Tosca* at the Festival Theatre – *till 10 Jan* (0131) 529 6000

31 **Aberdeen** Hogmanay (01224) 522190; **Biggar** Ne'erday Bonfire: Druid ceremony, torchlight procession, pipe band (01899) 220661; **Comrie** Flambeaux Procession: traditional pagan event (01764) 652578; **Stonehaven** Fireball Festival: old tradition of swinging fireballs (01569) 762635

WALES

The scenery of North Wales is glorious, including the Snowdonia National Park with the highest mountains in Wales or England; it also has plenty of places to visit – and gets the lion's share of summer visitors. West Wales has the most attractive coastline, with some lovely walks along it – even in bad weather, when upland areas are more or less a write-off, the coast preserves a gloomy magnificence. Mid-Wales has fewer tourist attractions: its strength is the unspoilt feel of its grand scenery, which includes the Brecon Beacons National Park, the empty and lonely Cambrian Mountains (wonderful high-level drives here), and the 'Welsh lake district' of the Elan Valley reservoirs. The chief appeal of South Wales is its good choice of interesting days out, but here too there is fine scenery – especially parts of the Gower peninsula, and the gorge of the lower Wye Valley, graced by Tintern Abbey.

The Welsh hills are almost synonymous with sheep – indeed, the present EU price support structure has if anything encouraged farmers to keep rather too many of them. A record 11 million (outnumbering humans four to one) now range the hills and valleys, and some conservationists are expressing concern about the effects.

Wales is of course also famous for its medieval castles and scenic private railways; less obviously, a good few mines have been turned into really interesting family days out. There are several good National Trust properties here too.

We have mentioned a handful of the Roman and prehistoric sites in which the area abounds. You can get more information from CADW (Welsh Historic Monuments Commission), (01222) 500200, which is also responsible for the care of the great majority of the historic castles and other monuments here: if you plan to visit many of their sites, an Explorer Pass (about £15 for a week, less for three days) from tourist information centres or CADW direct is good value as it admits to all.

You can cut down on transport costs with a seven-day Freedom of Wales Rover train pass (around £55), covering train trips round the whole of Wales and out to Chester.

NORTH WALES

Glorious scenery, lots to do and see.

With a splendid range of places to stay, many in superb countryside, this part has a great deal going for it. The coast has good long beaches and attractive traditional family resorts, though also plenty of places where you can get away from the crowds even at the height of summer – particularly on the deserted shores of the very Welsh Lleyn Peninsula. There is a remarkable variety of inland scenery, from majestic expanses of hill and mountain to the intricate and rather intimate landscapes of Clwyd, the luscious Vale of Conwy and the peace of Anglesey – twice the size of the Isle of Wight with just half the population. The dramatic mountain scenery of Snowdonia is justly famous, and the much less visited Berwyn Hills further inland also give memorable scenic drives.

Apart from the mighty castles, a wide choice of places to visit and things to do includes lots of picturesque railway lines – the one up Snowdon is the most stunning journey. Among great houses, Erddig is really memorable and particularly enjoyed by readers, Bodelwyddan Castle makes for a very good family visit, and the remarkable Plas Mawr in Conwy has reopened after painstaking restoration. There are some grand gardens (Bodnant is outstanding), and many other enjoyable family days out such as the gold mine on the edge of Dolgellau.

Where to stay

Abersoch SH3225 PORTHTOCYN Bwlchtocyn, Abersoch, Pwllheli, Gwynedd LL53 7BU (01758) 713303 **£95**, plus special breaks; 17 attractive rms, some with sea views. On a headland overlooking Cardigan Bay, this is a lovely place to stay – with a refreshingly sensible and helpful approach to families (though it isn't solely a family hotel), very friendly hard-working owners and staff, and a happy atmosphere; several cosy interconnecting sitting rooms with antiques and fresh flowers, most enjoyable traditional cooking in the restaurant (lots of options such as light lunches, high teas for children (they must be over 7 for dinner in the restaurant), and imaginative Sun lunches); lots of space in the pretty garden, heated swimming pool in summer, and a hard tennis court; cl mid Nov-wk before Easter; disabled access.

Beaumaris SH6076 OLDE BULLS HEAD Castle St, Beaumaris, Isle of Anglesey LL58 8AP (01248) 810329 *£79, plus special breaks; 15 rms with antiques and brass bedsteads. Partly 15th-c pub nr the castle, with snug alcoves, low beams and an open fire in the quaint rambling bar, and interesting decorations; popular bar food, very good restaurant food (especially fish), fine wines, and cheery service; the entrance to the pretty courtyard is closed by biggest single-hinged door in Britain; cl 25 Dec–1 Jan; children over 7 in restaurant at night.

Beddgelert SH5948 SYGUN FAWR COUNTRY HOUSE Beddgelert, Caernarfon, Gwynedd LL55 4NE (01766) 890258 £53, plus special breaks; 8 rms. Marvellous views of the Gwynant Valley and the Snowdon range from this secluded 17th-c hotel, and lots of surrounding walks; comfortable sitting room, a well-stocked bar, and home cooking in the candlelit traditionally furnished dining room; sauna; cl Nov–Feb.

Betws-y-coed SH7956 TY GWYN Betws-y-coed, Gwynedd LL24 0SG (01690) 710383 *£54 plus special breaks; 13 lovely rms, most with own bthrm. Welcoming 17th-c coaching inn with interesting old prints, furniture and bric-à-brac (the owners own the antique shop next door); good food and friendly service; pleasant setting overlooking the river and a very good base for the area; discounts for children sharing parents' room; dogs welcome; disabled access.

Brynsiencyn SH4868 PLAS TREFARTHEN Brynsiencyn, Llanfairpwllgwyngyll, Isle of Anglesey, Gwynedd LL61 6SJ (01248) 430379 *£42; 9 rms, 7 with own bthrm. Happy and comfortable family house with panoramic views of Caernarfon Castle and the Snowdonia mountain range; guest lounge, full-size snooker table, and table tennis; home-cooked food using produce grown on the farm; Mrs Roberts is a well known soprano soloist for Welsh choirs; cl Christmas.

Caernarfon SH5163 SEIONT MANOR Llanrug, Caernarfon, Gwynedd LL55 2AQ (01286) 673366 £130, plus special breaks; 28 luxurious rms. Fine hotel built from the original farmstead of a Georgian manor house, standing in 150 acres of mature parkland; open fires and comfortable sofas in the lounge, and a restful atmosphere in the library and drawing room; imaginative food in the 4 interconnecting areas of the restaurant; leisure suite with swimming pool, gym, sauna and solarium.

Capel Coch SH4682 TRE-YSGAWEN HALL Capel Coch, Llangefni, Isle of Anglesey, Gwynedd LL77 7UR (01248) 750750 £109.50, plus special breaks; 19 luxurious rms. Handsome Victorian stone mansion with landscaped gardens; a plushly comfortable bar, carefully decorated lounge, and friendly staff; fine food in the conservatory-style restaurant; clay pigeon shooting; disabled access.

Capel Garmon SH8156 TAN-Y-FOEL COUNTRY HOUSE Capel Garmon, Llannust, Gwynedd LL26 0RE (01690) 710507 *£120, plus special breaks; 7 spotlessly clean rms. Charming, partly 16th-c, no smoking manor house N of the village, with mature gardens and marvellous surrounding countryside; lounge with winter log fire, summer conservatory, and a warm, friendly, relaxing atmosphere; good food using the freshest produce inc local lamb and home-made bread; heated outdoor swimming pool (Jun–Sept); cl mid-Dec–mid-Jan; children over 7; no pets.

Capel Garmon SH8155 WHITE HORSE Capel Garmon, Llanrwst, Gwynedd LL26 0RW (01690) 710271 *£48, plus special breaks; 6 simple rms (those in the newish part are quietest). Comfortable, homely, low-beamed inn with a friendly atmosphere, and winter log fires; very good home-made food in both the bar and little no smoking restaurant (some traditional Welsh meals), and marvellous breakfasts; magnificent views, and delightful surrounding countryside; children over 12.

Conwy SH7877 CASTLE High St, Conwy, Gwynedd LL32 8DB (01492) 592324 £93.50, plus special breaks; 29 rms. In the heart of the historic town, this early 16th-c inn has fine original oil paintings in the public rooms, good food in the pretty restaurant, a proper pubby bar (popular with locals), friendly helpful staff, decent breakfasts, and car parking.

Ffordd-las SJ0771 BERLLAN BACH Ffordd-las, Llandyrnog, Denbigh, Clwyd LL16 4LR (01824) 790732 £40, plus special breaks; 3 rms with French windows onto individual patios. Carefully converted cottage and barns at the foot of hills in the lovely Vale of Clwyd; with a woodburner in the comfortable sitting room and good food in the dining conservatory; marvellous walks, well behaved dogs welcome.

Gellilydan SH6839 TYDDYN DU FARM Gellilydan, Ffestiniog, Gwynedd LL41 4RB (01766) 590281 *£38; 5 rms with views of hills and mountains, most with own bthrms, 1 in private cottage suite. 400-year-old farmhouse on a working farm in the heart of Snowdonia National Park; with beams and exposed stonework, and big inglenook fireplaces in the residents' lounge; wholesome home-made food using their own free-range eggs; you can help with the lambs, goats, ducks, sheep and pony; fine walks, inc a short one to their own Roman site; cl 25–26 Dec; some disabled access.

Hanmer SJ4639 BUCK FARM Hanmer, Whitchurch, Shropshire SY14 7LX (01948) 830339 *£36, plus special breaks; 3 rms, with shared bthrms. 16th-c half-timbered farmhouse in rolling dairy country; with a well stocked library and very good imaginative food using only fresh produce, often organic; lots to do in the area; no smoking.

Llanaber SH5919 LLWYNDU FARMHOUSE Llanaber, Barmouth, Gwynedd LL42 1RR (01341) 280144 *£52, plus special breaks; 7 charming rms, some in nicely converted 18th-c barn. Most attractive, 16th-c farmhouse set just above Cardigan Bay; with a warm welcome, big inglenook fireplaces, oak beams, little mullioned windows, and a relaxing lounge; enjoyable breakfasts, and good imaginative food in the candlelit dining room.

Llanarmon D C SJ1633 WEST ARMS Llanarmon D C, Llangollen, Clwyd LL20 7LD (01691) 600665 £90, plus special breaks; 12 rms. Charming and civilised old place with heavy beams and timbers, log fires in inglenook fireplaces, a lounge bar interestingly furnished with antique settles, sofas in the old-fashioned entrance hall, a comfortable locals' bar, good food, and a friendly, quiet atmosphere; the lawn runs down to the River Ceiriog (fishing for residents); disabled access.

Llandrillo SJ0337 TYDDYN LLAN Llandrillo, Corwen, Clwyd LL21 0ST (01490) 440264 *£98, plus special breaks; 10 pretty rms. Restful Georgian house with fresh flowers and antiques in the elegantly furnished and comfortable public rooms; charming staff, and very good inventive food (using their own herbs); 3 acres of lovely gardens, fishing on 4 miles of the River Dee (ghillies available) and fine forest walks (guides are available) – they can arrange riding and shooting too; dogs by prior arrangement.

Llandudno SH7979 BODYSGALLEN HALL Pentywyn Rd, Llandudno, Gwynedd LL30 1RS (01492) 584466 £156, plus special breaks; 29 deeply comfortable rms, 19 in hotel, the rest in cottages in the grounds. Fine 17th-c house in its own parkland, with mullioned windows, oak panelling, a lovely entrance hall and first-floor drawing room, and open fires; very good imaginative food in no smoking dining room; 18th-c walled rose garden and knot garden; tennis, croquet, swimming pool, sauna, gym and beauty salon; children over 8.

Llanerchymedd SH4284 LLWYDIARTH FAWR FARM Llanerchymedd, Isle of Anglesey, Gwynedd LL71 8DF (01248) 470321 *£50, plus special breaks; 3 rms in main house, 2 cottage suites in grounds. Handsome Georgian farmhouse on 850-acre cattle and sheep farm; with a particularly warm, homely atmosphere and welcome; comfortable lounge with antiques, log fire, books and lovely views, and very good home-made food using farm and other fresh local produce; terrace, a lake for private fishing, nature walks, and bird watching; no smoking; cl Christmas.

Llanerchymedd SH3981 TRE'R DDOL FARM Llandrygan, Llanerchymedd, Isle of Anglesey, Gwynedd LL71 7AR (01248) 470278 *£42; 3 rms with original features. Neatly kept 400-year-old farmhouse on a working mixed farm of 200 acres; with original staircase, log fire in the cosy lounge, a homely relaxed atmosphere and good farmhouse cooking; you can help with day-to-day farmwork, free riding for children, nature trails and bird watching; cl Christmas.

Llanfair D C SJ1358 EYARTH STATION Llanfair D C, Ruthin, Clwyd LL15 2EE (01824) 703643 £46, plus special breaks; 6 pretty rms. Carefully converted old railway station with quiet gardens and wonderful views; a friendly relaxed atmosphere, and a log fire in the airy and comfortable beamed lounge; good breakfasts and enjoyable suppers in the dining room (more lovely views); sun terrace and heated swimming pool, and lots of walks; dogs welcome by prior arrangement; disabled access.

Llanfihangel-yng-Ngwynfa SJ0814 CYFIE FARM Llanfihangel, Llanfyllin, Powys SY22 5JE (01691) 648451 £45; 4 rms incl 3 suites with lovely views. Carefully restored, 17th-c Welsh stone longhouse on 178 acres of cattle and sheep farm (guests are welcome to take an interest in the lambs, shearing and haymaking); timbered and beamed rms with fine family furniture, a log fire in the residents' lounge, hearty farmhouse cooking in an attractive dining conservatory, and a relaxed friendly atmosphere; cl Jan–Feb.

Llanfyllin SJ1320 BODFACH HALL Llanfyllin, Powys SY22 5HS (01691) 648272 *£72 plus special breaks; 9 quiet rms. Elegant house in 4 acres of mature garden; with a restful friendly atmosphere, a residents' drawing room, and a spacious lounge bar; simple food in the oak-panelled dining room, and very good service; cl Nov–Feb.

Llangollen SJ2044 ABBEY GRANGE Llantisilio, Llangollen, Clwyd LL20 8DD (01978) 860753 *£42; 8 comfortable rms. Cosily converted, former quarrymaster's house in a beautiful spot with superb views nr Valle Crucis Abbey; decent food, a good wine list and efficient, courteous service.

Llangollen SJ1945 BRITANNIA (Horseshoe Pass; on the A542 N) Llangollen, Clwyd LL20 8DW (01978) 860144 *£52, plus special breaks; 5 clean and pretty rms, all with 4-posters. Picturesque inn based on 15th-c core (though much extended and comfortably modernised), with traditional 17th-c Welsh elm furniture, a dining area and 2 bars; pleasant staff, lovely views, and an attractive garden; cl 25 Dec.

Llangollen SJ2541 BRYN HOWEL Llangollen, Clwyd LL20 7UW (01978) 860331 *£99, plus special breaks; 35 rms. Extended Victorian mansion in the lovely Vale of Llangollen, with comfortable lounges, a panelled bar, small cocktail bar, and open fires; good food using home-grown herbs and fresh local produce in the restaurant; neat grounds, sauna and solarium, and private salmon and trout fishing on the River Dee; cl 25–27 Dec; disabled access.

Llannefydd SH9770 HAWK & BUCKLE Llaneffyd, Denbigh, Clwyd LL16 5ED (01745) 540249 *£55; 10 modern rms, lovely views. Pleasant 17th-c stone inn, 215 metres (700 ft) up in the hills, with remarkable vistas; decent choice of food using fresh local produce, and a neatly kept, beamed and knocked-through lounge bar; a good base for exploring the area – by horse, car or on foot; cl 25 Dec; no children or dogs.

Llanrwst SH7965 PRIORY Maenan, Llanrwst, Gwynedd LL26 0UL (01492) 660247 £49, plus special breaks; 12 rms. Stately Victorian hotel with a battlemented tower; an elegant lounge, welcoming bar, good restaurant, and Welsh singing Sat evenings; attractive gardens; 11 acres of woodland across the road, and close to fishing; disabled access to bar and restaurant only.

Llansanffraid Glan Conwy SH8075 OLD RECTORY Llanrwst Rd, Llansanffraid Glan Conwy, Gwynedd LL28 5LF (01492) 580611 *£99, plus special breaks; 6 deeply comfortable rms. Georgian house in pleasant gardens with fine views over the Conwy estuary, Conwy castle and Snowdonia; delightful public rooms with flowers, antiques and family photos; after introductions over cocktails you can eat the delicious food either around a long, communal table or at separate tables; marvellous wine list, good Welsh breakfasts, and warm, friendly staff; mostly no smoking; cl Dec–Jan; children over 5; small, well behaved dogs welcome.

Llanwddyn SJ0219 LAKE VYRNWY Llanwddyn, Oswestry, Powys SY10 0LY (01691) 870692 £105; 35 rms, the ones overlooking the lake are the nicest – and quietest. Large, impressive, Tudor-style mansion on a hillside in 24,000 acres of forestry and looking over the lake, with lots of sporting activities (especially fishing); log fires and sporting prints in the comfortable and elegant public rooms, a relaxed atmosphere, clubby bar, and good food using home-made preserves, chutneys, mustards and vinegars and home-grown produce from their own kitchen garden; nice teas too.

Maentwrog SH6741 GRAPES Maentwrog, Blaenau Ffestiniog, Gwynedd LL41 4HN (01766) 590208 *£55; 8 rms. Bustling and cheery, 17th-c, family-run pub with interesting lamps, guns and blowlamps, old pine furniture, and stripped stone walls in the relaxed friendly bars; hearty, wholesome bar food, and big breakfasts; good views from terrace and garden.

Nant Gwynant SH6655 PEN-Y-GWYRD (junction of the A498 and the A4086) Nant Gwynant, Llanberis, Caernarfon, Gwynedd LL55 4NT (01286) 870211 £50; 16 comfortably basic rms, some with own bthrm (one with an unusual Edwardian bath). Wonderfully cheery climbers' inn in a magnificent setting below the mountains, with a rugged, slate-floored bar that doubles as a mountain rescue post; lots of climbing mementos and equipment, and a charming panelled sitting room; good lunches ordered through a hatch, hearty communal evening meals in the no smoking restaurant, and sherry from their own solera; sauna in the trees, table tennis; book well ahead; cl Nov–1 Jan, wkdys Jan and Feb; disabled access.

Penmaenpool SH6918 George III Penmaenpool, Dolgellau, Gwynedd LL40 1YD (01341) 422525 *£88, plus special breaks; 11 low-beamed rms, some in award-winning converted railway station. Cosy 17th-c inn on the Mawddach estuary with good lunchtime food, imaginative evening restaurant, snug lounge with log fire, and a beamed and partly panelled bar (real ales); fine nearby walks, and free salmon and trout fishing permits for residents; disabled access.

Portmeirion SH5937 Portmeirion Hotel Portmeirion, Penrhyndeudraeth, Porthmadog, Gwynedd LL48 6ET (01766) 770228 *£135 in hotel (14 rms), £90 in village (17 rms), plus special breaks. On the edge of an estuary and surrounded by beaches and woods (and traffic-free), this is a remarkable place; the hotel down by the water is quite luxurious – elegant rooms with marble, gilt, and rich, colourful fabrics – while behind and in the steeply landscaped grounds above it is a well dispersed very colourful Italianate village, luscious to look at, inc all sorts of characterful cottage bedrooms tucked into the hillside; very romantic when the day visitors have left; lots to do; cl 11 Jan–6 Feb. See Portmeirion entry in **To see and do** section on p.920.

Pwllheli SH3535 Yoke House Farm Pwllheli, Gwynedd LL53 5TY (01758) 612621 *£34; 1 rm. Warmly welcoming, Georgian farmhouse on 290-acre working farm; you can watch milking, calf-feeding, and there's a nature trail; cl Oct–Apr.

Saron SH4559 Pengwern Caernarfon, Gwynedd LL54 5UH (01286) 831500 *£50, plus special breaks; 3 rms. In 130 acres of land running down to Foryd Bay, this spacious, no smoking farmhouse has marvellous views of Snowdonia; delicious food using home-produced beef and lamb, in the attractive dining rm; cl Dec–Jan.

Talsarnau SH6135 Maes-y-Neuadd Talsarnau, Gwynedd LL47 6YA (01766) 780200 £125, plus special breaks; 16 luxurious rms. Looking out across Snowdonia National Park, this attractive, extended 14th-c mansion is set in 8 acres of landscaped hillside; flowers, plants, antiques and open fires, and a peaceful atmosphere; very good food (with herbs and vegetables from their own garden); friendly dogs and cats, and charming staff; children over 7 in evening restaurant; disabled access.

Tal-y-Bont SH7669 Lodge Tal-y-Bont, Conwy, Gwynedd LL32 8YX (01492) 660766 £70, plus special breaks; 10 rms. Friendly little modern hotel in the Conwy Valley with an open fire, books and magazines in the comfortable lounge; generous helpings of popular food using lots of home-grown produce in the no smoking restaurant, and good service; lots of walks; well behaved pets welcome; good disabled access.

Tremeirchion SJ0771 Bach-y-Graig Tremeirchion, St Asaph, Clwyd LL17 0UH (01745) 730627 £42; 3 rms, 2 with brass beds. Wales's first brick-built house with a date-stone of 1567, this is set in a 200-acre dairy farm at the foot of the Clwydian Range; an inglenook fireplace in the big lounge, home cooking using home-produced beef and lamb and their own free-range eggs, and a warm welcome; you can join in farm activities or walk along their woodland trail; cl Christmas–New Year.

Tudweiliog SH2437 Lion Tudweiliog, Pwllheli, Gwynedd LL53 8ND (01758) 770244 £38; 4 basic rms. Extended, 300-year-old village pub with good-value home-made food in the comfortable bar and dining rooms; a welcome for families, play area, lovely views, and 10 minutes' walk to the beach.

Please let us know what you think of places in the *Guide*. Use the report forms at the back of the book or simply send a letter.

To see and do

🏛 **Aberffraw** SH3371 BARCLODIAD Y GAWRES Some 5,000 years old, this 6-metre (20-ft) underground passage tomb at the top of the cliff is notable for the patterns carved by the entrance and in the side chambers, shown up by a good torch; it's sealed, but you can ask for a key at the Wayside Café in Llanfaelog, about a mile away. Hard to believe now, but Aberffraw was once the Welsh capital. There are some lovely unspoilt coves and beaches nearby; the beach up the road at Rhosneigr SH3273 is particularly good (and clean).

† 👁 🏠 ⚘ **Bangor** SH5771 Quiet university town with a pedestrianised High St and a yacht harbour that adds a lively touch in summer; the pier was restored with an EU grant. A CATHEDRAL was founded here 70 years before the one at Canterbury; the present building is restored 13th–15th c, and has an interesting 16th-c carving of Christ bound and seated on a rock, as well as some fine Victorian stained glass. The Bible Garden outside contains only plants mentioned in the Scriptures. Opposite is a little museum of Welsh rural life (cl Sun and Mon; free), and the Nelson nr the harbour has decent food, as do the Antelope and Union. PENRHYN CASTLE 🎫 (1m E) Splendid 19th-c neo-Norman fantasy built by a slate magnate: the interior is in suitably grand style, with quite remarkable – and often bizarre – panelling, decoration and furnishings. The cathedral-like great hall is heated by the Roman method of hot air under the floor, and one of the beds weighs over a ton – carved from slate. An unexpectedly rich collection of paintings includes works by Rembrandt and Canaletto. In the stableyard is a museum of unique early locomotives, and there's a walled garden and adventure playground. Meals, snacks, shop, disabled access; cl am (exc July and Aug), Tues, Nov–Mar; (01248) 353084; £5, garden only £3; NT.

★ 🏰 🏠 👁 ♪ † **Beaumaris** SH6076 The most attractive town on Anglesey, with a good deal of character, several old buildings, a busy waterfront, and a 15th-c church. The CASTLE is one of the most impressive and complete of those built by Edward I, despite the struggle over it with Owain Glyndwr in the early 1400s, and the plundering of its lead, timber and stone in later ages. Beautifully symmetrical, it took from 1295 to 1312 to build (though the money ran out before it could be finished). Shop, good disabled access; cl 24–26 Dec, 1 Jan; (01248) 810361; £2.20. Opposite the castle, the COURTHOUSE is a unique Victorian survival. You can stand in the dock and imagine you're just about to be sentenced. Open May–Sept, exc when court is in session; (01248) 811691; *£1.35. Down the road the GAOL paints a vivid picture of the harshness of the 19th-c prison system, especially in the dank, poky cells. Shop, limited disabled access; open as courthouse, or by appointment, (01248) 810921; £2.75, joint with courthouse £2.80. MARINE WORLD 🎫 (Seafront) has displays of the sea life of the Menai Strait; cl 25 Dec; (01248) 810072; £2.25; and the CHURCH of St Mary and St Nicholas – easy to spot by its robust square tower – houses the stone coffin of Joan, daughter of King John and wife of the Welsh leader Llewelyn the Great. The Olde Bull's Head and Sailors Return are excellent for lunch.

★ ⚓ **Beddgelert** SH5948 A quiet village which dreamed up the myth that it was the resting place of Llewelyn's faithful mastiff over a hundred years ago and has been living off it ever since. The Prince Llewelyn does good-value food. SYGUN COPPER MINE 🎫 (on the A498) Interesting tours through often spectacular underground mine workings, with magnificent stalactites and stalagmites and traces of gold and silver in the copper ore veins. You're greeted by a wonderful view of the mountains when you

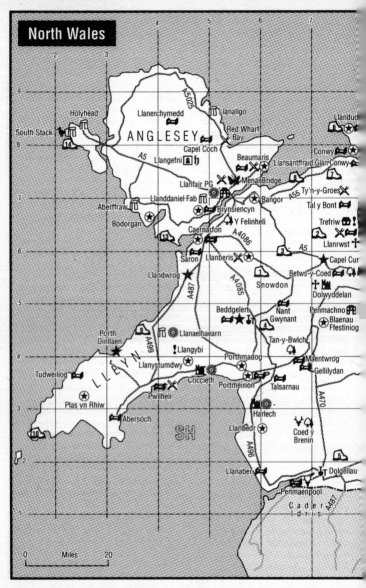

North Wales

come out at the end. Snacks, shop, some disabled access; cl 25 Dec; (01766) 510101; £4.50.

Betws-y-coed SH7956 19th-c inland resort village in a beautiful wooded gorge at the head of the Vale of Conwy, on the road to Bangor (and thence Ireland) as well as to Snowdon. Surrounded by

picturesque woodland and river walks, the village has over a century of catering to visitors behind it. The raging Swallow Falls and Fairy Glen just W of the village itself are deservedly regarded as 2 of the area's finest beauty spots. Several interesting bridges nearby, as well as the bizarre Ugly House, which looks

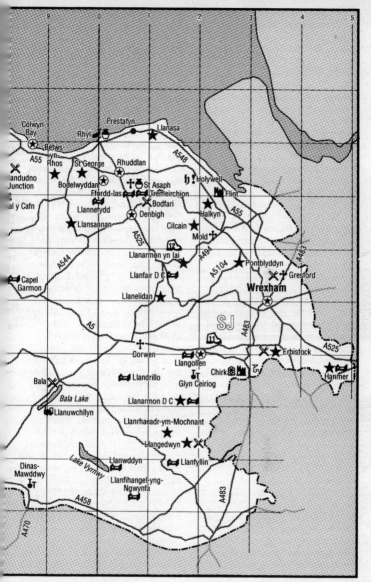

like a series of boulders thrown haphazardly together. CONWY VALLEY RAILWAY MUSEUM (Old Goods Yard) Good look at the narrow and standard gauge railways of North Wales, with railway stock and other memorabilia, model railway layouts, a steam-hauled model railway in the 4-acre grounds, and a 15in-gauge

tramway to the woods. Meals, snacks, shop, disabled access; cl wkdys Nov–Feb; (01690) 710568; site free, *£1 museum. The Royal Oak Hotel (open all day – afternoon teas, too), Glan Aber Hotel and Ty Gwyn have good food.
☎ ⅃ᴛ ❋ **Blaenau Ffestiniog** SH7045 This straggle of a village is completely

dwarfed by the vast spoil slopes from the slate mines all around it – once the slate capital of Wales, now with the passing of the industry like a living museum. GLODDFA GANOL SLATE MINE (on the A470) Reputedly the largest slate mine in the world, with guided tours by Land Rover. You can walk through the spectacular underground chambers, or watch the blasting operations from the safety of the museum. Above ground there's a little narrow-gauge railway, as well as 3 period furnished quarrymen's cottages. Meals, snacks, shop, disabled access; cl wknds (exc Sun mid-July–Aug), and all Oct–Easter; (01776) 830664; £5.50. LLECHWEDD SLATE CAVERNS ⚅ (on the A470) Very busy and popular, with particularly exciting underground train journeys through the caverns; one of the 2 routes recreates the world of the Victorian miner, while the other (along Britain's steepest railway) ends with a walk through 10 atmospheric chambers, each with its own sound and light show. Plenty on the surface too, inc a railway museum, slate mill and complete Victorian village. Meals, snacks, shop, disabled access with prior warning; cl 25–26 Dec, 1 Jan; (01766) 830306; single tour £6.25, both £9.50, surface attractions free. PUMPED STORAGE POWER STATION (Tanygrisiau, off the A496 S) Guided tours of the first hydro-electric pumped storage scheme in the country, with dramatic views towards the peaks of Snowdonia. Meals, snacks, shop; cl Sat, Nov–Easter; (01766) 830310; £2.50. From the information centre there's an attractive (if slightly hairy) drive into the mountains to Stwlan Dam, which also gives super views. The Grapes at Maentwrog is fairly handy for lunch.

🏠🏚️🖼️✝ **Bodelwyddan** SH9974 BODELWYDDAN CASTLE ⚅ (off the A55) The walled gardens surrounding this showy white limestone castle include a glorious mix of woodland walks, flowering plants, aviary and water features. The house (older than its 19th-c exterior suggests) has been very well restored

as a Victorian mansion, with furniture from the Victoria & Albert Museum, and photographs and portraits from the National Portrait Gallery. Plenty for children, inc a woodland adventure playground, and entertaining exhibitions of puzzles, games and optical illusions. Snacks, shop, disabled access; cl Fri (exc July and Aug), Mon Nov–Mar; (01745) 584060; £4.50, grounds only £2. In the village itself the 19th-c MARBLE CHURCH, built entirely of locally quarried stone, is an unusual and quite splendid sight. The Kinmel Arms at St George has good, interesting food.

☺🐄🖼️ **Bodorgan** SH3868 HENBLAS PARK Good range of family activities, from sheep shearing, falconry and farm animals, through magic shows and juggling workshops, to a tractor ride to a Neolithic burial chamber. Meals, snacks, shop, disabled access (but no facilities); open Easter hols, May bank hol wknd, late May–Sept; (01407) 840440; £3.75.

🎣🐄🖼️ **Brynsiencyn** SH4867 ANGLESEY SEA ZOO ⚅ (discount voucher not valid on bank hols; on the A4080 just S) Excellent collection of local marine life, housed in tanks specially designed to provide as unrestricted and natural an environment as possible. Also walk-through shipwreck, touch pools, adventure playground, and home-made fudge and ice-cream. Meals and snacks (their oysters are guaranteed to contain a pearl), shop, disabled access; cl 23 Dec–2 Jan; (01248) 430411; £4.95. Nearby the FOEL FARM PARK is a friendly working farm with daily sheep milking, tractor rides, and more home-made ice-cream. Snacks, shop, disabled access; cl Nov–Mar; (01248) 430646; £3.50. Another farm here, Gwydryn Hir, lets you PICK YOUR OWN fruit and vegetables while taking in the view of Snowdonia; open Jun–Oct; (01248) 430344. A couple of miles NW of the village by the back road towards Llangaffo is what looks like a Stone Age hut, but is actually a burial chamber from which the covering earth has been eroded over the millennia. The Mermaid at Foel Ferry is quite useful for lunch.

🏰 🏛 ✝ **Caernarfon** SH4862 Surviving lengths of the 13th-c town walls still crowd in its quaintly narrow streets (quaint, that is, unless you're trying to drive through them). The CASTLE is the largest of Edward I's Welsh castles, built after the defeat of Llewelyn the Last, and still quite spectacular. Finished in 1328, it's unusual both for its octagonal towers and for the bands of colour decorating the walls. Edward's son was born here and presented to the people, setting the precedent for future Princes of Wales. Shop, some disabled access; cl 24–26 Dec, 1 Jan; (01286) 677617; £3.80. In the square outside, around the statue of former PM David Lloyd George, they still have a busy Saturday market. The castle walls were thought to be modelled partly on the walls of Constantinople – reflecting the tradition that Constantine the Great was born at nearby SEGONTIUM (on the A4085), a Roman fort dating from AD78. Excavations at the fort have exposed the remains of various rebuildings during its 3 centuries of importance, and there's a museum with some of the finds. Shop, disabled access; cl Nov–Feb; (01286) 675625; £1.25. The harbour is busy with yachts in summer, and you can explore a restored steam-powered dredger moored here. The Black Boy and Palace Vaults do decent food. AIR WORLD 🟦 (Airport) They encourage you to climb aboard some of the helicopters and aeroplanes here; also a great many model aeroplanes, and pleasure flights. Meals, snacks, shop, disabled access; cl Nov–Jan (exc by appointment); (01286) 830800; £3.50.

🏰 ❀ **Chirk** SJ2638 The quiet little town, important as a staging post on the former road to Ireland, has something of a bypassed-by-time feel now; the Hand and (on the B5070 S) Bridge are quite useful for lunch. CHIRK CASTLE (just W of town) One of the lucky few of Edward I's castles to survive as an occupied home rather than fall to ruin. The exterior is still

much as it was when built 700 years ago, with its high walls and drum towers, though there have been lots of alterations inside: most of the medieval-looking decorations were by Pugin in the 19th c, the elegant stone staircase dates from the 18th c, and the Long Gallery is 17th c. The wrought-iron entrance gates are particularly fine, and the formal gardens are magnificent. Meals, snacks, shop, some disabled access; cl am, Mon (exc bank hols) and Tues, Nov–Mar; (01691) 777701; £4.40; NT. It's right by a well preserved stretch of the earthworks of Offa's Dyke.

🔦 ⚘ **Coed-y-Brenin** SH7326 The name means King's Forest, and it was so called to commemorate the Silver Jubilee of King George V. Some beautifully varied sights and landscapes, as well as wildlife observation hides, and over 50 miles of walks. The FOREST PARK AND VISITOR CENTRE (Maesgwn) is an excellent introduction. Snacks, shop, disabled access; cl wkdys Nov–Easter; (01341) 422289; free, £1 parking. You can hire bikes.

☺ 🎏 ❁ **Colwyn Bay** SH8678 Though this busy summer seaside resort has all that's wanted for a family beach holiday, it's rather eclipsed by Llandudno just along the coast. The quieter end at Rhos-on-Sea has a PUPPET THEATRE; mainly open just school hols; (01492) 548166 for programme. The Rhos Fynach opposite the small harbour at this end, once Capt Morgan's home, does decent food. WELSH MOUNTAIN ZOO (Flagstaff Gardens, Old Highway) Lots of exotic animals in natural-looking habitats, but what really distinguishes this 37-acre zoo from any other is the quite magnificent view over the bay. Meals, snacks, shop, mostly disabled access; cl 25 Dec; (01492) 532938; £5.75. In summer a free minibus service usually runs here from the town station. The Mountain View at Mochdre has good-value food.

★ 🏰 🏛 ✂ ☛ **Conwy** SH7777 Cheerful old town dominated by its CASTLE, one of the best-known in

Wales and one of the most important examples of military architecture in the whole of Europe. Built for Edward I in 1283–9, it's very well preserved, still looking exactly as a medieval fortress should – despite the ravages of the Civil War and beyond. There's an exhibition on Edward and the other castles he built, as well as a scale model of the castle and the town in the early 14th c. The tops of the turrets offer fine panoramic views; the most dramatic views of the castle itself are from the other side of the estuary. Shop; cl 24–26 Dec, 1 Jan; (01492) 592358; £3. The castle was the key part of the town's elaborate defensive system – 21 (originally 22) towers linked by walls some 9 metres (30 ft) high, the most complete town wall in Wales, with craggy old town gates. You can walk along some parts, looking down over the narrow little streets that still follow their medieval layout. The bridges spanning the river are also worth a second glance – the tubular one was built by Stephenson in 1848, and the suspension bridge by Telford in 1826. The latter has been restored by the National Trust, who have also opened up its TOLL HOUSE, the rooms furnished as they would have been in the last century; open Apr–Oct; (01492) 573282; £1. The only house in the town which survives from the 14th c is ABERCONWY HOUSE, once the home of a prosperous merchant. Rooms are furnished in period style and there's an interesting audiovisual show. Shop; cl Tues, Nov–Mar; (01492) 592246; £2; NT. The elaborate Tudor mansion PLAS MAWR (High St) has reopened after a lengthy restoration, its splendid plasterwork, stone-flagged floors, and huge fireplaces all now looking as good as when they were new. Shop; cl Mon (exc bank hols); (01222) 500200; £3. Nicely placed on the quayside is Britain's SMALLEST HOUSE, barely 2 metres (6 ft) wide and its front wall only 3 metres (10 ft) high. Squeezed into the 2 rooms (one up, one down) are all the comforts of home, or at least most – there's no lavatory. Shop, limited disabled

access; cl Nov–Mar; (01492) 593484; *50p. There's a little aquarium nearby, and you can usually go on summer boat trips. By the river in Bodlondeb Park, the BUTTERFLY JUNGLE has butterflies and exotic plants and birds in a recreated jungle environment. Snacks, shop, disabled acess; cl Nov–Mar; (01492) 593149; *£3. TEAPOT WORLD (Castle St) Splendidly silly collection of unusually shaped teapots from the last 300 years – everything from wigwams to cabbages. Shop; cl Nov–Easter; (01492) 593429; *£1.50. The Castle Hotel is a civilised place for lunch.

✝ **Corwen** SJ0843 RHUG CHAPEL (1m N of Corwen) 17th-c, is not inspiring from the outside, but a riot of colour inside, almost every available piece of woodwork covered with cheery patterns and paintwork. Cl 2–3pm, Sun and Mon (exc bank hol wknds), Oct–Mar; (01490) 412025; £1.70. A mile or so down the road lies LLANGAR CHURCH (on the B4401 S of Corwen) Built in the 13th c, with remarkable paintings of the 7 deadly sins; it's usually visited only at 2pm, from Rhug chapel (and covered by the same ticket). The Crown in Corwen has good-value food. DERWEN CHURCH SJ0751 (off the A494 a few miles N of Corwen) Interesting medieval building with an elaborately carved rood screen and loft, some old wall paintings, and an excellent Celtic cross in the churchyard.

Criccieth SH5038 Restrained resort with a good, sheltered sandy beach. The remains of its 13th-c CASTLE stand on a rocky, mounded peninsula above the little town, giving superb views over Tremadog Bay. Parts of the inner walls are well preserved, and there's an impressive gatehouse. A cartoon video looks at Gerald of Wales and other Welsh princes. Shop, disabled access; cl 24–26 Dec, 1 Jan; (01766) 522227; £2.20. The Prince of Wales is a reliable food pub.

✝ **Denbigh** SJ0566 The gatehouse of the ruined 13th-c CASTLE is still impressive, with its trio of towers and a superb archway; the figure on the summit is thought to represent Edward I. Among the remains are one of the gateways, and what's left of an ambitious church built by the Earl of Leicester, favourite of Elizabeth I. Limited disabled access; free. A museum in the High St has interesting finds from nearby Bronze Age sites, and the riverside Brookhouse Mill is popular for lunch, as is the Lion out at Gwytherin (on the B5384 W).

⛨ **Dinas-Mawddwy** SH8513 Nestling among riverside woods below the mountains on the S fringes of Snowdonia, this is a charming setting for MEIRION MILL, a working woollen mill, in the grounds of the old Mawddwy railway station. Meals, snacks, shop (lots of locally made goods), disabled access; cl Jan–Feb; (01650) 531311; free. Nearby is a picturesque packhorse bridge, and the waterside Dolbrodmaeth has decent food.

⛨ **Dolgellau** SH7318 GWYNFYNYDD GOLD MINE (Marian Mawr) Dark, noisy and quite fascinating tours of working gold mine, once one of the richest in Britain, when it employed over 500 men. You can see craftsmen turning the gold into jewellery in the visitor centre, and have a go at panning for gold yourself; from here a bus takes you to the mine proper, where they provide protective clothing, helmet and lamp. You'll need around 3 hours for the full tour (which takes in a unique underground mill). Shop, disabled access to visitor centre only; cl winter Sun, best to book for tours (no under 5s); (01341) 423332; visitor centre free, panning £2.50, full tour (inc panning) £9.50.

⛫ ✝ **Dolwyddelan** SH7352 DOLWYDDELAN CASTLE Picturesquely set on a lightly wooded crag, these old ruins were reputedly the birthplace of Llewelyn the Great. You can still see a restored keep from around 1200 and a 13th-c curtain wall. Cl 24–26 Dec, 1 Jan; (01690) 750366; £1.70. The parish church is attractive.

⛫ **Flint** SJ2472 Another fine 13th-c CASTLE, one of the earliest built by Edward I to subdue the natives. Parts of the walls and corner towers survive, but the most impressive bit is the great tower or donjon, which is separated by the moat. Overlooking the River Dee, it has a role in Shakespeare's *Richard II*. Cl 24–26 Dec, 1 Jan; free. The Britannia in nearby Halkyn is good for lunch, with fine Dee estuary views from its conservatory.

⛨ **Glyn Ceiriog** SJ2038 CHWAREL WYNNE MINE In beautiful surroundings, an 18th-c slate mine with entertaining ½-hour guided tours of the underground workings. The 12-acre landscaped grounds have won several awards, and there are nature trails and walks through the adjacent old woodland. Snacks, shop (selling alpines and evergreens in season), disabled access; open only summer wknds; (01691) 718343; £2.50. The Woolpack right by the slate tramway in the attractively unspoilt village is handy for lunch, and the valley's remote landscape is popular with walkers.

✝ **Gresford** SJ3555 The parish CHURCH has some wonderful medieval stained glass, and its bells are often described as one of the Seven Wonders of Wales. A yew tree outside is reputed to be 1,400 years old. The Pant-yr-Ochain has good food.

⛫ ✿ **Harlech** SH5831 CASTLE Splendid-looking structure built in 1283–90 by Edward I, its rugged glory the massive twin-towered gatehouse. It was starved into capitulation by Owain Glyndwr in 1404, and later, dogged defence inspired the song *Men of Harlech*. Before the sea retreated there was a sheer drop into the water on one side, but the castle now stands above dunes, with wonderful views of Snowdonia from the battlements. Shop; cl 24–26 Dec, 1 Jan; (01766) 780552; £3. The village around it has all that the crowds of summer visitors to the castle and the good beach could want. The riverside Victoria at Llanbedr does decent food.

⛫ **Holyhead** SH2582 Long-established fishing town on little Holy Island, now an unassuming resort with some burial chambers and ancient sites not far away. The Victorian breakwater protecting the harbour is Britain's longest. Across the old Four Mile Bridge at Valley the Bull has good-value food.

! ♄ Holywell SJ1876 ST WINEFRIDE'S WELL Source of the holy spring that turned the spot into a centre of pilgrimage – it's supposed to have healing powers. There are pleasant walks from here through the valley to the coast. GREENFIELD VALLEY HERITAGE PARK (on the A458) Farm museum, and an increasing number of buildings rescued from their original sites and rebuilt here. These include a 17th-c cottage, Victorian farmhouse, and a school, all furnished in period style. Also the remains of a Cistercian abbey and a good few relics of the Industrial Revolution. Snacks, shop, disabled access; cl Nov–Mar; (01352) 714172; £1.60.

🏛 ❀ Llanaelhaearn SH3744 Off the B4417, just up the hill from here, a signed path leads to the TRE'R CEIRI HILL FORT, occupied from the Bronze Age through to the Dark Ages; a massive stone wall, lots of hut foundations, and fine views. At Morfa Nefyn nearby the Bryncynan and (overlooking a lovely sandy bay) Cliff Hotel do good lunches.

🏛 Llanallgo SH4985 DIN LLUGWY ANCIENT VILLAGE The remains of a 4th-c village: a pentagonal stone wall surrounds 2 circular and 7 rectangular buildings; free. The Parciau Arms at Marianglas is the best place for a meal.

♄ ↗ ♨ Llanbedr SH5826 MAES ARTRO (on the A496) Imaginatively converted wartime RAF camp, with an original air raid shelter complete with light and sound effects, a 'Village of Yesteryear', log fort playground, marine aquarium, and nature trails through the woodland. Meals, snacks, shop, disabled access; cl Sept–Easter; (01341) 241467; £3. The Victoria in the village is useful for a family lunch. SHELL ISLAND A causeway leads over the sands to this near-island, appropriately named – after winter storms and high tides it's excellent for beach-combing; there

are also wild birds and flowers, and you can fish here. Snacks, shop; cl Dec–Feb; (01341) 241453; £4 per car.

🏖 ❀ ↗ ♨ ✗ Llanberis SH5760 Plenty of B & Bs, small hotels, shops and cafés for the summer visitors here for Snowdon, and there are quite a few craft shops dotted along the High St. Sherpa Buses run a good service up the mountain (you can get it from several of the North Wales resorts), but the best ascent is via the SNOWDON MOUNTAIN RAILWAY (on the A4086), Britain's only public rack-and-pinion railway, operated by vintage Swiss steam and modern diesel locomotives. It follows the route of an old pony track, and on a good day takes passengers up over 915 metres (3,000 ft) right to the summit – where in clear weather glorious breathtaking views might include the Isle of Man and the Wicklow Mountains in Ireland. It's without a doubt one of the most spectacular train journeys in the country. Trains leave when there are more than a couple of dozen people on board – so if there aren't many people about you may have to wait for it to start, and if there are you may have to queue (there is a sort of booking service). When trains are running to the summit, you can visit the highest postbox in Britain. It can be chilly, so wrap up well. Meals, snacks, shop, disabled access (with notice); open mid-Mar–Oct, though always best to ring first – of the 241 operational days in 1996, it was only possible to reach the summit on 138; (01286) 870223; £14.50 return. The mountain summit is crowned by a café that Prince Charles dubbed 'the highest slum in Wales'; certainly one of the less successful works of Portmeirion architect Sir Clough Williams-Ellis, it's likely to be replaced in the next few years. LAKE RAILWAY 🚂 (Padarn Country Park, off the A4086) 4-mile trips along the shore of Llyn Padarn, using steam locomotives dating from 1889 to 1948. Ideal for those who want the steamtrain experience but don't want to spend too long getting it. Snacks, shop, disabled access; cl Nov–Feb; (01286) 870549 for timetable; £3.90. The station is set in a super lakeside park with walks through ancient woodland, also home to the WELSH SLATE MUSEUM, once one of the biggest quarries in the country. The quarry workshop has been preserved largely in its original state – complete with working craftsmen and machinery. Its waterwheel is one of the largest in the world. Shop, disabled access; cl wknds Oct–Apr; (01286) 870360; £3. ELECTRIC MOUNTAIN Various changing exhibitions, then a coach whisks you off for a tour of the spectacular Dinorwic hydro-electric power station (one of Europe's biggest), deep in the mountain. Best to book, (01286) 870636. Snacks, shop, disabled access (with notice); cl Dec–Jan; £5. DOLBADARN CASTLE (on the A4086, at the foot of Llanberis Pass) Built in the early 13th c by Llywelyn the Great – it has a fine round keep; free. Just N of town is a modern working POTTERY; cl 2 wks at Christmas; (01286) 872529; free. Another good spot for Snowdon walks is the Pen-y-Gwryd at Nant Gwynant to the E; also a useful place for lunch.

🏚 **Llandaniel fab** SH5070 BRYN CELLI DDU Restored Neolithic passage burial chamber built over a previous stone circle, at the end of a long tunnel, with a carved stone over a burial pit; locked, but key at nearby farmhouse; free. Take a torch.

★ ♨ ♿ **Llandudno** SH7881 The main holiday town in the area, and though it does have a long, well sheltered curve of good pebbly beach, a prom and a range of resort entertainments, it doesn't feel at all brash. There are charming little shops and boutiques, a well restored pier (from where you can fish), and cable-cars as well as the famous tramway up the massive Great Orme headland which protects the main beach – there's a quieter but more exposed beach on the far side. Climbing up to the Orme's summit yourself is much more satisfying; a café en route has views to justify stopping. At the top there's a 12th-c

church, a visitor centre with local geology, and the GREAT ORME MINES, a 4,000 yr-old copper mine that's the biggest such site so far discovered. It's also the only prehistoric mine open to the public, with displays of finds, and guided underground walks through the cavernous workings themselves. Teas, shop; cl Nov–Jan; (01492) 870447; £4.20. On the way down a dry ski slope also has a toboggan run. Back in town, the RABBIT HOLE 🔤 (Trinity Sq) is a jolly exhibition devoted to Alice in Wonderland, with life-size animated tableaux; the real Alice holidayed in Llandudno as a child. Shop, disabled access; cl winter Suns; (01492) 860082; £2.75. The CONWY VALLEY RAILWAY, a BR line from here to Blaenau Ffestiniog, runs through magnificent scenery and has several useful stops en route. The Queen's Head at Glanwydden, off the Colwyn Bay road, does very good food.

❋ 🏚 **Llanfairpwllgwyngyllgogerychwyrnd robwllllantysiliogogogoch** SH5372 Locals generally shorten their village's remarkable name to Llanfair P G, or Llanfairpwll. Excellent views of Snowdonia and the Menai Strait from the top of the Marquess of Anglesey's Column, built in 1816 to commemorate the military achievements of Wellington's second in command at the Battle of Waterloo. Fine mountain views, too, from his creeper-covered former home PLAS NEWYDD (2m S on the A4080), an elegant 18th-c mansion best known for its mural by Rex Whistler. Other works by the painter as well, along with a collection of relics from Waterloo, and a good spring garden with rhododendrons (Apr–Jun only). Meals, snacks, shop, disabled access; cl Fri and Sat, Nov–Mar; (01248) 714795; £4.20; NT. The nearby village of Penmynydd was the ancient home of the Tudor family. The Liverpool Arms at Menai Bridge is the nearest good place for lunch.

🔲 ♭ **Llangefni** SH4676 Right in the centre of Anglesey, with a big open-air market every Thurs. ORIEL YNYS

Mon (Rhosmeirch, on the B5111) Excellent gallery with imaginative, changing displays on the history of Anglesey, as well as a collection of wildlife paintings by C F Tunnicliffe. You can spend a surprising amount of time here. Snacks, shop, disabled access; cl Mon (exc bank hols), Christmas wk; (01248) 724444; *£2.

🏔 🏮 🛴 ❈ ♨ Llangollen SJ2141 Not special in itself despite a good few solid and gracious Georgian and Victorian villas; what makes it attractive is its charming valley setting above the River Dee. It has discreet hotels that cater for the generally older people to whom the area most appeals – though it comes vividly alive during the Eisteddfod. VALLE CRUCIS ABBEY (on the A542 2m N) Substantial remains of the early 13th-c abbey church, and some beautifully carved grave slabs. Shop, limited disabled access; cl Nov–Mar; (01978) 860326; £1.70. The ruins stand at the bottom of the Horseshoe Pass, a nerve-wrackingly steep but extremely scenic mountain drive; the Britannia Inn just above the abbey has exceptional views. PLAS NEWYDD Lady Eleanor Butler and Sarah Ponsonby, the 'Ladies of Llangollen', lived here from 1780 to 1831. The beautiful, half-timbered house has stained glass, leather wall coverings and domestic paraphernalia of the period. Pleasant gardens. Shop; cl Nov–Mar; (01978) 861314; £2. LLANGOLLEN RAILWAY (Abbey Rd) Now running 8 miles, this used to be part of the Great Western Railway; steam and diesel trains go from the pleasantly preserved station to the village of Glyndyfrdwy up the Dee (the Bedwyn Arms in a lovely setting above the river does food). Meals, snacks, shop, special coach for the disabled (you have to book); no trains Jan, wkdys Nov and Dec; (01978) 860951 for timetable; *£6.60 full return fare, less for shorter trips. On the Wharf a CANAL EXHIBITION CENTRE has displays on the history of Welsh canals, and organises HORSE-DRAWN BOAT TRIPS along the Vale of Llangollen 🚂. Meals, snacks, shop; cl Weds Apr, Thurs and Fri Oct,

Nov–Mar; (01978) 860584; *£1. The Sarah Ponsonby (by the canal museum), Abbey Grange, Royal and Wild Pheasant hotels do decent lunches. The Pontcysyllte aqueduct (off the A5/A539 E) is very spectacular to cross – by boat or on foot; the Sun Trevor at Trevor Uchaf above here has good food and spectacular views.

! Llangybi SH4241 ST CYBI'S WELL Known to the Welsh as Fynnon Gybi, this has been reckoned to have healing properties for over a thousand years. Look out for the corbelled beehive vaulting inside the roofless stone structure, which is ancient Irish in style.

✝ Llanrwst SH8061 Pretty little town with old stone bridge over the Conwy river, said to be the work of Inigo Jones. GWYDIR CHAPEL, added by the influential Wynn family to the parish church in the 17th c, has a stone coffin reputedly that of Llewelyn the Great, as well as a magnificent rood screen from the ruins of Maenan Abbey. The Wynns also constructed the nearby GWYDIR UCHAF CHAPEL, with intriguing ceiling paintings.

🛴 Llanuwchllyn SH8730 BALA LAKE RAILWAY 🚂 Some of the carriages on trains using this delightful 4½-mile route are open to the elements, which seems to make the views of the lake and mountains more vivid. The locomotives were once used to haul slate in the local quarries. Snacks, shop, disabled access (but no facilities); cl most Mon and Fri Apr–Jun and Sept, Oct–Mar; (01678) 540666 for timetable; £6. The Eryrod, with panoramic views, has good-value food.

🕯 🏮 🚍 Llanystumdwy SH4738 LLOYD GEORGE MEMORIAL MUSEUM (on the A497) Audio-visual displays and memorabilia relating to the life of Lloyd George, whose family moved here from Manchester when he was a boy. They lived in nearby Highgate Cottage, which has been restored to the way it was then, and has a neat Victorian garden. Shop, disabled access; cl wknds (exc in summer), Nov–Mar (exc by appointment); (01766) 522071; £2.50. It's a short stroll from here to the site where he's buried. Just up the hill, children should enjoy the RABBIT FARM which, as well as around 700 rabbits, has other animals and pony rides. Open Easter–Sept; (01766) 523136; £2.50.

🦋 **Menai Bridge** SH5572 The village takes its name from Thomas Telford's magnificent iron suspension bridge linking Anglesey to the mainland, the first such bridge in the world. BUTTERFLY PALACE Exotic butterflies from all corners of the globe, as well as bird house, insectarium, reptile house, and adventure playground. Meals, snacks, shop, disabled access; cl Jan and Feb; (01248) 712474; £3.75. The waterside Liverpool Arms has decent fresh food.

✝ **Mold** SJ2464 A very good theatre, and a richly decorated parish CHURCH built to commemorate the victory of Henry Tudor at Bosworth Field in 1485. The Druid Arms in a lovely setting at Llanferres out on the Ruthin road has good food.

↧ 🏚 **Penmachno** SH7950 PENMACHNO WOOLLEN MILL Timeless watermill powered by the River Machno, with local weavers explaining and demonstrating the history and craft of the cottage weaving industry. The setting is lovely. Snacks, good shop; cl 25 Dec; (01690) 710545; free. TY'N Y COED Reached by a pleasant walk along the river from the Woollen Mill's car park, a fully furnished 19th-c farmhouse, good for showing the traditional way of life in this area. Open pm Thurs, Fri and Sun Apr–Oct; (01690) 760229; *£1.80; NT. TY MAWR (Wybrnant, on the forest road W of village) Picturesque, lonely thick-walled medieval cottage, birthplace of Bishop William Morgan who first translated the Bible into Welsh (see St Asaph entry on p.920). Shop; open pm Thurs–Sun Apr–Oct; (01690) 760213; *£1.80 NT.

⋎ **Penmaenpool** SH6918 Its small waterside nature reserve has a very useful nature information centre pointing out promising places throughout this whole area, a good region for walks. About a mile away,

Abergwynant Farm (on the A493) has a PONY TREKKING CENTRE which will take beginners out for an hour over scenic routes; (01341) 422377; from £8.50. You can stay at the farm too. The George III is a pleasant place for lunch.

🏚 ⊛ 🐸 **Plas yn Rhiw** SH2328 PLAS YN RHIW Charming if unassuming little manor house, worth a visit for the gardens and woodland, inc a waterfall, spring snowdrop wood and subtropical specimens. Shop, very limited disabled access; open pm daily exc Tues Apr–Sept; (01758) 780219; £2.60; NT. The setting is lovely, overlooking one of the area's wildest coasts. The beautifully placed Sun over at Llanengan does decent food.

🛏 ↧ 🐾 **Porthmadog** SH5638 Quite a busy shopping town of low slate-roofed houses, with a spacious harbour. The famous narrow-gauge FFESTINIOG RAILWAY (Harbour Station) opened in 1836 to carry slate from Blaenau Ffestiniog to Porthmadog by gravity. Closed in 1946, it reopened in 1955 and has gradually been extended to climb the 13¼ miles to Blaenau Ffestiniog; further extensions are planned. Stop off at stations along the way for good walks and views. Meals, snacks, shop, some disabled access; cl wkdys Nov–late Mar (exc school hols); (01766) 512340; full fare £12.40. The adjacent FFESTINIOG RAILWAY MUSEUM tells the story of the railway, with exhibits inc a four-wheeled hearse converted from an old quarryman's coach, and one of the original steam locos from 1863; cl wkdys Nov–Mar; donations. The railway links with the British Rail Cambrian Coast Line, hugging the coast from Pwllheli to Machynlleth, with many stops along the way. Overshadowed by its more famous neighbour in size but certainly not in spirit is the WELSH HIGHLAND RAILWAY (opposite the BR station), an enthusiastically restored line that currently runs trains daily in the summer hols and most Suns Apr–Oct; (01766) 513402 for timetable; *£1.75. This railway's ownership of some of the track that the Ffestiniog Railway plans to develop to Caernarfon caused a bit of a dispute between the 2 companies – which was confused still further by the Ffestiniog Railway Co's use of the name Welsh Highland Railway in some of their literature. A POTTERY at Snowdon Mill has demonstrations and the chance to make a pot yourself, as well as other crafts, and a mural illustrating the town's history. Snacks, shop, very good disabled access; cl wknds exc July, Aug and bank hols, best to check winter opening; (01766) 512137; free, though may be charges for some activities. The Ship has decent food (and a Chinese restaurant), and nearby Black Rock Golden Sands is one of the area's finest beaches.

★ ᠿ ❀ **Portmeirion** ⊞ SH5937 On the steep wooded shores of an inlet from Tremadog Bay, this fairy-tale holiday village, designed by Welsh architect Sir Clough Williams Ellis, is set in 175 acres of lush coastal cliff and woodland gardens. Quite charming, it's an Italianate folly – pastel-washed cottages interlaced with grottoes and cobbled squares, a bell tower, castle and lighthouse, and long picturesque flights of steps zigzagging down to the water, which at low tide dries to miles of sand. Enveloping the village are the 60 acres of Gwyllt gardens, with fine displays of rhododendrons, azaleas, hydrangeas and subtropical flora; good wild woodlands, too. You have to pay a toll to enter the village, but once in you can see the house where Noel Coward wrote *Blithe Spirit* and the locations for the cult TV series *The Prisoner*; children can play in the playground, on a make-believe schooner apparently moored by the hotel, or, tide permitting, on the beach. A lovely relaxing place, quite unlike anywhere else. Meals, snacks, shops (one specialising in Portmeirion pottery), some disabled access; cl 25 Dec; (01766) 770228; £3.80, less Nov–Mar. No dogs – though there's a touching dog cemetery in the woods nearby. PLAS BRONDANW SH6142 (Llanfrothen)

The ancestral home of Clough Williams Ellis, and you can visit the architectural garden he designed there – great views; (01766) 771136; £1.50.

Prestatyn SJ0783 Bustling seaside resort standing at one end of the 168-mile route of Offa's Dyke, marked by a stone pillar above the main beach.

🏰 ᠿ ✝ **Rhuddlan** SJ0278 Once a busy port, now a sleepy little town with a fine old CASTLE adapted by Edward I from an earlier Norman structure. Overlooking the river, it's a pretty spot. Cl Oct–Apr; (01745) 590777; £1.70. BODRHYDDAN HALL (on the A5151 Rhuddlan–Dyserth road) Lovely doll's-house front, and some wonderfully elaborate fireplaces in the drawing room. Also formal French garden and an interesting well-house built by Inigo Jones. Teas, shop, disabled access to ground floor only; open pm Tues and Thurs Jun–Sept; (01745) 590414; *£3. Follow the road through to Dyserth and there's a partly 13th-c CHURCH (with Jesse window), and a plunging 18-metre (60-ft) waterfall.

⛄ ♪ **Rhyl** SJ0181 Rather brash seaside resort, but if you're passing with children, the Knight's Cavern, a lively interpretation of Welsh history, should amuse them. On East Parade, there's also one of the very good SEA LIFE CENTRES that we've described in several English resorts, with a dramatic Shark Encounter as well as the usual walk-through underwater tunnel. Meals, snacks, shop, disabled access; cl 25 Dec; (01745) 344660; £4.50.

✝ ⛄ **St Asaph** SJ0475 Tiny city with the smallest CATHEDRAL in Britain, founded in 537. A column in the grounds commemorates its most famous cleric Bishop Morgan (see Penmachno entry on p.919) and his work translating the Bible into Welsh. There's a little museum with finds from the site, open by appointment, Shop, disabled access; (01745) 583429; free. The Farmers Arms (The Waen) does proper food.

🦜 ᠿ **South Stack** SH2082 The spectacular cliffs nr the lighthouse are full of seabird breeding colonies, and there's a 780-acre RSPB RESERVE, where you may be able to see guillemots, razorbills and puffins (especially around May, Jun and July). Lots of colourful wild flowers too, and maybe the odd seal. The visitor centre has closed-circuit TV pictures of nesting birds; guided walks leave here at 2pm Tues and Sat May–Aug. Visitor centre cl mid-Sept–Easter; (01407) 764973; free. Nearby is a large group of the foundations of HUT CIRCLES, probably around 2,000 years old, still with some visible traces of stone sleeping slabs.

🎗 **Tal-y-Cafn** SH8072 BODNANT GARDEN (off the A470) Started in

---

Days Out

Medieval town planning and seaside Victoriana
Conwy; lunch at Castle Hotel there, or Queen's Head, Llandudno Junction; tram up the Great Ormes Head from Llandudno, or visit Bodnant Garden, Tal-y-Cafn.

Around the Welsh Everest
Caernarfon Castle; lunch at Y Bistro, Llanberis; Snowdon Mountain Railway, Electric Mountain or Welsh Slate Museum there; drive to Beddgelert, if time walk along the old railway track through Aberglaslyn Pass

Italianate fantasy and slate city
Ffestiniog Railway, Porthmadog; lunch at the Ship there; Portmeirion, or Llechwedd Slate Caverns, Blaenau Ffestiniog.

Beside the Menai Strait
Beaumaris; lunch at Sailor's Return or Olde Bull's Head there, or Jodie's Bistro, Menai Bridge; Plas Newydd, Llanfair P G.

To the tip of the Lleyn peninsula
Tre'r Ceiri hill fort, Llanaelhaearn; lunch at the Sun, Llanengan; Plas yn Rhiw (limited opening); stroll at the end of the Lleyn peninsula.

Panning for gold
Precipice Walk (see △-5 in **Walks** section on p.923), or walk across the railway bridge over the Mawddach estuary from Barmouth; lunch at the Last Inn, Barmouth; Gwynfynydd gold mine, Dolgellau.

Anglesey adventure
Bryn Celli Ddu burial chamber, Llandaniel Fab; walk from Newborough Warren along the beach to Llanddwyn Island; picnic on the beach; Barclodiad y Gawres burial chamber, Aberffraw, and beach nearby; Henblas Park, Bodorgan, or walk on Holyhead Mountain.

Canal-age wonder
Walk over Pontcysyllte aqueduct nr Llangollen; lunch at the Sun Trevor, Trevor Uchaf; Plas Newydd, Llangollen, or walk up to Castell Dinas Bran (easiest access from the high level road); horse-drawn canal boat trip or train ride, Llangollen.

North Marches panorama
Walk to Moel Famau's viewpoint tower (see △-12 in **Walks** section on p.923); lunch at the Dinorben Arms, Bodfari; Bodelwyddan Castle, or Rhuddlan castle and Bodrhyddan Hall (limited opening).

1875 but improved in 1900 (and indeed ever since, in the hands of the green-fingered family which has owned them), these gardens are among Britain's greatest. Part of the 80-acre grounds has a beautiful woodland garden in a sheltered valley, notable for its rhododendrons and azaleas, while below the house are 5 terraces in the Italian style, with a canal pool, reconstructed pin mill and an open-air stage on the lowest. Many fine rare plants inc unusual trees and shrubs. Meals, snacks, shop, disabled access (but it is steep in places); cl Nov–mid-Mar; (01492) 650460; £4.20; NT. The Tal y Cafn Inn is useful for lunch, and the Olde Bull, in a delightful setting on the hillside opposite at Llanbedr y Cennin, does good imaginative food; the Holland Arms at Trofarth is also useful.

Tan-y-Bwlch SH6641 (off the A487) The grounds of the Snowdonia National Park's study centre at PLAS TAN-Y-BWLCH have rewarding strolls through extensive woodland; in places the paths cross the Ffestiniog Railway (and you can buy tickets for it here). Woods open all year, gardens summer only; (01766) 590324; donations.

Trefriw SH7863 TREFRIW WOOLLEN MILL (on the B5106) The same family have run this woollen mill for 135 years; 2 hydro-electric turbines are driven by the fast-flowing Afon Crafnant, and there's a weaver's garden (best Jun–Sept). Weaving demonstrations in the turbine house wkdys all year (even Nov–Easter when the mill itself is closed), plus wknds in summer. Maybe spinning demonstrations too in summer, so worth checking first to see exactly what's going on. Snacks, shop (selling tapestries and tweeds made here), disabled access; cl Sun (exc bank hols and late May–Sept); (01492) 640462; free. Trefriw used to be a spa, and you can still see the WELLS on the N outskirts of the village (the water is said to treat rheumatism, indigestion, and homesickness). The village also has a 14th-c church; the Prince's Arms has decent food.

Wrexham SJ3250 Mostly an industrial town, but its 15th-c CHURCH is worth a look, with its magnificent steeple. ERDDIG (well signed S of Wrexham) Superb late 17th-c house, especially interesting for the way you can explore the life of those 'upstairs' and 'downstairs' equally as thoroughly; the gallery of servants' portraits is especially touching. Enlarged and improved in the early 18th c, the house is filled with splendid original furnishings, inc a magnificent state bed in Chinese silk. Restored outbuildings include a laundry, bakehouse, estate smithy and sawmill, and the surrounding parkland is very pleasant to stroll through. It's one of the most attractive places to visit in all of Wales. Meals, snacks, shop, disabled access with prior notice; open pm Sat–Weds Easter–Sept; (01978) 313333; £5.40, garden and below-stairs tour only £3.60; NT. Adjacent FARM WORLD is well liked by readers, a 300-acre working dairy farm with all the necessary ingredients. Cl Nov–Feb; (01978) 840697; £3.60. The Boat at Erbistock, a few miles S of Erddig, is a beautifully placed dining pub. BERSHAM INDUSTRIAL HERITAGE CENTRE (on the B5099/B5098 W of Wrexham) Well recreated 18th-c ironworks, with a good overview of other local industries, and demonstrations of various traditional skills. Snacks, shop, limited disabled access; cl 25–26 Dec, 1 Jan; (01978) 261529; heritage centre free, ironworks £1.

Y Felinheli SH5365 GREENWOOD CENTRE ■ (off the B4366 NE of Caernarfon) An unexpected delight, a lively look at trees and wood from trunks and rainforests to Ethiopian wooden pillows. You can handle most of the exhibits, and there are 17 acres of woodland to explore. Mostly indoors so ideal for rainy days, but worth popping into at any time. Teas, shop, disabled access; open daily in summer, best to ring for winter opening; (01248) 671493; £3.75. The Vaynol Arms at Pentir has good food.

★ **Attractive villages** in the area, all

with decent pubs but in general tending to appeal for their surroundings more than for the beauty of their buildings, include Betws-yn-Rhos SH9174, Capel Curig SH7258 (excellent walks here), Cilcain SJ1865, Erbistock SJ3542, Halkyn SJ2172, Hanmer SJ4639, Llanarmon D C SJ1633, Llanarmon yn Ial SJ1956, Llanasa SJ1082, Llandwrog SH4456, Llanelidan SJ1150, Llangedwyn SJ1924 in the Tanat valley, Llanrhaeadr ym Mochnant SJ1226 (where *An Englishman Who Went Up A Hill* was filmed), Llansannan SH9466, Pontblyddyn SJ2761, Porth Dinllaen SH2741 (an idyllic seaside spot, but you have to walk to it) and St George SH9776.

Other pubs and inns in attractive areas or with notable views include the Porth Tocyn Hotel above the sea at Abersoch SH3226 (excellent clean beach for families here), Castell Cidwm at Betws Garmon SH5458, Sportsman's Arms up on the A543 S of Bylchau SH9863, White Horse and Bryn Tyrch at Capel Garmon SH8255, Grouse at Carrog SJ1144, T'yn y Groes at Ganllwyd SH7224, Eagle & Child in the hilltop village of Gwaenysgor SJ0881, Druid at Llanferres SJ1961 (doing well under new management), Cross Foxes on the Dee at Overton Bridge SJ3643, the Ship by acres of sand on the shore of Red Wharf Bay SH5281, Cwellyn Arms at Rhyd-Ddu SH5753 (big playground), White Eagle on Holy Island at Rhoscolyn SH2676 and Caerffynon Hall at Talsarnau SH6236.

Walks

This area has plenty of fine walking, both gentle and taxing – somewhere to justify a walking holiday.

Snowdonia's main mountain group soars dramatically, many of its peaks having easily identifiable shapes (when you can see them through the mist). **Snowdon** SH6054 ⌂-1, the highest mountain in England or Wales, has a number of ways up, ranging from the easy path alongside the mountain railway to the enthralling Horseshoe Route, which makes its way along knife-edge ridges; the Pyg Track and Watkin Path are among the favourites. For a taste of the mountain without actually going up it, follow the start of the Miners' Track (from the Pen-y-pass car park on the A4086), which really is a track as far as Glaslyn, the last of 4 lakes passed. Recommended lower-level rambles include the reservoirs N of **Capel Curig** SH7258 ⌂-2, the nature trail around **Llyn Idwal** SH6459 ⌂-3 (a superbly sited lake beneath Glyder Fach), the **Aberglaslyn Pass** SH5947 ⌂-4 S of Beddgelert, and the signposted **Precipice Walk** SH7321 ⌂-5 N of Dolgellau SH7318. There's a pleasant riverside stroll along the old railway track by the Afon Llugwy W from Betws-y-coed SH7956, and you can walk along the shores of Bala Lake SH9134.

Much of the coast is built up or ribboned by roads. Notable exceptions giving good walks are **Great Ormes Head** SH7683 ⌂-6 (quaintly reachable by a steep tram from Llandudno), **Conwy Mountain** SH7577 ⌂-7 (not a real mountain but with views of Anglesey worthy of mountain status), and **Lavan Sands** SH6376 ⌂-8 nr Aber SH6573. The very unspoilt **Lleyn Peninsula** ⌂-9 has a 563-metre (1,849-ft) mountain, Yr Eifl SH3644 (the Rivals) close to the coast. The **peninsula tip** ⌂-10 has some good coastal walks starting W from Aberdaron SH1726, with fine windswept views from Mynydd Mawr SH1325 (bird reserve nearby), and E of here is the spectacular bay of Hell's Mouth SH2626; the beaches along here have clean bathing water.

Castell Dinas Bran SJ2243 ⌂-11 in Clwyd is the place to head for from Llangollen SJ2142. This hill fort commands views over the vale and is close by the Panorama Walk (actually a surfaced minor road); walks can be tied in with the canal towpath below. **Moel Fammau** SJ1663 ⌂-12 is the highest point of the Clwydian Range, a bulging massif with clearly marked paths; walk up from the car park on the minor road E of Llanbedr D C SJ1359 through colour-coded forest trails or over open land, for views of much of Snowdonia, the edge of the Peak district and the Wirral.

Anglesey is too flat to offer much interest inland, but its lovely beaches, as at Newborough Warren SH4263 (giving a walk to peninsular **Llanddwyn Island**) ⌂-13, are satisfying enough. Paths intermittently follow the indented coastline around Amlwch SH4493. **Holyhead Mountain** SH2182 ⌂-14 is a dramatic hill, with an Iron Age fort and Roman watchtower site, at the W tip of Holy Island.

Where to eat

Bala SH9236 NEUADD-Y-CYFNOD (Old School Restaurant) High St (01678) 521269 Relaxed and informal restaurant with huge helpings of good-value food (morning coffee, lunch, tea and dinner), pleasant service, and attractive furnishings; Welsh lamb a speciality; disabled access; cl 25–26 Dec, 1 Jan. £12|£5.

Beaumaris SH6076 SAILORS RETURN Church St (01248) 811314 Bright and cheerful place, more or less open-plan, with a collection of car-shaped teapots, naval memorabilia and maps and old prints, comfortable furnishings in rich colours, and a good mix of customers; well kept real ales, and enjoyable food inc daily specials. £17|£6.

Bodfari SJ0970 DINORBEN ARMS (01745) 710309 Carefully extended building with warmly welcoming beamed rooms, 3 open fires, a huge collection of whiskies, well kept real ales and plenty of good wines, a popular lunchtime smorgasbord, Fri–Sat carvery, and help-yourself farmhouse buffet on Weds and Thurs; disabled access. £14|£4.45.

Erbistock SJ3542 BOAT (01978) 780143 Popular 16th-c dining pub in an enchanting setting looking out over the sleepy River Dee; with a comfortable no smoking beamed dining room, a restaurANTY feel, 2 well kept real ales, and good enjoyable lunchtime bar food; old-fashioned seats on a gravel terrace surrounded by flowers and charming up-and-down lawns. £16.45|£5.95.

Gresford SJ3555 PANT-YR-OCHAIN (01978) 853525 Attractively and interestingly decorated spacious pub with country furnishings, good open fires, a big dining area set out as a library, and a no smoking room; consistently good interesting food, a decent range of wines, well kept real ales, polite efficient service, and a civilised atmosphere. £21|£5.95.

Llanberis SH5760 Y BISTRO 43–45 High St (01286) 871278 Friendly no smoking restaurant with good local produce used in the Welsh and English cooking – fine fish and enjoyable puddings; cl Sun, Mon in winter. £28.

Llandudno Junction SH8180 QUEENS HEAD Glanwydden (01492) 546570 Busy but comfortable dining pub, lots of very good seafood, excellent home-made puddings, good daily specials, interesting evening extras, and decent wines; cl 25 Dec; children over 7. £18|£5.

Llangedwyn SJ1924 GREEN (01691) 828234 Very well run, ancient place in a lovely spot in the Tanat valley, with lots of nooks, alcoves and crannies, a blazing log fire, and a good mix of furnishings; a pleasant upstairs no smoking restaurant, an impressive range of good, tasty bar food, half-a-dozen real ales, and a good choice of malt whiskies and wines; attractive garden over road with picnic sets by the river, and fishing permits. £16.45|£5.50.

Llanrwst SH8062 TY-HWNT-I'R-BONT(01492) 640138 Charming little 500-year-old cottage by the bridge, run by the Holt family for 25 years; filled rolls and sandwiches, salads, home-made cakes, shortbread, and scones, enjoyable afternoon teas, and quite a choice of teas, coffees and milk shakes; home-made mustards to take away, and old books and bric-à-brac upstairs; cl 2 Nov–7 Apr; partial disabled access. |£2.70.

Menai Bridge SH5572 Jodies's Bistro Telford Rd (01248) 714864 Fine views of the old suspension bridge and Menai Strait as well as very good varied light lunchtime snacks and meals; and interesting evening meals; no smoking room, decent wines, and friendly service; cl 25 Dec, 1 Jan. £19|£4.50.

Pwllheli SH3535 Plas Bodegroes off the A497 (01758) 612363 Lovely Georgian manor house surrounded by tree-filled grounds, with comfortably restful rooms; good food using superb fresh local produce (especially fish) and very good wine list; bedrooms; cl Mon, Nov–Feb. £38.50 for 5 courses.

Red Wharf Bay SH5281 Ship (01248) 852568 Solidly built old pub looking over miles of cockle sands, with enterprising bar food, big old-fashioned bars, coal fires, and friendly cheerful service; no smoking dining room and cellar room, well kept real ales, quite a few whiskies, and plenty of seats outside; disabled access. £18|£6.70.

Ty'n-y-Groes SH7672 Groes (01492) 650545 Family-run pub with wonderful views from the airy, no smoking conservatory, rambling, low-beamed and thick-walled rooms with a welcoming atmosphere and interesting old furnishings, winter log fires, good traditional country cooking, well kept real ales, and efficient friendly service; bedrms; children over 11 in restaurant; disabled access. £25|£7.

WEST WALES

Lovely unspoilt coast, interesting places to potter around – great for a quiet holiday.

The coast has the best of the scenery here. It's relatively gentle in the south, with level cliffs, intricate estuaries and some lovely sandy beaches; Tenby, showing its medieval origins still, is an enjoyably civilised small resort. In the west and north it's much more rugged, with seals and dolphins. Outstanding stretches are between St David's and Strumble Head near Fishguard – largely unspoilt, full of rocky coves and exhilarating cliff walks; around St Brides Bay – low cliffs flanking surfing beaches; by the attractive fishing villages of Solva and Little Haven; and in the wild places around Marloes.

Inland, the most scenic parts are around Brechfa and Abergorlech, with steep forests and plunging ravines, and other good spots include the blustery Prescelly Hills and the secluded and intimate Gwaun Valley; but other parts of Wales are better for scenic drives.

St David's is the most interesting place to visit, with its cathedral a real surprise in such rural surroundings, and a good few things to look at nearby. There are lots of castles, a fair spread of other places to visit, and though the area has virtually no bright-lights attractions, families will find quite a lot to keep children amused – the leisure park near Narberth is particularly good, with a really scary new ride.

Where to stay

Broad Haven SM8614 Druidstone Broad Haven, Haverfordwest, Dyfed SA62 3NE (01437) 781221 £56, plus special breaks; 9 rms sharing bthrms (and 4 holiday cottages, 2 with wheelchair access). Alone on the coast above an effectively private beach with exhilarating cliff walks, this roomy and very informally friendly hotel, with something of a folk-club and Outward Bound feel at times, is extremely winning and relaxing if you take to its unique combination of good wholesome and often memorably inventive food, slightly fend-for-yourself approach amid elderly furniture, and glorious seaside surroundings. All sorts of unusual sporting activities inc sand-yachting; cl Mon–Weds 10 Nov–18 Dec (fully open from then on), cl Mon–Weds 5 Jan–12 Feb; disabled access (see above).

Carew SN0403 OLD STABLE COTTAGE Carew, Tenby, Dyfed SA70 8SL (01646) 651889 £48; 3 rms. Originally a stable and carthouse for the castle, this attractive place has an inglenook fireplace and original bread oven, games room, and a conservatory overlooking the garden; good Aga-cooked food; cl Dec–Feb; children over 3.

Crugybar SN6437 GLANRANNELL PARK Crugybar, Llanwrda, Dyfed SA19 8SA (01558) 685230 *£72, plus special breaks; 8 rms. Surrounded by lawns and overlooking a small private lake in 23 acres of parkland, this peaceful hotel has 2 comfortable lounges and a small library, a well stocked bar, good food using fresh local produce where possible, and friendly helpful staff; excellent area for walks and especially birdwatching, also lots of wildlife, pony-trekking, and fishing nearby; cl Nov–Mar.

Fishguard SM9736 GILFACH GOCH FARM Fishguard, Dyfed SA65 9SR (01348) 873871 *£50, plus special breaks; 6 rms. Traditional, carefully modernised, 18th-c Welsh stone farmhouse on a 10-acre smallholding with sheep, donkeys, Vietnamese pot-bellied pig, dogs, cats, and fowl; with lovely views and nr Pembrokeshire coastal path; log fires, and a homely lounge; good country cooking using many home-produced ingredients; a safe garden for children; no smoking; cl Nov–Feb; children over 5; disabled access.

Fishguard SM9537 MANOR HOUSE Fishguard, Dyfed SA65 9HG (01348) 873260 £48, plus special breaks; 6 comfortable rms, most with sea views. Georgian house with fine views of harbour from the sheltered garden; well planned basement restaurant with a good choice of international home-made food using fresh local produce; cl Christmas.

Llandeloy SM8527 LOCHMEYLER FARM Llandeloy, Haverfordwest, Dyfed SA62 6LL (01348) 837724 £50, plus special breaks; 12 rms. Attractive 16th-c farmhouse in mature gardens on 220-acre working dairy farm; 2 lounges (one no smoking), log fires; traditional farmhouse cooking in pleasant dining room, and Welsh cakes on arrival; you can walk around the farm trails; disabled access.

Nevern SN0840 TREWERN ARMS Nevern, Newport, Dyfed SA42 0NB (01239) 820395 *£45; 9 rms. Welcoming creeper-clad old inn in a pleasant riverside hamlet nr interesting pilgrims' church; a very warm welcome, interestingly decorated slate-floored bar, decent food, and well kept real ales.

Penally SS1199 PENALLY ABBEY Penally, Tenby, Dyfed SA70 7PY (01834) 843033 £96; 12 pretty rms, many with 4-poster beds, and 4 in coach house. 'Gothick'-style country-house hotel in 5 acres of gardens and woodland, with fine views across the golf course and Carmarthen Bay; open fire in the comfortable lounge, tiny bar, and conservatory; very good food in the elegant candlelit restaurant, delicious breakfasts; small indoor swimming pool, snooker and croquet; children over 7 in restaurant, disabled access.

Pontfaen SN0533 TREGYNON COUNTRY FARMHOUSE Pontfaen, Gwaun Valley, Fishguard, Dyfed SA65 9TU (01239) 820531 £48, plus special breaks; 8 rms. Peacefully set 16th-c farmhouse on valley edge in lovely unspoilt countryside with lots of wildlife and walks; big inglenook fireplace in beamed lounge, and a friendly welcome; very good, imaginative, additive-free food using produce from their own own and neighbouring farms, home-smoked meats, and home-made preserves.

Rhydlewis SN3447 BRONIWAN Rhydlewis, Llandysul, Dyfed SA44 5PF (01239) 851261 £37; 3 pretty rms, 2 with own bthrm. Grey stone house with pine-panelled windows, on small farm surrounded by beech and pine trees; fine views of the Prescelly Hills in the distance, and lots of wildlife; you can help with the calves, hens, and cows; stone barn with games, table tennis and books, woodburner in comfortable sitting room; separate dining room; and good naturally produced food from garden and farm; no smoking; children over 5.

St David's SM7525 WARPOOL COURT St David's, Haverfordwest, Dyfed SA62 6BN (01437) 720300 *£130, plus special breaks; 25 rms. Originally built as St David's cathedral school in the 1860s and bordering NT land, this popular hotel has lovely views over St Brides Bay; Ada Williams's collection of lovely hand-painted tiles can be seen in the public rooms; food in the spacious elegant restaurant is imaginative (good for vegetarians too), and staff are helpful and friendly; quiet gardens, heated summer swimming pool, tennis, exercise room, table tennis, pool, croquet, and free golf at St David's golf club; cl Jan.

Spittal SM9822 LOWER HAYTHOG Spittal, Haverfordwest, Dyfed SA62 5QL (01437) 731279 *£50; 6 rms. Centuries-old farmhouse on working dairy farm in 250 acres of unspoilt countryside; with comfortable lounge, log fire, books and games; traditional breakfasts, good cooking in the dining room, and friendly owners; swing and slide in the garden, trout ponds in the woods.

Whitemill SN4622 PANTGWYN FARM Whitemill, Carmarthen, Carmarthenshire SA32 7ES (01267) 290247 £50; 3 rms. Traditional, 18th-c no smoking farmhouse with sheep, donkey, pony, free-range chickens and lots of wildlife; open fire in inglenook fireplace, and residents' lounge; lovely food (at least one Welsh dish) in dining room using their own or local farm produce, proper breakfasts with hand-churned butter and their own honey; self-catering in converted barn; many surrounding walks; good disabled access.

To see and do

WALES FAMILY ATTRACTION OF THE YEAR

☺ **Narberth** SN0615 OAKWOOD The only real theme park in Wales, and a good one too, especially in the summer holidays when they stay open till 10pm, rounding off every night with a firework display. Though there's a real mix of things to do, from Europe's biggest wooden rollercoaster to live Wild West saloon shows, it's not the kind of place where you'll have to dash round trying to cram everything in; a day here is rather less manic than at several theme parks we know, and you won't come across as many crowds or queues. The most popular rides are the water-coaster and the bobsleigh run, with things like putting and boating for those with gentler tastes; you can have a go at panning for gold. Younger children have their own little roller-coaster (there's another medium-sized one aimed at families), as well as a small farm area, and carousels and the like. But the real talking point is the new sky-coaster, Vertigo, quite the most unpleasant-looking ride we've ever seen: you're strapped in a harness and winched to a height of up to 42 metres (140 ft), then freefall at 60 mph back towards the ground – just before which you'll start swinging like a frantic pendulum. A nightmare cross between bungee-jumping and a parachute drop, this obviously wouldn't suit everyone, so rather than bump up the entry price, there's an extra charge (£30 for up to 3 people, the maximum number that can go on it at once). This has proved enormously popular, so if you want to try it in peak periods you'll need to get there fairly early to book in. Otherwise, for the rest of the park, we'd recommend coming after lunch and staying through the evening rather than arriving first thing. Meals, snacks, shop, disabled access; cl Oct–Easter (exc around Christmas, when special events); (01834) 891373; £9.45.

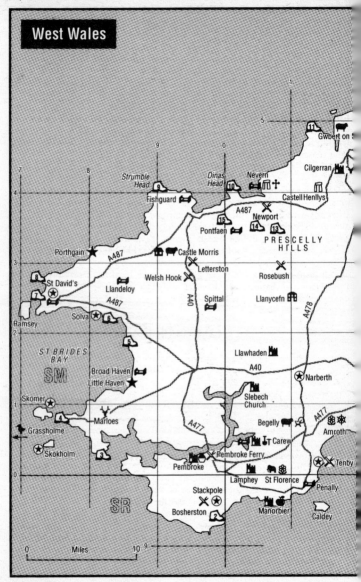

West Wales

✤ 🐝 **Amroth** SN1508 The beach here is lovely, and the New Inn facing it has good home cooking inc local seafood. COLBY WOODLAND GARDEN (off the A477) Beautiful woodland gardens in sheltered valley with pretty cascading stream – very pleasant and colourful, especially in autumn. A walled garden has a gothic gazebo

and colourful herbaceous plants. Snacks, shop; cl Nov–Mar; (01834) 811885; £2.60; NT.

🐑 🐾 **Begelly** SN1107 FOLLY FARM (on the A478) Busy working dairy farm, with the chance to milk a cow – or watch the more modern methods in the milking parlour. Everyone gets a chance to bottle-feed some of the

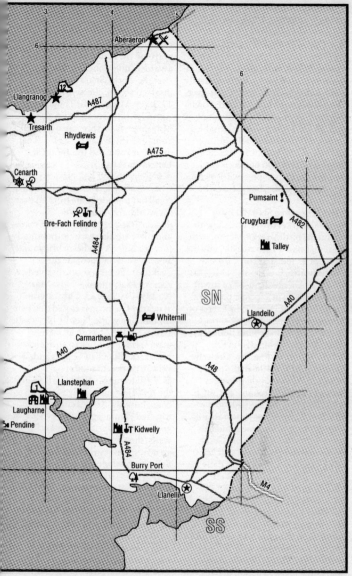

friendly animals. Meals, snacks, shop, disabled access; cl Nov–Mar; (01834) 812731; £3.50. A working POTTERY is nearby, (01834) 811204. There's good fresh fish at the Royal Oak down in the quiet extended seaside village of Saundersfoot, which has a lighthouse on the spit sheltering the harbour and sandy beach.

⚄ **Burry Port** SN4400 PEMBREY COUNTRY PARK Good for families to unwind, with 100 acres of woodland, summer falconry and orienteering, adventure playground, visitor centre, dry ski slope, and 8 miles of clean sandy beach (no dogs in summer). Meals, snacks, shop, disabled access; park open all year, though most attractions cl winter; (01554) 833913; parking £3, less winter, charges for some attractions.

🎃 ⬇︎T **Carew** SN0403 CAREW CASTLE AND TIDAL MILL Magnificent Norman castle (the setting for the Great Tournament of 1507), with especially handsome ivy-clad – southeast tower. The mill is one of just 3 restored tidal mills in Britain, with records dating back to 1558. Shop, limited disabled access; cl Nov-Easter; (01646) 651782; £2.50 both, £1.70 each. By the good Carew Inn nearby is the Carew Cross, an impressive 4-metre (13-ft) Celtic cross dating from the 11th c.

♨ 🌼 **Carmarthen** SN4120 Busy regional market town, according to legend the birthplace of Merlin, with the remains of a 13th-c castle, and on Priory St an unusual 2nd-c Roman amphitheatre. CARMARTHEN MUSEUM SN4321 (Abergwili, just E of town) Good museum in a former palace of the Bishop of St David's, in 7 acres of attractive grounds. Snacks, shop, disabled access to ground floor only; cl Sun, 24 Dec–1 Jan, Good Fri; (01267) 231691; free. The Cresselly Arms along the A40 E in the pretty village of Pont ar Gothi (pleasant riverside walks) is reliable for lunch. GWILI RAILWAY (Bronwydd, on the 484 N of Carmarthen) Short steam train trips along a scenic standard-gauge branch line of the old Great Western Railway. Meals, snacks, shop, disabled access; trains daily in Aug, most Suns and some Weds May–Sept; (01267) 230666; *£3.

🏛 **Castell Henllys** SN1139 (signed off the A487 E of Newport – where the Llwyngwair Arms surprises with its authentic Indian food) Iron Age hill fort in beautiful countryside overlooking River Gwaun, with interesting reconstruction of 3 big conical roundhouses. Also a forge, smithy, primitive looms and herb garden. Snacks, shop, some disabled access; cl Nov–Mar; (01239) 891319; £2.50.

🐂 🏛 **Castle Morris** SM9031 LLANGLOFFAN FARMHOUSE CHEESE (Llangloffan Farm, just N) Delicious traditional farmhouse hard cheeses

are hand-made here, and you can watch them do it. Before Mr Downey set up the farm (run entirely on organic principles) he was a viola player in the Hallé orchestra; his award-winning cheeses now go all over the world. Snacks, shop, disabled access; cheesemaking 10am-12.30pm Mon, Weds, Thurs, and Sat Apr–Oct, plus Tues and Fri May–Sept; (01348) 891241; *£1.75. The excellent-value fish restaurant at Letterston is handy.

✿ ✗ᐟ **Cenarth** SN2641 NATIONAL CORACLE CENTRE Unique collection of small hand-made boats from all over the world; they may have demonstrations of how they're made, and there are also various tools used for poaching. A medieval bridge and a pretty waterfall provide the backdrop. Snacks, shop, disabled access; cl Sat, and all – Nov–Mar; (01239) 710980; £2. The watermill at nearby Cwmcou is closed this year for building work. Nearby Newcastle Emlyn SN3042 has an attractive main st leading down to an ancient bridge; the Bunch of Grapes and Pelican do decent food.

🎃 Ψ **Cilgerran** SN1943 CASTLE (off the A484) Picturesquely placed on a crag above the River Teifi, this twin-towered Plantagenet fortress has good views from its towers and high walls, though, as usual, you have to go up a spiral staircase. Shop (not Sat), disabled access; cl 24–26 Dec, 1 Jan; (01239) 615007; *£1.70. WELSH WILDLIFE CENTRE Covering 350 acres, this is one of the richest areas of wetland in the district; the reed bed is the second biggest in Wales. You'll probably see more towards dusk, but even then some bashful creatures might not emerge; a video shows the species you may have missed. Meals, snacks, shop, disabled access; Cl Oct–Mar; (01239) 621600; *£2.40. The ancient Pendre is good for lunch.

⬇︎T ✗ᐟ **Dre-Fach Felindre** SN3538 MUSEUM OF THE WELSH WOOLLEN INDUSTRY (off the A484) Working museum with textile machinery and tools dating back to the 18th c. Also factory trails, and demonstrations of fabric-making – you may be able to try your hand at spinning. Snacks, shop, disabled access to ground floor; cl 24–26 Dec, 1 Jan; (01559) 370929; *£2.50. There are decent places to eat in Newcastle Emlyn.

Fishguard SM9537 The old fishing harbour is surrounded by appropriately small streets of terraced cottages (the Ship here has lots of atmosphere); there's an entirely separate big commercial harbour used by the Irish ferries. In between, the upper town has some attractive old buildings and is pleasant to saunter through. In 1997 a 30-metre (100-ft) long tapestry went on show to commemorate the 200th anniversary of the defeat here of the last army to invade mainland Britain. The Royal Oak (scene of the final surrender) has enjoyable food. You can drive or walk up on to the high headland which protects the harbour; its cliffs are quite grand, particularly where the seas boil through the narrow neck cutting off the rock on which Strumble Head lighthouse stands. Down on the rocks there you quite often see seals even in the spring, though they're more common in late summer.

☷ Gwbert on Sea SN1649 COASTAL FARM PARK Most notable for its fine clifftop setting overlooking Cardigan Island; there are a good few friendly animals for children, as well as plenty of wild flowers, and a coastal walk to caves where seals breed (best Mar–Nov). You may even see dolphins leaping out of the sea. Open all year; (01239) 612196; £1.

☷ ↥ Kidwelly SN4006 When the impressive CASTLE was built in the 12th c the sea used to wash against the steep slope below it. 4 massive towers, the tremendous gatehouse and much of the outer walls still remain, with steps up to the battlements and turrets. From the walls, the narrow medieval street layout of Kidwelly itself is very obvious. Shop, some disabled access; (01554) 890104; £2.20. INDUSTRIAL MUSEUM (Mynyddygarreg, NE of Kidwelly) Looks at 2 great Welsh industries, coal and tin mining. The original tinplate working buildings are still here, and there's an exhibition of coal mining with pithead gear and a winding engine. Snacks, shop, disabled access; open Easter, spring and May bank hols, wkdys and pm wknds Jun–Sept; (01554) 891078; free. The riverside Gwenllian Court Hotel out this way has decent food.

☷ Lamphey SN0100 LAMPHEY PALACE (A4139) Ruined 13th-c palace once belonging to the Bishops of St David's. Some disabled access; (01222) 500200; free.

☷☷ Laugharne SN2910 (pronounced 'Larn') DYLAN THOMAS'S BOAT HOUSE (Dylan's Walk) Wales's best known recent poet lived here while he was writing *Under Milk Wood*, and there are still some of his family photographs and furniture. The writing shed he used for so many poems is nearby. Snacks, shop; (01994) 427420; *£2. Thomas and his wife are buried in the village churchyard, their grave marked by a simple white cross. The ruined CASTLE he described as 'brown as owls' is a massive battlemented compilation of styles from the 12th to 16th c; it has good views over the estuary. Cl Oct–Apr; (01222) 500200; £1.70.

★ ☷☷ Llandeilo SN6222 An attractive, sloping town; the Plough at Rhosmaen just N is a favourite local dining pub. DINEFWR PARK (20 minutes' walk from riverside lodge at S edge of town; follow Dyfed Wildlife Trust path) Pleasant walks through wooded Capability Brown parkland around isolated, largely 13th-c castle. Plenty of deer, but no trace of the medieval town which is known to have stood outside the walls. Meals, snacks, disabled access; cl Tues, Weds, Nov–Mar; (01558) 823902; £2.60. GELLI AUR COUNTRY PARK (3m W, off the B4300) Very relaxing: 90 acres of wooded parkland around a splendid mansion, with an arboretum, nature trails, and specimen trees and shrubs. Meals, snacks, shop, disabled access; cl 25–26 Dec; (01558) 668885; £1.10 parking charge.

☷☷ Llanelli SN5000 PARC

HOWARD ART GALLERY AND MUSEUM
Set in pleasant parkland, the largest
collection of the distinctive local
pottery in existence, as well as local
history, and pictures by local artist
J Dickson Innes. Snacks; cl 1–2pm,
25–26 Dec; (01554) 772029; free.
The Stepney (Park St) is handy for
lunch. WILDFOWL AND WETLANDS
TRUST (3m E) Set beside Wales's main
estuary for wildfowl and waders,
with plenty of observation hides and
special walkways. Many of the birds
will feed from your hand, and at their
summer Duckery you can hear
ducklings calling from inside their
eggs. Meals, snacks, shop, disabled
access; cl 24–25 Dec; (01554)
741087; £3.75.

Llanstephan SN3510 LLANSTEPHAN
CASTLE Sprawling 11th to 13th-c ruin,
majestically overlooking the Tywi
estuary and Carmarthen Bay from an
isolated ridge high over the water.
Impressive gatehouse with fine
vaulted ceiling, and you can still see
the slots for drenching intruders with
boiling fat or lead; free.

Llanycefn SN0923 PENRHOS
COTTAGE (off the B4313) There can't
have been many housing problems
around here if local tradition is to be
believed; anyone who built a house
overnight on common land was
entitled to claim it, and this old
cottage was such a one, frantically
constructed by friends and family.
Small shop, disabled access; open by
appointment only, (01437) 731328;
free.

Llawhaden SN0617 CASTLE 12th-c
ruins, surrounded by a deep moat,
with the remains of the 13th–14th-c
bishop's hall, kitchen and bakehouse;
free. The post office nearby sells
guides and postcards.

Manorbier SS0697 MANORBIER
CASTLE Still in the hands of the family
who have owned it for over 300
years, this impressive partly 12th-c
fortress looking down to the beach
has massive medieval outer walls and
an early round tower, with a 13th-c
chapel and other buildings, and more
modern constructions within the
walls. Snacks, shop; cl Oct–Easter;
(01834) 871394; *£2. The quiet

village is attractive, with a
particularly good clean beach, and
there's a striking view of the castle
from the church. Springfields Farm
(off the A4139) has PICK-YOUR-OWN
strawberries and a decent farm shop;
(01834) 871746. The Castle Inn
(open all day in summer) is useful for
lunch.

Marloes SM7908 DEER PARK Not
actually a deer park, but a wild cliffy
headland a couple of miles W, joined
to the mainland by quite a narrow
isthmus showing steep Iron Age
defences; a place to watch birds
(choughs breed here) and maybe seals
on the offshore rocks. The Lobster
Pot in Marloes is a useful informal
family pub, and the beaches are safe
for bathing as well as gloriously
remote.

Narberth SN0615 Pleasant
little town standing on the imaginary
Landsker line separating the 'Little
England' of South Pembrokeshire
from the more properly Welsh areas
to the N. The LANDSKER VISITOR
CENTRE (High St) is enjoyable (one of
its local yarns involves a man who
tried to hang a pregnant mouse), but
as we went to press its future was
uncertain; best to check on (01834)
860061. The Angel and Coach &
Horses are useful for lunch.
BLACKPOOL MILL (Canaston Bridge,
3m W of Narberth) Striking 3-
storeyed former corn mill with
working machinery, and pleasant
walks along the fish-filled river that
powers it. More likely to appeal to
children are the caves with life-size
mock-ups of prehistoric life; a huge
Welsh dragon is thrown in for good
measure. Meals, snacks, shop; cl
Nov–Easter; (01437) 541233; £2.
For the OAKWOOD amusement park
just along the A4075 from here *see
separate Family Panel on p927*; more
family activities at the CANASTON
CENTRE next door, which includes a
reconstruction of TV's *Crystal Maze*;
cl 25–26 Dec; (01834) 891622;
separate charges for individual
attractions. CWM DERI VINEYARD
SN0310 (Martletwy, off the A4075
SW of Narberth) Self-guided walks,
rare breeds, a small collection of

teddy bears hidden in a shed, and tastings. Cl winter wkdys, Jan–Feb (though worth giving them a ring if you're passing); (01834) 891274; free, 20p for each tasting.

✝ 🏛 **Nevern** SN0840 Interesting old riverside village with a medieval bridge over the Nyfer. The CHURCH has a tall 10th-c carved Celtic cross and other carved stones, some with Viking patterns, in the graveyard, where the massive yew trees are reputed to weep tears of blood if the priest is not Welsh-speaking. The Trewern Arms is handy for lunch. PENTRE IFAN BURIAL CHAMBER SN0937 (SE of Nevern, towards Brynberian) One of the most impressive ancient monuments in Wales: a striking former long barrow with the enormous capstone still held up by three of the four surviving great upright megaliths. Great views over the Nyfer valley.

🏛 👁 **Pembroke** SM9801 PEMBROKE CASTLE The birthplace of Henry VII and thus the Tudor dynasty, this impressive 13th-c castle is largely intact, and its endless passages, tunnels and stairways are great fun to explore. The 23-m (75-ft) tower is one of the finest in Britain. Summer snacks, shop, disabled access; cl 25–26 Dec, 1 Jan; (01646) 684585; *£2.95 (guided tours by arrangement, Jun–Aug exc Sat, 50p extra). MUSEUM OF THE HOME (Westgate Hill) Intriguing private collection of all sorts of everyday objects from the past 300 years, in a pleasant domestic setting. No under 5s; open Mon–Thurs May–Sept; (01646) 681200; *£1.20. The Pembroke Ferry by the water at the foot of the bridge over the estuary does good fresh fish.

👁 **Pendine** SN2308 The hard flat sand on the beaches here made it a favourite spot for attempting new speed records; in 1926 J G Parry Thomas and his 27-litre car *Babs* set a short-lived land-speed record of 168mph, but the careers of both ended the following year in a grisly accident. The car spent the next 40 years buried in the sand but has now been restored, and in July and Aug (maybe longer) forms the centrepiece of the small MUSEUM OF SPEED overlooking the beach. Also local and natural history; (01994) 453488; free.

❗ **Pumsaint** SN6640 DOLAUCOTHI GOLD MINES (off the A482) 2,000 years of gold-mining are the focus of this unusual mine, in use since Roman times; tours of both the Roman adits and the deeper 1930s workings, complete with miners' lamps and helmets. Good visitor centre, woodland walks, and the chance to have a go at panning for gold. Stout footwear recommended. Meals, snacks, shop, disabled access; site open Apr–Sept, underground tours (no under 5s) mid-May–late Sept; (01558) 650359; £3, or less for individual parts; NT. Get there early for the underground tours, especially in summer hols. The nearby Brunant Arms in fine scenery at Caio has decent food.

★ ✝ 🏛 ✎ 🐂 ☺ 👁 🏛 **St David's** SM7525 The Norman CATHEDRAL here has had a community in residence around it for longer than any other in Britain, but thanks to the relative isolation of the place it's stayed undeveloped, so that St David's today is little more than a village. The church had largely collapsed by the 15th c and elaborate repairs had to be made; the resulting roof is an impressive lace-like oak affair, and oak features in most of the rest of the church too. There's a fine collection of Celtic sculptured crosses. Shop, disabled access; £2 suggested donation. Lots of colourful flowers in spring. Now a series of impressive ruins, the BISHOP'S PALACE was once the clearly rather grand main residence of the local bishops. Plenty of quadrangles, stairways and splendid arcaded walls, with all sorts of intricate and often entertaining details (like the carvings below the arcaded parapets). Very atmospheric and tranquil, particularly out of season when you may have it largely to yourself. Shop, limited disabled access; cl am winter Sun, 25–26 Dec, 1 Jan; (01437) 720517; £1.70. OCEANARIUM (New St) Excellent insight into sea and shore life; highlights include the shark tank and rock pool. Snacks, shop, limited disabled access; cl 25–26 Dec; (01437) 720453; *£3. St David's Farm Park (NE edge of town, off the A487) Big collection of rare breeds, as well as rides on either a tractor or one of their shire horses. Highly praised by readers. Meals, snacks, shop (with their own wool, and spinning demonstrations), disabled access; cl Nov–Mar; (01437) 721601; £3.50. Adventure Days can organise well supervised abseiling, canoeing, rock-climbing and other activities – ideal for off-loading active children for the day; (01437) 721611. In summer there are BOAT TRIPS from the lifeboat station to rocky Ramsey Island, where seabirds nest in great numbers. About half a mile away is the reputed birthplace of St Non, the mother of St David; there are lovely sea views from the very scant ruins of the chapel here, signed down a track from the useful St Non's Hotel, with a holy well nearby. It's a good area for coastal walks, perhaps to ANCIENT SITES such as the neolithic burial chambers up by St David's Head or over towards Solva, or the ramparts of the coastal hill forts right on the point of St David's Head and overlooking Caerfai Bay just S of the town. The Old Cross Hotel nr the cathedral is a civilised place for lunch, and the Farmers Arms is cheap and cheerful. The beach at Whitesand Bay is good.

🐾 🐝 **St Florence** SN0801 Manor House Wildlife and Leisure Park 🔲 (on the B4318) Around 35 acres of wooded grounds and gardens with exotic birds, reptiles and fish, a pets corner, playground, model railway and twice-daily falconry displays (not Sat). Meals, snacks, shop, disabled access; cl Oct–Easter; (01646) 651201; £3.50. The Old Parsonage Farm does quick family food.

🏚 **Slebech Church** SN0313 (off the A40 5m E of Haverfordwest) Gloriously isolated ruined 12th-c church, formerly a temple of the Knights Hospitaller, by the tidal waters of the East Cleddau. Though there is a track from the main road, it's more enjoyable to turn down the A4075, take the next right turn and park by the mill, walk over the bridge and down the track through the woods above the river. In Haverfordwest, George's (Market St) does good food.

★ 🌸 🏛 **Solva** SM8024 One of the prettiest villages on the coast, with a great deal of character. On the opposite bank from the harbour a high crag (enclosed by the ramparts of an Iron Age fort) gives pretty views of the attractive little fishing village and the coast. The Cambrian Arms does decent food.

🐾 🐝 🏚 **Stackpole** SR9896 (off the B4319) This spectacular 2,000 acre estate is a real delight to wander through, with lakes, woodlands, cliffs, dunes and beaches offering a range of landscapes to suit every taste and mood. Barafundle Bay is a lovely, relatively undiscovered beach. Footpaths lead past a quarry and assorted wildlife over the lake to Bosherston SR9694 (or you can drive round – there are several car parks), where the ancient LILY PONDS are a fine sight when in bloom in summer. A little further down towards St Govan's Head SR9792, St Govan's Chapel is a simple reroofed 14th-c ruin, dramatically set halfway down the sea cliffs, and reached via rough rock steps; the former holy well just below has now dried up. Snacks (at Stackpole Quay); (01646) 661359; free, NT. The Armstrong Arms does good food, and the St Govan's pub is useful too.

🏚 **Talley** SN6332 Talley Abbey (off the B4302) Ruins of once-magnificent 12th-c abbey, still looking good, especially the 2 pointed archways; (01558) 685444; £1.20.

🏠 🏚 ♨ 🖼 ✝ ⚓ 🐤 **Tenby** SN1300 Pleasantly restrained family seaside resort, with sheltered beaches and rock coves. It's a walled town, the splendidly preserved 13th-c wall still with many of its towers left, as well as a magnificent 14th-c arched barbican gateway; a moat used to run the whole length of what is now a tree-lined street. There are some remains of the 13th-c CASTLE on the headland above the yachting harbour. Within the castle site is a local history and geology MUSEUM, with prehistoric finds and an art gallery with a collection of Augustus and Gwen John. Shop; cl winter wknds; (01834) 842809; *£1.50. TUDOR MERCHANTS HOUSE (Quay Hill) Fine example of gabled 15th-c architecture, with a good Flemish chimney and the remains of frescoes on 3 walls. Shop; cl Weds, Nov–Mar; (01834) 842279; *£1.60; NT. ST MARY'S CHURCH Interesting 13th-c building with a huge steeple and a plaque commemorating a local invention that many of us use every day – the equals sign. The medieval Plantagenet House, and Coach & Horses and Lamb are all pleasant lunch places. CALDEY ISLAND 🏆 Reached by summer boat trips from the harbour (wkdys May–Sept, poss plus Sat in summer hols, £6), still a monastic island, where the Cistercian monks have good cream and honey for sale, as well as more durable crafts and old-fashioned perfume. Besides the modern abbey, there's a 13th-c church with a simple cobbled floor,

still in use, on one side of the small cloister of the original priory; these ancient priory buildings (which you can see from outside but not enter) give a better sense of the past than almost anywhere else in West Wales. Sailing times from the tourist information centre, (01834) 842404. HOYLES MOUTH CAVE (off the A4139 just SW of Tenby, Trefloyne Lane towards St Florence; short path through wood on left after 500 yds) Running more than 30 metres (100 ft) back into the hillside, this spooky place has yielded Ice Age mammoth bones, as well as human tools dating back over 10,000 years. Take a torch, but don't go in winter – you'd disturb the hibernating bats. DINO'S DEN SN1001 (Great Wedlock Farm, Gumfreston on the B4318 W of Tenby) Fun for families, and an unusual example of farm diversification. The woods are filled with very well constructed life-size dinosaurs, some of which roar or spit. A visitor centre is designed to look like fossilised dinosaur ribs. Meals, snacks, shop, disabled access; open daily Apr–Sept, and wknds and school hols in Oct; (01834) 845272; £3.50.

Days Out

Cathedral village
Solva; lunch at Cambrian Arms there, or Old Cross Hotel or Farmers Arms, St David's; St David's cathedral and bishop's palace; boat trip to Ramsey Island, or walk from Whitesand Bay to St David's Head.

Lily ponds behind the beach
Pembroke Castle; lunch at Armstrong Arms, Stackpole, or the ferry, Pembroke Ferry; Bosherston lily ponds, St Govan's Chapel.

Primeval Pembrokeshire
Nevern Cross (in churchyard), Pentre Ifan burial chamber; drive over the Prescelly Hills via the B4329; lunch at New Inn or Old Post Office, Rosebush; Castell Henllys, or explore more of the E end of Prescelly (e.g. Carn Arthur).

Harnessing the tide
Tenby; lunch at Carew Inn, Carew; Carew castle and tidal mill; bishop's palace, Lamphey.

Welsh gold
Dolaucothi gold mines, Pumsaint; lunch at Black Lion, Abergorlech; Llandeilo; Carreg Cennen castle (see entry in **Mid-Wales** section on p.941).

♣ ⚥ ⚘ Particularly worth a visit are the 3 islands of **Skomer** SM7209, **Skokholm** SM7305 and, much further out to sea, **Grassholme** SM5909, all of which can be reached by boats run by the national parks. Skomer has 720 acres of spectacular wild scenery with countless birds (including breeding pairs of short-eared owls) and flowers, as well as seals playing on the shore – maybe common seals briefly in Jun or July, more likely grey seals and their pups in Sept and Oct; it's also remarkable for the easily traced remains of the Iron Age settlement here – there's a well laid out trail. Grassholme is notable for its 30,000 pairs of gannets: on a clear sunny morning even from the coast you can see it's white with them. Skokholm has Britain's first bird observatory. Sailing times (usually Apr–Oct only) from Dale Sailing Co, (01646) 601636. In Dale SM8005, where the boats usually start, the Griffin overlooking the anchorage is useful for lunch.

Other **seaside villages** well worth visiting, all with decent pubs right by the sea, are Little Haven SM8512, Llangranog SN3154 (fishing village with nice family beach backed by cliffs), Porthgain SM8132 and Tresaith SN2751 (with a waterfall to its beach). The line of colourwashed houses facing the harbour at Aberaeron SN4462 is very pretty; there's a good craft centre here too, and the Harbourmaster is a useful stop.

Pubs and inns doing food elsewhere that are noteworthy for their fine positions include the Black Lion at Abergorlech SN5833 (lots of good walks nearby), Forest Arms at Brechfa SN5230, Cresselly Arms by the water at Cresswell Quay SN0406, Denant Mill at Dreenhill SM9214 (includes a Goan restaurant), Stanley Arms on the Cleddau estuary opposite Picton Castle at Landshipping SN0111, and Cennen Arms at Trap SN6518. The Teifi Netpool at St Dogmaels SN1645 is handy for a walk along to Poppitt Sands.

Walks

Laugharne SN2910 ⌂-1 with its setting on the Taf estuary makes a rewarding spot for wandering – past Laugharne Castle, Dylan Thomas's Boat House and along the cliff walk (known as Dylan's Walk); in the other direction there's a pleasant walk via Roche Castle.

Sections of the Pembrokeshire Coast Path, which snakes around the intricate Pembrokeshire seaboard, make for notable walks. The lily ponds at **Bosherston** SR9694 ⌂-2 merit a diversion off the path. The **Dale peninsula** SM8103 ⌂-3 at the entrance to the huge natural harbour of Milford Haven has gentle level-topped terrain looking down on the shipping activities, reducing the giant oil tankers to a pleasantly toy-like scale. With the **Marloes peninsula** SM7708 ⌂-4 to the W, similarly gentle above its cliffs, it supplies memorable walkers' routes that need only minimal inland walking to complete the circuit – from Marloes peninsula, Skomer Island is in sight.

Little Haven SM8512 ⌂-5 has attractive sandy-floored rock coves to explore at low tide, with more around the Druidstone Hotel SM8616 to the N; there's a good cliff walk northwards to the long sweep of sand and surf at Newgale Sands SM8421 (food all day from the Duke of Edinburgh). **Solva** SM8024 ⌂-6 has a good interesting shortish path running E to Dinas Fawr SM8122, the opposite headland.

St David's SM7525 ⌂-7 has paths leading S to St Non's chapel on the coast; W, St Justinian SM7225 (there is yet another chapel here) looks over Ramsey Island. **St David's Head** SM7227 ⌂-8 is noticeably more rugged, spectacular in autumn with both heather and gorse out; from the top of Carn Ledi, the moorland hill close by the coast path, you can often see Ireland.

Strumble Head SM8941 ⌂-9 typifies the rocky, big-dipper coastline of northern Pembrokeshire; there is a car park nr the lighthouse. **Dinas Head** SN0041 ⌂-10 is a nice miniature headland which takes about an hour to tour.

Cemaes Head SN1350 ⌂-11 in Cardigan Bay gives good views over the mouth of the Teifi estuary and out over the Irish Sea. Cardiganshire lacks a coast path for much of the way, but **Llangranog** SN3154 ⌂-12 offers a pleasant stroll to a headland to the N.

Inland, the Mynydd Preseli or **Prescelly Hills** SN1032 ⌂-13 and Mynydd Carningli or **Carningli Common** SN0537 ⌂-14 S of Newport each give pleasant walks with some interesting views, on largely unspoilt moors capped by ancient cairns and other antiquities – on Prescelly for example, the intriguing Carn Arthur SN1332 and a hill fort SN1533, both reached from the back road along the E side. The lusher **Gwaun Valley** ⌂-15 offers pretty walks along the wooded river either upstream or downstream of Pontfaen SN0234.

Where to eat

Aberaeron SN4462 Hive on the Quay Cadwgan Pl (01545) 570445 Cheery harbourside place on the wharf, based around family honey business (their home-made honey ice-cream is delicious), with lunchtime buffet, popular café, and good unfussy evening meals relying heavily on organic produce – quite an emphasis on fish from their own boat; also bee exhibition and shop; cl mid-Sept–Spring bank hol. £19|£5.

Letterston SM9429 Something Cooking (on the A40 5m S of Fishguard) (01348) 840621 Cheerful and enthusiastically run fish restaurant with truly outstanding fresh fish, served by neat uniformed waitresses – very reasonable prices too; cl am Sun, 2 wks Christmas; disabled access. £12.75.

Newport SN0539 Cnapan East St (01239) 820575 Friendly country house with a relaxed atmosphere, a cosy bar, good, hearty home-made lunchtime food with more elaborate, imaginative evening meals (delicious puddings), and popular roast Sun lunch; super breakfasts (they are also a guest house), and plenty of books and games; cl Jan–Feb; partial disabled access. £25|£4.50.

Pembroke Ferry SM9603 Ferry (01646) 682947 Former sailors' haunt set by the water's edge below Cleddau Bridge (not by the new ferry), with simply cooked, very good fish dishes (and meaty ones too), a nautical decor, good views, a relaxed pubby atmosphere, well kept real ales, decent malt whiskies, and efficient service; restaurant cl Sun, pm Mon, 25–26 Dec; children allowed in restaurant only. £19.50|£4.95.

Rosebush SN0529 New Inn B4329 (01437) 532542 Attractively restored 17th-c drovers' inn on the edge of the Prescelly Hills, with a quiet relaxed atmosphere, coal fires, flagstones and antique furniture in the cosy bar rooms, and a small garden room; a good range of enjoyable bar food, 6 real ales, a well chosen wine list, friendly staff; tables outside and plenty of walks. £24.25|£5.50.

Rosebush SN0729 Old Post Office (01437) 532205 Quaint bistro with lots of local photos, farming tools and teapots on the ceiling; good-value lunches (some tasty filled Yorkshire puddings), and well prepared traditional cooking in the evening; bedrooms too; cl pm Sun; some disabled access. £15|£4.95.

Stackpole SR9896 Armstrong Arms Jasons Corner (01646) 672324 Charming rather Swiss-looking dining pub with neat oak furnishings and glossy beams in 4 rambling areas; particularly good interesting food (more elaborate in the evening), well kept real ales, and cheerful uniformed waitresses; seats in the flower-filled garden; must book pm Sat, am Sun; cl winter pm Sun. £17|£5.75.

Tenby SN1300 Celtic Fare Tea Rooms Vernon House, St Julian St (01834) 845258 Cosy tea room with jugs and teapots hanging from the beams, an open fire, and gas lamps; quite a few teas, and really good home-made cakes, scones, and pastries; disabled access. |£5.25.

Welsh Hook SM9327 STONE HALL (01348) 840212 Imaginative French food and fine wines in the beamed restaurant of this 14th-c house; characterful bar, lovely grounds and bedrooms; open pm only. £25.

MID WALES

The quietest part of Wales, with splendid unspoilt scenery.

Sparsely populated, with far more sheep than people, this is undiscovered Wales, with glorious scenic drives and well above-average walking in scenery that's spectacular (if not quite up to the very best of Snowdonia and the West Wales coast). It's one of the best parts of Britain for really getting away from it all. There aren't that many places to visit, but those we include do suit the distinctive character of this part of Wales. Celtica in Machynlleth is particularly worth going to, and families find King Arthur's Labyrinth at Corris fun. The towns are friendly and untouristy, and include a string of dignified, slightly old-fashioned inland spa towns.

But it's the scenery which counts for most here. Little-used former drovers' roads thread through the huge tracts of forest and moorland around the Llyn Briane reservoir, the Cambrian Mountains and the reservoirs above the Elan valley. Other, kinder ranges of hills tempt more people out, most notably the western Black Mountain, the Brecon Beacons and the eastern Black Mountains, as well as the range stretching all the way up the borders from Brecon to the Kerry hills and beyond. The area's river valleys are among the finest in Wales: the friendly Usk, the rather more imposing Upper Wye and, above Aberystwyth, the beautiful Vale of Rheidol.

There are some very comfortable places to stay, with glorious countryside more or less on their doorsteps.

Where to stay

Aberdovey SN6195 BODFOR Bodfor Terrace, Aberdovey, Gwynedd LL35 0EA (01654) 767475 *£47; 16 rms with showers, most with sea views. Small family-run hotel on sea front, with a bar, and comfortable lounge; good restaurant food, and helpful service; dogs welcome.

Aberdovey SN6195 PENHELIG ARMS Terrace Rd, Aberdovey, Gwynedd LL35 0LT (01654) 767215 *£70, plus special breaks; 10 comfortable rms. Carefully refurbished building in fine position overlooking the sea, with cosy bar, pleasant dining room, and open fires; very good food (especially local fish), extensive wine list, splendid breakfasts, and friendly service; lovely views of Dyfy Estuary; cl 25 Dec.

Aberhafesp SO0692 DYFFRYN Aberhafesp, Newtown, Powys SY16 3JD (01686) 688817 *£46; 3 rms. Carefully restored half-timbered barn on 100-acre sheep and beef-cattle farm, with a residents' lounge overlooking the stream; traditional cooking in the dining room, and friendly owners; no smoking; baby-sitting by arrangement, children's play area and nature trail.

Carno SN9697 ALEPPO MERCHANT Carno, Caersws, Powys SY17 5LL (01686) 420210 *£45; 5 rms, some with shower. Warm and friendly 17th-c inn in rural setting, with comfortably modernised beamed lounge bar, and an open fire in the small adjoining lounge; a fair choice of well liked food, helpful service, and well kept real ales; children over 12.

Church Stoke SO2794 DREWIN FARM Church Stoke, Montgomery, Powys SY15 6TW (01588) 620325 *£38; 2 rms, 1 with own bthrm. Attractive 17th-c farmhouse with lovely views, warm welcome, comfortable lounge, dining room and games room with snooker table in converted granary; Offa's Dyke footpath runs through the mixed farm of sheep, cattle and crops; cl Nov–Feb.

Crickhowell SO2118 BEAR Crickhowell, Powys NP8 1BW (01873) 810408 £56; 29 rms, the back ones are the best, and some have Jacuzzis. Particularly friendly coaching inn with good, civilised atmosphere; excellent food using local produce and home-grown herbs (some Welsh specialities), fine wines and ports, well kept real ales, and prompt attentive service; lots of antiques, deeply comfortable seats, and a roaring log fire in the heavily beamed lounge; children over 5 in restaurant; disabled access; dogs welcome.

Crickhowell SO1719 GLIFFAES COUNTRY HOUSE Crickhowell, Powys NP8 1RH (01874) 730371 £73, plus special breaks; 22 rms. Run by the same family for over 40 years and set in wonderfully quiet, peaceful grounds of 33 acres (lovely rare trees); an enjoyably informal and relaxed atmosphere, comfortable big sitting room, elegant drawing room, pleasant conservatory, and glorious Usk Valley views from the terrace; good cooking, and cheerful staff; fishing, hard tennis court, golf practice net, and a putting and croquet lawn.

Eglwysfach SN6796 YNYSHIR HALL Eglwysfach, Machynlleth, Powys SY20 8TA (01654) 781209 *£100, plus special breaks; 8 individually decorated rms. Carefully run old manor house in 14 acres of landscaped gardens adjoining the Ynyshir coastal bird reserve; with antiques, log fires and paintings in the light and airy public rooms; extremely good food using home-grown vegetables, and thoughtful service; children over 9; cl Jan.

Felinfach SO0833 TREHENRY FARM Felinfach, Brecon LD3 0UN (01874) 754312 *£40; 4 rms. 18th-c farmhouse on 200-acre farm with lovely views of the Black Mountains and Brecon Beacons; inglenook fireplaces, beams, TV lounge, good food, and a large garden; self-catering also; cl Christmas–New Year.

Gladestry SO2355 ROYAL OAK Gladestry, Kington, Herefordshire HR5 3NR (01544) 370669 *£35 plus special breaks; 5 well equipped rms, some with own bthrm. Unpretentious, welcoming, beamed and flagstoned inn on Offa's Dyke, quiet and relaxing; good home-cooked bar food (inc nice breakfasts), comfortable lounge, separate bar, and picnic-table sets in lovely secluded garden behind.

Guilsfield SJ2212 LOWER TRELYDAN Guilsfield, Welshpool, Powys SY21 9PH (01938) 553105 £42; 3 rms. Charming black and white farmhouse on beef and sheep farm, with lovely heavily beamed ceilings, fine antiques and comfortable seating; a cosy licensed bar, warm and friendly atmosphere, and delicious farmhouse cooking; pretty garden; self-catering also in barn conversion; cl Christmas.

Hay-on-Wye SO2342 OLD BLACK LION Hay-on-Wye, Hereford, Herefordshire HR3 5AD (01497) 820841 *£52, plus special breaks; 10 rms, some in modern annexe. Smartly civilised old hotel with low beams and black panelling, and a convivial bar; a wide choice of carefully prepared food in bar and candlelit, no smoking, cottagey restaurant, and an extensive wine list; close to fishing (private salmon and trout fishing) and riding; disabled access; children over 5.

Llandegley SO1462 FFALDAU COUNTRY HOUSE Llandegley, Llandrindod Wells, Powys LD1 5UD (01597) 851421 *£40; 4 rms. Carefully restored, heavily beamed 16th-c country house with flower-filled landscaped gardens, log fire in comfortable lounge, residents' bar, and upstairs sitting room with games and books; enjoyable dinners in charming dining room, and good breakfasts; dogs by prior arrangement; children over 10.

Llyswen SO1337 GRIFFIN Llyswen, Brecon, Powys LD3 0UR (01874) 754241 **£70**, plus special breaks; 7 rms. Old-fashioned and warmly welcoming, family-run sporting inn, very well run, with imaginative fresh food in no smoking restaurant (brook trout and salmon caught by the family, local game in season), and good breakfasts; an interesting, comfortable bar with huge inglenook, and helpful service; fishing and shooting courses.

Llyswen SO1239 LLANGOED HALL Llyswen, Brecon, Powys LD3 0YP (01874) 754525 **£165**, plus special breaks; 23 very pretty rms with luxurious touches. Fine, partly 16th-c house, beautifully converted into a first-class hotel with lovely house-party atmosphere; handsome hall, elegant and spacious public rooms with antiques, fresh flowers and views over the grounds; imaginative modern cooking, and very good Welsh breakfasts; marvellous surrounding countryside; children over 8.

Montgomery SO2296 DRAGON The Square, Montgomery, Powys SY15 6PA (01686) 668359 **£72**, plus special breaks; 15 rms. Attractive black and white timbered small hotel with a pleasant grey-stone tiled hall, comfortable residents' lounge, and beamed bar; good food using local produce in the restaurant, and welcoming licensees; indoor swimming pool.

Newtown SO1292 LOWER GWESTYDD Aberbechan, Newtown, Powys SY16 3AY (01686) 626718 ***£38**; 2 rms. Traditional 17th-c black and white half-timbered house on 200 acres of mainly sheep and arable farmland in lovely countryside; comfortable lounge and dining room, and good food using their own home-grown fruit and vegetables, chicken and Welsh lamb; you can wander around the farm; cl Christmas.

Pennal SH6799 GOGARTH HALL FARM Pennal, Machynlleth, Powys SY20 9LB (01654) 791235 ***£36**; 2 rms. 17th-c house on working farm of suckler cows and sheep with marvellous views of Dovey estuary; dining room and lounge, and guests are welcome to walk around the farm; babysitting available; dogs by arrangement; self-catering also.

Presteigne SO3265 RADNORSHIRE ARMS Presteigne, Powys LD8 2BE (01544) 267406 **£86.50**; 16 rms. Rambling, handsomely timbered 17th-c hotel with old-fashioned charm and an unchanging atmosphere, elegantly moulded beams and fine dark panelling in the lounge bar, and latticed windows; enjoyable food (inc morning coffee and afternoon tea), separate no smoking restaurant, well kept real ales, and politely attentive service.

Rhandirmwyn SN7843 ROYAL OAK Rhandirmwyn, Llandovery, Dyfed SA20 0NY (01550) 760201 **£56**; 5 rms, most with own bthrm. Homely, friendly, family-run pub in the foothills of the Cambrian Mountains with fine views, superb walking and the RSPB Dinas Bird Reserve nearby; simple furnishings, log fire, well kept real ale, decent food, and a warm welcome; dogs by prior arrangement.

Rhayader SN9969 BEILI NEUADD Rhayader, Powys LD6 5NS (01597) 810211 **£37**, plus special activity breaks; 3 rms. Charming partly 16th-c stone-built farmhouse in quiet countryside (they have their own trout pools and woodland), with log fires in renovated rooms; golf, pony-trekking and guided walks nearby; cl Christmas; children over 8.

Tal-y-llyn SH7210 MINFFORDD HOTEL Tal-y-llyn, Tywyn, Gwynedd LL36 9AJ (01654) 761665 ***£72**, plus special breaks; 6 rms. 17th-c drovers' inn in a lovely valley at the base of Cader Idris mountain, and surrounded by fields of sheep; warmly welcoming and relaxed, open fires in cosy little rooms, good Aga-cooked food in beamed dining room, and super breakfasts; lots of outdoor pursuits; cl Dec–Feb; children over 5.

Please let us know what you think of places in the *Guide*. Use the report forms at the back of the book or simply send a letter.

To see and do

Aberdovey SN6195 Attractive, restrained resort with very pleasant sheltered beaches but none of the crowds or tat they usually bring. Legend has it there's a lost city beneath the sea, inundated by the crashing waves in a great storm 1,500 years ago. Sometimes at night imaginative people can hear the mournful tolling of its bells. Besides the Penhelig Arms Hotel, the Britannia does good food and has great views.

◨ ▣ ⛰ ᴘ **Aberystwyth** SN5881 Low-key resort, scarcely changed in 20 years, with long shingle beaches and sedate cliff railway to large camera obscura high above. Quite a scholarly town too, with a university, and the NATIONAL LIBRARY OF WALES, which has exhibitions of fine early Welsh and Celtic manuscripts and art; cl Sun, bank hols and 1st full wk Oct; 01970 623816; free. Also a good museum, and one of the very few of Edward I's castles in this part of Wales. You can hire bikes from the Cycle Doctor on Llanbadarn Rd. VALE OF RHEIDOL RAILWAY (next to main line station, Alexander Rd) The town's main attraction for families, with steam trains for several miles along the picturesque twists of the Rheidol Valley to the dramatic beauty-spot gorge of Devils Bridge (see entry below). Snacks, limited disabled access; trains run most days Easter–Oct, (01970) 625819 for timetable; *£10 full return fare.

▣ **Brecon** SO0428 Enjoyable and interesting small town, with some fine old buildings around its main square and narrow streets, and a bustling livestock market on Tues and Fri. The striking Norman priory was grandly restored in the 19th c and became a cathedral in 1923. Also the rather sad remnants of a castle, and a couple of decent little museums, the best of which, the BRECKNOCK MUSEUM (Captain's Walk), contains the town's excellently preserved assize court, as well as plenty of love spoons and some interesting Celtic crosses. Cl 1–2pm wknds, winter

Suns, Good Fri, 25–26 Dec, 1 Jan; (01874) 624121; £1. The George (George St) has good-value food. Some of the highest peaks in the area are a short drive away, and there's a useful National Parks Visitor Centre just S in the BRECON BEACONS MOUNTAIN CENTRE; they can advise on local walks, inc how to get to the spectacular waterfalls nr Glyn Neath (see ⌂-5 in **Walks** section on p.947). The CANTREF RIDING CENTRE can organise pony-trekking through this attractive landscape, and does B & B too; ring Mrs Evans on (01874) 665223.

⛰ ⛩ **Carreg Cennen Castle** SN6619 (nr Trap, SE of Llandeilo) Few castles can boast as excellent a setting as these old ruins, dramatically dominating their limestone crag high above the river, and overlooking the unspoilt countryside towards the Black Mountains. Rebuilt in the 13th c (and again in the 19th – you can easily distinguish the new stonework), the castle has a mysterious passage in the side of the cliff, and there's a working farm with rare breeds. Readers find the people who look after the site quite charming. Meals, snacks, shop, some disabled access; cl 25 Dec; (01558) 822291; £2.20. The Cennen Arms nearby has good simple food.

⚘ ♣ **Corris** SH7608 Attractive and nicely set beneath the towering crags of Cader Idris (see ⌂-15 in **Walks** section on p.948), with lakes and pine forests in the surrounding valley. The whole village seems to be made of slate. A CRAFT CENTRE (off the A487 towards Corris Uchaf) has a working potter, toymaker, and candlemaker, with a restaurant and picnic area; best to check winter opening; (01341) 423588; free. KING ARTHUR'S LABYRINTH Fun for families; a boat trip takes you to the heart of the underground tunnels and caverns, then it's a half-mile walk through passageways punctuated with scenes from the local version of the Arthurian legends. Wrap up well: it can get cold down here. Shop; cl

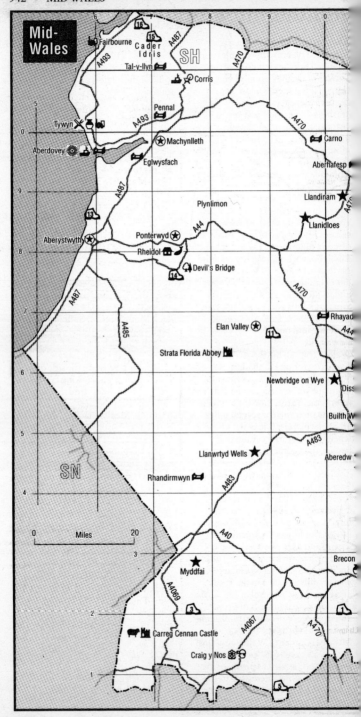

Nov–Easter; (01654) 761584; £4.

🏕 🕸 **Craig y Nos** SN8315 DAN YR OGOF SHOWCAVES 🔳 (on the A4067 just N) Fascinating series of caves, well lit to bring out the extraordinary rock formations. The Cathedral Cave is the largest single chamber open to the public in any British showcave, while 3,000 years ago Bone Cave was lived in by humans. There's also a dinosaur park, Iron Age farm, shire horse centre, and artificial ski-slope, so lots to see. Meals, snacks, shops; cl Nov–Mar; (01639) 730284; £6. The Tafarn y Garreg just N does decent food. Down the road, CRAIG Y NOS COUNTRY PARK is ideal for a picnic or a stroll: 40 acres of woodland, lake and meadow, landscaped and developed in the last century by the opera singer Adelina Patti. Interactive displays in the visitor centre, and a wild-flower maze. Shop, disabled access; cl 25 Dec; (01639) 730395; park free, though car park £1.

🍴 **Devil's Bridge** SN7477 Pretty bridges and dramatic waterfall, tucked away in an atmospheric wooded gorge. The oldest bridge gave this beauty spot its name, when it was built by the Devil in order to trap an old woman into giving him her soul; she outwitted him. Wordsworth was inspired to write a sonnet after a visit here. The entertaining Halfway Inn at Pisgah on the A4120 to Aberystwyth is good for lunch.

🐦 🚌 🐄 **Elan Valley** SN9365 These 4 man-made lakes are the best and most famous of the many reservoirs in Wales. Even the dams look good, and there are splendid views. It's a good spot for bird-watching, especially in summer, and among the many species you may see red kites. The VISITOR CENTRE in Elan village is the best place to start, with an audio visual show and various walks and displays. Cl Nov–Easter; (01597) 810880; free. Outside is a statue of Shelley, who lived in a house now lost beneath the water. The Elan Valley Hotel (on the B4518) has decent food, and at nearby Rhayader SN9768, where the Bear, Castle and Cornhill are useful food stops, you can tour the workshops of WELSH ROYAL CRYSTAL;

no glassmaking wknds, or some wkdys, best to check first on (01597) 811005, shop cl 25 Dec, 1 Jan; £1.50. There are excellent views from the farm trail at GIGRIN FARM (South Rd, just out of town), which from Nov–Easter also has a red kite centre with hides. (01597) 810243; *£2.50.

🕭 **Fairbourne** SH6114 FAIRBOURNE AND BARMOUTH STEAM RAILWAY (Beach Rd) Running the spectacular 2½ miles to the end of the peninsula and the ferry for Barmouth, this started life in 1890 as a horse-drawn railway used to carry building materials for the seaside resort of Fairbourne. Meals, snacks, shop, good disabled access; cl Nov–Easter, (01341) 250362 for timetable; £3.80. The Fairbourne Hotel is quite useful for lunch, as is the 15th-c Last Inn on Barmouth Harbour. The attractively set George III along the estuary at Penmaenpool (see entry in **North Wales** section, above) is quite handy too. Fairbourne and Barmouth both have good clean beaches.

★ **Hay-on-Wye** SO2342 This pleasant small town has become a world centre for secondhand and antiquarian books. There is a growing number of antique shops too, as well as a rather jolly puzzle and teddy bear shop on Broad St. Hay Bluff nearby has lovely walks, and the town's within easy reach of the Black Mountains, the Golden Valley over the English border, and the attractive unspoilt countryside just over the Gwent border that we mention in the **South Wales Walks** section on p.961. Besides the fine Old Black Lion, the Kilvert Court (01497) 821042 can be recommended both for food and as a place to stay. Black Mountain Activities just up the road (technically in Herefordshire) can arrange all sorts of exertions; (01497) 847897.

✝ **Llanbister** SO1173 The CHURCH here is interesting, with a chimney instead of the usual tower, and there's an even better one a mile away at Llananno, with an astonishingly elaborate rood screen that wouldn't be out of place in a cathedral.

★ 🛁 **Llandrindod Wells** SO0561 Civilised inland resort sheltering below the hills, a largely intact gem of the railway age, with imposing buildings on broad avenues and terraces, wrought-iron frills everywhere, elegant flower displays and Victorian parks, antique shop fronts and little canopies along the shopping streets. It was clearly a resort for temperance – though there are places to drink, they're tucked discreetly away. The former spa pump room has been reopened, and there's a very old-fashioned boating lake, as well as a charming district MUSEUM on Temple St; cl 12.30–2pm, Weds, winter wknds exc am Sat; 01597 824513; £1. The atmospheric old Llanerch has good home cooking, and the Metropole Hotel generally does some food all day. The summer Victorian Festival is fun.

🕭 **Llanfair Caereinion** SJ1006 WELSHPOOL & LLANFAIR LIGHT RAILWAY 🏆 (on the A458) Colonial and Austrian steam locomotives are among the wide variety of engines that run along this pretty 8-mile line, and the Welshpool end has an award-winning station reconstruction. Snacks, shop, disabled access (with prior notice); cl Oct–Mar exc Dec Santa Specials, (01938) 810441 for timetable; £7.30. The Goat is useful for lunch.

🍴 🛁 👪 **Machynlleth** SH7400 A couple of hundred yards away from the wide main street's handsome 24-metre (78-ft) 19th-c clock tower, an 18th-c mansion is the home of CELTICA 🏆, a very enjoyable look at the history and legends of the Celts. There's a traditionalish museum upstairs, but more fun is the lively walk-through exhibition on the ground floor, special effects bringing ancient villages and druids' prophecies vividly to life. It's popular with school trips the last couple of weeks of term. Good shop, disabled access; cl one wk in Jan, 24–25 Dec; (01654) 702702; exhibition *£4.65. A local history museum in the 16th-c PARLIAMENT HOUSE has a particular emphasis on the rebellion of Owain Glyndwr (it's on the spot where he held parliament). Shop, disabled access; cl 1–1.30pm, Sun,

Oct–Easter, exc by appointment; (01654) 702827; free. The White Lion does decent lunches, inc vegetarian. You can hire bikes at the Old Station. CENTRE FOR ALTERNATIVE TECHNOLOGY (on the A487 3m N) Technologies for the improvement of the environment have been researched and displayed at this enthusiastic place for over 20 years now, with constantly updated demonstrations of wind power, organic gardening and solar energy – you can even ride a water-powered cliff railway (Easter–Oct). There's a fun exhibition on what it's like in a mole-hole. The site, an old slate quarry, overlooks the Snowdonia National Park, and they look after children well. Wholesome restaurant, good bookshop, disabled access; cl 24–26 Dec, 1 Jan, and 3 wks mid-Jan; (01654) 702400; *£5.50 inc cliff railway, *£4.95 without (less if come by bike).

♨ ☎ 🅿 **Ponterwyd** SN7380 LLYWERNOG SILVER-LEAD MINE (on the A44 just W) A busy lively place, set against a beautiful sweeping mountainside backdrop. Regular displays of silver panning, sound and light tableaux in the caves and tunnels, and working waterwheels. This year they're adding a narrow gauge railway, and you can try panning for fool's gold or dowsing for mineral veins. Wear sensible shoes in wet weather. Snacks, shop, disabled access (exc underground); open Easter–Oct; (01970) 890620; £4.50. BWLCH NANT-YR-ARIAN FOREST VISITOR CENTRE SN7281 (on the A44 just W) Good starting point for exploring the forest, with walks and a few activities for children. Snacks, shop, disabled access; cl Nov–Easter; (01974) 261404; free. The Dyffryn Castell in the spectacular valley to the E is good for lunch, and there's an eye-opening mountain drive N past the partly wooded Nant-y-moch reservoir SN7586 below the slopes of Plynlimon, and on to Tal-y-bont.

☎ 🎣 **Rheidol** SN7178 HYDRO-ELECTRIC SCHEME (off the A44 at Capel Bangor) Guided tours of power station with unexpected fish farm.

Good nature trails, scenic lakes and reservoirs, trout fishing. Snacks, disabled access; cl Nov–Mar; (01970) 880667; free, fishing permits from £6.

🏛 **Strata Florida Abbey** SN7566 Little is left of this once-important centre of learning, except the ruined church and cloister, but the surroundings are lovely. 14th-c poet Dafyd ap Gwilym is thought to be buried here. Teas, shop, disabled access; cl Oct–Mar; (01974) 831261; £1.70. From Tregaron down the B4343 a steep road climbs through the pine forests into the mountains, eventually reaching the Llyn Brianne reservoir.

🏚 🏛 **Tretower** SO1821 TRETOWER COURT AND CASTLE (off the A40) The medieval manor house dates from the 14th c, though it has been developed over the centuries; beside it is the substantial ruin of an 11th-c motte and bailey, with massively thick walls and a 3-storey tower. Shop, limited disabled access; cl Nov–Feb; (01222) 500200; £2.20. The Nantyffin Cider Mill is a good handy place for lunch. Crickhowell further down the road is a pleasant village-sized 'town', with an excellent inn in the Bear, and a fine ancient bridge over the Usk (which the good Bridge End Inn overlooks).

🚂 👃 **Tywyn** SH5800 TAL-Y-LLYN RAILWAY This railway journey affords glorious views, climbing from the little seaside resort up the steep sides of the Fathew valley and stopping for passengers to admire Dolgoch Falls and visit the Nant Gwernol Forest (there's a waterfall 2 minutes away from the platform at this end). The 27in-gauge railway, the oldest of this gauge in the world, was built in 1865 to serve the slate mine at Abergynolwyn SH6807 (where the Railway Inn does decent food in a lovely setting). Snacks, shop, disabled access with prior notice; cl Nov–mid-Feb (exc Dec Santa specials); (01654) 710472 for timetable; *£8 full return journey. A museum at the Tywyn Station shows locomotives, wagons and signalling equipment whenever the railway is running.

🏛 🥨 👃 **Welshpool** SJ2106 POWIS

CASTLE (1m S on the A483) Set in magnificent gardens with splendid 18th-c terraces, this dramatic-looking castle was built in the 13th c, but far from falling into decay like so many others, has developed into a grand house over the years. It's been constantly occupied since its construction, once by the son of Clive of India – there are displays about his father's life. Meals, snacks, shop; cl Mon (exc bank hols), Tues (exc July and Aug), Nov–Mar; (01938) 554336; £6, Clive museum and garden only £4; NT. The Raven and Royal Oak both have decent food, and the main BR station is rather unusual. There's a respectable local history MUSEUM on the Canal Wharf (cl 1–2pm, Weds; £1). The King's Head at Guilsfield does good home cooking.

★ **Attractive villages and small towns** in the area, all with decent pubs, include Berriew SJ1801, Llandinam SO0388, Llangenny SO2417, Llanidloes SN9584 (unique Elizabethan timbered market hall), Llyswen SO1337, Montgomery SO2296, Myddfai SN7730, Newbridge on Wye SO0158, Presteigne SO3164 and Talybont-on-Usk SO1122 (the White Hart by the canal is on the Taff Trail); the small spa towns of Builth Wells SO0351 and Llanwrtyd Wells SN8746 (said to be Britain's smallest town, with good walks nearby) are pleasant.

Other pubs doing food that are particularly worth noting for their positions include the Admiral Rodney at Criggion SJ2915, Farmers Arms at Cwmdu SO1823, Dolfor Inn at Dolfor SO1187, White Swan at

Days Out

The railway that served the mines
Aberystwyth; snack at Mill (Mill St) there; Devil's Bridge by the Vale of Rheidol Railway; or by car, then drive via Llywernog silver mine, Ponterwyd, and on past Nant-y-Moch reservoir to Talybont – if time, stroll on the nearby Ynyslas seaside nature reserve.

Drovers' roads over the Cambrians
Drive from Rhayader through the Elan valley; picnic there, or lunch at the Elan Valley Hotel; take the mountain road to Cwmystwyth, B4343 S past the turning to Strata Florida abbey, return E by the road from Tregaron to Beulah.

The red-brick spa amid the green Welsh hills
Presteigne; New Radnor; take the A44 past start of walk to Water-break-its-neck (see ⌂-9 in **Walks** section on p.948); Llandrindod Wells; lunch at Llanerch there; drive through back lanes via Hundred House and Glascwm to Gladestry; Old Radnor church.

Ascent from bookshop town
Hay-on-Wye; drive up Gospel Pass (see ⌂-2 in **Walks** section on p.947; lunch at Abbey Hotel, Llanthony; walk there (leaflets in car park); Cwmyoy and Partrishow churches.

Brecon Beacons waterfall country
Brecon; take the A470 past the slopes of Pen-y-fan; walk from Brecon Beacons Mountain Centre on to Mynydd Illtud common, or in the Mellte on Hepste gorges, with a picnic en route; Dan yr Ogof caves.

Through the Usk valley
Drive up from Talybont past the reservoirs; Crickhowell; lunch at the Bear there or Nantyffin Cider Mill nearby; Tretower Court and castle.

Llanfrynach SO0725, Coach & Horses above the canal at Llangynidr SO1519 (lovely walks), Stables Hotel at Neuadd Fawr SO2322 (good hill walking), Harp at Old Radnor SO2559 (another good base for walks) and canalside Royal Oak at Pencelli SO0925.

✝ Fine **churches** can be found at Old Radnor SO2559 (handsome screen and roof, Britain's oldest organ-case and font) and Presteigne SO3164. But the speciality of the area is unspoilt and humble rustic churches in beautiful settings, such as Aberedw SO0847, Bleddfa SO2168 (the Hundred House is a good base for walkers), Disserth SO0358, Llanbadarn-y-garreg SO1148, Maesyronnen Chapel SO1740 SW of Hay, and Rhulen SO1349.

Walks

The **Brecon Beacons** △-1 proper are a pair of graceful pointed summits connected by a short ridge that seems to be visible from most of South Wales, and that gives a magnificent high-level walk along the crest, with massive drops on the northern side. Pen-y-Fan SO0121 (886 metres, 2,906 ft) is the highest Welsh summit outside Snowdonia, and the main E–W upland spine effectively stretches about 5 miles. The most popular route up from Pont ar Daf SN9819, from the A470 to the W, is straightforward enough although there has been some serious footpath erosion, but the N approaches are more exciting and surprisingly little walked.

The **Black Mountains** △-2, making up the E part of the Brecon Beacons National Park, are a range of finger-shaped ridges bordering on Herefordshire (and shared with South Wales), with steep-sided valleys in between. Most of the best views are from the Offa's Dyke Path along the E flanks: the land eastwards slopes abruptly down to low-lying agricultural Herefordshire, and views far into England give you a feeling of true border country. Circular walks here tend to be long and hefty, often with 2 major ascents to get you up on to the different ridges, but the scenic Gospel Pass road from Hay-on-Wye SO2342 lets you drive to within reasonable striking distance of Hay Bluff SO2436 (670 metres, 2,200 ft). Twmpa SO2234 (690 metres, 2,263 ft) is better known by its intriguing English name of Lord Hereford's Knob; though it's not itself on the Offa's Dyke Path, it is nearby, and you can combine it with Hay Bluff in a longer walk. Llanthony Priory (described in **South Wales To see and do** section on p.956), with a pub, makes a beautiful objective in the valley below, where diligent map-reading is needed for a cross-fields route from Cwmyoy SO2923, with extensions on to the Offa's Dyke Path on the ridge to complete a satisfying circuit.

Confusingly, the westernmost range in the national park is called **Black Mountain** SN7417 △-3. Much of the high terrain is a long way from the road, so this part is more the preserve of the committed long-distance walker. The craggy ridge known as Carmarthen Fan protrudes dramatically above the moors and provides the high point of a long but rewarding walk from the N.

The southern parts of the Brecon Beacons National Park, within easy reach of South Wales, have gentler walking in the form of forest walks in the large conifer plantations there, where waterfalls and a series of attractive reservoirs are the main features.

The lusher swathes of the **Usk Valley** △-4 can be enjoyed by walks along the towpath of the 33-mile Monmouthshire & Brecon canal.

A series of mighty **waterfalls** △-5 with few rivals in Britain grace the deep wooded gorges of the Nedd, Hepste and Mellte, just inside the southern park boundary (within easy reach of South Wales, too). An easy path from Pontneddfechan SN9007 nr Glyn Neath leads along the River Nedd, while Porth yr Ogof car park SN9212 nr Ystradfellte is convenient for the Mellte.

Dire warning notices ward you off getting too close to the edge (it is certainly hazardously slippery), but you can accompany the river most of the way to its junction with the Hepste. Here, a path actually crosses the river by going behind the curtain of Sgwd yr Eira waterfall – a rock ledge holds you in safely, but it's an excitingly damp experience.

The Offa's Dyke Path again provides the major walkers' attraction further N; on its coast-to-coast route over the Welsh Marches it takes in some very attractive hill-farm country between Hay-on-Wye and Knighton SO2872, including **Hergest Ridge** ⌂-6 (in Herefordshire, but easily reached from the Welsh side) and some well preserved stretches of Offa's 9th-c boundary marker between Knighton and Kington SO2956.

Away from Offa's Dyke, Radnorshire is less well known than it deserves to be, with old drovers' tracks providing some enjoyable escapist walking, and a reasonable network of field paths. There are few major objectives, but it is all very pleasant: the best bets include the **River Wye** ⌂-7 around Aberedw SO0847 and Boughrood SO1339, the **hills** ⌂-8 between Aberedw, Glascwm SO1553 and Gladestry SO2355 (where the Royal Oak is on the Offa's Dyke Path), and the upland massif of **Radnor Forest** ⌂-9 (open country for the most part, with conifers on the northern slopes), where walks include New Radnor SO2160 to the modest summit of the quaintly named Whimble SO2062, and from the A44 between Llanfihangel-nant-Melan SO1858 and New Radnor to Water-break-its-neck waterfall SO1860 (don't miss the path at the top of the fall).

From Llandrindod Wells SO0561, a sedate walk around the town's lake can extend into an expedition E of **Cefnllys Castle** SO0861 ⌂-10, an impressively sited hill fort with a lonely church below, close to Shaky Bridge (no longer shaky); a nature trail here takes you along the banks of the River Ithon.

W of Rhayader, some high-level trackways afford magnificent views over the Cambrian Mountains and adjacent **Elan valley** SN9768 ⌂-11; lower-level options start from the Elan valley visitor centre and neighbouring reservoirs, and include forest walks and strolls along the old railway track by the water's edge – very attractive, as the lakes built at the turn of the century have weathered in well now, and there's quite a bit of wildlife.

Montgomeryshire consists of the quintessential sheep-grazed lands of rural Wales. Much of it lacks major objectives for walkers, with few major peaks and fair distances between villages, but **Montgomery** SO2296 ⌂-12, with great views from its castle perched above, is rewarding for a short exploration on foot, and the windswept (often boggy) uplands of Plynlimon and the Cambrian Mountains, though not endowed with the friendliest of climates, can be magnificently exhilarating.

On the **coast** ⌂-13, you can do a one-way walk along the straight stretch between Aberystwyth SN5881 and Borth SN6189, using the train service between the two for the other half of the round trip. Just N of Borth is the Ynyslas nature reserve SN6094, with broad sands, lots of birds. Similarly, walks in or above the pretty **Vale of Rheidol** ⌂-14 between Aberystwyth and Devil's Bridge SN7477 can be aided by the private railway between the two. The most dramatic parts here are around Devil's Bridge.

Cader Idris SH7113 ⌂-15, a great peak in the Snowdonia of the National Park, offers various ways up its friendly slopes. The **estuary walk** ⌂-16 along the old railway track beside the Mawddach Estuary between Penmaenpool SH6918 and Fairbourne SH6114 gives magnificent views; you can detour to the Arthog waterfalls SH6414 and nearby lakes on the lower slopes of Cader Idris.

Where to eat

Crickhowell SO1920 NANTYFFIN CIDER MILL (on the A40 NW) (01873) 801775 Handsome pink-washed dining pub with a striking raftered restaurant, smart relaxed atmosphere, fresh and dried flowers, a woodburner, and comfortable tables and chairs; beautifully presented imaginative food (much organic produce), well kept real ales, and good wines; charming views; cl Mon, 2 wks Jan, 1 wk Nov; disabled access. £20.25|£7.95.

Llandrindod Wells SO0561 LLANERCH Waterloo Rd (01597) 822086 Cheerful old town local with old-fashioned settles in beamed main bar, and communicating lounges (one is no smoking); good-value straightforward bar food, well kept real ales, and prompt service; peaceful mountain views from the back terrace, and boules and an orchard in the garden; disabled access. £20|£3.50.

Llangattock SO2117 VINE TREE (01873) 810514 Friendly, well run dining pub with comfortable bar, carefully prepared often imaginative food, and well kept real ales; seats outside. £18|£3.85.

Llangynidr SO1519 COACH & HORSES (01874) 730245 Friendly, well run and bustling pub with tables on a small lawn running down to a lock on the narrow Monmouth and Brecon Canal (moorings); spacious lounge with a big winter fire, and a no smoking area in the restaurant; enjoyable food inc lots of fresh fish, and well kept real ales; bdrms. £19|£8.

Llowes SO1941 RADNOR ARMS (01497) 847460 Small, modest and very old place with a log fire in the bar, a neat little cottagey dining room, and tables in imaginatively planted garden; enjoyable food (nice puddings), and friendly staff; cl pm Sun, Mon (exc bank hols). £17|£7.

Tywyn SH5800 PROPER GANDER High St (01654) 711270 Well liked by contributors, with morning coffee, lunches, and good afternoon teas, and more elaborate evening restaurant; disabled access. £21|£5.20.

Many of the places listed in the **Where to Stay** section serve very good food, too.

SOUTH WALES

The best part of Wales for sightseeing.

South Wales has the principality's best variety of interesting and enjoyable places to visit – with plenty to suit all age groups and tastes, including spectacular medieval castles and great art collections. We'd particularly pick out the excellent Techniquest in Cardiff, the very entertaining Llancaiach Fawr at Nelson, the Welsh Folk Museum just outside, and the Rhondda Heritage Park at Porth (perhaps the best of all the mining places for family visits; the Big Pit at Blaenavon is also a very good 'tourist mine'). Monmouth and Chepstow are small towns of great character.

This area includes the most built-up and industrialised parts of Wales, but there are attractive and unspoilt parts too, for example around the further edges of the Gower peninsula (almost like a mini-Pembrokeshire), the cliffs at Nash Point near St Donats, the hills on the edge of the Brecon Beacons above the former mining valleys (which themselves are more appealing than many might think, with a strong sense of place), the fine gorge of the lower Wye Valley (magnificent in autumn) and the edge of the Black Mountains (which are discussed in the **Mid Wales** section).

Where to stay

Gilwern SO2413 WENALLT FARM Twyn-Wenallt, Gilwern, Abergavenny, Gwent NP7 OHP (01873) 830694 *£40; 10 rms. Friendly and relaxing 16th-c Welsh longhouse on 50 acres of farmland, with oak beams and inglenook fireplace in the big drawing room, and a TV room; good food in dining room, and lots to do nearby; disabled access.

Govilon SO2513 LLANWENARTH HOUSE Govilon, Abergavenny, Gwent NP7 9SF (01873) 830289 *£78, plus special breaks; 4 spacious, comfortable rms. Fine family-run 16th-c manor house in quiet grounds within Brecon Beacons National Park; with gracious sitting room, log fires, antiques and fresh flowers; fine food using local game and fish and home-produced meat, poultry and garden vegetables in elegant candlelit dining room, and friendly helpful staff; lots to do nearby; croquet; cl mid-Jan–Feb; children over 10; disabled access.

Little Mill SO3203 PENTWYN FARM Little Mill, Pontypool, Gwent NP4 0HQ (01495) 785249 *£40; 4 rms, 2 with own bthrm. Most attractive pink-washed 16th-c longhouse on mixed farm of 120 acres; open fire in big sitting room, lots of books and games, and good country cooking around large table in beamed dining room; large garden with swimming pool, table tennis in barn, and rough shooting in woods; cl Christmas–New Year; children over 4.

Llanvihangel Crucorney SO3321 PENYCLAWDD COURT Llanfihangel Crucorney, Abergavenny, Gwent NP7 7LB (01873) 890719 *£73, plus special breaks; 3 rms with mountain views. Interesting Tudor manor house, at the foot of Bryn Arw mountain in the Brecon Beacons National Park; with an Elizabethan knot garden, herb garden, a listed Norman motte and bailey, and a developing yew hedge maze; careful renovation, underfloor heating (to avoid unsightly radiators) and no electricity in the dining room (breakfast and dinner are by candlelight), as well as flagstones, beams and sloping floors; decent breakfasts, good evening meals (and Tudor feasts), and a friendly, relaxed atmosphere; children over 12.

Monmouth SO5113 RIVERSIDE Cinderhill Street, Monmouth, Gwent NP5 3EY (01600) 715577 *£68, plus special breaks; 17 rms. Comfortably refurbished bustling hotel overlooking River Monnow and the 13th-c fortified gatehouse; with good-value bar meals, extensive restaurant menu, conservatory, and a warm welcome; disabled access.

The Mumbles SS6087 HILLCREST HOUSE Higher Lane, Langland, Swansea SA3 4NS (01792) 363700 *£65, plus special breaks; 7 individually decorated rms, each themed to represent a different country. Friendly white house with stone terrace 2 minutes from beach yet handy for Swansea; informal welcoming atmosphere, thoughtful individual service, and comfortable lounge; imaginative seasonal dishes in restaurant (not pm Sun); cl 23 Dec–16 Jan, exc 31 Dec–1 Jan.

Oxwich SS5086 OXWICH BAY Oxwich, Swansea, W Glamorgan SA3 1LS (01792) 390329 £65, plus special breaks; 13 rms. Comfortable hotel on the edge of a beach in a lovely area, with dedicated friendly staff, and food served all day; restaurant/lounge bar with panoramic views, summer outdoor dining area with wknd barbecues, and a welcome for families; cl 24–25 Dec; disabled access.

Reynoldston SS4691 FAIRYHILL Reynoldston, Swansea, W Glamorgan SA3 1BS (01792) 390139 *£120, plus special breaks; 8 rms. 18th-c hotel in 24 acres of wooded grounds with croquet, a trout stream, and wild duck on the lake; a log fire in the comfortable drawing room, and a cosy bar; lovely food in attractive dining room, hearty breakfasts, afternoon tea on leafy terrace, and personal friendly service; children over 8; cl 3 days at Christmas.

St Brides Wentlooge ST2982 WEST USK LIGHTHOUSE St Brides Wentlooge, Newport, Gwent NP1 9SF (01633) 810126 *£65; 3 rms. Unusual ex-lighthouse – squat rather than tall – that was on an island in the Bristol channel (the land has since been reclaimed); modern, stylish furnishings, lots of framed record sleeves (Mr Sheahan used to work for a record company), and an informal atmosphere; good big breakfasts, and small dinner-partyish vegan restaurant; flotation tank, aromatherapy and psychotherapy sessions, and lots of walks.

Tintern Parva SO5301 PARVA FARMHOUSE Tintern Parva, Chepstow, Gwent NP6 6SQ (01291) 689411 *£64, plus special breaks; 9 comfortable rms. Friendly stone farmhouse, rebuilt in mid-17th c, with leather chesterfields, woodburner and honesty bar in large beamed lounge, and books (no TV downstairs); very good food and wine (inc wine using home-grown grapes) in cosy newly refurbished restaurant; 50 yds from River Wye and lovely surrounding countryside.

Whitebrook SO5306 CROWN AT WHITEBROOK Whitebrook, Monmouth, Gwent NP5 4TX (01600) 860254 *£80, plus special breaks; 12 neat rms. Small modernised hotel with 17th-c heart in the beautiful Wye Valley, friendly caring service, relaxed atmosphere, comfortable lounge and bar; small cosy restaurant with fine wines and excellent food combining Welsh ingredients and French style, very good breakfasts; cl 2 wks Jan and 2 wks Aug.

To see and do

♣† **Aberdulais** SS7799 ABERDULAIS FALLS (on the A465) Since the 16th c this splendid waterfall has been used to power a range of industries from copper smelting to tinplate. A magnificent antique waterwheel now generates electricity. Wknd snacks, shop, disabled access (right to the top of the falls thanks to a lift powered by the electricity generated on site); open Apr–Oct; (01639) 636674; £2.80 (one child free per adult); NT.

† 🏰 **Abergavenny** SO2914 There are some attractive ancient buildings in Nevill St and particularly Market St – where there's a busy Tues and Fri market. The CHURCH has a remarkable collection of memorials. The remains of the 12th- and 14th-c CASTLE include the walls, towers and rebuilt gatehouse; the early 19th-c keep and an adjoining house now contain a local history museum. Shop; cl 1–2pm, Sun (exc pm in summer), 24–26 Dec, 1 Jan; (01873) 854282; £1. The Greyhound is a good dining pub, while outside the town the Lamb & Flag (on the B4598 SE) and Llanwenarth Arms (on the Brecon road) are also popular.

♣ **Barry** ST1268 Lively seaside resort which, along with its jutting-out peninsula Barry Island, grew as a centre for the coal industry. Remains of 13th-c castle, and usual fairground attractions for children. WELSH HAWKING CENTRE 🦅 (Weycock Rd) Cheery centre with over 200 birds of prey. Regular flying demonstrations, adventure playground, and animals for children to fuss. Snacks, shop, some disabled access; cl 25 Dec; (01446) 734687; £3. Nearby, the Star in Dinas Powis is good for lunch.

♣† **Blaenavon** SO2508 BIG PIT MINING MUSEUM (on the B4248) Sample the life of a miner by donning a safety helmet and descending 90 metres (300 ft) in the cage into the Big Pit, which closed as a working coal mine in 1980. Also a reconstructed miner's cottage, and an exhibition in the old pithead baths. Good fun – the guides are former miners so have plenty of anecdotes; you'll need sensible shoes and warm clothing. No under 5s underground. Meals, snacks, shop, disabled access with prior warning; usually cl Dec–Feb – but worth checking; (01495) 790311; £5.50. Nearby are some pretty much perfectly preserved 18th-c IRONWORKS; open Easter and Apr–Sept; (01495) 752036; £1.20. The Goose & Cuckoo over the hill at Rhyd-y-Meirch just off the A4042 does good home cooking.

🏰 ⚔ 🏛 **Bridgend** SS9079 NEWCASTLE Ruined 12th-c castle with surviving rectangular tower, richly carved Norman gateway and massive

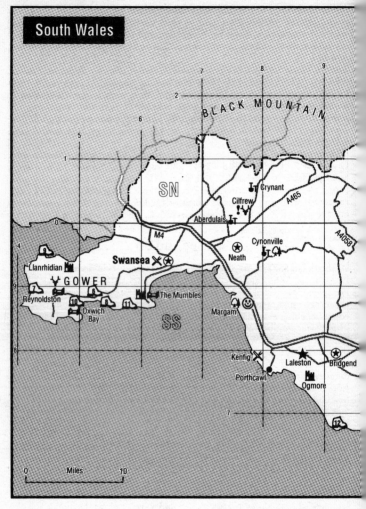

South Wales

curtain walls; collect key from nearby
corner shop. The prosperous
industrial town below isn't much of a
place for visitors, but nearby Merthyr
Mawr SS8877, with its interesting
warren of high sandhills, is attractive,
as are Southerndown and Ogmore
(see Ogmore entry below). The
ruined PRIORY at Ewenny SS9077 is
one of the finest fortified religious
buildings in Britain, and there's a
working POTTERY close by; cl 1–2pm,
Sun exc pm in summer; free. Slightly
N, BRYNGARW COUNTRY PARK is an
unexpectedly tranquil refuge from

the M4, with woodland walks,
formal gardens, ornamental lakes
and a Japanese garden. Snacks, shop,
disabled access; cl 25–26 Dec;
(01656) 725155; free.
Caerleon ST3490 FORTRESS
BATHS, AMPHITHEATRE AND BARRACKS
One of the best examples of an
amphitheatre in the country,
alongside a similarly well preserved
bath-house, now under cover. Also
the foundations of barrack lines and
parts of the ramparts, and the
remains of the cookhouse and
latrines. Shop, disabled access; cl am

Sun, 24–26 Dec, 1 Jan, Good Fri; (01222 500200); £2.85. The adjacent ROMAN LEGIONARY MUSEUM (High St) gives some idea of the daily life of the garrison; quite a few hands-on activities at wknds. Shop, disabled access; (01633) 423134; *£2. You can get a joint ticket for the museum and the baths. Caerleon is reckoned in these parts to have been the site of the court of King Arthur. The Tourist Information Centre on the High St has a little art gallery and various craft workshops; the Hanbury Arms has generous food.

Caerphilly ST1587 Oddly strung-out small town, dominated by the CASTLE, the largest in Wales, with extensive land and water defences. Rising sheer from its broad outer moat, it's a proper picture-book castle, pleasing for this reason to the most casual visitor. It also enthrals serious students of castle architecture with its remarkably complex design of concentric defences. Look out for the incredible leaning tower, which appears ready to topple any second. Shop, some disabled access; cl 24–26 Dec, 1 Jan; (01222) 883143; £2.20.

The ancient Courthouse overlooking the castle has a good quick carvery, while the thatched Travellers' Rest is worthwhile.

🏛 **Caerwent** ST4791 ROMAN WALLS These massive walls, still some 4½ metres (15 ft) high in places, enclosed the large site of Venta Silurum – over 40 acres, enough for a sizeable town, though none of that's left now; free. The Carpenters Arms up in the attractive village of Shirenewton does good-value food.

🏰 ⚱ **Caldicot** ST4888 The well preserved 12th–14th-c CASTLE (off the B4245) was restored as a family home in the 1880s, and lived in until 20 years ago – since when it's been a local museum, surrounded by a country park. Snacks, shop, limited disabled access; cl am Sun, lunchtimes Oct and Mar, Nov–Feb; (01291) 424447; *£1.50.

🏰 ⚱ ♨ ✿ † **Cardiff** ST1876 The civic centre has a range of grand 20th-c white stone civic or governmental buildings around a formal park. The old city centre is closer to Cardiff Castle, which has Capability Brown's 18th-c landscaped park between it and the river. In the centre, parts are pedestrianised (for example around the fine church of St John the Baptist), and there are many covered shopping arcades, Victorian and modern; multi-ride bus tickets are good value for getting around. CARDIFF CASTLE (Castle St) Despite their fairy-tale medieval appearance, the main buildings are largely 19th c, when the Marquess of Bute employed William Burges to rebuild and restore the place, adding richly romantic wall paintings, tapestries and carvings. Some parts are much older, and in the grounds there's even a piece of a 3-metre (10-ft) thick Roman wall. The Norman keep survives, and there's a 13th-c tower – these two look like proper castle architecture, perched on a little mound. Snacks, shop; cl 25 Dec, 1 Jan; (01222) 878100; £4.80 for full guided tour, £2.40 grounds only. NATIONAL MUSEUM OF WALES (Cathays Park) Considerably enlivened in recent years, with interactive displays and exhibitions on subjects as diverse as ceramics, coins and prehistoric sea monsters. The east wing has an impressive collection of paintings, with notable French Impressionists, and there's an excellent section on the evolution of the Welsh landscape. Meals, snacks, shop, disabled access; cl Mon exc bank hols, 24–25 Dec; (01222) 397951; £3.25. WELSH INDUSTRIAL AND MARITIME MUSEUM (Bute St) Exhaustive exploration of Welsh industrial and maritime development, spread over 5 former dockland buildings. One gallery houses ancient trams, cars and so forth, another various industrial engines (many of which may clank, whirr, thud or grind noisily into life), another locomotives, full size or model, yet another ships and shipping, and there's more outside. Steam days 1st Sat of the month Apr–Oct. Snacks, shop, disabled access; cl Mon (exc bank hols), 24–26 Dec, 1 Jan; (01222) 481919; *£2.25. TECHNIQUEST 🆓 (Stuart St) Fun as well as interest at this hi-tech science centre, with around 160 hands-on exhibits and activities, a planetarium, and even a realistic dragon conjured up by laser. All exceptionally well done, it's an excellent family excursion. Meals, snacks, shop, very good disabled access; cl 24–26 Dec; (01222) 475475; *£4.50. These last two attractions are at the heart of the Cardiff Bay Development Area, an ambitious rejuvenation of the Inner Harbour and Docklands. There's also a space-age-looking VISITOR CENTRE explaining the project (cl 25–26 Dec; free), and a slightly incongruous Norwegian timbered church; the docklands New Sea Lock (Harrowby St) may be Cardiff's most unspoilt pub, the smarter Wharf (Atlantic Wharf) is right on the water's edge. Llandaff is a mile or two out from the centre, where the CATHEDRAL has been rebuilt several times; it includes some delightful medieval masonry, Pre-Raphaelite works, a marvellous modern timber roof, and a central concrete arch that you may think a mistake. The nearby green has an attractive collection of buildings around it. WELSH FOLK MUSEUM (St Fagans, 4m W on the A4232) Excellent 100-acre open-air museum, with a variety of reconstructed buildings from castles to cottages illustrating styles and living conditions throughout the ages. Buildings have come from all over Wales, and there are some remarkable exhibits, inc a homely gas-lit Edwardian farmhouse and an entire Celtic village. You can buy things from a period grocery store. Also crafts and lots of seasonal events – there's plenty to fascinate here. Meals and snacks (in 1920s tearoom), shop, disabled access; cl 25–26 Dec, 1 Jan; (01222) 573500; £5.25. In Cardiff centre the Cottage and Philharmonic both in St Marys St and Golden Cross in Custom House St are quite useful for lunch.

🎿 ☷ ⚒ **Chepstow** ST5393 A steep but civilised small town, still with its battlemented 13th-c town gate. CHEPSTOW CASTLE The first recorded Norman stone castle, proudly standing on an easily defended spot above the Wye, overlooking the harbour. Splendid gatehouse with portcullis grooves and ancient gates, and exhibitions on siege warfare and the English Civil War. Shop, limited disabled access; cl 24–26 Dec, 1 Jan; *£3. STUART CRYSTAL have a museum and workshop opposite, and there's a working pottery on Lower Church St (cl 1–2pm). Bridge St has a good local history MUSEUM (cl 1–2pm, am Sun; £1). The civilised Bridge and Castle View are both good for lunch.

✌ ! **Cilfrew** SN7700 PENSCYNOR WILDLIFE PARK 🐾 (off the A465) Lots of animals in a charming setting, inc meerkats, parrots, tropical birds and 25 species of monkey. You can feed rainbow trout or take a ride in the chairlift to the clifftop – coming down again on an exciting bobsleigh ride. Meals, snacks, shop, disabled access; cl 25 Dec; (01639) 642189; £5.

⚒ **Crynant** SN7904 CEFN COED COLLIERY MUSEUM (Blaenant Colliery, on the A4109) On the site of a former colliery, the story of mining in the Dulais Valley. It still has a steam winding-engine, though the winding gear is now run by electricity. Also a simulated underground mining gallery, boiler house and compressor house. Summer snacks, shop, disabled access; cl Nov–Mar; (01639) 750556; £2.50.

🐖 **Cwmbran** ST2995 GREENMEADOW COMMUNITY FARM 🐾 (1m W) Founded to protect one of the encroaching new town's last green areas, this friendly farm has a wide range of animals – traditional, rare and cuddly – as well as a deer enclosure, bluebell wood, and craft workshops. Meals, snacks, shop, disabled access; cl 25 Dec; (01633) 862202; *£2.75. Up towards Pontypool the canalside Open Hearth (Griffithstown) has good food.

🐾 ⚒ **Cynonville** SS8294 AFAN FOREST PARK (on the A4107) 9,000 tranquil acres of forest, with trails for walking or cycling (you can hire mountain bikes in summer), visitor centre, and the WELSH MINERS MUSEUM, illustrating life as a miner with coal faces, pit gear and mining equipment among the displays. Meals, snacks, shop, disabled access; cl 25–26 Dec; (01639) 850564; *60p museum, park free, though £1.10 parking charge wknds, bank hols Apr–Aug, and school hols.

❀ **Ebbw Vale** SO1609 VICTORIA PARK (Victoria, 2m S on the A4046) The site of the 1992 Garden Festival, still full of the lakes, gardens, wetlands and woodland from then. Much of the site is being developed as an ambitious garden village, and it's fascinating watching the project's progress. Pleasant walks and trails, interesting exhibitions, and some quite extraordinary sculptures, one made from 30,000 individually modelled clay bricks. A factory shopping centre opened last year. Snacks, shop, disabled access; centre cl 25 Dec; (01495) 350010; free.

✌ **The Gower** This peninsula stretching W of Swansea has quite a bit of off-putting ribbon development along the roads entering it, but it's well worth persevering, as the further parts are full of interest around the coast: the long glistening cockle sands below Llanrhidian SS4992, the dunes and marshy slacks of the Whiteford Burrows nature reserve SS4495, the islet of Burry Holms SS4092 with its ruined chapel and Iron Age fort (you can walk out at low tide), the long surfers' sands of Rhossili Bay SS4090 below rough-cropped windswept open moorland that seems a million miles from Swansea yet as the crow flies is only about 10 from the outskirts, the tidal rocks of Worms Head nature reserve SS3887 where you may see seals in late summer, Port Eynon Point SS4884 with its huge medieval rock-dove dovecot in the cliff and cliff walks on either side, and the dunes and broad sands of Oxwich Bay SS5286. These last two are good for wind-surfing – you can hire wetsuits from a wind-surfing school at Oxwich Bay – though the the water will never be more than what might euphemistically be called invigorating. Busy in summer (quite a young feel in parts), these places all tend to be virtually empty out of season. There's an informative NT visitor centre at Rhossili, cl Mon–Tues Nov–Dec, wkdys Feb–Mar, Jan. See entries below for Llanrhidian and the Mumbles. The King Arthur at Reynoldston, Joiners Arms at Bishopston and Greyhound at Oldwalls are well placed for food.

Llanrhidian SS4792 WEOBLEY CASTLE 12th–14th-c fortified manor house with an exhibition on the area's history, and superb views. Cl am Sun in winter, 24–26 Dec, 1 Jan; (01792) 390012; £1.70. The Welcome to Town is in a lovely spot above the estuary.

† Llanthony SO2827 LLANTHONY PRIORY Graceful ruins of 12th-c priory, the money for its construction put up by Hugh de Lacey when he decided he'd had enough of being a bold bad baron and was thinking of retiring into these lonely hills. It's a very romantic spot, with nothing much but the noise of the sheep to disturb the peace. The remains cover a variety of architectural styles; free. The very ancient crypt bar below the Abbey Hotel, right among the priory buildings, is useful for a snack lunch – a most unusual place. On the way up

the valley, turn off to see medieval CWMYOY CHURCH SO2923: repeated landslips have left the whole church twisted, and its tower leans at an angle that makes the Tower of Pisa look positively sober.

Llantilio Crosseny SO3915 Attractive village with a lovely view of the 13th-c church from the former moat of Hen Gwrt nearby; the Halfway House and Hostry are good for lunch. The remains of the WHITE CASTLE (NW of the village) are the most substantial of the trio of moated castles Hubert de Burgh built to defend the Welsh Marches; £1.70. The other ruins stand at Skenfrith SO4621 (the Bell has good value food) and Grosmont SO4024, an attractive hillside village with another 13th-c church (the Angel here is also good value).

Margam SS8186 MARGAM PARK (on the A48) Pretty country park based around splendid 'gothick' mansion, its 850 acres full of natural and historic features and various themed areas, inc a scaled-down nursery-rhyme village for young children. Also a ruined abbey and Iron Age hill fort, marked walks among the parkland and forests, giant maze, deer and cattle, and an adventure playground. Meals, snacks, shop, disabled access; cl winter Mon and Tues; (01639) 871131; £3.50, less in winter, when none of the attractions are open (though they have various special events).

Merthyr Tydfil SO0707 BRECON MOUNTAIN RAILWAY (off the A465) The route of this narrow-gauge railway starts at Pant Station, 3 miles N of Merthyr Tydfil, where there's a display of various engines inc vintage locomotives and others from around the world. The journey takes you into the beautiful Brecon Beacons as far as the Taf Fechan reservoir. Snacks, shop, disabled access; cl Nov–Easter exc over Christmas; (01685) 722988 for timetable; £5.80. On a disused railway line, the Dowlais Viaduct is a striking sight, well worth a detour. CYFARTHFA CASTLE (Cyfarthfa Park)

Impressive early 19th-c castellated Gothic mansion, set in beautiful gardens. Recently restored to their full Regency glory, the state rooms contain a museum with displays on Egyptology and archaeology. Meals, snacks, shop, disabled access; cl 24 Dec–2 Jan; (01685) 723112; £1.30. JOSEPH PARRY'S COTTAGE (Chapel Row, Georgetown) The composer of *Myfanwy* was born here, and the ground floor has been restored and decorated in the style of the 1840s. Shop, limited disabled access; open pm Easter–Oct; (01685) 725142; *60p. The Butchers Arms up at Pontsticill has good home cooking. GARWNANT FOREST CENTRE SN9913 (5 m NW, off A470) Looking out over the Llwyn-On reservoir on the S edge of the National Park, carefully restored old farm buildings with displays on forestry, wildlife and conservation, and information on nature trails and cycle routes (you can hire bikes). Meals, snacks, shop, disabled access; (01639) 710221; £1 car parking charge.

★ ♨ Monmouth SO5012 Attractive market town of considerable character; below the remains of the 12th-c castle where Henry V was born, and the 17th-c Great Castle House (built with enormous blocks of masonry in its precincts), the main Agincourt Square is surrounded by handsome buildings, inc the imposing central Shire Hall with its arcaded market floor. The town nestles in the crook formed by the River Wye and the River Monnow, with a splendid 13th-c gatehouse bridge over the Monnow. NELSON MUSEUM (Priory St) Tremendous collection relating to Nelson, inc letters, medals and best of all his fighting sword. Nelson had nothing to do with Monmouth, but the collection was originally put together by Lady Llangattock who lived nearby. Shop, limited disabled access; cl 1–2pm, 24–26 Dec, 1 Jan; (01600) 713519; £1. The Punch House is the most enjoyable place here for lunch, and the Gockett (B4293 towards Trelleck) is also good.

♨ The Mumbles SS6188 Pleasantly unspoilt resort with a collection of traditional Welsh love spoons (cl Sun), and a surprisingly active night-life; 14 pubs line the stretch of Mumbles Rd nr Mumbles Head, and students like to 'go mumbling' between them. OYSTERMOUTH CASTLE Very complete ruins of the de Breose family castle, in a small park overlooking the bay. The gatehouse, chapel and great hall date from the 13th–14th c. Cl Oct–Mar; £1. The White Rose does good-value food.

🏠 Nantgarw ST1285 NANTGARW CHINA WORKS (Treforest Industrial estate, off the A470) For a brief period early in the 19th c, Nantgarw porcelain was among the finest in the world. They still make pots and clay pipes, and you can watch the craftsmen at work. Snacks, shop; cl Mon, plus winter Tues and Weds; (01443) 841703; *£1.

🏰 ♨ 🏵 Neath SS7597 NEATH ABBEY Remains of Cistercian abbey founded in 1130 by Richard de Grainville. Disabled access; cl am Sun, 25–26 Dec; free. The BOROUGH MUSEUM (Gwyn Hall, Orchard St) includes finds from a nearby Roman fort. Shop, disabled access; cl Sun, Mon (exc bank hols); (01639) 645741; free. GNOLL ESTATE (on the B4434 NE of Neath) Landscaped grounds beautifully restored by the borough council. The visitor centre will have you believe they're the finest in Europe, and though this is something of an exaggeration, with some of the features it's not too wide of the mark. Snacks, shop, disabled access; cl 24 Dec–2 Jan; (01639) 635808; free.

🏠 ♨ Nelson ST1195 LLANCAIACH FAWR 🏯 (on the B4254) Splendidly entertaining and carefully organised living history museum, the Elizabethan manor's Civil War days brought vividly to life by costumed guides who rarely step out of character – they even speak in 17th-c style. Children don't mind visiting a stately home when it's like this – not only are there no ropes or barriers (it's all firmly hands-on), but they can try on historic clothes, handle armour, or even languish in the stocks for a while. Extra activities summer wknds. Meals, snacks, shop, some disabled access (not to upper floors of house); cl am Sun in winter, and Christmas wk; (01443) 412248; £4.10.

🔥🅐🏠⚜ **Newport** ST3189 Industrial town, with a decent MUSEUM AND ART GALLERY on John Frost Square showing off plenty of teapots (cl Sun and bank hols; free). TREDEGAR HOUSE 🔲 (Coedkernew; off the A48, SW edge of Newport) Magnificent 17th-c house and gardens set in 90-acre landscaped park. The Morgans, later Lords Tredegar, lived here for 5 centuries, and the household's above and below stairs activities are well illustrated in the 30 or so rooms on show. In the grounds are carriage rides, self-guided trails, craft workshops, an Edwardian sunken garden, as well as boating and an adventure playfarm. Meals, snacks, shop, disabled access; cl Mon and Tues (exc Aug), Oct wkdys, and all Nov–Easter; (01633) 815880; £3.95. Past here on the B4239 the Lighthouse Inn at St Brides Wentlooge has good food upstairs, and great Severn views.

🏰 **Ogmore** SS8675 OGMORE CASTLE 3-storeyed 12th-c keep with a preserved hooded fireplace, a dry moat surrounding the inner ward and a surviving 12-metre (40-ft) W wall. The setting of this ruin is attractive: odd to think that this impressive fortress was built to defend the row of stepping stones which still cross the river; free. The Pelican is good for lunch, and the cheery Three Golden Cups along the road at Southerndown gives sea views to Devon on a clear day. Just past it there's a car park by the interestingly preserved remains of the seaside gardens of the entirely demolished Dunraven Castle SS8873, with walks by the cliffs over the sands and rock pools, and around to the fragmentary remains of an Iron Age promontory hill fort above the sea.

🔥♓ **Penarth** ST1871 An unspoilt seaside resort of some charm, with the usual attractions – and changing exhibits from the National Museum of Wales at TURNER HOUSE on Plymouth Rd; limited disabled access; cl 12.45–2pm, am Sun, Mon (exc bank hols), and between exhibitions; (01222) 708870; *£1.25 (free Sun pms). COSMESTON MEDIEVAL VILLAGE (Cosmeston Lakes Country Park, Lavernock Rd, S of Penarth towards Sully) Living museum of medieval life, reconstructed on the site of an actual village which was deserted during the 14th c. Hens and sheep wander between the cottages. Meals, snacks, shop, disabled access; cl 25 Dec; (01222) 708686; *£2.50. It's set in the Cosmeston Lakes country park, with lakes, woodland and wildlife.

🏰 **Penhow** ST4290 PENHOW CASTLE 🔲 (on the A48) The oldest lived-in castle in Wales, with tours of the restored rooms taking you from the 12th-c ramparts and Norman bedchamber through the 15th-c great hall with its minstrels' gallery to the Victorian housekeeper's room. There's a choice of several good Walkman tours, one specially for children, and others concentrating on a particular topic, such as the musical or domestic history of the building. You can stay here. Snacks, shop; cl Mon (exc bank hols), Tues, Oct–Mar exc Weds and pm occasional Suns; (01633) 400800; £3.35.

♓ **Pontypool** SO2800 VALLEY INHERITANCE (Pontypool Park, off the A4042) The story of a typical South Wales valley, well shown in the Georgian stable block of Pontypool Park House. Snacks, shop, disabled access; cl am Sun, Jan; (01495) 752036; £1.20. Pleasant wood and moorland walks in the surrounding country park. The Open Hearth just below the canal at Griffithstown is good for lunch.

♓ **Porth** ST0491 RHONDDA HERITAGE PARK (off the A470) Based in the last colliery buildings in the area, a very good developing centre with lively multi-media exhibitions re-creating the days when coal was king. Sights, sounds and smells from the life and work of the miners, and an excellent underground tour showing what it was like to work a shift; the noise and heat are uncannily realistic. It ends with an exciting dark ride back to the surface. Unusual features include the gallery with art by locals, a section on the role of women, and an authentic Valley chapel. With a good themed play area for children, this is a fulfilling family day out. Meals, snacks, shop, disabled access; cl winter Mons, and 25–26 Dec; (01443) 682036; £4.95. The Bunch of Grapes in Pontypridd (Ynysangharad Rd) is useful for food.

Porthcawl SS8177 Still developing summer resort, with broad sandy beaches, well placed golf club, fairground, fishing from the pier, and what's said to be the largest caravan park in Wales (some say Europe); it's quieter on the W side of the harbour.

Raglan SO4107 RAGLAN CASTLE Quite magnificent ruins of 15th-c castle, particularly notable for its Yellow Tower of Gwent. Its intricate history is displayed in the closet tower and 2 rooms of the gatehouse. Cl 24–26 Dec, 1 Jan; (01291) 690228; £2.20. The Clytha Arms (on the Abergavenny road) has good food.

St Hilary ST0173 BEAUPRE CASTLE Well preserved ruined Elizabethan courtyard mansion with an extraordinarily elaborate 3-storey Italianate porch. Cl Sun, Christmas

Days Out

Gower seascapes
Threecliff Bay/Cefn Bryn (see △-6 and △-8 in **Walks** section below); lunch at Beaufort Arms, Kittle, or King Arthur, Reynoldston; Rhossili Down and Mewslade Bay (see △-7 in **Walks** section below); Weobley Castle, Llanrhidian.

Industrial legacies
Aberdulais Falls; Penscynor Wildlife Park, Cilfrew; picnic or snack in Gnoll Estate nr Neath; Cefn Coed Colliery Museum, Crynant, or Afan Forest Park, Cynonville.

Lower Wye tour
Chepstow Castle; lunch at Castle Hotel or Bridge Hotel there; view from Wynd Cliff (see △-1 in **Walks** section below); Tintern Abbey; Monmouth.

Castles for free
Dyffryn Gardens, St Nicholas; Beaupre Castle (cl Sun), St Hilary; lunch at Bush there; Nash Point and cliffs; Ogmore and Dunraven Castles.

The great buildings collection
Castell Coch, Tongwynlais; Llandaff cathedral; lunch at Maltsters Arms there; Welsh Folk Museum, St Fagans (like Llandaff, described under Cardiff).

Cultural Cardiff
Cardiff Castle; lunch at Le Monde (cl Sun) or Cottage, both St Mary St; National Museum of Wales.

Cardiff's baytown
Visitor Centre for harbour and docklands; lunch at Wharf, Atlantic Wharf; Techniquest.

An industrious past
Stroll along Monmouthshire & Brecon Canal between Gilwern and Govilon, back along old railway track; lunch at Drum & Monkey, Clydach; Big Pit mining museum, Blaenavon.

and Easter; free. The Bush is good for lunch, and the village with its thatched houses is pretty.

🏵 **St Nicholas** ST0972 DYFFRYN GARDENS (off the A48) Small themed gardens and seasonal bedding displays help break up the 50 acres of rare plants and shrubs which make up these lovely gardens. Also extensive plant houses, inc a large temperate house and a succulent house, and an arboretum. Summer snacks (open-air theatre then too), shop; open daily; (01222) 593328; *£2 in season.

🏠🖼🎏⚓♨�·🚻 🏵 **Swansea** SS6592 Largely post-industrial and commercial, so there are few buildings of any age or great appeal to visitors, but there's a good fresh-food covered market with cockles and laverbread, and long sandy beaches have made it something of a family summer resort. Among some high spots is the 1934 GUILDHALL, containing the Brangwyn Hall with its 16 huge British Empire murals painted by Sir Frank Brangwyn for the House of Lords – Wales's gain, as they were judged too controversial. There are some castle ruins (you can't go inside, but can see them from outside), inc a striking 14th-c 1st-floor arcade. The town's local history MUSEUM (Victoria Rd, Maritime Quarter) is the oldest in Wales (cl Mon exc bank hols; free). MARITIME AND INDUSTRIAL MUSEUM (Museum Sq, Maritime Quarter) In the heart of the revitalised docks, with its summer collection of historic ships the biggest and most varied assemblage of floating maritime exhibits in Wales. Also a complete working woollen mill. Lots of thought is put into the displays. Summer snacks, shop, disabled access; cl Mon (exc bank and school hols), 25–26 Dec, 1 Jan; (01792) 650351; free. TY LLEN (Somerset Place, Marina) Centre devoted to Welsh literature, with exhibitions, restaurant, and a good bookshop. GLYNN VIVIAN ART GALLERY AND MUSEUM (Alexandra Rd) Displays of porcelain from Swansea's all-too-brief but brilliant period of production between 1814 and 1824,

and paintings, drawings and sculptures by British, French and, above all, Welsh artists – especially the locally born Ceri Richards. Good changing exhibitions. Shop, some disabled access; cl Mon (exc bank hols), 25–26 Dec, 1 Jan; (01792) 655006; free. PLANTASIA (Parc Tawe) Tropical and desert plants in big futuristic landscaped glasshouse, also aviary and various creepy-crawlies. Snacks, shop, disabled access; (01792) 474555; cl Mon, 25–26 Dec; *£1.70. The Hanbury in Kingsway is popular for lunch.

🏰 🎏 **Tintern** SO5200 TINTERN ABBEY (off the A466) Remarkably well preserved, these 14th-ruins were considered an essential spot for 18th-c artists and poets to visit, lying as they do in a lovely part of the steeply wooded Wye Valley. Wordsworth was just one of many to find inspiration here. Shop, disabled access; cl 24–26 Dec, 1 Jan; (01291) 689251; £2.20. The ABBEY MILL nearby has been converted into a little craft centre, with demonstrations and a decent coffee shop; cl Mon; free. A VISITOR CENTRE at Tintern Old Station can help you make the most of the surrounding hills and woodland.

🏰 **Tongwynlais** ST1382 CASTELL COCH (off the A470) This spectacular triangular hillside landmark, designed in 1875 by William Burges for the Marquis of Bute, is actually based on a 13th-c castle in spite of its improbable appearance, something by Disney out of Wagner – red sandstone, conical towers, drawbridge and portcullis. Though never finished, it's a very successful pastiche, and inside is just as impressive: an astonishly elaborate mock-medieval idyll of gilt, gorgeous colours, statues, murals and carvings. The bedroom of Lady Bute is decorated on the theme of Sleeping Beauty. Shop, disabled access to ground floor only; cl 24–26 Dec, 1 Jan; (01222) 810101; £2.20.

★ **Attractive villages or small towns,** all with decent pubs, include Bedwellty SO1600, Cowbridge SS9974, Laleston SS8879 and Usk SO3801, which also has a decent rural life museum in an old barn (cl Nov–Mar; *£1.50).

Pubs or inns elsewhere which are particularly useful for their attractive surroundings or views include the Lamb & Flag out on the Brecon road from Abergavenny SO2515, Bridgend by the canal at Gilwern SO2414, Old Glais at Glais SN7000, Prince of Wales nr the sand dune nature reserve at Kenfig SS8081, Old House at Llangynwyd SS8588, Greyhound at Llantrisant ST3997, Brynfynnon at Llanwonno ST0295, Plough & Harrow at Monknash SS9270, Rowan Tree at Nelson ST1195, Halfway House at Tal-y-coed SO4115, Trekkers at The Narth SO5206 and Fountain at Trelleck Grange SO4902.

✝ **Notable churches** include the one at Partrishow SO2722 in the Black Mountains not far from Llanthony, a remarkable building, with a musicians' gallery and a mural of a figure of Death wielding a shovel. The church at Bettws-Newydd SO3605, largely unaltered from the 15th c, also has a gallery and fine screen. The church and churchyard of Llancarfan ST0570 are worth a look, and the one in the interesting village of Llanvapley SO3714 dates from 860.

Walks

Part of Gwent's boundary with England is made up of the picturesque Lower Wye gorge. The **Wye valley walk** ☼-1 connects Chepstow ST5393 with Tintern SO5200 – there are only occasional views down to the river, but the short detour up steps to the Wynd Cliff viewpoint ST5297 gets an extensive panorama. Further good sections of the gorge can be walked from **Monmouth** SO5012 ☼-2 to Fairview Rock SO5514, a lofty crag nr the Biblins suspension bridge; a level track supplies an easy riverside route.

The industrial valleys have rather scrappy moorland and patches of conifer plantation rising high above the towns; it's not a pretty scene, but its gruff sense of place appeals to some. There are some interesting examples of post-mining land reclamation, including **Parc Cwm Darran** ☼-3 in the Rhymney valley nr Bargoed ST1499, which now provides a wide variety of natural habitats for wildlife and plants, with scenery ranging from the valley floor through forest areas to upland moors with superb views of the Brecon Beacons; and the **Afon Lwyd valley** ☼-4 between Cwmbran New Town ST2995 and Blaenavon SO2509.

The abrupt transition from here into the empty wildness of the Brecon Beacons National Park (described in the **Mid Wales** section on p.947 but very easily reached from here) is startling. The Black Mountains, too, are discussed in the **Mid Wales** section, p.947, though the valleys stretching up into them from Gwent, for instance past **Llanthony** SO2827 ☼-5, offer some of the best approaches.

The Gower Peninsula encapsulates on a small scale many different types of Welsh landscape, once beyond the creeping urbanisation W of Swansea. It rises to rounded moorland hills such as **Cefn Bryn** SS4989 ☼-6 and **Rhossili Down** SS4190 ☼-7, which offer breathtaking views of both – or all three – coasts. From Rhossili you can also take in Mewslade Bay SS4187, where the sands are enclosed by limestone cliffs. From **Penmaen** SS5388 ☼-8 (NT car park nr the church) a good walk follows the lane to Threecliff Bay, then heads W along the coast as far as Nicholaston Farm to end with the mild ascent of Cefn Bryn ridge. **Whiteford Burrows** SS4495 ☼-9 (pine trees and sand dunes), **Oxwich Bay** SS5086 ☼-10 (more dunes, presided over by Oxwich Point on its S side), and tiny **Brandy Cove** SS5887 ☼-11 (walk down the wooded Bishopston valley to get there) are among other highlights. The N coast is attractive only at its western end.

Closer to Cardiff, the curious striped cliffs of the Glamorgan coast·look over the Bristol Channel to Exmoor. **Nash Point** SS9168 ⌂-12 is the best access point, as it is worth getting to shore level to see the cliffs in their full glory.

Where to eat

Cardiff ST1876 LE MONDE 60 St Mary St (01222) 387376 Bustling open-plan restaurant with a big choice of delicious fish and shellfish dishes, decent wines, and friendly efficient service; cl Sun, 25–26 Dec. **£22.**

Clydach SO2213 DRUM & MONKEY (01873) 831980 Attractively set old pub with good, interesting food in pretty bar and restaurant, helpful friendly staff, and real ales; cl first 2 wks Jan; disabled access. **£20|£8.**

Kenfig SS8081 PRINCE OF WALES (01656) 740356 Unspoilt and unpretentious old local with a warm open fire, small storm windows, and a friendly atmosphere; good simple home-made bar food using home-grown vegetables and their own eggs, a fine range of real ales, and decent malt whiskies; lots of walks. **|£4.95.**

Llandewi Skirrid SO3416 WALNUT TREE (01873) 852797 Comfortable, stylish dining pub run by the same licensees for over 27 years, with a marvellously relaxed atmosphere (you can pop in for just a drink or one-course meal); outstanding imaginative and carefully prepared food using tip-top quality produce (wonderful puddings and fine cheeses), an attractive choice of wines (particularly strong on Italian ones), and efficient friendly service; cl Sun, Mon, 2 wks Feb; disabled access. **£35|£14.**

Raglan SO3608 CLYTHA ARMS (01873) 840206 Fine old country inn with a tastefully and solidly comfortable bar, and cheerful helpful staff; good, carefully prepared food inc delicious puddings and good-value Sun lunch in no smoking restaurant, log fires, well kept real ales, and neat garden; bdrms. **£18|£6.25.**

Swansea SS6592 NUMBER ONE RESTAURANT 1 Wind St (01792) 456996 Small bistro-style restaurant with a relaxed friendly atmosphere, helpful staff, and really good food using local produce – lots of fish and game and lovely puddings; cl Sun, Mon, 24 Dec–1 Jan. **£15.95 lunch, £23 dinner|£7.**

Tal-y-coed SO4115 HALFWAY HOUSE (01600) 780269 Pretty, neat and clean 17th-c cottage with huge wisteria, cosy little no smoking dining room, a snug main bar, lots of Wills cigarette cards; well kept real ales, carefully presented bar food, and welcoming service; a tidy garden. **£17.70|£6.20.**

Special thanks to Howard James, Francine Lewis, Mrs S C Cartwright, Margaret Haycock, Mrs M A Hill, Pam Goodfellow, Mr and Mrs T Pitwell, B Lees, Mr and Mrs M Ruth, Mr and Mrs R S Blake, Ian Phillips, Mary McCann.

We welcome reports from readers . . .

This *Guide* depends on readers' reports. Do help us if you can – in return, we offer a discount on the next edition to people who've helped us with reports for it. Tell us what you think about places already in it, and any-thing extra you think we should say about them. And send us your ideas for inclusion in the next edition: places to visit, eat at or stay in, attractive drives or walks, maybe even unusual interesting shops you know of. Use the card in the middle, the report forms at the end, or just write – no stamp needed: *The Good Guide to Britain*, FREEPOST TN1569, Wadhurst, E Sussex TN5 7BR.

WALES CALENDAR

Some of these dates were provisional as we went to press. Please check information with the telephone numbers provided.

JANUARY

1 **Cardiff** BBC National Orchestra of Wales New Year's Day Concert at St David's Hall (01222) 878500; **Saundersfoot** New Year's Day Swim from the beach (01834) 813039

9 **Llanwrtyd Wells** Roman festival: chariot race, Screaming Lord Such as Lord of Misrule at the Neuadd Arms – *till Sun 11* (01591) 610236

FEBRUARY

7 **Cardiff** Wales v Italy at Cardiff Arms Park (01222) 781700

MARCH

6 **Llanwrtyd Wells** Folk Weekend – *till Sun 8* (01591) 610666

13 **Llandudno** North Wales Country Music Festival – *till Sun 15* (01492) 879771

APRIL

12 **Newport** 1920s Event: music, costumes, fashion show at Tredegar House – *till Mon 13* (01633) 815880

19 **Llanelwedd** Working Breeds Dog Show at the Showground (01639) 823078

MAY

1 **South Pembrokeshire** Landsker Walking Festival – *till Mon 4* (01834) 860965

2 **Porthmadog** Gala Weekend at Ffestiniog Railway – *till Mon 4* (01766) 512340

3 **Gwernesney** Welsh Festival of Dressage at Usk Showground (01222) 885697

4 **Holywell** Carnival (01352) 715056; **Newport** 1920s Event at Tredegar House (01633) 815880

8 **Llangollen** International Jazz Festival – *till Sun 10* (0151) 339 3367

15 **Newport** Folk Festival at Tredegar House – *till Sun 17* (01633) 815880

22 **Hay-on-Wye** Literature Festival – *till Sun 31* (01497) 820144

23 **Hay-on-Wye** Children's Festival of the Arts – *till Mon 25* (01544) 328424; **St David's** St David's Cathedral Music Festival – *till Sun 31* (01437) 720271

24 **Newport** Rare Plant Sale at Tredegar House (01633) 815880

25 **Merthyr Tydfil** Fête and Gala (01685) 725000

JUNE

6 **Llangollen** Choral Festival (01625) 502600

13 **Chepstow** Horse Trials – *till Sun 14* (01291) 628982; **Llanwrtyd Wells** Man v Horse Race (01591) 610236; **Rhydyfelin** Aberystwyth Agricultural Show at Tanycastell Park (01970) 820030

19 **Burry Port** Welsh Open Play Golf Stroke Play Championship – *till Sun 21* (01633) 430830; **Wrexham** Craft Show at Erddig (01978) 313333

20 **Barmouth** Start of Yacht Race to Fort William (01341) 280298; **Llanwrtyd Wells** Drovers Challenge Walk (01591) 610236

21 **Colwyn Bay** North Wales Motor Show (01492) 516140

22 **Cardiff** International Animation Festival – *till Sun 28* (01222) 667773

WALES CALENDAR

JUNE cont

25 **Gregynog** Festival – *till Sun 28* (01686) 625007
26 **Cardiff** Folk Dance Festival – *till Sun 28* (01222) 653989
27 **Trellech** Festival of Music and Flowers at St Nicholas Church – *till Sun 28* (01600) 860433

JULY

3 **Aberystwyth** Poetry Festival *till Sat 11* (01970) 622889; **Conwy** North Wales Bluegrass Music Festival – *till Sun 5* (01492) 580454; **Llanwrtyd Wells** Morris in the Forest Festival – *till Sun 5* (01591) 610666; **St Donats Castle** Welsh International Festival of Storytelling at St Donats Arts Centre – *till Sun 5* (01446) 794848
7 **Llangollen** International Musical Eisteddfod: cosmopolitan gathering at Royal International Pavilion – *till Sun 12* (01978) 860236
10 **Ffostrasol** Folk Festival – *till Sat 11* (01559) 384551
11 **Newport** Fireworks Concert at Tredegar House (01633) 815880; **Welshpool** Festival of Transport at Powys Castle Showground – *till Sun 12* (01938) 553680
11 **Gwalchmai** Anglesey Show at the Showground – *till Wed 15* (01407) 720072
18 **Aberystwyth** International Music Festival and Summer School – *till Fri 31* (01970) 622889; **Llanfairpwll** Open-air Concert at Plas Newydd (01248) 714795
20 **Llanelwedd** Royal Welsh Show at the Showground – *till Thurs 23* (01982) 553683; **Newport** Open-air Shakespeare at Tredegar House – *till Sat 25* (01633) 815880
22 **Llanfairpwll** Open-air Jazz at Plas Newydd (01248) 714795
25 **Caernarfon** North Wales Agricultural Show at Wern Ddu Fields (01286) 881632; **Fishguard** Music Festival – *till 1 Aug* (01348) 873612

AUGUST

1 **Bridgend** Royal National Eisteddfod of Wales – *till Sat 8* (01222) 763777; **Brecon** County Show (01568) 708760;
5 **Aberaeron** Sheepdog Trials at Drenewydd Fields (01545) 570534
6 **Llanwrtyd Wells** Mountain Bike Festival – *till Sun 9* (01591) 610236; **Newport** National Sheepdog Trials (01234) 352672
7 **Brecon** Jazz Festival: over 80 international performers – *till Sun 9* (01874) 625557; **Fishguard** Show (01348) 873484; **Hay-on-Wye** Vintage Steam Rally at Boatside Farm (01874) 711110
9 **Hay-on-Wye** Vintage Rally at Boatside Farm (01497) 820144
13 **Carmarthen** United Counties Agricultural Show – *till Fri 14* (01267) 232141
14 **Cardigan Bay** Regatta – *till Sun 16* (01545) 561019
19 **Fonmon** Vale of Glamorgan Agricultural Show at Fonmon Castle Park (01446) 772027
22 **Talybont** and North Cardiganshire Agricultural and Horticultural Show
26 **LLangeitho** Agricultural and Horticultural Annual Show – (01974) 821259
27 **Monmouthshire** Show at Vauxhall Fields (01291) 691160
31 **Llanwrtyd Wells** World Bog Snorkling Championship and Mountain Bike Bog Leaping (01591) 610236; **Merthyr Tydfil** Show (01685) 725000

WALES CALENDAR

SEPTEMBER

1 **Llanarthney** Sheepdog Trials at Wernbongam Farm (01267) 290282
4 **Barmouth** Arts Festival – *till Sat 12* (01341) 280392
5 **Llandysul** Agricultural Show (01559) 362850; **Vale of Glamorgan** Festival of Contemporary Music – *till Tues 15* (01222) 667773
9 **Porthcawl** Home International Golf Championship at the Royal Porthcawl Golf Club – *till Fri 11* (01633) 430830
12 **Gwermesney** Usk Show (01291) 672379
14 **Conwy** Honey Fair (01492) 650851
15 **Llanwrtyd Wells** Welsh International Four Days Walks – *till Fri 18* (01591) 610236
18 **Tenby** Arts Festival – *till Sat 26* (01834) 842291
19 **St Asaph** North Wales Music Festival in the cathedral – *till Sat 26* (01745) 584508

OCTOBER

3 **Swansea** Festival – *till Sat 24* (01792) 205318
10 **Porthcawl** South Wales Miner's Eisteddfod at Grand Pavilion – *till Sun 11* (01656) 642684
15 **Llanwrtyd Wells** Welsh International Four Day Cycle Rides – *till Sun 18* (01591) 610236
25 **Snowdonia** Marathon (01492) 860123
31 **Newport** Halloween at Tredegar House – *till 1 Nov* (01633) 815880

NOVEMBER

13 **Aberystywth** Welsh International Film Festival – *till Sun 22* (01970) 617995; **Llanwrtyd Wells** Mid Wales Beer Festival at the Neuadd Arms inc real ale ramble – *till Sun 22* (01591) 610236

DECEMBER

8 **Llanelwedd** Royal Welsh Agricultural Winter Fair at the Royal Welsh Showground (01982) 553683
31 **Llanwrtyd Wells** New Year Walk In, *11pm* The Square: torchlight walk with a horse's skull (Welsh tradition) (01591) 610236

INDEX

This index includes the main places in the **To See and Do** sections. Please let us know if you feel we should also include a 'thematic' index (eg. showing all the page numbers on which castles, say, are mentioned), and/or an index of the names of places to stay in – bearing in mind that adding to the book's length in that way might mean we'd have to cut somewhere else.

LONDON INDEX

Report forms

Please report to us: you can use the card in the middle of the book, tear-out forms on the following pages, or just plain paper – whichever's easiest for you. We need to know what you think of the places mentioned in this edition – especially, whether you think we should add to or change our descriptions of them. We need to know about other places worthy of inclusion. We need to know about ones that should not be included. We try to answer all letters, and readers who send us reports will be offered a discount on the price of the next edition that benefits from their help.

If you are recommending a new entry, the more detail you can put into your description, the better. This will help not just us but also your fellow-readers gauge its appeal. A description of its character and even furnishings is a tremendous boon. Imagine you're writing about it for the *Guide* itself, and put in the sorts of things you'd want to know yourself before deciding whether to choose it.

The atmosphere and character of a holiday hotel or simpler place to stay, or of a restaurant, are very important to us – why it would, or would not, appeal to people who don't know it. But of course the quality and type of its food matters a lot, too, so please tell us about that as well. A full address and telephone number is an enormous help.

We'd also very much like you to let us know of places you've enjoyed visiting – anything from a little village to a stately home, from a shop selling unusual things to a factory visit, from an outstanding plant nursery to a hot-air balloon festival, from a hidden-away country church to a cathedral, from a peaceful wood or a nature reserve or a stretch of unspoilt coastal cliff to a theme park or a zoo or a pleasure beach. We're also particularly interested in enjoyable walks. Whatever it is, if you've enjoyed it, please tell us about it.

The card in the middle of the book is a general purpose one for any recommendation. There are also different forms on the following pages: one for endorsement of existing entries; and two forms for more detailed descriptions of places to visit, hotels or restaurants.

When you go to a hotel, restaurant, or anywhere else, don't tell them you're a reporter for *The Good Guide to Britain*; we do make clear that all inspections are anonymous, and if you declare yourself as a reporter you risk getting special treatment – for better or for worse!

When you write to *The Good Guide to Britain*, FREEPOST TN1569, WADHURST, E. Sussex, TN5 7BR, you don't need a stamp in the UK. We'll gladly send you more forms (free) if you wish. The information you send us will be stored in our computer files.

Though we try to answer letters, we do have other work to do, besides producing this guide. So please understand if there's a delay. And from June well into autumn, when we are fully extended getting the next edition to the printers, we put all letters and reports aside, not answering them until the rush is over (and after our post-press-day autumn holiday). The end of May is pretty much the cut-off date for reasoned consideration of reports for the next edition – and the earlier the better, if they're suggestions of new entries.

We'll assume we can print your name or initials as a recommender unless you tell us otherwise.

The Good Guide to Britain: Endorsement Form

I have been to the following hotels/restaurants/attractions/places in *The 1998 Good Guide to Britain* in the last few months, found them as described, and confirm that they deserve continued inclusion:

Your own name and address (*block capitals please*)

Please return to:
The Good Guide to Britain
FREEPOST TN1569
WADHURST
E. Sussex
TN5 7BR

The Good Guide to Britain: New Report Form

Please use this form to tell us about anything which *you* think should or should not be included in the next edition of *The Good Guide to Britain*. Just fill it in and return it to us – no stamp or envelope needed.

ALISDAIR AIRD

☐ *Please tick this box if you would like extra report forms*

REPORT ON (*its name*)

Its address:

Postcode: Telephone:

What is this? (e.g. *hotel, restaurant, garden, village, drive, walk*)

Description/why it appeals

PLEASE GIVE YOUR NAME AND ADDRESS ON THE BACK OF THIS FORM

Your own name and address (*block capitals please*)

Please return to:
The Good Guide to Britain
FREEPOST TN1569
WADHURST
E. Sussex
TN5 7BR

The Good Guide to Britain: New Report Form

Please use this form to tell us about anything which *you* think should or should not be included in the next edition of *The Good Guide to Britain*. Just fill it in and return it to us – no stamp or envelope needed.

ALISDAIR AIRD

☐ *Please tick this box if you would like extra report forms*

REPORT ON (*its name*)

Its address:

Postcode: Telephone:

What is this? (e.g. *hotel, restaurant, garden, village, drive, walk*)

Description/why it appeals

PLEASE GIVE YOUR NAME AND ADDRESS ON THE BACK OF THIS FORM

Your own name and address (*block capitals please*)

Please return to:
The Good Guide to Britain
FREEPOST TN1569
WADHURST
E. Sussex
TN5 7BR